UNIVERSITY CASEBOOK SERIES

FEDERAL CRIMINAL LAW

by

PETER W. LOW
Vice President and Provost of the University
Hardy Cross Dillard Professor of Law
University of Virginia

and

JOSEPH L. HOFFMANN
Professor of Law
Indiana University
Bloomington

WESTBURY, NEW YORK
THE FOUNDATION PRESS, INC.
1997

COPYRIGHT © 1997 By THE FOUNDATION PRESS, INC.
615 Merrick Ave.
Westbury, N.Y. 11590–6607
(516) 832–6950

Library of Congress Cataloging-in-Publication Data
Low, Peter W., 1937–
    Federal criminal law / by Peter W. Low, Joseph L. Hoffmann.
      p.   cm. — (University casebook series)
    Includes index.
    ISBN 1–56662–346–4 (hard cover)
    1. Criminal law—United States. 2. Mail fraud—United States.
  3. Racketeering—United States. 4. Organized crime—United States.
I. Hoffmann, Joseph L., 1957–   . II. Title. III. Series.
KF9370.L69 1996
345.73—dc20
[347.305]   96–33057

 *TEXT IS PRINTED ON 10% POST CONSUMER RECYCLED PAPER*

PREFACE

Our primary goal in writing this book has been to emphasize those aspects of federal criminal law that make it different from state criminal law. Drawing on our respective scholarly backgrounds in the areas of federal jurisdiction and criminal procedure, we have sought to identify and discuss those major themes that are uniquely—or at least predominantly— raised by federal crimes and federal prosecutions. Thus, unlike prior casebooks in the area, ours is not a survey book. Indeed, a number of important federal criminal statutes are addressed herein only in passing, if at all. (All major statutes, however, are reproduced in full in a separate supplement to this book, for those teachers who wish to cover them.) Instead, we have focused our attention on helping students understand the concepts, issues, and problems that are special to federal criminal law. By so doing, we hope better to prepare students to deal with an ever-changing area of the law that grows in scope and significance with each passing year.

In keeping with our goal, each of the five chapters in this book uses one or more of the major federal criminal statutes to illustrate a particular theme that distinguishes federal criminal law from state criminal law:

Chapter I, "Jurisdiction of the Federal Government Over Crimes," deals with the evolution of federal jurisdiction from its earliest and most limited bases (such as the customs power and the maritime and territorial jurisdiction), through the modern expansion of the commerce clause, to the U.S. Supreme Court's partial reinvigoration of constitutional limits in the 1994 case of United States v. Lopez. This chapter introduces federal jurisdiction as a current and vital aspect of federal criminal law, not merely an historical artifact. The chapter integrates well with the treatment of federal jurisdiction in basic constitutional law courses, although it does not assume prior coverage of such materials.

Chapter II, "Mail Fraud," presents this classic federal crime as a prime example of Congress's troubling tendency to enact extremely broad criminal statutes and then rely on the discretion of federal prosecutors to ensure that only the proper persons are charged.

Chapter III, "Racketeering: Illustrative Statutes Aimed at Organized Crime," highlights the importance of legislative history—usually much more extensive, but often more ambiguous, at the federal level than at the state level—in the interpretation of expansive federal criminal statutes like the Hobbs Act and the Travel Act. The chapter focuses especially on the Hobbs Act as it has been applied to labor relations and to bribery of public officials. Excerpts from the legislative history of the Hobbs Act are included in the chapter. Additional materials are contained in the Appendices.

Chapter IV, "Enterprise Criminality—RICO and CCE," addresses these two new favorite tools of the federal prosecutor (and, in the case of RICO, civil plaintiffs as well). The chapter contains full treatment of not only the basic concept of "enterprise criminality," but also the interactions between this new concept and traditional doctrines such as double jeopardy and accomplice liability. The chapter also includes extensive materials on forfeiture as a special sanction aimed at organized crime.

Finally, Chapter V, "Sentencing for Federal Crimes," recognizes that crime issues and sentencing issues often are inextricably intertwined. The Federal Sentencing Guidelines severely restrict judicial discretion and give federal prosecutors tremendous leverage over members of criminal enterprises. The chapter concludes with a discussion of the recently expanded federal death penalty.

In the first three chapters of the book, we have provided extensive notes designed to help students acquire a sense of the historical evolution of federal statutes like the Mann Act, the mail fraud statute, and the Hobbs Act. By contrast, RICO, CCE, and the Sentencing Guidelines are still in the formative stages of their doctrinal development. Thus, in the last two chapters, we have chosen primarily to let the recent case law speak for itself.

We have tried to build as much flexibility as possible into the book. We have included a number of sections that may be omitted to fit the course into a limited schedule or to create room for coverage of specific federal criminal statutes that are not discussed in the book. In particular, sections two and three of Chapter III ("Bribery Under the Travel Act" and "Bribery Under the Hobbs Act"), section four of Chapter IV ("Enterprise Criminality and 'Aider and Abettor' Liability"), the last subsection of section five of Chapter IV ("Forfeiture and the First Amendment"), and section four of Chapter V ("The Federal Death Penalty"), may be covered or omitted at the discretion of the teacher. It is also possible to omit section three of Chapter IV ("Enterprise Criminality and Double Jeopardy"), but that would likely necessitate also omitting the "Note on Forfeiture and the Double Jeopardy Clause," which appears in the first subsection of section five of Chapter IV.

Throughout the preparation of this book, we have placed the highest priority on making the book easy for students to read and understand. Consistent with this philosophy, we have conformed all citations to our usage, which is standard except that we omit citations to subsequent history, such as certiorari or rehearing denied. Citations and footnotes have been omitted without specific indication; in the text, deletion of anything more than bare citation to authority has been indicated by brackets or ellipses. The original footnote numbers have been retained in all excerpted materials; footnotes by the editors are lettered rather than numbered.

PWL

Charlottesville, Virginia
November, 1996

JLH

Bloomington, Indiana
November, 1996

*

SUMMARY OF CONTENTS

TABLE OF CONTENTS

TABLE OF CASES

Principal cases are in bold type. Non-principal cases are in roman type. References are to Pages.

xvii

*

FEDERAL CRIMINAL LAW

*

CHAPTER I

JURISDICTION OF THE FEDERAL GOVERNMENT OVER CRIMES

INTRODUCTORY NOTES ON THE PREMISES OF FEDERAL JURISDICTION OVER CRIMES

1. Jurisdictional Elements. Typically, a 19th century state legislature would approach the job of defining a criminal offense either by describing its elements in language reminiscent of the common law or by incorporating the common law definition with a summary reference. The statute thus might have said that "larceny" is the "taking and carrying away of the personal property of another with intent to deprive" or, simply, that "larceny" is punishable by such and such a penalty. New crimes that had no common law counterpart would be defined by detailed description of the departures from the social norm they were designed to punish, but still would be likely to use terminology familiar to the common law. In any of these situations, the traditions of the common law would give important content to the substance of the criminal law. They would provide background meaning for the words used by the legislature, and would also provide principles for decision when issues arose that were not covered by legislation.

Modern federal crimes share with state crimes this common law heritage. They too have traditionally been defined—and by and large still are—in terminology familiar to the common law. They too are interpreted against the background of that tradition, and gaps are filled by reference to common law principles. There is, however, an important difference between the traditional definition of a state crime and the traditional definition of a federal crime. Federal crimes usually will include what will be called in these materials a "jurisdictional" element. This "jurisdictional element" is almost always a prominent, often dominant, feature of the definition of a federal offense. Thus, theft is not punished as such by the federal government, but the federal criminal code punishes theft from an interstate shipment, or theft from a military base, or theft of government property. Consider, for example, the following statute:

> "Whoever embezzles, steals, or unlawfully takes by any fraudulent device, scheme, or game, from any railroad car, bus, vehicle, steamboat, vessel, or aircraft operated by any common carrier moving in interstate or foreign commerce or from any passenger thereon any money, baggage, goods, or chattels, or whoever buys, receives, or has in his possession any such money, baggage, goods, or chattels, knowing the same to have been embezzled or stolen

[s]hall ... be fined under this title or imprisoned not more than ten years, or both; but if the amount or value of such money, baggage, goods or chattels does not exceed $100, he shall be fined under this title or imprisoned not more than one year, or both."
18 U.S.C. § 659.

Notice that the language describing the theft-like behavior covered by this statute draws heavily on the common law. How are the courts to give content to words like "embezzle" or "steal"? How is a court to determine the mental elements (or mens rea) required for "stealing"? The answer to both questions is that a federal court, like its state counterpart, will follow the admonition of Justice Jackson in Morissette v. United States, 342 U.S. 246, 263 (1952):

> "[W]here Congress borrows terms of art in which are accumulated the legal tradition and meaning of centuries of practice, it presumably knows and adopts the cluster of ideas that were attached to each borrowed word in the body of learning from which it was taken and the meaning its use will convey to the judicial mind unless otherwise instructed."

Notice in addition that most of § 659 is addressed to its jurisdictional features, that is, to the occasions when theft can be prosecuted by the federal government. The statute is violated by theft from an interstate carrier, but is not violated by theft from a military base. It is violated by theft from an airline passenger, but not by theft from a private car heading for another state on an interstate highway. It is this focus on "jurisdictional" elements that is the distinctive feature of most federal crimes. As will be illustrated in materials to follow, moreover, these jurisdictional ingredients normally must be proved beyond a reasonable doubt to the same extent as any other element of the offense. Often they require culpability, just as with most elements of most criminal offenses.

2. The Constitutional Structure. Why are federal statutes drafted with such concern for jurisdictional features? The answer lies in the nature of our constitutional structure. In basic outline, the federal government is a government of limited, enumerated powers. Congress can enact legislation only with respect to those subjects falling within its specifically delegated powers, most of which are found in article I, § 8 of the Constitution. Legislative authority not delegated to the federal government is retained by the states.

Fidelity to this structure has led to the ordinary, though—as will be seen—not invariable, practice of drafting criminal offenses by including specific elements that confine the offense to the constitutional authority of the federal government. If Congress wanted to punish all theft within the territorial confines of the United States, there are arguments that it has the constitutional authority to do so.[a] But in general Congress has not

---

a The argument would be that thefts in the aggregate have a substantial impact on interstate commerce. United States v. Lo- pez, ___ U.S. ___, 115 S.Ct. 1624 (1995), considered later in this Chapter, casts doubt

followed this approach, and instead has defined federal crimes by reference to specific interests that it wished to address. As will be illustrated, congressional focus on jurisdictional elements matters a great deal in the interpretation and reach of the federal criminal law.

This does not mean, however, that the reach of the federal criminal law is narrow, or that there are but a few offenses that can be prosecuted by the federal government. To the contrary, the reach of the federal criminal law is enormous. Many offenses, moreover, create expansive opportunities for the exercise of federal prosecutorial authority, cabined only by the exercise of restraint in the selection of targets for prosecution.

3. Common Law Crimes. A second premise of the federal criminal law should also be highlighted at the outset. It is that there are no federal common law crimes. Federal courts have authority to punish criminal behavior only if, and to the extent that, Congress has by statute identified the behavior as a federal crime.

There was debate on this point early in the Nation's history. But it was settled in United States v. Hudson & Goodwin, 11 U.S. (7 Cranch) 32 (1812), that the fact that behavior was recognized as criminal by the common law did not in itself authorize federal prosecution. It follows that the early practice of the common law courts of exerting criminal jurisdiction over matters not yet defined as criminal—of, not to put too fine a point on it, creating new crimes as the occasion seemed to warrant—has never been followed by the federal courts.[b] Federal crimes are defined by statute. There are no federal crimes other than those that have been created by Congress in enacted legislation.

It should be emphasized again that this does not mean that the common law is irrelevant to the federal criminal law. Quite the contrary is true. As the quotation above from Justice Jackson's opinion in *Morissette* implies, Congress often uses common law terms and these terms are interpreted within the tradition of their common law meanings. Moreover, the enactment of a federal criminal statute invariably will leave gaps to be filled by the federal courts. Until recently, for example, Congress had never spoken to the substantive standards governing the insanity defense.[c] Similarly, there are no general federal statutory standards governing issues of culpability or the entire range of justification defenses. When Congress

on how far this line of argument can be taken.

[b] Later materials will question the extent to which this statement is true. There are occasions, as with the conspiracy and mail fraud statutes, 18 U.S.C. §§ 371, 1341, where one might argue that in substance the federal courts are engaging in what amounts to retroactive crime creation. But what the federal courts will not do is recognize a federal crime that is not tied, at least as a formal matter, to a specific statute. The issues raised by §§ 371 and 1341 concern when

statutory "interpretation" is extended to the point that in effect amounts to unwarranted judicial crime creation. For a discussion of this problem, see John C. Jeffries, Jr., Legality, Vagueness, and the Construction of Penal Statutes, 71 Va. L. Rev. 189 (1985).

[c] Congress first enacted an insanity defense in 1984 (18 U.S.C. § 17) following the acquittal by reason of insanity of John Hinckley for the attempted assassination of President Reagan.

has not spoken to such matters, the gaps are filled in by the courts. And it is to principles developed by the common law that the courts look for guidance.

4. Exclusivity of Federal–Court Jurisdiction Over Federal Crimes. The jurisdiction of the federal courts over federal crimes is exclusive:

> "The district courts of the United States shall have original jurisdiction, exclusive of the courts of the States, of all offenses against the laws of the United States.

> "Nothing in this title shall be held to take away or impair the jurisdiction of the courts of the several States under the laws thereof." 18 U.S.C. § 3231.

As the second paragraph of § 3231 suggests, however, federal crimes are generally not pre-emptive; that is, they do not preclude state prosecution for offenses against state law even though the behavior might also fit within the definition of a federal crime.

5. Questions and Comments on the Objectives of the Federal Criminal Law. The tradition in this country is that state and local government provides the primary protection from the kinds of predators that most of us think about when we think of crime. Street crimes, bank robbery, rape, housebreaking, murder, and the like, are punished by the criminal codes of every state. The police who are visible to most of us work for either state or local government. The first line of defense to which we look for basic order and safety in our lives is provided by state and local authorities.

Against this background, one might ask why there is a need for a separate level of federal crimes? Are state criminal laws inadequate or insufficient? If so, in what respects? What justifications could one advance for federal criminal laws in general or for particular federal crimes?

The remainder of these materials will provide background for consideration of these questions. Chapter I begins the inquiry by considering the primary objectives of a federal criminal law. Section 1 illustrates two situations where there can hardly be much debate. The first involves "direct federal interests." It concerns the entitlement of the federal government to investigate and prosecute offenses against federal sovereignty. Laws against treason or assassinating the President fit comfortably within the scope of "direct" federal interests. The second part of Section 1 deals with territories over which the federal government has exclusive jurisdiction—cases where if there is no federal criminal law there will be no law of crimes at all. Here too, the justification for a federal criminal law seems clear.

Section 2 moves on to what are called "auxiliary" or "supplementary" offenses. These terms are used to describe situations where the federal government has chosen to supplement—and perhaps overlap—the coverage of state law. Bank robbery, for example, is a crime in every state. But robbery of a bank holding federally insured deposits (how many banks are excluded?) is also a federal crime. Many federal crimes, and virtually all that are controversial, fall within this category. It is here that the justification for invoking the federal law enforcement machinery often becomes more tentative.

There will be no suggestion in these pages that this "auxiliary" or "supplementary" function of federal law enforcement is always inappropriate, or that redundancy of coverage in our complex federal system is necessarily a bad thing. To the contrary, many "supplementary" federal offenses seem plainly desirable. The tougher question, to be suggested by many of the examples considered below, is where to draw the line of appropriate federal involvement.[d]

INTRODUCTORY NOTES ON THE EVOLUTION OF THE FEDERAL CRIMINAL LAW

1. The Special Part.[e] The best single word to describe the evolution of the federal criminal law is "accretion." Beginning with a revenue fraud provision enacted by the first Congress, the federal criminal law in the early years of the Republic was limited to protecting the "direct" interests of the federal government. "Not until after the Civil War did the federal criminal law make its first substantial ventures beyond the punishment of acts directly injurious to the central government." The earliest statutes designed "to protect private individuals from invasion of their rights by other private individuals—a traditional function of state law" were the Post Office Code of 1872, which contained the predecessor of the modern mail fraud statute (18 U.S.C. § 1341), and two civil rights statutes (now 18 U.S.C. §§ 241, 242) enacted in 1866 and 1870.[f]

It was not until the 20th century that Congress began the expansion of the federal criminal law that led to its present bulk. Early statutes were

[d] For some thoughtful recent answers to this question, see Franklin E. Zimring and Gordon Hawkins, "Toward a Principled Basis for Federal Criminal Legislation," 543 Annals of the Am. Acad. of Pol. & Soc. Sci.15 (1996); Philip B. Heymann and Mark H. Moore, "The Federal Role in Dealing with Violent Street Crime: Principles, Questions, and Cautions," 543 Annals of the Am. Acad. of Pol. & Soc. Sci. 103 (1996); Sara Sun Beale, "Too Many and Yet Too Few: New Principles to Define the Proper Limits for Federal Criminal Jurisdiction," 46 Hastings L.J. 979 (1995); Rory K. Little, "Myths and Principles of Federalization," 46 Hastings L.J. 1029 (1995); John C. Jeffries, Jr., and the Honorable John Gleeson, "The Federalization of Organized Crime: Advantages of Federal Prosecution," 46 Hastings L.J. 1095 (1995); Kathleen F. Brickey, "Criminal Mischief: The Federalization of American Criminal Law," 46 Hastings L.J. 1135 (1995); and

Sara Sun Beale, "Reporter's Draft for the Working Group on Principles to Use When Considering the Federalization of Criminal Law," 46 Hastings L.J. 1277 (1995).

[e] The term "special part", a word of art in the vernacular of the criminal law, refers to the law associated with specific substantive offenses, *e.g.*, the law of murder, the law of theft, etc. It is to be contrasted to the "general part" of the criminal law, which consists of those principles of general application that cut across particular crimes. The insanity defense, principles of mistake or justification, and general principles of causation are examples.

[f] The quotations and illustrations in this paragraph are taken from Louis B. Schwartz, Federal Criminal Jurisdiction and Prosecutors' Discretion, 13 Law & Contemp. Probs. 64, 65 (1948).

the Mann Act in 1910 (transporting a woman in interstate commerce for prostitution or other immoral purposes, now contained in revised form in 18 U.S.C. §§ 2421, 2422) and the Dyer Act in 1919 (interstate transportation of a stolen motor vehicle, now contained in revised form in 18 U.S.C. § 2312). A sense for the evolution of successor provisions is revealed in the following comments:

"Nothing has so distorted federal criminal law as the habit of defining federal crimes in such a way as to make jurisdictional requirements appear to be penologically significant elements of the offense. This confuses federal power to prohibit certain conduct with the nature of the crime itself. This confusion is a hangover from the 18th century when the states exercised virtually exclusive responsibility for law enforcement within their territories, and the federal government dealt with a narrow range of offenses of peculiarly national concern, e.g., treason, piracy, revenue and customs offenses. It was natural, under those circumstances, to think that the federal feature of the offense, was central to the exercise of federal penal power. But the 19th and 20th centuries saw a vast expansion of federal criminal legislation directed against common crimes. 'Private' conventional offenses like theft, fraud, prostitution, obscenity, extortion, usury, narcotics, illegal possession and use of weapons were brought within the federal ken by a myriad of statutes, based on Congress' powers in the areas of interstate commerce, mails, taxation, etc. Federal power was invoked because state power proved increasingly inadequate to deal with crime extending beyond state borders. The federal program was 'auxiliary' to state law enforcement. . . .

"The expansion of federal auxiliary jurisdiction took place gradually, step-by-step, the steps being spread over more than a century. Each new statute, although dealing with the same misconduct, would incorporate an additional jurisdictional base. Statutes passed at different times would carry quite different penalties for the same misconduct, reflecting chiefly the current level of anti-crime feeling. Little regard was given to the fact that the same misconduct was differently penalized under earlier federal legislation based on a different jurisdictional element." National Commission on Reform of Federal Criminal Laws, Study Draft of a New Federal Criminal Code xxviii (1970).

Under the caption "The Chaos of Existing Law," the same commentary also states:

"Title 18 of the United States Code, entitled 'Crimes and Criminal Procedure,' was established in its present form in 1948, following upon earlier 'codes' of 1909 and 1877. These codes were essentially compilations of existing laws brought together in one place with only the grossest inconsistencies eliminated. The statutes thus brought together were of varying antiquity, from the 14th century formulation of treason in terms of adhering 'to their enemies, giving them aid and comfort,' to a 19th century enactment penalizing seduction of female steamship passengers, regardless of age or consent, by 'solicitation or the making of gifts or presents,' to 20th century formulations dealing with racketeering, riot, and civil rights. Trivial offenses, like misuse of the Swiss Confederation coat of arms, are found in title 18, while many grave felonies, including capital offenses, do not appear in this compilation of 'Crimes and Criminal Procedure,' but are found scattered throughout the 50 titles of the U.S. Code under such headings as Transportation (49 U.S.C. § 1472(i)—aircraft piracy) and Public Health and Welfare (42 U.S.C. § 2272—Atomic Energy Act violations).

"Within title 18 itself, chaos reigns. Modern penal codes arrange offenses according to the harm done or threatened by the offender. Thus, there are ordinarily chapters dealing with offenses against the person, ranging from murder to assault, offenses against property ranging from arson to malicious mischief, offenses against the state, etc. Title 18, however, knows no such logical ordering. It is alphabetical, running 'Aircraft,' 'Animals,' 'Arson', through 'White Slave Traffic.' Such an organization of the material is consistent with the limited objective of the 1948 revision—to bring together scattered legislative enactments where they could readily be found—but it plays hob with any effort to make consistent legislative policy. For example, conspiracy to defraud the United States carries a maximum imprisonment of five years under 'Conspiracy' (chapter 19, § 371), and a maximum of 10 years under 'Claims and Services' (chapter 15, § 286).

"Some of the chaos of existing law comes from making the circumstances which support federal jurisdiction part of the definition of the crime itself. Thus, there are a number of statutes in title 18 which prohibit burglary, each applicable within a narrow range of federal power, e.g., burglary of a post office (18 U.S.C. § 2115—five years), burglary of an interstate pipeline (18 U.S.C. § 2117—10 years). Similarly, 18 U.S.C. § 1341 prohibits *use of mails* to defraud, not *theft* in the course of which the mails were used. The federal government has the power to punish because the mails are used, but the criminologically significant conduct is not the mailing of a letter, but the stealing." Id. at xxvi-vii.

A related study found "well over 100 separate [federal] statutes [dealing] with theft or some other theft-related activity." II Working Papers of the National Commission on Reform of Federal Criminal Laws 913 (1970). The study continued:

"Present federal law includes a wide and unmanageable variety of overlapping and confusing terms to deal with various forms of acquisitive conduct—'embezzle,' 'steal,' 'purloin,' 'convert,' 'conceal,' 'retain,' 'take,' 'carry away,' 'abstract,' 'misapply,' 'use,' 'buy,' 'secrete,' 'possess,' 'receive,' 'obtain by fraud or deception,' 'take by device, scheme, or game,' 'obtain, dispose of, commit or attempt an act of extortion'—and so on at considerable length. Such variety adds nothing but color to the law, and at the same time builds in serious disadvantages. It is practically impossible to develop an overview of the kinds of conduct reached by federal law, for the purpose of measuring the extent to which it is in accord with modern economic circumstances or for the purpose of assuring consistency of sanction for comparable conduct. Such diversity is an open invitation to the technical defense—to the argument that 'the indictment charges stealing but what I was really doing was purloining and therefore my conviction should be reversed.'[1] There are undoubtedly hidden gaps in coverage as well, gaps which would be apparent if there were some consistency of language and approach.[2]"   Id. at 914.

The picture that emerges is a Congress that adds periodically to an alphabetical list of offenses as new forms of criminality or new occasions for the exercise of federal authority come to its attention. Little effort is made each successive year to coordinate the new with the old; each year's approach to drafting follows the penological preferences and linguistic conventions that suit that year's style. After 200 years or so of a statute here and a statute there, what results is a hodge-podge, a chaotic collection of criminal offenses, some in title 18 and some in others of the 49 additional titles of the federal code, that achieve a substantial federal presence in the criminal law of the country. Just how substantial will be illustrated in the materials that follow.

2. The General Part. The commentary to the Study Draft quoted above continued:

"Important sections of the federal criminal law do not appear at all in statutory form, i.e., have never been the subject of congressional consideration and enactment. The law of insanity,[g] self-defense, and entrapment is all judge-made. No statute sets forth a general rule on the liability of a corporation for the crimes of its agents. The result is that on some issues different circuit courts of appeals apply different 'federal' law. On other issues, no court has spoken and it is thus impossible to say what the federal law is." National Commission on Reform of Federal Criminal Laws, Study Draft of a New Federal Criminal Code xxvii (1970).

[1] "See, e.g., Bennett v. United States, 399 F.2d 740 (9th Cir.1968), where an offender was saved from a conviction for 'stealing' because he swindled the bank instead. See also United States v. Kubacki, 237 F.Supp. 638 (E.D.Pa.1965), where a conviction under 18 U.S.C. § 1951 for extortion was set aside because the defendant proved that he was guilty of bribery rather than extortion."

[2] "In addition to the cases cited in note 1, compare 18 U.S.C. § 659 ('with intent to convert to his own use') with 18 U.S.C. § 641 ('converts to his own use or the use of another')."

[g] A federal insanity defense was enacted after this was written. See 18 U.S.C. § 17.—[Footnote by eds.]

Nowhere is the resulting law more chaotic than in the law relating to standards of culpability for federal crimes. The problem starts with the statutes:

"The 'mental element' of federal crimes is specified in the definitions of the crimes,[h] which definitions are frequently modified, if not indeed distorted, in judicial decisions. If one looks to the statutes alone, the specifications of mental states form a staggering array:

[Here some 78 different combinations of words are extracted from various federal statutes in title 18 alone. Examples are 'willfully,' 'willfully and corruptly,' 'willfully and maliciously,' 'willfully or maliciously,' 'willfully and unlawfully,' 'willfully and knowingly,' 'willfully, deliberate, malicious, and premeditated,' 'unlawfully and willfully,' 'knowingly and willfully,' 'knowingly or willfully,' 'fraudulently or wrongfully,' 'from a premeditated design unlawfully and maliciously to,' 'knowingly, willfully, and corruptly,' 'willfully neglects,' 'feloniously,' and 'improperly.']

"Unsurprisingly, the courts have been unable to find substantive correlates for all of these varied descriptions of mental states, and, in fact, the opinions display far fewer mental states than the statutory language. Not only does the statutory language not reflect accurately or consistently what are the mental elements of the various crimes; there is no discernible pattern or consistent rationale which explains why one crime is defined or understood to require one mental state and another crime another mental state or indeed no mental state at all.

"Perhaps the best illustration of the confusion engendered by existing statutory formulations of the mental element in federal crimes is that surrounding the word 'willfully.' [T]he courts, including the Supreme Court, have endowed the requirement of willfulness with the capacity to take on whatever meaning seems appropriate in the statutory context." I Working Papers of the National Commission on Reform of Federal Criminal Laws 119–20 (1970).

Not only, therefore, is the special part of the federal criminal law a chaotic mess, the statutory contribution to the general part is no better. And by and large, the general part is left to judicial development on a case-by-case basis. Given the demands on its time from other quarters, it is not surprising, moreover, that the Supreme Court has yet to develop a mature, complete jurisprudence filling all of the gaps left in the general principles that govern federal criminal litigation. The surprising thing, by contrast, is how little—even given the institutional constraints on its time—the

[h] Rather than in a single, generally applicable provision, such as ALI, Model Penal Code § 2.02.—[Footnote by eds.]

Supreme Court has in fact contributed to a coherent philosophy of federal crimes.

3. The Brown Commission. Congress responded to the chaos in 1966 by creating the National Commission on Reform of Federal Criminal Laws. The Commission consisted of three members of the Senate, three members of the House, three federal judges, and three members of the public. It had a Director and a full-time staff, as well as a number of consultants. It took its name from the Chairman, Edmund G. (Pat) Brown, a former Governor of California (whose son was later to succeed him as Governor). Professor Louis B. Schwartz of the University of Pennsylvania Law School was the Director.

The Commission was charged to:

"make a full and complete review and study of the statutory and case law of the United States which constitutes the federal system of criminal justice for the purpose of formulating and recommending to the Congress legislation which would improve the federal system of criminal justice. It shall be the further duty of the Commission to make recommendations for revision and recodification of the criminal laws of the United States, including the repeal of unnecessary or undesirable statutes and such changes in the penalty structure as the Commission may feel will better serve the ends of justice." Pub. Law 89–801, 89th Cong., H.R. 15766 (1966).

The Commission was established four years after the American Law Institute had published the final version of its influential Model Penal Code, which sought to encourage each American jurisdiction to engage in comprehensive revision of its penal statutes. The need for revision was reflected in the fact that virtually all state criminal codes—only one had been significantly revised in the 20th century—were in the same condition as the federal code. A few states—most notably New York—had revised their criminal codes based on the American Law Institute's model at the time the federal Commission was established and a number of other states had established Commissions (as was the process in New York) to study the question. The federal commission, it was hoped at the time, would lead to a bi-partisan effort to accomplish the same objective at the federal level.

The Commission completed the first draft of its statute in 1970. This "Study Draft" of the proposed new federal code, from the introduction to which extensive quotations have been reproduced above, was accompanied by three volumes of "Working Papers," consisting mainly of staff memoranda and consultants reports on various sections of the proposed new code. The Final Report of the Commission was transmitted to Congress in 1971. Although there were differences in detail, the Brown Commission's Final Report looked a lot like the Model Penal Code. Part A consisted of General Provisions covering matters such as culpability, responsibility, complicity, causation, and justification and excuse. Part B covered specific offenses, categorized by the nature of the harm inflicted. Part C dealt with sentencing.

The most innovative feature of the proposal was its approach to federal jurisdiction. A single section (§ 201) was drafted that contained every basis of jurisdiction Congress had employed over the years. For example, § 201(c) covered situations where the victim was a federal public servant (from the President on down); § 201(d) covered situations involving federal property; § 201(e) covered use of the mails or other interstate facilities; § 201(g) covered matters affecting interstate or foreign commerce; etc. The crimes were then defined to look like any other crimes, e.g., theft in terms of the kinds of property and the methods of taking that amounted to stealing, criminal homicide in terms of the normal grading of that offense into various levels depending on culpability (murder, manslaughter, etc.), and so on. Each substantive crime then had a section that triggered appropriate provisions of § 201. The jurisdictional part of the crime thus was not part of the definition of the offense itself, but a separate statement, e.g., "there is federal jurisdiction over [name of offense] under paragraphs c, d, and e of § 201." The culpability structure of the proposed new code, which closely resembled that of the Model Penal Code, specifically did not apply to the jurisdictional components of offenses. The federal jurisdictional component of a given offense was not an "element" of the offense, although it was required that jurisdiction be established by proof beyond a reasonable doubt.[i]

Publication of the Brown Commission's Final Report led to a flurry of executive and legislative activity. The Justice Department, not wholly enamored of the Brown Commission product, got to work on its own version of a new federal criminal code. So did the staff of the Senate

[i] The most controversial portion of § 201 was the so-called "piggyback" provision in § 201(b). Subsection (b) authorized federal jurisdiction in any case where "the offense is committed in the course of committing or in immediate flight from the commission of any other offense defined in this Code over which federal jurisdiction exists." The rationale for this provision was rooted, essentially, in appropriate principles of grading. Present 18 U.S.C. § 242, for example, provides for a one year maximum sentence for certain violations of civil rights, but "if bodily injury results" the defendant can receive up to ten years in prison, and "if death results" the maximum changes to life imprisonment. (The death penalty is also authorized "if death results," but only if the defendant intended to kill, intended to inflict serious bodily injury, contemplated the use of lethal force, or acted with reckless disregard for human life. See 18 U.S.C. § 3591(a)(2).) Thus, life imprisonment is appropriately authorized for a murder that occurs during the course of a civil rights violation. But life imprisonment is also authorized for a reckless, negligent, or accidental (or perhaps even justified) killing that occurs during a civil rights offense that violates § 242. The approach of the Brown Commission was to make the penalty for the civil rights violation commensurate with the seriousness of the civil rights component of that offense. In cases where death resulted, the provisions of the new Code on criminal homicide were in effect incorporated by reference by making § 201(b) a jurisdictional basis for the federal criminal homicide laws. A death occurring during the course of a civil rights violation thus would be murder, manslaughter, negligent homicide, or no homicide offense depending on the defendant's culpability with respect to the death.

The "piggyback" provision was the focus of intense criticism as the Commission's proposals were debated, and indeed most likely played a substantial part in the failure of the Commission's product to achieve enactment. The criticism did not focus on the grading feature of the provision, but rather on the perception that § 201(b) was a major and unwarranted expansion of federal jurisdiction.

Committee on the Judiciary. Eventually, three separate Codes were presented to various House and Senate Committees, and over the years many more versions were produced. After a decade or so of legislative activity, the Brown Commission proposals, and more importantly the idea of a comprehensive revision of the federal criminal code, quietly died away. The result is that the descriptions of the federal criminal law reproduced above are still accurate. Title 18 is a chaotic, alphabetically organized amalgam of 200+ years of legislation, and other federal crimes remain randomly scattered throughout the other 49 titles of the federal code. The opportunity for reform appears to have been lost.

SECTION 1: ORDINARY CRIME

SUBSECTION A: DIRECT FEDERAL INTERESTS

INTRODUCTORY NOTES ON CRIMES PROTECTING DIRECT FEDERAL INTERESTS

1. **Typical Offenses**. There are numerous offenses in title 18 of the United States Code that are designed to protect the direct interests of the federal government. Section 2381 implements the constitutional definition of treason contained in art. III, § 3, followed in §§ 2382–91 with a series of related offenses covering sedition and other subversive activities. These provisions are designed to protect the integrity of government itself. Other provisions are aimed at protecting the functioning of the various components of the national government. For example, §§ 111, 351, 1114, and 1751 cover assaulting, attempting to kill, or killing federal officials, § 201 covers bribery of federal officials and witnesses, § 1361 destruction of government property, § 1367 interfering with the operation of a satellite, § 1381 enticing or harboring a deserter from the military, §§ 1425–26 unlawful procurement of citizenship and forgery of citizenship papers, §§ 1501–15 obstruction of justice (e.g., assaulting a process server, jury tampering, retaliating against a witness), §§ 1541–46 offenses associated with passports and visas, and §§ 1691–1738 crimes related to the postal service (e.g., destruction or theft of mail, obstruction of the mails).

There are many similar provisions in title 18 and elsewhere in the federal code. They range from the serious crimes illustrated above to offenses that achieve such a level of detailed regulation as (almost?) to be trivial. Consider the following:

"Whoever, except as authorized under rules and regulations issued by the Secretary, knowingly and for profit manufactures, reproduces, or uses the character 'Woodsy Owl', the name 'Woodsy Owl', or the associated slogan, 'Give a Hoot, Don't Pollute' shall be fined under this title or imprisoned not more than six months, or both."

18 U.S.C. § 711a. Cf. 18 U.S.C. § 711 ("Smokey Bear").

Although one could debate the need for invoking the majesty of the federal criminal process to protect Woodsy Owl and Smokey Bear, there can be little doubt as a general matter that protection of the direct governmental interests of the United States is an appropriate function for a federal criminal law. A dramatic illustration is provided by comparison of the assassination of President Kennedy with the attempt to assassinate President Reagan. When Lee Harvey Oswald shot President Kennedy in November, 1963, Oswald was taken into custody by the Dallas police, a situation that led to the tragic confrontation in the local police station between Jack Ruby and Oswald. By contrast, when John Hinckley attempted to assassinate President Reagan in March, 1981, Hinckley was immediately spirited by the FBI to a secure federal facility where he was removed from public view and from possible contact by a Jack Ruby.

Why the difference? Why didn't the FBI take Oswald into secure custody? The answer lies at least in part in the configuration of the federal criminal code at the time. When President Kennedy was assassinated, §§ 111 and 1114 of title 18 punished the assault, attempted killing, or killing of a long list of federal officials that did *not* include the President, Vice–President, President-elect, Vice–President-elect, or (in case there was no Vice–President) the next person in the line of succession to the presidency. Thus, the murder of President Kennedy was a local crime, falling within the jurisdiction of the Dallas police and not the FBI. Not surprisingly, in August of 1965—some twenty-one months after the assassination—Congress enacted 18 U.S.C. § 1751, making presidential assassination (and assassination, kidnaping, or assault of the list of top officials recited above) a federal crime. Thus, when Hinckley shot President Reagan, a federal crime was committed. Investigation and prosecution fell within the authority of the federal government, not only within the authority of local District of Columbia officials as would have been the case prior to the enactment of § 1751.

The reasons why the federal police and prosecutorial authorities would wish to have control over situations like these—as well as other cases where the direct interests of the federal government are at stake—are obvious, and seem hardly debatable. Accordingly, only a small portion of the materials that follow will be devoted to crimes of this nature.

2. Overlap with State Offenses; Multiple State and Federal Prosecutions. One question suggested by overlapping federal and state jurisdiction is whether criminal behavior that violates the laws of both the federal government and a state can be prosecuted by *both* sovereigns. If President Kennedy had been assassinated after the passage of § 1751, it is clear that both state and federal law would have been violated.[a] Could Oswald have been convicted under *both* state and federal law? If he had been tried by the state and acquitted, could he then have been retried by the federal government?

[a] It is also clear that § 1751 would not have preempted the state murder offense. See 18 U.S.C. § 3231.

These questions must be analyzed at two levels. The first is whether the Constitution *permits* double prosecution in such cases. It does, as is elaborated below. Since it does, the second question is how it works out as a matter of policy, that is, whether such double prosecution is a frequent occurrence and the circumstances under which it might be undertaken.

(i) **The Constitutional Landscape**. The Constitution has not been interpreted to forbid multiple prosecution by state and federal government for the same criminal act. The two leading cases are Bartkus v. Illinois, 359 U.S. 121 (1959), and Abbate v. United States, 359 U.S. 187 (1959). *Bartkus* involved a state conviction for bank robbery after the defendant had been acquitted for the same bank robbery in federal court.[b] *Abbate* involved the reverse situation. The defendants, who had agreed to dynamite telephone company facilities, pled guilty in state court and were sentenced to three months' imprisonment for conspiring to destroy the property of another. Based on the same acts, they were subsequently convicted in federal court of conspiring to destroy communications facilities operated or controlled by the United States.

In both cases the Supreme Court held that, since the double jeopardy clause only prohibits multiple prosecutions by the same sovereign, the second prosecution did not violate the Constitution. Although the decisions have been criticized, the Court still adheres to what has come to be known as the doctrine of "dual sovereignty."[c]

Why did the Supreme Court come to this conclusion? Part of the reason is revealed in the following passage from *Bartkus*:

"A practical justification for rejecting [a contrary reading of the constitutional limits] commends itself..... In Screws v. United States, 325 U.S. 91 (1945), defendants were tried and convicted in a federal court under federal statutes with maximum sentences of a year and two years respectively. But the state crime there involved was a capital offense. Were the federal prosecution of a comparatively minor offense to prevent state prosecution of so grave an infraction of state law, the result would be a shocking and untoward deprivation of the historic right and obligation of the states to maintain peace and order within their confines. It would be in derogation of our federal system to displace the reserved power of states over state offenses by reason of prosecution of minor federal offenses by federal authorities beyond the control of the states."

There is a similar passage in *Abbate*:

"[U]ndesirable consequences would follow [if we were to prohibit federal prosecution after a state prosecution. I]f the states

[b] The federal charge was robbing a federally insured bank.

[c] The Court has not applied the same principle to successive prosecutions by state and municipal government. See Waller v. Florida, 397 U.S. 387 (1970). But it has applied the "dual sovereignty" principle to permit successive prosecutions by two different states. See Heath v. Alabama, 474 U.S. 82 (1985).

are free to prosecute criminal acts violating their laws, and the resultant state prosecutions bar federal prosecutions on the same acts, federal law enforcement must necessarily be hindered. For example, the petitioners in this case insist that their [state] convictions resulting in three months' prison sentences should bar this federal prosecution which could result in a sentence of up to five years. Such a disparity will very often arise when, as in this case, the defendants' acts impinge more seriously on a federal interest than on a state interest. But no one would suggest that, in order to maintain the effectiveness of federal law enforcement, it is desirable completely to displace state power to prosecute crimes based on acts which might also violate federal law. This would bring about a marked change in the distribution of powers to administer criminal justice, for the states under our federal system have the principal responsibility for defining and prosecuting crimes. Thus, unless the federal authorities could somehow insure that there would be no state prosecutions for particular acts that also constitute federal offenses, the efficiency of federal law enforcement must suffer if the double jeopardy clause prevents successive state and federal prosecutions. Needless to say, it would be highly impractical for the federal authorities to attempt to keep informed of all state prosecutions which might bear on federal offenses."

One can imagine situations where a prior state court acquittal would seriously undermine appropriate federal prosecutorial interests. Civil rights offenses, for example, have sometimes involved the violation of constitutional rights by local governmental officials, who might be in a position to "arrange" a swift acquittal of any wrongdoing in a state court. Should a subsequent federal prosecution for a civil rights offense be barred in this circumstance? Could a similar situation suggest the need for a state prosecution following federal proceedings? Is solution of the practical problems that might arise between state and federal law enforcement authorities—and that would allow each sovereign to pursue its own legitimate interests—difficult enough to justify retention of the present rules? If not, what approach should be substituted?

(ii) Operative Policies. Many states prohibit state prosecution following a federal prosecution, some under an interpretation of the state constitution and others by applying a state statutory limitation. Otherwise, successive prosecution by state authorities is a matter of state prosecutorial discretion.

At the federal level, Attorney General William Rogers published a memorandum shortly after the decisions in *Bartkus* and *Abbate* which still represents Justice Department policy. He wrote:

"After a state prosecution there should be no federal trial for the same act or acts unless the reasons are compelling. [N]o federal case should be tried when there has already been a state prosecution for substantially the same act or acts without the United

States Attorney first submitting a recommendation to the appropriate Assistant Attorney General in the Department. No such recommendation should be approved by the Assistant Attorney General in charge of the Division without having it first brought to my attention."

In Petite v. United States, 361 U.S. 529 (1960), a federal conviction had been obtained following state court proceedings. In the Supreme Court, the Solicitor General moved to vacate the judgment with directions to dismiss the indictment on the ground that the Attorney General's policy had been violated. The Court granted the motion and since that decision the statements quoted above have come to be known as the "*Petite* policy." Other similar convictions have been set aside since then on the government's motion,[d] but it seems clear that the *Petite* policy is an internal Justice Department matter and that it cannot be asserted by an indicted or convicted defendant as the basis for avoiding federal prosecution.[e] The *Petite* policy does not, in other words, establish a legally enforceable immunity from federal prosecution. Nonetheless, the government normally will refrain from prosecution in such circumstances. If there is a prosecution, it will, on occasion, confess error and seek dismissal for the violation of its own internal operating procedures.

(iii) Questions and Comments. In the infamous Rodney King beating case, four Los Angeles police officers who participated in the 1991 attack on Mr. King (a black motorist who was stopped by police after a high-speed chase and whose brutal beating was secretly videotaped by an eyewitness) were first tried under state law for various assault-related crimes, including assault with a deadly weapon. The police officers were initially acquitted by an all-white jury,[f] touching off riots in portions of Los Angeles which caused more than 40 deaths and millions of dollars in property damage. Later, in a separate federal criminal trial based on the same incident, two of the same police officers were convicted by a multi-racial jury of committing federal civil-rights crimes against Mr. King. See Los Angeles Times Magazine, "Case History: The Strategy, The Fights, The Setbacks," June 27, 1993; Los Angeles Times, "Two Officers Guilty, Two Acquitted," April 18, 1993, p. 1; Los Angeles Times, "U.S. Files Civil Rights Charges Against Four Officers in King Case," August 6, 1992, p. 1; Los Angeles Times, "All Four in King Beating Acquitted; Violence Follows Verdicts," April 30, 1992, p. 1.

The American Civil Liberties Union (ACLU), a well-known organization devoted to the protection of civil rights and liberties, had long opposed the "dual sovereignty" doctrine and argued that successive prosecutions by state and federal authorities were improper, regardless of the Supreme Court's resolution of the constitutional issue in *Bartkus* and *Abbate*. After the acquittal of the police officers in the first Rodney King trial, however,

[d] See, e.g., Rinaldi v. United States, 434 U.S. 22 (1977).

[e] See, e.g., Haley v. United States, 394 F.Supp. 1022 (W.D.Mo.1975).

[f] The jury acquitted the police officers on all but one of the counts charged; with respect to one defendant, and one count, the jury deadlocked 8–4 in favor of acquittal.

the ACLU membership became deeply divided over whether or not the organization should publicly support a second, federal prosecution of the police officers. The national board of the ACLU originally decided to "suspend" its opposition to the "dual sovereignty" doctrine and support the federal prosecution. See Wall Street Journal, "Asides: The ACLU's New Cut," July 20, 1992, p. A14. During the federal trial, however, the national board reversed itself in a close, racially divided vote, and condemned the federal prosecution. See Wall Street Journal, "Split Decision: Verdict in King Case Owes Much to Lessons of State–Court Trial," April 19, 1993, p. A1. Meanwhile, the local Southern California ACLU chapter broke ranks with the national board, and continued to support the federal prosecution. See Los Angeles Daily News, "Opinion: King Beating Trial is Not a Case of Double Jeopardy," April 14, 1993.

In light of what you have learned about multiple state and federal prosecutions, do you see any problems with the exercise of federal criminal jurisdiction in the Rodney King case? Assuming that the "dual sovereignty" doctrine of *Bartkus* and *Abbate* eliminates any possible constitutional objections, do you agree with the discretionary decision by federal prosecutors to subject the defendants to a second criminal trial for the same act or acts?

Note that—because of the aforementioned constitutional limitations on federal power—there is no general federal crime of "assault" that could have been applied to the police officers in the Rodney King case. Rather, the police officers were subject to federal criminal prosecution *only* because the evidence (i.e., the videotape) tended to prove that they acted with the *intent,* or the *conscious objective,* to violate Mr. King's civil rights. Congress acquired the power to criminalize certain civil-rights violations (but *not* all "assaults") through the 13th, 14th, and 15th amendments to the Constitution, which were ratified shortly after the Civil War. Does this information change your view about the propriety of the decision to proceed with a second, federal prosecution in the Rodney King case?

Liparota v. United States

United States Supreme Court, 1985.
471 U.S. 419.

■ JUSTICE BRENNAN delivered the opinion of the Court.

The federal statute governing food stamp fraud provides that "whoever knowingly uses, transfers, acquires, alters, or possesses coupons or authorization cards in any manner not authorized by [the statute] or the regulations" is subject to a fine and imprisonment. 7 U.S.C. § 2024(b).[g] The

---

[g] Violation of this statute is a felony if the value of the coupons or authorization cards is $100 or more. The maximum sentence for a first conviction in such a case is a fine of not more than $10,000 or imprisonment for not more than five years, or both. If the value of the coupons or cards is less than $100, the offense is a misdemeanor with a maximum penalty of a fine of not more

question presented is whether in a prosecution under this provision the government must prove that the defendant knew that he was acting in a manner not authorized by statute or regulations.

I

Petitioner Frank Liparota was the co-owner with his brother of Moon's Sandwich Shop in Chicago, Illinois. He was indicted for acquiring and possessing food stamps in violation of § 2024(b). The Department of Agriculture had not authorized petitioner's restaurant to accept food stamps.[2] At trial, the government proved that petitioner on three occasions purchased food stamps from an undercover Department of Agriculture agent for substantially less than their face value. On the first occasion, the agent informed petitioner that she had $195 worth of food stamps to sell. The agent then accepted petitioner's offer of $150 and consummated the transaction in a back room of the restaurant with petitioner's brother. A similar transaction occurred one week later, in which the agent sold $500 worth of coupons for $350. Approximately one month later, petitioner bought $500 worth of food stamps from the agent for $300.

In submitting the case to the jury, the District Court rejected petitioner's proposed "specific intent" instruction, which would have instructed the jury that the government must prove that "the defendant knowingly did an act which the law forbids, purposely intending to violate the law."[3] Concluding that "[t]his is not a specific intent crime" but rather a "knowledge case," the District Court instead instructed the jury as follows:

> "When the word 'knowingly' is used in these instructions, it means that the defendant realized what he was doing, and was aware of the nature of his conduct, and did not act through ignorance, mistake, or accident. Knowledge may be proved by defendant's conduct and by all the facts and circumstances surrounding the case."

The District Court also instructed that the government had to prove that "the defendant acquired and possessed food stamp coupons for cash in a

than $1,000 and imprisonment for not more than one year, or both.—[Footnote by eds.]

[2] Food stamps are provided by the government to those who meet certain need-related criteria. They generally may be used only to purchase food in retail food stores. If a restaurant receives proper authorization from the Department of Agriculture, it may receive food stamps as payment for meals under certain special circumstances not relevant here.

[3] The instruction proffered by petitioner was drawn from 1 E. Devitt & C. Blackmar, Federal Jury Practice and Instructions § 14.03 (1977). The instruction read in its entirety:

> "The crime charged in this case is a serious crime which requires proof of specific intent before the defendant can be convicted. Specific intent, as the term implies, means more than the general intent to commit the act. To establish specific intent the government must prove that the defendant knowingly did an act which the law forbids, purposely intending to violate the law. Such intent may be determined from all the facts and circumstances surrounding the case."

manner not authorized by federal statute or regulations" and that "the defendant knowingly and wilfully acquired the food stamps." Petitioner objected that this instruction required the jury to find merely that he knew that he was acquiring or possessing food stamps; he argued that the statute should be construed instead to reach only "people who knew that they were acting unlawfully." The judge did not alter or supplement his instructions, and the jury returned a verdict of guilty.

Petitioner appealed his conviction to the Court of Appeals for the Seventh Circuit, arguing that the District Court erred in refusing to instruct the jury that "specific intent" is required in a prosecution under 7 U.S.C. § 2024(b). The Court of Appeals rejected petitioner's arguments. Because this decision conflicted with recent decisions of three other Courts of Appeals, we granted certiorari. We reverse.

II

The controversy between the parties concerns the mental state, if any, that the government must show in proving that petitioner acted "in any manner not authorized by [the statute] or the regulations." The government argues that petitioner violated the statute if he knew that he acquired or possessed food stamps and if in fact that acquisition or possession was in a manner not authorized by statute or regulations. According to the government, no mens rea, or "evil-meaning mind," Morissette v. United States, 342 U.S. 246, 251 (1952), is necessary for conviction. Petitioner claims that the government's interpretation, by dispensing with mens rea, dispenses with the only morally blameworthy element in the definition of the crime. To avoid this allegedly untoward result, he claims that an individual violates the statute if he knows that he has acquired or possessed food stamps and if he also knows that he has done so in an unauthorized manner.[5] Our task is to determine which meaning Congress intended.

The definition of the elements of a criminal offense is entrusted to the legislature, particularly in the case of federal crimes, which are solely creatures of statute.[6] With respect to the element at issue in this case, however, Congress has not explicitly spelled out the mental state required.

[5] The required mental state may of course be different for different elements of a crime. In this case, for instance, both parties agree that petitioner must have known that he acquired and possessed food stamps. They disagree over whether any mental element at all is required with respect to the unauthorized nature of that acquisition or possession.

We have also recognized that the mental element in criminal law encompasses more than the two possibilities of "specific" and "general" intent. The Model Penal Code, for instance, recognizes four mental states—purpose, knowledge, recklessness, and negligence. ALI, Model Penal Code § 2.02. In this case, petitioner argues that with respect to the element at issue, knowledge is required. The government contends that no mental state is required with respect to that element.

[6] Of course, Congress must act within any applicable constitutional constraints in defining criminal offenses. In this case, there is no allegation that the statute would be unconstitutional under either interpretation.

Although Congress certainly intended by use of the word "knowingly" to require *some* mental state with respect to *some* element of the crime defined in § 2024(b), the interpretations proffered by both parties accord with congressional intent to this extent. Beyond this, the words themselves provide little guidance. Either interpretation would accord with ordinary usage.[7] The legislative history of the statute contains nothing that would clarify the congressional purpose on this point.

Absent indication of contrary purpose in the language or legislative history of the statute, we believe that § 2024(b) requires a showing that the defendant knew his conduct to be unauthorized by statute or regulations.[9] "The contention that an injury can amount to a crime only when inflicted by intention is no provincial or transient notion. It is as universal and persistent in mature systems of law as belief in freedom of the human will and a consequent ability and duty of the normal individual to choose between good and evil." *Morissette v. United States*, supra, at 250. Thus, in United States v. United States Gypsum Co., 438 U.S. 422, 438 (1978), we noted that "[c]ertainly far more than the simple omission of the appropriate phrase from the statutory definition is necessary to justify dispensing with an intent requirement" and that criminal offenses requiring no mens rea have a "generally disfavored status." Similarly, in this case, the failure of Congress explicitly and unambiguously to indicate whether mens rea is required does not signal a departure from this background assumption of our criminal law.

This construction is particularly appropriate where, as here, to interpret the statute otherwise would be to criminalize a broad range of

---

[7] One treatise has aptly summed up the ambiguity in an analogous situation:

"Still further difficulty arises from the ambiguity which frequently exists concerning what the words or phrases in question modify. What, for instance, does 'knowingly' modify in a sentence from a ... criminal statute punishing one who 'knowingly sells a security without a permit' from the securities commissioner? To be guilty must the seller of a security without a permit know only that what he is doing constitutes a sale, or must he also know that the thing he sells is a security, or must he also know that he has no permit to sell the security he sells? As a matter of grammar the statute is ambiguous; it is not at all clear how far down the sentence the word 'knowingly' is intended to travel—whether it modifies 'sells,' or 'sells a security' or 'sells a security without a permit.' "

W. LaFave & A. Scott, Criminal Law 193 (1972).

[9] The dissent repeatedly claims that our holding today creates a defense of "mistake of law." Our holding today no more creates a "mistake of law" defense than does a statute making knowing receipt of stolen goods unlawful. In both cases, there is a legal element in the definition of the offense. In the case of a receipt of stolen goods statute, the legal element is that the goods were stolen; in this case, the legal element is that the "use, transfer, acquisition," etc., were in a manner not authorized by statute or regulations. It is not a defense to a charge of receipt of stolen goods that one did not know that such receipt was illegal, and it is not a defense to a charge of a § 2024(b) violation that one did not know that possessing food stamps in a manner unauthorized by statute or regulations was illegal. It is, however, a defense to a charge of knowing receipt of stolen goods that one did not know that the goods were stolen, just as it is a defense to a charge of a § 2024(b) violation that one did not know that one's possession was unauthorized.

apparently innocent conduct. For instance, § 2024(b) declares it criminal to use, transfer, acquire, alter, or possess food stamps in any manner not authorized by statute or regulations. The statute provides further that "[c]oupons issued to eligible households shall be used by them only to purchase food in retail food stores which have been approved for participation in the food stamp program *at prices prevailing in such stores*." 7 U.S.C. § 2016(b)(emphasis added). This seems to be the only authorized use. A strict reading of the statute with no knowledge of illegality requirement would thus render criminal a food stamp recipient who, for example, used stamps to purchase food from a store that, unknown to him, charged higher than normal prices to food stamp program participants. Such a reading would also render criminal a nonrecipient of food stamps who "possessed" stamps because he was mistakenly sent them through the mail due to administrative error, "altered" them by tearing them up, and "transferred" them by throwing them away. Of course, Congress could have intended that this broad range of conduct be made illegal, perhaps with the understanding that prosecutors would exercise their discretion to avoid such harsh results. However, given the paucity of material suggesting that Congress did so intend, we are reluctant to adopt such a sweeping interpretation.

In addition, requiring mens rea is in keeping with our long-standing recognition of the principle that "ambiguity concerning the ambit of criminal statutes should be resolved in favor of lenity." Rewis v. United States, 401 U.S. 808, 812 (1971). Application of the rule of lenity ensures that criminal statutes will provide fair warning concerning conduct rendered illegal and strikes the appropriate balance between the legislature, the prosecutor, and the court in defining criminal liability. Although the rule of lenity is not to be applied where to do so would conflict with the implied or expressed intent of Congress, it provides a time-honored interpretive guideline when the congressional purpose is unclear. In the instant case, the rule directly supports petitioner's contention that the government must prove knowledge of illegality to convict him under § 2024(b).

The government argues, however, that a comparison between § 2024(b) and its companion, § 2024(c), demonstrates a congressional purpose not to require proof of the defendant's knowledge of illegality in a § 2024(b) prosecution. Section 2024(c) is directed primarily at stores authorized to accept food stamps from program participants. It provides that "[w]hoever presents, or causes to be presented, coupons for payment or redemption ... *knowing* the same to have been received, transferred, or used in any manner in violation of [the statute] or the regulations" is subject to fine and imprisonment (emphasis added). The government contrasts this language with that of § 2024(b), in which the word "knowingly" is placed differently: "whoever *knowingly* uses, transfers ..." (emphasis added). Since § 2024(c) undeniably requires a knowledge of illegality, the suggested inference is that the difference in wording and structure between the two sections indicates that § 2024(b) does not.

The government urges that this distinction between the mental state required for a § 2024(c) violation and that required for a § 2024(b) violation is a sensible one. Absent a requirement of mens rea, a grocer presenting food stamps for payment might be criminally liable under § 2024(c) even if his customer or employees have illegally procured or transferred the stamps without the grocer's knowledge. Requiring knowledge of illegality in a § 2024(c) prosecution is allegedly necessary to avoid this kind of vicarious, and non-fault-based, criminal liability. Since the offense defined in § 2024(b)—using, transferring, acquiring, altering, or possessing food stamps in an unauthorized manner—does not involve this possibility of vicarious liability, argues the government, Congress had no reason to impose a similar knowledge of illegality requirement in that section.

We do not find this argument persuasive.... Grocers are participants in the food stamp program who have had the benefit of an extensive informational campaign concerning the authorized use and handling of food stamps. Yet the government would have to prove knowledge of illegality when prosecuting such grocers, while it would have no such burden when prosecuting third parties who may well have had no opportunity to acquaint themselves with the rules governing food stamps. It is not immediately obvious that Congress would have been so concerned about imposing strict liability on grocers, while it had no similar concerns about imposing strict liability on nonparticipants in the program. Our point once again is not that Congress could not have chosen to enact a statute along these lines, for there are no doubt policy arguments on both sides of the question as to whether such a statute would have been desirable. Rather, we conclude that the policy underlying such a construction is neither so obvious nor so compelling that we must assume, in the absence of any discussion of this issue in the legislative history, that Congress *did* enact such a statute.

The government advances two additional arguments in support of its reading of the statute. First, the government contends that this Court's decision last Term in United States v. Yermian, 468 U.S. 63 (1984), supports its interpretation. *Yermian* involved a prosecution for violation of the federal false statement statute, 18 U.S.C. § 1001.[14] All parties agreed that the statute required proof at least that the defendant "knowingly and willfully" made a false statement. Thus, unlike the instant case, all parties in *Yermian* agreed that the government had to prove the defendant's mens rea.[15] The controversy in *Yermian* centered on whether the government

---

[14] The statute provides:

"Whoever, in any matter within the jurisdiction of any department or agency of the United States knowingly and willfully ... makes any false ... statements or representations ... shall be fined not more than $10,000 or imprisoned not more than five years, or both."

[15] The fact that both parties in *Yermian* agreed that the government had to prove that the defendant had "knowingly and willfully" made a false statement does not of course indicate that the parties agreed on the mental state applicable to other elements of the offense. What it does mean is that in *Yermian*, unlike this case, all parties agreed that an

also had to prove that the defendant knew that the false statement was made in a matter within the jurisdiction of a federal agency. With respect to this element, although the Court held that the government did not have to prove actual knowledge of federal agency jurisdiction, the Court explicitly reserved the question whether some culpability was necessary with respect even to the jurisdictional element. 468 U.S., at 75, n.14. In contrast, the government in the instant case argues that *no* mens rea is required with respect to any element of the crime. Finally, *Yermian* found that the statutory language was unambiguous and that the legislative history supported its interpretation. The statute at issue in this case differs in both respects.

Second, the government contends that the § 2024(b) offense is a "public welfare" offense, which the Court defined in *United States v. Morissette*, 342 U.S., at 252–53, to "depend on no mental element but consist only of forbidden acts or omissions." Yet the offense at issue here differs substantially from those "public welfare offenses" we have previously recognized. In most previous instances, Congress has rendered criminal a type of conduct that a reasonable person should know is subject to stringent public regulation and may seriously threaten the community's health or safety. Thus, in United States v. Freed, 401 U.S. 601 (1971), we examined the federal statute making it illegal to receive or possess an unregistered firearm. In holding that the government did not have to prove that the recipient of unregistered hand grenades knew that they were unregistered, we noted that "one would hardly be surprised to learn that possession of hand grenades is not an innocent act." See also United States v. International Minerals & Chemical Corp., 402 U.S. 558, 564–65 (1971). Similarly, in United States v. Dotterweich, 320 U.S. 277, 284 (1943), the Court held that a corporate officer could violate the Food and Drug Act when his firm shipped adulterated and misbranded drugs, even "though consciousness of wrongdoing be totally wanting." See also United States v. Balint, 258 U.S. 250 (1922). The distinctions between these cases and the instant case are clear. A food stamp can hardly be compared to a hand grenade, nor can the unauthorized acquisition or possession of food stamps be compared to the selling of adulterated drugs.

III

We hold that in a prosecution for violation of § 2024(b), the government must prove that the defendant knew that his acquisition or possession of food stamps was in a manner unauthorized by statute or regulations.[16] This holding does not put an unduly heavy burden on the government in prosecuting violators of § 2024(b). To prove that petitioner

"evil-meaning mind" was required with respect at least to one element of the crime.

[16] Although we agree with petitioner concerning his interpretation of the statute, we express no opinion on the "specific intent" instruction he tendered, see n.2, supra. This instruction has been criticized as too general and potentially misleading, see United States v. Arambasich, 597 F.2d 609, 613 (7th Cir.1979). A more useful instruction might relate specifically to the mental state required under § 2024(b) and eschew use of difficult legal concepts like "specific intent" and "general intent."

knew that his acquisition or possession of food stamps was unauthorized, for example, the government need not show that he had knowledge of specific regulations governing food stamp acquisition or possession. Nor must the government introduce any extraordinary evidence that would conclusively demonstrate petitioner's state of mind. Rather, as in any other criminal prosecution requiring mens rea, the government may prove by reference to facts and circumstances surrounding the case that petitioner knew that his conduct was unauthorized or illegal.[17]

Reversed.

JUSTICE POWELL took no part in the consideration or decision of this case.

JUSTICE WHITE, with whom THE CHIEF JUSTICE joins, dissenting.

Forsaking reliance on either the language or the history of § 2024(b), the majority bases its result on the absence of an explicit rejection of the general principle that criminal liability requires not only an actus reus, but a mens rea. In my view, the result below is in fact supported by the statute's language and its history, and it is the majority that has ignored general principles of criminal liability.

I

The Court views the statutory problem here as being how far down the sentence the term "knowingly" travels. See n.7. Accepting for the moment that if "knowingly" does extend to the "in any manner" language today's holding would be correct—a position with which I take issue below—I doubt that it gets that far. The "in any manner" language is separated from the litany of verbs to which "knowingly" is directly connected by the intervening nouns. We considered an identically phrased statute last Term in *United States v. Yermian*. We found that under the "most natural reading" of the statute, "knowingly and willfully" applied only to the making of false ... statements and not to the fact of jurisdiction. By the same token, the "most natural reading" of § 2024(b) is that knowingly modifies only the verbs to which it is attached.[1]

---

[17] In this case, for instance, the government introduced evidence that petitioner bought food stamps at a substantial discount from face value and that he conducted part of the transaction in a back room of his restaurant to avoid the presence of the other patrons. Moreover, the government asserts that food stamps themselves are stamped "nontransferable." A jury could have inferred from this evidence that petitioner knew that his acquisition and possession of the stamps was unauthorized.

[1] The majority's efforts to distinguish *Yermian* are unavailing. First, it points out that under the statute at issue there, the prosecution had to establish some mens rea because it had to show a knowing falsehood. However, as the majority itself points out elsewhere, see n.5, different mental states can apply to different elements of an offense. The fact that in *Yermian* mens rea had to be proved as to the first element was irrelevant to the Court's holding that it did not with regard to the second. There is no reason to read this statute differently. Second, the majority states that the language in *Yermian* was "unambiguous." Since it is identical, the language at issue in this case can be no less so. Finally, the majority notes that the Court in *Yermian* did not decide whether the prosecution might have to prove that the defendant "should have known" that his

In any event, I think that the premise of this approach is mistaken. Even accepting that "knowingly" does extend through the sentence, or at least that we should read § 2024(b) as if it does, the statute does not mean what the Court says it does. Rather, it requires only that the defendant be aware of the relevant aspects of his conduct. A requirement that the defendant know that he is acting in a particular manner, coupled with the fact that that manner is forbidden, does not establish a defense of ignorance of the law. It creates only a defense of ignorance or mistake of fact. Knowingly to do something that is unauthorized by law is not the same as doing something knowing that it is unauthorized by law.

This point is demonstrated by the hypothetical statute referred to by the majority, which punishes one who "knowingly sells a security without a permit." See n.7. Even if "knowingly" does reach "without a permit," I would think that a defendant who knew that he did not have a permit though not that a permit was required, could be convicted.

Section 2024(b) is an identical statute, except that instead of detailing the various legal requirements, it incorporates them by proscribing use of coupons "in any manner not authorized" by law. This shorthand approach to drafting does not transform knowledge of illegality into an element of the crime. As written, § 2024(b) is substantively no different than if it had been broken down into a collection of specific provisions making crimes of particular improper uses. For example, food stamps cannot be used to purchase tobacco. The statute might have said, inter alia, that anyone "who knowingly uses coupons to purchase cigarettes" commits a crime. Under no plausible reading could a defendant then be acquitted because he did not know cigarettes are not "eligible food." But in fact, that is exactly what § 2024(b) does say, it just does not write it out longhand.

The Court's opinion provides another illustration of the general point: someone who used food stamps to purchase groceries at inflated prices without realizing he was overcharged. I agree that such a person may not be convicted, but not for the reason given by the majority. The purchaser did not "knowingly" use the stamps in the proscribed manner, for he was unaware of the circumstances of the transaction that made it illegal.

The majority and I would part company in result as well as rationale if the purchaser knew he was charged higher than normal prices but not that overcharging is prohibited. In such a case, he would have been aware of the nature of his actions, and therefore the purchase would have been "knowing." I would hold that such a mental state satisfies the statute. Under the Court's holding, as I understand it, that person could not be convicted because he did not know that his conduct was illegal.[3]

statements were within the agency's jurisdiction. However, that passing statement was irrelevant to the interpretation of the statute's language the Court did undertake.

[3] The appropriate prosecutorial target in such a situation would of course be the seller rather than the purchaser. I have no doubt that every prosecutor in the country would agree. The discussion of this hypothetical is wholly academic.

For similar reasons, I am unmoved by the spectre of criminal liability for someone

Much has been made of the comparison between § 2024(b) and § 2024(c). The government ... argues that the express requirement of knowing illegality in subsection (c) supports an inference that the absence of such a provision in subsection (b) was intentional. ... I view most of this discussion as beside the point. The government's premise seems to me mistaken. Subsection (c) does not impose a requirement of knowing illegality. The provision is much like statutes that forbid the receipt or sale of stolen goods. Just as those statutes generally require knowledge that the goods were stolen, so § 2024(c) requires knowledge of the past impropriety. But receipt of stolen goods statutes do not require that the defendant know that receipt itself is illegal, and similarly § 2024(c) plainly does not require that the defendant know that it is illegal to present coupons that have been improperly used in the past. It is not inconceivable that someone presenting such coupons—again, like someone buying stolen goods—would think that his conduct was above board despite the preceding illegality. But that belief, however sincere, would not be a defense. In short, because § 2024(c) does not require that the defendant know that the conduct for which he is being prosecuted was illegal, it does not create an ignorance of the law defense.[5]

I therefore cannot draw the government's suggested inference. The two provisions are nonetheless fruitfully compared. What matters is not their difference, but their similarity. Neither contains any indication that "knowledge of the law defining the offense [is] an element of the offense." See ALI, Model Penal Code § 2.02, Comment p. 131 (Tent. Draft No. 4, 1955). A requirement of knowing illegality should not be read into either provision....

II

The broad principles of the Court's opinion are easy to live with in a case such as this. But the application of its reasoning might not always be so benign. For example, § 2024(b) is little different from the basic federal prohibition on the manufacture and distribution of controlled substances. 21 U.S.C. § 841(a) provides:

"Except as authorized by this subchapter, it shall be unlawful for any person knowingly or intentionally—

who is mistakenly mailed food stamps and throws them out, and do not think the hypothetical offers much of a guide to congressional intent. We should proceed on the assumption that Congress had in mind the run-of-the-mill situation, not its most bizarre mutation. Arguments that presume wildly unreasonable conduct by government officials are by their nature unconvincing, and reliance on them is likely to do more harm than good. No rule, including that adopted by the Court today, is immune from such contrived defects.

[5] Similarly, it is a valid defense to a charge of theft that the defendant thought the property legally belonged to him, even if that belief is incorrect. But this is not because ignorance of the law is an excuse. Rather, "the legal element involved is simply an aspect of the attendant circumstances, with respect to which knowledge ... is required for culpability. ... The law involved is not the law defining the offense; it is some other legal rule that characterizes the attendant circumstances that are material to the offense." ALI, Model Penal Code § 2.02, Comment p. 131 (Tent. Draft No. 4, 1955).

"(1) to manufacture, distribute, or dispense, or possess with intent to manufacture, distribute or dispense, a controlled substance...."

I am sure that the members of the majority would agree that a defendant charged under this provision could not defend on the ground that he did not realize his manufacture was unauthorized or that the particular substance was controlled. See United States v. Balint, 258 U.S. 250 (1922). On the other hand, it would be a defense if he could prove he thought the substance was something other than what it was. By the same token, I think, someone in petitioner's position should not be heard to say that he did not know his purchase of food stamps was unauthorized, though he may certainly argue that he did not know he was buying food stamps. I would not stretch the term "knowingly" to require awareness of the absence of statutory authority in either of these provisions.

These provisions might be distinguished because of the different placements of the "except as authorized" and the "in any manner not authorized" clauses in the sentences. However, nothing in the majority's opinion indicates that this difference is relevant. Indeed, the logic of the Court's opinion would require knowledge of illegality for conviction under any statute making it a crime to do something "in any manner not authorized by law" or "unlawfully." I suspect that if a case rises in the future where such a result is unacceptable, the Court will manage to distinguish today's decision. But I will be interested to see how it does so.

III

In relying on the "background assumption of our criminal law" that mens rea is required, the Court ignores the equally well-founded assumption that ignorance of the law is no excuse. It is "the conventional position that knowledge of the existence, meaning or application of the law determining the elements of an offense is not an element of that offense...." ALI, Model Penal Code § 2.02, Comment, p. 130 (Tent. Draft No. 4, 1955).

This Court's prior cases indicate that a statutory requirement of a "knowing violation" does not supersede this principle. For example, under the statute at issue in United States v. International Minerals & Chemical Corp., 402 U.S. 558 (1971), the Interstate Commerce Commission was authorized to promulgate regulations regarding the transportation of corrosive liquids, and it was a crime to "knowingly violat[e] any such regulation." Viewing the word "regulations" as "a shorthand designation for specific acts or omissions which violate the act," we adhered to the traditional rule that ignorance of the law is not a defense. The violation had to be "knowing" in that the defendant had to know that he was transporting corrosive liquids and not, for example, merely water. But there was no requirement that he be aware that he was violating a particular regulation. Similarly, in this case the phrase "in any manner not authorized by" the statute or regulations is a shorthand incorporation of a variety of legal requirements. To be convicted, a defendant must have been aware of what he was doing, but not that it was illegal.

[T]he statutory language [in *International Minerals*] lent itself to the approach adopted today if anything more readily than does § 2024(b).[6] I would read § 2024(b) like [that statute], to require awareness of only the relevant aspects of one's conduct rendering it illegal, not the fact of illegality. This reading does not abandon the "background assumption" of mens rea by creating a strict liability offense, and is consistent with the equally important background assumption that ignorance of the law is not a defense.

IV

I wholly agree that "[t]he contention that an injury can amount to a crime only when inflicted by intention is no provincial or transient notion." Morissette v. United States, 342 U.S. 246, 250 (1952). But the holding of the court below is not at all inconsistent with that longstanding and important principle. Petitioner's conduct was intentional; the jury found that petitioner "realized what he was doing, and was aware of the nature of his conduct, and did not act through ignorance, mistake, or accident" (trial court's instructions). Whether he knew which regulation he violated is beside the point.

NOTES ON *LIPAROTA* v. *UNITED STATES*

1. Interpreting Federal Criminal Statutes. It is not surprising that the federal government would choose to protect the integrity of its food stamp program by criminal legislation. Note that it did so not by integrating the prohibition with other fraud provisions in title 18, but by adding a provision specifically related to food stamp fraud in title 7, the repository of the statutes establishing the food stamp program. This is a fairly typical congressional approach to protection of the interests involved in a federal program. It has resulted in the location of literally hundreds of federal criminal statutes outside of title 18.

Liparota presents an intriguing problem of statutory interpretation that illustrates several features of the judiciary's approach to federal crimes. Notice first the common law origins of the language in the instruction offered by the defendant (footnote 3) and the response by the District Court. Justice Brennan's reference to the "background assumption of our criminal law" that mens rea is normally assumed to be a part of

[6] The Court distinguishes [*International Minerals*] as [a] "public welfare offense" . . . involving inherently dangerous articles of commerce whose users should have assumed were subject to regulation. But see United States v. Freed, 401 U.S., at 612 (Brennan, J., concurring in judgment). Apart from the fact that a reasonable person would also assume food stamps are heavily regulated and not subject to sale and exchange, this distinction is not related to the actual holdings in those cases. The . . . concurrence in *Freed* [did] not discuss this consideration. And the Court's references to the dangerousness of the goods in *International Minerals* were directed to possible due process challenges to convictions without notice of criminality. As today's majority acknowledges, n.6, there is no constitutional defect with the holding of the court below. The only issue here is one of congressional intent.

a federal crime also reflects a fidelity to common law principles. Note too, though, the reference to the Model Penal Code in footnote 5. Increasingly in federal courts, as well as in state courts that have not enacted comprehensive revisions of their penal codes, the Model Penal Code culpability structure is exerting an influence on the vocabulary and approach to problems of culpability.

On the merits, the question of "how far down the sentence the word 'knowingly' is intended to travel" (see footnote 7) is a problem encountered in many statutes drafted in the common law tradition. Once this issue is resolved, however, the difficult question in *Liparota* emerges: what the word "knowingly" means in this context. Should it mean, as White contends, that the defendant must "know that he is acting in a particular manner, coupled with the fact that that manner is forbidden"? Or should it mean, as Brennan would have it, that the defendant must know "that he was acting in a manner not authorized by statute or regulations"? Does the majority give Liparota an ignorance of the law defense? If so, is this a context in which such a defense is warranted?

The overriding point, in any event, is that the federal criminal law, while presenting a number of unique problems on which the remainder of these materials will largely focus, yields many questions that are not so very different from those that would be encountered in a typical state that has not adopted a Model Penal Code approach to its criminal law. It is important to understand this point as a background assumption of the federal criminal law.

2. Recent Supreme Court Mens Rea Decisions. Mens rea issues like the one addressed in *Liparota* also arise in a variety of other federal statutory contexts, and continue to plague the Court. In Cheek v. United States, 498 U.S. 192 (1991), for example, the defendant was charged with nine counts of tax-related federal crimes; six alleged violations of 26 U.S.C. § 7201, which provides that any person "who willfully attempts in any manner to evade or defeat any tax imposed by this title or the payment thereof shall be guilty of a felony," while the other three alleged violations of 26 U.S.C. § 7203, which provides that "[a]ny person required under this title ... or by regulations made under authority thereof to make a return ... who willfully fails to ... make such return" shall be guilty of a misdemeanor. Cheek, a professional airline pilot, admitted that he had not filed tax returns for the years in question.[h] He claimed, however, that his actions were prompted by the advice he had received at seminars held by a group (which included several lawyers) that believed the federal tax laws were unconstitutional as applied to wages received from a private employer. He claimed that this advice, along with his own study of the law, instilled in him a sincere belief that (1) wages were not "income" within the meaning of the Internal Revenue Code, (2) he was not a "taxpayer" within the meaning of the Code, and (3) the tax laws were being unconstitutional-

---

[h] Cheek also admitted claiming up to 60 withholding allowances, which resulted in a substantial under-withholding of federal income tax from his wages.

ly enforced and, therefore, his actions were lawful.[i] The Supreme Court reversed Cheek's convictions and remanded for a new trial, explaining:

> "Willfulness, as construed by our prior decisions in criminal tax cases, requires the government to prove that the law imposed a duty on the defendant, that the defendant knew of this duty, and that he voluntarily and intentionally violated that duty. ... In this case, if Cheek asserted that he truly believed that the Internal Revenue Code did not purport to treat wages as income, and the jury believed him, the government would not have carried its burden to prove willfulness, however unreasonable a court might deem such a belief. Of course, in deciding whether to credit Cheek's good-faith belief claim, the jury would be free to consider any admissible evidence from any source showing that Cheek was aware of his duty to file a return and to treat wages as income...." Id., at 201–02.

The Court also cautioned, however:

> "Claims that some of the provisions of the tax code are unconstitutional are submissions of a different order. They do not arise from innocent mistakes caused by the complexity of the Internal Revenue Code. Rather, they reveal full knowledge of the provisions at issue and a studied conclusion, however wrong, that those provisions are invalid and unenforceable.... We thus hold that in a case like this, a defendant's views about the validity of the tax statutes are irrelevant to the issue of willfulness and need not be heard by the jury, and, if they are, an instruction to disregard them would be proper. For this purpose, it makes no difference whether the claims of invalidity are frivolous or have substance." Id., at 205–06.

See also Staples v. United States, 511 U.S. 600, 114 S.Ct. 1793 (1994)(conviction under National Firearms Act, 26 U.S.C. § 5861(d), for possessing unregistered "machine gun," requires that defendant knew his rifle had characteristics that brought it within statutory definition of "machine gun"); Ratzlaf v. United States, 510 U.S. 135, 114 S.Ct. 655 (1994)(conviction under 31 U.S.C. § 5322(a) for "willfully violating" statute, 31 U.S.C. § 5324, that prohibits structuring cash transactions exceeding $10,000 for the purpose of avoiding requirement of filing report with Secretary of the Treasury, requires that defendant knew about anti-structuring provision); Money Laundering Suppression Act of 1994, P.L. No. 103–325 (amendment to 31 U.S.C. § 5324 designed to overrule *Ratzlaf* by allowing conviction based on defendant's knowledge of reporting requirement, rather than on defendant's knowledge of anti-structuring provision).

---

[i] Cheek apparently adhered to these beliefs despite the fact that he had been involved in four unsuccessful civil lawsuits challenging various aspects of the federal income tax system, and had also attended at least two previous criminal trials of persons who were charged with similar tax offenses.

SUBSECTION B: THE SPECIAL MARITIME AND TERRITORIAL JURISDICTION

INTRODUCTORY NOTES ON THE SPECIAL MARITIME AND TERRITORIAL JURISDICTION

1. Background. The "special maritime and territorial jurisdiction" of the United States consists of geographic areas as to which, by and large, the criminal laws of the various states cannot operate directly. Typical places that might fall within this designation are national parks, post offices, military reservations, airports, and the like. Generally speaking, if there is no federal law of crimes in such areas, there will be no criminal law at all. State law is either preempted by superior federal authority or nonexistent because the area in question falls within no state. As a matter of terminology, such places are often referred to as "federal enclaves."

The scope of the special maritime and territorial jurisdiction of the United States is defined in 18 U.S.C. § 7, which provides:

"The term 'special maritime and territorial jurisdiction of the United States', as used in this title, includes:

"(1) The high seas, any other waters within the admiralty and maritime jurisdiction of the United States and out of the jurisdiction of any particular State, and any vessel belonging in whole or in part to the United States or any citizen thereof, or to any corporation created by or under the laws of the United States, or of any State, Territory, District, or possession thereof, when such vessel is within the admiralty and maritime jurisdiction of the United States and out of the jurisdiction of any particular State.

"(2) Any vessel registered, licensed, or enrolled under the laws of the United States, and being on a voyage upon the waters of any of the Great Lakes, or any of the waters connecting them, or upon the St. Lawrence River where the same constitutes the International Boundary Line.

"(3) Any lands reserved or acquired for the use of the United States, and under the exclusive or concurrent jurisdiction thereof, or any place purchased or otherwise acquired by the United States by consent of the legislature of the State in which the same shall be, for the erection of a fort, magazine, arsenal, dockyard, or other needful building.

"(4) Any island, rock, or key containing deposits of guano, which may, at the discretion of the President, be considered as appertaining to the United States.

"(5) Any aircraft belonging in whole or in part to the United States, or any citizen thereof, or to any corporation created by or under the laws of the United States, or any State, Territory, district, or possession thereof, while such aircraft is in flight over the high seas, or over any other waters within the admiralty and maritime jurisdiction of the United States and out of the jurisdiction of any particular State.

"(6) Any vehicle used or designed for flight or navigation in space and on the registry of the United States pursuant to the Treaty on Principles Governing the Activities of States in the Exploration and Use of Outer Space, Including the Moon and Other Celestial Bodies and the Convention on Registration of Objects Launched into Outer Space, while that vehicle is in flight, which is from the moment when all external doors are closed on Earth following embarkation until the moment when one such door is opened on Earth for disembarkation or in the case of a forced landing, until the competent authorities take over the responsibility for the vehicle and for persons and property aboard.

"(7) Any place outside the jurisdiction of any nation with respect to an offense by or against a national of the United States.

"(8) To the extent permitted by international law, any foreign vessel during a voyage having a scheduled departure from or arrival in the United States with respect to an offense committed by or against a national of the United States."

2. Specific Offenses. Over the years Congress has enacted a number of specific criminal offenses that apply only to the special maritime and territorial jurisdiction. For example, 18 U.S.C. §§ 1111 and 1112 define murder and manslaughter in terms reminiscent of many early American statutes on the subject. Both statutes are specifically confined to offenses that occur "[w]ithin the special maritime and territorial jurisdiction of the United States." Section 113 covers assault with intent to commit murder (20–year maximum), as well as a range of other assaults, again all confined to the special maritime and territorial jurisdiction. Section 1113 applies to attempted murder and manslaughter[a] (three-year maximum) in a federal enclave.[b] In 1986, Congress enacted a comprehensive range of sexual

---

[a] Can there be such an offense as attempted manslaughter?

[b] Perhaps surprisingly, there is no general federal statute dealing with attempts. There are, instead, specific attempt statutes scattered throughout the federal code, of which § 1113 is an illustration. Additionally, Congress often includes attempts in the definition of a substantive offense. For example, 18 U.S.C. § 1951 (the Hobbs Act) covers one who "obstructs, delays, or affects commerce . . . by robbery or extortion or attempts or conspires so to do."

The result of this piecemeal approach to attempts is that there is no unified law of attempt in the federal courts and, in particular, no unified approach to the penalty for attempt. The Hobbs Act, for example, punishes attempts at the same level (20–year maximum) as the completed offense, whereas assault with intent to murder and attempted murder are punished significantly less severely than murder. While particular disparities such as these might be rationalized, the scattering of attempt crimes throughout the federal code prevents the implementation of any comprehensive policy.

Conspiracy offenses, incidentally, are treated only slightly differently. There is a general federal conspiracy offense. 18 U.S.C.

abuse statutes (18 U.S.C. §§ 2241–45) applicable to persons who commit those offenses "in the special maritime and territorial jurisdiction of the United States or in a Federal prison." Among the other offenses that apply to federal enclaves are arson (18 U.S.C. § 81), kidnaping (18 U.S.C. § 1201), malicious mischief (18 U.S.C. § 1363), receiving stolen property (18 U.S.C. § 662), robbery (18 U.S.C. § 2111), and theft (18 U.S.C. § 661).

3. The Assimilative Crimes Act. Congress has not, however, enacted a comprehensive criminal code for federal enclaves. There are gaps in coverage—substantial areas of criminal behavior that would not be punished if the list of specific offenses contained in the federal code were the exclusive bases for federal prosecution. Congress foresaw this problem as early as 1825, when it enacted the first Assimilative Crimes Act. Successor provisions have been in force since that time. Today, 18 U.S.C. § 13(a) provides:

> "Whoever within or upon any of the places now existing or hereafter reserved or acquired as provided in section 7 of this title, is guilty of any act or omission which, although not made punishable by any enactment of Congress, would be punishable if committed or omitted within the jurisdiction of the State, Territory, Possession, or District in which such place is situated, by the laws thereof in force at the time of such act or omission, shall be guilty of a like offense and subject to a like punishment."[c]

The next two cases and accompanying notes deal with the interpretation and application of this provision.

Williams v. United States

Supreme Court of the United States, 1946.
327 U.S. 711.

■ Justice Burton delivered the opinion of the Court.

This case turns upon the applicability of the Assimilative Crimes Act, § 289 of the Criminal Code, 18 U.S.C. § 468,[d] which reads:

> "Whoever, within the territorial limits of any State, organized Territory, or district, but within or upon any of the places now

§ 371. But there are also specific conspiracy offenses scattered throughout the federal code, as well as conspiracies covered (as in the Hobbs Act quoted above) in particular substantive definitions. There is again, therefore, the same potential for inconsistency of penalty and definition that exists with respect to attempt.

c Subsection (b) of 18 U.S.C. § 13, added in 1988, contains a special provision treating any "judicial or administrative action . . . for a conviction for operating a motor vehicle under the influence of a drug or alcohol,"

including suspension of driving privileges, as "punishment" for purposes of subsection (a). Subsection (b) also authorizes the imposition of additional fines and terms of imprisonment if a minor (other than the defendant) was present in the motor vehicle at the time of the offense, and if the relevant state law does not already provide for such added punishment.

d The present section numbers in title 18 were assigned in 1948. The reference here is to the pre–1948 counterpart to 18 U.S.C. § 13.—[Footnote by eds.]

existing or hereafter reserved or acquired, described in section 272 of the Criminal Code (18 U.S.C. § 451),[1] shall do or omit the doing of any act or thing which is not made penal by any laws of Congress, but which if committed or omitted within the jurisdiction of the State, Territory, or district in which such place is situated, by the laws thereof in force on February 1, 1940, and remaining in force at the time of the doing or omitting the doing of such act or thing, would be penal, shall be deemed guilty of a like offense and be subject to a like punishment.''

The petitioner, a married white man, was convicted in the District Court of the United States for the District of Arizona, of having had sexual intercourse in 1943, within the Colorado River Indian Reservation in Arizona, with an unmarried Indian girl who was then over 16, but under 18 years of age. There was no charge or evidence of use of force by the petitioner or of lack of consent by the girl. The Circuit Court of Appeals affirmed the judgment by a divided court. We granted certiorari ... because of the importance of the case in interpreting the Assimilative Crimes Act.

It is not disputed that this Indian reservation is "reserved or acquired for the use of the United States, and under the exclusive or concurrent jurisdiction thereof,"[2] or that it is "Indian country" within the meaning of Rev. Stat. § 2145.[3] This means that many sections of the federal criminal code apply to the reservation, including not only the Assimilative Crimes Act, but also those making penal the offenses of rape,[4] assault with intent to commit rape,[5] having carnal knowledge of a girl,[6] adultery[7] and fornica-

---

[1] "**Sec. 272.** The crimes and offenses defined in this chapter [§§ 272–289, 18 U.S.C. §§ 451–468] shall be punished as herein prescribed:

"Third. *When committed within or on any lands reserved or acquired for the use of the United States, and under the exclusive or concurrent jurisdiction thereof*, or any place purchased or otherwise acquired by the United States by consent of the legislature of the State in which the same shall be, for the erection of a fort, magazine, arsenal, dockyard, or other needful building." 18 U.S.C. § 451 (Italics supplied).

[2] See note 1.

[3] "Except as to [certain crimes not material here] the general laws of the United States as to the punishment of crimes committed in any place within the sole and exclusive jurisdiction of the United States, ... shall extend to the Indian country." Rev. Stat. § 2145, 25 U.S.C. § 217.

[4] "Whoever shall commit the crime of rape shall suffer death." Criminal Code § 278, 18 U.S.C. § 457.

[5] "Whoever shall assault another with intent to commit ... rape, shall be imprisoned not more than twenty years. ..." Criminal Code § 276, 18 U.S.C. § 455.

[6] "Whoever shall carnally and unlawfully know any female under the age of sixteen years, or shall be accessory to such carnal and unlawful knowledge before the fact, shall, for a first offense, be imprisoned not more than fifteen years, and for a subsequent offense be imprisoned not more than thirty years." Criminal Code § 279, 18 U.S.C. § 458.

[7] " ... the offenses defined in this chapter [§§ 311–322, 18 U.S.C. §§ 511–522] shall be punished as hereinafter provided, when committed within any Territory or District, or within or upon any place within the exclusive jurisdiction of the United States." Criminal Code § 311, 18 U.S.C. § 511.

"Whoever shall commit adultery shall be imprisoned not more than three years; ... and when such act is committed between a married man and a woman who is unmarried,

tion.[8]

While the laws and courts of the state of Arizona may have jurisdiction over offenses committed on this reservation between persons who are not Indians, the laws and courts of the United States, rather than those of Arizona, have jurisdiction over offenses committed there, as in this case, by one who is not an Indian against one who is an Indian.

The conviction cannot be sustained under the federal definitions of rape or assault with intent to rape, because the federal crime of rape carries with it the requirement of proof of the use of force by the offender and of an absence of consent by the victim. Neither of these elements was charged or proved here. The federal crime of having carnal knowledge of a girl requires proof that she was under 16 years of age at the time of the offense, whereas here the indictment charged merely that she was under 18 and the proof showed that she was between 16 and 18. While the indictment did not state whether or not the petitioner was an Indian or whether or not he was married, the undisputed evidence showed that he was a married white man.

However, the offense charged comes within the statutory definition of "rape" in § 43–4901 of the Arizona Code.[11] That section expands the crime of "statutory rape" so as to include sexual intercourse with a girl under 18 instead of merely with a girl under 16. Accordingly, the question here is whether or not the Assimilative Crimes Act makes this section

the man shall be deemed guilty of adultery." Criminal Code § 316, 18 U.S.C. § 516.

[8] "If any unmarried man or woman commits fornication, each shall be fined not more than one hundred dollars, or imprisoned not more than six months." Criminal Code § 318, 18 U.S.C. § 518.

[11] Arizona's definition of rape and the punishment that Arizona prescribes for its commission differ from those relating either to rape or carnal knowledge under the Federal Criminal Code. These differences well illustrate the confusing variations from the definition of a federal crime and from provisions for its punishment which would have to be considered if indictments were permitted under the Assimilative Crimes Act for every act committed within a federal enclave and which might come within a state's enlargement of the federal definition of the same offense. Section 43–4901 of the Arizona Code of 1939 provides:

"Rape is an act of sexual intercourse accomplished with a female, not the wife of the perpetrator, under any of the following circumstances:

"Where the female is under the age of eighteen [18] years;

"Where she is incapable, through lunacy or any other unsoundness of mind, whether temporary or permanent, of giving legal consent;

"Where she resists, but her resistance is overcome by force or violence;

"Where she is prevented from resisting by threats of immediate and great bodily harm, accompanied by apparent power of execution, or by any intoxicating, narcotic, or anaesthetic substance, administered by or with the privity of the accused;

"Where she submits under a belief that the person committing the act is her husband, and this belief is induced by any artifice, pretense or concealment practiced by the accused, with intent to induce such belief . . .

"Rape is punishable by imprisonment in the state prison for life or for any term of years not less than five [5]."

applicable to Indian reservations in Arizona. The question extends not only to the definition of the offense but also to the punishment prescribed. The Arizona Code fixes the punishment for its violation in those instances where violations would not come within § 279 of the Federal Criminal Code. Under those circumstances, on an Indian reservation in Arizona, the statutory punishment, fixed by § 279 of the Federal Criminal Code, for a man, not an Indian, who had carnal knowledge of an Indian girl under 16, would be imprisonment for not more than 15 years for the first offense and not more than 30 years for a subsequent offense, with no minimum sentence specified. On the same facts, except that the girl be between 16 and 18, the punishment, fixed by the Arizona Code, would be imprisonment for life or for any term not less than five years. This would impose a more stringent range of punishment, including the minimum sentence of five years imposed in this case, upon what Congress in its Criminal Code evidently had treated as a lesser offense.

We hold that the Assimilative Crimes Act does not make the Arizona statute applicable in the present case because (1) the precise acts upon which the conviction depends have been made penal by the laws of Congress defining adultery and (2) the offense known to Arizona as that of "statutory rape" has been defined and prohibited by the Federal Criminal Code, and is not to be redefined and enlarged by application to it of the Assimilative Crimes Act. The fact that the definition of this offense as enacted by Congress results in a narrower scope for the offense than that given to it by the state, does not mean that the congressional definition must give way to the state definition. This is especially clear in the present case because the specified acts which would come within the additional scope given to the offense by the state through its postponement of the age of consent of the victim from 16 to 18 years of age, are completely covered by the federal crimes of adultery or fornication. This interesting legislative history of the Assimilative Crimes Act discloses nothing to indicate that, after Congress has once defined a penal offense, it has authorized such definition to be enlarged by the application to it of a state's definition of it. It has not even been suggested that a conflicting state definition could give a narrower scope to the offense than that given to it by Congress. We believe that, similarly, a conflicting state definition does not enlarge the scope of the offense defined by Congress. The Assimilative Crimes Act has a natural place to fill through its supplementation of the Federal Criminal Code, without giving it the added effect modifying or repealing existing provisions of the Federal Code.

Where offenses have been specifically defined by Congress and the public has been guided by such definitions for many years, it is not natural for Congress by general legislation to amend such definitions or the punishments prescribed for such offenses, without making clear its intent to do so.[17] On the other hand, it is natural for Congress from time to time,

---

[17] ...In Franklin v. United States, 216 U.S. 559, 568 (1910), in referring to the Assimilative Crimes Act, it was said, "by this act Congress adopted for the government of the designated places, ... the criminal laws then existing in the several States within which

through renewals of the Assimilative Crimes Act, to use local statutes to fill in gaps in the Federal Criminal Code where no action of Congress has been taken to define the missing offenses.

That the attorneys for the government have recognized the force of some of these considerations is apparent from the following statement at the close of their brief:

"Congress, of course, was free to fix policy for areas of federal jurisdiction even though it might conflict with local policy, and we think it has done so in respect of the instant situation. These considerations, we think, outweigh the considerations in support of the judgment of the court below."

The first Federal Crimes Act, approved April 30, 1790, 1 Stat. 112, dealt primarily with subjects over which the Constitution had expressly given jurisdiction to the federal government. For example, it dealt with treason, crimes upon the high seas and counterfeiting of securities of the United States. In so far as it related to federal enclaves, it recognized and provided punishment for the offenses of "wilful murder" and manslaughter if committed "within any fort, arsenal, dock-yard, magazine, or in any other place or district of country, under the sole and exclusive jurisdiction of the United States. . . ." It contained nothing corresponding directly to the Assimilative Crimes Act.

On February 10, 1823, James Buchanan, then serving his first term in the House of Representatives, clearly stated the need for the recognition of additional federal crimes. He secured the adoption of a Resolution "That the Committee on the Judiciary be instructed to inquire whether there be any, and, if any, what, crimes not now punishable by law, to which punishments ought to be affixed." Annals of Congress, 17th Cong., 2d Sess. 929 (1822–1823).[19]

In the second session of the next Congress, Daniel Webster, Chairman of the Committee of the Judiciary of the House of Representatives, sponsored the bill which became the Federal Crimes Act of March 3, 1825.

---

such places were situated, *in so far as said laws were not displaced by specific laws enacted by Congress."* (Italics supplied.)

[19] "In offering this resolution, Mr. B. said, it had been decided that the courts of the United States had no power to punish any act, no matter how criminal in its nature, unless Congress have declared it to be a crime, and annexed a punishment to its perpetration. Offences at the common law, not declared such by acts of Congress, are therefore not within the range of the jurisdiction of the federal courts. Congress have annexed punishments but to a very few crimes, and those all of an aggravated nature. The consequence is, that a great variety of actions, to which a high degree of moral guilt

is attached, and which are punished as crimes at the common law, and by every state in the Union, may be committed with impunity on the high seas, and in any place where Congress has exclusive jurisdiction. To afford an example: An assault and battery, with intent to commit murder, may be perpetrated, either on the high seas, or in a fort, magazine arsenal, or dockyard, belonging to the United States, and there exists no law to punish such an offence.

"This is a palpable defect in our system, which requires a remedy; and it is astonishing that none has yet ever been supplied." Annals of Congress, 17th Cong., 2d Sess. 929 (1822–1823).

After extended debate, Congress expanded the list of enumerated federal crimes. It also added the § 3 which became the basis of the Assimilative Crimes Act of today:

> " ... If any offence shall be committed in any of the places aforesaid,[22] the punishment of which offence is not specially provided for by any law of the United States, such offence shall, upon a conviction in any court of the United States having cognisance thereof, be liable to, and receive the same punishment as the laws of the state in which such fort, dock-yard, navy-yard, arsenal, armory, or magazine, or other place, ceded as aforesaid, is situated, provide for the like offence when committed within the body of any county of such state." 4 Stat. 115.

This was amended in 1866, 14 Stat. 13, and in 1874 it was incorporated in the Revised Statutes as § 5391 in substantially its then existing form. For many years it thus referred to an "offense" which is not prohibited or the punishment of which "is not specially provided for, by any law of the United States ..."[23] A similar provision was enacted in 1898 in 30 Stat. 717. In 1909, however, in codifying the Federal Criminal Code, this section was slightly changed when it was incorporated in that Code as § 289 in substantially its present form. The word "offense" was changed so as to avoid the use of it as referring to an action which had not been prohibited and, therefore, technically could not be an "offense." Possibly this change of the old phrase into the phrase "any act or thing which is not made penal by any laws of Congress" led to the present attempt to interpret it in a specific sense as referring to individual acts of the parties rather than in a generic sense referring to acts of a general type or kind. The new words, in the light of the Congressional Committee's explanation of them,[24] cannot, however, be regarded as changing the scope of the act so substantially as to make it amend and enlarge the definition of an existing federal

---

[22] " ... any fort, dock-yard, navy-yard, arsenal, armory, or magazine, the site whereof is ceded to, and under the jurisdiction of, the United States, or on the site of any lighthouse, or other needful building belonging to the United States ..."

[23] "If any offense be committed in any place which has been or may hereafter be, ceded to and under the jurisdiction of the United States, which offense is not prohibited, or the punishment thereof is not specifically provided for, by any law of the United States, such offense shall be liable to, and receive, the same punishment as the laws of the State in which such place is situated, now in force, provide for the like offense when committed within the jurisdiction of such State; and no subsequent repeal of any such State law shall affect any prosecution for such offense in any court of the United States." Rev. Stat. § 5391.

[24] The Committee's statement as to the new section was:

"Section 5391, Revised Statutes, provides that if any 'offense' be committed, etc., which 'offense' shall receive the same punishment as is attached thereto by the law of the State within which the place upon which it is committed is situated.

"An act which is not forbidden by law and to the commission of which no penalty is attached in no legal sense can be denominated an 'offense.' The section has therefore been rewritten so as to correctly express what Congress intended when it enacted the section referred to." H.R. Rep. No. 2, 60th Cong., 1st Sess., p. 25.

offense as well as to cover the case where an "offense" had not been prohibited. To do so would be contrary to the expressed purpose of the Committee to continue, rather than to change, its original meaning. In the instant case not only has the generic act been covered by the definition of having carnal knowledge, but the specific acts have been made "penal" by the definition of adultery. The subsequent amendments have been made merely to advance the dates as of which the assimilated local statutes must have been in force. The last amendment, in 1940, followed an explanation of the bill in identical letters from the Attorney General to the Speaker of the House of Representatives and to the Chairman of the Senate Committee on the Judiciary. These letters adopted the view that the act was to cover crimes on which Congress had not legislated and did not suggest that the act was to enlarge or otherwise amend definitions of crimes already contained in the Federal Code.[26]

As to the particular offense involved in this case, the legislative history shows an increasing purpose by Congress to cover rape and all related offenses fully with penal legislation. In the Federal Crimes Act of 1825, rape was prohibited and made punishable only within certain areas under the admiralty and maritime jurisdiction of the United States. In the same act, the assimilative crimes section was applied to federal enclaves. It thus provided the original federal prohibition of such conduct in those areas. If Congress had been satisfied to continue to apply local law to this and related offenses it would have been simple for it to have left the offense to the Assimilative Crimes Act. A contrary intent of Congress has been made obvious. Congress repeatedly has increased its list of specific prohibitions of related offenses and has enlarged the areas within which those prohibitions are applicable. It has covered the field with uniform federal legislation affecting areas within the jurisdiction of Congress.

When Congress thus enacted the statute as to carnal knowledge in 1889 it gave special attention to the age of consent. The House of Representatives fixed the age at 14 and the Senate changed it to 16.[29]

For these reasons, we believe that the Assimilative Crimes Act does not make the Arizona Code applicable to the facts of this case. The judgment of the Court of Appeals accordingly is

Reversed.

[26] "Certain crimes committed on Federal reservations are expressly defined in the Criminal Code. This is true of grave offenses, such as murder, manslaughter, rape, assault, mayhem, robbery, arson, and larceny (18 U.S.C. §§ 451–467). The Congress has not, however, legislated as to other crimes committed on federal reservations, but has provided generally that as to them, the law of the state within which the reservation is situated, shall be applicable (Criminal Code, § 289, 18 U.S.C. § 468)." Quoted in H. Rep. No. 1584, 76th Cong., 3d Sess., p. 2 and S. Rep. No. 1699, 76th Cong., 3d Sess., p. 1.

[29] Senator Faulkner, in charge of the bill, said: " ... the age was fixed by the committee after considerable discussion and an examination of the laws of the several states. Some of the states have changed their laws. A number of the States have fixed the age of 16. Some of them have fixed as high as 18. Mississippi, Colorado, and Alabama have fixed as high as 18." 19 Cong. Rec. 6501.

JUSTICE RUTLEDGE concurs in the result.

JUSTICE JACKSON took no part in the consideration or decision of this case.

NOTES ON THE ASSIMILATIVE CRIMES ACT

1. Background. The original Assimilative Crimes Act enacted in 1825 made no reference to what would happen if a state amended or added an offense after passage of the federal act. New York added a new offense to its code in 1829 (third degree burglary), and the question arose in United States v. Paul, 31 U.S. (6 Pet.) 141 (1832), whether Paul could be convicted of that offense for conduct committed on the federal enclave at West Point. The Supreme Court said "no," that the 1825 statute was meant to incorporate only the state laws in force at the time the Assimilative Crimes Act was enacted.

Paul led to a period of "static conformity" of the federal and state law, that is, the state laws borrowed by the Assimilative Crimes Act were frozen in time as of 1825. Congress sought to remedy this built-in obsolescence of assimilated state laws by periodically reenacting the Act. Revisions of the Assimilative Crimes Act were enacted in 1866, 1874, 1898, 1909, 1933, 1935, 1940, and 1948. The first four of these statutes expressly limited the assimilation to state laws "now in force," or words to that effect. The next three statutes assimilated the state laws in force on a particular date, conditioned upon the laws "remaining in force at the time of the doing or omitting the doing of such act or thing."[a]

Congress changed its approach in 1948. The present statute, pursuant to the 1948 revision, assimilates state laws "in force at the time of such act or omission." This provision leads to what has been called the "dynamic" conformity of federal to state law, that is, the federal law changes automatically in response to changes in the state law; the operative question is, what is the state law in force at the time the criminal act is committed? As the Reviser's Note to the 1948 revision stated:

> "The revised section omits the specification of any date as unnecessary in a revision, which speaks from the date of its enactment. Such omission will not only make effective within federal reservations, the local state laws in force on the date of the enactment of the revision, but will authorize the federal courts to apply the same measuring stick to such offenses as is applied in the adjoining state under future changes of the state law and will make unnecessary periodic pro forma amendments of this section to keep abreast of changes of local laws. In other words, the revised section makes applicable to offenses committed on such reservations, the law of the place that would govern if the reservation had not been ceded to the United States."

[a] The prosecution in *Williams* was based on the 1940 Act.

2. Constitutionality; *United States v. Sharpnack*. The constitutionality of the present regime was challenged in United States v. Sharpnack, 355 U.S. 286 (1958). The defendant was charged with committing sex crimes involving two boys in violation of Texas law, as assimilated by 18 U.S.C. § 13. The offenses were alleged to have been committed in 1955 at Randolph Air Force base, a federal enclave in Texas. The Texas statutes involved had been enacted in 1950. The District Court dismissed the indictment because "Congress may not legislatively assimilate and adopt criminal statutes of a state which are enacted by the state subsequent to the enactment of the Federal Assimilative Statute."

The Supreme Court reversed. Justice Burton, writing for the Court, described the effect of the 1948 revision of the federal statute:

"This assimilation applies whether the state laws are enacted before or after the Federal Assimilative Crimes Act and at once reflects every addition, repeal or amendment of a state law. Recognizing its underlying policy of 123 years' standing, Congress has thus at last provided that within each federal enclave, to the extent that offenses are not pre-empted by congressional enactments, there shall be complete current conformity with the criminal laws of the respective states in which the enclaves are situated.

"There is no doubt that Congress may validly adopt a criminal code for each federal enclave. It certainly may do so by drafting new laws or by copying laws defining the criminal offenses in force throughout the state in which the enclave is situated. As a practical matter, it has to proceed largely on a wholesale basis. Its reason for adopting local laws is not so much because Congress has examined them individually as it is because the laws are already in force throughout the state in which the enclave is situated.[9] The basic legislative decision made by Congress is its decision to conform the laws in the enclaves to the local laws as to all offenses not punishable by any enactment of Congress. Whether Congress sets forth the assimilated laws in full or assimilates them by reference, the result is as definite and as ascertainable as are the state laws themselves.

"Having the power to assimilate the state laws, Congress obviously has like power to renew such assimilation annually or daily in order to keep the laws in the enclaves current with those in the states. That being so, we conclude that Congress is within its constitutional powers and legislative discretion when, after 123 years of experience with the policy of conformity, it enacts that policy in its most complete and accurate form. Rather than being a delegation by Congress of its legislative authority to the states, it is a deliberate continuing adoption by Congress for federal en-

---

[9] "We do not now pass upon the effect of the Assimilative Crimes Act where an assimilated state law conflicts with a specific feder- al criminal statute, cf. Williams v. United States, 327 U.S. 711 (1946), or with a federal policy."

claves of such unpre-empted offenses and punishments as shall have been already put in effect by the respective states for their own government. Congress retains power to exclude a particular state law from the assimilative effect of the act. This procedure is a practical accommodation of the mechanics of the legislative functions of state and nation in the field of police power where it is especially appropriate to make the federal regulation of local conduct conform to that already established by the state."

Justice Douglas, joined by Justice Black, dissented. He thought the 1948 version of the Assimilative Crimes Act an unconstitutional delegation of legislative authority to the states:

"It is . . . the Congress, and the Congress alone, that has the power to make rules governing federal enclaves. . . . The power to make laws under which men are punished for crimes calls for . . . serious . . . deliberation. . . . [It calls] for the exercise of legislative judgment; and I do not see how that requirement can be satisfied by delegating the authority . . . to the states. . . .

"Of course Congress can adopt as federal laws the laws of a state; and it has often done so. . . . Also Congress could, I think, adopt as federal law, governing an enclave, the state law governing speeding as it may from time to time be enacted. The Congress there determines what the basic policy is. Leaving the details to be filled in by a state is analogous to the scheme of delegated implementation of congressionally adopted policies with which we are familiar in the field of administrative law. But it is Congress that must determine the policy, for that is the essence of lawmaking. Under the scheme now approved, a state makes such federal law, applicable to the enclave, as it likes, and that law becomes federal law, for the violation of which the citizen is sent to prison.

"[A law enacted by a state] may be a law that could never command a majority in the Congress or that in no sense reflected its will. [The citizen] is entitled to the considered judgment of Congress whether the law applied to him fits the federal policy. That is what federal lawmaking is. It is that policy which has led the Court heretofore to limit these Assimilative Crimes Acts to those state laws in force at the time of enactment of the federal act.

"There is some convenience in doing what the Court allows today. Congress is saved the bother of enacting new Assimilative Crimes Acts from time to time. Federal laws grow like mushrooms without Congress passing a bill. But convenience is not material to the constitutional problem. With all due deference to those who are convinced the other way, I am forced to conclude that under this Assimilative Crimes Act it is a state, not the Congress, that is exercising the legislative power. . . . . That may not constitutionally be done."

3. Questions and Comments. The first Assimilative Crimes Act incorporated state crimes "the punishment of which offence is not specifically provided for by any law of the United States." By the time of *Williams*, the statute covered state crimes punishing "the doing of any act or thing which is not made penal by any laws of Congress." The current statute borrows state offenses which are "not made punishable by any enactment of Congress." The suggestion of these various statements is that some state laws are not to be assimilated. Where Congress has already enacted a relevant penal statute, that statute will govern. The purpose of the Assimilative Crimes Act is to fill any remaining gaps.

By what test does the Court in *Williams* determine what constitutes a "gap" that can be filled by state law? More specifically, of what relevance are the then-existing federal enclave adultery and fornication offenses? These two offenses (see footnotes 7 and 8 in *Williams*) were repealed after *Williams* was decided. Would their repeal have changed the outcome in *Williams*? Congress changed the law again in 1986 with the passage of 18 U.S.C. §§ 2241–45. What result in *Williams* today?

In *Sharpnack*, see Note 2, supra, the Court described the effect of existing federal enclave laws as follows: "Recognizing its underlying policy of 123 years' standing, Congress has thus at last provided that within each federal enclave, *to the extent that offenses are not pre-empted by congressional enactments*, there shall be complete current conformity with the criminal laws of the respective states in which the enclaves are situated." (Emphasis added.) Does the concept of "pre-emption" accurately describe the effect given to existing federal law in *Williams*?

United States v. Eades

United States Court of Appeals, Fourth Circuit, 1980.
615 F.2d 617.

■ Before HAYNSWORTH, CHIEF JUDGE, WINTER, CIRCUIT JUDGE, and PERRY, DISTRICT JUDGE.

WINTER, CIRCUIT JUDGE:

These consolidated appeals present the question of whether, under the Assimilative Crimes Act, one may be charged and convicted of a third degree sexual offense in violation of Art 27, § 464B(a)(1)(iii), Ann. Code of Md. (1976 Repl. Vol. and 1978 Cum. Supp.) which occurred on a federal reservation, when Congress has enacted 18 U.S.C. § 113 making simple assault and more aggravated forms of assault federal offenses. We hold that Congress has preempted the Maryland statute and that one may not be charged and convicted of the Maryland crime perpetrated on a federal reservation in that state. . . .

I

John Herbert Eades was charged in a 9–count indictment with a variety of offenses arising out of the following three major incidents which occurred at the United States Naval Academy, a federal reservation at Annapolis, Maryland:

On January 28, 1978, a female officer who was a member of the faculty, returned to the ladies locker room at McDonough Hall after having been swimming in the pool located in that building. She was standing in the shower room, wrapped in a towel, when she noticed a man, later identified as Eades, looking at her through a window in the shower room. Eades entered the room, approached her and backed her into a shower stall. He started to kiss her neck and forced her down on a ledge in the stall. While she sought to defend herself and to keep the towel wrapped around her, he placed his arm around her and started to move his hand down her side and leg. He succeeded in touching her left buttock through the towel and ran his hand down to her knee. When Eades started to place his hand under the towel, she screamed, and Eades fled.

On January 30, 1978, Eades was apprehended in another locker room on the Academy grounds cutting the locks off lockers.

On February 4, 1978, a female cadet who was to be a member of the next entering class was in the ladies locker room at McDonough Hall. She was standing in front of her locker changing from her sweatshirt and bathing suit into her blouse. While only partially clothed, she noticed Eades standing but two feet from her. When she screamed, he grabbed her, threw her to the floor and banged her head on the floor. He continued to bang her head as she continued to scream, then he pulled down her lower undergarment and rubbed her genital area with both hands. Eventually, Eades abruptly left.[1]

Counts 1–4 of the indictment involved the incident on January 28, 1978, counts 5–8 concerned the second locker room assault on February 4, and count 9 referred to January 30. Eades was indicted for assault with intent to commit rape in violation of 18 U.S.C. § 113(a)[a] (count 1), a third

[1] Eades also surprised the date of a midshipman and another young woman in the ladies room in a building at the Academy on February 3, 1978, when he opened the door apparently preparatory to entering. When Eades saw both, he closed the door and left. He was seen again on the morning of February 4, 1978, in the vicinity of the ladies locker room by a member of the faculty and his wife.

[a] At the time, 18 U.S.C. § 113 provided:

"§ 113. Assaults within maritime and territorial jurisdiction.

"Whoever, within the special maritime and territorial jurisdiction of the United States, is guilty of an assault shall be punished as follows:

"(a) Assault with intent to commit murder or rape, by imprison-

ment for not more than twenty years.

"(b) Assault with intent to commit any felony, except murder or rape, by fine of not more than $3,000 or imprisonment for not more than ten years, or both.

"(c) Assault with a dangerous weapon, with intent to do bodily harm, and without just cause or excuse, by fine of not more than $1,000 or imprisonment for not more than five years, or both.

"(d) Assault by striking, beating, or wounding, by fine of not more than $500 or imprisonment for not more than six months, or both.

"(e) Simple assault, by fine of not more than $300 or imprison-

degree sexual offense in violation of Maryland law with respect to the first victim (count 2), simple assault of his first victim in violation of 18 U.S.C. § 113(e)(count 3), entry upon the Naval Academy for the purpose of committing assault with intent to rape, to engage in unlawful sexual conduct, and to commit assault with respect to his first victim in violation of 18 U.S.C. § 1382[b] (count 4), assault with intent to rape in violation of 18 U.S.C. § 113(a) with respect to his second victim (count 5), a third degree sexual offense in violation of Maryland law with respect to his second victim (count 6), assault by striking of his second victim in violation of § 113(d)(count 7), entry upon the Naval Academy for the purpose of committing a crime against his second victim in violation of 18 U.S.C. § 1382 (count 8), and entry upon the Naval Academy for the purpose of committing theft in violation of 18 U.S.C. § 1382 (count 9).

At trial, the jury acquitted Eades of the charges contained in counts 1 and 5 (assault with intent to rape) and counts 4 and 8 (unlawful entry for the purpose of committing sex crimes). He was convicted, however, on counts 2 and 6, charging the Maryland third degree sex offense with respect to both victims, counts 3 and 7, charging simple assault, and assault by striking, respectively, and count 9, entry upon the Academy grounds for the purpose of theft.

Prior to trial, Eades ... sought to dismiss counts 2 and 6 on the grounds of improper use of the Assimilative Crimes Act, 18 U.S.C. § 13. The District Court held this motion sub curia until after the jury's verdicts, but denied it in a published opinion, United States v. Eades, 455 F.Supp. 436 (D.Md.1978).

Larry F. Wilson was charged with six offenses arising from his actions when he persuaded a young woman who was standing on the street in the District of Columbia at night awaiting a taxicab to accept his offer to drive her home in his car. After the young woman entered the car, he drove not to her home but to the Suitland Parkway, which is constructed on land acquired for the use of the United States and under its jurisdiction. While still driving the car, Wilson put his hand down his companion's skirt touching her sexual organs and said that he was going to have intercourse with her. Eventually the young woman was successful in grabbing the steering wheel and steering the car off of the road to the side where it became mired. While Wilson was seeking to extricate the car, the young woman jumped from it and was rescued by a United States Park Policeman.

ment for not more than three months, or both.

"(f) Assault resulting in serious bodily injury, by fine of not more than $10,000 or imprisonment for not more than ten years, or both."—[Footnote by eds.]

[b] At the time, Section 1382 provided:

"Whoever, within the jurisdiction of the United States, goes upon any military, naval, or Coast Guard reservation, post, fort, arsenal, yard, station, or installation, for any purpose prohibited by law or lawful regulation [s]hall be fined not more than $500 or imprisoned not more than six months, or both."—[Footnote by eds.]

Although Wilson was charged, inter alia, with kidnaping and several sexual offenses, he was convicted only of assault with intent to commit rape in violation of 18 U.S.C. § 113(a) and a third degree sexual offense in violation of Maryland law. A mistrial was declared with respect to the other charges.

In this appeal, Wilson raises no question about the correctness of his conviction under federal law of assault with intent to rape. Nor does he question that the evidence was legally sufficient to support his conviction of the Maryland third degree sexual offense if that charge were proper. But Wilson does contend that he was improperly charged and convicted of the Maryland crime because application of the state law to federal reservations in Maryland through the Assimilative Crimes Act has been preempted by the federal law on assault. Wilson unsuccessfully sought dismissal of the count of the indictment charging this crime prior to trial, but the District Judge, relying upon *United States v. Eades*, supra, denied his motion to dismiss.

II.

The Assimilative Crimes Act, 18 U.S.C. § 13, makes punishable the doing of acts or the omission to do acts on federal reservations which, "although not made punishable by an enactment of Congress, would be punishable if committed or omitted" within the jurisdiction of the state in which the reservation is situated. Upon conviction of a violation of such an assimilated state law, the offender shall be subject to the punishment prescribed by the state.

The Maryland statute under which both defendants were convicted proscribes as a "third degree sexual offense" sexual contact by one against the will and without the consent of another where the accused threatens or places the victim in fear of, inter alia, death, serious physical injury or kidnaping.[2] Art. 27, § 461, Ann. Code of Md. (1976 Repl. Vol. and 1978 Cum. Supp.) defines "sexual contact" to include the intentional touching of the anal or genital area for the purposes of sexual arousal or gratification.

The common question that these appeals present is whether the Assimilative Crimes Act makes the Maryland statute applicable to a federal reservation in Maryland when Congress has enacted 18 U.S.C. § 113, a comprehensive statute with respect to assaults. Stated otherwise, the

---

[2] The pertinent portions of the text of § 464B follow:

"§ 464B. Third degree sexual offense.

"(a) What constitutes.—A person is guilty of a sexual offense in the third degree if the person engages in sexual contact:

"(1) With another person against the will and without the consent of the other person, and . . .

"(iii) Threatens or places the victim in fear that the victim . . . will be imminently subjected to death, suffocation, strangulation, disfigurement, serious physical injury, or kidnaping. . . .

"(b) Penalty.—A person violating the provisions of this section is guilty of a felony and upon a conviction is subject to imprisonment for a period of not more than 10 years."

question is has there been a failure by Congress, notwithstanding the enactment of § 113, to make punishable the acts constituting the commission of a Maryland third degree sexual offense—the necessary premise for making § 464B(a)(1)(iii) applicable to a federal reservation in Maryland under the Assimilative Crimes Act.

In denying Eades' pretrial motion to dismiss the counts of the indictment grounded on the Maryland statute as made applicable by the Assimilative Crimes Act, the District Court confined its consideration to the question of whether the enactment of federal § 113(a)(assault with intent to rape) constituted congressional occupation of the subject matter so as to render § 464B(a)(1)(iii) inapplicable under the terms of the Assimilative Crimes Act. The District Court ruled that it did not on the theory that only a conviction under § 113(a) required proof of an intent to rape; a conviction under § 464B(a)(1)(iii) could be had even where the accused had no intent to rape if it were shown that there was a touching of the anal or genital area without the consent of the victim accompanied by a threat or fear of serious physical injury. The ruling of the District Court on Wilson's pretrial motion to dismiss also focused upon § 113(a) alone. Unquestionably, the District Court restricted its examination of § 113, because counsel for both defendants, in their written motions, claimed only that § 113(a) preempted § 464B(a)(1)(iii).

We find it unnecessary to say that either ruling of the District Court, limited to the effect of § 113(a), standing alone, on § 464B(a)(1)(iii), was legally incorrect, because we think that the other provisions of § 113 should also have been considered. When all of the provisions of § 113 are considered, we conclude that the Assimilative Crimes Act does not make § 464B(a)(1)(iii) applicable to federal reservations in Maryland.[4]

The seminal case on the reach of the Assimilative Crimes Act is Williams v. United States, 327 U.S. 711 (1946). There the accused was convicted of having carnal knowledge of an unmarried female over the age of 16 but under the age of 18 on a federal reservation in Arizona, in violation of Arizona law. The offense was not prohibited as carnal knowledge under federal law because federal law requires proof that the victim was under 16 at the time of the offense. It also was not rape or assault with intent to rape under federal law because the required element of force was absent.

The Court held the Arizona law was not applicable under the Assimilative Crimes Act and that the defendant could not be punished thereunder for the following reasons:

---

[4] It is an accepted rule of appellate procedure that ordinarily an appellate court will not consider an issue not raised in the court from which the appeal is taken. The rule, however, is not inflexible, and we think that we are justified in departing from the rule in this case for two reasons. First, the various subsections of § 113 are so related to § 113(a) that a contention that they render § 464B(a)(1)(iii) inapplicable is not totally new and different from the contention that was advanced. Second, we are so persuaded that the Maryland statute is inapplicable that to permit the convictions thereunder to stand would result in manifest injustice.

"We hold that the Assimilative Crimes Act does not make the Arizona statute applicable in the present case because (1) the precise acts upon which the conviction depends have been made penal by the laws of Congress defining adultery and (2) the offense known to Arizona as that of 'statutory rape' has been defined and prohibited by the Federal Criminal Code, and is not to be redefined and enlarged by application to it of the Assimilative Crimes Act. The fact that the definition of this offense as enacted by Congress results in a narrower scope for the offense than that given to it by the state, does not mean that the congressional definition must give way to the state definition. This is especially clear in the present case because the specified acts which would come within the additional scope given to the offense by the state through its postponement of the age of consent of the victim from 16 to 18 years of age, are completely covered by the federal crimes of adultery or fornication."

We think that under *Williams* neither defendant can properly be convicted of a violation of the Maryland third degree sexual offense. Viewed in its entirety, federal § 113 covers the entire range of assaults from simple assault to assault by striking, assault with a dangerous weapon, assault with intent to commit a felony other than murder or rape, assault resulting in serious bodily injury, and assault with intent to commit murder or rape.[5] The Maryland third degree sexual offense is merely a special form of assault and battery. It is an unwanted touching of the genital or anal area of a person's body under circumstances causing fear for the purpose of sexual arousal or sexual gratification. One cannot possibly commit a Maryland third degree sexual offense without committing a violation of some portion of federal § 113. Indeed, Eades was convicted of violating § 113(d)[6] with respect to his second victim for the very acts upon which he was twice convicted of violating § 464B(a)(1)(iii), and Wilson was convicted of a violation of § 113(a) for the acts for which he was also convicted under the Maryland statute. Thus "the precise acts upon which the convictions of both defendants depend have been made penal" by a congressional enactment proscribing various assaults, and the Maryland statute merely redefines certain types of assaults and establishes a more severe permissible penalty for them. Therefore, the Assimilative Crimes Act does not make the Maryland statute applicable to federal reservations.

We think that our application of the *Williams* case and the conclusion that we reach in these cases accords with the weight of authority. In

---

[5] At common law, an assault did not necessarily require a touching; assault by touching was termed battery. From the language of § 113, it is manifest that Congress employed the word "assault" to include battery. "[A]n assault is an attempted battery and proof of a battery will support conviction of assault." United States v. Dupree, 544 F.2d 1050, 1052 (9th Cir.1976).

[6] Of course Eades could have been convicted of a violation of § 113(d) for the head banging alone without proof that he touched the genital or anal area of his victim; but more significantly, had there been no head banging, Eades could have been convicted of a violation of § 113(e), the lesser included offense, merely upon proof of unwanted touching.

United States v. Butler, 541 F.2d 730 (8th Cir.1976), it was held that a federal statute punishing acquisitions and receipt by felons of firearms that have traveled in interstate commerce preempted a state law proscribing the same type of conduct that had no interstate nexus requirement. The District Court had ruled that the phrase "any enactment" in the Assimilated Crimes Act referred to statutes applicable only to a federal enclave, thus the state act was assimilated since the only federal statute applied to persons both off and on a federal enclave. The Court of Appeals rejected this interpretation. It reads *Williams* to be concerned primarily with whether Congress had intended to punish the generic conduct in question, not whether Congress had made the precise acts penal. In the instant cases, the conclusion that the Assimilated Crimes Act does not make the Maryland statute applicable is even more compelling, because, as has been shown, it is impossible to violate the Maryland statute without transgressing some provision of federal § 113. Thus, Congress has evidenced an intent to proscribe the precise acts made penal by Maryland. ...

In urging affirmance, the government places principal reliance on United States v. Smith, 574 F.2d 988 (9th Cir.1978). There, three inmates of a federal penitentiary committed forcible acts of sodomy upon another male prisoner. They were convicted under the Assimilative Crimes Act by application of a state statute which defines the crime of rape to include such acts. On appeal, they unsuccessfully urged that Congress did not intend to permit reference to state law for punishment of the sexual conduct in question. Specifically, they asserted that federal § 113(b) (assault with intent to commit a felony) precluded application of the state statute.

Their contention was rejected. First, the court noted that "[t]here is no federal statute punishing the specific acts perpetrated by a homosexual rapist." The court then read *Williams* to require the federal assault statute to punish the precise acts upon which the Assimilative Crimes Act conviction depends in order to oust application of the state statute. In applying that test, the court said that the state statute required sexual contact between the perpetrator and the victim, while the federal statute does not require physical contact. Even where the victim is physically touched, the federal statute does not require the contact to be a sexual one. Thus, the court concluded that the state statute was not precluded and the convictions should stand.

We express no view as to whether *Smith* should be followed because we think that is distinguishable from the instant appeals. Unlike the Ninth Circuit in *Smith*, we are dealing with conduct in each case which, if it constitutes a violation of Maryland law, necessarily constitutes a violation of some subsection of federal § 113. In short, there is a federal statute which punishes the precise conduct proscribed by Maryland law. The government's reliance on the principle in *Smith* might be persuasive were we dealing only with § 113(a) as did the District Court in both of the instant cases. But, as we have said earlier, we think that all of the subsections of § 113 should be considered in determining whether

§ 464B(a)(1)(iii) has been precluded, not merely § 113(a). So considered, we think that the Maryland statute has been precluded and the convictions thereunder must be reversed. . . .

HAYNSWORTH, CHIEF JUDGE, dissenting:

I agree that Wilson's conviction under the Assimilative Crimes Act of a violation of Maryland's § 464B should not be allowed to stand. He was convicted of an assault with intent to commit rape in violation of 18 U.S.C. § 113(a), a greater offense than a third degree sexual offense under the Maryland statute. I think there was preemption there.

I cannot agree, however, that 18 U.S.C. § 113 preempted the convictions of Eades under the Maryland statute.

If 18 U.S.C. § 113 may be viewed as a generally comprehensive proscription of assaults within the federal maritime and territorial jurisdiction, it surely is not a comprehensive federal statute dealing with the particular problem of sexual assaults. It literally proscribes assaults with intent to commit rape, but there is no other reference to sexual offenses. I agree that an aggravated sexual assault would be a violation of 18 U.S.C. § 113(e) proscribing simple assault punishable by the imposition of a fine of not more than $300 or imprisonment of not more than three months or both. It seems plain to me, however, that Congress intended in that subsection to deal only with minor offenses and not with aggravated sexual assaults. United States v. Smith, 574 F.2d 988 (9th Cir.1978), is illustrative. I cannot ascribe to the Congress, in the enactment of § 113(e) dealing with simple assault, an intention to preclude prosecution under the Assimilative Crimes Act for the serious, forcible sodomy offenses of which the three defendants in that case were convicted.

In contrast to § 113 of the federal statute, the Maryland sexual offense statutes deal comprehensively with such offenses. They are classified into six separate degrees. Some acts may be prosecuted under more than one section, leaving prosecutor and jury some room for leniency, but substantial gradations of offenses is surely appropriate to the problem. There are no such gradations under the federal statute.

As the majority notices, Eades could have been convicted of assault by striking in violation of § 113(d) when he banged the victim's head on the floor, but the sexual offense would be wholly irrelevant to a conviction under that subsection. At most, it could be treated in the sentencing as an aggravating circumstance.

In short, I do not see § 113 as a comprehensive treatment of the problem of sex offenses on federal enclaves. Some sex offenses are serious and widely regarded as felonious, though not assaults with an actual intent to commit rape. I cannot believe that Congress, in enacting a simple assault statute providing punishment appropriate to a minor misdemeanor, could have intended to prohibit prosecution under the Assimilative Crimes Act of serious sex offenses.

I respectfully dissent.

United States v. Eades

United States Court of Appeals, Fourth Circuit, 1980.
633 F.2d 1075.

■ Before HAYNSWORTH, CHIEF JUDGE, and WINTER, BUTZNER, RUSSELL, WIDENER, HALL, PHILLIPS, MURNAGHAN, SPROUSE and ERVIN, CIRCUIT JUDGES, sitting en banc.

HAYNSWORTH, CHIEF JUDGE:

A divided panel of this court reversed the defendant's conviction on two counts under the Assimilative Crimes Act, 18 U.S.C. § 13, of third degree sexual offenses in violation of Article 27, § 464B(a)(1)(iii) of the Annotated Code of Maryland. The government filed a petition for rehearing en banc, which was granted. Now, after oral argument before the en banc court, a majority of the judges in regular active service holds that the defendant's conviction on Counts 2 and 6 of the third degree sexual offenses was not precluded by 18 U.S.C. § 113. The reasons for the majority's conclusion are adequately stated in the opinion of the dissenting judge. United States v. Eades, 615 F.2d 617, 624 (4th Cir.1980)(Haynsworth, C.J., dissenting).

The suggestion in the dissenting opinion after the en banc rehearing of inconsistency requires a further word.

The problem is one of preemption by a comprehensive federal assault statute, 18 U.S.C. § 113, of a comprehensive Maryland sexual offense statute, Article 27, § 461, et seq., Annotated Code of Maryland. The key to the answer is our perception of congressional intention. That perception is enlightened by a consideration of the apparent purpose of the Congress in the enactment of § 113.

The Congress had been concerned with some sexual offenses committed within the special territorial maritime jurisdiction of the United States. Rape is a serious offense made unlawful by 18 U.S.C. § 2031, while carnal knowledge of a female under the age of 16 years and not married to the defendant is proscribed by 18 U.S.C. § 2032. Section 113, however, deals entirely with assaults. In it there is only one reference to a sexual offense. Assault with the intent to commit murder or rape is made unlawful by § 113(a), but that does not suggest that in the enactment of § 113 Congress intended to deal comprehensively, or even generally, with sexual offenses. That it did not have such an intention is strongly suggested by its enactment of separate statutes dealing with carnal knowledge of a female without her consent or under the age of 16 years.

Under common law concepts, Wilson's conduct was appropriately catalogued as assault with intent to commit rape. He touched the victim's sex organ without her consent and told her that he intended to have intercourse with her, provoking her reaction to effect her escape. It was conduct specifically proscribed by § 113(a). It was conduct which also falls within the more generalized language of Maryland's § 464B(a)(1)(iii), but surely Congress could not have intended that conduct specifically proscribed by § 113(a) be again punishable under the Assimilative Crimes Act.

To that extent, there is an overlap of the federal assault statute with Maryland's sexual offense statute, but we are unaware of any rule that any such slight touching of federal and state statutes, generally having different purposes, means that the state statute cannot be assimilated in other contexts in which there is no relevant federal statute proscribing the specific conduct in which the defendant has engaged.

There is also a slight touching of the two statutes in the sense that the great majority of the offenses proscribed by Maryland's sexual offense statutes may be said to encompass simple assault as a lesser included offense. The fact that simple assault is made unlawful by § 113(e), however, does not convert the federal assault statute into a general sexual offense statute. One asked to catalogue the conduct of Eades in forcefully fondling the genitals of his second victim and banging her head on the floor, would hardly entitle it "simple assault." There is simply no indication that Congress, in the enactment of § 113, intended to deal with that kind of offense.

We conclude that federal preemption of a state statute in one context when the defendant's conduct is clearly proscribed by a federal statute does not necessarily preempt the state statute in other contexts when the defendant's conduct is nowhere addressed by any federal statute. It is a matter of congressional intention.[2] We find no congressional intention to preempt the prosecution under the Assimilative Crimes Act and Maryland § 464B(a)(1)(iii) of Eades for the sexual conduct in which he engaged, which is not proscribed by § 113 or any other federal statute, unless it is treated as only a simple assault. . . .

Accordingly, the defendant's conviction of the third degree sexual offense charged in Counts 2 and 6, as well as his convictions upon charges in Counts 3, 7 and 9, are all affirmed.

Winter, Circuit Judge, dissenting:

I dissent from the [affirmance] of Eades' conviction for the reasons expressed in the panel majority opinion. United States v. Eades, 615 F.2d 617 (4th Cir.1980). I would write no more except that I am constrained to call attention to the fact that, in my view, the dissenting panel opinion on which the en banc court relies contains an internal inconsistency. That inconsistency is one which was adopted by the government and, notwithstanding its protestations to the contrary, appears to be adopted by the majority of the en banc court.[2] As a consequence, I believe that the district

---

[2] The problem arises most frequently when the federal statute is a comprehensive one covering a wide range of criminal activity, as § 113 does. It is perhaps exacerbated if the state statute is a comprehensive one. Maryland's sexual offense statutes are certainly comprehensive. Even if attention is focused upon § 464B(a)(1)(iii) its general terms reach varied conduct, including Wilson's assault with intent to commit rape, since there was sexual contact, and the kind of offensive touching committed by Eades, though there was no apparent intention of committing rape.

[2] Accepting the correctness of the panel's decision with respect to Wilson, the government sought rehearing only as to Eades. Although the court granted rehearing en banc as to Eades, it did not on its own motion grant rehearing as to Wilson. I interpret this

courts and the United States Attorneys of this circuit will be hard pressed to fathom what prosecutions are authorized under the Assimilative Crimes Act for acts in violation of Maryland's Third Degree Sexual Offense statute.

In the panel opinion, the panel unanimously reversed the conviction of Wilson, and the majority of the panel reversed the conviction of Eades, with Chief Judge Haynsworth in dissent. With regard to Wilson who was convicted of assault with intent to commit rape in violation of 18 U.S.C. § 113(a) and of a third degree sexual offense under the Maryland statute, it was Judge Haynsworth's view that, because the former offense is "a greater offense than" the latter, Congress preempted the state crime and rendered it inapplicable. With regard to Eades, however, it was Judge Haynsworth's view, now adopted by the majority of the en banc court, that Congress did not preempt his conviction under the Maryland statute because he was convicted only of simple assault under 18 U.S.C. § 113(e).

A state statute may not be incorporated through the Assimilative Crimes Act if Congress has preempted the punishment of conduct under that statute by enacting a federal criminal statute that proscribes the same conduct. Williams v. United States, 327 U.S. 711 (1946). The reach Congress intended the federal criminal statute to have is thus determinative of whether a similar state statute may be assimilated. It is illogical and inconsistent to affirm Eades' conviction if that of Wilson is reversed. Conversely, if it is correct to reverse Wilson's conviction because § 113(a)—the section proscribing assault with intent to rape—preempted the Maryland sexual offense statute, Eades' conviction must be reversed also. Once preemption as to Wilson is found, there is preemption as to Eades. If the state statute is preempted, it is preempted as to all defendants charged under that state statute regardless of which, if any, section of the federal assault statute they may be charged with violation. The distinction between Eades and Wilson—that one was convicted of simple assault and the other of assault with intent to rape—is simply irrelevant to the determination of whether the Maryland sexual offense statute was preempted by federal criminal law.

When the majority asserts that federal preemption of a state statute in one context when the defendant's conduct is clearly proscribed by a federal statute does not necessarily preempt the state statute in other contexts, it cites no authority to support it. It seems to me that the majority is speaking of merger and confusing merger with preemption.[3] In my view the very concept of preemption is that, if a state statute is preempted by

inaction as implying approval of the decision as to Wilson notwithstanding what is said in the ... opinion of the en banc court.

[3] The rationale of the panel dissenting opinion that Wilson was convicted under federal law of "a greater offense than a third degree sexual offense under the Maryland statute" and therefore there was preemption suggests the notion of merger. The correct test is not whether the federal offense is greater than the state offense; the test is whether the precise acts have been made penal by an Act of Congress, irrespective if the "offense as enacted by Congress results in a narrower scope for the offense than that given to it by the state ..." Williams v. United States, 327 U.S. 711, 717 (1946).

any federal statute, it is totally preempted and is not available for any other federal prosecution.

NOTES ON APPLICATION OF THE ASSIMILATIVE CRIMES ACT

1. ***United States v. Smith***.   The government relied in *Eades* on United States v. Smith, 574 F.2d 988 (9th Cir.1978).   In *Smith*, three male inmates of the federal penitentiary at McNeil Island in the state of Washington committed forcible acts of sodomy upon another male prisoner. Washington had a sex-neutral rape statute that specifically covered such acts.   The defendants were convicted under this rape statute as assimilated by 18 U.S.C. § 13 (which carried a maximum sentence of 20 years) *and* of violating 18 U.S.C. § 113(b)("Assault with intent to commit any felony"; 10–year maximum).[c]

At the time, 18 U.S.C. § 2031 punished rape on a federal enclave, but that statute, the *Smith* court noted, "has been interpreted to punish rape as defined at common law, that is, carnal knowledge of a female by force or threat of force."   The court thought *Williams* distinguishable because "[t]he federal statutory scheme with respect to the conduct punished in this case differs from the relevant scheme in *Williams*."   Here,

> "Congress has neither proscribed the specific acts committed by these defendants nor the generic conduct in which they engaged in such a way as to indicate an intent to '[cover] the field with uniform federal legislation'.... There is no federal statute punishing the specific acts perpetrated by a homosexual rapist.

> "In arguing that Congress did act with reference to the type of conduct in question here when it passed the statute proscribing rape, appellants rely upon the policy reflected by the Washington statute, which defines rape of a female and the act of sodomy as one and the same offense.   [T]he act of rape is not, for federal purposes, generically the same as the acts of sodomy committed here.   ... Sodomy has traditionally been defined as an offense generically distinct from the crime of rape.   Congress enacted the Assimilative Crimes Act against this background.   We conclude that enactment of the federal rape statute does not constitute legislative action with reference to acts of sodomy.   Therefore, Congress did not intend to bar incorporation through the Assimilative Crimes Act of a state statute which makes the act of sodomy a criminal offense.

> "Appellants contend that since their conduct is proscribed by 18 U.S.C. § 113(b)(assault with intent to commit a felony), the reasoning of *Williams* precludes application of the Assimilative Crimes Act.   We reject this argument because the federal assault

---

[c] Do the words "any felony" in § 113(b) include felonies under state law?   If not, what *federal* felony might the defendants in *Smith* have committed?   The opinion in *Smith* is silent on these questions.

statute does not punish the 'precise acts upon which the [Assimilative Crimes Act] conviction depends. . . .' Rape as defined by the Washington statute requires sexual contact between perpetrator and victim, whereas the federal statute prohibiting assault does not require physical contact, and in cases where the victim is physically touched does not require the contact to be a sexual one. The two crimes are readily distinguishable. Congressional specificity with respect to assault does not preclude incorporation of the offense in question here under the Assimilative Crimes Act."[d]

2. Questions and Comments. Both *Eades* and *Smith* involve applications of the Assimilative Crimes Act to state sex offenses under circumstances where arguably the Supreme Court's analysis in *Williams* required a different result.

(i) *Eades*. Consider the *Eades* case first. Judge Winter suggests that Eades could not be convicted of the Maryland offense because "[o]ne cannot possibly commit a Maryland third degree sexual offense without committing a violation of some portion of federal § 113." To paraphrase *Williams*, "the precise acts upon which the conviction depends have been made penal by the laws of Congress defining" assault. Since Congress has provided criminal punishment for the "precise acts" in which Eades engaged, the Maryland law cannot be assimilated. It is, in the words of *Sharpnack*, preempted by the existing federal law. Nor is it an answer to this line of argument, Judge Winter might have added, that § 133(e)(simple assault) is a much lesser offense or protects a different victim interest than the Maryland law. The same was true in *Williams*, where the "precise acts" in which Williams engaged were covered by an adultery statute, a lesser offense protecting different victim interests than the Arizona statute sought to be assimilated there. It follows, Judge Winter would conclude, that Eades cannot be convicted of the Maryland offense.

Is there anything wrong with this reasoning? Does Judge Haynsworth have an effective answer? Does the problem lie with the reasoning (though perhaps not the ultimate conclusion) in *Williams*? Does it lie in talk about preemption? Judge Haynsworth reasons, essentially, that Congress has not comprehensively addressed the victim interest protected by laws against sexual assault. It has spoken to the most serious offenses—rape and assault with intent to rape—but has left a "gap" in the law, to be filled with appropriate state offenses, for lesser intrusions against the victim's

[d] The Court added that "[t]here is also some question as to whether assault with intent to commit a felony as applied to the acts perpetrated in this case is a lesser included offense with respect to a charge of rape." The court refused to reach the issue because it was not adequately raised below and was therefore waived and because the sentences under the federal assault statute and the state rape statute were to run concurrently and "the concurrent sentence rule makes our consideration of this issue unnecessary."

Under the "concurrent sentence rule," if the total sentence received by the defendant is supported by an affirmed conviction, the court will not review convictions on other counts for which the defendant received a concurrent sentence.

sexual integrity. Is it fair to say that Judge Winter refuses to borrow state law based on a formal, "is it covered at all by federal law" analysis, whereas Judge Haynsworth borrows state law based on an analysis of relevant criminal law policies? Which is the better approach?

If Judge Haynsworth is right, why is Eades guilty of violating *both* the Maryland statute *and* § 113(e)? To borrow Judge Winter's phrase, shouldn't a conviction of both offenses be barred by the doctrine of merger?

(ii) Smith. Is *Smith* consistent with *Williams*? There are at least two arguments that it is not. The first is that Congress has by its rape statute "occupied the field" of rape law on federal enclaves and that any state law expressing an inconsistent policy about the reach of the law of rape cannot be assimilated. The analogy is to the inconsistency in the "age of discretion" between the Arizona and federal laws in *Williams*. Second, since the "precise acts" committed by the defendants in *Smith* are covered by § 113(b), the state law cannot be assimilated.

Judge Winter distinguished *Smith*. Is his distinction persuasive? From his point of view, should he have said simply that *Smith* was wrong? On the other hand, is it *Smith* and *Eades* that were correctly decided? If so, how can *Williams* be distinguished?

(iii) The Federal Sexual Abuse Statutes. Congress has now resolved the problems on the facts of both *Eades* and *Smith*. In 1986 it enacted a modern, comprehensive, sex-neutral sexual abuse law (18 U.S.C. §§ 2241–45) applicable to federal enclaves.[e] It seems clear, under any analysis of the Assimilative Crimes Act, that Eades and Smith today would be prosecuted under appropriate sections of this statute and that state law could not be applicable. But of course cases like *Williams*, *Eades*, and *Smith* remain the source of the principles by which the Assimilative Crimes Act will be interpreted in other contexts.

3. *United States v. Butler*. *Williams*, *Eades*, and *Smith* involve situations where federal statutes that applied only to federal enclaves arguably precluded the assimilation of state law. Is the analysis different when the arguably preclusive federal statute is not limited to federal enclaves but applies throughout the country? Such a situation was presented in United States v. Butler, 541 F.2d 730 (8th Cir.1976).

Butler, an Indian, was observed by FBI agents on a reservation in South Dakota. The agents knew that Butler had previously been convicted of a felony. At the time, Butler was wearing a .45 caliber revolver in a hip holster. He was arrested and charged in a two-count indictment for unlawful possession of the gun. The first count, which was voluntarily dismissed by the government before trial, charged a violation of 18 U.S.C.

---

[e] At the same time, it eliminated the words "or rape" in § 113(a) as it existed at the time of *Eades* (see footnote f to the first *Eades* opinion). It also added the words "or a felony under chapter 109A" to § 113(b).

App. § 1202(a)(1).[f] The second count charged a violation of South Dakota law under the Assimilative Crimes Act (ACA).

(i) The District Court Decision. Butler was convicted and sentenced to a term of imprisonment for two years. In response to a motion for an arrest of judgment, the District Court first noted the difference between § 1202(a)(1)(applying "to all persons within the geographic area of the United States") and statutes, such as 18 U.S.C. § 113, that are limited in their application to federal enclaves. It then held:

> "If a person is charged, while *not* on a federal enclave, for both a violation of a federal and state criminal statute, even though both arise from the same act or omissions, he may be tried for either or both. Since the Assimilated Crimes Act is designed to equalize the rights and duties of a person on a federal enclave and a person in the state containing the federal enclave, a person in a federal enclave should also be subject to prosecution from both the general federal criminal statute and the assimilated state statute. The difficulty arises, however, when Congress has passed a specific federal enclave law, e.g., 18 U.S.C. § 113, that vitiates the need for the assimilated state statute. To prevent a person on a federal enclave from being subject to prosecution under general federal criminal laws, the federal enclave law, and the assimilated state law, Congress made a wise legislative decision to exempt a person on a federal enclave from the assimilation of a state statute if a federal enclave law on the same subject or course of conduct applies. To allow the language of the Assimilated Crimes Act to do more than this, i.e., to exempt persons on federal enclaves from [state laws because of] general criminal statutes as well as federal enclave laws, would be to overbalance the equities in favor of the person on the federal enclave. Such a result would be contrary to the intent behind the act itself, i.e., to equalize the duties of persons on a federal enclave with those of persons in the same

The new sexual abuse provisions are codified in chapter 109A.

[f] 18 U.S.C. App. § 1202(a)(1), since repealed, provided:

> "Any person who ... has been convicted by a court of the United States or of any State or any political subdivision thereof of a felony ... and who receives, possesses or transports in commerce or affecting commerce ... any firearm shall be fined not more than $10,000, or imprisoned for not more than two years, or both."

The Supreme Court held in United States v. Bass, 404 U.S. 336 (1971), that the words "in commerce or affecting commerce" modified "receives," "possesses," and "transports." Thus, the government must prove (although the requirement is not onerous) the commerce nexus in each case brought under § 1202(a)(1). *Bass* is a main case in Section 3 of this Chapter, infra. The question of how onerous the proof requirement of the government is also dealt with in the materials following *Bass*.

At the time of this prosecution, 18 U.S.C. § 922(h) made it a criminal offense for any convicted felon "to receive any firearm ... which has been shipped or transported in interstate or foreign commerce." Violation of § 922(h) carried a five-year maximum sentence. When § 1202(a)(1) was repealed, the coverage of § 922 was enlarged to remove the inconsistency and redundancy between the two statutes.

governmental unit that geographically surrounds the enclave. Defendant's motion must fail."

(ii) The Circuit Court Decision. The Circuit Court reversed. It held that the "enactments" of Congress that could foreclose the assimilation of state laws were not limited to federal enclave laws, but extended to "any" act of Congress:

"The district court based its interpretation of the ACA upon a supposed purpose to equalize the rights and duties of persons on and off federal enclaves. We find no history or precedent to support this interpretation. The legislative history of the ACA demonstrates that its purpose was not to equalize, but to fill the voids in the criminal law applicable to federal enclaves created by the failure of Congress to pass specific criminal statutes. . . .

"We conclude that the district court erred in its construction of the Assimilative Crimes Act and that the plain meaning of the act requires that state law not be 'assimilated' where '*any* enactment of Congress' punished the conduct. We turn then to the question of whether *any* enactment of Congress covers the acts of the defendant thereby precluding the use of the ACA to apply state law."

The Court then held, after a long discussion of *Williams*, that the "receipt" provisions in §§ 922(h) and 1202(a)(1)

"constitute laws of the United States which . . . proscribe the *generic* conduct of acquisition and possession of firearms by irresponsible persons, including felons on federal enclaves.[13] . . .

"The added requirement[ ] of proof of an interstate nexus . . . under a federal receipt charge do not serve to make the state law applicable and the federal law inapplicable under the ACA. If they did the test of applicability of the ACA would be whether the exact same elements of proof are required under the state and federal laws. *Williams* holds directly to the contrary. The test is not whether the same elements of proof are contained in both state and federal statutes, but whether the acts of the defendant are made punishable under *any* enactment of Congress. As *Williams* makes clear, 'acts' under the ACA does not refer to 'individual acts of the parties' but, rather, in a 'generic sense' to acts of a specific type or kind which are prohibited. In addition, Congress in enacting the ACA did not intend that the assimilation of state law

---

[13] "If Butler was moving the gun in interstate commerce, . . . then the assimilation of state law under the ACA would not be proper. However, the fact that such factual proof is not in the record should have little relevance. Otherwise, the government could avoid the congressional requirement, that prosecution proceed under the applicable federal criminal statute, by simply selecting to proceed under the ACA and the lesser burden of proof required by state law. This, of course, is contrary to the reasoning of *Williams*."

was to depend on a prosecutor's selection of a statute under which it would be easier to obtain a conviction.

"In summary, we hold that the generic conduct of acquisition and receipt of firearms by felons is punishable under § 1202(a)(1) and § 922(h), and the fact that the federal statutes are narrower in scope does not allow the federal government to use state law to broaden the definition of a federal crime."

(iii) Questions and Comments. Did the Eighth Circuit reach the right decision in *Butler*? Suppose another convicted felon possessed (or received) a firearm three feet outside a federal enclave. Such a person, as the District Court pointed out, could have been prosecuted in state court for a state firearms offense, or in federal court for a violation of § 1202(a)(1) or § 922(h). Is it a plausible purpose of the Assimilative Crimes Act, as the District Court thought, to treat persons who commit crimes on an enclave the same way they would be treated just outside of the enclave? Are there elements of comity, equality of right and obligation, or cooperation with state law enforcement policy involved in the Assimilative Crimes Act? Or is the purpose, as the Circuit Court thought, simply to fill gaps in the federal law—to allow for prosecution of persons who otherwise would be guilty of no offense at all? Are there problems with both views?

Did the Circuit Court in *Butler* interpret *Williams* correctly? If so, does *Butler* mean that if *any* general federal offense is potentially available, prosecution in a federal court under an assimilated state statute is foreclosed? Even if the "general" federal statute contains a jurisdictional prerequisite that can't be satisfied? [g]

NOTE ON THE ASSIMILATIVE CRIMES ACT AND THE SENTENCING
REFORM ACT OF 1984

Recall that the Assimilative Crimes Act provides that, whenever the defendant commits an act that, although not punishable by an Act of Congress, would be punishable under state law, then the defendant "shall be guilty of a like offense *and subject to a like punishment*." 18 U.S.C. § 13(a)(emphasis added).

In the Sentencing Reform Act of 1984, Congress created the United States Sentencing Commission and ordered the Commission to write a systematic, comprehensive set of guidelines to govern sentencing in federal criminal cases. (The subject of sentencing for federal crimes is discussed in greater detail in Chapter V.) The Sentencing Reform Act of 1984 instructed federal courts to sentence all defendants according to these new guidelines. The Act also provided as follows, 18 U.S.C. Sec. 3553(b):

[g] It is likely that the government could have satisfied the jurisdictional element on the facts of *Butler* had it chosen to do so. Section 1202(a)(1) could have been satisfied by proof that the gun had previously traveled in interstate commerce (what gun hasn't?). See Scarborough v. United States, 431 U.S. 563 (1977). Section 922(h) could have been satisfied by the same proof. See Barrett v. United States, 423 U.S. 212 (1976).

> "In the absence of an applicable sentencing guideline ..., the
> court shall also have due regard for the relationship of the sen-
> tence imposed to sentences prescribed by guidelines applicable to
> similar offenses and offenders, and to the applicable policy state-
> ments of the Sentencing Commission."

In the original set of federal sentencing guidelines, which became effective
in 1987, the United States Sentencing Commission included the following
provision, Section 2X5.1:

> "Other Offenses. If the offense is a felony or Class A misdemean-
> or for which no guideline expressly has been promulgated, apply
> the most analogous offense guideline. If there is not a sufficiently
> analogous guideline, the provisions of [18 U.S.C. § 3553(b), as
> quoted above] shall control."

Under the Sentencing Reform Act of 1984 and the federal sentencing
guidelines, it is now possible for a federal court to "find" an appropriate
sentence—defined as appropriate by the United States Sentencing Commission, which is the federal agency with the delegated authority to establish
and implement federal sentencing policy—for *any* federal crime. To put it
a little differently, one might say that there are no longer any "gaps" in
the federal criminal law *of sentencing* (even though "gaps" continue to
exist in the definitions of federal *crimes*). If the Commission has written
no specific guideline for the particular federal crime at issue, then the
federal court simply applies the "most analogous offense" guideline (under
§ 2X5.1), or applies whatever guidelines would apply to "similar offenses
and offenders" (under 18 U.S.C. § 3553(b)).

To what extent, if any, does the Sentencing Reform Act of 1984
effectively repeal the portion of the Assimilative Crimes Act that deals with
sentencing for assimilated state-law crimes? Can you foresee any problems
this might create? Imagine, for example, a defendant who is convicted in
federal court of an assimilated state-law crime for which the punishment
under state law would be 2 to 4 years in prison. Now suppose that either
the "most analogous offense" guideline (under § 2X5.1), or the guidelines
for "similar offenses and offenders" (under 18 U.S.C. § 3553(b)), would
suggest a federal sentence of 3 to 6 years in prison. May (or must?) the
federal court sentence the defendant according to the "most analogous
offense" or "similar offenses and offenders" approach, even though such an
approach might produce a sentence longer than the maximum sentence
authorized by the assimilated state law? Could the defendant argue that
he or she has some kind of reliance interest in the punishment scheme set
out in the state statute?

This situation has already caused difficulties for the lower federal
courts. See, e.g., United States v. Garcia, 893 F.2d 250 (10th
Cir.1989)(holding that the federal sentencing guidelines apply to violations
of the Assimilated Crimes Act, but that the sentence imposed by the federal
court may not exceed the maximum sentence, nor fall below any minimum
mandatory sentence, that is authorized by the relevant state law).

Section 2: "Auxiliary" or Supplemental Offenses

INTRODUCTORY NOTE ON "AUXILIARY" OR SUPPLEMENTAL OFFENSES

The most controversial category of federal crimes contains offenses that are "auxiliary to state law enforcement."[a] These crimes cover behavior that is within the reach of state laws but that, for one reason or another over the years, Congress has been persuaded to criminalize. Normally such laws are not justified because of the desire to protect some direct federal interest or function, but because of some perceived deficiency in state or local law enforcement. When Bonnie and Clyde are able to rob a bank and escape pursuing officers by crossing a state line, a case is made for a criminal law covering their behavior that need not accord significance to the state border. When organized criminal activity has spread its tentacles across numerous jurisdictional boundaries, a case is made for a national law enforcement effort that is not limited by territorial constraints. When local officials are so corrupt as to reach the very institutions of law enforcement that might bring them to justice, a case is made for a law enforcement effort that is independent of local influence. When state or local government officials are involved in the denial of civil rights, a case is made for independent enforcement by authorities that are not subject to regional prejudice.

As these examples illustrate, it is not difficult to come up with situations that arguably justify the enactment of a federal criminal law even though the same behavior is already punished by state law. The most pervasive problem arises from the breadth with which such federal laws are often drafted. Consider, for example, the Hobbs Act, 18 U.S.C. § 1951, which punishes "[w]hoever in any way or degree ... affects commerce ... by robbery ..." where the term "commerce" is defined to include "all ... commerce over which the United States has jurisdiction." Use of the Hobbs Act to reach multistate activity by large organizations is unlikely to lead to serious controversy, but—because the commerce power of the United States is so broad—the act seems literally to apply to the robbery of a candy store by a local hoodlum, indeed to any robbery within the territorial limits of the United States. One might take the position that there is plenty of crime to go around, and that it is a matter of indifference whether a particular criminal is prosecuted by federal, state, or local government; the important thing is that criminals be prosecuted somewhere. Many, however, would disagree, arguing that important values are preserved by keeping the federal government out of purely local situations.

The distinction between crimes that protect "direct" federal interests and crimes where the federal law enforcement presence is "auxiliary" is a slippery one. There are clear cases of "direct" federal interests (assassina-

[a] Louis B. Schwartz, Federal Criminal Jurisdiction and Prosecutors' Discretion, 13 Law & Contemp. Probs. 64, 70 (1948).

tion of a President) where the behavior is also covered by state law. There are also clear cases of "auxiliary" federal laws (robbery of a federally insured bank), where the crime could be considered purely local but where there is nonetheless a federal value at stake (the financial integrity of the federal insurance program). It can nonetheless be asserted that the more remote the federal interest and the more broadly the federal crime is defined, the more the controversy it is likely to engender. As a practical matter, in many situations it is the discretion of state and federal prosecutors that determines where a given offense will be prosecuted. Whether this is healthy or harmful is an issue near the surface of most of the remaining materials in this book.

Caminetti v. United States

Supreme Court of the United States, 1917.
242 U.S. 470.

■ JUSTICE DAY delivered the opinion of the Court.

[T]hree cases were argued together, and may be disposed of in a single opinion. In each of the cases there was a conviction and sentence for violation of the so-called White Slave Traffic Act of June 25, 1910, 36 Stat. 825 [today known as the Mann Act, after its principal sponsor], the judgments were affirmed by the Circuit Courts of Appeals, and writs of certiorari bring the cases here.

In the *Caminetti* case, the petitioner was indicted in the United States District Court for the Northern District of California. . . . The indictment . . . charged him with transporting and causing to be transported and aiding and assisting in obtaining transportation for a certain woman from Sacramento, California, to Reno, Nevada, in interstate commerce for the purpose of debauchery, and for an immoral purpose, to wit, that the aforesaid woman should be and become his mistress and concubine. [The] defendant was found guilty and sentenced to imprisonment for 18 months and to pay a fine of $1,500.00. Upon writ of error to the United States Circuit Court of Appeals for the Ninth Circuit, that judgment was affirmed.

Diggs was indicted at the same time as was Caminetti. . . . The first count charged the defendant with transporting and causing to be transported and aiding and assisting in obtaining transportation for a certain woman from Sacramento, California, to Reno, Nevada, for the purpose of debauchery, and for an immoral purpose, to wit, that the aforesaid woman should be and become his concubine and mistress. The second count charged him with a like offense as to another woman (the companion of Caminetti) in transportation, etc., from Sacramento to Reno that she might become the mistress and concubine of Caminetti. The third count charged him (Diggs) with procuring a ticket for the first mentioned woman from Sacramento to Reno in interstate commerce, with the intent that she should become his concubine and mistress. The fourth count made a like charge as to the girl companion of Caminetti. Upon trial and verdict of guilty on these four counts, he was sentenced to imprisonment for two years and to pay fine of

$2,000.00. As in the Caminetti case, that judgment was affirmed by the Circuit Court of Appeal.

In the *Hays* case, . . . an indictment was returned in the United States District Court for the Western District of Oklahoma against Hays and another, charging violations of the act. The first count charged the said defendants with having, on March 17th, 1914, persuaded, induced, enticed and coerced a certain woman, unmarried and under the age of 18 years, from Oklahoma City, Oklahoma, to the city of Wichita, Kansas, in interstate commerce and travel, for the purpose and with intent then and there to induce and coerce the said woman, and intending that she should be induced and coerced to engage in prostitution, debauchery and other immoral practices, and did then and there, in furtherance of such purposes, procure and furnish a railway ticket entitling her to passage over a line of railway . . ., and did then and there and thereby knowingly entice, and cause the said woman to go and to be carried and transported as a passenger in interstate commerce upon said line of railway. The second count charged that on the same date the defendants persuaded, induced, enticed and coerced the same woman to be transported from Oklahoma City to Wichita, Kansas, with the purpose and intent to induce and coerce her to engage in prostitution, debauchery and other immoral practices at and within the state of Kansas, and that they enticed her and caused her to go and be carried and transported as a passenger in interstate commerce from Oklahoma City, Oklahoma, to Wichita, Kansas, upon a line and route of a common carrier. . . . Defendants were found guilty by a jury upon both counts, and Hays was sentenced to imprisonment for 18 months. Upon writ of error to the Circuit Court of Appeals for the Eighth Circuit, judgment was affirmed.

It is contended that the act of Congress is intended to reach only "commercialized vice," or the traffic in women for gain, and that the conduct for which the several petitioners were indicted and convicted, however reprehensible in morals, is not within the purview of the statute when properly construed in the light of its history and the purposes intended to be accomplished by its enactment. In none of the cases was it charged or proved that the transportation was for gain or for the purpose of furnishing women for prostitution for hire, and it is insisted that, such being the case, the acts charged and proved, upon which conviction was had, do not come within the statute.

It is elementary that the meaning of a statute must, in the first instance, be sought in the language in which the act is framed, and if that is plain, and if the law is within the constitutional authority of the law-making body which passed it, the sole function of the courts is to enforce it according to its terms.

Where the language is plain and admits of no more than one meaning the duty of interpretation does not arise and the rules which are to aid doubtful meanings need no discussion. There is no ambiguity in the terms of this act. It is specifically made an offense to knowingly transport or cause to be transported, etc., in interstate commerce, any woman or girl for the purpose of prostitution or debauchery, or for "any other immoral purpose," or with the intent and purpose to induce any such woman or girl to become a prostitute or to give herself up to debauchery, or to engage in any other immoral practice.

Statutory words are uniformly presumed, unless the contrary appears, to be used in their ordinary and usual sense, and with the meaning commonly attributed to them. To cause a woman or girl to be transported for the purposes of debauchery, and for an immoral purpose, to-wit, becoming a concubine or mistress, for which Caminetti and Diggs were convicted; or to transport an unmarried woman, under 18 years of age, with the intent to induce her to engage in prostitution, debauchery and other immoral practices, for which Hays was convicted, would seem by the very statement of the facts to embrace transportation for purposes denounced by the act, and therefore fairly within its meaning.

While such immoral purpose would be more culpable in morals and attributed to baser motives if accompanied with the expectation of pecuniary gain, such considerations do not prevent the lesser offense against morals of furnishing transportation in order that a woman may be debauched, or become a mistress or a concubine from being the execution of purposes within the meaning of this law. To say the contrary would shock the common understanding of what constitutes an immoral purpose when those terms are applied, as here, to sexual relations.

In United States v. Bitty, 208 U.S. 393 (1908), it was held that the act of Congress against the importation of alien women and girls for the purpose of prostitution "and any other immoral purpose" included the importation of an alien woman to live in concubinage with the person importing her. In that case this Court said:

> "All will admit that full effect must be given to the intention of Congress as gathered from the words of the statute. There can be no doubt as to what class was aimed at by the clause forbidding the importation of alien women for purposes of 'prostitution.' It refers to women who for hire or without hire offer their bodies to indiscriminate intercourse with men. The lives and example of such persons are in hostility to 'the idea of the family, as consisting in and springing from the union for life of one man and one woman in the holy estate of matrimony; the sure foundation of all that is stable and noble in our civilization; the best guaranty of that reverent morality which is the source of all beneficent progress in social and political improvement.' Murphy v. Ramsey, 114 U.S. 15, 45 (1885). ... Now the addition in the last statute of the words, 'or for any other immoral purpose,' after the word 'prostitution,' must have been made for some practical object. Those added words show beyond question that Congress had in view the protection of society against another class of alien women other than those who might be brought here merely for purposes of 'prostitution.' In forbidding the importation of alien women 'for any other immoral purpose,' Congress evidently thought that there

were purposes in connection with the importations of alien women which, as in the case of importations for prostitution, were to be deemed immoral. It may be admitted that in accordance with the familiar rule of ejusdem generis, the immoral purpose referred to by the words 'any other immoral purpose,' must be one of the same general class or kind as the particular purpose 'prostitution' specified in the same clause of the statute. But that rule cannot avail the accused in this case; for, the immoral purpose charged in the indictment is of the same general class or kind as the one that controls in the importation of an alien woman for the purpose strictly of prostitution. The prostitute may, in the popular sense, be more degraded in character than the concubine, but the latter none the less must be held to lead an immoral life, if any regard whatever he had to the views that are almost universally held in this country as to the relations which may rightfully, from the standpoint of morality, exist between man and woman in the matter of sexual intercourse."

This definition of an immoral purpose was given prior to the enactment of the act now under consideration, and must be presumed to have been known to Congress when it enacted the law here involved. (See the sections of the act[1] set forth in the margin.)

[1] Sections 2, 3, and 4 of the act are as follows:

"Sec. 2. That any person who shall knowingly transport or cause to be transported, or aid or assist in obtaining transportation for, or in transporting, in interstate or foreign commerce, or in any Territory or in the District of Columbia, any woman or girl for the purpose of prostitution or debauchery, or for any other immoral purpose, or with the intent and purpose to induce, entice, or compel such woman or girl to become a prostitute or to give herself up to debauchery, or to engage in any other immoral practice; or who shall knowingly procure or obtain, or cause to be procured or obtained, or aid or assist in procuring or obtaining, any ticket or tickets, or any form of transportation or evidence of the right thereto, to be used by any woman or girl in interstate or foreign commerce, or in any Territory or the District of Columbia, in going to any place for the purpose of prostitution or debauchery, or for any other immoral purpose, or with the intent or purpose on the part of such person to induce, entice, or compel her to give herself up to the practice of prostitution, or to give herself up to debauchery, or any other immoral practice, whereby any such woman or girl shall be transported in interstate or foreign com- merce, or in any Territory or the District of Columbia, shall be deemed guilty of a felony, and upon conviction thereof shall be punished by a fine not exceeding five thousand dollars, or by imprisonment of not more than five years, or by both such fine and imprisonment, in the discretion of the court.

"Sec. 3. That any person who shall knowingly persuade, induce, entice, or coerce, or cause to be persuaded, induced enticed, or coerced, or aid or assist in persuading, inducing, enticing, or coercing any woman or girl to go from one place to another in interstate or foreign commerce, or in any Territory or the District of Columbia, for the purpose of prostitution or debauchery, or for any other immoral purpose, or with the intent and purpose on the part of such person that such woman or girl shall engage in the practice of prostitution or debauchery, or any other immoral practice, whether with or without her consent, and who shall thereby knowingly cause or aid or assist in causing such woman or girl to go and to be carried or transported as a passenger upon the line or route of any common carrier or carriers in interstate or foreign commerce, or any Territory or the District of Columbia, shall be deemed guilty of a felony and on conviction thereof shall be punished by a fine of not more than five

But it is contended that though the words are so plain that they cannot be misapprehended when given their usual and ordinary interpretation, and although the sections in which they appear do not in terms limit the offense defined and punished to acts of "commercialized vice," or the furnishing or procuring of transportation of women for debauchery, prostitution or immoral practices for hire, such limited purpose is to be attributed to Congress and engrafted upon the act in view of the language of § 8 and the report which accompanied the law upon its introduction into and subsequent passage by the House of Representatives.

In this connection, it may be observed that while the title of an act cannot overcome the meaning of plain and unambiguous words used in its body, the title of this act embraces the regulation of interstate commerce "by prohibiting the transportation therein for immoral purposes of women and girls, and for other purposes." It is true that § 8 of the act provides that it shall be known and referred to as the "White-slave traffic Act," and the report accompanying the introduction of the same into the House of Representatives set forth the fact that a material portion of the legislation suggested was to meet conditions which had arisen in the past few years, and that the legislation was needed to put a stop to a villainous interstate and international traffic in women and girls. Still, the name given to an act by way of designation or description, or the report which accompanies it, cannot change the plain import of its words. If the words are plain, they give meaning to the act, and it is neither the duty nor the privilege of the courts to enter speculative fields in search of a different meaning.

Reports to Congress accompanying the introduction of proposed laws may aid the courts in reaching the true meaning of the legislature in cases of doubtful interpretation. But, as we have already said, and it has been so often affirmed as to become a recognized rule, when words are free from doubt they must be taken as the final expression of the legislative intent, and are not to be added to or subtracted from by considerations drawn from titles or designating names or reports accompanying their introduction, or from any extraneous source. In other words, the language being plain, and not leading to absurd or wholly impracticable consequences, it is the sole evidence of the ultimate legislative intent.

The fact, if it be so, that the act as it is written opens the door to blackmailing operations upon a large scale, is no reason why the courts

thousand dollars, or by imprisonment for a term not exceeding five years, or by both such fine and imprisonment, in the discretion of the court.

"Sec. 4. That any person who shall knowingly persuade, induce, entice, or coerce any woman or girl under the age of eighteen years, from any State or Territory or the District of Columbia, to any other State or Territory or the District of Columbia, with the purpose and intent to induce or coerce her, or that she shall be induced or coerced to engage in prostitution or debauchery, or any other immoral practice, and shall in furtherance of such purpose knowingly induce or cause her to go and to be carried or transported as a passenger in interstate commerce upon the line or route of any common carrier or carriers, shall be deemed guilty of a felony, and on conviction thereof shall be punished by a fine of not more than ten thousand dollars, or by imprisonment for a term not exceeding ten years, or by both such fine and imprisonment, in the discretion of the court."

should refuse to enforce it according to its terms, if within the constitutional authority of Congress. Such considerations are more appropriately addressed to the legislative branch of the government, which alone had authority to enact and may if it sees fit amend the law.[b]

It is further insisted that a different construction of the act than is to be gathered from reading it is necessary in order to save it from constitutional objections, fatal to its validity. The act has its constitutional sanction in the power of Congress over interstate commerce. The broad character of that authority was declared once for all in the judgment pronounced by this court, speaking by Chief Justice Marshall, in Gibbons v. Ogden, 22 U.S. (9 Wheat.) 1 (1824), and has since been steadily adhered to and applied to a variety of new conditions as they have arisen.

It may be conceded, for the purpose of the argument, that Congress has no power to punish one who travels in interstate commerce merely because he has the intention of committing an illegal or immoral act at the conclusion of the journey. But this act is not concerned with such instances. It seeks to reach and punish the movement in interstate commerce of women and girls with a view to the accomplishment of the unlawful purposes prohibited.

The transportation of passengers in interstate commerce, it has long been settled, is within the regulatory power of Congress, under the commerce clause of the Constitution, and the authority of Congress to keep the channels of interstate commerce free from immoral and injurious uses has been frequently sustained, and is no longer open to question.

Moreover, this act has been sustained against objections affecting its constitutionality of the character now urged. Hoke v. United States, 227 U.S. 308 (1913); Athanasaw v. United States, 227 U.S. 326 (1913); Wilson v. United States, 232 U.S. 563 (1914). In the *Hoke* case, the constitutional objections were given consideration and denied upon grounds fully stated in the opinion. It is true that the particular case arose from a prosecution of one charged with transporting a woman for the purposes of prostitution in violation of the act. But, holding as we do, that the purposes and practices for which the transportation in these cases was procured are equally within the denunciation of the act, what was said in the *Hoke* case as to the power of Congress over the subject is an applicable now as it was then[:]

> "The principle established by the cases is the simple one, when rid of confusing and distracting considerations, that Congress has power over transportation 'among the several States': that the

---

[b] Caminetti's lawyer had argued:

"We cannot suppose that those who drafted this law, or that those who enacted it upon a full consideration, could not foresee its consequences, and we must, therefore, suppose that the Congress of the United States knew that it was arming blackmailers, both male and female, with such an effective instrument as this act furnishes them, if construed to embrace mere escapades. It is a part of the history of our time that the Department of Justice is even now covering this Republic with a dragnet in an effort to apprehend those who have been preying upon the weaknesses and vices of men and women."—[Footnote by eds.]

power is complete in itself, and that Congress, as an incident to it, may adopt not only means necessary but convenient to its exercise, and the means may have the quality of police regulations. We have no hesitation, therefore, in pronouncing the act of June 25, 1910, a legal exercise of the power of Congress." . . .

The judgment in each of the cases is affirmed.

JUSTICE MCREYNOLDS took no part in the consideration or decision of these cases.

JUSTICE MCKENNA, with whom concurred CHIEF JUSTICE WHITE and JUSTICE CLARKE, dissenting.

Undoubtedly in the investigation of the meaning of a statute we resort first to its words, and when clear they are decisive. The principle has attractive and seemingly disposing simplicity, but that it is not easy of application or, at least, encounters other principles, many cases demonstrate. The words of a statute may be uncertain in their signification or in their application. If the words be ambiguous, the problem they present is to be resolved by their definition; the subject-matter and the lexicons become our guides. But here, even, we are not exempt from putting ourselves in the place of the legislators. If the words be clear in meaning but the objects to which they are addressed be uncertain, the problem then is to determine the uncertainty. And for this a realization of conditions that provoked the statute must inform our judgment. Let us apply these observations to the present case.

The transportation which is made unlawful is of a woman or girl "to become a prostitute or to give herself up to debauchery, or to engage in any other immoral practice." Our present concern is with the words "any other immoral practice," which, it is asserted, have a special office. The words are clear enough as general descriptions; they fail in particular designation; they are class words, not specification. Are they controlled by those which precede them? If not, they are broader in generalization and include those that precede them, making them unnecessary and confusing. To what conclusion would this lead us? "Immoral" is a very comprehensive word. It means a dereliction of morals. In such sense it covers every form of vice, every form of conduct that is contrary to good order. It will hardly be contended that in this sweeping sense it is used in the statute. But if not used in such sense, to what is it limited and by what limited? If it be admitted that it is limited at all, that ends the imperative effect assigned to it in the opinion of the Court. But not insisting quite on that, we ask again, By what is it limited? By its context, necessarily, and the purpose of the statute.

For the context I must refer to the statute; of the purpose of the statute Congress itself has given us illumination. It devotes a section to the declaration that the "Act shall be known and referred to as the 'White-slave traffic Act.' " And its prominence gives it prevalence in the construction of the statute. It cannot be pushed aside or subordinated by indefinite words in other sentences, limited even there by the context. It is a peremptory rule of construction that all parts of a statute must be taken into account in ascertaining its meaning, and it cannot be said that § 8 has no object. Even if it gives only a title to the act it has especial weight. But it gives more than a title; it makes distinctive the purpose of the statute. The designation "White-slave traffic" has the sufficiency of an axiom. If apprehended, there is no uncertainty as to the conduct it describes. It is commercialized vice, immoralities having a mercenary purpose, and this is confirmed by other circumstances.

The author of the bill was Mr. Mann, and in reporting it from the House Committee on Interstate and Foreign Commerce he declared for the Committee that it was not the purpose of the bill to interfere with or usurp in any way the police power of the states, and further that it was not the intention of the bill to regulate prostitution or the places where prostitution or immorality was practiced, which were said to be matters wholly within the power of the states and over which the federal government had no jurisdiction. And further explaining the bill, it was said that the sections of the act had been "so drawn that they are limited to cases in which there is the act of transportation in interstate commerce of women for purposes of prostitution." And again:

> "The White Slave Trade. A material portion of the legislation suggested and proposed is necessary to meet conditions which have arisen within the past few years. The legislation is needed to put a stop to a villainous interstate and international traffic in women and girls. The legislation is not needed or intended as an aid to the states in the exercise of their police powers in the suppression or regulation of immorality in general. It does not attempt to regulate the practice of voluntary prostitution, but aims solely to prevent panderers and procurers from compelling thousands of women and girls against their will and desire to enter and continue in a life of prostitution." House Report No. 47, 61st Cong., 2d Sess., pp. 9, 10.

In other words, it is vice as a business at which the law is directed, using interstate commerce as a facility to procure or distribute its victims.

In 1912 the sense of the Department of Justice was taken of the act in a case where a woman of 24 years went from Illinois, where she lived, to Minnesota at the solicitation and expense of a man. She was there met by him and engaged with him in immoral practices like those for which petitioners were convicted. The district attorney forwarded her statement to the Attorney General, with the comment that the element of traffic was absent from the transaction and that therefore, in his opinion, it was not "within the spirit and intent of the Mann Act."[1] Replying, the Attorney

---

[1] "Careful consideration of the facts and circumstances as related by Miss Cox fails to convince me that her case came within the spirit and intent of the Mann Act. The element of traffic is entirely absent from this transaction. It is not a case of prostitution or debauchery and the general words 'or other immoral practice' should be qualified by the particular preceding words and be read in the light of the rule of ejusdem generis. This

General expressed his concurrence in the view of his subordinate.[2]

Of course, neither the declarations of the report of the Committee on Interstate Commerce of the House nor the opinion of the Attorney General are conclusive of the meaning of the law, but they are highly persuasive. The opinion was by one skilled in the rules and methods employed in the interpretation or construction of laws, and informed besides of the conditions to which the act was addressed. The report was by the committee charged with the duty of investigating the necessity for the act and to inform the House of the results of that investigation, both of evil and remedy. The report of the committee, has, therefore, a higher quality than debates on the floor of the House. The representatives of the latter may indeed be ascribed to the exaggerations of advocacy or opposition. The report of a committee is the execution of a duty and has the sanction of duty. There is a presumption, therefore, that the measure it recommends has the purpose it declares and will accomplish it as declared.

This being the purpose, the words of the statute should be construed to execute it, and they may be so construed even if their literal meaning be otherwise. In Holy Trinity Church v. United States, 143 U.S. 457 (1892), there came to this Court for construction an act of Congress which made it unlawful for any one in any of the United States "to prepay the transportation, or in any way assist or encourage the importation or migration of any alien or aliens, any foreigner or foreigners, into the United States ... under contract or agreement ... to perform labor or *service of any kind* [italics mine] in the United States, its Territories or the District of Columbia." The Trinity Church made a contract with one E. W. Warren, a resident of England, to remove to the City of New York and enter its service as rector and pastor. The church was proceeded against under the act and the Circuit Court held that it applied and rendered judgment accordingly.

It will be observed that the language of the statute is very comprehensive, fully as much so as the language of the act under review, having no limitation whatever from the context; and the Circuit Court, in submission to what the court considered its imperative quality, rendered judgment against the church. This Court reversed the judgment, and, in an elaborate opinion by Mr. Justice Brewer, declared that "It is a familiar rule, that a thing may be within the letter of the statute and yet not within the statute, because not within its spirit, nor within the intention of its makers." And the learned Justice further said: "This has been often asserted, and the reports are full of cases illustrating its application."

view of the statute is the more reasonable when considered in connection with § 8 where Congress employs the terms 'slave' and 'traffic' as indicative of its purpose to suppress certain forms of abominable practice connected with the degradation of women for gain."

[2] "I agree with your conclusion that the facts and circumstances set forth in your letter and its enclosure do not bring the matter within the true intent of the White Slave Traffic Act, and that no prosecution against Edwards should be instituted in the federal courts unless other and different facts are presented to you."

It is hardly necessary to say that the application of the rule does not depend upon the objects of the legislation, to be applied or not applied as it may exclude or include good things or bad things. Its principle is the simple one that the words of a statute will be extended or restricted to execute its purpose.

Another pertinent illustration of the rule is Reiche v. Smythe, 80 U.S. (13 Wall.) 162 (1871), in which the court declared that if at times it was its duty to regard the words of a statute, at times it was also its duty to disregard them, limit or extend them, in order to execute the purpose of the statute. And applying the principle, it decided that in a tariff act the provision that a duty should be imposed on horses, etc., and other *live animals* imported from foreign countries should not include canary birds, ignoring the classification of nature. And so again in Silver v. Ladd, 74 U.S. (7 Wall.) 219 (1868), where the benefit of the Oregon Donation Act was extended by making the words "single man" used in the statute mean an unmarried woman, disregarding a difference of genders clearly expressed in the law.

The rule that these cases illustrate is a valuable one and in varying degrees has daily practice. It not only rescues legislation from absurdity (so far the opinion of the Court admits its application), but it often rescues it from invalidity, a useful result in our dual form of governments and conflicting jurisdictions. It is the dictate of common sense. Language, even when most masterfully used, may miss sufficiency and give room for dispute. Is it a wonder therefore, that when used in the haste of legislation, in view of conditions perhaps only partly seen or not seen at all, the consequences, it may be, beyond present foresight, it often becomes necessary to apply the rule? And it is a rule of prudence and highest sense. It rescues from crudities, excesses and deficiencies, making legislation adequate to its special purpose, rendering unnecessary repeated qualifications and leaving the simple and best exposition of a law the mischief it was intended to redress. Nor is this judicial legislation. It is seeking and enforcing the true sense of a law notwithstanding its imperfection or generality of expression.

There is much in the present case to tempt to a violation of the rule. Any measure that protects the purity of women from assault or enticement to degradation finds an instant advocate in our best emotions; but the judicial function cannot yield to emotion—it must, with poise of mind, consider and decide. It should not shut its eyes to the facts of the world and assume not to know what everybody else knows. And everybody knows that there is a difference between the occasional immoralities of men and women and that systematized and mercenary immorality epitomized in the statute's graphic phrase "White-slave traffic." And it was such immorality that was in the legislative mind and not the other. The other is occasional, not habitual—inconspicuous—does not offensively obtrude upon public notice. Interstate commerce is not its instrument as it is of the other, nor is prostitution its object or its end. It may, indeed, in instances, find a convenience in crossing state lines, but this is its accident, not its aid.

There is danger in extending a statute beyond its purpose, even if justified by a strict adherence to its words. The purpose is studied, all effects measured, not left at random—one evil practice prevented, opportunity given to another. The present case warns against ascribing such improvidence to the statute under review. Blackmailers of both sexes have arisen, using the terrors of the construction now sanctioned by this court as a help—indeed, the means—their brigandage. The result is grave and should give us pause. It certainly will not be denied that legal authority justifies the rejection of a construction which leads to mischievous consequences, if the statute be susceptible of another construction.

United States v. Bitty, 208 U.S. 393 (1908), is not in opposition. The statute passed upon was a prohibition against the importation of alien women or girls, a statute, therefore, of broader purpose than the one under review. Besides, the statute finally passed upon was an amendment to a prior statute and the words construed were an addition to the prior statute and necessarily, therefore, had an added effect. The first statute prohibited the importation of any alien woman or girl into the United States "*for the purposes of prostitution.*" The second statute repeated the words and added "*or for any other immoral purpose*" (italics mine). Necessarily there was an enlargement of purpose, and besides the act was directed against the importation of foreign corruption and was construed accordingly. The case, therefore, does not contradict the rule; it is an example of it.

For these reasons I dissent from the opinion and judgment of the Court. . . .

NOTES ON *CAMINETTI* AND THE MANN ACT

1. Background. The Mann Act is of historic importance for at least two reasons. The first is its role in the development of the modern commerce clause. It had been established in Champion v. Ames (The Lottery Case), 188 U.S. 321 (1903), that Congress had the power, in effect, to prohibit interstate traffic in "polluted" goods. Hoke v. United States, 227 U.S. 308 (1913), involved the constitutionality of the Mann Act, and the Court took one more incremental step in expansion of the congressional power. Effie Hoke had been convicted of persuading Annette Baden to travel from New Orleans to Beaumont, Texas, "for the purpose of prostitution." The power of Congress to regulate the interstate movement of people, she argued, was different from its power to regulate traffic in goods. The Court responded that "surely if the facility of interstate transportation can be taken away from the demoralization of lotteries, the debasement of obscene literature, the contagion of diseased cattle or persons, the impurity of food and drugs, the like facility can be taken away from the systematic enticement to and the enslavement in prostitution and debauchery of women, and, more insistently, of girls."

Second, the Mann Act is the first of many efforts by Congress to combat organized crime:

> "The social evil at which the Mann Act was aimed seems to have been real enough. The white slave traffic was regarded as one of the big criminal rackets of the period before the prohibition era, the Age of the Red Light District, and it was widely believed that professional procurers operated on a large scale to supply the established houses of prostitution. One of them was shown to have had an income of $102,000 a year.

> "The white slave gangs operated in a manner strongly reminiscent of the methods of the gangs who impressed seamen in an early period of our history. They sought their victims in both town and country and to get them employed liquor, trickery, fraud and deceit, and often sheer force. They were particularly active in ports of entry where they could prey upon the large number of female immigrants coming into the country in pursuit of the American Dream.

> "Indeed, at the turn of the century the white slave traffic was an international problem, and many European countries had entered into an international convention for its suppression, the Paris Agreement of May 18, 1904, to which the United States adhered. The Mann Act was the culmination of the effort to suppress the white slave traffic. As early as March 3, 1875, Congress had adopted an act prohibiting the importation into the United States of alien women for the purpose of prostitution, and on February 20, 1907, the act had been amended to prohibit such importation not only 'for the purpose of prostitution' but also 'for any other immoral purpose.'

> "It is apparent that this statute furnished the model for the Mann Act...." William Seagle, The Twilight of the Mann Act, 55 A.B.A.J. 641–42 (1969).

2. Questions and Comments on *Caminetti*. The operative words of the Mann Act at stake in *Caminetti* were "for the purpose of prostitution or debauchery, or for any other immoral purpose." One could read these words (as appears to have been the dominant legislative objective) as limited to transportations for the purpose of promoting large-scale commercialized vice or, perhaps more narrowly, as limited to transportations that facilitated coercive or involuntary participation in organized commercial vice. A broader reading would include all commercial sexual arrangements, even though not part of a larger organization. A still broader reading would include all "immoral" sexual behavior. Broader yet would be all "immoral" purposes having to do with sex or sexual stimulation. The broadest reading would be any "immoral" act, whether or not having sexual connotations.

All of these readings are plausible; no one of them is demanded or foreclosed by the language used by Congress. And surely the dissenters in

Caminetti are right that the problem before the Court cannot be resolved by analysis of the "plain meaning" of the words of the act. But recognition of this point does not resolve the case. How should the Court have interpreted the statute? Are there principles to which one can look that are of any help? Did either the majority or the dissent discover any? On a fresh slate, would one expect the present Court to reach the conclusion reached in 1917?

Of what relevance is the decision in *Bitty*? *Bitty* involved an interpretation of the statute enacted in 1875, and amended in 1907, referred to in the passage from the Seagle article quoted above. At one point in *Bitty*, the Court said that "[t]he statute in question, it must be remembered, was intended to keep out of this country immigrants whose permanent residence here would not be desirable or for the common good, and we cannot suppose either that Congress intended to exempt from the operation of the statute the importation of an alien woman brought here only that she might live in a state of concubinage with the man importing her, or that it did not regard such an importation as being for an immoral purpose." Which side of the *Caminetti* debate does this passage support? Does Congress have the same power (or incentive) to police the character of persons entering a state as it does persons entering the country? Note that *Bitty* was on the books when the Mann Act was passed. Does the dissent effectively distinguish the case? Or does it, as the majority contends, predetermine *Caminetti*'s fate?

3. Prosecutorial Discretion. It is fair to say, given *Caminetti* at least, that the Mann Act literally prohibits a broader range of conduct than Congress explicitly considered in the legislative records that are available. It is also fair to surmise that *not all* people who violate the Mann Act as interpreted in *Caminetti* are brought to federal justice. This characteristic, a statute with a broad—indeed huge—reach that is selectively enforced is typical of federal criminal legislation. What this means is that the Justice Department, and more particularly the individual United States Attorneys around the country, determine what might be called the "real" content of the federal criminal law. The Justice Department has adopted guidelines for prosecution, but they are not judicially enforceable nor is there any formal sanction if an individual United States Attorney institutes a prosecution in violation of the guidelines.[c]

With respect to the Mann Act, "the Department of Justice hardly waited for the ink to dry on the *Caminetti* decision before it reaffirmed the

---

[c] There were some political overtones to *Caminetti*. Caminetti's father was Commissioner of Immigration in a Democratic administration. The U.S. Attorney was a Republican. But there were also some aggravating factors. Caminetti and Diggs were both married, and both had children. They seduced two young women, aged 19 and 20. After the truth became public, they told the women that their wives would take them to juvenile court and have them sent to a reformatory if they didn't run away with the men to Reno. For elaboration of the facts of the case, see William Seagle, The Twilight of the Mann Act, 55 A.B.A.J. 641, 642 (1969); Note, Interstate Immorality: The Mann Act and the Supreme Court, 56 Yale L.J. 718, 727–28 (1946).

enforcement policy which it had followed in the first six years during which the Mann Act was in force." Specifically, and "[f]rom that day to this," Mann Act prosecutions are supposed to be restricted to cases of commercial sex and "only such noncommercial cases as involve a fraudulent over-reaching; previously chaste or very young women or girls (when state laws are inadequate); or married women, with young children, then living with their husbands."[d]

For a more recent example of the use of the Mann Act, see United States v. Fowler, 608 F.2d 2 (D.C.Cir.1979). Two men were convicted of three counts of Mann Act violations for inducing two young women (one was 20 and the other, who had just finished high school, was 17 or 18; neither had previously engaged in prostitution) to come from Buffalo to Washington, D.C., "to 'make some money' from prostitution '[b]ecause it was easier down here.'" When the two women were picked up in Buffalo, two other women were in the car. The four women were driven to a house in Maryland. That evening they were taken to 14th Street in Washington. On the way, they were instructed on how much to charge for various services. As soon as they were deposited on the street, they were told that a woman would approach them with further instructions on "working on the street in D.C."

The court described these facts as "typical of those in the reported Mann Act cases," though particularly egregious. It summed up the situation as follows:

> "Fowler and Gibson involved very young women, one just graduated from high school, in commercial prostitution. This was not merely a personal venture with two young friends. When appellants 'surprised' [the two women] by showing up with [two others] for the trip to Washington, it became apparent that they had recruited a 'stable' and that for them prostitution was big business. Appellants' knowledge of 'white slave' traffic was corroborated by the rapidity with which they dumped the four victims at 14th and K Streets, the local center for on-street prostitution. In addition, most telling is appellants' apparent relationship with an on-street representative of the local organization, whom the victims were told would meet and instruct them in the local modus operandi. The victims were met and instructed as promised, and it would be naive to think that this 'service' was performed without prior understanding that the instructor was to be compensated from the proceeds of the prostitution. In short, Fowler and Gibson were engaged in supplying young women for what appears to be organized prostitution in Washington...."

4. Count Stacking. *Caminetti* and *Fowler* both illustrate another common feature of federal criminal prosecutions. Recall that Diggs, Cami-

---

[d] The quotations in this paragraph are taken from William Seagle, The Twilight of the Mann Act, 55 A.B.A.J. 641, 643 (1969).

netti's companion, was charged with four violations of the Mann Act: transporting his own companion; assisting in the transportation of Caminetti's companion; buying a ticket for his own companion; and buying a ticket for Caminetti's companion. In *Fowler*, the two defendants were charged with three violations: transporting three women from Buffalo to Washington on March 29, 1978; transporting two women from Maryland to Washington on March 30; and transporting two women from Maryland to Washington on March 31.[e] Each "jurisdictional act," as it were, constitutes a separate offense, although typically convictions on such multiple counts do not lead to consecutive sentences. The federal mail fraud statute (18 U.S.C. § 1341) provides another example where the same possibility frequently arises. Since the offense is "use of the mails with intent to defraud" rather than "defrauding someone," *each letter* mailed during the course of a single fraudulent transaction is a separate federal offense.

5. Subsequent Supreme Court Decisions. There have been two major decisions interpreting the Mann Act since *Caminetti*. The first hints that *Caminetti*'s days may be numbered. The second recants the hint.

(i) *Mortensen v. United States*. The defendants in Mortensen v. United States, 322 U.S. 369 (1944), were a husband and wife who operated a house of prostitution in Grand Island, Nebraska. They drove to Yellowstone and Salt Lake City on a short vacation. Two of their prostitutes asked to come along for a little R & R. No "business" was conducted on the trip. It was business as usual, however, after the four travelers returned to Grand Island.

The Mortensens were charged with violations of the Mann Act based on their return trip. As the Supreme Court described the instructions, the jury was charged that "purpose was an essential ingredient of the crime" and that if "the transportation from Salt Lake City to Grand Island was planned with no immoral purpose" they should acquit. However, the jury should convict if it found that the Mortensens "transported the girls from Salt Lake City to Grand Island for the purpose of prostitution and debauchery." The jury convicted and the convictions were sustained by the Circuit Court.

The Supreme Court reversed:

"To constitute a violation of the act, it is essential that the interstate transportation have for its object or be the means of effecting or facilitating the proscribed activities. An intention that the women or girls shall engage in the conduct outlawed by [the act] must be found to exist before the conclusion of the interstate journey and must be the dominant motive of such interstate movement. And the transportation must be designed to bring about such result. Without the necessary intention and motiva-

[e] The second and third counts involved the same two women; these two women were also involved in the first count, along with a third woman (the recent high school graduate) who was arrested on her first night out.

tion, immoral conduct during or following the journey is insufficient to subject the transporter to the penalties of the act."

The question, then, was what was the "dominant motive" of the return trip? On this question, the Court, speaking through Justice Murphy, had two things to say. First, it analyzed the record and found "a complete lack of relevant evidence from which the jury could properly find ... that petitioners transported the girls in interstate commerce 'for the purpose of prostitution or debauchery' within the meaning of the Mann Act":

> "It may be assumed that petitioners anticipated that the two girls would resume their activities as prostitutes upon their return to Grand Island. But we do not think it is fair or permissible under the evidence adduced to infer that this interstate vacation trip, or any part of it, was undertaken by petitioners for the purpose of, or as a means of effecting or facilitating, such activities. The sole purpose of the journey from beginning to end was to provide innocent recreation and a holiday for petitioners and the two girls. It was a complete break or interlude in the operation of petitioners' house of ill fame and was entirely disassociated therefrom. There was no evidence that any immoral acts occurred on the journey or that petitioners forced the girls against their will to return to Grand Island for immoral purposes. What Congress has outlawed by the Mann Act, however, is the use of interstate commerce as a calculated means for effectuating sexual immorality. In ordinary speech an interstate trip undertaken for an innocent vacation purpose constitutes to use of interstate commerce for that innocent purpose. Such a trip does not lose that meaning when viewed in light of a criminal statute outlawing trips for immoral purposes.
>
> "The fact that the two girls actually resumed their immoral practices after their return to Grand Island does not, standing alone, operate to inject a retroactive illegal purpose into the return trip to Grand Island. Nor does it justify an arbitrary splitting of the round trip into two parts so as to permit an inference that the purpose of the drive to Salt Lake City was innocent while the purpose of the homeward journey to Grand Island was criminal. The return journey under the circumstances of this case cannot be considered apart from its integral relation with the innocent round trip as a whole. . . . ."

The Court also added some comments of potentially wider import:

> "We do not here question or reconsider any previous construction placed on the act which may have led the federal government into areas of regulation not originally contemplated by Congress. But experience with the administration of the law admonishes us against adding another chapter of statutory construction and application which would have a similar effect and which would make possible even further justification of the fear expressed at the time of the adoption of the legislation that its broad provisions 'are

liable to furnish boundless opportunity to hold up and blackmail and make unnecessary trouble, without any corresponding benefits to society.' [45 Cong. Rec. 1033.]

"To punish those who transport inmates of a house of prostitution on an innocent vacation trip in no way related to the practice of their commercial vice is consistent neither with the purpose nor with the language of the act. Congress was attempting primarily to eliminate the 'white slave' business which uses inter state and foreign commerce as a means of procuring and distributing its victims and 'to prevent panderers and procurers from compelling thousands of women and girls against their will and desire to enter and continue in a life of prostitution.' [H.Rep. No. 47, p. 10, (61st Cong., 2d Sess.). The same statement appears in S.Rep. No. 886, p. 10 (61st Cong., 2d Sess.). See also 45 Cong. Rec. 805, 821, 1035, 1037.] Such clearly was not the situation revealed by the facts of this case. To accomplish its purpose the statute enumerates the prohibited acts in broad language capable of application beyond that intended by the legislative framers. But even such broad language is conditioned upon the use of interstate transportation for the purpose of, or as a means of effecting or facilitating, the commission of the illegal acts. Here the interstate round trip had no such purpose and was in no way related to the subsequent immoralities in Grand Island. In short, we perceive no statutory purpose or language which prohibits petitioners under these circumstances from using interstate transportation for a vacation or for any other innocent purpose."

Chief Justice Stone, joined by Justices Black, Reed, and Douglas, dissented. The Chief Justice thought that "the policy and wisdom of the Mann Act" was a matter for "Congress to determine, not the courts." As for the evidence in the record:

"The fact that petitioners, who were engaged in an established business of operating a house of prostitution in Nebraska, took some of its women inmates on a transient and innocent vacation trip to other states, is in no way incompatible with the conclusion that petitioners, in bringing them back to Nebraska, purposed and intended that they should resume there the practice of commercialized vice, which in fact they did promptly resume in petitioners' establishment. . . ."

Note that the conduct prohibited by the Mann Act—two or more people crossing a state line; purchasing a railroad ticket for another person—is by any measure entirely innocent. What makes the behavior criminal is the *purpose* with which the conduct is undertaken. And after *Mortensen*, it is the "dominant" purpose that counts, "the use of interstate commerce as a calculated means for effecting sexual immorality." Is the form of the Mann Act (innocent conduct undertaken with culpable intent) subject to criticism? It is undoubtedly preoccupation with the jurisdictional question that led Congress to this form of prohibition. Quite apart from the ultimate reach of the Mann Act, can a case be made that the preoccupation in this instance produced an undesirable approach to defining the offense? Given the definition, moreover, how is one to determine "dominant," as opposed (one would guess) to "subsidiary," motives of interstate travel? Is the requirement that such issues be litigated an efficient approach to the definition of crime?

The Chief Justice suggested that it was contrary to the Court's proper function for the majority to concern itself with the "policy and wisdom" of the act. In what respects did the Court concern itself with the "policy and wisdom" of the act? Suppose the crime were "interstate transportation for the purpose of engaging in bank robberies." If the Mortensen gang returned to Grand Island after their vacation and resumed their commission of bank robberies the next day, would the result have been the same? Should it have been?

(ii) *Cleveland v. United States*. Any implication in *Mortensen* that a narrower approach would be taken to interpretation of the Mann Act was countermanded in Cleveland v. United States, 329 U.S. 14 (1946). The defendants were members of a fundamentalist Mormon sect that "not only believe in polygamy; ... they practice it." Each was convicted of transporting at least one wife across state lines for the purpose of cohabiting with her. The question was whether this objective constituted an "immoral purpose." In an opinion by Justice Douglas, the Supreme Court held that it did. As to the meaning of the statute, Justice Douglas observed:

> "While *Mortensen v. United States* rightly indicated that the act was aimed 'primarily' at the use of interstate commerce for the conduct of the white slave business, we find no indication that a profit motive is a sine qua non to its application. Prostitution, to be sure, normally suggests sexual relations for hire. But debauchery has no such implied limitation. In common understanding the indulgence which that term suggests may be motivated solely by lust. And so we start with words which by their natural import embrace more than commercialized sex. What follows is 'any other immoral purpose.' Under the ejusdem generis rule of construction the general words are confined to the class and may not be used to enlarge it. But we could not give the words a faithful interpretation if we confined them more narrowly than the class of which they are a part.

> "That was the view taken by the Court in the *Bitty* and *Caminetti* cases. We do not stop to reexamine the *Caminetti* case to determine whether the act was properly applied to the facts there presented. But we adhere to its holding, which has been in force for almost 30 years, that the act, while primarily aimed at the use of interstate commerce for the purpose of commercialized sex, is not restricted to that end."

"We conclude," Justice Douglas continued, "that polygamous practices are not excluded from the act." Polygamy "is a practice with far more pervasive influences in society than the casual, isolated transgressions involved in the *Caminetti* case" and represents "a notorious example of promiscuity" that has "long been branded as immoral in the law." Justice Douglas also held both that the requisite purpose as elaborated in *Mortensen* had been sufficiently proved (one woman was transported for the purpose of entering into a plural marriage) and that it was no defense that the defendants were "motivated by a religious belief." On this latter point, Justice Douglas said:

> "That defense claims too much. If upheld, it would place beyond the law any act done under claim of religious sanction. But it has long been held that the fact that polygamy is supported by a religious creed affords no defense in a prosecution for bigamy. Whether the act is immoral within the meaning of the statute is not to be determined by the accused's concepts of morality. Congress has provided the standard."

Justice Rutledge concurred in a separate opinion. Justices Black and Jackson voted to reverse. They said, without elaboration, that "affirmance requires extension of the rule announced in the *Caminetti* case and . . . the correctness of that rule is so dubious that it should at least be restricted to its particular facts." Justice Murphy also dissented. He disagreed with the majority's characterization of polygamy as "'in the same genus' as prostitution and debauchery." He also pointed out that a different part of the statute at issue in *Bitty* specifically excluded "polygamists, or persons who admit their belief in the practice of polygamy" and thus, he concluded, "the phrase 'for any other immoral purpose' . . . certainly did not comprehend polygamy." He concluded:

> "The result here reached is but another consequence of this Court's long-continued failure to recognize that the White Slave Traffic Act, as its title indicates, is aimed solely at the diabolical interstate and international trade in white slaves, 'the business of securing white women and girls and of selling them outright, or of exploiting them for immoral purposes.' H. Rep. No. 47, 61st Cong., 2d Sess., p. 11. The act was suggested and proposed to meet conditions which had arisen in the years preceding 1910 and which had revealed themselves in their ugly details through extensive investigations. The framers of the act specifically stated that it is not directed at immorality in general; it does not even attempt to regulate the practice of voluntary prostitution, leaving that problem to the various states. Its exclusive concern is with those girls and women who are 'unwillingly forced to practice prostitution' and to engage in other similar immoralities' and 'whose lives are lives of involuntary servitude.' Ibid. A reading of the legislative reports and debates makes this narrow purpose so clear as to remove all doubts on the matter. And it is a purpose that has absolutely no relation to the practice of polygamy, however much that practice may have been considered immoral in 1910.

> "Yet this Court in *Caminetti* . . . closed its eyes to the obvious and interpreted the broad words of the statute without regard to

the express wishes of Congress. I think the *Caminetti* case can be factually distinguished from the situation at hand, since it did not deal with polygamy. But the principle of the *Caminetti* case is still with us today, the principle of interpreting the White Slave Traffic Act in disregard of the specific problem with which Congress was concerned. I believe the issue should be met squarely and the *Caminetti* case overruled. It has been on the books for nearly 30 years and its age does not justify its continued existence. Stare decisis certainly does not require a court to perpetuate a wrong for which it was responsible, especially when no rights have accrued in reliance on the error. . . .

"The consequence of prolonging the *Caminetti* principle is to make the federal courts the arbiters of the morality of those who cross state lines in the company of women and girls. They must decide what is meant by 'any other immoral purpose' without regard to the standards plainly set forth by Congress. I do not believe that this falls within the legitimate scope of the judicial function. . . ."

Is Justice Murphy right? He quoted the legislative history in *Mortensen* to the effect that a broad construction of the statute is "liable to furnish boundless opportunity to hold up and blackmail and make unnecessary trouble, without any corresponding benefits to society." Is this an additional reason to exclude cases such as *Caminetti* from the statute? Cases such as *Cleveland*?

6. The Amended Statute. The Mann Act was amended in 1986. It now reads:

"Whoever knowingly transports any individual in interstate or foreign commerce, or in any Territory or Possession of the United States, with intent that such individual engage in prostitution, or in any sexual activity for which any person can be charged with a criminal offense, shall be fined under this title or imprisoned not more than five years, or both." 18 U.S.C. § 2421.

Related provisions deal with a person who "knowingly persuades, induces, entices, or coerces any individual to travel in interstate . . . commerce . . . to engage in prostitution, or in any sexual activity for which any person can be charged with a criminal offense" (18 U.S.C. § 2422(a); five-year maximum); a person who, "using any facility or means of interstate commerce . . . or within the special maritime and territorial jurisdiction . . . knowingly persuades, induces, entices, or coerces" anyone under 18 "to engage in prostitution or any sexual act for which any person may be criminally prosecuted" (18 U.S.C. § 2422(b); ten-year maximum); and a person who "knowingly transports any individual under the age of 18 years in interstate . . . commerce" for the purposes prohibited in § 2421 or who "travels in interstate commerce, or conspires to do so . . . for the purpose of engaging in any sexual act (as defined in section 2245) with a person under 18 years of age that would be a violation of [§§ 2241–45] if the sexual act occurred in the special maritime or territorial jurisdiction of the United States" (18 U.S.C. § 2423; 10-year maximum).

There is no legislative history describing the purpose of these provisions. One objective, plainly, was to describe the Mann Act offense in sex-neutral terms, as is common today in sex-related offenses and as was done at the same time in a comprehensive revision of the rape and sexual assault laws applicable in the special maritime and territorial jurisdiction and in federal prisons.[f] But has the substantive scope of the offense been altered? What is the referent for the term "criminal offense"? Any federal crime? Any federal crime punished by §§ 2241–45? Any crime in the state into which (or from which?) the transportation is made? Any crime in any state? Could there be a prosecution today on the facts of *Caminetti*? *Cleveland*? If Congress wanted to amend the Mann Act, why would it care to preserve these decisions? Is it that hard to come up with language that restricts the coverage of the statute to commercial sex or to coerced prostitution?

SECTION 3: INTERPRETATION OF JURISDICTIONAL ELEMENTS

PRELIMINARY NOTES ON THE TECHNICALITIES OF FEDERAL JURISDICTION

1. Definitions of "Interstate Commerce". Section 10 of title 18 contains a definition of interstate commerce that is generally applicable to federal crimes:

> "The term 'interstate commerce', as used in this title, includes commerce between one State, Territory, Possession, or the District of Columbia and another State, Territory, Possession, or the District of Columbia. ..."[a]

There are also a number of specific offenses that contain their own definitions of interstate commerce. For example, the firearms offenses proscribed in 18 U.S.C. §§ 921–28 are governed by the following definition:

> "The term 'interstate or foreign commerce' includes commerce between any place in a State and any place outside of that State, or within any possession of the United States (not including the Canal Zone) or the District of Columbia, but such term does not include commerce between places within the same State but through any place outside of that State. The term 'State' includes the District of Columbia, the Commonwealth of Puerto Rico, and the possessions of the United States (not including the Canal Zone)." 18 U.S.C. § 921(2).

The Hobbs Act defines commerce as follows:

> "The term 'commerce' means commerce within the District of Columbia, or any Territory or Possession of the United States; all commerce between any point in a State, Territory, Possession, or the District of Columbia and any point outside thereof; all com-

---

[f] See 18 U.S.C. §§ 2241–45.

[a] Section 10 also defines foreign commerce to include "commerce with a foreign country."

merce between points within the same State through any place outside such State; and all other commerce over which the United States has jurisdiction." 18 U.S.C. § 1951(b)(3).

2. Illustrative Issues. The concentration on jurisdiction in federal criminal offenses can lead to some fine splitting of hairs. Consider, for example, the contrast between United States v. Wilson, 266 F. 712 (E.D.Tenn.1920), and Batsell v. United States, 217 F.2d 257 (8th Cir.1954).

(i) *United States v. Wilson.* *Wilson* was a Mann Act prosecution in which the defendant transported a woman from one point in Tennessee to another point in Tennessee. However, the train on which they were traveling passed through a small part of Alabama on the way. The question was whether this conduct constituted transportation "in interstate . . . commerce".

The original Mann Act (notice the date of the case) contained a definition of transportation in interstate commerce stating that it included "transportation from any State or Territory . . . to any other State or Territory." The court said that:

> "This definition necessarily excludes, by implication, transportation from one point in a state to another point in the same state; the words "from" and "to" as used in the act manifestly referring to two different States or Territories as the respective points of origin and final destination of the transportation, and not to a state through which the woman is carried as a mere incident of the through transportation. Hence, as the indictment merely charges transportation of the woman from one point to another in Tennessee, through Alabama, and does not charge that she was transported from Alabama as the point of origin to Tennessee, it necessarily follows that it does not state a case of transportation in interstate commerce, as defined in the White Slave Traffic Act."

(ii) *Batsell v. United States.* When title 18 was recodified in 1948, the Mann Act was revised to cover, in relevant part, anyone who "knowingly transports in interstate . . . commerce . . . any woman or girl for the purpose of prostitution or debauchery, or for any other immoral purpose. . . ." The special definition of interstate commerce was omitted. The revisers notes included the following cryptic comment:

> "Section 397 of title 18, U.S.C., 1940 ed., containing a definition of the terms 'interstate commerce' and 'foreign commerce' was omitted as unnecessary in view of the definition of those terms in section 10 of this title."

Batsell was a post–1948 prosecution under the Mann Act. Gloria Jordell was a prostitute operating in Minneapolis, Minnesota. Batsell told her that he knew someone in Duluth, Minnesota, who might be able to get her into a house of prostitution in Superior, Wisconsin, which is only a short distance from Duluth. They accordingly set off for Duluth by car. They apparently ran into road construction on the way, and took a detour that crossed the state line into Wisconsin. They then passed through

Superior, and recrossed the state line into Duluth. At that point it turned out that there was no job in Superior after all. Batsell was convicted, and on appeal his conviction was affirmed:

"Appellant complains that even if the facts as must have been found by the jury were correct, they do not spell out a violation of the Mann Act. [H]is contention is that the detour from Minnesota into Wisconsin and back into Minnesota again was merely a matter of necessity caused by road conditions and that there was no improper purpose in going into the state of Wisconsin. He relies upon Mortensen v. United States, 322 U.S. 369 (1944). . . .

"[*Mortensen* is not] in point here. The main purpose of this trip so far as the appellant and Gloria Jordell were concerned was to obtain work for her as a prostitute in Superior, Wisconsin. That was the ultimate objective. While it had been first intended that they would cross no state lines and would merely telephone while in Duluth, Minnesota, exigencies of the situation made it necessary for them to cross into Wisconsin, pass through the City of Superior, Wisconsin, and return again into Minnesota. This, in the opinion of the [trial] court, constituted interstate commerce and established a violation of the act. What was said by this court in Neff v. United States, 105 F.2d 688, 691 (8th Cir.1939), is appropriate to the present situation:

'The gist . . . of the offense with which the defendant was charged is the interstate transportation of a female for immoral purposes, and the offense is complete the moment the female has been transported across the state line with the immoral purpose or intent in the mind of the person responsible for her transportation.'

"The accomplishment of the illicit purpose is not necessary to the establishment of guilt. The offense is complete upon the transportation in interstate commerce of a female as a result of the illicit motive. Thus, in the instant case, the act of crossing the state line from Minnesota into Wisconsin, done in furtherance of the illicit motive, is sufficient to establish a violation of the Mann Act, even though the immoral purpose was never achieved. . . ."

(iii) Questions and Comments. In view of the reviser's comment on the reenactment of the Mann Act in 1948, could it be argued that the court in *Batsell* was wrong? Does the definition in 18 U.S.C. § 10 provide a basis for distinguishing *Wilson*? Could the problem in *Wilson* have been cured if the indictment had ignored the actual origin of the trip and charged that the defendant transported the woman "from Alabama to Tennessee"? If the facts of *Wilson* and *Batwell* were revised so that the defendants could be charged with violations of the federal firearms laws and the Hobbs Act, would convictions be upheld?

Hypertechnical questions such as these are common in federal criminal litigation. The focus on jurisdictional elements in the definition of criminal offenses is a defense lawyer's paradise, a device by which the focal point of a case can be deflected from the underlying moral transgression of which the defendant may very well be guilty to a technical defense that, while it may seem diversionary and beside the point to the lay person, is made central to federal guilt by a fetish of long tradition. Litigation is diverted from the iniquitous nature of the underlying activity to whether some technical element of federal jurisdiction can be satisfied. Cases turn not on penological policy, but on how the jurisdictional ingredient of the federal offense happens to have been defined by the Congress on a particular occasion. How likely is it, moreover, that the particular jurisdictional reach of each federal criminal statute fits a coherent conception of the role of the federal government in our criminal justice system? And how many prosecutorial resources are wasted?

(iv) Bribery of Local Officials. Other examples of the centrality of technical questions of jurisdiction to guilt of a federal crime will come up from time to time in the materials to follow. For now, consider one further illustration. The Hobbs Act punishes one who "affects commerce . . . by robbery or extortion." 18 U.S.C. § 1951. The Travel Act applies to one who "travels in interstate . . . commerce . . . with intent to . . . carry on . . . any unlawful activity, and thereafter performs . . . any [unlawful activity]." 18 U.S.C. § 1952(a)(3). "Unlawful activity" is defined to include, inter alia, "extortion, bribery, or arson in violation of the laws of the State in which committed or of the United States." The Hobbs Act has a 20–year maximum sentence; the Travel Act, a five-year maximum.

One of the substantive questions to be dealt with in subsequent materials is whether the Hobbs Act covers bribery of state and local public officials. As will be seen, its definition of "extortion" can arguably be so read. But since the Travel Act explicitly covers such bribery (see the definition of "unlawful activity" quoted above), why would the federal prosecutor care whether the Hobbs Act also applied? One answer, of course, might be the higher maximum penalty provided by the Hobbs Act. But a more likely response is the difference in jurisdictional reach of the two statutes. Under the Travel Act, it must be proved not only that the defendant committed the offense, but also that she or he also traveled in interstate commerce with intent to commit that offense. Under the Hobbs Act it must only be shown that the offense was committed and that it "affected" interstate commerce. Clearly, the Travel Act presents more of a jurisdictional hurdle—one that, in many instances of local bribery, will be difficult if not impossible to satisfy. Thus whether an instance of local bribery is a federal offense at all may turn on whether the Hobbs Act is applicable. Again, therefore, the technical definition of a jurisdictional ingredient has an important practical consequence, in this instance inviting the courts to stretch one offense (the Hobbs Act) in order to overcome a perceived jurisdictional inadequacy of another (the Travel Act).

Moreover, the sentencing consequences of a Hobbs Act as opposed to a Travel Act conviction are not trivial—20 year maximum versus five. If both statutes cover local bribery, the difference between these authorized sentences turns on a technicality of federal jurisdiction. Differential grading of the same type of offense normally should turn, one would think, on factors such as the harm caused and the moral depravity of the defendant. Is there a sensible grading policy that would turn such a difference in penalty on the jurisdictional nuance that separates the Hobbs Act and the Travel Act?

3. Other Bases of Federal Jurisdiction. The commerce power is perhaps the most frequently used basis for federal criminal jurisdiction over offenses that are "auxiliary" or supplementary to state criminal law. There are, however, many other sources of constitutional authority that have been used in service of the "direct" and "auxiliary" interests of the federal government in prosecuting criminal behavior. The bankruptcy power, for example, is the support for the crimes defined in 18 U.S.C. §§ 151–55 (concealment of assets; bribery of trustee; and the like). The postal power is the basis of 18 U.S.C. § 1341 (mail fraud) and the range of offenses covered by 18 U.S.C. §§ 1691–1738 (theft of mail; nonmailable matter; embezzlement of postal funds; and the like). The power to coin money provides the authority, for example, for 18 U.S.C. §§ 471–513, which punish counterfeiting and related offenses. Section 5 of the 14th amendment justifies the civil rights offenses covered by 18 U.S.C. §§ 241–42. And of course there are numerous tax offenses incidental to exercises by Congress of the power to raise revenues.

Technical questions can of course arise with respect to the jurisdictional reach of these offenses. However, most of the offenses of concern in these materials relate to the commerce clause, and it is to the elaboration of that basis of Congressional power that the remainder of this Chapter is devoted.

United States v. Bass

Supreme Court of the United States, 1971.
404 U.S. 336

■ JUSTICE MARSHALL delivered the opinion of the Court.

Respondent was convicted in the Southern District of New York of possessing firearms in violation of title VII of the Omnibus Crime Control and Safe Streets Act of 1968, 18 U.S.C. App. § 1202(a). In pertinent part, that statute reads:

"Any person who—

"(1) has been convicted by a court of the United States or of a State or any political subdivision thereof of a felony . . . and who receives, possesses, or transports in commerce or affecting commerce . . . any firearm shall be fined not more than $10,000 or imprisoned for not more than two years, or both."

The evidence showed that respondent, who had previously been convicted of a felony in New York state, possessed on separate occasions a pistol and then a shotgun. There was no allegation in the indictment and no attempt by the prosecution to show that either firearm had been possessed "in commerce or affecting commerce." The government proceeded on the assumption that § 1202(a)(1) banned all possessions and receipts of firearms by convicted felons, and that no connection with interstate commerce had to be demonstrated in individual cases.

After his conviction, respondent unsuccessfully moved for arrest of judgment on two primary grounds: that the statute did not reach possession of a firearm not shown to have been "in commerce or affecting commerce," and that, if it did, Congress had overstepped its constitutional powers under the commerce clause. The Court of Appeals reversed the conviction, being of the view that if the government's construction of the statute were accepted, there would be substantial doubt about the statute's constitutionality. We granted certiorari [and now] affirm the judgment of the court below....[4] We conclude that § 1202 is ambiguous in the critical respect. Because its sanctions are criminal and because, under the government's broader reading, the statute *would* mark a major inroad into a domain traditionally left to the states, we refuse to adopt the broad reading in the absence of a clearer direction from Congress.

I

Not wishing "to give point to the quip that only when legislative history is doubtful do you go to the statute,"[5] we begin by looking to the text itself. The critical textual question is whether the statutory phrase "in commerce or affecting commerce" applies to "possesses" and "receives" as well as to "transports." If it does, then the government must prove as an essential element of the offense that a possession, receipt, or transportation was "in commerce or affecting commerce"—a burden not undertaken in this prosecution for possession.

While the statute does not read well under either view, "the natural construction of the language" suggests that the clause "in commerce or affecting commerce" qualifies all three antecedents in the list. Porto Rico Railway, Light & Power Co. v. Mor, 253 U.S. 345, 348 (1920). Once "in commerce or affecting commerce" undeniably applies to at least one antecedent, and since it makes sense with all three, the more plausible construction here is that it in fact applies to all three. But although this is a beginning, the argument is certainly neither overwhelming nor decisive.[6]

---

[4] In light of our disposition of the case, we do not reach the question whether, upon appropriate findings, Congress can constitutionally punish the "mere possession" of firearms; thus, we need not consider the relevance, in that connection of our recent decision in Perez v. United States, 402 U.S. 146 (1971). ...

[5] Felix Frankfurter, Some Reflections on the Reading of Statutes, 47 Colum. L. Rev. 527, 543 (1947).

[6] ... The government, noting that there is no comma after "transports," argues that the punctuation indicates a congressional intent to limit the qualifying phrase to the last antecedent. But many leading grammarians, while sometimes noting that commas at the end of series can avoid ambiguity, concede that use of such commas is discretionary. When grammarians are divided, and surely where they are cheerfully tolerant, we will not attach significance to an omitted comma. It is enough to say that the statute's punctu-

In a more significant respect, however, the language of the statute does provide support for respondent's reading. Undeniably, the phrase "in commerce or affecting commerce" is part of the "transports" offense. But if that phrase applies *only* to "transports," the statute would have a curious reach. While permitting transportation of a firearm unless it is transported "in commerce or affecting commerce," the statute would prohibit all possessions of firearms, and both interstate and intrastate receipts. Since virtually all transportations, whether interstate or intrastate, involve an accompanying possession or receipt, it is odd indeed to argue that on the one hand the statute reaches all possessions and receipts, and on the other hand outlaws only interstate transportations. Even assuming that a person can "transport" a firearm under the statute without possessing or receiving it, there is no reason consistent with any discernible purpose of the statute to apply an interstate commerce requirement to the "transports" offense alone.[7] In short, the government has no convincing explanation for the inclusion of the clause "in commerce or affecting commerce" if that phrase only applies to the word "transports." It is far more likely that the phrase was meant to apply to "possesses" and "receives" as well as "transports." As the court below noted, the inclusion of such a phrase "mirror[s] the approach to federal criminal jurisdiction reflected in many other federal statutes."

Nevertheless, the government argues that its reading is to be preferred because the defendant's narrower interpretation would make title VII redundant with title IV of the same act. Title IV, inter alia, makes it a crime for four categories of people—including those convicted of a crime punishable for a term exceeding one year—"to ship or transport any firearm or ammunition in interstate or foreign commerce [or] to receive any firearm or ammunition which has been shipped or transported in interstate or foreign commerce." 18 U.S.C. §§ 922(g) and (h). As Senator Long, the sponsor of title VII, represented to Senator Dodd, the sponsor of title IV, title VII indeed does complement title IV. Respondent's reading of title VII is fully consistent with this view. First, although subsections of the two titles do address their prohibitions to some of the same people, each statute also reaches substantial groups of people not reached by the other.[9]

ation is fully consistent with the respondent's interpretation, and that in this case grammatical expertise will not help to clarify the statute's meaning.

[7] The government urges that "transports" includes the act of "causing a firearm to be transported," and therefore would connote an offense separate in some cases from "receives" or "possesses." From this, the government argues that "Congress might have felt that the broader scope of the term 'transports,' as compared to the terms 're-ceives' or 'possesses,' justified its qualification by the interstate commerce requirement." Brief for the United States 14–15.

The government's view about the comparative breadth of the various offenses certainly does not follow from its definition of "transports." But beyond that, its argument about what Congress "might have felt" is purely speculative, and finds no support in any arguable purpose of the statute. There is certainly no basis for concluding that Congress was less concerned about the transporting and supplying of guns than their acquisition.

[9] Title VII limits the firearm-related activity of convicted felons, dishonorable discharges from the Armed Services, persons adjudged "mentally incompetent," aliens illegally in the country, and former citizens who

Secondly, title VII complements title IV by punishing a broader class of behavior. Even under respondent's view, a title VII offense is made out if the firearm was possessed or received "in commerce or affecting commerce"; however, title IV apparently does not reach possessions or intrastate transactions at all, even those with an interstate commerce nexus, but is limited to the sending or receiving of firearms as part of an interstate transportation.[10]

In addition, whatever reading is adopted, title VII and title IV are, in part, redundant. The interstate commerce requirement in title VII minimally applies to transportation. Since title IV also prohibits convicted criminals from transporting firearms in interstate commerce, the two titles overlap under both readings. The government's broader reading of title VII does not eliminate the redundancy, but simply creates a larger area in which there is no overlap. While the government would be on stronger ground if its reading were necessary to give title VII some unique and independent thrust, this is not the case here. In any event, circumstances surrounding the passage of title VII make plain that title VII was not carefully molded to complement title IV. Title VII was a last-minute Senate amendment to the Omnibus Crime Control and Safe Streets Act. The amendment was hastily passed, with little discussion, no hearings, and no report.[11] The notion that it was enacted to dovetail neatly with title IV

have renounced their citizenship. A felony is defined as "any offense punishable by imprisonment for a term exceeding one year, but does not include any offense (other than one involving a firearm or explosive) classified as a misdemeanor under the laws of a State and punishable by a term of imprisonment of two years or less...." 18 U.S.C. § 1202(c)(2).

Title IV reaches persons "under indictment for, or ... convicted in any court of, a crime punishable by imprisonment for a term exceeding one year"; fugitives from justice; users or addicts of various drugs; persons adjudicated as "mental defective[s] or ... committed" to a mental institution. 18 U.S.C. §§ 922(g) and (h).

10 Title IV is a modified and recodified version of [a statute passed in 1961], which in turn amended the original statute passed in 1938. Each amendment enlarged the group of people coming within the act's substantive prohibitions against transportation or receipt of firearms in interstate commerce. The wording of the substantive offense has remained identical, although the original act had a provision that possession of a firearm "shall be presumptive evidence that such firearm or ammunition was shipped or transported or received [in interstate or foreign commerce]." That presumption was struck

down in Tot v. United States, 319 U.S. 463 (1943), and the Court there noted:

"[T]he act is confined to the receipt of firearms or ammunition as a part of interstate transportation and does not extend to the receipt, in an intrastate transaction, of such articles which, at some prior time, have been transported interstate."

While the reach of title IV itself is a question to be decided finally some other day, the government has presented here no learning or other evidence indicating that the 1968 act changed the prior approach to the "receipt" offense.

11 The Omnibus Crime Control and Safe Streets Act of 1968 started its life as a measure designed to aid state and local governments in law enforcement by means of financial and administrative assistance. The bill passed the House on August 8, 1967, and went to the Senate. A similar bill was introduced in the Senate (S. 917) and went to the Committee on the Judiciary, which rewrote it completely. The amendments included the much debated provisions regarding the admissibility of confessions, wiretapping, and state firearm control.

On May 17, 1968, Senator Long introduced on the floor his amendment to S. 917,

rests perhaps on a conception of the model legislative process; but we cannot pretend that all statutes are model statutes. While courts should interpret a statute with an eye to the surrounding statutory landscape and an ear for harmonizing potentially discordant provisions, these guiding principles are not substitutes for congressional lawmaking. In our view, no conclusion can be drawn from title IV concerning the correct interpretation of title VII.

Other aspects of the meager legislative history, however, do provide some significant support for the government's interpretation. On the Senate floor, Senator Long, who introduced § 1202, described various evils that prompted his statute. These evils included assassinations of public figures and threats to the operation of businesses significant enough in the aggregate to affect commerce. Such evils, we note, would be most thoroughly mitigated by forbidding every possession of any firearm by specified classes of especially risky people, regardless of whether the gun was possessed, received, or transported "in commerce or affecting commerce." In addition, specific remarks of the Senator can be read to state that the amendment reaches the mere possession of guns without any showing of an interstate commerce nexus.[13] But Senator Long never specifically says that no connection with commerce need be shown in the individual case. And nothing in his statements explains why, if an interstate commerce nexus is irrelevant in individual cases, the phrase "in commerce or affecting commerce" is in the statute at all.[14] But even if Senator Long's

which he designated as title VII. His introductory remarks set forth the purpose of the amendment. About a week later he explained his amendment once again. There was a brief debate; the reaction was favorable but cautious, with "further thought" and "study" being suggested by several favorably inclined Senators who observed some problems with the bill as drafted. Unexpectedly, however, there was a call for a vote and title VII passed without modification. The amendment received only passing mention in the House discussion of the Bill, and never received committee consideration or study in the House either.

[13] For example, Senator Long began his floor statement by announcing: "I have prepared an amendment which I will offer at an appropriate time, simply setting forth the fact that anybody who has been convicted of a felony [or comes within certain other categories] is not permitted to possess a firearm...." 114 Cong. Rec. 13868.

[14] For the same, and additional reasons, § 1201, which contains the congressional "findings" applicable to § 1202(a), is not decisive support for the government. That section reports that:

"The Congress hereby finds and declares that the receipt, possession, or transportation of a firearm by felons, veterans who are discharged under dishonorable conditions, mental incompetents, aliens who are illegally in the country, and former citizens who have renounced their citizenship, constitutes—

"(1) a burden on commerce or threat affecting the free flow of commerce,

"(2) a threat to the safety of the President of the United States and Vice President of the United States,

"(3) an impediment or a threat to the exercise of free speech and the free exercise of a religion guaranteed by the first amendment to the Constitution of the United States, and

"(4) a threat to the continued and effective operation of the Government of the United States and of the government of each State guaranteed by article IV of the Constitution."

The government argues that these findings would have been "wholly unnecessary" un-

remarks were crystal clear to us, they were apparently not crystal clear to his congressional colleagues. Meager as the discussion of title VII was, one of the few Congressmen who discussed the amendment summarized title VII as "mak[ing] it a federal crime to take, possess, or receive a firearm across state lines...." 114 Cong. Rec. 16298 (statement of Rep. Pollock).

In short, "the legislative history of [the] act hardly speaks with that clarity of purpose which Congress supposedly furnishes courts in order to enable them to enforce its true will." Universal Camera Corp. v. NLRB, 340 U.S. 474, 483 (1951). Here, as in other cases, the various remarks by legislators "are sufficiently ambiguous insofar as this narrow issue is concerned ... to invite mutually destructive dialectic," and not much more. FCC v. Columbia Broadcasting System, 311 U.S. 132, 136 (1940). Taken together, the statutory materials are inconclusive on the central issue of whether or not the statutory phrase "in commerce or affecting commerce" applies to "possesses" and "receives" as well as "transports." While standing alone, the legislative history might tip in the government's favor, the respondent explains far better the presence of critical language in the statute. The government concedes that "the statute is not a model of logic or clarity." After "seiz[ing] everything from which aid can be derived," we are left with an ambiguous statute.

II

Given this ambiguity, we adopt the narrower reading: the phrase "in commerce or affecting commerce" is part of all three offenses, and the present conviction must be set aside because the government has failed to show the requisite nexus with interstate commerce. This result is dictated by two wise principles this Court has long followed.

First, as we have recently reaffirmed, "ambiguity concerning the ambit of criminal statutes should be resolved in favor of lenity." Rewis v. United States, 401 U.S. 808, 812 (1971). In various ways over the years, we have stated that "when choice has to be made between two readings of what conduct Congress has made a crime, it is appropriate, before we choose the harsher alternative, to require that Congress should have spoken in language that is clear and definite." United States v. Universal C.I.T. Credit Corp., 344 U.S. 218, 221–22 (1952). This principle is founded on two policies that have long been part of our tradition. First, "a fair warning should be given to the world in language that the common world will understand, of what the law intends to do if a certain line is passed. To make the warning fair, so far as possible the line should be clear."

less Congress intended to prohibit all receipts and possessions of firearms by felons. But these findings of "burdens" and "threats" simply state Congress' view of the constitutional basis for its power to act; the findings do not tell us how much of Congress' perceived power was in fact invoked. That the findings in fact support a statute broader than the one actually passed is suggested by the fact that "in commerce or affecting commerce" does not appear at all in the introductory clause to the "findings," even though § 1202(a) contains the phrase and concededly reaches only transportations "in commerce or affecting commerce."

McBoyle v. United States, 283 U.S. 25, 27 (1931)(Holmes, J.).[15] Second, because of the seriousness of criminal penalties, and because criminal punishment usually represents the moral condemnation of the community, legislatures and not courts should define criminal activity. This policy embodies "the instinctive distaste against men languishing in prison unless the lawmaker has clearly said they should." H. Friendly, Mr. Justice Frankfurter and the Reading of Statutes, in Benchmarks 196, 209 (1967). Thus, where there is ambiguity in a criminal statute, doubts are resolved in favor of the defendant. Here, we conclude that Congress has not "plainly and unmistakably" made it a federal crime for a convicted felon simply to possess a gun absent some demonstrated nexus with interstate commerce.

There is a second principle supporting today's result: unless Congress conveys its purpose clearly, it will not be deemed to have significantly changed the federal-state balance. Congress has traditionally been reluctant to define as a federal crime conduct readily denounced as criminal by the states. This congressional policy is rooted in the same concepts of American federalism that have provided the basis for judge-made doctrines. As this Court emphasized only last term in *Rewis v. United States*, supra, we will not be quick to assume that Congress has meant to effect a significant change in the sensitive relation between federal and state criminal jurisdiction. In traditionally sensitive areas, such as legislation affecting the federal balance, the requirement of clear statement assures that the legislature has in fact faced, and intended to bring into issue, the critical matters involved in the judicial decision. In *Rewis*, we declined to accept an expansive interpretation of the Travel Act. To do so, we said then, "would alter sensitive federal-state relationships [and] could over-extend limited federal police resources." While we noted there that "[i]t is not for us to weigh the merits of these factors," we went on to conclude that "the fact that they are not even discussed in the legislative history . . . strongly suggests that Congress did not intend that [the statute have the broad reach]." In the instant case, the broad construction urged by the government renders traditionally local criminal conduct a matter for federal enforcement and would also involve a substantial extension of federal police resources. Absent proof of some interstate commerce nexus in each case, § 1202(a) dramatically intrudes upon traditional state criminal jurisdiction. As in *Rewis* the legislative history provides scanty basis for concluding that Congress faced these serious questions and meant to affect

---

[15] Holmes prefaced his much-quoted statement with the observation that "it is not likely that a criminal will carefully consider the text of the law before he murders or steals. . . ." But in the case of gun acquisition and possession it is not unreasonable to imagine a citizen attempting to "[steer] a careful course between violation of the statute [and lawful conduct]." Of course, where there is a state law prohibiting felons from possessing firearms, as in New York State, it may be unreal to argue that there are notice problems under the federal law. There are many states, however, that do not have their own laws prohibiting felons from possessing firearms. See Martin S. Geisel, Richard Roll & R. Stanton Wettick, Jr., The Effectiveness of State and Local Regulation of Handguns: A Statistical Analysis, 1969 Duke L.J. 647, 652–53. Since ex-offenders in these states are limited only by the federal gun control laws, the notice problem of that law may be quite real.

the federal-state balance in the way now claimed by the government. Absent a clearer statement of intention from Congress than is present here, we do not interpret § 1202(a) to reach the "mere possession" of firearms.

III

Having concluded that the commerce requirement in § 1202(a) must be read as part of the "possesses" and "receives" offenses, we add a final word about the nexus with interstate commerce that must be shown in individual cases. The government can obviously meet its burden in a variety of ways. We note only some of these. For example, a person "possesses . . . in commerce or affecting commerce" if at the time of the offense the gun was moving interstate or on an interstate facility, or if the possession affects commerce. Significantly broader in reach, however, is the offense of "receiv[ing] . . . in commerce or affecting commerce," for we conclude that the government meets its burden here if it demonstrates that the firearm received has previously traveled in interstate commerce.[18] This is not the narrowest possible reading of the statute, but canons of clear statement and strict construction do "not mean that every criminal statute must be given the narrowest possible meaning in complete disregard of the purpose of the legislature." United States v. Bramblett, 348 U.S. 503, 510 (1955). We have resolved the basic uncertainty about the statute in favor of the narrow reading, concluding that "in commerce or affecting commerce" is part of the offense of possessing or receiving a firearm. But, given the evils that prompted the statute and the basic legislative purpose of restricting the firearm-related activity of convicted felons, the readings we give to the commerce requirement, although not all narrow, are appropriate. And consistent with our regard for the sensitive relation between federal and state criminal jurisdiction, our reading preserves as an element of all the offenses a requirement suited to federal criminal jurisdiction alone.

The judgment is affirmed.

JUSTICE BRENNAN joins the judgment of the Court and the opinion except for Part III. No question of the quantum of evidence necessary to establish the government's prima facie case is before the Court and he would await a case properly presenting that question before deciding it.

JUSTICE BLACKMUN, with whom CHIEF JUSTICE BURGER joins, dissenting.

I cannot join the Court's opinion and judgment. Five of the six United States Courts of Appeals that have passed upon the issue presented by this case have decided it adversely to the position urged by the respondent here.
. . .

1. The statute, 18 U.S.C. App. § 1202(a), when it speaks of one "who receives, possesses, or transports in commerce or affecting commerce," although arguably ambiguous and, as the government concedes, "not a

---

[18] This reading preserves a significant difference between the "receipt" offenses under title IV and title VII.

model of logic or clarity," is clear enough. The structure of the vital language and its punctuation make it refer to one who receives, to one who possesses, and to one who transports in commerce. If one wished to say that he would welcome a cat, would welcome a dog, or would welcome a cow that jumps over the moon, he would likely say "I would like to have a cat, a dog, or a cow that jumps over the moon." So it is here.

2. The meaning the Court implants on the statute is justified only by the addition and interposition of a comma after the word "transports." I perceive no warrant for this judicial transfiguration.

3. In the very same statute the phrase "after the date of enactment of this act" is separated by commas and undeniably modifies each of the preceding words, "receives," "possesses," and "transports." Obviously, then, the draftsman—and the Congress—knew the use of commas for phrase modification. We should give effect to the only meaning attendant upon that use.

4. The specific finding in 18 U.S.C. App. § 1201[3] clearly demonstrates that Congress was attempting to reach and prohibit every possession of a firearm by a felon; that Congress found that such possession, whether interstate or intrastate, affected interstate commerce; and that Congress did not conclude that intrastate possession was a matter of less concern to it than interstate possession. That finding was unnecessary if Congress also required proof that each receipt or possession of a firearm was in or affected interstate or foreign commerce.

5. Senator Long's explanatory comments reveal clearly the purpose, the intent, and the extent of the legislation:

> "I have prepared an amendment which I will offer at an appropriate time, simply setting forth the fact that anybody who has been convicted of a felony ... is not permitted to *possess* a firearm. . . .

> "It might be well to analyze, for a moment, the logic involved. When a man has been convicted of a felony, unless—as this bill sets forth—he has been expressly pardoned by the President and the pardon states that the person is to be permitted to *possess* firearms in the future, that man would have no right to *possess* firearms. He would be punished criminally if he is found in *possession* of them." 14 Cong. Rec. 13868 (emphasis supplied).

> "So Congress simply finds that the *possession* of these weapons by the wrong kind of people is either a burden on commerce or a threat that affects the free flow of commerce.

---

[3] "§ 1201. Congressional findings and declaration.

"The Congress hereby finds and declares that the receipt, possession, or transportation of a firearm by felons ... constitutes—

"(1) a burden on commerce or threat affecting the free flow of commerce. ..."

"You cannot do business in an area, and you certainly cannot do as much of it and do it as well as you would like, if in order to do business you have to go through a street where there are burglars, murderers, and arsonists armed to the teeth against innocent citizens. So the threat certainly affects the free flow of commerce." 114 Cong. Rec. 13869 (emphasis supplied).

"What the amendment seeks to do is to make it unlawful for a firearm—be it a handgun, a machine gun, a long-range rifle, or any kind of firearm—to be in the *possession* of a convicted felon who has not been pardoned and who has therefore lost his right to *possess* firearms. ... It also relates to the transportation of firearms. ...

"Clauses 1–5 describe persons who, by their actions, have demonstrated that they are dangerous, or that they may become dangerous, Stated simply, they may not be trusted to *possess* a firearm without becoming a threat to society. This title would apply both to hand guns and to long guns. ...

"All of these murderers had shown violent tendencies before they committed the crime for which they are most infamous. They should not have been permitted to *possess* a gun. Yet, there is no federal law which would deny *possession* to these undesirables.

"The killer of Medgar Evers, the murderer of the three civil rights workers in Mississippi, the defendants who shot Captain Lemuel Penn (on a highway while he was driving back to Washington after completion of reserve military duty) would all be free under present federal law to acquire another gun and repeat those same sorts of crimes in the future. ...

"So, under title VII, every citizen could *possess* a gun until the commission of his first felony. Upon his conviction, however, title VII would deny every assassin, murderer, thief and burglar of *the right to possess* a firearm in the future except where he has been pardoned by the President or a state Governor and has been expressly authorized by his pardon to possess a firearm.

"It has been said that Congress lacks the power to outlaw *mere possession* of weapons. ...

" ... The important point is that this legislation demonstrates that *possession* of a deadly weapon by the wrong people can be controlled by Congress, without regard to where the police power resides under the Constitution.

"Without question, the federal government does have power to control *possession* of weapons where such *possession* could become a threat to interstate commerce. ...

"State gun control laws where they exist have proven inadequate to bar *possession* of firearms from those most likely to use them for unlawful purposes. ...

"Nor would title VII impinge upon the rights of citizens generally to *possess* firearms for legitimate and lawful purposes. It deals solely with those who have demonstrated that they cannot be trusted to *possess* a firearm—those whose prior acts—mostly voluntary—have placed them outside of our society. ...

" ... I am convinced that we have enough constitutional power to prohibit these categories of people from *possessing*, receiving, or transporting a firearm. ...

"This amendment would provide that a convicted felon who participates in one of these marches and *is carrying a firearm* would be violating the law...." 114 Cong. Rec. 14773–74 (emphasis supplied).

One cannot detect in these remarks any purpose to restrict or limit the type of possession that was being considered for proscription.

6. The Court's construction of § 1202(a), limiting its application to interstate possession and receipt, shrinks the statute into something little more than a duplication of 18 U.S.C. §§ 922(g) and (h). I cannot ascribe to Congress such a gesture of nonaccomplishment.

I thus conclude that § 1202(a) was intended to and does reach all possessions and receipts of firearms by convicted felons, and that the Court should move on and decide the constitutional issue present in this case.

NOTES ON THE INTERPRETATION OF JURISDICTIONAL ELEMENTS

1. *Rewis v. United States*. Rewis v. United States, 401 U.S. 808 (1971), is often cited for the proposition that "ambiguity concerning the ambit of criminal statutes should be resolved in favor of lenity." In *Rewis*, two defendants, James Rewis and Mary Lee Williams, ran a "lottery, or numbers operation" in Yulee, Florida. Yulee is located only a few miles south of the Florida–Georgia state line. Operation of the lottery was a violation of state law, as was patronizing such a lottery. Two other defendants, Georgia residents, traveled to Yulee from their homes in Georgia to place bets. All four were convicted of violating the Travel Act, 18 U.S.C. § 1952, which in relevant part provides:

"(a) Whoever travels in interstate ... commerce ... with intent to ... promote, manage, establish, carry on, or facilitate the promotion, management, establishment, or carrying on, of any unlawful activity, and thereafter performs or attempts to perform [such unlawful activity] shall be fined under this title, imprisoned for not more than five years, or both.

"(b) As used in this section ... 'unlawful activity' means ... any business enterprise involving gambling ... in violation of the laws of the State ... or of the United States...."

The Court of Appeals reversed the conviction of the two Georgia residents, holding that § 1952 "did not make it a federal crime merely to cross a state line for the purpose of placing a bet."[b] The Court of Appeals affirmed the convictions of Rewis and Williams, however, "on the grounds that operators of gambling establishments are responsible for the interstate travel of their customers." There was no evidence that Rewis or Williams had ever crossed a state line in connection with the operation of the lottery.

The Supreme Court, Justice Marshall writing, unanimously reversed:[c]

"We agree with the Court of Appeals that it cannot be said, with certainty sufficient to justify a criminal conviction, that Congress intended that interstate travel by mere customers of a gambling establishment should violate the Travel Act. But we are also unable to conclude that conducting a gambling operation frequented by out-of-state betters, by itself, violates the act. Section 1952 prohibits interstate travel with the intent to 'promote, manage, establish, carry on, or facilitate' certain kinds of illegal activity; and the ordinary meaning of this language suggests that the traveler's purpose must involve more than the desire to patronize the illegal activity. Legislative history of the act is limited, but does reveal that § 1952 was aimed primarily at organized crime and, more specifically, at persons who reside in one state while operating or managing illegal activities located in another.[6] In addition, we are struck by what Congress did not say. Given the ease with which citizens of our nation are able to travel and the existence of many multi-state metropolitan areas,

[b] The government did not appeal this ruling.

[c] Justice White did not participate in the decision.

[6] "Incorporated in the Senate Report (Report No. 644, 87th Cong., 1st Sess., dated July 27, 1961) the following appears:

'The bill ... was introduced by the Chairman of the Committee, Senator James O. Eastland, on April 18, 1961, on the recommendation of the Attorney General, Robert F. Kennedy, as a part of the Attorney General's legislative program to combat organized crime and racketeering.

'The Attorney General testified before the committee in support of the bill ... and commented:

' "[W]e are seeking to take effective action against the racketeer who conducts an unlawful business but lives far from the scene in comfort and safety, as well as against other hoodlums.

' "Let me say from the outset that we do not seek or intend to impede the travel of anyone except persons engaged in illegal businesses as spelled out in the bill. ...

' "The target clearly is organized crime. The travel that would be banned is travel 'in furtherance of a business enterprise' which involves gambling, liquor, narcotics, and prostitution offenses or extortion or bribery. Obviously, we are not trying to curtail the sporadic, casual involvement in these offenses, but rather a continuous course of conduct sufficient for it to be termed a business enterprise. ...

' "Our investigations also have made it quite clear that only the federal government can shut off the funds which permit the top men of organized crime to live far from the scene and, therefore, remain immune from the local officials." ' "

substantial amounts of criminal activity, traditionally subject to state regulation, are patronized by out-of-state customers. In such a context, Congress would certainly recognize that an expansive Travel Act would alter sensitive federal-state relationships, could overextend limited federal police resources, and might well produce situations in which the geographic origin of customers, a matter of happenstance, would transform relatively minor state offenses into federal felonies. It is not for us to weigh the merits of these factors, but the fact that they are not even discussed in the legislative history of § 1952 strongly suggests that Congress did not intend that the Travel Act should apply to criminal activity solely because that activity is at times patronized by persons from another state. In short, neither statutory language nor legislative history supports such a broad ranging interpretation of § 1952. And even if this lack of support were less apparent, ambiguity concerning the ambit of criminal statutes should be resolved in favor of lenity, Bell v. United States, 349 U.S. 81 (1955)."

The government responded that the Travel Act should be applied either when the "operator can reasonably foresee that customers will cross state lines for the purpose of patronizing the illegal operation" or "whenever the operator actively seeks to attract business from another state." The first construction was rejected because "there is little, if any, evidence that Congress intended that foreseeability should govern criminal liability under § 1952" and because such an interpretation "is almost as expansive as interpretations that we have already rejected." "Whenever individuals actually cross state lines for the purpose of patronizing a criminal establishment," Justice Marshall continued, "it will almost always be reasonable to say that the operators of the establishment could have foreseen that some of their customers would come from out-of-state." As to the government's second construction, the Court responded:

"There may, however, be greater support for the second half of the government's proposed interpretation—that active encouragement of interstate passage violates the act. Of course, the conduct deemed to constitute active encouragement must be more than merely conducting the illegal operation; otherwise, this interpretation would only restate other constructions which we have rejected. Still, there are cases in which federal courts have correctly applied § 1952 to those individuals whose agents or employees cross state lines in furtherance of illegal activity, and the government argues that the principles of those decisions should be extended to cover persons who actively seek interstate patronage. Although we are cited no cases which have gone so far and although much of what we have said casts substantial doubt on the government's broad argument, there may be occasional situations in which the conduct encouraging interstate patronage so closely approximates the conduct of a principal in a criminal agency relationship that the Travel Act is violated."

The Court declined to explore the applicability of this theory on these facts, however, because "we are not informed of any action by petitioners, other than actually conducting their lottery, that was designed to attract out-of-state customers" and because, in any event, the jury was not asked to find "that petitioners actively sought interstate patronage."

2. *McBoyle v. United States*. McBoyle v. United States, 283 U.S. 25 (1931), was decided by a well-known opinion by Justice Holmes for a unanimous Court. The defendant was convicted of interstate transportation of an airplane that he knew to have been stolen. Prosecution was based on the Dyer Act, now 18 U.S.C. § 2311–12, which at the time provided a five-year maximum sentence for anyone who "shall transport or cause to be transported in interstate or foreign commerce a motor vehicle, knowing the same to have been stolen...." "Motor vehicle" was defined as "an automobile, automobile truck, automobile wagon, motor cycle, or any other self-propelled vehicle not designed for running on rails." "The question," Justice Holmes said, "is the meaning of the word 'vehicle' in the phrase 'any other self-propelled vehicle not designed for running on rails.'" The answer was as follows:

> "No doubt etymologically it is possible to use the word to signify a conveyance working on land, water or air..... But in everyday speech 'vehicle' calls up the picture of a thing moving on land. [H]ere, the phrase under discussion calls up the popular picture. For after including automobile truck, automobile wagon and motor cycle, the words 'any other self-propelled vehicle not designed for running on rails' ... indicate that a vehicle in the popular sense, that is a vehicle running on land, is the theme. It is a vehicle that runs, not something, not commonly called a vehicle, that flies. Airplanes were well known in 1919, when this statute was passed; but it is admitted that they were not mentioned in the reports or in the debates in Congress. It is impossible to read words that so carefully enumerate the different forms of motor vehicles and have no reference of any kind to aircraft, as including airplanes under a term that usage more and more precisely confines to a different class. The counsel for the petitioner have shown that the phraseology of the statute as to motor vehicles follows that of earlier statutes of [several states and the District of Columbia], none of which can be supposed to leave the earth.

> "Although it is not likely that a criminal will carefully consider the text of the law before he murders or steals, it is reasonable that a fair warning should be given to the world in language that the common world will understand, of what the law intends to do if a certain line is passed. To make the warning fair, so far as possible the line should be clear. When a rule of conduct is laid down in words that evoke in the common mind only the picture of vehicles moving on land, the statute should not be extended to aircraft, simply because it may seem to us that a similar policy

applies, or upon the speculation that, if the legislature had thought of it, very likely broader words would have been used."

3. Questions and Comments. The first part of the Court's opinion in *Bass* is devoted to a demonstration that the statute is ambiguous, hardly a debatable proposition. Part II resolves the ambiguity by resort to "two wise principles this Court has long followed." Do these principles demand that *all* cases resolving ambiguity in criminal statutes be decided in favor of the defendant? Plainly not, which might lead a cynic to suggest that the principles offer a convenient explanation when the Court has decided for other reasons to reject the broader of two plausible interpretations of a criminal statute. If this cynical comment is right, what might those other reasons be? If it is wrong, what means of distinction do the principles offer for deciding when to accept and when to reject a defendant's argument?

In Part III of its opinion, the Court says that the interstate commerce requirement of the "receiving" part of the offense in § 1202(a) is satisfied if "the firearm received has previously traveled in interstate commerce." "This is not the narrowest possible reading of the statute," the Court continues, "but canons of clear statement and strict construction do 'not mean that every criminal statute must be given the narrowest possible meaning in complete disregard of the purpose of the legislature.'" Why not? Because "the readings we give to the commerce requirement, although not all narrow, are appropriate"? What makes them more appropriate than dispensing with the commerce requirement entirely? As a practical matter, it would save significant prosecutorial time and money if the commerce element were abandoned for the possession offense. What, exactly, justifies the imposition of those costs?

Notice in connection with these questions that *McBoyle* did not involve the interstate commerce aspect of the Dyer Act, but instead its substantive reach, that is, the kinds of stolen property to which the act extended. Does this difference make a difference? Are the "wise principles" of *Bass* equally, or more or less, applicable to the facts of *McBoyle*?

On the general topic of lenity in federal criminal law, Dan M. Kahan has suggested that the "rule of lenity" can best be explained as a "nondelegation doctrine" designed to prevent federal courts from exercising discretion in the interpretation of federal criminal statutes. See Dan M. Kahan, "Lenity and Federal Common Law Crimes," 1994 Supreme Ct. Rev. 345 (1995). Kahan notes that, despite the claim that there are no federal common law crimes, see United States v. Hudson & Goodwin, 11 U.S. (7 Cranch) 32, 34 (1812), the federal courts have long engaged in interstitial lawmaking, even in the criminal law context. He contends that the lenity has usually been invoked in an effort to block such judicial lawmaking, but has largely failed to constrain the courts (or at least has not constrained them on a consistent basis). Kahan concludes that the "rule of lenity" should be abolished, and that we should develop a new theory of federal common law crimes (i.e., a theory about the proper role of the federal courts in interpreting federal criminal statutes, including resolving ambiguities and filling in gaps in statutes).

Does Kahan's explanation suggest that "judicial conservatives"—i.e., those who believe that judges should resist the urge to be lawmakers—should favor lenity, while "judicial activists"—i.e., those who advocate judicial lawmaking—should oppose it? There is some recent evidence of this. See, e.g., Moskal v. United States, 498 U.S. 103 (1990), in which Justice Marshall, writing for the Court, refused to apply the "rule of lenity," while Justice Scalia, in dissent, forcefully defended the rule. Is there any reason to prefer Kahan's proposed alternative approach? Would it make any of the difficult questions of statutory interpretation easier?

Scarborough v. United States

Supreme Court of the United States, 1977.
431 U.S. 563.

■ JUSTICE MARSHALL delivered the opinion of the Court.

Petitioner was convicted of possessing a firearm in violation of title VII of the Omnibus Crime Control and Safe Streets Act of 1968 (Omnibus Crime Control Act), 18 U.S.C. App. §§ 1201–03. The statute provides, in pertinent part:

"Any person who—

"(1) has been convicted by a court of the United States or of a State or any political subdivision thereof of a felony ... and who receives, possesses, or transports in commerce or affecting commerce ... any firearm shall be fined not more than $10,000 or imprisoned for not more than two years, or both." 18 U.S.C. App. § 1202(a).[1]

The issue in this case is whether proof that the possessed firearm previously traveled in interstate commerce is sufficient to satisfy the statutorily required nexus between the possession of a firearm by a convicted felon and commerce.

I

In 1972 petitioner pleaded guilty in the Circuit Court of Fairfax County, Va., to the felony of possession of narcotics with intent to distrib-

---

[1] Section 1202(a) reads in full:

"(a) Any person who—

"(1) has been convicted by a court of the United States or of a State or any political subdivision thereof of a felony, or

"(2) has been discharged from the Armed Forces under dishonorable conditions, or

"(3) has been adjudged by a court of the United States or of a State or any

political subdivision thereof of being mentally incompetent, or

"(4) having been a citizen of the United States has renounced his citizenship, or

"(5) being an alien is illegally or unlawfully in the United States,

"who receives, possesses, or transports in commerce or affecting commerce, after the date of enactment of this Act, any firearm shall be fined not more than $10,000 or imprisoned not more than two years, or both."

ute. A year later, in August 1973, law enforcement officials, in the execution of a search warrant for narcotics, seized four firearms from petitioner's bedroom. Petitioner was subsequently charged with both receipt and possession of the four firearms in violation of 18 U.S.C. App. § 1202(a)(1).

In a jury trial in the Eastern District of Virginia, the government offered evidence to show that all of the seized weapons had traveled in interstate commerce. All the dates established for such interstate travel were prior to the date petitioner became a convicted felon. The government made no attempt to prove that the petitioner acquired these weapons after his conviction. Holding such proof necessary for a receipt conviction, the judge, at the close of the government's case, granted petitioner's motion for a judgment of acquittal on that part of the indictment charging receipt.

Petitioner's defense to the possession charge was twofold. As a matter of fact, he contended that by the time of his conviction he no longer possessed the firearms. His claim was that, to avoid violating this statute, he had transferred these guns to his wife prior to pleading guilty to the narcotics felony. Secondly, he argued that, as a matter of law, proof that the guns had at some time traveled in interstate commerce did not provide an adequate nexus between the possession and commerce. In furtherance of this defense, petitioner requested that the jury be instructed as follows:

> "In order for the defendant to be found guilty of the crime with which he is charged, it is incumbent upon the government to demonstrate a nexus between the 'possession' of the firearms and interstate commerce. For example, a person 'possesses' in commerce or affecting commerce if at the time of the offense the firearms were moving interstate or on an interstate facility, or if the 'possession' affected commerce. It is not enough that the government merely show that the firearms at some time had traveled in interstate commerce. . . ."

The judge rejected this instruction. Instead he informed the jury:

> "The government may meet its burden of proving a connection between commerce and the possession of a firearm by a convicted felon if it is demonstrated that the firearm possessed by a convicted felon had previously traveled in interstate commerce. . . .
>
> "It is not necessary that the government prove that the defendant purchased the gun in some state other than that where he was found with it or that he carried it across the state line, nor must the government prove who did purchase the gun."

Petitioner was found guilty and he appealed. The Court of Appeals for the Fourth Circuit affirmed. It held that the interstate commerce nexus requirement of the possession offense was satisfied by proof that the firearm petitioner possessed had previously traveled in interstate commerce. [W]e granted certiorari. We affirm.

II

Our first encounter with title VII of the Omnibus Crime Control Act came in United States v. Bass, 404 U.S. 336 (1971). There we had to decide whether the statutory phrase "in commerce or affecting commerce" in § 1202(a) applied to "possesses" and "receives" as well as to "transports." We noted that the statute was not a model of clarity. On the one hand, we found "significant support" in the legislative history for the contention that the statute "reaches the mere possession of guns without any showing of an interstate commerce nexus" in individual cases. On the other hand, we could not ignore Congress' inserting the phrase "in commerce or affecting commerce" in the statute. The phrase clearly modified "transport" and we could find no sensible explanation for requiring a nexus only for transport. Faced with this ambiguity, the Court adopted the narrower reading that the phrase modified all three offenses.[6] We found this result dictated by two principles of statutory interpretation: First, that "ambiguity concerning the ambit of criminal statutes should be resolved in favor of lenity," Rewis v. United States, 401 U.S. 808, 812 (1971), and second, that "unless Congress conveys its purpose clearly, it will not be deemed to have significantly changed the federal-state balance," Bass, supra, at 349. Since "[a]bsent proof of some interstate commerce nexus in each case § 1202(a) dramatically intrudes upon traditional state criminal jurisdiction," we were unwilling to conclude, without a "clearer statement of intention," that Congress meant to dispense entirely with a nexus requirement in individual cases.

It was unnecessary in Bass for us to decide what would constitute an adequate nexus with commerce as the government had made no attempt to show any nexus at all. While we did suggest some possibilities, the present case presents the first opportunity to focus on the question with the benefit of full briefing and argument.

The government's position is that to establish a nexus with interstate commerce it need prove only that the firearm possessed by the convicted felon traveled at some time in interstate commerce. The petitioner contends, however, that the nexus must be "contemporaneous" with the possession, that the statute proscribes "only crimes with a present connection to commerce." He suggests that at the time of the offense the possessor must be engaging in commerce or must be carrying the gun at an interstate facility. At oral argument he suggested an alternative theory—that one can be convicted for possession without any proof of a present connection with commerce so long as the firearm was acquired after conviction.

In our effort to resolve the dispute, we turn first to the text of the statute. Petitioner contends that the meaning can be readily determined from the face of the statute, at least when it is contrasted with title IV of

---

[6] As one commentator described our dilemma: "[T]he legislative history looked one way and the logic and structure of the statute another, while the language was not clear." Robert L. Stern, The Commerce Clause Revisited—The Federalization of Intrastate Crime, 15 Ariz. L. Rev. 271, 281 (1973).

the Omnibus Crime Control Act, another title dealing with gun control. He points to one section of title IV, 18 U.S.C. § 922(h), arguing, in reliance on our decision in Barrett v. United States, 423 U.S. 212 (1976), that this section shows how Congress can, if it chooses, specify an offense based on firearms that have previously traveled in commerce. In § 922(h), Congress employed the present perfect tense, as it prohibited a convicted felon from receiving a firearm "which has been shipped or transported in interstate or foreign commerce." This choice of tense led us to conclude in *Barrett* that Congress clearly "denot[ed] an act that has been completed." Thus, petitioner argues, since Congress knows how to specify completed transactions, its failure to use that language in the present statute must mean that it wanted to reach only ongoing transactions.

The essential difficulty with this argument is that it is not very meaningful to compare title VII with title IV. Title VII was a last-minute amendment to the Omnibus Crime Control Act enacted hastily with little discussion and no hearings. The statute, as we noted in *Bass*, is not the product of model legislative deliberation or draftsmanship. Title IV, on the other hand, is a carefully constructed package of gun control legislation. It is obvious that the tenses used throughout title IV were chosen with care. For example, in addition to the prohibition in § 922(h) on receipt by convicted felons, Congress also made it illegal in § 922(g) for such person to "ship or transport any firearm or ammunition in interstate or foreign commerce." In § 922(j), Congress made it unlawful for "any person to receive ... any stolen firearm ..., which is moving as, which is part of, or which constitutes, interstate or foreign commerce." And § 922(k) makes it illegal for "any person knowingly to transport, ship, or receive, in interstate or foreign commerce, any firearm which has had [its] serial number removed, obliterated or altered." In view of such fine nuances in the tenses employed in the statute, the Court could easily conclude in *Barrett* that "Congress knew the significance and meaning of the language it employed." The language it chose was "without ambiguity." "Had Congress intended to confine § 922(h) to direct interstate receipts, it would have so provided, just as it did in other sections of [title IV]."

In the present case, by contrast, Congress' choice of language was ambiguous at best. While it is true that Congress did not choose the precise language used in § 922(h) to indicate that a present nexus with interstate commerce is not required, neither did it use the language of § 922(j) to indicate that the gun must have a contemporaneous connection with commerce at the time of the offense. Thus, while petitioner is correct in noting that Congress has the skills to be precise, the fact that it did not employ those skills here helps us not at all.

While Congress' choice of tenses is not very revealing, its findings and its inclusion of the phrase "affecting commerce" are somewhat more helpful. In the findings at the beginning of title VII, Congress expressly declared that "the receipt, possession, or transportation of a firearm by felons ... constitutes ... a burden on commerce or threat affecting the free flow of commerce," 18 U.S.C. App. § 1201(1).[10] It then implemented those findings by prohibiting possessions "in commerce and affecting commerce." As we have previously observed, Congress is aware of the "distinction between legislation limited to activities 'in commerce' and an assertion of its full commerce clause power so as to cover all activity substantially affecting interstate commerce." United States v. American Bldg. Maintenance Industries, 422 U.S. 271, 280 (1975). Indeed, that awareness was explicitly demonstrated here. In arguing that Congress could, consistent with the Constitution, "outlaw the mere possession of weapons," Senator Long, in introducing title VII, pointed to the fact that "many of the items and transactions reached by the broad swath of the Civil Rights Act of 1964 were reached by virtue of the power of Congress to regulate matters affecting commerce, not just to regulate interstate commerce itself." He advised a similar reliance on the power to regulate matters affecting commerce and urged that "Congress simply [find] that the possession of these weapons by the wrong kind of people is either a burden on commerce or a threat that affects the free flow of commerce." While in *Bass* we noted that we could not be sure that Congress meant to do away entirely with a nexus requirement, it does seem apparent that in implementing these findings by prohibiting both possessions in commerce and those affecting commerce, Congress must have meant more than to outlaw simply those possessions that occur in commerce or in interstate facilities. And we see no basis for contending that a weapon acquired after a conviction affects commerce differently from one acquired before and retained.

The legislative history in its entirety, while brief, further supports the view that Congress sought to rule broadly—to keep guns out of the hands of those who have demonstrated that "they may not be trusted to possess a firearm without becoming a threat to society." There is simply no indication of any concern with either the movement of the gun or the possessor or with the time of acquisition.

In introducing the amendment, Senator Long stated:

[10] Title 18 U.S.C. App. § 1201 reads in its entirety:

"Congressional findings and declaration.

"The Congress hereby finds and declares that the receipt, possession, or transportation of a firearm by felons, veterans who are discharged under dishonorable conditions, mental incompetents, aliens who are illegally in the country, and former citizens who have renounced their citizenship, constitutes—

"(1) a burden on commerce or threat affecting the free flow of commerce,

"(2) a threat to the safety of the President of the United States and Vice President of the United States,

"(3) an impediment or a threat to the exercise of free speech and the free exercise of a religion guaranteed by the first amendment to the Constitution of the United States, and

"(4) a threat to the continued and effective operation of the Government of the United States and of the government of each State guaranteed by article IV of the Constitution."

"I have prepared an amendment which I will offer at an appropriate time, simply setting forth the fact that anybody who has been convicted of a felony . . . is not permitted to possess a firearm. . . .

"It might be well to analyze, for a moment, the logic involved. When a man has been convicted of a felony, unless—as this bill sets forth—he has been expressly pardoned by the President and the pardon states that the person is to be permitted to possess firearms in the future, that man would have no right to possess firearms. He would be punished criminally if he is found in possession of them. . . .

"It seems to me that this simply strikes at the possession of firearms by the wrong kind of people. It avoids the problem of imposing on an honest hardware store owner the burden of keeping a lot of records and trying to keep up with the ultimate disposition of weapons sold. It places the burden and the punishment on the kind of people who have no business possessing firearms in the event they come into possession of them." 114 Cong. Rec. 13868–69.

The purpose of the amendment was to complement title IV. Senator Long noted:

"Of all the gun bills that have been suggested, debated, discussed, and considered, none except this title VII attempts to bar possession of a firearm from persons whose prior behaviors have established their violent tendencies. . . .

". . . Under title VI, every citizen could possess a gun until the commission of his first felony. Upon his conviction, however, title VII would deny every assassin, murderer, thief and burglar . . . the right to possess a firearm in the future. . . .

"Despite all that has been said about the need for controlling firearms in this country, no other amendment heretofore offered would get at the Oswalds or the Galts. They are the types of people at which title VII is aimed." Ibid., at 14773–74.

He proposed this amendment to remedy what he thought was an erroneous conception of the drafters of title IV that there was "a constitutional doubt that the federal government could outlaw the mere possession of weapons." Ibid., at 13868.

The intent to outlaw possession without regard to movement and to apply it to a case such as petitioner's could not have been more clearly revealed than in a colloquy between Senators Long and McClellan:

"Mr. McClellan. I have not had an opportunity to study the amendment. . . . The thought that occurred to me, as the Senator explained it, is that if a man has been in the penitentiary, had been a felon, and had been pardoned, without any condition in his pardon to which the able Senator referred, granting him the right to bear arms, could that man own a shotgun for the purpose of hunting?

"Mr. Long of Louisiana. No, he could not. He could own it, but he could not possess it.

"Mr. McClellan. I beg the Senator's pardon?

"Mr. Long of Louisiana. This amendment does not seek to do anything about who owns a firearm. He could not carry it around; he could not have it.

"Mr. McClellan. *Could he have it in his home?*

"Mr. Long of Louisiana. *No, he could not.*" Ibid., at 14774 (emphasis added).

It seems apparent from the foregoing that the purpose of title VII was to proscribe mere possession but that there was some concern about the constitutionality of such a statute. It was that observed ambivalence that made us unwilling in *Bass* to find the clear intent necessary to conclude that Congress meant to dispense with a nexus requirement entirely. However, we see no indication that Congress intended to require any more than the minimal nexus that the firearm have been, at some time, in interstate commerce.[11] In particular, we find no support for petitioner's theories.

Initially, we note our difficulty in fully comprehending petitioner's conception of a nexus with commerce. In his view, if an individual purchases a gun before his conviction, the fact that the gun once traveled in commerce does not provide an adequate nexus. It is necessary, in addition, that the person also carry it in an interstate facility. If, however, one purchases the same gun from the same dealer one day after the conviction as opposed to one day before, somehow the nexus magically appears, regardless of whether the purchaser carries the gun in any particular place. Such an interpretation strains credulity. We find no evidence in either the language or the legislative history for such a construction.[12]

---

[11] In *Bass*, the Court suggested that there might be a distinction between receipt and possession and that possession might require a stricter nexus with commerce. While such a requirement would make sense, further consideration has persuaded us that that was not the choice Congress made. Congress was not particularly concerned with the impact on commerce except as a means to insure the constitutionality of title VII. State gun control laws were found "inadequate to bar possession of firearms from those most likely to use them for unlawful purposes" and Congress sought to buttress the states' efforts. All indications are that Congress meant to reach possessions broadly.

[12] The argument sounds more like an effort to define possession, but the only issue before us is the nexus requirement. Petitioner has raised no objections to the trial court's definition of possession. Even as a proposed definition of possession, however, there is no support for it in the history or text. While Senator Long used the word "acquire" a few times in discussing the amendment, it is clear his concern was with the dangers of certain people having guns, not with when they obtained them. Furthermore, his use of the term "acquire" is better explained as a synonym for "receive" than "possess."

More significantly, these theories create serious loopholes in the congressional plan to "make it unlawful for a firearm ... to be in the possession of a convicted felon." A person who obtained a firearm prior to his conviction can retain it forever so long as he is not caught with it in an interstate facility. Indeed, petitioner's interpretation allows an individual to go out in the period between his arrest and conviction and purchase and stockpile weapons with impunity. In addition, petitioner's theories would significantly impede enforcement efforts. Those who do acquire guns after their conviction obviously do so surreptitiously and as petitioner concedes, it is very difficult as a practical matter to prove that such possession began after the possessor's felony conviction.

Petitioner responds that the government's reading of the statute fails to give effect to all three terms of the statute—receive, possess, transport. He argues that someone guilty of receipt or transport will necessarily be guilty of possession and that, therefore, there was no need to include the other two offenses in the statute. While this contention is not frivolous,[13] the fact is that petitioner's theory is similarly vulnerable. By his proposed definitions, there are essentially only two crimes—receipt and transport. The possessor who acquires the weapon after his conviction is guilty of receipt and the one who is carrying the gun in commerce or at an interstate facility presumably is guilty of transporting.[14] Thus, the definitions offered by both sides fail to give real substance to all three terms. The difference, however, is that the government's definition captures the essence of Congress' intent, striking at the possession of weapons by people "who have no business possessing [them]." Petitioner's version, on the other hand, fails completely to fulfill the congressional purpose. It virtually eliminates the one offense on which Congress focused in enacting the law.

Finally, petitioner seeks to invoke the two principles of statutory construction relied on in *Bass*—lenity in construing criminal statutes and caution where the federal-state balance is implicated. Petitioner, however, overlooks the fact that we did not turn to these guides in *Bass* until we had concluded that "[a]fter 'seizing everything from which aid can be derived,' ... we are left with an ambiguous statute." The principles are applicable only when we are uncertain about the statute's meaning and are not to be used "in complete disregard of the purpose of the legislature." United States v. Bramblett, 348 U.S. 503, 510 (1955). Here, the intent of Congress is clear. We do not face the conflicting pull between the text and the history that confronted us in *Bass*. In this case, the history is unambiguous and the text consistent with it. Congress sought to reach possessions broadly, with little concern for when the nexus with commerce occurred. Indeed, it was a close question in *Bass* whether § 1202(a) even required proof of any nexus at all in individual cases. The only reason we

---

[13] We note, however, that it is also arguable that one could receive and perhaps transport a weapon without necessarily exercising dominion and control over it.

[14] Petitioner suggests that a possessor's simply waiting in an interstate facility is not transporting. Even if that is true, we find it inconceivable, in view of the legislative history, that Congress intended the possession offense to have so limited a scope.

concluded it did was because it was not "plainly and unmistakably" clear that it did not. But there is no question that Congress intended no more than a minimal nexus requirement.

Since the District Court and the Court of Appeals employed the proper standard, we affirm the conviction of petitioner.

It is so ordered.

JUSTICE REHNQUIST took no part in the consideration or decision in this case.

JUSTICE STEWART, dissenting.

So far as the record reflects, the petitioner in this case acquired the four weapons in question before he was convicted of a felony in August 1972. Until that time, his possession of the guns was entirely legal under federal law. Under the Court's construction of 18 U.S.C. App. § 1202(a)(1), however, the petitioner was automatically guilty of a serious federal criminal offense at the moment he was convicted in the state felony case. This result is in my view inconsistent with the time-honored rule of lenity in construing federal criminal statutes. I would hold that § 1202(a)(1) does not come into play unless and until a person first comes into possession of a firearm *after* he is convicted of a felony.

The language of § 1202(a)(1) does not compel the construction that the Court adopts. The statute covers "[a]ny person who . . . has been convicted . . . of a felony . . . and who receives, possesses, or transports . . . any firearm. . . ." Plainly the acts of receiving and transporting are prohibited only if they occur after the defendant's conviction. The language does not indicate, however, whether the illegal possession must also first begin after conviction, or whether a prior possession becomes illegal at the moment the possessor is adjudged guilty of a felony. And, as the Court observes, any reading of the statute makes one or another part of it redundant. If § 1202(a) makes criminal any postconviction possession of a gun by a convicted felon, then there will almost never be a situation where the government would need to rely on the prohibition against receipt of the gun, for in most cases receipt would result in possession, and the latter is generally easier to prove. On the other hand, if the prohibition against possession refers to a possession that begins only after a felony conviction, the government presumably could proceed on a receipt charge in such cases, without relying on the possession offense (or vice versa).

The legislative history does not provide much help. There are statements suggesting that Congress meant to proscribe any possession of a firearm by a convicted felon. Other statements, however, intimate that the statute's purpose was to prevent a convicted felon from *coming into possession* of a weapon after his conviction. For instance, Senator Long, the drafter and sponsor of § 1202, stated that the statute "places the burden and the punishment on the kind of people who have no business possessing firearms *in the event they come into possession of them*." Later he added that § 1202(a) "would deny every assassin, murderer, thief and burglar . . . the right to possess a firearm in the future. . . ."

In short, I disagree with the Court that the scope of § 1202(a) is so crystal clear that there is no room for the operation of the rule of lenity. In my view, we are under no mandate to construe this statute so that a person in lawful possession of a firearm, and presumed to be innocent of a felony until proved guilty, must upon his conviction of a felony also be automatically and instantly guilty of a wholly different serious criminal offense.[1] The statute could equally be read to apply only when a person first comes into possession of a firearm after his felony conviction.[2] That being so, I would choose the latter alternative, for "it is appropriate, before we choose the harsher alternative, to require that Congress should have spoken in language that is clear and definite. We should not derive criminal outlawry from some ambiguous implication." United States v. Universal C.I.T. Credit Corp., 344 U.S. 218, 222 (1952).

Since the petitioner in this case came into possession of the firearms before he was convicted of any felony, I would hold that he did not violate § 1202(a)(1). Accordingly, I respectfully dissent from the opinion and judgment of the Court.

FURTHER NOTES ON THE INTERPRETATION OF JURISDICTIONAL ELEMENTS

1. Questions and Comments. Is it fair to say that the government lost the battle in *Bass* but won the war in *Scarborough*? How expensive was the victory? That is, what is the practical effect of the net result on the number of people who can be prosecuted and the costs to the government and the courts of prosecution, compared to the result if *Bass* had gone the other way?

Notice also the Court's treatment of *Bass*. The legislative history quoted in the *Bass* dissent is a featured part of the *Scarborough* majority opinion, prefaced by a statement that the "legislative history . . . supports the view that Congress sought to rule broadly—to keep guns out of the hands of" certain people. Moreover, in *Bass*, according to the Court in the next-to-last paragraph of its opinion, there was an "ambiguous" statute and a "conflicting pull between the text and the history." Did the text in *Bass* pull *against* the history? Or might one have said that, given the

---

[1] Under this construction, for example, a bookkeeper who owns a hunting rifle and who later commits embezzlement will, immediately upon his embezzlement conviction, also be guilty of violating § 1202(a). At oral argument the government agreed that such a person should have a reasonable time to relinquish possession without being automatically in violation of the statute, and suggested that prosecutorial discretion would take care of the problem. Proper construction of a criminal statute, however, cannot depend upon the good will of those who must enforce it.

[2] Contrary to the Court's suggestion, this reading would not allow a person "to go out in the period between his arrest and conviction and purchase and stockpile weapons with impunity." Title 18 U.S.C. § 922(h) makes it unlawful for any person who is under indictment for a crime punishable by imprisonment for a term exceeding one year to receive any firearm or ammunition that has been shipped or transported in interstate or foreign commerce.

history, the ambiguity should have been resolved consistently with it? By contrast, is the statute in *Scarborough* completely unambiguous? Is something funny going on here, or is the Court's explanation of the difference between the two cases sufficient and persuasive?

Finally, does Justice Stewart's dissent turn on an interpretation of the commerce requirement or the meaning of the word "possession"? Is the Court's response to Justice Stewart persuasive?

2. "In" Commerce v. "Affecting" Commerce. The Court observed in *Scarborough* that "Congress is aware of the 'distinction between legislation limited to activities "in commerce" and an assertion of its full commerce clause power so as to cover all activity substantially affecting interstate commerce.' " The case cited for this proposition, United States v. American Bldg. Maintenance Industries, 422 U.S. 271 (1975), said that the phrase "in" commerce " 'appears to denote only persons or activities within the flow of interstate commerce—the practical, economic continuity in the generation of goods and services for interstate markets and their transport and distribution to the consumer.' " In contrast, the phrase "affecting" commerce was at least in that case "specifically designed to expand . . . jurisdiction [by making] it coextensive with the constitutional power of Congress under the commerce clause."

It may be an excessive generalization to suggest that the phrase "affects commerce" always means the full extent of Congress' constitutional power under the commerce clause, but it is at least clear that "affects commerce" signals a broad exercise of congressional power. Scarborough was guilty of violating § 1202(1)(a) because the gun he possessed had previously traveled in interstate commerce. Would he have been guilty if the gun had been manufactured in-state, but several parts from another state were used? Suppose only local parts were used, but the manufacturer used tools or supplies (oil, screwdrivers, lathes, water coolers for its workers) that were manufactured out-of-state. If these cases are covered, why retain the requirement of a jurisdictional showing? Would proof of the commerce element of the offense then be simply a jurisdictional fetish requiring the prosecutor to jump through undemanding hoops that are more time-consuming and institutionally expensive than they are worth? If the cases hypothesized above are not covered by § 1202(1)(a), on the other hand, where is the line to be drawn? More importantly, what policies are likely to be reflected in the location of the line?

Consider the "affecting commerce" requirement in *Scarborough* from another angle. Exactly how does the possession of this weapon by Scarborough "affect" commerce? Is there any continuing or future effect from his possession? If there is, is there any relation between that effect[d] and the fact that the gun once traveled in interstate commerce? Is "effect on commerce" like a scarlet letter, that is, once the gun has passed through interstate commerce it is forever tainted and anyone who later possesses it

---

[d] Or potential effect—he might use the gun to rob someone who might have bought something in interstate commerce with the money.

is therefore within the jurisdiction of the federal government?   Isn't all this silly?   But is it irrelevant as the law now stands?

3. *Barrett v. United States*.   Subtleties can still arise in situations where the statute speaks to transactions "in" commerce.   An example is Barrett v. United States, 423 U.S. 212 (1976).

The facts were succinctly stated by Justice Stewart:

> "The petitioner bought a revolver from the Western Auto Store in Booneville, Ky., in an over-the-counter retail sale.   Within an hour, he was arrested for driving while intoxicated and the revolver was found on the floorboard of his car.   The revolver had been manufactured in Massachusetts and shipped to the Booneville retailer from a North Carolina distributor.   The prosecution submitted no evidence of any kind that the petitioner had participated in any interstate activity involving the revolver, either before or after its purchases.   On these facts, he was convicted of violating 18 U.S.C. § 922(h), which makes it unlawful for a former criminal offender like the petitioner, 'to receive any firearm or ammunition which has been shipped or transported in interstate or foreign commerce.' "[e]

Justice Stewart explained that, in his view, the conviction should be reversed because:

> "This clause first appeared in the . . . Federal Firearms Act of 1938.   In Tot v. United States, 319 U.S. 463 (1943), the Court interpreted this statutory language to prohibit only receipt of firearms or ammunition as part of an interstate transaction:
>
> > 'Both courts below held that the offense created by the act is confined to the receipt of firearms or ammunition as a part of interstate transportation and does not extend to the receipt, in an intrastate transaction, of such articles which, at some prior time, have been transported interstate.   The government agrees that this construction is correct.' . . .
>
> "The *Tot* case did not go unnoticed when 18 U.S.C. § 922(h) was enacted in its present form in 1968, as the legislative history clearly reveals.   [It was explained in hearings on the bill that] 'in order to establish a violation of this statute, it is necessary to prove that a convicted felon found in possession of a firearm

---

[e] Prior to amendments enacted in 1986, 18 U.S.C. § 922(h) provided in full:

"It shall be unlawful for any person—

"(1) who is under indictment for, or who has been convicted in any court of, a crime punishable by imprisonment for a term exceeding one year;

"(2) who is a fugitive from justice;

"(3) who is an unlawful user of or addicted to marihuana or any depressant or stimulant drug (as defined in section 201(v) of the Federal Food, Drug, and Cosmetic Act) or narcotic drug (as defined in section 4731(a) of the Internal Revenue Code of 1954); or

"(4) who has been adjudicated as a mental defective or who has been committed to any mental institution;

to receive any firearm or ammunition which has been shipped or transported in interstate or foreign commerce."

actually received it in the course of an interstate shipment.' . . .
Just four years ago, in United States v. Bass, 404 U.S. 336, 343 n.
10 (1971), the Court expressly stated that it found nothing to
indicate 'that the 1968 act changed the prior approach to the
"receipt" offense.' "

Justice Stewart, however, was writing in dissent. The majority opinion was written by Justice Blackmun.[f] He began by pointing out that the
jurisdictional language of the statute:

"is without ambiguity. It is directed unrestrictedly at the felon's
receipt of any firearm that 'has been' shipped in interstate commerce. It contains no limitation to a receipt which itself is part of
the interstate movement. [T]he language 'means exactly what it
says.' . . . There is no occasion here to resort to a rule of lenity,
see Rewis v. United States, 401 U.S. 808, 812 (1971); United
States v. Bass, 404 U.S. 336, 347 (1971), for there is no ambiguity
that calls for a resolution in favor of lenity. A criminal statute, to
be sure, is to be strictly construed, but it is 'not to be construed so
strictly as to defeat the obvious intention of the legislature.'
American Fur Co. v. United States, 27 U.S. (2 Pet.) 358, 367
(1829)."

Justice Blackmun further defended the Court's conclusion by resort to the
structure of the statute and the "manifest purpose" of the Congress in
enacting it. On the first point, he said that the "very structure of the Gun
Control Act demonstrates that Congress did not intend merely to restrict
interstate sales but sought broadly to keep firearms away from the persons
Congress classified as potentially irresponsible and dangerous. These
persons are comprehensively barred by the act from acquiring firearms by
any means." He also pointed out that the "proposed narrow construction
of § 922(h) would [create an] anomaly: if a prohibited person seeks to buy
from his local dealer a firearm that is not currently in the dealer's stock,
and the dealer then orders it interstate, that person violates § 922(h), but
under the suggested construction, he would not violate § 922(h) if the
firearm were already on the dealer's shelf." As to the legislative history,
he found it "fully supportive of our construction." The statute was
intended to deny certain classes of persons the right to receive firearms.
Congress could not have intended to "remove from the statute the most
usual transaction, namely, the felon's purchase or receipt from his local
dealer."[g]

---

[f] Justice White wrote a separate concurrence. Justice Rehnquist joined Justice
Stewart's dissent. Justice Stevens did not
participate.

[g] As to the quotation from *Tot* on which
Justice Stewart relied, Justice Blackmun replied: "The fact that the government long
ago took a narrow position on the reach of
the 1938 act may not serve to help its posture

here, when it seemingly argues to the contrary, but it does not prevent the government
from arguing that the current gun control
statute is broadly based and reaches a purchase such as that made by Barrett." He
added in a footnote that: "There is, of
course, no rule of law to the effect that the
government must be consistent in its stance
in litigation over the years. It has changed

4. The Amended Statutes. Sections 1202 and 922 were consolidated in 1986. Section 1202 was repealed. The new § 922 provided:

"(g) It shall be unlawful for any person—

"(1) who has been convicted in any court of a crime punishable by imprisonment for a term exceeding one year;

"(2) who is a fugitive from justice;

"(3) [who] is an unlawful user of or addicted to any controlled substance (as defined in section 102 of the Controlled Substances Act (21 U.S.C. 802));

"(4) who has been adjudicated as a mental defective or who has been committed to a mental institution;

"(5) who, being an alien, is illegally or unlawfully in the United States;

"(6) who has been discharged from the Armed Forces under dishonorable conditions; or

"(7) who, having been a citizen of the United States, has renounced his citizenship;[h]

to ship or transport in interstate or foreign commerce, or possess in or affecting commerce, any firearm or ammunition; or to receive any firearm or ammunition which has been shipped or transported in interstate or foreign commerce."

As can be seen by comparing old § 1202(a)(1)[i] with old § 922(h),[j] subsections (1) through (7) consolidate, with minor modifications, the classes of people covered by the former provisions.

---

position before." As to the statements from *Bass*, they were "just another observation made in passing as the Court proceeded to consider" the interpretation of another statute. The Court's observation in *Bass* "reserved the question of the reach of title IV for 'some other day.' That day is now at hand..... And it is at hand with the benefit of full briefing and an awareness of the plain language of § 922(h), of the statute's position in the structure of the entire act, and of the legislative aims and purpose."

[h] A new subsection (8) was added in 1994. It added to the list a person:

"who is subject to a court order that—

"(A) was issued after a hearing of which such person received actual notice, and at which such person had an opportunity to participate;

"(B) restrains such person from harassing, stalking, or threatening an intimate partner of such person or child of such intimate partner or person, or en-

gaging in other conduct that would place an intimate partner in reasonable fear of bodily injury to the partner or child; and

"(C)(i) includes a finding that such person represents a credible threat to the physical safety of such intimate partner or child; or

"(ii) by its terms explicitly prohibits the use, attempted use, or threatened use of physical force against such intimate partner or child that would reasonably be expected to cause bodily injury."

[i] Old § 1202(a)(1) is reproduced in footnote 1 of *Scarborough*.

[j] Old § 922(h) is reproduced in the note on *Barrett*, supra. The 1986 amendments also consolidated former §§ 922(g) and (h). Section 922(h) had made it unlawful for the listed class of persons "to receive any firearm or ammunition which has been shipped or transported in interstate or foreign commerce." Section 922(g) had made it unlawful

Is the jurisdictional reach of the former provisions preserved in § 922(g)? Would *Bass*, *Barrett*, and *Scarborough* be decided the same way today? Suppose a convicted felon transported a weapon (but did not receive or possess it, if that is possible) solely intrastate. Of what offense, if any, would she or he be guilty prior to the 1986 amendments? Of what offense, if any, after the amendments?

Section 924(b) of the federal gun control legislation provides:

"Whoever, with intent to commit therewith an offense punishable by imprisonment for a term exceeding one year, or with knowledge or reasonable cause to believe that an offense punishable by imprisonment for a term exceeding one year is to be committed therewith, ships, transports, or receives a firearm or any ammunition in interstate or foreign commerce shall be fined under this title, or imprisoned not more than ten years, or both."

Suppose a person with no prior convictions buys a gun that has previously traveled in interstate commerce and "transports" it to the site of a 7–Eleven store with intent to rob the store. Would a conviction under § 924(b) be upheld?

SECTION 4: CONSTITUTIONAL LIMITS

INTRODUCTORY NOTES ON THE CONSTITUTIONAL REACH OF FEDERAL CRIMINAL STATUTES

1. Introductory Comment. Typically, as the preceding materials reveal, federal criminal statutes contain jurisdictional elements that define their reach. Guns may not be possessed by a felon "in or affecting commerce." Individuals may not be transported "in" interstate commerce for the purpose of prostitution or criminal sexual activities. Arson, bribery, and extortion are punishable as federal crimes if committed by a person who traveled "in" interstate commerce with intent to commit the offense. What would happen if Congress were not to require findings in the particular case that connected the offense to an enumerated constitutional power? Could Congress justify a federal criminal statute by making an explicit (or implicit) finding that a particular kind of activity, at least in cumulative effect, *always* affects commerce? More broadly, are there serious limits on the reach of the federal power to prosecute criminal behavior? These are the questions now to be addressed.

2. *United States v. Five Gambling Devices*. The Court walked up to these issues but did not resolve them in United States v. Five Gambling Devices, 346 U.S. 441 (1953). Congress passed a statute in 1951 prohibit-

for the same persons "to ship or transport any firearm or ammunition in interstate or foreign commerce."

ing the transportation of gambling devices in interstate commerce.[a]   It provided in the same law that all manufacturers and dealers in gambling devices must register their business by name and file monthly reports listing each device sold and delivered during the preceding month.   Gambling devices were required to be marked and numbered so they could be traced.   Violation of any of these provisions was a felony punishable by up to two years in prison.   Unmarked machines were to be forfeited.

Unlike the transportation offense, the information, registration, and reporting requirements were not explicitly limited to persons who had a connection to interstate commerce.   *Five Gambling Devices* involved a criminal prosecution for failure to abide by the registration and reporting requirements and a forfeiture proceeding involving five unmarked slot machines.   The government took the position that it was not required to allege and prove a connection to interstate commerce in either case.   But a minority of three Justices interpreted the statute to require a case-specific commerce nexus in spite of the statutory silence.   Since two other Justices thought the statute unconstitutional for an unrelated reason, the Court did not reach a decision on the constitutional question the government sought to raise.

Justice Jackson announced the judgment of the Court in an opinion joined by Justices Frankfurter and Minton.   He began by summarizing the issues:

> "Appellees contend, first, that the act should not be construed to reach dealers, transactions or machines unless shown to have some relation to interstate commerce;   second, construed otherwise, the act exceeds the power delegated to Congress under the commerce clause of the Constitution.....   The government answers, first, that the statute, literally read, reaches all dealers and transactions and the possession of all unreported devices without reference to interstate commerce;   second, to make effective the prohibition of transportation in interstate commerce, Congress may constitutionally require reporting of all intrastate transactions...."

Justice Jackson proceeded as follows:

> "We do not intimate any ultimate answer to the appellees' constitutional questions other than to observe that they cannot be dismissed as frivolous, nor as unimportant to the nature of our federation.   No precedent of this Court sustains the power of Congress to enact legislation penalizing failure to report information concerning acts not shown to be in, or mingled with, or found to affect commerce.   [W]e find no instance where Congress has attempted under the commerce power to impose reporting duties under penal sanction which would raise the question posed by

---

[a] 15 U.S.C. §§ 1171–77, 64 Stat. 1134.   States could permit interstate transportation to places within their borders specifically exempted by state law.

these proceedings. It is apparent that the government's pleadings raise, and no doubt were intended to raise, a far-reaching question as to the extent of congressional power over matters internal to the individual states. Of course, Congress possesses not only power to regulate commerce among the several states but also an inexact power 'to make all laws which shall be necessary and proper for carrying into execution' its enumerated powers. ... While general statements, [made in other] contexts, might bear upon the subject one way or another, it is apparent that the precise question tendered to us now is not settled by any prior decision.

"The principle is old and deeply imbedded in our jurisprudence that this Court will construe a statute in a manner that requires decision of serious constitutional questions only if the statutory language leaves no reasonable alternative. This is not because we would avoid or postpone difficult decisions. The predominant consideration is that we should be sure Congress has intentionally put its power in issue by the legislation in question before we undertake a pronouncement which may have far-reaching consequences upon the powers of the Congress or the powers reserved to the several states. To withhold passing upon an issue of power until we are certain it is knowingly precipitated will do no great injury, for Congress once we have recognized the question, can make its purpose explicit and thereby necessitate or avoid decision of the question. Judicial abstention is especially wholesome where we are considering a penal statute. Our policy in constitutional cases is reinforced by the long tradition and sound reasons which admonish against enlargement of criminal statutes by interpretation. ...

"We do not question that literal language of this act is capable of the broad, unlimited construction urged by the government. Indeed, if it were enacted for a unitary system of government, no other construction would be appropriate. But we must assume that the implications and limitations of our federal system constitute a major premise of all congressional legislation, though not repeatedly recited therein. ... We find in the text no unmistakable intention of Congress to raise the constitutional questions implicit in the government's effort to apply the act in its most extreme impact upon affairs considered normally reserved to the states. [R]eference to legislative history is conspicuously meager and unenlightening. ... The committee handling the bill reported: '... the committee desires to emphasize that federal law enforcement in the field of gambling cannot and should not be considered a substitute for state and local law enforcement in this field.' But here it was the Federal Bureau of Investigation which entered a country club and seized slot machines not shown ever to have had any connection with interstate commerce in any manner whatever. If this is not substituting federal for state enforcement, it is difficult to know how it could be accomplished. A more local and detailed act of enforcement is hardly conceivable. These cases, if sustained, would substantially take unto the federal government the entire pursuit of the gambling device.

"... All that we would decide at present is a question of statutory construction. We think the act does not have the explicitness necessary to sustain the pleadings which the government has drafted in these cases. ..."

Justice Black, joined by Justice Douglas, concurred in the result on the ground that the statute was unconstitutionally vague.

Justice Clark was joined in dissent by Chief Justice Warren and Justices Reed and Burton. Justice Clark thought the statutory language plain and the legislative history "almost totally unenlightening." He also thought it plain that "to give the provision its literal meaning affords far more effective enforcement with respect to other sections of the act than would be the case if any of the other suggested interpretations were applied. For these reasons I am unable to agree with the solution of these cases offered by Justice Jackson." He then addressed the merits of the constitutional issue:

"The ultimate question presented by these cases is whether Congress has exceeded its constitutional power. I think it has not.

"It appears that Congress in this act has embarked on what it deemed the most effective course of action possible to eliminate one of the major sources of income to organized crime, while at the same time yielding to the policy of Nevada and a few other states where slot machines are legal and the underworld's control and profit are correspondingly minimized. The act prohibits shipment of gambling devices into any state except those which act to exempt themselves from the statute. [T]he registration and filing requirements here in issue [were] designed to make effective and enforceable the interstate shipment ban. It was thought that a report on each transfer of each machine before and after interstate shipment would enable enforcement officials to ascertain who transported the machine across state lines and thereby violated the law. Unless all such local sales were reported, it was thought that it would be an easy matter to conceal the identity of the interstate transporter by resorting to straw-man transactions, coverup intrastate 'sales' before and after interstate shipment, and the like. In view of the established tie-up between slot machines and 'nation-wide crime syndicates,' more stringent methods of enforcement were deemed necessary to accomplish the ban on interstate transportation of the machines than would be needed to control an activity in which dealers and manufacturers could be presumed to be law-abiding citizens who kept accurate books and accounts. The net effect of these considerations is to clearly establish that the registration and filing requirements of the act amount to reasonably necessary, appropriate, and probably essential means for enforcing the ban on interstate transportation of gambling devices.

"The question presented, then, is whether Congress is empowered by the Constitution to require information, reasonably necessary and appropriate to make effective and enforceable a concededly valid ban on interstate transportation of gambling devices, from persons not shown to be themselves engaged in interstate activity. I think that an affirmative answer is not inevitably dictated by prior decisions of the Court; but, more important, no decision precludes an affirmative answer. The question has not been previously decided because the legislative scheme utilized here apparently has not been heretofore attempted. But its novelty should not suggest its unconstitutionality.

"In the body of decisional law defining the scope of Congress' powers in regard to interstate commerce, it has been clearly established that activities local in nature may be *regulated* if they can fairly be said to 'affect' commerce, or where local goods are commingled with goods destined for interstate commerce, or were previously in interstate commerce. For present purposes, these cases at least establish that activities or goods intrastate in nature are not immune from congressional control where they are sufficiently related to interstate activities or goods controlled by Congress. ... I think it may accurately be said that every sale of slot machines affects the exercise of the power of Congress over commerce, in view of the elusive nature of the object whose interstate shipment is being controlled. ...

"In their brief appellees attack the power of Congress under the Constitution solely on the basis that the registration and filing requirements are not reasonable means of enforcing the provision against interstate transportation of slot machines. I believe that the reasonableness and the necessity of the requirements have already been adequately demonstrated. ... If Congress ... had sought to *regulate* local activity, its power would no doubt be less clear. But here there is no attempt to regulate; all that is required is information in aid of enforcement of the conceded power to ban interstate transportation. The distinction is substantial.

"In my view Congress has power to require the information ... since the requirement is a means reasonably necessary to effectuate the prohibition of transporting gambling devices interstate. If it be suggested that such a holding would open possibilities for widespread congressional encroachment upon local activities whose regulation has been reserved to the states, I would point out, first, that power of *regulation* heretofore exclusively vested in the states remains there; and second, that the situation here is unique: the commodity involved is peculiarly tied to organized interstate crime and is itself illegal in the great majority of the states, and the federal law in issue was actively sought by local and state law enforcement officials as a means to assist them, not supplant them, in local law enforcement. ..."

Perez v. United States

Supreme Court of the United States, 1971.
402 U.S. 146.

■ JUSTICE DOUGLAS delivered the opinion of the Court.

The question in this case is whether Title II of the Consumer Credit Protection Act, 18 U.S.C. § 891 et seq., as construed and applied to petitioner, is a permissible exercise by Congress of its powers under the commerce clause of the Constitution. Petitioner's conviction after trial by jury and his sentence were affirmed by the Court of Appeals, one judge dissenting.[b] We granted the petition for a writ of certiorari because of the importance of the question presented. We affirm that judgment.

Petitioner is one of the species commonly known as "loan sharks" which Congress found are in large part under the control of "organized crime."[1] "Extortionate credit transactions" are defined as those character-

---

[b] Perez was convicted of five counts of using extortionate means to collect or attempt to collect extensions of credit in violation of 18 U.S.C. §§ 891, 894. Section 894(a) provided:

"Whoever knowingly participates in any way, or conspires to do so, in the use of any extortionate means

(1) to collect or attempt to collect any extension of credit, or

(2) to punish any person for the nonrepayment thereof,

shall be fined not more than $10,000 or imprisoned not more than 20 years, or both."

Section 891 defined the term "extortionate means." The definition is quoted in footnote 2 of the Court's opinion.

Section 892(a), not at issue in *Perez* but controlled by its principle, authorized the same fine and imprisonment for anyone who "makes any extortionate extension of credit, or conspires to do so."

The defendant's argument, as stated by the Court of Appeals, was "that the statute under which he was convicted is unconstitutional in prohibiting all extortionate credit transactions, without requiring a showing in a particular case of effect on interstate commerce...."—[Footnote by eds.]

[1] Section 201(a) of Title II contains the following findings by Congress:

"(1) Organized crime is interstate and international in character. Its activities involve many billions of dollars each year. It is directly responsible for murders, willful injuries to person and property, corruption of officials, and terrorization of countless citizens. A substantial part of the income of organized crime is generated by extortionate credit transactions.

"(2) Extortionate credit transactions are characterized by the use, or the express or implicit threat of the use, of violence or other criminal means to cause harm to persons, reputation, or property as a means of enforcing repayment. Among the factors which have rendered past efforts at prosecution almost wholly ineffective has been the existence of exclusionary rules of evidence stricter than necessary for the protection of constitutional rights.

"(3) Extortionate credit transactions are carried on to a substantial extent in interstate and foreign commerce and through the means and instrumentalities of such commerce. Even where extortionate credit transactions are purely intrastate in character, they nevertheless

ized by the use or threat of the use of "violence or other criminal means" in enforcement.[2] There was ample evidence showing petitioner was a "loan shark" who used the threat of violence as a method of collection. He loaned money to one Miranda, owner of a new butcher shop, making a $1,000 advance to be repaid in installments of $105 per week for 14 weeks. After paying at this rate for six or eight weeks, petitioner increased the weekly payment to $130. In two months Miranda asked for an additional loan of $2,000 which was made, the agreement being that Miranda was to pay $205 a week. In a few weeks petitioner increased the weekly payment to $330. When Miranda objected, petitioner told him about a customer who refused to pay and ended up in a hospital. So Miranda paid. In a few months petitioner increased his demands to $500 weekly which Miranda paid, only to be advised that at the end of the week petitioner would need $1,000. Miranda made that payment by not paying his suppliers; but, faced with a $1,000 payment the next week, he sold his butcher shop. Petitioner pursued Miranda, first making threats to Miranda's wife and then telling Miranda he could have him castrated. When Miranda did not make more payments, petitioner said he was turning over his collections to people who would not be nice but who would put him in the hospital if he did not pay. Negotiations went on, Miranda finally saying he could only pay $25 a week. Petitioner said that was not enough, that Miranda should steal or sell drugs if necessary to get the money to pay the loan, and that if he went to jail it would be better than going to a hospital with a broken back or legs. He added, "I could have sent you to the hospital, you and your family, any moment I want with my people."

Petitioner's arrest followed. Miranda, his wife, and an employee gave the evidence against petitioner who did not testify or call any witnesses. Petitioner's attack was on the constitutionality of the act, starting with a motion to dismiss the indictment.

The constitutional question is a substantial one.

Two "loan shark" amendments to the bill that became this act were proposed in the House—one by Congressman Poff of Virginia and another one by Congressman McDade of Pennsylvania. The House debates include a long article from the New York Times Magazine for January 28, 1968, on the connection between the "loan shark" and organized crime. The gruesome and stirring episodes related have the following as a prelude:

directly affect interstate and foreign commerce."

[2] Section 891 of 18 U.S.C. provides in part:

"(6) An extortionate extension of credit is any extension of credit with respect to which it is the understanding of the creditor and the debtor at the time it is made that delay in making repayment or failure to make repayment could

result in the use of violence or other criminal means to cause harm to the person, reputation, or property of any person.

"(7) An extortionate means is any means which involves the use, or an express or implicit threat of use, of violence or other criminal means to cause harm to the person, reputation, or property of any person."

"The loan shark, then, is the indispensable 'money-mover' of the underworld. He takes 'black' money tainted by its derivation from the gambling or narcotics rackets and turns it 'white' by funneling it into channels of legitimate trade. In so doing, he exacts usurious interest that doubles the black-white money in no time; and, by his special decrees, by his imposition of impossible penalties, he greases the way for the underworld takeover of entire businesses."

There were objections on constitutional grounds. Congressman Eckhardt of Texas said:

"Should it become law, the amendment would take a long stride by the federal government toward occupying the field of general criminal law and toward exercising a general federal police power; and it would permit prosecution in federal as well as state courts of a typically state offense. . . .

"I believe that Alexander Hamilton, though a federalist, would be astonished that such a deep entrenchment on the rights of the states in performing their most fundamental function should come from the more conservative quarter of the House."

Senator Proxmire presented to the Senate the Conference Report approving essentially the "loan shark" provision suggested by Congressman McDade, saying:

"Once again these provisions raised serious questions of federal-state responsibilities. Nonetheless, because of the importance of the problem, the Senate conferees agreed to the House provision. Organized crime operates on a national scale. One of the principal sources of revenue of organized crime comes from loan sharking. If we are to win the battle against organized crime we must strike at their source of revenue and give the Justice Department additional tools to deal with the problem. The problem simply cannot be solved by the states alone. We must bring into play the full resources of the federal government."

The commerce clause reaches, in the main, three categories of problems. First, the use of channels of interstate or foreign commerce which Congress deems are being misused, as, for example, the shipment of stolen goods (18 U.S.C. §§ 2312–15) or of persons who have been kidnaped (18 U.S.C. § 1201). Second, protection of the instrumentalities of interstate commerce, as, for example, the destruction of an aircraft (18 U.S.C. § 32), or persons or things in commerce, as, for example, thefts from interstate shipments (18 U.S.C. § 659). Third, those activities affecting commerce. It is with this last category that we are here concerned.

Chief Justice Marshall in Gibbons v. Ogden, 22 U.S. (9 Wheat.) 1, 195 (1824) said:

"The genius and character of the whole government seem to be, that its action is to be applied to all the external concerns of the nation, and to those internal concerns which affect the states generally; but not to those which are completely within a particular state, which do not affect other states, and with which it is not necessary to interfere, for the purpose of executing some of the general powers of the government. The completely internal commerce of a state, then, may be considered as reserved for the state itself.''

Decisions which followed departed from that view; but by the time of United States v. Darby, 312 U.S. 100 (1941), and Wickard v. Filburn, 317 U.S. 111 (1942), the broader view of the commerce clause announced by Chief Justice Marshall had been restored. Chief Justice Stone wrote for a unanimous Court in 1942 that Congress could provide for the regulation of the price of intrastate milk, the sale of which, in competition with interstate milk, affects the price structure and federal regulation of the latter. United States v. Wrightwood Dairy Co., 315 U.S. 110, 119 (1942). The commerce power, he said, "extends to those activities intrastate which so affect interstate commerce, or the exertion of the power of Congress over it, as to make regulation of them appropriate means to the attainment of a legitimate end, the effective execution of the granted power to regulate interstate commerce.''

Wickard v. Filburn soon followed in which a unanimous Court held that wheat grown wholly for home consumption was constitutionally within the scope of federal regulation of wheat production because, though never marketed interstate, it supplied the need of the grower which otherwise would be satisfied by his purchases in the open market. We said:

"[E]ven if appellee's activity be local and though it may not be regarded as commerce, it may still, whatever its nature, be reached by Congress if it exerts a substantial economic effect on interstate commerce, and this irrespective of whether such effect is what might at some earlier time have been defined as 'direct' or 'indirect.' ''

In *United States v. Darby*, the decision sustaining an act of Congress which prohibited the employment of workers in the production of goods "for interstate commerce" at other than prescribed wages and hours, *a class of activities* was held properly regulated by Congress without proof that the particular intrastate activity against which a sanction was laid had an effect on commerce. A unanimous Court said:

"Congress has sometimes left it to the courts to determine whether the intrastate activities have the prohibited effect on the commerce, as in the Sherman Act. It has sometimes left it to an administrative board or agency to determine whether the activities sought to be regulated or prohibited have such effect, as in the case of the Interstate Commerce Act, and the National Labor Relations Act, or whether they come within the statutory definition of the prohibited act, as in the Federal Trade Commission Act. And sometimes Congress itself has said that a particular activity affects the commerce, as it did in the present act, the Safety Appliance Act and the Railway Labor Act. In passing on the validity of legislation of the *class* last mentioned the only function of courts is to determine whether the particular activity regulated or prohibited is within the reach of the federal power.''

That case is particularly relevant here because it involved a criminal prosecution, a unanimous Court holding that the act was "sufficiently definite to meet constitutional demands." Petitioner is clearly *a member of the class* which engages in "extortionate credit transactions" as defined by Congress and the description of that class has the required definiteness.

It was the "class of activities" test which we employed in Heart of Atlanta Motel v. United States, 379 U.S. 241 (1964), to sustain an act of Congress requiring hotel or motel accommodations for Negro guests. The act declared that "'any inn, hotel, motel, or other establishment which provides lodging to transient guests' affects commerce per se." That exercise of power under the commerce clause was sustained.

> "[O]ur people have become increasingly mobile with millions of people of all races traveling from state to state; . . . Negroes in particular have been the subject of discrimination in transient accommodations, having to travel great distances to secure the same; . . . often they have been unable to obtain accommodations and have had to call upon friends to put them up overnight . . . and . . . these conditions had become so acute as to require the listing of available lodging for Negroes in a special guidebook. . . ."

In a companion case, Katzenbach v. McClung, 379 U.S. 294 (1964), we ruled on the constitutionality of the restaurant provision of the same Civil Rights Act which regulated the restaurant "if . . . it serves or offers to serve interstate travelers or a substantial portion of the food which it serves . . . has moved in commerce." Apart from the effect on the flow of food in commerce to restaurants, we spoke of the restrictive effect of the exclusion of Negroes from restaurants on interstate travel by Negroes.

> "[T]here was an impressive array of testimony that discrimination in restaurants had a direct and highly restrictive effect upon interstate travel by Negroes. This resulted, it was said, because discriminatory practices prevent Negroes from buying prepared food served on the premises while on a trip, except in isolated and unkempt restaurants and under most unsatisfactory and often unpleasant conditions. This obviously discourages travel and obstructs interstate commerce for one can hardly travel without eating. Likewise, it was said, that discrimination deterred professional, as well as skilled, people from moving into areas where such practices occurred and thereby caused industry to be reluctant to establish there."

In emphasis of our position that it was the *class of activities* regulated that was the measure, we acknowledged that Congress appropriately considered the "total incidence" of the practice on commerce.

Where the *class activities* is regulated and that *class* is within the reach of federal power, the courts have no power "to excise, as trivial, individual instances" of the class. Maryland v. Wirtz, 392 U.S. 183, 193 (1968).

Extortionate credit transactions, though purely intrastate, may in the judgment of Congress affect interstate commerce. In an analogous situation, Mr. Justice Holmes, speaking for a unanimous Court, said: "[W]hen it is necessary in order to prevent an evil to make the law embrace more than the precise thing to be prevented it may do so." Westfall v. United States, 274 U.S. 256, 259 (1927). In that case an officer of a state bank which was a member of the Federal Reserve System issued a fraudulent certificate of deposit and paid it from the funds of the state bank. It was argued that there was no loss to the Reserve Bank. Mr. Justice Holmes replied, "But every fraud like the one before us weakens the member bank and therefore weakens the system." In the setting of the present case there is a tie-in between local loan sharks and interstate crime.

The findings by Congress are quite adequate on that ground. The McDade Amendment in the House, as already noted, was the one ultimately adopted. As stated by Congressman McDade it grew out of a "profound study of organized crime, its ramifications and its implications" undertaken by some 22 Congressmen in 1966–1967. The results of that study were included in a report, The Urban Poor and Organized Crime, submitted to the House on August 29, 1967, which revealed that "organized crime takes over $350 million a year from America's poor through loan-sharking alone." Congressman McDade also relied on The Challenge of Crime in a Free Society, A Report by the President's Commission on Law Enforcement and Administration of Justice (February 1967) which stated that loan sharking was "the second largest source of revenue for organized crime," and is one way by which the underworld obtains control of legitimate businesses.

The Congress also knew about New York's Report, An Investigation of the Loan Shark Racket (1965). That report shows the loan shark racket is controlled by organized criminal syndicates, either directly or in partnership with independent operators; that in most instances the racket is organized into three echelons, with the top underworld "bosses" providing the money to their principal "lieutenants," who in turn distribute the money to the "operators" who make the actual individual loans; that loan sharks serve as a source of funds to bookmakers, narcotic dealers, and other racketeers; that victims of the racket include all classes, rich and poor, businessmen and laborers; that the victims are often coerced into the commission of criminal acts in order to repay their loans that through loan sharking the organized underworld has obtained control of legitimate businesses, including securities brokerages and banks which are then exploited; and that "[e]ven where extortionate credit transactions are purely intrastate in character, they nevertheless directly affect interstate and foreign commerce." . . .

The essence of all these reports and hearings was summarized and embodied in formal congressional findings. They supplied Congress with the knowledge that the loan shark racket provides organized crime with its second most lucrative source of revenue, exacts millions from the pockets of people, coerces its victims into the commission of crimes against property, and causes the takeover by racketeers of legitimate businesses.

We have mentioned in detail the economic, financial, and social setting of the problem as revealed to Congress. We do so not to infer that Congress need make particularized findings in order to legislate. We relate the history of the act in detail to answer the impassioned plea of petitioner that all that is involved in loan sharking is a traditionally local activity. It appears, instead, that loan sharking in its national setting is one way organized interstate crime holds its guns to the heads of the poor and the rich alike and syphons funds from numerous localities to finance its national operations.

Affirmed.

JUSTICE STEWART, dissenting.

Congress surely has power under the commerce clause to enact criminal laws to protect the instrumentalities of interstate commerce, to prohibit the misuse of the channels or facilities of interstate commerce, and to prohibit or regulate those intrastate activities that have a demonstrably substantial effect on interstate commerce. But under the statute before us a man can be convicted without any proof of interstate movement, of the use of the facilities of interstate commerce, or of facts showing that his conduct affected interstate commerce. I think the Framers of the Constitution never intended that the national government might define as a crime and prosecute such wholly local activity through the enactment of federal criminal laws.

In order to sustain this law we would, in my view, have to be able at the least to say that Congress could rationally have concluded that loan sharking is an activity with interstate attributes that distinguish it in some substantial respect from other local crime. But it is not enough to say that loan sharking is a national problem, for all crime is a national problem. It is not enough to say that some loan sharking has interstate characteristics, for any crime may have an interstate setting. And the circumstance that loan sharking has an adverse impact on interstate business is not a distinguishing attribute, for interstate business suffers from almost all criminal activity, be it shoplifting or violence in the streets.

Because I am unable to discern any rational distinction between loan sharking and other local crime, I cannot escape the conclusion that this statute was beyond the power of Congress to enact. The definition and prosecution of local, intrastate crime are reserved to the state under the ninth and 10th amendments.

NOTES ON THE POWER OF CONGRESS TO DISPENSE WITH PROOF OF JURISDICTION

1. Questions and Comments on *Perez*. In his dissent to the Circuit Court decision in *Perez*, Judge Hays called the loan-shark statute "unprecedented" in that "[e]very trivial, insignificant and purely local act of the kind condemned is made a federal crime without any requirement of showing any connection with or effect upon interstate commerce. It is quite clear that not every extortionate act, no matter how small the debt involved, has any significant effect on interstate commerce. There is no reason to believe that using threats to collect debts has any more effect on interstate commerce than any other crime involving property. If extortionate conduct unrelated to interstate commerce can be made a federal crime, so can such crimes as robbery, burglary and larceny."

Both Judge Hays and Justice Stewart were concerned that the principle underlying the Court's decision in *Perez* might have no logical stopping point. If Congress can prohibit all instances of *this* crime, it can prohibit all instances of *any* crime. To this, one might respond "so what"? Do the precedents cited and discussed in *Perez* provide any basis for concluding that the commerce power has a relevant stopping point? Is the power as sustained in *Wickard v. Filburn* and other modern commerce clause cases fundamentally different from *Perez*?

2. Federalism and Congressional Use of the *Perez* Approach. Compare the Hobbs Act, 18 U.S.C. § 1951, which punishes "whoever in any way or degree obstructs, delays, or affects commerce or the movement of any article or commodity in commerce, by robbery or extortion or attempts or conspires so to do...." "Commerce" is defined to include "all ... commerce over which the United States has jurisdiction." Does the Hobbs Act extend, as a practical matter, to *all* robbery?[c] Does it matter that the Hobbs Act requires formal proof of an effect on commerce? Within the limits of *Wickard*, is such proof ever unavailable? One difference, to be sure, is the symbolic effect of going through the motions of establishing a logical link between a given robbery and an impact on interstate commerce. But it is worth the time and effort devoted to developing and litigating the proof? Why not follow the *Perez* model when the offense is to be defined so broadly?

Perhaps surprisingly, Congress has rarely used the power established in *Perez*.[d] Until recently, this phenomenon suggested the following possible generalization: Federalism may not be important as a constitutional

[c] See United States v. Collins, 40 F.3d 95 (5th Cir.1994), in which the defendant was convicted of, inter alia, violating the Hobbs Act by robbing a man at gunpoint of cash, jewelry, clothes, and a Mercedes–Benz containing a cellular telephone. The defendant argued on appeal that the robbery, which occurred at the victim's home, did not obstruct interstate commerce; the government responded that the victim's loss of his car and cellular telephone temporarily prevented him from conducting his interstate computer business, and that the car itself had previous-ly traveled in interstate commerce. The Fifth Circuit reversed the defendant's Hobbs Act conviction, holding that both of the government's contentions were "too attenuated to satisfy the interstate commerce requirement."

[d] One example of its use is the so-called Gambling Business Statute, 18 U.S.C. § 1955. See Iannelli v. United States, 420 U.S. 770 (1975). Another is the money-laundering activity covered by 18 U.S.C. § 1956(a)(1).

limitation on what Congress *can* do. But it may be an important constraint on what Congress is *likely* to do and on the extent to which the Court will actively collaborate with Congress in altering the federal-state balance. Even after *Perez*, there appear to be important arenas within which federalism operates. It seems to serve as an important *political* constraint on Congress and an important *judicial* restraint on the Court, even though it may not seriously limit the *constitutional* authority of a Congress determined to act.

Does this view of federalism make sense as a way of doing business? Does it represent an acceptable way of accommodating both the original intent of the Framers and the practical needs of a modern, globally interconnected, industrialized society?

Despite the apparent breadth of the Court's *Perez* ruling, Justice Stewart's somber declaration of federalism's demise as a constitutional limit on Congress's commerce clause power turned out to be premature. On April 26, 1995, the Supreme Court handed down *United States v. Lopez*, the first Court decision to strike down a federal statute on commerce clause grounds since the 1930's. *Lopez* has certainly changed the game. The question is, by how much?

United States v. Lopez

United States Supreme Court, 1995.
___ U.S. ___, 115 S.Ct. 1624.

■ CHIEF JUSTICE REHNQUIST delivered the opinion of the Court.

In the Gun–Free School Zones Act of 1990, Congress made it a federal offense "for any individual knowingly to possess a firearm at a place that the individual knows, or has reasonable cause to believe, is a school zone." 18 U.S.C. § 922(q)(1)(A)(1988 ed., Supp. V). The act neither regulates a commercial activity nor contains a requirement that the possession be connected in any way to interstate commerce. We hold that the act exceeds the authority of Congress "to regulate Commerce . . . among the several States" U.S. Const., Art. I, § 8, cl. 3.

On March 10, 1992, respondent, who was then a 12th-grade student, arrived at Edison High School in San Antonio, Texas, carrying a concealed .38 caliber handgun and five bullets. Acting upon an anonymous tip, school authorities confronted respondent, who admitted that he was carrying the weapon. He was arrested and charged under Texas law with firearm possession on school premises. The next day, the state charges were dismissed after federal agents charged respondent by complaint with violating the Gun–Free School Zones Act of 1990.[1]

A federal grand jury indicted respondent on one count of knowing possession of a firearm at a school zone, in violation of § 922(q). Respon-

---

[1] The term "school zone" is defined as "in, or on the grounds of, a public, parochial or private school" or "within a distance of 1,000 feet from the grounds of a public, parochial or private school." § 921(a)(25).

dent moved to dismiss his federal indictment on the ground that § 922(q) [is unconstitutional]. The District Court denied the motion..... Respondent waived his right to a jury trial. The District Court conducted a bench trial, found him guilty of violating § 922(q), and sentenced him to six months' imprisonment and two years' supervised release. On appeal, respondent challenged his conviction based on his claim that § 922(q) exceeded Congress' power to legislate under the commerce clause. The Court of Appeals for the Fifth Circuit agreed and reversed respondent's conviction. ... Because of the importance of the issue, we granted certiorari and we now affirm.

We start with first principles. The Constitution creates a federal government of enumerated powers. ... This constitutionally mandated division of authority "was adopted by the Framers to ensure protection of our fundamental liberties." Gregory v. Ashcroft, 501 U.S. 452, 458 (1991). "Just as the separation and independence of the coordinate branches of the federal government serves to prevent the accumulation of excessive power in any one branch, a healthy balance of power between the states and the federal government will reduce the risk of tyranny and abuse from either front."

... The Court, through Chief Justice Marshall, first defined the nature of Congress' commerce power in Gibbons v. Ogden, 22 U.S. (9 Wheat.) 1 (1824). ... For nearly a century thereafter, the Court's commerce clause decisions dealt but rarely with the extent of Congress' power, and almost entirely with the commerce clause as a limit on state legislation that discriminated against interstate commerce. ... In 1887, Congress enacted the Interstate Commerce Act, and in 1890, Congress enacted the Sherman Antitrust Act. These laws ushered in a new era of federal regulation under the commerce power.

[I]n the watershed case of NLRB v. Jones & Laughlin Steel Corp., 301 U.S. 1 (1937), the Court upheld the National Labor Relations Act against a commerce clause challenge..... The Court held that intrastate activities that "have such a close and substantial relation to interstate commerce that their control is essential or appropriate to protect that commerce from burdens and obstructions" are within Congress' power to regulate.

In United States v. Darby, 312 U.S. 100, 118 (1941), the Court upheld the Fair Labor Standards Act, stating:

"The power of Congress over interstate commerce is not confined to the regulation of commerce among the states. It extends to those activities intrastate which so affect interstate commerce or the exercise of the power of Congress over it as to make regulation of them appropriate means to the attainment of a legitimate end, the exercise of the granted power of Congress to regulate interstate commerce." ...

In Wickard v. Filburn, 317 U.S. 111 (1942), the Court upheld the application of amendments to the Agricultural Adjustment Act of 1938 to the production and consumption of home-grown wheat. The *Wickard*

Court explicitly rejected earlier distinctions between direct and indirect effects on interstate commerce, stating:

> "[E]ven if appellee's activity be local and though it may not be regarded as commerce, it may still, whatever its nature, be reached by Congress if it exerts a substantial economic effect on interstate commerce, and this irrespective of whether such effect is what might at some earlier time have been defined as 'direct' or 'indirect.' "

The *Wickard* Court emphasized that although Filburn's own contribution to the demand for wheat may have been trivial by itself, that was not "enough to remove him from the scope of federal regulation where, as here, his contribution, taken together with that of many others similarly situated, is far from trivial."

Jones & Laughlin Steel, *Darby*, and *Wickard* ushered in an era of commerce clause jurisprudence that greatly expanded the previously defined authority of Congress under that clause. In part, this was a recognition of the great changes that had occurred in the way business was carried on in this country. Enterprises that had once been local or at most regional in nature had become national in scope. But the doctrinal change also reflected a view that earlier commerce clause cases artificially had constrained the authority of Congress to regulate interstate commerce.

But even these modern-era precedents which have expanded congressional power under the commerce clause confirm that this power is subject to outer limits. In *Jones & Laughlin Steel*, the Court warned that the scope of the interstate commerce power "must be considered in the light of our dual system of government and may not be extended so as to embrace effects upon interstate commerce so indirect and remote that to embrace them, in view of our complex society, would effectually obliterate the distinction between what is national and what is local and create a completely centralized government." . . . Since that time, the Court has heeded that warning and undertaken to decide whether a rational basis existed for concluding that regulated activity sufficiently affected interstate commerce. See, e.g., Hodel v. Virginia Surface Mining & Reclamation Assn., Inc., 452 U.S. 264, 276–80 (1981); Perez v. United States, 402 U.S. 146, 155–56 (1971); Katzenbach v. McClung, 379 U.S. 294, 299–301 (1964); Heart of Atlanta Motel, Inc. v. United States, 379 U.S. 241, 252–53 (1964).

Similarly, in Maryland v. Wirtz, 392 U.S. 183, 196 (1968), the Court reaffirmed that "the power to regulate commerce, though broad indeed, has limits" that "the Court has ample power" to enforce. In response to the dissent's warnings that the Court was powerless to enforce the limitations on Congress' commerce powers because "all activities affecting commerce, even in the minutest degree, [*Wickard*], may be regulated and controlled by Congress," 392 U.S., at 204 (Douglas, J., dissenting), the *Wirtz* Court replied that the dissent had misread precedent as "neither here nor in *Wickard* has the Court declared that Congress may use a relatively trivial impact on commerce as an excuse for broad general regulation of state or private activities." Rather, "the Court has said only that where *a general regulatory statute bears a substantial relation to commerce*, the de minimis character of individual instances arising under that statute is of no consequence."

Consistent with this structure, we have identified three broad categories of activity that Congress may regulate under its commerce power. First, Congress may regulate the use of the channels of interstate commerce. ... Second, Congress is empowered to regulate and protect the instrumentalities of interstate commerce, or persons or things in interstate commerce, even though the threat may come only from intrastate activities. ... Finally, Congress' commerce authority includes the power to regulate those activities having a substantial relation to interstate commerce, i.e., those activities that substantially affect interstate commerce.

Within this final category, admittedly, our case law has not been clear whether an activity must "affect" or "substantially affect" interstate commerce in order to be within Congress' power to regulate it under the commerce clause. We conclude, consistent with the great weight of our case law, that the proper test requires an analysis of whether the regulated activity "substantially affects" interstate commerce.

We now turn to consider the power of Congress, in the light of this framework, to enact § 922(q). The first two categories of authority may be quickly disposed of: § 922(q) is not a regulation of the use of the channels of interstate commerce, nor is it an attempt to prohibit the interstate transportation of a commodity through the channels of commerce; nor can § 922(q) be justified as a regulation by which Congress has sought to protect an instrumentality of interstate commerce or a thing in interstate commerce. Thus, if § 922(q) is to be sustained, it must be under the third category as a regulation of an activity that substantially affects interstate commerce.

First, we have upheld a wide variety of congressional acts regulating intrastate economic activity where we have concluded that the activity substantially affected interstate commerce. Examples include the regulation of intrastate coal mining, *Hodel*, supra; intrastate extortionate credit transactions, *Perez*, supra; restaurants utilizing substantial interstate supplies, *McClung*, supra; inns and hotels catering to interstate guests, *Heart of Atlanta Motel*, supra; and production and consumption of home-grown wheat, *Wickard*, supra. These examples are by no means exhaustive, but the pattern is clear. Where economic activity substantially affects interstate commerce, legislation regulating that activity will be sustained.

Even *Wickard*, which is perhaps the most far reaching example of commerce clause authority over intrastate activity, involved economic activity in a way that the possession of a gun in a school zone does not. Roscoe Filburn operated a small farm in Ohio, on which, in the year involved, he raised 23 acres of wheat. It was his practice to sow winter wheat in the fall, and after harvesting it in July to sell a portion of the crop, to feed part of it to poultry and livestock on the farm, to use some in making flour for home consumption, and to keep the remainder for seeding future crops. The Secretary of Agriculture assessed a penalty against him under the

Agricultural Adjustment Act of 1938 because he harvested about 12 acres more wheat than his allotment under the act permitted. The act was designed to regulate the volume of wheat moving in interstate and foreign commerce in order to avoid surpluses and shortages, and concomitant fluctuation in wheat prices, which had previously obtained. The Court said, in an opinion sustaining the application of the act to Filburn's activity:

> "One of the primary purposes of the act in question was to increase the market price of wheat and to that end to limit the volume thereof that could affect the market. It can hardly be denied that a factor of such volume and variability as home-consumed wheat would have a substantial influence on price and market conditions. This may arise because being in marketable condition such wheat overhangs the market and, if induced by rising prices, tends to flow into the market and check price increases. But if we assume that it is never marketed, it supplies a need of the man who grew it which would otherwise be reflected by purchases in the open market. Home-grown wheat in this sense competes with wheat in commerce."

Section 922(q) is a criminal statute that by its terms has nothing to do with "commerce" or any sort of economic enterprise, however broadly one might define those terms.[3] Section 922(q) is not an essential part of a larger regulation of economic activity, in which the regulatory scheme could be undercut unless the intrastate activity were regulated. It cannot, therefore, be sustained under our cases upholding regulations of activities that arise out of or are connected with a commercial transaction, which viewed in the aggregate, substantially affects interstate commerce.

Second, § 922(q) contains no jurisdictional element which would ensure, through case-by-case inquiry, that the firearm possession in question affects interstate commerce. For example, in United States v. Bass, 404 U.S. 336 (1971), the Court interpreted former 18 U.S.C. § 1202(a), which made it a crime for a felon to "receive, possess, or transport in commerce or affecting commerce . . . any firearm." The Court interpreted the possession component of § 1202(a) to require an additional nexus to interstate commerce both because the statute was ambiguous and because "unless

---

[3] Under our federal system, the " 'states possess primary authority for defining and enforcing the criminal law.' " Brecht v. Abrahamson, 507 U.S. 619 (1993). When Congress criminalizes conduct already denounced as criminal by the states, it effects a " 'change in the sensitive relation between federal and state criminal jurisdiction.' " United States v. Enmons, 410 U.S. 396, 411–12 (1973)(quoting United States v. Bass, 404 U.S. 336, 349 (1971)). The government acknowledges that § 922(q) "displaces state policy choices in . . . that its prohibitions apply even in states that have chosen not to outlaw the conduct in question." Brief for United States 29, n.18; see also Statement of President George Bush on Signing the Crime Control Act of 1990, 26 Weekly Comp. of Pres. Doc. 1944, 1945 (Nov. 29, 1990)("Most egregiously, section [922(q)] inappropriately overrides legitimate state firearms laws with a new and unnecessary federal law. The policies reflected in these provisions could legitimately be adopted by the states, but they should not be imposed upon the states by Congress").

Congress conveys its purpose clearly, it will not be deemed to have significantly changed the federal-state balance." The *Bass* Court set aside the conviction because although the government had demonstrated that Bass had possessed a firearm, it had failed "to show the requisite nexus with interstate commerce." The Court thus interpreted the statute to reserve the constitutional question whether Congress could regulate, without more, the "mere possession" of firearms. See id., at 339, n.4. ... Unlike the statute in *Bass*, § 922(q) has no express jurisdictional element which might limit its reach to a discrete set of firearm possessions that additionally have an explicit connection with or effect on interstate commerce.

Although as part of our independent evaluation of constitutionality under the commerce clause we of course consider legislative findings, and indeed even congressional committee findings, regarding effect on interstate commerce, the government concedes that "neither the statute nor its legislative history contains express congressional findings regarding the effects upon interstate commerce of gun possession in a school zone." Brief for United States 5–6. We agree with the government that Congress normally is not required to make formal findings as to the substantial burdens that an activity has on interstate commerce. But to the extent that congressional findings would enable us to evaluate the legislative judgment that the activity in question substantially affected interstate commerce, even though no such substantial effect was visible to the naked eye, they are lacking here.[4]

The government argues that Congress has accumulated institutional expertise regarding the regulation of firearms through previous enactments. We agree, however, with the Fifth Circuit that importation of previous findings to justify § 922(q) is especially inappropriate here because the "prior federal enactments or Congressional findings [do not] speak to the subject matter of section 922(q) or its relationship to interstate commerce. Indeed, section 922(q) plows thoroughly new ground and represents a sharp break with the long-standing pattern of federal firearms legislation."

The government's essential contention, in fine, is that we may determine here that § 922(q) is valid because possession of a firearm in a local school zone does indeed substantially affect interstate commerce. The government argues that possession of a firearm in a school zone may result in violent crime and that violent crime can be expected to affect the functioning of the national economy in two ways. First, the costs of violent crime are substantial, and, through the mechanism of insurance, those

---

[4] We note that on September 13, 1994, President Clinton signed into law the Violent Crime Control and Law Enforcement Act of 1994, 108 Stat. 1796. Section 320904 of that Act, id., at 2125, amends § 922(q) to include congressional findings regarding the effects of firearm possession in and around schools upon interstate and foreign commerce. The government does not rely upon these subsequent findings as a substitute for the absence of findings in the first instance. Tr. of Oral Arg. 25 ("We're not relying on them in the strict sense of the word, but we think that at a very minimum they indicate that reasons can be identified for why Congress wanted to regulate this particular activity").

costs are spread throughout the population. Second, violent crime reduces the willingness of individuals to travel to areas within the country that are perceived to be unsafe. The government also argues that the presence of guns in schools poses a substantial threat to the educational process by threatening the learning environment. A handicapped educational process, in turn, will result in a less productive citizenry. That, in turn, would have an adverse effect on the nation's economic well-being. As a result, the government argues that Congress could rationally have concluded that § 922(q) substantially affects interstate commerce.

We pause to consider the implications of the government's arguments. The government admits, under its "costs of crime" reasoning, that Congress could regulate not only all violent crime, but all activities that might lead to violent crime, regardless of how tenuously they relate to interstate commerce. Similarly, under the government's "national productivity" reasoning, Congress could regulate any activity that it found was related to the economic productivity of individual citizens: family law (including marriage, divorce, and child custody), for example. Under the theories that the government presents in support of § 922(q), it is difficult to perceive any limitation on federal power, even in areas such as criminal law enforcement or education where states historically have been sovereign. Thus, if we were to accept the government's arguments, we are hard-pressed to posit any activity by an individual that Congress is without power to regulate.

Although Justice Breyer argues that acceptance of the government's rationales would not authorize a general federal police power, he is unable to identify any activity that the states may regulate but Congress may not. Justice Breyer posits that there might be some limitations on Congress' commerce power such as family law or certain aspects of education. These suggested limitations, when viewed in light of the dissent's expansive analysis, are devoid of substance.

Justice Breyer focuses, for the most part, on the threat that firearm possession in and near schools poses to the educational process and the potential economic consequences flowing from that threat. Specifically, the dissent reasons that (1) gun-related violence is a serious problem; (2) that problem, in turn, has an adverse effect on classroom learning; and (3) that adverse effect on classroom learning, in turn, represents a substantial threat to trade and commerce. This analysis would be equally applicable, if not more so, to subjects such as family law and direct regulation of education.

For instance, if Congress can, pursuant to its commerce clause power, regulate activities that adversely affect the learning environment, then, a fortiori, it also can regulate the educational process directly. Congress could determine that a school's curriculum has a "significant" effect on the extent of classroom learning. As a result, Congress could mandate a federal curriculum for local elementary and secondary schools because what is taught in local schools has a significant "effect on classroom learning" and that, in turn, has a substantial effect on interstate commerce.

Justice Breyer rejects our reading of precedent and argues that "Congress . . . could rationally conclude that schools fall on the commercial side of the line." Again, Justice Breyer's rationale lacks any real limits because, depending on the level of generality, any activity can be looked upon as commercial. Under the dissent's rationale, Congress could just as easily look at child rearing as "falling on the commercial side of the line" because it provides a "valuable service—namely, to equip [children] with the skills they need to survive in life and, more specifically, in the workplace." We do not doubt that Congress has authority under the commerce clause to regulate numerous commercial activities that substantially affect interstate commerce and also affect the educational process. That authority, though broad, does not include the authority to regulate each and every aspect of local schools.

Admittedly, a determination whether an intrastate activity is commercial or noncommercial may in some cases result in legal uncertainty. But, so long as Congress' authority is limited to those powers enumerated in the Constitution, and so long as those enumerated powers are interpreted as having judicially enforceable outer limits, congressional legislation under the commerce clause always will engender "legal uncertainty." . . . See . . . Gibbons v. Ogden, 22 U.S. (9 Wheat.) 1, 195 ("The enumeration presupposes something not enumerated"). The Constitution mandates this uncertainty by withholding from Congress a plenary police power that would authorize enactment of every type of legislation. Congress has operated within this framework of legal uncertainty ever since this Court determined that it was the judiciary's duty "to say what the law is." Marbury v. Madison, 5 U.S. (1 Cranch.) 137, 177 (1803)(Marshall, C. J.). Any possible benefit from eliminating this "legal uncertainty" would be at the expense of the Constitution's system of enumerated powers. In *Jones & Laughlin Steel*, we held that the question of congressional power under the commerce clause "is necessarily one of degree." . . .

These are not precise formulations, and in the nature of things they cannot be. But we think they point the way to a correct decision of this case. The possession of a gun in a local school zone is in no sense an economic activity that might, through repetition elsewhere, substantially affect any sort of interstate commerce. Respondent was a local student at a local school; there is no indication that he had recently moved in interstate commerce, and there is no requirement that his possession of the firearm have any concrete tie to interstate commerce.

To uphold the government's contentions here, we would have to pile inference upon inference in a manner that would bid fair to convert congressional authority under the commerce clause to a general police power of the sort retained by the states. Admittedly, some of our prior cases have taken long steps down that road, giving great deference to congressional action. The broad language in these opinions has suggested the possibility of additional expansion, but we decline here to proceed any further. To do so would require us to conclude that the Constitution's enumeration of powers does not presuppose something not enumerated, and that there never will be a distinction between what is truly national and what is truly local. This we are unwilling to do.

For the foregoing reasons the judgment of the Court of Appeals is Affirmed.

JUSTICE KENNEDY, with whom JUSTICE O'CONNOR joins, concurring.

The history of the judicial struggle to interpret the commerce clause during the transition from the economic system the founders knew to the single, national market still emergent in our own era counsels great restraint before the Court determines that the clause is insufficient to support an exercise of the national power. That history gives me some pause about today's decision, but I join the Court's opinion with these observations on what I conceive to be its necessary though limited holding.
. . .

The history of our commerce clause decisions contains at least two lessons of relevance to this case. The first . . . is the imprecision of content-based boundaries used without more to define the limits of the commerce clause. The second, related to the first but of even greater consequence, is that the Court as an institution and the legal system as a whole have an immense stake in the stability of our commerce clause jurisprudence as it has evolved to this point. Stare decisis operates with great force in counseling us not to call in question the essential principles now in place respecting the congressional power to regulate transactions of a commercial nature. That fundamental restraint on our power forecloses us from reverting to an understanding of commerce that would serve only an 18th-century economy, dependent then upon production and trading practices that had changed but little over the preceding centuries; it also mandates against returning to the time when congressional authority to regulate undoubted commercial activities was limited by a judicial determination that those matters had an insufficient connection to an interstate system. Congress can regulate in the commercial sphere on the assumption that we have a single market and a unified purpose to build a stable national economy.

. . . It does not follow, however, that in every instance the Court lacks the authority and responsibility to review congressional attempts to alter the federal balance. This case requires us to consider our place in the design of the government and to appreciate the significance of federalism in the whole structure of the Constitution.

. . . Though on the surface the idea may seem counterintuitive, it was the insight of the Framers that freedom was enhanced by the creation of two governments, not one. . . . The theory that two governments accord more liberty than one requires for its realization two distinct and discernable lines of political accountability: one between the citizens and the federal government; the second between the citizens and the states. If . . . the federal and state governments are to control each other and hold each other in check by competing for the affections of the people, those citizens must have some means of knowing which of the two governments to hold accountable for the failure to perform a given function. ... Were the federal government to take over the regulation of entire areas of traditional state concern, areas having nothing to do with the regulation of commercial activities, the boundaries between the spheres of federal and state authority would blur and political responsibility would become illusory. The resultant inability to hold either branch of the government answerable to the citizens is more dangerous even than devolving too much authority to the remote central power.

To be sure, one conclusion that could be drawn ... is that the balance between national and state power is entrusted in its entirety to the political process. ... Whatever the judicial role, it is axiomatic that Congress does have substantial discretion and control over the federal balance. [I]t would be mistaken and mischievous for the political branches to forget that the sworn obligation to preserve and protect the Constitution in maintaining the federal balance is their own in the first and primary instance. ... The political branches of the government must fulfill this grave constitutional obligation if democratic liberty and the federalism that secures it are to endure.

At the same time, the absence of structural mechanisms to require those officials to undertake this principled task, and the momentary political convenience often attendant upon their failure to do so, argue against a complete renunciation of the judicial role. Although it is the obligation of all officers of the government to respect the constitutional design, the federal balance is too essential a part of our constitutional structure and plays too vital a role in securing freedom for us to admit inability to intervene when one or the other level of government has tipped the scales too far.

In the past this Court has participated in maintaining the federal balance through judicial exposition of doctrines such as abstention, the rules for determining the primacy of state law, the doctrine of adequate and independent state grounds, the whole jurisprudence of pre-emption, and many of the rules governing our habeas jurisprudence. Our ability to preserve this principle under the commerce clause has presented a much greater challenge. But as the branch whose distinctive duty it is to declare "what the law is," Marbury v. Madison, 5 U.S. (1 Cranch) 137, 177 (1803), we are often called upon to resolve questions of constitutional law not susceptible to the mechanical application of bright and clear lines. The substantial element of political judgment in commerce clause matters leaves our institutional capacity to intervene more in doubt than when we decide cases, for instance, under the Bill of Rights even though clear and bright lines are often absent in the latter class of disputes. But our cases do not teach that we have no role at all in determining the meaning of the commerce clause. ...

Our position in enforcing the dormant commerce clause is instructive. ... Distinguishing between regulations that do place an undue burden on interstate commerce and regulations that do not depends upon delicate judgments. True, if we invalidate a state law, Congress can in effect overturn our judgment, whereas in a case announcing that Congress has transgressed its authority, the decision is more consequential, for its stands unless Congress can revise its law to demonstrate its commercial character. This difference no doubt informs the circumspection with which we invalidate an act of Congress, but it does not mitigate our duty to recognize meaningful limits on the commerce power of Congress.

The statute before us upsets the federal balance to a degree that renders it an unconstitutional assertion of the commerce power, and our intervention is required. As the Chief Justice explains, unlike the earlier cases to come before the Court here neither the actors nor their conduct have a commercial character, and neither the purposes nor the design of the statute have an evident commercial nexus. The statute makes the simple possession of a gun within 1,000 feet of the grounds of the school a criminal offense. In a sense any conduct in this interdependent world of ours has an ultimate commercial origin or consequence, but we have not yet said the commerce power may reach so far. If Congress attempts that extension, then at the least we must inquire whether the exercise of national power seeks to intrude upon an area of traditional state concern.

An interference of these dimensions occurs here, for it is well established that education is a traditional concern of the states. The proximity to schools, including of course schools owned and operated by the states or their subdivisions, is the very premise for making the conduct criminal. In these circumstances, we have a particular duty to insure that the federal-state balance is not destroyed. . . .

While it is doubtful that any state, or indeed any reasonable person, would argue that it is wise policy to allow students to carry guns on school premises, considerable disagreement exists about how best to accomplish that goal. In this circumstance, the theory and utility of our federalism are revealed, for the states may perform their role as laboratories for experimentation to devise various solutions where the best solution is far from clear.

If a state or municipality determines that harsh criminal sanctions are necessary and wise to deter students from carrying guns on school premises, the reserved powers of the states are sufficient to enact those measures. Indeed, over 40 states already have criminal laws outlawing the possession of firearms on or near school grounds.

Other, more practicable means to rid the schools of guns may be thought by the citizens of some states to be preferable for the safety and welfare of the schools those states are charged with maintaining. See Brief for National Conference of State Legislatures et al., as Amici Curiae 26–30 (injection of federal officials into local problems causes friction and diminishes political accountability of state and local governments). These might include inducements to inform on violators where the information leads to arrests or confiscation of the guns; programs to encourage the voluntary surrender of guns with some provision for amnesty; penalties imposed on parents or guardians for failure to supervise the child; laws providing for suspension or expulsion of gun-toting students; or programs for expulsion with assignment to special facilities.

The statute now before us forecloses the states from experimenting and exercising their own judgment in an area to which states lay claim by right of history and expertise, and it does so by regulating an activity beyond the realm of commerce in the ordinary and usual sense of that term. The tendency of this statute to displace state regulation in areas of traditional state concern is evident from its territorial operation. There are over 100,000 elementary and secondary schools in the United States. Each of these now has an invisible federal zone extending 1,000 feet beyond the (often irregular) boundaries of the school property. In some communities no doubt it would be difficult to navigate without infringing on those zones. Yet throughout these areas, school officials would find their own programs for the prohibition of guns in danger of displacement by the federal authority unless the state chooses to enact a parallel rule.

... Absent a stronger connection or identification with commercial concerns that are central to the commerce clause, that interference contradicts the federal balance the Framers designed and that this Court is obliged to enforce.

For these reasons, I join in the opinion and judgment of the Court.

JUSTICE THOMAS, concurring.

The Court today properly concludes that the commerce clause does not grant Congress the authority to prohibit gun possession within 1,000 feet of a school..... Although I join the majority, I write separately to observe that our case law has drifted far from the original understanding of the commerce clause. In a future case, we ought to temper our commerce clause jurisprudence in a manner that both makes sense of our more recent case law and is more faithful to the original understanding of that clause.

We have said that Congress may regulate not only "Commerce ... among the several states," U.S. Const., Art. I, § 8, cl. 3, but also anything that has a "substantial effect" on such commerce. This test, if taken to its logical extreme, would give Congress a "police power" over all aspects of American life. Unfortunately, we have never come to grips with this implication of our substantial effects formula. Although we have supposedly applied the substantial effects test for the past 60 years, we always have rejected readings of the commerce clause and the scope of federal power that would permit Congress to exercise a police power; our cases are quite clear that there are real limits to federal power. Indeed, on this crucial point, the majority and Justice Breyer agree in principle: the federal government has nothing approaching a police power.

While the principal dissent concedes that there are limits to federal power, the sweeping nature of our current test enables the dissent to argue that Congress can regulate gun possession. But it seems to me that the power to regulate "commerce" can by no means encompass authority over mere gun possession, any more than it empowers the federal government to regulate marriage, littering, or cruelty to animals, throughout the 50 states.

Our Constitution quite properly leaves such matters to the individual states, notwithstanding these activities' effects on interstate commerce. Any interpretation of the commerce clause that even suggests that Congress could regulate such matters is in need of reexamination.

In an appropriate case, I believe that we must further reconsider our "substantial effects" test with an eye toward constructing a standard that reflects the text and history of the commerce clause without totally rejecting our more recent commerce clause jurisprudence.

Today, however, I merely support the Court's conclusion with a discussion of the text, structure, and history of the commerce clause and an analysis of our early case law. My goal is simply to show how far we have departed from the original understanding and to demonstrate that the result we reach today is by no means "radical." I also want to point out the necessity of refashioning a coherent test that does not tend to "obliterate the distinction between what is national and what is local and create a completely centralized government." NLRB v. Jones & Laughlin Steel Corp., 301 U.S. 1, 37 (1937).

[At this point, Justice Thomas engaged in an extensive analysis of the pre–1930's case law. He concluded:]

These cases all establish a simple point: from the time of the ratification of the Constitution to the mid–1930's, it was widely understood that the Constitution granted Congress only limited powers, notwithstanding the commerce clause. Moreover, there was no question that activities wholly separated from business, such as gun possession, were beyond the reach of the commerce power. If anything, the "wrong turn" was the Court's dramatic departure in the 1930's from a century and a half of precedent. . . .

Apart from its recent vintage and its corresponding lack of any grounding in the original understanding of the Constitution, the substantial effects test suffers from the further flaw that it appears to grant Congress a police power over the nation. When asked at oral argument if there were any limits to the commerce clause, the government was at a loss for words. Likewise, the principal dissent insists that there are limits, but it cannot muster even one example. Indeed, the dissent implicitly concedes that its reading has no limits when it criticizes the Court for "threatening legal uncertainty in an area of law that . . . seemed reasonably well settled." The one advantage of the dissent's standard is certainty: it is certain that under its analysis everything may be regulated under the guise of the commerce clause.

The substantial effects test suffers from this flaw, in part, because of its "aggregation principle." Under so-called "class of activities" statutes, Congress can regulate whole categories of activities that are not themselves either "interstate" or "commerce." In applying the effects test, we ask whether the class of activities as a whole substantially affects interstate commerce, not whether any specific activity within the class has such effects when considered in isolation.

The aggregation principle is clever, but has no stopping point. Suppose all would agree that gun possession within 1,000 feet of a school does not substantially affect commerce, but that possession of weapons generally (knives, brass knuckles, nunchakus, etc.) does. Under our substantial effects doctrine, even though Congress cannot single out gun possession, it can prohibit weapon possession generally. But one always can draw the circle broadly enough to cover an activity that, when taken in isolation, would not have substantial effects on commerce. Under our jurisprudence, if Congress passed an omnibus "substantially affects interstate commerce" statute, purporting to regulate every aspect of human existence, the act apparently would be constitutional. Even though particular sections may govern only trivial activities, the statute in the aggregate regulates matters that substantially affect commerce. . . .

This extended discussion of the original understanding and our first century and a half of case law does not necessarily require a wholesale abandonment of our more recent opinions.[8] It simply reveals that our substantial effects test is far removed from both the Constitution and from our early case law and that the Court's opinion should not be viewed as "radical" or another "wrong turn" that must be corrected in the future. The analysis also suggests that we ought to temper our commerce clause jurisprudence.

Unless the dissenting Justices are willing to repudiate our long-held understanding of the limited nature of federal power, I would think that they too must be willing to reconsider the substantial effects test in a future case. If we wish to be true to a Constitution that does not cede a police power to the federal government, our commerce clause's boundaries simply cannot be "defined" as being " 'commensurate with the national needs' " or self-consciously intended to let the federal government " 'defend itself against economic forces that Congress decrees inimical or destructive of the national economy.' " Such a formulation of federal power is no test at all: it is a blank check.

At an appropriate juncture, I think we must modify our commerce clause jurisprudence. Today, it is easy enough to say that the clause certainly does not empower Congress to ban gun possession within 1,000 feet of a school.

JUSTICE STEVENS, dissenting.

The welfare of our future "Commerce with foreign Nations, and among the several States," U.S. Const., Art. I, § 8, cl. 3, is vitally dependent on the character of the education of our children. I therefore agree entirely with Justice Breyer's explanation of why Congress has ample power to prohibit the possession of firearms in or near schools—just as it may protect the school environment from harms posed by controlled substances

---

[8] Although I might be willing to return to the original understanding, I recognize that many believe that it is too late in the day to undertake a fundamental reexamina- tion of the past 60 years. Consideration of stare decisis and reliance interests may convince us that we cannot wipe the slate clean.

such as asbestos or alcohol.   I also agree with Justice Souter's exposition of the radical character of the Court's holding and its kinship with the discredited, pre-Depression version of substantive due process.   I believe, however, that the Court's extraordinary decision merits this additional comment.

Guns are both articles of commerce and articles that can be used to restrain commerce.   Their possession is the consequence, either directly or indirectly, of commercial activity.   In my judgment, Congress' power to regulate commerce in firearms includes the power to prohibit possession of guns at any location because of their potentially harmful use; it necessarily follows that Congress may also prohibit their possession in particular markets.   The market for the possession of handguns by school-age children is, distressingly, substantial.*   Whether or not the national interest in eliminating that market would have justified federal legislation in 1789, it surely does today.

JUSTICE SOUTER, dissenting.

In reviewing congressional legislation under the commerce clause, we defer to what is often a merely implicit congressional judgment that its regulation addresses a subject substantially affecting interstate commerce "if there is any rational basis for such a finding."   Hodel v. Virginia Surface Mining & Reclamation Assn., Inc., 452 U.S. 264, 276 (1981).   If that congressional determination is within the realm of reason, "the only remaining question for judicial inquiry is whether 'the means chosen by Congress [are] reasonably adapted to the end permitted by the Constitution.' "   Id., at 276.

The practice of deferring to rationally based legislative judgments "is a paradigm of judicial restraint."   FCC v. Beach Communications, Inc., 508 U.S. 307, 314 (1993).   In judicial review under the commerce clause, it reflects our respect for the institutional competence of the Congress on a subject expressly assigned to it by the Constitution and our appreciation of the legitimacy that comes from Congress's political accountability in dealing with matters open to a wide range of possible choices.

It was not ever thus, however, as even a brief overview of commerce clause history during the past century reminds us.   The modern respect for the competence and primacy of Congress in matters affecting commerce developed only after one of this Court's most chastening experiences, when it perforce repudiated an earlier and untenably expansive conception of judicial review in derogation of congressional commerce power.   A look at history's sequence will serve to show how today's decision tugs the Court off course, leading it to suggest opportunities for further developments that would be at odds with the rule of restraint to which the Court still wisely states adherence.

---

* Indeed, there is evidence that firearm manufacturers—aided by a federal grant— are specifically targeting school children as consumers by distributing, at schools, hunting-related videos styled "educational materials for grades four through 12," Herbert, Reading, Writing, Reloading, N.Y. Times, Dec. 14, 1994, p. A23, col. 1.

[After reviewing the early commerce clause and substantive due process cases and their repudiation in the mid–30's, Justice Souter continued:] [U]nder commerce, as under due process, adoption of rational basis review expressed the recognition that the Court had no sustainable basis for subjecting economic regulation as such to judicial policy judgments, and for the past half-century the Court has no more turned back in the direction of formalistic commerce clause review (as in deciding whether regulation of commerce was sufficiently direct) than it has inclined toward reasserting the substantive authority of *Lochner* due process (as in the inflated protection of contractual autonomy). . . .

There is today, however, a backward glance at both the old pitfalls, as the Court treats deference under the rationality rule as subject to gradation according to the commercial or noncommercial nature of the immediate subject of the challenged regulation. The distinction between what is patently commercial and what is not looks much like the old distinction between what directly affects commerce and what touches it only indirectly. And the act of calibrating the level of deference by drawing a line between what is patently commercial and what is less purely so will probably resemble the process of deciding how much interference with contractual freedom was fatal. Thus, it seems fair to ask whether the step taken by the Court today does anything but portend a return to the untenable jurisprudence from which the Court extricated itself almost 60 years ago. The answer is not reassuring. To be sure, the occasion for today's decision reflects the century's end, not its beginning. But if it seems anomalous that the Congress of the United States has taken to regulating school yards, the act in question is still probably no more remarkable than state regulation of bake shops 90 years ago. In any event, there is no reason to hope that the Court's qualification of rational basis review will be any more successful than the efforts at substantive economic review made by our predecessors as the century began. Taking the Court's opinion on its own terms, Justice Breyer has explained both the hopeless porosity of "commercial" character as a ground of commerce clause distinction in America's highly connected economy, and the inconsistency of this categorization with our rational basis precedents from the last 50 years.

Further glosses on rationality review, moreover, may be in the offing. Although this case turns on commercial character, the Court gestures toward two other considerations that it might sometime entertain in applying rational basis scrutiny (apart from a statutory obligation to supply independent proof of a jurisdictional element): does the congressional statute deal with subjects of traditional state regulation, and does the statute contain explicit factual findings supporting the otherwise implicit determination that the regulated activity substantially affects interstate commerce? Once again, any appeal these considerations may have depends on ignoring the painful lesson learned in 1937, for neither of the Court's suggestions would square with rational basis scrutiny. . . .

The Court observes that the Gun–Free School Zones Act operates in two areas traditionally subject to legislation by the states, education and enforcement of criminal law. The suggestion is either that a connection between commerce and these subjects is remote, or that the commerce power is simply weaker when it touches subjects on which the states have historically been the primary legislators. Neither suggestion is tenable. As for remoteness, it may or may not be wise for the national government to deal with education, but Justice Breyer has surely demonstrated that the commercial prospects of an illiterate state or nation are not rosy, and no argument should be needed to show that hijacking interstate shipments of cigarettes can affect commerce substantially, even though the states have traditionally prosecuted robbery. And as for the notion that the commerce power diminishes the closer it gets to customary state concerns, that idea has been flatly rejected, and not long ago. The commerce power, we have often observed, is plenary. ...

Nor is there any contrary authority in the reasoning of our cases imposing clear statement rules in some instances of legislation that would significantly alter the state-national balance. [W]hen faced with two plausible interpretations of a federal criminal statute, [for example,] we generally will take the alternative that does not force us to impute an intention to Congress to use its full commerce power to regulate conduct traditionally and ably regulated by the states. See United States v. Enmons, 410 U.S. 396, 411–12 (1973); United States v. Bass, 404 U.S. 336, 349–50 (1971); Rewis v. United States, 401 U.S. 808, 812 (1971).

These clear statement rules, however, are merely rules of statutory interpretation, to be relied upon only when the terms of a statute allow, and in cases implicating Congress's historical reluctance to trench on state legislative prerogatives or to enter into spheres already occupied by the states. They are rules for determining intent when legislation leaves intent subject to question. But our hesitance to presume that Congress has acted to alter the state-federal status quo (when presented with a plausible alternative) has no relevance whatever to the enquiry whether it has the commerce power to do so or to the standard of judicial review when Congress has definitely meant to exercise that power. Indeed, to allow our hesitance to affect the standard of review would inevitably degenerate into the sort of substantive policy review that the Court found indefensible 60 years ago. The Court does not assert (and could not plausibly maintain) that the commerce power is wholly devoid of congressional authority to speak on any subject of traditional state concern; but if congressional action is not forbidden absolutely when it touches such a subject, it will stand or fall depending on the Court's view of the strength of the legisla-tion's commercial justification. And here once again history raises its objections that the Court's previous essays in overriding congressional policy choices under the commerce clause were ultimately seen to suffer two fatal weaknesses: ... nothing in the clause compelled the judicial activism, and nothing about the judiciary as an institution made it a superior source of policy on the subject Congress dealt with. There is no reason to expect the lesson would be different another time. ...

There remain questions about legislative findings. ... The question for the courts, as all agree, is not whether as a predicate to legislation Congress in fact found that a particular activity substantially affects interstate commerce. The legislation implies such a finding, and there is no reason to entertain claims that Congress acted ultra vires intentionally. Nor is the question whether Congress was correct in so finding. The only question is whether the legislative judgment is within the realm of reason. Congressional findings do not, however, directly address the question of reasonableness; they tell us what Congress actually has found, not what it could rationally find. If, indeed, the Court were to make the existence of explicit congressional findings dispositive in some close or difficult cases something other than rationality review would be afoot. The resulting congressional obligation to justify its policy choices on the merits would imply either a judicial authority to review the justification (and, hence, the wisdom) of those choices, or authority to require Congress to act with some high degree of deliberateness, of which express findings would be evidence. But review for congressional wisdom would just be the old judicial pretension discredited and abandoned in 1937, and review for deliberateness would be as patently unconstitutional as an act of Congress mandating long opinions from this Court. Such a legislative process requirement would function merely as an excuse for covert review of the merits of legislation under standards never expressed and more or less arbitrarily applied. Under such a regime, in any case, the rationality standard of review would be a thing of the past. ... I would not allow for the possibility, as the Court's opinion may, that the addition of congressional findings could in principle have affected the fate of the statute here. ...

I respectfully dissent.

JUSTICE BREYER, with whom JUSTICE STEVENS, JUSTICE SOUTER, and JUSTICE GINSBURG join, dissenting.

... In my view, the statute [before the Court] falls well within the scope of the commerce power as this Court has understood that power over the last half-century. ... In reaching this conclusion, I apply three basic principles of commerce clause interpretation. First, the power to "regulate Commerce ... among the several States," U.S. Const., Art. I, § 8, cl. 3, encompasses the power to regulate local activities insofar as they significantly affect interstate commerce. ... Second, in determining whether a local activity will likely have a significant effect upon interstate commerce, a court must consider, not the effect of an individual act (a single instance of gun possession), but rather the cumulative effect of all similar instances (i.e., the effect of all guns possessed in or near schools). Third, the Constitution requires us to judge the connection between a regulated activity and interstate commerce, not directly, but at one remove. Courts must give Congress a degree of leeway in determining the existence of a significant factual connection between the regulated activity and interstate commerce—both because the Constitution delegates the commerce power directly to Congress and because the determination requires an empirical judgment of a kind that a legislature is more likely than a court to make with accuracy.   The traditional words "rational basis" capture this leeway. Thus, the specific question before us, as the Court recognizes, is not whether the "regulated activity sufficiently affected interstate commerce," but, rather, whether Congress could have had "a rational basis" for so concluding. . . .

Applying these principles to the case at hand, we must ask whether Congress could have had a rational basis for finding a significant (or substantial) connection between gun-related school violence and interstate commerce.   Or, to put the question in the language of the explicit finding that Congress made when it amended this law in 1994: Could Congress rationally have found that "violent crime in school zones," through its effect on the "quality of education," significantly (or substantially) affects "interstate" or "foreign commerce"?   18 U.S.C. §§ 922(q)(1)(F), (G)(Nov. 1994 Supp.).   As long as one views the commerce connection, not as a "technical legal conception," but as "a practical one," Swift & Co. v. United States, 196 U.S. 375, 398 (1905)(Holmes, J.), the answer to this question must be yes.   Numerous reports and studies—generated both inside and outside government—make clear that Congress could reasonably have found the empirical connection that its law, implicitly or explicitly, asserts.

For one thing, reports, hearings, and other readily available literature make clear that the problem of guns in and around schools is widespread and extremely serious.   These materials report, for example, that four percent of American high school students (and six percent of inner-city high school students) carry a gun to school at least occasionally; that 12 percent of urban high school students have had guns fired at them; that 20 percent of those students have been threatened with guns; and that, in any six-month period, several hundred thousand schoolchildren are victims of violent crimes in or near their schools.   And, they report that this widespread violence in schools throughout the nation significantly interferes with the quality of education in those schools.   Based on reports such as these, Congress obviously could have thought that guns and learning are mutually exclusive.   And, Congress could therefore have found a substantial educational problem—teachers unable to teach, students unable to learn—and concluded that guns near schools contribute substantially to the size and scope of that problem.

Having found that guns in schools significantly undermine the quality of education in our nation's classrooms, Congress could also have found, given the effect of education upon interstate and foreign commerce, that gun-related violence in and around schools is a commercial, as well as a human, problem.   Education, although far more than a matter of economics, has long been inextricably intertwined with the nation's economy. When this nation began, most workers received their education in the workplace, typically (like Benjamin Franklin) as apprentices.   As late as the 1920's, many workers still received general education directly from their employers—from large corporations, such as General Electric, Ford, and Goodyear, which created schools within their firms to help both the worker and the firm. ... As public school enrollment grew in the early 20th century, the need for industry to teach basic educational skills diminished. But, the direct economic link between basic education and industrial productivity remained. Scholars estimate that nearly a quarter of America's economic growth in the early years of this century is traceable directly to increased schooling; that investment in "human capital" (through spending on education) exceeded investment in "physical capital" by a ratio of almost two to one; and that the economic returns to this investment in education exceeded the returns to conventional capital investment.

In recent years the link between secondary education and business has strengthened, becoming both more direct and more important. Scholars on the subject report that technological changes and innovations in management techniques have altered the nature of the workplace so that more jobs now demand greater educational skills. ... Increasing global competition also has made primary and secondary education economically more important. The portion of the American economy attributable to international trade nearly tripled between 1950 and 1980, and more than 70 percent of American-made goods now compete with imports. Yet, lagging worker productivity has contributed to negative trade balances and to real hourly compensation that has fallen below wages in 10 other industrialized nations. At least some significant part of this serious productivity problem is attributable to students who emerge from classrooms without the reading or mathematical skills necessary to compete with their European or Asian counterparts and, presumably, to high school dropout rates of 20 to 25 percent (up to 50 percent in inner cities). Indeed, Congress has said, when writing other statutes, that "functionally or technologically illiterate" Americans in the work force "erode" our economic "standing in the international marketplace," Pub. L. 100–418, § 6002(a)(3), 102 Stat. 1469, and that "our nation is ... paying the price of scientific and technological illiteracy, with our productivity declining, our industrial base ailing, and our global competitiveness dwindling." H. R. Rep. No. 98–6, pt. 1, p. 19 (1983).

Finally, there is evidence that, today more than ever, many firms base their location decisions upon the presence, or absence, of a work force with a basic education. Scholars on the subject report, for example, that today, "high speed communication and transportation make it possible to produce most products and services anywhere in the world"; that "modern machinery and production methods can therefore be combined with low wage workers to drive costs down"; that managers can perform " 'back office functions anywhere in the world now,' " and say that if they " 'can't get enough skilled workers here' " they will " 'move the skilled jobs out of the country' "; with the consequence that "rich countries need better education and retraining, to reduce the supply of unskilled workers and to equip them with the skills they require for tomorrow's jobs." [Citations omitted.] In light of this increased importance of education to individual firms, it is no surprise that half of the nation's manufacturers have become involved with setting standards and shaping curricula for local schools, that

88 percent think this kind of involvement is important, that more than 20 states have recently passed educational reforms to attract new business, and that business magazines have begun to rank cities according to the quality of their schools.

The economic links I have just sketched seem fairly obvious. Why then is it not equally obvious, in light of those links, that a widespread, serious, and substantial physical threat to teaching and learning also substantially threatens the commerce to which that teaching and learning is inextricably tied? That is to say, guns in the hands of six percent of inner-city high school students and gun-related violence throughout a city's schools must threaten the trade and commerce that those schools support. The only question, then, is whether the latter threat is (to use the majority's terminology) "substantial." And, the evidence of (1) the extent of the gun-related violence problem, (2) the extent of the resulting negative effect on classroom learning, and (3) the extent of the consequent negative commercial effects, when taken together, indicate a threat to trade and commerce that is "substantial." At the very least, Congress could rationally have concluded that the links are "substantial." . . .

To hold this statute constitutional is not to "obliterate" the "distinction of what is national and what is local"; nor is it to hold that the commerce clause permits the federal government to "regulate any activity that it found was related to the economic productivity of individual citizens," to regulate "marriage, divorce, and child custody," or to regulate any and all aspects of education. For one thing, this statute is aimed at curbing a particularly acute threat to the educational process—the possession (and use) of life-threatening firearms in, or near, the classroom. The empirical evidence that I have discussed above unmistakably documents the special way in which guns and education are incompatible. [T]he immediacy of the connection between education and the national economic well-being is documented by scholars and accepted by society at large in a way and to a degree that may not hold true for other social institutions. It must surely be the rare case, then, that a statute strikes at conduct that (when considered in the abstract) seems so removed from commerce, but which (practically speaking) has so significant an impact upon commerce.

In sum, a holding that the particular statute before us falls within the commerce power would not expand the scope of that clause. Rather, it simply would apply pre-existing law to changing economic circumstances. It would recognize that, in today's economic world, gun-related violence near the classroom makes a significant difference to our economic, as well as our social, well-being. In accordance with well-accepted precedent, such a holding would permit Congress "to act in terms of economic . . . realities," would interpret the commerce power as "an affirmative power commensurate with the national needs," and would acknowledge that the "commerce clause does not operate so as to render the nation powerless to defend itself against economic forces that Congress decrees inimical or destructive of the national economy." North American Co. v. SEC, 327 U.S. 686, 705 (1946). . . .

The majority's holding ... creates three serious legal problems. First, the majority's holding runs contrary to modern Supreme Court cases that have upheld congressional actions despite connections to interstate or foreign commerce that are less significant than the effect of school violence. In Perez v. United States, 402 U.S. 146 (1971), the Court held that the commerce clause authorized a federal statute that makes it a crime to engage in loansharking ("extortionate credit transactions") at a local level. The Court said that Congress may judge that such transactions, "though purely *intra*state, ... affect *inter*state commerce." Presumably, Congress reasoned that threatening or using force, say with a gun on a street corner, to collect a debt occurs sufficiently often so that the activity (by helping organized crime) affects commerce among the states. But, why then cannot Congress also reason that the threat or use of force—the frequent consequence of possessing a gun—in or near a school occurs sufficiently often so that such activity (by inhibiting basic education) affects commerce among the states? The negative impact upon the national economy of an inability to teach basic skills seems no smaller (nor less significant) than that of organized crime.

In Katzenbach v. McClung, 379 U.S. 294 (1964), this Court upheld, as within the commerce power, a statute prohibiting racial discrimination at local restaurants, in part because that discrimination discouraged travel by African–Americans and in part because that discrimination affected purchases of food and restaurant supplies from other states. In Daniel v. Paul, 395 U.S. 298 (1969), this Court found an effect on commerce caused by an amusement park located several miles down a country road in the middle of Alabama—because some customers (the Court assumed), some food, 15 paddleboats, and a juke box had come from out of state. In both of these cases, the Court understood that the specific instance of discrimination (at a local place of accommodation) was part of a general practice that, considered as a whole, caused not only the most serious human and social harm, but had nationally significant economic dimensions as well. It is difficult to distinguish the case before us, for the same critical elements are present. Businesses are less likely to locate in communities where violence plagues the classroom. Families will hesitate to move to neighborhoods where students carry guns instead of books. ... And (to look at the matter in the most narrowly commercial manner), interstate publishers therefore will sell fewer books and other firms will sell fewer school supplies where the threat of violence disrupts learning. Most importantly, like the local racial discrimination at issue in *McClung* and *Daniel*, the local instances here, taken together and considered as a whole, create a problem that causes serious human and social harm, but also has nationally significant economic dimensions.

In Wickard v. Filburn, 317 U.S. 111 (1942), this Court sustained the application of the Agricultural Adjustment Act of 1938 to wheat that Filburn grew and consumed on his own local farm because, considered in its totality, (1) home-grown wheat may be "induced by rising prices" to "flow into the market and check price increases," and (2) even if it never actually enters the market, home-grown wheat nonetheless "supplies a need of the man who grew it which would otherwise be reflected by purchases in the open market" and, in that sense, "competes with wheat in commerce." To find both of these effects on commerce significant in amount, the Court had to give Congress the benefit of the doubt. Why would the Court, to find a significant (or "substantial") effect here, have to give Congress any greater leeway?

The second legal problem the Court creates comes from its apparent belief that it can reconcile its holding with earlier cases by making a critical distinction between "commercial" and noncommercial "transactions." That is to say, the Court believes the Constitution would distinguish between two local activities, each of which has an identical effect upon interstate commerce, if one, but not the other, is "commercial" in nature. As a general matter, this approach fails to heed this Court's earlier [cases.] More importantly, if a distinction between commercial and noncommercial activities is to be made, this is not the case in which to make it. The majority clearly cannot intend such a distinction to focus narrowly on an act of gun possession standing by itself, for such a reading could not be reconciled with either the civil rights cases (*McClung* and *Daniel*) or *Perez*—in each of those cases the specific transaction (the race-based exclusion, the use of force) was not itself "commercial." And, if the majority instead means to distinguish generally among broad categories of activities, differentiating what is educational from what is commercial, then, as a practical matter, the line becomes almost impossible to draw. Schools that teach reading, writing, mathematics, and related basic skills serve both social and commercial purposes, and one cannot easily separate the one from the other. American industry itself has been, and is again, involved in teaching. When, and to what extent, does its involvement make education commercial? Does the number of vocational classes that train students directly for jobs make a difference? Does it matter if the school is public or private, nonprofit or profit-seeking? Does it matter if a city or state adopts a voucher plan that pays private firms to run a school? Even if one were to ignore these practical questions, why should there be a theoretical distinction between education, when it significantly benefits commerce, and environmental pollution, when it causes economic harm?

Regardless, if there is a principled distinction that could work both here and in future cases, Congress (even in the absence of vocational classes, industry involvement, and private management) could rationally conclude that schools fall on the commercial side of the line. In 1990, the year Congress enacted the statute before us, primary and secondary schools spent $230 billion—that is, nearly a quarter of a trillion dollars—which accounts for a significant portion of our $5.5 trillion Gross Domestic Product for that year. The business of schooling requires expenditure of these funds on student transportation, food and custodial services, books, and teachers' salaries. And, these expenditures enable schools to provide a valuable service—namely, to equip students with the skills they need to survive in life and, more specifically, in the workplace. Certainly, Congress has often analyzed school expenditure as if it were a commercial investment, closely analyzing whether schools are efficient, whether they justify the significant resources they spend, and whether they can be restructured to achieve greater returns. Why could Congress, for commerce clause purposes, not consider schools as roughly analogous to commercial investments from which the nation derives the benefit of an educated work force?

The third legal problem created by the Court's holding is that it threatens legal uncertainty in an area of law that, until this case, seemed reasonably well settled. Congress has enacted many statutes (more than 100 sections of the United States Code), including criminal statutes (at least 25 sections), that use the words "affecting commerce" to define their scope , see, e.g., 18 U.S.C. § 844(i)(destruction of buildings used in activity affecting interstate commerce), and other statutes that contain no jurisdictional language at all, see, e.g., 18 U.S.C. § 922(*o*)(1)(possession of machine guns). Do these, or similar, statutes regulate noncommercial activities? If so, would that alter the meaning of "affecting commerce" in a jurisdictional element? More importantly, in the absence of a jurisdictional element, are the courts nevertheless to take *Wickard* (and later similar cases) as inapplicable, and to judge the effect of a single noncommercial activity on interstate commerce without considering similar instances of the forbidden conduct? However these questions are eventually resolved, the legal uncertainty now created will restrict Congress' ability to enact criminal laws aimed at criminal behavior that, considered problem by problem rather than instance by instance, seriously threatens the economic, as well as social, well-being of Americans. ...

In sum, to find this legislation within the scope of the commerce clause would permit "Congress ... to act in terms of economic ... realities." North American Co. v. SEC, 327 U.S. 686, 705 (1946). It would interpret the clause as this Court has traditionally interpreted it, with the exception of one wrong turn subsequently corrected. See Gibbons v. Ogden, 22 U.S. (9 Wheat.) 1, 195 (holding that the commerce power extends "to all the external concerns of the nation, and to those internal concerns which affect the states generally"); United States v. Darby, 312 U.S. 100, 116–17 (1941)("The conclusion is inescapable that *Hammer v. Dagenhart* [the child labor case], was a departure from the principles which have prevailed in the interpretation of the commerce clause both before and since the decision..... It should be and now is overruled"). Upholding this legislation would do no more than simply recognize that Congress had a "rational basis" for finding a significant connection between guns in or near schools and (through their effect on education) the interstate and foreign commerce they threaten. For these reasons, I would reverse the judgment of the Court of Appeals. Respectfully, I dissent.

NOTES ON THE SIGNIFICANCE OF *LOPEZ*

1. The Future of the Gun–Free School Zones Act of 1990. Shortly after the Supreme Court's decision in *Lopez*, President Clinton announced his intention to ask Congress to fix the constitutional problem with the statute. The President's proposal, which was introduced in the Senate on June 7, 1995, as the "Gun–Free School Zones Act of 1995," would leave the original statute entirely unchanged except for a simple amendment providing that the statute applies only to a firearm "that has moved in or that otherwise affects interstate or foreign commerce." See S. 890, 104th Congress, 1st Sess. (1995). As of January, 1996, the President's proposal was still awaiting action by the Senate Judiciary Committee.

Of course, S. 890 involves the same kind of case-specific jurisdictional element previously relied upon by the Court in construing 18 U.S.C. § 1202(a), the statute at issue in *Bass* and *Scarborough*, and 18 U.S.C. § 922(h), the statute at issue in *Barrett*. In light of its decision in *Lopez*, however, do you think that the Court would uphold § 922(q) with only the minimal statutory change proposed by President Clinton? What about the statement in the majority opinion in *Lopez*—which is mirrored in Justice Kennedy's concurring opinion—that § 922(q) fails to pass muster in part because "by its terms it has nothing to do with 'commerce' or any sort of economic enterprise"? Would the additional requirement, that the gun—at some time in the past—moved in or otherwise affected interstate commerce, be sufficient to overcome the majority's apparent view that Congress's power under the commerce clause is limited to the regulation of "commercial" or "economic" actors or activities? Did the Court in *Bass*, *Barrett*, or *Scarborough* ever squarely face the constitutional question addressed in *Lopez*, or did those prior decisions ultimately involve only issues of statutory interpretation? Is it significant that the majority opinion in *Lopez* cites with apparent approval *Bass* (where, you may recall, the government *lost*), but makes no explicit mention of either *Barrett* or *Scarborough*? Does this suggest that *Barrett* and *Scarborough*, both of which relied heavily on the fact that the gun at issue had previously traveled in interstate commerce, might be on shaky ground?

What do you make of the majority's conclusion that, henceforth, the test for commerce clause validity will not be whether the regulated activity "affects interstate commerce," but instead will be whether the regulated activity "*substantially* affects interstate commerce" (emphasis added)? Does this subtle change in commerce clause jurisprudence portend further trouble for the government in cases involving firearms possession statutes?

2. ***United States v. Robertson***. The Supreme Court decided United States v. Robertson, ___ U.S. ___, 115 S.Ct. 1732 (1995)(per curiam), just five days after *Lopez*. Robertson was convicted of a series of narcotics offenses and of violating 18 U.S.C. § 1962(a)(RICO) by investing the proceeds of his criminal activity in the "acquisition of any interest in, or the establishment or operation of, any enterprise which is engaged in, or the activities of which affect, interstate or foreign commerce." The Circuit Court reversed his conviction on the ground that the commerce nexus required by the statute had not been proved. The Supreme Court reinstated the conviction in a unanimous per curiam opinion. The Court stated the facts and its rationale as follows:

> "The facts relevant to the 'engaged in or affecting interstate commerce' issue were as follows: Some time in 1985, Robertson entered into a partnership agreement with another man, whereby

he agreed to finance a goldmining operation in Alaska. In fulfillment of this obligation, Robertson, who resided in Arizona, made a
cash payment of $125,000 for placer gold mining claims near
Fairbanks. He paid approximately $100,000 (in cash) for mining
equipment and supplies, some of which were purchased in Los
Angeles and transported to Alaska for use in the mine. Robertson
also hired and paid the expenses for seven out-of-state employees
to travel to Alaska to work in the mine. The partnership dissolved
during the first mining season, but Robertson continued to operate
the mine through 1987 as a sole proprietorship. He again hired a
number of employees from outside Alaska to work in the mine.
During its operating life, the mine produced between $200,000 and
$290,000 worth of gold, most of which was sold to refiners within
Alaska, although Robertson personally transported approximately
$30,000 worth of gold out of the state.

"Most of the parties' arguments, here and in the Ninth
Circuit, were addressed to the question whether the activities of
the gold mine 'affected' interstate commerce. We have concluded
we do not have to consider that point. The 'affecting commerce'
test was developed in our jurisprudence to define the extent of
Congress's power over purely *intra*state commercial activities that
nonetheless have substantial *inter*state effects. The proof at Robertson's trial, however, focused largely on the *inter*state activities
of Robertson's mine. For example, the government proved that
Robertson purchased at least $100,000 worth of equipment and
supplies for use in the mine. [A]ll of those items were not
purchased locally ...; the government proved that some of them
were purchased in California and transported to Alaska for use in
the mine's operations. Cf. United States v. American Building
Maintenance Industries, 422 U.S. 271, 285 (1975)(allegation that
company had made *local* purchases of equipment and supplies that
were merely *manufactured* out of state was insufficient to show
that company was 'engaged in commerce' within the meaning of
§ 7 of the Clayton Act). The government also proved that, on
more than one occasion, Robertson sought workers from out of
state and brought them to Alaska to work in the mine. Furthermore, Robertson, the mine's sole proprietor, took $30,000 worth of
gold, or 15 percent of the mine's total output, with him out of the
state.

"Whether or not these activities met (and whether or not, to
bring the gold mine within the 'affecting commerce' provision of
RICO, they would *have* to meet) the requirement of substantially
affecting interstate commerce, they assuredly brought the gold
mine within § 1962(a)'s alternative criterion of 'any enterprise ...
engaged in ... interstate or foreign commerce.' As we said in
American Building Maintenance, a corporation is generally 'engaged "in commerce"' when it is itself 'directly engaged in the

production, distribution, or acquisition of goods and services in interstate commerce.' "

3. Subsequent Litigation. *Lopez* has already unleashed a flood of litigation calling into question the validity of completed and prospective federal criminal prosecutions.   Five early Court of Appeals examples follow:

(i) *United States v. Murphy*. United States v. Murphy, 53 F.3d 93 (5th Cir.1995), was decided about two weeks after *Lopez*. It too involved a prosecution under the Gun–Free School Zones Act. The government sought to cure the *Lopez* problem by charging in the information that the "defendant ... did knowingly possess, *in and affecting interstate commerce*, in an area that the defendant knew or should have known was a school zone, a firearm—specifically, a Mossberg 12 gauge pistol grip shotgun; in violation of Title 18, United States Code, Section 922(q)." (Italics added.) The court held the allegation to no avail:

> "The Supreme Court ... held that the Gun–Free School Zones Act of 1990 is not within the constitutional power of Congress under the commerce clause. The Supreme Court decided that '[t]he possession of a gun in a local school zone is in no sense an economic activity that might, through repetition elsewhere, substantially affect any sort of interstate commerce.' In light of this decision, we ... affirm the decision of the district court [dismissing the information]."

(ii) *United States v. Hanna*. United States v. Hanna, 55 F.3d 1456 (9th Cir.1995), involved a prosecution under the current version of the statute involved in *Bass* and *Scarborough*, 18 U.S.C. § 922(g). Do the jurisdictional findings resulting from those decisions pass muster under *Lopez*? The Ninth Circuit said yes:

> "... Hanna argues 18 U.S.C. § 922(g)(1) is unconstitutional both on its face and as applied..... These arguments are meritless. In Scarborough v. United States, 431 U.S. 563 (1977), the United States Supreme Court concluded that 18 U.S.C. App. § 1202(a), the predecessor of § 922(g)(1), required only 'the minimal nexus that the firearm have been, at some time, in interstate commerce.' ... As the Supreme Court noted in discussing § 1202(a), 'Congress sought to reach possessions broadly, with little concern for when the nexus with commerce occurred.' In amalgamating §§ 922(g), 922(h), and 1202(a), Congress gave no indication that it meant to narrow the statutory reach with respect to possession. Accordingly, we hold that the *Scarborough* minimal nexus standard applies to § 922(g) and that a past connection is enough. Therefore, Hanna's contention that 18 U.S.C. § 922(g)(1) is facially unconstitutional must fail.

> "The serial number of the gun confiscated from Hanna in San Francisco revealed it had been stolen in Sparks, Nevada. This history is sufficient to establish a past connection between the gun

and interstate commerce. Therefore, § 922(g)(1) is not unconstitutional as applied to Hanna."

The court added in a footnote:

"We have read and considered United States v. Lopez, ___ U.S. ___, 115 S.Ct. 1624 (1995), holding 18 U.S.C. § 922(q) to be unconstitutional on commerce clause grounds, but it does not alter our analysis. The Supreme Court distinguished § 922(q) from 18 U.S.C. App. § 1202(a), the predecessor of § 922(g), stating '§ 922(q) contains no jurisdictional element which would ensure, through case-by-case inquiry, that the firearm possession in question affects interstate commerce.' Section 922(g)'s requirement that the firearm have been, at some time, in interstate commerce is sufficient to establish its constitutionality under the commerce clause."

(iii) *United States v. Wilks*. United States v. Wilks, 58 F.3d 1518 (10th Cir.1995), involved a conviction for violating 18 U.S.C. § 922(*o*), which makes it illegal to transfer or possess a machinegun manufactured after 1986. Like the Gun–Free School Zones Act, § 922(*o*) contains no case-specific jurisdictional element. Nevertheless, the Tenth Circuit upheld the constitutionality of the statute:

"*Lopez* does not dictate a similar result in the instant case. ...Whereas § 922(q) sought to regulate an activity which by its nature was purely intrastate and could not substantially affect commerce even when incidents of those activities were aggregated together, ... § 922(*o*) regulates machineguns, which by their nature are 'a commodity ... transferred across state lines for profit by business entities.' United States v. Hunter, 843 F.Supp. 235, 249 (E.D.Mich.1994). The interstate flow of machineguns 'not only has a substantial effect on interstate commerce; it is interstate commerce.' Id. Section 922(*o*) regulates this 'extensive, intricate, and definitively *national* market for machineguns,' id. (emphasis added).... As such, § 922(*o*) represents Congressional regulation of an item bound up with interstate attributes and thus differs in substantial respect from legislation concerning possession of a firearm within a purely local school zone."

(iv) *United States v. Stillo*. United States v. Stillo, 57 F.3d 553 (7th Cir.1995), involved a Cook County judge who was convicted of violating RICO and the Hobbs Act. The facts are elaborate, but interesting:

"Defense attorney Robert Cooley first met Judge Stillo at a party in 1976. Cooley asked the judge whom he should see to fix a criminal case assigned to Judge Stillo. Judge Stillo, knowing that Cooley was a frequent supplier of bribes to other judges and public officials, told Cooley that he would deal with him directly. Not long after the party, Judge Stillo accepted a bribe from Cooley to fix a misdemeanor case. Judge Stillo met with Cooley before trial and agreed to find Cooley's client not guilty. After the trial

Cooley met with Judge Stillo in his chambers. Cooley asked the judge whether $100 was an appropriate payment. Judge Stillo responded: 'Whatever you think' and accepted the $100 in cash.

"Between 1977 and 1983, Cooley bribed Stillo in five or six cases. Cooley would meet with the judge before trial and after a favorable disposition, Cooley would visit the judge in his chambers and pay him $100–$200 for fixing a misdemeanor and $1000–$2000 for fixing a felony. After the federal investigation into corruption among Chicago public officials became known in 1983, Cooley ceased paying bribes to Judge Stillo.

"On August 4, 1986, Cooley, now working with the FBI, inquired of Judge Stillo if he was still accepting bribes for favorable rulings. The judge said yes and that the system was the same as before. In order to catch Judge Stillo in the act, the FBI filed the fictitious case of People v. Hess on August 20, 1986. According to the fictional court papers, James Hess—played by an undercover FBI agent—had been stopped for speeding and an illegal lane change by an Illinois state trooper. Noticing open beer cans, the trooper had searched the car and discovered marijuana.

"The Hess trial was set for October 21, 1986, before Judge Stillo. On October 6, Cooley visited the judge in his chambers and asked whether he would suppress the marijuana in exchange for a bribe to which Judge Stillo agreed. Judge Stillo told Cooley that to 'make it look better' he should file a memorandum of law in support of his motion to suppress. Judge Stillo told Cooley not to worry and to speak to his nephew attorney Joseph Stillo. Thereafter, Cooley telephoned Joseph Stillo and arranged a meeting. On October 10, 1986, the two met. Joseph Stillo told Cooley that he had spoken to his uncle, Judge Stillo. Joseph Stillo and Cooley then went to lunch to arrange to fix the Hess case.

"Over lunch, Cooley explained the 'facts' of the Hess case to Joseph Stillo and that he wanted to have the marijuana suppressed. Joseph Stillo agreed. Cooley also told Joseph Stillo that he would pay any amount the Stillos deemed fair, to which Joseph Stillo also agreed. Cooley and Joseph Stillo arranged for Cooley to call Joseph Stillo the day before Hess was to go to trial and say 'The party is tomorrow night. Are you gonna go?' to alert Joseph Stillo that Hess would be tried the following day and to confirm the fix. As they parted following lunch, Stillo reassured Cooley, saying, 'I'll make the call.... Don't worry about it.'

"Cooley called Joseph Stillo the day before Hess was scheduled to go to trial to verify that the 'benefit' was still on for the following day. Joseph Stillo answered affirmatively but the Hess trial was postponed.

"Hess was finally tried to the court on November 5, 1986. A few days before, Cooley visited Judge Stillo to confirm that the bribe scheme was in place. Contrary to the agreement, however, Judge Stillo denied Cooley's motion to suppress the marijuana, found Hess guilty, and sentenced him to six months' supervision.

"That afternoon Cooley visited Joseph Stillo's law office and was told that Judge Stillo had found Hess guilty because he looked like an undercover FBI agent. Joseph Stillo agreed to ask his uncle whether Cooley could seek a reduced sentence for Hess. On November 7, Cooley spoke directly with Judge Stillo who reiterated that he found Hess guilty because he looked like an FBI 'plant.'

"On December 16, Cooley again spoke with Joseph Stillo, who told Cooley not to drop his attempt to seek favorable treatment for Hess because at the end of six months Judge Stillo could expunge Hess's conviction from his record. Six months thereafter, Cooley asked Judge Stillo to expunge Hess's supervision, and the judge issued an order to that effect."

Of present relevance, Judge Stillo and his nephew were convicted of conspiring to violate 18 U.S.C. § 1951 based on the "Hess episode." The Judge was sentenced to four years and his nephew to two years and a $10,000 fine.

A number of issues were raised on appeal, among them the argument that the government proved an insufficient relationship to interstate commerce. On this point, the court responded:

"The Hobbs Act prohibits extortion which 'in any way or degree ... affects [interstate] commerce.' 18 U.S.C. § 1951(a). Because the Supreme Court has interpreted this statute to reach the limits of the commerce clause, Stirone v. United States, 361 U.S. 212, 215 (1960), the burden on the government to establish this element is slight or de minimis. In this case ..., the government relied on a 'depletion of assets theory.' If Judge Stillo had accepted a bribe from Cooley, the assets of Cooley's law firm, which it was established purchased items in interstate commerce, would have been depleted. Payment of the bribe thus would have the potential to affect the firm's ability to purchase goods in interstate commerce—a nexus which this court has held sufficient on numerous occasions.

"Defendants argue that the connection between potential bribe payments and the law firm's participation in interstate commerce fails at three points. None of their contentions, however, casts doubt on the jury's verdict. First, defendants question the connection between Cooley's assets and the purchase of goods by his law firm in interstate commerce. But the government presented numerous items purchased by the law firm in interstate commerce, including a calculator and will covers, and an office employee of Cooley's firm testified that such supplies were purchased from a common account to which the three members of the firm, including Cooley, made weekly contributions. Though the government did not trace the purchase of a particular out-of-state calculator to Cooley's contribution to the account, the general set-up was sufficient to support the jury's finding that the payment of a bribe by Cooley could potentially deplete the assets with which the firm purchased goods and services in interstate commerce.

"Defendants next contend that based on Cooley's statement to Joseph Stillo at lunch that his client would be paying the bribe, Cooley's assets were not implicated. This argument fails for two reasons. First, the extortion conspiracy was already in place at the time of the luncheon conversation. It is the potential effect on interstate commerce at the time of the offense which is relevant. Later developments which negate or lower the potential effect on interstate commerce do not undermine the jurisdictional element. United States v. Staszcuk, 517 F.2d 53, 60 (7th Cir.1975). Second, even if the Stillos believed from the start that the fictional Hess would ultimately be footing the bill, the temporary depletion of Cooley's assets until repayment and the risk of non-payment would be sufficient to satisfy the de minimis interstate commerce requirement.

"Defendants' final argument is that because the Hess case was a sham, the FBI and not Cooley or his law firm would ultimately have paid any bribe. This court rejected an identical argument in [a prior case], in which Cooley again working with the FBI attempted to bribe another Cook County Circuit Court judge. The ultimate source of potential bribe money was found irrelevant because 'the Hobbs Act proscribes not just successful extortion schemes but attempts to induce a victim engaged in interstate commerce to part with property' and the intended victim was Cooley, not the FBI."

The court added a footnote on the significance of *Lopez* to this reasoning:

"Following oral argument, Joseph Stillo submitted the Supreme Court's recent decision in United States v. Lopez, 115 S.Ct. 1624 (1995), in support of his argument on the insufficiency of the government's evidence linking defendants' actions to interstate commerce. In invalidating the federal ban on guns in school zones, *Lopez* made clear that not everything is possible under the commerce clause. In so holding the Court did not call into question the Hobbs Act which—unlike the school gun ban—is aimed at a type of economic activity, extortion, and contains an express jurisdictional element. Nor did the *Lopez* decision undermine this Court's precedents that minimal potential effect on commerce is all that need be proven to support a conviction. 'Where a general regulatory statute bears a substantial relation to commerce, the de minimis character of individual instances arising under that statute is of no consequence.' *Lopez*, at ___, quoting Maryland v. Wirtz, 392 U.S. 183, 197 n. 27 (1968). More relevant than *Lopez*, though not brought to our attention by defendants, was the Court's decision five days later in United States v. Robertson, ___ U.S. ___, 115 S.Ct. 1732 (1995)(per curiam). In *Robertson*, the Court in a per curiam opinion reinstated the defendant's RICO conviction, holding that defendant's Alaskan silver mine was engaged in interstate commerce because it purchased supplies from out of state."

(v) *United States v. Oliver*. United States v. Oliver, 60 F.3d 547 (9th Cir.1995), involved a post-*Lopez* prosecution under 18 U.S.C. § 2119, which punished "[w]hoever, possessing a firearm as defined in section 921 of this title, takes a motor vehicle that has been transported, shipped, or received in interstate or foreign commerce from the person or presence of another by force and violence or by intimidation, or attempts to do so."[e] The court adhered to its pre-*Lopez* view that the anti-carjacking statute is within Congress's commerce clause power:

"In *Lopez*, the Supreme Court held that Congress exceeded its power under the commerce clause when it made it a federal offense for a person to possess a firearm within 1000 feet of a school. ... The Court noted that '§ 922(q) contains no jurisdictional element which would ensure, through a case-by-case inquiry, that the firearm possession in question affects interstate commerce.' ... It also explained that the statute does not seek to protect 'an instrumentality of interstate commerce.' ... Finally, the Court pointed out that there was no showing of a substantial effect of the prohibited activity on interstate commerce, and Congress had made no findings that there was such an effect....

"The carjacking statute has a very different background. First, it applies only to the forcible taking of a car 'that has been transported, shipped, or received in interstate commerce.' 18 U.S.C. § 2119. ... Second, cars are themselves instrumentalities of interstate commerce, which Congress may protect....

"Lastly, we note that Congress was not silent regarding the effect of carjacking on interstate commerce. ... Congress relied on, among other things, 'the emergence of carjacking as a "high-growth industry" that involves taking stolen vehicles to different states to retitle, exporting vehicles abroad, or selling cars to "chop shops" to distribute various auto parts for sale.' United States v. Martinez, 49 F.3d 1398, 1400 n. 2 (9th Cir.1995), (citing legislative history). That Congress was addressing economic evils of an interstate nature differentiates the carjacking statute from the firearms statute invalidated in *Lopez*."

Is the end in sight?

---

[e] The words "possessing a firearm as defined in section 921 of this title" were deleted by a 1994 amendment and replaced with the words "with the intent to cause death or serious bodily harm." See 108 Stat. 1970. The amendment was not applicable to *Oliver* because it was adopted after the events at issue.

CHAPTER II

MAIL FRAUD

SECTION 1: INTRODUCTION

INTRODUCTORY NOTES ON THE DEVELOPMENT OF THE MAIL FRAUD
OFFENSE

1. Background. In a fascinating article describing the early history
of the enforcement of the mail fraud statute, Jed S. Rakoff, a former Chief
of Business Frauds Prosecutions of the United States Attorney's Office for
the Southern District of New York, wrote:

> "To federal prosecutors of white collar crime, the mail fraud
> statute is our Stradivarius, our Colt 45, our Louisville Slugger, our
> Cuisinart—and our true love. We may flirt with RICO, show off
> with 10–b5, and call the conspiracy law 'darling,' but we always
> come home to the virtues of 18 U.S.C. § 1341, with its simplicity,
> adaptability, and comfortable familiarity. It understands us and,
> like many a foolish spouse, we like to think we understand it."
> Jed S. Rakoff, The Federal Mail Fraud Statute (Part I), 18 Du-
> quesne L. Rev. 771 (1980)(hereafter cited as Rakoff).

Later he said:

> "First enacted in 1872, the mail fraud statute, together with its
> lineal descendant, the wire fraud statute, has been characterized
> as the 'first line of defense' against virtually every new area of
> fraud to develop in the United States in the past century. Its
> applications, too numerous to catalog, cover not only the full range
> of consumer frauds, stock frauds, land frauds, bank frauds, insur-
> ance frauds, and commodity frauds, but have extended even to
> such areas as blackmail, counterfeiting, election fraud, and brib-
> ery. In many of these and other areas, where legislatures have
> sometimes been slow to enact specific prohibitory legislation, the
> mail fraud statute has frequently represented the sole instrument
> of justice that could be wielded against the ever-innovative practi-
> tioners of deceit." Rakoff, p. 772.

The mail fraud statute has been truly remarkable. It is in one sense
hopelessly vague. The courts have never come to grips with a satisfactory
definition of what constitutes "fraud"[a] and, as Rakoff says, federal prosecutors have effectively invented new crimes as they went along in response to

---

[a] Cf. Milton D. Green, Fraud, Undue Influence and Mental Incompetency, 43 Colum.
L. Rev. 176, 177 (1943): "Fraud, like many
familiar concepts, is one which seems to have
a perfectly obvious meaning until we try to
define it."

innovative ways of deceit crafted by inventive swindlers. Nor has the statute been limited to those who would obtain another's property in deceitful ways. The mail fraud statute has been the source of prosecutions for corporate and government corruption that have deprived stockholders and the public, respectively, of their right to "honest services" by those who are expected to attend their interests. Called the "intangible rights" doctrine, this interpretation of the mail fraud statute has permitted the federal courts to monitor corporate and government ethics through the creative application of a criminal statute designed ostensibly to prevent pollution of the mails.

But this is not all. Because of its focus on use of the mails as the federal jurisdictional event, *each separate use of the mails*—either by sending or receiving a letter—constitutes a separate offense, no matter that the letters were part of the same transaction or event, no matter that there were one or many victims, and no matter the amount of harm done. Thus the possibilities of count-multiplication are enormous, and there need be no relationship between the number of counts and the culpability of the defendant or the injury caused by the fraud. Since the enactment of the RICO statute, moreover, two counts of mail fraud create the possibility of the invocation of that statute—which carries a 20–year maximum sentence and forfeiture of all property related to the criminal offense. And civil RICO may permit ordinary commercial disputes over the enforcement of contracts to be turned into treble damage suits, with attorney's fees for the victorious plaintiff, if by creative pleading the dispute can be characterized as a form of "fraud".

Yet in spite of the doctrine that the federal courts are not to create new crimes, and in spite of the requirement of fair notice and protections against the vagueness of criminal statutes, the only constitutional challenge to the mail fraud statute that has been seriously entertained by the Supreme Court involved the extent of the federal postal powers, and in that case, summarized below (*Badders*), the Court thought the argument essentially frivolous. In another case, which appears as a main case below (*McNally*), the Supreme Court dramatically limited the scope of the statute, effectively confining it to situations where the property of another was obtained by deceit. But Congress promptly responded by amending the statute to overrule the Court's decision and reinstate the mail fraud statute in its full flower. Thus, mail fraud continues to be the "true love" of the federal prosecutor, a broad, self-defining statute that can be used to get crooks whose behavior falls between the cracks of other statutes. And because of civil RICO, mail fraud is becoming the "true love" of the commercial plaintiff's bar as well.

2. Text of the Original Statute. The mail fraud statute was first enacted on June 8, 1872, as part of a broader series of provisions containing 327 sections that revised laws relating to the post office. It provided:

"Sec. 301. That if any person having devised or intending to devise any scheme or artifice to defraud, [to][b] be effected by either opening or intending to open correspondence or communication with any other person (whether resident within or outside of the United States), by means of the post-office establishment of the United States, or by inciting such other person to open communication with the person so devising or intending, shall, in and for executing such scheme or artifice (or attempting so to do), place any letter or packet in any post-office of the United States, or take or receive any therefrom, such person, so misusing the post-office establishment, shall be guilty of a misdemeanor, and shall be punished with a fine of not more than five hundred dollars, with or without such imprisonment, as the court shall direct, not exceeding eighteen calendar months. The indictment, information, or complaint may severally charge offences to the number of three when committed within the same six calendar months; but the court thereupon shall give a single sentence, and shall proportion the punishment especially to the degree in which the abuse of the post-office establishment enters as an instrument into such fraudulent scheme and device." 17 Stat. 323.

As Rakoff reports, this provision "generated no congressional debate or other legislative history explaining its origins and purpose."

   3. Judicial Interpretation of the 1872 Statute. Notice the structure of the 1872 statute. The only behavior required is that the defendant mail or receive a letter. The rest of the offense is in the defendant's mind, that is, in its simplest terms, the defendant must mail or receive the letter intending to execute a scheme to defraud by use of the mails.[c] Though the statute has undergone four major revisions, each summarized below, this pattern of a seemingly innocuous act accompanied by a pernicious intent has been a consistent feature. The act may not, of course, be as innocuous as first appears, for the *content* of the letter may be important evidence of the fraud. And the relationship of the mailing to execution of the scheme to defraud—a matter further developed below—may provide further evidence that the act was not innocuous. In any event, one issue to watch for as these materials develop is the extent to which the offense of mail fraud ignores the traditional function of the "act requirement" in the criminal

---

[b] The original statute said "or" at this point, but the courts assumed that "to" was meant. See Rakoff, p. 783 n.55.

[c] In Stokes v. United States, 157 U.S. 187, 188–89 (1895), the Court set forth the elements that must be proved to establish a violation of the statute:

"[T]hree matters of fact must be charged in the indictment and established by the evidence. (1) That the persons charged must have devised a scheme to defraud. (2) That they must have intended to effect this scheme, by opening or intend-

ing to open correspondence with some other persons through the post office establishment, or by inciting such other person to open communication with them. (3) And that, in carrying out such scheme, such person must have either deposited a letter or packet in the post office, or taken or received one therefrom."

The Court was speaking specifically of the 1899 amendment to the statute, but its recitation is equally relevant to the original statute.

law, the extent to which, to put it bluntly, it punishes criminal intent without requiring sufficient corroborative behavior to justify the imposition of criminal sanctions.

There were three specific judicial developments with respect to the 1872 statute that deserve elaboration:

(i) Constitutional Concerns; *Ex parte Jackson*. Note that the 1872 statute emphasizes the connection of the offense with the mails in at least four places. First, the scheme to defraud must be intended to be effected by opening mail communication with the victim. Second, a letter or packet must be mailed. Third, the defendant "so misusing the post-office establishment" is guilty of a misdemeanor. And fourth, the sentence in the case of multiple counts shall be proportioned "especially to the degree in which the abuse of the post-office establishment enters as an instrument into such fraudulent scheme and device." Why did Congress place so much emphasis on the use of the mails?

Rakoff speculates that what he calls the "mail-emphasizing" language of the statute may have been an effort by Congress to "dress up" the statute "in such a way as to preserve it from judicial override" on constitutional grounds. It was not clear in 1872 how far the postal power[d] extended, and quite plausible to argue that Congress lacked the authority to punish schemes to defraud on the ground that such offenses, cognizable by state criminal provisions, were exclusively to be prosecuted under state law.

Any concern about the constitutionality of the statute was, however, short lived. In 1868 Congress had passed a "lottery law" making it unlawful to mail circulars or letters concerning illegal lotteries. The constitutionality of this statute came before the Supreme Court five years after the mail fraud statute was enacted, and in Ex parte Jackson, 96 U.S. 727 (1877), the Supreme Court unanimously upheld its validity. The Court spoke broadly of the postal power, and of the authority of Congress to regulate what kinds of matter could be mailed. The constitutionality of the mail fraud statute seemed so clear after *Jackson* that it was not until 1916, after the "mail-emphasizing" language had been removed, that constitutional questions about the statute were raised before the Supreme Court.[e]

Thus the "mail-emphasizing" language of the statute turned out not to be important to sustaining its constitutionality. But, as Rakoff develops, it was important to its interpretation.

(ii) Division in the Lower Courts. Rakoff observes that "the early interpretations [of the mail fraud statute] range to such extremes and seemingly reflect so many personal viewpoints that it is difficult to categorize them in any meaningful way." He does, however, suggest that the cases fell into two broad camps. The first, which he calls the "strict construction" cases, read the mail-emphasizing language as evidencing a

---

[d] "The Congress shall have power ... [t]o establish Post Offices and Post Roads...." U.S. Const., art. I, sec. 8.

[e] See Badders v. United States, 240 U.S. 391 (1916), discussed below.

congressional intent to limit the statute to those frauds that were "necessarily dependent on use of the mails for their success." The second, which he calls the "broad construction" cases, read the mail-emphasizing language as evidencing an intent "to punish any intentional 'abuse' of the mails in furtherance of fraud, regardless of the kind of fraud involved or how essential the use of the mails is to its success." "In other words," he concludes, "the 'strict-constructionists' saw the statute as being aimed at a particular kind of fraud—mail-dependent fraud—while the 'broad constructionists' viewed the statute as being directed against any misuse of the mails in furtherance of any kind of fraud."

Rakoff gives a paradigm example of each judicial camp:

(a) *United States v. Owens*. His "strict construction" example is United States v. Owens, 17 F. 72 (E.D. Mo.1883), which though decided 11 years after the statute was enacted, he states was "only the fourth reported decision of any kind dealing with the mail fraud statute." Owens owed a distillery $162.50. He mailed a letter to the distillery containing 50¢ in coin, stating that he was remitting the entire amount he owed in cash. His intent, apparently, was lay a basis for claiming that he had paid the full amount.

The court dismissed the indictment against Owens in reliance on the mail-emphasizing language of the statute, stating that the statute was "designed to strike at common schemes of fraud, whereby, through the post-office, circulars, etc., are distributed generally to entrap and defraud the unwary, and not [designed to invite] the supervision of commercial correspondence solely between a debtor and creditor." Thus, Rakoff concludes, "the court interpreted the mail-emphasizing language of the statute as setting forth a substantive qualification on the phrase 'any scheme or artifice to defraud'. . . ."

Other decisions of this genre limited mail fraud to schemes where the fraud itself was perpetrated by the use of the mails. Thus, the "strict construction" approach was a double-edged sword. The mail-emphasizing language both required that the mail be central to the perpetration of the fraud and limited the kinds of schemes to which the statute applied.

(b) *United States v. Jones*. The first case taking the "broad construction" approach was United States v. Jones, 10 F. 469 (C.C.S.D.N.Y. 1882). *Jones* involved a quaint expression of the day, a "green article" scheme. This involved the mailing of letters to persons offering to sell them counterfeit money ("green articles") at a small percentage of face value. The purchaser could then pass the money and realize the difference between face value and purchase price.[f] Rakoff speculates that under the "strict construction" view this could not have

---

[f] A "sawdust swindle" was a variant on this theme. The same letters were distributed, but the sender had no intention of providing the counterfeit money after receiving the purchase price. Persons who engaged in this practice relied on the obvious disincentive of the victim to report the fraud—how could the victim complain to the police that counterfeit money was paid for with the intent to use it as genuine but was never received?

been mail fraud, since the fraud would occur when the counterfeit money was passed and this act had no relationship to the use of the mails.[g]

But the *Jones* court held that a "green article" scheme was covered by the statute.[h] "[T]he gist of the offense," the court said, "consists in the abuse of the mail. The corpus delicti was the mailing of the letter ... and the letter itself showed its unlawful character."[i] Moreover, the court held, "[a]ny scheme, the necessary result of which would be the defrauding of somebody, is a scheme to defraud ... and a scheme to put counterfeit money in circulation is such a scheme." Thus, as Rakoff points out, an intentional use of the mails as part of a "scheme to defraud" was sufficient, even though the fraud was not perpetrated *by* the use of the mails. The umbilical connection between the mailing and the fraud was cut, but it didn't matter. So long as there was mailing and an intent to defraud, any connection between the two would suffice. The "broad constructionists," moreover, were not concerned with the kind of fraud being perpetrated.

"Accordingly," Rakoff concludes, "by a kind of dynamic complementarity, the narrow, conceptualistic emphasis on the misuse of the mails as the 'gist' of the crime afforded the courts that took this approach a certain freedom to embrace the most sweeping definitions of 'scheme to defraud' without appearing to expand federal jurisdiction." Other decisions of this genre held, for example, that since the essence of the offense was misuse of the mails, common law limitations on what constituted "fraud" did not qualify the concept of "scheme to defraud."

(iii) Supreme Court Cases; *In re Henry*. It was 15 years before any case involving the mail fraud statute reached the Supreme Court.[j] The first such case to do so was In re Henry, 123 U.S. 372 (1887).

Henry came before the Court on a motion to show cause why an original writ of habeas corpus should not issue. Henry had been convicted in a South Carolina District Court of mail fraud following an indictment that charged, as permitted by the statute, three separate and distinct offenses committed within a six month period. He was sentenced to a year in jail. Thereafter, he was indicted for three different offenses committed

---

[g] One could analyze these cases in terms of causation. The "strict constructionists" held, in effect, that the mail had to be the "direct," "immediate," or "indispensable" cause of the fraud (as well as that only certain kinds of frauds counted). The "broad constructionists" held, as the decision in *Jones* will reveal, that a more "indirect" or "proximate" causal relationship between the mailing and the fraud was sufficient.

[h] Rakoff points out, p. 797 n.106, that a "green articles" scheme was difficult to prosecute under the counterfeiting statutes of the day, since the only crimes were passing the money, attempting to do so, or conspiring to do so. If the recipient of the letter did noth-

ing, it was doubtful whether the sender's behavior had gone far enough to constitute an attempt and, if the sender had no confederates, a conspiracy charge would not lie.

[i] Whether or not *Jones* was the origin of the thought, this passage reflects lore that has passed down to the present day. It is frequently said that the "gist" of the mail fraud offense is the mailing—not, perhaps surprisingly, the fraud.

[j] Part of the reason for this undoubtedly was that the Supreme Court had very limited jurisdiction over criminal appeals prior to 1891. See Rakoff, p. 808 n.155, citing R. Stern & E. Gressman, Supreme Court Practice 38–41 (5th ed. 1978).

within the same six-month period. He was convicted and sentenced to a 15–month term of imprisonment for these violations of the statute, to be served consecutively to the first sentence.[k] After he completed the first sentence, he sought to overturn the second sentence, which he was then serving, by filing for a writ of habeas corpus in the Supreme Court. His argument was based on the last sentence of the mail fraud statute:

"The indictment, information, or complaint may severally charge offences to the number of three when committed within the same six calendar months; but the court thereupon shall give a single sentence, and shall proportion the punishment especially to the degree in which the abuse of the post-office establishment enters as an instrument into such fraudulent scheme and device."

He contended that the effect of this language was to preclude conviction for more than one series of offenses committed within the same six month period.

The Supreme Court unanimously disagreed:

"We ... are unable to agree ... that there can be but one punishment for all the offences committed by a person under this statute within any one period of six calendar months. As was well said by the District Judge on the trial of the indictment, 'the act forbids, not the general use of the post-office for the purposes of carrying out a fraudulent scheme or device, but the putting in the post-office of a letter or packet, or the taking out of a letter or packet from the post-office in furtherance of such a scheme. Each letter so taken out or put in constitutes a separate and distinct violation of the act.' It is not, as in [another case], a continuous offence, but it consists of a single isolated act, and is repeated as often as the act is repeated.

"It is indeed provided that three distinct offences, committed within the same six months, may be joined in the same indictment; but this is no more than allowing the joinder of three offences for the purposes of a trial. In its general effect this provision is not materially different from [another statute], which allows the joinder in one indictment of charges against a person 'for two or more acts or transactions of the same class of crimes or offenses,' and the consolidation of two or more indictments found in such cases. Under the present statute three separate offences, committed in the same six months, may be joined, but not more, and when joined there is to be a single sentence for all. That is the whole

[k] The Court's opinion does not reveal whether the second indictment was for offenses committed as part of the same transaction that produced the first indictment. One fact that suggests a different episode is that he was sentenced to serve the first term in a South Carolina prison and the second term in a New York prison. But both convictions were during the same term of the same South Carolina federal District Court, and the place of imprisonment could have had to do with an allocative decision independent of the nature of the offenses. In any event, the Supreme Court paid no attention to the matter.

scope and meaning of the provision, and there is nothing whatever in it to indicate an intention to make a single continuous offence, and punishable only as such, out of what, without it, would have been several distinct offences, each complete in itself.''

The last sentence of the statute was thus a permissive joinder provision and it did not affect the fact that mail fraud is committed with each mailing (or receipt of mail), apparently irrespective of whether successive mailings were part of the same scheme to defraud.[1]

4. Text of the 1889 Amendment. Congress amended the mail fraud statute on March 2, 1889, so that it then read:

"Sec. 5480. If any person having devised or intending to devise any scheme or artifice to defraud, or to sell, dispose of, loan, exchange, alter, give away, or distribute, supply, or furnish, or procure for unlawful use any counterfeit or spurious coin, bank notes, paper money, or any obligation or security of the United States or of any State, Territory, municipality, company, corporation, or person, or anything represented to be or intimated or held out to be such counterfeit or spurious articles, or any scheme or artifice to obtain money by or through correspondence, by what is commonly called the 'sawdust swindle', or 'counterfeit money fraud', or by dealing or pretending to deal in what is commonly called 'green articles,' 'green coin,' 'bills', 'paper goods,' 'spurious Treasury notes,' 'United States goods', 'green cigars', or any other names or terms intended to be understood as relating to such counterfeit or spurious articles, to be effected by either opening or intending to open correspondence or communication with any person, whether resident within or outside the United States, by means of the Post–Office Establishment of the United States, or by inciting such other person or any person to open communication with the person so devising or intending, shall, in and for executing such scheme or artifice or attempting so to do, place or cause to be placed, any letter, packet, writing, circular, pamphlet, or advertisement in any post-office, branch post-office, or street or hotel letter-box of the United States, to be sent or delivered by the said post-office establishment, or shall take or receive any such therefrom, such person so misusing the post-office establishment shall, upon conviction, be punishable by a fine of not more than five hundred dollars and by imprisonment for not more than eighteen months, or by both such punishments, at the discretion of the court. The indictment, information, or complaint may severally charge offenses to the number of three when committed within

---

[1] There was one additional decision by the Supreme Court concerning the 1872 version of the mail fraud statute, but it shed no light on the substantive meaning of the act. United States v. Hess, 124 U.S. 483 (1888), held that an indictment that simply recited the language of the statute and provided no particulars of the mailing or the scheme to defraud was defective. Otherwise, the Court noted, the defendant could not rely on the indictment for double jeopardy protection.

the same six calendar months; but the court thereupon shall give
a single sentence, and shall proportion the punishment especially
to the degree in which the abuse of the post-office establishment
enters as an instrument into such fraudulent scheme and device."
25 Stat. 873.

As Rakoff points out, there was "no express legislative history relating to
the 1889 amendment" either.

5. Judicial Interpretation of the 1889 Amendment. The 1889
amendment of the mail fraud statute made two clear changes. It recited a
laundry list of counterfeit schemes—tied to the slang of the day—that were
meant to be included in the statute, thus specifically embracing the *Jones*
decision summarized above. And it elaborated on the types of mailing that
counted, as well as where the mailing could occur. Since Congress retained
the last sentence of the statute after the *Henry* interpretation, the revision
also, it appears, indicated congressional acceptance of the idea that each
mailing constituted a separate violation of the statute and that there was
no substantive limit on the number of offenses that could be spun out of a
single scheme to defraud.

Did the amendment do any more than these things? Did it indicate
that Congress meant for the statute to be interpreted broadly? Or could
the strict constructionists continue to adhere to their interpretation of the
statute?

(i) Continued Division in the Lower Courts. After reviewing
the decisions under the 1889 amendment, Rakoff concludes that "neither
the amendment itself [nor] the Supreme Court decisions that shortly
followed its enactment ended the controversy between strict and broad
construction of the mail fraud statute. If anything, the divergence grew
greater." Earlier he had said:

"Thus, while the broad constructionists viewed the amendment as
vindication for their view that the now-specified schemes were
among the kinds of schemes Congress intended to cover from the
beginning, the strict constructionists viewed the amendment as
Congress' tacit concurrence that 'scheme to defraud' did not
extend to such schemes unless Congress specifically amended the
statute to include them."

Again, Rakoff gives a paradigm example of each judicial camp:

(a) *United States v. Beach*. In what Rakoff says was the
first reported decision under the amended statute, "a strict constructionist
court managed to read the amendment as narrowing the coverage of the
statute from what it had been before the amendment." In United States v.
Beach, 71 F. 160 (D.Colo.1895), the victim had been induced by the
defendant to travel a long way and spend a lot of money under the false
impression that he could get a job by doing so. The court said that this
might be within the ordinary meaning of the phrase "scheme to defraud,"
but that the "general language of the act must be limited to such schemes
and artifices as are ejusdem generis with those named." Since the defen-

dant's fraud, if such it was, was not of "the kind which are gainful to the wrongdoer," the prosecution was dismissed.

Notice that the new laundry list of offenses is stated in the disjunctive. That is, the statute now prohibits a "scheme to defraud" *or* one of the types of practices on the list. This was taken by the strict constructionists to mean that the laundry list was not within the original meaning of the phrase "scheme to defraud." Thus, the new statute did not prohibit schemes to defraud *such as* a sawdust swindle, but a scheme to defraud *and also* a sawdust swindle. The narrow meaning of "scheme to defraud" to which they adhered before the amendment thus was not affected when Congress added "green article" schemes and "sawdust swindles" to the act.

(b) *Horman v. United States*. This period also produced one of the broadest interpretations of the maul fraud statute in its history. In Horman v. United States, 116 F. 350 (6th Cir.1902), Judge Day (later appointed to the Supreme Court) wrote an opinion affirming a mail fraud conviction on a theory broader than the facts required. The defendant was charged, essentially, with blackmail. He mailed letters to three people, telling them that unless they paid him $7,000 he would disclose to the press and the public criminal offenses that he claimed to know about. In fact, the indictment charged, he knew of no such crimes. The District Court held, in effect, that any blackmail was within the statute, whether or not the defendant sought to acquire the money by deception: "[A]ny scheme by which it is sought to obtain another man's money wrongfully, without giving him any equivalent for it, is a scheme to defraud." On appeal, the Circuit Court agreed:

> "[T]o come within the terms of the statute under consideration, the artifice or scheme must be designed to defraud. We think, bearing in mind that the term is used to characterize the guilty purpose and wrongful intent with which the scheme or artifice has been formed by the accused, there is no difficulty in understanding the legislative purpose in using the term. ... The acts are required to be done with intent to injure or defraud, as distinguished from an innocent purpose in the doing of the same. We think the term in this statute ... is intended to define the wrongful purpose in injuring another, which must accompany the thing done to make it criminal within the meaning of the statute.
>
> ...
>
> "... To 'deprive of something dishonestly' is to defraud. ...
>
> "... That this scheme was not innocent, but intended for a wrongful purpose,—'to defraud' in the language of the statute,—is shown in the charge that these alleged crimes were to be published to the world in default of the payment of a large sum of money to the accused."

Notice that neither the District Court nor the Court of Appeals in *Horman* were concerned with the fact that the defendant lied when he claimed to know about crimes committed by his victims. Instead, *any* wrongful acquisition of the money of another was sufficient.   Deceit played no part in the theory of either court.

Rakoff criticizes the decision on this ground, arguing that "scheme to defraud," no matter the "vague meanings it may be given in other contexts, clearly denotes an element of deception."   As summarized below, he was reinforced in this observation by the holding of the Supreme Court expressly disavowing *Horman* in Fasulo v. United States, 272 U.S. 620 (1926).

(ii) Supreme Court Cases; *Durland v. United States*.   The Supreme Court decided three cases under the 1889 amendment.   Two involved technical questions of no importance to the substantive reach of the statute.[m]   The third, however, directly concerned the meaning of "scheme to defraud."

The question in Durland v. United States, 161 U.S. 306 (1896), was whether two indictments against Durland stated offenses under the mail fraud statute.   The first indictment alleged that Durland solicited 20 people by mail to purchase bonds for "a large sum of money, to wit, the sum of fifty dollars each" to be paid at $5 per month after an initial investment of $10.   A scale of redemption values was included in the solicitation, showing that profits in excess of 50 per cent could be obtained in less than a year.   The indictment further alleged that Durland had no intention of honoring the redemption schedule and that he meant instead to obtain the money "for his own use."   The second indictment was similar, in this case involving the solicitation by mail of a named person for $60 containing the same misrepresentations.

The Court began by observing that Durland "was trying to trap the unwary, and to secure money from them on the faith of a scheme glittering and attractive in form, yet unreal and deceptive in fact, and known to him to be such.   So far as the moral element is concerned it must be taken that the defendant's guilt was established."   Durland argued, however, that the mail fraud statute was limited to cases which at common law would come within the notion of "false pretenses," which required that there "be a misrepresentation as to some existing fact and not a mere promise as to the future."   Durland's brief elaborated:

> "[The indictment] discloses on its face absolutely nothing but an intention to commit a violation of a contract.   If there be one principle of criminal law that is absolutely settled by an over-whelming avalanche of authority it is that fraud either in the civil courts or in the criminal courts must be the misrepresentation of an existing or a past fact, and cannot consist of the mere intention not to carry out a contract in the future."

The Court answered:

---

[m] Stokes v. United States, 157 U.S. 187 (1895)(sufficiency of indictment and admissibility of evidence); Streep v. United States, 160 U.S. 128 (1895)(statute of limitations). In *Stokes*, the Court did set forth the elements that had to be proved in a mail fraud prosecution.   See footnote c, supra.

"We cannot agree with counsel. The statute is broader than is claimed. Its letter shows this: 'Any scheme or artifice to defraud.' Some schemes may be promoted through mere representations and promises as to the future, yet are none the less schemes and artifices to defraud. ...

"But beyond the letter of the statute is the evil sought to be remedied. It is common knowledge that nothing is more alluring than the expectation of receiving large returns on small investments. Eagerness to take the chances of large gains lies at the foundation of all lottery schemes, and, even when the matter of chance is eliminated, any scheme or plan which holds out the prospect of receiving more than is parted with appeals to the cupidity of all.

"In the light of this the statute must be read, and so read it includes everything designed to defraud by representations as to the past or present, or suggestions and promises as to the future. The significant fact is the intent and purpose. The question presented by this indictment to the jury was not, as counsel insist, whether the business scheme suggested in this bond was practicable or not. If the testimony had shown that this ... company, and the defendant, as its president, had entered in good faith upon that business, believing that out of the moneys received they could by investment or otherwise make enough to justify the promised returns, no conviction could be sustained, no matter how visionary might seem the scheme. The charge is that in putting forth this scheme it was not the intent of the defendant to make an honest effort for its success, but that he resorted to this form and pretence of a bond without a thought that he or the company would ever make good its promises. It was with the purpose of protecting the public against all such intentional efforts to despoil, and to prevent the post office from being used to carry them into effect, that this statute was passed; and it would strip it of value to confine it to such cases as disclose an actual misrepresentation as to some existing fact, and exclude those in which is only the allurement of a specious and glittering promise. This, which is the principal contention of counsel, must be overruled."[n]

Rakoff commented that "the broad and conclusory language" used in *Durland* "exemplifies reasoning typical of the broad constructionists' decisions and gives not the slightest hint of support for the strict constructionists' approach." To this could be added the fact that *Durland* was in the forefront of early decisions establishing that false promises could amount to

[n] Durland also argued that the first indictment was defective in other ways not material to the "false promises" issue. One of his claims was that it was "multifarious" in that it included too many offenses, citing *Henry*. The Court held that since this objection was not made until after the verdict, it "was presented too late."

fraud.°

Yet *Durland* did not settle the approach to be taken to mail fraud by the lower courts. As Rakoff observed:

"Having thus come close to the point of endorsing, in *Durland*, the broad constructionist point of view, the Supreme Court retreated once again into silence, and did not deliver another opinion dealing with the scope of the mail fraud statute until nearly 18 years later. In the interim, the strict constructionists renewed their assault upon a broad application of the mail fraud statute. Indeed, at the same time that the broad constructionists were extending the application of the mail fraud statute even further, the strict constructionists were busy shackling it with even more narrowing limitations." Rakoff, p. 812.

The result was that Congress was again persuaded to enter the fray.

6. Text and Effect of the 1909 Amendment. Congress amended the mail fraud statute again on March 4, 1909, this time more dramatically:

"Sec. 215. Whoever, having devised or intending to devise any scheme or artifice to defraud, or for obtaining money or property by means of false or fraudulent pretenses, representations, or promises, or to sell, dispose of, loan, exchange, alter, give away, distribute, supply, or furnish or procure for unlawful use any counterfeit or spurious coin, bank note, paper money, or any obligation or security of the United States, or of any State, Territory, municipality, company, corporation, or person or anything represented to be or intimated or held out to be such counterfeit or spurious article, or any scheme or artifice to obtain money by or through correspondence, by what is commonly called the 'saw-dust swindle,' or 'counterfeit-money fraud,' or by dealing or pretending to deal in what is commonly called 'green articles,' 'green coin,' 'green goods,' 'bills,' 'paper goods,' 'spurious Treasury notes,' 'United States goods,' 'green cigars,' or any other names or terms intended to be understood as relating to such counterfeit or spurious articles, shall, for the purpose of executing such scheme or artifice or attempting so to do, place, or cause to be placed, any letter, postal card, package, writing, circular, pamphlet, or advertisement, whether addressed to any person residing within or outside the United States, in any post-office, or station thereof, or street or other letter box of the United States, or authorized depository for mail matter, to be sent or delivered by the post-office establishment of the United States, or shall take or receive any such therefrom whether mailed within or without the United

_____

° For an article placing *Durland* in the context of other decisions recognizing false promises as the basis for theft by false pretenses (and rejecting the so-called "existing fact" doctrine), see Arthur R. Pearce, Theft by False Promises, 101 U. Pa. L. Rev. 967, 978–80 (1953). Pearce describes *Durland* as a leading and innovative case in the law of fraud.

States, or shall knowingly cause to be delivered by mail according to the direction thereon, or at the place at which it is directed to be delivered by the person to whom it is addressed, any such letter, postal card, package, writing, circular, pamphlet, or advertisement, shall be fined not more than one thousand dollars, or imprisoned not more than five years, or both." 35 Stat. 1130–31.

Gone was the "mail-emphasizing" language, and specifically ratified was the decision in *Durland*.[p] The offense was now reduced to two elements, a scheme to defraud and a mailing "for the purpose of executing such scheme."[q] Although again there was "virtually no direct legislative history,"[r] the statute appears, as Rakoff says, to be "clear in both intent and effect." Rakoff reasons:

"Bereft of [the] mail-emphasizing provisions, the statute ceased to afford any genuine support for the arguments developed by the strict constructionists over the previous 37 years. With the very mention of mailing now reduced to ... the requirement that in execution of the scheme to defraud there occur at least one mailing ... no court could seriously argue that the language of the statute dictated the substantive limitation of the statute's coverage to mail-dependent schemes whose very 'essence' was the use of the mails. ... Congress' elimination from the statute of nearly every vestige of the language upon which the strict constructionists had based their constructions could ... be interpreted only as a flat rejection of the strict constructionist approach." Rakoff, pp. 816–17.

But is the revision this clear? As Rakoff himself notes, the mailing must be "for the purpose of executing" the fraudulent scheme, and it could thus still be argued that the fraud and the mailing must be closely connected. And there was still the ambiguity reflected in the disjunctive phrasing of the statute. There were now three forms of fraudulent schemes covered: a "scheme to defraud" *or* obtaining money by false pretense or promise *or* one of the forms of counterfeiting schemes. *Durland* held that obtaining money by a false promise *was* a scheme to defraud. Could the Congress have meant to ratify this result, but to indicate that the Court was wrong in holding it embraced within the original concept of "scheme to defraud"? Could a court still reason that "scheme to defraud" is to be narrowly construed, and that two additional forms of fraud are now specifically included?

Rakoff asserts that the 1909 amendment was not the end of the strict construction approach, but that the force of this movement was diminished dramatically. Rather than a sharp continuation of the two prior camps, the cases following the 1909 amendment reflected the narrower approach

[p] Notice also that the maximum penalty was increased from 18 months to five years.

[q] Compare the *Stokes* recitation of the elements in footnote c, supra.

[r] Rakoff, p. 816 n.205.

far less frequently and far less dramatically. In fact, the most dramatic vestige of the strict construction approach was not to come until many years later, 1987 to be precise, in a decision by the Supreme Court (*McNally*) reproduced below as a main case.

Rakoff concludes his discussion of the early development of the mail fraud statute by making three points. First, "one lesson" to be learned from the history, he says, is that "continued emphasis upon the mailing aspects in interpreting the mail fraud statute is misplaced and serves no useful function." This follows, he asserts, from the reliance of many early interpretations of the statute on the misuse of the mails as the central feature of the statute, and the rejection of the basis for those decisions in the 1909 amendment. Second, and "contrary to common belief," he asserts that the substantive reach of the statute, at least by those in the broad construction camp, "was virtually as broad in the early days of the statute's application as it is today...." Moreover, it appears that Congress "intended from the beginning" that the statute be construed broadly, and "approved and fostered this broad application at every opportunity." Finally, he observes that the emphasis of the early versions of the statute on the mail-emphasizing language deflected the courts from undertaking their most important task in construing the statute, namely defining with some precision the meaning of "scheme to defraud."

7. *United States v. Young*. In the first case to reach the Supreme Court after the 1909 amendment, United States v. Young, 232 U.S. 155 (1914), the District Court had dismissed an indictment because, inter alia, it did not contain a specific allegation that the scheme was intended to be executed through the mails. "The gist of the offense," the District Court said, "is the use of the United States mails in the execution of the scheme, or in attempting so to do. It is not an unlawful scheme unless the use of the mails was a part of the scheme...." The District Court had thus read the 1909 statute as though it still contained the "mail-emphasizing" requirement that gave rise to the second element of the offense recited by the Supreme Court in *Stokes*.[s]

On direct appeal, the government argued that the District Court had failed to "note the essential differences" between the old and the new statutes. The Supreme Court agreed:

"There is a distinction between the [old and the new provisions], and the elements of an offense under [the 1909 amendment] are (a) a scheme devised or intended to be devised to defraud, or for obtaining money or property by means of false pretenses, and, (b) for the purpose of executing such scheme or attempting to do so, the placing of any letter in any post office of the United States to be sent or delivered by the Post Office Establishment. The District Court apparently overlooked the distinction between the [old and new provisions] and was of

[s] See footnote c, supra.

175

opinion that something more was necessary to an offense under [the revised statute]."

It was enough if the scheme to defraud was in fact sought to be executed by means of a mailing. The scheme itself need not have been "mail-dependent," that is, a scheme that depended on use of the mails for its execution. Thus, one of the specific props of the "strict constructionist" view was held no longer a part of the statute.

8. ***Badders v. United States***. In Badders v. United States, 240 U.S. 391 (1916), the defendant had been convicted on seven counts (involving seven letters) for "placing letters in the mail for the purpose of executing a scheme to defraud...." He was sentenced to five years imprisonment on each count, to be served concurrently, and to a $1,000 fine on each count, cumulated to $7,000. He argued that the mail fraud statute was unconstitutional because "beyond the power of Congress as applied to what may be a mere incident of a fraudulent scheme that itself is outside the jurisdiction of Congress to deal with." He also argued that if the statute "makes the deposit of each letter a separate offense subject to such punishment as [he] received in this case it imposes cruel and unusual punishment and excessive fines."

In perfunctory fashion, Justice Holmes rejected both arguments for a unanimous Court:

> "These contentions need no extended answer. The overt act of putting a letter into the postoffice of the United States is a matter that Congress may regulate. Ex parte Jackson, 96 U.S. 727 (1877). Whatever the limits of its power, it may forbid any such acts done in furtherance of a scheme that it regards as contrary to public policy, whether it can forbid the scheme or not. Intent may make an otherwise innocent act criminal, if it is a step in a plot. The acts alleged have been found to have been done for the purpose of executing the scheme, and there would be no ground for contending, if it were argued, that they were too remotely connected with the scheme for the law to deal with them. The whole matter is disposed of by United States v. Young, 232 U.S. 155 (1914). As to the other point, there is no doubt that the law may make each putting of a letter into the postoffice a separate offense. In re Henry, 123 U.S. 372, 374 (1887). And there is no ground for declaring the punishment unconstitutional."

And that was that. The rest of the opinion dealt with several other contentions, in an equally perfunctory manner.

Justice Harlan packed a great deal into his short response to the defendant's contentions. Congress can regulate mailings, and can forbid mailings for what it regards as objectionable purposes, even if it lacks authority to regulate the purposes directly. The absence of the "mail-emphasizing" language, perhaps originally put in the statute to save its constitutionality, was by 1916 not even worth mention. Moreover, the centrality of the mailing to execution of the scheme also seems irrelevant, thus removing another prop from the "strict constructionist" decisions under the 1872 and 1889 statutes. And the fact that each mailing is a separate offense and that, here, the fines had been cumulated for each mailing, did not raise a constitutional question worth discussing.

9. *Fasulo v. United States*. Fasulo v. United States, 272 U.S. 620 (1926), was the first decision by the Supreme Court in which it narrowed the potential scope of the mail fraud statute. The defendant was convicted of a conspiracy to violate the statute. The Court described the issue before it as follows:

> "The question for decision is whether the use of the mails for the purpose of obtaining money by means of threats of murder or bodily harm is a scheme to defraud within the meaning of that section. Petitioner contends that sending threatening letters for that purpose involves coercion and not fraud. The government insists that in a broad sense threats constitute fraud, and that the section covers the obtaining of money or property of another by dishonest means. ... On the basis of [Horman v. United States, 116 F. 350 (6th Cir.1902), and one other case] the government argues that the statute embraces all dishonest methods of deprivation the gist of which is the use of the mails."

The Court referred to another case in which it had said that *Horman* "went to the verge" and that the words "to defraud" "primarily mean to cheat; that they usually signify the deprivation of something of value by trick, deceit, chicane or overreaching, and that they do not extend to theft by violence, or to robbery or burglary." It then held that the defendant's conviction must be reversed:

> "Undoubtedly the obtaining of money by threats to injure or kill is more reprehensible than cheat, trick, or false pretenses; but that is not enough to require the court to hold that a scheme based on such threats is one to defraud within [the mail fraud statute]. While, for the ascertainment of the true meaning and intention of the words relied on, regard is to be had to the evils that called forth the enactment, and to the rule that a strict construction of penal statutes does not require the words to be so narrowed as to exclude cases that fairly may be said to be covered by them, it is not permissible for the court to search for an intention that the words themselves do not suggest.

> "If threats to kill or injure unless money is forthcoming do not constitute a scheme to defraud within the statute, there is none in this case. The only means employed by petitioner and his co-conspirators to obtain the money demanded was the coercion of fear. A comprehensive definition of 'scheme or artifice to defraud' need not be undertaken. The phrase is a broad one and extends to a great variety of transactions. But broad as are the words 'to defraud,' they do not include threat and coercion through fear or force. The rule laid down in the *Horman* case includes every

scheme that in its necessary consequences is calculated to injure another or to deprive him of his property wrongfully. That statement goes beyond the meaning that justly may be attributed to the language used. The purpose of the conspirators was to compel action in accordance with their demand. The attempt was by intimidation and not by anything in the nature of deceit or fraud as known to the law or as generally understood. The words of the act suggest no intention to include the obtaining of money by threats. There are no constructive offenses; and, before one can be punished, it must be shown that his case is plainly within the statute. ...

"The threats in question cannot fairly be held to constitute a scheme to defraud."

10. The 1948 Amendment and the Current Mail Fraud Statute. The mail fraud statute was amended again in 1948 as part of a recodification of the federal criminal laws. This time the 19th century references to "green articles" and "sawdust swindles" were dropped, but not in a manner to suggest any diminution of the coverage of the statute; the goal was to simplify the statute, not change its meaning, and the 1948 amendment preserved the three forms of fraudulent schemes listed in the 1909 amendment.

Although there have been several subsequent amendments, the current mail fraud statute remains largely the same as the 1948 amended version (amendments to the statute since 1948 are indicated in brackets):

"§ 1341. FRAUDS AND SWINDLES

"Whoever, having devised or intending to devise any scheme or artifice to defraud, or for obtaining money or property by means of false or fraudulent pretenses, representations, or promises, or to sell, dispose [of],[t] loan, exchange, alter, give away, distribute, supply, or furnish or procure for unlawful use any counterfeit or spurious coin, obligation, security, or other article, or anything represented to be or intimated or held out to be such counterfeit or spurious article, for the purpose of executing such scheme or artifice or attempting so to do, places in any post office or authorized depository for mail matter, any matter or thing whatever to be sent or delivered by the [Postal Service],[u] [or deposits or causes to be deposited any matter or thing whatever to be sent or delivered by any private or commercial interstate carrier,][v] or

[t] The statute as enacted in 1948 said "or" here. The correction to "of" was made in 1949. 63 Stat. 94.

[u] The 1948 statute said "Post Office Department." "Postal Service" was substituted in 1970. 84 Stat. 778.

[v] This language was added by the Violent Crime Control and Law Enforcement Act of 1994. 108 Stat. 2087. Can this amendment be based on the same postal power that was used to uphold the constitutionality of the lottery law in *Ex parte Jackson*, discussed supra at Note 3(i), and the entire mail fraud statute in *Badders v. United States*, discussed supra at Note 8? What other constitutional provision might authorize Congress to enact a criminal statute prohibiting the use of pri-

takes or receives therefrom, any such matter or thing, or knowing-ly causes to be delivered by mail [or such carrier]ʷ according to the direction thereon, or at the place at which it is directed to be delivered by the person to whom it is addressed, any such matter or thing, shall be fined [under this title]ˣ or imprisoned not more than five years, or both. [If the violation affects a financial institution, such person shall be fined not more than $1,000,000 or imprisoned for not more than 30 years, or both.]ʸ" 62 Stat. 763.

11. Conclusion. The history of the mail fraud statute until 1948 is an interesting mixture of judicial interpretation and congressional re-sponse. The net result of the first 75 years of its life was that a statute of uncertain scope when enacted still remained in many respects of uncertain scope, and that many issues remained for more modern litigation as prosecutors continued to press their "first line of defense" against the ingenuity of swindlers and thieves and, today, corrupt corporate executives and public officials. Still to come, as indicated above, was the Supreme Court's most dramatic narrowing of the lengths to which the statute had been taken by the lower courts. This occurred in *McNally v. United States*, the next main case. Congress overruled *McNally* by adding a new section to the chapter of the U.S. Code containing the mail fraud statute—this new statute, no matter the ambiguity of previous amendments, clearly designed to invite a broad definition of "scheme to defraud" by the courts, a definition the outer perimeters of which remain to be discovered.

After the treatment of *McNally* below, Section 2 turns to a series of recent Supreme Court decisions on the required relation between the mailing and the fraud. In these decisions will be found a rerun of the "strict construction-broad construction" debate of an earlier time. For it is not the case today that any "incidental" mailing associated with a scheme to defraud will suffice for conviction under the statute, and to the extent that the relation between the mailing and the fraud is tightened the decisions are reminiscent of the older cases that relied on the "mail-emphasizing" features of the statute to limit its reach to "mail-dependent" fraud. Section 3 then returns to the meaning of "scheme to defraud" by presenting several far-reaching lower court decisions to illustrate the modern direction of the courts and the modern meaning of the mail fraud statute.

---

vate delivery services, such as Federal Ex-press or United Parcel Service, to commit fraud? The commerce clause? Is it signifi-cant that the mail fraud statute does not require any showing that the alleged fraud affected interstate commerce? Cf. *United States v. Lopez*, ___ U.S. ___, 115 S.Ct. 1624 (1995), discussed in Chapter I, Section 4, supra.

ʷ Ibid.

ˣ In 1994, this language was substituted for "not more than $1,000." 108 Stat. 2147.

ʸ This language was added by amend-ments in 1989, 103 Stat. 500, and 1990, 104 Stat. 4861.

McNally v. United States

Supreme Court of the United States, 1987.
483 U.S. 350.

■ JUSTICE WHITE delivered the opinion of the Court.

This action involves the prosecution of petitioner Gray, a former public official of the commonwealth of Kentucky, and petitioner McNally, a private individual, for alleged violation of the federal mail fraud statute, 18 U.S.C. § 1341.[1] The prosecution's principal theory of the case, which was accepted by the courts below, was that petitioners' participation in a self-dealing patronage scheme defrauded the citizens and government of Kentucky of certain "intangible rights," such as the right to have the commonwealth's affairs conducted honestly. We must consider whether the jury charge permitted a conviction for conduct not within the scope of the mail fraud statute.

We accept for the sake of argument the government's view of the evidence, as follows. The petitioners and a third individual, Howard P. "Sonny" Hunt, were politically active in the Democratic Party in the commonwealth of Kentucky during the 1970's. After Democrat Julian Carroll was elected Governor of Kentucky in 1974, Hunt was made chairman of the state Democratic Party and given de facto control over selecting the insurance agencies from which the state would purchase its policies. In 1975, the Wombwell Insurance Company of Lexington, Kentucky (Wombwell), which since 1971 had acted as the commonwealth's agent for securing a workmen's compensation policy, agreed with Hunt that in exchange for a continued agency relationship it would share any resulting commissions in excess of $50,000 a year with other insurance agencies specified by him. The commissions in question were paid to Wombwell by the large insurance companies from which it secured coverage for the state.

From 1975 to 1979, Wombwell funneled $851,000 in commissions to 21 separate insurance agencies designated by Hunt. Among the recipients of these payments was Seton Investments, Inc. (Seton), a company controlled by Hunt and petitioner Gray and nominally owned and operated by petitioner McNally.

Gray served as Secretary of Public Protection and Regulation from 1976 to 1978 and also as Secretary of the Governor's Cabinet from 1977 to 1979. Prior to his 1976 appointment, he and Hunt established Seton for the sole purpose of sharing in the commissions distributed by Wombwell. Wombwell paid some $200,000 to Seton between 1975 and 1979, and the money was used to benefit Gray and Hunt. Pursuant to Hunt's direction,

---

[1] Section 1341 provides in pertinent part:

"Whoever, having devised or intending to devise any scheme or artifice to defraud, or for obtaining money or property by means of false or fraudulent pretenses, representations, or promises, ...

for the purpose of executing such scheme or artifice or attempting so to do [uses the mails or causes them to be used,] shall be fined not more than $1,000 or imprisoned not more than five years, or both."

Wombwell also made excess commission payments to the Snodgrass Insurance Agency, which in turn gave the money to McNally.

On account of the foregoing activities, Hunt was charged with and pleaded guilty to mail and tax fraud and was sentenced to three years' imprisonment. The petitioners were charged with one count of conspiracy and seven counts of mail fraud, six of which were dismissed before trial.[2] The remaining mail fraud count was based on the mailing of a commission check to Wombwell by the insurance company from which it had secured coverage for the state. This count alleged that petitioners had devised a scheme (1) to defraud the citizens and government of Kentucky of their right to have the commonwealth's affairs conducted honestly, and (2) to obtain, directly and indirectly, money and other things of value by means of false pretenses and the concealment of material facts.[3] The conspiracy count alleged that petitioners had (1) conspired to violate the mail fraud statute through the scheme just described and (2) conspired to defraud the United States by obstructing the collection of federal taxes.

After informing the jury of the charges in the indictment,[4] the District Court instructed that the scheme to defraud the citizens of Kentucky and

[2] The six counts dismissed were based on the mailing of Seton's tax returns. The Court of Appeals held that mailings required by law cannot be made the basis for liability under § 1341 unless the documents are themselves false, see Parr v. United States, 363 U.S. 370 (1960), and that the six counts were properly dismissed since the indictment did not allege that Seton's tax returns were false. The government has not sought review of this holding.

[3] The mail fraud count also alleged that petitioners' fraudulent scheme had the purpose of defrauding the citizens and government of Kentucky of their right to be made aware of all relevant facts when selecting an insurance agent to write the commonwealth's workmen's compensation insurance policy. The District Court did not instruct on this purpose, holding that it was subsumed in the purpose to deny the right to honest government.

[4] The instruction summarized the charge as follows:

"Count 4 of the indictment charges in part that the defendants devised a scheme or artifice to:

"(a)(1) defraud the citizens of the commonwealth of Kentucky and its governmental departments, agencies, officials and employees of their right to have the commonwealth's business and its affairs conducted honestly, impartially, free from corruption, bias, dishonesty, deceit, official misconduct, and fraud; and,

"(2) obtain (directly and indirectly) money and other things of value, by means of false and fraudulent pretenses, representations, and promises, and the concealment of facts.

"And for the purpose of executing the aforesaid scheme, the defendants, James E. Gray and Charles J. McNally, and Howard P. 'Sonny' Hunt, Jr., and others, did place and cause to be placed in a post office or authorized deposit for mail matter, matters and things to be sent and delivered by the Postal Service, and did take and receive and cause to be taken and received therefrom such matters and things and did knowingly cause to be delivered thereon and at the place at which it was directed to be delivered by the person to whom it was addressed, matters and things.

"(b) Defraud the United States by impeding, impairing, and obstructing and defeating the lawful governmental functions of the Internal Revenue Service of the Treasury Department of the United States of America in the ascertainment, computation, assessment and collection of federal taxes."

The government concedes that it was error for the District Court to include the

to obtain money by false pretenses and concealment could be made out by either of two sets of findings: (1) that Hunt had de facto control over the award of the workmen's compensation insurance contract to Wombwell from 1975 to 1979; that he directed payments of commissions from this contract to Seton, an entity in which he had an ownership interest, without disclosing that interest to persons in state government whose actions or deliberations could have been affected by the disclosure; and that petitioners, or either of them, aided and abetted Hunt in that scheme; or (2) that Gray, in either of his appointed positions, had supervisory authority regarding the commonwealth's workmen's compensation insurance at a time when Seton received commissions; that Gray had an ownership interest in Seton and did not disclose that interest to persons in state government whose actions or deliberations could have been affected by that disclosure; and that McNally aided and abetted Gray (the latter finding going only to McNally's guilt).

The jury convicted petitioners on both the mail fraud and conspiracy counts, and the Court of Appeals affirmed the convictions. In affirming the substantive mail fraud conviction, the court relied on a line of decisions from the Courts of Appeals holding that the mail fraud statute proscribes schemes to defraud citizens of their intangible rights to honest and impartial government. Under these cases, a public official owes a fiduciary duty to the public, and misuse of his office for private gain is a fraud. Also, an individual without formal office may be held to be a public fiduciary if others rely on him " 'because of a special relationship in the government' " and he in fact makes governmental decisions. The Court of Appeals held that Hunt was such a fiduciary because he "substantially participated in governmental affairs and exercised significant, if not exclusive, control over awarding the workmen's compensation insurance contract to Wombwell and the payment of monetary kick-backs to Seton."

We granted certiorari and now reverse.

The mail fraud statute clearly protects property rights, but does not refer to the intangible right of the citizenry to good government. As first enacted in 1872, as part of a recodification of the postal laws, the statute contained a general proscription against using the mails to initiate correspondence in furtherance of "any scheme or artifice to defraud." The sponsor of the recodification stated, in apparent reference to the anti-fraud provision, that measures were needed "to prevent the frauds which are mostly gotten up in the large cities ... by thieves, forgers, and rapscallions generally, for the purpose of deceiving and fleecing the innocent people in the country."[5] Insofar as the sparse legislative history reveals anything, it

instruction on tax fraud in the substantive mail fraud instruction, but the effect of that error is not now at issue.

[5] Cong. Globe, 41st Cong., 3d Sess., 35 (1870)(remarks of Rep. Farnsworth). These remarks were made during the debate on H.R. 2295, the recodification legislation introduced during the 41st Congress. Representative Farnsworth proceeded to describe a scheme whereby the mail was used to solicit the purchase by greedy and unwary persons of counterfeit bills, which were never delivered.

indicates that the original impetus behind the mail fraud statute was to protect the people from schemes to deprive them of their money or property.

Durland v. United States, 161 U.S. 306 (1896), the first case in which this Court construed the meaning of the phrase "any scheme or artifice to defraud," held that the phrase is to be interpreted broadly insofar as property rights are concerned, but did not indicate that the statute had a more extensive reach. The Court rejected the argument that "the statute reaches only such cases as, at common law, would come within the definition of 'false pretenses,' in order to make out which there must be a misrepresentation as to some existing fact and not a mere promise as to the future." Instead, it construed the statute to "includ[e] everything designed to defraud by representations as to the past or present, or suggestions and promises as to the future." Accordingly, the defendant's use of the mails to sell bonds which he did not intend to honor was within the statute. The Court explained that "[i]t was with the purpose of protecting the public against all such intentional efforts to despoil, and to prevent the post office from being used to carry them into effect, that this statute was passed. . . ."

Congress codified the holding of *Durland* in 1909, and in doing so gave further indication that the statute's purpose is protecting property rights.[6] The amendment added the words "or for obtaining money or property by means of false or fraudulent pretenses, representations, or promises" after the original phrase "any scheme or artifice to defraud." Act of Mar. 4, 1909, ch. 321, § 215, 35 Stat. 1130.[7] The new language is based on the statement in *Durland* that the statute reaches "everything designed to defraud by representations as to the past or present, or suggestions and promises as to the future." However, instead of the phrase "everything

---

The recodification bill was not passed by the 41st Congress, but was reintroduced and passed by the 42nd Congress with the anti-fraud section intact. Act of June 8, 1872, ch. 335, §§ 149 and 301, 17 Stat. 302 and 323.

[6] Prior to *Durland* Congress had amended the statute to add language expressly reaching schemes of the period, many of the same nature as those mentioned by Representative Farnsworth in 1870, see n.5, supra, dealing or pretending to deal in counterfeit currency under such names as "green coin" or "green cigars." Act of March 2, 1889, ch. 393, § 1, 25 Stat. 873. The addition of this language appears to have been nothing more than a reconfirmation of the statute's original purpose in the face of some disagreement among the lower federal courts as to whether the statute should be broadly or narrowly read. See Jed S. Rakoff, The Federal Mail Fraud Statute (Part 1), 18 Duquesne L. Rev. 771, 790–99, 808–09 (1980). Some of the

language added in 1889 was removed in 1948 in an amendment (Act of June 25, 1948, ch. 645, § 1341, 62 Stat. 763) designed to remove surplusage without changing the meaning of the statute. See H.R. Rep. No. 304, 80th Cong., 1st Sess., A100 (1947). Post–1948 amendments to the statute have been technical in nature. The last substantive amendment of the statute, then, was the codification of the holding of *Durland*, and other changes not relevant here, in 1909.

[7] The new language was suggested in the Report of the Commission to Revise and Codify the Criminal and Penal Laws of the United States, which cited *Durland* in the margin of its Report. See S. Doc. No. 68, pt. 2, 57th Cong., 1st Sess., 63, 64 (1901). The sponsor of the 1909 legislation did not address the significance of the new language, stating that it was self-explanatory. 42 Cong. Rec. 1026 (1908)(remarks of Sen. Heyburn).

designed to defraud" Congress used the words "[any scheme or artifice] for obtaining money or property."

After 1909, therefore, the mail fraud statute criminalized schemes or artifices "to defraud" or "for obtaining money or property by means of false or fraudulent pretenses, representation, or promises...." Because the two phrases identifying the proscribed schemes appear in the disjunctive, it is arguable that they are to be construed independently and that the money-or-property requirement of the latter phrase does not limit schemes to defraud to those aimed at causing deprivation of money or property. This is the approach that has been taken by each of the Courts of Appeals that has addressed the issue: schemes to defraud include those designed to deprive individuals, the people or the government of intangible rights, such as the right to have public officials perform their duties honestly.

As the Court long ago stated, however, the words "to defraud" commonly refer "to wronging one in his property rights by dishonest methods or schemes," and "usually signify the deprivation of something of value by trick, deceit, chicane or overreaching." Hammerschmidt v. United States, 265 U.S. 182 (1924).[8] The codification of the holding in *Durland* in 1909 does not indicate that Congress was departing from this common understanding. As we see it, adding the second phrase simply made it unmistakable that the statute reached false promises and misrepresentations as to the future as well as other frauds involving money or property.

---

[8] *Hammerschmidt* concerned the scope of the predecessor of 18 U.S.C. § 371, which makes criminal any conspiracy "to defraud the United States, or any agency thereof in any manner or for any purpose." *Hammerschmidt* indicates, in regard to that statute, that while "[t]o conspire to defraud the United States means primarily to cheat the government out of property or money, ... it also means to interfere with or obstruct one of its lawful governmental functions by deceit, craft or trickery, or at least by means that are dishonest." Other cases have held that § 371 reaches conspiracies other than those directed at property interests. See, e.g., Haas v. Henkel, 216 U.S. 462 (1910)(predecessor of § 371 reaches conspiracy to defraud the government by bribing a government official to make an advance disclosure of a cotton crop report); Glasser v. United States, 315 U.S. 60 (1942)(predecessor of § 371 reaches conspiracy to defraud the United States by bribing a United States attorney). However, we believe that this broad construction of § 371 is based on a consideration not applicable to the mail fraud statute.

In Curley v. United States, 130 F. 1 (1st Cir.1904), cited with approval in *Haas v. Henkel*, supra, the court stated:

"Quite likely the word 'defraud,' as ordinarily used in the common law, and as used in English statutes and in the statutes of our states, enacted with the object of protecting property and property rights of communities and individuals, as well as of municipal government, which exist largely for the purpose of administering local financial affairs, has reference to frauds relating to money and property."

The court concluded, however, that

"[a] statute which ... has for its object the protection of the individual property rights of the members of the civic body, is one thing; a statute which has for its object the protection and welfare of the government alone, which exists for the purpose of administering itself in the interests of the public, [is] quite another."

Section 371 is a statute aimed at protecting the federal government alone; however, the mail fraud statute, as we have indicated, had its origin in the desire to protect individual property rights, and any benefit which the government derives from the statute must be limited to the government's interests as property-holder.

We believe that Congress' intent in passing the mail fraud statute was to prevent the use of the mails in furtherance of such schemes. The Court has often stated that when there are two rational readings of a criminal statute, one harsher than the other, we are to choose the harsher only when Congress has spoken in clear and definite language. United States v. Bass, 404 U.S. 336, 347 (1971). See also Rewis v. United States, 401 U.S. 808, 812 (1971). As the Court said in a mail fraud case years ago, "There are no constructive offenses; and before one can be punished, it must be shown that his case is plainly within the statute." Fasulo v. United States, 272 U.S. 620, 629 (1926). Rather than construe the statute in a manner that leaves its outer boundaries ambiguous and involves the federal government in setting standards of disclosure and good government for local and state officials, we read § 1341 as limited in scope to the protection of property rights. If Congress desires to go further, it must speak more clearly than it has.

For purposes of this action, we assume that Hunt, as well as Gray, was a state officer. The issue is thus whether a state officer violates the mail fraud statute if he chooses an insurance agent to provide insurance for the state but specifies that the agent must share its commissions with other named insurance agencies, in one of which the officer has an ownership interest and hence profits when his agency receives part of the commissions. We note that as the action comes to us, there was no charge and the jury was not required to find that the commonwealth itself was defrauded of any money or property. It was not charged that in the absence of the alleged scheme the commonwealth would have paid a lower premium or secured better insurance. Hunt and Gray received part of the commissions but those commissions were not the commonwealth's money. Nor was the jury charged that to convict it must find that the commonwealth was deprived of control over how its money was spent. Indeed, the premium for insurance would have been paid to some agency, and what Hunt and Gray did was to assert control that the commonwealth might not otherwise have made over the commissions paid by the insurance company to its agent.[9] Although the government now relies in part on the assertion that

[9] Justice Stevens would affirm the conviction even though it was not charged that requiring the Wombwell agency to share commissions violated state law. We should assume that it did not. For the same reason we should assume that it was not illegal under state law for Hunt and Gray to own one of the agencies sharing in the commissions and hence to profit from the arrangement, whether or not they disclosed it to others in the state government. It is worth observing as well that it was not alleged that the mail fraud statute would have been violated had Hunt and Gray reported to state officials the fact of their financial gain. The violation asserted is the failure to disclose their financial interest, even if state law did

not require it, to other persons in the state government whose actions could have been affected by the disclosure. It was in this way that the indictment charged that the people of Kentucky had been deprived of their right to have the commonwealth's affairs conducted honestly.

It may well be that Congress could criminalize using the mails to further a state officer's efforts to profit from governmental decisions he is empowered to make or over which he has some supervisory authority, even if there is no state law proscribing his profiteering or even if state law expressly authorized it. But if state law expressly permitted or did not forbid a state officer such as Gray to

the petitioners obtained property by means of false representations to Wombwell, there was nothing in the jury charge that required such a finding. We hold, therefore, that the jury instruction on the substantive mail fraud count permitted a conviction for conduct not within the reach of § 1341.

The government concedes that if petitioners' substantive mail fraud convictions are reversed their conspiracy convictions should also be reversed.

The judgment of the Court of Appeals is reversed and the case remanded for proceedings consistent with this opinion.

It is so ordered.

JUSTICE STEVENS, with whom JUSTICE O'CONNOR joins as to Parts I, II and III, dissenting.

Congress has broadly prohibited the use of the United States mails to carry out "any scheme or artifice to defraud." 18 U.S.C. § 1341. The question presented is whether that prohibition is restricted to fraudulent schemes to deprive others of money or property, or whether it also includes fraudulent schemes to deprive individuals of other rights to which they are entitled. Specifically, we must decide whether the statute's prohibition embraces a secret agreement by state officials to place the state's workmen's compensation insurance with a particular agency in exchange for that company's agreement to share a major portion of its commissions with a list of agents provided by the officials, including sham agencies under the control of the officials themselves.

The same question of statutory construction has arisen in a variety of contexts over the past few decades. In the public sector, judges, state governors, chairmen of state political parties, state cabinet officers, city aldermen, congressmen and many other state and federal officials have been convicted of defrauding citizens of their right to the honest services of their government officials.[1] In most of these cases, the officials have

have an ownership interest in an insurance agency handling the state's insurance, it would take a much clearer indication than the mail fraud statute evidences to convince us that having and concealing such an interest defrauds the state and is forbidden under federal law.

[1] [Here Justice Stevens listed 12 Circuit Court decisions involving the array of public officials he summarized in the text of his opinion. Specifically, they involved a county judge, a city budget director, a State Alcoholic Beverage Control commissioner, a party leader, a Congressman, a Governor of Maryland (Mandel), a city building commissioner, a city Director of Public Relations, two cases involving city aldermen, an ex-Governor of Illinois (Kerner) and an ex-Director of Illinois

Department of Revenue, and an election commissioner. He added that "[s]ome private defendants have also been convicted of devising schemes through which public servants defraud the public." Here, he cited four cases involving bribing a mayor, bribing a judge, bribing a state Secretary of State, and a "scheme to bribe state officials." He then said:]

In Shushan v. United States, 117 F.2d 110 (5th Cir.1941), the Fifth Circuit upheld the mail fraud prosecution of a member of a Louisiana parish levy board for receiving kickbacks from the underwriters of a plan to refund outstanding bonds of the levy district. Explaining why it rejected the argument that no actual fraud had occurred because the

secretly made governmental decisions with the objective of benefiting themselves or promoting their own interests, instead of fulfilling their legal commitment to provide the citizens of the state or local government with their loyal service and honest government. Similarly, many elected officials and their campaign workers have been convicted of mail fraud when they have used the mails to falsify votes, thus defrauding the citizenry of its right to an honest election.[2] In the private sector, purchasing agents, brokers, union leaders, and others with clear fiduciary duties to their employers or unions have been found guilty of defrauding their employers or unions by accepting kickbacks or selling confidential information.[3] In other cases, defendants have been found guilty of using the mails to defraud individuals of their rights to privacy, and other nonmonetary rights.[4] All of these cases have something in common—they involved what the Court now refers to as "intangible rights." They also share something else in common. The many federal courts that have confronted the question whether these sorts of schemes constitute a "scheme or artifice to defraud" have uniformly and consistently read the statute in the same, sensible way. They have realized that nothing in the words "any scheme or artifice to defraud," or in the purpose of the statute, justifies limiting its application to schemes intended to deprive victims of money or property.

I

The mail fraud statute sets forth three separate prohibitions. It prohibits the use of the United States mails for the purpose of executing

"[1] any scheme or artifice to defraud, [2] or for obtaining money or property by means of false or fraudulent pretenses, representations, or promises, [3] or to sell, dispose of, loan, exchange, alter, give away, distribute, supply, or furnish or procure for unlawful use any counterfeit or spurious coin, obligation, security, or other article, or anything represented to be or intimated or held out to be such counterfeit or spurious article ..." 18 U.S.C. § 1341 (brackets added).

As the language makes clear, each of these restrictions is independent. One can violate the second clause—obtaining money or property by false pretenses—even though one does not violate the third clause—counterfeit-

---

refunding operation had actually been profitable to the levy board, the court stated:

> "No trustee has more sacred duties than a public official and any scheme to obtain an advantage by corrupting such a one must in the federal law be considered a scheme to defraud."

[2] [Here Justice Stevens cited four Circuit Court opinions involving a candidate for a state legislature, a sheriff, a party chairman, and candidates for city office.]

[3] [Here Justice Stevens cited nine cases. Seven of them involved a chairman of a political action committee, an attorney, a securities trader, an insurance manager, two cases involving purchasing agents, and an attempt to bribe a competitor's employee.]

[4] [Here Justice Stevens cited three cases. They involved a wire fraud conviction related to a bogus talent agency designed to seduce women, a scheme to fraudulently obtain confidential personal information, and fraudulent information on an application for a liquor license.]

ing. Similarly, one can violate the first clause—devising a scheme or artifice to defraud—without violating the counterfeiting provision. Until today it was also obvious that one could violate the first clause by devising a scheme or artifice to defraud, even though one did not violate the second clause by seeking to obtain money or property from his victim through false pretenses. Every court to consider the matter had so held. Yet, today, the Court, for all practical purposes, rejects this longstanding construction of the statute by imposing a requirement that a scheme or artifice to defraud does not violate the statute unless its purpose is to defraud someone of money or property. I am at a loss to understand the source or justification for this holding. Certainly no canon of statutory construction requires us to ignore the plain language of the provision.

In considering the scope of the mail fraud statute it is essential to remember Congress' purpose in enacting it. Congress sought to protect the integrity of the United States mails by not allowing them to be used as "instruments of crime." See Durland v. United States, 161 U.S. 306 (1896); Parr v. United States, 363 U.S. 370, 389 (1960). "The focus of the statute is upon the misuse of the Postal Service, not the regulation of state affairs, and Congress clearly has the authority to regulate such misuse of the mails. See Badders v. United States, 240 U.S. 391 (1916)." United States v. States, 488 F.2d 761, 767 (8th Cir.1973). Once this purpose is considered, it becomes clear that the construction the Court adopts today is senseless. Can it be that Congress sought to purge the mails of schemes to defraud citizens of money but was willing to tolerate schemes to defraud citizens of their right to an honest government, or to unbiased public officials? Is it at all rational to assume that Congress wanted to ensure that the mails not be used for petty crimes, but did not prohibit election fraud accomplished through mailing fictitious ballots? Given Congress' "broad purpose," I "find it difficult to believe, absent some indication in the statute itself or the legislative history, that Congress would have undercut sharply that purpose by hobbling federal prosecutors in their effort to combat" use of the mails for fraudulent schemes. McElroy v. United States, 455 U.S. 642, 655 (1982).

The limitation the Court adopts today shows no fidelity to Congress' words or purpose. The Court recognizes that the "money or property" limitation of the second clause does not actually apply to prosecutions under the first clause. But where else can such a limitation be derived from? A few examples of the types of frauds that have been prosecuted under the "intangible right" theory reveals that these schemes constitute "fraud" in every sense of the word, and that the "intangible right" theory plays an indispensable role in effectuating Congress' goal of preserving the integrity of the Postal Service.

In *States*, supra, two candidates running for the office of Committeemen in St. Louis, Missouri, used the United States mails in their scheme to falsify voter registration affidavits in order to carry out an extensive fraudulent write-in scheme. The candidates had their campaign workers fill in the affidavits with fictitious names and addresses, making sure that the mailing addresses were accessible to the campaign. Applications for absentee ballots were filed, and when they arrived through the mail, they were filled in with the candidates' names and mailed back. The candidates and one of their aides were convicted of mail fraud for having devised a scheme to defraud the voters, the residents, and the Board of Election Commissioners. The Court of Appeals affirmed the convictions, rejecting the defendants' arguments that they had not defrauded anyone since they never sought money or property. The court explained that the term "defraud" must be "construed to further the purpose of the statute; namely, to prohibit the misuse of the mails to further fraudulent enterprises."

In United States v. Rauhoff, 525 F.2d 1170 (7th Cir.1975), the defendant was part of a scheme that used the United States mail to facilitate its paying the Illinois Secretary of State approximately $50,000 a year in return for the Secretary's awarding the state's license plate contract to a certain company. In response to the argument that all parties to the scheme were reaping profits, and that nobody was defrauded, the Court of Appeals explained that the victims of the scheme were the "people of Illinois, who were defrauded of their right to have the business of the office of the Secretary of State conducted free from bribery." Although it was not proven that the state or its citizens lost any money, it was and is clear that this was a scheme to defraud under § 1341.

There are scores of other examples of such schemes which, although not depriving anyone of money or property, are clearly schemes to defraud, and are clearly within the scope of Congress' purpose in enacting the mail fraud statute. Discussing the peculiar facts of each of them would only confirm the observation that fraud if "as old as falsehood and as versable as human ingenuity." Weiss v. United States, 122 F.2d 675, 681 (5th Cir.1941). But, taken as a whole, these cases prove just how unwise today's judicial amendment of the mail fraud state is.

II

The cases discussed above demonstrate that the construction the courts have consistently given the statute is consistent with the common understanding of the term "fraud," and Congress' intent in enacting the statute. It is also consistent with the manner in which the term has been interpreted in an analogous federal statute; the way the term was interpreted at the time of this statute's enactment; and the statute's scant legislative history. There is no reason, therefore, to upset the settled, sensible construction that the federal courts have consistently endorsed.

The term "defraud" is not unique to § 1341. Another federal statute, 18 U.S.C. § 371, uses the identical term in prohibiting conspiracies to "defraud the United States," and the construction we have given to that statute should be virtually dispositive here. In Haas v. Henkel, 216 U.S. 462 (1910), the Court, dealing with the predecessor to § 371, rejected the argument that there could be no conspiracy to defraud in the absence of contemplated monetary or property loss. "The statute is broad enough in its terms to include any conspiracy for the purpose of impairing, obstructing or defeating the lawful function of any department of government." Again, in Hammerschmidt v. United States, 265 U.S. 182 (1924), the Court described the scope of the statute as prohibiting not only conspiracies to "cheat the government out of property or money, but it also means to interfere with or obstruct one of its lawful governmental functions by deceit, craft or trickery, or at least by means that are dishonest."[6] It is thus clear that a conspiracy to defraud the United States does not require any evidence that the government has suffered any property or pecuniary loss. See also United States v. Barnow, 239 U.S. 74, 79 (1915).

There is no basis for concluding that the term "defraud" means something different in § 1341 (first enacted in 1872) than what it means in § 371 (first enacted in 1867). Although § 371 includes the words "in any manner or for any purpose," those words only modify the underlying act— fraud, and if that term does not include nonproperty interests then our longstanding interpretation of § 371 is unjustified. In any event, § 1341 itself includes the expansive phrase "any scheme or artifice to defraud."

The Court nonetheless suggests that interpreting the two statutes differently can be justified because § 371 applies exclusively to frauds against the United States, while § 1341 benefits private individuals. This argument is wide of the mark. The purpose of § 1341 is to protect the integrity of the United States Postal Service, and, as I have explained, it is ludicrous to think that a Congress intent on preserving the integrity of the Postal Service would have used the term "defraud" in a narrow sense so as to allow mailings whose purpose was merely to defraud citizens of rights other than money or property. There is, therefore, no reason to believe that Congress used the term "defraud" in a more limited way in § 1341 than it did in § 371.[7] The Court is correct in pointing out that Congress intended to go beyond any common-law meaning of the word "defraud" in enacting § 371. But we have also rejected the argument that the common-law meaning of the term "defraud" confines the scope of § 1341. See Durland v. United States, 161 U.S. 306 (1896).

[6] "To conspire to defraud the United States means primarily to cheat the government out of property or money, but it also means to interfere with or obstruct one of its lawful governmental functions by deceit, craft or trickery, or at least by means that are dishonest. It is not necessary that the government shall be subjected to property or pecuniary loss by the fraud, but only that its legitimate official action and purpose shall be defeated by misrepresentation, chicane or the overreaching of those charged with carrying out the governmental intention." Hammerschmidt v. United States, 265 U.S., at 188.

It is extraordinary that the only support the Court presents for its narrow definition is some language in Hammerschmidt, even though Hammerschmidt itself goes on to expressly reject the notion that fraud is limited to interference with monetary or property rights.

[7] The prohibition against employing "any device, scheme, or artifice to defraud" in connection with transactions on a National Securities Exchange similarly does not require proof that specific individuals have suffered tangible losses. See SEC v. Texas Gulf Sulphur Co., 401 F.2d 833, 848 (2d Cir.1968). By its terms, that language is broad enough to "reach any person engaged in any fraudulent scheme." Chiarella v. United States, 445 U.S. 222, 240 (1980)(Burger, C.J., dissenting).

Examination of the way the term "defraud" has long been defined, and was defined at the time of the statute's enactment, makes it clear that Congress' use of the term showed no intent to limit the statute to property loss. For example, Justice Story cites the definition of "fraud" as "applied to every artifice made use of by one person for the purpose of deceiving another," or as "any cunning, deception, or artifice used to circumvent[,] cheat, or deceive another." 1 J. Story, Equity Jurisprudence § 186, pp. 189–90 (1870). Similarly, the law dictionaries of the era broadly defined the type of interests subject to deprivation by fraudulent action. One leading dictionary stated that "[t]o defraud is to withhold from another that which is justly due to him, or to deprive him of a right by deception or artifice." 1 Bouvier's Law Dictionary 530 (1897). Another dictionary defined "defraud" as "[t]o cheat; to deceive; to deprive of a right by an act of fraud . . . to withhold from another what is justly due him, or to deprive him of a right, by deception or artifice." W. Anderson, A Dictionary of Law 474 (1893). See also 1 Burrill's Law Dictionary 658–59 (1859).[8]

It is, in fact, apparent that the common law criminalized frauds beyond those involving "tangible rights." For example, in a case remarkably similar to the one before us, a public official was convicted for depriving the government of his honest services. See Trial of Regina v. Valentine Jones, 31 How. St. Tr. 251 (1809). The case has been abstracted as follows:

> "A, a commissary-general of stores in the West Indies, makes contracts with B to supply stores, on the condition that B should divide the profits with A. A commits a misdemeanor." J. Stephen, Digest of The Criminal Law, Art. 121, p. 85 (3d ed. 1883).

By the same token, the crime of fraud has often included deceptive seduction, although that crime often includes no property or monetary loss. See State v. Parker, 114 Wash. 428, 195 P. 229 (1921); cf. United States v. Condolon, 600 F.2d 7 (4th Cir.1979)(fraudulent scheme to seduce women supported wire fraud conviction). Of course, even if the term was not that expansively defined at common law, we have held that Congress went beyond the common-law definitions in enacting this statute. *Durland*, 161 U.S., at 313–14.

In a recent decision upholding the mail fraud conviction of an Illinois judge, despite the absence of proof that anyone suffered loss of tangible property, the Court of Appeals for the Seventh Circuit reaffirmed the broad meaning of the word "defraud." United States v. Holzer, 816 F.2d 304, 307–08 (7th Cir.1987). Writing for the court, Judge Posner explained:

> "Fraud in its elementary common law sense of deceit—and this is one of the meanings that fraud bears in the statute— includes the deliberate concealment of material information in a

---

[8] Although there are surely cases and commentaries to be found which describe "fraud" in a more limited manner, none have been brought to our attention that reject the broader interpretations cited here. There is, of course, no doubt that the term "defraud" includes money and property interests, and the cases referring to such interests do not conflict with my understanding of the statute.

setting of fiduciary obligation. A public official is a fiduciary toward the public, including, in the case of a judge, the litigants who appear before him, and if he deliberately conceals material information from them he is guilty of fraud. When a judge is busily soliciting loans from counsel to one party, and not telling the opposing counsel (let alone the public), he is concealing material information in violation of his fiduciary obligations. ...

"Second, the systematic and long-continued receipt of bribes by a public official, coupled with active efforts to conceal the bribe-taking from the public and the authorities ... is fraud (again in its elementary sense of deceit, and quite possibly in other senses as well), even if it is the public rather than counsel that is being kept in the dark. It is irrelevant that, so far as appears, Holzer never ruled differently in a case because of a lawyer's willingness or unwillingness to make him a loan, so that his conduct caused no demonstrable loss either to a litigant or to the public at large. How can anyone prove how a judge would have ruled if he had not been bribed?"

The general definition of the term "defraud" does not support, much less compel, today's decision.

Even if there were historical evidence of a limited definition of "fraud," the Court's holding would reflect a strange interpretation of legislation enacted by the Congress in the 19th Century. Statutes like the Sherman Act, the civil rights legislation, and the mail fraud statute were written in broad general language on the understanding that the courts would have wide latitude in construing them to achieve the remedial purposes that Congress had identified. The wide open spaces in statutes such as these are more appropriately interpreted as implicit delegations of authority to the courts to fill in the gaps in the common-law tradition of case by case adjudication. The notion that the meaning of the words "any scheme or artifice to defraud" was frozen by a special conception of the term recognized by Congress in 1872 is manifestly untenable. As Judge Posner put it:

"The argument depends on the view that the meaning of fraud in the mail-fraud statute was frozen by the conception of fraud held by the framers of the statute when it was first passed back in the 19th century. This seems to us the opposite and equally untenable extreme from arguing that fraud is whatever strikes a judge as bad, but in any event the 'intangible rights' concept that the argument attacks is too well established in the courts of appeals for us to disturb." *Holzer*, 816 F.2d, at 310.

Finally, there is nothing in the legislative history of the mail fraud statute that suggests that Congress intended the word "fraud" to have a narrower meaning in that statute than its common meaning and the meaning that it has in § 371. As originally enacted in 1872, the statute had but one class of prohibition: use of the mails as part of "any scheme or artifice to defraud." Act of June 8, 1872, ch. 335, § 301, 17 Stat. 323. The second clause, which prohibits "any scheme ... for obtaining money or property by means of false or fraudulent pretenses, representations, or promises," was added in 1909. Act of Mar. 4, 1909, ch. 321, § 215, 35 Stat. 1130. The purpose of the second clause was to codify this Court's holding in *Durland* that the act prohibits false promises even if they did not qualify as "fraud" at common law. See *Durland*, 161 U.S., at 312–14. There is no evidence to suggest that Congress sought to limit the scope of the original prohibition, and its use of the disjunctive "or" demonstrates that it was adding to, not modifying, the original prohibition.

Reviewing the general history of Congress' reactions to the Courts' decisions interpreting the mail fraud statute also supports the reading the lower courts have attributed to § 1341. The general language in the mail fraud statute has repeatedly been construed to cover novel species of fraud, and Congress has repeatedly amended the statute in ways that support a broad interpretation of its basic thrust. That long history is accurately summarized in the following observations:

> "First enacted in 1872, the mail fraud statute, together with its lineal descendant, the wire fraud statute, has been characterized as the 'first line of defense' against virtually every new area of fraud to develop in the United States in the past century. Its applications, too numerous to catalog, cover not only the full range of consumer frauds, stock frauds, land frauds, bank frauds, insurance frauds, and commodity stock frauds, but have extended even to such areas as blackmail, counterfeiting, election fraud, and bribery. In many of these and other areas, where legislatures have sometimes been slow to enact specific prohibitory legislation, the mail fraud statute has frequently represented the sole instrument of justice that could be wielded against the ever-innovative practitioners of deceit.

> "During the past century, both Congress and the Supreme Court have repeatedly placed their stamps of approval on expansive use of the mail fraud statute. Indeed, each of the five legislative revisions of the statute has served to enlarge its coverage." Jed S. Rakoff, The Federal Mail Fraud Statute (Part I), 18 Duquesne L.Rev. 772–73 (1980).

III

To support its crabbed construction of the act, the Court makes a straight-forward but unpersuasive argument. Since there is no explicit, unambiguous evidence that Congress actually contemplated "intangible rights" when it enacted the mail fraud statute in 1872, the Court explains, any ambiguity in the meaning of the criminal statute should be resolved in favor of lenity. The doctrine of lenity is, of course, sound, for the citizen is entitled to fair notice of what sort of conduct may give rise to punishment. But the Court's reliance on that doctrine in this case is misplaced for several reasons.

To begin with, "although 'criminal statutes are to be construed strictly ... this does not mean that every criminal statute must be given the narrowest possible meaning in complete disregard of the purpose of the legislature.'" McElroy v. United States, 455 U.S. 642, 658 (1982), quoting United States v. Bramblett, 348 U.S. 503, 509–10 (1955). Especially in light of the statutory purpose, I believe that § 1341 unambiguously prohibits all schemes to defraud that use the United States mails—whether or not they involve money or property.

In any event, this asserted ambiguity in the meaning of the word "defraud," if it ever existed, was removed by judicial construction long ago. Even if Chief Justice Taft's opinion for the Court in the *Hammerschmidt* case was not sufficient to make it perfectly clear that a fraud on the public need not deprive it of tangible property, the series of Court of Appeals' opinions applying this very statute to schemes to defraud a state and its citizens of their intangible right to honest and faithful government, notwithstanding the absence of evidence of tangible loss, removed any relevant ambiguity in this statute. Surely these petitioners knew that it would be unlawful to place Kentucky's insurance coverage with an agent who would secretly make hundreds of thousands of dollars available for the private use of petitioners, their relatives, and their paramours. This is, indeed, a strange application of the doctrine of lenity.[9]

I recognize that there may have been some overly expansive applications of § 1341 in the past. With no guidance from this Court, the Courts of Appeals have struggled to define just when conduct which is clearly unethical is also criminal. In some instances, however, such as voting fraud cases, the criminality of the scheme and the fraudulent use of the mails could not be clearer. It is sometimes difficult to define when there has been a scheme to defraud someone of intangible rights. But it is also sometimes difficult to decide when a tangible loss was caused by fraud. The fact that the exercise of judgment is sometimes difficult is no excuse for rejecting an entire doctrine that is both sound and faithful to the intent of Congress.

IV

Perhaps the most distressing aspect of the Court's action today is its casual—almost summary—rejection of the accumulated wisdom of the many distinguished federal judges who have thoughtfully considered and correctly answered the question this case presents. The quality of this Court's work is most suspect when it stands alone, or virtually so, against a tide of well-considered opinions issued by state or federal courts. In this

---

[9] When considering how much weight to accord to the doctrine of lenity, it is appropriate to identify the class of litigants that will benefit from the Court's ruling today. They are not uneducated, or even average, citizens. They are the most sophisticated practitioners of the art of government among us. There is an element of fiction in the presumption that every citizen is charged with a responsibility to know what the law is. But the array of government executives, judges, and legislators who have been accused, and convicted, of mail fraud under the well-settled construction of the statute that the Court renounces today are people who unquestionably knew that their conduct was unlawful.

case I am convinced that those judges correctly understood the intent of the Congress that enacted this statute. Even if I were not so persuaded, I could not join a rejection of such a long-standing, consistent interpretation of a federal statute.

In the long run, it is not clear how grave the ramifications of today's decision will be. Congress can, of course, negate it by amending the statute. Even without Congressional action, prosecutions of corrupt officials who use the mails to further their schemes may continue since it will frequently be possible to prove some loss of money or property.[10] But many other types of fraudulent use of the mail will now be immune from prosecution. The possibilities that the decision's impact will be mitigated do not moderate my conviction that the Court has made a serious mistake. Nor do they erase my lingering questions about why a Court that has not been particularly receptive to the rights of criminal defendants in recent years has acted so dramatically to protect the elite class of powerful individuals who will benefit from this decision.

I respectfully dissent.

NOTES ON THE IMPACT AND FATE OF *McNALLY*

1. Questions and Comments on *McNally*. The Court holds that the mail fraud statute applies only to deprivations of "property." The 1909 amendment in codifying the *Durland* decision added the words "or for obtaining money or property by means of false or fraudulent pretenses, representations, or promises." Given that this is in the disjunctive, what room is left for the operation of the words "scheme or artifice to defraud"? Presumably there is some form of criminal behavior to which they apply and which is not covered by the other provisions of the statute. Or is there? Did the Court make these words redundant? Is it likely that Congress meant for the 1909 amendment to add words to the statute that completely described the forms of behavior covered by a "scheme to defraud"? What would be the purpose of such an amendment?

Recall that a "green articles" scheme, while it had the deprivation of property as its ultimate objective, did not itself involve "fraud" in the sense that any deprivation was visited upon the recipient of the mailing. The actual fraud occurred later, when the counterfeit money sold to the mail recipient was passed on to the unsuspecting public. Does the fact that Congress specifically included such behavior in the mail fraud statute in the 1899 amendment, and has carried it forward in substance ever since, indicate that Congress did not mean the mail fraud statute to be restricted

---

[10] When a person is being paid a salary for his loyal services, any breach of that loyalty would appear to carry with it some loss of money to the employer—who is not getting what he paid for. Additionally, "[i]f an agent receives anything as a result of his violation of a duty of loyalty to the principal, he is subject to a liability to deliver it, its value, or its proceeds, to the principal." Restatement (Second) of Agency § 403 (1958). This duty may fulfill the Court's "money or property" requirement in most kickback schemes.

only to situations where the mail recipient was defrauded of specific "property"? Wherein lies the fraud in a "green articles" scheme? Is the "intangible rights" doctrine different?

On the other hand, should a criminal statute be construed "in a manner that leaves its outer boundaries ambiguous and involves the federal government in setting standards of disclosure and good government for local and state officials"? For these reasons, are the fair warning and federalism arguments in cases like *Bass* and *Rewis* persuasive here? Suppose, as Justice White hypothesizes in footnote 9, the behavior of McNally and his cohorts was lawful under state law. Would that matter to the interpretation of a *federal* criminal statute that does not, in terms, incorporate state law? Should it? What is the appropriate role of the United States Attorney (and the federal judiciary) in assuring good government to the citizens of states and localities?

Section 371 of title 18 provides:

> "If two or more persons conspire either to commit any offense against the United States, or to defraud the United States, or any agency thereof in any manner or for any purpose, and one or more of such persons do any act to effect the object of the conspiracy, each shall be fined under this title or imprisoned not more than five years, or both."

It is well established, as the opinions in *McNally* recognize, that the words "to defraud the United States" in this statute, enacted at roughly the same time as the mail fraud statute, are not limited to deprivations of "property." Is Justice White persuasive that Congress would have intended to protect the interests of the United States by one concept of fraud in this statute and to protect the integrity of the mail system by another concept of fraud in the mail fraud statute? Do the words "in any manner and for any purpose" in § 371 serve to distinguish the two situations?

Finally, what is the relevance of the consistent line of Circuit Court opinions referred to by Justice Stevens? He is right that the Supreme Court virtually "stands alone" in its reading of the statute. Should that matter? The prohibition of this form of fraud by the mail fraud statute was not "discovered" by the Circuit Courts, at least in substantial numbers, until the mid-to-late 1970s. Should that matter?

2.   Retroactivity of *McNally*. The courts were quickly deluged with claims by defendants previously convicted on an "intangible rights" theory of mail fraud that their convictions should be set aside in light of *McNally*. For those defendants on direct appeal at the time *McNally* was decided, application of the decision proved straightforward. Just prior to *McNally*, the Supreme Court, in Griffith v. Kentucky, 479 U.S. 314 (1987), had held that *all* new constitutional rulings should be applied to the benefit of defendants whose cases are still pending on direct appeal. For those defendants whose convictions had already been affirmed on direct appeal, however, the situation was a little more complicated. Defendants still imprisoned based on an "intangible rights" theory sought relief under 28

U.S.C § 2255. See, e.g., Toulabi v. United States, 875 F.2d 122 (7th Cir.1989)(granting such relief). Defendants whose sentences had been fully served generally sought a writ of error coram nobis. See, e.g., United States v. Bush, 888 F.2d 1145 (7th Cir.1989)(denying such relief); United States v. Mandel, 862 F.2d 1067 (4th Cir.1988)(granting such relief).

The premise of collateral attacks based on *McNally* was that the decision should be retroactively applied. The standards for retroactive application of new constitutional rulings in habeas corpus and § 2255 proceedings are now governed by Teague v. Lane, 489 U.S. 288 (1989), and its progeny. See Joseph L. Hoffmann, "The Supreme Court's New Vision of Federal Habeas Corpus for State Prisoners," 1989 Supreme Ct. Rev. 165. Virtually all courts that have addressed the issue under § 2255 have ruled in favor of retroactive application of *McNally*. For a pre-*Teague* example, see United States v. Shelton, 848 F.2d 1485 (10th Cir.1988)(en banc). Coram nobis claims are more difficult. Generally speaking, coram nobis is available to remedy errors in a conviction "of the most fundamental character" where the defendant is not in "custody" but where the conviction has some lingering effect beyond its mere stigma. As the debate between *Bush* and *Mandel* illustrates, the circuits are split as to whether the *McNally* situation meets this standard.

An even more sticky question is whether a defendant whose mail fraud conviction was overturned in light of *McNally* may be retried for the same "fraud," with the prosecution attempting at the retrial to satisfy the Court's new "tangible rights" theory of mail fraud. Pre-*McNally* double jeopardy law held that, in general, a defendant may not be retried if his or her conviction is overturned on grounds of insufficiency of the evidence. See Burks v. United States, 437 U.S. 1 (1978). The idea was that the prosecution should not get a second chance to produce sufficient evidence for a conviction. But should the *Burks* rule apply to this situation, in which the prosecution may have produced more than enough evidence to sustain a conviction under the "intangible rights" theory of mail fraud, only to have the Supreme Court (disagreeing with every Court of Appeals that had addressed the issue) later invalidate that theory?

3. *Carpenter v. United States*. The Court had an opportunity to flesh out the impact of *McNally* on the mail fraud statute the next Term. Carpenter v. United States, 484 U.S. 19 (1987), involved convictions under the wire, mail, and securities fraud statutes. Winans was a reporter for the Wall Street Journal, one of two responsible for writing the column "Heard on the Street," which reviewed positive and negative factors about particular stocks and which, the District Court found, had "an impact on the market, difficult though it may be to quantify in a particular case." It was the official policy of the Journal that the contents of the column were the Journal's confidential information prior to publication. Nevertheless, Winans entered into an arrangement with two stockbrokers at Kidder Peabody to provide them with advance information about the column. When the scheme came to light, they, and a client, had netted $690,000 in profits during a four-month period based on their advance knowledge of the contents of 27 columns.

One of the stockbrokers pleaded guilty under a plea agreement and testified for the government in the trial of Winans, the other stockbroker, and Carpenter, who was Winans roommate. Winans and the stockbroker were convicted as principals, and Carpenter as an aider and abettor. The Court of Appeals affirmed and the Supreme Court granted certiorari. It was equally divided on the securities fraud issues, and thus affirmed. In an opinion by Justice White, it unanimously affirmed the mail and wire fraud convictions.

Three issues were addressed. The first was whether, under *McNally*, the scheme to defraud deprived anyone of "property." On this point the Court held:

> "This is not a case like *McNally*..... The Journal, as Winans employer, was defrauded of much more than its contractual right to honest and faithful service, an interest too ethereal in itself to fall within the protection of the mail fraud statute, which 'had its origin in the desire to protect individual property rights.' *McNally*, supra at n. 8. Here, the object of the scheme was to take the Journal's confidential business information—the publication schedule and contents of the 'Heard' column—and its intangible nature does not make it any less 'property' protected by the mail and wire fraud statutes. *McNally* did not limit the scope of § 1341 to tangible as distinguished from intangible property rights. ... The confidential information was generated from the business and the business had a right to decide how to use it prior to disclosing it to the public."

Second, the Court held that Winans and the other defendants had engaged in a "scheme to defraud" within the statute. "The concept of 'fraud' includes the act of embezzlement," the Court said, and "Winans' undertaking at the Journal was not to reveal prepublication information about his column, a promise that became a sham when in violation of his duty he passed along to his co-conspirators confidential information belonging to the Journal...." Moreover, "Winans continued in the employ of the Journal, appropriating its confidential business information for his own use, all the while pretending to perform his duty of safeguarding it." He had even reported two "leaks" not related to his own scheme, which the Court regarded as demonstrating that he was well aware of the confidential nature of the column and "his deceit as he played the role of loyal employee."

Finally, the Court addressed the issue, dealt with in the next section of these materials, of the required relationship between the mailing and the fraud, whether the mails (and wires in this case) were used "for the purpose of executing" the scheme to defraud. Here the wires and mail were used to print and send the Journal to its customers. This was sufficient because "circulation of the 'Heard' column was not only antici-pated but an essential part of the scheme. Had the column not been made available to Journal customers, there would have been no effect on stock prices and no likelihood of profiting from the information leaked by Winans.''

4. Congressional Reaction to *McNally*. Congressional reaction to *McNally* was swift. As a miscellaneous section added to the comprehensive Drug–Abuse Act of 1988, it added a new section to chapter 63 of title 18:

"§ 1346. Definition of 'scheme or artifice to defraud'

"For the purpose of this chapter, the term 'scheme or artifice to defraud' includes a scheme or artifice to deprive another of the intangible right of honest services.''

Thus, with one stroke of the congressional pen, *McNally* was overruled (with respect to fraudulent schemes that occurred after the effective date of the new statute) and the line of Court of Appeals decisions that it set aside was reinstated. It is for this reason that the thrust of those Court of Appeals decisions is examined in Section 3 of this Chapter.

SECTION 2: RELATION OF THE MAILING TO THE FRAUD

INTRODUCTORY NOTES ON THE RELATION OF THE MAILING TO THE FRAUD

1. Background. As the preceding materials reveal, the mail fraud statute requires proof of two elements: a scheme to defraud (or one of the two alternative forms of fraud) and a mailing "for the purpose of executing such scheme." The second of these two elements has received far more Supreme Court attention than the first. *McNally*, in fact, was the first time since *Durland* that the Court had addressed the first element, and *McNally* is no longer with us.

This section presents two main cases in which the Supreme Court addressed the second element. Before consideration of those cases, however, four prior cases must be examined. As will be seen, the meaning of these four cases figures prominently in the main cases to come.

2. *Kann v. United States*. Triumph Explosives, Inc., was a public corporation that made munitions for the government. Two banks had lent large sums to Triumph under a written agreement under which Triumph was limited in the salaries and bonuses it could pay. In order to get around this limitation, the defendants created the Elk Mills Loading Corporation to act as a subcontractor of Triumph. Forty-nine per cent of the stock in Elk Mills was distributed to the defendants without consideration. The remaining 51 per cent was sold to Triumph in exchange for profitable subcontracts. Salaries, bonuses, and dividends were then paid by Elk Mills to the defendants. The defendants did no substantial work for Elk Mills.

Kann was convicted of two counts of mail fraud.[a] His convictions were affirmed on appeal and the Supreme Court granted certiorari. Each count

---

[a] His codefendants pleaded nolo contendere.

was based on mailings that occurred during the bank collection procedures that followed the cashing of a check. The defendant argued that there was no fraud, but the Court found it unnecessary to reach this question. He also argued that he did not "cause" the checks to be mailed. This question the Court resolved against him. The defendant's third contention was "that the checks were not mailed in the execution of, or for the purpose of executing, the scheme." In Kann v. United States, 323 U.S. 88 (1944), the Court accepted this argument and reversed the convictions.

(i) **The Majority Opinion**. Justice Roberts wrote the opinion for the Court. He began by observing that the checks delivered to the defendants were cashed at a local bank. They received the money it was intended they should receive, and the banks became the owners of the checks. He continued:

"The banks which cashed or credited the checks, being holders in due course, were entitled to collect from the drawee bank in each case and the drawer had no defense to payment. The scheme in each case had reached fruition. The persons intended to receive the money had received it irrevocably. It was immaterial to them, or to any consummation of the scheme, how the bank which paid or credited the check would collect from the drawee bank. It cannot be said that the mailings in question were for the purpose of executing the scheme, as the statute requires.

"The case is to be distinguished from those where the mails are used prior to, and as one step toward, the receipt of the fruits of the fraud..... Also to be distinguished are cases where the use of the mails is a means of concealment so that further frauds which are part of the scheme may be perpetrated. In these the mailing has ordinarily had a much closer relation to further fraudulent conduct than has the mere clearing of a check, although it is conceivable that this alone, in some settings, would be enough. The federal mail fraud statute does not purport to reach all frauds, but only those limited instances in which the use of the mails is a part of the execution of the fraud, leaving all other cases to be dealt with by appropriate state law.

"The government argues that the scheme was not complete, that so long as Elk Mills remained a subcontractor the defendants expected to receive further bonuses and profits and that the clearing of these checks in the ordinary course was essential to its further prosecution. But, even in that view, the scheme was completely executed as respects the transactions in question when the defendants received the money intended to be obtained by their fraud, and the subsequent banking transactions between the banks concerned were merely incidental and collateral to the scheme and not a part of it.

"We hold, therefore, that one element of the offense defined by the statute, namely, that the mailing must be for the purpose of executing the fraud, is lacking in the present case. The judgment must be reversed."

(ii) The Dissent. Justice Douglas, joined by Justices Black, Jackson, and Rutledge, dissented. Justice Douglas said:

"I hardly think we would set this conviction aside if the collecting bank instead of cashing the checks took them for collection only and refused to pay the defendants until the checks had been honored by the drawee. It is plain that the mails would then be used to obtain the fruits of the fraud. And I do not see why the fraud fails to become a federal offense merely because the collecting bank cashes the checks. That would seem to be irrelevant under these circumstances. [T]he object of the scheme was to defraud Triumph; and the use of the mails was an essential step to that end. It is true that the collecting bank was a holder in due course against whom the drawer had no defense. But that does not mean that the fraudulent scheme had reached fruition at that point of time. Yet if legal technicalities rather than practical considerations are to decide that question it should be noted that the defendants were payee-indorsers of the checks. They had received only a conditional credit, or payment as the case may be. It took payment by the drawee to discharge them from their liability as indorsers. Not until then would the defendants receive irrevocably the proceeds of their fraud.

"Moreover, this was not the last step in the fraudulent scheme. It was a continuing venture. Smooth clearances of the checks were essential lest these intermediate dividends be interrupted and the conspirators be called upon to disgorge. Different considerations would be applicable if we were dealing with incidental mailings. But we are not. To obtain money was the sole object of this fraud. The use of the mails was crucial to the total success of the fraudulent project. We are not justified in chopping up the vital banking phase of the scheme into segments and isolating one part from the others. That would be warranted if the scheme were to defraud the collecting bank. But it is plain that these plans had a wider reach and that but for the use of the mails they would not have been finally consummated."

3. *Pereira v. United States*. Pereira v. United States, 347 U.S. 1 (1954), involved a classic confidence game. Pereira and an accomplice met two women as they were checking into a hotel. Pereira, who was 33 years old, declared his attraction for one of them, a wealthy widow, aged 56, later that evening after the two men had persuaded the women to join them for dinner and a round of night clubs. One thing led to another, to the conclusion that Pereira and the widow were married slightly more than a month later. By clever manipulation, Pereira persuaded his wife to come up with $7,000 for a cadillac, which Pereira bought for $4,750 (the events occurred in 1951) and "kept the change." Later, he persuaded her to advance $35,000 towards a hotel venture. Once he obtained the money, he got into his cadillac and left. She got a divorce, and next saw him at his criminal trial.

Pereira was convicted of mail fraud and a violation of the National Stolen Property Act, which at the time provided:

> "§ 2314. Transportation of stolen goods, securities, monies, or articles used in counterfeiting.
>
> "Whoever transports in interstate or foreign commerce any goods, wares, merchandise, securities, or money, of the value of $5,000 or more, knowing the same to have been stolen, converted, or taken by fraud ... [s]hall be fined not more than $10,000 or imprisoned not more than ten years, or both."[b]

In an opinion unanimous as to Pereira, the Supreme Court affirmed. The mail fraud conviction was based on the $35,000 check, which was written on a California bank by a securities broker in Los Angeles and apparently mailed to the widow in Texas. She gave it to Pereira, who endorsed it for collection to an El Paso bank. Three days later, after the check had cleared, Pereira obtained a cashier's check from the El Paso bank and began his journey in the cadillac.

Chief Justice Warren's reasoning for the Court was brief:

> "Petitioners do not deny that the proof offered establishes that they planned to defraud Mrs. Joyce. Collecting the proceeds of the check was an essential part of the scheme. For this purpose, Pereira delivered the check drawn on a Los Angeles bank to the El Paso bank. There was substantial evidence to show that the check was mailed from Texas to California, in the ordinary course of business.
>
> "The elements of the offense of mail fraud ... are (1) a scheme to defraud, and (2) a mailing of a letter, etc., for the purpose of executing the scheme. It is not necessary that the scheme contemplate the use of the mails as an essential element. United States v. Young, 232 U.S. 155 (1914). Here, the scheme to defraud is established, and the mailing of the check by the bank, incident to an essential part of the scheme, is established. There remains only the question whether Pereira 'caused' the mailing. Where one does an act with knowledge that the use of the mails will follow in the ordinary course of business, or where such use can reasonably be foreseen, even though not actually intended, then he 'causes' the mails to be used. The conclusion that Pereira's conviction under this count was proper follows naturally from this factor."

Kann was not mentioned.

---

[b] The Act was recently amended to substitute "transports, transmits, or transfers" for "transports," and "fined under this title" for "fined not more than $10,000." See 102 Stat. 4402, 108 Stat. 2147.

Several other questions were addressed by the Court. The first was whether Pereira could also be convicted under the National Stolen Property Act, for the same behavior, without violating double jeopardy. (The subject of double jeopardy will be discussed in greater detail in Chapter IV, Section 3, infra.) The Court answered in the affirmative, "so long as each [statute] requires proof of a fact not essential to the other," citing Blockburger v. United States, 284 U.S. 299 (1932). The elements of the stolen property offense were "(1) knowledge that certain property has been stolen or obtained by fraud, and (2) transporting it, or causing it to be transported, in interstate commerce." The Court reasoned:

> "It is obvious that the mail fraud offense requires different proof. The transporting charge does not require proof that any specific means of transporting were used, or that the acts were done pursuant to a scheme to defraud, as is required for the mail fraud charge. When Pereira delivered the check, drawn on an out-of-state bank, to the El Paso bank for collection, he 'caused' it to be transported in interstate commerce. It is common knowledge that such checks must be sent to the drawee bank for collection, and it follows that Pereira intended the El Paso bank to send this check across state lines."

The Court then turned to whether there was sufficient evidence to convict Pereira's accomplice as an aider and abettor of the scheme. The Court found that there was. It was this issue that produced a dissent by three Justices.[c]

4. *Parr v. United States*. Parr v. United States, 363 U.S. 370 (1960), involved a pervasive fraud perpetrated over a five-year period by nine individuals and two banks. Essentially, the evidence showed that they did three kinds of things: (1) they misappropriated approximately $185,000 of the funds of a school district by causing its checks to be issued in small amounts over the years to fictitious persons, or to members of their families, checks which they then cashed and the proceeds of which they kept; (2) they forged endorsements on district checks, cashed them, and kept proceeds totaling approximately another $25,000; and (3) they obtained gas and oil on credit cards issued to the district. One of them, a lawyer, also remodeled his office at district expense to the extent of around $2,500. The defendants were in a position to do all these things because three of them were on the District Board (out of seven members), one was the tax assessor-collector, one the Board secretary, one the Board lawyer, and three were in control of the banks in which Board money was deposited.

---

[c] Two other issues were discussed. One was whether the conviction of the defendants on the substantive counts and a conspiracy to commit the crimes underlying those substantive counts "constitutes double jeopardy." Following well-established precedent, the Court said that it did not. The other was whether there was sufficient evidence to support the conspiracy conviction that they *agreed* to use the mails or to transport stolen property in interstate commerce. It was clear from the facts that Pereira know that an out-of-state bank would be involved in getting the money and that, the Court said, was sufficient.

Nineteen counts of mail fraud were based on these activities and a twentieth count charged a conspiracy to commit the offense outlined in one of the counts. The defendants were convicted on all counts and their convictions were affirmed by the Court of Appeals. Parr, the ringleader, was sentenced to 10 years imprisonment and a fine of $20,000. Four of the other individuals were sentenced to prison terms ranging from five to three years, and four were given suspended sentences and put on probation. The two corporate defendants were fined modest amounts ($2,000 and $900, respectively). The Supreme Court granted certiorari and reversed.

(i) The Majority Opinion. There were, undoubtedly, numerous mailings over the years in connection with such massive fraud, but the government chose to rest its case on 19 such acts, each occurring within a particular division of the District Court in Houston, Texas.[d] The tone of the majority's reaction to the government's approach is revealed in its concluding paragraph:

> "The strongest element in the government's case is that petitioners' behavior was shown to have been so bad and brazen, which, coupled with the inability or at least the failure of the state authorities to bring them to justice, doubtless persuaded the government to undertake this prosecution.[e] But the showing, however convincing, that state crimes of misappropriation, conversion, embezzlement and theft were committed does not establish the federal crime of using the mails to defraud, and, under our vaunted legal system, no man, however bad his behavior, may be convicted of a crime of which he was not charged, proven and found guilty in accordance with due process."

(a) The First 16 Counts. The mailings in the first 16 counts were summarized by the Court as "the letter notice of a modification in assessed valuation, two letters giving notice of hearings before the Board of Equalization to determine taxable value of property, one letter complying with a property owner's request for an 'auxiliary tax notice,' and 12 checks of taxpayers and their letters of transmittal." Each of these letters, in other words, was associated with the collection of real estate taxes, the level of which was determined by the District Board and the income from which supplied the major source of revenue for the School District.

The Court, in a lengthy opinion by Justice Whittaker, laboriously summarized the indictments and the 6,000 pages of evidence received at the trial. It began its analysis by observing:

[d] The government had in mind the requirement of Rule 18 of the Federal Rules of Criminal Procedure, which says that venue for a federal criminal case shall lie in "the district in which the offense was committed," but where there are two or more divisions, "in a division in which the offense was committed."

[e] There had been numerous prosecutions of some of the defendants under state law, but each successful conviction had been reversed on appeal.—[Footnote by eds.]

"There can be no doubt that the indictment charged and the
evidence tended strongly to show that petitioners devised and
practiced a brazen scheme to defraud by misappropriating, converting and embezzling the District's moneys and property. Counsel for petitioners concede that this is so. But, as they correctly
say, these were essentially state crimes and could become federal
ones, under the mail fraud statute, only if the mails were used 'for
the purpose of executing such scheme.' "

The defendants' argument was that the Board was required by Texas
law to assess and collect taxes and that the taxes themselves were not
shown in any way to be unlawful. The letters enumerated in the indictment, they continued, were mailed pursuant to this lawful function and
were not themselves part of the fraud or sent "for the purpose of executing" the fraud.

The government responded with three theories. First, the mailings
associated with the tax collection process were nonetheless a "step in the
scheme" to defraud the School District even though they were lawful.
Second, the taxes were in fact unlawful because they were padded, that is,
the defendants were able to induce the Board to set the tax rate higher
than was necessary to meet the expenses of the School District, thus
allowing an excess which they were able to appropriate over time. Thus
the mailings in the first 16 counts were a necessary part of the scheme,
since they were part of a process that produced "excess" funds that were
there for the taking. Third, not only was the property of the School
District obtained by fraud, so was the property of the taxpayers. The tax
assessments and mailings were in effect a representation to the taxpayers
that the rates were lawfully set and the moneys would be used for lawful
purposes. Thus, in effect false promises were made, and the mailings in
the first 16 counts were an essential part of this scheme.

The Court responded to the government's second theory first, observing that

"after a most careful examination we are compelled to say that the
indictment did not expressly or impliedly charge, and there was no
evidence tending to show, that the taxes assessed were excessive,
'padded' or in any way illegal. Nor did the court submit any such
issue to the jury."

In fact, the Court added, the *defendants* asked for such an instruction and
it was refused. Instead, the government's position at the trial, the Court
said, was that the taxes were lawful and that the defendants' fraud left the
School Board in debt—that is, the money taken was not from "excess"
funds generated by overtaxation, but in effect was diverted from projects on
which it could lawfully have been spent by the School Board. The
government's second theory, the Court said, was injected into the case by
the Court of Appeals in an effort to save the case. In effect, the argument
came too late.

The Court then turned to the government's first theory. It said:

"The crucial question, respecting Counts 1 through 16 of the indictment, then comes down to whether the legally compelled mailings of the lawful—or, more properly, what are not charged or shown to be unlawful—letters, tax statements, checks and receipts, complained of in those counts, properly may be said to have been for the purpose of executing a scheme to defraud because those legally compelled to cause and causing those mailings planned to steal an indefinite part of the receipts.

"The fact that a scheme may violate state laws does not exclude it from the proscriptions of the federal mail fraud statute, for Congress 'may forbid any [mailings] in furtherance of a scheme that it regards as contrary to public policy, whether it can forbid the scheme or not.' Badders v. United States, 240 U.S. 391, 393 (1916). In exercise of that power, Congress enacted § 1341 forbidding and making criminal any use of the mails 'for the purpose of executing [a] scheme' to defraud or to obtain money by false representations—leaving generally the matter of what conduct may constitute such a scheme for determination under other laws. Its purpose was 'to prevent the post office from being used to carry [such schemes] into effect....' Durland v. United States, 161 U.S. 306, 314 (1896). Thus, as its terms and purpose make clear, '[t]he federal mail fraud statute does not purport to reach all frauds, but only those limited instances in which the use of the mails is a part of the execution of the fraud, leaving all other cases to be dealt with by appropriate state law.' Kann v. United States, 323 U.S. 88, 95 (1944). Therefore, only if the mailings were 'a part of the execution of the fraud,' or, as we said in Pereira v. United States, 347 U.S. 1, 8 (1954), were 'incident to an essential part of the scheme,' do they fall within the ban of the federal mail fraud statute. ...

"[I]n light of the particular circumstances of this case, and especially of the facts (1) that the School Board was legally required to assess and collect taxes, (2) that the indictment did not charge nor the proofs show that the taxes assessed and collected were in excess of the District's needs or that they were 'padded' or in any way unlawful, (3) that no such issue was submitted to, nor, hence, determined by the jury, (4) that the Board was compelled to collect and receipt for the taxes by state law, which, in the circumstances here, compelled it to use and *cause* (here, principally by permitting) the use of the mails for those purposes, we must conclude that the legally compelled mailings, complained of in the first 16 counts of the indictment, were not shown to have been unlawful 'step[s] in a plot,' *Badders v. United States*, supra, 240 U.S., at 394, 'part[s] of the execution of the fraud,' *Kann v. United States*, supra, 323 U.S., at 95, 'incident to an essential part of the scheme,' *Pereira v. United States*, supra, 347 U.S., at 8, or to have been made 'for the purpose of executing such scheme,' within the meaning of § 1341, for we think it cannot be said that mailings made or caused to be made under the imperative command of duty imposed by state law are criminal under the federal mail fraud statute, even though some of those who are so required to do the mailing for the District plan to steal, when or after received, some indefinite part of its moneys."[f]

The Court then turned to the government's third theory. It was a sufficient basis to reject this theory, the Court said, that the letters on which the first 16 counts relied did not themselves contain any misrepresentations.

(b) The Remaining Counts. As to counts 17 through 19, which charged the obtaining of gasoline and other filling station products on credit cards issued to the School District, the analysis was different. The Court said:

> "The mailings complained of in those counts were two invoices, said to contain amounts for items so procured ..., mailed by the oil company ... to the District ... and the District's check mailed to the oil company ... in payment of the latter invoice. We think these counts are ruled by *Kann v. United States*, supra. Here, as in *Kann*, '[t]he scheme in each case had reached fruition' when [the defendants] received the goods and services complained of. 'The persons intended to receive the [goods and services] and received [them] irrevocably. It was immaterial to them, or to any consummation of the scheme, how the [oil company] would collect from the [District]. It cannot be said that the mailings in question were for the purpose of executing the scheme, as the statute requires.' 323 U.S., at 94 [brackets in the internal quotations by the Court]."

Count 20, which charged a conspiracy to commit the substantive offense underlying the first count, fell with the count on which it was based.

(ii) The Dissent. Justice Frankfurter, not to be outmatched, wrote a lengthy, if less convoluted, dissent. He was joined by Justices Harlan and Stewart.

(a) The First 16 Counts. Frankfurter saw the question presented as to the first 16 counts as:

> "whether the act is violated by a public officer vested by law with a discretionary power to levy taxes for the purpose of providing funds estimated to meet projected expenditures for a statutorily defined public need for the satisfaction of which the power is entrusted to him, who exercises that power over several years to collect through the mails sums which could as a matter of law be so expended, but a portion of which he at all times, throughout successive years of fixing the tax rate and utilizing the proceeds, actually intends to and does appropriate to his own uses."

---

[f] Yes, this paragraph *is* all one sentence.

He thought it "established beyond peradventure that [the defendants'] abuse of the District's powers was a seamless fraudulent scheme, conceived and executed as such with every element of the enterprise interdependent with every other." He pointed out that the defendants, who effectively controlled the School District, "raised the tax rate to the statutory maximum," and then "regularly spent less than the amount collected on the schools, created no reserves, and appropriated a portion of the proceeds to their own use." For him it was critical that the tax rate, up to the statutory maximum, was discretionary: "No Texas statute required them to collect what they intended to spend to keep the schools running, plus an amount which they intended to misappropriate, and that is precisely what the proof established and the jury found that they did." He continued:

> "Petitioners' claim raises the further question whether, even if the mailings were not immune in themselves, they were too remote from the purpose of the fraudulently designed scheme to be deemed in 'execution' of it. Whether a mailing which occurs in discernable relation to a scheme to defraud is an execution of it is a question of the degree of proximity of the mailing to the scheme. The statute was enacted 'with the purpose of protecting the public against all such intentional efforts to despoil, and to prevent the post office from being used to carry them into effect....' " Durland v. United States, 161 U.S. 306, 314 (1896). Whether the post office was so used must be the Court's central inquiry. If the use of the mails occurred not as a step in but only after the consummation of the scheme, the fraud is the exclusive concern of the states. Kann v. United States, 323 U.S. 88 (1944). The adequate degree of relationship between a mailing which occurs during the life of a scheme and the scheme is of course not a matter susceptible of geometric determination. ... The determining question is whether the mailing was designed materially to aid the consummation of the scheme....

> "For the purposes of the statute, the significance of the relationship between scheme and mailing depends on the interconnection of the parts in a particular scheme. Ordinarily, once the fraud is proved, its scope is not a matter of dispute. But when, as here, the fraud involves the abuse of a position of public trust, closer analysis is required. Petitioners seek to denude their scheme of its range and pervasiveness. They construct an artifact whereby their fraudulent scheme was, as it were, intramural, unrelated to taxpayers to whom they sent the tax bills, and so the mails, the ingenuous argument runs, were not used in the fraud because the wrongdoing only arose after the mails had fulfilled their function by bringing the returns. The wrong is thus nicely pigeonholed as embezzlement, without any prior scheme.

> "The fraudulent, episodic, petty-cash peculations of a clerk at a regulatory agency are frauds upon that agency, and although taxpayers generally are injured by the fraud and in that sense are

the ultimate objects of it, the mailings by which the tax proceeds are collected which constitute the vast government funds out of which the agency's funds are taken, are, as a matter of practical good sense by which law determines such issues of causation too remote from the scheme to be deemed in execution of it. But to analogize petitioners' scheme to a conventional case of peculation by an employee, whether public or private, is to disregard the facts of this case.

"The petitioners themselves controlled the entire conduct of the District's fiscal affairs, and their own decision, limited only by a statutory ceiling, determined the amount of the tax that would be collected. Petitioners' exercise of their power to fix the amount of the tax, an exercise which ultimately assured to themselves an excess of funds over their intended expenditures or reserves for school purposes, was necessarily central to their scheme. Such control obliterates the line they seek to draw between themselves and the entity it was their duty to serve. By demanding and collecting what they intended to misappropriate they made the process of collection an inseparable element of their scheme."

"The petitioners' control of the District and therefore of its tax rate, similarly disposes of their contentions that one or another element of a technical fraud upon the taxpayers of the District is absent. The suggestion that in the collection of taxes there was no representation by petitioners to the taxpayers of the District might be pertinent were the system a self-executing tax structure under which the time for, and amount of, the payment due and the payee to whom it is to be made are designated by statute, so that the tax collector, serving as an automatic conduit, does nothing to cause collection of the tax. These collectors, however, were the prime actors in the structure. They not only billed the taxpayers but also fixed the rate of the tax itself. For that reason it cannot be said that the taxpayers paid their taxes solely under compulsion of Texas law, and not at all in reliance upon the implied false representation of petitioners that the amounts assessed were collected to meet projected expenditures. . . .

"[T]hey urge an absence of detriment to the taxpayers . . . since their payments were ordinarily credited to them on the District's books. The claim is frivolous. Whether they are viewed as having overpaid for school services, or having been deprived of services for which they paid, the detriment to the taxpayers is self-evident. . . . Here inescapably the bills were padded by the predetermined increase, which, though within technical legal limits, was for fraudulent ends. . . . If the fraudulent enterprise of which this record reeks is not a scheme essentially to defraud the taxpayers who constitute the District rather than a disembodied, abstract entity called the District, English words have lost their meaning."

Justice Frankfurter then argued that the indictment, the way the case was tried, and the trial court's charge "adequately placed" these theories before the jury.

(b) **The Remaining Counts**. On counts 17 through 19, Frankfurter responded to the majority's reliance on *Kann*:

"[I]t is urged that, under the rationale of Kann v. United States, 323 U.S. 88 (1944), the mailings, even if caused by petitioners, were not in execution of a scheme to defraud because the scheme was consummated once they received the gasoline. *Kann v. United States* found an appropriate instance of such a limitation; but it also expressly excepted from the force of the rule situations in which the subsequent mailing has the function of affording 'concealment so that further frauds which are part of the scheme may be perpetrated.' Here the jury might properly have found that consumption of gasoline for private purposes was but one device of petitioners for turning their control of the District to their personal advantage, and that the continuing presentation and payment of the bills, and not merely the receipt of the gasoline, was the purpose of the scheme."

As to the conspiracy count, "no substantial objections" were raised "that are not disposed of by what has already been said."

5. *United States v. Sampson*. In United States v. Sampson, 371 U.S. 75 (1962), 43 substantive counts of mail fraud were stated in an indictment against officers, directors and employees of a nationwide corporation, with regional offices in various states. The corporation was also a defendant. The District Court dismissed 34 of the substantive counts. The case came to the Supreme Court on the government's direct appeal.

The allegations were that the ostensible purpose of the corporation was to help clients obtain loans or sell their businesses. Salesmen secured "contracts" with prospective clients by representing the services to be performed, but the defendants "did not intend to and did not in fact make any substantial efforts to perform these promised services." The clients were persuaded to give their check for an "advance fee," refundable if their "contracts" were not accepted by the home office. These fees were immediately converted into cashiers' checks and forwarded to the appropriate regional office. All contracts were then "accepted" and an acceptance letter was mailed to the victims together with a form letter stating that the services would be performed. Various perfunctory acts thereafter occurred to assure the victims that progress was being made. Complaints by victims were met with further false representations that efforts would continue and the services would be performed. The indictment alleged, in short, "that the scheme, as originally planned by the defendants and as actually carried out, included fraudulent activities both before and after the victims had actually given over their money to the defendants."

The use of the mails relied on in the dismissed counts of the indictment "was the mailing by the defendants of their acceptances of the victims' applications for their services."   The government conceded that the defendants had obtained all the money they expected to get from that victim *before* these mailings occurred.   The District Court relied on *Kann* and *Parr* in holding that, since the money had already been received, any subsequent mailings could not have been "for the purpose of executing" the fraudulent scheme.

(i) **The Majority Opinion**.   In an opinion by Justice Black, the Supreme Court reversed.   After summarizing the holdings of *Kann* and *Parr*, it said:

"We are unable to find anything in either the *Kann* or the *Parr* case which suggests that the Court was laying down an automatic rule that a deliberate, planned use of the mails after the victims' money had been obtained can never be 'for the purpose of executing' the defendants' scheme.   Rather the Court found only that under the facts in those cases the schemes had been fully executed before the mails were used. . . .

"Moreover, . . . the indictment in this case alleged that the defendant's scheme contemplated from the start the commission of fraudulent activities which were to be and actually were carried out both before and after the money was obtained from the victims.   The indictment specifically alleged that the signed copies of the accepted applications and the covering letters were mailed by the defendants to the victims for the purpose of lulling them by assurances that the promised services would be performed.   We cannot hold that such a deliberate and planned use of the United States mails by defendants engaged in a nationwide, fraudulent scheme in pursuance of a previously formulated plan could not, if established by evidence, be found by a jury under proper instructions to be 'for the purpose of executing' a scheme within the meaning of the mail fraud statute.   For these reasons, we hold that it was error for the District Court to dismiss these 34 substantive counts."

(ii) **The Dissent**.   Justice Douglas dissented.   He that thought the Court's decision "materially qualifies" *Parr*:

"There, in the face of the jury's verdict, we held that a check on a third party's funds, mailed to pay for property after the property had been fraudulently 'obtained,' could not be 'for the purpose of executing' a scheme to obtain the property.   As the statute makes clear, there is only one foundation for prosecution under the statute and that is using the mails 'for the purpose of executing' the various schemes described in the act.   So far as is relevant here, those schemes are either to defraud or to obtain money by false or fraudulent representations.

"It is possible that in this case indictments could be drawn which charge the use of mails *to lull existing victims* into a feeling of security so that a scheme to obtain money *from other victims* could be successfully consummated. The opinion does not so construe the indictment but concludes, as I read it, that the mere lulling of existing victims into a sense of security is enough.[2] If that is enough, then in the *Parr* case it would seem that we should have sustained the conviction because the defendants there may well have wanted the third party to pay for the property that had been fraudulently obtained so that they would not be apprehended. In the *Parr* case, as here, there was 'a continuing course of conduct' (to borrow a phrase from the dissent) not only to obtain money fraudulently but also to conceal the fraud so that future peculations might be possible. In *Parr*, future peculations from the same taxpayers were part of the scheme. Here there is no suggestion that those previously defrauded were to be defrauded a second time. The mails were used only to tranquilize those already defrauded. Or at least that is the only way I can read this indictment. It is therefore a much weaker case than *Parr*.

"We should not struggle to uphold poorly drawn counts. To do so only encourages more federal prosecution in fields that are essentially local."

6. Questions and Comments on the Relationship of the Mailing to the Fraud. Has the Supreme Court been consistent in applying the "for the purpose of executing [the] scheme or artifice" language of the statute? Specifically, what is the difference between *Kann* and *Pereira*? In *Kann*, the defendants received cash for their checks, which then went through the collection process. In *Pereira*, the defendant had to wait three days for the check to clear before he obtained the money. If this is the relevant difference, does it make any sense for the availability of a federal mail fraud conviction to turn on such technicalities of the bank collection process? Does a trusting bank as opposed to a cautious bank have any bearing on any issue that should rightfully determine the federal criminal liability of a swindler? Is the problem with the way the statute is written, or with the way the Court has interpreted it?

Now compare *Parr* and *Sampson*. Can one reconcile *Parr*'s treatment of counts 17 through 19 with the decision in *Sampson*? Or is Douglas right that *Sampson* "materially qualifies" *Parr*? Or is the answer that the government got its theory straight in *Sampson* having learned its lesson in *Parr*? Notice in any event the critical nature of the government's theory and proof. It seems clear that the government could have prevailed on the first 16 counts in *Parr*, had it alleged and proved "padding" of the tax bills. If this is right, on what grounds are such jurisdictional esoterica justified? Does it make any sense, or in any material way change the underlying offense to federal interests of the defendants' behavior, for criminality in a case like *Parr* to turn on such niceties of pleading?

---

[2] "The indictment, as I read it, charges on this phase only 'lulling said victims' into a sense of security."

Consider, in this respect, one further aspect of *Parr*. Did the defendants defraud the School District or the taxpayers? Couldn't the answer be "both"? If so, is the Court's analysis of the issue of taxpayer-fraud persuasive? It said, simply, that there were no misrepresentations in the letters to or from the taxpayers. Does this matter? Is it required that the mailing itself contain fraudulent statements?

Consider also the mens rea requirements the Court is imposing. The statute says "for the *purpose* of executing" the fraudulent scheme. In what sense is the word "purpose" used? Does it mean "use the mails with the conscious objective of promoting the scheme"? Chief Justice Warren said in *Pereira* that it was not necessary that the scheme "contemplate" use of the mails. It was enough that the scheme to defraud was established, and that the mailing was "incident to an essential part of the scheme". What kind of "purpose" is this? Do the other cases agree on this point? The issue in *Pereira* was "causation," which was established if one "knows" that the use of the mails will follow, "or where such use can reasonably be foreseen". The statute says that one must mail or "knowingly cause" a mailing. What kind of "knowledge" is this? Do the other cases agree on this point?

It is also useful to compare the language of the National Stolen Property Act to the mail fraud statute. In 1956, just two years after the *Pereira* decision, Congress added a provision to the stolen property statute virtually tracking the mail fraud statute, albeit with a different jurisdictional trigger.[g] Notice, however, that the transportation under the stolen property statute must be "in the execution *or concealment* of a scheme or artifice" to defraud. Presumably this would make a case like *Sampson* easy, if one substituted "transportation" for "use of the mails" on the facts. The "acceptance letter" and its accompanying form assurances were certainly part of an effort to "conceal" the fraud. Did *Sampson* in effect read the "concealment" language into the mail fraud statute? If so, do the other cases agree?

At a broader level, as raised by some of the questions above, these cases raise substantial concerns about the wisdom of the jurisdictional fetish that so dominates the federal criminal law. As with other statutes that have been examined to this point, the focus of debate is shifted from the essential criminality of the defendants' behavior to technical niceties of pleading and proof that must focus on the satisfaction of esoteric jurisdictional predicates. A great deal of pressure is placed on United States

---

[g] The provision added in 1956, with subsequent amendments indicated by brackets, now reads as follows:

"Whoever, having devised or intending to devise any scheme or artifice to defraud, or for obtaining money or property by means of false or fraudulent pretenses, representations, or promises, transports or causes to be transported, or induces any person [or persons] to travel in, or to be transported in interstate [or foreign] commerce in the execution or concealment of a scheme or artifice to defraud that person [or those persons] of money or property having a value of $5,000 or more ... [s]hall be fined [under this title] or imprisoned not more than ten years, or both." 18 U.S.C. § 2314.

Attorneys, at the outset of the case, to contort the facts to meet jurisdictional pressures. Is this any way to run a railroad?

United States v. Maze

Supreme Court of the United States, 1974.
414 U.S. 395.

■ JUSTICE REHNQUIST delivered the opinion of the Court.

In February 1971 respondent Thomas E. Maze moved to Louisville, Kentucky, and there shared an apartment with Charles L. Meredith. In the spring of that year respondent's fancy lightly turned to thoughts of the sunny Southland, and he thereupon took Meredith's BankAmericard and his 1968 automobile and headed for Southern California. By presenting the BankAmericard and signing Meredith's name, respondent obtained food and lodging at motels located in California, Florida, and Louisiana. Each of these establishments transmitted to the Citizens Fidelity Bank & Trust Co. in Louisville, which had issued the BankAmericard to Meredith, the invoices representing goods and services furnished to respondent. Meredith, meanwhile, on the day after respondent's departure from Louisville, notified the Louisville bank that his credit card had been stolen.

Upon respondent's return to Louisville he was indicted on four counts of violation of the federal mail fraud statute, 18 U.S.C. § 1341, and one count of violation of the Dyer Act, 18 U.S.C. § 2312. The mail fraud counts of the indictment charged that respondent had devised a scheme to defraud the Louisville bank, Charles L. Meredith, and several merchants in different states by unlawfully obtaining possession of the BankAmericard issued by the Louisville bank to Meredith, and using the card to obtain goods and services. The indictment charged that respondent had obtained goods and services at four specified motels by presenting Meredith's BankAmericard for payment and representing himself to be Meredith, and that respondent knew that each merchant would cause the sales slips of the purchases to be delivered by mail to the Louisville bank which would in turn mail them to Meredith for payment. The indictment also charged that the delay in this mailing would enable the respondent to continue purchasing goods and services for an appreciable period of time.

Respondent was tried by a jury in the United States District Court for the Western District of Kentucky. At trial, representatives of the four motels identified the sales invoices from the transactions on Meredith's BankAmericard which were forwarded to the Louisville bank by their motels. An official of the Louisville bank testified that all of the sales invoices for those transactions were received by the bank in due course through the mail, and that this was the customary method by which invoices representing BankAmericard purchases were transmitted to the Louisville bank. The jury found respondent guilty as charged on all counts, and he appealed the judgment of conviction to the Court of Appeals for the Sixth Circuit. That court reversed the judgment as to the mail fraud statute, but affirmed it as to the Dyer Act.[1] Because of an apparent conflict among the courts of appeals as to the circumstances under which the fraudulent use of a credit card may violate the mail fraud statute, we granted the government's petition for certiorari. For the reasons stated below, we affirm the judgment of the Court of Appeals.

The applicable parts of the mail fraud statute provide as follows:[3]

"Whoever, having devised or intending to devise any scheme or artifice to defraud, or for obtaining money or property by means of false or fraudulent pretenses, representations, or promises ... for the purpose of executing such scheme or artifice or attempting so to do ... knowingly causes to be delivered by mail according to the direction thereon, or at the place at which it is directed to be delivered by the person to whom it is addressed, any [matter or thing whatever to be sent or delivered by the Postal Service] shall be fined not more than $1,000 or imprisoned not more than five years, or both." 18 U.S.C. § 1341.

In Pereira v. United States, 347 U.S. 1, 8–9 (1954), the Court held that one "causes" the mails to be used where he "does an act with knowledge that the use of the mails will follow in the ordinary course of business, or where such use can reasonably be foreseen, even though not actually intended...." We assume, as did the Court of Appeals, that the evidence would support a finding by the jury that Maze "caused" the mailings of the invoices he signed from the out-of-state motels to the Louisville bank. But the more difficult question is whether these mailings were sufficiently closely related to respondent's scheme to bring his conduct within the statute.[4]

[1] The Court of Appeals determined that even though it affirmed respondent's Dyer Act conviction, for which he had received a concurrent five-year sentence, it should also consider the mail fraud convictions as well. There is no jurisdictional barrier to such a decision, Benton v. Maryland, 395 U.S. 784 (1969), and the court decided that "no considerations of judicial economy or efficiency have been urged to us that would outweigh the interest of appellant in the opportunity to clear his record of a conviction of a federal felony." We agree that resolution of the mail fraud questions presented by this case is appropriate.

[3] The full text of the section reads as follows:

"Whoever, having devised or intending to devise any scheme or artifice to defraud, or for obtaining money or property by means of false or fraudulent pretenses, representations, or promises, or to sell, dispose of, loan, exchange, alter, give away, distribute, supply, or furnish or procure for unlawful use any counterfeit or spurious coin, obligation, security, or other article, or anything represented to be or intimated or held out to be such counterfeit or spurious article, for the purpose of executing such scheme or artifice or attempting so to do, places in any post office or authorized depository for mail matter, any matter or thing whatever to be sent or delivered by the Postal Service, or takes or receives therefrom, any such matter or thing, or knowingly causes to be delivered by mail according to the direction thereon, or at the place at which it is directed to be delivered by the person to whom it is addressed, any such matter or thing, shall be fined not more than $1,000 or imprisoned not more than five years, or both." 18 U.S.C. § 1341.

[4] The government indicates that in 1969 it was estimated that more than 300 million consumer credit cards were in circulation,

Under the statute, the mailing must be "for the purpose of executing the scheme, as the statute requires," Kann v. United States, 323 U.S. 88, 94 (1944), but "[i]t is not necessary that the scheme contemplate the use of the mails as an essential element," *Pereira v. United States*, supra, at 8. The government relies on *Pereira*, supra, and United States v. Sampson, 371 U.S. 75 (1962), to support its position, while respondent relies on *Kann v. United States*, supra, and Parr v. United States, 363 U.S. 370 (1960).

In *Kann*, supra, corporate officers and directors were accused of having set up a dummy corporation through which to divert profits of their own corporation to their own use. As a part of the scheme, the defendants were accused of having fraudulently obtained checks payable to them which were cashed or deposited at a bank and then mailed for collection to the drawee bank. This Court held that the fraud was completed at the point at which defendants cashed the checks:

> "The scheme in each case had reached fruition. The persons intended to receive the money had received it irrevocably. It was immaterial to them, or to any consummation of the scheme, how the bank which paid or credited the check would collect from the drawee bank. It cannot be said that the mailings in question were for the purpose of executing the scheme, as the statute requires."

In *Parr*, supra, the defendants were charged, inter alia, with having obtained gasoline and other products and services for their own purposes by the unauthorized use of a gasoline credit card issued to the school district which employed them. The oil company which furnished products and services to the defendants would mail invoices to the school district for payment, and the school district's payment was made by check sent in the mail. Relying on *Kann*, the Court again found that there was not a sufficient connection between the mailing and the execution of the defendants' scheme, because it was immaterial to the defendants how the oil company went about collecting its payment.

The defendant in *Pereira*, supra, was charged with having defrauded a wealthy widow of her property after marrying her. The Court describes the conduct of defendant in these words:

> "Pereira asked his then wife if she would join him in the hotel venture and advance $35,000 toward the purchase price of $78,-000. She agreed. It was then agreed, between her and Pereira, that she would sell some securities that she possessed in Los Angeles, and bank the money in a bank of his choosing in El Paso. On June 15, she received the check for $35,000 on the Citizens National Bank of Los Angeles from her brokers in Los Angeles, and gave it to Pereira, who endorsed it for collection to the State

with annual charges between $40 billion and $60 billion. It was also estimated that, in 1969, 1.5 million cards were lost or stolen, and that losses due to fraud had risen from $20 million in 1966 to $100 million in 1969.

The mail fraud statute, first enacted in 1872, while obviously not directed at credit card frauds as such, is sufficiently general in its language to include them if the requirements of the statute are otherwise met.

National Bank of El Paso. The check cleared, and on June 18, a cashier's check for $35,000 was drawn in favor of Pereira.''

Thus the mailings in *Pereira* played a significant part in enabling the defendant in that case to acquire dominion over the $35,000, with which he ultimately absconded.[5] Unlike the mailings in *Pereira*, the mailings here were directed to the end of adjusting accounts between the motel proprietor, the Louisville bank, and Meredith, all of whom had to a greater or lesser degree been the victims of respondent's scheme. Respondent's scheme reached fruition when he checked out of the motel, and there is no indication that the success of his scheme depended in any way on which of his victims ultimately bore the loss.[6] Indeed, from his point of view, he probably would have preferred to have the invoices misplaced by the various motel personnel and never mailed at all.

The government, however, relying on *United States v. Sampson*, supra, argues that essential to the success of any fraudulent credit-card scheme is the "delay" caused by use of the mails "which aids the perpetrator ... in the continuation of a fraudulent credit card scheme and the postponement of its detection." In *Sampson*, various employees of a nationwide corporation were charged with a scheme to defraud businessmen by obtaining advance fees on the promise that the defendants would either help the businessmen to obtain loans or to sell their businesses. Even after the checks representing the fees had been deposited to the accounts of the defendants, however, the plan called for the mailing of the accepted application together with a form letter assuring the victims that the services for which they had contracted would be performed. The Court found that *Kann* and *Parr* did not preclude the application of the mail fraud statute to "a deliberate, planned use of the mails after the victims' money had been obtained."

We do not believe that *Sampson* sustains the government's position. The subsequent mailings there were designed to lull the victims into a false sense of security, postpone their ultimate complaint to the authorities, and therefore make the apprehension of the defendants less likely than if no mailings had taken place. But the successful completion of the mailings

---

[5] While it is clearly implied in this Court's opinion in *Pereira* that the El Paso bank did not immediately credit the account of the defendant, but instead awaited advice from the Los Angeles bank to which it had mailed the check, the opinion of the Court of Appeals for the Fifth Circuit in *Pereira* makes that fact abundantly clear:

"The return of [the] check from Texas to California constitutes the mailing referred to in the first count..... In mailing the check back to the bank in California on which it was drawn, the El Paso, Texas, bank sent 'instructions to wire fate,' meaning to wire whether the item was paid or not. Upon receiving a

telegram stating that the check had been paid, the bank in El Paso gave Pereira its cashier's check for $35,286.01, which Pereira promptly cashed on June 19, 1951.''

[6] Mr. Justice White's dissenting opinion indicates that respondent engaged in a "two-week, $2,000 transcontinental spending spree." While we are not sure of the legal significance of the amounts fraudulently charged on the credit card by the respondent, we note that the four counts of mail fraud charged in the indictment were based on charges on Meredith's credit card totaling $301.85.

from the motel owners here to the Louisville bank increased the probability that respondent would be detected and apprehended.   There was undoubtedly delay in transmitting invoices to the Louisville bank, as there is in the physical transmission of any business correspondence between cities separated by large distances.   Mail service as a means of transmitting such correspondence from one city to another is designed to overcome the effect of the distance which separates the places.   But it is the distance, and not the mail service,[7] which causes the time lag in the physical transmission of such correspondence.[8]

Congress has only recently passed an amendment to the Truth in Lending Act[9] which makes criminal the use of a fraudulently obtained credit card in a "transaction affecting interstate or foreign commerce."   15 U.S.C. § 1644.   Congress could have drafted the mail fraud statute so as to require only that the mails be in fact used as a result of the fraudulent scheme.[10]   But it did not do this; instead, it required that the use of the

---

[7] Since we are admonished that we may not as judges ignore what we know as men, we do not wish to be understood as suggesting that delays in mail service are solely attributable to the distance involved.   If the Postal Service appears on occasion to be something less than a 20th century version of the wing-footed Mercury, the fact remains that the invoices were mailed to and were ultimately received by the Louisville bank.

[8] Distance is not the only cause of delay. The Court of Appeals noted that BankAmericard had a billing system in which billing was accomplished by collecting receipts over a one-month period and then billing the card holder.   It might reasonably be argued that respondent himself used facilities of interstate travel for the purpose of executing his scheme, since the large distances separating the defrauded motels from one another and from the Louisville bank probably did make it more difficult to apprehend him than if he had simply defrauded local enterprises in Louisville.   But the statute is cast, not in terms of use of the facilities of interstate travel, but in terms of use of the mails.

[9] 15 U.S.C. § 1644 provides:

"Whoever, in a transaction affecting interstate or foreign commerce, uses any counterfeit, fictitious, altered, forged, lost, stolen, or fraudulently obtained credit card to obtain goods or services, or both, having a retail value aggregating $5,000 or more, shall be fined not more than $10,000 or imprisoned not more than five years, or both."

The Court of Appeals felt that the enactment by Congress of the above amendment to the Truth in Lending Act manifested a legislative judgment that credit card fraud schemes were to be excluded from the application of the mail fraud statute "unless the offender makes a purposeful use of the mails to accomplish his scheme."

Respondent contends that the passage of the amendment indicates that Congress believed in 1970 that credit card fraud was not a federal crime under 18 U.S.C. § 1341 or otherwise.   Respondent also notes that the legislative history of the passage of the amendment indicates that the original bill, as enacted by the Senate, contained no jurisdictional amount limitation.   The Senate–House conferees, at the request of the Department of Justice, later added the limitation of federal jurisdiction under the section to purchases exceeding $5,000.

The government contends that the Court of Appeals erred in attaching significance to the 1970 amendment, urging that there is no indication that Congress intended its provisions to be the sole vehicle for the federal prosecution of credit card frauds.

We deem it unnecessary to determine the significance of the passage of the amendment, since we conclude without resort to that fact that the mail fraud statute does not cover the respondent's conduct in this case.

[10] We are admonished by The Chief Justice in dissent that the "mail fraud statute must remain strong to be able to cope with the new varieties of fraud" which threaten "the financial security of our citizenry" and

mails be "for the purpose of executing such scheme or artifice. . . ." Since the mailings in this case were not for that purpose, the judgment of the Court of Appeals is

Affirmed.

CHIEF JUSTICE BURGER, with whom JUSTICE WHITE joins, dissenting.

I join in the dissent of Justice White which follows but add a few observations on an aspect of the Court's holding which seems of some importance. Section 1341 of Title 18 U.S.C. has traditionally been used against fraudulent activity as a first line of defense. When a "new" fraud develops—as constantly happens—the mail fraud statute becomes a stop-gap device to deal on a temporary basis with the new phenomenon, until particularized legislation can be developed and passed to deal directly with the evil. "Prior to the passage of the 1933 [Securities] Act, most criminal prosecutions for fraudulent securities transactions were brought under the federal mail fraud statute." Arthur F. Mathews, Criminal Prosecutions Under the Federal Securities Laws and Related Statutes: The Nature and Development of SEC Criminal Cases, 39 Geo. Wash. L. Rev. 901, 911 (1971). Loan sharks were brought to justice by means of 18 U.S.C. § 1341, Stewart Lynch, Prosecuting Loan Sharks Under the Mail Fraud Statute, 14 Ford. L. Rev. 150 (1945), before Congress in 1968, recognized the interstate character of loansharking and the need to provide federal protection against this organized crime activity, and enacted 18 U.S.C. § 891 et seq., outlawing extortionate extensions of credit. Although inadequate to protect the buying and investing public fully, the mail fraud statute stood in the breach against frauds connected with the burgeoning sale of undeveloped real estate, until Congress could examine the problems of the land sales industry and pass into law the Interstate Land Sales Full Disclosure Act, 82 Stat. 590, 15 U.S.C. § 1701 et seq. Ronald J. Coffey & James d'A. Welch, Federal Regulation of Land Sales: Full Disclosure Comes Down to Earth, 21 Case W. Res. L. Rev. 5 (1969). Similarly, the mail fraud statute was used to stop credit card fraud, before Congress moved to provide particular protection by passing 15 U.S.C. § 1644.

The mail fraud statute continues to remain an important tool in prosecuting frauds in those areas where legislation has been passed more directly addressing the fraudulent conduct. Mail fraud counts fill pages of securities fraud indictments even today. Mathews, supra, 39 Geo. Wash. L. Rev., at 911. Despite the pervasive government regulation of the drug industry, postal fraud statutes still play an important role in controlling the solicitation of mail-order purchases by drug distributors based upon fraudulent misrepresentations. Frederick M. Hart, The Postal Fraud Statutes: Their Use and Abuse, 11 Food Drug Cosm. L.J. 245, 247, 261 (1956). Maze's interstate escapade—of which there are numberless counterparts—

which "the federal government must be ever alert to combat." We believe that under our decision the mail fraud statute remains a strong and useful weapon to combat those evils which are within the broad reach of its language. If the federal government is to engage in combat against fraudulent schemes not covered by the statute, it must do so at the initiative of Congress and not of this Court.

demonstrates that the federal mail fraud statute should have a place in dealing with fraudulent credit card use even with 15 U.S.C. § 1644 on the books.

The criminal mail fraud statute must remain strong to be able to cope with the new varieties of fraud that the ever-inventive American "con artist" is sure to develop. Abuses in franchising and the growing scandals from pyramid sales schemes are but some of the threats to the financial security of our citizenry that the federal government must be ever alert to combat. Comment, Multi-Level or Pyramid Sales Systems: Fraud or Free Enterprise, 18 S.D. L. Rev. 358 (1973).

The decision of the Court in this case should be viewed as limited to the narrow facts of Maze's criminal adventures on which the Court places so heavy a reliance, and to the Court's seeming desire not to flood the federal courts with a multitude of prosecutions for relatively minor acts of credit card misrepresentation considered as more appropriately the business of the states. The Court of Appeals, whose judgment is today affirmed, was careful to state that "[w]e do not hold that the fraudulent use of a credit card can never constitute a violation of the mail fraud statute." The Court's decision, then, correct or erroneous, does not mean that the United States ought, in any way, to slacken its prosecutorial efforts under 18 U.S.C. § 1341 against those who would use the mails in schemes to defraud the guileless members of the public with worthless securities, patent medicines, deeds to arid and inaccessible tracts of land, or other empty promises of instant wealth and happiness. I agree with Justice White that the judgment of the Court of Appeals was error and should be reversed.

JUSTICE WHITE, with whom THE CHIEF JUSTICE, JUSTICE BRENNAN, and JUSTICE BLACKMUN concur, dissenting.

Until today the acts charged in the indictment in this case—knowingly causing four separate sales invoices to be mailed by merchants to the bank that had issued the stolen BankAmericard in furtherance of a scheme to defraud the bank by using the credit card without authorization and by falsely securing credit—would have been a criminal offense punishable as mail fraud under 18 U.S.C. § 1341.[1] But no more. By misreading this Court's prior decisions and giving an unambiguous federal criminal statute an unrealistic reading, the majority places beyond the reach of the statute a fraudulent scheme that by law is not consummated until after the mails have been used, that utilizes the mails as a central necessary instrumentality in its perpetration, and that demands federal investigatory and prosecutorial resources if it is to be effectively checked. Because I cannot subscribe to the majority's reasoning or the result it reaches, I dissent.

As "part of his scheme and artifice to defraud," respondent was charged with "obtain[ing] property and services on credit through the use

---

[1] The majority recognizes [in citations omitted from the Court's opinion] that prior to this decision at least five courts of appeals had taken a view contrary to that reached by the court below. [Addition to footnote by eds.]

of" an unlawfully possessed BankAmericard and "by means of false and fraudulent pretenses, representations and promises...." The property and services were obtained from Citizens Fidelity Bank and Trust Company of Louisville, Kentucky, a BankAmericard licensee, Charles Meredith, the authorized card holder and user, and various persons and business concerns "which had previously entered into agreements with BankAmericard to furnish property and services on credit to the holders of BankAmericards...." The indictment also charged that the mails played an indispensable role in respondent's fraudulent activities:

> "It was a further part of his scheme and artifice to defraud that the defendant would and did obtain property and services on credit through the use of [the] BankAmericard ... by charging purchases on credit, well knowing at the time that the bank copies of the sales invoices recording these purchases would be, and were, delivered by mail to Citizens Fidelity Bank and Trust Company, Louisville, Kentucky, according to the directions thereon for posting to the BankAmericard account of Charles L. Meredith, that copies of these sales invoices, together with a bill for the accumulated charges, would subsequently be mailed in the normal course of business to Charles L. Meredith; and that the delay inherent in this posting and mailing would enable the defendant to continue to make purchases with [the] BankAmericard ... before his scheme and artifice to defraud could be detected."

I

Section 1341 proscribes use of the mails "for the purpose of executing" a fraudulent scheme. The trial court had instructed the jury that it could convict on the four mail fraud counts only if it found, inter alia, that

> "the mails were in fact used to *carry out* the scheme and that the use of the mails was reasonably foreseeable. The mail matter need not disclose on its face a fraudulent representation or purpose, but need only be intended to *assist in carrying out* the scheme to defraud." (Emphasis added.)

Viewing each fraudulent transaction as consummated at the time respondent received goods in exchange for signing the BankAmericard sales drafts, the Court of Appeals held that respondent did not cause the subsequent mailings "for the *purpose* of executing his fraudulent scheme." (Emphasis in original.) The court below acknowledged that "the fraud was directed against the card issuer and the card holder," but it nevertheless concluded that the relevant perspective was respondent's. "As far as [respondent] was concerned, his transaction was complete when he checked out of each motel; the subsequent billing was merely 'incidental and collateral to the scheme and not a part of it.' " [Quoting Kann v. United States, 323 U.S. 88, 95 (1944).]

The majority has uncritically embraced this unnecessarily restrictive approach to construing the statute. Like the Court of Appeals, it has selectively seized upon language in our prior decisions in pursuit of its notion that the fraudulent scheme ended when respondent duped the motels into giving him goods and services on credit. We are told, for example, as in *Kann*, supra, where the mails were used to deliver checks drawn from a dummy corporation as part of a scheme by corporate officers to defraud their own corporation, that the scheme here "had reached fruition," that the person "intended to receive the [goods and services] had received [them] irrevocably," that it was "immaterial . . . to any consummation of the scheme" how the sales invoices were forwarded by the motels to the issuing bank for payment and billing to the card holder, and that the so-called billing process was, as previously noted, "incidental and collateral to the scheme and not a part of it." "Therefore, only if the mailings were 'a part of the execution of the fraud,' or, as we said in Pereira v. United States, 347 U.S. 1, 8 (1954), were 'incident to an essential part of the scheme,' do they fall within the ban of the federal mail fraud statute." Parr v. United States, 363 U.S. 370, 390 (1960).

What the majority overlooks is the salient fact that the fraud in this case—and most others involving unauthorized use of credit cards—was practiced on the card issuer and not on the individual merchants who furnished lodgings and meals to respondent. As the Court of Appeals itself recognized, "[t]he merchants who honored the BankAmericard were likely insulated from loss under the agreements with BankAmericard. See Roland E. Brandel & Carl A. Leonard, Bank Charge Cards: New Cash or New Credit, 69 Mich. L. Rev. 1033, 1040 (1971)."[2] Here, then, the fraud was

[2] Almost all of the bank credit card systems presently in operation in this country rely upon a three-way transaction between the card issuer, the cardholder, and a subscribing retailer. This tripartite credit card arrangement basically entails three separate contractual agreements: (1) between the bank issuing the credit card and the individual cardholder; (2) between one of the banks in the system and a local merchant; and (3) between the merchant and the cardholder. See generally Comment, The Tripartite Credit Card Transaction: A Legal Infant, 48 Calif. L. Rev. 459 (1960).

"The most important of the many parties to such a system is the bank which issues the charge cards to the public. The issuer-bank establishes an account on behalf of the person to whom the card is issued, and the two enter into an agreement which governs their relationship. This agreement establishes a line of credit under which the cardholder may incur obligations to the issuer by a cash advance or through a purchase of goods or services from one of the merchant-members.

"These merchants also have an agreement with the banks requiring them to honor all charge cards issued by a member-bank, and enabling them to deposit slips evidencing sales to cardholders in an ordinary checking account at the bank with which he has reached an agreement in return for a discounted credit to that account. These slips are then cleared and forwarded through an interchange system to the member-bank which originally issued the card and from which the cardholder will be billed periodically. The cardholder must then decide whether to make payment in full within a specified period, free of finance charges, or to defer payment and ultimately be charged an extra percentage of the amount billed." Comment, Bank Credit Cards—Contemporary Problems, 41 Fordham L. Rev. 373, 374 (1972).

Because the legal relationship between the parties is dictated by the terms of their respective agreements, the contract governs the distribution of risk for credit card frauds between the merchant and the issuer. Under most systems, with certain exceptions for negligence on the part of the merchant if he

ultimately perpetrated upon the credit card issuer and not the merchant.[3] The mails thus became "part of the execution of the fraud...." *Kann v. United States*, supra, at 95. Indeed, they were "an essential element" and not merely "incident to an essential part of the scheme...." Pereira v. United States, 347 U.S. 1, 8 (1954).

Nor had respondent's plan reached fruition. For his part, he may very well not have schemed beyond obtaining the goods and services under false pretenses with a stolen credit card. But from a legal standpoint of criminal fraud, this was only the first and certainly

> "not the last step in the fraudulent scheme. It was a continuing venture. ... The use of the mails was crucial to the total success of the fraudulent project. We are not justified in chopping up ... the scheme into segments and isolating one part from the others. That would be warranted if the scheme were to defraud [only the merchants]. But it is plain that these plans had a wider reach and that but for the use of the mails they would not have been finally consummated." *Kann v. United States*, supra, at 96 (Douglas, J., dissenting).

Since it was the card-issuing bank that was actually defrauded, the mails were employed "for the purpose of executing [the] scheme...."

II

The mails further contributed to the realization of respondent's fraudulent scheme by creating the delay in detecting the fraud that necessarily

honors an expired card or one appearing on the current "stop list" or if he makes a sale for an amount in excess of the cardholder's credit line, the issuer assumes all risks for frauds. Daniel E. Murray, A Legal–Empirical Study of the Unauthorized Use of Credit Cards, 21 U. Miami L. Rev. 811, 813 (1967); Note, Credit Cards: Distributing Fraud Loss, 77 Yale L. J. 1418, 1420 (1968); Comment, The Tripartite Credit Card Transaction, 48 Calif. L. Rev., at 464–65.

> " 'As far as the merchant is concerned, he is in the same financial and legal position as if he were receiving certified checks on a bank that does not clear at par, with no risk that the check will be returned or payment stopped, or as if he were receiving cash at a small discount for the bank's services. This firm bank commitment is what makes the merchant willing to accept a bank card as freely as cash and what makes the bank card as good as cash to its holder (and without the risks of carrying cash).

> " 'Under these arrangements, the card-issuing bank takes all the credit

risk, which is appropriate to the banking function it performs, the cardholder selects the merchant with whom he will deal, and the bank and the cardholder-purchaser expect the merchant to assume the merchandise risk. It is this division and allocation of risks between merchant and bank which permits the bank card to be used as though it were cash with hundreds of thousands of participating merchants throughout the country and abroad.' " A.G. Cleveland, Jr., Bank Credit Cards: Issuers, Merchants, and Users, 90 Banking L.J. 719, 723–24 (1973), quoting Statement of the American Bankers Association, the Consumers Bankers Association, Interbank Card Association, and National Bank-Americard, Inc. to the Federal Trade Commission in the matter of Revised Proposed Trade Regulation Rule on Preservation of Consumers' Claims and Defenses, 4–5 (Mar. 5, 1973).

[3] Section 133(a) of the Truth in Lending Act limited the card-holder's liability for the unauthorized use of his credit card to $50. 15 U.S.C. § 1643(a).

results from the time-consuming processing of credit card invoices by mail. During his two-week, $2,000 transcontinental spending spree, respondent took full advantage of this inevitable delay to continue his unlawful activities. If the motel owners had employed an instantaneous identification or verification system, respondent's fraudulent scheme would most likely have been nipped in the bud. But the simple truth of the matter is that they did not. As a direct consequence of the prevailing business practice of mailing invoices to the issuer for subsequent billing to the card holder and the system's attendant time delays, respondent was able to buy valuable time to postpone detection and thereby execute his scheme.

The majority mysteriously ignores prior decisions that 18 U.S.C. § 1341 reaches "cases where the use of the mails is a means of concealment so that further frauds which are part of the scheme may be perpetrated." *Kann v. United States*, supra, at 94–95. Moreover, it fails to take appropriate account of our most recent decision construing § 1341. In United States v. Sampson, 371 U.S. 75 (1962), an indictment for mail fraud had been dismissed by the District Court on the ground that the mailings after the money had already been obtained from the victims were not "for the purpose of executing" the scheme to defraud. We reversed.

> "We are unable to find anything in either the *Kann* or the *Parr* case which suggests that the Court was laying down an automatic rule that a deliberate, planned use of the mails after the victims' money had been obtained can never be 'for the purpose of executing' the defendants' scheme. Rather the Court found only that under the facts in those cases the schemes had been fully executed before the mails were used. And Court of Appeals decisions rendered both before and after *Kann* have followed the view that subsequent mailings can in some circumstances provide the basis for an indictment under the mail fraud statutes." Id., at 80.

As previously indicated, the indictment here charged that respondent knew that the delay inherent in the posting and mailing of the credit invoices would enable him to continue making purchases with the purloined card before his criminal conduct could be detected. Respondent engaged in a criminal enterprise that is by its very nature short-lived. Every time delay in the card holder's receipt of the forged credit card slips allows the scheme to continue that much longer. For my part, the indictment charged a crime under 18 U.S.C. § 1341, and the government established respondent's guilt beyond a reasonable doubt.

III

The majority's decision has ramifications far beyond the mere reversal of a lone criminal conviction. In this era of the "cashless" society, Americans are increasingly resorting to the use of credit cards in their day-to-day consumer purchases. Today well over 300 million credit cards are in circulation, and annual charges exceed $60 billion. In 1969, alone, 1.5 million credit cards were lost or stolen, resulting in fraud losses exceeding

$100 million.   115 Cong. Rec. 38987 (1969).   Current estimates of annual credit card fraud losses are put as high as $200 million. A.G. Cleveland, Jr., Bank Credit Cards: Issuers, Merchants, and Users, 90 Banking L.J. 719, 729 (1973).   Under the result reached by the majority, only those credit card frauds exceeding $5,000 covered by 15 U.S.C. § 1644 will be subject to federal criminal jurisdiction.

Yet this burgeoning criminal activity, as evidenced by the very facts of this case, does not recognize artificial state boundaries.   In the future, nationwide credit card fraud schemes will have to be prosecuted in each individual state in which a fraudulent transaction transpired.   Here, for example, respondent must now be charged and tried in California, Louisiana, and Florida.   This result, never intended by Congress, may precipitate a widespread inability to apprehend and/or prosecute those who would hijack the credit card system.

I dissent.

NOTES ON *UNITED STATES v. MAZE*

1.   Questions and Comments on *United States v. Maze*.   Who was the "victim" of the defendant's fraud in *Maze*?   The persons who provided goods and services to Maze were not in any meaningful sense defrauded.   They were paid full value, less the discount to which they agreed in their arrangement with the credit card company.   The "victim" must therefore have been Meredith or the bank.   In either case, no property was obtained *from them* until the mails were used.   Thus, on this view, the mails were "essential" to the scheme to defraud.   This view is, moreover, consistent with the cases.   *Sampson*, and to some extent *Pereira*, invite the government to develop a theory under which the mails played a part in the scheme, and suggests that it is that theory which will control the analysis rather than an arbitrarily selected view of what "really" happened.   It follows, therefore, that Maze's conviction should have been affirmed.

What is wrong with the above analysis?   Why did it not carry the day in the Supreme Court?

The majority had a contrary characterization of the facts.   Maze's scheme "reached fruition" when he "acquired" the property, not when his victims lost it.   Since use of the mails came after he had accomplished his objective, and merely sorted out between the potential victims who would bear the loss, the mails were not an integral part of the scheme.   His fraud in no way "depended ... on which of his victims ultimately bore the loss."   But weren't the mails nonetheless "essential" to the scheme?   Would Maze have been able to perpetrate the fraud without a credit card system in place to which use of the mails was essential?   Why isn't this factor significant?   And how "essential" must the mails be to the success of the scheme anyway?   Do the prior cases establish that the success of the scheme must "depend" on use of the mails?

The majority and the dissent disagree as to the application of the Court's precedents to the *Maze* facts. Which side has the better view? Do the precedents clearly point one way or the other? If not, on what basis should a case like *Maze* be resolved?

Consider, in this respect, the relevance of the Truth in Lending Act. Congress plainly adopted 15 U.S.C. § 1644 to deal with the *Maze* problem, but limited the application of the statute to situations where $5,000 or more was involved. Justice White argues that this gap should be filled by the mail fraud statute. Without federal prosecution there will be no way in multi-state spree cases in which to aggregate in one court the individual petty frauds perpetrated by a credit card thief. Maze responds that Congress created the gap and meant for there to be no federal prosecution—under § 1644 or any other statute—in cases that fall below the Truth in Lending Act ceiling. The Court (in footnote 9) thought it unnecessary to resolve the question, since the mail fraud statute did not apply anyway. Which is the better view? Does the fact that Congress has spoken to a particular form of fraud in another statute mean that the mail fraud statute cannot apply? Or is the matter to be resolved on the basis of "mail fraud" policies independently of anything Congress may have said elsewhere?

The majority and the dissent also disagree as to the significance of the processing delay in the credit card system. Which has the better view of this factor? Is Justice White right that *Sampson* holds that the government may rely on this factor in a case like this, or is Justice Rehnquist right that, from Maze's point of view, he would be better off if no mailing occurred and that therefore it is hardly proper to use the mailing as the basis for prosecuting him?

Finally, consider the Chief Justice's comments. Does he mean to suggest that the government may, in spite of *Maze*, continue to use the mail fraud statute to prosecute some credit card frauds? If so, under what circumstances? Also, is it appropriate for the government to use the mail fraud statute as a "first line of defense" against newly hatched fraudulent schemes that Congress has not specifically made criminal? What is the difference between such use of the mail fraud statute and a statute that says "whenever anybody thinks of a new crime that hasn't been invented yet, the courts should invent one"?

2. Amendments to the Truth in Lending Act. Congress amended § 1644 in 1974. The new statute provides:

"§ 1644. Fraudulent use of credit cards; penalties

> Use, attempt or conspiracy to use card in transaction
> affecting interstate or foreign commerce

"(a) Whoever knowingly in a transaction affecting interstate or foreign commerce, uses or attempts or conspires to use any counterfeit, fictitious, altered, forged, lost, stolen, or fraudulently obtained credit card to obtain money, goods, services, or anything else of value which within any one-year period has a value aggregating $1,000 or more; or

Transporting, attempting or conspiring to transport card in interstate commerce

"(b) Whoever, with unlawful or fraudulent intent, transports or attempts or conspires to transport in interstate or foreign commerce a counterfeit, fictitious, altered, forged, lost, stolen, or fraudulently obtained credit card knowing the same to be counterfeit, fictitious, altered, forged, lost, stolen, or fraudulently obtained; or

Use of interstate commerce to sell or transport card

"(c) Whoever, with unlawful or fraudulent intent, uses any instrumentality of interstate or foreign commerce to sell or transport a counterfeit, fictitious, altered, forged, lost, stolen, or fraudulently obtained credit card knowing the same to be counterfeit, fictitious, altered, forged, lost, stolen, or fraudulently obtained; or

Receipt, concealment, etc., of goods obtained by use of card

"(d) Whoever knowingly receives, conceals, uses, or transports money, goods, services, or anything else of value (except tickets for interstate or foreign transportation) which (1) within any one-year period has a value aggregating $1,000 or more, (2) has moved in or is part of, or which constitutes interstate or foreign commerce, and (3) has been obtained with a counterfeit, fictitious, altered, forged, lost, stolen, or fraudulently obtained credit card; or

Receipt, concealment, etc., of tickets for interstate or foreign transportation obtained by use of card

"(e) Whoever knowingly receives, conceals, uses, sells, or transports in interstate or foreign commerce one or more tickets for interstate or foreign transportation, which (1) within any one-year period have a value aggregating $500 or more, and (2) have been purchased or obtained with one or more counterfeit, fictitious, altered, forged, lost, stolen, or fraudulently obtained credit cards; or

Furnishing of money, etc., through use of card

"(f) Whoever in a transaction affecting interstate or foreign commerce furnishes money, property, services, or anything else of value, which within any one-year period has a value aggregating $1,000 or more, through the use of any counterfeit, fictitious, altered, forged, lost, stolen, or fraudulently obtained credit card knowing the same to be counterfeit, fictitious, altered, forged, lost, stolen, or fraudulently obtained—

"shall be fined not more than $10,000 or imprisoned not more than ten years, or both."

With what crimes could Maze be charged today? Suppose a person mails an application for a credit card containing lies as to credit status and income. After receiving the card, the person then buys a camera from one store for $500 and a car stereo from another for $750, and then—properly outfitted—drives to another state and charges a resort bill for $1500 to the account. How many federal crimes could realistically be charged?

Schmuck v. United States

Supreme Court of the United States, 1989.
489 U.S. 705.

■ JUSTICE BLACKMUN delivered the opinion of the Court.

I

In August 1983, petitioner Wayne T. Schmuck, a used-car distributor, was indicted in the United States District Court for the Western District of Wisconsin on 12 counts of mail fraud, in violation of 18 U.S.C. §§ 1341 and 2.

The alleged fraud was a common and straightforward one. Schmuck purchased used cars, rolled back their odometers, and then sold the automobiles to Wisconsin retail dealers for prices artificially inflated because of the low-mileage readings. These unwitting car dealers, relying on the altered odometer figures, then resold the cars to customers, who in turn paid prices reflecting Schmuck's fraud. To complete the resale of each automobile, the dealer who purchased it from Schmuck would submit a title-application form to the Wisconsin Department of Transportation on behalf of his retail customer. The receipt of a Wisconsin title was a prerequisite for completing the resale; without it, the dealer could not transfer title to the customer and the customer could not obtain Wisconsin tags. The submission of the title-application form supplied the mailing element of each of the alleged mail frauds.

Before trial, Schmuck moved to dismiss the indictment on the ground that the mailings at issue—the submissions of the title-application forms by the automobile dealers—were not in furtherance of the fraudulent scheme and, thus, did not satisfy the mailing element of the crime of mail fraud. Schmuck also moved under Federal Rule of Criminal Procedure 31(c) for a jury instruction on the then misdemeanor offense of tampering with an odometer, 15 U.S.C. §§ 1984 and 1990c(a)(1982 ed.).[2] The District Court denied both motions.[3] After trial, the jury returned guilty verdicts on all 12 counts.

---

[2] In 1986, Congress made odometer tampering a felony. 18 U.S.C. § 1990c(a)(1982 ed., Supp. IV).

[3] The District Court concluded that whether the mailings alleged in the indictment furthered the fraudulent scheme was a "matter to be determined at trial." The

A divided panel of the United States Court of Appeals for the Seventh Circuit reversed and remanded the case for a new trial. Although the panel rejected Schmuck's claim that he was entitled to a judgment of acquittal because the mailings were not made in furtherance of his scheme, it ruled that under Criminal Rule 31(c) the District Court should have instructed the jury on the lesser offense of odometer tampering. The panel applied the so-called "inherent relationship" test for determining what constitutes a lesser included offense for the purpose of Rule 31(c). See, e.g., United States v. Whitaker, 144 U.S.App.D.C. 344, 349, 447 F.2d 314, 319 (1971). Under that test, one offense is included in another when the facts as alleged in the indictment and proved at trial support the inference that the defendant committed the less serious offense, and an "inherent relationship" exists between the two offenses. This relationship arises when the two offenses relate to the protection of the same interests and the proof of the greater offense can generally be expected to require proof of the lesser offense. Applying this test, the court concluded that both the mail fraud and odometer tampering statutes protect against fraud, and that the proof of mail fraud generally entails proving the underlying fraudulent conduct.[4] The panel then held that Schmuck was entitled to the lesser offense instruction because a rational jury could have found him guilty of odometer tampering, yet acquitted him of mail fraud on the ground that the mailings were too tangential to the fraudulent scheme to satisfy the requirements of mail fraud.

The Court of Appeals vacated the panel decision and ordered the case to be reheard en banc. On rehearing, by a divided vote, the en banc court rejected the "inherent relationship" test for defining lesser included offenses, and adopted instead the "elements test" whereby one offense is necessarily included within another only when the elements of the lesser offense form a subset of the elements of the offense charged. The Court of Appeals found that the elements test "is grounded in the terms and history of Rule 31(c), comports with the constitutional requirement of notice to the defendant of the potential for conviction of an offense not separately charged, permits a greater degree of certainty in the application of Rule 31(c), and harmonizes the concept of 'necessarily included' under Rule 31(c) with that of a lesser included offense where the issue is double jeopardy." Applying the elements test, the Court of Appeals held that Schmuck was not entitled to a jury instruction on the offense of odometer

court concluded that Schmuck was not entitled to the lesser offense instruction because odometer tampering was not a necessarily included offense of mail fraud. Schmuck raised these objections again in support of a motion for acquittal at the close of the government's case. That motion was denied.

The District Court instructed the jury that in order to find Schmuck guilty of mail fraud the jury had to find beyond a reasonable doubt that he knowingly devised a scheme to defraud, and that he caused matter to be sent in the mail for the purpose of executing that scheme. The court also told the jury that it could find Schmuck guilty if the use of the mails was reasonably foreseeable.

[4] One judge, concurring in part and dissenting in part, agreed with the panel's application of the inherent relationship test, but found no such relationship between mail fraud and odometer tampering.

tampering because he could have been convicted of mail fraud without a showing that he actually altered the odometers, but could not have been convicted of odometer tampering absent such a showing. Since the elements of odometer tampering are not a subset of the elements of mail fraud, odometer tampering did not qualify as a lesser included offense of mail fraud and, accordingly, the District Court was not required under Rule 31(c) to instruct the jury on the odometer-tampering offense.

We granted certiorari to define further the scope of the mail fraud statute and to resolve a conflict among the circuits over which test to apply in determining what constitutes a lesser included offense for the purposes of Criminal Rule 31(c).

II

"The federal mail fraud statute does not purport to reach all frauds, but only those limited instances in which the use of the mails is a part of the execution of the fraud, leaving all other cases to be dealt with by appropriate state law." Kann v. United States, 323 U.S. 88, 95 (1944).[6] To be part of the execution of the fraud, however, the use of the mails need not be an essential element of the scheme. Pereira v. United States, 347 U.S. 1, 8 (1954). It is sufficient for the mailing to be "incident to an essential part of the scheme," ibid., or "a step in [the] plot," Badders v. United States, 240 U.S. 391, 394 (1916).

Schmuck, relying principally on this Court's decisions in *Kann*, supra, Parr v. United States, 363 U.S. 370 (1960), and United States v. Maze, 414 U.S. 395 (1974), argues that mail fraud can be predicated only on a mailing that affirmatively assists the perpetrator in carrying out his fraudulent scheme. The mailing element of the offense, he contends, cannot be satisfied by a mailing, such as those at issue here, that is routine and innocent in and of itself, and that, far from furthering the execution of the fraud, occurs after the fraud has come to fruition, is merely tangentially related to the fraud, and is counterproductive in that it creates a "paper trail" from which the fraud may be discovered. We disagree both with this characterization of the mailings in the present case and with this description of the applicable law.

We begin by considering the scope of Schmuck's fraudulent scheme. Schmuck was charged with devising and executing a scheme to defraud Wisconsin retail automobile customers who based their decisions to purchase certain automobiles at least in part on the low-mileage readings provided by the tampered odometers. This was a fairly large-scale opera-

---

[6] The statute provides in relevant part:

"Whoever, having devised or intending to devise any scheme or artifice to defraud, or for obtaining money or property by means of false or fraudulent pretenses, representations, or promises ... for the purpose of executing such scheme or artifice or attempting so to do ... knowingly causes to be delivered by mail according to the direction thereon, or at the place at which it is directed to be delivered by the person to whom it is addressed, any such matter or thing, shall be fined not more than $1,000 or imprisoned not more that five years or both." 18 U.S.C. § 1341.

tion. Evidence at trial indicated that Schmuck had employed a man known only as "Fred" to turn back the odometers on about 150 different cars. Schmuck then marketed these cars to a number of dealers, several of whom he dealt with on a consistent basis over a period of about 15 years. Indeed, of the 12 automobiles that are the subject of the counts of the indictment, five were sold to "P & A Sales," and four to "Southside Auto." Thus, Schmuck's was not a "one-shot" operation in which he sold a single car to an isolated dealer. His was an ongoing fraudulent venture. A rational jury could have concluded that the success of Schmuck's venture depended upon his continued harmonious relations with and good reputation among retail dealers, which in turn required the smooth flow of cars from the dealers to their Wisconsin customers.

Under these circumstances, we believe that a rational jury could have found that the title-registration mailings were part of the execution of the fraudulent scheme, a scheme which did not reach fruition until the retail dealers resold the cars and effected transfers of title. Schmuck's scheme would have come to an abrupt halt if the dealers either had lost faith in Schmuck or had not been able to resell the cars obtained from him. These resales and Schmuck's relationships with the retail dealers naturally depended on the successful passage of title among the various parties. Thus, although the registration-form mailings may not have contributed directly to the duping of either the retail dealers or the customers, they were necessary to the passage of title, which in turn was essential to the perpetuation of Schmuck's scheme. As noted earlier, a mailing that is "incident to an essential part of the scheme," *Pereira*, 347 U.S., at 8, satisfies the mailing element of the mail fraud offense. The mailings here fit this description.

Once the full flavor of Schmuck's scheme is appreciated, the critical distinctions between this case and the three cases in which this Court has delimited the reach of the mail fraud statute—*Kann*, *Parr*, and *Maze*—are readily apparent. The defendants in *Kann* were corporate officers and directors accused of setting up a dummy corporation through which to divert profits into their own pockets. As part of this fraudulent scheme, the defendants caused the corporation to issue two checks payable to them. The defendants cashed these checks at local banks, which then mailed the checks to the drawee banks for collection. This Court held that the mailing of the cashed checks to the drawee banks could not supply the mailing element of the mail fraud charges. The defendants' fraudulent scheme had reached fruition. "It was immaterial to them, or to any consummation of the scheme, how the bank which paid or credited the check would collect from the drawee bank."

In *Parr*, several defendants were charged, inter alia, with having fraudulently obtained gasoline and a variety of other products and services through the unauthorized use of a credit card issued to the school district which employed them. The mailing element of the mail fraud charges in *Parr* was purportedly satisfied when the oil company which issued the credit card mailed invoices to the school district for payment, and when the district mailed payment in the form of a check. Relying on *Kann*, this Court held that these mailings were not in execution of the scheme as required by the statute because it was immaterial to the defendants how the oil company went about collecting its payment.[7]

Later, in *Maze*, the defendant allegedly stole his roommate's credit card, headed south on a winter jaunt, and obtained food and lodging at motels along the route by placing the charges on the stolen card. The mailing element of the mail fraud charge was supplied by the fact that the defendant knew that each motel proprietor would mail an invoice to the bank that had issued the credit card, which in turn would mail a bill to the card owner for payment. The Court found that these mailings could not support mail fraud charges because the defendant's scheme had reached fruition when he checked out of each motel. The success of his scheme in no way depended on the mailings; they merely determined which of his victims would ultimately bear the loss.

The title-registration mailings at issue here served a function different from the mailings in *Kann*, *Parr*, and *Maze*. The intrabank mailings in *Kann* and the credit card invoice mailings in *Parr* and *Maze* involved little more than post-fraud accounting among the potential victims of the various schemes, and the longterm success of the fraud did not turn on which of the potential victims bore the ultimate loss. Here, in contrast, a jury rationally could have found that Schmuck by no means was indifferent to the fact of who bore the loss. The mailing of the title-registration forms was an essential step in the successful passage of title to the retail purchasers. Moreover, a failure in this passage of title would have jeopardized Schmuck's relationship of trust and goodwill with the retail dealers upon whose unwitting cooperation his scheme depended. Schmuck's reliance on our prior cases limiting the reach of the mail fraud statute is simply misplaced.

To the extent that Schmuck would draw from these previous cases a general rule that routine mailings that are innocent in themselves cannot supply the mailing element of the mail fraud offense, he misapprehends this Court's precedents. In *Parr* the Court specifically acknowledged that "innocent" mailings—ones that contain no false information—may supply the mailing element. In other cases, the Court has found the elements of

---

[7] *Parr* also involved a second fraudulent scheme through which the defendant school board members misappropriated school district tax revenues. The government argued that the mailing element of the mail fraud charges was supplied by the mailing of tax statements, checks, and receipts. This Court held, however, that in the absence of any evidence that the tax levy was increased as part of the fraud, the mailing element of the offense could not be supplied by mailings "made or caused to be made under the im-perative command of duty imposed by state law." No such legal duty is at issue here. Whereas the mailings of the tax documents in *Parr* were the direct product of the school district's state constitutional duty to levy taxes and would have been made regardless of the defendants' fraudulent scheme, the mailings in the present case, though in compliance with Wisconsin's car-registration procedure, were derivative of Schmuck's scheme to sell "doctored" cars and would not have occurred but for that scheme.

mail fraud to be satisfied where the mailings have been routine. See, e.g., Carpenter v. United States, 484 U.S. 19 (1987)(mailing newspapers).

We also reject Schmuck's contention that mailings that someday may contribute to the uncovering of a fraudulent scheme cannot supply the mailing element of the mail fraud offense. The relevant question at all times is whether the mailing is part of the execution of the scheme as conceived by the perpetrator at the time, regardless of whether the mailing later, through hindsight, may prove to have been counterproductive and return to haunt the perpetrator of the fraud. The mail fraud statute includes no guarantee that the use of the mails for the purpose of executing a fraudulent scheme will be risk free. Those who use the mails to defraud proceed at their peril.

For these reasons, we agree with the Court of Appeals that the mailings in this case satisfy the mailing element of the mail fraud offenses.

III

Federal Rule of Criminal Procedure 31(c) provides in relevant part: "The defendant may be found guilty of an offense necessarily included in the offense charged." As noted above, the Courts of Appeals have adopted different tests to determine when, under this Rule, a defendant is entitled to a lesser included offense instruction. The Seventh Circuit's original panel opinion applied the "inherent relationship" approach formulated in United States v. Whitaker, 144 U.S.App.D.C. 344, 349, 447 F.2d 314, 319 (1971):

> "[D]efendant is entitled to invoke Rule 31(c) when a lesser offense is established by the evidence adduced at trial in proof of the greater offense, with the caveat that there must also be an 'inherent' relationship between the greater and lesser offenses, i.e., they must relate to the protection of the same interests, and must be so related that in the general nature of these crimes, though not necessarily invariably, proof of the lesser offense is necessarily presented as part of the showing of the commission of the greater offense."

The en banc Seventh Circuit rejected this approach in favor of the "traditional," or "elements" test. Under this test, one offense is not "necessarily included" in another unless the elements of the lesser offense are a subset of the elements of the charged offense. Where the lesser offense requires an element not required for the greater offense, no instruction is to be given under Rule 31(c).

We now adopt the elements approach to Rule 31(c). As the Court of Appeals noted, this approach is grounded in the language and history of the Rule and provides for greater certainty in its application. It, moreover, is consistent with past decisions of this Court, which, though not specifically endorsing a particular test, employed the elements approach in cases involving lesser included offense instructions.[8]

---

[8] Our decision in no way alters the independent prerequisite for a lesser included offense instruction that the evidence at trial must be such that a jury could rationally

First, the wording of Rule 31(c), although not conclusive, supports the application of the elements approach. The Rule speaks in terms of an offense that is "necessarily included in the offense charged." This language suggests that the comparison to be drawn is between *offenses*. Since offenses are statutorily defined, that comparison is appropriately conducted by reference to the statutory elements of the offenses in question, and not, as the inherent relationship approach would mandate, by reference to conduct proved at trial regardless of the statutory definitions. Furthermore, the language of Rule 31(c) speaks of the necessary *inclusion* of the lesser offense in the greater. While the elements test is true to this requirement, the inherent relationship approach dispenses with the required relationship of necessary inclusion: the inherent relationship approach permits a lesser included offense instruction even if the proof of one offense does not invariably require proof of the other as long as the two offenses serve the same legislative goals.

In addition, the inherent relationship approach, in practice, would require that Rule 31(c) be applied in a manner inconsistent with its language. The Rule provides that a defendant "may be found guilty" of a lesser included offense, without distinguishing between a request for jury instructions made by the government and one made by the defendant. In other words, the language of the Rule suggests that a lesser included offense instruction is available in equal measure to the defense and to the prosecution.[9] Yet, under the inherent relationship approach, such mutuality is impossible.

It is ancient doctrine of both the common law and of our Constitution that a defendant cannot be held to answer a charge not contained in the indictment brought against him. This stricture is based at least in part on the right of the defendant to notice of the charge brought against him. Were the prosecutor able to request an instruction on an offense whose elements were not charged in the indictment, this right to notice would be placed in jeopardy. Specifically, if, as mandated under the inherent-relationship approach, the determination whether the offenses are sufficiently related to permit an instruction is delayed until all the evidence is developed at trial, the defendant may not have constitutionally sufficient notice to support a lesser included offense instruction requested by the

---

find the defendant guilty of the lesser offense, yet acquit him of the greater. Keeble v. United States, 412 U.S. 205, 208 (1973).

[9] This reading of the Rule is consistent with its origins. The Rule "developed as an aid to the prosecution in cases in which the proof failed to establish some element of the crime charged." Beck v. Alabama, 447 U.S. 625, 633 (1980).

Of course, it is now firmly established that Rule 31(c)'s provision for lesser offense

instructions benefits the defendant as well. The Court recognized in *Keeble v. United States*, supra, that where the jury suspects that the defendant is plainly guilty of *some* offense, but one of the elements of the charged offense remains in doubt, in the absence of a lesser offense instruction, the jury will likely fail to give full effect to the reasonable doubt standard, resolving its doubts in favor of conviction. The availability of a lesser included offense instruction protects the defendant from such improper conviction.

prosecutor if the elements of that lesser offense are not part of the indictment. Accordingly, under the inherent relationship approach, the defendant, by in effect waiving his right to notice, may obtain a lesser offense instruction in circumstances where the constitutional restraint of notice to the defendant would prevent the prosecutor from seeking an identical instruction. The elements test, in contrast, permits lesser offense instructions only in those cases where the indictment contains the elements of both offenses and thereby gives notice to the defendant that he may be convicted on either charge. This approach preserves the mutuality implicit in the language of Rule 31(c).

Second, the history of Rule 31(c) supports the adoption of the elements approach. The Rule, which has not been amended since its adoption in 1944, is the most recent derivative of the common-law practice that permitted a jury to find a defendant "guilty of any lesser offense necessarily included in the offense charged." Beck v. Alabama, 447 U.S. 625, 633 (1980). Over a century ago, Congress codified the common law for federal criminal trials, providing in the Act of June 1, 1872, ch. 255, § 9, 17 Stat. 198, that "in all criminal causes the defendant may be found guilty of any offence the commission of which is necessarily included in that with which he is charged in the indictment." Rule 31(c) was intended to be a restatement of this "pre-existing law." Accordingly, prevailing practice at the time of the Rule's promulgation informs our understanding of its terms, and, specifically, its limitation of lesser included offenses to those "necessarily included in the offense charged."

The nature of that prevailing practice is clear. In Giles v. United States, 144 F.2d 860, 861 (9th Cir.1944), decided just three months before the adoption of Rule 31(c), the Court of Appeals for the Ninth Circuit unequivocally applied the elements test to determine the propriety of a lesser included offense instruction: " 'To be necessarily included in the greater offense the lesser must be such that it is impossible to commit the greater without first having committed the lesser.' " This approach, moreover, was applied consistently by state courts. Indeed, in State v. Henry, 98 Me. 561, 564, 57 A. 891, 892 (1904), the Supreme Judicial Court of Maine concluded that "a practically universal rule prevails, that the verdict may be for a lesser crime which is included in a greater charged in the indictment, the test being that the evidence required to establish the greater would prove the lesser offense as a necessary element." The California Supreme Court in People v. Kerrick, 144 Cal. 46, 47, 77 P. 711, 712 (1904), stated: "To be 'necessarily included' in the offense charged, the lesser offense must not only be part of the greater in fact, but it must be embraced within the legal definition of the greater as a part thereof." This Court's decision in Stevenson v. United States, 162 U.S. 313 (1896), reflects the "practically universal" practice. There, in holding that the defendant in a murder charge was entitled to a lesser included offense instruction on manslaughter under the statutory predecessor to Rule 31(c), the Court engaged in a careful comparison of the statutory elements of murder and manslaughter to determine if the latter was a lesser included offense of the former. In short, the elements approach was settled doctrine at the time of the Rule's promulgation and for more than two decades thereafter. In its restatement of "pre-existing law," Rule 31(c) incorporated this established practice.[11]

Third, the elements test is far more certain and predictable in its application than the inherent relationship approach. Because the elements approach involves a textual comparison of criminal statutes and does not depend on inferences that may be drawn from evidence introduced at trial, the elements approach permits both sides to know in advance what jury instructions will be available and to plan their trial strategies accordingly. The objective elements approach, moreover, promotes judicial economy by providing a clearer rule of decision and by permitting appellate courts to decide whether jury instructions were wrongly refused without reviewing the entire evidentiary record for nuances of inference.

The inherent relationship approach, in contrast, is rife with the potential for confusion. Finding an inherent relationship between offenses requires a determination that the offenses protect the same interests and that "in general" proof of the lesser "necessarily" involves proof of the greater. In the present case, the Court of Appeals appropriately noted: "These new layers of analysis add to the uncertainty of the propriety of an instruction in a particular case: not only are there more issues to be resolved, but correct resolution involves questions of degree and judgment, with the attendant probability that the trial and appellate courts may differ." This uncertainty was illustrated here. The three judges of the original appellate panel split in their application of the inherent relationship test to the offenses of mail fraud and odometer tampering. In the context of rules of criminal procedure, where certainty and predictability are desired, we prefer the clearer standard for applying Rule 31(c).

IV

Turning to the facts of this case, we agree with the Court of Appeals that the elements of the offense of odometer tampering are not a subset of the elements of the crime of mail fraud. There are two elements in mail fraud: (1) having devised or intending to devise a scheme to defraud (or to perform specified fraudulent acts), and (2) use of the mail for the purpose of executing, or attempting to execute, the scheme (or specified fraudulent acts). The offense of odometer tampering includes the element of knowingly and willfully causing an odometer to be altered. This element is not a subset of any element of mail fraud. Knowingly and willfully tampering

---

[11] This Court's decisions after the adoption of Rule 31(c), while not formally adopting the elements approach, reflect adherence to it. Those decisions have focused on the statutory elements of individual offenses when considering the propriety of lesser included offense instructions. In *Keeble*, for example, we held that the defendant was entitled to an instruction on the lesser offense of simple assault:

"[A]n intent to commit serious bodily injury is a necessary element of the crime with which petitioner was charged, but not of the crime of simple assault. Since the nature of petitioner's intent was very much in dispute at trial, the jury could rationally have convicted him of simple assault if that option had been presented."

with an odometer is not identical to devising or intending to devise a fraudulent scheme.

V

We conclude that Schmuck's conviction was consistent with the statutory definition of mail fraud and that he was not entitled to a lesser included offense instruction on odometer tampering. The judgment of the Court of Appeals, accordingly, is affirmed.

It is so ordered.

JUSTICE SCALIA, with whom JUSTICE BRENNAN, JUSTICE MARSHALL, and JUSTICE O'CONNOR join, dissenting.

The Court today affirms petitioner's mail fraud conviction under 18 U.S.C. § 1341. A jury found that petitioner had defrauded retail automobile purchasers by altering odometer readings on used cars and then selling the cars to unwitting dealers for resale. The scheme was a continuing one, and some dealers bought a number of the cars from petitioner over a period of time. When the dealers sold the cars, state law required them to submit title application forms to the appropriate state agency. The Court concludes that the dealers' compliance with this requirement by mail caused the scheme to constitute mail fraud, because "a failure of this passage of title would have jeopardized Schmuck's relationship of trust and goodwill with the retail dealers upon whose unwitting cooperation his scheme depended." In my view this is inconsistent with our prior cases' application of the statutory requirement that mailings to be "for the purpose of executing" a fraudulent scheme.

The purpose of the mail fraud statute is "to prevent the post office from being used to carry [fraudulent schemes] into effect." Durland v. United States, 161 U.S. 306, 314 (1896); Parr v. United States, 363 U.S. 370, 389 (1960). The law does not establish a general federal remedy against fraudulent conduct, with use of the mails as the jurisdictional hook, but reaches only "those limited instances in which the use of the mails is *a part of the execution of the fraud*, leaving all other cases to be dealt with by appropriate state law." Kann v. United States, 323 U.S. 88, 95 (1944)(emphasis added). In other words, it is mail fraud, not mail and fraud, that incurs liability. This federal statute is not violated by a fraudulent scheme in which, at some point, a mailing happens to occur—nor even by one in which a mailing predictably and necessarily occurs. The mailing must be in furtherance of the fraud.

In *Kann v. United States*, we concluded that even though defendants who cashed checks obtained as part of a fraudulent scheme knew that the bank cashing the checks would send them by mail to a drawee bank for collection, they did not thereby violate the mail fraud statute, because upon their receipt of the cash "[t]he scheme ... had reached fruition," and the mailing was "immaterial ... to any consummation of the scheme." We held to the same effect in United States v. Maze, 414 U.S. 395, 400–02 (1974), declining to find that credit-card fraud was converted into mail fraud by the certainty that, after the wrongdoer had fraudulently received his goods and services from the merchants, they would forward the credit charges by mail for payment. These cases are squarely in point here. For though the government chose to charge a defrauding of retail customers (to whom the innocent dealers resold the cars), it is obvious that, regardless of who the ultimate victim of the fraud may have been, the fraud was complete with respect to each car when petitioner pocketed the dealer's money. As far as each particular transaction was concerned, it was as inconsequential to him whether the dealer resold the car as it was inconsequential to the defendant in *Maze* whether the defrauded merchant ever forwarded the charges to the credit-card company.

Nor can the force of our cases be avoided by combining all of the individual transactions into a single scheme, and saying, as the Court does, that if the dealers' mailings obtaining title for each retail purchaser had not occurred then the dealers would have stopped trusting petitioner for future transactions. (That conclusion seems to me a non sequitur, but I accept it for the sake of argument.) This establishes, at most, that the scheme could not technically have been consummated if the mechanical step of the mailings to obtain conveyance of title had not occurred. But we have held that the indispensability of such mechanical mailings, not strictly in furtherance of the fraud, is not enough to invoke the statute. For example, when officials of a school district embezzled tax funds over the course of several years, we held that no mail fraud had occurred even though the success of the scheme plainly depended on the officials' causing tax bills to be sent by mail (and thus tax payments to be received) every year. *Parr v. United States*, 363 U.S., at 388–92. Similarly, when those officials caused the school district to pay by mail credit card bills—a step plainly necessary to enable their continued fraudulent use of the credit card—we concluded that no mail fraud had occurred.

I find it impossible to escape these precedents in the present case. Assuming the Court to be correct in concluding that failure to pass title to the cars would have threatened the success of the scheme, the same could have been said of failure to collect taxes or to pay the credit card bills in *Parr*. And I think it particularly significant that in *Kann* the government proposed a theory *identical* to that which the Court today uses. Since the scheme was ongoing, the government urged, the fact that the mailing of the two checks had occurred after the defendants had pocketed the fraudulently obtained cash made no difference. "[T]he defendants expected to receive further bonuses and profits," and therefore "the clearing of these checks in the ordinary course was essential to [the scheme's] further prosecution." The dissenters in *Kann* agreed. "[T]his," they said, "was not the last step in the fraudulent scheme. It was a continuing venture. Smooth clearances of the checks were essential lest these intermediate dividends be interrupted and the conspirators be called upon to disgorge." The Court rejected this argument, concluding that "the subsequent banking transactions between the banks concerned were merely incidental and collateral to the scheme and not a part of it." I think the mailing of the title application forms equivalently incidental here.

What Justice Frankfurter observed almost three decades ago remains true: "The adequate degree of relationship between a mailing which occurs during the life of a scheme and the scheme is ... not a matter susceptible of geometric determination." *Parr v. United States*, supra, at 397 (Frankfurter, J., dissenting). All the more reason to adhere as closely as possible to past cases. I think we have not done that today, and thus create problems for tomorrow.

NOTE ON *SCHMUCK v. UNITED STATES*

Res ipsa loquitur.

SECTION 3: SCHEME OR ARTIFICE TO DEFRAUD

United States v. Newman

United States Court of Appeals, Second Circuit, 1981.
664 F.2d 12.

■ VAN GRAAFEILAND, CIRCUIT JUDGE.

The United States appeals from an order of the United States District Court for the Southern District of New York which dismissed an indictment charging James Mitchell Newman with securities fraud, § 10(b) of the Securities and Exchange Act of 1934 (15 U.S.C. § 78j(b))[a] and Rule 10b–5 (17 C.F.R. § 240.10b–5),[b] mail fraud, 18 U.S.C. § 1341, and conspiracy to commit securities and mail fraud, 18 U.S.C. § 371. The District

---

[a] Section 10(b) of the 1934 Act, codified at 15 U.S.C. § 78j, provides:

"It shall be unlawful for any person, directly or indirectly, by the use of any means or instrumentality of interstate commerce or of the mails, or of any facility of any national securities exchange—

"(b) To use or employ, in connection with the purchase or sale of any security registered on a national securities exchange or any security not so registered, any manipulative or deceptive device or contrivance in contravention of such rules and regulations as the [Securities and Exchange] Commission may prescribe as necessary or appropriate in the public interest or for the protection of investors."—[Footnote by eds.]

[b] Rule 10b–5, 17 C.F.R. § 240.10b–5, provides:

"It shall be unlawful for any person, directly or indirectly, by the use of any means or instrumentality of interstate commerce, or of the mails or of any facility of any national securities exchange,

"(a) To employ any device, scheme, or artifice to defraud,

"(b) To make any untrue statement of a material fact or to omit to state a material fact necessary in order to make the statements made, in the light of the circumstances under which they were made, not misleading, or

"(c) To engage in any act, practice, or course of business which operates or would operate as a fraud or deceit upon any person, in connection with the purchase or sale of any security."—[Footnote by eds.]

Court dismissed the securities fraud charge because it concluded that "there was no 'clear and definite statement' in the federal securities laws which both antedated and proscribed the acts alleged in [the] indictment" so as to give the defendant a reasonable opportunity to know that his conduct was prohibited. The District Court held that the allegations of mail fraud failed as a matter of law to charge a crime. The conspiracy count, the District Court said, fell with the two substantive counts. We reverse.

Although the indictment names appellee Newman and E. Jacques Courtois, Jr., Franklin Carniol, and Constantine Spyropoulos as defendants, only Newman was within the jurisdiction of the District Court and a party to the proceedings below. The allegations of the indictment refer to all defendants, however, and, for purposes of this opinion, we assume the following summary of facts to be true.

Morgan Stanley & Co., Inc. and Kuhn Loeb & Co., now known as Lehman Brothers Kuhn Loeb, Inc., are investment banking firms which represent companies engaged in corporate mergers, acquisitions, tender offers, and other takeovers. From 1972 to 1975, Courtois and an alleged but unindicted co-conspirator, Adrian Antoniu, were employed by Morgan Stanley. In 1975, Antoniu left Morgan Stanley and went to work for Kuhn Loeb. Between January 1, 1973 and December 31, 1978, Courtois and Antoniu misappropriated confidential information concerning proposed mergers and acquisitions that was entrusted to their employers by corporate clients. This information was conveyed surreptitiously to Newman, a securities trader and manager of the over-the-counter trading department of a New York brokerage firm. Newman passed along the information to two confederates, Carniol, a resident of Belgium, and Spyropoulos, a Greek citizen who lived in both Greece and France. Using secret foreign bank and trust accounts and spreading their purchases among brokers, all for the purpose of avoiding detection, the three conspirators purchased stock in companies that were merger and takeover targets of clients of Morgan Stanley and Kuhn Loeb.[1] They then reaped substantial gains when the mergers or takeovers were announced and the market price of the stocks rose. These profits were shared with Courtois and Antoniu, the sources of the wrongfully-acquired information.

We believe that these allegations of wrongdoing were sufficient to withstand challenge in all three counts.

THE SECURITIES FRAUD

In preparing the indictment, the government attempted to remedy a deficiency that led to the Supreme Court's reversal of a conviction in

---

[1] In two instances the targets themselves were clients of the investment banking firms. The government belatedly suggests that the indictment should be construed to allege securities laws violations in these two instances, on the theory that the defendants, by purchasing stock in the target companies, defrauded the shareholders of those companies. Whatever validity that approach might have, it is not fairly within the allegations of the indictment, which allege essentially that the defendants defrauded the investment banking firms and the firms' takeover clients.

Chiarella v. United States, 445 U.S. 222 (1980). In that case, the defendant secured confidential information concerning proposed corporate takeovers through his position as a mark-up in a financial printing establishment doing work for companies planning takeovers. He, too, prospered by purchasing stock in target companies. His conviction for § 10(b) and Rule 10b–5 violations was affirmed by this court, United States v. Chiarella, 588 F.2d 1358 (2d Cir.1978), but reversed by the Supreme Court because that Court found no fiduciary relationship between Chiarella and the sellers of stock which imposed upon him a duty to speak. 445 U.S. at 231–35.

The thrust of the government's case in *Chiarella* was that the defendant violated § 10(b) and Rule 10(b)–5 by failing to disclose material, nonpublic information to the shareholders of target companies from whom he purchased stock. As the Court observed, "[t]he jury was not instructed on the nature or elements of a duty owed by petitioner to anyone other than the sellers." To remedy the deficiency in *Chiarella*, the government here has pointed its charge of wrongdoing in a different direction. The indictment charges that Courtois and Antoniu breached the trust and confidence placed in them and their employers by the employers' corporate clients and the clients' shareholders, and the trust and confidence placed in Courtois and Antoniu by their employers. The indictment charges further that Newman, Carniol, and Spyropoulos "aided, participated in and facilitated Courtois and Antoniu in violating the fiduciary duties of honesty, loyalty and silence owed directly to Morgan Stanley, Kuhn Loeb, and clients of those investment banks." The indictment also charges that Courtois, Newman, and Carniol "did directly and indirectly, (a) employ devices, schemes, and artifices to defraud and (b) engage in acts, practices, and courses of business which operated as a fraud and deceit on Morgan Stanley, Kuhn Loeb, and those corporations and shareholders on whose behalf Morgan Stanley or Kuhn Loeb was acting, and to whom Morgan Stanley or Kuhn Loeb owed fiduciary duties, in connection with the purchase of securities. . . ."

Then Chief Judge Kaufman, writing for this court in *Chiarella*, stated that violation of an agent's duty to respect client confidences was a clear transgression of Rule 10b–5 "where, as here, the converted information both concerned securities and was used to purchase and sell securities."[2] The Supreme Court majority found it unnecessary to decide whether this theory had merit, because it was not presented to the jury. Justice Stevens stated in his concurring opinion that a legitimate argument could be made that Chiarella's conduct constituted a fraud or deceit upon his employer's clients but that it could also be argued that there was no actionable violation of Rule 10b–5 because the clients were neither purchasers nor sellers of target company securities. He added that the Court "wisely leaves the resolution of this issue for another day." For this court, that day has now come.

[2] Although Judge Meskill dissented in *United States v. Chiarella*, his dissent seems to be based primarily upon the absence of a special relationship between Chiarella and the sellers of the stock, the point which the Supreme Court held to be determinative.

We hold that appellee's conduct as alleged in the indictment could be found to constitute a criminal violation of § 10(b) and Rule 10b–5[3] despite the fact that neither Morgan Stanley, Kuhn Loeb nor their clients was at the time a purchaser or seller of the target company securities in any transaction with any of the defendants.

Because enforcement of § 10(b) and Rule 10b–5 has been largely by means of civil litigation, it is easy to forget that § 10(b) was written as both a regulatory and criminal piece of legislation. Looking at the language of the statute, the "starting point in every case involving construction," Blue Chip Stamps v. Manor Drug Stores, 421 U.S. 723, 756 (1975)(Powell, J. concurring), we find no express provision for a private civil remedy. Section 21 of the Securities and Exchange Act of 1934, 15 U.S.C. § 78u, gives the SEC broad investigatory powers and access to the district court for injunctive and mandamus help in preventing illegal practices. Section 32, 15 U.S.C. § 78ff, provides criminal penalties for willful violation of the act or rules thereunder, violation of which is made unlawful or the observance of which is required under the act. There is nothing in the history of the act to indicate that Congress intended any remedies other than these. *Blue Chip Stamps v. Manor Drug Stores*, supra, 421 U.S., at 729.

Rule 10b–5 makes it unlawful for any person to engage in any act or practice which operates as a fraud or deceit upon any person "in connection with the purchase or sale of any security." When litigation under this Rule is instituted by the SEC under § 21 or by a United States Attorney under § 32, the court's concern must be with the scope of the Rule, not plaintiff's standing to sue. See SEC v. National Securities, Inc., 393 U.S. 453, 467 n. 9 (1969); United States v. Naftalin, 441 U.S. 768, 774 n. 6 (1979). It is only because the judiciary has created a private cause of action for damages the "contours" of which are not described in the statute, that standing in such cases has become a pivotal issue. *Blue Chip Stamps v. Manor Drug Stores*, supra, 421 U.S. at 737, 749. The courts, not the Congress, have limited Rule 10b–5 suits for damages to the purchasers and sellers of securities. The District Court's statement that fraud perpetrated upon purchasers or sellers of securities is a "requisite element under the securities laws" is, therefore, an overbroad and incorrect summary of the law.

Long before appellee undertook to participate in the fraudulent scheme alleged in the indictment, this court, and other Courts of Appeals as well, had held that a plaintiff need not be a defrauded purchaser or seller in order to sue for injunctive relief under Rule 10b–5. See Crane Co. v. Westinghouse Air Brake Co., 419 F.2d 787, 798 (2d Cir.1969); Mutual Shares Corp. v. Genesco Inc., 384 F.2d 540, 546–47 (2d Cir.1967); Kahan v. Rosenstiel, 424 F.2d 161, 173 (3d Cir.1970); Britt v. Cyril Bath Co., 417 F.2d 433, 436 (6th Cir.1969). These holdings were consistent with the

[3] The acts covered by the indictment occurred prior to promulgation of Rule 14e–3, dealing specifically with insider trading in connection with tender offers. 17 C.F.R. § 240.14e–3.

language of Rule 10b–5, which contains no specific requirement that fraud be perpetrated upon the seller or buyer of securities. Appellee reasonably should have anticipated that in a criminal action the courts likewise would follow the language of the Rule.

In determining whether the indictment in the instant case charges a violation of Rule 10b-5, we need spend little time on the issue of fraud and deceit. The wrongdoing charged against appellee and his cohorts was not simply internal corporate mismanagement. See Superintendent of Insurance v. Bankers Life & Casualty Co., 404 U.S. 6, 12 (1971). In *United States v. Chiarella*, supra, 445 U.S., at 245, Chief Justice Burger, in dissenting, said that the defendant "misappropriated—stole to put it bluntly—valuable nonpublic information entrusted to him in the utmost confidence." See, also, the dissenting opinion of Justice Blackmun in which Justice Marshall concurred. Id. at 245–46. That characterization aptly describes the conduct of the connivers in the instant case.

Had appellant used similar deceptive practices to mulct Morgan Stanley and Kuhn Loeb of cash or securities, it could hardly be argued that those companies had not been defrauded. See *Superintendent of Insurance v. Bankers Life & Casualty Co.*, supra, 404 U.S. at 10–11. By sullying the reputations of Courtois' and Antoniu's employers as safe repositories of client confidences, appellee and his cohorts defrauded those employers as surely as if they took their money.

Appellee and his cohorts also wronged Morgan Stanley's and Kuhn Loeb's clients, whose takeover plans were keyed to target company stock prices fixed by market forces, not artificially inflated through purchases by purloiners of confidential information.

> "In a tender-offer situation, the effect of increased activity in purchases of target company's shares is, similarly, to drive up the price of the target company's shares; but this effect is damaging to the offering company because the tender offer will appear commensurately less attractive and the activity may cause it to abort."

13A B. Fox & E. Fox, Business Organizations, Corporate Acquisitions and Mergers § 27.05[4] (1981).

In other areas of the law, deceitful misappropriation of confidential information by a fiduciary, whether described as theft, conversion, or breach of trust, has consistently been held to be unlawful. Appellee would have had to be most ingenuous to believe that Congress intended to establish a less rigorous code of conduct under the Securities Acts.

Appellee is left, then, with the argument that his fraud had no connection with the purchase or sale of securities. However, since appellee's sole purpose in participating in the misappropriation of confidential takeover information was to purchase shares of the target companies, we find little merit in his disavowal of a connection between the fraud and the purchase.

In 1972, the year preceding the one in which appellee's fraudulent scheme was hatched, the Supreme Court decided Superintendent of Insurance v. Bankers Life & Casualty Co., supra, 404 U.S. 6 (1971). The Court construed the phrase "in connection with" flexibly to include deceptive practices "touching" the sale of securities, a relationship which has been described as "very tenuous indeed". 1 A. Bromberg & L. Lowenfels, Securities Fraud and Commodity Fraud § 4.7(574)(3) at 88.34 (1979). This Court and others have followed the teachings of the *Bankers Life* case.

In Competitive Associates, Inc. v. Laventhol, Krekstein, Horwath & Horwath, 516 F.2d 811, 815 (2d Cir.1975), which involved the allegedly fraudulent certification of financial statements, we said:

> "The broad 'touch' test enunciated in *Bankers Life* is certainly met by plaintiff's allegations that the very purpose of defendants' certification of Takara's financial statement was to aid in placing Yamada in a position where he could manipulate securities prices and sell these securities to investors attracted by Yamada's reputation and performance."

We reversed summary judgment in defendants' favor because, we said, that "[p]laintiff has alleged a fraudulent scheme the accomplishment of which is directly related to the trading process."

In *United States v. Naftalin*, supra, 441 U.S. 768, where the defendant was convicted of violating § 17(a)(1) of the Securities Act of 1933, 15 U.S.C. § 77q(a)(1), by defrauding his broker-agent, the Court held that investor protection was not the sole purpose of the act. Justice Brennan, writing for the Court, said that a "key part" of the program evidenced by enactment of the federal securities statutes was the "effort 'to achieve a high standard of business ethics ... *in every facet of the securities industry.*' "

The court below, in holding that appellee could not be held criminally liable for violating Rule 10b–5 unless he defrauded a purchaser or seller, misconstrued the thrust of the Securities Acts. Moreover, putting aside the question of standing, as we must in this criminal case, we believe that Rule 10b–5's proscription of fraudulent and deceptive practices upon any person in connection with the purchase or sale of a security provided clear notice to appellee that his fraudulent conduct was unlawful.

THE MAIL FRAUD

The indictment charges appellee and his cohorts with devising a scheme and artifice to defraud and with misappropriating confidential information concerning mergers and acquisitions and covertly using that information to buy stock in target companies. It clearly charges appellee with fraudulent misappropriation of property that did not belong to him. Intangibles such as "confidential and nonpublic commercial information" fall within the definition of "property" under the mail fraud statute.[4]

---

[4] Confidential business secrets are specifically protected in a number of criminal statutes. See, e.g., 18 U.S.C. § 1702; N.Y. Penal Law, §§ 155.00, 155.30(3).

We believe the District Court misconstrued the law of this Circuit concerning fraudulent breaches of fiduciary obligations under the statute. United States v. Von Barta, 635 F.2d 999 (2d Cir.1980), upon which the District Court relied, did not involve fraudulent misappropriation of confidential information entrusted to an employer. *Von Barta* concerned an employee's failure to disclose material information to his employer, allegedly in breach of a fiduciary duty of honesty and loyalty. The fraudulent scheme in the instant case ... was more egregious. Its "object was to filch from [the employer] its valuable property by dishonest, devious, reprehensible means." Abbott v. United States, 239 F.2d 310, 314 (5th Cir.1956).

However, in addition to alleging fraudulent misappropriation of an employer's secret information, this indictment also alleges that the scheme included breach of the employees' fiduciary duties by material misrepresentations to the employer and non-disclosure of material information required to be disclosed. In *Von Barta* the government had asserted the broad claim that every employee breach of a fiduciary duty of honesty and loyalty violates the mail fraud statute. Although we rejected that sweeping claim, we concluded that an employee's breach of his fiduciary obligations is actionable under the statute when it encompasses the violation of a "duty to disclose material information to his employer." If *Von Barta* left any doubt in the matter, and we do not believe that it did, United States v. Bronston, 658 F.2d 920, 926 (2d Cir., 1981), decided after the District Court's ruling in this case, clearly spelled out that "the concealment by a fiduciary of a material information which he is under a duty to disclose to another under circumstances where the non-disclosure could or does result in harm to another is a violation of the [mail fraud] statute." We do not intend, of course, that this rule be used in bootstrap fashion by finding an obligation to disclose in every breach of fiduciary duty. However, the indictment charges that Courtois and Antoniu were specifically required to report the buying activity which they concealed and that they falsely and fraudulently asserted that they maintained no direct or indirect interests in securities trading accounts. This was a sufficient averment of wrongdoing under *United States v. Bronston*, supra, and *United States v. Von Barta*, supra.[5]

---

[5] The District Court feared that the indictment here was an attempt to revive the broad theory of employee fiduciary liability rejected in *Von Barta*. The court cited the following portion of ¶ 10(d) of the indictment:

"In so doing, and by sharing profits from the sale of those securities with Courtois and Antoniu, Newman, Carniol and Spyropoulos aided, participated in and facilitated Courtois and Antoniu in violating the fiduciary duties of honesty, loyalty and silence owed directly to Morgan Stanley, Kuhn Loeb, and clients of those investment bankers."

However, this allegation does not rest on a theory that every employee fiduciary breach is actionable. On the contrary, the allegation is far narrower. The introductory words, "In so doing," refer to the immediately preceding allegations, which charge that Newman, along with Carniol and Spyropoulos:

"received covert information and advice from Antoniu and (through Antoniu) from Courtois. Based on that information and advice, Newman, Carniol and Spyropoulos opened and maintained secret foreign accounts and purchased target companies' securities through those secret foreign accounts."

The District Court erred in holding that, in every mail fraud case based upon a breach of fiduciary duty by a private employee, there must be proof of "direct, tangible, economic loss to the victim, actual or contemplated." Assuming, however, that such proof would be required in the instant case, the indictment fairly informed appellee that this was part of the charge against which he must defend. Appellee could not have been unaware that confidential information, such as that involved here, has a "negative" value which is diminished when confidentiality is lost. As discussed above, Morgan Stanley and Kuhn Loeb, and their clients as well, would almost surely be prejudiced if the veil of secrecy surrounding contemplated tender offers was fraudulently and surreptitiously lifted. At least, the jury could so find.

THE CONSPIRACY

Because dismissal of the substantive counts led to the dismissal of the conspiracy count, reinstatement of the former requires the reinstatement of the latter.

DISPOSITION

The order dismissing the indictment is reversed, and the matter is remanded to the District Court for further proceedings consistent with this opinion.

DUMBAULD, SENIOR DISTRICT JUDGE, concurring and dissenting.

I am not certain that the deceptive practice engaged in by defendant and his confederates was a fraud "in connection with the purchase or sale of any security" and hence violative of § 10(b) of the Securities Exchange Act of 1934. Chiarella v. United States, 445 U.S. 222 (1980), and Blue Chip Stamps v. Manor Drug Stores, 421 U.S. 723 (1975), seem to evince a trend to confine the scope of § 10(b) to practices harmful to participants in actual purchase-sale transactions.

The culprits in the case at bar (as in *Chiarella*) owed no duty to the sellers of the target company securities which they purchased. Though they deceptively and improperly violated a fiduciary duty to their employers and customers of their employers, those parties had not at that time actually purchased or sold any target company securities. All that can be said is, as Mr. Justice Stevens judiciously observes, that respectable arguments could be made in support of either position (445 U.S. at 238).

Hence I prefer to rest my concurrence in the reversal of the District Court's exculpation of defendant from trial for his reprehensible activities upon the more solid ground that he has clearly violated the Mail Fraud statute, 18 U.S.C. § 1341. As required by that provision, defendant is a person who "having devised . . . a scheme . . . to defraud," for the purpose of "executing such scheme" makes use of the mails.

In view of the sophisticated mechanisms employed for concealment of defendant's activities by use of foreign bank accounts, distribution of purchase orders, and utilization of confederates abroad, it is plain that the fraudulent scheme contemplated use of the mails as an integral feature of its operation and an essential incident to its successful consummation. Pereira v. United States, 347 U.S. 1, 8–9 (1954). That defendant's scheme was one to defraud is explicitly demonstrated by United States v. Von Barta, 635 F.2d 999, 1006–07 (2d Cir.1980).

Accordingly, I concur in reversal of the order of the District Court.

NOTES ON THE MEANING OF "SCHEME OR ARTIFICE TO DEFRAUD"

1. ***United States v. States***. The case often cited as giving impetus, if not birth, to the "intangible rights" theory of mail fraud is United States v. States, 488 F.2d 761 (8th Cir.1973). Isaac States was a candidate for Democratic Committeeman from a ward in the city of St. Louis. Robert Morgan was a candidate for Republican Committeeman from a different ward in the same city. Morgan and his campaign manager devised a scheme to invent some phantom voters who could then engage in extensive write-in voting for Morgan. They invited States to join in their scheme, after which Morgan and States came up with a more elaborate plan. They applied by mail for absentee ballots in the names of the made-up voters. When the Board of Elections mailed out the ballots, Michael McCoy, an accomplice, filled them out and returned the fake votes. Twenty-one such ballots were actually delivered by the Post Office, but postal authorities caught on to the scheme when route mail carriers recognized that the nonexistent persons listed on the envelope did not live at the address to which the mail was to be delivered. A "multi-count" indictment for mail fraud, using a fictitious name for the purpose of carrying out a scheme to defraud (18 U.S.C. § 1342), and conspiracy to commit mail fraud in violation of 18 U.S.C. § 371 was returned. The District Court (William J. Webster, J.) denied motions to dismiss the indictments and, after a bench trial, the defendants were convicted. On appeal, they argued that no mail fraud was committed, and that the other charges fell with the mail fraud charge. The Circuit Court, Judge Matthes writing for the panel, agreed that the other charges were contingent on a violation of the mail fraud statute. But the court affirmed the convictions because it found mail fraud to have been committed.

The defendants argued that the mail fraud statute applied only to cases where "money or property" was the object of the fraud. Specifically, they contended that when Congress added the words "or for obtaining money or property by means of false or fraudulent pretenses, representations, or promises" to the already existing "scheme or artifice to defraud" language, it meant to add to the types of fraudulent activity reached by the statute and to express its belief that "money or property" were the forbidden objectives. But the court held that "the more natural construction of the wording of the statute is to view the two phrases independently, rather than complementary of one another." Other courts, it noted, had construed the words "scheme or artifice to defraud" without reference to the later-enacted language. "Consequently, we hold," the court said, "that the language of the statute on its face does not preclude a finding that a 'scheme or artifice to defraud' need not concern money or property." Since it found no help in the statutory text, and "since the legislative history does not deal with the scope and meaning of the provision of the statute in issue," the court turned to prior judicial constructions to resolve the case.

It began by noting that "the concept of fraud in § 1341 is to be construed very broadly," citing Durland v. United States, 161 U.S. 306 (1896). It also cited Shushan v. United States, 117 F.2d 110 (5th Cir. 1941)(about which more below), and the following language from Blachly v. United States, 380 F.2d 665 (5th Cir.1967):

> "The crime of mail fraud is broad in scope. ... The fraudulent aspect of the scheme to 'defraud' is measured by a nontechnical standard. ... Law puts its imprimatur on the accepted moral standards and condemns conduct which fails to match the 'reflection of moral uprightness, of fundamental honesty, fair play and right dealing in the general and business life of the members of society.' This is indeed broad. For as Judge Holmes once observed, '[t]he law does not define fraud; it needs no definition. It is as old as falsehood and as versable as human ingenuity.'"

"Likewise," the court added, "the definition of fraud in § 1341 is to be broadly and liberally construed to further the purpose of the statute; namely, to prohibit the misuse of the mails to further fraudulent enterprises," citing *Durland* again.

"Here, we have a scheme by the appellants," the court next observed, "to deceive and defraud the public and the Board of Election Commissioners of certain intangible political and civil rights." The court found one district court decision (United States v. Classic, 35 F.Supp. 457 (E.D.La. 1940)) that had agreed in the context of election fraud, and then turned to cases involving bribery of public officials. *Shushan* was the first such case. It found in *Shushan* "the implication that a scheme to gain personal favors from public officials is a scheme to defraud the public, although the interest lost by the public can be described no more concretely than as an intangible right to the proper and honest administration of government." It also found "[t]his concept, that a scheme to defraud of certain intangible rights is grounds for prosecution under § 1341 if the mails are used ... more explicitly stated in United States v. Faser, 303 F.Supp. 380 (E.D.La.1969)." In that case, the court refused to dismiss an indictment against officials who accepted bribes to deposit public funds in a particular bank. Finally, the court found precedent for mail fraud indictments to prosecute "a scheme to defraud a corporation of the 'honest and faithful services' of one or more employees," United States v. Procter & Gamble Co., 47 F.Supp. 676 (D.Mass.1942),[c] and a "scheme 'to defraud the public' by issuing false

---

[c] This case involved a demurrer, overruled by the trial judge, to an indictment alleging that bribes were paid by Proctor & Gamble and some of its employees to "certain employees of Lever Brothers Company" in order to obtain "certain experimental cakes of soap, secret processes, formulas, facts and figures, etc." The Court quoted another case to the effect that "[t]o try to delimit 'fraud' by definition would tend to

medical diplomas and licenses to persons without medical education,'' Alexander v. United States, 95 F.2d 873 (8th Cir.1938).

The Court then concluded:

"Nevertheless, the appellants argue that the application of the mail fraud statute to the facts of this case will result in a 'policing' of state election procedure, and that Congress has never explicitly authorized such widespread intervention into state affairs. The appellants' argument misinterprets the purpose of the mail fraud legislation. The focus of the statute is upon the misuse of the Postal Service, not the regulation of state affairs, and Congress clearly has the authority to regulate such misuse of the mails. See Badders v. United States, 240 U.S. 391, 393 (1916): 'The overt act of putting a letter into the post-office of the United States is a matter that Congress may regulate. ... Whatever the limits to its power, it may forbid any such acts done in furtherance of a scheme it regards as contrary to public policy, whether it can forbid the scheme or not.' The purpose of 18 U.S.C. § 1341 is to prevent the Postal Service from being used to carry out fraudulent schemes, regardless of what is the exact nature of the scheme and regardless of whether it happens to be forbidden by state law. See Parr v. United States, 363 U.S. 370, 389, 390 (1960). 'Congress definitely intends that the misuse of the mails shall be controlled even though it be its policy to leave the control of elections to the several states.' *United States v. Classic*, supra, 35 F.Supp. at 458.

"The appellants' argument presents no justification for refusing to apply the mail fraud statutes to the facts of this case. The prosecution of appellants in federal court for mail fraud does not interfere with the state's enforcement of its election laws. There are no grounds for dismissing the indictment under the principles of comity or the abstention doctrine or under any other principle of federalism.''

The Court accordingly held that "the indictment alleged a federal offense and the evidence proved every element thereof.''

Judge Ross wrote a separate concurring opinion:

"I reluctantly concur. The law, as capably expressed by Judge Matthes, leaves us no other alternative.

"However, I cannot believe that it was the original intent of Congress that the federal government should take over the prosecution of every state crime involving fraud just because the mails have been used in furtherance of that crime. The facts in this case show that this election fraud was purely a state matter. It

reward subtle and ingenious circumvention and is not done," and then said that "the normal relationship of employer and employee implies that the employee will be loyal and honest ... and that he will not wrongfully divulge ... confidential information....'' Given this, "[w]hen one tampers with that relationship for the purpose of causing the employee to breach his duty he in effect is defrauding the employer of a lawful right.''

should have been prosecuted in state court. The Assistant United States Attorney conceded in oral argument that the case was not the type of mail fraud case covered by written instructions contained in the United States Attorneys' manual. In spite of this, the decision was made by the United States Attorney to prosecute the case without asking or receiving the approval of the Department of Justice. In so doing, he relieved the state of its duty to police the violation of its local election laws and helped create a precedent which will encourage the same sort of unwarranted federal preemption in the future."

2. *United States v. Isaacs*. United States v. Isaacs, 493 F.2d 1124 (7th Cir.1974), is a well known application of the "intangible rights" theory, if only because of the identity of one of the defendants. A 29–count indictment, followed by a six-week trial, resulted in the conviction of Theodore Isaacs and Otto Kerner for a variety of offenses, including mail fraud.[d] Isaacs was the Illinois Director of Revenue at the time of the offense. Kerner was Governor at that time and at the time of the trial and appeal was a sitting Judge on the Seventh Circuit Court of Appeals. Their conviction of mail fraud was affirmed, and Kerner was later impeached.[e]

It took the appellate court more than eight pages to describe the complex financial arrangements that led to the convictions, but essentially they boil down to accepting bribes (of $178,000 in Kerner's case) for favorable consideration of horse racing dates and other related actions to protect the interests of private tracks. As the court described it, the defendants "were charged with defrauding the state of Illinois and its citizens of the honest and faithful services of Kerner as governor, failing to administer the laws of the state in an impartial manner, obtaining secret profits as a result of the bribery scheme in which they actively participated, and defrauding the racing associations of Illinois of the right to obtain racing dates free from corruption and bribery." They argued on appeal that the indictment was defective because it did not charge that they defrauded anyone "out of something of definable value, money or property." Absent a monetary loss, they contended, there was merely a breach of fiduciary duty that did not violate § 1341.

The court held that "[t]he mail fraud statute is not restricted in its application to cases in which the victim has suffered actual monetary or property loss." It supported this assertion with discussions of the parallel line of cases under 18 U.S.C. § 371 (conspiracy to defraud the United States) and two Circuit Court cases, *Shushan* and United States v. George,

---

[d] The other offenses ranged from violations of the Travel Act to perjury before the grand jury and a series of income tax offenses.

[e] One of the questions argued on the appeal was whether the federal courts could exercise criminal jurisdiction over a sitting federal judge. The Court held that such jurisdiction was appropriate: "Otherwise, a person upon assuming federal judicial office would receive amnesty and would not be accountable for his misdeeds, whenever they occurred. We believe that the framers of the Constitution did not intend such a result." Isaacs and Kerner were sentenced to three years' imprisonment and fines totaling $50,-000.

477 F.2d 508 (7th Cir.1973).[f] It then concluded that there was sufficient evidence in the record that "the state of Illinois and its citizens were deprived of the loyal and honest services of their governor, Kerner" and "that the defendants actually did exert special influence in favor of and bestowed preferential treatment on" horse racing interests.

3. *United States v. Mandel*. Another well known application of the "intangible rights" theory of mail fraud involved a former Governor of Maryland, Marvin Mandel. Mandel and five other defendants were convicted of 15 counts of mail fraud and one RICO count.[g] Mandel was sentenced to four years in prison. The facts involved a complicated series of events concerning the allocation of racing days to horse tracks in Maryland. There was evidence that Governor Mandel received bribes for his part in legislation that expanded the racing days allocated to a particular track and that he participated in a scheme to hide the true ownership of the racing interests involved (and his business dealings with the owners) from the Maryland legislature and other state officials.

In United States v. Mandel, 591 F.2d 1347 (4th Cir.1979), a panel of the Fourth Circuit broadly described the scope of the mail fraud statute. It rejected the argument that some violation of state law must be shown, stating that "[a]s a result of the failure to limit the term 'scheme or artifice to defraud' to common law definitions of fraud and false pretenses and schemes prohibited by state law, the mail fraud statute generally has been available to prosecute a scheme involving deception that employs the mails in its execution that is contrary to public policy and conflicts with accepted standards of moral uprightness, fundamental honesty, fair play and right dealing." It held that there were two theories on which Mandel could have been convicted. The first was that Mandel received bribes: "[w]hen a public official has been bribed, he breaches his duty of honest, faithful and disinterested services." The second was that he failed to disclose material information to relevant public officials. Nondisclosure or concealment, in turn, could be based on either of two types of behavior: "the official's failure to disclose the existence of a direct interest in a matter he is passing on defrauds the public and pertinent public bodies of their intangible right to honest, loyal, faithful and disinterested government." Alternatively, the statute is violated "when there has been a fraudulent statement of facts, or a deliberate concealment thereof, to a public body, in order to receive a benefit by action of a public body." This latter form of behavior consti-

[f] In *George*, an employee of Zenith Radio Corporation took kickbacks from a supplier of radio cabinets. The supplier was the only available source at the time and the price paid by Zenith was fair and reasonable. Nonetheless, as the *Isaacs'* court quoted, "[i]f there was intent . . . to deprive Zenith of [its employee's] honest and loyal services in the form of his giving [the supplier] preferential treatment, it is simply beside the point that [the employee] may not have had to (or had occasion to) exert special influence in favor of [the supplier] or that Zenith was satisfied with [the supplier's] product and prices."

[g] The RICO statute is dealt with in detail in Chapter IV, infra. For now, it is sufficient to know that the RICO charge was predicated on the mail fraud counts and that it stood or fell with the outcome on those counts of the indictment.

tutes "the deprivation of the public of the right to have its officials act on other than false information."

The panel majority (Judge Widener writing) reversed the conviction, however, because it thought the jury had not been properly instructed. The defect in the instructions on the bribery theory was that bribery was not defined, that is, the jury was not told that bribery is distinguished from "legally innocent benefits" by the existence of some expected quid pro quo. The problem with the nondisclosure theory was that Mandel claimed that he did not know the information it was claimed he withheld from the legislature and others and the jury was not asked to make a specific finding that he was aware of the information. Plainly, the panel majority thought, "[i]f Governor Mandel did not know who any of the real owners of Marlboro were ..., he could hardly have participated with specific intent ... in a scheme to defraud that involved the misrepresentation or concealment of the names...."

Judge Butzner dissented. He did not dispute the necessity of charging the jury in the terms required by the majority. But he read the charge as a whole as clearly satisfying the majority's objective. The alleged bribes were discussed at length by the trial judge in context and, Judge Butzner concluded, the court "repeatedly stressed the legal requirement of a quid pro quo when discussing the contentions of the individual defendants." And the trial court defined fraud to include the "intentional use of false or fraudulent representations" and "told the jury that Mandel could not be convicted unless he had knowingly participated in the scheme to defraud...." The additional instruction sought by Mandel thus was duplicative of instructions already in substance given, and need not have been given.

The government motion for a rehearing en banc was granted, but the court that heard the case was reduced by recusals to six members. In United States v. Mandel, 602 F.2d 653 (4th Cir.1979), the judges set aside the panel decision and affirmed the conviction by an equally divided court. The one paragraph opinion stated that a majority would affirm the convictions against all arguments "except the claim of error in the charge to the jury which was the point upon which there was equal division." A second rehearing was denied, and the Supreme Court denied certiorari.

Mandel served 19 months of his four-year sentence. The remainder was commuted. He was also disbarred. When the Supreme Court in McNally v. United States, 483 U.S. 350 (1987), decided that the "intangible rights" theory could not be used as the basis for a mail fraud conviction, Mandel returned to court. He could not seek habeas corpus because he was no longer in "custody" as a result of his conviction. But there was federal precedent supporting the award of a writ of error coram nobis in similar circumstances. A federal District Court granted him such a writ, setting aside the conviction in light of McNally. In United States v. Mandel, 862 F.2d 1067 (4th Cir.1988), a divided panel of the Fourth Circuit affirmed. The court, per Judge Widener, found the case indistinguishable from McNally, in spite of two theories the government advanced to distinguish the two cases. The government's first theory was that the state was deprived of "property" because the bribes given to Mandel belonged to the state under a constructive trust. The second theory was that the state was deprived of the racing days that were allocated as a result of the bribes. But even if these theories were sound, the court concluded, the jury was not instructed as to them, and they thus came too late.

In dissent, Judge K.K. Hall argued that granting the coram nobis remedy was inappropriate. That remedy, he asserted, was available only to redress an error "of the most fundamental character" where "there has been a complete breakdown in the legal system." Since the record revealed facts and circumstances under which Mandel could have been convicted under proper post-*McNally* instructions, he would have been content to let the conviction stand because:

> "Marvin Mandel, then governor of Maryland, took bribes totalling at least $380,000 to manipulate the workings of state government, which had been entrusted to him by the people of Maryland, to divert extremely valuable racing days to his cohorts. His motive, their motive, was profit—profit proven to be at the expense of the people of the state of Maryland. Although their trial included an erroneous jury instruction [when tested against *McNally*], the proceedings were replete with evidence of bribery and manipulation. Their actions were and are patently illegal. My sense of justice does not compel me to set aside these convictions."[h]

4. ***United States v. Von Barta***. United States v. Von Barta, 635 F.2d 999 (2d Cir.1980), was said by the *Newman* court not to have foreclosed its decision. The court in *Von Barta* stated the task before it as follows:

> "In this case, we are asked to construe two seemingly limitless provisions, the mail and wire fraud statutes, in the context of the employer-employee relationship. The government urges us to hold that these statutes are violated whenever an employee, acting to further a scheme for pecuniary gain, intentionally breaches a fiduciary duty of honesty or loyalty he owes his employer. The defendant decries this 'overcriminalization' of the employment relationship, and asks us to declare his alleged conduct exempt from criminal sanction. While we reject the sweeping theory advanced by the government, we find that the mail and wire fraud statutes do reach the conduct with which the defendant is charged."

Von Barta had been charged with seven counts of mail fraud, seven counts of wire fraud, and one count of conspiracy to commit those offenses. The District Court dismissed the indictment on the ground that it failed to

[h] There is now a conflict in the circuits over the availability of coram nobis in "intangible rights" mail fraud cases where the sentence has been completely served. In contrast to *Mandel*, see United States v. Bush, 888 F.2d 1145 (7th Cir.1989).

charge a "scheme or artifice to defraud." On the government's appeal, the Circuit Court reversed.

The indictment alleged that Von Barta was employed as a salesman and trader of government bonds at a small securities firm in New York City. He was specifically told never to jeopardize the firm's banking relationships and always to advise his superior if the firm's repurchase agreements were in trouble. He was also given considerable discretion to open new customer accounts and knew that his decisions in that respect would not be re-examined by other members of the firm. Together with another person employed at a larger brokerage firm, Von Barta formed the Piwacket Corp. Von Barta and his cohort each contributed $5,000 to the corporate coffers. Von Barta, without telling anyone of his interest in Piwacket or its meager capitalization, then opened an account for Piwacket at his firm. Piwacket became one of Von Barta's best "clients," generating substantial commissions and, using the firm's credit, eventually speculated in more than $50 million in government bonds. It incurred liabilities in excess of the combined ability of Piwacket and the securities firm itself to cover. When the volume of Piwacket's trading came to the attention of his superior, the indictment alleged, Von Barta lied about his involvement and about Piwacket's assets.

Von Barta made money (about $200,000) at first, but the market weakened and the scheme came to ground. The two securities firms (that is, Von Barta's and his confederate's) eventually had to pick up a loss in the range of $2 million. The government's theory of why this constituted mail fraud was broad:

> "In setting out its theory of the indictment, the government has repeatedly refused to rely on allegations that Von Barta intended to defraud [his firm] of any tangible interest. Rather, the government charges that 'Von Barta, by abusing his fiduciary position as an employee . . . , and concealing material information, defrauded [his firm] of the right to his honest and faithful services, as well as of its right to decide what business risks to bear with all the facts before it.' "

"Thus," the court observed, "we are asked to decide whether Von Barta's alleged scheme to defraud his employer of only these intangible interests violates the mail and wire fraud statutes."

The Court held that the allegations summarized above were sufficient:

> "The absence of legislative guidance has left the courts with broad discretion to apply the mail fraud statute to the myriad fraudulent schemes devised by unscrupulous entrepreneurs. This process of case-by-case development has produced several limiting principles.[14] But not all the rules the courts have fashioned

[14] "Thus, to make out a mail fraud violation, the government must show that the scheme was devised with the specific intent to defraud. . . . To prove mail fraud, the prosecution must also demonstrate that the use of the mails in furtherance of the scheme

narrow the statute's scope. For example, it is now generally accepted that the object of the fraudulent scheme need not be the deprivation of a tangible interest. Artifices designed to cause losses of an intangible nature also violate the statute. ... Recognizing that § 1341 reaches some schemes causing intangible loss, we must determine whether 'mail fraud' encompasses all fraudulent schemes involving an employer's deprivation of his right to his employee's loyal and honest services.

"Despite the broad language contained in some opinions, several courts have held that the breach of an employee's fiduciary duty, without more, does not violate the mail fraud statute. The additional element which frequently transforms a mere fiduciary breach into a criminal offense is a violation of the employee's duty to disclose material information to his employer. ...

"Our discussion is not to be construed as holding that an employee's duty to disclose material information to his employer must be imposed by state or federal statute. Indeed, the employment relationship, by itself, may oblige an employee not to conceal, and in fact to reveal, information he has reason to believe is material to the conduct of his employer's business.

"[W]e have no difficulty holding that Von Barta was under a duty to apprise [his firm] of material information concerning Piwacket's trading in government bonds. [W]e need not decide whether all employees risk prosecution for mail fraud if they fail to reveal material information to their employers. Nor must we express any opinion as to what constitutes material information. We simply hold that on the facts alleged by the government, Von Barta's breach of his duty of disclosure subjects him to prosecution for mail fraud."

5. *United States v. Bronston*. In United States v. Bronston, 658 F.2d 920 (2d Cir.1981), an attorney was convicted of mail fraud for representing two clients with inconsistent interests. Two venture capital companies had engaged a law firm to assist in a $1.3 million investment in BusTop, the then-holder of a bus stop construction and maintenance contract with the city of New York. BusTop's contract was up for renewal, and it was important to the value of the investment that BusTop be successful in a continuation of its business with the city. Bronston, a Senator in the state legislature and a partner in the law firm, went to another partner (Lindenbaum) *before* the firm had agreed to represent the investors in BusTop with a proposal that the firm represent Steinberg, an existing client of the firm, in his efforts to compete with BusTop for the franchise. The lawyer declined because of personal friendships with Bus-

was reasonably foreseeable. Furthermore, the deceit must have gone to the nature of the bargain; that is, any nondisclosures or affirmative misrepresentations must have been material. And although the govern- ment need not show that the scheme's victims were in fact defrauded, the prosecution must prove that some actual harm or injury was at least contemplated." [Citations in support of these propositions omitted.]

Top's public relations consultant and attorney. Bronston went ahead himself anyway, however, and had an associate of the firm set up a corporation (C & S) through which Steinberg could compete for the franchise. A week later, *after* the firm had been retained by the BusTop investors, Bronston wrote a memorandum to the firm's new business committee proposing that they represent Steinberg and C & S in the upcoming competition for the franchise. His memo noted that the proposed representation "may involve conflict with other clients and should be discussed." It was indeed discussed, and the firm declined to undertake a representation of C & S. Bronston was involved in specific discussions in which conflict of interest was relied upon as the basis for the decision.

Bronston nevertheless continued to represent Steinberg and C & S, even filling out law firm time sheets for his efforts. He was elected assistant secretary of C & S, and participated in at least 21 billable meetings on C & S business. C & S retained another law firm, and Bronston also participated in a number of meetings with members of that firm on C & S business. During this period, Lindenbaum, who was the principal partner of Bronston's firm working on the BusTop investors' business, consulted with Bronston about the BusTop investors. Lindenbaum billed the time for these discussions to the BusTop investors. Unknown to Lindenbaum, Bronston talked with Steinberg about these meetings and billed the time to C & S.

Bronston's mail fraud conviction was based on two letters. One was from C & S's law firm to the franchise granting agency announcing that C & S would compete for the franchise. Bronston reviewed the contents of the letter, and billed C & S for five hours for time that included the review. The second letter was written by Bronston on his official New York State Senate stationery to a city official in which Bronston enclosed "some figures in connection with the existing franchise" and said, among other things, that a renewal of BusTop's franchise "[o]bviously ... would not appear in the public interest since it might be taken for a reward for non-performance." The letter was a paraphrase of an internal C & S document prepared well after Bronston's law firm had agreed to represent the BusTop investors and had declined to represent C & S on conflict of interest grounds.

Bronston's firm was paid $52,000 for its representation of the BusTop investors. Bronston was paid $12,500 by Steinberg for his activities on behalf of C & S. This payment was not recorded on the C & S books.

In an opinion by Judge Mansfield, Bronston's conviction of mail fraud was affirmed on appeal:

> "Bronston's principal contention is that in order to show a violation of the mail fraud statute based on a fraudulent breach of fiduciary duty, the government must prove that the defendant used his breach in some way that would benefit himself or harm the victim of the fraud and that the trial judge erred in failing to instruct the jury accordingly. Under this test, Bronston argues, the conviction must be reversed since the evidence was insufficient

to permit the jury to find that he used his fiduciary status as a partner of Rosenman Colin to benefit himself or C & S at the expense of the BusTop investors. We disagree.

"Although a mere breach of fiduciary duty, standing alone, may not necessarily constitute a mail fraud, the concealment by a fiduciary of material information which he is under a duty to disclose to another under circumstances where the non-disclosure could or does result in harm to the other is a violation of the statute. As we noted in United States v. Von Barta, 635 F.2d 999, 1005–06 & n. 24 (2d Cir.1980), proof that the fiduciary relationship was used or manipulated in some way is not necessary. ...

"In the present case the indictment charged that Bronston, in disregard of the fiduciary duty he owed as a member of the Rosenman Colin firm to the BusTop investors and for the purpose of benefiting Steinberg and C & S to their detriment, promoted the interests of Steinberg and C & S in their efforts to obtain a bus shelter franchise from the city of New York and 'did conceal from, and fail to disclose to, the BusTop minority investors and BusTop the fact that he was advising and promoting the interests of Steinberg and C & S.' These allegations, coupled with the charge that Rosenman Colin received $50,000 from BusTop for services to it, that Bronston received a check for $12,500 from Steinberg for promoting the interests of Steinberg and C & S with the intent of harming BusTop, and that Bronston caused two letters to be mailed in furtherance of the scheme, were sufficient to state a violation of the mail fraud statute.

"Applying these standards, the evidence before the jury was sufficient to support a conviction for the alleged mail fraud. It is clear beyond doubt that as a member of the Rosenman Colin firm Bronston owed a fiduciary duty to its clients, the BusTop investors, and that in promoting the interests of Steinberg and C & S in competition and conflict with those of his firm's clients, Bronston violated that duty. Having retained the Rosenman Colin firm as their counsel, the BusTop investors were entitled to the undivided loyalty of its partners.

"The element of specific intent to defraud was likewise established. There was ample evidence that Bronston, with knowledge that his law firm was representing investors who had entered into a long-term financial commitment to BusTop, which was dependent upon BusTop's success in securing renewal of its franchise, was secretly engaged, without disclosure to his firm's clients, in an ongoing and significant role in C & S's efforts to obtain the franchise for itself, which would cause serious harm to the clients. Despite his firm's explicit prohibition against any further involvement on behalf of C & S, he attended frequent meetings at which the C & S bid for the New York franchise was discussed. By filling out time tickets showing C & S as the client whenever he attended such a meeting or engaged in other activities in connection with C & S, Bronston gave the jury ample ground for finding that he perceived himself as acting on behalf of C & S, even though he was professionally obligated to remain loyal to the interests of the BusTop investors.[5] Finally, by writing an anti-BusTop letter to [a city official] and by participating in the preparation of another letter to city officials in support of C & S's bid, Bronston was engaging in furthering the scheme to defraud BusTop and its investors.

"The element of concealment of a material fact, necessary to prove the alleged scheme to defraud, was also established. At no time did Bronston reveal to the BusTop investors that he was working hand in glove with Steinberg and C & S to obtain the franchise for C & S to their detriment. The materiality of this fact is self-evident. This was no mere technical failure on a law firm's part to disclose all potential conflicts of interest to its clients. One can imagine few nondisclosures more crucial to an attorney-client relationship than the fact that the law firm which the client has retained is actively engaged in efforts designed to frustrate the precise endeavor which the client had engaged the firm to pursue. . . .

"Bronston argues that a decision upholding his conviction 'would render every disloyal or ethically questionable act which is accompanied by the mailing of a letter a crime.' We disagree. Although a hypothetical can be posed in which one could be prosecuted for mail fraud on the basis of a breach of fiduciary duty accompanied by little more than a failure to disclose the breach to the person to whom the duty was owed, without any prospect of substantial economic harm to the victim, this is not such a case. Here we are faced with a straight-forward economic fraud in which the object of the scheme was not merely to deprive the victims of a law firm's undivided loyalty, for which they paid $52,000 but to deprive BusTop and its minority investors of the BusTop franchise. A partner in a law firm used the mails with the specific

[5] "Bronston argues that, had he intended to conceal his C & S activities from his partners and the BusTop investors, he would never have filled out time tickets listing C & S as the client and then sent them to the firm's accounting office for registry on the firm's books. However, there is no evidence of any in-house mechanism which would have brought the time charges to the attention of anyone at Rosenman Colin who would have recognized their impropriety; in fact, they were only turned up after Bronston's activities on behalf of C & S had been uncovered through other means.

"In any case we find Bronston's time ticket entries principally probative not of his intent to deceive his partners and the Bus-Top investors but rather of his state of mind as he met with Steinberg and associates during 1977 and 1978. By noting that his time would at some future time be billed to the C & S account, Bronston was declaring in a most graphic fashion that he conceived of his efforts on behalf of Steinberg and the others as being professional rather than social and as redounding to C & S's benefit. The fact that under the circumstances it may have been foolish for Bronston to have made the entries does not render them exculpatory."

intent of defrauding one of his firm's own clients of the precise interest which it had been retained to defend. This falls within the ambit of the mail fraud statute."

Judge Van Graafeiland dissented based upon "prejudicial errors" he thought were made in the trial. He particularly criticized the District Court's "emasculation of the defense of good faith":

"The present mail fraud statute is the successor to . . . the 1872 Act . . . . While legislative history is sparse, what there is indicates that the statute was originally aimed at flimflam artists who use the mails to defraud the gullible. Durland v. United States, 161 U.S. 306, 314 (1896); Note, The Intangible–Rights Doctrine and Political–Corruption Prosecutions under the Federal Mail Fraud Statute, 47 U. Chi. L. Rev. 562, 568 (1980). In contravention of the general rule that 'ambiguity concerning the ambit of criminal statutes should be resolved in favor of lenity', § 1341 has been broadly interpreted to apply to fiduciaries who use their position for personal pecuniary gain. Where liability has been found, however, it was inevitably because the fiduciary relationship enabled the defendant to commit the wrongful acts for which he was convicted.

"Where, as here, liability is predicated upon the vicarious fiduciary responsibility of an individual lawyer in a large, modern-day law firm and there is no evidence that the defendant exploited the vicarious relationship for personal gain, the statute should be applied with careful attention to its basic purpose. . . .

"This is not a case in which the defendant took advantage of or used his fiduciary relationship with firm clients to do them harm. Judge Mansfield's statement that there was sufficient evidence to support an inference of 'use of or manipulation of Bronston's breach of fiduciary relationship' is completely without support in the record. The government took the position at the outset of the trial that it was not required to prove that any confidential information was wrongfully utilized or leaked by Bronston, and the government did not prove it. The government did not even prove that there was information of a confidential nature that might have been wrongfully disclosed. Every witness who was queried on the matter testified that there was no misuse of confidential information. The prosecution did not say one word in support of this contention in summation, and the District Court did not discuss it in its charge. Violation of 18 U.S.C. § 1341 could not be predicated upon misuse of confidential information; proof of other wrongful conduct was required.

"The trial court told counsel and jurors on numerous occasions that whether or not there was a breach of ethics was not an issue in the case. I disagree. The essence of the crime of mail fraud is wrongful intent. For there to have been a violation of the mail fraud statute, there must have been a 'conscious knowing intent to defraud', United States v. Kyle, 257 F.2d 559, 564 (2d Cir.1958), a conscious knowing violation of defendant's ethical fiduciary obligations. Evidence concerning the defendant's motives and his belief in the propriety of his conduct was material, because it might have tended to repel the inference of fraudulent intent. ...

"... Although the court charged the jury that good faith on the part of the defendant in urging competitive bidding was a complete defense, other rulings and instructions by the court made this a meaningless sop for the defense. The defense contended that what my colleagues term a 'quick, unopposed renewal' of the BusTop franchise was in fact a 'rip-off' of the people of the city of New York. The letter from the defendant to the [city official], which was the linchpin in the government's case, stated that BusTop was in default under its short-term contract with the city, that BusTop had built less than half of the shelters it had agreed to build, and had erected almost none of them in the disadvantaged areas of the Bronx. After this agreement had been terminated, BusTop attempted to push through a 'quick, unopposed' 20–year renewal without any competitive bidding by other companies.

"Are my colleagues now prepared to say that if the 'quick, unopposed' renewal of BusTop's contract had taken place, the city would not have been ripped off? I doubt it. Should not the jury have been given all the facts so that it could have made a fair, even-handed determination whether the defendant, a State Senator representing the Borough of Queens, was acting in good faith in attempting to prevent a rip-off? The jury was not given all the facts. The District Court prevented it.

"Defendant's letter stated that BusTop was in default under its contract. The truth or falsity of this statement goes directly to the heart of the government's claim of bad faith. Where lies the truth? The jury doesn't know, and neither do we. Questions dealing with the impropriety and harmful effects of BusTop's conduct were held not to be pertinent. After sustaining the government's objections to defense questions aimed at developing the facts, the court charged the jury:

'You must keep your attention riveted on the issue on trial. We are trying the terms of the indictment, the accusation. We are not trying here the question of which competitor was entitled to a franchise or on what terms, nor are we trying whether Bus Top Shelters, Inc. was or was not in compliance with the original agreement with the city. Those are not the matters you are here to decide. Don't be sidetracked thereby.'

"I suggest that the truth or falsity of defendant's letter was not a 'sidetrack' but was a fundamental issue in the case. If the defendant acted with an honest intent to accomplish a laudable object, there was no crime. Durland v. United States, 161 U.S. 306, 313–14 (1896).

"Since the jury was required to weigh defendant's bona fides with only half of the facts before it, I cannot agree with my colleagues that defendant had a fair trial."

6. **Questions and Comments on** *Newman*. Are the federal courts doing the right thing in the mail fraud holding of *Newman* and the line of mail fraud cases summarized above? Consider in connection with this question the comments by Judge Posner in United States v. Holzer, 816 F.2d 304, 309 (7th Cir.1987):[i]

"Holzer argues that he could not be deemed to have acted fraudulently when there was no clear-cut ethical rule prohibiting him from receiving loans from lawyers with business before him. This thrust is wide of the mark, since even if the receipt of the loans were not prohibited, the failure to disclose their receipt, at the very least to counsel opposing the lenders, would be fraudulent in the circumstances. But this point to one side, we do not agree that the absence of an explicit rule should make a difference. We do agree that the words 'scheme or artifice to defraud' don't reach everything that might strike a court as unethical conduct or sharp dealing, despite broad language to this effect in [some] cases. . . . . The frequently quoted suggestion in Gregory v. United States, 253 F.2d 104, 109 (5th Cir.1958), that whatever is not a 'reflection of moral uprightness, of fundamental honesty, fair play and right dealing in the general and business life of members of society' is fraud ... cannot have been intended, and must not be taken literally. It is much too broad, and given the ease of satisfying the mailing requirement ... would put federal judges in the business of creating what in effect would be common law crimes, i.e., crimes not defined by statute. However, ... elaborate efforts at conceal-ment ... are powerful evidence that a defendant's conduct violates an ethical standard well known to him and to the whole communi-ty, and not just something thought up after the fact by a perhaps overly sensitive federal judge. [T]he meaning of fraud in the mail fraud statute was [not] frozen by the conception of fraud held by the framers of the statute when it was first passed back in the 19th century. This seems to us the opposite and equally untena-ble extreme from arguing that fraud is whatever strikes a judge as bad. . . ."

Given the *McNally* holding, and the reinstatement of the "intangible rights" theory by the Congress in reaction to that decision, it can no longer be argued, it would seem, that the courts should reject the *States-Newman*

i *Holzer* was a case where a judge was convicted of mail fraud (and a violation of the Hobbs Act) for accepting, indeed actively seeking, loans from some lawyers who were appearing before him and from other lawyers who were interested in receivership appoint-ments.

line of decisions because they are unsound policy. But there are at least two important questions that remain.

The first is whether what Congress has commanded, and the decisions have held, is constitutionally permitted. This question, in turn, could be divided into at least two inquiries. Are there federalism or separation of powers limitations on the Congress, reflected in the long-accepted principle that federal courts are not to create common law crimes, that prohibit Congress from delegating to the courts the kind of crime creation reflected in the "intangible rights" decisions under the mail fraud statute? If not, are there personal rights of individual defendants, reflected in important premises of the criminal law protected by the due process clause, that are violated by these decisions?

It is of course an independent matter how far the federal courts now should take the invitation issued by the Congress in the 1988 amendment of the mail fraud statute. The second question that must be addressed, therefore, concerns matters of policy. It too has several aspects. Should Congress have been taken to have indicated its approval of *all* of the "intangible rights" decisions of the Circuit Courts? Did any of the decisions summarized above go too far, even given general approval of the concept of "intangible rights"? The *Gregory* principle, quoted by Judge Posner in the excerpt from *Holzer* above, could, as Judge Posner notes, be taken to prohibit anything a federal judge thinks is "bad". How far should the federal courts take the "intangible rights" idea? Is there any logical stopping point? Do the cases reflect any meaningful limitations? Consider also the relevance of whether a state crime was committed by the federal defendant. Should this make it *more* or *less* appropriate for the federal government to prosecute?

CHAPTER III

Racketeering: Illustrative Statutes Aimed at Organized Crime

Section 1: The Hobbs Act

INTRODUCTORY NOTES ON THE ANTI–RACKETEERING ACT OF 1934

1. Text. Effective June 18, 1934, Congress passed "An Act To protect trade and commerce against interference by violence, threats, coercion, or intimidation," otherwise known as the Anti–Racketeering Act of 1934:

> "*Be it enacted by the Senate and House of Representatives of the United States of America in Congress assembled*, That the term 'trade or commerce', as used herein, is defined to mean trade or commerce between any States, with foreign nations, in the District of Columbia, in any Territory of the United States, between any such Territory or the District of Columbia and any State or other Territory, and all other trade or commerce over which the United States has constitutional jurisdiction.

> "Sec. 2. Any person who, in connection with or in relation to any act in any way or in any degree affecting trade or commerce or any article or commodity moving or about to move in trade or commerce—

>> (a) Obtains or attempts to obtain, by the use of or attempt to use or threat to use force, violence, or coercion, the payment of money or other valuable considerations, or the purchase or rental of property or protective services, not including, however, the payment of wages by a bona-fide employer to a bona-fide employee; or

>> (b) Obtains the property of another, with his consent, induced by wrongful use of force or fear, or under color of official right; or

>> (c) Commits or threatens to commit an act of physical violence or physical injury to a person or property in furtherance of a plan or purpose to violate sections (a) or (b); or

>> (d) Conspires or acts concertedly with any other person or persons to commit any of the foregoing acts;

shall upon conviction thereof, be guilty of a felony and shall be punished by imprisonment from one to ten years or by a fine of $10,000 or both.

"Sec. 3.   (a) As used in this Act the term 'wrongful' means in violation of the criminal laws of the United States or of any State or Territory.

(b) The terms 'property', 'money', or 'valuable considerations' used herein shall not be deemed to include wages paid by a bona-fide employer to a bona-fide employee.

"Sec. 4.   Prosecutions under this Act shall be commenced only upon the express direction of the Attorney General of the United States.

"Sec. 5.   If any provisions of this Act or the application thereof to any person or circumstances is held invalid, the remainder of the Act, and the application of such provision to other persons or circumstances, shall not be affected thereby.

"Sec. 6.   Any person charged with violating this Act may be prosecuted in any district in which any part of the offense has been committed by him or by his actual associates participating with him in the offense or by his fellow conspirators: *Provided*, That no court of the United States shall construe or apply any of the provisions of this Act in such manner as to impair, diminish, or in any manner affect the rights of bona-fide labor organizations in lawfully carrying out the legitimate objects thereof, as such rights are expressed in existing statutes of the United States." 48 Stat. 979.

2. Legislative History. In June of 1933, by Senate Resolution 74 of the 73rd Congress, a subcommittee of the Committee on Commerce was authorized "to investigate rackets and racketeering in the United States, and to report to the Senate the results of such investigation, together with recommendations for the enactment of legislation designed to check the spread of racketeering." Report of the Copeland Committee, S. Rep. No. 1189, 75th Cong., 1st Sess., p. 1 (1937). In February of 1934, the authorization was broadened "to include crime and criminal practices generally." Ibid. By June, the Copeland Committee, as it was called after its Chairman, Senator Royal S. Copeland of New York, was ready to make an "interim report." See S. Rep. No. 1440, 73rd Cong., 2d Sess. (1934). Senator Copeland reported that some 105 bills had been introduced between January and June, 1934, that were "designed to close the gaps in existing federal laws and to render more difficult the activities of predatory criminal gangs of the Kelly and Dillinger types." The report listed 11 bills that had passed the Senate, including provisions on killing or assaulting federal officers, transportation of kidnapped persons in interstate commerce (a revision of the "Lindberg kidnapping law" enacted in 1932), extortion by use of interstate facilities, interstate flight to avoid prosecution, bank robbery, and transportation of stolen property. Also among the bills was S. 2248, later to become known as the Anti–Racketeering statute. No substantive comments were included in the Report on any of these provisions.

(i) The Senate.   The legislative history of S. 2248 is spotty.   In March of 1934, the Senate Judiciary Committee released a report under the caption "To Protect Trade and Commerce Against Interference by Violence, Threats, Coercion, or Intimidation."   S. Rep. No. 532, 73rd Cong., 2d Sess. (1934).   The report noted that the Judiciary Committee "reports [the bill] favorably to the Senate and recommends that the bill do pass."   Its only substantive comments recited that "[t]he purpose and need of this legislation" was set out in a memorandum from the Department of Justice. That memorandum is not without interest, but it is of little help in understanding the substantive limits of the statute.   It reads in full:

"S. 2248 (H.R. 6926), a bill to protect trade and commerce against interference by violence, threats, coercion, or intimidation. This is a proposed federal anti-racketeering statute based on the interstate commerce power.

"In the past such persons have been prosecuted in the federal courts for incidental violations of law, such as mail frauds or income-tax evasions.   The nearest approach to prosecution of racketeers as such has been under the Sherman Antitrust Act. This act, however, was designed primarily to prevent and punish capitalistic combinations and monopolies, and because of the many limitations engrafted upon the act by interpretations of the courts, the act is not well suited for prosecution of persons who commit acts of violence, intimidation, and extortion.   Furthermore, the Sherman Act requires proof of a conspiracy, combination, or monopoly, and it is often difficult to prove that the acts of racketeers affecting interstate commerce amount to a conspiracy in restraint of such commerce, or a monopoly.   Moreover, a violation of the Sherman Act is merely a misdemeanor, punishable by one year in jail plus $5,000 fine, which is not a sufficient penalty for the usual acts of violence and intimidation affecting interstate commerce.

"The accompanying proposed statute is designed to avoid many of the embarrassing limitations in the wording and interpretation of the Sherman Act, and to extend federal jurisdiction over all restraints of any commerce within the scope of the federal government's constitutional powers.   Such restraints if accompanied by extortion, violence, coercion, or intimidation, are made felonies, whether the restraints are in form of conspiracies or not. The proposed statute also makes it a felony to do any act 'affecting' or 'burdening' such trade or commerce if accompanied by extortion, violence, coercion, or intimidation.

"The provisions of the proposed statute are limited so as not to include the usual activities of capitalistic combinations, bona fide labor unions and ordinary business practices which are not accompanied by manifestations of racketeering.

"Offenses of the character designed to be prohibited are of such a serious nature that it is believed improper [sic] to make them felonies, punishable by imprisonment for not less than one year and for as long as the court, in its discretion, shall determine, and in addition by a fine at least commensurate with the amount of the unlawful gain. In one racketeering case prosecuted under criminal provisions of the Sherman Act, the unlawful gain was estimated to exceed $10,000,000 per year, but the fine was limited by the act to $5,000 for each person convicted. Under such circumstances it might be said that crime does pay. The penalty here suggested would cancel the benefits derived from the unlawful venture."

The Senate Report does not contain the proposed text of the bill to which these comments were directed, but presumably it was the same as the text of S. 2248 when it was considered by the Senate on March 29, 1934:

"*Be it enacted, etc.*, That the term 'trade and commerce', as used herein, shall include trade or commerce between any States, with foreign nations, in the District of Columbia, in any Territory of the United States, between any such Territory or the District of Columbia and any State or other Territory, and all other trade or commerce over which the United States has constitutional jurisdiction.

"Sec. 2. Any person who, in connection with or in relation to any act in any way or to any degree affecting burdening, hindering, destroying, stifling, or diverting trade or commerce or any article or commodity moving or about to move in trade or commerce—

(1) commits or threatens to commit any act of violence, intimidation, or injury to a person or property, or commits any act which is declared to be unlawful by the criminal laws of the State, District, or Territory where the act is committed; or

(2) Extorts or attempts to extort money or other valuable considerations; or

(3) Coerces or attempts to coerce any person, firm, association, or corporation to join or not to join an association, firm, corporation, or group, or to buy or rent commodities or services from particular sources, persons, firms, or corporations, or to make payments directly or indirectly to any person, association, firm, corporation, or group except for a bona fide consideration; or

(4) Coerces or attempts to coerce any person, firm, association, or corporation to do an act which such person, firm,

association, or corporation has a legal right not to do, or to abstain from doing an act which such person, firm, association, or corporation has a legal right to do—

shall, upon conviction thereof, be guilty of a felony and shall be punished by imprisonment from 1 to 99 years, and in addition, by a fine which shall be at least commensurate with the amount of the unlawful gain.

"Sec. 3.   Any person charged with violating this act may be punished in any district in which any part of the offense has been committed by him or his associates or his conspirators."   78 Cong. Rec. 5734–35 (Senate, March 29, 1934).

After the bill was read, a Senator said that he "should like an explanation of that bill."   The response was given by Senator Stephens from Mississippi on behalf of the Judiciary Committee:

"Mr. President, it is recognized that crime has reached very large proportions and because of that condition a resolution submitted by the Senator from New York [Mr. Copeland] was reported by the Committee on the Judiciary, and a very interesting investigation on this subject was had.   Based on that, and other considerations as well, seven or eight bills were introduced, some at the suggestion of the Department of Justice, some by individual Senators.   All such bills were referred to the Committee on the Judiciary.   We had before that Committee the Attorney General and one of his assistants.   Each one of the bills was gone over very carefully.   The Department of Justice through the Attorney General submitted a memorandum in which it was stated as follows:"

At this point Senator Stephens read the first three paragraphs of the Justice Department memorandum quoted above.   He then continued:

"In the hearings to which I have referred it was stated that the tax on the American public, resulting from crimes of this character and others closely related, is about $13,000,000,000 a year.   That is why the Attorney General is so very much interested and that is why the committee, after giving full consideration, unanimously adopted a favorable report.

"If there is any particular feature of the bill about which any Senator would like to inquire, I shall be glad to answer if I can."

Apparently, the 13 *billion* dollar figure (remember, this is 1934) was a show-stopper.[a]   The next entry in the Congressional Record is that "[t]he

---

[a] This figure was derived from the work of the Copeland Committee.   The Final Report of the Committee, published several years later, elaborated on what $13 billion meant in 1934:

"Viewed in another way, the total cost of crime ($12,933,000,000) is six times the cost of education.   It represents far more than the value of our exports.   It is 10 times as much as the combined cost of maintaining the Army and Navy and is four times as much as the cost of the normal operations of the federal government.   It is more than suf-

bill was ordered to be engrossed for a third reading, read the third time, and passed.''

On April 2, however, the subject was reopened. See 78 Cong. Rec. 5859. Senator Robinson of Indiana noted that S. 2248 was "passed unanimously and without opposition," but said that "[r]epresentatives of the American Federation of Labor informed me this afternoon that [the bill] might be very discriminatory against labor in this country, and that they wanted to be heard...." He added that labor had no opportunity to appear before the Judiciary Committee, and moved to reconsider the bill. The presiding officer (Senator Copeland, by coincidence), said that the bill had already gone to the House. There followed some wrangling over the proper procedure in such a situation. The motion to reconsider was entered, but there were no further comments on the substance of labor's complaint.

(ii) The House. The report by the House Judiciary Committee, H.R. Rep. No. 1833, 73rd Cong., 2d Sess. (1934), was issued in May. The Committee favorably reported the bill and recommended that it pass, in somewhat of an understatement, "with an amendment." The "amendment" was to "[s]trike out all after the enacting clause, and insert in lieu thereof" an entirely redrafted provision. Aside from a few unimportant variations in punctuation[b] and in wording here and there,[c] and aside from two major substantive differences, the amended bill recommended by the House Judiciary Committee is the same as the statute as it was eventually enacted. The two substantive differences are, first, the House version retained the penalty structure of S. 2248 as originally drafted and, second, § 2(a) of the House version included punishment under the statute for one who:

> "(a) Commits or threatens or attempts to commit an act of physical violence or personal injury to a person or to the property of another, in furtherance of a plan, purpose, or attempt to fix or increase prices, or restrict or allocate production, purchases, or sales, or suppress competition; or"[d]

The complete comments on the redrafted bill in the House Report were as follows:

> "This is the so-called 'antiracketeering bill' for the suppression of racketeering in interstate commerce. In explanation of the

ficient to pay the annual total of federal, state, and local taxes in normal times. It represents about one-fourth of the annual national income." Crime and Criminal Practices (Report of the Copeland Committee), S. Rep. No. 1189, 75th Cong., 1st Sess., p. 13 (1937).

[b] For example, § 2 of the enacted statute reads "Any person who, in connection with ..." whereas the House version reads "Any person, who in connection with ...".

[c] As examples, the word "herein" appeared in the House version just before the semi-colon at the end of § 2(c) of the enacted bill and the word "bona-fide" appeared without the hyphen in the House version.

[d] Subsections (b) through (e) of the House version were substantially identical to subsections (a) through (d) of the enacted legislation.

bill there is attached hereto, and made a part of this report, communication addressed to the Chairman of the Committee on the Judiciary, by the Attorney General, as follows:

"DEPARTMENT OF JUSTICE

"*Washington, D.C., May 18, 1934*

"HON. HATTON W. SUMNERS,

"*Chairman of the Judiciary Committee,*

"*House of Representatives, Washington, D.C.*

"DEAR MR. SUMNERS: I am enclosing herewith a new draft of the antiracketeering bill, S. 2248, which has been prepared upon the informal suggestion of your committee as a substitute for the bill which your committee has under consideration.

"After a series of conferences with Mr. Keenan and Mr. Rice, this draft has been definitely approved by Mr. William Green, president of the American Federation of Labor, and James B. Easby–Smith, Esq., counsel for Mr. Green.

"We believe that the bill in this form will accomplish the purposes of such legislation and at the same time meet the objections made to the original bill.

"The original bill was susceptible to the objection that it might include within its prohibition the legitimate and bona fide activities of employers and employees. As the purpose of the legislation is not to interfere with such legitimate activities but rather to set up severe penalties for racketeering by violence, extortion, or coercion, which affects interstate commerce, it seems advisable to definitely exclude such legitimate activities.

"As the typical racketeering activities affecting interstate commerce are those in connection with price fixing and economic extortion directed by professional gangsters, we have inserted subparagraphs (a) and (b), making such activities unlawful when accompanied by violence and affecting interstate commerce.

"The Sherman Antitrust Act is too restricted in its terms and the penalties thereunder are too moderate to make that act an effective weapon in prosecuting racketeers. The antiracketeering bill would extend the federal jurisdiction to those cases where racketeering acts are related to interstate commerce and are therefore of concern to the Nation as a whole.

"We have added a new provision prohibiting conspiracy as well as the substantive acts and we have also added a separability clause to make certain that the entire act will not be declared unconstitutional in the event that its application to any circumstances is held invalid.

"We feel that this bill is a vital part of any federal program to suppress so-called 'racketeering' activities which have assumed nation-wide proportions.

"Sincerely yours,

"HOMER CUMMINGS, *Attorney General"*

The bill first came before the floor of the House on June 8. It was passed over without prejudice after a colloquy about whether organized labor had in fact agreed to its wording. After the clerk called the bill, the following exchange occurred:

"MR. SCHULTE. Mr. Speaker, I object.

"MR. OLIVER of New York. Mr. Speaker, will the gentleman withhold his objection?

"MR. SCHULTE. I reserve the right to object, Mr. Speaker.

"MR. OLIVER of New York. This is the noted racketeering bill recommended here and agreed upon by organized labor and by the Department of Justice. It has been agreed upon by every factor involved in this kind of controversy. We have Mr. Green on record—

"MR. SCHULTE. Has the gentleman a letter from Mr. Green which states he is on record in favor of this bill?

"MR. OLIVER of New York. Yes.

"MR. SCHULTE. If so, I shall withdraw my objection, if the gentleman will show me the letter.

"MR. OLIVER of New York. I cannot show the gentleman the letter, but Mr. Green specifically agreed to it and it is stated in the report that there is a letter from the Attorney General embodying the agreement—

"MR. SCHULTE. I do not care anything about the Attorney General.

"MR. OLIVER of New York. And Mr. Green appeared before our committee and stated before our committee that he intended to go into a further conference—

"MR. SCHULTE. Will the gentleman give me his assurance that he has a letter from Mr. Green stating he has agreed to this bill?

"MR. OLIVER of New York. I will not say I have a letter—

"MR. SCHULTE. Has the gentleman seen such a letter from Mr. Green?

"MR. OLIVER of New York. No; but I have seen an agreement in which the Attorney General said that Mr. Green had agreed to it.

"MR. SCHULTE. I object, but I will agree to having it passed over without prejudice.

"MR. SUMNERS of Texas. Mr. Speaker, if the gentleman will bear with me a moment I do not know whether I can satisfy the gentleman or not. The members of the committee are very much concerned to have this matter straightened out if it can be done. Conferences have been had by the Attorney General with Mr. Green and with Mr. Easby–Smith, attorney for organized labor, and all the gentlemen of the committee believe the matter is entirely straightened and this bill is satisfactory to all those concerned.

"MR. SCHULTE. I am going to object at this time until you get in contact with Mr. Green.

"MR. ZIONCHECK. Mr. Speaker, I ask unanimous consent that this bill be passed over without prejudice.

"The SPEAKER. Is there objection to the request of the gentleman from Washington?

"There was no objection." 78 Cong. Rec. 10867 (House, June 8, 1934).

The bill then returned to the floor of the House on June 13. See 78 Cong. Rec. 11403. Mr. Oliver brought the "bill up for immediate consideration." The Speaker asked if there was any objection, and hearing none, asked the clerk to read the bill. The clerk then read both the Senate bill (S. 2248) and the House amendment. Mr. Oliver then offered two amendments to the House version of the bill: first, to eliminate § 2(a)(quoted above) and, second, to revise the penalty provisions to eliminate the one to 99–year sentence and fine up to the amount unlawfully gained and substitute imprisonment "up to 10 years or by a fine of $10,000 or both." Both amendments were agreed to without discussion, and the House thus passed a version of the bill virtually identical to the form in which it eventually became law.

(iii) Reconsideration by the Senate. The House version of the statute came before the Senate on June 14, 1934. See 78 Cong. Rec. 11482. The comments on the floor were brief:

"MR. COPELAND. Mr. President, I should like to call the attention of the Senator from Indiana [Mr. Robinson] to this matter. This bill passed the Senate and went to the House, and the provisions in the bill which were criticized have been corrected by the amendment. Therefore, if it is agreeable to the Senator from Indiana to withdraw his proposal for a reconsideration, I will ask that the Senate concur in the amendment of the House.

"MR. ROBINSON of Indiana. Mr. President, I asked for a reconsideration originally because those interested in American labor were opposed to the bill as drafted. I should like to ask the Senator from New York now whether or not labor is satisfied with the bill?

"MR. COPELAND. I am assured by the Attorney General that the Federation of Labor is now satisfied.

"I move that the Senate concur in the amendment of the House."

It is then noted, without further elaboration, that "[t]he motion was agreed to."

(iv) Final Report of the Copeland Committee. The final report of the Copeland Committee, entitled Crime and Criminal Practices, S. Rep. No. 1189, 75th Cong., 1st Sess., was not issued until 1937, three years after the Anti–Racketeering bill was enacted. Since the bill was initiated by the Committee—even though the final version appears to have been drafted by the Justice Department in consultation with representatives of organized labor—what the Copeland Committee has to say about the scope and purpose of its investigation may be of some relevance to proper interpretation of the enacted legislation.

"At the outset of its work," the Report states, "the subcommittee adopted a working definition of the terms 'racket' and 'racketeering.'" That definition, derived from the work of a special committee "for the repression of racketeering" of the Federal Bar Association of New York, New Jersey, and Connecticut, provided:

"Racketeering is an organized conspiracy to commit the crimes of extortion or coercion, or attempts to commit extortion or coercion, within the definition of these crimes found in the penal law of the state of New York and other jurisdictions. Racketeering, from the standpoint of extortion, is the obtaining of money or property from another with his consent, induced by the wrongful use of force or fear. The fear which constitutes the legally necessary element in extortion is induced by oral or written threats to do an unlawful injury to the property of the threatened person by means of explosives, fire, or otherwise; and to kill, kidnap, or injure him or a relative of his or some member of his family.

"Racketeering from the standpoint of coercion usually takes the form of compelling, by use of similar threats to person or property, a person to do or abstain from doing an act which such other person had a legal right to do or abstain from doing, such as joining a so-called protective association to protect his right to conduct a business or trade. Coercion as such does not necessarily involve the payment of money, but frequently both extortion and coercion are involved in racketeering."

This definition, the Report concluded, "was used by the committee throughout the investigation, and may be regarded as the official definition of the term 'racketeering.'"

Later in the Report, under the heading "Rackets," the Committee described "typical" behavior:

"Persons who had taken money to smuggle aliens into this country, forced the aliens to work out sums claimed to be due them, and in addition extorted further sums by threatening disclosure of the illegal entry.

"Dairy markets, fruit produce companies, and other food industries were forced to pay tribute, so that their merchandise (in most instances, highly perishable) as well as their equipment would not be damaged.

"Many industries in the city of New York had so-called 'unions'—that is, organizations for levying tribute upon employees by threatening to prevent them from working by the use of violence. These 'unions' are of course to be distinguished from legitimate trade-unions.

"Employees were forced to turn back part of their wages to unscrupulous foremen and others under threat of being kept from working—a form of extortion known as the 'kick-back.'

"Thousands of businessmen were compelled to join self-styled 'associations', and compelled to pay dues for 'protection' from injury to person and property by gangsters allied with those affording the 'protection.'

"The description of these few rackets is sufficient to illustrate the methods employed by racketeers, and to show the variety and range of the devices evolved for the purpose of exacting tribute from their victims. They also indicate the possibilities afforded to the unscrupulous for building large and powerful underworld organizations—one of the characteristics of rackets not usually found in other forms of criminal activity."

Under the heading "Racketeering," the Committee commented upon the implications of its findings on the need for supplementing local enforcement with a federal presence. It also talked about some of the factors that hampered all enforcement efforts in this area, concluding that:

"The testimony at the committee's hearings tended to establish that in some instances two serious conditions contribute to the difficulty of meeting the crime problem—first, corrupt police and prosecutors, and second, the influence of politicians who interfere with the administration of criminal justice and the enforcement of the laws. The extent to which these practices exist is, in the nature of things, impossible of exact determination. But that they sometimes exist, at least to a sufficient extent to hamper law enforcement, is clear. The very fact that the average man believes there is corruption of police, prosecutors, and the courts, is, in and of itself and apart from whether or not the belief is sound, a factor which aids the spread of racketeering. It emboldens the racketeer, puts fear into the victim, and thus depriving the authorities of the aid to which they are entitled, makes it more difficult for honest officials to perform their duties."

Part II of the Report contains a summary of the Committee's findings on enacted and proposed legislation. Specific proposals were made, and legislation enacted, on a number of topics, including efforts to control abuses in the poultry industry in New York, kickbacks, kidnapping, transportation of stolen property, bank robbery, wire frauds, fictitious checks, gambling devices, fugitive felons, killing or assaulting federal officers, firearms control, and a host of procedural topics related to the enforcement of laws enacted to deal with such problems. In its discussion of many of these subjects, the Committee recites detailed practices of the sort it would seek to punish. Its comments directly related to the Anti–Racketeering bill, however, are brief. Under the heading "Extortion—Coercion," the report states:

"Although of all of the types of crimes investigated, kidnapping had attracted the most public attention, it was by no means the most widespread form of racketeering. The type of racket which affects industries, particularly in the large cities, and the different types of rackets perpetrated in the field of transportation, are the most common. The definition of racketeering adopted by the committee states, as already noted, that racketeering is an organized conspiracy to commit crime through extortion, coercion, intimidation, or violence. While these efforts are usually against individuals, yet trade and commerce suffer from the same evil. The prevalence and nature of this type of racketeering are too familiar to require further discussion."

At this point, the Report describes two statutes addressed to the "protection of property and trade against interference by violence and coercion." The first addressed coercion through the use of telephone or telegraph facilities. As to the second, S. 2248, the Committee's comments in full are as follows:

"As a further protection to property, as well as trade and commerce, the committee introduced two bills in the 73rd Congress. These bills, originally numbered S. 2247 and S. 2248, were consolidated and renumbered S. 2248, entitled 'An act to protect trade and commerce against interference by violence, threats, or coercion, or intimidation.' The consolidated bill was amended in the House of representatives by a provision that all prosecutions thereunder shall be commenced only upon the express direction of the Attorney General of the United States. This amendment was intended to expedite legal procedure in cases coming under the act. The bill as amended passed both Houses and became Public Law No. 376 of the 73rd Congress.

"After further study, the committee introduced a bill during the 74th Congress to repeal the provision inserted in Public Law No. 376 by the House, requiring all prosecution under the act to be commenced on the express direction of the Attorney General of the United States, since it is believed that no sound reason exists why this law should be enforced in any different manner that other federal statutes. This bill, which was numbered S. 2789, was not reported from committee."

There is no comment in the Report on the other changes made by the House "amendment" of S. 2248.

Finally, in Part III of its report, the Committee quoted the text of all bills enacted and pending that resulted from its work. In all, 18 statutes were enacted, and many more awaited further action. S. 2248, in its enacted version, is included under the heading "Racketeering Bill, Public, No. 376 (S. 2247–48 Consolidated)."

3. Comments and Questions. It appears that organized labor was successful in getting three separate exemptions written into the Anti–Racketeering Act of 1934. Section 2(a) excepts "the payment of wages by a bona-fide employer to a bona-fide employee" from the strictures of § 2. Section 3(b) states that it is not illegal to obtain "wages paid by a bona-fide employer to a bona-fide employee" by the means proscribed by the act. And § 6 contains a proviso protecting "the rights of bona-fide labor organizations in lawfully carrying out the legitimate objects thereof." To what extent do these provisions exempt activities of the members of a labor union from criminal conviction under the act?

Specifically, consider several scenarios:

(i) A union leader says to a company president with whom the union has a contract: "If you do not raise the pay of the hourly employees by $1.00 an hour when the contract expires, I will call the troops out on strike." The president pays. Has the union leader violated the act?

(ii) A union leader says to a company president with whom the union has a contract: "If you do not raise the pay of the hourly employees by $1.00 an hour when the contract expires, I will bomb your plant." The president pays. Has the union leader violated the act?

(iii) A union leader says to a company president with whom the union has a contract: "If you do not hire 12 more employees named by my union, I will bomb your plant." The president responds "But we don't need these new employees." The union leader responds: "Tough." The president hires the new employees. Has the union leader violated the act?

(iv) A union leader says to a company president with whom the union has a contract: "If you do not pay me $100 a week, I will call the troops out on strike." The president pays. Has the union leader violated the act?

(v) A union leader says to a company president with whom the union has a contract: "If you do not pay me $100 a week, I will bomb your plant." The president pays. Has the union leader violated the act?

The following case involves a prosecution under the Anti–Racketeering Act of 1934 for a variation of the themes raised by these hypotheticals.

United States v. Local 807

Supreme Court of the United States, 1942.
315 U.S. 521.

■ JUSTICE BYRNES delivered the opinion of the Court.

This case comes here on cross-petitions for certiorari to review a judgment of the Circuit Court of Appeals reversing the conviction of Local 807 and 26 individuals on charges of conspiracy to violate §§ 2(a), 2(b) and 2(c) of the Anti–Racketeering Act of June 18, 1934. The government asks that the judgments of conviction be reinstated. In their cross-petition the defendants seek dismissal of the indictment. We do not regard this as a correct disposition of the case. Since the correctness of the views concerning the meaning of the statute on which the trial court submitted the case to the jury goes to the root of the convictions and their reversal by the Circuit Court of Appeals, we shall confine our consideration of these cases to that issue. Consequently, we are concerned only with whether the defendants were tried in a manner consistent with the proper meaning and scope of the pertinent provisions of § 2 of the act, which provide:

"Any person who, in connection with or in relation to any act in any way or in any degree affecting trade or commerce or any article or commodity moving or about to move in trade or commerce—

"(a) Obtains or attempts to obtain, by the use of or attempt to use or threat to use force, violence, or coercion, the payment of money or other valuable considerations, or the purchase or rental of property or protective services, not including, however, the payment of wages by a bona-fide employer to a bona-fide employee; or

"(b) Obtains the property of another, with his consent, induced by wrongful use of force or fear, or under color of official right; or

"(c) Commits or threatens to commit an act of physical violence or physical injury to a person or property in furtherance of a plan or purpose to violate sections (a) or (b);...."

The proof at the trial showed that the defendant Local 807 includes in its membership nearly all the motor truck drivers and helpers in the city of New York, and that during the period covered by the indictment defendants Campbell and Furey held office in the Local as delegates in charge of the west side of Manhattan and the other defendants were members. Large quantities of the merchandise which goes into the city from neighboring states are transported in "over-the-road" trucks, which are usually manned by drivers and helpers who reside in the localities from which the shipments are made and who are consequently not members of Local 807. Prior to the events covered by this indictment, it appears to have been customary for these out-of-state drivers to make deliveries to the warehouses of consignees in New York and then to pick up other merchandise from New York shippers for delivery on the return trip to consignees in the surrounding states.

There was sufficient evidence to warrant a finding that the defendants conspired to use and did use violence and threats to obtain from the owners of these "over-the-road" trucks $9.42 for each large truck and $8.41 for each small truck entering the city. These amounts were the regular union rates for a day's work of driving and unloading. There was proof that in some cases the out-of-state driver was compelled to drive the truck to a point close to the city limits and there to turn it over to one or more of the defendants. These defendants would then drive the truck to its destination, do the unloading, pick up the merchandise for the return trip and surrender the truck to the out-of-state driver at the point where they had taken it over. In other cases, according to the testimony, the money was demanded and obtained, but the owners or drivers rejected the offers of the defendants to do or help with the driving or unloading. And in several cases the jury could have found that the defendants either failed to offer to work, or refused to work for the money when asked to do so. Eventually many of the owners signed contracts with Local 807 under whose terms the defendants were to do the driving and unloading within the city and to receive regular union rates for the work. No serious question is raised by the evidence as to the ability of the defendants to perform the labor involved in these operations.

The first count of the indictment was based upon § 2(a) of the act and charged a conspiracy "to obtain the payment of money [from the owners] by the use of, attempt to use and threat to use, force, violence and coercion." The second count accused the defendants of conspiring to obtain the property of the owners "with their consent induced by wrongful use of force and of fear," in violation of § 2(b). The third and fourth counts alleged a conspiracy to violate § 2(c), in that the defendants agreed "to commit and threatened to commit acts of physical violence and of physical injury to the persons and property" of their victims, in furtherance of the general scheme to violate §§ 2(a) and 2(b). Local 807 and all of the individual defendants were convicted on the first count; the Local and 17 individuals on the second; and the Local and 11 individuals on the third and fourth.

The question in the case concerns that portion of § 2(a) which excepts from punishment any person who "obtains or attempts to obtain, by the use of or attempt to use or threat to use force, violence, or coercion, . . . the payment of wages by a bona-fide employer to a bona-fide employee."[2] The Circuit Court of Appeals reversed because it believed that the trial court had failed to instruct the jury properly with respect to this exception.

To ascertain the limits of the exception is a difficult undertaking. Always assuming the presence of violence and threats, as we must in the face of this record, three interpretations of varying restrictive force require consideration: (1) The exception applies only to a defendant who has enjoyed the status of a bona fide employee prior to the time at which he obtains or attempts to obtain the payment of money by the owner. (2) Assuming that this is incorrect and that the exception may affect a defendant who has not been a bona fide employee prior to the time in question, it does not apply if the owner's intention in making the payment is to buy "protection" and not buy service, even though the defendant may intend to perform the service or may actually perform it. We understand this to be the position adopted by the government in its brief and argument in this Court. (3) Assuming that both (1) and (2) are incorrect, the exception is not applicable to a defendant who obtains the payment of money if the owner rejects his genuine offer of service. We understand this to be the theory of the dissenting judge below.

Confronted with these various interpretations, we turn for guidance to the legislative history of the statute. Pursuant to a Senate Resolution of May 8, 1933, a sub-committee of the Senate Committee on Interstate Commerce which became known as the Copeland Committee, undertook an investigation of "rackets" and "racketeering" in the United States. After conducting hearings in several large cities, the committee introduced 13 bills, of which S. 2248 was one. As introduced, as reported by the Senate Judiciary Committee,[5] and as passed without debate by the Senate, S. 2248 embodied very general prohibitions against violence or coercion in connection with interstate commerce and contained no specific mention of wages or labor. After the bill had passed the Senate, however, representatives of the American Federation of Labor expressed fear that the bill in its then form might result in serious injury to labor, and the measure was redrafted by officials of the Department of Justice after conferences with the President of the Federation. In the course of this revision, the bill assumed substantially the form in which it was eventually enacted. In particular, the exception concerning "the payment of wages by a bona-fide employer to a bona-fide employee" was added, and a proviso preserving "the rights of bona-fide labor organizations" was incorporated in what became § 6 of the

[2] This exception does not appear in § 2(b). But we agree with the Circuit Court of Appeals that it too is subject to the exception. The trial judge's instructions show that he shared this view. And the definition of terms in § 3(b) was apparently intended to achieve this result.

[5] S. Rep. No. 532, 83d Cong., 2d Sess. The report included a memorandum from the Department of Justice in which it was stated: "The provisions of the proposed statute are limited so as not to include the usual activities of capitalistic combinations, bona fide labor unions, and ordinary business practices which are not accompanied by manifestations of racketeering."

act as finally passed.[8] In its favorable reports on this revised bill, the House Committee on the Judiciary set forth without comment a letter from the Attorney General to the Committee, dated May 18, 1934. In this letter the Attorney General informed the Committee that the draft of the substitute bill had been "definitely approved" by the President of the American Federation of Labor and his counsel. The letter continued:

"We believe that the bill in this form will accomplish the purposes of such legislation and at the same time meet the objections made to the original bill.

"The original bill was susceptible to the objection that it might include within the prohibition the legitimate and bona fide activities of employers and employees. As the purpose of the legislation is not to interfere with such legitimate activities but rather to set up severe penalties for racketeering by violence, extortion, or coercion, which affects interstate commerce, it seems advisable to definitely exclude such legitimate activities.

"As the typical racketeering activities affecting interstate commerce are those in connection with price fixing and economic extortion directed by professional gangsters, we have inserted subparagraphs (a) and (b), making such activities unlawful when accompanied by violence and affecting interstate commerce."

The substitute was agreed to by both the House and Senate without debate, when assurances were given that the approval of organized labor had been obtained. Thereafter, while the bill awaited the signature of the President, Senator Copeland submitted a report in which he referred to S. 2248 as one of 11 bills which had been enacted "to close gaps in existing federal laws and to render more difficult the activities of predatory criminal gangs of the Kelly and Dillinger types."

This account of the legislative proceedings obviously does not provide specific definition of "wages," "bona-fide employer," or "bona-fide employee," as those terms are used in § 2(a). But it does contain clear declarations by the head of the department which drafted the section and by the sponsor of the bill in Congress, first, that the elimination of terroristic activities by professional gangsters was the aim of the statute, and second, that no interference with traditional labor union activities was intended.

It may be true that professional rackets have sometimes assumed the guise of labor unions, and, as the Circuit Court of Appeals observed, that they may have "covered their practices by the pretence that the tribute collected was pay for services rendered." And it may also be true that labor organizations of good repute and honest purpose can be misdirected and become agencies of blackmail. Nevertheless, Congress plainly attempt-

[8] "*Provided*, That no court of the United States shall construe or apply any of the provisions of this Act in such manner as to impair, diminish, or in any manner affect the rights of bona-fide labor organizations in lawfully carrying out the legitimate objects thereof, as such rights are expressed in existing statutes of the United States." 18 U.S.C. § 420(d).

ed to distinguish militant labor activity from the other and to afford it ample protection. With this legislative purpose uppermost in mind, we return to test the three theories of interpretation of § 2(a) to which we have referred.

(1) We hold that the exemption is not restricted to a defendant who has attained the status of an employee prior to the time at which he obtains or attempts or conspires to obtain the money. In the first place, we agree with the observation of the court below that "practically always the crux of a labor dispute is who shall get the job, and what the terms shall be ..." To exclude this entire class of disputes from the protection of the exception would be unjustifiably to thwart the purpose of Congress as we understand it. In the second place, the structure and language of § 2(a) itself is persuasive against so narrow an interpretation. It does not except "*a bona fide employee* who obtains or attempts to obtain the payment of wages from a bona-fide employer." Rather, it excepts "*any person* who ... obtains or attempts to obtain .... the payment of wages from a bona-fide employer to a bona-fide employee." Certainly, an outsider who "attempts" unsuccessfully by violent means to achieve the status of an employee and to secure wages for services falls within the exception. And where, as here, the offense charged is conspiracy to violate the section, the defendants are entitled to immunity if their objective is to become bona fide employees and to obtain wages in that capacity, even though they may fail of their purpose.

(2) The government contends, as we have said, that the test is "whether, under all the circumstances, it appears that the money has been paid for labor or for protection." If the defendants do not offer to work, or if they refuse to work, or if their offer to work is rejected by the owners, the government argues that any payment made to them must be for protection rather than for services. And even if the defendants actually perform some work, it is said, this circumstance should be regarded as relevant but not controlling in determining "the one crucial issue in every case such as this—namely, whether the money was paid for labor or for protection."

We take this to mean that the intent of the owners in making the payment is to be regarded as controlling. We cannot agree. The state of mind of the truck owners cannot be decisive of the guilt of these defendants. On the contrary, their guilt is determined by whether or not their purpose and objective was to obtain "the payment of wages by a bona-fide employer to a bona-fide employee." And, of course, where the defendants are charged with conspiracy as they were here, it is particularly obvious that the nature of their plan and agreement is the crux of the case. The mischief of a contrary theory is nowhere better illustrated than in industrial controversies. For example, the members of a labor union may decide that they are entitled to the jobs in their trade in a particular area. They may agree to attempt to obtain contracts to do the work at the union wage scale. They may obtain the contracts, do the work, and receive the money. Certainly Congress intended that these activities should be excepted from the prohibitions of this particular act, even though the agreement may have contemplated the use of violence. But it is always an open question whether the employers' capitulation to the demands of the union is prompted by a desire to obtain services or to avoid further injury or both. To make a fine or prison sentence for the union and its members a contingent upon a finding by the jury that one motive or the other dominated the employers' decision would be a distortion of the legislative purpose.

We are told, however, that under this view such a common law offense as robbery would become an innocent pastime, inasmuch as it is an essential element of that crime that the victim be moved by fear of violence when he parts with his money or property. This objection mistakes the significance of this requirement of proof in the case of robbery. Its true significance is that it places an added burden upon the prosecutor rather than upon the accused. That is, the prosecutor must first establish a criminal intent upon the part of the defendant and he must then make a further showing with respect to the victim's state of mind. The effect of this rule is to render conviction of robbery more, rather than less, difficult. There is no such restrictive evidentiary requirement in prosecutions under this act. If the objective that these defendants sought to attain by the use of force and threats is not the objective to which the exception in § 2(a) affords immunity, they are guilty and nothing further need be shown concerning the actual motive of the owners in handing over the money. On the other hand, if their objective did enjoy the protection of that exception, they are innocent and their innocence is not affected by the state of mind of the owners. We shall consider in a moment, in point (3) below, the legal consequences which flow from the owners' actual rejection of proffered services. But it needs to be emphasized here that for the owners to reject an offer of services amounts to an overt act on their part. It is conduct or behavior as distinct from intention or state of mind. It is an event which alters the external situation in which the defendants find themselves. The latter must then decide whether they will continue to push their demands for the money. Whether or not they are guilty of an offense under this act if they choose to do so we shall presently discuss. But that decision must be made in terms of their motives and purposes and objectives rather than those of the owners.

We do not mean that an offer to work or even the actual performance of some services necessarily entitles one to immunity under the exception. A jury might of course find that such an offer or performance was no more than a sham to disguise an actual intention to extort and to blackmail. But the inquiry must nevertheless be directed to whether this was the purpose of the accused or whether they honestly intended to obtain a chance to work for a wage.

(3) There remains to be considered the difficult issue which divided the court below. The whole court agreed that the payment of money to one who refuses to perform the services is not "the payment of wages by a bona-fide employer to a bona-fide employee," within the meaning of § 2(a); it also agreed that payments to one who has been permitted actually to

perform the services do fall within the exception. But it divided over the question whether the payment of money to one whose sincere offer to work is rejected constitutes the payment of "wages" to a "bona-fide employee." Since the offence charged here is conspiracy, these questions must be put somewhat differently. Thus, there is no conspiracy to violate the act if the purpose of the defendants is actually to perform the services in return for the money, but there is a punishable conspiracy if their plan is to obtain money without doing the work. The doubtful case arises where the defendants agree to tender their services in good faith to an employer and to work if he accepts their offer, but agree further that the protection of their trade union interests requires that he should pay an amount equivalent to the prevailing union wage even if he rejects their proffered services.

We think that such an agreement is covered by the exception. The terms "wages," "bona-fide employee" and "bona-fide employer" are susceptible of more than one meaning, and the background and legislative history of this act require that they be broadly defined. We have expressed our belief that Congress intended to leave unaffected the ordinary activities of labor unions. The proviso in § 6 safeguarding "the rights of bona-fide labor organizations in lawfully carrying out the legitimate objects thereof," although obscure indeed, strengthens us somewhat in that opinion.[12] The test must therefore be whether the particular activity was among or is akin to labor union activities with which Congress must be taken to have been familiar when this measure was enacted. Accepting payments even where services are refused is such an activity. The Circuit Court has referred to the "stand-by" orchestra device, by which a union local requires that its members be substituted for visiting musicians, or, if the producer or conductor insists upon using his own musicians, that the members of the local be paid the sums which they would have earned had they performed. That similar devices are employed in other trades is well known. It is admitted here that the stand-by musician has a "job" even though he renders no actual service. There can be no question that he demands the payment of money regardless of the management's willingness to accept his labor. If, as it is agreed, the musician would escape punishment under this act even though he obtained his "stand-by job" by force or threats, it is certainly difficult to see how a teamster could be punished for engaging in the same practice. It is not our province either to approve or disapprove such tactics. But we do believe that they are not "the activities of predatory criminal gangs of the Kelly and Dillinger types" at which the act was aimed, and that on the contrary they are among those practices of labor unions which were intended to remain beyond its ban.

This does not mean that such activities are beyond the reach of federal legislative control. Nor does it mean that they need go unpunished. The power of state and local authorities to punish acts of violence is beyond question. It is not diminished or affected by the circumstance that the violence may be the outgrowth of a labor dispute. The use of violence disclosed by this record is plainly subject to the ordinary criminal law.

---

[12] See note 8, supra.

As we have said, the evidence with respect to the crucial issues was conflicting. Thus, the jury might have believed that in some instances the defendants refused to do any driving or unloading when requested to do so, that in other cases they did not offer to work, that in other cases their offers were rejected, and that in still other cases they actually did some or all of the driving and unloading. In the early stages, written contracts were not in existence; later, a number of the owners signed contracts and the defendants performed the services for which they called.

The jury's task was difficult. The trial lasted six weeks. The jury required two days in which to reach a verdict, and twice during that period it sought further instructions from the court, particularly with reference to the law relating to labor activity. In such circumstances, where acts of violence naturally would influence the minds of the jury, the instructions were of vital importance, especially as they affected the question of whether the payments which the defendants conspired to obtain fell within the exception contained in § 2(a). The trial judge made a number of statements which were relevant to this issue, but we agree with the Circuit Court that the following were decisive:

> "If the jury find that the sums of money paid by the truck operators were not wages so paid in return for services performed by such defendants, but were payments made by the operators in order to induce the defendants to refrain from interfering unlawfully with the operation of their trucks, then the sums in question may not be regarded as wages paid by a bona fide employer to a bona fide employee.

> "The fact that any defendant may have done some work on a truck of an operator is not conclusive as to whether payments received by such defendants were wages; the jury may consider the performance of work by a defendant as evidence of the nature of the relationship between the defendant and the operator as establishing the status of a bona fide employer and a bona fide employee. If, however, what the operator was paying for was not labor performed but merely for protection from interference by the defendants with the operation of operator's trucks, the fact that a defendant may have done some work on an operator's truck is not conclusive."

These instructions embody the rule for which the government contends, and which we think is erroneous for the reasons we have given. Under them the jury was free to return a verdict of guilty if it found that the motive of the owners in making the payments was to prevent further damage and injury rather than to secure the services of the defendants. Whether or not the defendants were guilty of conspiracy thus became contingent upon the purposes of others and not upon their own aims and objectives. Moreover, the charge failed correctly to explain the legal consequences of proof that the owners had rejected bona fide offers by the defendants to perform the services. As we have said, the jury was bound to acquit the defendants if it found that their objective and purpose was to obtain by the use or threat of violence the chance to work for the money but to accept the money even if the employers refused to permit them to work. While the 48th, 49th and 58th instructions requested by the defendants, all of which were refused, do not constitute a complete exposition of the rules which we regard as applicable to this case, they cover a good deal of the ground and should have been granted. The 48th states that "it is not an offense under the Anti–Racketeering Act for anyone to obtain employment by the use or threat of violence if the intention is to actually work for the pay received, and to give an honest day's work for a day's wage." The 49th declared that "it is not the purpose of the Anti–Racketeering Act to prevent labor unions from attempting to obtain employment for their members, . . . and that the use of violence or the threat of violence for such purposes, while punishable under the laws, is not punishable under the Anti–Racketeering Act." The 58th requested charge read as follows:

> "I charge you that in order that the defendants herein may be convicted under any one of the four counts of the Anti–Racketeering indictment, you must find a conspiracy under such counts; and that in order to sustain the charge of conspiracy under any one of the counts under the Anti–Racketeering indictment, the proof must show not only that individual defendants obtained money without rendering adequate service, but that it was the aim and object of the conspiracy that [they][13] should obtain money without rendering adequate service therefor."

Since the instructions denied, and the misleading instructions actually given, go to what is indeed the heart of the case, we hold that the convictions cannot stand and that the judgment of the Circuit Court of Appeals must be

Affirmed.

JUSTICE ROBERTS and JUSTICE JACKSON took no part in the consideration or decision of this case.

CHIEF JUSTICE STONE, dissenting:

I think the judgment should be reversed, and the convictions affirmed, subject only to an examination of the sufficiency of the evidence as to some of the respondents, and to a consideration of whether the union itself is a "person" within the meaning of the statute.

Respondents, who are members of a labor union, were convicted of conspiracy to violate the Anti–Racketeering Act. They, or some of them, lay in wait for trucks passing from New Jersey to New York, forced their way onto the trucks, and by beating or threats of beating the drivers procured payments to themselves from the drivers or their employers of a sum of money for each truck, $9.42 for a large truck and $8.41 for a small

---

[13] The words "all of the conspirators," rather than "they," appeared in the requested instruction as submitted to the trial judge. We think that as so expressed the charge would have been erroneous, but that with this change it states the correct rule.

one, said to be the equivalent of the union wage scale for a day's work. In some instances they assisted or offered to assist in unloading the trucks; and in others they disappeared as soon as the money was paid, without rendering or offering to render any service.

The Anti–Racketeering Act condemns the obtaining or conspiracy to obtain the payment of money or delivery of property by "the use of ... force, violence, or coercion ... '' To this definition of the offense Congress added two—and only two—qualifications. It does not embrace the "payment of wages by a bona-fide employer to a bona-fide employee," and the provisions of the act are not to be applied so as to "affect the rights of bona-fide labor organizations in lawfully carrying out the legitimate objects thereof, as such rights are expressed in existing statutes of the United States.''

There is abundant evidence in the record from which the jury could have concluded that respondents, or some of them, conspired to compel by force and violence the truck drivers or their employers to pay the sums of money to respondents or some of them; that the payments were made by the drivers or truck owners to purchase immunity from the violence of respondents and for no other reason; and that this was the end knowingly sought by respondents.

I can only conclude that such conduct accompanied by such a purpose constitutes a violation of the statute even though the defendants stood ready to unload the trucks in the event that they were hired to do so. Unless the language of the statute is to be disregarded, one who has rejected the proffered service and pays money only in order to purchase immunity from violence is not a bona fide employer and is not paying the extorted money as wages. The character of what the drivers or owners did and intended to do—pay money to avoid a beating—was not altered by the willingness of the payee to accept as wages for services rendered what he in fact intentionally exacted from the driver or owner as the purchase price of immunity from assault, and what he intended so to exact whether the proffered services were accepted or not. It is no answer to say that the guilt of a defendant is personal and cannot be made to depend upon the acts and intention of another. Such an answer if valid would render common law robbery an innocent pastime. For there can be no robbery unless the purpose of the victim in handing over the money is to avoid force. Precisely as under the present statute, the robber's use of force and its intended effect on the victim are essential elements of the crime both of which the prosecutor must prove. Under this statute when both are present the crime is complete, irrespective of other motives which may actuate the offender, if he is also aware, as we must take it the jury found, that the money is not in fact paid as wages by a bona fide employer. It is a contradiction in terms to say that the payment of money forcibly extorted by a payee who is in any case a lawbreaker, and paid only to secure immunity from violence, without establishment of an employment relationship or the rendering of services, is a good faith payment or receipt of wages.

Even though the procuring of jobs by violence is not within the act, and though this includes the "stand-by" job where no actual service is rendered, the granted immunity, unless its words be disregarded, does not extend to the case where the immediate objective is to force the payment of money regardless of the victim's willingness to accept and treat the extortioner as an employee. It was for the jury to say whether such was the objective of respondents and whether they were aware that the money was paid because of their violence and not as wages.

When the Anti–Racketeering Act was under consideration by Congress, no member of Congress and no labor leader had the temerity to suggest that such payments, made only to secure immunity from violence and intentionally compelled by assault and battery, could be regarded as the payment of "wages by a bona-fide employer" or that the compulsion of such payments is a legitimate object of a labor union, or was ever made so by any statute of the United States. I am unable to concur in that suggestion now. It follows that all the defendants who conspired to compel such payments by force and violence, regardless of the willingness of the victims to accept them as employees, were rightly convicted.

If I am right in this conclusion, there was no error in the instructions to the jury. All the counts of the indictment were for conspiracy to violate the statute. The jury was told that to convict it must find conspiracy or agreement by respondents to violate the statute and that they must have the purpose or intention to commit the crime which it defined. As I have said, the intention to commit the offense includes the intention to use force and violence on the victim and the intention that the victim shall pay because of it. The jury was then instructed that the offense defined by the statute was the obtaining of money or property by force and violence but that

> "the jury may not find the defendants guilty on any count of the Anti-Racketeering Act indictment if the money which they are charged with having obtained from truck owners through the use of force and violence or threats of force and violence was paid as wages, and if the defendants who received the money were bona fide employees and the truck operators who paid the money were bona fide employers. ... If the jury find that the sums of money paid by the truck operators were not wages so paid in return for services performed by such defendants, but were payments made by the operators in order to induce the defendants to refrain from interfering unlawfully with the operation of their trucks, then the sums in question may not be regarded as wages paid by a bona fide employer to a bona fide employee. ... If, however, what the operator was paying for was not labor performed but merely for protection from interference by the defendants with the operation of the operator's trucks, the fact that a defendant may have done some work on an operator's truck is not conclusive."

Respondents' 48th and 49th requests were rightly refused. So far as they involved a ruling that the obtaining of employment by force and violence does not constitute the offense, the court had already ruled specifically that there could be no substantive offense unless the payment of money or property had been obtained by force. But, in any case, both requests were erroneous because they made respondents' willingness to work the test of guilt, regardless of the intended and actual effect of the violence on the victims in compelling them to pay the money not as wages but in order to secure immunity from assault. The first part of the 58th request likewise had already been charged. The rest was plainly defective, since it required an acquittal unless it was the aim and object of the conspiracy that "all of the conspirators should obtain money without rendering adequate service therefor." Upon any theory of the meaning of the statute, it was not necessary for the government to show that it was the object of the conspiracy that "all the conspirators" should receive payments of money. They would be equally guilty if they had conspired to procure the payments to some.

NOTES ON THE ANTI–RACKETEERING ACT OF 1934

1. **The Court of Appeals Decision**. The Court of Appeals decision in *Local 807*, reported at 118 F.2d 684 (2d Cir.1941), was written by Learned Hand. He was joined by Judge Charles Clark, who also wrote separately. Augustus Hand dissented.

(i) **The Majority Opinion**. The majority opinion first rejected an interpretation of § 2(a) that would have limited the wages exception "to situations in which an employee procured by threats the payment of wages due under a contract which the employer had made without coercion." This, said the opinion, would deny the wages exclusion all meaningful effect:

"[I]t would be an extremely rare occasion when coercion would be applied merely to collecting the wage upon a contract freely made. Practically always the crux of a labor dispute is who shall get the job and what the terms shall be; and such pressure—lawful or unlawful—as is put upon the employer is at the time the contract is made. After that it is seldom necessary to renew the pressure; its effect usually continues.... To confine the exception to cases where the original contract was voluntary would therefore leave out the great mass of instances in which the issue would ever arise."

Instead, the words of the statute "had quite another meaning in our opinion":

"[T]hey were designed to limit the exception to cases in which the employee really did the work for which he was paid, however he might secure the job; and to exclude cases where he disguised the levy of blackmail by a pretext of service never in fact rendered. [W]e do not believe that the act made it a crime for a labor union to get jobs or an increase in wages for its members, even by threats or violence."

In this case, the "question is whether the act applies in case the employee is ready and able to do the work, but the employer, although coerced into paying the wage, prefers to employ a substitute to do the work." It would be "incredible," the court continued,

"that, when Congress gave immunity to employees who succeeded in coercing their employer into giving them the job, it should have made it criminal to take the pay when he refused to let them work. The wrong is the extortion of money without quid pro quo, and a bona fide tender is the only step that the putative employee can ever take towards performance. ... Hence, we hold that, if the employee in good faith actually proffers his services, it is the same whether or not they are accepted. In the case at bar, the accused were for the most part willing to do the work...."

There was, to be sure, evidence as to some of the union members (at least some of the time) that they would not have accepted employment even if it was offered, that they accepted the money without exhibiting a willingness to work for it. As to them the court was prepared to assume, arguendo, that there was sufficient evidence in the record to support a conviction had the issue been properly presented to the jury. The problem, however, lay in the jury instructions:

"The jury was in substance told that the only payments which were immune were wages paid for work actually done. ... A verdict should not stand when the jury has been so far misdirected upon the very kernel of the case; it is not only possible, but likely, that here they supposed many—perhaps all—of the accused were ready, as they certainly were able, to drive and unload the trucks. If they attended at all to what the judge told them, they must have thought this immaterial, and there was really nothing left for them to decide if they concluded that the payments had been extorted by threats."

Finally, the court concluded:

"In conclusion we may add that a consideration of the evil at which Congress was aiming, seems to us to confirm the construction we are putting upon what it said. For a number of years before 1934—at least in the City of New York—the levy of blackmail upon industry, especially upon relatively small shops, had become very serious, and the local authorities either would not, or could not, check it. The courts were powerless, because the witnesses were terrorized and could not be protected if they told what they knew; the public felt themselves at the mercy of organized gangs of bandits and became much wrought up over the situation. It was, at least primarily, to check such Camorras that Congress passed this measure. Some of these offenders had been members of labor unions, real or pretended, and at times it may be that they covered their practices by the pretence that the tribute collected was to pay for services rendered.... Congress might indeed have gone further than it did; it might have included payments extorted by threats for services rendered or offered; that too is a grave evil. But grave as it is, it is of a different kind from that at which this act was aimed. The history of labor disputes is studded with violence which unhappily is not yet obsolete; but, although the means employed may be the same as those here condemned, the end is always different, for it is to secure work on better terms. That purpose may indeed lead far afield, even to the domination of a whole industry, but the stake is always the same; and it is toto coelo a different thing to seek to secure work or higher wages, from extorting money without proposing to give anything in return. Nor is that difference obliterated even though it was unreasonable to exact a full day's wage for services which would have taken much less than a day to perform. It is not unreasonable to ascribe to Congress the purpose of observing this distinction and of leaving to the states the maintenance of order in cases of disorders in labor disputes. True, it may be asked why Congress should not also have left to the states the suppression of such disorders as the act indubitably does forbid. That we cannot answer, and indeed it would not be proper for us to import the distinction which we have, if the language used did not demand it. We have tried to show how that was the inevitable consequence of what was said; and it fortifies our conclusion that there was a possible purpose for the distinction. Furthermore, the proviso [in § 6 of the act], although that too is most obscure, at least shows a vague intention to discriminate between violence in labor disputes and elsewhere."

(ii) The Concurrence. Judge Clark raised two points in his concurrence. The first questioned whether the union itself was a "person" as contemplated by the act. His second point elaborated on the meaning of the proviso in § 6 of the act:

"I agree that it is 'most obscure,' and also that it 'at least shows a vague intention to discriminate between violence in labor disputes and elsewhere.' It may therefore mean in effect that the acts of violence here made a federal crime do not include such acts when occurring in otherwise legitimate activities of bona fide (i.e., non-outlaw) labor organizations. If the word 'otherwise' should be omitted from this statement, if the acts of violence themselves render the union activities not legitimate, then the proviso becomes wholly meaningless, since it would then say that union activities are excepted only when they do not violate the act. Yet it was clear legislative history that this and the exceptions of [§§ 2(a) and 3(b)] were drafted by or for the great labor organizations, and the original bill was held up in both House and Senate until these provisions satisfactory to labor interests could be prepared and added. This is not to legitimatize violence; for the legislative issue was whether the federal criminal jurisdiction should be greatly expanded—in ways unknown to the founding fathers or their descendants prior to 1934—because state processes were ineffective or had broken down. To meet what was thought to be an emergency, there were passed the series of about a dozen acts, among which were this act and the amended kidnapping, the fugitive felon, and the stolen property acts. The proviso therefore may simply mean in effect that the emergency did not extend to even violent acts in furthering legitimate union activities; control or punishment of them should still remain with the states.... Perhaps final interpretation should not now be attempted, but as at present advised I think conviction cannot be had where the acts or threats complained of are part of an endeavor of members of bona fide labor organizations to carry out their otherwise legitimate objects.''

(iii) The Dissent. Judge Augustus Hand dissented only in part because he thought the evidence with respect to some of the defendants might have been insufficient. But he disagreed with the majority that the instructions of the trial judge were deficient.

He thought the exemption in § 2(a) ''is not such as to relieve defendants from prosecution who obtained money by threats without earning wages for any real work even though they might have been willing to accept employment if the operators of the trucks had consented to engage them.'' He elaborated:

''[T]he employee is ex hypothesi a law breaker who has used violence or coercion to extort money and that money which he has not worked to earn is not wages or paid as such. Only 'payment of wages' is excepted under [§ 2(a)] from the penalties of the act. He does not come within the terms of the [section]. I see no reason for enlarging its terms by implication for his benefit even if some other person, who had gone far enough through the same unlawful means to obtain the status of an employee, would come within the exemption.

''It may be added that Congress may have determined to exempt men from prosecution under the Anti–Racketeering Act who actually obtain a status as employees, even though the status is secured by coercion, but not to grant exemption to men who have done nothing but 'shake down' prospective employers without rendering any service. The one policy would tend to preserve an employer-employee relationship when once established, while the other would involve toleration of intermittent acts of brigandage resulting in no ascertainable advantage.''

2. Questions and Comments on *United States v. Local 807*. The Supreme Court considered three possible interpretations of the Anti–Racketeering Act that would have led to affirmance of the convictions. All three assume that the defendants obtained money by violence or threats of violence, that is, that the substantive prohibition of the act occurred. The question, then, is what the exemption in § 2(a)[e] means, who among those

---

[e] One of the charges was filed under § 2(b) of the act, which does not in terms contain a ''wages'' exemption. But as the Court noted in footnote 2 of its opinion, it

who have otherwise violated the statute should nonetheless be excluded from conviction.

The first possible interpretation is that the exemption applied only to existing employees, that is, to persons who were already employees of the "victim" of the offense prior to the conduct on which the charge is based. The next two assumed that this was wrong, and that the exemption could be claimed by persons who were not already employees at the time of the alleged offense but who wanted to become employees. The Court's second hypothesis was that the case should turn on the intent of the victim—if the victim sought to buy "protection" then an offense was committed; if the victim sought to hire an employee then no offense was committed. The third possibility was that the exemption is unavailable if money is accepted without employment, that is, if the putative employee offers services, but nonetheless accepts money even though those services are refused.

Before addressing the Court's resolution of these three possible constructions of the statute, it may help to consider some clearer cases. It appears that all of the judges who participated in the *Local 807* decision at both the Court of Appeals and Supreme Court levels would agree that it would violate the statute (and the exemption would not apply) if money was obtained by threat of violence and *no* services were offered in return (a classic shakedown or "protection" racket). The same result should follow if sham or fictitious services were offered ("I'll keep your place from being burned down and your employees from being beaten up (by me if you do not pay, it is the unmistakable implication)"). It is also probable that the statute would be violated in some situations where a "service" was actually performed. Consider, for example, a case where a union official promises to prevent a strike over a grievance issue if the official personally is paid $10,000. That such a payment may save the employer a great deal of money, and in that sense be considered a valuable "service" by the employer, would not seem to insulate the union official from prosecution under the act. Indeed, such personal payoffs to union officials appear to constitute one of the paradigm situations that Congress sought to reach by the Anti–Racketeering Act.

seems clear that § 2(b) should also be read to exempt the same class of payments as does § 2(a). As the Court of Appeals observed, indeed, it is unclear—aside from one context not involved here—what difference in substantive coverage is achieved by the addition of § 2(b):

> "The whole statute is very loosely drawn and we are not sure what [§ 2(b)] does add to [§ 2(a)], beyond making it an offense to extort 'property . . . under color of official right.' 'Property' in [§ 2(b)] presumably includes 'money' in [§ 2(a)]

and, the phrase, 'consent induced by wrongful use of force or fear' in [§ 2(b)] must include a 'threat to use force,' in [§ 2(a)]; if so, the two subdivisions to some extent appear to overlap. However that may be, we cannot suppose that the exaction of wages by a 'bona-fide employee' is forbidden by [§ 2(b)] after being expressly exempted from [§ 2(a)]."

The Court of Appeals accordingly concluded that the count charging a violation of § 2(b) "added nothing of substance" to the count charging a violation of § 2(a). Apparently the Supreme Court agreed.

One cannot say, however, that all coercion of employers fits within the statute. The difficulties arise because in some sense, indeed in a federally protected sense, unions are in the business of coercing employers to do things they don't want to do. And the legitimate objectives of concerted union activity—for example, a strike for higher wages or better working conditions—would literally violate the affirmative prohibition of the statute: the "payment of money or other valuable considerations" would be "obtained" "by [economic] coercion." Plainly, however, the wage exclusion would exempt the strikers from criminal liability in such a case. Is the situation changed if the picketing is accompanied by violence? Learned Hand pointed out that "[p]ractically always the crux of a labor dispute is who shall get the job and what the terms shall be", and added: "The history of labor disputes is studded with violence which unhappily is not yet obsolete; but, although the means employed may be the same as those here condemned, the end is always different, for it is to secure work on better terms." Does the legitimacy of the union objective bring the use of illegitimate means within the "wage" exclusion? Or does the use of illegitimate means preclude reliance on the wage exclusion and permit a criminal conviction under the statute?

If the answer is that violence on the picket line *is* punished by the Anti–Racketeering Act, then *Local 807* would seem be wrong. If the pursuit of lawful objectives by striking employees is criminalized because of the use of unlawful means, it would be hard for the Local 807 members to argue that their behavior is excluded from the statute. On the other hand, if the answer is that violence on the picket line *is not* criminal under the Anti–Racketeering Act, then the *Local 807* case poses more difficulty. The question presented is different from violent picketing at least in two respects. First, the Local 807 members were not already employed by the truck owners. They were union members who were seeking employment, not existing employees who were seeking higher pay or better working conditions. Second, while they were, in the main, offering "real" and "lawful" services which they were qualified to provide, the prospective employer did not want or need those services. The services were superfluous from the employer's perspective. Do these factors change the analysis?

Consider these two differences separately. If *some* payments obtained by violence are excluded from the statute (namely those obtained by striking employees), is it reasonable, as Augustus Hand seems to have asserted, to read the exemption as limited to existing employees and not applicable to persons seeking employment? Isn't it unlikely that the appeasement of labor that was a part of the drafting of the statute could have been bought if labor understood that such a narrow meaning was intended? What, on the other hand, was labor trying to buy? The right to continue to engage in violence free of a federal criminal sanction?[f] If put in these terms, is it likely that Congress would have concurred? But what else could the exemption have meant?

[f] State criminal laws of course remained available, then as now, for assaults and other violent behavior committed during otherwise lawful union activity.

Now consider the second difference. Is there any practical way Local 807 could have engaged in peaceful picketing in order to achieve its goals? If it could have done so, would its objectives then have been lawful even if the truck owners ultimately were forced to pay for labor they did not want or need? If so, does it follow that both the Court of Appeals and Supreme Court were right to read the exemption as applicable to the same sort of behavior accompanied by violence? Does Judge Clark's reading of the proviso in § 6 add an important argument in support of this conclusion? On the other hand, if there was no practical way in which the union could have achieved its objective by peaceful means, or if the objective of compelling the truck owners to pay for services which they did not want or need was itself unlawful, does it follow that the Court of Appeals and the Supreme Court were wrong?

In any event, does it help, as the government sought to do, to characterize the issue as whether the payments of the employer were "for labor or for protection"? If an employer capitulates and agrees to higher wages in the face of violent picketing, what is being purchased: labor, or protection from further violence? Is the answer to this question any easier on the *Local 807* facts?

Finally, consider the case from one further perspective. In the end, the Supreme Court's decision turns on the adequacy of the jury instructions. What exactly was the error made by the trial judge? Did the Court of Appeals and the Supreme Court agree as to the nature of the error?

The reason all this matters, as the following material reveals, is that Congress reacted to the *Local 807* case by replacing the Anti–Racketeering Act of 1934 with the Hobbs Act. While the legislative history of the Hobbs Act is somewhat murky, the one thing that is clear is that Congress disagreed with the result and wanted to overrule the decision. One question to be explored below is exactly how the Hobbs Act was meant to change the federal criminal law applicable to union activity of the sort involved in *Local 807*. Another, which reached the Supreme Court in a case reproduced below, is whether the Hobbs Act was meant to apply to violence that occurs during picketing for what would otherwise be legitimate union objectives.

INTRODUCTORY NOTES ON THE HOBBS ACT

1. Text. On July 3, 1946, an act "[t]o amend the Act entitled 'An Act to protect trade and commerce against interference by violence, threats, coercion, or intimidation'" became law. The new statute has become known as the Hobbs Act, and is now codified (with only one minor amendment, enacted in 1994, changing the maximum fine of $10,000 to a fine "under this title") at 18 U.S.C. § 1951:

> *Be it enacted by the Senate and House of Representatives of the United States of America in Congress assembled,* That the Act entitled "An Act to protect trade and commerce against interference by violence, threats, coercion, or intimidation", approved June 18, 1934 (48 Stat. 979), be, and it is hereby, amended to read as follows:

"TITLE I

"Sec. 1. As used in this title—

"(a) The term 'commerce' means (1) commerce between any point in a State, Territory, or the District of Columbia and any point outside thereof, or between points within the same State, Territory, or the District of Columbia but through any place outside thereof, and (2) commerce within the District of Columbia or any Territory, and (3) all other commerce over which the United States has jurisdiction; and the term 'Territory' means any Territory or possession of the United States.

"(b) The term 'robbery' means the unlawful taking or obtaining of personal property, from the person or in the presence of another, against his will, by means of actual or threatened force, or violence, or fear of injury, immediate or future, to his person or property, or property in his custody or possession, or the person or property of a relative or member of his family or anyone in his company at the time of the taking or obtaining.

"(c) The term 'extortion' means the obtaining of property from another, with his consent, induced by wrongful use of actual or threatened force, violence, or fear, or under color of official right.

"Sec. 2. Whoever in any way or degree obstructs, delays, or affects commerce, or the movement of any article or commodity in commerce, by robbery or extortion, shall be guilty of a felony.

"Sec. 3. Whoever conspires with another or with others, or acts in concert with another or with others to do anything in violation of section 2 shall be guilty of a felony.

"Sec. 4. Whoever attempts or participates in an attempt to do anything in violation of section 2 shall be guilty of a felony.

"Sec. 5. Whoever commits or threatens physical violence to any person or property in furtherance of a plan or purpose to do anything in violation of section 2 shall be guilty of a felony.

"Sec. 6. Whoever violates any section of this title shall, upon conviction thereof, be punished by imprisonment for not more than twenty years or by a fine of not more than $10,000, or both.

TITLE II

"Nothing in this Act shall be construed to repeal, modify, or affect either section 6 or section 20 of an Act entitled 'An Act to supplement existing laws against unlawful restraints and monopolies, and for other purposes', approved October 15, 1914 [the Clayton Act], or an Act entitled 'An Act to amend the judicial code and to define and limit the jurisdiction of the courts in equity, and for other purposes', approved March 23, 1932 [the Norris–LaGuardia Act], or an Act entitled 'An Act to provide for the prompt disposition of disputes between carriers and their employees, and for other purposes', approved May 20, 1926, as amended [the Railway Labor Act], or an Act entitled 'An Act to diminish the causes of labor disputes burdening or obstructing interstate or foreign commerce, to create a National Labor Relations Board, and for other purposes', approved July 5, 1935 [the National Labor Relations Act]." 60 Stat. 420.

2. Legislative History. Congress did not wait long to react to the *Local 807* decision. Several bills designed to overrule the decision were promptly introduced. It was four years, however, before the Hobbs Act was enacted. The intervening legislative history makes it clear that Congress was disturbed about the *Local 807* result. But, as the following material reveals, the precise substantive scope of the enacted substitute was far from clear.

(i) The First House Report. The *Local 807* case was decided on March 2, 1942. On May 27 of that year, the House Judiciary Committee reported out a bill, H.R. 7067, itself the successor to another bill, H.R. 6872, to replace the Anti–Racketeering Act of 1934. See H.R. Rep. No. 2176, 77th Cong., 2d Sess. The text of the bill was substantially identical to title I of the Hobbs Act as eventually enacted. The purpose of the proposed legislation was stated as "to prevent interference with interstate commerce by robbery or extortion, as defined in the bill." The substantive comments of the Committee on the proposal are reproduced below in full:

"This [bill] is an amendment of the existing antiracketeering law which was enacted in 1934. It was passed in an effort to eliminate racketeering in relation to interstate commerce, of concern to the Nation as a whole. That statute came under examination of the Supreme Court recently in *United States v. Local 807* and the opinion in that case is set out in full, both the majority opinion and the dissent: [Here the opinion was quoted.]

"The objective of [the bill] is to prevent anyone from obstructing, delaying, or affecting commerce, or the movement of any article of commodity in commerce by robbery or extortion as defined in the bill. A conspiracy or attempt to do anything in violation of section 2 is likewise made punishable, as is the commission or threat of physical violence to any person or property in furtherance of a plan to violate section 2.

"A penalty is prescribed of imprisonment for not more than 10 years or a fine of not more than $10,000, or both, upon conviction of violating any section."

A minority report was filed by Congressmen Celler (New York) and Eliot (Massachusetts). Their report read in full:

"The original Antiracketeering Act of 1934 was expressly aimed at 'the elimination of terroristic activities by professional gangsters' and intended 'no interference with traditional labor

union activities' (*U.S. v. Local 807*).   The only case under this act
which reached the Supreme Court was one involving labor union
activities.   The committee hearings on the bill were largely addressed to alleged evils committed by labor unions, particularly the
Teamsters' Union.   Therefore, it is clear that the sole intention of
the instant proposal is not further to curb racketeering activities
by professional gangsters, but rather to impose severe criminal
restrictions upon the activities of labor unions.

"We do not approve of or condone the activities of the local
Teamster Union involved in the *Local 807* case, nor do we approve
of the activities of other locals which were described in the course
of the hearings on this bill.   On the contrary, it is our own belief
that these activities are in the long run disadvantageous to those
comparatively few locals who engage in them and to the organized
labor movement in general.

"It is interesting to note that Daniel Tobin, general president
of the Teamsters' Union, not only disavowed the practices of the
local Teamsters' Union involved in the *Local 807* case and the
similar practices of the other locals, but actually issued an order
prohibiting in the future such outrageous conduct on the part of
unions under his jurisdiction.

"However, even if these were normal peacetimes there has, in
our opinion, been a complete failure of any showing requiring so
drastic a federal police measure affecting all labor unions throughout the country.   [Please note penalties of not more than 20 years
imprisonment are prescribed.[a]]   In this period of grave national
emergency the bill is not only unnecessary to meet any alleged
evils; it would, if passed, make serious inroads in our constructive
labor policy with a consequent interference with full war production.   In brief, the bill is at best dangerously ill-timed.

"Organized labor has voluntarily and patriotically given its
solemn pledge not to strike.   By so doing, it has abandoned its
most effective instrument for security and advancement.   That
pledge has been fulfilled to a surprisingly high degree.   Since
December 7, 1941, there has not been a single authorized strike
affecting war production.   The comparatively few unauthorized
strikes that have taken place have been of very brief duration—
their prompt settlement in most cases having been accomplished
by the vigorous intervention of labor leaders.

"The success of the 'no strike' pledge has been truly amazing.
Since Pearl Harbor, there has been only 1 day lost per man in 30
years of work.   The following statistics are contained in an official

---

[a] This sentence, as explained below, was
added in a subsequent restatement of the
minority report.—[Footnote by eds.]

release of the Nation War Labor Board, and they include all strikes which appear to affect the war effort.

'Strike idleness in relation to war production during first quarter of 1942 was one–15th of the corresponding period of 1941,....

'There were approximately 332,000 man-days of idleness due to strikes affecting the war effort during the first quarter of 1942 or about one-fourth of the approximately 1,384,000 man-days idle for the first quarter of 1941. At the same time, employment on war materials has increased three and two-thirds times since the first quarter of 1941—from about 156 million man-days in the first quarter of 1941 to about 552 million for the first quarter of 1942.

'Expressed as a percentage of war employment, idleness in strikes related to war production was approximately .9 of one percent in the first quarter of 1941 and only .06 of one percent for the first quarter of 1942.'

"In brief, the pledge has virtually been 100 percent fulfilled. Stoppages of war production due to labor disputes have ceased to give any concern. This record is a tribute to democracy. The organized American workingman has conclusively shown the superiority of voluntary patriotic cooperation over dictatorial compulsion.

"This alone, namely the success of the 'no strike' pledge, removes whatever alleged evils are said to require the passage of this bill. It is a simple fact that interstate commerce is not being seriously interfered with by any labor unions. Whatever the evils of extortion and robbery, whether committed by professional gangsters or others, there are ample statutes with appropriate penalties in every state of the Union. States, and not the federal government, are the proper sovereignties to cope with such problems. That has not only been traditional in our country, it conforms with and is necessary to our federal system of government. The proponents of the bill are in the main upholders of the doctrine of states' rights. There has been no showing whatever that the states have been unable fully to deal with the crimes of extortion and robbery. The congressional action proposed by this bill is entirely excessive and threatens unnecessarily to undermine states' rights.

"The basic objection to the bill, however, lies in its wholly unwarranted reflection on the organized millions of working men and women in the country. Unstintingly, they have been given [sic] their skill, energies, and spirit to the end that liberty and democracy survive. Labor unions have been in the forefront in making constructive suggestions to our administrative war agencies so that war production be improved and increased. They have been carrying on gigantic and effective campaigns for the purchase of war bonds. They have at their own expense supplied and transported vast numbers of skilled workers to distant places where they were required for the war effort. They have voluntarily given up contractual wage benefits such as double time for holiday work. They have, in short, shown every willingness and ability to cooperate to the utmost with the President and the government of the United States in this great emergency.

"To imply, therefore, as enactment of this bill necessarily does imply that strong criminal measures are necessary to restrain the excesses of labor unions, is wholly without foundation or cause.

"More important, it will inevitably disturb and disrupt the high morale of millions of organized workers of this country. Theirs has been a necessary and greatly effective contribution to the national war program. Criminal antilabor legislation is hardly the appropriate reward."

(ii) The Second House Report. Apparently H.R. 7067 went no further. But the House Judiciary Committee submitted another report on January 28, 1943, on a successor bill, H.R. 653. See H.R. Rep. No. 66, 78th Cong., 1st Sess. The proposed statute was again substantially identical to title I of the Hobbs Act as ultimately enacted.[b] The report is virtually word-for-word the same as H.R. Rep. No. 2176 as quoted above. Again a minority report was submitted, this time by Congressmen Celler and Lane (Massachusetts). The minority report was also virtually identical to the previous minority report quoted above, with the addition of the sentence in brackets accompanying footnote a, supra, and an elaboration of the strike statistics supplied in a letter from an official of the National War Labor Board showing that by December, 1942, the percentage of time lost due to strikes was down to .03 of one percent.

(iii) Supplemental Report to the Second House Report. On April 7, 1943, the House Judiciary Committee issued a Supplemental Report on H.R. 653. See H.R. Rep. No. 66, Part 2, 78th Cong., 1st Sess. The report offered an amendment to the bill that added, in identical wording, what was to become title II of the Hobbs Act as enacted. The Committee offered the following comments in justification for the recommendation:

"It is considered by the committee that the provisions of title I were not intended to prevent the doing of acts authorized under the [Clayton Act, the Norris–LaGuardia Act, the Railway Labor Act, and the National Labor Relations Act] but in order to remove any question the committee has agreed to the ... amendment..... The proposed ... amendment is not intended to be interpreted as authorizing any unlawful acts, particularly those amounting to robbery or extortion. The need for the legislation was emphasized

[b] The maximum authorized imprisonment was raised from 10 years in H.R. 7067 to 20 years in H.R. 653. It remained at 20 years in the enacted statute.

by the opinion of the Supreme Court in the case of United States v. Local 807 (315 U.S. 521)."

(iv) The First House Debate. H.R. 653 went to the floor of the House on April 9 and was the subject of extensive debate, extending for some 38 pages[c] in the Congressional Record. See 89 Cong. Rec. 3192–3230. Significant portions of the debate[d] are reproduced, in full, in Appendix A to this book. A taste of the debate can be experienced by reading the following brief passages.

There was much vilification of the result in the *Local 807* case, but little specific elaboration of the intended substantive scope of the new provisions and, in spite of their broad wording, almost no discussion of the possible application of the bill outside the labor context. Most of the generalizations in the House Reports were repeated often and at length. It is clear that Congress regarded the behavior in *Local 807* as "highway robbery" or some equally nefarious practice, but no enlightenment on whether there might have been any legitimacy to any of the union objectives reflected in the case. In short, Congress expressed its outrage but did so in essentially uninformative statements.

Two major amendments to the bill were before the House. The first (the Committee amendment) was the amendment proposed in the Supplemental Report summarized above. Congressman Celler offered alternative language (the Celler or A.F. of L. amendment):

"That no acts, conduct, or activities which are lawful under section 6 or section 20 of an act entitled 'An Act to supplement existing laws against unlawful restraints and monopolies, and for other purposes', approved October 15, 1914 [the Clayton Act], or under an act entitled 'An Act to amend the judicial code and to define and limit the jurisdiction of the courts in equity, and for other purposes', approved March 23, 1932 [the Norris–LaGuardia Act], or under an act entitled 'An Act to provide for the prompt disposition of disputes between carriers and their employees, and for other purposes', approved May 20, 1926, as amended [the Railway Labor Act], or under an act entitled 'An Act to diminish the causes of labor disputes burdening or obstructing interstate or foreign commerce, to create a National Labor Relations Board, and for other purposes', approved July 5, 1935 [the National Labor Relations Act], shall constitute a violation of this act." (3220)

The first speaker was Congressman Halleck:

"Mr. HALLECK. ... I shall try in a few words to give ... some idea of what I think this is about.

---

[c] Each page is three columns of small type that would print out to about 3½ pages in the type face used in this book.

[d] Particular attention has been paid in selecting these excerpts to colloquies or statements that may be relevant to the intended substantive scope of the statute. The page numbers from which quotations have been taken appear in parenthesis following each statement.

"In 1934 Congress enacted a so-called Anti–Racketeering Act. It was designed to bring about federal prosecution of people obtaining money or property by violence and threats of violence in connection with the movement of goods in interstate commerce. An exception was written into the law which provided it should not apply to a situation where there existed a bona fide relationship of employer and employee.

"The celebrated *807* case in New York came on for decision by the Supreme Court. The case involved the conduct of individuals who stopped trucks going into the city of New York and in effect hijacked the drivers out of $8 or $9 per truck. The Supreme Court held that under the exception heretofore referred to by me, relative to the relationship of employer and employee, the prosecution would not lie in that case. I know a lot of good lawyers who disagree with that decision, and personally I disagree with it....

"This bill seeks to supply the deficiency created by that decision. In a word, what this bill seeks to do is to superimpose federal jurisdiction or federal prosecution for robbery and extortion committed in connection with the movement of goods in interstate commerce. I say that is the objective, and as far as I have ever heard that is the sole objective of the bill. It is to stop the so-called hijacking and racketeering that has prevailed...." (3192–93)

"Mr. HOBBS. [T]he decision of the Supreme Court in the *Local 807* case ... has ... decided that no matter how much violence a union man might use in seeking employment, he could not be punished under the 1934 Anti-Racketeering Act. If he commits murder, or if he commits assault with a weapon, it is all right under the antiracketeering law.

"Mr. HALLECK. [I]s it not true that that decision of the Supreme Court in the *807* case hinged upon the exception written into the act in reference to the bona fide relationship of employer to employee, and is it not also true that if this act becomes the law those words will be repealed, which will mean that the words upon which that decision depended will no longer be in the law?

"Mr. HOBBS. No. I do not so construe the opinion.... If I read that opinion correctly, and I have read it a hundred times, ... the opinion is based on both of the exceptions ..., the latter one of which is substantially in blanket form what is detailed in the committee amendment and what is also detailed in the A.F. of L. amendment. ...

"Mr. WRIGHT. I want to know how the gentleman can argue that both of these amendments are substantially the same, then say in the next breath that the Celler amendment emasculates the act and at least infer that the other one does not.

"Mr. HOBBS. I never said that. I said they seemed so at first reading. I submit that there is within the essence of the Celler amendment a phrase which seems to be in accord with our wishes as to stamping out the racket, but which does not result in that. It permits robbery or extortion because it does not deal truly with the status. It says that no acts, conduct or activity which are lawful under the four laws therein cited should constitute guilt under this law. And it implies that this is to be taken as true, no matter how unlawfully any of those lawful acts may be done. The four laws cited in the Celler amendment require the lawful acts in them enumerated to be done in a peaceful, lawful way. The Celler amendment, quite cleverly, omits any such requirement. ...

"Mr. COLMER. Will the gentleman explain how one can do an act lawfully and at the same time do it unlawfully?

"Mr. HOBBS. Of course, the question as framed contains a contradiction in terms. No one can act lawfully and unlawfully at the same time. But no such case is presented by the Celler amendment or its underlying meaning. There we have a lawful act done unlawfully. [T]hat is the effect of the construction put upon robbery committed while engaged in otherwise lawful conduct by the Supreme Court decision. No matter how much force is used, robbery is a perfectly innocent pastime, as Chief Justice Stone said, if the perpetrator be a labor-union member seeking employment." (3195)

"Mr. HANCOCK. ... This is a bill of general application. It covers the most heinous crimes the criminal statute book contemplates. It had its origin in the activities of the Dillinger gang. All this bill does is abolish the double standard which Justice Byrnes established and makes labor responsible for crimes just as well as those who are not laborers. That is all it does.

"Mr. CELLER. I wish the gentleman's interpretation were correct, but I fear that he is woefully in error. This bill is primarily aimed at labor. It has a label of racketeering, it has a label of extortion, it has a label of robbery, but it is an antilabor bill. Let us not delude ourselves, because were it not for the so-called Teamsters' Local decision by Mr. Justice Byrnes, a labor decision, we would not have had this bill. ...

"This bill is not properly called an antiracketeering bill. Those opposing the bill, unamended, and labor opposing the bill cannot and should not be said to be in favor of racketeering. We disfavor any bill that interferes with legitimate labor acts under the guise of preventing racketeering. The language is broad and sweeping and is as broad as a barn door and may permit simple assaults to be converted into felonies." (3201)

After almost twenty additional pages of remarks, including a lengthy statement by Congressman Hobbs which concluded with quotes from the Star Spangled Banner and Elijah on Mount Carmel, the bill was read and a series of motions and amendments were formally presented. The Celler amendment was the most vigorously debated, and was ultimately rejected by a vote of 167 to 126. After the Celler amendment was rejected, the Committee amendment was adopted without further debate and without a recorded vote. Further debate on other proposed amendments followed. One, to eliminate the words "or under color of official right" from the definition of "extortion," was rejected following a debate that is dealt with in connection with other materials below. Another, to reduce the authorized maximum punishment from 20 years to 10, was also rejected. A vote on the bill, as amended by adding the Committee amendment, was then held. H.R. 635 passed by a vote of 270 to 107, with 57 members not voting.

But the saga was not over. After all this, no action was taken on the bill in the Senate, and it accordingly failed to become law.

(v) The Third House Report. On February 27, 1945, almost two years later, the House Judiciary Committee reported favorably on H.R. 32, which was worded identically to H.R. 653 as it had previously passed the House. See H.R. Rep. No. 238, 79th Cong., 1st Sess. The Report was virtually word-for-word the same as the report that had ushered H.R. 653 to the House floor. This time there was no minority report, and the bill itself contained the language that became title II of the Hobbs Act. On that provision, the Committee's comments in full were:

> "The purpose of this title is to make clear that the provisions of title I were not intended to prevent the doing of acts authorized under sections 6 to 20 of the act popularly known as the Clayton Act, or of the Norris–LaGuardia Act, the Railway Labor Act, or the National Labor Relations Act. It is not the intention of the committee that title [II] be interpreted as authorizing any unlawful acts, particularly those amounting to robbery or extortion. The need for the legislation was emphasized by the opinion of the Supreme Court in the case of United States v. Local 807 (315 U.S. 521)."

(vi) The Second House Debate. H.R. 32, which was destined to become the Hobbs Act as enacted, came to the House floor for debate almost nine months later, on December 11–12, 1945. This time the debate continued for some 31 pages[e] in the Congressional Record. See 91 Cong. Rec. 11839–48, 11899–922.

Again, the debate is reproduced in relevant part in Appendix B to this book. The flavor of the debate was much the same as the debate on H.R. 635 two years earlier. There was much haranguing of the Supreme Court's decision in *Local 807*, and the same sort of general talk about hijacking and racketeering. A minority complained that the rights of labor were being undermined; the majority responded that no one should be able to commit robbery and extortion. Precious little time was spent, as in the

---

[e] See footnote c, supra.

prior debate, on the specifics, that is, on exactly what the rights of labor were or exactly what types of union activity (beyond the "outrage" presented by the "facts" of *Local 807*) constituted "robbery" or "extortion." There were numerous references to the source of the definitions of "robbery" and "extortion" in the then-current law of New York, and to the prevalence of the tactics used by Local 807 in other parts of the country.

During the course of the lengthy debate, Congressman Celler offered an amendment that would have added both the definition of "property" from § 3(b) of the 1934 statute and the proviso from § 6 of that statute to H.R. 32. This amendment was rejected. Congressman Celler then proceeded to offer the same amendment he had offered to H.R. 653; it, too, was rejected. Congressman LaFollette then suggested that the original 1934 Act be retained with the following addition:

> "Sec. 7. The following definitions shall be binding upon all courts in construing this act:
>
> > "(a) The term 'the payment of wages by a bona fide employer to a bona fide employee' shall not be construed so as to include the payment of money or the transfer of a thing of value by a person to another when the latter shall use or attempt to use or threaten to use force or violence against the body or to the physical property (as distinguished from intangible property) of the former or against the body of anyone having the possession, custody, or control of the physical property of the former, in attempting to obtain or obtaining such payment or transfer.
>
> > "(b) The term 'the rights of a bona fide labor organization in lawfully carrying out the legitimate objects thereof, as such rights are expressed in existing statutes of the United States' shall not be construed so as to ignore, void, set aside, or nullify the definitions set out or the words used in or the plain meaning of subsection (a) hereof."

He explained that this was his attempt "in good faith ... to prevent a reoccurrence of what happened in the Supreme Court opinion" and added:

> "Of course, there is an element of coercion in strikes. It is the only right that labor has. I am not going to stand in the well of this House and affect that right in any way. But I am also not going to vote in this House for language which I am convinced can be construed against the organizing activities of labor. ..."
> (11920)

After the LaFollette amendment was defeated, the bill itself was passed. There was no recorded vote.

(vii) The President's Veto of the Case Bill. A month later, on January 14, 1946, H.R. 4908 (known as the Case Bill) was certified as passed by both the House and Senate and sent to President Truman for signature. The statute was a long (6½ pages of small print) and complicated measure whose objectives as stated in the preamble were "to encourage settlement of disputes between labor and management by collective bargaining and by conciliation, mediation and voluntary arbitration, thereby minimizing industrial strife, strikes and lock-outs." It established a Federal Mediation Board to assist in the accomplishment of these purposes, and contained a melange of other provisions dealing with a wide range of labor-management issues. Section 7 incorporated H.R. 32 as adopted by the House.

On June 11, 1946, the President transmitted to Congress a nine-page message outlining his reasons for vetoing the Case Bill. See H.R. Doc. No. 651, 79th Cong., 2d Sess. His comments on § 7 were brief:

"Section 7: Reenacts in amended form the so-called Antiracketeering Act. On its face, this section does no more than prohibit all persons, whether union representatives or employees or others, from interfering with interstate commerce by robbery or extortion.

"I am in full accord with the objectives which the Congress here had in mind.

"However, it has already been suggested that some question may arise from the fact that § 7 omits from the original act the provision that it was not to be construed so as to—

'impair, diminish, or in any manner affect the rights of bona-fide labor organizations in lawfully carrying out the legitimate objects thereof.'

"It should be made clear in express terms that § 7 does not make it a felony to strike and picket peacefully, and to take other legitimate and peaceful concerted action."

(viii) The Senate Report. On June 18, 1946—seven days after the President's veto of the Case Bill—the Senate Judiciary Committee issued S.R. No. 1516, 79th Cong., 2d Sess., in which it reported H.R. 32 favorably to the floor of the Senate. The report is no more than a paraphrase of some of the comments in the House report. It adds nothing of substance on the meaning of the bill.

(ix) Adoption of the Hobbs Act. On June 24, 1946, it was announced to the House that the Senate had passed H.R. 32 "without amendment." 92 Cong. Rec. 7398. There was no recorded debate. This time there was no Presidential veto, and the Hobbs Act became law on July 3.

NOTES ON FEATHERBEDDING

1. Background. "Featherbedding" is a term used to describe efforts by labor to "feather their beds" by exacting from employers unnecessary work or jobs. Typical is the practice before the Supreme Court in American Newspaper Publishers Ass'n v. National Labor Relations Board, 345 U.S. 100 (1953):

"Printers in newspaper composing rooms have long sought to retain the opportunity to set up in type as much as possible of whatever is printed by their respective publishers. In 1872, when printers were paid on a piecework basis, each diversion of composition was at once reflected by a loss in their income. Accordingly, ITU [the International Typographical Union], which had been formed in 1852 from local typographical societies, began its long battle to retain as much type-setting work for printers as possible.

"With the introduction of the linotype machine in 1890, the problem took on a new aspect. When a newspaper advertisement was set up in type, it was impressed on a cardboard matrix, or 'mat.' These mats were used by their makers and also were reproduced and distributed, at little or no cost, to other publishers who used them as molds for metal castings from which to print the same advertisement. This procedure by-passed all compositors, except those who made up the original form. Facing this loss of work, ITU secured the agreement of newspaper publishers to permit their respective compositors, at convenient times, to set up duplicate forms for all local advertisements in precisely the same manner as though the mat had not been used. For this reproduction work the printers received their regular pay. The doing of this 'made work' came to be known as 'setting bogus.' It was a wasteful procedure. Nevertheless, it has become a recognized idiosyncracy of the trade and a customary feature of the wage structure and work schedule of newspaper printers.

"By fitting the 'bogus' work into slack periods, the practice interferes little with 'live' work. The publishers who set up the original composition find it advantageous because it burdens their competitors with costs of mat making comparable to their own. Approximate time limits for setting 'bogus' usually have been fixed by agreement at from four days to three weeks. On rare occasions the reproduced compositions are used to print the advertisements when rerun, but, ordinarily, they are promptly consigned to the 'hell box' and melted down. Live matter has priority over reproduction work but the latter usually takes from two to five per cent of the printers' time.[5]"

Justice Clark in dissent in that case had a more colorful description:

"Those 'services,' no more and no less, consist of setting 'bogus' type, then proofread and reset for corrections, only to be

---

[5] "In metropolitan areas, only the printers on the 'ad side' of a composing room, as contrasted with those on the 'news side,' take part in the reproduction work and never on a full-time basis. Such work is not done at overtime rates but when there is an accumulation of it, the newspaper is not permitted to reduce its work force or decline to hire suitable extra printers applying for employment. The trial examiner, in the instant case, found that reproduction work at the Rochester Democrat and Chronicle cost over $5,000 a year, at the Chicago Herald–American, about $50,000, and at the New York times, about $150,000."

immediately discarded and never used. Instead, this type is consigned to waste to a 'hell box' which feeds the 'melting pot'; and that, in turn, oozes fresh lead then molded into 'pigs' which retravel the same Sisyphean journey."

One could describe the activities of Local 807 in New York as an effort to secure "featherbedding" work for the union members. The farmers were perfectly capable of driving their own trucks to market, and neither wanted nor needed the extra "help" afforded by a union driver. But the union wanted the work for its members, and insisted—by violence in that case—that union drivers be employed. To the extent that money was obtained without a genuine offer to work, one might call what they did "extortion" (or "hijacking"). But to the extent that the union members were willing to drive and unload the truck for their pay, is there a difference between what they wanted and the setting of "bogus" type?

2. The Lea Act. The Lea Act, otherwise known as the Petrillo Act,[a] was adopted on April 16, 1946. It was an amendment to the Communications Act of 1934:

> "Sec. 506. It shall be unlawful, by the use or express or implied threat of the use of force, violence, intimidation, or duress, or by the use or express or implied threat of the use of other means, to coerce, compel or constrain or attempt to coerce, compel, or constrain a licensee—
>
> > "(1) to employ or agree to employ, in connection with the conduct of the broadcasting business of such licensee, any person or persons in excess of the number of employees needed by such licensee to perform actual services...."

Violation of the prohibition was a misdemeanor, punishable by imprisonment for not more than one year, by a fine of not more than $1000, or both.

The constitutionality of this statute was challenged in United States v. Petrillo, 332 U.S. 1 (1947). The argument that the words "number of such employees needed by such licensee" were unwarrantedly vague and could not support a criminal prosecution. Although the Court upheld the statute,[b] no conviction was obtained because the District Judge held that it was

---

[a] Petrillo was the head of the American Federation of Musicians, and the statute was aimed at "stand-by orchestras" insisted upon by that union.

[b] The Court said:

> "Clearer and more precise language might have been framed by Congress to express what it meant by 'number of employees needed.' But none occurs to us, nor has any better language been suggested, effectively to carry out what appears to have been the congressional purpose. The argument really seems to be that it is impossible for a jury or court

ever to determine how many employees a business needs, and that, therefore, no statutory language could meet the problem Congress had in mind. If this argument should be accepted, the result would be that no legislature could make it an offense for a person to compel another to hire employees, no matter how unnecessary they were, and however desirable a legislature might consider suppression of the practice to be.

> "The Constitution presents no such insuperable obstacle to legislation. We think that the language Congress used

not shown that Petrillo knew that the extra musicians were not needed. United States v. Petrillo, 75 F.Supp. 176 (N.D.Ill.1948). There are no other reported instances of an effort to enforce this statute.

3. The Taft–Hartley Act. The National Labor Relations Act, originally adopted in 1935, was amended by the Taft–Hartley Act (otherwise known as the Labor Management Relations Act) in 1947. The Taft–Hartley Act added as an unfair labor practice the following language in § 8(b)(6):

> "It shall be an unfair labor practice for a labor organization or its agents ... to cause or attempt to cause an employer to pay or deliver or agree to pay or deliver any money or other thing of value, in the nature of an exaction, for services which are not performed or not to be performed."

The Taft–Hartley bill was pending in Congress when the *Petrillo* decision was before the Supreme Court. The House version of the bill made it an unfair labor practice to engage in a strike or other concerted activity "an object of which is to compel an employer to accede to featherbedding practices." H.R. 3020, 80th Cong. 1st Sess. "Featherbedding practice" was then defined to include, inter alia, requiring an employer "to employ or agree to employ any person or persons in excess of the number of employees reasonably required by such employer to perform actual services." Senator Taft explained on the floor of the Senate the reason the Senate version of the bill was worded in the fashion quoted above:

> "There is one further provision which may possibly be of interest, which was not in the [original] Senate bill. The House had rather elaborate provisions prohibiting so-called featherbedding practices and making them unlawful labor practices. The Senate conferees, while not approving of feather-bedding practices, felt that it was impracticable to give to a board or a court the power to say that so many men are all right, and so many men are too many. It would require a practical application of the law by the courts in hundreds of different industries, and a determination of facts which it seemed to me would be almost impossible. So we declined to adopt the provisions which are now in the Petrillo Act. After all, that statute applies to only one industry. Those provisions are now the subject of court procedure. Their constitutionality has been questioned. We thought that probably we had better wait and see what happened, in any event, even though we

provides an adequate warning as to what conduct falls under its ban, and marks boundaries sufficiently distinct for judges and juries fairly to administer the law in accordance with the will of Congress. That there may be marginal cases in which it is difficult to determine the side of the line on which a particular fact situation falls is no sufficient reason to hold the language too ambiguous to define a criminal offense. ... The Constitution has erected procedural safeguards to protect against conviction for crime except for violation of laws which have clearly defined conduct thereafter to be punished; but the Constitution does not require impossible standards."

were in favor of prohibiting all feather-bedding practices. However, we did accept one provision which makes it an unlawful labor
practice for a union to accept money for people who do not work.
That seemed to be a fairly clear case, easy to determine, and we
accepted that additional unfair labor practice on the part of
unions...." 93 Cong. Rec. 6441.

4. *American Newspaper Publishers Ass'n v. National Labor Relations Board*. Application of § 8(b)(6) of the Taft–Hartley Act to the practice of setting "bogus" type described above came before the Supreme Court in American Newspaper Publishers Ass'n v. National Labor Relations Board, 345 U.S. 100 (1953). The plaintiff was an association of newspaper publishers representing more than 90% of the circulation of daily and Sunday newspapers in the United States. It filed unfair labor practice charges with the National Labor Relations Board (NLRB). The Board dismissed the § 8(b)(6) charges, and an appeal was taken to the Seventh Circuit Court of Appeals. That court upheld the Board decision, and the Supreme Court granted certiorari in this case and in a companion case described below.

The Supreme Court affirmed, with three Justices dissenting. After describing the legislative history of the statute, the Court said:

"The act now limits its condemnation to instances where a labor organization or its agents exact pay from an employer in return for services not performed or not to be performed. Thus, where work is done by an employee, with the employer's consent, a labor organization's demand that the employee be compensated for time spent in doing the disputed work does not become an unfair labor practice. The transaction simply does not fall within the kind of featherbedding defined in the statute. ... Section 8(b)(6) leaves to collective bargaining the determination of what, if any, work, including bona fide 'made work,' shall be included as compensable services and what rate of compensation shall be paid for it."

5. *National Labor Relations Board v. Gamble Enterprises, Inc*. To the same effect was the Court's decision in National Labor Relations Board v. Gamble Enterprises, Inc., 345 U.S. 117 (1953), decided on the same day. "The question here," the Court said, is whether § 8(b)(6) is violated when a union "insists that the management of one of an interstate chain of theaters shall employ a local orchestra to play in connection with certain programs, although that management does not need or want to employ that orchestra." The Court held § 8(b)(6) not violated, again over three dissents.[c]

The facts in *Gamble Enterprises* were described by the Court as follows:

[c] Two of the dissenters were the same, but Justice Douglas dissented from the *American Newspaper Publishers* decision and Justice Jackson from the result in *Gamble Enterprises*.

"For generations professional musicians have faced a shortage in the local employment needed to yield them a livelihood. They have been confronted with the competition of military bands, traveling bands, foreign musicians on tour, local amateur organizations and, more recently, technological developments in reproduction and broadcasting. To help them conserve local sources of employment, they developed local protective societies. Since 1896, they also have organized and maintained on a national scale the American Federation of Musicians, affiliated with the American Federation of Labor. By 1943, practically all professional instrumental performers and conductors in the United States had joined the Federation, establishing a membership of over 200,000, with 10,000 more in Canada.

"The Federation uses its nationwide control of professional talent to help individual members and local unions. It insists that traveling band contracts be subject to its rules, laws and regulations. Article 18, § 4, of its By–Laws provides: 'Traveling members cannot, without the consent of a Local, play any presentation performances in its jurisdiction unless a local house orchestra is also employed.'

"From this background we turn to the instant case. For more than 12 years the Palace Theater in Akron, Ohio, has been one of an interstate chain of theaters managed by respondent, Gamble Enterprises, Inc., which is a Washington corporation with its principal office in New York. Before the decline of vaudeville and until about 1940, respondent employed a local orchestra of nine union musicians to play for stage acts at that theater. When a traveling band occupied the stage, the local orchestra played from the pit for the vaudeville acts and, at times, augmented the performance of the traveling band.

"Since 1940, respondent has used the Palace for showing motion pictures with occasional appearances of traveling bands. Between 1940 and 1947, the local musicians, no longer employed on a regular basis, held periodic rehearsals at the theater and were available when required. When a traveling band appeared there, respondent paid the members of the local orchestra a sum equal to the minimum union wages for a similar engagement but they played no music.

"The Taft–Hartley Act, containing § 8(b)(6), was passed, over the President's veto, June 23, 1947, and took effect August 22. Between July 2 and November 12, seven performances of traveling bands were presented on the Palace stage. Local musicians were neither used nor paid on those occasions. They raised no objections and made no demands for 'stand-by' payments. However, in October, 1947, the American Federation of Musicians, Local No. 24 of Akron, Ohio, here called the union, opened negotiations with respondent for the latter's employment of a pit orchestra of local musicians whenever a traveling band performed on the stage. The pit orchestra was to play overtures, 'intermissions' and 'chasers' (the latter while patrons were leaving the theater). The union required acceptance of this proposal as a condition of its consent to local appearances of traveling bands. Respondent declined the offer and a traveling band scheduled to appear November 20 canceled its engagement on learning that the union had withheld its consent.

"May 8, 1949, the union made a new proposal. It sought a guaranty that a local orchestra would be employed by respondent on some number of occasions having a relation to the number of traveling band appearances.[4] This and similar proposals were declined on the ground that the local orchestra was neither necessary nor desired. Accordingly, in July, 1949, the union again declined to consent to the appearance of a traveling band desired by respondent and the band did not appear. In December an arrangement was agreed upon locally for the employment of a local orchestra to play in connection with a vaudeville engagement on condition that the union would consent to a later traveling band appearance without a local orchestra. Respondent's New York office disapproved the plan and the record before us discloses no further agreement."

The Court held:

"We accept the finding of the Board, made upon the entire record, that the union was seeking actual employment for its members and not mere 'stand-by' pay. The Board recognized that, formerly, before § 8(b)(6) had taken effect, the union had received 'stand-by' payments in connection with traveling band appearances. Since then, the union has requested no such payments and has received none. It has, however, requested and consistently negotiated for actual employment in connection with traveling band and vaudeville appearances. It has suggested various ways in which a local orchestra could earn pay for performing competent work and, upon those terms, it has offered to consent to the appearance of traveling bands which are Federation-controlled. Respondent, with equal consistency, has declined these offers as it had a right to do.

"Since we and the Board treat the union's proposals as in good faith contemplating the performance of actual services, we agree that the union has not, on this record, engaged in a practice proscribed by § 8(b)(6).... We are not dealing here with offers of

---

[4] "The union suggested four plans. Each called for actual playing of music by a local union orchestra in connection with the operation of the theater: (1) to play overtures, intermissions and chasers; (2) to play the music required for vaudeville acts not an integral part of a traveling band ensemble; (3) to perform on stage with vaudeville acts booked by respondent; or (4) to play at half of the total number of respondent's stage shows each year."

mere 'token' or nominal services. The proposals before us were appropriately treated by the Board as offers in good faith of substantial performances by competent musicians. There is no reason to think that sham can be substituted for substance under § 8(b)(6) any more than under any other statute. Payments for 'standing-by,' or for the substantial equivalent of 'standing-by,' are not payments for services performed, but when an employer receives a bona fide offer of competent performance of relevant services, it remains for the employer, through free and fair negotiation, to determine whether such offer shall be accepted and what compensation shall be paid for the work done.[5]"

6. *United States v. Green*. In United States v. Green, 350 U.S. 415 (1956), charges had been filed under the Hobbs Act against an individual and a union. There were two counts against each defendant, charging extortion against two different employers in the same language. The defendants were alleged to have attempted to obtain from the employer in question:

> "his money, in the form of wages to be paid for imposed, unwanted, superfluous and fictitious services of laborers commonly known as swampers, in connection with the operation of machinery and equipment then being used and operated by said [employer] in the execution of his said contract for maintenance work on said levee, the attempted obtaining of said property from said [employer] as aforesaid being then intended to be accomplished and accomplished with the consent of said [employer], induced and obtained by the wrongful use, to wit, the use for the purposes aforesaid, of actual and threatened force, violence and fear made to said [employer], and his employees and agents then and there being; in violation of § 1951 of title 18, United States Code."

The defendants were found guilty under each count, and their motions for acquittal or in the alternative for a new trial were denied. The trial court granted their motions in arrest of judgment, however, in an opinion saying that the action was taken "solely" on the following grounds:

---

[5] "In addition to the legislative history cited in the *American Newspaper* case, the following explanation by Senator Ball emphasizes the point that § 8(b)(6) proscribes *only* payments where *no work is done*. As a member of the Senate Committee on Labor and Public Welfare, and as one who had served as a Senate conferee, he made it on the floor of the Senate immediately preceding the passage of the bill, over the President's veto, June 23, 1947:

> " 'There is not a word in that [§ 8(b)(6)], Mr. President, about "featherbedding." It says that it is an unfair practice for a union to force an employer

to pay for *work which is not performed*. In the colloquy on this floor between the Senator from Florida [Mr. Pepper] and the Senator from Ohio [Mr. Taft], before the bill was passed, it was made abundantly clear that it did not apply to rest periods, it did not apply to speed-ups or safety provisions, or to anything of that nature; it applied *only* to situations, for instance, where the Musicians' Federation forces an employer to hire one orchestra and then to pay for another *stand-by orchestra, which does not work at all*.' (Emphasis supplied.) 93 Cong. Rec. 7529."

"This court is without jurisdiction of the offense.

"(b) The facts alleged in the indictment failed to set forth an offense against the United States such as to give this court jurisdiction.

"(c) A proper construction of the statute in question clearly indicates that it does not cover the type of activity charged in this indictment; to interpret the act in question as covering the type of activity charged in this indictment is to extend the jurisdiction of this court and the power of Congress beyond their Constitutional limits."

The court, as the Supreme Court described it, "thought persuasive our recent cases which held union efforts to secure 'made work' for their members were not unfair labor practices," citing *American Newspaper Publishers* and *Gamble Enterprises*. The trial court reasoned, as the Supreme Court quoted:

"In the usual extortion case, the extorter is obtaining money or property of another for his own benefit. ... In the case at hand, I conclude that Green's original activity in 'attempting to obtain from Arthur W. Terry, Jr., his money in the form of wages to be paid for imposed, unwanted, superfluous and fictitious services of laborers' which said charge was seriously controverted, was of itself not a violation of this statute, and within his rights and responsibilities as a union representative, which was not prohibited this statute.

"... I conclude that the trouble in this community and on this particular job was caused by a disagreement between the contractor and labor, and was in no wise an attempt to extort for the use of either the union or the defendant Green, any money or property of the contractor."

The government took a direct appeal to the Supreme Court from the trial court's order.

The Supreme Court reversed. After reviewing the *Local 807* case and noting that it relied on the "wages" exclusion, the Court noted that the exclusion clause was dropped in the Hobbs Act and that "[t]he legislative history makes it clear that the new act was meant to eliminate any grounds for future judicial conclusions that Congress did not intend to cover the employer-employee relationship. The words were defined to avoid any misunderstanding."[d] The Court then said:

"Title II of the Hobbs Act provides that the provisions of the act shall not affect the Clayton Act; the Norris–LaGuardia Act;

[d] At this point, the Court quoted H.R. Rep. No. 238 to the effect that "[i]t is not the intention of the committee that title [II] be interpreted as authorizing any unlawful acts, particularly those amounting to robbery or extortion." The Court added that "[e]ach of the prior bills [i.e., those that preceded H.R. 32] had the same purpose—amending the Anti-Racketeering Act so as to change the terms which brought about the result reached in the *Local 807* case."

the Railway Labor Act; or the National Labor Relations Act.[6] There is nothing in any of those acts, however, that indicates any protection for unions or their officials in attempts to get personal property through threats of force or violence. Those are not legitimate means for improving labor conditions. If the trial court intended by its references to the Norris–LaGuardia and Wagner Acts to indicate any such labor exception, which we doubt, it was in error. Apparently what the court meant is more clearly expressed by its statement, set out . . . above, that the charged acts would be criminal only if they were used to obtain property for the personal benefit of the union or its agent, in this case Green. This latter holding is also erroneous. The city truckers in the *Local 807* case similarly were trying by force to get jobs and pay from the out-of-state truckers by threats and violence. The Hobbs Act was meant to stop just such conduct. And extortion as defined in the statute in no way depends upon having a direct benefit conferred on the person who obtains the property.

"It is also stated in the opinion below that to interpret the act as covering the activity charged would 'extend the jurisdiction of the court, and the power of Congress beyond their Constitutional limits.' The same language is in the order. Since in our view the legislation is directed at the protection of interstate commerce against injury from extortion, the court's holding is clearly wrong. We said in the *Local 807* case that racketeering affecting interstate commerce was within federal legislative control.

"On this appeal the record does not contain the evidence upon which the court acted. The indictment charges interference with commerce by extortion in the words of the act's definition of that crime. We rule only on the allegations of the indictment and hold that the acts charged against appellees fall within the terms of the act. The order in arrest of judgment is reversed and the cause remanded to the District Court."[e]

Three Justices dissented on the ground that, since the district court had relied in its order on evidence outside the indictment, no direct appeal to the Supreme Court was permitted.

---

[6] "The Hobbs Act was enacted prior to the Labor Management Relations Act of 1947."

[e] The original District Court decision in *Green* appears at 135 F.Supp. 162 (S.D.Ill. 1955). The proceedings on remand are reported at 143 F.Supp. 442 (S.D.Ill.1956), aff'd, 246 F.2d 155 (7th Cir.). The objective in *Green* was to force a construction firm to hire "swampers", that is, men who scouted ahead of bulldozers and warned of approaching pitfalls. The employer did not wish to hire anyone to perform such services. In response to a question from one of the employers as to whether he was going to call a strike, Green said "Never you mind, I will stop you." At the construction site, Green and a large number of his men appeared and said to those who were working there such things as "[w]e ought to bash his head in" and "[w]e ought to throw his car into the canal."

7. Questions and Comments. What exactly is the holding in *Green*? Because of the procedural posture of the case, the issue before the Court was confined to the allegations in the indictment, which were that money was sought to be obtained for "imposed, unwanted, superfluous and fictitious services" and that "actual and threatened force, violence and fear" were used to get it. Which factor was critical to the Court's decision—the nature of the services sought, or the fact that violence was used? More specifically, does *Green* hold that violence used to gain lawful union objectives violates the Hobbs Act? Or does it hold that featherbedding violates the Hobbs Act? Or is the key word "fictitious"? Could the indictment be construed to allege a protection racket, that is, essentially a scheme to get money without offering any services at all? If so, does the Court seem to have so construed it?

Notice also the Court's reference to the Taft–Hartley Act in footnote 6. Does the Court mean to imply that this statute is not relevant to the meaning of title II of the Hobbs Act? Is it irrelevant? Or should behavior not prohibited by the Taft–Hartley Act, as featherbedding now seems to be after the *American Newspaper Publishers* and *Gamble Enterprises* decisions, be viewed as among the legitimate objectives of labor within the spirit of title II of the Hobbs Act? If so, does this mean that the problem in *Green* was not that the union sought to obtain money for unwanted, superfluous, and unneeded services, but that violence was the alleged means? Note the Court's comment on the meaning of title II:

"There is nothing in any of those acts, however, that indicates any protection for unions or their officials in attempts to get personal property through threats of force or violence. Those are not legitimate means for improving labor conditions. If the trial court intended by its references to the Norris–LaGuardia and Wagner Acts to indicate any such labor exception, which we doubt, it was in error."

How else could this language be read?

Does all this mean that violence would also be the key characteristic if the facts of *Local 807* were to arise again today? With respect to those situations on the *Local 807* facts where actual services were offered (even though unwanted, superfluous, and unneeded), and laying aside for the moment the use of violence, the union objectives in *Local 807* would arguably be lawful under modern labor law. Did the Congress that enacted the Hobbs Act think so? If so, then the criminal activity reached by the Hobbs Act must be either (a) obtaining money without offering any services in return, or (b) obtaining money by violence, or both. Is this a reasonable construction of the statute?

Finally, note the Court's response to the reasoning of the District Court: "[E]xtortion as defined in the statute in no way depends upon having a direct benefit conferred on the person who obtains the property." Extortion is defined by the act as "the obtaining of property from another, with his consent, induced by wrongful use of actual or threatened force, violence, or fear...." The Court apparently reads these words as signifying that the person who obtains the property need not be the same person as the one who "induced" the payment by force, violence, or fear. Does this make sense? If not, then how is the tension between the Hobbs Act and the Taft–Hartley Act to be resolved? How would *Local 807* be decided under the Hobbs Act?

United States v. Enmons

United States Supreme Court, 1973.
410 U.S. 396.

■ JUSTICE STEWART delivered the opinion of the Court.

A one-count indictment was returned in the United States District Court for the Eastern District of Louisiana charging the appellees with a violation of the Hobbs Act, 18 U.S.C. § 1951. In pertinent part, that act provides:

> "(a) Whoever in any way or degree obstructs, delays, or affects commerce or the movement of any article or commodity in commerce, by robbery or extortion or attempts or conspires so to do, or commits or threatens physical violence to any persons or property in furtherance of a plan or purpose to do anything in violation of this section shall be fined not more than $10,000 or imprisoned not more than twenty years, or both."

"Extortion" is defined in the act, as "the obtaining of property from another, with his consent, induced by wrongful use of actual or threatened force, violence, or fear. . . ." 18 U.S.C. § 1951(b)(2).

At the time of the alleged conspiracy, the employees of the Gulf States Utilities Company were out on strike. The appellees are members and officials of labor unions that were seeking a new collective-bargaining agreement with that company. The indictment charged that the appellees and two named co-conspirators conspired to obstruct commerce, and that as part of that conspiracy, they

> "would obtain the property of the Gulf States Utilities Company in the form of wages and other things of value with the consent of the Gulf States Utilities Company . . . , such consent to be induced by the wrongful use of actual force, violence and fear of economic injury by [the appellees] and co-conspirators, in that [the appellees] and the co-conspirators did commit acts of physical violence and destruction against property owned by the Gulf States Utilities Company in order to force said company to agree to a contract with Local 2286 of the International Brotherhood of Electrical Workers calling for higher wages and other monetary benefits."

Five specific acts of violence were charged to have been committed in furtherance of the conspiracy—firing high-powered rifles at three company transformers, draining the oil from a company transformer, and blowing up a transformer substation owned by the company. In short, the indictment charged that the appellees had conspired to use and did in fact use violence to obtain for the striking employees higher wages and other employment benefits from the company.

The District Court granted the appellees' motion to dismiss the indictment for failure to state an offense under the Hobbs Act. The court noted that the appellees were union members on strike against their employer, Gulf States, and that both the strike and its objective of higher wages were legal. The court expressed the view that if "the wages sought by violent acts are wages to be paid for unneeded or unwanted services, or for no services at all," then that violence would constitute extortion within the meaning of the Hobbs Act. But in this case, by contrast, the court noted that the indictment alleged the use of force to obtain legitimate union objectives:

> "The union had a right to disrupt the business of the employer by lawfully striking for higher wages. Acts of violence occurring during a lawful strike and resulting in damage to persons or property are undoubtedly punishable under state law. To punish persons for such acts of violence was not the purpose of the Hobbs Act."

The court found "no case where a court has gone so far to hold the type of activity involved here to be a violation of the Hobbs Act."

We noted probable jurisdiction of the government's appeal, to determine whether the Hobbs Act proscribes violence committed during a lawful strike for the purpose of inducing an employer's agreement to legitimate collective-bargaining demands.

I

The government contends that the statutory language unambiguously and without qualification proscribes interference with commerce by "extortion," and that in terms of the statute, "extortion" is "the obtaining of property from another, with his consent, induced by wrongful use of actual or threatened force, violence, or fear...." Wages are the "property" of the employer, the argument continues, and strike violence to obtain such "property" thus falls within the literal proscription of the act. But the language of the statute is hardly as clear as the government would make it out to be. Its interpretation of the act slights the wording of the statute that proscribes obtaining property only by the "wrongful" use of actual or threatened force, violence, or fear. The term "wrongful," which on the face of the statute modifies the use of each of the enumerated means of obtaining property—actual or threatened force, violence, or fear[2]—would be superfluous if it only served to describe the means used. For it would be redundant to speak of "wrongful violence" or "wrongful force" since, as

[2] Congressman Hobbs indicated that "wrongful" was to modify the entire section. 91 Cong. Rec. 11908.

the government acknowledges, any violence or force to obtain property is "wrongful."[3] Rather, "wrongful" has meaning in the act only if it limits the statute's coverage to those instances where the obtaining of the property would itself be "wrongful" because the alleged extortionist has no lawful claim to that property.

Construed in this fashion, the Hobbs Act has properly been held to reach instances where union officials threatened force or violence against an employer in order to obtain personal payoffs, and where unions used the proscribed means to exact "wage" payments from employers in return for "imposed, unwanted, superfluous and fictitious services" of workers.[5] For in those situations, the employer's property has been misappropriated. But the literal language of the statute will not bear the government's semantic argument that the Hobbs Act reaches the use of violence to achieve legitimate union objectives, such as higher wages in return for genuine services which the employer seeks. In that type of case, there has been no "wrongful" taking of the employer's property; he has paid for the services he bargained for, and the workers receive the wages to which they are entitled in compensation for their services.

II

The legislative framework of the Hobbs Act dispels any ambiguity in the wording of the statute and makes it clear that the act does not apply to the use of force to achieve legitimate labor ends. The predecessor of the Hobbs Act, § 2 of the Anti–Racketeering Act of 1934,[6] proscribed, in connection with interstate commerce, the exaction of valuable consideration by force, violence, or coercion, "not including, however, the payment

---

[3] The government suggests a convoluted construction of "wrongful." It concedes that when the means used are not "wrongful," such as where fear of economic loss from a strike is employed, then the objective must be illegal. If, on the other hand, "wrongful" force and violence are used, even for a legal objective, the government contends that the statute is satisfied. But that interpretation simply accepts the redundancy of the term "wrongful" whenever it applies to "force" and "violence" in the statute.

[5] See, e.g., United States v. Green, 350 U.S. 415, 417 (1956).

[6] Section 2 of the act provided:

"Any person who, in connection with or in relation to any act in any way or in any degree affecting trade or commerce or any article or commodity moving or about to move in trade or commerce—

"(a) Obtains or attempts to obtain, by the use of or attempt to use or threat to use force, violence, or coercion, the payment of money or other valuable considerations, or the purchase or rental of property or protective services, not including, however, the payment of wages by a bona-fide employer to a bona-fide employee; or

"(b) Obtains the property of another, with his consent, induced by wrongful use of force or fear, or under color of official right; or

"(c) Commits or threatens to commit an act of physical violence or physical injury to a person or property in furtherance of a plan or purpose to violate sections (a) or (b); or

"(d) Conspires or acts concertedly with any other person or persons to commit any of the foregoing acts;

shall, upon conviction thereof, be guilty of a felony and shall be punished by imprisonment from one to ten years or by a fine of $10,000, or both."

of wages by a bona-fide employer to a bona-fide employee.''[7]   In United States v. Local 807, 315 U.S. 521 (1942), the Court held that this exception covered the members of a New York City truck drivers union who, by violence or threats, exacted payments for themselves from out-of-town truckers in return for the unwanted and superfluous service of driving out-of-town trucks to and from the city.   The New York City teamsters would lie in wait for the out-of-town trucks, and then demand payment from the owners and drivers in return for allowing the trucks to proceed into the city.   The teamsters sometimes drove the arriving trucks into the city, but in other instances, the out-of-town truckers paid the fees but rejected the teamsters' services and drove the trucks themselves.   In several cases there was evidence that, having exacted their fees, the city drivers disappeared without offering to perform any services at all.   The Court held that the activities of the city teamsters were included within the wage exception to the Anti–Racketeering Act although what work they performed was unneeded and unwanted, and although in some cases their work was rejected.

Congressional disapproval of this decision was swift.   Several bills were introduced with the narrow purpose of correcting the result in the *Local 807* case.[9]   H.R. 32, which became the Hobbs Act, eliminated the wage exception that had been the basis for the *Local 807* decision.[10]   But, as frequently emphasized on the floor of the House, the limited effect of the bill was to shut off the possibility opened up by the *Local 807* case, that union members could use their protected status to exact payments from employers for imposed, unwanted, and superfluous services.   As Congressman Hancock explained:

"This bill is designed simply to prevent both union members and nonunion people from making use of robbery and extortion under the guise of obtaining wages in the obstruction of interstate commerce.   That is all it does.   . . .

"[T]his bill is made necessary by the amazing decision of the Supreme Court in the case of the United States against Teamsters' Union 807, three years ago.   That decision practically nullified the anti-racketeering bill of 1934.   . . .   In effect the Supreme Court held that . . . members of the Teamsters' Union . . . were exempt

[7] See § 2(a), quoted in n.6, supra.   While the specific wage exception was found only in § 2(a) of the act, § 3(b) excluded "wages paid by a bona-fide employer to a bona-fide employee" from the definition of "property," "money," or other "valuable considerations." The wage exception thus permeated the entire act.   United States v. Green, 350 U.S. 415, 419 n. 4 (1956); United States v. Local 807, 315 U.S. 521, 527 n. 2 (1942).

[9] See United States v. Green, 350 U.S. 415, 419 n. 5 (1956); Note, Labor Faces the Amended Anti–Racketeering Act, 101 U. Pa. L. Rev. 1030, 1033–34 (1953).

[10] The Hobbs Act also eliminated the proviso in § 6 of the Anti–Racketeering Act of 1934: "That no court of the United States shall construe or apply any of the provisions of this Act in such manner as to impair, diminish, or in any manner affect the rights of bona-fide labor organizations in lawfully carrying out the legitimate objects thereof, as such rights are expressed in existing statutes of the United States."   That proviso was one of the supports for the *Local 807* decision.

from the provisions of that law when attempting by the use of force or the threat of violence to obtain wages for a job whether they rendered any service or not."   91 Cong. Rec. 11900.

Congressman Hancock proceeded to read approvingly from an editorial which characterized the teamsters' action in the *Local 807* case as "compelling the truckers to pay day's wages to local union drivers whose services were neither wanted nor needed." Ibid. Congressman Fellows stressed the fact that the facts of the *Local 807* case showed that "these stick-up men disappeared as soon as the money was paid without rendering or offering to render any service." Id., at 11907. And Congressman Rivers characterized the facts of the *Local 807* case as "nothing short of hijacking, intimidation, extortion, and out-and-out highway robbery." Id., at 11917.[11]

But by eliminating the wage exception to the Anti–Racketeering Act, the Hobbs Act did not sweep within its reach violence during a strike to achieve legitimate collective-bargaining objectives. It was repeatedly emphasized in the debates that the bill did not "interfere in any way with any legitimate labor objective or activity";[12] "there is not a thing in it to interfere in the slightest degree with any legitimate activity on the part of labor people or labor unions."[13] And Congressman Jennings, in responding to a question concerning the act's coverage, made it clear that the act "does not have a thing in the world to do with strikes." Id., at 11912.

Indeed, in introducing his original bill, Congressman Hobbs[14] explicitly refuted the suggestion that strike violence to achieve a union's legitimate objectives was encompassed by the act:

"Mr. MARCANTONIO. All right. In connection with a strike, if an incident occurs which involves—

"Mr. HOBBS. The gentleman need go no further. This bill does not cover strikes or any question relating to strikes.

"Mr. MARCANTONIO. Will the gentleman put a provision in the bill stating so?

"Mr. HOBBS. We do not have to, because a strike is perfectly lawful and has been so described by the Supreme Court and by the

---

[11] ... In its report on the bill, the House Committee on the Judiciary reproduced this Court's decision in the *Local 807* case and concluded that "[t]he need for the legislation was emphasized by the opinion of the Supreme Court in ... *United States v. Local 807....*" H.R. Rep. No. 238, 79th Cong., 1st Sess., 10. See also S. Rep. No. 1516, 79th Cong., 2d Sess.

[12] 91 Cong. Rec. 11841 (Remarks of Rep. Walter).

[13] Id., at 11908 (Remarks of Rep. Sumners).

[14] The remarks with respect to that bill, H.R. 653, 78th Cong., 1st Sess., which passed

only the House, are wholly relevant to an understanding of the Hobbs Act, since the operative language of the original bill was substantially carried into the act. The congressional debates on the Hobbs Act in the 79th Congress repeatedly referred to the legislative history of the original bill. Surely an interpretation placed by the sponsor of a bill on the very language subsequently enacted by Congress cannot be dismissed out of hand, as the dissent would have it, simply because the interpretation was given two years earlier.

statutes we have passed. This bill takes off from the springboard that the act must be unlawful to come within the purview of this bill.

"Mr. MARCANTONIO. That does not answer my point. My point is that an incident such as a simple assault which takes place in a strike could happen. Am I correct?

"Mr. HOBBS. Certainly.

"Mr. MARCANTONIO. That then could become an extortion under the gentleman's bill, and that striker as well as his union officials could be charged with violation of sections in this bill.

"Mr. HOBBS. I disagree with that and deny it in toto." 89 Cong. Rec. 3213.[16]

The government would derive a different lesson from the legislative history. It points to statements made during the floor debates that the act was meant to have "broad coverage" and, unlike its predecessor, to encompass the "employer-employee" relationship. But that proves no more than that the achievement of illegitimate objectives by employees or their representatives, such as the exaction of personal payoffs, or the pursuit of "wages" for unwanted or fictitious services, would not be exempted from the act solely because the extortionist was an employee or union official and the victim an employer.[17] The government would also

---

[16] The proponents of the Hobbs Act defended the act as no encroachment on the legitimate activities of labor unions on the ground that the statute did no more than incorporate New York's conventional definition of extortion—"the obtaining of property from another ... with his consent, induced by a wrongful use of force or fear, or under color of official right." N.Y. Penal Law § 850 (1909).

Judicial construction of the New York statute reinforces the conclusion that, however militant, union activities to obtain higher wages do not constitute extortion. For extortion requires an intent " 'to obtain that which in justice and equity the party is not entitled to receive.' " People v. Cuddihy, 151 Misc. 318, 324, 271 N.Y.S. 450, 456 (1934). An accused would not be guilty of extortion for attempting to achieve legitimate labor goals; he could not be convicted without sufficient evidence that he "was actuated by the purpose of obtaining a financial benefit for himself ... and was not attempting in good faith to advance the cause of unionism...." People v. Adelstein, 9 App. Div. 2d 907, 908, 195 N.Y.S.2d 27, 28 (1959), aff'd sub nom. People v. Squillante, 8 N.Y.2d 998, 169 N.E.2d 425 (1960).

Hence, New York's highest court has interpreted its extortion statute to apply to a case where the accused received a payoff to buy an end to labor picketing. People v. Dioguardi, 8 N.Y.2d 260, 271, 168 N.E.2d 683, 690–91 (1960):

"The picketing here ... may have been perfectly lawful in its inception (assuming it was part of a bona fide organizational effort) and may have remained so—despite its potentially ruinous effect on the employers' businesses—so long as it was employed to accomplish the legitimate labor objective of organization. Its entire character changed from legality to criminality, however, when it was used as a pressure device to exact the payment of money as a condition of its cessation...."

In short, when the objectives of the picketing changed from legitimate labor ends to personal payoffs, then the actions became extortionate.

[17] The government relies heavily on a statement by Congressman Michener, in a dialogue with two of his colleagues, to the effect that union members who "by robbery or exploitation collect a day's wage—a union

find support for its expansive interpretation of the statute in the rejection of two amendments, one proposed by Congressman Celler, the other by Congressman LaFollette, which would have inserted in the act an exception for cases where violence was used to obtain the payment of wages by a bona-fide employer to a bona-fide employee. But both amendments were rejected solely because they would have operated to continue the effect of the *Local 807* case. Their rejection thus proves nothing more than that Congress was intent on undoing the restrictive impact of that case.

III

In the nearly three decades that have passed since the enactment of the Hobbs Act, no reported case has upheld the theory that the act proscribes the use of force to achieve legitimate collective-bargaining demands.

The only previous case in this Court relevant to the issue, United States v. Green, 350 U.S. 415 (1956), held no more than that the Hobbs Act had accomplished its objective of overruling the *Local 807* case. The alleged extortions in that case, as in *Local 807*, consisted of attempts to obtain so-called wages for "imposed, unwanted, superfluous and fictitious services of laborers...." The indictment charged that the employer's consent was obtained "by the wrongful use, to wit, the use for the purposes aforesaid, of actual and threatened force, violence and fear...." The government thus did not rely, as it does in the present case, solely on the use of force in an employer-employee relationship; it alleged a wrongful purpose—to obtain money from the employer that the union officials had no legitimate right to demand. We concluded that the Hobbs Act could reach extortion in an employer-employee relationship and that personal profit to the extortionist was not required, but our holding was carefully limited to the charges in that case: "We rule only on the allegations of the indictment and hold that the acts charged against appellees fall within the terms of the act."

A prior decision in the Third Circuit, United States v. Kemble, 198 F.2d 889 (3d Cir.1952), on which the government relied in *Green,* also concerned the exaction, by threats and violence, of wages for superfluous services. In affirming a conviction under the Hobbs Act of a union business agent for using actual and threatened violence against an out-of-town driver in an attempt to force him to hire a local union member, the Court of Appeals carefully limited its holding:

"We need not consider the normal demand for wages as compensation for services desired by or valuable to the employer. It is

wage—they are not exempted from the law solely because they are engaging in a legitimate union activity." 91 Cong. Rec. 11843–44. But Congressman Michener was referring to the activity of "robbery or exploitation," and his statement continued: "I cannot understand how any union man can claim that the conduct described by Justice Stone is a legitimate union activity." Id., at 11844. Justice Stone's dissenting opinion in the *Local 807* case described payoffs for the superfluous and unwanted work involved in that case.

enough for this case, and all we decide, that payment of money for imposed, unwanted and superfluous services ... is within the language and intendment of the statute.''

Most recently, in United States v. Caldes, 457 F.2d 74 (9th Cir.1972), the Court of Appeals for the Ninth Circuit was squarely presented with the question at issue in this case. Two union officials were convicted of Hobbs Act violations in that they damaged property of a company with which they were negotiating for a collective-bargaining agreement, in an attempt to pressure the company into agreeing to the union contract. Concluding that the act was not intended to reach militant activity in the pursuit of legitimate union ends, the court reversed the convictions and ordered the indictment dismissed.

Indeed, not until the indictments were returned in 1970 in this and several other cases has the government even sought to prosecute under the Hobbs Act actual or threatened violence employed to secure a union contract "calling for higher wages and other monetary benefits." Yet, throughout this period, the Nation has witnessed countless economic strikes, often unfortunately punctuated by violence. It is unlikely that if Congress had indeed wrought such a major expansion of federal criminal jurisdiction in enacting the Hobbs Act, its action would have so long passed unobserved.

IV

The government's broad concept of extortion—the "wrongful" use of force to obtain even the legitimate union demands of higher wages—is not easily restricted. It would cover all overtly coercive conduct in the course of an economic strike, obstructing, delaying, or affecting commerce. The worker who threw a punch on a picket line, or the striker who deflated the tires on his employer's truck would be subject to a Hobbs Act prosecution and the possibility of 20 years' imprisonment and a $10,000 fine.[20]

Even if the language and history of the act were less clear than we have found them to be, the act could not properly be expanded as the government suggests—for two related reasons. First, this being a criminal statute, it must be strictly construed, and any ambiguity must be resolved in favor of lenity. Rewis v. United States, 401 U.S. 808, 812 (1971). Secondly, it would require statutory language much more explicit than that before us here to lead to the conclusion that Congress intended to put the federal government in the business of policing the orderly conduct of strikes. Neither the language of the Hobbs Act nor its legislative history can justify the conclusion that Congress intended to work such an extraor-

[20] Realizing the breadth of its argument, the government's brief concedes that there might be an exception for "the incidental injury to person or property that not infrequently occurs as a consequence of the charged atmosphere attending a prolonged labor dispute." But nothing, either in the language or the history of the act, justifies any such exception.

Similarly, there is nothing to support the dissent's exception for "mischievous" conduct, post, at n.17, even if we could begin to define the meaning and limits of such a term.

dinary change in federal labor law or such an unprecedented incursion into the criminal jurisdiction of the States.

As we said last Term:

"[U]nless Congress conveys its purpose clearly, it will not be deemed to have significantly changed the federal-state balance. Congress has traditionally been reluctant to define as a federal crime conduct readily denounced as criminal by the states. [W]e will not be quick to assume that Congress has meant to effect a significant change in the sensitive relation between federal and state criminal jurisdiction." United States v. Bass, 404 U.S. 336, 349 (1971).

The District Court was correct in dismissing the indictment. Its judgment is affirmed.

It is so ordered.

JUSTICE BLACKMUN, concurring.

I join the Court's opinion. I readily concede that my visceral reaction to immaturely conceived acts of violence of the kind charged in this indictment is that such acts deserve to be dignified as federal crimes. That reaction on my part, however, is legislative in nature rather than judicial. If Congress wishes acts of that kind to be encompassed by a federal statute, it has the constitutional power in the interstate context to effect that result. The appellees so concede. Tr. of Oral Arg. 18–19. But Justice Stewart has gathered the pertinent and persuasive legislative history demonstrating that Congress did not intend to exercise its power to reach these acts of violence.

The government's posture, with its concession that certain strike violence (which it would downgrade as "incidental" and the dissent as "low level," post, at n.17), although aimed at achieving a legitimate end, is not covered by the act, necessarily means that the legislation would be enforced selectively or, at the least, would embroil all concerned with drawing the distinction between major and minor violence. That, for me, is neither an appealing prospect nor solid support for the position taken.

This type of violence, as the Court points out, is subject to state criminal prosecution. That is where it must remain until the Congress acts otherwise in a manner far more clear than the language of the Hobbs Act.

JUSTICE DOUGLAS, with whom THE CHIEF JUSTICE, JUSTICE POWELL, and JUSTICE REHNQUIST concur, dissenting.

The Court today achieves by interpretation what those who were opposed to the Hobbs Act were unable to get Congress to do. The Court considers primarily the legislative history of a predecessor bill considered by the 78th Congress. The bill before us was considered and enacted by the 79th Congress; and, as I read the debates, the opposition lost in the 79th Congress what they win today. All of which makes pertinent Justice Holmes' admonition in Missouri, K. & T.R. Co. v. May, 194 U.S. 267, 270

(1904) that "it must be remembered that legislatures are ultimate guardians of the liberties and welfare of the people in quite as great a degree as the courts."

In United States v. Local 807, 315 U.S. 521 (1942), we had before us the Anti-Racketeering Act of 1934, which made it a crime to use violence respecting interstate trade or commerce to obtain the "payment of money or other valuable considerations," excluding "the payment of wages by a bona-fide employer to a bona-fide employee." We held that the exception included demands for unwanted or superfluous services and covered those who wanted jobs, not only those who presently had them.

Congress in the Hobbs Act changed the law. The critical change was the exclusion of the employer-employee clause. The Court said in United States v. Green, 350 U.S. 415, 419 (1956):

"In the Hobbs Act, carried forward as 18 U.S.C. § 1951, which amended the Anti-Racketeering Act, the exclusion clause involved in the *Local 807* decision was dropped. The legislative history makes clear that the new act was meant to eliminate any grounds for future judicial conclusions that Congress did not intend to cover the employer-employee relationship. The words were defined to avoid any misunderstanding."

In *Green*, the Court held that it was an extortion within the meaning of the act to use force to obtain payment of wages for unwanted and superfluous services.

Here, the services were not unwanted or superfluous; they were services being negotiated under a collective-bargaining agreement.

The Court relies mostly on the legislative history of a measure covering the same topic which was passed by the previous House but on which the Senate did not act. Two years later, the bill in its present form was enacted. It was a differently constituted House that debated it and the year was 1945 rather than 1943. So the most relevant legislative history, in my view, concerns the 79th Congress, not the 78th.

The fear was expressed in the House that the elimination of the Exception Clause would open up the prospect of labor's being prosecuted.[1] As a consequence, Congressman Celler sought to amend the measure so as to exempt the use of violence to exact "wages paid by a bona fide employer to a bona fide employee."[2] His precise amendment in that regard would define "property" in the act as not including "wages paid by a bona fide employer to a bona fide employee."[3] Those who objected said that it would substantially restore the 1934 Act.[4]

Congressman Biemiller, in speaking for the Celler Amendment said:

[1] 91 Cong. Rec. 11914 (Remarks of Rep. Marcantonio).

[2] Id., at 11913.

[3] Ibid.

[4] Id., at 11914–15, 11918.

"We fear, for example, under the bill as it now stands that a simple, unfortunate altercation on a picket line—and we all know that human beings are frail and when tempers are hot some trouble may develop—under such a situation you may send a man to jail for 20 years or fine him $10,000."[5]

The Celler Amendment was rejected.[6]

As I read the Congressional Record, Congressman Baldwin spoke for the consensus when he said:

"This bill would not have been presented to the House if organized labor had recognized law and order in striking and in establishing their rights, as they have a right to do. Everyone can remember the taxicab strike in the city of Baltimore, which does not pertain to this bill, where cabs were overthrown, bricks thrown through the windows endangering the lives of people, innocent victims. Those were the tactics of organized labor which you people support outright and which organized labor sanctioned. The leaders were locked up and put in jail for participating in those activities. Yet you stand here on the floor of this House and , say they did not do it or they did not know anything about it.

"Mr. Chairman, labor has a right to strike, but when labor perpetrates that sort of thing, they are going far beyond the bounds of reason. Certainly, I do not take the position that labor has not the right to organize or to strike, but when they do so they should abide by the laws of the land and the laws of decency. If they had done that, we would not have this legislation before the House today."[7]

Congressman Whittington voiced the same sentiments:

"The pending bill will provide for punishing racketeers who rob or extort. There is no justification for labor unions opposing the bill as it constitutes no invasion of the legitimate rights of labor. Robbery and extortion by members of labor unions must be punished. Labor unions owe that much to the public. In demanding the protection of laws, labor unions should urge that those engaged in legitimate interstate commerce be protected from robbery and extortion."[8]

Congressman Celler offered another amendment which would give as a defense to a charge under the Hobbs Act that the employee "did not violate the provisions of the Norris-LaGuardia Act, the Clayton Act, or the Railway Labor Act, or the National Labor Relations Act."[9] But that amendment was also voted down;[10] the only provision of the Hobbs Act which touched on that problem was 18 U.S.C. § 1951(c), which stated that this section

[5] Id., at 11916.
[6] Id., at 11917.
[7] Id., at 11918.
[8] Id., at 11913.
[9] Id., at 11919.
[10] Ibid.

"shall not be construed to repeal, modify or affect" those laws. References were made in the House debates to the trucking problem in New York, where farmers bringing their produce to market in trucks were held up and money was extorted "from the drivers in order that the shipments might enter the Holland Tunnel and be delivered to their respective destinations in New York."[11]

Congressman LaFollette offered an amendment which would keep the 1934 Act intact but would bar the use of violence by a person not a bona fide employee to obtain property from a bona fide employer.[12] That, too, was defeated.[13]

In the present case, violence was used during the bargaining—five acts of violence involving the shooting and sabotage of the employer's transformers and the blowing up of a company transformer substation. The violence was used to obtain higher wages and other benefits for union members. The acts literally fit the definition of extortion used in the Hobbs Act, 18 U.S.C. § 1951. The term "extortion" means the use of violence to obtain "property" from another. The crime is the use of "extortion" in furtherance of a plan to do anything in violation of the section. The prior exception covering those who seek "the payment of wages by a bona-fide employer to a bona-fide employee" was taken out of the act by Congress. Hence, the use of violence to obtain higher wages is plainly a method of obtaining "property from another" within the meaning of § 1951(b)(2).

Seeking higher wages is certainly not unlawful. But using violence to obtain them seems plainly within the scope of "extortion" as used in the act, just as is the use of violence to exact payment for no work or the use of violence to get a sham substitution for no work. The regime of violence, whatever its precise objective, is a common device of extortion and is condemned by the act.

Congressman Lemke said in the House debates on the Hobbs Act, which he opposed, "The minority is generally right."[14]

[11] Id., at 11917.

[12] Id., at 11919. The proposed amendment read as follows:

"(a) The term 'the payment of wages by a bona fide employer to a bona fide employee' shall not be construed so as to include the payment of money or the transfer of a thing of value by a person to another when the latter shall use or attempt to use or threaten to use force or violence against the body or to the physical property (as distinguished from intangible property) of the former or against the body of anyone having the possession, custody, or control of the physical property of the former, in attempting to obtain or obtaining such payment or transfer.

"(b) The term 'the rights of a bona fide labor organization in lawfully carrying out the legitimate objects thereof, as such rights are expressed in existing statutes of the United States' shall not be construed so as to ignore, void, set aside, or nullify the definitions set out or the words used in or the plain meaning of subsection (a) hereof."

[13] Id., at 11922.

[14] Ibid.

Whatever may be thought of the policy which the Court today embroiders into the act, it was the minority view in the House and clearly did not represent the consensus of the House. No light is thrown on the matter by the Senate, for it summarily approved the House version of the bill.[15]

It is easy in these insulated chambers to put an attractive gloss on an act of Congress if five votes can be obtained. At times, the legislative history of a measure is so clouded or obscure that we must perforce give some meaning to vague words. But where, as here, the consensus of the House is so clear, we should carry out its purpose no matter how distasteful or undesirable that policy may be to us,[17] unless of course the act oversteps constitutional boundaries. But none has been so hardy as even to suggest that.

While we said in Kirschbaum v. Walling, 316 U.S. 517, 522 (1942), that it is "retrospective expansion of meaning which properly deserves the stigma of judicial legislation," the same is true of retrospective contraction of meaning.

I would reverse.

NOTE ON *UNITED STATES v. ENMONS*

What happened to *Green*? Is it now the legitimacy of the union's objective that counts rather than the fact that it engaged in violence? And are efforts to obtain "imposed, unwanted, and superfluous" services now an illegitimate union objective? Put another way, does the Hobbs Act make kinds of featherbedding not reached by the Taft–Hartley Act illegal? If so, isn't it strange that Congress went further in a 1946 criminal statute with a 20–year maximum penalty than it was willing to go in defining an unfair labor practice a year later in the Taft–Hartley Act?

Perhaps the answer is that it is only the confluence of violence and featherbedding that violates the Hobbs Act, although this still would not explain why, in the Court's terms, the union objective would be "wrongful". Would a peaceful strike to obtain featherbedding objectives violate the Hobbs Act? Would the consent of the employer in that case have been induced by "force" or "fear"? The Court's dilemma, it might be argued, is that it cannot limit the Hobbs Act to cases where no services or where only

---

[15] 92 Cong. Rec. 7308.

[17] The fear was expressed in the House debates by opponents of the measure that a fistfight on a picket line during a strike could bring down on the offender a $10,000 fine and 20 years in jail or both. See 91 Cong. Rec. 11916. And the government actually argued in one case, United States v. Caldes, 457 F.2d 74, 78 (9th Cir.1972), that a union and its members were guilty of extortion if they used the coercion of a strike to obtain economic benefits from the employer. That, however, is nonsense, as the court in *Caldes* ruled, for the Hobbs Act specifically does not touch collective bargaining of which the strike is a component part. 18 U.S.C. § 1951(c). Moreover, the court in *Caldes* held that "mischievous" conduct during a strike and actions which are "the by-product of frustration engendered by a prolonged, bona fide collective bargaining negotiation," are often only low-level acts of violence that may be unfair labor practices or, at best, subject to state, not federal, prosecution. That is my view.

sham or fictitious services are offered. That, the argument would continue, would reinstate the holding of *Local 807* and would be inconsistent with the legislative history of the Hobbs Act. On this line of reasoning, has the Court made the best of a confusing and difficult, no-win situation?

In addition to these general questions, several observations and questions are in order about the specific reasoning of the Court and of the dissent.

The Court begins its analysis in Part I of its opinion with an examination of the text of the Hobbs Act, and turns the case on its reading of the word "wrongful." This, it appears, turns the statute into a theft-by-violence provision, that is, it is a "property-protection" statute rather than only a "protection of the person" statute. And this is consistent, one might conclude, with the history of the crime of extortion. Extortion has never been solely aimed at accomplishing legitimate objectives by the use of violence; statutes aimed at preventing violence (assault, murder) are thought sufficient to achieve those ends. Are these conclusions consistent with the legislative history of the Hobbs Act? Are they right?

The Court next turns in Part II to an examination of the legislative history of the act. Does the debate between Stewart and Douglas on this point have a winner? Is it *clear* from the legislative history that the Hobbs Act was not aimed at the illegitimate use of force by labor unions, for whatever objective? Or, as suggested above, does Congress' reliance on the traditional concepts of robbery and extortion suggest that the Court is right, even though the legislative history is typically murky? Does Douglas's quotation of Congressman Whittington (see the text accompanying his footnote 8) aid his argument? Which way does the rejection of the LaFollette amendment cut?

Parts III and IV of the Court's opinion discuss prior Hobbs Act precedent and general principles about the interpretation of criminal statutes. For openers, does the Court adequately distinguish *Green*? For closers, isn't the case over by this point? What do these portions of the Court's opinion add to the debate?

NOTES ON POST-*ENMONS* DECISIONS

1. ***United States v. Russo***. United States v. Russo, 708 F.2d 209 (6th Cir.1983), involved the J & J Cartage Company, a corporation engaged in the business of hauling raw steel from the Detroit waterfront to various plants and warehouses in the Detroit area. It employed about 40 truck drivers for this purpose. The drivers, some of whom owned their own equipment, were paid a percentage of the gross amount paid to J & J for the loads hauled. They were members of Local 299 of the International Brotherhood of Teamsters, and worked pursuant to a collective bargaining contract that provided, inter alia, that it was the obligation of J & J to pay certain amounts to a health and welfare plan and to a pension plan.

The Company didn't pay these benefits. The drivers responded by forming a grievance committee to object, among other things, to the nonpayment. Management in turn responded by calling a general meeting of the drivers in which it proposed that 15 per cent of the gross earnings of each driver be deducted to cover the cost of the payments. The drivers objected, and no compromise was reached. A second meeting was later called at which the Company proposed that if the drivers submitted to an 11 per cent "service charge" it would meet its obligations under the contract. The drivers rejected this proposal too.

After the second meeting, the Company president called each of the drivers individually into his office and, as the court described it, "through promises, threats of economic loss, and misrepresentation" persuaded each to sign a "Supplementary Agreement" in which the driver agreed to the 11 per cent charge against earnings. The service charge then remained in effect for about 10 months.

Four defendants were indicted for violating the Hobbs Act. The first count charged an overall conspiracy, the second a substantive violation of the act by each of the defendants. Cusmano, the president of the Company, was tried separately and convicted. His conviction was set aside on appeal because of a technical variation between the indictment and the evidence offered at trial. His case was remanded for a new trial. United States v. Cusmano, 659 F.2d 714 (6th Cir.1981). The other three defendants, Russo (a co-owner of the Company), Meli (a public relations employee and "negotiator" for the Company[a]), and Smith (a business agent of Local 299, in effect the union representative for the employees[b]), were also convicted. On their appeal, a panel of the Sixth Circuit affirmed.

(i) The Majority Opinion. Judge Brown wrote the majority opinion. To the argument by the defendants that their conduct was not an offense under the Hobbs Act, he noted that the argument had been rejected "by inference" in the decision of Cusmano's appeal, even though it had not been expressly discussed, because the same argument was made there and the case had been remanded for a new trial rather than remanded for dismissal. Then he described *Enmons* and responded on the merits:

"In the instant case, the Company, for which the appellants acted, had no legitimate claim to the 'service charge' of 11 per cent of the gross revenues. This is true because the existing contracts expressly required the Company to make the payments to the welfare and pension funds out of the Company's own funds. ... Moreover, the provision requiring the Company to make payments to the welfare and pension funds was ... contained in a collective bargaining contract, and yet the agreement to shift this burden to the drivers did not result from collective bargaining. It is true that defendant and co-appellant Smith, the business agent for the local, signed the agreement, but this was done after it had been

[a] There was evidence at the trial that "Meli had a reputation as being a part of the Mafia," offered by the drivers to show their state of mind when they agreed to the "service charge."

[b] Smith was indicted because he signed the "service charge" agreement entered into by the drivers, thus indicating the union's assent to the contract variation.

individually signed by the drivers as a result of individual negotiation with and pressure exerted upon them by representatives of the Company. As we see it, the situation for purposes of the applicability of the Hobbs Act would not have been different had the drivers, as a result of threats of economic loss, been forced to take money out of their pockets and pay it to the Company to be used to satisfy the Company's legal obligation to the pension and welfare funds.

"While it is not necessary to our decision here, we further point out that the *Enmons* exception to the application of the Hobbs Act has been held to be confined to payments gained or sought in furtherance of legitimate *labor* objectives. United States v. Quinn, 514 F.2d 1250, 1257 (5th Cir.1975). . . .

"We therefore conclude that the indictment charges crimes under the Hobbs Act and that, under the government's view of the evidence, a case was made for submission to the jury."

(ii) The Concurrence in the Opinion. Judge Martin wrote a separate concurring opinion. He agreed that the Cusmano appeal resolved the Hobbs Act question on the merits, albeit by implication. He agreed with the analysis of *Enmons* reflected in the concurrence in the result by Judge Holschuh, but said that "we part company, however, over its application to the facts of this case." He added:

"In *Enmons*, in the context of a lawful strike by a union in pursuit of a collective bargaining agreement, the Court held that the utilization of wrongful means in pursuit of legitimate labor objectives, although punishable by other laws, did not violate the Hobbs Act. The distinguishing factor in this case, it seems to me, is the objective. Here the employer, outside the collective bargaining context, attempted to obtain by wrongful means and under the guise of a 'service charge' an objective which the parties' own contract specified would be 'unlawful and illegal'—the shifting of responsibility for welfare and pension fund payments to the employees. It seems to me that under these circumstances *Enmons* is no bar to application of the act."

(iii) The Concurrence in the Result. Judge Holschuh dissented from the application of the Hobbs Act in the majority opinion but, for reasons noted below, he nonetheless concurred in the result. He began:

"This case, in my view, is of great significance because of its potential impact on the activities of both labor and management in the resolution of industrial disputes. It squarely presents the important question of the extent to which the Hobbs Act, a criminal statute with severe penalties for its violation, applies to disputes between labor and management over the terms and conditions of employment, a subject that is already extensively regulated by other federal statutes.

"In labor's struggle for higher wages and better working conditions and in management's efforts to minimize labor costs, the use of threats of economic loss is commonplace. Employees threaten to shut down an employer's plant by strike if their demands for higher wages are not met; employers in today's economy have threatened to shut down their own plants if employees do not agree to reduce their wages. Threats of economic loss take many forms, of course, and occur in many different settings. Some are properly made across a conference room table during collective bargaining negotiations; some are surreptitiously and improperly made and clearly constitute unfair labor practices. The question of when a threat of economic loss made during the course of a labor dispute between an employer and the employer's own employees becomes not just an unfair labor practice but a violation of the Hobbs Act, the critical issue on this appeal, is neither well settled nor easily resolved. This case, with its *Cusmano* companion, may be the first case in which the Hobbs Act has been held to apply to activities between an employer and the employer's own employees while engaged in an attempt to resolve a labor dispute over terms and conditions of employment. The ramifications of the majority opinion are both far-reaching and, to me, troublesome for both labor and management."

Judge Holschuh then examined the *Local 807* case and the legislative history of the Hobbs Act. He concluded that the Hobbs Act "made it clear that Congress did not regard obtaining money for no work or for superfluous and rejected services to be a legitimate objective of a labor union." He continued:

"The important point is that neither the Anti–Racketeering Act nor the Hobbs Act was intended to make criminal the use of violence or threats of economic loss if such activities had a legitimate labor goal..... The means used to obtain such [a] goal[] may well constitute an unfair labor practice under the extensive federal statutes governing the conduct of labor, and the use of violence may be punishable as a crime under local statutes. However, insofar as the Hobbs Act is concerned, its legislative background reveals no intention of Congress to impose the severe criminal sanctions of that act upon activities of labor aimed at achieving a legitimate labor objective. If Congress did not intend to impose the severe criminal sanctions of the Hobbs Act on activity of labor having a legitimate labor objective, then it must follow that it did not intend to impose those sanctions on activity of management having a legitimate management objective."

Green, for Judge Holschuh, was easy to explain: "The extraction of money for superfluous services rejected by the prospective employer could not be considered a legitimate function of labor." *Enmons* too was not difficult: the term "wrongful" applied to the *objective*, not the *means* used to attain the objective; and it is the *objective* that must be unlawful in order for the Hobbs Act to apply:

"Thus, as I read *Enmons*, use of wrongful *means*—and the use of violence on a picket line is clearly wrongful—is not enough to come within the coverage of the act. To come within the prohibitions of the act the *objective* must be wrongful, i.e., the use of robbery or extortion to obtain property to which the defendant 'has no lawful claim.' Because striking employees may lawfully claim higher wages, this is a legitimate labor objective, and the Hobbs Act does not apply to the conduct of such employees regardless of how reprehensible it may be and regardless of the fact that such conduct may violate other state and federal laws.

"If, then, the act does not apply to a labor union's use of wrongful means to achieve legitimate labor objectives, then certainly the same construction applies to management, and the act should not apply to management's use of wrongful means to achieve legitimate management objectives. If management in the *Enmons* case, for example, had retaliated by violently assaulting the strikers in an effort to break the strike and to force acceptance of management's wage offer, would management have been guilty of a violation of the Hobbs Act? Clearly such conduct would have violated other laws, but under the Supreme Court's interpretation of the Hobbs Act I do not believe such conduct would have come under the coverage of the act. Although the means employed in my hypothetical case are just as deplorable as the means employed by the striking workers in *Enmons*, Congress did not intend the Hobbs Act to regulate the *means* employed by either labor or management when they are seeking the *legitimate objectives of labor or the legitimate objectives of management.*"

Judge Holschuh then turned to the application of his analysis to the facts of the case before him. He did not disagree as to the facts on which the analysis turned. But he was "unable to conclude that the defendants' actions fall within the scope of the Hobbs Act" because "an attempt by management to reduce its labor costs through a modification of a collective bargaining agreement is a legitimate management objective." He elaborated:

"Section 8(d) of the National Labor Relations Act, 29 U.S.C. § 158(d), explicitly sets forth the means by which a mid-term modification of a collective bargaining agreement may be obtained. Failure to comply with the procedures set forth in § 8(d) constitutes an unfair labor practice. Section 8(d), therefore, is a recognition by Congress of the right of labor and management to seek modifications of a collective bargaining agreement during the life of that agreement and prescribes the procedures to be followed for obtaining such modifications. Thus, the fact that a collective bargaining agreement is in effect does not mean that labor and management cannot seek changes in that agreement or that demands for concessions are in any sense unlawful. Those demands, of course, do not have to be accepted, but the demands of labor in seeking greater benefits and the objective of management in seeking lower labor costs are legitimate objectives even though the parties are contractually bound at that time by a previously executed collective bargaining agreement.

"I recognize that the evidence in the present case established without question that the defendants (1) breached the [agreement], and (2) committed an unfair labor practice in obtaining a modification of the [agreement] through the tactics resorted to by defendants. However, while the *means* employed by the defendants to obtain a modification of the compensation agreement were highly improper, the fact that the defendants employed such improper means does not establish that the defendants violated the Hobbs Act. ... The objective of management in the present case—reduction of its labor costs in the form of lower wages—is just as legitimate an *objective* as was the objective of labor in the *Enmons* case—increased labor costs in the form of higher wages. While the use of wrongful means in both *Enmons* and the present case is deplorable, the use of the wrongful means does not by itself constitute a violation of the Hobbs Act."

Judge Holschuh then responded at length to the points made in the majority opinion. In the main, he repeated the above analysis. As to the majority's point that the case is no different from one where the drivers were "forced to take money out of their pockets and pay it to the Company," he responded that the same point could be made in *Enmons*: management in that case "may well have been forced to take money out of the company's 'pockets' and pay it to the employees to satisfy the employees' demands for higher wages." He also agreed that *Enmons* was a "labor" case. But this case too, he said, is a "labor case": "While caution should be exercised in extending *Enmons* too far—especially to cases outside the labor context—equal, if not greater, caution should be exercised in *not* applying *Enmons* to cases such as ours which *do* involve labor disputes."

Next, Judge Holschuh turned to the implications of the majority opinion as he read it. He said:

"I see little, if any, difference between the present case and one in which the management of a company that has suffered severe financial loss attempts, without success, to have its employees by vote reduce their contract wages and, having failed in this attempt, then tells its employees that unless they agree to management's requested reduction the company will shut down its operation and lay off all its employees. As I understand the majority opinion, if management in such a situation makes that threat to the union representative it would be considered in the context of a collective bargaining negotiation and, therefore, it would not be a violation of the Hobbs Act. However, if management makes the identical threat to any of its employees it would be a violation of the Hobbs Act and a criminal offense. In my view, the Hobbs Act should not be construed to convert what might be an unfair labor practice into a severe criminal offense involving a possible term of imprisonment of 20 years.

"If the Hobbs Act is construed in the manner adopted by the majority, the resulting Damoclean sword would hang as much over the head of labor as it would over the head of management. If, in the present case, the contract had exempted the company from making contributions to the benefit funds, but the employees, disgruntled by the exemption, threatened to strike if the employer did not make such benefit payments, then under the rationale of the majority opinion I assume the employees would be guilty of a Hobbs Act violation on the theory that they have no 'legitimate' claim to those increased benefits. Similarly, under the majority rationale, employees would be guilty of this criminal offense whenever a wildcat strike occurs as a result of the employees demanding more than the employer is contractually obligated to provide. Even more troublesome would be those cases in which ambiguous contract language makes it difficult to discern whether the employees' or employer's demands for concessions are 'legitimate' or 'not legitimate.' The spectre of a possible federal grand jury indictment would be present in all such cases and would be an unwarranted and unwelcome intruder in the resolution of industrial disputes between an employer and its employees over the terms and conditions of employment."

Having said all this, Judge Holschuh nonetheless concluded that he was required to concur in the majority result. He agreed that "the *Cusmano* panel implicitly decided that the indictment involved in this case states a violation of the Hobbs Act when that panel remanded the *Cusmano* case for a new trial." He then said that "I reluctantly concur in the result reached by the majority" because, in his view, only an en banc circuit court should be able to overrule a panel decision. Such a rule, he concluded, was the best approach because "it should lead to consistency in panel decisions and would discourage unwarranted appeals."

2. Questions and Comments on *Russo*. Both the majority opinion and Judge Martin's concurrence seem to turn on two main characteristics of the case: the fact that the Company had no legitimate claim to the "service charge"; and the fact that the agreement to shift this cost to the drivers did not result from collective bargaining. For good measure, the court added that the *Enmons* exception to Hobbs Act liability was limited to cases where the defendants sought legitimate *labor* objectives.

Consider the last point first. Judge Holschuh says that "[i]f Congress did not intend to impose the severe criminal sanctions of the Hobbs Act on activity of labor having a legitimate labor objective, then it must follow that it did not intend to impose those sanctions on activity of management having a legitimate management objective." Is he right that what is sauce for the goose should be sauce for the gander?   Does the *Enmons* rationale apply to management as well as labor?   If not, of course, the case is over. If so, however, there is more to it.

If Judge Holschuh is right that management too can rely on *Enmons*, which of the remaining two factors on which the majority relies seems the more critical?   More specifically, if the dispute arose in a "collective bargaining context," could management make a "legitimate claim" to a service charge for the benefits at stake?   How does one tell whether a dispute between management and employees who are represented by a union is or is not part of the collective bargaining between them?   Judge Holschuh reads the majority to say that it would be ok to threaten a *union representative* with a shut-down to obtain mid-contract concessions, but would become a violation of the Hobbs Act to threaten the *employees* individually.   Is this a correct reading of the majority?   If so, does such a distinction make sense?   Or is Judge Holschuh right that since obtaining a mid-contract concession is expressly recognized by the federal labor laws as a legitimate management objective, *Enmons* exempts *any* means used to accomplish that objective from Hobbs Act criminalization?

Consider also Judge Holschuh's discussion of the implications of the majority opinion.   Is he right that labor too has much to fear from this decision?   He poses the following possibility: "If, in the present case, the contract had exempted the company from making contributions to the benefit funds, but the employees, disgruntled by the exemption, threatened to strike if the employer did not make such benefit payments, then under the rationale of the majority opinion I assume the employees would be guilty of a Hobbs Act violation on the theory that they have no 'legitimate' claim to those increased benefits."   How would the majority respond to this case?   Would collective action by the employees make their strike part of the "collective bargaining" process and therefore not criminal under the Hobbs Act?   Would the form of coercion chosen (a strike) not have amounted to the "force or fear" required by the Hobbs Act?   In this connection, consider also the method of coercion used by the employer on the facts of *Russo*.   Does the Hobbs Act require violence?   Or are "promises, threats of economic loss, and misrepresentation" sufficient?

Judge Holschuh also poses a hypothetical variation of *Enmons* in his opinion: "If management in the *Enmons* case . . . had retaliated by violently assaulting the strikers in an effort to break the strike and to force acceptance of management's wage offer, would management have been guilty of a violation of the Hobbs Act?"   How should this situation be analyzed?   Would management have obtained any "property" of the employees in this scenario?

In the end, how should *Russo* have been decided?   If the Supreme Court had granted certiorari, what would it have done?

3.   *United States v. Culbert*.   The most recent Supreme Court opinion on the Hobbs Act involved another issue.   It illustrates the broad potential of the act outside the labor context.

The defendant and an accomplice were convicted of bank robbery in violation of 18 U.S.C. § 2113(a)[c] and of a Hobbs Act violation for attempting to obtain $100,000 from a federally insured bank by threatening physical violence against the bank's president. The Court of Appeals reversed the Hobbs Act conviction because " 'although an activity may be within the literal language of the Hobbs Act, it must constitute "racketeering" to be within the perimeters of the act.' "[d] The Supreme Court granted certiorari and in United States v. Culbert, 435 U.S. 371 (1978), unanimously reversed.[e]

The Court began its analysis by observing that "[n]othing on the face of the statute suggests a congressional intent to limit its coverage to persons who have engaged in 'racketeering.' " To the contrary, the words of the statute "do not lend themselves to restrictive interpretation; as we have recognized, they 'manifest ... a purpose to use all the constitutional power Congress has to punish interference with interstate commerce by extortion, robbery or physical violence.' Stirone v. United States, 361 U.S. 212, 215 (1960)." The Court noted that reading a "racketeering" requirement into the statute might, given the lack of an available definition of the term, create serious vagueness problems. "But we need not concern ourselves with these potential constitutional difficulties," the Court concluded, "because a construction that avoids them is virtually compelled by the language and structure of the statute."

At this point the Court examined the legislative history of the statute in detail. It recognized that the title of the predecessor statute indicated that Congress was concerned with racketeering, and that there was much talk in the Hobbs Act debates about the effort to control racketeers. But neither the language of the 1934 statute nor the language of the Hobbs Act included a specific "racketeering" element and, the Court noted, Congress' reason for replacing the 1934 statute with the Hobbs Act had nothing to do with any element of racketeering but concerned its dissatisfaction with the Local 807 decision. The primary focus of the debates on the Hobbs Act, the Court added, "was on whether the bill was designed as an attack on

[c] Section 2113(a) provides:

"Whoever, by force and violence, or by intimidation, takes, or attempts to take, from the person or presence of another ... any ... money ... belonging to ... any bank ... [s]hall be fined under this title, or imprisoned not more than twenty years, or both."
The term "bank" is defined in § 2113(f) to include "any institution the deposits of which are insured by the Federal Deposit Insurance Corporation."

[d] The Court of Appeals also set aside the bank robbery conviction. It did so because the government confessed error on the ground that § 2113(a) requires that the taking be "from the person or presence of another." On the facts here, the defendant's plan required the bank president to deliver the money to a parking lot and the taking, the government accordingly conceded, was not from his "person" or in his "presence."

In its brief before the Supreme Court, the government disavowed the concession below and said that it did not represent the position of the Department of Justice on the interpretation of § 2113. But the issue was not before the Supreme Court and it expressed no opinion on its proper resolution.

[e] Justice Marshall wrote the Court's opinion. Justice Brennan did not participate.

organized labor," and supports no implication that Congress meant to define a crime that required proof of who was and who was not a racketeer.

The Court then said:

"We therefore conclude that respondent's position has no support in either the statute or its legislative history. Respondent also invokes, as did the court below, two maxims of statutory construction, but neither is applicable here. It is true that 'ambiguity concerning the ambit of criminal statutes should be resolved in favor of lenity,' Rewis v. United States, 401 U.S. 808, 812 (1971), and that 'unless Congress conveys its purpose clearly, it will not be deemed to have significantly changed the federal-state balance,' United States v. Bass, 404 U.S. 336, 349 (1971). But here Congress has conveyed its purpose clearly, and we decline to manufacture ambiguity where none exists. The two maxims only apply 'when we are uncertain about the statute's meaning'; they are 'not to be used' in complete disregard of the purpose of the legislature.'" Scarborough v. United States, 431 U.S. 563, 577 (1977).

"With regard to the concern about disturbing the federal-state balance, moreover, there is no question that Congress intended to define as a federal crime conduct that it knew was punishable under state law. The legislative debates are replete with statements that the conduct punishable under the Hobbs Act was already punishable under state robbery and extortion statutes. [Citing, e.g., the remarks of Rep. Hancock at 91 Cong. Rec. 11900.] Those who opposed the act argued that it was a grave interference with the rights of the states. [Citing, e.g., the remarks of Rep. Resa, id. at 11913.] Congress apparently believed, however, that the states had not been effectively prosecuting robbery and extortion affecting interstate commerce and that the federal government had an obligation to do so. See, e.g., id., at 11911 (remarks of Rep. Jennings); id., at 11904, 11920 (remarks of Rep. Gwynne).

"Our examination of the statutory language and the legislative history of the Hobbs Act impels us to the conclusion that Congress intended to make criminal all conduct within the reach of the statutory language. We therefore decline the invitation to limit the statute's scope by reference to an undefined category of conduct termed 'racketeering.' The judgment of the Court of Appeals is, accordingly, reversed."

4. Questions and Comments on *Culbert*. One can have some sympathy with the Court's explicit reluctance to read a vague, undefined "racketeering" element into the Hobbs Act, as well as with its implied reluctance to undertake the difficult task of resolving the vagueness of such a concept by coming up with a suitable definition of the term. It could be added that these difficulties would be just as severe in the application of the Hobbs Act to the paradigm cases that Congress had in mind in enacting the statute.

But, by contrast, one can also have some sympathy with the underlying point of the defendant's argument. Without some limitation of the language of the statute, it literally covers, given the modern breadth of the commerce power, *all* extortion and *all* robbery, committed *anywhere* within the United States and committed against *any* victim, no matter how trivial the amount involved and no matter how far afield the facts seem to be from the problems Congress explicitly addressed in the debates on the Hobbs Act.

Note the breadth of the Court's conclusion: "Our examination of the statutory language and the legislative history of the Hobbs Act impels us to the conclusion that *Congress intended to make criminal all conduct within the reach of the statutory language*." (Emphasis added.) Was the Court required to adopt an "all or nothing" solution to the problem before it? Has it foreclosed any similar effort to confine the application of the Hobbs Act to behavior short of any robbery or extortion the government chooses to prosecute? Is it now up to federal prosecutorial authorities to exclude "low-level violence" (see the discussion in *Enmons*) in situations to which the Hobbs Act applies?

Of what relevance is the statute's legislative history to the issue put in these terms? Congress was quite single-minded, it appears, in the problem it sought to solve in enacting the Hobbs Act. It meant to continue the reach of the 1934 statute (aimed at "organized crime"?), and to blunt the effect of one particular application by the Supreme Court of that statute to "egregious" labor activity. Did it mean to do more? Did it mean to criminalize at the federal level *all* robbery and *all* extortion?

Consider in this respect the Court's reference to the remarks of Representatives Jennings and Gwynne at the end of the second paragraph quoted above. The Court apparently had in mind the following statements:

"Mr. JENNINGS. Mr. Chairman, this bill is designed to protect trade and commerce against interference by violence, threat, coercion, or intimidation. It is brought before the Congress under and pursuant to the commerce clause of the federal constitution which gives Congress the power to regulate commerce among the states. The necessity for this measure grows out of the misconstruction placed upon the antiracketeering law enacted in 1934 by what is popularly known as the Byrnes opinion in the case of United States against Local 807.

"Let us get right down to what this bill is designed to do. In response to the statement that it is a booby trap, I have this to say: it is a trap for a man who is boob enough to go out and undertake to trample the rights of American citizens under his feet and commit highway robbery and interfere with them in their right to market their products across state lines. Properly, Congress could, if it so desired, occupy the whole field with respect to legislation affecting interstate commerce, but we do not choose to do that. It is true that the statutes of most states denounce robbery and extortion as crimes but this act is peculiarly appropriate because these offenses many times are committed at state lines and may, in the perpetration and consummation of the crime, cross and recross state lines. ...

"I have always been taught that a curved line is the beautiful thing in art but that a straight line is the beautiful thing in morals and in good conduct. We are just undertaking to draw a straight line here, not capable of misinterpretation or distortion, between the right which belongs to the man on his legitimate mission to market and the misconduct of a robber who undertakes to take away from him his property at the point of a gun or with a blackjack on a public thoroughfare of this country."

"Mr. GWYNNE of Iowa. Of course, the state law prohibits robbery and extortion. Unquestionably state indictments could have been returned against the members of this union. The fact is, however, such indictments were not returned. It is a breakdown of law enforcement reminding the Congress of its duty to protect interstate commerce by the enactment of this bill.

"Mr. Chairman, I have been amazed and disappointed at the attitude of certain labor leaders in regard to this proposed legislation. Many of them have labelled this as antilabor legislation. That is not true. This bill would simply protect interstate commerce from robbery and extortion, no matter by whom these crimes were committed." (11904)

"Mr. GWYNNE of Iowa. ... What was the situation before we passed the law originally? Prior to 1934 every state in the Union had laws against robbery and extortion. The purpose of the antiracketeering law was to create the federal offenses of robbery and extortion if those crimes interfered with or affected interstate commerce...." (11920)

Do these statements, or any of the other excerpts from the legislative history reproduced above or in Appendix B, support the result that any effort to limit the statute should be abandoned? How might the statute be limited? Does it contain any words that would provide a convenient hook for a rule of law that limits its apparent breadth? Or did the Court have no choice but to reject the argument presented in *Culbert* and, since no other principled limitation was suggested, to interpret the statute literally?

SECTION 2: BRIBERY UNDER THE TRAVEL ACT

Perrin v. United States

Supreme Court of the United States, 1979.
444 U.S. 37.

■ CHIEF JUSTICE BURGER delivered the opinion of the Court.

We granted certiorari to resolve a Circuit conflict on whether commercial bribery of private employees prohibited by a state criminal statute constitutes "bribery ... in violation of the laws of the State in which committed" within the meaning of the Travel Act, 18 U.S.C. § 1952.

I

Petitioner Vincent Perrin and four codefendants[2] were indicted in the Eastern District of Louisiana for violating the Travel Act, 18 U.S.C. § 1952, and for conspiring to violate the Act, 18 U.S.C. § 371. The Travel Act provides in part:

"(a) Whoever travels in interstate or foreign commerce or uses any facility in interstate or foreign commerce, including the mail, with intent to—

"(1) distribute the proceeds of any unlawful activity; or

"(2) commit any crime of violence to further any unlawful activity; or

"(3) otherwise promote, manage, establish, carry on, or facilitate the promotion, management, establishment, or carrying on, of any unlawful activity,

and thereafter performs or attempts to perform any of the acts specified in subparagraphs (1), (2), and (3), shall be fined not more than $10,000 or imprisoned for not more than five years, or both.[a]

"(b) As used in this subsection 'unlawful activity' means (1) any business enterprise involving gambling, liquor on which the Federal excise tax has not been paid, narcotics or controlled substances (as defined in section 102(6) of the Controlled Substances Act), or prostitution offenses in violation of the laws of the State in which they are committed or of the United States, or (2) extortion, bribery, or arson in violation of the laws of the State in which committed or of the United States."

The indictment charged that Perrin and his codefendants used the facilities of interstate commerce for the purpose of promoting a commercial bribery scheme in violation of the laws of the State of Louisiana.[3]

[2] Also indicted with petitioner were Duffy LaFont, Jr., David Levy, Albert Izuel, and Jim Haddox. Proceedings against Izuel and Haddox were severed by the trial court, and the charges were subsequently dismissed.

[a] The sentencing provision of the Travel Act was amended in 1994. It now authorizes a maximum sentence of 20 years in prison for violations of subparagraph (2), involving crimes of violence. The maximum sentence remains five years in prison under subparagraphs (1) and (3). 108 Stat. 2147.—[Footnote by eds.]

[3] Louisiana's commercial bribery statute, La. Rev. Stat. Ann. § 14.73 (West 1974), provides in part:

"Commercial bribery is the giving or offering to give, directly or indirectly, anything of apparent present or prospective value to any private agent, employee, or fiduciary, without the knowledge and consent of the principal or employer, with the intent to influence such agent's, employee's, or fiduciary's action in relation to the principal's or employer's affairs."

Following a jury trial, Perrin was convicted on the conspiracy count and two substantive Travel Act counts. He received a one-year suspended sentence on each of the three counts.

The government's evidence at trial was that Perrin, David Levy, and Duffy LaFont engaged in a scheme to exploit geological data obtained from the Petty–Ray Geophysical Co. Petty–Ray, a Louisiana-based company, was in the business of conducting geological explorations and selling the data to oil companies. At trial, company executives testified that confidentiality was imperative to the conduct of their business. The economic value of exploration data would be undermined if its confidentiality were not protected. Moreover, public disclosure after sale would interfere with the contractual rights of the purchaser and would otherwise injury Petty–Ray's relationship with its customers.

In June 1975 LaFont importuned Roger Willis, an employee of Petty–Ray, to steal confidential geological exploration data from his employer. In exchange, LaFont promised Willis a percentage of the profits of a corporation which had been created to exploit the stolen information. Willis' position as an analyst of seismic data gave him access to the relevant material, which he in turn surreptitiously provided to the conspirators. Perrin, a consulting geologist, was brought into the scheme to interpret and analyze the data.

In late July 1975 Perrin met with Willis, LaFont, and Levy. Perrin directed Willis to call a firm in Richmond, Tex., to obtain gravity maps to aid him in his evaluation.[4] After the meeting, Willis contacted the Federal Bureau of Investigation and disclosed the details of the scheme. Willis agreed to permit conversations between himself and the other participants to be recorded. Forty-seven tapes were made, a large number of which were played to the jury.

The United States Court of Appeals for the Fifth Circuit affirmed Perrin's conviction, rejecting his contention that Congress intended "bribery" in the act to include only bribery of public officials. The court also rejected challenges to the constitutionality of the Louisiana commercial bribery statute, to the sufficiency of the interstate nexus to establish jurisdiction under the Travel Act,[5] and to the failure of the trial judge to sever petitioner's trial from that of his codefendants.[6]

II

Petitioner argues that Congress intended "bribery" in the Travel Act to be confined to its common-law definition, i.e., bribery of a public official.

---

[4] The government claimed at trial that Perrin purposefully chose an out-of-state supplier because it would be less likely to notice leasing activities in Louisiana.

[5] Phone calls from Louisiana to Richmond, Tex., by Willis and Levy, and the subsequent shipment of materials by the Richmond firm to Louisiana by Continental Bus were held to provide the interstate nexus jurisdictionally required to support the Travel Act prosecutions.

[6] LaFont and Levy were also convicted; the Court of Appeals affirmed. Petitions for certiorari have been filed by both LaFont and Levy and are pending before this Court.

He contends that because commercial bribery was not an offense at common law, the indictment fails to charge a federal offense.[7]

The Travel Act was one of several bills enacted into law by the 87th Congress as part of the Attorney General's 1961 legislative program directed against "organized crime." Then Attorney General Robert Kennedy testified at Senate and House hearings that federal legislation was needed to aid state and local governments which were no longer able to cope with the increasingly complex and interstate nature of large scale, multiparty crime. The stated intent was to "dry up" traditional sources of funds for such illegal activities.

To remedy a gap in the authority of federal investigatory agencies, Congress employed its now familiar power under the commerce clause of the federal Constitution to prohibit activities of traditional state and local concern that also have an interstate nexus. That Congress was consciously linking the enforcement powers and resources of the federal and state governments to deal with traditional state crimes is shown by its definition of "unlawful activity" as an "enterprise involving gambling, liquor ..., narcotics or controlled substances ..., or prostitution offenses in violation of the laws of the State in which they are committed or of the United States." The statute also makes it a federal offense to travel or use a facility in interstate commerce to commit "extortion [or] bribery ... in violation of the laws of the State in which committed or of the United States." Because the offenses are defined by reference to existing state as well as federal law, it is clear beyond doubt that Congress intended to add a second layer of enforcement supplementing what it found to be inadequate state authority and state enforcement.

We begin with the language of the Travel Act itself. A fundamental canon of statutory construction is that, unless otherwise defined, words will be interpreted as taking their ordinary, contemporary, common meaning. Therefore, we look to the ordinary meaning of the term "bribery" at the time Congress enacted the statute in 1961. In light of Perrin's contentions we consider first the development and evolution of the common-law definition.

At early common law, the crime of bribery extended only to the corruption of judges. 3 E. Coke, Institutes *144, *147 (1628). By the time of Blackstone, bribery was defined as an offense involving a judge or "other person concerned in the administration of justice" and included the giver as well as the receiver of the bribe. 4 W. Blackstone, Commentaries *139–*140 (1765). The writings of a 19th-century scholar inform us that by that time the crime of bribery had been expanded to include the corruption of any public official and the bribery of voters and witnesses as well. J. Stephen, Digest of the Criminal Law 85–87 (1877). And by the 20th century, England had adopted the Prevention of Corruption Act making

---

[7] Perrin's other contentions, including a claim that the asserted ambiguity of the Travel Act resulted in failure to provide adequate notice that his conduct violated federal as well as Louisiana laws, do not merit discussion.

criminal the commercial bribery of agents and employees.   Act of 1906, 6 Edw. 7, ch. 34, amended by the Prevention of Corruption Act of 1916, 6 & 7 Geo. 5, ch. 64.

In this country, by the time the Travel Act was enacted in 1961, federal and state statutes had extended the term bribery well beyond its common-law meaning.   Although Congress chose not to enact a general commercial bribery statute, it perceived abuses in the areas it found required particular legislation.   Federal statutes specifically using "bribery" in the sense of payments to private persons to influence their actions are the Transportation Act of 1940, 49 U.S.C. § 1(17)(b) (prohibiting the "bribery" of agents or employees of common carriers), and the 1960 Amendments to the Communications Act, 47 U.S.C. § 509(a)(2) (prohibiting the "bribery" of television game show contestants).[8]

A similar enlargement of the term beyond its common-law definition manifested itself in the states prior to 1961.   Fourteen states had statutes which outlawed commercial bribery generally.[9]   An additional 28 had adopted more narrow statutes outlawing corrupt payments to influence private duties in particular fields, including bribery of agents, common carrier and telegraph company employees, labor officials, bank employees, and participants in sporting events.[10]

In sum, by 1961 the common understanding and meaning of "bribery" had extended beyond its early common-law definitions.   In 42 states and in federal legislation, "bribery" included the bribery of individuals acting in a private capacity.[11]   It was against this background that the Travel Act was passed.

III

On a previous occasion we took note of the sparse legislative history of the Travel Act. Rewis v. United States, 401 U.S. 808, 811 (1971).   The record of the hearings and floor debates discloses that Congress made no attempt to define the statutory term "bribery," but relied on the accepted contemporary meaning.   There are ample references to the bribery of state

[8] Examples of federal statutes which make illegal the giving or receiving of payments to influence private duties but without using the word bribery are found at 18 U.S.C. § 215 (prohibiting payments to bank officers to influence their consideration of loans); 41 U.S.C. § 51 (prohibiting payments to contractors to secure subcontracts); and 29 U.S.C. § 186 (prohibiting payments to labor union officials).

[9] [Citations omitted.]   Of these 14, most had also enacted other private bribery statutes reaching labor, banking, or sports bribery.

[10] [Citations omitted.]   Since 1961, of the eight states which had not adopted non-public official bribery statutes, Georgia, Kansas, New Hampshire, New Mexico, North Dakota, and Wyoming now have such statutes.   Moreover, a number of the states which did not have a commercial bribery statute in 1961 do so today.

[11] See also ALI, Model Penal Code § 223.10, pp. 113–17, Comments (Tent. Draft No. 11, 1960)("all relations which are recognized in a society as involving special trust should be kept secure from the corrupting influence of bribery"); ALI, Model Penal Code § 224.8 (P.O.D. 1962)(containing a specific prohibition against commercial bribery).

and local officials, but there is no indication that Congress intended to so limit its meaning. Indeed, references in the legislative history to the purposes and scope of the Travel Act, as well as other bills under consideration by Congress as part of the package of "organized crime" legislation aimed at supplementing state enforcement, indicate that Members, Committees, and draftsmen used "bribery" to include payments to private individuals to influence their actions.

Senator Keating, for instance, expressed concern about the influence of gamblers and racketeers on athletics. He indicated his belief that the sports bribery scandals could be dealt with under the Travel Act. See The Attorney General's Program to Curb Organized Crime and Racketeering: Hearings on S. 1653, S. 1654, etc., before the Senate Committee on the Judiciary, 87th Cong., 1st Sess. 327–28 (1961)(hereinafter Senate Hearings). Attorney General Kennedy in his opening statement in both the Senate and House hearings in 1961 expressed his concern that "gamblers have bribed college basketball players to shave points on games." Legislation Relating to Organized Crime: Hearings on H.R. 468, H.R. 1246, etc., before Subcommittee No. 5 of the House Committee on the Judiciary, 87th Cong., 1st Sess. 25 (1961)(hereinafter House Hearings); Senate Hearings 6. In the consideration of a related bill to grant immunity to witnesses testifying in labor racketeering cases, repeated reference was made to the need to curb "bribery" of labor and management officials involved in labor disputes. See House Hearings 84. It is not suggested that the references to the immunity bill were intended to define the content of "bribery" in the Travel Act, yet they do indicate that Congress did not use the word in the narrow, common-law sense.

Petitioner also contends that commercial bribery is a "management" or "white-collar" offense not generally associated with organized criminal activities. From this, he argues that Congress could not have intended to encompass commercial bribery within § 1952.

The notion that bribery of private persons is unrelated or unknown to what is called "organized crime" has no foundation. The hearings on the Travel Act make clear that a major area of congressional concern was with the infiltration by organized crime into legitimate activities. Legitimate businesses had come to be used as a means for highly organized criminal activities to hide income derived from illegal sources. Moreover, Committees investigating these activities found that those who infiltrated legitimate businesses often used the same criminal techniques to expand their operations and sales in the legitimate enterprises. Thus, in discussing the infiltration of organized groups into nongambling amusement games, the McClellan Committee reported that the organization achieved its holdings in legitimate business by "force, terror and the corruption of management, union and public officials." Final Report of the Select Committee on Improper Activities in the Labor or Management Field, S. Rep. No. 1139, 86th Cong., 2d Sess., 856 (1960).

Indeed, the McClellan Committee in 1960, like the Kefauver Committee in 1950–1951, documented numerous specific instances of the use of commercial bribery by these organized groups to control legitimate businesses. The McClellan Committee, for example, reported that a particular "shylocking" operation began in New York when persons were able to obtain a substantial unsecured line of credit at a New York bank "by making gifts to two of the bank officials." Id., at 772–73. The Kefauver Committee explored, among numerous others, the relationship between a high-ranking official of the Ford Motor Co. and persons believed to be members of organized illegal groups. Its evidence suggested that organized crime had exploited that relationship to obtain Ford dealerships and hauling contracts. Third Interim Report of the Special Committee to Investigate Organized Crime in Interstate Commerce S. Rep. No. 307, 82d Cong., 1st Sess., 75 (1951). See also id., at 160–61 (expressing concern about "corruption of college basketball players who could be talked into controlling the score of a game").[12]

There can be little doubt that Congress recognized in 1961 that bribery of private persons was widely used in highly organized criminal efforts to infiltrate and gain control of legitimate businesses, an area of special concern of Congress in enacting the Travel Act.

Our approach to ascertaining the meaning of "bribery" must be guided by our holding in United States v. Nardello, 393 U.S. 286 (1969), where the same provision of the act under review in this case was before the Court. There, the respondents were charged with traveling in interstate commerce with the intent to engage in extortion contrary to the laws of Pennsylvania in violation of § 1952. Pennsylvania's "extortion" statute applied only to acts committed by public officials. However, the state had outlawed the particular conduct engaged in by the appellees under a statute entitled "blackmail." Nardello and his codefendants argued, as Perrin does here, that Congress intended to use the word "extortion" in its common-law sense, which would be limited to conduct by public officials.

An opinion by Chief Justice Warren for a unanimous Court rejected the argument limiting the definition of extortion to its common-law meaning, holding that Congress used the term in a generic and contemporary sense. The Court noted that in 1961 the Attorney General had pressed Congress to include "shakedown rackets," "shylocking," and labor extor-

---

[12] Although congressional hearings subsequent to the passage of the Travel Act are not relied on, they do support the conclusion that bribery of private persons is a familiar tool of organized criminal groups. See Organized Crime, Stolen Securities: Hearings before the Subcommittee on Investigations of the Senate Committee on Government Operations, 92d Cong., 1st Sess., 675–83 (1971)(bribing of employees of banking institutions to accept pledges of worthless and stolen securities and of employees of brokerage houses to steal securities); Organized Crime, Techniques for Converting Worthless Securities into Cash: Hearings before the House Select Committee on Crime, 92d Cong., 1st Sess., 3, 242, 292–93, 361 (1971)(bribing of insurance company presidents to buy worthless securities for the company); Organized Crime, Securities: Thefts and Frauds: Hearings before the Permanent Subcommittee on Investigations of the Senate Committee on Government Operations, 93d Cong., 1st Sess., 183, 239–40, 467–68, 475–76 (1973)(bribing of certified public accountants and employees in financial institutions and brokerage houses).

tion, which were methods frequently used by organized groups to generate income and infiltrate legitimate activities.

In rejecting Nardello's argument that Congress intended to adopt the common-law meaning of the term "extortion" the Court stated:

> "In light of the scope of the congressional purpose we decline to give the term 'extortion' an unnaturally narrow reading ... and thus conclude that the acts for which appellees have been indicted fall within the generic term extortion as used in the Travel Act."

We are similarly persuaded that the generic definition of bribery, rather than a narrow common-law definition, was intended by Congress.[13]

IV

Petitioner also contends that a broad interpretation of the meaning of bribery will have serious federalism implications. He relies particularly on Rewis v. United States, 401 U.S. 808 (1971). See also United States v. Bass, 404 U.S. 336, 349–50 (1971). The factual setting in *Rewis* was very different from this case. There, we were confronted with a Travel Act prosecution of the proprietors of a gambling establishment located a few miles south of the Georgia–Florida state line. There was no evidence that Rewis had employed interstate facilities to conduct him numbers operation; moreover, he could not readily identify which customers had crossed state lines. The District Court had instructed the jury that if it found that third persons traveled from Georgia to Florida to place bets, that would be sufficient to supply the interstate commerce element necessary to sustain the conviction of the proprietors under the act. In reversing, we cautioned that in that setting "an expansive Travel Act would alter sensitive federal-state relationships, could overextend limited federal police resources, and ... would transform relatively minor state offenses into federal felonies."

Reliance on the federalism principles articulated in *Rewis* to dictate a narrow interpretation of "bribery" is misplaced. Our concern there was with the tenuous interstate commerce element. Looking at congressional intent in that light, we held that Congress did not intend that the Travel Act should apply to criminal activity within one state solely because that activity was sometimes patronized by persons from another state.

Here, the sufficiency of the interstate nexus is no longer at issue. Rather, so long as the requisite interstate nexus is present, the statute reflects a clear and deliberate intent on the part of Congress to alter the federal-state balance in order to reinforce state law enforcement. In defining an "unlawful activity," Congress has clearly stated its intention to

---

[13] Our analysis leads us to reject the application of the maxim of statutory construction that ambiguity concerning the ambit of criminal statutes should be resolved in favor of lenity. Bell v. United States, 349 U.S. 81, 83 (1955). Although *Bell* states the general rule in cases where the courts are faced with genuine ambiguity, the rule of lenity applies " 'when we are uncertain about the statute's meaning,' " and is " 'not to be used in complete disregard of the purpose of the legislature.' " United States v. Culbert, 435 U.S. 371, 379 (1978), quoting Scarborough v. United States, 431 U.S. 563, 577 (1977). *Nardello* leaves little room for uncertainty about the statute's meaning.

include violations of state as well as federal bribery law. Until statutes such as the Travel Act contravene some provision of the Constitution, the choice is for Congress, not the courts.

We hold that Congress intended "bribery ... in violation of the laws of the State in which committed" as used in the Travel Act to encompass conduct in violation of state commercial bribery statutes. Accordingly, the judgment of the Court of Appeals is

Affirmed.

JUSTICE WHITE took no part in the decision of this case.

NOTES ON THE TRAVEL ACT

1. Legislative History. As the Chief Justice said in *Perrin*, the legislative history of the Travel Act is "sparse." It was enacted on a relatively hurried timetable in 1961 as part of a package of "organized crime" legislation proposed by then-Attorney General Robert Kennedy. The package included, in addition to what was to become the Travel Act, such diverse measures as the creation of an office of "syndicated crime" in the Justice Department, extension of the fugitive felon act, provisions on the interstate transportation of wagering paraphernalia and the transmission of gambling information, immunity-for-testimony provisions, and a provision on conspiracy to commit an "organized crime" offense.[a]

Seven days of hearings, the transcript of which extends for 388 pages, were held in the House on the Attorney General's proposed package of legislation from May 17 to May 31, 1961. As then drafted, the House predecessor to the Travel Act, H.R. 6572, read:

"§ 1952. Interstate and foreign travel in aid of racketeering enterprises

"(a) Whoever travels in interstate or foreign commerce with intent to—

"(1) distribute the proceeds of any unlawful activity; or

"(2) commit any crime of violence to further any unlawful activity; or

"(3) otherwise promote, manage, establish, carry on, or facilitate the promotion, management, establishment, or carrying on, of any unlawful activity

[a] The term "organized crime" offense was defined to mean:

"any offense proscribed by the laws of or the common law as recognized in any State relating to gambling, narcotics, extortion, intoxicating liquor, prostitution, criminal fraud, or false pretenses, or murder, maiming, or assault with intent to inflict great bodily harm, and punishable by imprisonment in a penitentiary or by death." H.R. 5230, reproduced in House Hearings 8.

Citations below to the House and Senate Hearings will follow the form used by the Chief Justice in *Perrin*. The full citations can be found in his *Perrin* opinion.

shall be fined not more than $10,000 or imprisoned for not more than five years, or both.

"(b) As used in this section 'unlawful activity' means

"(1) any business enterprise involving gambling, liquor, narcotics, or prostitution offenses in violation of the laws of the state in which they are committed or of the United States, or

"(2) extortion or bribery in violation of the laws of the state in which committed or of the United States...." House Hearings 9.

The Hearings began with a statement by the Attorney General, who spoke in support of "proposed legislation which we, in the Department of Justice believe can be extremely effective in combatting organized crime and racketeering." See House Hearings 18–24. After some introductory remarks, he went through the proposals one by one. He began with H.R. 6572:

"Organized crime is nourished by a number of activities, but the primary source of its growth is illicit gambling. From huge gambling profits flow the funds to bankroll ... other illegal activities ... including the bribery of local officials. ...

"The main target of our bill is interstate travel to promote gambling. It is also aimed at the huge profits in the traffic in liquor, narcotics, prostitution, as well as the use of these funds for corrupting local officials and for their use in racketeering in labor and management. Thus, when we speak of unlawful business it is business engaged in the aforementioned improper activities.

"A brief explanation of the method by which the funds are obtained by the big time gambling operator may be useful at this time."

At this point, the Attorney General described the way numbers operations and illegal off-track betting worked. The person who takes an off-track bet at track odds, he explained, takes a profit and, since his "action" may not reflect the "action" at the track, "reinsures" his risk by "laying off" to a person who, for a commission, accepts the excess wager. This "lay-off man", in turn, protects his risks by laying off any excess to a nationwide "syndicate or combine" of gamblers who are able to balance the bets nationwide. Thus,

"[w]ith a balanced book at the handbook [or local bookmaker], layoff, or syndicate level, the edge is divided and no one loses except the man who places the original bet. As an indication of the volume of business I am talking about, one of the largest operators in the combine does a layoff business of $18 million a year. His net profit is $720,000 a year. This is a four per cent return on volume with relatively no risk as a result of the balancing of the books on each event.

> "The term 'gambler' is a misnomer for these people. They accept money that small gamblers wager but they do not gamble at all. ..."

Kennedy continued to state that the numbers racket was generating about $300,000 per day in New York City at $1 per ticket. "With that background on the type of business done by these persons," Kennedy continued, "let me now move on to their interstate travel activities to show how we hope to be of aid and assistance to local law authorities."

He then gave some examples. The common theme is reflected in the first one. Some "notorious individuals" whom Kennedy offered to name in executive session lived in Miami but had an interest in the numbers racket in New York City:

> "Every month a messenger carried the profits of the numbers racket from the scene of operations to the resort town. One of the payments was in excess of $250,000. Thus, the persons reaping the profit from the illegal activity remained beyond the reach of the law enforcement officials at the place of operation and committed no crime in the state where they lived. Only the federal government can curtail the flow of funds which permit the kingpins to live far from the scene, preventing the local officials, burdened by the gambling activity, from punishing them.
>
> "If our bill is enacted we will be able to prosecute the courier who carries the funds across state lines and in conjunction with the aiding and [abetting] statute, we will be able to prosecute the person who caused the courier to travel—namely the kingpin. This example illustrates what we have found to be a pattern around the country where the apparent innocuous 10–cent numbers bet in a large city turns into tremendous profits in the hands of bigtime hoodlums."

After giving several similar examples, Kennedy concluded his comments on H.R. 6572 as follows:

> "None of the activities of which I have just spoken, that is, interstate travel to carry on a racketeering enterprise, travel to deliver the profits of an illegal enterprise, or travel to commit a crime of violence and furtherance of the activities of an illegal business is now per se, a violation of state or federal law. The travel is performed by these persons with impunity, but because of that travel and the interstate aspects of the activities, the task of the local law enforcement officials is staggering.
>
> "I am not now discussing isolated instances, Mr. Chairman, but what we have found to be a pattern of behavior in a number of geographic areas.
>
> "We have skirted the area of social gambling by limiting the proposed statute to gambling, as a business, which violates state or federal law. In this limited aspect, the enactment of the bill will

be a tremendous tool for stamping out the vicious and dangerous criminal combinations.

"Mr. Chairman, this bill is vital. We need it. Local law enforcement officials need it. The country needs it."

In the questioning of the Attorney General that followed this statement, the Chairman of the Committee, Emanuel Celler from New York, raised a theme that recurred throughout the hearings. He asked Kennedy whether the bill would reach isolated instances of travel for purposes of prostitution or travel by the owner of a small liquor store to keep the store open beyond the required closing time (a technical violation of the liquor laws). Kennedy answered "yes," but said, in effect, that there would be no prosecution in such cases:

"Mr. KENNEDY. We are relying on the good judgment of law enforcement officials, Mr. Chairman, just as the Congress did when they passed the Mann Act. ... We have the authority to [prosecute], Mr. Chairman, but we don't intend to. ... It seems to me that, based on the history of statutes that have been enacted in the past, this can be administered properly." House Hearings 35–36.

Another theme that emerged in the testimony was that the bill as drafted focused solely on intent. Typical was the criticism of Harris Steinberg, a New York criminal lawyer:

"Mr. STEINBERG. It seems to me [that H.R. 6572] comes dangerously close to thought control. This [bill] penalizes and makes criminal a man's intent, which is something that is in his mind. It has never been the policy of our law to make criminal what is in a man's mind unless he externalizes it with some act, which is immediately dangerous to public welfare. ...

"The CHAIRMAN. In other words, we have the bill that whoever travels with intent—that is mental—to do certain things, all he does is to travel and he has that intent and then he violates the law.

"Mr. STEINBERG. That to me is a terrible thing, Mr. Chairman. That is what this law says. ...

"The CHAIRMAN. Even if ... he changes his mind after he gets to the place of destination, will he have committed the crime?

"Mr. STEINBERG. Under this bill he would have committed the crime. ..." House Hearings 145.

On the last day of the Hearings, Herbert J. Miller, Assistant Attorney General in charge of the Criminal Division, defended the bill against this charge:

"I do not believe that H.R. 6572 can be properly criticized as a 'thought control' proposal because of its emphasis on the intent of the person travelling in interstate or foreign commerce. Intent is a key element of proof in most of our criminal statutes. As with these other statutes, successful prosecution under the proposed bill would require proof of the defined intent by reference to some overt conduct. Under H.R. 6572, the government would have to link the interstate travel with the furtherance of the specified unlawful activity in such a way as to prove that the defendant was traveling with [the] requisite intent. Far from being a 'thought control' bill, H.R. 6572 requires an imposing burden of proof before the sanctions of the bill would apply." House Hearings 336–37.

The last day of hearings in the House was May 31, 1961. Beginning on June 6 and extending until June 26, five days of hearings were held in the Senate. The transcript of the Senate Hearings extends for 329 pages. Again Attorney General Kennedy led off. In his prepared statement and extemporaneous comments, he repeated, virtually verbatim, his testimony in the House. Most of the other testimony was also duplicative of matters covered in the House Hearings.

On July 27, the Senate Judiciary Committee issued its favorable report on S. 1653, its version of what was to become the Travel Act. See S. Rep. No. 644, 87th Cong., 1st Sess. In substance, it recommended an amendment to the House bill as reproduced above by adding the words "and thereafter performs or attempts to perform any of the acts specified in subparagraphs (1), (2), and (3)" after the list of prohibited purposes in § 1952(a).[b] The substantive comments in the Senate Report were sparse, consisting in the main of a quotation from Kennedy's testimony, several unrevealing letters, and a statement of the purpose of the bill in such general terms as to be uninformative:

> "The purpose of the bill, as amended, is to amend chapter 95 of title 18, United States Code, by adding a new § 1952, to prohibit travel or transportation in aid of racketeering enterprises, subject to a fine of not more than $10,000 or imprisonment for not more than five years, or both."

Less than a month later, on August 17, after the Senate had passed its bill, the House Judiciary Committee reported favorably on S. 1653 with House amendments. See H.R. Rep. No. 966, 87th Cong., 1st Sess. The reported bill included the "and thereafter performs" language recommended by the Senate Judiciary Committee. The major difference between the two bills was in the House definition of "unlawful activity", which

---

[b] The matter was slightly more complicated than suggested in the text. The Senate bill had two sections, the first of which prohibited travel with intent to do the things listed in subsections (a)(1), (a)(2), and (a)(3) and the second of which prohibited using any facility for transportation, including the mail, for the same three purposes. The two sections were consolidated in the House bill and minor differences in wording between them were reconciled.

The Senate bill also contained the words "liquor on which the Federal excise tax has not been paid" which appeared in the statute as enacted but were not contained in the House bill. The purpose of these words, according to the Senate Report, was to narrow the scope of liquor law violations "so as not to involve the federal government in petty offenses at the state or local level which may involve the sale of liquor."

restricted the covered extortion and bribery offenses to "extortion or bribery in connection with such offenses", i.e., in connection with gambling, liquor, narcotics, or prostitution.[c] There were no comments of substance on the bill, beyond a summary of Attorney General Kennedy's testimony and a statement that "[n]othing in this bill is to be construed as immunizing any violator of state law from state prosecution."

The House bill passed as reported. A Conference Report, issued by the respective House and Senate Managers on September 11, reconciled the differences between the two bills. See H.R. Rep. No. 1161, 87th Cong., 1st Sess. Essentially, the Senate coverage of extortion and bribery was accepted, the two sections of the Senate bill were consolidated into one, and the "thereafter" clause was retained to require "that an act be performed subsequent to the travel in or the use of the interstate or foreign commerce facility. Thus, there is required the commission of an overt act after having traveled or after having used the facilities of interstate or foreign commerce."

The conference bill became law on September 13. At the suggestion of the Justice Department, arson was added to the list of "unlawful activities" in § 1952(b)(2) in 1965. See H.R. Rep. No. 264, 89th Cong., 1st Sess. (April, 1965); S. Rep. No. 351, 89th Cong., 1st Sess. (June, 1965). Several additional offenses were added to subsection (b) in a new subpart (3) in 1986.

2. *United States v. Nardello*. Chief Justice Burger relies in *Perrin* on Chief Justice Warren's opinion for a unanimous Court[d] in United States v. Nardello, 393 U.S. 286 (1969). *Nardello* was a direct appeal to the Supreme Court from the dismissal of an indictment by a District Court. The "[a]ppellees were indicted under § 1952," the Court explained, "for their alleged participation in a 'shakedown' operation whereby individuals would be lured into a compromising homosexual situation and then threatened with exposure unless appellees' silence was purchased." The District Court examined Pennsylvania statutes which classified certain acts as "extortion" and others as "blackmail." "Extortion" was limited to acts by public officials, whereas "blackmail", defined, inter alia, as conduct with an intent "to extort", reached private behavior of the sort alleged here. The

---

[c] Byron White, then Deputy Attorney General, expressed the opposition of the Justice Department to this limitation in a letter to Representative Celler dated August 7, 1961. He opposed the change because it:

"eliminated from the purview of the bill extortions not related to the four above offenses but which are, and have historically been, activities which involve organized crime. Such activities are the 'shakedown racket,' 'shylocking' (where interest of 20 per cent per week is charged and which is collected by means of force and violence, since in most states the loans are uncollectible in court) and labor extortion. It also removes from the purview of the bill the bribery of state, local and federal officials by the organized criminals unless we can prove that the bribery is directly attributable to gambling, liquor, narcotics, or prostitution."

Quoted in Martin R. Pollner, Attorney General Robert F. Kennedy's Legislative Program to Curb Organized Crime and Racketeering, 28 Brooklyn L. Rev. 37, 41 (1961).

[d] Justice White did not participate.

District Court thought the limitation of the crime of extortion to acts by public officials dispositive.

The Supreme Court reversed. It first noted that there was wide variation in the labels the states used to punish extortionate behavior. Faced with this diversity, the Solicitor General argued, as the Court explained, "that Congress intended that extortion [in the Travel Act] should refer to those acts prohibited by state law which would be generically classified as extortionate, i.e., obtaining something of value from another with his consent induced by the wrongful use of force, fear, or threats."[e] The Court agreed with the Solicitor General's construction.

It began by reviewing the legislative history, focusing particularly on the letter from then-Justice White opposing the narrower definition of extortion in the House version of the bill. It then said:

"The Travel Act ... thus reflects a congressional judgment that certain activities of organized crime which were violative of state law had become a national problem. The legislative response was to be commensurate with the scope of the problem. Appellees suggest, however, that Congress intended that the common-law meaning of extortion—corrupt acts by a public official—be retained. If Congress so intended, then § 1952 would cover extortionate acts only when the extortionist was also a public official. Not only would such a construction conflict with the congressional desire to curb the activities of organized crime rather than merely organized criminals who were also public officials, but also § 1952 imposes penalties upon any individual crossing state lines or using interstate facilities for any of the statutorily enumerated offenses. The language of the Travel Act, 'whoever' crosses state lines or uses interstate facilities, includes private persons as well as public officials.[11]

"Appellees argue that Congress' decision not to define extortion combined with its decision to prohibit only extortion in violation of state law compels the conclusion that peculiar versions of state terminology are controlling. Since in Pennsylvania a distinction is maintained between extortion and blackmail with only the latter term covering appellees' activities,[12] it follows that

---

[e] The Court had previously noted that extortion in the Travel Act was undefined and had, by way of contrast, set forth the definition in the Hobbs Act. As can be seen, it closely tracked the Hobbs Act definition in describing the "generic" nature of the offense.

[11] "The government notes that subsection (b)(2) prohibits bribery as well as extortion. Bribery has traditionally focused upon corrupt activities by public officials. Since Pennsylvania's extortion statute covers corrupt acts by public officials, the government

suggests that appellees' construction of 'extortion' renders the bribery prohibition superfluous."

[12] "Several cases cast some doubt upon the vitality of this distinction as they indicate that in Pennsylvania the terms extortion and blackmail are considered synonymous. [Citations omitted.] Federal criminal statutes have also used the terms interchangeably. For example, 18 U.S.C. § 250 (1940 ed.) was entitled 'Extortion by informer'; today sub-

the Travel Act does not reach the conduct charged.   The fallacy of this contention lies in its assumption that, by defining extortion with reference to state law, Congress also incorporated state labels for particular offenses.   Congress' intent was to aid local law enforcement officials, not eradicate only those extortionate activities which any given state denominated extortion.   Indiana prohibits appellees' type of conduct under the heading of theft; Kansas terms such conduct robbery in the third degree; Minnesota calls it coercion; and Wisconsin believes that it should be classified under threats.   States such as Massachusetts, Michigan, and Oregon have enacted measures covering similar activities; each of these statutes contains in its title the term extortion.   Giving controlling effect to state classifications would result in coverage under § 1952 if appellees' activities were centered in Massachusetts, Michigan, or Oregon, but would deny coverage in Indiana, Kansas, Minnesota, or Wisconsin although each of these states prohibits identical criminal activities.   ...

"... We therefore conclude that the inquiry is not the manner in which states classify their criminal prohibitions but whether the particular state involved prohibits the extortionate activity charged.

"Appellees do not dispute that Pennsylvania prohibits the conduct for which they were indicted.   Accepting our conclusion that Congress did not intend to limit the coverage of § 1952 by reference to state classifications, appellees nevertheless insist that their activities were not extortionate.   The basis for this contention is an asserted distinction between blackmail and extortion: the former involves two private parties while the latter requires the participation of a public official.   As previously discussed, revenue-producing measures such as shakedown rackets and loan-sharking were called to the attention of Congress as methods utilized by organized crime to generate income.   These activities are traditionally conducted between private parties whereby funds are obtained from the victim with his consent produced by the use of force, fear, or threats.[13]   Prosecutions under the Travel Act for extortionate offenses involving only private individuals have been consistently maintained.   [Citations omitted.]   Appellees, according to the court below, attempted to obtain money from their victims by threats to expose alleged homosexual conduct.   Although only private individuals are involved, the indictment encompasses a type of activity generally known as extortionate since money was to be obtained from the victim by virtue of fear and

stantially the same provision is captioned 'Blackmail.'   See 18 U.S.C. § 873."

[13] "Extortion is typically employed by organized crime to enforce usurious loans, infiltrate legitimate businesses, and obtain control of labor unions.   See President's Commission on Law Enforcement and Administration of Justice, Task Force Report: Organized Crime 3–5 (1967)."

threats of exposure. In light of the scope of the congressional purpose we decline to give the term 'extortion' an unnaturally narrow reading, and thus conclude that the acts for which appellees have been indicted fall within the generic term extortion as used in the Travel Act."

3. Questions and Comments on *Perrin* and the Travel Act. Several technical aspects of the problem presented by *Perrin* should first be noticed. At the outset, is there any evidence recited by the Court that Perrin himself made any payments to Willis? Is any evidence recited that Perrin personally engaged in the jurisdictional acts which sufficed to satisfy those elements of the Travel Act charge? Does it matter whether the answer to either of these questions is "no"?

Consider also the argument made by Perrin that the asserted ambiguity in the Travel Act about whether it encompassed commercial bribery situations denied him fair notice that federal law might have been violated. The Court said in footnote 7 that the argument did "not merit discussion." Is there more to it than that? Should the Court have taken the argument seriously?

The Court observed in footnote 10 that several states had adopted commercial bribery statutes *after* the Travel Act was enacted in 1961. It does not appear to have been concerned with when the Louisiana statute was enacted. Is this a fatal flaw in the Court's analysis? Can Congress use subsequently enacted state criminal laws as the basis for prosecution under a federal statute?

On the merits of the inclusion of commercial bribery in the Travel Act, did the Court get the right answer? The Court began its analysis of the issue by referring to the legislative history, particularly to the fact that the objective of the statute was to get at "organized crime." Is there any evidence that this prosecution was against "organized crime"? Does the answer to this question matter? The Court also relied on the holding in *Nardello*. Does *Nardello* support its conclusion? Was *Nardello* itself correctly decided? Should the Court have paid more attention in *Perrin* and *Nardello* to the principles of fairness and federalism underlying *Rewis*, *Bass*, and related decisions?

Finally, consider the relevance of these decisions to the meaning of the concept of extortion in the Hobbs Act. The issue in the cases to be considered in the next section is whether bribery of local public officials can be prosecuted under the Hobbs Act. Given the explicit coverage of bribery in the Travel Act, why would federal prosecutors want to use the Hobbs Act? Could it be argued that the differences between extortion and bribery reflected in *Nardello* and, perhaps by implication in *Perrin*, preclude a Hobbs Act charge of bribery? By contrast, could it be argued that the Travel Act cases reinforce application of the Hobbs Act to bribery? Should the Hobbs Act be construed to permit the conviction of state and local officials who have taken bribes but who have not used their office or threats of "force, violence, or fear" to induce consensual payments?

SECTION 3: BRIBERY UNDER THE HOBBS ACT

McCormick v. United States

Supreme Court of the United States, 1991.
500 U.S. 257.

■ JUSTICE WHITE delivered the opinion of the Court.

This case requires us to consider whether the Court of Appeals properly affirmed the conviction of petitioner, an elected public official, for extorting property under color of official right in violation of the Hobbs Act, 18 U.S.C. § 1951. We also must address the affirmance of petitioner's conviction for filing a false income tax return.

I

Petitioner Robert L. McCormick was a member of the West Virginia House of Delegates in 1984. He represented a district that had long suffered from a shortage of medical doctors. For several years, West Virginia had allowed foreign medical school graduates to practice under temporary permits while studying for the state licensing exams. Under this program, some doctors were allowed to practice under temporary permits for years even though they repeatedly failed the state exams. McCormick was a leading advocate and supporter of this program.

In the early 1980's, following a move in the House of Delegates to end the temporary permit program, several of the temporarily licensed doctors formed an organization to press their interests in Charleston. The organization hired a lobbyist, John Vandergrift, who in 1984 worked for legislation that would extend the expiration date of the temporary permit program. McCormick sponsored the House version of the proposed legislation and a bill was passed extending the program for another year. Shortly thereafter, Vandergrift and McCormick discussed the possibility of introducing legislation during the 1985 session that would grant the doctors a permanent medical license by virtue of their years of experience. McCormick agreed to sponsor such legislation.

During his 1984 reelection campaign, McCormick informed Vandergrift that his campaign was expensive, that he had paid considerable sums out of his own pocket, and that he had not heard anything from the foreign doctors. Vandergrift told McCormick that he would contact the doctors and see what he could do. Vandergrift contacted one of the foreign doctors and later received from the doctors $1,200 in cash. Vandergrift delivered an envelope containing nine $100 bills to McCormick. Later the same day, a second delivery of $2,000 in cash was made to McCormick. During the fall of 1984, McCormick received two more cash payments from the doctors.

McCormick did not list any of these payments as campaign contributions[1] nor did he report the money as income on his 1984 federal income tax return. And although the doctors' organization kept detailed books of its expenditures, the cash payments were not listed as campaign contributions. Rather, the entries for the payments were accompanied only by initials or other codes signifying that the money was for McCormick.

In the spring of 1985, McCormick sponsored legislation permitting experienced doctors to be permanently licensed without passing the state licensing exams. McCormick spoke at length in favor of the bill during floor debate and the bill ultimately was enacted into law. Two weeks after the legislation was enacted, McCormick received another cash payment from the foreign doctors.

Following an investigation, a federal grand jury returned an indictment charging McCormick with five counts of violating the Hobbs Act, by extorting payments under color of official right, and with one count of filing a false income tax return in violation of 26 U.S.C. § 7206(1),[3] by failing to report as income the cash payments he received from the foreign doctors. At the close of a six-day trial, the jury was instructed that to establish a Hobbs Act violation the government had to prove that McCormick induced a cash payment and that he did so knowingly and willfully by extortion. [T]he court defined "extortion" and other terms and elaborated on the proof required with respect to the extortion counts.

[At this point, the Court reproduced several pages from the trial judge's instructions to the jury. The most significant instructions were as follows:

"Extortion means the obtaining of property from another, with his consent, either induced by the wrongful use of fear or induced under color of official right. The term 'wrongful' means the obtaining of property unfairly and unjustly by one having no lawful claim thereto. As to inducement, the United States must prove that the defendant induced the person or persons described in the indictment to part with property, a term which includes money. It is charged that the defendant did so under color of official right. In proving this element, it is enough that the government prove beyond a reasonable doubt that the benefactor transferred something of significant value, here alleged to be money, to the public official with the expectation that the public official would extend to him some benefit or refrain from some harmful action, and the public official accepted the money knowing it was being transferred to him with that expectation by the

[1] West Virginia law prohibits cash campaign contributions in excess of $50 per person.

[3] Section 7206 of the Internal Revenue Code provides in part:

"Any person who—(1) ... Willfully makes and subscribes any return ... which contains or is verified by a written declaration that it is made under the penalties of perjury, and which he does not believe to be true and correct as to every material matter ... shall be guilty of a felony...."

benefactor and because of his office. [I]nducement can be in the overt form of a demand, or in a more subtle form such as custom or expectation such as might have been communicated by the nature of the defendant's prior conduct of his office. ... If the public official knows the motivation of the victim to make any payment focuses on the public official's office, and money is obtained by the public official which was not lawfully due and owing to him or the office he represented, that is sufficient to satisfy the government's burden of showing a misuse of office and extortion under color of official right. The mere voluntary payment of money, however, does not constitute extortion. ... Many public officials receive legitimate political contributions from individuals who, the official knows, are motivated by a general gratitude toward him because of his position on certain issues important to them, or even in the hope that the good will generated by such contributions will make the official more receptive to their cause. The mere solicitation or receipt of such political contributions is not illegal. ... When a public official accepts the payment for an implicit promise of fair treatment ... there is an inherent threat that without the payment, the public official would exercise his discretion in an adverse manner. [I]t is not necessary that the government prove that the defendant committed or promised to commit a quid pro quo, that is, consideration in the nature of official action in return for the payment of the money not lawfully owed. Such a quid pro quo may, of course, be forthcoming in an extortion case or it may not. In either event it is not an essential element of the crime."]

The next day the jury informed the court that it "would like to hear the instructions again with particular emphasis on the definition of extortion under the color of official right and on the law as regards the portion of moneys received that does not have to be reported as income." The court then reread most of the extortion instructions to the jury, but reordered some of the paragraphs and made the following significant addition: "Extortion under color of official right means the obtaining of money by a public official when the money obtained was not lawfully due and owing to him or to his office. Of course, extortion does not occur where one who is a public official receives a legitimate gift or a voluntary political contribution even though the political contribution may have been made in cash in violation of local law. Voluntary is that which is freely given without expectation of benefit."

It is also worth noting that with respect to political contributions, the last two paragraphs of the supplemental instructions on the extortion counts were as follows:

"It would not be illegal, in and of itself, for Mr. McCormick to solicit or accept political contributions from foreign doctors who would benefit from this legislation.

"In order to find Mr. McCormick guilty of extortion, you must be convinced beyond a reasonable doubt that the payment alleged in a given count of the indictment was made by or on behalf of the doctors with the expectation that such payment would influence Mr. McCormick's official conduct, and with knowledge on the part of Mr. McCormick that they were paid to him with that expectation by virtue of the office he held."

The jury convicted McCormick of the first Hobbs Act count (charging him with receiving the initial $900 cash payment) and the income tax violation but could not reach verdicts on the remaining four Hobbs Act counts. The District Court declared a mistrial on those four counts.

The Court of Appeals affirmed [McCormick's two convictions]. Because of disagreement in the Courts of Appeals regarding the meaning of the phrase "under color of official right" as it is used in the Hobbs Act,[5] we granted certiorari. We reverse and remand for further proceedings.

[5] Until the early 1970's, extortion prosecutions under the Hobbs Act rested on allegations that the consent of the transferor of property had been "induced by wrongful use of actual or threatened force, violence, or fear—"; public officials had not been prosecuted under the "color of official right" phrase standing alone. Beginning with the conviction involved in United States v. Kenny, 462 F.2d 1205 (3d Cir.1972), however, the federal courts accepted the government's submission that because of the disjunctive language of § 1951(b)(2), allegations of force, violence or fear were not necessary. Only proof of the obtaining of property under claims of official right was necessary. Furthermore, every Court of Appeals to have construed the phrase held that it did not require a showing that the public official "induced" the payor's consent by some affirmative act such as a demand or solicitation. Although there was some difference in the language of these holdings, the "color of official right" element required no more than proof of the payee's acceptance knowing that the payment was made for the purpose of influencing his official actions.

In 1984, however, the Court of Appeals for the Second Circuit, en banc, held that some affirmative act of inducement by the official had to be shown to prove the government's case. United States v. O'Grady, 742 F.2d 682 (1984). In 1988, the Ninth Circuit, en banc, agreed with the Second Circuit, overruling a prior decision expressing the majority rule. United States v. Aguon, 851 F.2d 1158 (1988). Other courts have been unimpressed with the view expressed in O'Grady and Aguon. See, e.g., United States v. Evans, 910 F.2d 790 (11th Cir.1990), cert. pending....

The conflict on this issue is clear, but this case is not the occasion to resolve it. The trial court instructed that proof of inducement was essential to the government's case, but stated that the requirement could be satisfied by showing the receipt of money by McCormick knowing that it was proffered with the expectation of benefit and on account of his office, proof that would be inadequate under the O'Grady view of inducement. McCormick did not challenge this instruction in the trial court or the Court of Appeals; nor does he here.

We do address, however, the issue of what proof is necessary to show that the receipt of a campaign contribution by an elected official is violative of the Hobbs Act. The trial court and the Court of Appeals were of the view that it was unnecessary to prove that, in exchange for a campaign contribution, the official specifically promised to perform or not to perform an act incident to his office. Other Courts of Appeals appear to require proof of a quid pro quo. [See, e.g.,] United States v. Dozier, 672 F.2d 531 (5th Cir.1982).

Justice Stevens in dissent makes the bald assertion that "[i]t is perfectly clear ... that the evidence presented to the jury was adequate to prove beyond a reasonable doubt that petitioner knowingly used his public office to make or imply promises or threats to his constituents for purposes of pressuring

II

McCormick's challenge to the judgment below affirming his conviction is limited to the Court of Appeals' rejection of his claim that the payments made to him by or on behalf of the doctors were campaign contributions, the receipt of which did not violate the Hobbs Act. Except for a belated claim not properly before us,[6] McCormick does not challenge any rulings of the courts below with respect to the application of the Hobbs Act to payments made to nonelected officials or to payments made to elected officials that are properly determined not to be campaign contributions. Hence, we do not consider how the "under color of official right" phrase is to be interpreted and applied in those contexts. In two respects, however, we agree with McCormick that the Court of Appeals erred.

A

First, we are quite sure that the Court of Appeals affirmed the conviction on legal and factual grounds that were never submitted to the jury. Although McCormick challenged the adequacy of the jury instructions to distinguish between campaign contributions and payments that are illegal under the Hobbs Act, the Court of Appeals' opinion did not examine or mention the instructions given by the trial court. The court neither dealt with McCormick's submission that the instructions were too confusing to give adequate guidance to the jury, nor, more specifically, with the argument that although the jury was instructed that voluntary campaign contributions were not vulnerable under the Hobbs Act, the word "voluntary" as used "in several places during the course of these instructions," was defined as "that which is freely given without expectation of benefit." Neither did the Court of Appeals note that the jury was not instructed in accordance with the court's holding that the difference between legitimate and illegitimate campaign contributions was to be determined by the

them to make payments that were not lawfully due him." Contrary to Justice Stevens' apparent suggestion, the main issue throughout this case has been whether under proper instructions the evidence established a Hobbs Act violation and, as our opinion indicates, it is far from "perfectly clear" that the government has met its burden in this regard.

[6] In briefing the merits in this Court, McCormick has argued that the Hobbs Act was never intended to apply to corruption involving local officials and that in any event an official has not acted under color of official right unless he falsely represents that by virtue of his office he has a legal right to the money or property he receives. These arguments were not presented to the courts below. They are not expressly among the questions presented in the petition for certiorari and are only arguably subsumed by the questions presented. Nor in view of the language

of the Hobbs Act and the many cases approving the conviction of local officials under the act can it be said that plain error occurred in the lower courts for failure to recognize that the act was inapplicable to the extortion charges brought against McCormick. As for the false-pretenses argument, [several Courts of Appeals] have rejected the claim and many other convictions have been affirmed where it is plain that there was no misrepresentation of legal right. In view of these cases and the origin of the phrase "under color of official right", see James Lindgren, The Elusive Distinction Between Bribery and Extortion: From the Common Law to the Hobbs Act, 35 U.C.L.A. L. Rev. 815 (1988), no plain error occurred below in failing to interpret the phrase as McCormick argues. Accordingly, the submission does not comply with our rules, is untimely, and we do not address it further.

intention of the parties after considering specified factors.[7] Instead, the Court of Appeals, after announcing a rule of law for determining when payments are made under color of official right, went on to find sufficient evidence in the record to support findings that McCormick was extorting money from the doctors for his continued support of the 1985 legislation, and further that the parties never intended any of the payments to be a campaign contribution.

It goes without saying that matters of intent are for the jury to consider. It is also plain that each of the seven factors that the Court of Appeals thought should be considered in determining the parties' intent presents an issue of historical fact. Thus even assuming the Court of Appeals was correct on the law, the conviction should not have been affirmed on that basis but should have been set aside and a new trial ordered. If for no other reason, therefore, the judgment of the Court of Appeals must be reversed and the case remanded for further proceedings.[8]

B

We agree with the Court of Appeals that in a case like this it is proper to inquire whether payments made to an elected official are in fact campaign contributions, and we agree that the intention of the parties is a relevant consideration in pursuing this inquiry. But we cannot accept the Court of Appeals' approach to distinguishing between legal and illegal campaign contributions. The Court of Appeals stated that payments to elected officials could violate the Hobbs Act without proof of an explicit quid pro quo by proving that the payments "were never intended to be *legitimate* campaign contributions" (emphasis added).[9] This issue, as we

[7] "Some of the circumstances that should be considered in making this determination include, but are not limited to, (1) whether the money was recorded by the payor as a campaign contribution, (2) whether the money was recorded and reported by the official as a campaign contribution, (3) whether the payment was in cash, (4) whether it was delivered to the official personally or to his campaign, (5) whether the official acted in his official capacity at or near the time of the payment for the benefit of the payor or supported legislation that would benefit the payor, (6) whether the official had supported similar legislation before the time of the payment, and (7) whether the official had directly or indirectly solicited the payor individually for the payment."

[8] Justice Stevens apparently refuses to recognize that the Court of Appeals affirmed McCormick's conviction on legal and factual theories never tried to the jury. As indicated above, for that reason alone, and without dealing with the Court of Appeals' other er-

rors, the judgment must be reversed. [I]n a criminal case a defendant is constitutionally entitled to have the issue of criminal liability determined by a jury in the first instance. ... This Court has never held that the right to a jury trial is satisfied when an appellate court retries a case on appeal under different instructions and on a different theory than was ever presented to the jury. Appellate courts are not permitted to affirm convictions on any theory they please simply because the facts necessary to support the theory were presented to the jury.

[9] The record shows that McCormick did not ask for an instruction to the effect that proof of an explicit quid pro quo was necessary to convict an elected official under the Hobbs Act for extorting a campaign contribution. Indeed, at one point McCormick's counsel stated that there was no such requirement. ... In the Court of Appeals, however, McCormick argued that such an undertaking by the official was essential. The Court of Appeals chose to address the

read the Court of Appeals' opinion, actually involved two inquiries; for after applying the factors the Court of Appeals considered relevant, it arrived at two conclusions: first, that McCormick was extorting money for his continued support of the 1985 legislation and "[f]urther," that the money was never intended by the parties to be a campaign contribution at all. The first conclusion, especially when considered in light of the second, asserts that the campaign contributions were illegitimate, extortionate payments.

This conclusion was necessarily based on the factors that the court considered, the first four of which could not possibly by themselves amount to extortion. Neither could they when considered with the last three more telling factors, namely, whether the official acted in his official capacity at or near the time of the payment for the benefit of the payor; whether the official had supported legislation before the time of the payment; and whether the official had directly or indirectly solicited the payor individually for the payment. Even assuming that the result of each of these seven inquiries was unfavorable to McCormick, as they very likely were in the Court of Appeals' view, we cannot agree that a violation of the Hobbs Act would be made out, as the Court of Appeals' first conclusion asserted.

Serving constituents and supporting legislation that will benefit the district and individuals and groups therein is the everyday business of a legislator. It is also true that campaigns must be run and financed. Money is constantly being solicited on behalf of candidates, who run on platforms and who claim support on the basis of their views and what they intend to do or have done. Whatever ethical considerations and appearances may indicate, to hold that legislators commit the federal crime of extortion when they act for the benefit of constituents or support legislation furthering the interests of some of their constituents, shortly before or after campaign contributions are solicited and received from those beneficiaries, is an unrealistic assessment of what Congress could have meant by making it a crime to obtain property from another, with his consent, "under color of official right." To hold otherwise would open to prosecution not only conduct that has long been thought to be well within the law but also conduct that in a very real sense is unavoidable so long as election campaigns are financed by private contributions or expenditures, as they have been from the beginning of the Nation. It would require statutory language more explicit than the Hobbs Act contains to justify a contrary conclusion. Cf. United States v. Enmons, 410 U.S. 396 (1973).

This is not to say that it is impossible for an elected official to commit extortion in the course of financing an election campaign. Political contributions are of course vulnerable if induced by the use of force, violence, or fear. The receipt of such contributions is also vulnerable under the act as having been taken under color of official right, but only if the payments are made in return for an explicit promise or undertaking by the official to

submission and, as we understand it, rejected it. The issue is fairly subsumed in the questions presented here and is argued in the briefs. Hence, we reach and decide the question.

perform or not to perform an official act. In such situations the official asserts that his official conduct will be controlled by the terms of the promise or undertaking. This is the receipt of money by an elected official under color of official right within the meaning of the Hobbs Act.

This formulation defines the forbidden zone of conduct with sufficient clarity. As the Court of Appeals for the Fifth Circuit observed in United States v. Dozier, 672 F.2d 531, 537 (1982): "A moment's reflection should enable one to distinguish, at least in the abstract, a legitimate solicitation from the exaction of a fee for a benefit conferred or an injury withheld. Whether described familiarly as a payoff or with the Latinate precision of quid pro quo, the prohibited exchange is the same: a public official may not demand payment as inducement for the promise to perform (or not to perform) an official act."

The United States agrees that if the payments to McCormick were campaign contributions, proof of a quid pro quo would be essential for an extortion conviction, and quotes the instruction given on this subject in Department of Justice Manual § 9–85A.306: "campaign contributions will not be authorized as the subject of a Hobbs Act prosecution unless they can be proven to have been given in return for the performance of or abstaining from an official act; otherwise any campaign contribution might constitute a violation."

We thus disagree with the Court of Appeals' holding in this case that a quid pro quo is not necessary for conviction under the Hobbs Act when an official receives a campaign contribution.[10] By the same token, we hold, as McCormick urges, that the District Court's instruction to the same effect was error.

III

The government nevertheless insists that a properly instructed jury in this case found that the payment at issue was not a campaign contribution at all and that the evidence amply supports this finding. The instructions given here are not a model of clarity, and it is true that the trial court instructed that the receipt of voluntary campaign contributions did not violate the Hobbs Act. But under the instructions a contribution was not "voluntary" if given with any expectation of benefit; and as we read the instructions, taken as a whole, the jury was told that it could find McCormick guilty of extortion if any of the payments, even though a campaign contribution, was made by the doctors with the expectation that McCormick's official action would be influenced for their benefit and if McCormick knew that the payment was made with that expectation. It may be that the jury found that none of the payments was a campaign contribution, but it is mere speculation that the jury convicted on this basis rather than on the impermissible basis that even though the first payment

---

[10] As noted previously, McCormick's sole contention in this case is that the payments made to him were campaign contributions. Therefore, we do not decide whether a quid pro quo requirement exists in other contexts, such as when an elected official receives gifts, meals, travel expenses, or other items of value.

was such a contribution, McCormick's receipt of it was a violation of the Hobbs Act.

The United States submits that McCormick's conviction on the tax count plainly shows that the jury found that the first payment was not a campaign contribution. Again, we disagree, for the instruction on the tax count told the jury, among other things, that if the money McCormick received "constituted voluntary political contributions ... it was ... not taxable income," and failure to report it was not illegal. The jury must have understood "voluntary" to mean what the Court had said it meant, i.e., as "that which is freely given without expectation of benefit." The jury might well have found that the payments were campaign contributions but not voluntary because they were given with an expectation of benefit. They might have inferred from this fact, although they were not instructed to do so, that the payments were taxable even though they were contributions. Furthermore, the jury was instructed that if it found that McCormick did not use the money for campaign expenses or to reimburse himself for such expenses, then the payments given him by the doctors were taxable income even if the jury found that the doctors intended the payments to be campaign contributions. Contrary to the government's contention, therefore, by no means was the jury required to determine that the payments from the doctors to McCormick were not campaign contributions before it could convict on the tax count. The extortion conviction cannot be saved on this theory.

IV

The Court of Appeals affirmed McCormick's conviction for filing a false return on the sole ground that the jury's finding that McCormick violated the Hobbs Act "under these facts implicitly indicates that it rejected his attempts to characterize at least the initial payment as a campaign contribution." This conclusion repeats the error made in affirming the extortion conviction. The Court of Appeals did not examine the record in light of the instructions given the jury on the extortion charge but considered the evidence in light of its own standard under which it found that the payments were not campaign contributions. Had the court focused on the instructions actually given at trial, it would have been obvious that the jury could have convicted McCormick of the tax charge even though it was convinced that the payments were campaign contributions but was also convinced that the money was received knowing that it was given with an expectation of benefit and hence was extorted. The extortion conviction does not demonstrate that the payments were not campaign contributions and hence taxable.

Of course, the fact that the Court of Appeals erred in affirming the extortion conviction and erred in relying on that conviction in affirming the tax conviction does not necessarily exhaust the possible grounds for affirming on the tax count. But the Court of Appeals did not consider the verdict on that count in light of the instructions thereon and then decide whether, in the absence of the Hobbs Act conviction, McCormick was properly convicted for filing a false income tax return. That option will be open on remand.

V

Accordingly we reverse the judgment of the Court of Appeals and remand for further proceedings consistent with this opinion.

So ordered.

JUSTICE SCALIA, concurring.

I agree with the Court's conclusion and, given the assumption on which this case was briefed and argued, with the reasons the Court assigns. If the prohibition of the Hobbs Act, 18 U.S.C. § 1951, against receipt of money "under color of official right" includes receipt of money from a private source for the performance of official duties, that ambiguously described crime assuredly need not, and for the reasons the Court discusses should not, be interpreted to cover campaign contributions with anticipation of favorable future action, as opposed to campaign contributions in exchange for an explicit promise of favorable future action.

I find it unusual and unsettling, however, to make such a distinction without any hint of a justification in the statutory text: § 1951 contains not even a colorable allusion to campaign contributions or quid pro quos. I find it doubly unsettling because there is another interpretation of § 1951, contrary to the one that has been the assumption of argument here, that would render the distinction unnecessary. While I do not feel justified in adopting that interpretation without briefing and argument, neither do I feel comfortable giving tacit approval to the assumption that contradicts it. I write, therefore, a few words concerning the text of this statute, and the history that has produced the unexamined assumption underlying our opinion.

Section 1951(a) provides: "Whoever in any way or degree obstructs, delays, or affects commerce or the movement of any article or commodity in commerce, by robbery or extortion ... shall be fined not more than $10,000 or imprisoned not more than twenty years, or both." Section 1951(b)(2) defines "extortion" as "the obtaining of property from another, with his consent, induced by wrongful use of actual or threatened force, violence, or fear, or under color of official right." The relevant provisions were enacted as part of the Anti–Racketeering Act of 1934, and were carried forward without change in the Hobbs Act of 1948. For more than 30 years after enactment, there is no indication that they were applied to the sort of conduct alleged here.

When, in the 1960's, it first occurred to federal prosecutors to use the Hobbs Act to reach what was essentially the soliciting of bribes by state officials, courts were unimpressed with the notion. They thought that public officials were not guilty of extortion when they accepted, or even when they requested, voluntary payments designed to influence or procure their official action. Not until 1972 did any court apply the Hobbs Act to bribery. See United States v. Kenny, 462 F.2d 1205, 1229 (3d

Cir.1972)("kickbacks" by construction contractors to public officials established extortion "under color of official right," despite absence of "threat, fear, or duress"). That holding was soon followed by the Seventh Circuit in United States v. Braasch, 505 F.2d 139, 151 (1974), which said that "[s]o long as the motivation for the payment focuses on the recipient's office, the conduct falls within the ambit of 18 U.S.C. § 1951." While *Kenny*, *Braasch*, and subsequent cases were debated in academic writing, compare Charles F.C. Ruff, Federal Prosecution of Local Corruption: A Case Study in the Making of Law Enforcement Policy, 65 Geo. L.J. 1171 (1977)(criticizing *Kenny*), with James Lindgren, The Elusive Distinction between Bribery and Extortion: From the Common Law to the Hobbs Act, 35 U.C.L.A. L. Rev. 815 (1988)(defending *Kenny*), the Courts of Appeals accepted the expansion with little disagreement, and this Court has never had occasion to consider the matter.

It is acceptance of the assumption that "under color of official right" means "on account of one's office" that brings bribery cases within the statute's reach, and that creates the necessity for the reasonable but textually inexplicable distinction the Court makes today. That assumption is questionable. "The obtaining of property . . . under color of official right" more naturally connotes some false assertion of official entitlement to the property. This interpretation might have the effect of making the § 1951 definition of extortion comport with the definition of "extortion" at common law. One treatise writer, describing "extortion by a public officer," states: "At common law it was essential that the money or property be obtained under color of office, that is, under the pretense that the officer was entitled thereto by virtue of his office. The money or thing received must have been claimed or accepted in right of office, and the person paying must have yielded to official authority." 3 R. Anderson, Wharton's Criminal Law and Procedure 790–91 (1957).

It also appears to be the case that under New York law, which has long contained identical "under color of official right" language and upon which the Hobbs Act is said to have been based, see Ruff, supra, at 1183, bribery and extortion were separate offenses. An official charged with extortion could defend on the ground that the payment was voluntary and thus he was guilty only of bribery. People v. Feld, 262 A.D. 909 (Sup. Ct. 1941). I am aware of only one pre-Hobbs Act New York prosecution involving extortion "under color of official right," and there the defendant, a justice of the peace, had extracted a payment from a litigant on the false ground that it was due him as a court fee. People v. Whaley, 6 Cow. (N.Y.) 661, 661–63 (Sup. Ct. 1827).

Finally, where the United States Code explicitly criminalizes conduct such as that alleged in the present case, it calls the crime bribery, not extortion—and like all bribery laws I am aware of (but unlike § 1951 and all other extortion laws I am aware of) it punishes not only the person receiving the payment but the person making it. See 18 U.S.C. § 201(b) (criminalizing bribery of and by federal officials).[1] Compare 18 U.S.C. § 872 (criminalizing extortion by federal officials, making no provision for punishment of person extorted). McCormick, though not a federal official, is subject to federal prosecution for bribery under the Travel Act, 18 U.S.C. § 1952, which criminalizes the use of interstate commerce for purposes of bribery—and reaches, of course, both the person giving and the person receiving the bribe.

I mean only to raise this argument, not to decide it, for it has not been advanced and there may be persuasive responses. See, e.g., Lindgren, supra, at 837–89 (arguing that under early common law bribery and extortion were not separate offenses and that extortion did not require proof of a coerced payment). But unexamined assumptions have a way of becoming, by force of usage, unsound law. Before we are asked to go further down the road of making reasonable but textually unapparent distinctions in a federal "payment for official action" statute—as we unquestionably will be asked, see ante n. 5—I think it well to bear in mind that the statute may not exist.

JUSTICE STEVENS, with whom JUSTICE BLACKMUN and JUSTICE O'CONNOR join, dissenting.

An error in a trial judge's instructions to the jury is not ground for reversal unless the defendant has made, and preserved, a specific objection to the particular instruction in question. Rule 30 of the Federal Rules of Criminal Procedure provides, in part: "No party may assign as error any portion of the charge or omission therefrom unless that party objects thereto before the jury retires to consider its verdict, stating distinctly the matter to which that party objects and the grounds of the objection."

This Court's disapproval of portions of the reasoning in the Court of Appeals' opinion is not a sufficient ground for reversing its judgment. It is perfectly clear that the indictment charged a violation of the Hobbs Act and that the evidence presented to the jury was adequate to prove beyond a reasonable doubt that petitioner knowingly used his public office to make or imply promises or threats to his constituents for purposes of pressuring them to make payments that were not lawfully due him. Apart from its criticism of the Court of Appeals' opinion, the Court's reversal of petitioner's conviction, in the final analysis, rests on its view that the jury instructions were incomplete because they did not adequately define the concept of "voluntary" contribution in distinguishing such contributions from extorted payments, and because the instructions did not require proof

---

[1] Section 201(b)(2) prescribes penalties for anyone who "being a public official or person selected to be a public official, directly or indirectly, corruptly demands, seeks, receives, accepts, or agrees to receive or accept anything of value personally or for any other person or entity, in return for: (A) being influenced in performance of any official act; (B) being influenced to commit or aid in committing, or to collude in, or allow, any fraud, or make opportunity for the commission of any fraud on the United States; or (C) being induced to do or omit to do any act in violation of the official duty of such official or person." Section 201(b)(1) provides penalties for anyone who "corruptly gives, offers or promises anything of value to any public official or person who has been selected to be a public official" for the same three purposes.

that petitioner made an "explicit" promise (or threat) in exchange for a campaign contribution. In my opinion the instructions were adequate and, in any event, to the extent that they were ambiguous, petitioner failed to preserve a proper objection.

In the Court of Appeals, petitioner argued that his conviction under the Hobbs Act was not supported by sufficient evidence. In reviewing such a contention, the appellate court must, of course, view the evidence in the light "most favorable to the government." Glasser v. United States, 315 U.S. 60, 80 (1942). So viewed, it is perfectly clear that petitioner could properly have been found by the jury to be guilty of extortion.

Petitioner's crime was committed in two stages. Toward the end of May 1984, petitioner held an "unfriendly" conversation with Vandergrift, the representative of the unlicensed doctors, which the jury could have interpreted as an implied threat to take no action on the licensing legislation unless he received a cash payment as well as an implicit promise to support the legislation if an appropriate cash payment was made. Because the statute applies equally to the wrongful use of political power by a public official as to the wrongful use of threatened violence, that inducement was comparable to a known thug's offer to protect a storekeeper against the risk of severe property damage in exchange for a cash consideration. Neither the legislator nor the thug needs to make an explicit threat or an explicit promise to get his message across.

The extortion was completed on June 1, 1984, when Vandergrift personally delivered an envelope containing nine $100 bills to petitioner. The fact that the payment was not reported as a campaign contribution, as required by West Virginia law, or as taxable income, as required by federal law, together with other circumstantial evidence, adequately supports the conclusion that the money was intended as a payment to petitioner personally to induce him to act favorably on the licensing legislation. His covert acceptance of the cash—indeed, his denial at trial that he received any such payment—supports the conclusion that petitioner understood the payers' intention and that he had implicitly (at least) promised to provide them with the benefit that they sought.

As I understand its opinion, the Court would agree that these facts would constitute a violation of the Hobbs Act if the understanding that the money was a personal payment rather than a campaign contribution had been explicit rather than implicit and if the understanding that, in response to the payment, petitioner would endeavor to provide the payers with the specific benefit they sought had also been explicit rather than implicit. In my opinion there is no statutory requirement that illegal agreements, threats, or promises be in writing, or in any particular form. Subtle extortion is just as wrongful—and probably much more common—than the kind of express understanding that the Court's opinion seems to require.

Nevertheless, to prove a violation of the Hobbs Act, I agree with the Court that it is essential that the payment in question be contingent on a mutual understanding that the motivation for the payment is the payer's desire to avoid a specific threatened harm or to obtain a promised benefit that the defendant has the apparent power to deliver, either through the use of force or the use of public office. In this sense, the crime does require a "quid pro quo." Because the use of the Latin term "quid pro quo "tends to confuse the analysis, however, it is important to clarify the sense in which the term was used in the District Court's instructions.

As I have explained, the crime of extortion was complete when petitioner accepted the cash pursuant to an understanding that he would not carry out his earlier threat to withhold official action and instead would go forward with his contingent promise to take favorable action on behalf of the unlicensed physicians. What he did thereafter might have evidentiary significance, but could neither undo a completed crime or complete an uncommitted offense. When petitioner took the money, he was either guilty or not guilty. For that reason, proof of a subsequent quid pro quo— his actual support of the legislation—was not necessary for the government's case. And conversely, evidence that petitioner would have supported the legislation anyway is not a defense to the already completed crime. The thug who extorts protection money cannot defend on the ground that his threat was only a bluff because he would not have smashed the shopkeeper's windows even if the extortion had been unsuccessful. It was in this sense that the District Court correctly advised the jury that the government did not have to prove the delivery of a postpayment quid pro quo. ...

This Court's criticism of the District Court's instructions focuses on this single sentence: "Voluntary is that which is freely given without expectation of benefit." The Court treats this sentence as though it authorized the jury to find that a legitimate campaign contribution is involuntary and constitutes extortion whenever the contributor expects to benefit from the candidate's election. In my opinion this is a gross misreading of that sentence in the context of the entire set of instructions.

In context, the sentence in question advised the jury that a payment is voluntary if it is made without the expectation of a benefit that is specifically contingent upon the payment. An expectation that the donor will benefit from the election of a candidate who, once in office, would support particular legislation regardless of whether or not the contribution is made, would not make the payment contingent or involuntary in that sense; such a payment would be "voluntary" under a fair reading of the instructions, and the candidate's solicitation of such contributions from donors who would benefit from his or her election is perfectly legitimate. If, however, the donor and candidate know that the candidate's support of the proposed legislation is contingent upon the payment, the contribution may be found by a jury to have been involuntary or extorted.

In my judgment, the instructions, read as a whole, properly focused the jury's attention on the critical issue of the candidate's and contributor's intent at the time the specific payment was made. But even if they were ambiguous, or subject to improvement, they certainly do not provide a basis for reversing the conviction when the petitioner failed to advise the District Court of an error this Court now believes it has detected.

In the Court of Appeals, petitioner did not argue that any specific instruction was erroneous or that the District Court erred by refusing to give any instruction that petitioner had tendered. Nor, at trial, did petitioner request the judge to instruct the jury that any promise or threat in exchange for the payment had to be explicit or to clarify the meaning of a "voluntary" contribution as distinguished from an illegally induced payment. In fact, the District Court's instruction that a finding that an "implicit promise of fair treatment" on the part of petitioner in exchange for the contribution would support a Hobbs Act conviction came in part from petitioner's tendered instructions at trial.

Given that the District Court's instructions to the jury largely tracked the instructions requested by petitioner at trial, I can see no legitimate reason for this Court now to find these instructions inadequate. Because I am convinced that the petitioner was fairly tried and convicted by a properly instructed jury, I would affirm the judgment of the Court of Appeals. Of course, an affirmance of the Court of Appeals' judgment would not mean that we necessarily affirm the Court of Appeals' opinion. It is sufficient that an affirmance of McCormick's conviction rests on the legal and factual theories actually presented to the jury, whether or not these theories were the ones relied upon by the Court of Appeals.

I respectfully dissent.

Evans v. United States

Supreme Court of the United States, 1992.
504 U.S. 255.

■ JUSTICE STEVENS delivered the opinion of the Court.

We granted certiorari to resolve a conflict in the Circuits over the question whether an affirmative act of inducement by a public official, such as a demand, is an element of the offense of extortion "under color of official right" prohibited by the Hobbs Act, 18 U.S.C. § 1951. We agree with the Court of Appeals for the 11th Circuit that it is not, and therefore affirm the judgment of the court below.

I

Petitioner was an elected member of the Board of Commissioners of DeKalb County, Georgia. During the period between March 1985 and October 1986, as part of an effort by the Federal Bureau of Investigation (FBI) to investigate allegations of public corruption in the Atlanta area, particularly in the area of rezonings of property, an FBI agent posing as a real estate developer talked on the telephone and met with petitioner on a number of occasions. Virtually all, if not all, of those conversations were initiated by the agent and most were recorded on tape or video. In those conversations, the agent sought petitioner's assistance in an effort to rezone a 25–acre tract of land for high-density residential use. On July 25, 1986, the agent handed petitioner cash totaling $7,000 and a check, payable to petitioner's campaign, for $1,000. Petitioner reported the check, but not the cash, on his state campaign-financing disclosure form; he also did not report the $7,000 on his 1986 federal income tax return. Viewing the evidence in the light most favorable to the government, as we must in light of the verdict, we assume that the jury found that petitioner accepted the cash knowing that it was intended to ensure that he would vote in favor of the rezoning application and that he would try to persuade his fellow commissioners to do likewise. Thus, although petitioner did not initiate the transaction, his acceptance of the bribe constituted an implicit promise to use his official position to serve the interests of the bribe-giver.

In a two-count indictment, petitioner was charged with extortion in violation of 18 U.S.C. § 1951 and with failure to report income in violation of 26 U.S.C. § 7206(1). He was convicted by a jury on both counts. With respect to the extortion count, the trial judge gave the following instruction:

> "The defendant contends that the $8,000 he received from agent Cormany was a campaign contribution. The solicitation of campaign contributions from any person is a necessary and permissible form of political activity on the part of persons who seek political office and persons who have been elected to political office. Thus, the acceptance by an elected official of a campaign contribution does not, in itself, constitute a violation of the Hobbs Act even though the donor has business pending before the official.

> "However, if a public official demands or accepts money in exchange for [a] specific requested exercise of his or her official power, such a demand or acceptance does constitute a violation of the Hobbs Act regardless of whether the payment is made in the form of a campaign contribution."

In affirming petitioner's conviction, the Court of Appeals noted that the instruction did not require the jury to find that petitioner had demanded or requested the money, or that he had conditioned the performance of any official act upon its receipt. The Court of Appeals held, however, that "passive acceptance of a benefit by a public official is sufficient to form the basis of a Hobbs Act violation if the official knows that he is being offered the payment in exchange for a specific requested exercise of his official power. The official need not take any specific action to induce the offering of the benefit."[1]

This statement of the law by the Court of Appeals for the 11th Circuit is consistent with holdings in eight other Circuits. Two Circuits, however,

[1] The Court of Appeals explained its conclusion as follows: "[T]he requirement of inducement is automatically satisfied by the power connected with the public office. Therefore, once the defendant has shown that a public official has accepted money in return for a requested exercise of official power, no additional inducement need be shown. 'The coercive nature of the official office provides all the inducement necessary.'"

have held that an affirmative act of inducement by the public official is required to support a conviction of extortion under color of official right. United States v. O'Grady, 742 F.2d 682, 687 (2d Cir.1984)(en banc)("Although receipt of benefits by a public official is a necessary element of the crime, there must also be proof that the public official did something, under color of his public office, to cause the giving of benefits"); United States v. Aguon, 851 F.2d 1158, 1166 (9th Cir.1988)(en banc)("We find ourselves in accord with the Second Circuit's conclusion that inducement is an element required for conviction under the Hobbs Act"). Because the majority view is consistent with the common-law definition of extortion, which we believe Congress intended to adopt, we endorse that position.

II

It is a familiar "maxim that a statutory term is generally presumed to have its common-law meaning." Taylor v. United States, 495 U.S. 575 (1990). As we have explained, "where Congress borrows terms of art in which are accumulated the legal tradition and meaning of centuries of practice, it presumably knows and adopts the cluster of ideas that were attached to each borrowed word in the body of learning from which it was taken and the meaning its use will convey to the judicial mind unless otherwise instructed. In such case, absence of contrary direction may be taken as satisfaction with widely accepted definitions, not as a departure from them." Morissette v. United States, 342 U.S. 246, 263 (1952).[3]

At common law, extortion was an offense committed by a public official who took "by colour of his office"[4] money that was not due to him for the performance of his official duties.[5] A demand, or request, by the public official was not an element of the offense. Extortion by the public official was the rough equivalent of what we would now describe as "taking a

---

[3] Or, as Justice Frankfurter advised, "if a word is obviously transplanted from another legal source, whether the common law or other legislation, it brings the old soil with it." Felix Frankfurter, Some Reflections on the Reading of Statutes, 47 Colum.L.Rev. 527, 537 (1947).

[4] Blackstone described extortion as "an abuse of public justice, which consists in an officer's unlawfully taking, by colour of his office, from any man, any money or thing of value, that is not due to him, or more than is due, or before it is due." 4 W. Blackstone, Commentaries *141. He used the phrase "by colour of his office," rather than the phrase "under color of official right," which appears in the Hobbs Act. Petitioner does not argue that there is any difference in the phrases. Hawkins' definition of extortion is probably the source for the official right language used in the Hobbs Act. See James Lindgren, The

Elusive Distinction Between Bribery and Extortion: From the Common Law to the Hobbs Act, 35 U.C.L.A. L.Rev. 815, 864 (1988)(hereinafter Lindgren). Hawkins defined extortion as follows: "[I]t is said, That extortion in a large sense signifies any oppression under colour of right; but that in a strict sense, it signifies the taking of money by any officer, by colour of his office, either where none at all is due, or not so much is due, or where it is not yet due." 1 W. Hawkins, Pleas of the Crown 316 (6th ed. 1787).

[5] See Lindgren 882–89. The dissent says that we assume that "common law extortion encompassed any taking by a public official of something of value that he was not 'due.'" That statement, of course, is incorrect because, as stated in the text above, the payment must be "for the performance of his official duties."

bribe." It is clear that petitioner committed that offense.[7] The question is whether the federal statute, insofar as it applies to official extortion, has narrowed the common-law definition.

Congress has unquestionably expanded the common-law definition of extortion to include acts by private individuals pursuant to which property is obtained by means of force, fear, or threats. It did so by implication in the Travel Act, 18 U.S.C. § 1952, see United States v. Nardello, 393 U.S. 286 (1969), and expressly in the Hobbs Act. The portion of the Hobbs Act that is relevant to our decision today provides:

> "(a) Whoever in any way or degree obstructs, delays, or affects commerce or the movement of any article or commodity in commerce, by robbery or extortion or attempts or conspires so to do, or commits or threatens physical violence to any person or property in furtherance of a plan or purpose to do anything in violation of this section shall be fined not more than $10,000 or imprisoned not more than twenty years, or both.

> "(b) As used in this section—

> * * *

> "(2) The term 'extortion' means the obtaining of property from another, with his consent, induced by wrongful use of actual or threatened force, violence, or fear, or under color of official right." 18 U.S.C. § 1951.

The present form of the statute is a codification of a 1946 enactment, the Hobbs Act, which amended the federal Anti–Racketeering Act.[9] In crafting the 1934 Act, Congress was careful not to interfere with legitimate activities between employers and employees. The 1946 amendment was

---

[7] Petitioner argued to the jury, at least with respect to the extortion count, that he had been entrapped; however, in light of the jury's verdict on that issue, we must assume that he was predisposed to commit the crime.

[9] Section 2(b) of the 1934 Act read as follows:

"Sec. 2. Any person who, in connection with or in relation to any act in any way or in any degree affecting trade or commerce or any article or commodity moving or about to move in trade or commerce—

* * *

"(b) Obtains the property of another, with his consent, induced by wrongful use of force or fear, or under color of official right."

One of the models for the statute was the New York statute: "Extortion is the obtaining of property from another, or the obtaining the property of a corporation from an officer, agent or employee thereof, with his consent, induced by a wrongful use of force or fear, or under color of official right." Penal Law of 1909, § 850, as amended, Laws of 1917, ch. 518. The other model was the Field Code, a 19th century model code: "Extortion is the obtaining of property from another, with his consent, induced by a wrongful use of force or fear, or under color of official right." Commissioners of the Code, Proposed Penal Code of the State of New York § 613 (1865)(Field Code).

Lindgren points out that according to the Field Code, coercive extortion and extortion by official right are separate offenses..... Lindgren identifies early English statutes and cases to support his contention that official extortion did not require a coercive taking, nor did it under the early American statutes....

intended to encompass the conduct held to be beyond the reach of the 1934 Act by our decision in United States v. Teamsters, 315 U.S. 521 (1942). The amendment did not make any significant change in the section referring to obtaining property "under color of official right" that had been prohibited by the 1934 Act. Rather, Congress intended to broaden the scope of the Anti–Racketeering Act and was concerned primarily with distinguishing between "legitimate" labor activity and labor "racketeering," so as to prohibit the latter while permitting the former.

Although the present statutory text is much broader than the common-law definition of extortion because it encompasses conduct by a private individual as well as conduct by a public official,[13] the portion of the statute that refers to official misconduct continues to mirror the common-law definition. There is nothing in either the statutory text or the legislative history that could fairly be described as a "contrary direction," *Morissette v. United States*, 342 U.S., at 263, from Congress to narrow the scope of the offense.

The legislative history is sparse and unilluminating with respect to the offense of extortion. There is a reference to the fact that the terms "robbery and extortion" had been construed many times by the courts and to the fact that the definitions of those terms were "based on the New York law." 89 Cong.Rec. 3227 (1943)(statement of Rep. Hobbs). In view of the fact that the New York statute applied to a public officer "who asks, or receives, or agrees to receive" unauthorized compensation, N.Y. Penal Code § 557 (1881), the reference to New York law is consistent with an intent to apply the common-law definition. The language of the New York statute quoted above makes clear that extortion could be committed by one who merely received an unauthorized payment. This was the statute that was in force in New York when the Hobbs Act was enacted.

The two courts that have disagreed with the decision to apply the common-law definition have interpreted the word "induced" as requiring a wrongful use of official power that "begins with the public official, not with the gratuitous actions of another." *United States v. O'Grady*, 742 F.2d, at 691; see *United States v. Aguon*, 851 F.2d, at 1166 (" 'inducement' can be in the overt form of a 'demand,' or in a more subtle form such as 'custom' or 'expectation' "). If we had no common-law history to guide our interpretation of the statutory text, that reading would be plausible. For two reasons, however, we are convinced that it is incorrect.

First, we think the word "induced" is a part of the definition of the offense by the private individual, but not the offense by the public official. In the case of the private individual, the victim's consent must be "induced

---

[13] Several states had already defined the offense of extortion broadly enough to include the conduct of the private individual as well as the conduct of the public official. See, e.g., United States v. Nardello, 393 U.S. 286, 289 (1969)("In many states ... the crime of extortion has been statutorily ex- panded to include acts by private individuals under which property is obtained by means of force, fear, or threats"). At least one commentator has argued that at common law, extortion under color of official right could also be committed by a private individual. See Lindgren 875.

by wrongful use of actual or threatened force, violence or fear." In the case of the public official, however, there is no such requirement. The statute merely requires of the public official that he obtain "property from another, with his consent, . . . under color of official right." The use of the word "or" before "under color of official right" supports this reading.[14]

Second, even if the statute were parsed so that the word "induced" applied to the public officeholder, we do not believe the word "induced" necessarily indicates that the transaction must be initiated by the recipient of the bribe. Many of the cases applying the majority rule have concluded that the wrongful acceptance of a bribe establishes all the inducement that the statute requires. They conclude that the coercive element is provided by the public office itself. And even the two courts that have adopted an inducement requirement for extortion under color of official right do not require proof that the inducement took the form of a threat or demand.[17]

Petitioner argues that the jury charge with respect to extortion allowed the jury to convict him on the basis of the "passive acceptance of a contribution."[18] He contends that the instruction did not require the jury

[14] This meaning would, of course, have been completely clear if Congress had inserted the word "either" before its description of the private offense because the word "or" already precedes the description of the public offense. The definition would then read: "The term 'extortion' means the obtaining of property from another, with his consent, either induced by wrongful use of actual or threatened force, violence, or fear, or under color of official right."

[17] Moreover, we note that while the statute does not require that affirmative inducement be proven as a distinct element of the Hobbs Act, there is evidence in the record establishing that petitioner received the money with the understanding that he would use his office to aid the bribe-giver. Petitioner and the agent had several exchanges in which they tried to clarify their understanding with each other. For example, petitioner said to the agent: "I understand both of us are groping . . . for what we need to say to each other. . . . I'm gonna work. Let m[e] tell you I'm gonna work, if you didn't give me but three [thousand dollars], on this, I've promised to help you. I'm gonna work to do that. You understand what I mean. . . . If you gave me six, I'll do exactly what I said I was gonna do for you. If you gave me one, I'll do exactly what I said I was gonna do for you. I wanna make sure you're clear on that part. So it doesn't really matter. If I promised to help, that's what I'm gonna do." Petitioner instructed the agent on the form of the payment ("What you do, is make me out one, ahh, for a thousand. . . . And, and that means we gonna record it and report it and then the rest would be cash"), and agreed with the agent that the payment was being made, not because it was an election year, but because there was a budget to support petitioner's actions, and that there would be a budget either way ("Either way, yep. Oh, I understand that. I understand").

[18] Petitioner also makes the point that "[t]he evidence at trial against [petitioner] is more conducive to a charge of bribery than one of extortion." Brief for Petitioner 40. Although the evidence in this case may have supported a charge of bribery, it is not a defense to a charge of extortion under color of official right that the defendant could also have been convicted of bribery. Courts addressing extortion by force or fear have occasionally said that extortion and bribery are mutually exclusive, see, e.g., People v. Feld, 262 App. Div. 909 (1941); while that may be correct when the victim was intimidated into making a payment (extortion by force or fear), and did not offer it voluntarily (bribery), that does not lead to the conclusion that extortion under color of official right and bribery are mutually exclusive under either common law or the Hobbs Act. See, e.g., Herbert Stern, Prosecutions of Local Political Corruption Under the Hobbs Act: The Unnecessary Distinction Between Bribery and Extortion, 3 Seton Hall L.Rev. 1, 14 (1971)("If the [Hobbs] Act is read in full, the

to find "an element of duress such as a demand," and it did not properly describe the quid pro quo requirement for conviction if the jury found that the payment was a campaign contribution.

We reject petitioner's criticism of the instruction, and conclude that it satisfies the quid pro quo requirement of McCormick v. United States, 500 U.S. 257 (1991), because the offense is completed at the time when the public official receives a payment in return for his agreement to perform specific official acts; fulfillment of the quid pro quo is not an element of the offense. We also reject petitioner's contention that an affirmative step is an element of the offense of extortion "under color of official right" and need be included in the instruction.[19] As we explained above, our construction of the statute is informed by the common-law tradition from which the term of art was drawn and understood. We hold today that the government need only show that a public official has obtained a payment to which he was not entitled, knowing that the payment was made in return for official acts.[20]

Our conclusion is buttressed by the fact that so many other courts that have considered the issue over the last 20 years have interpreted the statute in the same way. Moreover, given the number of appellate court decisions, together with the fact that many of them have involved prosecutions of important officials well known in the political community, it is obvious that Congress is aware of the prevailing view that common-law extortion is proscribed by the Hobbs Act. The silence of the body that is empowered to give us a "contrary direction" if it does not want the common-law rule to survive is consistent with an application of the normal presumption identified in *Morissette*, supra.

III

An argument not raised by petitioner is now advanced by the dissent. It contends that common-law extortion was limited to wrongful takings under a false pretense of official right. It is perfectly clear, however, that although extortion accomplished by fraud was a well-recognized type of extortion, there were other types as well. As the court explained in Commonwealth v. Wilson, 30 Pa. Super. 26 (1906), an extortion case involving a payment by a would-be brothel owner to a police captain to ensure the opening of her house: "The form of extortion most commonly

distinction between bribery and extortion becomes unnecessary where public officials are involved"). ... We agree with the Seventh Circuit in United States v. Braasch, 505 F.2d 139, 151, n. 7 (1974), that "the modern trend of the federal courts is to hold that bribery and extortion as used in the Hobbs Act are not mutually exclusive. United States v. Kahn, 472 F.2d 272, 278 (2d Cir.1973)."

[19] We do not reach petitioner's second claim pertaining to the tax fraud count because, as petitioner conceded at oral argu-

ment, we would only have to reach that claim in the event that petitioner succeeded on his Hobbs Act claim.

[20] The dissent states that we have "simply made up" the requirement that the payment must be given in return for official acts. On the contrary, that requirement is derived from the statutory language "under color of official right," which has a well-recognized common-law heritage that distinguished between payments for private services and payments for public services.

dealt with in the decisions is the corrupt taking by a person in office of a fee for services which should be rendered gratuitously; or when compensation is permissible, of a larger fee than the law justifies, or a fee not yet due; but this is not a complete definition of the offense, by which I mean that it does not include every form of common-law extortion.''

The dissent's theory notwithstanding, not one of the cases it cites holds that the public official is innocent unless he has deceived the payor by representing that the payment was proper. Indeed, none makes any reference to the state of mind of the payor, and none states that a ''false pretense'' is an element of the offense. Instead, those cases merely support the proposition that the services for which the fee is paid must be official and that the official must not be entitled to the fee that he collected—both elements of the offense that are clearly satisfied in this case. The complete absence of support for the dissent's thesis presumably explains why it was not advanced by petitioner in the District Court or the Court of Appeals, is not recognized by any Court of Appeals, and is not advanced in any scholarly commentary.

The judgment is affirmed.

It is so ordered.

JUSTICE O'CONNOR, concurring in part and concurring in the judgment.

I join Parts I and II of the Court's opinion, because in my view they correctly answer the question on which the Court granted certiorari—whether or not an act of inducement is an element of the offense of extortion under color of official right. The issue raised by the dissent and discussed in Part III of the Court's opinion is not fairly included in this question, and sound prudential reasons suggest that the Court should not address it. Neither party in this case has briefed or argued the question. A proper resolution of the issue requires a detailed examination of common law extortion cases, which in turn requires intensive historical research. As there appear to be substantial arguments on either side, we would be far more assured of arriving at the correct result were we to await a case in which the issue had been addressed by the parties. It is unfair to the respondent to decide a case on a ground not raised by the petitioner and which the respondent has had no opportunity to address. For these reasons, I join neither the dissent nor Part III of the Court's opinion, and I express no view as to which is correct.

JUSTICE KENNEDY, concurring in part and concurring in the judgment.

The Court gives a summary of its decision in these words: ''We hold today that the government need only show that a public official has obtained a payment to which he was not entitled, knowing that the payment was made in return for official acts.'' In my view the dissent is correct to conclude that this language requires a quid pro quo as an element of the government's case in a prosecution under 18 U.S.C. § 1951, and the Court's opinion can be interpreted in a way that is consistent with this rule. Although the Court appears to accept the requirement of a quid pro quo as an alternative rationale, in my view this element of the offense is essential to a determination of those acts which are criminal and those which are not in a case in which the official does not pretend that he is entitled by law to the property in question. Here the prosecution did establish a quid pro quo that embodied the necessary elements of a statutory violation. I join part III of the Court's opinion and concur in the judgment affirming the conviction. I write this separate opinion to explain my analysis and understanding of the statute.

With regard to the question whether the word "induced" in the statutory definition of extortion applies to the phrase "under color of official right," 18 U.S.C. § 1951(b)(2), I find myself in substantial agreement with the dissent. Scrutiny of the placement of commas will not, in the final analysis, yield a convincing answer, and we are left with two quite plausible interpretations. Under these circumstances, I agree with the dissent that the rule of lenity requires that we avoid the harsher one. We must take as our starting point the assumption that the portion of the statute at issue here defines extortion as "the obtaining of property from another, with his consent, induced ... under color of official right."

I agree with the Court, on the other hand, that the word "induced" does not "necessarily indicat[e] that the transaction must be initiated by the" public official. Something beyond the mere acceptance of property from another is required, however, or else the word "induced" would be superfluous. That something, I submit, is the quid pro quo. The ability of the official to use or refrain from using authority is the "color of official right" which can be invoked in a corrupt way to induce payment of money or to otherwise obtain property. The inducement generates a quid pro quo, under color of official right, that the statute prohibits. The term "under color of" is used, as I think both the Court and the dissent agree, to sweep within the statute those corrupt exercises of authority that the law forbids but that nevertheless cause damage because the exercise is by a governmental official. Cf. Monroe v. Pape, 365 U.S. 167, 184 (1961)(" 'Misuse of power, possessed by virtue of state law and made possible only because the wrongdoer is clothed with the authority of state law, is action taken 'under color of state law' ").

The requirement of a quid pro quo means that without pretense of any entitlement to the payment, a public official violates § 1951 if he intends the payor to believe that absent payment the official is likely to abuse his office and his trust to the detriment and injury of the prospective payor or to give the prospective payor less favorable treatment if the quid pro quo is not satisfied. The official and the payor need not state the quid pro quo in express terms, for otherwise the law's effect could be frustrated by knowing winks and nods. The inducement from the official is criminal if it is express or if it is implied from his words and actions, so long as he intends it to be so and the payor so interprets it.

The criminal law in the usual course concerns itself with motives and consequences, not formalities. And the trier of fact is quite capable of deciding the intent with which words were spoken or actions taken as well as the reasonable construction given to them by the official and the payor.

See McCormick v. United States, 500 U.S. 257, 270 (1991)("It goes without saying that matters of intent are for the jury to consider"). In this respect a prosecution under the statute has some similarities to a contract dispute, with the added and vital element that motive is crucial. For example, a quid pro quo with the attendant corrupt motive can be inferred from an ongoing course of conduct. In such instances, for a public official to commit extortion under color of official right, his course of dealings must establish a real understanding that failure to make a payment will result in the victimization of the prospective payor or the withholding of more favorable treatment, a victimization or withholding accomplished by taking or refraining from taking official action, all in breach of the official's trust. See James Lindgren, The Elusive Distinction Between Bribery and Extortion: From the Common Law to the Hobbs Act, 35 U.C.L.A. L. Rev. 815, 887–88 (1988)(observing that the offense of official extortion has always focused on public corruption).

Thus, I agree with the Court, that the quid pro quo requirement is not simply made up, as the dissent asserts. Instead, this essential element of the offense is derived from the statutory requirement that the official receive payment under color of official right, see n.20, as well as the inducement requirement. And there are additional principles of construction which justify this interpretation. First is the principle that statutes are to be construed so that they are constitutional. As one Court of Appeals Judge who agreed with the construction the Court today adopts noted, "the phrase 'under color of official right,' standing alone, is vague almost to the point of unconstitutionality." *United States v. O'Grady*, supra, at 695 (Van Graafeiland, J., concurring in part and dissenting in part). By placing upon a criminal statute a narrow construction, we avoid the possibility of imputing to Congress an enactment that lacks necessary precision.

Moreover, the mechanism which controls and limits the scope of official right extortion is a familiar one: a state of mind requirement. See Morissette v. United States, 342 U.S. 246 (1952)(refusing to impute to Congress the intent to create a strict liability crime despite the absence of any explicit mens rea requirement in the statute). Hence, even if the quid pro quo requirement did not have firm roots in the statutory language, it would constitute no abuse of judicial power for us to find it by implication.

Morissette legitimates the Court's decision in an additional way. As both the Court and the dissent agree, Congress' choice of the phrase "under color of official right" rather than "by colour of his office" does not reflect a substantive modification of the common law. Instead, both the Court and dissent conclude that the language at issue here must be interpreted in light of the familiar principle that absent any indication otherwise, Congress meant its words to be interpreted in light of the common law. As to the meaning of the common law, I agree with the Court's analysis, and therefore join part III of the Court's opinion.

While the dissent may well be correct that prior to the enactment of the Hobbs Act a large number of the reported official extortion cases in the

United States happened to involve false pretenses, those cases do not so much as hint that a false pretense of right was ever considered as an essential element of the offense. See, e.g., People v. Whaley, 6 Cow. 661, 663–64 (N.Y.Sup.Ct.1827)("Extortion signifies, in an enlarged sense, any oppression under color of right. In a stricter sense, it signifies the taking of money by any officer, by color of his office; either, where none at all is due, or not so much due, or when it is not yet due"); Hanley v. State, 125 Wis. 396, 104 N.W. 57, 59 (1905)("The common-law offense of extortion is said 'to be an abuse of public justice,' which consists in any officer's unlawfully taking by color of his office, from any man, any money or thing of value that is not due him, or more than is due him, or before it is due")(quoting W. Blackstone, 4 Commentaries 141). Furthermore, as the Court demonstrates, during the same period other American courts affirmed convictions of public officials for extortion based upon corrupt receipt of payment absent any claim of right.

Morissette is relevant in one final respect. As I have indicated, and as the jury instructions in this case made clear, an official violates the statute only if he agrees to receive a payment not due him in exchange for an official act, knowing that he is not entitled to the payment. Modern courts familiar with the principle that only a clear congressional statement can create a strict liability offense understand this fundamental limitation. [E]ven if the rule had been otherwise at common law, our modern jurisprudence would require that there be a mens rea requirement now. In short, a public official who labors under the good-faith but erroneous belief that he is entitled to payment for an official act does not violate the statute. That circumstance is not, however, presented here.

The requirement of a quid pro quo in a § 1951 prosecution such as the one before us, in which it is alleged that money was given to the public official in the form of a campaign contribution, was established by our decision last term in McCormick v. United States, 500 U.S. 257 (1991). Readers of today's opinion should have little difficulty in understanding that the rationale underlying the Court's holding applies not only in campaign contribution cases, but all § 1951 prosecutions. That is as it should be, for, given a corrupt motive, the quid pro quo, as I have said, is the essence of the offense.

Because I agree that the jury instruction in this case complied with the quid pro quo requirement, I concur in the judgment of the Court.

JUSTICE THOMAS, with whom CHIEF JUSTICE REHNQUIST and JUSTICE SCALIA join, dissenting.

The Court's analysis is based on the premise, with which I fully agree, that when Congress employs legal terms of art, it " 'knows and adopts the cluster of ideas that were attached to each borrowed word in the body of learning from which it was taken and the meaning its use will convey to the judicial mind.' " (quoting Morissette v. United States, 342 U.S. 246, 263 (1952)). Thus, we presume, Congress knew the meaning of common-law extortion when it enacted the Hobbs Act, 18 U.S.C. § 1951. Unfortunately, today's opinion misapprehends that meaning and misconstrues the statute. I respectfully dissent.

I

Extortion is one of the oldest crimes in Anglo–American jurisprudence. See 3 E. Coke, Institutes *541. Hawkins provides the classic common-law definition: "[I]t is said, that Extortion in a large Sense signifies any Oppression under Colour of Right; but that in a strict Sense it signifies the Taking of Money by any Officer, by Colour of his Office, either where none at all is due, or not so much is due, or where it is not yet due." 1 W. Hawkins, Pleas of the Crown 170 (2d ed. 1724). Blackstone echoed that definition: "[E]xtortion is an abuse of public justice, which consists in any officer's unlawfully taking, by colour of his office, from any man, any money or thing of value, that is not due to him, or more than is due, or before it is due." 4 W. Blackstone, Commentaries on the Laws of England 141 (1769).

These definitions pose, but do not answer, the critical question: what does it mean for an official to take money "by colour of his office"? The Court fails to address this question, simply assuming that common-law extortion encompassed any taking by a public official of something of value that he was not "due."

The "under color of office" element of extortion, however, had a definite and well-established meaning at common law. "At common law it was essential that the money or property be obtained under color of office, that is, under the pretense that the officer was entitled thereto by virtue of his office. The money or thing received must have been claimed or accepted in right of office, and the person paying must have yielded to official authority." 3 R. Anderson, Wharton's Criminal Law and Procedure § 1393, pp. 790–791 (1957). Thus, although the Court purports to define official extortion under the Hobbs Act by reference to the common law, its definition bears scant resemblance to the common-law crime Congress presumably codified in 1946.

A

The Court's historical analysis rests upon a theory set forth in one law review article. See ante, nn. 4–6 (citing James Lindgren, The Elusive Distinction Between Bribery and Extortion: From the Common Law to the Hobbs Act, 35 U.C.L.A. L. Rev. 815 (1988)). Focusing on early English cases, the article argues that common-law extortion encompassed a wide range of official takings, whether by coercion, false pretenses, or bribery. Whatever the merits of that argument as a description of early English common law,[2] it is beside the point here—the critical inquiry for our

---

[2] Those merits are far from clear. Most commentators maintain that extortion and bribery were distinct crimes at early English common law. See, e.g., J. Noonan, Bribes 398, 585–87 (1984); Charles F.C. Ruff, Feder-al Prosecution of Local Corruption: A Case Study in the Making of Law Enforcement Policy, 65 Geo. L.J. 1171, 1179–80 (1977). While—as I explain below—Professor Lindgren may well be correct that common-law

purposes is the American understanding of the crime at the time the Hobbs Act was passed in 1946.

A survey of 19th and early 20th century cases construing state extortion statutes in light of the common law makes plain that the offense was understood to involve not merely a wrongful taking by a public official, but a wrongful taking under a false pretense of official right. A typical case is Collier v. State, 55 Ala. 125 (1877). The defendant there was a local prosecutor who, for a fee, had given legal advice to a criminal suspect. The Alabama Supreme Court rejected the state's contention that the defendant's receipt of the fee—even though improper—amounted to "extortion," because he had not taken the money "under color of his office." "The object of the [extortion] statute is . . . not the obtaining money by mere impropriety of conduct, or by fraud, by persons filling official position." Rather, the court explained, "[a] taking under color of office is of the essence of the offense. The money or thing received must have been claimed, or accepted, in right of office, and the person paying must have been yielding to official authority." That a public official took money he was not due was not enough. "[T]hough the defendant may have been guilty of official infidelity, the wrong was to the state only, and no wrong was done the person paying the money. That wrong is not punishable under this indictment. Private and public wrong must concur, to constitute extortion." Numerous decisions from other jurisdictions confirm that an official obtained a payment "under color of his office" only—as the phrase suggests—when he used the office to assert a false pretense of official right to the payment.

Because the Court misapprehends the "color of office" requirement, the crime it describes today is not the common-law crime that Congress presumably incorporated into the Hobbs Act. The explanation for this error is clear. The Court's historical foray has the single-minded purpose of proving that common-law extortion did not include an element of "inducement"; in its haste to reach that conclusion, the Court fails to consider the elements that common-law extortion did include. Even if the Court were correct that an official could commit extortion at common law simply by receiving (but not "inducing") an unlawful payment, it does not follow either historically or logically that an official automatically committed extortion whenever he received such a payment.

The Court, therefore, errs in asserting that common-law extortion is the "rough equivalent of what we would now describe as 'taking a bribe.'" Regardless of whether extortion contains an "inducement" requirement, bribery and extortion are different crimes. An official who solicits or takes a bribe does not do so "under color of office"; i.e., under any pretense of official entitlement. "The distinction between bribery and extortion seems to be that the former offense consists in offering a present or receiving one, the latter in demanding a fee or present by color of office." State v.

extortion did not contain an "inducement" element, in my view he does not adequately account for the crime's "by color of office" element. This latter element has existed since long before the founding of the Republic, and cannot simply be ignored.

Pritchard, 107 N.C. 921, 929, 12 S.E. 50, 52 (1890). Where extortion is at issue, the public official is the sole wrongdoer; because he acts "under color of office," the law regards the payor as an innocent victim and not an accomplice. See, e.g., 1 W. Burdick, Law of Crime §§ 273–75, pp. 392–96 (1946). With bribery, in contrast, the payor knows the recipient official is not entitled to the payment; he, as well as official, may be punished for the offense. See, e.g., id., §§ 288–92, pp. 426–36. Congress is well aware of the distinction between the crimes; it has always treated them separately. Compare 18 U.S.C. § 872 ("Extortion by officers or employees of the United States," which criminalizes extortion by federal officials, and makes no provision for punishment of the payor), with 18 U.S.C. § 201 ("Bribery of public officials and witnesses," which criminalizes bribery of and by federal officials). By stretching the bounds of extortion to make it encompass bribery, the Court today blurs the traditional distinction between the crimes.

B

Perhaps because the common-law crime—as the Court defines it—is so expansive, the Court, at the very end of its opinion, appends a qualification: "We hold today that the government need only show that a public official has obtained a payment to which he was not entitled, knowing that the payment was made in return for official acts." This quid pro quo requirement is simply made up. The Court does not suggest that it has any basis in the common law or the language of the Hobbs Act, and I have found no treatise or dictionary that refers to any such requirement in defining "extortion."

Its only conceivable source, in fact, is our opinion last Term in McCormick v. United States, 500 U.S. 257 (1991). Quite sensibly, we insisted in that case that, unless the government established the existence of a quid pro quo, a public official could not be convicted of extortion under the Hobbs Act for accepting a campaign contribution. We did not purport to discern that requirement in the common law or statutory text, but imposed it to prevent the Hobbs Act from effecting a radical (and absurd) change in American political life. "To hold otherwise would open to prosecution not only conduct that has long been thought to be well within the law but also conduct that in a very real sense is unavoidable so long as election campaigns are financed by private contributions or expenditures, as they have been from the beginning of the Nation. It would require statutory language more explicit than the Hobbs Act contains to justify a contrary conclusion." We expressly limited our holding to campaign contributions. See n.10 ("[W]e do not decide whether a quid pro quo requirement exists in other contexts, such as when an elected official receives gifts, meals, travel expenses, or other items of value").

Because the common-law history of extortion was neither properly briefed nor argued in McCormick, the quid pro quo limitation imposed there represented a reasonable first step in the right direction. Now that we squarely consider that history, however, it is apparent that that limitation was in fact overly modest: at common law, McCormick was innocent of extortion not because he failed to offer a quid pro quo in return for campaign contributions, but because he did not take the contributions under color of official right. Today's extension of *McCormick*'s reasonable (but textually and historically artificial) quid pro quo limitation to all cases of official extortion is both unexplained and inexplicable—except insofar as it may serve to rescue the Court's definition of extortion from substantial overbreadth.

II

As serious as the Court's disregard for history is its disregard for well-established principles of statutory construction. The Court chooses not only the harshest interpretation of a criminal statute, but also the interpretation that maximizes federal criminal jurisdiction over state and local officials. I would reject both choices.

A

The Hobbs Act defines "extortion" as "the obtaining of property from another, with his consent, induced by wrongful use of actual or threatened force, violence, or fear, or under color of official right." 18 U.S.C. § 1951(b)(2).[5] Evans argues, in part, that he did not "induce" any payment. The Court rejects that argument, concluding that the verb "induced" applies only to the first portion of the definition. Thus, according to the Court, the statute should read: " 'The term "extortion" means the obtaining of property from another, with his consent, either [1] induced by wrongful use of actual or threatened force, violence, or fear, or [2] under color of official right.' " That is, I concede, a conceivable construction of the words. But it is—at the very least—forced, for it sets up an unnatural and ungrammatical parallel between the verb "induced" and the preposition "under."

The more natural construction is that the verb "induced" applies to both types of extortion described in the statute. Thus, the unstated "either" belongs after "induced": "The term 'extortion' means the obtaining of property from another, with his consent, induced either [1] by wrongful use of actual or threatened force, violence, or fear, or [2] under color of official right." This construction comports with correct grammar and standard usage by setting up a parallel between two prepositional phrases, the first beginning with "by"; the second with "under."

Our duty in construing this criminal statute, then, is clear: "The Court has often stated that when there are two rational readings of a criminal statute, one harsher than the other, we are to choose the harsher only when Congress has spoken in clear and definite language." McNally

[5] I have no quarrel with the Court's suggestion that there is no difference of substance between the classic common-law phrase "by colour of his office" and the Hobbs Act's formulation "under color of official right." The act's formulation, of course, only underscores extortion's essential element of a false assertion of official right to a payment.

v. United States, 483 U.S. 350, 359–60 (1987). Because the Court's
expansive interpretation of the statute is not the only plausible one, the
rule of lenity compels adoption of the narrower interpretation. That rule,
as we have explained on many occasions, serves two vitally important
functions: "First, 'a fair warning should be given to the world in language
that the common world will understand, of what the law intends to do if a
certain line is passed. To make the warning fair, so far as possible the line
should be clear.' Second, because of the seriousness of criminal penalties,
and because criminal punishment usually represents the moral condemnation of the community, legislatures and not courts should define criminal
activity." United States v. Bass, 404 U.S. 336, 348 (1971). Given the text
of the statute and the rule of lenity, I believe that inducement is an
element of official extortion under the Hobbs Act.

Perhaps sensing the weakness of its position, the Court suggests an
alternative interpretation: even if the statute does set forth an "inducement" requirement for official extortion, that requirement is always satisfied, because "the coercive element is provided by the public office itself."
I disagree. A particular public official, to be sure, may wield his power in
such a way as to coerce unlawful payments, even in the absence of any
explicit demand or threat. But it ignores reality to assert that every public
official, in every context, automatically exerts coercive influence on others
by virtue of his office. If the Chairman of General Motors meets with a
local court clerk, for example, whatever implicit coercive pressures exist
will surely not emanate from the clerk. In Miranda v. Arizona, 384 U.S.
436 (1966), of course, this Court established a presumption of "inherently
compelling pressures" in the context of official custodial interrogation.
Now, apparently, we assume that all public officials exude an aura of
coercion at all places and at all times. That is not progress.

B

The Court's construction of the Hobbs Act is repugnant not only to the
basic tenets of criminal justice reflected in the rule of lenity, but also to
basic tenets of federalism. Over the past 20 years, the Hobbs Act has
served as the engine for a stunning expansion of federal criminal jurisdiction into a field traditionally policed by state and local laws—acts of public
corruption by state and local officials. See generally Charles F.C. Ruff,
Federal Prosecution of Local Corruption: A Case Study in the Making of
Law Enforcement Policy, 65 Geo. L.J. 1171 (1977). That expansion was
born of a single sentence in a Third Circuit opinion: "[The 'under color of
official right' language in the Hobbs Act] repeats the common law definition of extortion, a crime which could only be committed by a public
official, and which did not require proof of threat, fear, or duress." United
States v. Kenny, 462 F.2d 1205, 1229 (1972). As explained above, that
sentence is not necessarily incorrect in its description of what common-law
extortion did not require; unfortunately, it omits an important part of
what common-law extortion did require. By overlooking the traditional
meaning of "under color of official right," *Kenny* obliterated the distinction
between extortion and bribery, essentially creating a new crime encompass-

ing both. "As effectively as if there were federal common law crimes, the court in *Kenny* ... amend[ed] the Hobbs Act and [brought] into existence a new crime—local bribery affecting interstate commerce. Hereafter, for purposes of Hobbs Act prosecutions, such bribery was to be called extortion. The federal policing of state corruption had begun." J. Noonan, Bribes 586 (1984). After *Kenny*, federal prosecutors came to view the Hobbs Act as a license for ferreting out all wrongdoing at the state and local level—" 'a special code of integrity for public officials.' " United States v. O'Grady, 742 F.2d 682, 694 (2d Cir.1984)(en banc). In short order, most other circuits followed *Kenny*'s lead and upheld, based on a bribery rationale, the Hobbs–Act extortion convictions of an astonishing variety of state and local officials, from a state governor, see United States v. Hall, 536 F.2d 313, 320–21 (10th Cir.1976), down to a local policeman, see United States v. Braasch, 505 F.2d 139, 151 (7th Cir.1974).

Our precedents, to be sure, suggest that Congress enjoys broad constitutional power to legislate in areas traditionally regulated by the states—power that apparently extends even to the direct regulation of the qualifications, tenure, and conduct of state governmental officials. See, e.g., Garcia v. San Antonio Metropolitan Transit Authority, 469 U.S. 528, 547–54 (1985). As we emphasized only last term, however, concerns of federalism require us to give a narrow construction to federal legislation in such sensitive areas unless Congress' contrary intent is "unmistakably clear in the language of the statute." Gregory v. Ashcroft, 501 U.S. 452, 460 (1991). "This plain statement rule is nothing more than an acknowledgement that the states retain substantial sovereign powers under our constitutional scheme, powers with which Congress does not readily interfere." *Gregory*'s teaching is straightforward: because we "assume Congress does not exercise lightly" its extraordinary power to regulate state officials, we will construe ambiguous statutory provisions in the least intrusive manner that can reasonably be inferred from the statute.

Gregory's rule represents nothing more than a restatement of established law: "Congress has traditionally been reluctant to define as a federal crime conduct readily denounced as criminal by the states.... As this Court emphasized only last term in Rewis v. United States, 401 U.S. 808 (1971), we will not be quick to assume that Congress has meant to effect a significant change in the sensitive relation between federal and state criminal jurisdiction. In traditionally sensitive areas, such as legislation affecting the federal balance, the requirement of clear statement assures that the legislature has in fact faced, and intended to bring into issue, the critical matters involved in the judicial decision." *United States v. Bass*, 404 U.S., at 349. Similarly, in McNally v. United States, 483 U.S. 350 (1987)—a case closely analogous to this one—we rejected the government's contention that the federal mail fraud statute, 18 U.S.C. § 1341, protected the citizenry's "intangible right" to good government, and hence could be applied to all instances of state and local corruption. Such an expansive reading of the statute, we noted with disapproval, would "leav[e] its outer boundaries ambiguous and involv[e] the federal government in setting standards of disclosure and good government for local and state officials."[7] Cf. Andrew T. Baxter, Federal Discretion in the Prosecution of Local Political Corruption, 10 Pepp. L. Rev. 321, 336–43 (1983).

The reader of today's opinion, however, will search in vain for any consideration of the principles of federalism that animated *Gregory*, *Rewis*, *Bass*, and *McNally*. It is clear, of course, that the Hobbs Act's proscription of extortion "under color of official right" applies to all public officials, including those at the state and local level. As our cases emphasize, however, even when Congress has clearly decided to engage in some regulation of the state governmental officials, concerns of federalism play a vital role in evaluating the scope of the regulation. The Court today mocks this jurisprudence by reading two significant limitations (the textual requirement of "inducement" and the common-law requirement of "under color of office") out of the Hobbs Act's definition of official extortion.

III

I have no doubt that today's opinion is motivated by noble aims. Political corruption at any level of government is a serious evil, and, from a policy perspective, perhaps one well suited for federal law enforcement. But federal judges are not free to devise new crimes to meet the occasion. Chief Justice Marshall's warning is as timely today as ever: "It would be dangerous, indeed, to carry the principle that a case which is within the reason or mischief of a statute, is within its provisions, so far as to punish a crime not enumerated in the statute, because it is of equal atrocity, or of kindred character, with those which are enumerated." United States v. Wiltberger, 18 U.S. (5 Wheat.) 76, 96 (1820).

Whatever evils today's opinion may redress, in my view, pale beside those it will engender. "Courts must resist th[e] temptation [to stretch criminal statutes] in the interest of the long-range preservation of limited and even-handed government." United States v. Mazzei, 521 F.2d 639, 656 (3d Cir.1975)(en banc)(Gibbons, J., dissenting). All Americans, including public officials, are entitled to protection from prosecutorial abuse. The facts of this case suggest a depressing erosion of that protection.

Petitioner Evans was elected to the Board of Commissioners of DeKalb County, Georgia, in 1982. He was no local tyrant—just one of five part-time Commissioners earning an annual salary of approximately $16,000. The Board's activities were entirely local, including the quintessentially

---

[7] Prior to our decision in *McNally*, the government's theory had been accepted by every Court of Appeals to consider the issue. ... The interpretation given a statute by a majority of the Courts of Appeals, of course, is due our most respectful consideration. Ultimately, however, our attention must focus on the reasons given for that interpretation. Error is not cured by repetition, and we do not discharge our duty simply by counting up the circuits on either side of the split. ...

Moreover, I reject the notion—as this Court has on many occasions—that Congress, through its silence, implicitly ratifies judicial decisions. See, e.g., Patterson v. McLean Credit Union, 491 U.S. 164, 175, n. 1 (1989)("It is impossible to assert with any degree of assurance that congressional failure to act represents affirmative congressional approval" of judicial interpretation of a statute).

local activity of zoning property. The United States does not suggest that there were any allegations of corruption or malfeasance against Evans.

In early 1985, as part of an investigation into "allegations of public corruption in the Atlanta area," a Federal Bureau of Investigation agent, Clifford Cormany, Jr., set up a bogus firm, "WDH Developers," and pretended to be a land developer. Cormany sought and obtained a meeting with Evans. From March 1985 until October 1987, a period of some two and a half years, Cormany or one of his associates held 33 conversations with Evans. Every one of these contacts was initiated by the agents. During these conversations, the agents repeatedly requested Evans' assistance in securing a favorable zoning decision, and repeatedly brought up the subject of campaign contributions. Agent Cormany eventually contributed $8,000 to Evans' reelection campaign, and Evans accepted the money. There is no suggestion that he claimed an official entitlement to the payment. Nonetheless, he was arrested and charged with Hobbs Act extortion.

The Court is surely correct that there is sufficient evidence to support the jury's verdict that Evans committed "extortion" under the Court's expansive interpretation of the crime. But that interpretation has no basis in the statute that Congress passed in 1946. If the Court makes up this version of the crime today, who is to say what version it will make up tomorrow when confronted with the next perceived rascal? Until now, the Justice Department, with good reason, has been extremely cautious in advancing the theory that official extortion contains no inducement requirement. "Until the Supreme Court decides upon the validity of this type of conviction, prosecutorial discretion should be used to insure that any case which might reach that level of review is worthy of federal prosecution. Such restraint would require that only significant amounts of money and reasonably high levels of office should be involved." See U.S. Dept. of Justice, United States Attorneys' Manual § 9–131.180 (1984). Having detected no "[s]uch restraint" in this case, I certainly have no reason to expect it in the future.

Our criminal-justice system runs on the premise that prosecutors will respect and courts will enforce the boundaries on criminal conduct set by the legislature. Where, as here, those boundaries are breached, it becomes impossible to tell where prosecutorial discretion ends and prosecutorial abuse, or even discrimination, begins. The potential for abuse, of course, is particularly grave in the inherently political context of public-corruption prosecutions.

In my view, Evans is plainly innocent of extortion. With all due respect, I am compelled to dissent.

NOTES ON *McCORMICK* AND *EVANS*

1. Questions and Comments. In *McCormick*, the Court holds that a "quid pro quo" is required for a conviction under the Hobbs Act based on the receipt of a campaign contribution, regardless of whether it is a

legitimate contribution.   Justice White writes the majority opinion, and
Justice Stevens dissents.   In *Evans*, just a year later, Stevens writes the
majority opinion affirming a Hobbs Act conviction because the challenged
jury instructions satisfied the "quid pro quo" requirement of *McCormick*.
In dissent, Justice Thomas says that *Evans* overextends *McCormick*.

If Stevens didn't agree with the Court's decision in *McCormick*, why
would he write an opinion in *Evans* that extends it?   Or is Thomas wrong
to say that *Evans* extends *McCormick*?   Does Stevens actually manage
somehow to limit *McCormick* in his *Evans* opinion?   If so, then why does
White (who wrote *McCormick*) join the majority opinion in *Evans*?

2. Legislative History.   Does the legislative history of the Hobbs
Act indicate that Congress was concerned with non-coercive behavior by
state and local officials?   That it was concerned *at all* with the behavior of
state and local officials?

Recall that the Hobbs Act was a replacement for the Anti–Racketeering
Act of 1934, intended to *extend* the coverage of the 1934 statute to behavior
excluded by the Supreme Court and not, it at least could be argued, to
cover any less than the behavior in other respects criminalized by the 1934
statute.   Section 2(b) of the 1934 Act applied to one who "[o]btains the
property of another, with his consent, induced by wrongful use of force or
fear, or under color of official right."   This language obviously was the
model for the similar provision in the Hobbs Act.   Is there anything in the
legislative history of the 1934 Act indicating that it was designed to reach
bribery of state and local officials?

There was precious little discussion in the debates on the Hobbs Act of
the "under color of official right" language.   One colloquy that did occur
during the first debate in the House (on H.R. 653) was the following:

"Mr. DAY.   Mr. Chairman, I offer an amendment.

"The clerk read as follows:

"Amendment offered by Mr. DAY: [In section 1(c)], after
the word 'fear', strike out the comma and insert a period. . . .

"Mr. DAY.   Mr. Chairman, I wonder if the committee is not
guilty of some inadvertence in their definition of the word 'extortion'. . . . .   I ask the author of the bill to follow me closely.   I read:

'The term "extortion" means the obtaining of property
from another, with his consent, induced by wrongful use of
actual or threatened force, violence, or fear'—

"Up to that point it would amount to duress, it is clear
intimidation or extortion then it states: 'or under color of official
right.'

"I want to ask this, and if you do not mean this in the bill,
then so state in the interest of clarification of the future enforcement of this act and for the benefit of the House. . . .

"When you say that by extortion you mean getting money or property from a man with his consent or under color of official right, it would apply to an initiation fee in a labor union.

"Mr. HOBBS. Certainly not. 'Color of official right' means absence of right but pretended assertion of right.

"Mr. DAY. I know; but what do the words 'official right' mean?

"Mr. HOBBS. The same thing.

"Mr. DAY. It has not got to be by some authority?

"Mr. HOBBS. In other words, you pretend to be a police officer, you pretend to be a deputy sheriff, but you are not.

"Mr. DAY. I think the change should be made that I have mentioned.

"Mr. HOBBS. It could not possibly apply if there was any bona fide right; it applies only to pretended right.

"Mr. BRADLEY of Pennsylvania. Mr. Chairman, will the gentleman yield?

"Mr. DAY. I yield.

"Mr. BRADLEY of Pennsylvania. With reference to what the gentleman from Illinois said about union dues, suppose somebody should say that he paid union dues only because of fear or violence. I think the gentleman is right.

"Mr. DAY. That is just the point. A union official might be indicted and face a 20–year sentence in a federal penitentiary or $10,000 fine. Not only that, but there might be great hardship to himself and his family if there should be some careless construction of this language. I think this is very important. . . .

"Mr. SUMNERS of Texas. May I suggest to my friend that if he will examine the language carefully I believe he will conclude that it means money acquired by some person who claims to be a officer of the law who is trying to take his money.

"Mr. DAY. You say that.

"Mr. SUMNERS of Texas. That is the language.

"Mr. DAY. It is subject to the construction I have given it or I could not have arrived at it. This is a penal statute. Why do you not make it clear?

"Mr. SUMNERS of Texas. We believe we have. 'Officially' means an officer of the government.

"Mr. DAY. The gentleman knows there is a quibble in there or he would not be debating it. You are writing a statute here.

"Mr. SUMNERS of Texas. Would the gentleman accept the statement by the chairman of the Judiciary Committee that re-

ported the bill that the language means money acquired by somebody claiming to be a public officer?

"Mr. DAY.   You say that but why do you not say 'by some
public official'?

"Mr. SUMNERS of Texas.   That is it.

"Mr. DAY.   An officer of a union is a private official, not a
public official.

"Mr. SUMNERS of Texas.   No.

"Mr. DAY.   Why leave any doubt about it?   Let us write these
laws in clear language.

"The CHAIRMAN.   The time of the gentleman has expired.

"The question is on the amendment offered by the gentleman
from Illinois [Mr. DAY].

"The amendment was rejected."   89 Cong. Rec. 3228–29
(April 9, 1943).

Should anything be made of this?

3.   Rationale for Use of the Hobbs Act.   Why do federal prosecutors seek to use the Hobbs Act in bribery situations when other federal
laws, most prominently the Travel Act, wire fraud, or mail fraud, more
clearly reach such behavior?   One answer was suggested by United States
Attorney Herbert Stern in Prosecutions of Local Political Corruption Under
the Hobbs Act: The Unnecessary Distinction Between Bribery and Extortion, 3 Seton Hall L. Rev. 1, 9–11 (1971).   He noted first that the Travel
Act requires travel in or use of the facilities of interstate commerce,
whereas the Hobbs Act requires only an effect on commerce "in the
slightest degree."   He added:

"Moreover, there is a curious ambivalence between the way
the courts have construed the jurisdictional requirements under
the two statutes.   Under the Travel Act, the courts have required
deliberate, knowing interstate travel or the similar use of interstate facilities to achieve the illegal act.   However, under the
Hobbs Act it has been held that if, in fact the 'extortion' affected
interstate commerce, there is a violation of the Act notwithstanding the absence of an intent to have this effect, or even the
absence of any anticipation that such an effect might result.
Moreover, under the Travel Act the determination of whether or
not there was a knowing use of interstate travel or facilities is left
to the jury.   On the other hand, the courts have held that what
constitutes an effect on interstate commerce under the Hobbs Act
is a question of law for the court and not a question of fact for the
jury."

He concluded on this point that "in situations where interstate travel or
use of interstate facilities cannot be proven, or where the knowing use of
them by the public official cannot be demonstrated, the federal government

will often have to prosecute local political corruption under the Hobbs Act or not at all." To this might be added the availability of a wire or mail fraud prosecution, even under the expansive "intangible rights" theory, only when narrow jurisdictional requirements of the wire or mail fraud statutes can be met. And of course more serious sentences are often available under the Hobbs Act.[a]

4. Concluding Comments. Whether the bribery of state and local officials is an appropriate subject for federal prosecution is perhaps a debatable question, though one can begin to make a case for it at least in situations where the corruption reaches the very local agencies in charge of prosecutions under state law. But that question has been settled. It *is* the federal policy to prosecute accepting a bribe when travel in interstate commerce can be proved. It *is* the federal policy to prosecute accepting a bribe when interstate wire services or the mails are used. Why the question should be debatable when interstate commerce is merely *affected* seems an odd way to pose the question of the appropriate role of the federal government in prosecuting bribe-taking by state and local public officials. And why a five-year maximum sentence is the right answer when interstate travel is involved or the mails are used and a 20–year maximum sentence is the right answer when commerce is merely affected in some remote way is perhaps understandable, given the structure of the federal criminal code, but nonetheless seems a strange way to do business.

[a] See supra Section 2, n. a and accompanying text, for a discussion of the Travel Act's sentencing provisions.

CHAPTER IV

ENTERPRISE CRIMINALITY—RICO AND CCE

SECTION 1: INTRODUCTION TO ENTERPRISE CRIMINALITY

SUBSECTION A: THE RICO AND CCE STATUTES

Among the federal criminal statutes that Congress has enacted in an attempt to strike back at "organized crime," RICO and CCE are unique. They represent more than simply two new federal crimes; indeed, they represent an entirely new concept of criminality. Unlike most traditional crimes, which criminalize a particular act or series of acts by a defendant, RICO and CCE criminalize what might better be described as a defendant's "status"—in RICO, the status of being a "racketeer," and in CCE, the status of being a "drug kingpin." Under RICO and CCE, the focus is on the defendant's involvement in an "enterprise," rather than on the specific criminal acts of that defendant or "enterprise." In short, RICO and CCE rely on the concept of "enterprise criminality."

Sedima, S.P.R.L. v. Imrex Co., Inc.

Supreme Court of the United States, 1985.
473 U.S. 479.

◼ JUSTICE WHITE delivered the opinion of the Court.

The Racketeer Influenced and Corrupt Organizations Act (RICO) provides a private civil action to recover treble damages for injury "by reason of a violation of" its substantive provisions. 18 U.S.C. § 1964(c). The initial dormancy of this provision and its recent greatly increased utilization[1] are now familiar history.[2] In response to what it perceived to be misuse of civil RICO by private plaintiffs, the court below construed § 1964(c) to permit private actions only against defendants who had been convicted on criminal charges, and only where there had occurred a "racketeering injury." While we understand the court's concern over the

[1] Of 270 District Court RICO decisions prior to this year, only three per cent (nine cases) were decided throughout the 1970's, two per cent were decided in 1980, seven per cent in 1981, 13 per cent in 1982, 33 per cent in 1983, and 43 per cent in 1984. Report of the Ad Hoc Civil RICO Task Force of the ABA Section of Corporation, Banking and Business Law 55 (1985)(hereinafter ABA Report); see also id., at 53a (table).

[2] For a thorough bibliography of civil RICO decisions and commentary, see Anita C. Milner, A Civil RICO Bibliography, 21 C.W.L.R. 409 (1985).

consequences of an unbridled reading of the statute, we reject both of its holdings.

I

RICO takes aim at "racketeering activity," which it defines as any act "chargeable" under several generically described state criminal laws, any act "indictable" under numerous specific federal criminal provisions, including mail and wire fraud, and any "offense" involving bankruptcy or securities fraud or drug-related activities that is "punishable" under federal law. § 1961(1). Section 1962, entitled "Prohibited Activities," outlaws the use of income derived from a "pattern of racketeering activity" to acquire an interest in or establish an enterprise engaged in or affecting interstate commerce; the acquisition or maintenance of any interest in an enterprise "through" a pattern of racketeering activity; conducting or participating in the conduct of an enterprise through a pattern of racketeering activity; and conspiring to violate any of these provisions.

Congress provided criminal penalties of imprisonment, fines, and forfeiture for violation of these provisions. § 1963. In addition, it set out a far-reaching civil enforcement scheme, § 1964, including the following provision for private suits:

> "Any person injured in his business or property by reason of a violation of section 1962 of this chapter may sue therefor in any appropriate United States district court and shall recover threefold the damages he sustains and the costs of the suit, including a reasonable attorney's fee."

In 1979, petitioner Sedima, a Belgian corporation, entered into a joint venture with respondent Imrex Co. to provide electronic components to a Belgian firm. The buyer was to order parts through Sedima; Imrex was to obtain the parts in this country and ship them to Europe. The agreement called for Sedima and Imrex to split the net proceeds. Imrex filled roughly $8 million in orders placed with it through Sedima. Sedima became convinced, however, that Imrex was presenting inflated bills, cheating Sedima out of a portion of its proceeds by collecting for nonexistent expenses.

In 1982, Sedima filed this action in the Federal District Court for the Eastern District of New York. The complaint set out common-law claims of unjust enrichment, conversion, and breach of contract, fiduciary duty, and a constructive trust. In addition, it asserted RICO claims under § 1964(c) against Imrex and two of its officers. Two counts alleged violations of § 1962(c), based on predicate acts of mail and wire fraud. See 18 U.S.C. §§ 1341, 1343, 1961(1)(B). A third count alleged a conspiracy to violate § 1962(c). Claiming injury of at least $175,000, the amount of the alleged over-billing, Sedima sought treble damages and attorney's fees.

The District Court held that for an injury to be "by reason of a violation of § 1962," as required by § 1964(c), it must be somehow different in kind from the direct injury resulting from the predicate acts of racketeering activity. While not choosing a precise formulation, the District Court held that a complaint must allege a "RICO-type injury," which was either some sort of distinct "racketeering injury," or a "competitive injury." It found "no allegation here of any injury apart from that which would result directly from the alleged predicate acts of mail fraud and wire fraud," and accordingly dismissed the RICO counts for failure to state a claim.

A divided panel of the Court of Appeals for the Second Circuit affirmed. After a lengthy review of the legislative history, it held that Sedima's complaint was defective in two ways. First, it failed to allege an injury "by reason of a violation of § 1962." In the court's view, this language was a limitation on standing, reflecting Congress' intent to compensate victims of "certain specific kinds of organized criminality," not to provide additional remedies for already compensable injuries. Analogizing to the Clayton Act, which had been the model for § 1964(c), the court concluded that just as an antitrust plaintiff must allege an "antitrust injury," so a RICO plaintiff must allege a "racketeering injury"—an injury "different in kind from that occurring as a result of the predicate acts themselves, or not simply caused by the predicate acts, but also caused by an activity which RICO was designed to deter." Sedima had failed to allege such an injury.

The Court of Appeals also found the complaint defective for not alleging that the defendants had already been criminally convicted of the predicate acts of mail and wire fraud, or of a RICO violation. This element of the civil cause of action was inferred from § 1964(c)'s reference to a "violation" of § 1962, the court also observing that its prior-conviction requirement would avoid serious constitutional difficulties, the danger of unfair stigmatization, and problems regarding the standard by which the predicate acts were to be proved.

The decision below was one episode in a recent proliferation of civil RICO litigation within the Second Circuit[5] and in other Courts of Appeals.[6]

[5] The day after the decision in this case, another divided panel of the Second Circuit reached a similar conclusion. Bankers Trust Co. v. Rhoades, 741 F.2d 511 (2d Cir.1984). It held that § 1964(c) allowed recovery only for injuries resulting not from the predicate acts, but from the fact that they were part of a *pattern*. "If a plaintiff's injury is that caused by the predicate acts themselves, he is injured regardless of whether or not there is a pattern; hence he cannot be said to be injured *by* the pattern," and cannot recover.

The following day, a third panel of the same Circuit, this time unanimous, decided Furman v. Cirrito, 741 F.2d 524 (2d Cir. 1984). In that case, the District Court had dismissed the complaint for failure to allege a distinct racketeering injury. The Court of Appeals affirmed, relying on the opinions in *Sedima* and *Bankers Trust*, but wrote at some length to record its disagreement with those decisions. The panel would have required no injury beyond that resulting from the predicate acts.

[6] A month after the trio of Second Circuit opinions was released, the Eighth Circuit decided Alexander Grant & Co. v. Tiffany Industries, Inc., 742 F.2d 408 (8th Cir.1984). Viewing its decision as contrary to *Sedima* but consistent with, though broader than, *Bankers Trust*, the court held that a RICO claim does require some unspecified element beyond the injury flowing directly from the predicate acts. At the same time, it stood by a prior decision that had rejected any re-

In light of the variety of approaches taken by the lower courts and the importance of the issues, we granted certiorari. We now reverse.

II

As a preliminary matter, it is worth briefly reviewing the legislative history of the private treble-damages action. RICO formed title IX of the Organized Crime Control Act of 1970. The civil remedies in the bill passed by the Senate, S. 30, were limited to injunctive actions by the United States and became §§ 1964(a), (b), and (d). Previous versions of the legislation, however, had provided for a private treble-damages action in exactly the terms ultimately adopted in § 1964(c).

During hearings on S. 30 before the House Judiciary Committee, Representative Steiger proposed the addition of a private treble-damages action "similar to the private damage remedy found in the anti-trust laws. [T]hose who have been wronged by organized crime should at least be given access to a legal remedy. In addition, the availability of such a remedy would enhance the effectiveness of title IX's prohibitions." Hearings on S. 30, and Related Proposals, before Subcommittee No. 5 of the House Committee on the Judiciary, 91st Cong., 2d Sess., 520 (1970)(hereinafter House Hearings). The American Bar Association also proposed an amendment "based upon the concept of § 4 of the Clayton Act." Id., at 543–44, 548, 559.

Over the dissent of three members, who feared the treble-damages provision would be used for malicious harassment of business competitors, the Committee approved the amendment. In summarizing the bill on the House floor, its sponsor described the treble-damages provision as "another example of the antitrust remedy being adapted for use against organized criminality." 116 Cong. Rec. 35295 (1970). The full House then rejected a proposal to create a complementary treble-damages remedy for those injured by being named as defendants in malicious private suits. Representative Steiger also offered an amendment that would have allowed private injunctive actions, fixed a statute of limitations, and clarified venue and process requirements. The proposal was greeted with some hostility because it had not been reviewed in Committee, and Steiger withdrew it without a vote being taken. The House then passed the bill, with the treble-damages provision in the form recommended by the Committee.

The Senate did not seek a conference and adopted the bill as amended in the House. The treble-damages provision had been drawn to its attention while the legislation was still in the House, and had received the endorsement of Senator McClellan, the sponsor of S. 30, who was of the

quirement that the injury be solely commercial or competitive, or that the defendants be involved in organized crime.

Two months later, the Seventh Circuit decided Haroco, Inc. v. American National Bank & Trust Co. of Chicago, 747 F.2d 384 (7th Cir.1984). Dismissing *Sedima* as the resurrection of the discredited requirement of an organized crime nexus, and *Bankers Trust* as an emasculation of the treble-damages remedy, the Seventh Circuit rejected "the elusive racketeering injury requirement." ...

view that the provision would be "a major new tool in extirpating the baneful influence of organized crime in our economic life." Id., at 25190.

III

The language of RICO gives no obvious indication that a civil action can proceed only after a criminal conviction. The word "conviction" does not appear in any relevant portion of the statute. To the contrary, the predicate acts involve conduct that is "chargeable" or "indictable," and "offense[s]" that are "punishable," under various criminal statutes. As defined in the statute, racketeering activity consists not of acts for which the defendant has been convicted, but of acts for which he could be. See also S. Rep. No. 91–617, p. 158 (1969): "a racketeering activity . . . must be an act in itself *subject* to criminal sanction" (emphasis added). Thus, a prior-conviction requirement cannot be found in the definition of "racketeering activity." Nor can it be found in § 1962, which sets out the statute's substantive provisions. Indeed, if either § 1961 or § 1962 did contain such a requirement, a prior conviction would also be a prerequisite, nonsensically, for a criminal prosecution, or for a civil action by the government to enjoin violations that had not yet occurred.

The Court of Appeals purported to discover its prior-conviction requirement in the term "violation" in § 1964(c). However, even if that term were read to refer to a criminal conviction, it would require a conviction under RICO, not of the predicate offenses. That aside, the term "violation" does not imply a criminal conviction. It refers only to a failure to adhere to legal requirements. This is its indisputable meaning elsewhere in the statute. Section 1962 renders certain conduct "unlawful"; § 1963 and § 1964 impose consequences, criminal and civil, for "violations" of § 1962. We should not lightly infer that Congress intended the term to have wholly different meanings in neighboring subsections.[7]

The legislative history also undercuts the reading of the court below. The clearest current in that history is the reliance on the Clayton Act model, under which private and governmental actions are entirely distinct.[8]

---

[7] When Congress intended that the defendant have been previously convicted, it said so. [Section] 1963(f) states that "[u]pon conviction of a person under this section," his forfeited property shall be seized. Likewise, in title X of the same legislation Congress explicitly required prior convictions, rather than prior criminal activity, to support enhanced sentences for special offenders. See 18 U.S.C. § 3575(e).

[8] The court below considered it significant that § 1964(c) requires a "violation of § 1962," whereas the Clayton Act speaks of "anything forbidden in the antitrust laws." See 15 U.S.C. § 15(a). The court viewed this as a deliberate change indicating Congress' desire that the underlying conduct not only

be forbidden, but also have led to a criminal conviction. There is nothing in the legislative history to support this interpretation, and we cannot view this minor departure in wording, without more, to indicate a fundamental departure in meaning. Representative Steiger, who proposed this wording in the House, nowhere indicated a desire to depart from the antitrust model in this regard. To the contrary, he viewed the treble-damages provision as a "parallel private remedy." 116 Cong. Rec. 27739 (1970). Likewise, Senator Hruska's discussion of his identically worded proposal gives no hint of any such intent. See 115 Cong. Rec. 6993 (1969). In any event, the change in language does not support the court's drastic inference. It

The only specific reference in the legislative history to prior convictions of which we are aware is an objection that the treble-damages provision is too broad precisely because "there need *not* be a conviction under any of these laws for it to be racketeering." 116 Cong. Rec. 35342 (1970)(emphasis added). The history is otherwise silent on this point and contains nothing to contradict the import of the language appearing in the statute. Had Congress intended to impose this novel requirement, there would have been at least some mention of it in the legislative history, even if not in the statute.

The Court of Appeals was of the view that its narrow construction of the statute was essential to avoid intolerable practical consequences.[9] First, without a prior conviction to rely on, the plaintiff would have to prove commission of the predicate acts beyond a reasonable doubt. This would require instructing the jury as to different standards of proof for different aspects of the case. To avoid this awkwardness, the court inferred that the criminality must already be established, so that the civil action could proceed smoothly under the usual preponderance standard.

We are not at all convinced that the predicate acts must be established beyond a reasonable doubt in a proceeding under § 1964(c). In a number of settings, conduct that can be punished as criminal only upon proof beyond a reasonable doubt will support civil sanctions under a preponderance standard. That the offending conduct is described by reference to criminal statutes does not mean that its occurrence must be established by criminal standards or that the consequences of a finding of liability in a private civil action are identical to the consequences of a criminal conviction. But we need not decide the standard of proof issue today. For even if the stricter standard is applicable to a portion of the plaintiff's proof, the resulting logistical difficulties, which are accepted in other contexts, would not be so great as to require invention of a requirement that cannot be found in the statute and that Congress, as even the Court of Appeals had to

seems more likely that the language was chosen because it is more succinct than that in the Clayton Act, and is consistent with the neighboring provisions.

[9] It is worth bearing in mind that the holding of the court below is not without problematic consequences of its own. It arbitrarily restricts the availability of private actions, for lawbreakers are often not apprehended and convicted. Even if a conviction has been obtained, it is unlikely that a private plaintiff will be able to recover for all of the acts constituting an extensive "pattern," or that multiple victims will all be able to obtain redress. This is because criminal convictions are often limited to a small portion of the actual or possible charges. The decision below would also create peculiar in-

centives for plea bargaining to non-predicate-act offenses so as to ensure immunity for a later civil suit. If nothing else, a criminal defendant might plead to a tiny fraction of counts, so as to limit future civil liability. In addition, the dependence of potential civil litigants on the initiation and success of a criminal prosecution could lead to unhealthy private pressures on prosecutors and to self-serving trial testimony, or at least accusations thereof. Problems would also arise if some or all of the convictions were reversed on appeal. Finally, the compelled wait for the completion of criminal proceedings would result in pursuit of stale claims, complex statute of limitations problems, or the wasteful splitting of actions, with resultant claim and issue preclusion complications.

concede, did not envision.[10]

The court below also feared that any other construction would raise severe constitutional questions, as it "would provide civil remedies for offenses criminal in nature, stigmatize defendants with the appellation 'racketeer,' authorize the award of damages which are clearly punitive, including attorney's fees, and constitute a civil remedy aimed in part to avoid the constitutional protection of the criminal law." We do not view the statute as being so close to the constitutional edge. As noted above, the fact that conduct can result in both criminal liability and treble damages does not mean that there is not a bona fide civil action. The familiar provisions for both criminal liability and treble damages under the antitrust laws indicate as much. Nor are attorney's fees "clearly punitive." As for stigma, a civil RICO proceeding leaves no greater stain than do a number of other civil proceedings. Furthermore, requiring conviction of the predicate acts would not protect against an unfair imposition of the "racketeer" label. If there is a problem with thus stigmatizing a garden variety defrauder by means of a civil action, it is not reduced by making certain that the defendant is guilty of *fraud* beyond a reasonable doubt. Finally, to the extent an action under § 1964(c) might be considered quasi-criminal, requiring protections normally applicable only to criminal proceedings, the solution is to provide those protections, not to ensure that they were previously afforded by requiring prior convictions.[11]

Finally, we note that a prior-conviction requirement would be inconsistent with Congress' underlying policy concerns. Such a rule would severely handicap potential plaintiffs. A guilty party may escape conviction for any number of reasons—not least among them the possibility that the government itself may choose to pursue only civil remedies. Private attorney general provisions such as § 1964(c) are in part designed to fill prosecutorial gaps. This purpose would be largely defeated, and the need

[10] The Court of Appeals also observed that allowing civil suits without prior convictions "would make a hash" of the statute's liberal-construction requirement. See RICO § 904(a). Since criminal statutes must be strictly construed, the court reasoned, allowing liberal construction of RICO—an approach often justified on the ground that the conduct for which liability is imposed is "already criminal"—would only be permissible if there already existed criminal convictions. Again, we have doubts about the premise of this rather convoluted argument. The strict-construction principle is merely a guide to statutory interpretation. Like its identical twin, the "rule of lenity," it "only serves as an aid for resolving an ambiguity; it is not to be used to beget one." Callanan v. United States, 364 U.S. 587, 596 (1961); see also United States v. Turkette, 452 U.S. 576, 587–88 (1981). But even if that principle has some application, it does not support the court's holding. The strict-and liberal-construction principles are not mutually exclusive; § 1961 and § 1962 can be strictly construed without adopting that approach to § 1964(c). Indeed, if Congress' liberal-construction mandate is to be applied anywhere, it is in § 1964, where RICO's remedial purposes are most evident.

[11] Even were the constitutional questions more significant, any doubts would be insufficient to overcome the mandate of the statute's language and history. "Statutes should be construed to avoid constitutional questions, but this interpretative canon is not a license for the judiciary to rewrite language enacted by the legislature." United States v. Albertini, 472 U.S. 675, 680 (1985).

for treble damages as an incentive to litigate unjustified, if private suits could be maintained only against those already brought to justice.

In sum, we can find no support in the statute's history, its language, or considerations of policy for a requirement that a private treble-damages action under § 1964(c) can proceed only against a defendant who has already been criminally convicted. To the contrary, every indication is that no such requirement exists. Accordingly, the fact that Imrex and the individual defendants have not been convicted under RICO or the federal mail and wire fraud statutes does not bar Sedima's action.

IV

In considering the Court of Appeals' second prerequisite for a private civil RICO action—"injury ... caused by an activity which RICO was designed to deter"—we are somewhat hampered by the vagueness of that concept. Apart from reliance on the general purposes of RICO and a reference to "mobsters," the court provided scant indication of what the requirement of racketeering injury means. It emphasized Congress' undeniable desire to strike at organized crime, but acknowledged and did not purport to overrule Second Circuit precedent rejecting a requirement of an organized crime nexus. The court also stopped short of adopting a "competitive injury" requirement; while insisting that the plaintiff show "the kind of economic injury which has an effect on competition," it did not require "actual anticompetitive effect."

The court's statement that the plaintiff must seek redress for an injury caused by conduct that RICO was designed to deter is unhelpfully tautological. Nor is clarity furnished by a negative statement of its rule: standing is not provided by the injury resulting from the predicate acts themselves. That statement is itself apparently inaccurate when applied to those predicate acts that unmistakably constitute the kind of conduct Congress sought to deter. The opinion does not explain how to distinguish such crimes from the other predicate acts Congress has lumped together in § 1961(1). The court below is not alone in struggling to define "racketeering injury," and the difficulty of that task, itself cautions against imposing such a requirement.[12]

We need not pinpoint the Second Circuit's precise holding, for we perceive no distinct "racketeering injury" requirement. Given that "racketeering activity" consists of no more and no less than commission of a predicate act, we are initially doubtful about a requirement of a "racketeering injury" separate from the harm from the predicate acts. A reading of the statute belies any such requirement. Section 1964(c) authorizes a private suit by "[a]ny person injured in his business or property by reason

---

[12] The decision below does not appear identical to *Bankers Trust*. It established a standing requirement, whereas *Bankers Trust* adopted a limitation on damages. The one focused on the mobster element, the other took a more conceptual approach, distinguishing injury caused by the individual acts from injury caused by their cumulative effect. ... The evident difficulty in discerning just what the racketeering injury requirement consists of would make it rather hard to apply in practice or explain to a jury.

of a violation of § 1962." Section 1962 in turn makes it unlawful for "any person"—not just mobsters—to use money derived from a pattern of racketeering activity to invest in an enterprise, to acquire control of an enterprise through a pattern of racketeering activity, or to conduct an enterprise through a pattern of racketeering activity. If the defendant engages in a pattern of racketeering activity in a manner forbidden by these provisions, and the racketeering activities injure the plaintiff in his business or property, the plaintiff has a claim under § 1964(c). There is no room in the statutory language for an additional, amorphous "racketeering injury" requirement.[13]

A violation of § 1962(c), the section on which Sedima relies, requires (1) conduct (2) of an enterprise (3) through a pattern[14] (4) of racketeering activity. The plaintiff must, of course, allege each of these elements to state a claim. Conducting an enterprise that affects interstate commerce is obviously not in itself a violation of § 1962, nor is mere commission of the predicate offenses. In addition, the plaintiff only has standing if, and can only recover to the extent that, he has been injured in his business or property by the conduct constituting the violation. As the Seventh Circuit has stated, "[a] defendant who violates § 1962 is not liable for treble damages to everyone he might have injured by other conduct, nor is the defendant liable to those who have not been injured." Haroco, Inc. v.

[13] Given the plain words of the statute, we cannot agree with the court below that Congress could have had no "inkling of [§ 1964(c)'s] implications." Congress' "inklings" are best determined by the statutory language that it chooses, and the language it chose here extends far beyond the limits drawn by the Court of Appeals. Nor does the "clanging silence" of the legislative history justify those limits. For one thing, § 1964(c) did not pass through Congress unnoticed. In addition, congressional silence, no matter how "clanging," cannot override the words of the statute.

[14] As many commentators have pointed out, the definition of a "pattern of racketeering activity" differs from the other provisions in § 1961 in that it states that a pattern *requires* at least two acts of racketeering activity," § 1961(5)(emphasis added), not that it "means" two such acts. The implication is that while two acts are necessary, they may not be sufficient. Indeed, in common parlance two of anything do not generally form a "pattern." The legislative history supports the view that two isolated acts of racketeering activity do not constitute a pattern. As the Senate Report explained: "The target of [RICO] is thus not sporadic activity. The infiltration of legiti-

mate business normally requires more than one 'racketeering activity' and the threat of continuing activity to be effective. It is this factor of *continuity plus relationship* which combines to produce a pattern." S. Rep. No. 91-617, p. 158 (1969)(emphasis added). Similarly, the sponsor of the Senate bill, after quoting this portion of the Report, pointed out to his colleagues that "[t]he term 'pattern' itself requires the showing of a relationship.... So, therefore, proof of two acts of racketeering activity, without more, does not establish a pattern...." 116 Cong. Rec. 18940 (1970)(statement of Sen. McClellan). See also id., at 35193 (statement of Rep. Poff)(RICO "not aimed at the isolated offender"). Significantly, in defining "pattern" in a later provision of the same bill, Congress was more enlightening: "[C]riminal conduct forms a pattern if it embraces criminal acts that have the same or similar purposes, results, participants, victims, or methods of commission, or otherwise are interrelated by distinguishing characteristics and are not isolated events." 18 U.S.C. § 3575(e). This language may be useful in interpreting other sections of the act. Cf. Iannelli v. United States, 420 U.S. 770, 789 (1975).

American National Bank & Trust Co. of Chicago, 747 F.2d 384, 398 (7th Cir.1984).

But the statute requires no more than this. Where the plaintiff alleges each element of the violation, the compensable injury necessarily is the harm caused by predicate acts sufficiently related to constitute a pattern, for the essence of the violation is the commission of those acts in connection with the conduct of an enterprise. Those acts are, when committed in the circumstances delineated in § 1962(c), "an activity which RICO was designed to deter." Any recoverable damages occurring by reason of a violation of § 1962(c) will flow from the commission of the predicate acts.[15]

This less restrictive reading is amply supported by our prior cases and the general principles surrounding this statute. RICO is to be read broadly. This is the lesson not only of Congress' self-consciously expansive language and overall approach, see United States v. Turkette, 452 U.S. 576, 586–87 (1981), but also of its express admonition that RICO is to "be liberally construed to effectuate its remedial purposes," § 904(a). The statute's "remedial purposes" are nowhere more evident than in the provision of a private action for those injured by racketeering activity. Far from effectuating these purposes, the narrow readings offered by the dissenters and the court below would in effect eliminate § 1964(c) from the statute.

RICO was an aggressive initiative to supplement old remedies and develop new methods for fighting crime. While few of the legislative statements about novel remedies and attacking crime on all fronts were made with direct reference to § 1964(c), it is in this spirit that all of the act's provisions should be read. The specific references to § 1964(c) are consistent with this overall approach. Those supporting § 1964(c) hoped it would "enhance the effectiveness of title IX's prohibitions," House Hearings, at 520, and provide "a major new tool," 116 Cong. Rec. 35227 (1970). Its opponents, also recognizing the provision's scope, complained that it provided too easy a weapon against "innocent businessmen," H.R. Rep. No. 91–1549, p. 187 (1970), and would be prone to abuse, 116 Cong. Rec. 35342 (1970). It is also significant that a previous proposal to add RICO-like

---

[15] Such damages include, but are not limited to, the sort of competitive injury for which the dissenters would allow recovery. Under the dissent's reading of the statute, the harm proximately caused by the forbidden conduct is not compensable, but that ultimately and indirectly flowing therefrom is. We reject this topsy-turvy approach, finding no warrant in the language or the history of the statute for denying recovery thereunder to "the direct victims of the [racketeering] activity," while preserving it for the indirect. Even the court below was not that grudging. It would apparently have allowed recovery for both the direct and the ultimate harm flowing from the defendant's conduct, requiring injury "not *simply* caused by the predicate acts, but *also* caused by an activity which RICO was designed to deter."

The dissent would also go further than did the Second Circuit in its requirement that the plaintiff have suffered a competitive injury. Again, as the court below stated, Congress "nowhere suggested that actual anti-competitive effect is required for suits under the statute." The language it chose, allowing recovery to "[a]ny person injured in his business *or property*," § 1964(c)(emphasis added), applied to this situation, suggests that the statute is not so limited.

provisions to the Sherman Act had come to grief in part precisely because it "could create inappropriate and unnecessary obstacles in the way of . . . a private litigant [who] would have to contend with a body of precedent—appropriate in a purely antitrust context—setting strict requirements on questions such as 'standing to sue' and 'proximate cause.'" 115 Cong. Rec. 6995 (1969)(ABA comments on S. 2048). In borrowing its "racketeering injury" requirement from antitrust standing principles, the court below created exactly the problems Congress sought to avoid.

Underlying the Court of Appeals' holding was its distress at the "extraordinary, if not outrageous," uses to which civil RICO has been put. Instead of being used against mobsters and organized criminals, it has become a tool for everyday fraud cases brought against "respected and legitimate 'enterprises.' " Yet Congress wanted to reach both "legitimate" and "illegitimate" enterprises. *United States v. Turkette,* supra. The former enjoy neither an inherent incapacity for criminal activity nor immunity from its consequences. The fact that § 1964(c) is used against respected businesses allegedly engaged in a pattern of specifically identified criminal conduct is hardly a sufficient reason for assuming that the provision is being misconstrued. Nor does it reveal the "ambiguity" discovered by the court below. "[T]he fact that RICO has been applied in situations not expressly anticipated by Congress does not demonstrate ambiguity. It demonstrates breadth." *Haroco, Inc. v. American National Bank & Trust Co. of Chicago,* supra, at 398.

It is true that private civil actions under the statute are being brought almost solely against such defendants, rather than against the archetypal, intimidating mobster.[16] Yet this defect—if defect it is—is inherent in the statute as written, and its correction must lie with Congress. It is not for the judiciary to eliminate the private action in situations where Congress has provided it simply because plaintiffs are not taking advantage of it in its more difficult applications.

We nonetheless recognize that, in its private civil version, RICO is evolving into something quite different from the original conception of its enactors. Though sharing the doubts of the Court of Appeals about this increasing divergence, we cannot agree with either its diagnosis or its remedy. The "extraordinary" uses to which civil RICO has been put appear to be primarily the result of the breadth of the predicate offenses, in particular the inclusion of wire, mail, and securities fraud, and the failure of Congress and the courts to develop a meaningful concept of "pattern." We do not believe that the amorphous standing requirement imposed by

---

[16] The ABA Task Force found that of the 270 known civil RICO cases at the trial court level, 40 per cent involved securities fraud, 37 per cent common-law fraud in a commercial or business setting, and only nine per cent "allegations of criminal activity of a type generally associated with professional criminals." ABA Report, at 55–56. Another survey of 132 published decisions found that 57 involved securities transactions and 38 commercial and contract disputes, while no other category made it into double figures. American Institute of Certified Public Accountants, The Authority to Bring Private Treble–Damage Suits Under "RICO" Should be Removed 13 (Oct. 10, 1984).

the Second Circuit effectively responds to these problems, or that it is a form of statutory amendment appropriately undertaken by the courts.

V

Sedima may maintain this action if the defendants conducted the enterprise through a pattern of racketeering activity. The questions whether the defendants committed the requisite predicate acts, and whether the commission of those acts fell into a pattern, are not before us. The complaint is not deficient for failure to allege either an injury separate from the financial loss stemming from the alleged acts of mail and wire fraud, or prior convictions of the defendants. The judgment below is accordingly reversed, and the case is remanded for further proceedings consistent with this opinion.

It is so ordered.

■ JUSTICE MARSHALL, with whom JUSTICE BRENNAN, JUSTICE BLACKMUN, and JUSTICE POWELL join, dissenting.

The Court today recognizes that "in its private civil version, RICO is evolving into something quite different from the original conception of its enactors." The Court, however, expressly validates this result, imputing it to the manner in which the statute was drafted. I fundamentally disagree both with the Court's reading of the statute and with its conclusion. I believe that the statutory language and history disclose a narrower interpretation of the statute that fully effectuates Congress' purposes, and that does not make compensable under civil RICO a host of claims that Congress never intended to bring within RICO's purview.

I

The Court's interpretation of the civil RICO statute quite simply revolutionizes private litigation; it validates the federalization of broad areas of state common law of frauds, and it approves the displacement of well-established federal remedial provisions. We do not lightly infer a congressional intent to effect such fundamental changes. To infer such intent here would be untenable, for there is no indication that Congress even considered, much less approved, the scheme that the Court today defines.

The single most significant reason for the expansive use of civil RICO has been the presence in the statute, as predicate acts, of mail and wire fraud violations. Prior to RICO, no federal statute had expressly provided a private damages remedy based upon a violation of the mail or wire fraud statutes, which make it a federal crime to use the mail or wires in furtherance of a scheme to defraud. See 18 U.S.C. §§ 1341, 1343. Moreover, the Courts of Appeals consistently had held that no implied federal private causes of action accrue to victims of these federal violations. The victims normally were restricted to bringing actions in state court under common-law fraud theories.

Under the Court's opinion today, two fraudulent mailings or uses of the wires occurring within 10 years of each other might constitute a "pattern of racketeering activity" leading to civil RICO liability. The effects of making a mere two instances of mail or wire fraud potentially actionable under civil RICO are staggering, because in recent years the Courts of Appeals have "tolerated an extraordinary expansion of mail and wire fraud statutes to permit federal prosecution for conduct that some had thought was subject only to state criminal and civil law." United States v. Weiss, 752 F.2d 777, 791 (2d Cir.1985)(Newman, J., dissenting). In bringing criminal actions under those statutes, prosecutors need not show either a substantial connection between the scheme to defraud and the mail and wire fraud statutes, see Pereira v. United States, 347 U.S. 1, 8 (1954), or that the fraud involved money or property. Courts have sanctioned prosecutions based on deprivations of such intangible rights as a shareholder's right to "material" information, United States v. Siegel, 717 F.2d 9, 14–16 (2d Cir.1983); a client's right to the "undivided loyalty" of his attorney, United States v. Bronston, 658 F.2d 920, 927 (2d Cir.1981); an employer's right to the honest and faithful service of his employees, United States v. Bohonus, 628 F.2d 1167, 1172 (9th Cir.1980); and a citizen's right to know the nature of agreements entered into by the leaders of political parties, United States v. Margiotta, 688 F.2d 108, 123–25 (2d Cir.1982).

The only restraining influence on the "inexorable expansion of the mail and wire fraud statutes," United States v. Siegel, 717 F.2d, at 24 (Winter, J., dissenting in part and concurring in part), has been the prudent use of prosecutorial discretion. Prosecutors simply do not invoke the mail and wire fraud provisions in every case in which a violation of the relevant statute can be proved. For example, only where the scheme is directed at a "class of persons or the general public" and includes "a substantial pattern of conduct," will "serious consideration . . . be given to [mail fraud] prosecution." In all other cases, "the parties should be left to settle their differences by civil or criminal litigation in the state courts." U.S. Dept. of Justice, United States Attorney's Manual § 9–43.120 (Feb. 16, 1984).

The responsible use of prosecutorial discretion is particularly important with respect to criminal RICO prosecutions—which often rely on mail and wire fraud as predicate acts—given the extremely severe penalties authorized by RICO's criminal provisions. Federal prosecutors are therefore instructed that "[u]tilization of the RICO statute, more so than most other federal criminal sanctions, requires particularly careful and reasoned application." Id., § 9–110.200 (Mar. 9, 1984). The Justice Department itself recognizes that a broad interpretation of the criminal RICO provisions would violate "the principle that the primary responsibility for enforcing state laws rests with the state concerned." Ibid. Specifically, the Justice Department will not bring RICO prosecutions unless the pattern of racketeering activity required by 18 U.S.C. § 1962 has "some relation to the purpose of the enterprise." United States Attorney's Manual § 9–110.350 (Mar. 9, 1984).

Congress was well aware of the restraining influence of prosecutorial discretion when it enacted the criminal RICO provisions. It chose to confer broad statutory authority on the executive fully expecting that this authority would be used only in cases in which its use was warranted. See Measures Relating to Organized Crime, Hearings on S. 30 et al. before the Subcommittee on Criminal Laws and Procedures of the Senate Committee on the Judiciary, 91st. Cong., 1st Sess., 346–47, 424 (1969)(hereinafter cited as Senate Hearings). Moreover, in seeking a broad interpretation of RICO from this Court in United States v. Turkette, 452 U.S. 576 (1981), the government stressed that no "extreme cases" would be brought because the Justice Department would exercise "sound discretion" through a centralized review process.

In the context of civil RICO, however, the restraining influence of prosecutors is completely absent. Unlike the government, private litigants have no reason to avoid displacing state common-law remedies. Quite to the contrary, such litigants, lured by the prospect of treble damages and attorney's fees, have a strong incentive to invoke RICO's provisions whenever they can allege in good faith two instances of mail or wire fraud. Then the defendant, facing a tremendous financial exposure in addition to the threat of being labeled a "racketeer," will have a strong interest in settling the dispute. See Jed S. Rakoff, Some Personal Reflections on the *Sedima* Case and on Reforming RICO, in RICO: Civil and Criminal 400 (Law Journal Seminars–Press 1984). The civil RICO provision consequently stretches the mail and wire fraud statutes to their absolute limits and federalizes important areas of civil litigation that until now were solely within the domain of the states.

In addition to altering fundamentally the federal-state balance in civil remedies, the broad reading of the civil RICO provision also displaces important areas of federal law. For example, one predicate offense under RICO is "fraud in the sale of securities." By alleging two instances of such fraud, a plaintiff might be able to bring a case within the scope of the civil RICO provision. It does not take great legal insight to realize that such a plaintiff would pursue his case under RICO rather than do so solely under the Securities Act of 1933 or the Securities Exchange Act of 1934, which provide both express and implied causes of action for violations of the federal securities laws. Indeed, the federal securities laws contemplate only compensatory damages and ordinarily do not authorize recovery of attorney's fees. By invoking RICO, in contrast, a successful plaintiff will recover both treble damages and attorney's fees.

More importantly, under the Court's interpretation, the civil RICO provision does far more than just increase the available damages. In fact, it virtually eliminates decades of legislative and judicial development of private civil remedies under the federal securities laws. Over the years, courts have paid close attention to matters such as standing, culpability, causation, reliance, and materiality, as well as the definitions of "securities" and "fraud." See, e.g., Blue Chip Stamps v. Manor Drug Stores, 421 U.S. 723 (1975)(purchaser/seller requirement). All of this law is now an endangered species because plaintiffs can avoid the limitations of the securities laws merely by alleging violations of other predicate acts. For example, even in cases in which the investment instrument is not a "security" covered by the federal securities laws, RICO will provide a treble-damages remedy to a plaintiff who can prove the required pattern of mail or wire fraud. Before RICO, of course, the plaintiff could not have recovered under federal law for the mail or wire fraud violation.

Similarly, a customer who refrained from selling a security during a period in which its market value was declining could allege that, on two occasions, his broker recommended by telephone, as part of a scheme to defraud, that the customer not sell the security. The customer might thereby prevail under civil RICO even though, as neither a purchaser nor a seller, he would not have had standing to bring an action under the federal securities laws. See also Sedima, S.P.R.L. v. Imrex Co., Inc., 741 F.2d 482, 499 (2d Cir.)(1984)("two misstatements in a proxy solicitation could subject any director in any national corporation to 'racketeering' charges and the threat of treble damages and attorneys' fees"). . . . The list goes on and on.

The dislocations caused by the Court's reading of the civil RICO provision are not just theoretical. In practice, this provision frequently has been invoked against legitimate businesses in ordinary commercial settings. As the Court recognizes, the ABA Task Force that studied civil RICO found that 40 per cent of the reported cases involved securities fraud and 37 per cent involved common-law fraud in a commercial or business setting. Many a prudent defendant, facing ruinous exposure, will decide to settle even a case with no merit. It is thus not surprising that civil RICO has been used for extortive purposes, giving rise to the very evils that it was designed to combat. Report of the Ad Hoc Civil RICO Task Force of the ABA Section of Corporation, Banking and Business Law 69 (1985)(hereinafter cited as ABA Report).

Only nine per cent of all civil RICO cases have involved allegations of criminal activity normally associated with professional criminals. The central purpose that Congress sought to promote through civil RICO is now a mere footnote.

In summary, in both theory and practice, civil RICO has brought profound changes to our legal landscape. Undoubtedly, Congress has the power to federalize a great deal of state common law, and there certainly are no relevant constraints on its ability to displace federal law. Those, however, are not the questions that we face in this case. What we have to decide here, instead, is whether Congress in fact intended to produce these far-reaching results.

Established canons of statutory interpretation counsel against the Court's reading of the civil RICO provision. First, we do not impute lightly a congressional intention to upset the federal-state balance in the provision of civil remedies as fundamentally as does this statute under the Court's view. . . . Second, with respect to effects on the federal securities laws and other federal regulatory statutes, we should be reluctant to displace the well-entrenched federal remedial schemes absent clear direction from Congress.

In this case, nothing in the language of the statute or the legislative history suggests that Congress intended either the federalization of state common law or the displacement of existing federal remedies. Quite to the contrary, all that the statute and the legislative history reveal as to these matters is what Judge Oakes [in his opinion below] called a "clanging silence."

Moreover, if Congress has intended to bring about dramatic changes in the nature of commercial litigation, it would at least have paid more than cursory attention to the civil RICO provision. This provision was added in the House of Representatives after the Senate already had passed its version of the RICO bill; the House itself adopted a civil remedy provision almost as an afterthought; and the Senate thereafter accepted the House's version of the bill without even requesting a Conference. Congress simply does not act in this way when it intends to effect fundamental changes in the structure of federal law.

II

The statutory language and legislative history support the view that Congress did not intend to effect a radical alteration of federal civil litigation. In fact, the language and history indicate a congressional intention to limit, in a workable and coherent manner, the type of injury that is compensable under the civil RICO provision. As the following demonstrates, Congress sought to fill an existing gap in civil remedies and to provide a means of compensation that otherwise did not exist for the honest businessman harmed by the economic power of "racketeers."

A

I begin with a review of the statutory language. Section 1964(c) grants a private right of action to any person "injured in his business or property by reason of a violation of section 1962." Section 1962, in turn, makes it unlawful to invest, in an enterprise engaged in interstate commerce, funds "derived ... from a pattern of racketeering activity," to acquire or operate an interest in any such enterprise through "a pattern of racketeering activity," or to conduct or participate in the conduct of that enterprise "through a pattern of racketeering activity." Section 1961 defines "racketeering activity" to mean any of numerous acts "chargeable" or "indictable" under enumerated state and federal laws, including state-law murder, arson, and bribery statutes, federal mail and wire fraud statutes, and the antifraud provisions of federal securities laws. It states that "a pattern" of racketeering activity requires proof of at least two acts of racketeering within 10 years.

By its terms, § 1964(c) therefore grants a cause of action only to a person injured "by reason of a violation of *§ 1962*." The Court holds today that the only injury a plaintiff need allege is injury occurring by reason of a predicate, or racketeering, act—i.e., one of the offenses listed in § 1961.

But § 1964(c) does not by its terms provide a remedy for injury by reason of *§ 1961*; it requires an injury by reason of *§ 1962*. In other words:

> "While § 1962 prohibits the involvement of an 'enterprise' in 'racketeering activity,' racketeering *itself* is not a violation of § 1962. Thus, a construction of RICO permitting recovery for damages arising out of the racketeering acts simply does not comport with the statute as written by Congress. In effect, the broad construction replaces the rule that treble damages can be recovered only when they occur *'by reason of* a violation of section 1962,' with a rule permitting recovery of treble damages *whenever* there has been a violation of § 1962. Such unwarranted judicial interference with the act's plain meaning cannot be justified." Comment, 76 Nw. U. L. Rev. 100, 128 (1981).

See also Andrew P. Bridges, Private RICO Litigation Based Upon "Fraud in the Sale of Securities," 18 Ga. L. Rev. 43, 67 (1983).

In addition, the statute permits recovery only for injury to business or property. It therefore excludes recovery for personal injuries. However, many of the predicate acts listed in § 1961 threaten or inflict personal injuries—such as murder and kidnaping. If Congress in fact intended the victims of the predicate acts to recover for their injuries, as the Court holds it did, it is inexplicable why Congress would have limited recovery to business or property injury. It simply makes no sense to allow recovery by some, but not other victims of predicate acts, and to make recovery turn solely on whether the defendant has chosen to inflict personal pain or harm to property in order to accomplish its end.

In summary, the statute clearly contemplates recovery for injury resulting from the confluence of events described in § 1962 and not merely from the commission of a predicate act. The Court's contrary interpretation distorts the statutory language under the guise of adopting a plain-meaning definition, and it does so without offering any indication of congressional intent that justifies a deviation from what I have shown to be the plain meaning of the statute. However, even if the statutory language were ambiguous, the scope of the civil RICO provision would be no different, for this interpretation of the statute finds strong support in the legislative history of that provision.

B

In reviewing the legislative history of civil RICO, numerous federal courts have become mired in controversy about the extent to which Congress intended to adopt or reject the federal antitrust laws as a model for the RICO provisions. The basis for the dispute among the lower courts is the language of the treble-damages provision, which tracks virtually word for word the treble-damages provision of the antitrust laws, § 4 of the Clayton Act;[1] given this parallel, there can be little doubt that the latter

---

[1] Section 1964(c) provides:
"Any person injured in his business or property by reason of a violation of section 1962 of this chapter may sue

served as a model for the former. Some courts have relied heavily on this congruity to read an antitrust-type "competitive injury" requirement into the civil RICO statute. Other courts have rejected a competitive-injury requirement, or any antitrust analogy, relying in significant part on what they perceive as Congress' rejection of a wholesale adoption of antitrust precedent.

Many of these courts have read far too much into the antitrust analogy. The legislative history makes clear that Congress viewed the form of civil remedies under RICO as analogous to such remedies under the antitrust laws, but that it did not thereby intend the substantive compensable injury to be exactly the same. The legislative history also suggests that Congress might have wanted to avoid saddling the civil RICO provisions with the same standing requirements that at the time limited standing to sue under the antitrust laws. However, the Committee Reports and hearings in no way suggest that Congress considered and rejected a requirement of injury separate from that resulting from the predicate acts. Far from it, Congress offered considerable indication that the kind of injury it primarily sought to attack and compensate was that for which existing civil and criminal remedies were inadequate or nonexistent; the requisite injury is thus akin to, but broader than, that targeted by the antitrust laws and different in kind from that resulting from the underlying predicate acts.

A brief look at the legislative history makes clear that the antitrust laws in no relevant respect constrain our analysis or preclude formulation of an independent RICO-injury requirement. When Senator Hruska first introduced to Congress the predecessor to RICO, he proposed an amendment to the Sherman Act that would have prohibited the investment or use of intentionally unreported income from one line of business to establish, operate, or invest in another line of business. S. 2048, 90th Cong., 1st Sess. (1967). After studying the provision, the American Bar Association issued a report that, while acknowledging the effects of organized crime's infiltration of legitimate business, stated a preference for a provision separate from the antitrust laws. According to the report:

> "By placing the antitrust-type enforcement and recovery procedures in a separate statute, a commingling of criminal enforcement goals with the goals of regulating competition is avoided.
>
> . . .

therefor in any appropriate United States district court and shall recover threefold the damages he sustains and the cost of the suit, including a reasonable attorney's fee."

Section 4 of the Clayton Act, 15 U.S.C. § 15, provides in relevant part:

"[A]ny person who shall be injured in his business or property by reason of

anything forbidden in the antitrust laws may sue therefor in any district court of the United States in the district in which the defendant resides or is found or has an agent, without respect to the amount in controversy, and shall recover threefold the damages by him sustained, and the cost of suit, including a reasonable attorney's fee."

"Moreover, the use of antitrust laws themselves as a vehicle for combating organized crime could create inappropriate and unnecessary obstacles in the way of persons injured by organized crime who might seek treble damage recovery. Such a private litigant would have to contend with a body of precedent—appropriate in a purely antitrust context—setting strict requirements on questions such as 'standing to sue' and 'proximate cause.' " 115 Cong. Rec. 6995 (1969).

Congress subsequently decided not to pursue an addition to the antitrust laws but instead to fashion a wholly separate criminal statute. If in fact that decision was made in response to the ABA's statement and not to other political concerns, it may be interpreted at most as a rejection of antitrust *standing* requirements. Court-developed standing rules define the requisite proximity between the plaintiff's injury and the defendant's antitrust violation. See Blue Shield of Virginia v. McCready, 457 U.S. 465, 476 (1982)(discussing antitrust standing rules developed in the federal Circuits). Thus, at most we may read the early legislative history to eschew wholesale adoption of the particular nexus requirements that limit the class of potential antitrust plaintiffs. Courts that read this history to bar *any* analogy to the antitrust laws simply read too much into the scant evidence available to us. In particular, courts that read this history to bar an injury requirement akin to "antitrust" injury are in error. The requirement of antitrust injury, as articulated in Brunswick Corp. v. Pueblo Bowl–O–Mat, Inc., 429 U.S. 477 (1977), differs in kind from the standing requirement to which the ABA referred and, in fact, had not been articulated at the time of the ABA comments.

At the same time, courts that believe civil RICO doctrine should mirror civil antitrust doctrine also read too much into the legislative history. It is absolutely clear that Congress intended to adopt antitrust *remedies*, such as civil actions by the government and treble damages. The House of Representatives added the civil provision to title IX in response to suggestions from the ABA and Congressmen that there be a remedy "similar to the private damages remedy found in the anti-trust laws," Organized Crime Control: Hearings on S. 30 and Related Proposals, before Subcommittee No. 5 of the House Committee on the Judiciary, 91st Cong., 2d Sess., 520 (1970)(statement of Rep. Steiger)(hereinafter House Hearings). The decision to adopt antitrust remedies does not, however, compel the conclusion that Congress intended to adopt substantive antitrust doctrine. Courts that construe these references to the antitrust laws as indications of Congress' intent to adopt the substance of antitrust doctrine also read too much into too little language.

C

While the foregoing establishes that Congress sought to adopt remedies akin to those used in antitrust law—such as civil government enforcement—and to reject antitrust standing rules, other portions of the legislative history reveal just what Congress intended the substantive dimensions of the civil action to be. Quite simply, its principal target was the economic power of racketeers, and its toll on legitimate businessmen. To this end, Congress sought to fill a gap in the civil and criminal laws and to provide new remedies broader than those already available to private or government antitrust plaintiffs, different from those available to government and private citizens under state and federal laws, and significantly narrower than those adopted by the Court today.

In 1967, Senator Hruska proposed two bills, S. 2048 and S. 2049, 90th Cong., 1st Sess., which were designed in part to implement recommendations of the President's Commission on Law Enforcement and the Administration of Justice (the Katzenbach Commission) on the fight against organized crime. See 113 Cong. Rec. 17998–18001 (1967). The former bill proposed an amendment to the Sherman Act prohibiting the investment or use of unreported income derived from one line of business in another business. The latter bill, which was separate from the Sherman Act, prohibited the acquisition of a business interest with income derived from criminal activity. Representative Poff introduced similar bills in the House of Representatives. See H.R. 11266, H.R. 11268, 90th Cong., 1st Sess. (1967); 113 Cong. Rec. 17976 (1967).

Introducing S. 2048, Senator Hruska explained that "[b]y limiting its application to intentionally unreported income, this proposal highlights the fact that *the evil to be curbed is the unfair competitive advantage inherent in the large amount of illicit income available to organized crime.*" (Emphasis added.) He described how organized crime had infiltrated a wide range of businesses, and he observed that "[i]n each of these instances, large amounts of cash coupled with threats of violence, extortion, and similar techniques were utilized by mobsters *to achieve their desired objectives: monopoly control of these enterprises.*" (Emphasis added.) He identified four means by which control of legitimate business had been acquired:

> "First. Investing concealed profits acquired from gambling and other illegal enterprises.

> "Second. Accepting business interests in payment of the owner's gambling debts.

> "Third. Foreclosing on usurious loans.

> "Fourth. Using various forms of extortion."

The Senator then explained how this infiltration takes its toll:

> "The proper functioning of a free economy requires that economic decisions be made by persons free to exercise their own judgment. Force or fear limits choice, ultimately reduces quality, and increases prices. When organized crime moves into a business, it brings all the techniques of violence and intimidation which it used in its illegal businesses. Competitors are eliminated and customers confined to sponsored suppliers. Its effect is even more unwholesome than other monopolies because its position does not rest on economic superiority."

Congress never took action on these bills.

In 1969, Senator McClellan introduced the Organized Crime Control Act, which altered numerous criminal law areas such as grand juries, immunity, and sentencing, but which contained no provision like that now known as RICO. See S. 30, 91st Cong., 1st Sess.; 115 Cong. Rec. 769 (1969). Shortly thereafter, Senator Hruska introduced the Criminal Activities Profits Act. S. 1623, 91st Cong., 1st Sess.; 115 Cong. Rec. 6995–96 (1969). He explained that S. 1623 was designed to synthesize the earlier two bills (S. 2048 and S. 2049) while placing the "unified whole" outside the Sherman Act in response to the ABA's concerns. According to the Senator, the bill was meant to attack *the economic power of organized crime and its exercise of unfair competition with honest businessmen*," and to address "[t]he power of organized crime to establish a monopoly within numerous business fields" and the impact on the free market and honest competitors of "a racketeer dominated venture." (Emphasis added.)

As introduced, S. 1623 contained a provision for a private treble-damages action; the language of that provision was virtually identical to that in § 1964(c), and it likely served as the model for § 1964(c). Explaining this provision, Senator Hruska said:

"In addition to this criminal prohibition, the bill also creates civil remedies for the honest businessman who has been damaged by unfair competition from the racketeer businessman. Despite the willingness of the courts to apply the Sherman Anti–Trust Act to organized crime activities, *as a practical matter the legitimate businessman does not have adequate civil remedies available under that act. That bill fills that gap.*" (Emphasis added.)

The Senate did not act directly on either S. 30 or S. 1623. Instead, Senators McClellan and Hruska jointly introduced S. 1861, the Corrupt Organizations Act of 1969, 91st Cong., 1st Sess.; 115 Cong. Rec. 9568–71, which combined features of the two other bills and added to them. The new bill expanded the list of offenses that would constitute "racketeering activity" and required that the proscribed conduct be committed through a pattern of "racketeering activity." It did not, however, contain a private civil remedy provision, but only authorization for an injunctive action brought by the Attorney General. Senator McClellan thereafter requested that the provisions of S. 1861 be incorporated by amendment into the broad Organized Crime Control Act, S. 30. See 115 Cong. Rec. 9566–71 (1969).

In December 1969, the Senate Judiciary Committee reported on the Organized Crime Control Act, S. 30, as amended to include S. 1861 as title IX, "Racketeer Influenced and Corrupt Organizations." Title IX, it is clear, was aimed at precisely the same evil that Senator Hruska had targeted in 1967—the infiltration of legitimate business by organized crime. According to the Committee Report, the title

"has as its purpose the elimination of the infiltration of organized crime and racketeering into legitimate organizations operating in interstate commerce. It seeks to achieve this objective by the fashioning of new criminal and civil remedies and investigative procedures." S. Rep. No. 91–617, p. 76 (1969).

In language taken virtually verbatim from the earlier floor statements of Senator Hruska, the Report described the extraordinary range of legitimate businesses and unions that had been infiltrated by racketeers, and the means by which the racketeers sought to profit from the infiltration. It described "scams" involving bankruptcy and insurance fraud, and the use of "force or fear" to secure a monopoly in the service or product of the business, and it summed up: "When the campaign is successful, the organization begins to extract a premium price from customers."

Similarly, Senator Byrd spoke in favor of title IX and gave other examples of the "awesome power" of racketeers and their methods of operation. He described, for example, how one racketeer had gained a foothold in a detergent company and then had used arson and murder to try to get the A & P Tea Co. to buy a detergent that A & P had tested and rejected. 116 Cong. Rec. 607 (1970). As another example, he explained that racketeers would corner the market on a good or service and then withhold it from a businessman until he surrendered his business or made some other related economic concession. In each of these cases, I note, the racketeer engaged in criminal acts in order to accomplish a commercial goal—e.g., to destroy competition, create a monopoly, or infiltrate a legitimate business. ... In sum, "[s]crutiny of the Senate Report ... establishes without a doubt a single dominating purpose of the Senate in proposing the RICO statute: 'Title IX represents the committee's careful efforts to fashion new remedies to deal with the infiltration of organized crime into legitimate organizations operating in interstate commerce.'" ABA Report 105.

The bill passed the Senate after a short debate by a vote of 73 to one, without a treble-damages provision, and it was then considered by the House. In hearings before the House Judiciary Committee, it was suggested that the bill should include "the additional civil remedy of authorizing private damage suits based upon the concept of § 4 of the Clayton Act." House Hearings, at 543–44 (statement of Edward Wright, ABA president-elect). Before reporting the bill favorably in September 1970, the House Judiciary Committee made one change to the civil remedy provision—it added a private treble-damages provision to the civil remedies already available to the government; the Committee accorded this change only a single statement in the Committee Report: "The title, as amended, also authorizes civil treble damage suits on the part of private parties who are injured." H.R. Rep. No. 91–1549, p. 35 (1970). Three Congressmen dissented from the Report. Their views are particularly telling because, with language that is narrow compared to the extraordinary scope the civil provision has acquired, these three challenged the possible breadth and abuse of the private civil remedy by plaintiff-*competitors*:

> "Indeed, [§ 1964(c)] provides invitation for disgruntled and malicious *competitors* to harass innocent businessmen engaged in inter-

state commerce by authorizing private damage suits. A *competitor* need only raise the claim that his rival has derived gains from two games of poker, and, because this title prohibits even the 'indirect use' of such gains—a provision with tremendous outreach—litigation is begun. What a protracted, expensive trial may not succeed in doing, the adverse publicity may well accomplish—destruction of the rival's business." Id., at 187 (emphasis added).

The bill then returned to the Senate, which passed it without a conference, apparently to assure passage during the session. Thus, the private remedy at issue here slipped quietly into the statute, and its entrance evinces absolutely no intent to revolutionize the enforcement scheme, or to give undue breadth to the broadly worded provisions—provisions Congress fully expected government enforcers to narrow.

Putting together these various pieces, I can only conclude that Congress intended to give to businessmen who might otherwise have had no available remedy a possible way to recover damages for competitive injury, infiltration injury, or other economic injury resulting out of, but wholly distinct from, the predicate acts. Congress fully recognized that racketeers do not engage in predicate acts *as ends in themselves*; instead, racketeers threaten, burn, and murder in order to induce their victims to act in a way that accrues to the economic benefit of the racketeer, as by ceasing to compete, or agreeing to make certain purchases. Congress' concern was not for the direct victims of the racketeers' acts, whom state and federal laws already protected, but for the competitors and investors whose businesses and interests are harmed or destroyed by racketeers, or whose competitive positions decline because of infiltration in the relevant market. Its focus was on the victims of the extraordinary economic power that racketeers are able to acquire through a wide range of illicit methods. Indeed, that is why Congress provided for recovery only for injury to business or property—that is, commercial injuries—and not for personal physical or emotional injury.

The only way to give effect to Congress' concern is to require that plaintiffs plead and prove that they suffered RICO injury—injury to their competitive, investment, or other business interests resulting from the defendant's conduct of a business or infiltration of a business or a market, through a pattern of racketeering activity. As I shall demonstrate, this requirement is manageable, and it puts the statute to the use to which it was addressed. In addition, this requirement is faithful to the language of the statute, which does not appear to provide recovery for injuries incurred by reason of individual predicate acts. It also avoids most of the "extraordinary uses" to which the statute has been put, in which legitimate businesses that have engaged in two criminal acts have been labeled "racketeers," have faced treble-damages judgments in favor of the direct victims, and often have settled to avoid the destructive publicity and the resulting harm to reputation. These cases take their toll; their results distort the market by saddling legitimate businesses with uncalled-for punitive bills and undeserved labels. To allow punitive actions and significant damages for injury beyond that which the statute was intended to target is to achieve nothing the statute sought to achieve, and ironically to injure many of those lawful businesses that the statute sought to protect. Under such circumstances, I believe this Court is derelict in its failure to interpret the statute in keeping with the language and intent of Congress.

Several lower courts have remarked, however, that a "RICO injury" requirement, while perhaps contemplated by the statute, defies definition. I disagree. The following series of examples, culled in part from the legislative history of the RICO statute, illustrates precisely what does and does not fall within this definition.

First. If a "racketeer" uses "[t]hreats, arson and assault . . . to force competitors out of business and obtain larger shares of the market," House Hearings, at 106 (statement of Sen. McClellan), the threats, arson, and assault represent the predicate acts. The pattern of those acts is designed to accomplish, and accomplishes, the goal of monopolization. Competitors thereby injured or forced out of business could allege "RICO" injury and recover damages for lost profits. So, too, purchasers of the racketeer's goods or services, who are forced to buy from the racketeer/monopolist at higher prices, and whose businesses therefore are injured, might recover damages for the excess costs of doing business. The direct targets of the predicate acts—whether competitors, suppliers, or others—could recover for damages flowing from the predicate acts themselves, but under state or perhaps other federal law, not RICO.

Second. If a "racketeer" uses arson and threats to induce honest businessmen to pay protection money, or to purchase certain goods, or to hire certain workers, the targeted businessmen could sue to recover for injury to their business and property resulting from the added costs. This would be so if they were the direct victims of the predicate acts or if they had reacted to offenses committed against other businessmen. In each case, the predicate acts were committed in order to accomplish a certain end—e.g., to induce the prospective plaintiffs to take action to the economic benefit of the racketeer; in each case the result would have taken a toll on the competitive position of the prospective plaintiff by increasing his costs of doing business.

At the same time, the plaintiffs could not recover under RICO for the direct damages from the predicate acts. They could not, for example, recover for the cost of the building burned, or for personal injury resulting from the threat. Indeed, compensation for this latter injury is barred already by RICO's exclusion of personal injury claims. As in the previous example, these injuries are amply protected by state-law damages actions.

Third. If a "racketeer" infiltrates and obtains control of a legitimate business either through fraud, foreclosure on usurious loans, extortion, or acceptance of business interests in payment of gambling debts, the honest investor who is thereby displaced could bring a civil RICO action claiming infiltration injury resulting from the infiltrator's pattern of predicate acts that enabled him to gain control. Thereafter, if the enterprise conducts its business through a pattern of racketeering activity to enhance its profits or perpetuate its economic power, competitors of that enterprise could bring civil RICO actions alleging injury by reason of the enhanced commercial position the enterprise has obtained from its unlawful acts, and customers forced to purchase from sponsored suppliers could recovery their added costs of doing business. At the same time, the direct victims of the activity—for example, customers defrauded by an infiltrated bank—could not recover under civil RICO. The bank does not, of course, thereby escape liability. The customers simply must rely on the existing causes of action, usually under state law.

Alternatively, if the infiltrated enterprise operates a legitimate business to a businessman's competitive disadvantage because of the enterprise's strong economic base derived from perpetration of predicate acts, the competitor could bring a civil RICO action alleging injury to his competitive position. The predicate acts then would have enabled the "enterprise" to gain a competitive advantage that brought harm to the plaintiff-competitor. Again, the direct victims of the predicate acts whose profits were invested in the "legitimate enterprise," would not be able to recover damages under civil RICO for injury resulting from the predicate acts alone.

These examples are not exclusive, and if this formulation were adopted, lower courts would, of course, have the opportunity to smooth numerous rough edges. The examples are designed simply to illustrate the type of injury that civil RICO was, to my mind, designed to compensate. The construction I describe offers a powerful remedy to the honest businessmen with whom Congress was concerned, who might have had no recourse against a "racketeer" prior to enactment of the statute. At the same time, this construction avoids both the theoretical and practical problems outlined in part I. Under this view, traditional state-law claims are not federalized; federal remedial schemes are not inevitably displaced or superseded; and, consequently, ordinary commercial disputes are not misguidedly placed within the scope of civil RICO.[2]

III

The Court today permits two civil actions for treble damages to go forward that are not authorized either by the legislative history of the civil RICO statute, or by the policies that underlay passage of that statute. In so doing, the Court shirks its well-recognized responsibility to assure that Congress' intent is not thwarted by maintenance of unintended litigation, and it does so based on an unfounded and ill-considered reading of a statutory provision. Because I believe the provision at issue is susceptible of a narrower interpretation that comports both with the statutory language and the legislative history, I dissent.

---

[2] The analysis in my dissent would lead to the dismissal of the civil RICO claims at stake here. I thus do not need to decide whether a civil RICO action can proceed only after a criminal conviction.

■ JUSTICE POWELL, dissenting.

I agree with Justice Marshall that the Court today reads the civil RICO statute in a way that validates uses of the statute that were never intended by Congress, and I join his dissent. I write separately to emphasize my disagreement with the Court's conclusion that the statute must be applied to authorize the types of private civil actions now being brought frequently against respected businesses to redress ordinary fraud and breach-of-contract cases.[1]

I

In United States v. Turkette, 452 U.S. 576, 580 (1981), the Court noted that in construing the scope of a statute, its language, if unambiguous, must be regarded as conclusive *"in the absence* of a 'clearly expressed legislative intent to the contrary.' " Accord, Russello v. United States, 464 U.S. 16, 20 (1983). In both *Turkette* and *Russello*, we found that the "declared purpose" of Congress in enacting the RICO statute was " 'to seek the eradication of organized crime in the United States.' " That organized crime was Congress' target is apparent from the act's title, is made plain throughout the legislative history of the statute, and is acknowledged by all parties to these two cases. The legislative history cited by the Court today amply supports this conclusion, and the Court concedes that "in its private civil version, RICO is evolving into something quite different from the original conception of its enactors." Yet, the Court concludes that it is compelled by the statutory language to construe § 1964(c) to reach garden-variety fraud and breach of contract cases such as those before us today.

As the Court of Appeals observed in this case, "[i]f Congress had intended to provide a federal forum for plaintiffs for so many common law wrongs, it would at least have discussed it."[2] The Court today concludes that Congress *was* aware of the broad scope of the statute, relying on the fact that some Congressmen objected to the possibility of abuse of the RICO statute by arguing that it could be used "to harass innocent businessmen." H.R. Rep. No. 91–1549, p. 187 (1970)(dissenting views of Reps. Conyers, Mikva, and Ryan); 116 Cong. Rec. 35342 (1970)(remarks of Rep. Mikva).

In the legislative history of every statute, one may find critics of the bill who predict dire consequences in the event of its enactment. A court need not infer from such statements by opponents that Congress *intended* those consequences to occur, particularly where, as here, there is compelling evidence to the contrary. The legislative history reveals that Congress did not state explicitly that the statute would reach only members of the Mafia because it believed there were constitutional problems with establishing such a specific status offense. Nonetheless, the legislative history

[1] The Court says these suits are not being brought against the "archetypal, intimidating mobster" because of a "defect" that is "inherent in the statute." If RICO must be construed as the Court holds, this is indeed a defect that Congress never intended. I do not believe that the statute *must* be construed in what in effect is an irrational manner.

[2] The force of this observation is accented by RICO's provision for treble damages—an enticing invitation to litigate these claims in federal courts.

makes clear that the statute was intended to be *applied* to organized crime, and an influential sponsor of the bill emphasized that any effect it had beyond such crime was meant to be only incidental. Id., at 18914 (remarks of Sen. McClellan).

The ABA study concurs in this view. The ABA Report states [at 71–72]:

> "In an attempt to ensure the constitutionality of the statute, Congress made the central proscription of the statute the use of a 'pattern of racketeering activities' in connection with an 'enterprise,' rather than merely outlawing membership in the Mafia, La Cosa Nostra, or other organized criminal syndicates. 'Racketeering' was defined to embrace a potpourri of federal and state criminal offenses deemed to be the type of criminal activities frequently engaged in by mobsters, racketeers and other traditional members of 'organized crime.' The 'pattern' element of the statute was designed to limit its application to planned, ongoing, continuing crime as opposed to sporadic, unrelated, isolated criminal episodes. The 'enterprise' element, when coupled with the 'pattern' requirement, was intended by the Congress to keep the reach of RICO focused directly on traditional organized crime and comparable ongoing criminal activities carried out in a structured, organized environment. The reach of the statute beyond traditional mobster and racketeer activity and comparable ongoing structured criminal enterprises, was intended to be incidental, and only to the extent necessary to maintain the constitutionality of a statute aimed primarily at organized crime."

It has turned out in this case that the naysayers' dire predictions have come true. As the Court notes, RICO has been interpreted so broadly that it has been used more often against respected businesses with no ties to organized crime, than against the mobsters who were the clearly intended target of the statute. While I acknowledge that the language of the statute *may* be read as broadly as the Court interprets it today, I do not believe that it *must* be so read. Nor do I believe that interpreting the statutory language more narrowly than the Court does will "eliminate the [civil RICO] private action" in cases of the kind clearly identified by the legislative history. The statute may and should be read narrowly to confine its reach to the type of conduct Congress had in mind. It is the duty of this Court to implement the unequivocal intention of Congress.

II

The language of this complex statute is susceptible of being read consistently with this intent. For example, the requirement in the statute of proof of a "pattern" of racketeering activity may be interpreted narrowly. Section 1961(5), defining "pattern of racketeering activity," states that such a pattern "requires at least two acts of racketeering activity." This contrasts with the definition of "racketeering activity" in § 1961(1), stating that such activity "means" any of a number of acts. The definition of "pattern" may thus logically be interpreted as meaning that the presence of the predicate acts is only the beginning: something more is required for a "pattern" to be proved. The ABA Report concurs in this view. It argues persuasively that "[t]he 'pattern' element of the statute was designed to limit its application to planned, ongoing, continuing crime as opposed to sporadic, unrelated, isolated criminal episodes," ABA Report 72, such as the criminal acts alleged in the case before us today.

The legislative history bears out this interpretation of "pattern." Senator McClellan, a leading sponsor of the bill, stated that "proof of two acts of racketeering activity, without more, does not establish a pattern." 116 Cong. Rec. 18940 (1970). Likewise, the Senate Report considered the "concept of 'pattern' [to be] essential to the operation of the statute." S. Rep., at 158. It stated that the bill was not aimed at sporadic activity, but that the "infiltration of legitimate business normally requires more than one 'racketeering activity' *and* the threat of continuing activity to be effective. It is this factor of continuity *plus* relationship which combines to produce a pattern." (Emphasis added.) The ABA Report suggests that to effectuate this legislative intent, "pattern" should be interpreted as requiring that (i) the racketeering acts be related to each other, (ii) they be part of some common scheme, and (iii) some sort of continuity between the acts or a threat of continuing criminal activity must be shown. ABA Report, at 193–208. By construing "pattern" to focus on the manner in which the crime was perpetrated, courts could go a long way toward limiting the reach of the statute to its intended target—organized crime.

The Court concedes that "pattern" could be narrowly construed, ante n.14, and notes that part of the reason civil RICO has been put to such extraordinary uses is because of the "failure of Congress and the courts to develop a meaningful concept of 'pattern.'" The Court declines to decide whether the defendants' acts constitute such a pattern in this case, however, because it concludes that that question is not before the Court. I agree that the scope of the "pattern" requirement is not included in the questions on which we granted certiorari. I am concerned, however, that in the course of rejecting the Court of Appeals' ruling that the statute requires proof of a "racketeering injury" the Court has read the entire statute so broadly that it will be difficult, if not impossible, for courts to adopt a reading of "pattern" that will conform to the intention of Congress.

The Court bases its rejection of the "racketeering injury" requirement on the general principles that the RICO statute is to be read "broadly," that it is to be "'liberally construed to effectuate its remedial purposes,'" and that the statute was part of "an aggressive initiative to supplement old remedies and develop new methods for fighting crime." Although the Court acknowledges that few of the legislative statements supporting these principles were made with references to RICO's private civil action, it concludes nevertheless that all the act's provisions should be read in the "spirit" of these principles. By constructing such a broad premise for its rejection of the "racketeering injury" requirement, the Court seems to mandate that all future courts read the entire statute broadly.

It is neither necessary to the Court's decision, nor in my view correct, to read the civil RICO provisions so expansively. We ruled in *Turkette* and *Russello* that the statute must be read broadly and construed liberally to effectuate its remedial purposes, but like the legislative history to which the Court alludes, it is clear we were referring there to RICO's *criminal* provisions. It does not necessarily follow that the same principles apply to RICO's private civil provisions. The Senate Report recognized a difference between criminal and civil enforcement in describing proposed civil remedies that would have been available to the government. It emphasized that although those proposed remedies were intended to place additional pressure on organized crime, they were intended to reach "essentially an economic, *not* a punitive goal." S. Rep. at 81 (emphasis added). The Report elaborated as follows:

> "However remedies may be fashioned, it is necessary to free the channels of commerce from predatory activities, *but* there is no intent to visit punishment on any individual; the purpose is civil. Punishment as such is limited to the criminal remedies...." (Emphasis added.)

The reference in the Report to "predatory activities" was to organized crime. Only a small fraction of the scores of civil RICO cases now being brought implicate organized crime in any way. Typically, these suits are being brought—in the unfettered discretion of private litigants—in federal court against legitimate businesses seeking treble damages in ordinary fraud and contract cases. There is nothing comparable in those cases to the restraint on the institution of criminal suits exercised by government prosecutorial discretion. Today's opinion inevitably will encourage continued expansion of resort to RICO in cases of alleged fraud or contract violation rather than to the traditional remedies available in state court. As the Court of Appeals emphasized, it defies rational belief, particularly in light of the legislative history, that Congress intended this far-reaching result. Accordingly, I dissent.

INTRODUCTORY NOTES ON ENTERPRISE CRIMINALITY

1. *Sedima* and the Concept of Enterprise Criminality. *Sedima* was not the first "enterprise criminality" case to reach the U.S. Supreme Court, but it is certainly one of the most important ones. In *Sedima*, the Court effectively gave its stamp of approval to Congress's new method of dealing with organized crime. The Court did so in two ways. First, the Court refused to place significant limits on the scope of so-called "civil RICO," or that part of the RICO statute (not duplicated in the CCE statute) that provides private parties with a cause of action—for treble damages—if they have been injured "by reason of" a RICO violation. See 18 U.S.C. § 1964(c). Second, the Court stressed generally, pursuant to Congressional direction, that "RICO is to be read broadly" so as to "effectuate its remedial purposes." With few exceptions, this point of view has largely prevailed in the Court's post-*Sedima* RICO decisions.

Sedima is important for another reason. In footnote 14 of *Sedima*, the Court explained (in dictum) that the "pattern" element of RICO—which requires "at least two acts of racketeering activity," see 18 U.S.C. § 1961(5)—is not necessarily satisfied merely by proving the occurrence of any two or more of the specific criminal acts that the RICO statute identifies as "racketeering activity." However, the Court did not provide a precise definition of a RICO "pattern." Footnote 14 of *Sedima* has been cited and discussed by the Court in several subsequent RICO decisions, and has also been relied upon by dozens of lower federal courts. RICO's "pattern" element is addressed later in this Chapter.

2. The RICO Statute. The Racketeer Influenced and Corrupt Organizations Act (RICO) was enacted as title IX of the Organized Crime Control Act of 1970. It is codified in 18 U.S.C. §§ 1961–1968. Further details of the statute will be addressed in subsequent materials. For now, these provisions—including amendments to the statute enacted through 1996—are relevant:

§ 1961. Definitions

As used in this chapter—

(1) "racketeering activity" means (A) any act or threat involving murder, kidnapping, gambling, arson, robbery, bribery, extortion, dealing in obscene matter, or dealing in a controlled substance or listed chemical (as defined in section 102 of the Controlled Substances Act), which is chargeable under State law and punishable by imprisonment for more than one year, (B) any act which is indictable under any of the following provisions of title 18, United States Code: Section 201 (relating to bribery), section 224 (relating to sports bribery), sections 471, 472, and 473 (relating to counterfeiting), section 659 (relating to theft from interstate shipment) if the act indictable under section 659 is felonious, section 664 (relating to embezzlement from pension and welfare funds), sections 891–894 (relating to extortionate credit transactions), section 1029 (relating to fraud and related activity in connection with access devices), section 1084 (relating to the transmission of gambling information), section 1341 (relating to mail fraud), section 1343 (relating to wire fraud), section 1344 (relating to financial institution fraud), sections 1461–1465 (relating to obscene matter), section 1503 (relating to obstruction of justice), section 1510 (relating to obstruction of criminal investigations), section 1511 (relating to the obstruction of State or local law enforcement), section 1512 (relating to tampering with a witness, victim, or an informant), section 1513 (relating to retaliating against a witness, victim, or an informant), section 1951 (relating to interference with commerce, robbery, or extortion), section 1952 (relating to racketeering), section 1953 (relating to interstate transportation of wagering paraphernalia), section 1954 (relating to unlawful welfare fund payments), section 1955 (relating to the prohibition of illegal gambling businesses), section 1956 (relating

to the laundering of monetary instruments), section 1957 (relating to engaging in monetary transactions in property derived from specified unlawful activity), section 1958 (relating to use of interstate commerce facilities in the commission of murder-for-hire), sections 2251, 2251A, 2252, and 2258 (relating to sexual exploitation of children), sections 2312 and 2313 (relating to interstate transportation of stolen motor vehicles), sections 2314 and 2315 (relating to interstate transportation of stolen property), section 2318 (relating to trafficking in counterfeit labels for phonorecords, computer programs or computer program documentation or packaging and copies of motion pictures or other audiovisual works), section 2319 (relating to criminal infringement of a copyright), section 2319A (relating to unauthorized fixation of and trafficking in sound recordings and music videos of live musical performances), section 2320 (relating to trafficking in goods or services bearing counterfeit marks), section 2321 (relating to trafficking in certain motor vehicles or motor vehicle parts), sections 2341–2346 (relating to trafficking in contraband cigarettes), sections 2421–24 (relating to white slave traffic), (C) any act which is indictable under title 29, United States Code, section 186 (dealing with restrictions on payments and loans to labor organizations) or section 501(c)(relating to embezzlement from union funds), (D) any offense involving fraud connected with a case under title 11 (except a case under section 157 of that title [sic]), fraud in the sale of securities, or the felonious manufacture, importation, receiving, concealment, buying, selling, or otherwise dealing in a controlled substance or listed chemical (as defined in section 102 of the Controlled Substances Act), punishable under any law of the United States, or (E) any act which is indictable under the Currency and Foreign Transactions Reporting Act;

(2) "State" means any State of the United States, the District of Columbia, the Commonwealth of Puerto Rico, any territory or possession of the United States, any political subdivision, or any department, agency, or instrumentality thereof;

(3) "person" includes any individual or entity capable of holding a legal or beneficial interest in property;

(4) "enterprise" includes any individual, partnership, corporation, association, or other legal entity, and any union or group of individuals associated in fact although not a legal entity;

(5) "pattern of racketeering activity" requires at least two acts of racketeering activity, one of which occurred after the effective date of this chapter and the last of which occurred within ten years (excluding any period of imprisonment) after the commission of a prior act of racketeering activity;

(6) "unlawful debt" means a debt (A) incurred or contracted in gambling activity which was in violation of the law of the United States, a State or political subdivision thereof, or which is unenforceable under State or Federal law in whole or in part as to principal or interest because of the laws relating to usury, and (B)

which was incurred in connection with the business of gambling in violation of the law of the United States, a State or political subdivision thereof, or the business of lending money or a thing of value at a rate usurious under State or Federal law, where the usurious rate is at least twice the enforceable rate;

(7) "racketeering investigator" means any attorney or investigator so designated by the Attorney General and charged with the duty of enforcing or carrying into effect this chapter;

(8) "racketeering investigation" means any inquiry conducted by any racketeering investigator for the purpose of ascertaining whether any person has been involved in any violation of this chapter or of any final order, judgment, or decree of any court of the United States, duly entered in any case or proceeding arising under this chapter;

(9) "documentary material" includes any book, paper, document, record, recording, or other material; and

(10) "Attorney General" includes the Attorney General of the United States, the Deputy Attorney General of the United States, the Associate Attorney General of the United States, any Assistant Attorney General of the United States, or any employee of the Department of Justice or any employee of any department or agency of the United States so designated by the Attorney General to carry out the powers conferred on the Attorney General by this chapter. Any department or agency so designated may use in investigations authorized by this chapter either the investigative provisions of this chapter or the investigative power of such department or agency otherwise conferred by law.

§ 1962. Prohibited activities

(a) It shall be unlawful for any person who has received any income derived, directly or indirectly, from a pattern of racketeering activity or through collection of an unlawful debt in which such person has participated as a principal within the meaning of section 2, title 18, United States Code, to use or invest, directly or indirectly, any part of such income, or the proceeds of such income, in acquisition of any interest in, or the establishment or operation of, any enterprise which is engaged in, or the activities of which affect, interstate or foreign commerce. A purchase of securities on the open market for purposes of investment, and without the intention of controlling or participating in the control of the issuer, or of assisting another to do so, shall not be unlawful under this subsection if the securities of the issuer held by the purchaser, the members of his immediate family, and his or their accomplices in any pattern or racketeering activity or the collection of an unlawful debt after such purchase do not amount in the aggregate to one percent of the outstanding securities of any one class, and do not confer, either in law or in fact, the power to elect one or more directors of the issuer.

(b) It shall be unlawful for any person through a pattern of racketeering activity or through collection of an unlawful debt to acquire or maintain, directly or indirectly, any interest in or control of any enterprise which is engaged in, or the activities of which affect, interstate or foreign commerce.

(c) It shall be unlawful for any person employed by or associated with any enterprise engaged in, or the activities of which affect, interstate or foreign commerce, to conduct or participate, directly or indirectly, in the conduct of such enterprise's affairs through a pattern of racketeering activity or collection of unlawful debt.

(d) It shall be unlawful for any person to conspire to violate any of the provisions of subsection (a), (b), or (c) of this section.

§ 1963. Criminal penalties

(a) Whoever violates any provision of section 1962 of this chapter shall be fined under this title or imprisoned not more than 20 years (or for life if the violation is based on a racketeering activity for which the maximum penalty includes life imprisonment), or both, and shall forfeit to the United States, irrespective of any provision of State law—

 (1) any interest the person has acquired or maintained in violation of section 1962;

 (2) any—

 (A) interest in;

 (B) security of;

 (C) claim against; or

 (D) property or contractual right of any kind affording a source of influence over;

any enterprise which the person has established, operated, controlled, conducted, or participated in the conduct of, in violation of section 1962; and

 (3) any property constituting, or derived from, any proceeds which the person obtained, directly or indirectly, from racketeering activity or unlawful debt collection in violation of section 1962.

The court, in imposing sentence on such person shall order, in addition to any other sentence imposed pursuant to this section, that the person forfeit to the United States all property described in this subsection. In lieu of a fine otherwise authorized by this section, a defendant who derives profits or other proceeds from an offense may be fined not more than twice the gross profits or other proceeds.

(b) Property subject to criminal forfeiture under this section includes—

 (1) real property, including things growing on, affixed to, and found in land; and

(2) tangible and intangible personal property, including rights, privileges, interests, claims, and securities.

(c) All right, title, and interest in property described in subsection (a) vests in the United States upon the commission of the act giving rise to forfeiture under this section. Any such property that is subsequently transferred to a person other than the defendant may be the subject of a special verdict of forfeiture and thereafter shall be ordered forfeited to the United States, unless the transferee establishes in a hearing pursuant to subsection (*l*) that he is a bona fide purchaser for value of such property who at the time of purchase was reasonably without cause to believe that the property was subject to forfeiture under this section.

(d) (1) Upon application of the United States, the court may enter a restraining order or injunction, require the execution of a satisfactory performance bond, or take any other action to preserve the availability of property described in subsection (a) for forfeiture under this section—

(A) upon the filing of an indictment or information charging a violation of section 1962 of this chapter and alleging that the property with respect to which the order is sought would, in the event of conviction, be subject to forfeiture under this section; or

(B) prior to the filing of such an indictment or information, if, after notice to persons appearing to have an interest in the property and opportunity for a hearing, the court determines that—

(i) there is a substantial probability that the United States will prevail on the issue of forfeiture and that failure to enter the order will result in the property being destroyed, removed from the jurisdiction of the court, or otherwise made unavailable for forfeiture; and

(ii) the need to preserve the availability of the property through the entry of the requested order outweighs the hardship on any party against whom the order is to be entered:

Provided, however, that an order entered pursuant to subparagraph (B) shall be effective for not more than ninety days, unless extended by the court for good cause shown or unless an indictment or information described in subparagraph (A) has been filed.

(2) A temporary restraining order under this subsection may be entered upon application of the United States without notice or opportunity for a hearing when an information or indictment has not yet been filed with respect to the property, if the United States demonstrates that there is probable cause to believe that the

property with respect to which the order is sought would, in the event of conviction, be subject to forfeiture under this section and that provision of notice will jeopardize the availability of the property for forfeiture. Such a temporary order shall expire not more than ten days after the date on which it is entered, unless extended for good cause shown or unless the party against whom it is entered consents to an extension for a longer period. A hearing requested concerning an order entered under this paragraph shall be held at the earliest possible time, and prior to the expiration of the temporary order.

(3) The court may receive and consider, at a hearing held pursuant to this subsection, evidence and information that would be inadmissible under the Federal Rules of Evidence.

(e) Upon conviction of a person under this section, the court shall enter a judgment of forfeiture of the property to the United States and shall also authorize the Attorney General to seize all property ordered forfeited upon such terms and conditions as the court shall deem proper. Following the entry of an order declaring the property forfeited, the court may, upon application of the United States, enter such appropriate restraining orders or injunctions, require the execution of satisfactory performance bonds, appoint receivers, conservators, appraisers, accountants, or trustees, or take any other action to protect the interest of the United States in the property ordered forfeited. Any income accruing to, or derived from, an enterprise or an interest in an enterprise which has been ordered forfeited under this section may be used to offset ordinary and necessary expenses to the enterprise which are required by law, or which are necessary to protect the interests of the United States or third parties. . . .

§ 1964.   Civil remedies

(a) The district courts of the United States shall have jurisdiction to prevent and restrain violations of section 1962 of this chapter by issuing appropriate orders, including, but not limited to: ordering any person to divest himself of any interest, direct or indirect, in any enterprise; imposing reasonable restrictions on the future activities or investments of any person, including, but not limited to, prohibiting any person from engaging in the same type of endeavor as the enterprise engaged in, the activities of which affect interstate or foreign commerce; or ordering dissolution or reorganization of any enterprise, making due provision for the rights of innocent persons.

(b) The Attorney General may institute proceedings under this section. Pending final determination thereof, the court may at any time enter such restraining orders or prohibitions, or take such other actions, including the acceptance of satisfactory performance bonds, as it shall deem proper.

(c) Any person injured in his business or property by reason of a violation of section 1962 of this chapter may sue therefor in any appropriate United States district court and shall recover threefold the damages he sustains and the cost of the suit, including a reasonable attorney's fee, except that no person may rely upon any conduct that would have been actionable as fraud in the purchase or sale of securities to establish a violation of section 1962. The exception contained in the preceding sentence does not apply to an action against any person that is criminally convicted in connection with the fraud, in which case the statute of limitations shall start to run on the date on which conviction becomes final.

(d) A final judgment or decree rendered in favor of the United States in any criminal proceeding brought by the United States under this chapter shall estop the defendant from denying the essential allegations of the criminal offense in any subsequent civil proceeding brought by the United States.

In addition to the codified statutory provisions above, Section 1 of Public Law 91–452 (the bill containing RICO) set forth an explicit statement of legislative intent:

"Congressional Statement of Findings and Purpose

"The Congress finds that (1) organized crime in the United States is a highly sophisticated, diversified, and widespread activity that annually drains billions of dollars from America's economy by unlawful conduct and the illegal use of force, fraud, and corruption; (2) organized crime derives a major portion of its power through money obtained from such illegal endeavors as syndicated gambling, loan sharking, the theft and fencing of property, the importation and distribution of narcotics and other dangerous drugs, and other forms of social exploitation; (3) this money and power are increasingly used to infiltrate and corrupt legitimate business and labor unions and to subvert and corrupt our democratic processes; (4) organized crime activities in the United States weaken the stability of the Nation's economic system, harm innocent investors and competing organizations, interfere with free competition, seriously burden interstate and foreign commerce, threaten the domestic security, and undermine the general welfare of the Nation and its citizens; and (5) organized crime continues to grow because of defects in the evidence-gathering process of the law inhibiting the development of the legally admissible evidence necessary to bring criminal and other sanctions or remedies to bear the unlawful activities of those engaged in organized crime and because the sanctions and remedies available to the Government are unnecessarily limited in scope and impact.

"It is the purpose of this Act to seek the eradication of organized crime in the United States by strengthening the legal tools in the evidence-gathering process, by establishing new penal prohibitions, and by providing enhanced sanctions and new remedies to deal with the unlawful activities of those engaged in organized crime."

Also, in Section 904 of Public Law 91–452, Congress included the following clauses on "Liberal Construction" and "Supersedure of Federal or State Laws":

> "(a) The provisions of this title ... shall be liberally construed to effectuate its remedial purposes.

> "(b) Nothing in this title shall supersede any provision of Federal, State, or other law imposing criminal penalties or affording civil remedies in addition to those provided for in this title."

For excellent general discussions of RICO, see G. Robert Blakey & Brian Gettings, Racketeer Influenced and Corrupt Organizations (RICO): Basic Concepts, Criminal and Civil Remedies, 53 Temple L.Q. 1009 (1980); Gerard E. Lynch, RICO: The Crime of Being a Criminal, 87 Colum. L. Rev. 661 (1987)(in two parts); Barry Tarlow, RICO: The New Darling of the Prosecutor's Nursery, 49 Fordham L. Rev. 165 (1980); and the various articles contained in Symposium: Law and the Continuing Enterprise: Perspectives on RICO, 65 Notre Dame L. Rev. 873 (1990).

3. The CCE Statute. As part of the Comprehensive Drug Abuse Prevention and Control Act of 1970, Congress enacted 21 U.S.C. § 848, which prohibits the operation of a "continuing criminal enterprise" (CCE). This statute, often referred to as the "Drug Kingpin Statute," was designed to impose severe punishments (including a possible life sentence or even, under a subsequent amendment, the death penalty) against those who conduct major illegal drug operations "in concert with" five or more other persons and who occupy a "a position of organizer, a supervisory position, or any other position of management" with respect to those other persons. See 21 U.S.C. § 848(c)(2)(A).

The CCE statute provides, in relevant part:

§ 848. Continuing criminal enterprise

(a) Penalties; forfeitures

Any person who engages in a continuing criminal enterprise shall be sentenced to a term of imprisonment which may not be less than 20 years and which may be up to life imprisonment, to a fine not to exceed the greater of that authorized in accordance with the provisions of Title 18, or $2,000,000 if the defendant is an individual or $5,000,000 if the defendant is other than an individual, and to the forfeiture prescribed in section 853 of this title; except that if any person engages in such activity after one or more prior convictions of him under this section have become final, he shall be sentenced to a term of imprisonment which may not be less than 30 years and which may be up to life imprisonment, to a fine not to exceed the greater of twice the amount authorized in accordance with the provisions of Title 18, or $4,000,000 if the defendant is an individual or $10,000,000 if the defendant is other than an individual, and to the forfeiture prescribed in section 853 of this title.

(b) Life imprisonment for engaging in continuing criminal enterprise

Any person who engages in a continuing criminal enterprise shall be imprisoned for life and fined in accordance with subsection (a) of this section, if—

(1) such person is the principal administrator, organizer, or leader of the enterprise or is one of several such principal administrators, organizers, or leaders; and

(2) (A) the violation referred to in subsection (c)(1) of this section involved at least 300 times the quantity of a substance described in subsection 841(b)(1)(B) of this title, or

(B) the enterprise, or any other enterprise in which the defendant was the principal or one of several principal administrators, organizers, or leaders, received $10 million dollars in gross receipts during any twelve-month period of its existence for the manufacture, importation, or distribution of a substance described in section 841(b)(1)(B) of this title.

(c) "Continuing criminal enterprise" defined

For purposes of subsection (a) of this section, a person is engaged in a continuing criminal enterprise if—

(1) he violates any provision of this subchapter or subchapter II of this chapter the punishment for which is a felony, and

(2) such violation is a part of a continuing series of violations of this subchapter or subchapter II of this chapter—

(A) which are undertaken by such person in concert with five or more other persons with respect to whom such person occupies a position of organizer, a supervisory position, or any other position of management, and

(B) from which such person obtains substantial income or resources.

(d) Suspension of sentence and probation prohibited

In the case of any sentence imposed under this section, imposition or execution of such sentence shall not be suspended, [nor shall] probation ... be granted....

(e) Death penalty

(1) In addition to the other penalties set forth in this section—

(A) any person engaging in or working in furtherance of a continuing criminal enterprise, or any person engaging in an offense punishable under section 841(b)(1)(A) of this title or section 960(b)(1) of this title who intentionally kills or counsels, commands, induces, procures, or causes the intentional killing of an individual and such killing results, shall be sentenced to any term of imprisonment, which shall not be less than 20 years, and which may be up to life imprisonment, or may be sentenced to death; and

(B) any person, during the commission of, in furtherance of, or while attempting to avoid apprehension, prosecution or service of a prison sentence for, a felony violation of this subchapter or subchapter II of this chapter who intentionally kills or counsels, commands, induces, procures, or causes the intentional killing of any Federal, State, or local law enforcement officer engaged in, or on account of, the performance of such officer's official duties and such killing results, shall be sentenced to any term of imprisonment, which shall not be less than 20 years, and which may be up to life imprisonment, or may be sentenced to death.

(2) As used in paragraph (1)(b), the term "law enforcement officer" means a public servant authorized by law or by a Government agency or Congress to conduct or engage in the prevention, investigation, prosecution or adjudication of an offense, and includes those engaged in corrections, probation, or parole functions. . . .

SUBSECTION B: ENTERPRISE CRIMINALITY AND CONSPIRACY

The traditional crime that is probably the most similar to RICO and CCE is the crime of conspiracy. Conspiracy law, like RICO and CCE, prohibits criminal activity committed (or planned to be committed) by more than one person. Unlike RICO and CCE, however, conspiracy law relies on the traditional concept of criminalizing a particular act or series of acts— specifically, a conspiratorial "agreement."

The materials that follow are designed to address the relationship between crimes like RICO and CCE, on the one hand, and conspiracy, on the other. To what extent are the problems that arise under RICO and CCE analogous to those that arise under conspiracy law? To what extent does "enterprise criminality" create new problems that are different from those of conspiracy law?

These materials also raise an additional concern: Given that RICO and CCE closely resemble conspiracy crimes, does it make sense to talk about the crime of conspiring to violate RICO or CCE? If so, how would such a conspiracy be defined? What would be the nature of the conspiratorial agreement?

United States v. Elliott

United States Court of Appeals, Fifth Circuit, 1978.
571 F.2d 880.

Before AINSWORTH, SIMPSON, and MORGAN, CIRCUIT JUDGES.

■ SIMPSON, CIRCUIT JUDGE:

In this case we deal with the question of whether and, if so, how a free society can protect itself when groups of people, through division of labor, specialization, diversification, complexity of organization, and the accumulation of capital, turn crime into an ongoing business. Congress fired a telling shot at organized crime when it passed the Racketeer Influenced and Corrupt Organizations Act of 1970, popularly known as RICO. 18 U.S.C. §§ 1961 et seq. (1970). Since the enactment of RICO, the federal courts, guided by constitutional and legislative dictates, have been responsible for perfecting the weapons in society's arsenal against criminal confederacies.

Today we review the convictions of six persons accused of conspiring to violate the RICO statute, two of whom were also accused and convicted of substantive RICO violations. The government admits that in this prosecution it has attempted to achieve a broader application of RICO than has heretofore been sanctioned. Predictably, the government and the defendants differ as to what this case is about. According to the defendants, what we are dealing with is a leg, a tail, a trunk, an ear—separate entities unaffected by RICO proscriptions. The government, on the other hand, asserts that we have come eyeball to eyeball with a single creature of behemoth proportions, securely within RICO's grasp. After a careful, if laborious study of the facts and the law, we accept, with minor exceptions, the government's view. Because of the complicated nature of this case, both factually and doctrinally, a detailed explication of the facts and of the reasoning underlying our conclusions must be undertaken.

I. THE FACTS

Simply stated, this is a case involving a group of persons informally associated with the purpose of profiting from criminal activity. The facts giving rise to this generalization, however, are considerably more complex. Evidence presented during the 12 day trial implicated the six defendants and 37 unindicted co-conspirators in more than 20 different criminal endeavors. Because the jury found the defendants guilty as charged, with two exceptions, we proceed on the assumption that all relevant credibility choices were made in favor of the government. Glasser v. United States, 315 U.S. 60 (1942). The facts can most clearly be set forth by focusing on specific episodes, arranged in roughly chronological order.

A. 1970, Act One: Arson:

The history of the first Community Convalescent Nursing Home in Sparta, Georgia, began when defendant William Marion Foster encouraged a group of 34 blacks to invest in the project and ended several months later when the completed but unoccupied home was burned to the ground at Foster's behest. The second Community Convalescent Nursing Home was then built, at a profit, by Foster's construction company.

Foster, who had been in the construction and nursing home business, arranged for an SBA loan to the B. F. Hubert Development Corporation, comprised of 34 blacks. In expressing his willingness to help, Foster noted that SBA loans were available but that, tragically, many blacks did not know how to secure them. Foster set up a corporation, Community Convalescent Center, Inc., to lease the nursing home from the B. F. Hubert group. Construction on the home was completed in the summer of 1970, after which James E. McMullen, a coowner of the leasing corporation, worked to ready the home for its scheduled opening on December 4, 1970. On the evening of December 2, Foster ordered McMullen to fire the night watchman, Tommy Barnes. The next night McMullen and his wife worked at the home until 11:00 p.m., when they left, locking the doors behind them. Within hours, the front door of the home was unlocked, and gasoline and explosives were strewn through the halls and ignited. An investigation by the Georgia State Fire Marshal's Office reached the conclusion that the fire was intentionally set, but the perpetrators were never caught.

The crime might have remained unsolved had it not been for admissions made three years later by Foster and codefendant John Clayburn Hawkins, ironically nicknamed "J.C." Foster and J.C. had been attempting to elicit the cooperation of their friend and occasional business associate James Gunnells in the concealment of a stolen shipment of meat and dairy products (an incident discussed later in this opinion). To show that he and J.C. were serious, Foster told Gunnells that he had paid J.C. and his brother, Recea Hawkins—also a codefendant—$4500 to burn the Community Convalescent Nursing Home. Gunnells, who was also in the nursing home business, replied that there was nothing in a nursing home to burn. J.C. explained that he had used three 55 gallon drums of gasoline and one drum of naphtha and had no problem in starting the fire.

B.   Counterfeit Titles/Stolen Cars:

From mid–1971 until at least the end of 1974, J.C. Hawkins and codefendants Robert Ervin Delph, Jr., and John Frank Taylor furnished counterfeit titles to and helped sell cars stolen by a major car theft ring operating in and near Atlanta, Georgia.

J.C. procured 200 counterfeit Georgia certificates of title in mid–1971 by furnishing negatives of titles to a Macon printer, Marvin Farr. After printing the 200 titles, Farr destroyed the negatives and the plates and buried the remains in his back yard. J.C. had also commissioned Farr to print books of state vehicle inspection stickers, for which he again furnished the negatives. Farr, however, was unable to complete the order because he could not devise a way to apply adhesive to the stickers. After a visit from J.C. during which J.C. demanded the inspection stickers "or else," Farr left town. He was later arrested in Denton, Texas, and returned to Macon on state counterfeiting charges. In Macon he was contacted by Abe Crosby, an attorney and unindicted co-conspirator in this case. Crosby told Farr that he had been sent by people that Farr "was scared of" and that J.C. Hawkins wanted Farr to keep his mouth shut. After his release from jail, Farr was visited at his place of employment by J.C., who told him that he, Farr, was crazy "and that nobody talked about [J.C.] and got away with it."

The car theft ring was comprised of Billy Royce Jackson, James A. Green, and Kenneth Sutton Boyd, all convicted car thieves and key witnesses for the prosecution in this case. Each testified that on several occasions he purchased counterfeit certificates of title from Delph and Taylor for $25 or $50 apiece. Green and Boyd testified that Delph and Taylor more than once identified their source of counterfeit titles as a man named "J.C." in Macon. Similarly, Larry Estes, a cousin of James Gunnells, purchased several counterfeit titles from J.C., both directly and through a middleman, Joe Breland. Green testified that in 1972 and 1973, he stole cars on request for Delph and Taylor. In the late summer or early fall of 1974, J.C. visited Green at the furniture store where Green was employed and asked him to steal two cars. Over the next year, Green stole several cars for J.C., at $400 per car. Recea Hawkins often accompanied his brother to pick up and pay for the cars.

Titles printed by Farr and distributed by J.C. were recovered in Alabama, California, Florida, Georgia, North Carolina, and Texas in connection with investigations of car thefts. In some cases, however, J.C. was able to recapture both car and title before either fell into the hands of the police. One such episode involved Benjamin F. Chester, Jr., who leased from J.C. a lounge adjacent to a liquor store owned and run by J.C. In 1971, J.C. sold Chester three cars "wholesale" and furnished the certificates of title. Chester, in turn, sold one of the cars to Raymond Booker. Instead of having Chester sign his title over to Booker, J.C. simply furnished Booker with a new "title." In July 1972, J.C. met with Chester and Booker at the lounge and demanded that the cars and titles be returned because they had "got hot." Booker recalled no threats from J.C., only the statement, "I've got to have my car back so y'all don't be hard headed." Chester, however, was reluctant to return his cars and remembered that J.C. finally stated, "I tell you what, if you don't give me them cars back, I will kill you myself or I will have you killed." Both men returned their cars and titles.

C. Stolen Hormel Meat:

On March 30, 1972, a truckload of approximately 33,000 pounds of Hormel meat packed in cardboard boxes left the packing plant in Fremont, Nebraska, consigned to the Alterman Food Company in Atlanta, Georgia. The trailer carrying the shipment arrived in Smyrna, Georgia, late that night and was parked at the South Cobb Service Station to be picked up by another driver, Byron Moseley, for ultimate delivery on April 2. At 3:00 p.m. on April 1, Moseley observed the tractor-trailer parked at the service station. By 9:00 that evening, it had been stolen. The abandoned tractor was found beside a highway south of Atlanta the following day. About one month later, the empty trailer was recovered in Warner Robins, Georgia.

On the night of April 1, 1972, J.C. Hawkins visited Rudolph Flanders at Flanders' grocery store, the Pick and Carry. J.C. asked if he could store boxes of Hormel Meat in the cooler of the Pick and Carry, and Flanders consented. Over the next few days, J.C. stored 40 to 50 boxes of meat which he sold with some assistance from Flanders. At some point that month, J.C. offered to sell a "semi-trailer truck" of meat to Larry Sykes for $7,000. Sykes contacted his brother, who was in the meat packing busi-

434	CHAPTER 4 ENTERPRISE CRIMINALITY—RICO AND CCE

ness, and was advised to pass up the deal because the meat "was just too low priced." At about the same time, codefendant James Alford Elliott, Jr., sold a 50 pound piece of Hormel meat to Joe Fuchs, then a pharmacist in Macon. Fuchs returned the meat after he learned from a butcher friend that it was not "legitimate." A year later, shortly before Rudolph Flanders was tried in federal court for possession of the stolen Hormel meat, J.C. told James Gunnells that "it was his [J.C.'s] load of meat," that he had purchased it for approximately $10,000, and that Recea Hawkins was also involved in the transaction.

D. Efforts to Influence the Outcome of the Stolen Meat Trial:

Rudolph Flanders' trial for possession of the stolen interstate shipment of meat took place during the first week of May, 1973. Days before the trial, Flanders met with J.C., Gunnells, and others, in the coffee shop of the old Grady Hotel in Macon. At the meeting, the jury list for Flanders' trial was passed around to "see who we knew on it and who we could talk to." J.C. recognized one name on the list, James Elliott, as that of a young man who lived behind him. He indicated that he was certain Elliott would cooperate if he were on the jury. Elliott was selected as a juror at Flanders' trial and, alone among the other 11 jurors, voted for acquittal, causing a mistrial.[5]

E. September, 1973: A Truck Theft and Its Aftermath:

On September 24, 1973, a Caterpillar front-end loader and a Ford dump truck were stolen from a construction site near Atlanta. That night,

---

[5] This episode is mentioned twice in the indictment in this case, first as an overt act in the broad conspiracy charge in Count One, and again as the basis of the substantive charge of obstructing justice, in violation of 18 U.S.C. §§ 1503 and 2, Count Four. J. C. Hawkins and Elliott were named in both counts. Both were found guilty under Count One but were acquitted under Count Four, Hawkins by jury verdict, Elliott by directed verdict. Elliott now argues that his acquittal on the substantive offense precludes consideration of that offense as part of the conspiracy charge, citing United States v. Campanale, 518 F.2d 352, 358 (9th Cir.1975). Dicta in *Campanale* that acquittal on substantive offenses "presumably eliminate[s] those acts from consideration under the [RICO] conspiracy count" does not comport with prior case law in this and other circuits. "An acquittal on a substantive offense does not preclude a verdict of guilty on a count charging a conspiracy to commit such substantive offense." United States v. Carlton, 475 F.2d 104, 106 (5th Cir.1973). This principle applies with equal force where, as here, the alleged conspiracy had as its purpose far more than the commission of the single substantive offense of which a defendant was acquitted. "The overt act ... need not be a crime and is not a part of the offense charged, but simply something done in furtherance of the object of the conspiracy...." Castro v. United States, 296 F.2d 540, 542–43 (5th Cir.1961). Here, we are bound by the determination that J. C. and Elliott did not commit the crime of obstructing justice in violation of 18 U.S.C. § 1503. Nevertheless, we may infer that the jury, in finding J. C. and Elliott guilty on Count One, concluded that both engaged in acts "done in furtherance of the object of the conspiracy" but not criminal in themselves— that J. C. promised to contact Elliott in an effort to hang the Flanders jury, and that Elliott voted to acquit Flanders. We recognize that Elliott's vote to acquit is not unambiguously an act in furtherance of the conspiracy and might, as Elliott testified, have been based on a genuine conviction that the government had not proved Flanders guilty beyond a reasonable doubt. Interpretation of Elliott's acts was within the province of the jury and we assume ... that the jury chose not to believe Elliott's account.

J.C. Hawkins appeared at the Eubanks Tire and Battery Company near Macon to purchase a new tire for the stolen dump truck. He gave his name as "Roy Evans," and remained on the opposite side of the highway in a brown Buick while Tommy Ellison, an employee of Eubanks, changed the tire.

In the pre-dawn hours of the following day, September 25, Terry Singleton, a Bibb County Sheriff's Deputy, received a call from Jimmy Reeves. Reeves stated that J.C. had just telephoned him and asked him to go to the Waffle House at the intersection of I–475 and U.S. 80. Singleton and his partner, Jim Reid, conducted a surveillance of the Waffle House, where they observed J.C. with a light blue Continental Mark IV and Reeves, in his pick-up truck. Eventually, Reeves' truck left the Waffle House, proceeding west on U.S. 80. Singleton saw the truck slow down and flash its left turn signal near an underpass, but it never executed the turn. Within an hour, Singleton called Reeves to learn what had happened. Reeves reported that he drove J.C. along U.S. 80 so that J.C. could show him where the dump truck and front-end loader were hidden, but that just as he was about to turn left to reach the spot, J.C. observed a marked patrol car and was "spooked." Singleton drove to the area described by Reeves and found the stolen equipment. On January 21, 1974, J.C. was indicted in state court for the theft of the dump truck and front-end loader.

1. The Murder of Jimmy Reeves: In the spring of 1974, J.C. and Gunnells had discussed the purchase of antique watches and guns from Jimmy Reeves. One night in April or May of that year, J.C. received a call at his home in the presence of Gunnells. After the call, J.C. told Gunnells that they should be glad they had not done business with Reeves, whom J.C. then described as a "finking son of a bitch." Later that night, during a conversation about the state theft charges pending against him, J.C. commented to Gunnells that "they wouldn't have a witness." Early on the morning of May 27, 1974, Reeves received a telephone call. He left his home in his pick-up truck immediately after the call, explaining to his wife and children that he did not have time to eat breakfast. At 8:40 that morning, in a church yard not far from his home, Reeves' body was found lying on the floor board of his truck. He had been killed by three 16–gauge shotgun blasts using Number One buckshot. Extensive powder burns associated with two of Reeves' wounds indicated that they had been inflicted at a "very close" range.

Two or three days after the Reeves murder, Gunnells was present at J.C.'s house and overheard a conversation between J.C. and his brother, Recea. J.C. asked, "How did it go?," to which Recea responded, "First shot out of the barrel and he didn't even know what happened—didn't even see it coming." Recea explained that he was "real sure" because he was "close enough for powder burns." Other evidence circumstantially linking Recea to the Reeves murder came from an eyewitness who observed a dark blue car parked on a dirt road near the church yard shortly before 8:00 on the morning of the murder. In May, 1974, Recea owned a 1968 or 1969 dark blue Pontiac.

2. The Intimidation of Tommy Ellison: In September 1974, one year after he sold a tire to "Roy Evans," Ellison was approached at his place of work in Griffin, Georgia, by two black men who offered to drive him to Atlanta to "have some fun." Ellison explained that he could only go on a rainy day, when he would not be required to work. About a week later, on a rainy day, the men returned and drove Ellison to Atlanta in a Lincoln Continental with two pistols lying on the front seat. During the ride, the men offered Ellison $150 to make a statement that he did not know "a friend of theirs." Ellison agreed. In Atlanta, he was taken to the office of Charles E. Clark, an attorney, where he signed a sworn statement reading, in part, as follows:

> "Upon being introduced to a man called J.C. HAWKINS, I noticed immediately that this was not the man to whom I gave tire service on the night of September 24, 1973. The man that I observed at the Eubanks Tire Center was several inches taller and weighed more than this man. I have never seen the man introduced to me as J.C. Hawkins before in my life."

According to Ellison, this statement was false. After signing it, he was introduced to J.C., who had been waiting in another office. J.C. said, "I appreciate what you did and my friends will take care of you, what they promised you," and gave Ellison a drink of liquor. The two black men then drove Ellison back to Griffin, but paid him only $25.

F. Stolen Swift Meat and Dairy Products:

On October 19, 1973, a tractor-trailer load of swinging beef, pork, veal, and lamb, and boxes of butter and cheese was shipped from Nashville, Tennessee, aboard a Thompkins Motor Lines refrigerated trailer. The shipment was driven to a terminal in Decatur, Georgia, where it was parked temporarily. At some point over the next two days, the tractor and trailer were stolen by Milton Burnett and Bill Rainey. On October 24, the abandoned tractor was discovered near Forest Park, Georgia; the loaded trailer had been sold to J.C. in Macon.

The first problem confronting J.C. was where to store the large quantity of meat and dairy products that he had illicitly acquired. The stolen goods probably would have been kept at three nursing homes owned by Foster had it not been for a fortuitous series of events the month before. In September, 1973, Foster learned that the Georgia Bank was about to foreclose on his nursing homes in Sparta, Lumber City, and La Grange. To avoid losing the homes, Foster went into business with James Gunnells, who loaned him approximately $60,000. Foster, in turn, leased the homes to Gunnells, effective October 1, 1973. Consequently, before Foster could use the nursing homes for his own purposes, he had to secure Gunnells' permission.

On October 24, 1973, Foster and J.C. spoke to Gunnells in Foster's office. J.C. stated that he had "a semi-truckload of swinging beef" parked at a truck stop on Gray Highway and that he needed a place to store it. A "deal" that J.C. and Foster had on the meat had fallen through, and now they wanted Gunnells to release his leases on the nursing homes so that Foster could have access to their refrigeration units. Gunnells refused. J.C. told Gunnells that he was "a goddamn fool" and that, if he did not cooperate, he would lose $8,500 that he had loaned to Foster over the past two days. Foster called Gunnells "silly and explained that 'he could trust J.C. completely.' " At this point Foster related how he had paid J.C. and Recea Hawkins $4,500 to burn the Sparta nursing home in 1970. Finally, pressed by J.C. to come up with a place to put the meat, Gunnells suggested that they move the trailer to the farm of his friend, Howard Wooden.

That night, J.C. drove the tractor-trailer to Wooden's farm off Interstate Highway 75 near Perry, Georgia, south of Macon. There, J.C., Wooden, Gunnells, and Larry Estes tried unsuccessfully to back the trailer into Wooden's barn. At about 2:30 a.m. the next day, October 25, the four men drove the van to an open field adjoining I–75 farther south, and left it there for the night. After daybreak, J.C. and Estes drove the van back to Wooden's farm. With Wooden and Gunnells, they unloaded the stolen meat and dairy products into an old ice cream truck and a U–Haul van rented by J.C. that day in Macon.

On October 26, Estes drove the U–Haul van to a grocery store in Jeffersonville, Georgia, which was owned by Foster and had been closed for about one year. There he met Foster and Larry Hudson, a mechanic employed as Gunnells' "general flunky." After Hudson, at Foster's request, turned on the store's old freezers, the three men began unloading the U–Haul van. At that point, a state patrol or local police car pulled up outside the store. Foster spoke to the officer, who soon left. Foster then told Estes and Hudson that he did not want the meat and cheese at his store, so they reloaded the van and drove to J.C.'s house in Macon, where they were able to fit some of the goods into an old chest-type freezer on J.C.'s back porch. The next day Foster told Gunnells that a law enforcement officer had caught him with the meat but that he, Foster, had "outtalked him." The remainder of the stolen meat, butter, and cheese was sold to the owner of a supermarket in Charlotte, North Carolina, by Paul Moose, Jr., at the request of Leon Averett.

G.   Stolen Forklift and Ditchwitch: Honor Among Thieves:

J.C. believed that he had been shortchanged by Rainey and Burnett in that he paid for but did not receive a full trailer load of meat and dairy products. He demanded and received a partial refund. Instead of paying in cash, however, Rainey and Burnett made good on their obligation by delivering to J.C. a stolen forklift and ditchwitch. At about the same time in November, 1973, Foster told J.C. that he needed a forklift at one of his construction projects. In the presence of James Gunnells, J.C. told Foster that he could save money by buying the "hot" equipment, from him for $3,500. Foster bought the two pieces of equipment, knowing they were stolen. He got less than a bargain, however. The forklift developed mechanical problems, and remained at the construction site for only two months before Foster had it moved to his backyard in Jeffersonville, where his children used it as a springboard for their trampoline. The forklift remained at Foster's home for nine months until it was confiscated by the Georgia Bureau of Investigation.

H. Stolen "Career Club" Shirts:

On November 7, 1973, a trailer load of "Career Club" shirts consigned to an interstate shipment and valued in excess of $56,000 was stolen from the Roadway Express Terminal in Macon. The trailer, on which the name "Roadway" was painted in tall, bold letters along each side, wound up in an Atlanta warehouse built and owned by Foster.

The lessons of the stolen meat experience the month before apparently were not lost on Foster. Two years earlier he had entered into a business venture with Kenneth Lamar Keyes, a glass installer, to construct a warehouse-type building for Keyes to rent for use as a glass processing plant. The building, located in Atlanta, was completed during the summer of 1973 and had doors large enough for semi-trucks and trailers to pass through. As of November, 1973, no equipment had been installed. That month, Foster asked Keyes if he could rent the building to someone for two or three months, ostensibly to help defray interest payments on the money borrowed to finance the building. Keyes consented. A few days after he was contacted by Foster, Keyes, along with his stepson, Kenneth Horace Johnson, witnessed J.C. and two other men drive up to the warehouse, pry the locks off the surrounding gate with a crowbar, and replace them with new locks. Several days later Keyes and Johnson looked inside the warehouse and found the 40 foot Roadway trailer. Within a week the trailer was gone, a pile of U–Haul blankets left in its stead.

Gunnells, by his account, was unwittingly drawn into the stolen shirt episode by Foster. First, as a Christmas present, Foster gave Gunnells approximately 25 of the stolen shirts. When Gunnells later learned that the shirts were stolen, he returned all but one to J.C. and Recea Hawkins. The one remaining shirt, which he turned over to the Bibb County Police, was introduced into evidence in the instant case and was identified as a part of the stolen shipment. Second, Foster asked Gunnells to take some polaroid photographs of the outside of his Atlanta warehouse. Gunnells travelled to Atlanta with J.C. and Recea for this purpose. At the warehouse, J.C. unlocked the gate and the office door, showed Gunnells the trailer and its contents, and offered to sell him shirts for one dollar apiece. As they were leaving the warehouse, Gunnells noticed a police car parked across the street but was told by J.C. not to worry. On his return to Macon, Gunnells approached Foster to register his concern over what had happened in Atlanta. Foster explained that "there wasn't nothing to worry about, that he had a lease drawed up showing that he had leased it to somebody if anything ever happened."

Like the meat and dairy products the month before, the stolen shirts were eventually disposed of through Leon Averett and Paul Moose, Jr. in Charlotte, North Carolina. In connection with the sale of the shirts, Averett told Moose that "they" had a warehouse in Atlanta big enough to handle several tractor-trailers. Some of the shirts sold by Averett and Moose were recovered and identified as part of the stolen shipment.

I.   O False Apothecaries!:

With the exception of Foster, all defendants were implicated in a number of illegal drug transactions throughout the period covered by the indictment. We list those transactions chronologically.

1.   1971–72: Elliott Barters in Black Beauties: Early in 1971, Joe Fuchs, then a pharmacist in Macon, wished to have a screened enclosure built around his porch. According to Fuchs, James Elliott suggested that Joe Breland could do the work at a low price. He and Breland went to Fuchs' house, where Elliott negotiated a deal, requesting payment in amphetamine pills, popularly known as "black beauties." Fuchs agreed, and the work was completed over the period of a year, during which time Fuchs gave the pills to Elliott and Breland in installments of 400.

2.   1972–73: Amphetamine Sales: In early 1972, shortly after their counterfeit title transactions commenced, Robert Delph began selling amphetamines to car thief Jim Green. Green recalled approximately six occasions on which he purchased 1,000 pills from Delph for $150. Kenneth Boyd, also a member of the car theft ring, accompanied Green to Delph's house during the first transaction, and later became a steady customer. For a period of eight months beginning in the summer of 1972, Boyd bought somewhere between 1,000 and 10,000 pills from Delph at two week intervals. Boyd also purchased amphetamines from defendant Taylor in similar quantities at one month intervals for about one year, beginning in the summer of 1972. According to Boyd, both Delph and Taylor on several occasions identified their source of pills as J.C. Hawkins. Knowing that the pills supplied to him were not pharmaceutical, Boyd was concerned about their source because uniformity of quality was an important factor in their resale value. During one conversation, Boyd pressed Delph for details about his source of pills. Delph, who had been drinking, eventually stated that "he had a truck that he was running for J.C. and that they was partners in the deal or some kind of operation or setup."

3.   Winter 1973: The Jamaican Conspiracy: In November 1972, J.C. approached his friend Harry Randall in Macon about purchasing marihuana and amphetamines in Jamaica. Randall at the time owned a car rental business in Kingston, Jamaica. He contacted his Kingston associate, Dillon Barnes. Barnes flew to Macon where he, J.C. and Randall, after protracted negotiations, reached an agreement as to their general plan: Barnes would return to Kingston to set up the purchase of 300 pounds of marihuana and 200 pounds of amphetamine powder, Randall would then fly down to make

the purchase and arrange for transportation to the United States; J.C. would pay for and distribute the drugs. By coincidence, during this period, J.C. and James Gunnells were interested in purchasing a piece of property in Macon owned by the Tweedles, a couple who lived in Jamaica. When Randall finally flew to Jamaica in January, 1973, to purchase the drugs, J.C. asked him to contact the Tweedles to negotiate the sale of their Macon property. J.C. arranged for Randall's trip to be paid for by Gunnells, who knew nothing of the drug conspiracy. Randall travelled to Jamaica, set up the deal and wired home for $1,500, which was sent by Western Union but never received by Randall. The drug deal fell through when Randall learned that the pilot he had recruited to fly the illicit goods back to Macon was an agent for the Drug Enforcement Administration.

4. Spring 1973: The Canadian Conspiracy: During the spring of 1973, Delph and Taylor met with James Green to discuss a plan to bring large quantities of amphetamine powder and MDA into the United States from Canada. Delph and Taylor stated that they planned to travel to Canada where they knew a chemist who could supply the drugs, and asked Green to assist them in selling whatever they were able to bring back. Soon thereafter, Delph and Taylor drove to Canada and returned with powdered amphetamine and MDA which they sold to Green for $125 per ounce and which Green resold to a single individual for $150 per ounce.

5. Fall 1973: The Mexican Conspiracy: In late October or early November, 1973, William Maxwell Martin, who was peripherally involved in the car theft ring, was introduced to Taylor by Billy Royce Jackson, a member of the ring. After Jackson arranged to purchase a counterfeit certificate of title from Taylor, Martin asked Taylor if he would be interested in buying several tons of marihuana. Taylor stated that marihuana required too much space in transportation and asked if Martin could obtain heroin or cocaine, noting that others with whom he was involved "had just got through purchasing an airplane for $102,000 to bring heroin to this country." Martin and Jackson, already planning to go to Mexico in search of marihuana, agreed to look for heroin and cocaine for Taylor. The two never reached Mexico, however; they were arrested en route in Laredo, Texas, on Dyer Act charges of transporting a stolen vehicle across state lines. After his arrest, Martin agreed to cooperate with the Drug Enforcement Agency. From his hotel room in Laredo and in the presence of DEA agents, Martin called Taylor and stated that he was out of jail and in Mexico and that he could put a deal together as discussed. According to Martin, Taylor "said that he was hoping that we could, that he wanted to do some checking, and for me to get back with him later." Martin, however, was unable to contact Taylor again. The single telephone call from Martin's hotel room went unrecorded due to a malfunction in the DEA's recording equipment.

6. 1973: Miscellaneous Drug Transactions: In addition to the major drug deals, successful and unsuccessful, of 1973, the evidence disclosed several minor, isolated drug transactions that year. In the spring of 1973, Joe Breland purchased a bottle of "speed" from J.C. at one of Foster's

construction sites. At about the same time, J.C. invited Joe Fuchs to his house to rummage through his stash of illegally obtained prescription drugs. Fuchs noted that most of the drugs were "normal prescription type medication" with no street value and thus of no interest to him. J.C. explained that "Scooter" Herring had recently been through those drugs and had picked out what he wanted, so that only a few controlled drugs were left. Fuchs found four to six bottles of Ritalin, a Schedule II controlled substance, which he bought from J.C. for $250. Additionally, Billy Royce Jackson recalled that sometime in 1973 he was given about 25 amphetamine pills by Delph.

7. 1974: MDA: Early in 1974, J.C. approached Larry Estes and offered to sell him MDA, explaining that he had two pounds on hand and needed some money. Estes promised to check at a local nightclub to see if he could find a buyer. Within a week, Estes called J.C. and stated that he had found someone interested in purchasing MDA. At J.C.'s suggestion, Estes went to Recea's motorcycle shop in Macon and told Recea that he could sell one ounce of MDA for $350. Recea told Estes to walk down the road for a while and that when he returned, the MDA would be under the front seat of a particular car parked outside the shop. After picking up the MDA in this manner, Estes returned to his apartment, where his potential buyer sampled the product and paid $350 for the tiny plastic bag of grayish-brown powder. Estes then delivered the money to Recea. Over the next two weeks, Estes made two more sales for Recea using the same procedure. On April 27, 1974, Macon police raided the apartment of Recea's estranged wife, Patricia Thomas, and seized approximately 364 grams of 245 tri-methoxyamphetamine, a controlled substance similar to MDA. Although keys to the apartment were possessed by Recea Hawkins, Ricky Strozier and Patricia Thomas, the latter two denied any knowledge of the seized drugs.

8. 1976: Marihuana: In May, 1976, J.C. met with Bob Day, a pilot and an old friend. With Day's consent, the meeting was surreptitiously recorded by agents of the Georgia Bureau of Investigation, and relevant portions of the tape were admitted into evidence at the trial. At one point in this conversation, J.C. admitted to Day that three to five weeks earlier, "we got 200 pounds" of "goddamn, jamup good" marihuana. Soon thereafter, J.C.'s narrative statement continued, J.C. and his unnamed compatriots purchased but returned another 200 pounds which were not as good. They then purchased 300 pounds of marihuana, which they sold within two weeks although it too was of low quality.

9. 1976: The Hawkins–Day Conspiracy: In April, 1976, J.C. met with Day and Kevin Sapp at Day's home in Dawson, Georgia, to discuss two criminal schemes, one of which involved a marihuana deal J.C. claimed to be working on in "New Mexico." At the meeting, J.C. offered Day $10 per pound to fly a minimum of 500 pounds of marihuana from "New Mexico" to Georgia. The next month, Day, wired for sound, visited J.C. in Macon to discuss their plans. J.C. raised the possibility of importing a large quantity of marihuana from Colombia, South America, by ship because "the quality right now in Mexico is lousy." If Day knew of a ship that was available,

J.C. stated, he had someone willing to invest over a million dollars. As for airplanes, "I done blowed three or four years' salary in the last three or four years fucking with them airplanes. Almost everyone that's come from down there has got caught, has got jumped." When Day described a shrimp boat for sale, J.C. replied that such a boat "is not big enough to haul what I'm talking about, 50,000 pounds."

J.   Epilogue: The Bravo Plot:

Months after he knew that a federal grand jury was hot on his trail, J.C. continued to devise criminal money-making schemes, as his tape recorded conversation with Bob Day reveals. In addition to marihuana deals, J.C. planned to burglarize the Triangle Chemical Company in Macon and steal approximately 2,000 five gallon cans of "Bravo," a fungicide used to dust crops during the summer months. In April, 1976, J.C. solicited the help of Day and Kevin Sapp in this endeavor, the details of which were discussed the following month in the taped conversation between J.C. and Day. J.C. stated that he already had the trucks necessary to carry the 60 pound chemical drums—a tractor-trailer and two "six-wheelers." He then outlined a plan to assure that the eventual buyer would be unaware of J.C.'s and Kevin Sapp's involvement and that Sapp, apparently an employee of Triangle, would be unaware of the identity of the buyer.

J.C.'s modus operandi, as reflected in this arrangement, was based on the mistaken notion that a person could not be convicted on the basis of only one co-conspirator's testimony.[13] J.C. thus assumed—and often advised others—that he would be sheltered from liability if he could deal with only one other person at each phase of a particular transaction. His explanation to Day is illustrative:

"HAWKINS: They won't never be more than two people together on your end of it. So you and the guy you deal, you and me.

"DAY: I'd just rather deal with you . . .

"HAWKINS: You go deal with your man by yourself and you tell him what you want him to know.

"DAY: That's right. You just don't tell Calvin [sic] that I was nowhere around or nothing.

"HAWKINS: Naw, but he'll know in his own mind that you—

"DAY: I think he will too, but—

"HAWKINS: That don't mean nothing. Even in court if he said you was, that's nothing. Your word's as good as his."

As for his own liability, J.C. told Day that the buyer "can pay you direct and you can pay me, and you'll never see anybody else. That's my word

[13] Evidently, J. C. was unfamiliar with a line of cases in this Circuit holding that "the uncorroborated testimony of an accomplice is sufficient to support a conviction in the federal courts if it is not on its face incredible or otherwise insubstantial." United States v. Iacovetti, 466 F.2d 1147, 1153 (5th Cir.1972).

against yours . . . That don't even bother me . . . One on one ain't worth a shit."[14]

II. THE INDICTMENT

The eight count indictment in this case was returned on July 29, 1976, superseding an almost identical indictment filed on June 10, 1976. The indictment charged the following:

COUNT ONE: Conspiracy to Violate RICO: All six defendants, James Alford Elliott, Jr., Robert Ervin Delph, Jr., William Marion Foster, Recea Howell Hawkins, John Clayburn Hawkins, Jr. a/k/a J.C., and John Frank Taylor, were named in Count One as having conspired, from December 3, 1970, until the filing of the indictment, with each other, with 37 unindicted co-conspirators, and with "others to the grand jury known and unknown" to violate a substantive provision of the RICO statute, 18 U.S.C. § 1962(c), in violation of 18 U.S.C. § 1962(d).[15] The essence of the conspiracy charge was that the defendants agreed to participate, directly and indirectly, in the conduct of the affairs of an "enterprise" whose purposes were to commit thefts, "fence" stolen property, illegally traffic in narcotics, obstruct justice, and engage in "other criminal activities." The indictment listed 25 overt acts, beginning with the burning of the Community Convalescent Nursing Home in 1970 and culminating with J.C. Hawkins' marihuana transactions in the spring of 1976.

COUNT TWO: The Substantive RICO Charge: J.C. and Recea Hawkins only were charged with a substantive violation of the RICO statute, 18 U.S.C. § 1962(c), in that they conducted and participated, directly and indirectly, in the conduct of the affairs of an enterprise through a pattern of racketeering activity. The crimes alleged to satisfy the statutory requirements for "a pattern of racketeering activity" included those charged in Counts Three through Six and Count Eight, as well as the possession and sale of Ritalin and the distribution of MDA on three occasions, all in violation of 21 U.S.C. § 841, the murder of Jimmy Reeves, in violation of Ga. Code Ann. § 26–1101, and the burning of the Community Convalescent Nursing Home, in violation of Ga. Code Ann. § 26–1401.

COUNT THREE: J.C. Hawkins was charged with violating 18 U.S.C. §§ 659 and 2 in that he possessed and concealed with the intent to convert

---

[14] J. C.'s lecture to Joe Fuchs about the "one on one" principle is worth recording for the insight it provides into the rationale apparently behind most of the enterprise's activities:

"HAWKINS: That's one against one and which one wins? If they don't have the meat—so what's the deal? You're as good as he is or better. He said you did, you say you didn't. Who's going to believe what? You'll never be indicted on that shit. I been down them roads twenty-five years. It don't bother me—if a guy said well, J. C. sold me or stole or

sold or I saw or shit—that's unreal. If they catch me in the act or catch me with the goods or two or three guys tell them they bought it or seen it or I had it, then that's a different story. That's the story that will go down in the book, in the court and it'll convict your ass."

[15] The defendants were not charged under the general conspiracy statute, 18 U.S.C. § 371, which carries a maximum penalty less severe than does the specific RICO conspiracy provision.

to his own use a stolen interstate shipment of Hormel meat valued in excess of $100.

COUNT FOUR: J.C. Hawkins and James Elliott were charged with violating 18 U.S.C. §§ 1503 and 2 in that they corruptly endeavored to obstruct justice by "hanging" the jury in the trial of Rudolph Flanders for the possession and concealment of the stolen Hormel meat.

COUNT FIVE: J.C. Hawkins and William Marion Foster were charged with violating 18 U.S.C. §§ 659 and 2 in that they possessed and concealed with the intent to convert to their own use a stolen interstate shipment of Swift Premium meat and dairy products valued in excess of $100.

COUNT SIX: J.C. Hawkins, Recea Hawkins and Foster were charged with violating 18 U.S.C. §§ 659 and 2 in that they possessed and concealed with the intent to convert to their own use a stolen interstate shipment of "Career Club" shirts valued in excess of $100.

COUNT SEVEN: James Elliott was charged with violating 18 U.S.C. § 1503 in that he corruptly endeavored to obstruct justice by encouraging Joe Fuchs to lie to a federal grand jury "investigating theft from interstate shipment of Swift Premium boxed beef." The indictment's reference to "Swift" was erroneous; the boxed beef discussed by Elliott and Fuchs had been produced by Hormel.

COUNT EIGHT: J.C. Hawkins was charged with violating 18 U.S.C. § 2315 in that he knowingly received and disposed of a counterfeit security, a Georgia State Certificate of Title, moving in interstate commerce.

At the close of the government's case, the trial judge directed a verdict of acquittal on Count Four in favor of James Elliott. The jury acquitted J.C. Hawkins on Count Four and Elliott on Count Seven, thus eliminating all substantive obstruction of justice charges from the case. All remaining defendants were found guilty as charged by the jury under Counts One, Two, Three, Five, Six, and Eight, were adjudged guilty, and received the following sentences: J.C. Hawkins, 80 years imprisonment; Recea Hawkins, 50 years imprisonment; Delph and Taylor, each 10 years, with parole eligibility in 24 months; Foster, one year imprisonment, five years probation; James Elliott, five years probation.

In this appeal, the defendants have raised a myriad of issues, all of which we have considered at length. Some are too frivolous to warrant discussion. Others present serious and novel legal questions that we attempt to address and resolve by the discussion which follows.

III. THE SUBSTANTIVE RICO VIOLATION

J.C. and Recea Hawkins contend that their acts, while arguably violative of other criminal statutes, are not proscribed by the substantive RICO provision under which they were charged, 18 U.S.C. § 1962(c), in that they were not committed in furtherance of the affairs of an "enterprise" as required by the Act. At best, they say, the facts disclosed that two brothers confederated to commit a few, isolated criminal acts over a period of six years. Neither the facts nor the law support this contention.

Because this prosecution was based on a novel and recently enacted criminal statute, we must, at the outset, determine exactly what that statute denounces as illegal, as relevant to this case. Section 1962(c) provides:

"It shall be unlawful for any person employed by or associated with any enterprise engaged in, or the activities of which affect, interstate or foreign commerce, to conduct or participate, directly or indirectly, in the conduct of such enterprise's affairs through a pattern of racketeering activity or collection of unlawful debt."

This section must be read in the context of the statutory definitions of its key terms. "Enterprise," as used in the Act, "includes any individual, partnership, corporation, association, or other legal entity, and any union or group of individuals associated in fact although not a legal entity." 18 U.S.C. § 1961(4). As relevant to this case, a "pattern of racketeering activity" simply requires at least two acts of "racketeering activity" committed within ten years of each other. 18 U.S.C. § 1961(5). "Racketeering activity" includes three broad categories of crimes: (A) any of several specified "act[s] or threat[s] . . . chargeable under State law and punishable by imprisonment for more than one year," including, as relevant here, murder and arson, (B) any act which is indictable under any of several specified sections of Title 18, U.S.C., including, as relevant here, § 659 (felonious theft from interstate shipment), § 1503 (obstruction of justice), and § 2315 (interstate shipment of stolen or counterfeit securities) or (C) federal offenses involving narcotics or other dangerous drugs. 18 U.S.C. § 1961(1). Reduced to its bare essentials, the charge against J.C. and Recea may be restated as follows:[16]

"Being associated with a group of individuals who were associated in fact, J.C. and Recea Hawkins each directly and indirectly participated in the group's affairs through the commission of two or more predicate crimes."

The gist of J.C.'s and Recea's objection to their conviction on Count Two is that there was no group of individuals associated in fact—no enterprise—in whose affairs they could have participated, directly or indirectly. We disagree.

In United States v. Hawes, 529 F.2d 472, 479 (5th Cir.1976), we noted that "Congress gave the term 'enterprise' a very broad meaning." On its face and in light of its legislative history, the Act clearly encompasses "not only legitimate businesses but also enterprises which are from their inception organized for illicit purposes." United States v. McLaurin, 557 F.2d 1064, 1073 (5th Cir.1977). Similarly, we are persuaded that "enterprise" includes an informal, de facto association such as that involved in this case.

---

[16] To keep our restatement of the charge as simple as possible, we have omitted the interstate commerce element necessary to make out a RICO violation. With multiple thefts from interstate commerce, transportation of stolen cars and counterfeit titles across numerous state lines, and sales of stolen goods in several states, there is no question that this case involves an effect on interstate commerce more than adequate to satisfy RICO requirements.

In defining "enterprise," Congress made clear that the statute extended beyond conventional business organizations to reach "any . . . group of individuals" whose association, however loose or informal, furnishes a vehicle for the commission of two or more predicate crimes. The statute demands only that there be association "in fact" when it cannot be implied in law. There is no distinction, for "enterprise" purposes, between a duly formed corporation that elects officers and holds annual meetings and an amoeba-like infra-structure that controls a secret criminal network.

Here, the government proved beyond a reasonable doubt the existence of an enterprise comprised of at least five of the defendants.[18] This enterprise can best be analogized to a large business conglomerate. Meta-phorically speaking, J.C. Hawkins was the chairman of the board, function-ing as the chief executive officer and overseeing the operations of many separate branches of the corporation. An executive committee in charge of the "Counterfeit Title, Stolen Car, and Amphetamine Sales Department" was comprised of J.C., Delph, and Taylor, who supervised the operations of lower level employees such as Farr, the printer, and Green, Boyd, and Jackson, the car thieves. Another executive committee, comprised of J.C., Recea and Foster, controlled the "Thefts From Interstate Commerce De-partment," arranging the purchase, concealment, and distribution of such commodities as meat, dairy products, "Career Club" shirts, and heavy construction equipment. An offshoot of this department handled subsid-iary activities, such as murder and obstruction of justice, intended to facilitate the smooth operation of its primary activities. Each member of the conglomerate, with the exception of Foster, was responsible for procur-ing and wholesaling whatever narcotics could be obtained. The thread tying all of these departments, activities, and individuals together was the desire to make money. J.C. might have been voicing the corporation's motto when he told Bob Day, in May, 1976, "if it ain't a pretty damn good bit of money, I ain't going to fuck with it."

A jury is entitled to infer the existence of an enterprise on the basis of largely or wholly circumstantial evidence. Like a criminal conspiracy, a RICO enterprise cannot be expected to maintain a high profile in the community. Its affairs are likely to be conducted in secrecy and to involve a minimal amount of necessary contact between participants. Thus, direct evidence of association may be difficult to obtain; a jury should be permitted to draw the natural inference arising from circumstantial evi-dence of association.[19] In this case, persuasive circumstantial evidence of association was buttressed by direct evidence tending to prove the existence

[18] We treat the enterprise in this case as a group of people in light of the government's admission that its "theory of the case from beginning to end has been that the 'enter-prise' in this case was comprised of all six appellants as a group of individuals associat-ed in fact." The indictment charged only that each defendant was associated with the enterprise.

[19] In conspiracy cases, we allow the jury to infer agreement on the basis of "the acts and conduct of the alleged conspirators them-selves." United States v. Morado, 454 F.2d 167, 174 (5th Cir.1972). In this case, it is apparent that the enterprise operated in a manner calculated to minimize direct evi-dence of association. See notes 13 and 14, supra, and accompanying text.

of an enterprise. According to Boyd, defendant Delph stated that "he had a truck that he was running for J.C. and that they was partners in the deal or some kind of operation or setup." William Martin described defendant Taylor's admission that he and others "had just gotten through purchasing an airplane for $102,000 to bring heroin into this country," and J.C. told Day that he had virtually bankrupted himself by spending money on airplanes to import drugs. Leon Averett, in the course of selling a trailer load of stolen shirts, stated that his associates had a warehouse in Atlanta big enough to handle several tractor-trailers.

Additionally, although the target of the RICO statute is not "sporadic activity," we find nothing in the Act excluding from its ambit an enterprise engaged in diversified activity. Indeed, Congress expressly stated that the purpose of the Act was "to seek the eradication of organized crime," which it described as a "highly sophisticated, diversified, and widespread activity that annually drains billions of dollars from America's economy by unlawful conduct...." Pub.L. 91–452, § 1, 84 Stat. 922 (1970). To this end, it directed that "the provisions of this title shall be liberally construed to effectuate its remedial purposes." Id., § 904. While earlier cases have considered enterprises engaged in only one type of prohibited activity, a single enterprise engaged in diversified activities fits comfortably within the proscriptions of the statute and the dictates of common sense:

> "As in a firm with a real estate department and an insurance department, the fact that partners bring in two kinds of business on the basis of their different skills and connections does not affect the fact that they are partners in a more general business venture."

United States v. Mallah, 503 F.2d 971, 976 (2d Cir.1974). We would deny society the protection intended by Congress were we to hold that the Act does not reach those enterprises nefarious enough to diversify their criminal activity.[23]

The evidence in this case demonstrated the existence of an enterprise—a myriopod criminal network, loosely connected but connected nonetheless. By committing arson, actively assisting a car theft ring, fencing thousands of dollars worth of goods stolen from interstate commerce, murdering a key witness, and dealing in narcotics, J.C. and Recea Hawkins directly and indirectly participated in the enterprise's affairs through a pattern, indeed a plethora, of racketeering activity. We affirm their convictions on Count Two.

---

[23] We note that at least two district courts have construed "a pattern of racketeering activity," as used in the Act, to require that the two or more acts of "racketeering activity" be interrelated. On its face, however, the statute does not require such "interrelatedness," and we can perceive no reason for reading it into the statutory definition, 18 U.S.C. § 1961(5).... We note also that the Act does not criminalize either associating with an enterprise or engaging in a pattern of racketeering activity standing alone. The gravamen of the offense described in 18 U.S.C. § 1962(c) is the conduct of an enterprise's affairs through a pattern of racketeering activity. Thus, the Act does require a type of relatedness: the two or more predicate crimes must be related to the affairs of the enterprise but need not otherwise be related to each other.

IV. THE RICO CONSPIRACY COUNT

All six defendants were convicted under 18 U.S.C. § 1962(d) of having conspired to violate a substantive RICO provision, § 1962(c). In this appeal, all defendants, with the exception of Foster, argue that while the indictment alleged but one conspiracy, the government's evidence at trial proved the existence of several conspiracies, resulting in a variance which substantially prejudiced their rights and requires reversal, citing Kotteakos v. United States, 328 U.S. 750 (1946). Prior to the enactment of the RICO statute, this argument would have been more persuasive. However, as we explain below, RICO has displaced many of the legal precepts traditionally applied to concerted criminal activity. Its effect in this case is to free the government from the strictures of the multiple conspiracy doctrine and to allow the joint trial of many persons accused of diversified crimes.

A. Prior Law: Wheels and Chains

1. *Kotteakos* and the Wheel Conspiracy Rationale: The Court in *Kotteakos* held that proof of multiple conspiracies under an indictment alleging a single conspiracy constituted a material variance requiring reversal where a defendant's substantial rights had been affected. At issue was "the right not to be tried en masse for the conglomeration of distinct and separate offenses committed by others." 328 U.S. at 775. *Kotteakos* thus protects against the "spill-over effect," the transference of guilt from members of one conspiracy to members of another. United States v. Bertolotti, 529 F.2d 149, 156 (2d Cir.1975).

The facts of *Kotteakos* have been summarized by this court as follows:

"In that case, one where the indictment charged but one overall conspiracy, the government's proof at trial, by its own admission, showed that there were eight separate conspiracies involving some thirty-two persons. The key figure in the scheme, which involved the obtaining of government loans by making fraudulent representations, was a man named Brown, who was a part of, and directed each of the eight conspiracies. Brown was the only element common to the eight otherwise completely separate undertakings, no other person taking part in, nor having knowledge of the other conspiracies. Though each of the conspiracies had similar illegal objects, none depended upon, was aided by, or had any interest in the success of the others."

United States v. Perez, 489 F.2d 51, 60 (5th Cir.1973). These facts led the Court to speak in terms of a "wheel conspiracy," in which one person, the "hub" of the wheel, was accused of conspiring with several others, the "spokes" of the wheel. As we explained in United States v. Levine, 546 F.2d 658, 663 (5th Cir.1977):

"For a [single] wheel conspiracy to exist those people who form the wheel's spokes must have been aware of each other and must do something in furtherance of some single, illegal enterprise. Otherwise the conspiracy lacks 'the rim of the wheel to enclose the spokes.' If there is not some interaction between those conspirators who form the spokes of the wheel as to at least one common illegal object, the 'wheel' is incomplete, and two conspiracies rather than one are charged." [Citations omitted].

2. *Blumenthal* and the Chain Conspiracy Rationale: The impact of *Kotteakos* was soon limited by the Court in Blumenthal v. United States, 332 U.S. 539 (1947), where the indictment charged a single conspiracy to sell whiskey at prices above the ceiling set by the Office of Price Administration. The owner of the whiskey, through a series of middlemen, had devised an intricate scheme to conceal the true amount he was charging for the whiskey. Although some of the middlemen had no contact with each other and did not know the identity of the owner, they had to have realized that they were indispensible cogs in the machinery through which this illegal scheme was effectuated. The Court concluded that "in every practical sense the unique facts of this case reveal a single conspiracy of which the several agreements were essential and integral steps." Id. at 559. Thus the "chain conspiracy" rationale evolved.

The essential element of a chain conspiracy—allowing persons unknown to each other and never before in contact to be jointly prosecuted as co-conspirators—is interdependence. The scheme which is the object of the conspiracy must depend on the successful operation of each link in the chain." An individual associating himself with a 'chain' conspiracy knows that it has a 'scope' and that for its success it requires an organization wider than may be disclosed by his personal participation." United States v. Agueci, 310 F.2d 817, 827 (2d Cir.1962). "Thus, in a 'chain' conspiracy prosecution, the requisite element—knowledge of the existence of remote links—may be inferred solely from the nature of the enterprise." *United States v. Perez*, supra, 489 F.2d at 59 n. 10.

3. Limits of the Chain Conspiracy Rationale: The rationale of *Blumenthal* applies only insofar as the alleged agreement has "a common end or single unified purpose." United States v. Morado, 454 F.2d 167, 170–71 (5th Cir.1972). Generally, where the government has shown that a number of otherwise diverse activities were performed to achieve a single goal, courts have been willing to find a single conspiracy. This "common objective" test has most often been used to connect the many facets of drug importation and distribution schemes. The rationale falls apart, however, where the remote members of the alleged conspiracy are not truly interdependent or where the various activities sought to be tied together cannot reasonably be said to constitute a unified scheme. In United States v. Miley, 513 F.2d 1191, 1207 (2d Cir.1975), for example, the Second Circuit held that the value and quantity of drugs sold by the defendant-suppliers was insufficient to justify the inference that each knew his supplies were only a small part of the drugs handled by a larger operation. Similarly, in *United States v. Bertolotti*, supra, 529 F.2d at 155, the same Court focused on an alleged narcotics conspiracy that bore little resemblance to "the orthodox business operation" found to exist in other drug cases; many of the "narcotics transactions" involved amounted to "little more than simple

cash thefts" in which no drugs changed hands. The only factor that tied several isolated transactions together, the Court noted, was the presence of two of the defendants, Rossi and Coralluzzo, in each. In effect, "the scope of the operation was defined only by Rossi's resourcefulness in devising new methods to make money." Under these circumstances, the Court held that the government had failed to prove the existence of a single conspiracy.

Applying pre-RICO conspiracy concepts to the facts of this case, we doubt that a single conspiracy could be demonstrated. Foster had no contact with Delph and Taylor during the life of the alleged conspiracy. Delph and Taylor, so far as the evidence revealed, had no contact with Recea Hawkins. The activities allegedly embraced by the illegal agreement in this case are simply too diverse to be tied together on the theory that participation in one activity necessarily implied awareness of others. Even viewing the "common objective" of the conspiracy as the raising of revenue through criminal activity, we could not say, for example, that Foster, when he helped to conceal stolen meat, had to know that J.C. was selling drugs to persons unknown to Foster, or that Delph and Taylor, when they furnished counterfeit titles to a car theft ring, had to know that the man supplying the titles was also stealing goods out of interstate commerce. The enterprise involved in this case probably could not have been successfully prosecuted as a single conspiracy under the general federal conspiracy statute, 18 U.S.C. § 371.

B.   RICO to the Rescue: The Enterprise Conspiracy

In enacting RICO, Congress found that "organized crime continues to grow" in part "because the sanctions and remedies available to the Government are unnecessarily limited in scope and impact." Thus, one of the express purposes of the Act was "to seek the eradication of organized crime . . . by establishing new penal prohibitions, and by providing enhanced sanctions and new remedies to deal with the unlawful activities of those engaged in organized crime." Pub.L.91–452, § 1, 84 Stat. 922 (1970). Against this background, we are convinced that, through RICO, Congress intended to authorize the single prosecution of a multi-faceted, diversified conspiracy by replacing the inadequate "wheel" and "chain" rationales with a new statutory concept: the enterprise.

To achieve this result, Congress acted against the backdrop of hornbook conspiracy law. Under the general federal conspiracy statute,

> "the precise nature and extent of the conspiracy must be determined by reference to the agreement which embraces and defines its objects. Whether the object of a single agreement is to commit one or many crimes, it is in either case that agreement which constitutes the conspiracy which the statute punishes." Braverman v. United States, 317 U.S. 49, 53 (1942).

In the context of organized crime, this principle inhibited mass prosecutions because a single agreement or "common objective" cannot be inferred from the commission of highly diverse crimes by apparently unrelated individuals. RICO helps to eliminate this problem by creating a substantive offense which ties together these diverse parties and crimes. Thus, the object of a RICO conspiracy is to violate a substantive RICO provision—here, to conduct or participate in the affairs of an enterprise through a pattern of racketeering activity—and not merely to commit each of the predicate crimes necessary to demonstrate a pattern of racketeering activity. The gravamen of the conspiracy charge in this case is not that each defendant agreed to commit arson, to steal goods from interstate commerce, to obstruct justice, and to sell narcotics; rather, it is that each agreed to participate, directly and indirectly, in the affairs of the enterprise by committing two or more predicate crimes. Under the statute, it is irrelevant that each defendant participated in the enterprise's affairs through different, even unrelated crimes, so long as we may reasonably infer that each crime was intended to further the enterprise's affairs. To find a single conspiracy, we still must look for agreement on an overall objective. What Congress did was to define that objective through the substantive provisions of the Act.

C. Constitutional Considerations

The "enterprise conspiracy" is a legislative innovation in the realm of individual liability for group crime. We need to consider whether this innovation comports with the fundamental demand of due process that guilt remain "individual and personal." *Kotteakos*, supra, 328 U.S. at 772.

The substantive proscriptions of the RICO statute apply to insiders and outsiders—those merely "associated with" an enterprise—who participate directly and indirectly in the enterprise's affairs through a pattern of racketeering activity. 18 U.S.C. § 1962(c). Thus, the RICO net is woven tightly to trap even the smallest fish, those peripherally involved with the enterprise. This effect is enhanced by principles of conspiracy law also developed to facilitate prosecution of conspirators at all levels. Direct evidence of agreement is unnecessary: "proof of such an agreement may rest upon inferences drawn from relevant and competent circumstantial evidence—ordinarily the acts and conduct of the alleged conspirators themselves." *United States v. Morado*, supra, 454 F.2d at 174. Additionally, once the conspiracy has been established, the government need show only "slight evidence" that a particular person was a member of the conspiracy. Id. at 175. Of course, "a party to a conspiracy need not know the identity, or even the number, of his confederates." United States v. Andolschek, 142 F.2d 503, 507 (2d Cir.1944).

Undeniably, then, under the RICO conspiracy provision, remote associates of an enterprise may be convicted as conspirators on the basis of purely circumstantial evidence. We cannot say, however, that this section of the statute demands inferences that cannot reasonably be drawn from circumstantial evidence or that it otherwise offends the rule that guilt be individual and personal. The Act does not authorize that individuals "be tried en masse for the conglomeration of distinct and separate offenses committed by others." *Kotteakos*, supra. Nor does it punish mere association with conspirators or knowledge of illegal activity; its proscriptions are directed against conduct, not status. To be convicted as a member of an enterprise conspiracy, an individual, by his words or actions, must have objectively manifested an agreement to participate, directly or indirectly, in the affairs of an enterprise through the commission of two or more predicate crimes. One whose agreement with the members of an enterprise did not include this vital element cannot be convicted under the Act. Where, as here, the evidence establishes that each defendant, over a period of years, committed several acts of racketeering activity in furtherance of the enterprise's affairs, the inference of an agreement to do so is unmistakable.

It is well established that "the government is not required to prove that a conspirator had full knowledge of all the details of the conspiracy; knowledge of the essential nature of the plan is sufficient." United States v. Brasseaux, 509 F.2d 157, 160 n. 3 (5th Cir.1975). The Supreme Court explained the policy behind this rule in *Blumenthal v. United States*, supra, 332 U.S. at 556–57:

"For it is most often true, especially in broad schemes calling for the aid of many persons, that after discovery of enough to show clearly the essence of the scheme and the identity of a number participating, the identity and the fact of participation of others remain undiscovered and undiscoverable. Secrecy and concealment are essential features of successful conspiracy. The more completely they are achieved, the more successful the crime. Hence the law rightly gives room for allowing the conviction of those discovered upon showing sufficiently the essential nature of the plan and their connections with it, without requiring evidence of knowledge of all its details or of the participation of others. Otherwise the difficulties, not only of discovery, but of certainty in proof and of correlating proof with pleading would become insuperable, and conspirators would go free by their very ingenuity."

In the instant case, it is clear that "the essential nature of the plan" was to associate for the purpose of making money from repeated criminal activity. Defendant Foster, for example, hired J.C. Hawkins to commit arson, helped him to conceal large quantities of meat and shirts stolen from interstate commerce, and bought a stolen forklift from him. It would be "a perversion of natural thought and of natural language" to deny that these facts give rise to the inference that Foster knew he was directly involved in an enterprise whose purpose was to profit from crime. As we noted in United States v. Gonzalez, 491 F.2d 1202, 1206 (5th Cir.1974), "persons so associating and forming organizations for furthering such illicit purposes do not normally conceive of the association as engaging in one unlawful transaction and then disbanding. Rather the nature of such organizations seems to be an ongoing operation ..." Foster also had to know that the enterprise was bigger than his role in it, and that others unknown to him were participating in its affairs. He may have been unaware that others who had agreed to participate in the enterprise's affairs did so by selling drugs and murdering a key witness. That, however, is irrelevant to his own liability, for he is charged with agreeing to participate in the enterprise through his own crimes, not with agreeing to commit each of the crimes through which the overall affairs of the enterprise were conducted.[30] We perceive in this no significant extension of a co-conspirator's liability. When a person "embarks upon a criminal venture of indefinite outline, he takes his chances as to its content and membership, so be it that they fall within the common purposes as he understands them." *United States v. Andolschek*, supra, 142 F.2d at 507.[31]

Our society disdains mass prosecutions because we abhor the totalitarian doctrine of mass guilt. We nevertheless punish conspiracy as a distinct offense because we recognize that collective action toward an illegal end involves a greater risk to society than individual action toward the same end. That risk is greatly compounded when the conspirators contemplate not a single crime but a career of crime. "There are times when of necessity, because of the nature and scope of the particular federation, large numbers of persons taking part must be tried together or perhaps not at all.... When many conspire, they invite mass trial by their conduct." *Kotteakos*, supra, 328 U.S. at 773.

We do not lightly dismiss the fact that under this statute four defendants who did not commit murder have been forced to stand trial jointly with, and as confederates of, two others who did. Prejudice inheres in such a trial; great Neptune's ocean could not purge its taint.[33] But the Constitution does not guarantee a trial free from the prejudice that inevitably accompanies any charge of heinous group crime; it demands only that the potential for transference of guilt be minimized to the extent possible under the circumstances in order "to individualize each defendant in his relation to the mass." *Kotteakos*, supra, 328 U.S. at 773. The RICO statute does not offend this principle. Congress, in a proper exercise of its legislative power, has decided that murder, like thefts from interstate commerce and the counterfeiting of securities, qualifies as racketeering activity. This, of course, ups the ante for RICO violators who personally would not contemplate taking a human life. Whether there is a moral imbalance in the equation of thieves and counterfeiters with murderers is a question whose answer lies in the halls of Congress, not in the judicial conscience.

---

[30] These observations apply with equal, if not greater, force to defendants Delph and Taylor who, in addition to committing several acts of racketeering activity, actually admitted to others that they were part of an ongoing enterprise. Similarly, while Recea Hawkins' acts hardly establish him as the "brains" of the enterprise, his support for the enterprise's affairs was more than mere acquiescence or presence; among his other crimes, he committed murder for the enterprise.

[31] Although the evidence here supports the inference that each remote member of this enterprise knew he was a part of a much larger criminal venture, we do not wish to imply that each "department" of the enterprise was wholly independent of the others. A close look at the modus operandi of the enterprise reveals a pattern of interdependence which bolsters our conclusion that the functions of each "department" directly contributed to the success of the overall operation.

[33] Cf. Shakespeare, Macbeth, Act III, Scene I.

D. Other Issues Related to the Conspiracy Count

[The court proceeded to consider, and reject, several additional defense claims. One such claim was that the defense was entitled to a "bill of particulars" that would have given additional notice of the government's allegations. The court explained: "We are not unmindful of counsel's argument that notice and pleading requirements developed in the context of the general federal conspiracy statute may not pass constitutional muster under the RICO conspiracy statute. We do not reach this question, however, because we are satisfied that the indictment in this case afforded adequate notice under any reasonable test."

After reviewing the evidence in support of the convictions, the court reversed defendant Elliott's conviction on Count One, stating: "The evidence relevant to James Elliott as we view the record, was not sufficient to permit the jury to conclude that he conspired with the other five defendants to violate the RICO statute." The court rejected the defendants' remaining insufficiency-of-the-evidence claims.]

VII. CONCLUSION

Through RICO, Congress defined a new separate crime to help snare those who make careers of crime. Participation in the affairs of an enterprise through the commission of two or more predicate crimes is now an offense separate and distinct from those predicate crimes. So too is conspiracy to commit this new offense a crime separate and distinct from conspiracy to commit the predicate crimes. The necessity which mothered this statutory invention was caused by the inability of the traditional criminal law to punish and deter organized crime.

The realistic view of group crime which inspired Congress to enact RICO should also guide the courts in construing RICO. Thus, in this case, we are satisfied that the evidence, circumstantial and indirect though it largely was, proved the existence of both an enterprise committed to profiting from criminal activity and an agreement among five of the defendants to participate in the affairs of the enterprise through a pattern of racketeering activity.

As explained above, we find the evidence insufficient to sustain James Elliott's conviction on Count One and reverse as to him. We find that the other defendants were properly convicted and affirm in each of their cases. Those five, Delph, Foster, Recea Hawkins, John Clayburn Hawkins, Jr. a/k/a J.C., and Taylor received their just deserts by the verdict of the jury in a fair trial free from prejudicial error.

Affirmed in part, reversed in part.

NOTES ON ENTERPRISE CRIMINALITY AND CONSPIRACY

1. The Model Penal Code Conspiracy Offense. The typical contours of the crime of conspiracy are revealed by the Model Penal Code conspiracy offense:

"Section 5.03. Criminal Conspiracy.

"(1) *Definition of Conspiracy.* A person is guilty of conspiracy with another person or persons to commit a crime if with the purpose of promoting or facilitating its commission he:

"(a) agrees with such other person or persons that they or one or more of them will engage in conduct that constitutes such crime or an attempt or solicitation to commit such crime; or

"(b) agrees to aid such other person or persons in the planning or commission of such crime or of an attempt or solicitation to commit such crime.

"(2) *Scope of Conspiratorial Relationship.* If a person guilty of conspiracy, as defined by Subsection (1) of this Section, knows that a person with whom he conspires to commit a crime has conspired with another person or persons to commit the same crime, he is guilty of conspiring with such other person or persons, whether or not he knows their identity, to commit such crime.

"(3) *Conspiracy With Multiple Criminal Objectives.* If a person conspires to commit a number of crimes, he is guilty of only one conspiracy so long as such multiple crimes are the object of the same agreement or continuous conspiratorial relationship....

"(5) *Overt Act.* No person may be convicted of conspiracy to commit a crime, other than a felony of the first or second degree, unless an overt act in pursuance of such conspiracy is alleged and proved to have been done by him or by a person with whom he conspired.

"(6) *Renunciation of Criminal Purpose.* It is an affirmative defense that the actor, after conspiring to commit a crime, thwarted the success of the conspiracy, under circumstances manifesting a complete and voluntary renunciation of his criminal purpose.

"(7) *Duration of Conspiracy.* For purposes of Section 1.06(4):

"(a) conspiracy is a continuing course of conduct that terminates when the crime or crimes that are its object are committed or the agreement that they be committed is abandoned by the defendant and by those with whom he conspired; and

"(b) such abandonment is presumed if neither the defendant nor anyone with whom he conspired does any overt act in pursuance of the conspiracy during the applicable period of limitation; and

"(c) if an individual abandons the agreement, the conspiracy is terminated as to him only if and when he advises those with whom he conspired of his abandonment or he informs the law enforcement authorities of the existence of the conspiracy and of his participation therein."

The general federal conspiracy statute, 18 U.S.C. § 371, contains an explicit "overt act" requirement; in order to be convicted, a conspirator must "do any act to effect the object of the conspiracy." The federal drug conspiracy statute, 28 U.S.C. § 846, however, contains no such language, and the Supreme Court has recently held that no "overt act" is required for conviction under the federal drug conspiracy statute. See United States v. Shabani, ___ U.S. ___, 115 S.Ct. 382 (1994).

2. RICO and Conspiracy Compared; *United States v. Griffin.* Is the main difference between traditional conspiracy and RICO the fact that conspiracy law requires an "agreement" to commit specific crimes, whereas RICO requires only a loose "association" of individuals who happen to be engaged in related criminal activity? Consider the following comments from United States v. Griffin, 660 F.2d 996 (4th Cir.1981):

"The illegitimate, associated-in-fact RICO enterprise ... shares important characteristics with the traditional conspiracy of criminal law. Indeed, one of the avowed purposes of RICO was to relieve some of the deficiencies of the traditional conspiracy prosecution as a means for coping with contemporary organized crime. The increasing complexity of 'organized' criminal activity had made it difficult to show the single agreement or common objective essential to proof of conspiracy on the basis of evidence of the commission of highly diverse crimes by apparently unrelated individuals. Congress attempted through RICO to relieve this problem by creating a new substantive offense, association in fact in an enterprise whose affairs are conducted through a pattern of racketeering activity, 18 U.S.C. § 1962(c), in which 'association' is presumably easier to prove than conspiracy, while at the same time creating a RICO conspiracy offense, 18 U.S.C. § 1962(d), whose common objective is simply the commission of the substantive associational offense. United States v. Elliott, 571 F.2d 880, 902 (5th Cir.1978).

"While within the resulting statutory scheme conspiracy remains conspiracy and an associated-in-fact enterprise is plainly intended to be something different and less difficult of proof, they nevertheless continue to share the basic characteristic that each proscribes purposeful associations of individuals. It is this shared characteristic that has created the special danger that in conspiracy prosecutions guilt will not be assessed on an 'individual and personal' basis, Kotteakos v. United States, 328 U.S. 750, 772 (1946), but solely by association. Judge Learned Hand's admonition in the conspiracy context, see United States v. Falcone, 109 F.2d 579, 581 (2d Cir.1940), is therefore applicable as well to charge and proof of this kind of RICO enterprise: if the government must show that a defendant has participated in or conducted the affairs of an enterprise in order to hold him for associating with others in it, then it is essential to determine the purpose of the enterprise. The relevant analysis in United States v. Turkette, 452 U.S. 576 (1981), is precisely to this effect. Proof of the existence of an associated-in-fact enterprise requires proof of a 'common purpose' animating its associates, and this may be done by evidence of an 'ongoing organization, formal or informal,' of those associates in which they function as a 'continuing unit.' The ties between the individual associates that are implied by these concepts of continuity, unity, shared purpose and identifiable structure operate precisely to guard against the danger that guilt will be adjudged solely by virtue of associations not so related. They define the line between 'concerted action' through 'group association for criminal purposes,' for which 'combination in crime' may constitutionally be proscribed, Callanan v. United States, 364 U.S. 587, 593–94 (1961), and less clearly related conduct that may not be so proscribed and prosecuted.

"Critical therefore to charge and proof of the existence of an associated-in-fact enterprise under § 1962(c) is charge and proof of a common purpose for which the group of individuals alleged to constitute the enterprise have associated themselves. That proof may of course be direct but, as the *Turkette* Court pointed out, it may also be circumstantial, as by evidence that the group of individuals functions as a continuing unit in an informal or formal organization engaged in a course of conduct directed toward the accomplishment of the common purpose alleged."

Is the *Griffin* court's reassurance that RICO contains sufficient safeguards against overly broad application persuasive? Does RICO, unlike traditional conspiracy law, rely on the idea of "guilt by association?"

3. Questions and Comments on Conspiracy to Violate RICO. What are the elements of an ordinary conspiracy? How do the elements of a RICO conspiracy differ? Does it follow from the approach of the *Elliott* court that anyone guilty of violating RICO will also be guilty of conspiring to violate RICO? If so, note that this effectively ups the ante for those who violate one of the substantive RICO provisions from a potential of 20 to a potential of 40 years. Ask J.C. and Recea Hawkins whether this is a realistic possibility.

Consider also the joinder implications of a RICO conspiracy trial. Under Rule 8(b) of the Federal Rules of Criminal Procedure:

"Two or more defendants may be charged in the same indictment or prosecution if they are alleged to have participated in the same act or transaction or in the same series of acts or transactions constituting an offense or offenses. Such defendants may be charged in one or more counts together or separately and all of the defendants need not be charged in each count."

Is the prosecution opportunity for combining a large number of defendants into a single trial significantly expanded by the concept of a RICO conspiracy? Is this good or bad?

SECTION 2: ENTERPRISE CRIMINALITY AND LOSS OF PROSECUTORIAL CONTROL: THE ELEMENTS OF CRIMINAL AND CIVIL RICO

One of the recurring themes of federal criminal law is the tension between a Congress that enacts broad criminal statutes (in this context, in order to effectively combat "organized crime") and the impulse of the federal courts to impose reasonable limits on such statutes (in this context, in order to avoid overly broad applications to non-"organized crime" defendants). Often, the federal courts have relied heavily on prosecutorial discretion as a means to limit the scope of such statutes.

This theme is as relevant to RICO and CCE as it is to the Mann Act, the mail fraud statute, and the Hobbs Act. As *Sedima* points out, however, RICO adds an important new ingredient to the mix. In Section 1964 of the RICO statute, Congress created special civil remedies for racketeering activity that generally resemble those available under the federal antitrust laws. These civil remedies, including a treble damages remedy and attorneys' fees for prevailing plaintiffs, provide a strong incentive for "private attorneys general" to join with federal prosecutors in the battle against "organized crime." The availability of these civil remedies under RICO thus has meant the loss of prosecutorial control over RICO—and has made it increasingly difficult for the federal courts to rely on prosecutorial discretion as a limitation on the scope of RICO.

SUBSECTION A: "ENTERPRISE"

United States v. Turkette

Supreme Court of the United States, 1981.
452 U.S. 576.

■ JUSTICE WHITE delivered the opinion of the Court.

[The] Racketeer Influenced and Corrupt Organizations [Act (RICO)] was added to [the federal criminal law] by title IX of the Organized Crime Control Act of 1970. The question in this case is whether the term "enterprise" as used in RICO encompasses both legitimate and illegitimate enterprises or is limited in application to the former. The Court of Appeals ... held that Congress did not intend to include within the definition of "enterprise" those organizations which are exclusively criminal. ... We granted certiorari....

I

Count nine of a nine-count indictment charged respondent and 12 others with conspiracy to conduct and participate in the affairs of an enterprise engaged in interstate commerce through a pattern of racketeering activities, in violation of 18 U.S.C. § 1962(d). The indictment described the enterprise as "a group of individuals associated in fact for the purpose of illegally trafficking in narcotics and other dangerous drugs, committing arsons, utilizing the United States mails to defraud insurance companies, bribing and attempting to bribe local police officers, and corruptly influencing and attempting to corruptly influence the outcome of state court proceedings...." The other eight counts of the indictment charged the commission of various substantive criminal acts by those engaged in and associated with the criminal enterprise, including possession with intent to distribute and distribution of controlled substances, and several counts of insurance fraud by arson and other means. The common thread to all counts was respondent's alleged leadership of this criminal organization through which he orchestrated and participated in the commission of the various crimes delineated in the RICO count or charged in the eight preceding counts.

After a six-week jury trial, in which the evidence focused upon both the professional nature of this organization and the execution of a number of distinct criminal acts, respondent was convicted on all nine counts. He was sentenced to a term of 20 years on the substantive counts, as well as a two-year special parole term on the drug count. On the RICO conspiracy count he was sentenced to a 20–year concurrent term and fined $20,000.

On appeal, respondent argued that RICO was intended solely to protect legitimate business enterprises from infiltration by racketeers and that RICO does not make criminal the participation in an association which performs only illegal acts and which has not infiltrated or attempted to infiltrate a legitimate enterprise. The Court of Appeals agreed. We reverse.

II

In determining the scope of a statute, we look first to its language. If the statutory language is unambiguous, in the absence of "a clearly expressed legislative intent to the contrary, that language must ordinarily be regarded as conclusive." Consumer Product Safety Comm'n v. GTE Sylvania, Inc., 447 U.S. 102, 108 (1980). Of course, there is no errorless test for identifying or recognizing "plain" or "unambiguous" language. Also, authoritative administrative constructions should be given the deference to which they are entitled, absurd results are to be avoided and internal inconsistencies in the statute must be dealt with. We nevertheless begin with the language of the statute.

Section 1962(c) makes it unlawful "for any person employed by or associated with any enterprise engaged in, or the activities of which affect, interstate or foreign commerce, to conduct or participate, directly or indirectly, in the conduct of such enterprise's affairs through a pattern of racketeering activity or collection of unlawful debt." The term "enterprise" is defined as including "any individual, partnership, corporation, association, or other legal entity, and any union or group of individuals associated in fact although not a legal entity." § 1961(4). There is no restriction upon the associations embraced by the definition: an enterprise includes any union or group of individuals associated in fact. On its face, the definition appears to include both legitimate and illegitimate enterprises within its scope; it no more excludes criminal enterprises than it does legitimate ones. Had Congress not intended to reach criminal associations, it could easily have narrowed the sweep of the definition by inserting a single word, "legitimate." But it did nothing to indicate that an enterprise consisting of a group of individuals was not covered by RICO if the purpose of the enterprise was exclusively criminal.

The Court of Appeals, however, clearly departed from and limited the statutory language. It gave several reasons for doing so, none of which is adequate. First, it relied in part on the rule of ejusdem generis, an aid to statutory construction problems suggesting that where general words follow a specific enumeration of persons or things, the general words should be limited to persons or things similar to those specifically enumerated. The Court of Appeals ruled that because each of the specific enterprises enumerated in § 1961(4) is a "legitimate" one, the final catchall phrase—"any union or group of individuals associated in fact"—should also be limited to legitimate enterprises. There are at least two flaws in this reasoning. The rule of ejusdem generis is no more than an aid to construction and comes into play only when there is some uncertainty as to the meaning of a particular clause in a statute. Considering the language and structure of § 1961(4), however, we not only perceive no uncertainty in the meaning to be attributed to the phrase, "any union or group of individuals associated in fact" but we are convinced for another reason that ejusdem generis is wholly inapplicable in this context.

Section 1961(4) describes two categories of associations that come within the purview of the "enterprise" definition. The first encompasses organizations such as corporations and partnerships, and other "legal entities." The second covers "any union or group of individuals associated in fact although not a legal entity." The Court of Appeals assumed that the second category was merely a more general description of the first. Having made that assumption, the court concluded that the more generalized description in the second category should be limited by the specific examples enumerated in the first. But that assumption is untenable. Each category describes a separate type of enterprise to be covered by the statute—those that are recognized as legal entities and those that are not. The latter is not a more general description of the former. The second category itself not containing any specific enumeration that is followed by a general description, ejusdem generis has no bearing on the meaning to be attributed to that part of § 1961(4).[4]

---

[4] The Court of Appeals' application of ejusdem generis is further flawed by the assumption that "any individual, partnership, corporation, association or other legal entity" could not act totally beyond the pale of the law. The mere fact that a given enterprise is favored with a legal existence does not prevent that enterprise from proceeding along a wholly illegal course of conduct. Therefore, since legitimacy of purpose is not a universal characteristic of the specifically listed enterprises, it would be improper to engraft this characteristic upon the second category of enterprises.

A second reason offered by the Court of Appeals in support of its judgment was that giving the definition of "enterprise" its ordinary meaning would create several internal inconsistencies in the act. With respect to § 1962(c), it was said:

> "If 'a pattern of racketeering' can itself be an 'enterprise' for purposes of § 1962(c), then the two phrases 'employed by or associated with any enterprise' and 'the conduct of such enterprise's affairs through [a pattern of racketeering activity]' add nothing to the meaning of the section. The words of the statute are coherent and logical only if they are read as applying to legitimate enterprises."

This conclusion is based on a faulty premise. That a wholly criminal enterprise comes within the ambit of the statute does not mean that a "pattern of racketeering activity" is an "enterprise." In order to secure a conviction under RICO, the government must prove both the existence of an "enterprise" and the connected "pattern of racketeering activity." The enterprise is an entity, for present purposes a group of persons associated together for a common purpose of engaging in a course of conduct. The pattern of racketeering activity is, on the other hand, a series of criminal acts as defined by the statute. The former is proved by evidence of an ongoing organization, formal or informal, and by evidence that the various associates function as a continuing unit. The latter is proved by evidence of the requisite number of acts of racketeering committed by the participants in the enterprise. While the proof used to establish these separate elements may in particular cases coalesce, proof of one does not necessarily establish the other. The "enterprise" is not the "pattern of racketeering activity"; it is an entity separate and apart from the pattern of activity in which it engages. The existence of an enterprise at all times remains a separate element which must be proved by the government.[5]

Apart from § 1962(c)'s proscription against participating in an enterprise through a pattern of racketeering activities, RICO also proscribes [in § 1962(a)] the investment of income derived from racketeering activity in an enterprise engaged in or which affects interstate commerce as well as [in § 1962(b)] the acquisition of an interest in or control of any such enterprise through a pattern of racketeering activity. The Court of Appeals concluded that these provisions of RICO should be interpreted so as to apply only to legitimate enterprises. If these two sections are so limited, the Court of Appeals held that the proscription in § 1962(c), at issue here, must be similarly limited. Again, we do not accept the premise from which the Court of Appeals derived its conclusion. It is obvious that §§ 1962(a) and

---

[5] The government takes the position that proof of a pattern of racketeering activity in itself would not be sufficient to establish the existence of an enterprise: "We do not suggest that any two sporadic and isolated offenses by the same actor or actors ipso facto constitute an 'illegitimate' enterprise; rather, the existence of the enterprise as an independent entity must also be shown." But even if that were not the case, the Court of Appeals' position on this point is of little force. Language in a statute is not rendered superfluous merely because in some contexts that language may not be pertinent.

(b) address the infiltration by organized crime of legitimate businesses, but we cannot agree that these sections were not also aimed at preventing racketeers from investing or reinvesting in wholly illegal enterprises and from acquiring through a pattern of racketeering activity wholly illegitimate enterprises such as an illegal gambling business or a loan-sharking operation.   There is no inconsistency or anomaly in recognizing that § 1962 applies to both legitimate and illegitimate enterprises.   Certainly the language of the statute does not warrant the Court of Appeals' conclusion to the contrary.

Similarly, the Court of Appeals noted that various civil remedies were provided by § 1964, including divestiture, dissolution, reorganization, restrictions on future activities by violators of RICO, and treble damages. These remedies it thought would have utility only with respect to legitimate enterprises.   As a general proposition, however, the civil remedies could be useful in eradicating organized crime from the social fabric, whether the enterprise be ostensibly legitimate or admittedly criminal. The aim is to divest the association of the fruits of its ill-gotten gains. Even if one or more of the civil remedies might be inapplicable to a particular illegitimate enterprise, this fact would not serve to limit the enterprise concept.   Congress has provided civil remedies for use when the circumstances so warrant.   It is untenable to argue that their existence limits the scope of the criminal provisions.

Finally, it is urged that the interpretation of RICO to include both legitimate and illegitimate enterprises will substantially alter the balance between federal and state enforcement of criminal law.   This is particularly true, so the argument goes, since included within the definition of racketeering activity are a significant number of acts made criminal under state law.   But even assuming that the more inclusive definition of enterprise will have the effect suggested,[9] the language of the statute and its legislative history indicate that Congress was well aware that it was entering a new domain of federal involvement through the enactment of this measure. Indeed, the very purpose of the Organized Crime Control Act of 1970 was to enable the federal government to address a large and seemingly neglected problem.   The view was that existing law, state and federal, was not adequate to address the problem, which was of national dimensions.   That Congress included within the definition of racketeering activities a number of state crimes strongly indicates that RICO criminalized conduct that was also criminal under state law, at least when the requisite elements of a RICO offense are present.   As the hearings and legislative debates reveal, Congress was well aware of the fear that RICO would "mov[e] large

---

[9] RICO imposes no restrictions upon the criminal justice systems of the states.   See 84 Stat. 947 ("Nothing in this title shall supersede any provision of Federal, State, or other law imposing criminal penalties or affording civil remedies in addition to those provided for in this title").   Thus, under RICO, the states remain free to exercise their police powers to the fullest constitutional extent in defining and prosecuting crimes within their respective jurisdictions.   That some of those crimes may also constitute predicate acts of racketeering under RICO, is no restriction on the separate administration of criminal justice by the states.

substantive areas formerly totally within the police power of the state into the federal realm." 116 Cong. Rec. 35217 (1970)(remarks of Rep. Eckhardt). In the face of [this objection], Congress nonetheless proceeded to enact the measure, knowing that it would alter somewhat the role of the federal government in the war against organized crime and that the alteration would entail prosecutions involving acts of racketeering that are also crimes under state law. There is no argument that Congress acted beyond its power in so doing. That being the case, the courts are without authority to restrict the application of the statute. See United States v. Culbert, 435 U.S. 371, 379–80 (1978).

Contrary to the judgment below, neither the language nor structure of RICO limits its application to legitimate "enterprises." Applying it also to criminal organizations does not render any portion of the statute superfluous nor does it create any structural incongruities within the framework of the act. The result is neither absurd nor surprising. On the contrary, insulating the wholly criminal enterprise from prosecution under RICO is the more incongruous position.

Section 904(a) of RICO, 84 Stat. 947, directs that "[t]he provisions of this Title shall be liberally construed to effectuate its remedial purposes." With or without this admonition, we could not agree with the Court of Appeals that illegitimate enterprises should be excluded from coverage. We are also quite sure that nothing in the legislative history of RICO requires a contrary conclusion.[10]

III

The statement of findings that prefaces the Organized Crime Control Act of 1970 reveals the pervasiveness of the problem that Congress was addressing by this enactment:

> "The Congress finds that (1) organized crime in the United States is a highly sophisticated, diversified, and widespread activity that annually drains billions of dollars from America's economy by unlawful conduct and the illegal use of force, fraud, and corruption; (2) organized crime derives a major portion of its power through money obtained from such illegal endeavors as syndicated gambling, loan sharking, the theft and fencing of prop-

---

[10] We find no occasion to apply the rule of lenity to this statute. "[T]hat 'rule,' as is true of any guide to statutory construction, only serves as an aid for resolving an ambiguity; it is not to be used to beget one. . . . The rule comes into operation at the end of the process of construing what Congress has expressed, not at the beginning as an overriding consideration of being lenient to wrongdoers." Callanan v. United States, 364 U.S. 587, 596 (1961). There being no ambiguity in the RICO provisions at issue here, the rule of lenity does not come into play. See United States v. Moore, 423 U.S. 122, 145 (1975), quoting United States v. Brown, 333 U.S. 18, 25–26 (1948)(" 'The canon in favor of strict construction [of criminal statutes] is not an inexorable command to override common sense and evident statutory purpose. . . . Nor does it demand that a statute be given the "narrowest meaning"; it is satisfied if the words are given their fair meaning in accord with the manifest intent of the lawmakers' "); see also Lewis v. United States, 445 U.S. 55, 60–61 (1980).

erty, the importation and distribution of narcotics and other dangerous drugs, and other forms of social exploitation; (3) this money and power are increasingly used to infiltrate and corrupt legitimate business and labor unions and to subvert and corrupt our democratic processes; (4) organized crime activities in the United States weaken the stability of the Nation's economic system, harm innocent investors and competing organizations, interfere with free competition, seriously burden interstate and foreign commerce, threaten the domestic security, and undermine the general welfare of the Nation and its citizens; and (5) organized crime continues to grow because of defects in the evidence-gathering process of the law inhibiting the development of the legally admissible evidence necessary to bring criminal and other sanctions or remedies to bear on the unlawful activities of those engaged in organized crime and because the sanctions and remedies available to the Government are unnecessarily limited in scope and impact." 84 Stat. 922–23.

In light of the above findings, it was the declared purpose of Congress "to seek the eradication of organized crime in the United States by strengthening the legal tools in the evidence-gathering process, by establishing new penal prohibitions, and by providing enhanced sanctions and new remedies to deal with the unlawful activities of those engaged in organized crime." Id., at 923.[11] The various titles of the act provide the tools through which this goal is to be accomplished. Only three of those titles create substantive offenses, title VIII, which is directed at illegal gambling operations, title IX, at issue here, and title XI, which addresses the importation, distribution, and storage of explosive materials. The other titles provide various procedural and remedial devices to aid in the prosecution and incarceration of persons involved in organized crime.

Considering this statement of the act's broad purposes, the construction of RICO suggested by respondent and the court below is unacceptable. Whole areas of organized criminal activity would be placed beyond the substantive reach of the enactment. For example, associations of persons engaged solely in "loan sharking, the theft and fencing of property, the importation and distribution of narcotics and other dangerous drugs," id., at 922–23, would be immune from prosecution under RICO so long as the association did not deviate from the criminal path. Yet these are among the very crimes that Congress specifically found to be typical of the crimes committed by persons involved in organized crime, and as a major source of revenue and power for such organizations. Along these same lines, Senator McClellan, the principal sponsor of the bill, gave two examples of types of problems RICO was designed to address. Neither is consistent with the

[11] See also 116 Cong. Rec. 602 (1970)(remarks of Sen. Yarborough)("a full scale attack on organized crime"); id., at 819 (remarks of Sen. Scott)("purpose is to eradicate organized crime in the United States"); id., at 35199 (remarks of Rep. Rodino)("a truly full-scale commitment to destroy the insidious power of organized crime groups"); id., at 35300 (remarks of Rep. Mayne)(organized crime "must be sternly and irrevocably eradicated").

view that substantive offenses under RICO would be limited to legitimate enterprises: "Organized criminals, too, have flooded the market with cheap reproductions of hit records and affixed counterfeit popular labels. They are heavily engaged in the illicit prescription drug industry." 116 Cong. Rec. 592 (1970). In view of the purposes and goals of the act, as well as the language of the statute, we are unpersuaded that Congress nevertheless confined the reach of the law to only narrow aspects of organized crime, and, in particular, under RICO, *only* the infiltration of legitimate business.

This is not to gainsay that the legislative history forcefully supports the view that the major purpose of title IX is to address the infiltration of legitimate business by organized crime. The point is made time and again during the debates and in the hearings before the House and Senate.[13] But none of these statements requires the negative inference that Title IX did not reach the activities of enterprises organized and existing for criminal purposes.

On the contrary, these statements are in full accord with the proposition that RICO is equally applicable to a criminal enterprise that has no legitimate dimension or has yet to acquire one. Accepting that the primary purpose of RICO is to cope with the infiltration of legitimate businesses, applying the statute in accordance with its terms, so as to reach criminal enterprises, would seek to deal with the problem at its very source. Supporters of the bill recognized that organized crime uses its primary sources of revenue and power—illegal gambling, loan sharking and illicit drug distribution—as a springboard into the sphere of legitimate enterprise. The Senate Report stated:

> "What is needed here, the committee believes, are new approaches that will deal not only with individuals, but also with the economic base through which those individuals constitute such a serious threat to the economic well-being of the nation. In short, an attack must be made on *their source of economic power itself*, and the attack must take place on all available fronts." S. Rep. No. 91–617, p. 79 (1969)(emphasis supplied).

Senator Byrd explained in debate on the floor, that "loan sharking paves the way for organized criminals to gain access to and eventually take over the control of thousands of legitimate businesses." 116 Cong. Rec. 606 (1970). Senator Hruska declared that "the combination of criminal and civil penalties in this title offers an extraordinary potential for striking a mortal blow against the property interests of organized crime." Id., at

[13] 116 Cong. Rec. 591 (1970)(remarks of Sen. McClellan)("title IX is aimed at removing organized crime from our legitimate organizations"); id., at 602 (remarks of Sen. Hruska)("title IX of this act is designed to remove the influence of organized crime from legitimate business by attacking its property interests and by removing its members from control of legitimate businesses which have been acquired or operated by unlawful racke- teering methods"); id., at 607 (remarks of Sen. Byrd)("alarming expansion into the field of legitimate business"); id., at 953 (remarks of Sen. Thurmond)("racketeers ... gaining inroads into legitimate business"); id., at 845 (remarks of Sen. Kennedy)("title IX ... may provide us with new tools to prevent organized crime from taking over legitimate businesses and activities"); S. Rep. No. 91–617, p. 76 (1969).

602.[14] Undoubtedly, the infiltration of illegitimate businesses was of great concern, but the means provided to prevent that infiltration plainly included striking at the source of the problem. As Representative Poff, a manager of the bill in the House, stated: "[T]itle IX ... will deal not only with individuals, but also with the economic base through which those individuals constitute such a serious threat to the economic well-being of the nation. In short, an attack must be made on their source of economic power itself...." Id., at 35193.

As a measure to deal with the infiltration of legitimate businesses by organized crime, RICO was both preventive and remedial. Respondent's view would ignore the preventive function of the statute. If Congress had intended the more circumscribed approach espoused by the Court of Appeals, there would have been some positive sign that the law was not to reach organized criminal activities that give rise to the concerns about infiltration. The language of the statute, however—the most reliable evidence of its intent—reveals that Congress opted for a far broader definition of the word "enterprise," and we are unconvinced by anything in the legislative history that this definition should be given less than its full effect.

The judgment of the Court of Appeals is accordingly

Reversed.

■ JUSTICE STEWART agrees with the reasoning and conclusion of the Court of Appeals as to the meaning of the term "enterprise" in this statute. Accordingly, he respectfully dissents.

NOTE ON *UNITED STATES v. FRUMENTO*

In United States v. Frumento, 563 F.2d 1083 (3d Cir.1977), the Third Circuit addressed the application of RICO to a governmental "enterprise."

[14] See also, e.g., 115 Cong. Rec. 827 (1969)(remarks of Sen. McClellan)("Organized crime ... uses its ill-gotten gains ... to infiltrate and secure control of legitimate business and labor union activities"); 116 Cong. Rec. 591 (1970)(remarks of Sen. McClellan) ("illegally gained revenue also makes it possible for organized crime to infiltrate and pollute legitimate business"); id., at 603 (remarks of Sen. Yarborough) ("[RICO] is designed to root out the influence of organized crime in legitimate business, into which billions of dollars of illegally obtained money is channeled"); id., at 606 (remarks of Sen. Byrd)("loan sharking paves the way for organized criminals to gain access to and eventually take over the control of thousands of legitimate businesses"); id., at 35193 (remarks of Rep. Poff)("[T]itle IX ... will deal not only with individuals, but also with the economic base through which those individuals constitute such a serious threat to the economic well-being of the nation. In short, an attack must be made on their source of economic power itself...."); S. Rep. No. 91–617, supra, at 78–80; H.R. Rep. No. 1574, supra, at 5 ("The President's Crime Commission found that the greatest menace that organized crime presents is its ability through the accumulation of illegal gains to infiltrate into legitimate business and labor unions"); Hearings on Organized Crime Control before Subcommittee No. 5 of the House Committee on the Judiciary, 91st Cong., 2d Sess., 170 (1970)(Department of Justice Comments)("Title IX is designed to inhibit the infiltration of legitimate business by organized crime, and like the previous title, *to reach the criminal syndicates' major sources of revenue*")(emphasis supplied).

The case involved allegations that several defendants had engaged in various racketeering acts related to the operation of the Bureau of Cigarette and Beverage Taxes, an agency of the Commonwealth of Pennsylvania. The defendants argued that the agency could not be a RICO "enterprise." The court disagreed:

"Appellants vigorously assert on appeal that a reading of the statute supports their contention that the term 'enterprise' was never intended to include governmental organizations. First, they say violations of § 1962 not only gave rise to criminal penalties, but the district courts of the United States are also given extensive civil remedy powers in the event of violation of the statute, including the power to order dissolution or reorganization of any 'enterprise'; and that Congress could not have intended to give the courts the power to order dissolution or reorganization of a state agency. Secondly, appellants argue that since § 1964(c) permits private persons to sue and recover treble damages for violations of § 1962, Congress could not have intended, in view of the limitations of the 11th amendment, to allow suits against state governmental bodies. Finally, appellants argue that in construing the statutory definition of 'enterprise,' the phrase 'other legal entity' following nouns of narrow scope relating to different forms of business ventures, must be construed under the rule of ejusdem generis in the light of the narrow terms which follow. Thus, the words of the final clause in the definition dealing with nonlegal entities indicate Congress intended to limit the term 'enterprise' to private business or labor organizations.

"Appellants also take comfort in the absence of any reference to governmental bodies in the legislative history of the Organized Crime Control Act of 1970. In this respect, they rely heavily in support of their position on United States v. Mandel, 415 F.Supp. 997 (D.Md.1976). The District Court in that case concluded that the silence of the legislative history of title IX of the Organized Crime Control Act as to whether an enterprise may include such public entities as governments and states suggests a narrow construction of the statute. Since the major purpose of title IX is 'to rid racketeering influences from the commercial life of the nation,' the District Court believed that reading 'enterprise' to include public entities would do violence to the plain purpose of title IX. Thus, predicating its decision on its analysis of the legislative history, the purpose of title IX and the doctrine of ejusdem generis, the court held that the state of Maryland was not an 'enterprise' within the meaning of the racketeering statute. We disagree.

"We begin our discussion with an assessment of the ejusdem generis doctrine. It is not a rule of law but merely a useful tool of construction resorted to in ascertaining legislative intent. The rule should not be employed when the intention of the legislature is otherwise evident. Nor should it be applied to defeat the obvious purpose of the statute or to narrow the targets of Congressional concern. 'The rule of "ejusdem generis" is applied as an aid in ascertaining the intention of the legislature, not to subvert it when ascertained.' Texas v. United States, 292 U.S. 522, 534 (1934). For reasons to which we later advert, it is apparent that Congress intended the general words defining an 'enterprise' in § 1961(4) to go beyond the specific reference to private business or labor organizations.

"As we read the Organized Crime Control Act, Congress was not so much concerned with limiting the protective and remedial features of the act to business and labor organizations as it was with reducing the insidious capabilities of persons in organized crime to infiltrate the American economy. This accounts for the new civil remedies in the act which permit equitable restraint of economic activity engaged in by organized crime as a substitute for criminal prosecution with its attendant procedural and constitutional protection for defendants. See Note, Infiltration of Legitimate Business, 124 U. Pa. L. Rev. 192, 196 (1975). In other words, Congress' concern was enlarging the number of tools with which to attack the invasion of the economic life of the country by the cancerous influences of racketeering activity;[13] Congress did not confine its scrutiny to special areas of economic activity. Congress had no reason to adopt a constricted approach to the solution of the problem. Congress was concerned with the infiltration of organized crime into the American economy and to the devastating effects that racketeering activity had upon it.[14] Yet,

[13] Congress stated that the purpose of the act is "to seek the eradication of organized crime in the United States by strengthening the legal tools in the evidence-gathering process[,] by establishing penal prohibitions[,] and by providing sanctions and new remedies to deal with the unlawful activities of those engaged in organized crime." 84 Stat. 923.

[14] A recent report of the Advisory Commission on Intergovernmental Relations describes the pattern of cigarette bootlegging that has been developing for the past decade and the link between bootlegging and organized criminal elements. The Commission states inter alia:

"In [about a dozen states mainly in the East and Midwest] cigarette smuggling is a multi-million dollar business, organized crime syndicates are heavily involved, and there are many victims. State and local governments lose millions of dollars; taxpayers pay higher taxes or receive fewer services; cigarette wholesalers and retailers are driven out of business and jobs are lost; political and law enforcement officials are corrupted; trucks are hijacked and warehouses raided; and people are injured and even killed. . . .

"The profits from organized smuggling of cigarettes are enormous. The Council Against Cigarette Bootlegging estimates that the illegal profits in eight eastern states were about $97.9 million in fiscal year 1975–76. The profits from cigarette smuggling are used by organized crime to finance other illegal operations, such as drugs, loan sharking, and gambling. These profits are earned at the expense of state and local governments, which, according to the Council, lost an estimated $170.7 million in revenues in the eight eastern states (Connecticut, Delaware, Maryland, Massachusetts, New York, New Jersey, Pennsylvania, and Rhode Island), and the tobacco industry (wholesalers and retailers), which lost an estimated $470 million in sales." Advisory

we are asked to believe that Congress' approach to a monumental problem besetting the country was myopic and artificially contained. Is it conceivable that in considering the ever more widespread tentacles of organized crime in the nation's economic life, Congress intended to ignore an important aspect of the economy because it was state operated and state controlled? We think not. Congress declared that the provisions of title IX 'be liberally construed to effectuate its remedial purposes.' 84 Stat. 947.

"In its statement of the broad purposes of the act, Congress evinced no reason why governmental agencies which had been infiltrated by organized crime should be immune from the reach of the act. In fact, in Pennsylvania the Commonwealth is engaged in several of the largest and more affluent business operations in the state, each of which involve many millions of dollars. The Commonwealth of Pennsylvania purchases, distributes, and sells alcoholic beverages legally consumed among its more than 12,000,000 citizens;[15] it sells and distributes games of chance through its much touted lottery system.[16] The constricted reading of the statute advocated by the appellants makes little sense; private business organizations legitimately owned and operated by the states, even though their activities substantially affect interstate commerce, would be open game for racketeers. We refuse to believe that Congress had such 'tunnel-vision' when it enacted the racketeering statute or that it intended to exclude from the protective embrace of this broad statute, designed to curb organized crime, state operated commercial ventures engaged in interstate commerce, or other governmental agencies regulating commercial and utility operations affecting interstate commerce.

"We also find support for our view in the congressional findings underpinning the legislation. Although Congress does refer in one of its findings to the increasing use of money and power to infiltrate and corrupt legitimate business and labor unions, its findings also note concern for all of 'America's economy' from which organized crime in 'highly sophisticated, diversified, and widespread activity' annually drains billions of dollars and weakens 'the stability of the nation's economic system.' These findings sensibly dwell upon the total American economy, not segments of it. Furthermore, the House Report on § 1962

Commission on Intergovernmental Relations, Cigarette Bootlegging: A State and Federal Responsibility 20–20 (1977).

15 The Commonwealth of Pennsylvania operated 752 retail liquor stores from July 1, 1970 to June 29, 1971, inclusive and the store sales for that period amounted to $474,010,-000; it operated 757 stores from June 30, 1971 to June 27, 1972, inclusive and the store sales for that period amounted to $496,590,-

000. Table 40, Pennsylvania Statistical Abstract 1976, 18th ed.

16 The Commonwealth of Pennsylvania commenced its lottery operations in 1972. For its first fiscal year ending June 30, 1972, it generated ticket sales amounting to $50,-452,000. For its fiscal year ending June 30, 1973, its lottery ticket sales amounted to $118,801,000. Table 167, Pennsylvania Statistical Abstract 1976, 18th ed.

observes that through three subsections it establishes 'a threefold prohibition aimed at stopping the infiltration of racketeers into legitimate organizations.' House Report No. 1549, 91st Cong., 2d Sess. 39 (1970), U.S. Code Cong. & Admin. News, 1970, p. 4033. The report addresses not only private business organizations and unions, but speaks to legitimate organizations as a class. We therefore hold that a state agency charged with the responsibility of enforcing the tax laws on an interstate industry engaged in importing cigarettes from points outside the state is an enterprise within the meaning of 18 U.S.C. § 1961(4)."

United States v. Bledsoe

United States Court of Appeals, Eighth Circuit, 1982.
674 F.2d 647.

Before LAY, CHIEF JUDGE, and HEANEY and ROSS, CIRCUIT JUDGES.

■ LAY, CHIEF JUDGE.

The central issues in this case are (1) the requisite characteristics and proof of an "enterprise" under 18 U.S.C. § 1962(c), the Racketeer Influenced and Corrupt Organization Act (RICO) and (2) the propriety of joining charges of securities fraud against one defendant which are not alleged to be overt acts in furtherance of the conspiracy nor as predicate acts of racketeering in a RICO count with separate charges of securities fraud and conspiracy and RICO charges against four other defendants.

The government originally sought and obtained an indictment variously charging 22 defendants. Count one charged all 22 defendants with conspiracy to violate RICO in violation of 18 U.S.C. § 1962(d) and alleged the commission of 93 overt acts in furtherance of the conspiracy. Count two charged all defendants with violation of RICO, 18 U.S.C. § 1962(c). This count alleged that defendants were associated with an enterprise, described as a group of individuals associated in fact to fraudulently sell securities of agricultural cooperatives in Missouri, Oklahoma, and Arkansas, and that defendants participated in the affairs of this enterprise through a pattern of racketeering activity. Count two detailed the acts constituting the pattern of racketeering as to each defendant in paragraphs 159 through 209 and in separate counts three through 161 which were incorporated into count two by reference. The predicate acts of racketeering consisted of the fraudulent sale of securities of two Missouri cooperatives, United Farmers Association of America (UFA–Mo.) and Progressive Farmers Association (PFA); an Oklahoma cooperative, United Farmers Association of America (UFA–Ok.); and an Arkansas cooperative, Consumer–Farmers Association (CFA). Counts three through 68 charged all five appellants and 15 others with violating 15 U.S.C. §§ 77q (a) and 77x and 18 U.S.C. § 2 by fraudulently selling PFA securities. Counts 69 through 161 charged defendants Phillips, Cloninger, Bledsoe and two others, but not Moffitt and Stafford, with violating 18 U.S.C. §§ 2 and 1341 by devising a scheme to defraud in the sale of PFA securities.

Counts 162 through 169 charged Phillips with evading personal income taxes and failure to file corporate tax returns. Counts 170 through 175 charged Phillips with violating 15 U.S.C. §§ 77q(a) and 77x by fraudulently selling securities of a Missouri corporation, Progressive Investors (PI).

Trial of 11 defendants commenced on October 2, 1979. The government elected to try only Phillips, Bledsoe, Cloninger, and Donald Burks on counts 45 and 66 which were renumbered as counts three and four. However, original counts three through 161 remained incorporated in count two as predicate acts of racketeering. The government elected not to join any of the tax charges and only two of the fraud charges against Phillips alone, counts 172 and 174 which were renumbered as counts five and six. For various reasons, only five defendants remained when the case was submitted to the jury on August 14, 1980. On August 25, 1980, the remaining five defendants were found guilty under all the counts with which they were charged. All five have appealed.

I. Facts.

In May of 1972, Phillips incorporated Progressive Investors, an ordinary business corporation. Through PI, Phillips offered and sold a security called an Estate Builder. The Estate Builder was an unsecured annuity contract in which PI agreed to make a lump sum payment to an investor after a period of years provided the investor made certain installment payments. PI did not engage in any investment program or substantial business of any kind. Income raised from security sales was diverted primarily to Phillips' personal use through a number of personal corporations. Phillips, assisted by a small sales staff, made false statements and failed to disclose material facts in the sale of PI securities. Moffitt was involved in the sale of PI securities, but none of the other defendants were connected in any way to PI securities business nor was Moffitt named in counts five and six which charge Phillips with fraud in the sale of PI securities.

During the summer of 1972, Phillips consulted with Donald H. Gibson, an attorney who was an unindicted co-conspirator and the government's principal witness in this case, concerning the sale of securities through agricultural cooperatives. Phillips described PI's securities sales. Gibson advised that co-ops were exempt from various registration requirements. Defendant Cloninger was present at several of these meetings. However, Cloninger is not alleged to have had any interest in the cooperative which Phillips and Gibson eventually formed.

Phillips and Gibson agreed to form the cooperative and evenly share its profits. In October of 1972, UFA–Mo. was incorporated as a non-stock, not-for-profit, agricultural cooperative. UFA–Mo. had no significant business operations other than the sale of a security called an Estate Builder. In April of 1973, Phillips left UFA–Mo. Gibson continued to operate the cooperative until approximately June of 1975.

In May 1973, Phillips incorporated PFA, a Missouri agricultural cooperative. Phillips recruited a board of directors composed primarily of farmers with little business experience. PI entered into a consulting agreement with PFA. Cloninger came to PFA in the spring or summer of 1973 to assist in its sale of securities. In November 1973, defendants Bledsoe and Burks were hired to manage PFA's security sales. PI thereafter assigned 25 per cent of its interest in the consulting agreement to corporations controlled by Bledsoe, Burks, and Cloninger. Phillips, Bledsoe, Burks, and Cloninger made a secret agreement to evenly share all profits derived from PFA. Burks became president of PFA. Around the same time, PFA hired Moffitt and Stafford as salesmen. PFA originally sold Estate Builders and later also sold bonds and stock.

In April 1974, PI purchased a tract of land in Stone County, Missouri which was designated Table Rock Heights. Phillips obtained an inflated appraisal of the land. Phillips then began to contact PI investors to urge them to convert their securities into mortgage notes through additional payments. The mortgage note was a PI promissory note secured by a deed of trust for a lot in PI's tract. In actuality, no lots existed.

PFA had several legitimate business operations although evidence indicated that none proved profitable. In early 1975, PFA acquired land in Table Rock Heights through a merger with National Business Corporation (NBC). NBC was created to act as a conduit through which to move the land from PI to PFA. The merger also transformed PFA into a stock cooperative. Phillips, Bledsoe, Cloninger, and Stafford received substantial shares of the newly issued PFA stock.

In May 1975, Phillips suggested to Gibson that they form a partnership to organize cooperatives in other states. Phillips wanted Gibson to insulate him by not disclosing his interest in new co-ops and by serving as a channel through which Phillips would obtain his share of any profits. Gibson and Moffitt traveled to Arkansas, Texas, and Oklahoma to investigate the feasibility of organizing cooperatives in those states. Gibson, Moffitt, and Paul Canaday agreed to form UFA–Ok. and share its proceeds. Phillips and Gibson agreed to share Gibson's one-third interest, but Moffitt was unaware of Phillips' involvement. Phillips gave PFA materials to Gibson and UFA–Ok. as modeled after PFA. UFA–Ok. sold a security labeled Estate Builder. Stafford sold UFA–Ok. securities. Cloninger participated in one meeting with two officers of UFA–Ok. and Phillips at which the co-op's accounting procedures were discussed. He was not shown to have participated in any sales of UFA–Ok. securities or shared any of the co-op's profits.

In November of 1975, Gibson and Ron Elia agreed to share profits earned by an Arkansas cooperative. Gibson agreed to share his profits with Phillips. Consumer–Farmers Association was incorporated on January 23, 1976, as an Arkansas agricultural cooperative. Moffitt sold CFA securities called Estate Builders. UFA–Mo., UFA–Ok. and CFA each operated in tandem with separate "management companies" which played a role similar to that played by PI in relation to PFA. These companies were used to divert revenue to the principal operatives or their personal corporations. CFA's sale of securities was enjoined by the Arkansas

Securities Commission in the spring of 1976. UFA–Ok. was similarly restrained by the Oklahoma Securities Commission in October of 1976.

In the fall of 1975, Progressive Farmers Association–Farmers Marketing Association (PFA–FMA) was incorporated. Burks was PFA–FMA's original president and was succeeded by Bledsoe when Bledsoe succeeded Burks as president of PFA in January 1976. PFA transferred several of its assets to PFA–FMA in return for unsecured promissory notes. PFA also made cash advances to PFA–FMA. PFA–FMA stock was held by those who held PFA stock when PFA–FMA was formed. Bledsoe, Cloninger, Stafford, and Phillips owned substantial shares of this stock. PFA–FMA did agree to pay two per cent of its gross sales to PA, but these payments were diverted to Phillips, Bledsoe and Cloninger.

Phillips, Bledsoe, Cloninger, and Burks agreed to terminate their interest in PI's consulting agreement with PFA in November 1975. In return, PFA made substantial payments over a period of time to these individuals. However, PFA continued to make payments to Burks, Cloninger, Bledsoe, and Phillips as if the consulting agreement was still valid. In October 1976, Bledsoe resigned as president of PFA, but continued as president of PFA–FMA. Both PFA–FMA and PFA were declared bankrupt in May 1977.

II. Misjoinder.

Before trial commenced in this case, the trial court, the Honorable Warren K. Urbom presiding, responding to various motions from the defendants, expressed concern about the manageability and fairness of the trial. The court questioned the jurors' capacity to comprehend and separate the activities of and connections between individual defendants. In order to simplify the trial, the court directed the government to reduce the number of counts to six. Notwithstanding the court's effort, the government did not sever any of the allegations from counts three through 161 from the substantive RICO count, count two, in which each of these allegations was incorporated by reference as predicate acts of racketeering. Thus, in effect, the government submitted proof on 163 counts; the anticipated simplification and saving of time was not achieved.

Counts five and six charged only Phillips with securities fraud in the sale of PI Estate Builders and mortgage notes.[2] These counts were selected from among original counts 170–175. Several defendants moved to sever these counts before trial; during the trial the court granted all defendants a continuing motion to sever these counts. All motions were denied. On appeal, this objection is renewed.

[At this point, the court engaged in an extensive discussion of the complexities of the trial. It found that there was a misjoinder and that it was "clearly prejudicial." It concluded: "[T]he danger of jury confusion

---

[2] Specifically, count five involves the mailing of a PI mortgage note to Jerry F. Gallivan on or about October 23, 1974, and count six involves the mailing of a personal check from Hobart L. and Pauline Coffelt to PI on or about January 16, 1975.

was substantial. There were over 100 limitations of proof with regard to counts five and six, and sometimes the limitation would shift back and forth from question to question. An average juror cannot be expected to keep the evidence compartmentalized with so many defendants and in such a complex factual background."]

III. RICO Counts.

All of the original 22 defendants were indicted under count two for violation of RICO, 18 U.S.C. § 1962(c). Additionally, each defendant was charged in count one with conspiracy to violate RICO under 18 U.S.C. § 1962(d). The indictment charged that each of the 22 defendants were employed by or associated with an "enterprise," to wit, "a group of individuals associated in fact to offer and sell securities of corporations organized as agricultural cooperatives in order to obtain money and property by fraudulent means from residents of the states of Missouri, Oklahoma and Arkansas, which enterprise was engaged in, and the activities of which affected, interstate commerce." Each defendant was charged with having "willfully and knowingly conducted and participated, directly and indirectly, in the conduct of the enterprise's affairs through a pattern of racketeering activity." The government incorporated all of the original 159 substantive counts of mail and securities fraud as predicate acts constituting the pattern of racketeering alleged in count two.

RICO makes it a crime "for any person employed by or associated with any enterprise engaged in, or the activities of which affect, interstate or foreign commerce, to conduct or participate, directly or indirectly, in the conduct of such enterprise's affairs through a pattern of racketeering activity or collection of unlawful debt." 18 U.S.C. § 1962(c). The act defines enterprise to include "any individual, partnership, corporation, association, or other legal entity, and any union or group of individuals associated in fact although not a legal entity." 18 U.S.C. § 1961(4). The act defines a "pattern of racketeering activity" as the commission of any two of a specified number of federal and state crimes, including mail fraud under 18 U.S.C. § 1341 and security fraud under 15 U.S.C. § 77q(a), within 10 years of each other. 18 U.S.C. § 1961(1)(B) and (D).

Phillips, Bledsoe, and Cloninger do not now challenge the sufficiency of the evidence from which the jury found them guilty of the substantive crimes charged in counts three and four nor do any of the defendants challenge the sufficiency of the evidence of their commission of the alleged predicate acts of racketeering. We must recognize, however, that even if some of the defendants were guilty of securities fraud as charged in counts three and four or as predicate acts in count two, each was also charged with and convicted of a more serious crime under RICO. The maximum penalty under 18 U.S.C. § 1341 (mail fraud) is five years and $1,000. The maximum punishment for security fraud is five years and $10,000. 15 U.S.C. § 77x. By comparison, the maximum penalty under RICO is 20 years and $25,000 as well as potential criminal forfeitures. 18 U.S.C. § 1963(a). If, in fact, the government did not prove the defendants violated RICO, then it is fundamental to fair process of law, regardless of how much we condemn their wrongful conduct, that they cannot be convicted under the act.

We are satisfied that RICO was not designed to serve as a recidivist statute, imposing heavier sentences for crimes which are already punishable under other statutes. The act was not intended to be a catchall reaching all concerted action of two or more criminals involving two or more of the designated crimes.

The inclusion of the RICO and conspiracy counts allowed the government to join all of the original 22 defendants in the indictment even though not all of the defendants were involved in the formation and sale of securities of all of the various cooperatives. The vehicle which the government used to connect the five appellants, as well as the other 17 charged, and which enabled the government to utilize evidence of fraud involving all of the co-ops was RICO and the broad tentacles of the conspiracy charge. Under Fed. R. Crim. P. 8(b), the government was required to allege some type of overall scheme involving each of the defendants and all the fraud charges in order to join them under one indictment. This allegation of participation in an all-encompassing RICO enterprise was necessary even after the number of defendants was reduced to the present five. Without the broad allegation, the government could not have introduced evidence of all of the 209 alleged predicate acts of racketeering and 93 alleged overt acts in furtherance of the conspiracy, some of which related to only one of the defendants. The government concedes that had it alleged that the enterprise was a single cooperative, only evidence of mail and security fraud relating to that cooperative would have been admissible. More significantly, only those defendants who participated in the affairs of that co-op through a pattern of racketeering activity would have been susceptible to joint trial.

The government must and does now assert that the RICO counts allege an enterprise consisting of a multistate association of all of the 22 original defendants. The government specifically conceded at trial and now on appeal that the indictment does not charge that the enterprise through which the pattern of racketeering activities took place was PFA or any of the other agricultural cooperatives organized by the defendants. As the government repeatedly stated in its closing argument, "It's the people and not the co-ops that constitute the enterprise." This concession was acknowledged by the trial court.[5]

Although a co-op, as a legal entity, could clearly qualify as an enterprise under RICO, the government does not and cannot now argue that the enterprise was one or more of the cooperatives since the case was not tried on that theory. ... Thus the convictions can only be sustained if we find

---

[5] In its memorandum and order disposing of appellants' post-trial motions, the trial court stated, "the prosecution of the present case proceeded upon the theory that the enterprise was the association of individuals and not the cooperatives which were formed by those individuals."

sufficient evidence of a single enterprise composed of the various individual defendants associated in fact and distinct from the co-ops.

A.   Statutory Construction.

The government argues, citing United States v. Elliott, 571 F.2d 880, 902 (5th Cir.1978), that RICO was passed to obviate the difficulty of proving a conspiracy. It urges that all those who participate in the affairs of an enterprise need not enter into an agreement encompassing all of its affairs. Once an enterprise is formed, the government argues, any person who becomes associated with or employed by the enterprise and carries out its affairs through a pattern of racketeering can be convicted under RICO. The government asserts that defendants need not be aware of one another's activities, of the overall scope of the enterprise, or even of the existence of the enterprise. The argument is that conviction is predicated solely on defendants' relationship to the enterprise and commission of the predicate acts of racketeering.[6]

This construction of the requirements that a defendant be "employed by or associated with" an enterprise and that he or she "conduct or participate, directly or indirectly, in the conduct of such enterprise's affairs" through a pattern of racketeering has some support in the case law. Courts have held that predicate crimes which constitute "a pattern of racketeering" under 18 U.S.C. § 1961(5)(defining "pattern of racketeering activity" as two acts of racketeering within 10 years of each other) need not be related in any manner other than that they were perpetrated through an enterprise. United States v. Weisman, 624 F.2d 1118, 1122 (2d Cir.1980); United States v. Rone, 598 F.2d 564, 571 (9th Cir.1979). Some courts have interpreted the statutory language requiring that a person be "employed by or associated with" an enterprise and "conduct or participate, directly or indirectly, in the conduct of such enterprise's affairs" to require nothing more than any association with the individuals constituting the enterprise. In *Elliott*, the Fifth Circuit wrote:

> "The substantive proscriptions of the RICO statute apply to insiders and outsiders—those merely 'associated with' an enterprise—who participate directly and indirectly in the enterprise's affairs through a pattern of racketeering activity. 18 U.S.C. § 1962(c). Thus, the RICO net is woven tightly to trap even the smallest fish, those peripherally involved with the enterprise." 571 F.2d, at 903.

But see United States v. Mandel, 591 F.2d 1347, 1375 (4th Cir.1979)(operation or management of enterprise required); United States v. Forsythe, 429 F.Supp. 715, 725 (W.D.Pa.1977)(employment or similar relationship required). Courts have also held that participation in the conduct of an enterprise's affairs through a pattern of racketeering activity does not

---

[6] In the present case, there is added a conspiracy count (count one) alleging each of the defendants' general agreement to violate RICO. The government's argument is some- what vague as to whether knowledge of the enterprise or its essential purpose must be established to sustain the conspiracy charge. See note 12 infra.

involve any degree of scienter greater than that necessary to commit the crimes constituting the pattern of racketeering. United States v. Boylan, 620 F.2d 359, 361–62 (2d Cir.1980). We express grave doubts as to the propriety of the holdings in these cases, but given this loose conception of what it means to be "employed by or associated with" an enterprise and to "conduct or participate" in its affairs, it is more crucial for us to determine in this case what forms of organization or association in fact constitute an enterprise.

The government argues that any association of individuals can be an enterprise. Under this theory, in any security or mail fraud case wherein a conspiracy of two or more persons is formed and two or more overt acts of fraud occur, defendants may be prosecuted under RICO with its heightened punishment. Similarly, under the government's argument, any confederation, no matter how loose or temporary, of two or more individuals committing two or more sporadic crimes which are predicate crimes under RICO provides a basis for prosecution under the act. Cf. United States v. Aleman, 609 F.2d 298 (7th Cir.1979)(two defendants convicted under RICO after committing three home burglaries). Although several courts have accepted this loose construction of RICO, we believe that the legislative history of the statute and an analysis of the statute itself as well as the surrounding criminal law indicates that such a broad construction is not warranted.

The primary intent of Congress in enacting 18 U.S.C. § 1962(c) was to prevent organized crime from infiltrating businesses and other legitimate economic entities. See United States v. Turkette, 452 U.S. 576 (1981). The report of the Senate Committee on the Judiciary on the Organized Crime Control Act of 1969 states that 18 U.S.C. § 1961 et seq. (title IX of the act) has as its purpose the elimination of the infiltration of organized crime and racketeering into legitimate organizations operating in interstate commerce. S. Rep. No. 91–617; 91st Cong., 1st Sess. 76 (1969). When directed against infiltration of legitimate enterprises, the provisions have a relatively well defined scope of application. Legitimate businesses and other legitimate organizations tend to have a definite structure and clear boundaries which limit the applicability of a criminal statute aimed at the infiltration of criminal elements into these entities. Infiltration of legitimate entities also warrants the act's severe sanctions. The act's drafters perceived a distinct threat to the free market in organized criminal groups gaining control of enterprises operating in that market. These congressmen thought that organized criminal elements exert a monopoly-like power in the legitimate economic sphere. The bill's sponsors also believed that such infiltration was a source of power and protection for organized crime and gave it a permanent base from which it was more likely to perpetrate a continuing pattern of criminal acts.

But Congress did not draft the statute to apply solely to infiltration of legitimate enterprises. The statute also reaches wholly criminal organizations. However, the act was not intended to reach any criminals who merely associate together and perpetrate two of the specified crimes, rather it was aimed at "organized crime."[8] In *Turkette*, the Court upheld a RICO conviction of individuals who participated in a criminal enterprise which evidence revealed was of a "professional nature" and executed "a number of distinct criminal acts."

Obviously, no statute could and this statute was not intended to require direct proof that individuals are engaged in something as ill defined as "organized crime." The statute is an attack on organized crime, but it utilizes a per se approach. Thus Senator McClellan, the bill's principal sponsor, stated that the crimes enumerated in the definition of racketeering activity are not committed only by participants in organized crime, but argued that they are "characteristic of organized crime." John L. McClellan, The Organized Crime Act (S.30) or Its Critics: Which Threatens Civil Liberties?, 46 Notre Dame Law. 55, 142–43, 144 (1970). McClellan observes:

> "The danger that a commission of such offenses by other individuals would subject them to proceedings under title IX is [small] since commission of a crime listed under title IX provides only one element of title IX's prohibitions. Unless an individual not only commits such a crime but engages in a pattern of such violations, and uses that pattern to obtain or operate an interest in an interstate business, he is not made subject to proceedings under title IX."

Each element of the crime, that is, the predicate acts, the pattern of such acts, and the enterprise requirement, was designed to limit the applicability of the statute and separate individuals engaged in organized crime from ordinary criminals. The enterprise requirement must be interpreted in this light.

---

[8] The Chairman of the House Subcommittee which held hearings on The Organized Crime Control Act stated at the start of the hearings:

> "[W]e must take care to identify those types of criminal offense which we classify as 'organized crime.' The need to define the target of this legislation and to circumscribe the reach of the substantive as well as the procedural provisions is underscored by the following brief statement from the 1967 report of the President's Commission on Law Enforcement and Administration of Justice:

> > 'A skid-row drunk lying in a gutter is crime. So is the killing of an unfaithful wife. A Cosa Nostra conspiracy to bribe public officials is crime. So is a strong-arm robbery by a 15–year-old boy. The embezzlement of a corporation's funds by an executive is crime. So is the possession of marihuana cigarettes by a student. These crimes can no more be lumped together for purposes of analysis than can measles and schizophrenia, or lung cancer and a broken ankle. As with disease, so with crime: if causes are to be understood, if risks are to be evaluated, and if preventive or remedial actions are to be taken, each kind must be looked at separately. Thinking of "crime" as a whole is futile.'

> "Thus, when we speak of 'organized crime' we must not generalize—we must define our terms and focus on specifics. Comparable precision is essential in developing a federal legislative program to eradicate organized crime."

Organized Crime Control: Hearings on S. 30, and related proposals Before the Subcomm. No. 5 of the House Comm. on the Judiciary, 91st Cong., 2d Sess. 77 (1970).

The crime defined in 18 U.S.C. § 1962(c) involves two modes of association with an enterprise.[9] In order to violate the provision, an individual must be "employed by or associated with" an enterprise and must "participate, directly or indirectly, in the conduct of such enterprise's affairs through a pattern of racketeering activity." Construing the statute to give effect to all its words, it requires an association with an enterprise which is distinct from participation in the conduct of the enterprise through a pattern of racketeering activity. In order for such association, for example, formal membership in or employment by a legitimate organization or their equivalent in a criminal group, to exist, the enterprise must be more than an informal group created to perpetrate the acts of racketeering.

The Supreme Court, in *Turkette*, stated, "The 'enterprise' is not the 'pattern of racketeering activity'; it is an entity separate and apart from the pattern of activity in which it engages. The existence of an enterprise at all times remains a separate entity which must be proved by the government." This court, in United States v. Anderson, 626 F.2d 1358, 1365 (8th Cir.1980), wrote, "The term 'enterprise' must signify an association that is substantially different from the acts which form the 'pattern of racketeering activity.' A contrary interpretation would alter the essential elements of the offense as determined by Congress."

The word "enterprise" ordinarily means an undertaking or project or a unit of organization established to perform any such undertaking or project.[10] However, under RICO, an enterprise cannot simply be the undertaking of the acts of racketeering, neither can it be the minimal association which surrounds these acts. Any two criminal acts will necessarily be surrounded by some degree of organization and no two individuals will ever jointly perpetrate a crime without some degree of association apart from the commission of the crime itself. Thus unless the inclusion of the enterprise element requires proof of some structure separate from the racketeering activity and distinct from the organization which is a necessary incident to the racketeering, the act simply punishes the commission of two of the specified crimes within a 10–year period. Congress clearly did not intend such an application of the act.

[9] The definition of "enterprise" in 18 U.S.C. § 1961(4) is clearly incomplete. If only the literal terms of the definition were utilized, the act would apply both to "any individual" and to "any ... group of individuals associated in fact" and the "enterprise" element would be wholly eliminated.

[10] The term "enterprise" is also used in the Fair Labor Standards Act, 29 U.S.C. § 201 et seq. The act defines enterprise as follows:

" 'Enterprise' means the related activities performed (either through unified operation or common control) by any person or persons for a common business purpose, and includes all such activities whether performed in one or more establishments or by one or more corporate or other organizational units." 29 U.S.C. § 203(r).

The Supreme Court, in Brennan v. Arnheim & Neely, Inc., 410 U.S. 512, 518 (1973), identified the three main elements of an enterprise as related activities, unified operation or common control, and common business purpose.

A comparison of the severe penalties authorized by RICO with those for conspiracy indicates that the act must have been directed at participation in enterprises consisting of more than simple conspiracies to perpetrate the predicate acts of racketeering. Violation of RICO may be punished by a fine of up to $25,000 or imprisonment for up to 20 years or both, while conspiracy to commit an offense against the United States carries a maximum penalty of a $10,000 fine and five years imprisonment. Compare 18 U.S.C. § 1963(a) with 18 U.S.C. § 371. If the enterprise element is satisfied by proof of conspiracy or looser associations not characterized by conspiratorial consent, the heightened punishment can only be justified by the requirement of two acts of racketeering and thus the act is merely a recidivist statute. RICO provisions of the Organized Crime Control Act could not have been intended to punish recidivism because the act explicitly provided for such punishment in the following title (title X), now codified as 18 U.S.C. § 3575, which provides for heightened punishment of repeat offenders. See 18 U.S.C. § 3575(e)(1).

Because RICO does not require proof of a single agreement as in a conspiracy case, it creates a danger of guilt by association. See United States v. Griffin, 660 F.2d 996, 1000 (4th Cir.1981). The individuality of guilt is assured by requiring proof that the enterprise with which individuals associated had certain distinct characteristics. As the Fourth Circuit wrote in *Griffin*:

> "Proof of the existence of an associated-in-fact enterprise requires proof of a 'common purpose' animating its associates, and this may be done by evidence of an 'ongoing organization, formal or informal,' of those associates in which they function as a 'continuing unit.' *Turkette*, 452 U.S., at 583. The ties between the individual associates that are implied by these concepts of continuity, unity, shared purpose and identifiable structure operate precisely to guard against the danger that guilt will be adjudged solely by virtue of associations not so related. They define the line between 'concerted action' through 'group association for criminal purpose,' for which 'combination in crime' may constitutionally be proscribed, Callanan v. United States, 364 U.S. 587, 593–94 (1961), and less clearly related conduct that may not be so proscribed and prosecuted." 660 F.2d, at 1000.

Although commonality of purpose may be the sine qua non of a criminal enterprise, in many cases this singular test fails to distinguish enterprises from individuals merely associated together for the commission of sporadic crime. Any two wrongdoers who through concerted action commit two or more crimes share a purpose. This suggests that an enterprise must exhibit each of three basic characteristics.

In addition to having a common or shared purpose which animates those associated with it, it is fundamental that the enterprise "function as a continuing unit." In *Turkette*, the Supreme Court stated that an enterprise "is proved by evidence of an *ongoing* organization, formal or informal, and by evidence that the various associates function as a *continu-*

ing unit.'' (Emphasis added.) This does not mean the scope of the enterprise cannot change as it engages in diverse forms of activity nor does it mean that the participants in the enterprise cannot vary with different individuals managing its affairs at different times and in different places. What is essential, however, is that there is some continuity of both structure and personality. For example, the operatives in a prostitution ring may change through time, but the various roles which the old and new individuals perform remain the same. But if an entirely new set of people begin to operate the ring, it is not the same enterprise as it was before.

Finally, an enterprise must have an "ascertainable structure" distinct from that inherent in the conduct of a pattern of racketeering activity. This distinct structure might be demonstrated by proof that a group engaged in a diverse pattern of crimes or that it has an organizational pattern or system of authority beyond what was necessary to perpetrate the predicate crimes. The command system of a Mafia family is an example of this type of structure as is the hierarchy, planning, and division of profits within a prostitution ring.

B. Proof of Alleged Enterprise.

During the summer of 1972, Gibson and Phillips met to discuss the sale of securities through an agricultural cooperative. Although Cloninger was present at several of these meetings, he was not party to the agreement between Gibson and Phillips which resulted in the formation of UFA–Mo. in October of 1972. A management company, Midwest Investment Group, was used to divert funds from UFA–Mo. to Phillips and Gibson. The only identifiable association of individuals distinct from the pattern of racketeering in the operation of UFA-Mo. was the agreement between Gibson and Phillips to share the co-op's profits. This association arguably exhibits a distinct structure and the common purpose of Gibson and Phillips. However, the difficulty with the assertion that it represents the beginning of the charged enterprise is that this "enterprise" had a short life.

In April of 1973, Gibson and Phillips had a misunderstanding and dissolved their arrangement. Gibson stayed on and operated UFA–Mo. Moffitt became a salesman for UFA–Mo. In May of 1973, Phillips independently formed PFA. At this point in time, no entity existed which encompassed both UFA–Mo. and FA. Although they were operated in a similar manner, the only continuity between the original UFA–Mo. and PFA was Phillips' participation in both co-ops. The common purpose originally shared by Gibson and Phillips had broken down. An enterprise can grow and evolve, but it must be shown to have some continuity of structure and personality and the participants must maintain their common purpose.

Cloninger came to PFA sometime in the spring or summer of 1973. In November 1973, Phillips and Cloninger hired Bledsoe and Burks to manage PFA's security sales. Burks became president of PFA. The evidence shows that thereafter Phillips, Bledsoe, Burks, and Cloninger made an agreement to evenly share all profits derived from PFA. Moffitt and Stafford joined PFA as salesmen in the fall of 1973. Thus there is evidence of association among the five defendants in operating PFA and a shared purpose to profit from the fraudulent sale of PFA securities. Furthermore, the government argues, "The secrecy of the agreement among Phillips, Cloninger, Burks and Bledsoe proved the existence of an association separate from the PFA cooperative." However, this external association did not include Moffitt and Stafford. But even assuming this agreement was the basis of an enterprise, the enterprise was unrelated to UFA–Mo. which, until June of 1975, was operated by Gibson using Moffitt as a salesman (Stafford also signed a UFA–Mo. salesman's contract, but made no sales).

At best, the government has shown two separate associations of individuals without any overarching structure or common control. The evidence demonstrates only that the two schemes were conducted using the same modus operandi, that Phillips initiated both schemes, and that Moffitt and Stafford had some connection with both PFA and UFA–Mo.

The government charges that the purpose of the alleged enterprise was to sell securities of agricultural cooperatives by fraudulent means in several states. On this basis, proof of fraudulent sales in both Oklahoma and Arkansas was admitted into evidence. It is conceded that Bledsoe did not participate in the planning or operation and may not even have had any knowledge of the Oklahoma or Arkansas co-ops. Stafford was a salesman for UFA–Ok., but had no connection with the activities of CFA in Arkansas. Thus, in order to argue that all defendants were implicated in the fraudulent acts in Oklahoma and Arkansas, it was essential for the government to demonstrate the existence of an enterprise operating UFA–Ok. and CFA as well as UFA–Mo. and PFA in Missouri.

This court fails to find evidence of any association in fact exhibiting the requisite features which embraces the activities of all the co-ops. As in 1972, Phillips initiated the plan to organize co-ops in other states. Again, he returned to his old confederate, Gibson. Around this same time, UFA–Mo. became defunct. Gibson still had nothing to do with PFA in Missouri. Phillips discussed the plan with Gibson and the two of them formed a partnership to organize co-ops in other states. Thereafter, Gibson prevailed on Moffitt and Paul Canaday to form UFA–Ok. and share the proceeds. Unknown to Moffitt, Gibson had agreed to share his one-third interest with Phillips, his secret partner. Moffitt evidently had a falling out with Phillips and refused to participate in the new venture if Phillips had anything to do with UFA–Ok. The evidence shows that Cloninger's participation in UFA–Ok. amounted to his presence at one meeting with two officers of UFA–Ok. and Phillips at which the co-op's accounting procedures were discussed. There is no evidence indicating he participated in the operation of the co-op or received any of its profits.

In November of 1975, Gibson and another defendant charged in the indictment, Ron Elia, agreed to share profits earned by an Arkansas cooperative. Gibson once again agreed to share his profits with Phillips. Consumer–Farmers Association was thus incorporated on January 23,

1976, as an Arkansas agricultural cooperative. There is evidence that Moffitt sold CFA securities.

The only association which embraced the Arkansas and Oklahoma operations was the agreement between Gibson and Phillips. This agreement is temporally disjunct from their original agreement. The other defendants did not participate in this association except through their roles in the individual cooperatives. The new agreement did not relate to the operation of UFA–Mo. or PFA. There simply was no structured association, apart from the individual co-ops, which exhibited any degree of continuity over the period between 1972 and 1977 and which was concerned with the operation of all four co-ops.

Although many of the defendants played various roles in UFA–Mo., PFA, UFA–Ok., and CFA, these roles cannot be seen as constituent elements of a larger structure. Apart from the individual co-ops, the evidence reveals loose and discontinuous patterns of associations and agreements, primarily between Phillips and Gibson, contemplating the illegal use of the co-ops. We find no real evidence of a structure, a pattern of authority or control, or of continuity in the pattern of association or the common purpose of all of the defendants. At best, there is proof of various ventures initiated by Phillips and sometimes Phillips and Gibson in which many of the defendants from time to time participated. This evidence is not sufficient to support conviction under RICO. Thus we conclude the evidence in this case does not support the allegation that a single enterprise existed which was distinct from the individual co-ops, which operated in Missouri, Oklahoma, and Arkansas, and which continued to exist from mid–1972 until the spring of 1977.[12]

On this basis, we reverse the convictions of all defendants under counts one and two.

IV. Phillips' Remaining Issues.

[At this point, the court discussed a number of additional errors asserted by Phillips. After reviewing the "almost 200 volumes of trial transcript," the court concluded:]

___

[12] Assuming there was sufficient evidence to show a substantive violation of RICO, there is a further deficiency in the evidence on the conspiracy count. The government failed to show that all of the defendants, particularly Bledsoe, had sufficient knowledge of the enterprise charged. Assuming a separate, identifiable enterprise was shown to have formed and operated PFA, the only cooperative in which Bledsoe participated, Bledsoe did not knowingly agree or conspire to violate RICO since there is no evidence he knew of the enterprise alleged or that he ever agreed to participate in it.

Thus, at least as against Bledsoe, the conspiracy conviction could not stand. Cf. United States v. Winter, 663 F.2d 1120, 1136 (1st Cir.1981)(requiring that defendant "knowingly join an enterprise"); *Elliott*, 571 F.2d, at 903 ("knowledge of the essential nature of the plan is sufficient"). It is also questionable whether the men who served only as salesmen for the various cooperatives had sufficient knowledge to sustain a charge that they knew of and agreed to participate in a single enterprise encompassing all of the co-ops.

We affirm the convictions of Phillips under counts three, four, five, and six. Since we vacate his convictions on counts one and two, we deem it proper that Phillips be resentenced as to each of the counts for which we have affirmed his conviction.

The convictions of Bledsoe and Cloninger on counts three and four are vacated since we find they were misjoined with the separate counts five and six relating to Phillips only. These counts, as against Bledsoe and Cloninger, are remanded to the District Court for a new trial. The convictions of all of the defendants on counts one and two are ordered vacated and dismissed.

The cause is remanded for further proceedings before the trial court in accord with this court's direction.

■ Ross, Circuit Judge, dissenting.

In my view, the government proved that an enterprise existed through "evidence of an ongoing organization, formal or informal, and by evidence that the various associates function as a continuing unit." United States v. Turkette, 452 U.S. 576, 583 (1981). While the government must show that the enterprise "is an entity separate and apart from the pattern of [racketeering] activity, ... proof used to establish these separate elements may in particular cases coalesce, [but] proof of one does not necessarily establish the other." Id.

The facts in this case, construed in the light most favorable to the verdict, proved that under RICO these defendants and other persons charged in the indictment were "a group of persons associated together for a common purpose of engaging in a course of conduct." Id.

Congress in "§ 904(a) of RICO, 84 Stat. 947, direct[ed] that 'the provisions of this title shall be liberally construed to effectuate its remedial purposes.'" Id., at 587. Thus, the RICO definition of an enterprise as including "any union or group of individuals associated in fact," 18 U.S.C. § 1961(4), must be liberally construed.

Initially, I would emphasize my view of this case. This view is that it would be next to impossible to engage in the massive[2] sale of fraudulent securities to small investors through formation of seemingly legitimate businesses over a five year period without a "group of individuals associated in fact."

Beyond the predicate acts of racketeering, there is considerable evidence of an enterprise although, as noted in *Turkette*, the proof of each may at times coalesce. But proof of the predicate acts of securities mail fraud was sufficiently separate from the proof the government made regarding the enterprise. While some trappings of "legitimacy" may be necessary to any securities or mail fraud, this group of individuals went to great lengths to develop seemingly legitimate businesses and maintain their legitimacy

[2] The government indicates that when PFA was declared bankrupt on May 13, 1977, over $11 million had been raised from sales of PFA "estate builders," bonds and stock. After liquidation of PFA's assets only about $200,000 remained.

while draining the assets of the businesses through secret agreements.[3] If RICO was primarily enacted to eliminate infiltration of organized crime into legitimate businesses, I fail to see why RICO is not just as appropriate a weapon against a group of individuals who form and then use "legitimate" businesses as their vehicle for racketeering activity.

Applying the *Turkette* standards set forth above for proof of an enterprise, I believe the evidence, both direct and circumstantial, met those standards. As noted in United States v. Elliott, 571 F.2d 880, 898 (5th Cir.1978), "[a] jury is entitled to infer the existence of an enterprise on the basis of largely or wholly circumstantial evidence."

The following evidence satisfied the *Turkette* requirements that these defendants and others were an "ongoing organization, formal or informal" which "function[ed] as a continuing unit."[4]

The leader of this "enterprise" was Phillips. Gibson was a "partner" with Phillips in the formation of UFA–Mo. and the Arkansas and Oklahoma cooperatives. There is evidence that Phillips was the "instigator" of these schemes and Gibson joined in at the suggestion of Phillips.

Judge Lay argues that the dissolution of the UFA–Mo. arrangement between Phillips and Gibson caused one association of individuals to split

---

[3] The enterprise formed "legitimate" cooperatives, set up "sham" boards of directors, fraudulently inflated the businesses' assets through numerous schemes to provide an appearance of prosperity, used individual and multimember "shell" consulting corporations to drain the assets of the cooperatives without the knowledge of the boards of directors or investors, carried on "promotional" activities to appear to be undertaking legitimate business development, and arranged for their accountants to treat "estate builder" sales as "income" rather than "liabilities." On the other hand, the predicate acts relied upon were all specific instances of using the mail in furtherance of a scheme to defraud or fraud in the sale of securities.

[4] When the RICO enterprise is not a "legal entity," which may automatically provide an organization and continuity, then the proof of organization and continuity must of necessity be largely circumstantial. The jury must be allowed to look at the activities of the defendants which surround the predicate acts and draw reasonable inferences from that activity to determine whether a single enterprise exists. I believe that the Supreme Court's views regarding proof of a single "conspiracy" in Blumenthal v. United States, 332 U.S. 539, 556–57 (1947), are helpful when considering proof of a single "enterprise." In *Blumenthal* the Court stated:

"[C]onspiracies involving ... elaborate arrangements generally are not born full-grown. Rather they mature by successive stages which are necessary to bring in the essential parties. And not all of those joining in the earlier ones make known their participation to others later coming in. The law does not demand proof of so much. For it is most often true, especially in broad schemes calling for the aid of many persons, that after discovery of enough to show clearly the essence of the scheme and the identity of a number participating, the identity and the fact of participation of others remain undiscovered and undiscoverable. Secrecy and concealment are essential features of successful conspiracy. The more completely they are achieved the more successful the crime. Hence the law rightly gives room for allowing the conviction of those discovered upon showing sufficiently the essential nature of the plan and their connections with it, without requiring evidence of knowledge of all its details or of the participation of others. Otherwise the difficulties, not only of discovery, but of certainty in proof and of correlating proof with pleading would become insuperable, and conspirators would go free by their very ingenuity."

into two separate entities. While there may be no evidence of ongoing financial association between Gibson and Phillips, there is circumstantial and direct evidence that they continued to be associated, in fact, as leaders of the enterprise to protect the "legitimacy" of both UFA–Mo. and PFA so as to further their common purpose.

In April 1973 when Phillips left UFA–Mo. he remained in the same city, Springfield, Missouri, and started PFA. Charles Thrower who sold "estate builders" for UFA–Mo. joined with Phillips to recruit the PFA Board of Directors. In May 1973, Gibson, at the request of Phillips, signed the cover letter submitting the PFA Articles of Incorporation to the secretary of state and mailed them for Phillips. Also in May 1973, Moffitt joined UFA–Mo. as a salesman. Moffitt had previously sold "estate builders" with Phillips through Progressive Investors. In August 1973, there was a meeting between Gibson, Moffitt, Thrower and Phillips. Gibson arranged the meeting because he had found out that Thrower had been trying to sell PFA securities to his former UFA–Mo. customers. Phillips and Thrower agreed not to call on any of the UFA–Mo. investors.[5] In the early fall of 1973, Moffitt and Gibson used a PFA "certificate of participation" (another fraudulent security) as the model for a UFA–Mo. "certificate of participation." Sometime in the later part of 1973 Moffitt joined PFA as a salesman. In early 1974, Gibson and Phillips met and Gibson told Phillips that he SEC wanted Gibson to testify about "estate builders." Phillips advised Gibson to invoke the fifth amendment, or at least not to refer to PFA's sales of estate builders or to mention Phillips' name. In March 1974, the Missouri Commissioner of Securities directed PFA to halt sales of estate builders until a disclosure letter was prepared. Phillips went to see Gibson and obtained a UFA–Mo. disclosure document from Gibson. The UFA–Mo. document was used substantially in drafting the PFA offering letter and Phillips was able to resume sales of estate builders in about one week. Finally, in early 1975, UFA–Mo. was in financial trouble and Gibson was ready to file bankruptcy. Phillips met with Gibson and convinced him to hold off until Phillips could look into the situation. About three weeks later, the Phillips/Gibson agreement to form cooperatives in other states was made and as a result of this agreement the Arkansas and Oklahoma cooperatives were eventually formed. Gibson agreed to secretly divide the profits with Phillips and Phillips agreed to provide travel and front money for the expansion and to deal with the local banks who were putting pressure on Gibson.

In my view this evidence shows that Gibson and Phillips continued to associate together as leaders of the enterprise even during the time that Gibson ran UFA–Mo. and Phillips ran PFA. Their leadership roles went beyond the simple selling of fraudulent securities, their roles and efforts were to maintain the "legitimacy" of the cooperatives that had been

[5] While this agreement might be seen as evidence of separate associations, I believe the jury could permissibly infer that this agreement furthered the activities of the enterprise by assuring that UFA–Mo. and PFA would not compete for buyers or "oversell" any one buyer.

formed. The evidence supports the fact that each assisted the other in maintaining the legitimacy of not only their own cooperative but the other's cooperative. The evidence supports the inference that without the association between Gibson and Phillips in running two cooperatives in the same town, the common purpose of both may have been destroyed. Public financial ruin or public disclosure of securities violations of either of the cooperatives would very possibly have led to the downfall of the other cooperative. But this did not occur and later under their continuing leadership the affairs of the enterprise were expanded when Phillips and Gibson jointly formed the Arkansas and Oklahoma cooperatives.

Beyond the leadership of this enterprise is its ongoing organization in terms of management and operatives. Moffitt sold securities for both UFA–Mo. and later for PFA. Moffitt then became head of the UFA–Okla. sales force and later went on to sell "estate builders" for CFA–Ark.

Stafford signed a salesman contract with UFA–Mo. but did not sell for UFA–Mo. In late 1973, Stafford began selling for PFA and later in the spring of 1976 he sold for UFA–Okla. In midsummer of 1976, the Oklahoma Securities Commission filed a civil suit against UFA–Okla. and sales were halted. From late September 1976 until January 1977, Stafford sold his personal stock in PFA[6] to 19 investors who paid a total of $85,925. Cloninger told Stafford to sell the stock in the name of Consolidated Mortgage Corporation to avoid any panic by PFA shareholders that would result from a top salesman selling his own stock. Stafford told the investors that he was selling the stock of a widow.

Cloninger was not financially involved in UFA–Mo., however, he was present at Gibson's and Phillips' initial meetings and prepared a possible draft promotional brochure during one of these meetings. Gibson later adapted the brochure for use by UFA–Mo. Phillips brought Cloninger into PFA shortly after its incorporation. During the summer of 1973 Phillips and Cloninger prepared promotional materials for "estate builder" sales and a "pitchbook" for use by the PFA salesmen. The "pitchbook" is a mass of fraudulent information and omitted material facts. Cloninger helped Phillips bring into PFA the management team of Burks and Bledsoe. Each of the four took a 25 per cent interest in the PFA–Progressive Investors "consulting agreement." Large sums of money were channeled to the four under this "consulting agreement" and large payments were made upon "termination" of the agreement in November 1975. Cloninger hired Stafford as a salesman. Cloninger was also involved in the decisions regarding the PFA–NBC merger. See footnote 6. Cloninger

---

[6] In early 1975, PFA converted from a nonstock to a stock cooperative. The conversion occurred as part of one of the many schemes involving inflation of PFA's assets. PFA "merged" with National Business Corporation, a shell corporation involving Bledsoe, Phillips, Cloninger and Stafford. Stock and money were paid to NBC by PFA in the merger. NBC passed all the money through to Progressive Investors. Supposedly, PFA through the merger had acquired two and one-quarter million dollars worth of real estate. The land acquired was only part of 372 acres Phillips, through PI, had bought in April of 1974 for $29,000 cash and a $71,000 promissory note from Progressive Investors. In the "merger," PFA assumed Progressive Investors' liability on the note.

received payments from PFA that were channeled through five different corporations. He received payments through the Progressive Investors consulting agreement, through the PFA–NBC merger, through sale of PFA stock, and through a percentage of gross sales revenue from business operations. In early 1976, when a new type of "estate builder" was sold by PFA, Phillips' payments were funneled through one of Cloninger's corporations. Cloninger also personally bought land with his mother's PFA stock. In the last six months of PFA's "life," payments were still being made to Cloninger as an "assistant to the president" of PFA. Cloninger's grand total of monies received from PFA was $456,068. During 1975 Cloninger made one visit with Phillips to the UFA–Okla. offices. The government's evidence showed that Cloninger's main involvement was with PFA–Mo.

The government's evidence as to Bledsoe was that he was a management official of PFA–Mo. Bledsoe initially received a 25 per cent interest in the Progressive Investors' consulting agreement and was the head of the PFA–Mo. sales force. Bledsoe was involved in the PFA–NBC merger and received monies from the sale of PFA stock. The large checks to the secret partners upon termination of the Progressive Investors' consulting agreement were drawn upon Bledsoe's directions. In January 1976, Bledsoe became president of PFA and Bledsoe had PFA purchase the former president's (Burks) corporation which had no business operation but merely held PFA stock and a PFA note. Bledsoe became president of FMA in October 1976 and resigned as president of PFA. However, agreements between PFA and FMA continued the flow of monies from PFA to FMA and on to Bledsoe and others. Bledsoe's grand total for PFA involvement was $407,468 according to the government.

While these defendants were part of the enterprise, they were not the only persons involved. Other persons such as Elia and Canaday sold securities for UFA–Mo. and/or PFA–Mo. and later "graduated" to management roles in UFA–Okla. and CFA–Ark.

In my view the common purpose of this "ongoing organization," to engage in securities fraud, continued nonstop until the demise of PFA in May 1977.[7] The "continuing unit" which existed apart from the acts of securities fraud is exemplified by the activities of the "leadership" (Phillips and Gibson), the "management" (Cloninger, Bledsoe and later Moffitt) and the "salesmen" (Moffitt and Stafford). The *Turkette* requirements of an "ongoing association" and a "continuing unit" were satisfied by the proof, both direct and circumstantial, of the defendants' activities beyond the predicate acts.

---

[7] It is important to note that PFA continued to operate during the existence of both UFA–Okla. and CFA–Ark. Both Cloninger and Bledsoe were continuing "management" for PFA, while Moffitt and Stafford went to Arkansas and/or Oklahoma. In my view, the absence of some defendants from the Oklahoma and Arkansas ventures does not indicate "sporadic" involvement. Rather, there was a need to keep the most successful and long-running cooperative, PFA, alive and well. UFA–Okla. sold securities for about one year until the summer of 1976. CFA–Ark. sold securities for only about three months until April 1976. In both instances, the cooperatives were shut down by the state securities commissions.

[At this point, Judge Ross also stated his disagreement with the majority on the misjoinder point. He therefore concluded:]

For these reasons I would affirm the convictions of all defendants.

National Organization for Women, Inc. v. Scheidler

Supreme Court of the United States, 1994.
510 U.S. 249.

■ CHIEF JUSTICE REHNQUIST delivered the opinion of the Court.

We are required once again to interpret the provisions of the Racketeer Influenced and Corrupt Organizations (RICO) chapter of the Organized Crime Control Act of 1970 (OCCA), Pub.L. 91–452, Title IX, 84 Stat. 941, as amended, 18 U.S.C. §§ 1961–1968 (1988 ed. and Supp. IV). Section 1962(c) prohibits any person associated with an enterprise from conducting its affairs through a pattern of racketeering activity. We granted certiorari to determine whether RICO requires proof that either the racketeering enterprise or the predicate acts of racketeering were motivated by an economic purpose. We hold that RICO requires no such economic motive.

I

Petitioner National Organization For Women, Inc. (NOW) is a national nonprofit organization that supports the legal availability of abortion; petitioners Delaware Women's Health Organization, Inc. (DWHO) and Summit Women's Health Organization, Inc. (SWHO) are health care centers that perform abortions and other medical procedures. Respondents are a coalition of antiabortion groups called the Pro–Life Action Network (PLAN), Joseph Scheidler and other individuals and organizations that oppose legal abortion, and a medical laboratory that formerly provided services to the two petitioner health care centers.

Petitioners sued respondents in the United States District Court for the Northern District of Illinois, alleging violations of the Sherman Act, 26 Stat. 209, as amended, 15 U.S.C. § 1 et seq., and RICO's §§ 1962(a), (c), and (d), as well as several pendent state-law claims stemming from the activities of antiabortion protesters at the clinics. According to respondent Scheidler's congressional testimony, these protesters aim to shut down the clinics and persuade women not to have abortions. See, e.g., Abortion Clinic Violence, Oversight Hearings before the Subcommittee on Civil and Constitutional Rights of the House Committee on the Judiciary, 99th Cong., 1st and 2d Sess., 55 (1987)(statement of Joseph M. Scheidler, Executive Director, Pro–Life Action League). Petitioners sought injunctive relief, along with treble damages, costs, and attorneys' fees. They later amended their complaint, and pursuant to local rules, filed a "RICO Case Statement" that further detailed the enterprise, the pattern of racketeering, the victims of the racketeering activity, and the participants involved.

The amended complaint alleged that respondents were members of a nationwide conspiracy to shut down abortion clinics through a pattern of racketeering activity including extortion in violation of the Hobbs Act, 18 U.S.C. § 1951.[2] Section 1951(b)(2) defines extortion as "the obtaining of property from another, with his consent, induced by wrongful use of actual or threatened force, violence, or fear, or under color of official right." Petitioners alleged that respondents conspired to use threatened or actual force, violence or fear to induce clinic employees, doctors, and patients to give up their jobs, give up their economic right to practice medicine, and give up their right to obtain medical services at the clinics. Petitioners claimed that this conspiracy "has injured the business and/or property interests of the [petitioners]." According to the amended complaint, PLAN constitutes the alleged racketeering "enterprise" for purposes of § 1962(c).

The District Court dismissed the case pursuant to Federal Rule of Civil Procedure 12(b)(6). Citing Eastern Railroad Presidents Conference v. Noerr Motor Freight, Inc., 365 U.S. 127 (1961), it held that since the activities alleged "involve[d] political opponents, not commercial competitors, and political objectives, not marketplace goals," the Sherman Act did not apply. 765 F.Supp. 937, 941 (N.D.Ill.1991). It dismissed petitioners' RICO claims under § 1962(a) because the "income" alleged by petitioners consisted of voluntary donations from persons opposed to abortion which "in no way were derived from the pattern of racketeering alleged in the complaint." Ibid. The District Court then concluded that petitioners failed to state a claim under § 1962(c) since "an economic motive requirement exists to the extent that some profit-generating purpose must be alleged in order to state a RICO claim." Id., at 943. Finally, it dismissed petitioners' RICO conspiracy claim under § 1962(d) since petitioners' other RICO claims could not stand.

The Court of Appeals affirmed. 968 F.2d 612 (7th Cir.1992). As to the RICO counts, it agreed with the District Court that the voluntary contributions received by respondents did not constitute income derived from racketeering activities for purposes of § 1962(a). Id., at 625. It adopted the analysis of the Court of Appeals for the Second Circuit in United States v. Ivic, 700 F.2d 51 (2d Cir.1983), which found an "economic motive" requirement implicit in the "enterprise" element of the offense. The Court of Appeals determined that "non-economic crimes committed in furtherance of non-economic motives are not within the ambit of RICO." 968 F.2d, at 629. Consequently, petitioners failed to state a claim under § 1962(c). The Court of Appeals also affirmed dismissal of the RICO conspiracy claim under § 1962(d).

We granted certiorari to resolve a conflict among the courts of appeals on the putative economic motive requirement of 18 U.S.C. § 1962(c) and

---

[2] The Hobbs Act, 18 U.S.C. § 1951(a) provides: "Whoever in any way or degree obstructs, delays, or affects commerce or the movement of any article or commodity in commerce, by robbery or extortion or attempts or conspires so to do, or commits or threatens physical violence to any person or property in furtherance of a plan or purpose to do anything in violation of this section shall be fined not more than $10,000 or imprisoned not more than twenty years, or both." Respondents contend that petitioners are unable to show that their actions violated the Hobbs Act. We do not reach that issue, and express no opinion upon it.

(d). Compare *United States v. Ivic,* supra, and United States v. Flynn, 852 F.2d 1045, 1052 (8th Cir.1988), ("For purposes of RICO, an enterprise must be directed toward an economic goal"), with Northeast Women's Center, Inc. v. McMonagle, 868 F.2d 1342 (3d Cir.1989)(because the predicate offense does not require economic motive, RICO requires no additional economic motive).

II

We first address the threshold question raised by respondents of whether petitioners have standing to bring their claim. Standing represents a jurisdictional requirement which remains open to review at all stages of the litigation. Bender v. Williamsport Area School Dist., 475 U.S. 534, 546–547 (1986). Respondents are correct that only DWHO and SWHO, and not NOW, have sued under RICO.[3] Despite the fact that the clinics attempted to bring the RICO claim as class actions, DWHO and SWHO must themselves have standing. Simon v. Eastern Ky. Welfare Rights Organization, 426 U.S. 26, 40, n. 20 (1976), citing Warth v. Seldin, 422 U.S. 490, 502 (1975). Respondents are wrong, however, in asserting that the complaint alleges no "injury" to DWHO and SWHO "fairly traceable to the defendant's allegedly unlawful conduct." Allen v. Wright, 468 U.S. 737, 751 (1984).

We have held that "[a]t the pleading stage, general factual allegations of injury resulting from the defendant's conduct may suffice, for on a motion to dismiss we presume that general allegations embrace those specific facts that are necessary to support the claim." Lujan v. Defenders of Wildlife, 504 U.S. 555, 561 (1992)(citations omitted). The District Court dismissed petitioners' claim at the pleading stage pursuant to Federal Rule of Civil Procedure 12(b)(6), so their complaint must be sustained if relief could be granted "under any set of facts that could be proved consistent with the allegations." Hishon v. King & Spalding, 467 U.S. 69, 73 (1984). DWHO and SWHO alleged in their complaint that the respondents conspired to use force to induce clinic staff and patients to stop working and obtain medical services elsewhere. Petitioners claimed that this conspiracy "has injured the business and/or property interests of the [petitioners]." In addition, petitioners claimed that respondent Scheidler threatened DWHO's clinic administrator with reprisals if she refused to quit her job at the clinic. Paragraphs 106 and 110 of petitioners' complaint incorporate these allegations into the § 1962(c) claim. Nothing more is needed to confer standing on DWHO and SWHO at the pleading stage.

III

We turn to the question of whether the racketeering enterprise or the racketeering predicate acts must be accompanied by an underlying econom-

---

[3] NOW sought class certification for itself, its women members who use or may use the targeted health centers, and other women who use or may use the services of such centers. The District Court did not certify the class, apparently deferring its ruling until resolution of the motions to dismiss. All pending motions were dismissed as moot when the court granted respondents' motion to dismiss. 765 F.Supp. 937, 945 (N.D.Ill. 1991).

ic motive. Section 1962(c) makes it unlawful "for any person employed by or associated with any enterprise engaged in, or the activities of which affect, interstate or foreign commerce, to conduct or participate, directly or indirectly, in the conduct of such enterprise's affairs through a pattern of racketeering activity or collection of unlawful debt." Section 1961(1) defines "pattern of racketeering activity" to include conduct that is "chargeable" or "indictable" under a host of state and federal laws. RICO broadly defines "enterprise" in § 1961(4) to "includ[e] any individual, partnership, corporation, association, or other legal entity, and any union or group of individuals associated in fact although not a legal entity." Nowhere in either § 1962(c), or in the RICO definitions in § 1961, is there any indication that an economic motive is required.

The phrase "any enterprise engaged in, or the activities of which affect, interstate or foreign commerce" comes the closest of any language in subsection (c) to suggesting a need for an economic motive. Arguably an enterprise engaged in interstate or foreign commerce would have a profit-seeking motive, but the language in § 1962(c) does not stop there; it includes enterprises whose activities "affect" interstate or foreign commerce. Webster's Third New International Dictionary 35 (1969) defines "affect" as "to have a detrimental influence on—used especially in the phrase affecting commerce." An enterprise surely can have a detrimental influence on interstate or foreign commerce without having its own profit-seeking motives.

The Court of Appeals thought that the use of the term "enterprise" in §§ 1962(a) and (b), where it is arguably more tied in with economic motivation, should be applied to restrict the breadth of use of that term in § 1962(c). 968 F.2d, at 629. Respondents agree, and point to our comment in Sedima, S.P.R.L. v. Imrex Co., 473 U.S. 479, 489 (1985), regarding the term "violation," that "[w]e should not lightly infer that Congress intended the term [violation] to have wholly different meanings in neighboring subsections."

We do not believe that the usage of the term "enterprise" in subsections (a) and (b) leads to the inference that an economic motive is required in subsection (c). The term "enterprise" in subsections (a) and (b) plays a different role in the structure of those subsections than it does in subsection (c). Section 1962(a) provides that it "shall be unlawful for any person who has received any income derived, directly or indirectly, from a pattern of racketeering activity ... to use or invest, directly or indirectly, any part of such income, or the proceeds of such income, in acquisition of any interest in, or the establishment or operation of, any enterprise which is engaged in, or the activities of which affect, interstate or foreign commerce." Correspondingly, § 1962(b) states that it "shall be unlawful for any person through a pattern of racketeering activity or through collection of an unlawful debt to acquire or maintain, directly or indirectly, any interest in or control of any enterprise which is engaged in, or the activities of which affect, interstate or foreign commerce." The "enterprise" referred to in subsections (a) and (b) is thus something acquired through the use of illegal activities or by money obtained from illegal activities. The enterprise in these subsections is the victim of unlawful activity and may very well be a "profit-seeking" entity that represents a property interest and may be acquired. But the statutory language in subsections (a) and (b) does not mandate that the enterprise be a "profit-seeking" entity; it simply requires that the enterprise be an entity that was acquired through illegal activity or the money generated from illegal activity.

By contrast, the "enterprise" in subsection (c) connotes generally the vehicle through which the unlawful pattern of racketeering activity is committed, rather than the victim of that activity. Subsection (c) makes it unlawful for "any person employed by or associated with any enterprise . . . to conduct or participate . . . in the conduct of such enterprise's affairs through a pattern of racketeering activity. . . ." Consequently, since the enterprise in subsection (c) is not being acquired, it need not have a property interest that can be acquired nor an economic motive for engaging in illegal activity; it need only be an association in fact that engages in a pattern of racketeering activity.[5] Nothing in subsections (a) and (b) directs us to a contrary conclusion.

The Court of Appeals also relied on the reasoning of United States v. Bagaric, 706 F.2d 42 (2d Cir.1983), to support its conclusion that subsection (c) requires an economic motive. In upholding the dismissal of a RICO claim against a political terrorist group, the *Bagaric* court relied in part on the congressional statement of findings which prefaces RICO and refers to the activities of groups that " 'drain billions of dollars from America's economy by unlawful conduct and the illegal use of force, fraud, and corruption.' " 706 F.2d, at 57, n. 13 (quoting OCCA, 84 Stat. 922). The Court of Appeals for the Second Circuit decided that the sort of activity thus condemned required an economic motive.

We do not think this is so. Respondents and the two courts of appeals, we think, overlook the fact that predicate acts, such as the alleged extortion, may not benefit the protestors financially but still may drain money from the economy by harming businesses such as the clinics which are petitioners in this case.

We also think that the quoted statement of congressional findings is a rather thin reed upon which to base a requirement of economic motive neither expressed nor, we think, fairly implied in the operative sections of the Act. As we said in H.J. Inc. v. Northwestern Bell Telephone Co., 492 U.S. 229, 248 (1989), "[t]he occasion for Congress' action was the perceived need to combat organized crime. But Congress for cogent reasons chose to enact a more general statute, one which, although it had organized crime as its focus, was not limited in application to organized crime."

[5] One commentator uses the terms "prize," "instrument," "victim," and "perpetrator" to describe the four separate roles the enterprise may play in section 1962. See G. Robert Blakey, The RICO Civil Fraud Action in Context: Reflections on *Bennett v. Berg*, 58 Notre Dame L.Rev. 237, 307–25 (1982).

In United States v. Turkette, 452 U.S. 576 (1981), we faced the analogous question of whether "enterprise" as used in § 1961(4) should be confined to "legitimate" enterprises. Looking to the statutory language, we found that "[t]here is no restriction upon the associations embraced by the definition: an enterprise includes any union or group of individuals associated in fact." Id., at 580. Accordingly, we resolved that § 1961(4)'s definition of enterprise "appears to include both legitimate and illegitimate enterprises within its scope; it no more excludes criminal enterprises than it does legitimate ones." Id., at 580–581. We noted that Congress could easily have narrowed the sweep of the term "enterprise" by inserting a single word, "legitimate." Id., at 581. Instead, Congress did nothing to indicate that "enterprise" should exclude those entities whose sole purpose was criminal.

The parallel to the present case is apparent. Congress has not, either in the definitional section or in the operative language, required that an "enterprise" in § 1962(c) have an economic motive.

The Court of Appeals also found persuasive guidelines for RICO prosecutions issued by the Department of Justice in 1981. The guidelines provided that a RICO indictment should not charge an association as an enterprise, unless the association exists " 'for the purpose of maintaining operations directed toward an economic goal....' " The Second Circuit, in *United States v. Ivic,* supra, believed these guidelines were entitled to deference under administrative law principles. See 700 F.2d, at 64. Whatever may be the appropriate deference afforded to such internal rules, for our purposes we need note only that the Department of Justice amended its guidelines in 1984. The amended guidelines provide that an association-in-fact enterprise must be "directed toward an economic or other identifiable goal." U.S. Dept. of Justice, United States Attorney's Manual § 9–110.360 (Mar. 9, 1984).

Both parties rely on legislative history to support their positions. We believe the statutory language is unambiguous, and find in the parties' submissions respecting legislative history no such "clearly expressed legislative intent to the contrary" that would warrant a different construction. Reves v. Ernst & Young, 507 U.S. 170 (1993).

Respondents finally argue that the result here should be controlled by the rule of lenity in criminal cases. But the rule of lenity applies only when an ambiguity is present; "it is not used to beget one.... The rule comes into operation at the end of the process of construing what Congress has expressed, not at the beginning as an overriding consideration of being lenient to wrongdoers." *Turkette,* supra, 452 U.S., at 587–88, n. 10. We simply do not think there is an ambiguity here which would suffice to invoke the rule of lenity. "[T]he fact that RICO has been applied in situations not expressly anticipated by Congress does not demonstrate ambiguity. It demonstrates breadth." *Sedima,* 473 U.S., at 499.[6]

[6] Several of the respondents, and several amici argue that application of RICO to anti-abortion protesters could chill legitimate expression protected by the First Amendment.

We therefore hold that petitioners may maintain this action if respondents conducted the enterprise through a pattern of racketeering activity. The questions of whether the respondents committed the requisite predicate acts, and whether the commission of these acts fell into a pattern, are not before us. We hold only that RICO contains no economic motive requirement.

The judgment of the Court of Appeals is accordingly reversed.

■ JUSTICE SOUTER, with whom JUSTICE KENNEDY joins, concurring.

I join the Court's opinion and write separately to explain why the First Amendment does not require reading an economic-motive requirement into the RICO, and to stress that the Court's opinion does not bar First Amendment challenges to RICO's application in particular cases.

Several respondents and amici argue that we should avoid the First Amendment issues that could arise from allowing RICO to be applied to protest organizations by construing the statute to require economic motivation, just as we have previously interpreted other generally applicable statutes so as to avoid First Amendment problems. See, e.g., Eastern Railroad Presidents Conference v. Noerr Motor Freight, Inc., 365 U.S. 127, 138 (1961)(holding that antitrust laws do not apply to businesses combining to lobby the government, even where such conduct has an anticompetitive purpose and an anticompetitive effect, because the alternative "would raise important constitutional questions" under the First Amendment); see also Lucas v. Alexander, 279 U.S. 573, 577 (1929)(a law "must be construed with an eye to possible constitutional limitations so as to avoid doubts as to its validity"). The argument is meritless in this case, though, for this principle of statutory construction applies only when the meaning of a statute is in doubt, see *Noerr*, supra, and here "the statutory language is unambiguous," ante.

Even if the meaning of RICO were open to debate, however, it would not follow that the statute ought to be read to include an economic-motive requirement, since such a requirement would correspond only poorly to free-speech concerns. Respondents and amici complain that, unless so limited, the statute permits an ideological organization's opponents to label its vigorous expression as RICO predicate acts, thereby availing themselves of powerful remedial provisions that could destroy the organization. But an economic-motive requirement would protect too much with respect to First Amendment interests, since it would keep RICO from reaching ideological entities whose members commit acts of violence we need not fear chilling. An economic-motive requirement might also prove to be underprotective, in that entities engaging in vigorous but fully protected

However, the question presented for review asked simply whether the Court should create an unwritten requirement limiting RICO to cases where either the enterprise or racketeering activity has an overriding economic motive. None of the respondents made a constitutional argument as to the proper construction of RICO in the Court of Appeals, and their constitutional argument here is directed almost entirely to the nature of their activities, rather than to the construction of RICO. We therefore decline to address the First Amendment question argued by respondents and the amici.

expression might fail the proposed economic-motive test (for even protest movements need money) and so be left exposed to harassing RICO suits.

An economic-motive requirement is, finally, unnecessary, because legitimate free-speech claims may be raised and addressed in individual RICO cases as they arise. Accordingly, it is important to stress that nothing in the Court's opinion precludes a RICO defendant from raising the First Amendment in its defense in a particular case. Conduct alleged to amount to Hobbs Act extortion, for example, or one of the other, somewhat elastic RICO predicate acts may turn out to be fully protected First Amendment activity, entitling the defendant to dismissal on that basis. See NAACP v. Claiborne Hardware, Co., 458 U.S. 886, 917 (1982)(holding that a state common-law prohibition on malicious interference with business could not, under the circumstances, be constitutionally applied to a civil-rights boycott of white merchants). And even in a case where a RICO violation has been validly established, the First Amendment may limit the relief that can be granted against an organization otherwise engaging in protected expression. See NAACP v. Alabama ex rel. Patterson, 357 U.S. 449 (1958)(invalidating under the First Amendment a court order compelling production of the NAACP's membership lists, issued to enforce Alabama's requirements for out-of-state corporations doing business in the State). See also NAACP v. Claiborne Hardware, Co., supra, 458 U.S., at 930–932 (discussing First Amendment limits on the assessment of derivative liability against ideological organizations); Oregon Natural Resources Council v. Mohla, 944 F.2d 531 (9th Cir.1991)(applying a heightened pleading standard to a complaint based on presumptively protected First Amendment conduct).

This is not the place to catalog the speech issues that could arise in a RICO action against a protest group, and I express no view on the possibility of a First Amendment claim by the respondents in this case (since, as the Court observes, such claims are outside the question presented, see ante, at 806, n. 6). But I think it prudent to notice that RICO actions could deter protected advocacy and to caution courts applying RICO to bear in mind the First Amendment interests that could be at stake.

NOTE ON *NOW v. SCHEIDLER*

See Craig M. Bradley, *NOW v. Scheidler*: RICO Meets the First Amendment, 1994 Supreme Court Review 129 (1995). According to Professor Bradley, the Court was clearly correct in agreeing with NOW's contention that RICO contains no "economic motive" requirement. In the future, however, he points out that RICO plaintiffs like NOW will still have several difficult hurdles to overcome before they can turn RICO into an effective weapon against politically motivated opponents. For one thing, RICO plaintiffs will have difficulty establishing that non-violent picketing—for purposes unrelated to "obtaining property"—violates the Hobbs Act or any other RICO predicate crime statute. Moreover, established First Amendment doctrines will tend to shield organizations from broad liability for the politically motivated acts of their individual members. See NAACP v. Claiborne Hardware, Co., 458 U.S. 886 (1982)(NAACP cannot be held liable for damages resulting from non-violent boycott of white merchants; damages for violent acts related to boycott cannot be imposed against individuals solely because they belong to a group or association that includes some violent members; NAACP cannot be held liable for violent acts absent grant of actual or apparent authority from NAACP, or ratification by NAACP, for those acts). Finally, the First Amendment may also protect individual defendants from RICO prosecution based on non-violent, albeit economically coercive, conduct. See Organization for a Better Austin v. Keefe, 402 U.S. 415 (1971)(peaceful distribution of pamphlets, even if potentially damaging to economic interests of person criticized by pamphlets, cannot be subjected to prior restraint based on alleged invasion of privacy).

SUBSECTION B: "PATTERN"

United States v. Indelicato

United States Court of Appeals, Second Circuit, 1989.
865 F.2d 1370.

Before OAKES, CHIEF JUDGE, FEINBERG, MESKILL, NEWMAN, KEARSE, CARDAMONE, PIERCE, WINTER, PRATT, MINER, ALTIMARI, and MAHONEY, CIRCUIT JUDGES, sitting en banc.

■ KEARSE, CIRCUIT JUDGE:

Defendant Anthony Indelicato has appealed from a judgment ... convicting him of participating and conspiring to participate in the affairs of an enterprise through a pattern of racketeering activity, in violation of [RICO]. He was sentenced to two consecutive 20–year terms of incarceration and a $50,000 fine. His appeal and the appeals of his codefendants were heard by a panel of this court and remain pending before that panel. We granted this rehearing en banc in order to consider the limited question of whether Indelicato's participation in three murders as part of a single criminal transaction could constitute a "pattern of racketeering activity" within the meaning of RICO. For the reasons below, we answer that question in the affirmative, and we remand the matter to the panel for further proceedings consistent with this holding.

I. BACKGROUND

Indelicato was charged in two counts of a 25–count superseding indictment charging him and seven codefendants with various crimes arising out of operations of an organization known as the "Commission" of La Cosa Nostra, which was alleged to be the ruling body of the La Cosa Nostra organized crime families throughout the United States. The Commission was alleged to be a RICO enterprise, and Indelicato was charged with one count of participating in, and one count of conspiring to participate in, the affairs of the Commission through a pattern of racketeering activity, in violation of 18 U.S.C. §§ 1962(c) and (d), respectively.

To the extent pertinent to the question considered in this en banc rehearing, the evidence at trial, taken in the light most favorable to the government, revealed the following. The Commission had existed for decades as the governing body of the five La Cosa Nostra families in New York City and affiliated families in other cities. Each organized crime family included a "boss" or leader, assisted by an underboss and a counselor; beneath this level were "capos" or captains, who supervised a number of people who had been made "members" or "soldiers" of the family. To be made a member of such a family, one was required to vow obedience to the rules and orders of the Commission and to be personally approved by it for admission. The functions of the Commission included overseeing interfamily ventures and intrafamily leadership disputes. The prior approval of the Commission was required before any family boss could be killed.

The Commission consisted principally of the bosses of the five organized crime families in the New York City area. During most of the 1970's, however, it did not include a representative of one such family, the Bonanno organized crime family ("Bonanno family"), because of leadership disputes within that family. During this period, the Commission itself directly controlled the operations of the Bonanno family.

In 1979, the boss of the Bonanno family was Carmine Galante. Indelicato was a member of the family; his father was a capo; and an uncle, J.B. Indelicato, was a member. As part of an overall plan to end the factional disputes within the Bonanno family and to realign its leadership, the Commission planned and implemented the murder of Galante and two of his close associates.

In planning the murder of Galante, the Commission worked through Aniello Dellacroce, underboss of the Gambino organized crime family, Stefano Canone, the counselor of the Bonanno family, and several soldiers in the Bonanno family including Indelicato, Dominic Trinchera, and Cesare Bonventre. Thus, in May or June 1979, Trinchera introduced Indelicato to one Louis Giongetti, a lifelong felon. Indelicato asked Giongetti whether he had ever "hit," i.e., killed, anyone. Giongetti assured Indelicato that he was experienced and trustworthy. In early July, Indelicato and Trinchera met in a bar with Giongetti; Trinchera sent Giongetti to a "safe house" to retrieve a cache of shotguns and other weapons.

On July 12, 1979, Indelicato and two other men, all wearing ski masks, entered a restaurant in Brooklyn, New York, where Galante, his cousin Giuseppe Turano, and Galante's friend and associate Leonard Coppola were having lunch. Using guns of the type earlier amassed at the bar, Indelicato and his two companions shot and killed Galante, Turano, and Coppola. The victims were shot numerous times at close range with several weapons. The evidence also showed that two other men, including Bonventre, who had accompanied Coppola to lunch and were uninjured in the shootings, had joined in shooting Coppola, Turano, and Galante. Indelicato and his two companions fled in a car stolen a month earlier. After abandoning that car, Indelicato immediately went with his father, his uncle J.B., and

Phillip Giaccone, another Bonanno family capo, to a social club in Manhattan to report his success to Dellacroce and Canone. A surveillance videotape showed Indelicato being congratulated by Canone.

Thereafter, Indelicato remained involved with the Commission. He, Trinchera, and Bonventre were promoted to the rank of capo. Indelicato maintained that rank until at least 1981.

The three murders were the only RICO predicate acts alleged against Indelicato. He was not named in any of the remaining 23 counts of the indictment. The proof at trial relating to the three murders included, in addition to the above, ballistics and medical forensic evidence, eyewitness evidence, and Indelicato's palm print on an inside door handle of the getaway car. Indelicato was convicted on both of the counts against him. His appeal and the appeals of his codefendants were heard before a panel of this Court in September 1987, and those appeals remain pending.

Indelicato's principal argument on appeal is that proof of his commission of, or agreement to commit, three murders as part of a single criminal transaction is insufficient to establish a "pattern of racketeering activity" within the meaning of RICO. In April 1988, we agreed to rehear this issue en banc, in tandem with an en banc rehearing of Beauford v. Helmsley, 843 F.2d 103 (2d Cir.1988). For the reasons below, we conclude that the facts proven by the government are sufficient to establish a RICO pattern.

II. DISCUSSION

... Our assessment of Indelicato's contention that his commission of three murders as part of a single criminal episode or transaction cannot be considered a RICO "pattern" requires a review of the development of Second Circuit doctrine as to the RICO concept of pattern both before and after the Supreme Court's decision in Sedima, S.P.R.L. v. Imrex Co., 473 U.S. 479 (1985).

A. *Early Second Circuit Interpretations of "Pattern"*

Following the enactment of RICO, few cases in this Court required us to focus closely on the meaning and content of the statutory definition of "pattern of racketeering activity." In those that did, we generally gave "pattern" a generous reading.

In United States v. Parness, 503 F.2d 430 (2d Cir.1974), we considered a conviction under 18 U.S.C. § 1962(b), which makes it unlawful to, inter alia, acquire an interest in or control of an enterprise through a pattern of racketeering activity. A defendant convicted of gaining control of a hotel in violation of this section contended that there was insufficient proof of the requisite number of acts of racketeering activity to constitute a pattern. We affirmed the conviction, noting that on February 4, 1971, this defendant had caused the interstate transport of stolen funds, in violation of 18 U.S.C. § 2314 (1970); that on February 4, he had caused the victim of his scheme to travel in interstate commerce to pick up two checks representing the stolen funds, also in violation of § 2314; and that on February 9, the defendant had caused the interstate transport of an additional check representing stolen funds, in violation of the same section. We concluded that a RICO pattern had been adequately proven: "Parness was charged with and convicted of three separate violations of § 2314. ... Convictions on any two of these counts were sufficient under § 1961(5) to establish the 'pattern of racketeering activity' necessary for a conviction under § 1962(b)."

Shortly thereafter, the district court in United States v. Moeller, 402 F.Supp. 49 (D.Conn.1975), interpreting the statement that "any two" of the *Parness* acts sufficed to establish a RICO pattern as a ruling that even the very closely related acts that occurred on the same day constituted a pattern, expressed its skepticism: "While the statutory definition makes clear that a pattern can consist of only two acts, I would have thought the common sense interpretation of the word 'pattern' implies acts occurring in *different criminal episodes*, episodes that are at least somewhat separated in time and place yet still sufficiently related by purpose to demonstrate a continuity of activity." On the authority of *Parness*, however, the court concluded that the kidnaping of three employees who worked in a building, followed by arson on the building on the same day, could constitute a RICO pattern in a prosecution under § 1962(c). ...

In United States v. Weisman, 624 F.2d 1118, 1123 (2d Cir.1980), we ... rejected the defendants' contention that the jury should have been charged that it could not find a RICO pattern on the basis of two predicate acts "unless the predicate acts were also found to be 'related' to each other through a 'common scheme, plan or motive.'" Weisman was convicted of a number of offenses, including nine counts of securities fraud committed in 1973, nine counts of bankruptcy fraud in connection with the financial problems of a theatre opened in 1975, and one count of participating in the affairs of an enterprise through a pattern of racketeering, in violation of § 1962(c). He contended that no RICO pattern had been proven because, inter alia, the securities frauds (which the trial court had charged the jury could constitute only a single predicate act because they arose "out of the same episode") and the bankruptcy frauds were not related to each other. We rejected this contention both on the facts and in principle.

Without commenting on the trial court's "same episode" theory, we concluded that even counting the nine securities frauds as one act, the securities fraud and bankruptcy frauds were all related to the theatre and could "constitute 10 separate predicate acts of racketeering, any two of which would be sufficient to sustain the conviction on the RICO count." Noting that if a direct relationship between the acts were required, it had been amply proven by reason of similarity of victims, goals, and methods, we stated that "the statutory language does not expressly require that the predicate acts of racketeering be specifically 'related' to each other." We agreed with Weisman that RICO was not intended to apply to sporadic and unrelated criminal acts, but we concluded that where each act was related to the conduct of the affairs of a RICO enterprise, the jury was entitled to find a RICO pattern. Id. at 1122 ("the enterprise itself supplies a significant unifying link between the various predicate acts specified in section 1961(1) that may constitute a [RICO] 'pattern' "). . . .

B. Sedima*'s Footnote 14 and* Ianniello*'s Interpretation of It*

... In United States v. Ianniello, 808 F.2d 184 (2d Cir.1986), we affirmed convictions under § 1962(c) in connection with the defendants' skimming of profits from several New York City restaurants and bars and their fraudulent procurement of liquor licenses in aid of that practice. On appeal, the defendants argued, inter alia, (1) that our decision in *Weisman* should be reconsidered in light of *Sedima*'s statement in footnote 14 that two acts are necessary but not sufficient to constitute a RICO pattern, and (2) that two acts of mail fraud in the procurement of liquor license renewals in successive years were parts of a single scheme and thus could not, as a matter of law, constitute a pattern. We rejected both contentions.

... *Ianniello* ... stated its adherence to *Weisman*, which it read as holding "that two predicate acts can suffice to satisfy the pattern requirement of RICO." Since *Weisman* had indicated that the requisite relationship between racketeering acts could be found in the fact that each of them was related to a RICO enterprise, *Ianniello* concluded that "the inquiry as to relatedness and continuity," which *Sedima* suggested should be made in assessing whether there is a pattern, "is best addressed in the context of the concept of 'enterprise.' "

On the facts before us in *Ianniello*, we concluded that continuity of enterprise was adequately shown:

"an enterprise with 'a single purpose,' here fraud continuing indefinitely, can provide the basis for a § 1962(c) violation. The common purpose in this case was to skim profits and had no obvious terminating goal or date, clearly establishing the enterprise requirement."

We also rejected the contention that evidence of two racketeering acts in pursuit of a single unlawful goal is insufficient to prove a RICO pattern and that establishment of more than one unlawful scheme is necessary:

"Instead, we hold that when a person commits at least two acts that have the common purpose of furthering a continuing criminal enterprise with which that person is associated, the elements of relatedness and continuity which the *Sedima* footnote construes § 1962(c) to include are satisfied." ...

C. *This Circuit's Post*-Ianniello *Decisions*

In the wake of *Ianniello*, the district courts of this circuit divided over whether the *Ianniello* holding that two predicate acts sufficed to satisfy the pattern requirement applied in civil RICO actions. Some held that the same rules apply in both criminal and civil RICO cases, while others held that *Ianniello*'s holding was limited to cases involving wholly criminal enterprises.

In a series of appeals from dismissals of civil RICO complaints, we clarified that *Ianniello*'s ruling that two predicate acts suffice to establish a RICO pattern does apply to civil RICO actions. In addition, we added gloss to *Ianniello*'s imputation of the continuity requirement to the enterprise element.

In Beck v. Manufacturers Hanover Trust Co., 820 F.2d 46 (2d Cir. 1987), the plaintiffs brought a civil RICO action complaining that the defendant bank, an indenture trustee, had breached its fiduciary duties by fraudulently making certain interest payments, selling collateral at a reduced price, and disposing of the proceeds. As predicate acts of racketeering activity, the complaint alleged that the bank had committed numerous mail frauds ... and wire frauds.... The District Court dismissed the complaint for, inter alia, failure to plead a valid RICO pattern, on the ground that the alleged racketeering acts were part of a single episode and that *Sedima*'s footnote 14 interpretation of RICO pattern required proof of "multiple episodes." We rejected this interpretation of the pattern requirement as foreclosed by *Ianniello*:

> "It is clear after *Ianniello* that the District Court erred in interpreting 'pattern of racketeering activity' to require multiple episodes. *Ianniello* confirms that two related predicate acts will suffice to establish a pattern.... Plaintiffs' amended complaint pleads at least two related acts of mail and wire fraud with regard to the sale of the U.S. collateral and therefore satisfies the pleading requirement for 'pattern of racketeering activity'"

Nonetheless, noting that, "[a]s *Ianniello* recognized, whether one looks for the requisite continuity and relatedness by examining the pattern or the enterprise is really a matter of form, not substance," we affirmed the dismissal of the *Beck* complaint, concluding that it did not adequately allege a RICO enterprise. We noted that "*Ianniello* emphasizes that a plaintiff must prove the existence of a continuing enterprise" or "'*continuing operation*'" under § 1962(c), by showing "'an *ongoing organization*,'" and "'evidence that the various associates function as a continuing unit.'" We concluded that because the enterprise alleged by the *Beck* plaintiffs, insofar as the complaint adequately pleaded any fraud, had "had but one straightforward, short-lived goal," i.e., the sale of the collateral at a reduced price, and had ceased to function at the conclusion of that sale, the alleged "association is not sufficiently continuing to constitute an 'enterprise.'"
...

In United States v. Benevento, 836 F.2d 60 (2d Cir.1987), we affirmed a RICO conviction under § 1962(c) in which the enterprise was a corporation formed for the purpose of manufacturing and distributing narcotics, and two of the predicate acts alleged were a conspiracy to manufacture and distribute narcotics in violation of 21 U.S.C. § 846 (1982), and a conspiracy to import one of the necessary ingredients into the United States in violation of 21 U.S.C. § 963. Carmine Loiacono, the defendant thus convicted, contended that the two conspiracies could not be deemed separate acts of racketeering activity because they were part of the single overall narcotics scheme. We disagreed. Noting that the differences between the two conspiratorial offenses meant that a defendant could be held guilty of either, neither, or both, we concluded that

> "[t]he fact that Loiacono committed both crimes as part of a single plan does not invalidate the RICO conviction, since this circuit has rejected the view that a pattern of racketeering activity or a racketeering enterprise must consist of multiple ventures or plans. So long as the defendants commit at least two predicate acts, they have met the pattern requirement and, so long as the enterprise is long and elaborate enough to be considered continuing, the enterprise requirement is satisfied." . . .

Finally, in Beauford v. Helmsley, 843 F.2d 103 (2d Cir.1988), which was reheard en banc with the present case, we affirmed the dismissal of a civil RICO complaint alleging that the defendants had committed mail fraud in connection with offering for sale 8,286 apartments that were being converted into condominiums. The alleged racketeering activity was said to be the mailing of fraudulent offering plans to the tenants of the apartments, as well as to others, and the later mailing of plan amendments to those persons. We stated that our precedents were confusing but seemed to require the conclusion that "a single alleged scheme to defraud buyers, tenants, and the authorities overseeing the laws pertaining to" the conversion is not sufficient to allege a RICO enterprise "regardless of how many fraudulent acts it entails." We concluded that the *Beauford* complaint was properly dismissed for lack of a RICO enterprise because the scheme, though "widespread," was "discrete," and, though "continuing," was "finite."

[Part D, in which the court discussed the interpretation of "pattern" and "enterprise" in other circuits, has been omitted.]

E.   *"Pattern" and "Enterprise" Revisited*

It is in this posture that today's en banc issue arises. This circuit . . . has held that a RICO pattern of racketeering activity may be established simply by proof of two acts of racketeering activity, but that a RICO enterprise is not established unless there is proof that it is ongoing and that there is more than a single scheme having no demonstrable ending point. For the reasons below, we conclude today that proof of two acts of racketeering activity without more does not suffice to establish a RICO pattern; that the concepts of relatedness and continuity are attributes of activity, not of a RICO enterprise, and that a RICO pattern may not be established without some showing that the racketeering acts are interrelated and that there is continuity or a threat of continuity; that a pattern may be established without proof of multiple schemes, multiple episodes, or multiple transactions; and that racketeering acts that are not widely separated in time or space may nonetheless, given other evidence of the threat of continuity, constitute a RICO pattern.

[T]he *Sedima* dictum was entitled to far greater deference than *Ianniello* gave it. Moreover, the language of the statute and the legislative history support the essential point of that dictum. ... Accordingly, we abandon the *Ianniello* view that two acts, without more, suffice. ...

Further, we no longer adhere to the view of *Ianniello* and its progeny that relationship and continuity are necessary characteristics of a RICO enterprise. Neither the statutory definition of enterprise nor the legislative history suggests that those concepts pertain to the notion of enterprise. Rather, the language and the history suggest that Congress sought to define that term as broadly as possible, "includ[ing]" within it every kind of legal entity and any "group of individuals associated in fact although not a legal entity." 18 U.S.C. § 1961(4). To the extent that the legislative history discusses the concepts of relatedness and continuity, it does so in connection with proposed definitions of pattern of racketeering activity. We conclude that relatedness and continuity are essentially characteristics of activity rather than of enterprise.

An interrelationship between acts, suggesting the existence of a pattern, may be established in a number of ways. These include proof of their temporal proximity, or common goals, or similarity of methods, or repetitions. The degree to which these factors establish a pattern may depend on the degree of proximity, or any similarities in goals or methodology, or the number of repetitions. ...

We recognize that to the extent relatedness is to be shown by the acts' temporal proximity, there may well be a tension between relatedness and continuity, for obviously the shorter the elapsed time between the two acts, the less it can be said that the activity is continuing. Nonetheless, "[i]t is important to recognize that in footnote 14 the Supreme Court does not enshrine 'continuity plus relationship' as a determinative two-pronged test. Rather, the Court quotes this language to demonstrate how the pattern requirement should be interpreted to prevent the application of RICO to the perpetrators of 'isolated' or 'sporadic' criminal acts." Sun Savings & Loan Ass'n v. Dierdorff, 825 F.2d 187, 192 (9th Cir.1987). Further, we note that the legislative history referred not just to continuity but also to the threat of continuity. Therefore, where the virtual simultaneity of two acts suggests that they are related, the timing does not negate the existence of a pattern; rather, evidence of continuity or the threat of continuity will simply have to come from facts external to those two acts.

We do not agree with those courts that have in effect concluded that temporal proximity requires that two or more acts be counted as one. While temporal separation of events is a common feature of a pattern of action, it is not an essential; such a pattern may be found, for example, in the simultaneous commission of like acts for similar purposes against a number of victims.

Nor, with respect to the requirement of continuity or threat of continuity, do we see any basis in RICO or its legislative history for the proposition that a RICO violation cannot be established without proof of more than one scheme, episode, or transaction, or without proof that the scheme pursuant to which the racketeering acts were performed is a scheme with no apparent termination date.... There is no mention [in the statute] of schemes, episodes, or transactions. We doubt that Congress meant to exclude from the reach of RICO multiple acts of racketeering simply because they achieve their objective quickly or because they further but a single scheme. . . .

In sum, though we would disapprove any attempt by the government or a private plaintiff to go beyond Congress's intent and fragment an act that plainly is unitary into multiple acts in order to invoke RICO, we conclude that where in fact there are a number of different acts, each should be separately counted. If there are similarities between them with respect to victim, methodology, goal, etc., and if there is evidence of a threat of continuation of racketeering activity, we conclude that the acts may constitute a pattern even though they are nearly simultaneous.

In some cases both the relatedness and the continuity necessary to show a RICO pattern may be proven through the nature of the RICO enterprise. For example, two racketeering acts that are not directly related to each other may nevertheless be related indirectly because each is related to the RICO enterprise. The nature of the enterprise may also serve to show the threat of continuing activity. Where the enterprise is an entity whose business is racketeering activity, an act performed in furtherance of that business automatically carries with it the threat of continued racketeering activity. Even where the enterprise is legitimate, if the racketeering acts were performed at the behest of an organized crime group, that fact would tend to belie any notion that the racketeering acts were sporadic or isolated. We do not suggest that a defendant's association with an organized crime group is itself an act of racketeering activity, or that the defendant is to be held accountable for the racketeering acts of others. We simply note that such an association may reveal the threat of continued racketeering activity and thereby help to establish that the defendant's own acts constitute a pattern within the meaning of RICO.

Finally, we note that though the interrelatedness concept discussed above pertains to the predicate acts, it is plain that for establishment of a RICO violation there must also be some kind of relationship between the acts and the enterprise, for each of the substantive RICO subsections prohibits a specific type of interplay between a pattern of racketeering activity and the enterprise. Section 1962(a) prohibits use of income derived from a pattern of racketeering activity for the establishment of, or acquisition of an interest in, an enterprise engaged in or affecting interstate or foreign commerce. Section 1962(b) prohibits use of a pattern of racketeering activity to acquire an interest in, or control of, such an enterprise. And § 1962(c) prohibits use of a pattern of racketeering activity in the conduct of such an enterprise's affairs. Thus, no RICO violation can be shown unless there is proof of the specified relationship between the racketeering acts and the RICO enterprise. To the extent, therefore, that the relationship between acts necessary to establish a pattern depends on the relationships between individual acts and the enterprise, there will often be some overlap of proof and analysis. The degree of overlap will vary depending in part on the substantive RICO subsection at issue. The establishment of a subsection (a) violation, for example, will likely entail less overlap, since the acts by which the tainted income is acquired need have no logical relationship to the enterprise in which investment will thereafter be made. In contrast, establishment of a subsection (c) violation will often entail overlap, for each act of racketeering activity will be related to the enterprise since the latter's affairs are by hypothesis conducted through a pattern of such acts. The differences and overlap are simply a consequence of Congress's use of the same defined terms in fashioning different substantive prohibitions.

This is not to say that one should ever view the enterprise and the pattern as the same thing, for they are not. "[T]he concept 'enterprise' focuses on a group of people;.... The concept 'pattern' focuses on the relationship between acts of racketeering...." G. Robert Blakey & Brian Gettings, Racketeer Influenced and Corrupt Organizations (RICO): Basic Concepts—Criminal and Civil Remedies, 53 Temp. L.Q. 1009, 1026 n.91 (1980). But the difference in the nature of the two elements does not mean that the same piece of evidence may not help to establish both. See *Turkette*, 452 U.S., at 583 ("the proof used to establish these separate elements may in particular cases coalesce"). We conclude that evidence of the nature of the enterprise may be used to show the threat of continuity sufficient to establish a RICO pattern.

F. *Application of These Principles to Indelicato*

Under these standards, we have little difficulty in concluding that Indelicato's participation in the three Bonanno family murders as a representative of the Commission constituted a pattern of racketeering activity within the meaning of RICO. There were three persons targeted for assassination. Though the murders were virtually simultaneous, they plainly constituted more than one act. Further, the three murders were indisputably related since the purpose for each was facilitation of the desired change in leadership of the Bonanno crime family. Though the murders themselves were quickly completed, both the nature of the Commission, which was the alleged RICO enterprise, and the criminal nature of the Bonanno family, control of which the murders were designed to achieve, made it clear beyond peradventure that there was a threat of continuing racketeering activity. The evidence was plainly ample to permit the jury to infer that the murders were part of a RICO pattern.

CONCLUSION

We conclude that the nearly simultaneous murders of three persons as part of the conduct of the affairs of an organized crime enterprise constituted a "pattern of racketeering activity" within the meaning of § 1961(5). We remand the matter to the panel for further proceedings consistent with this ruling.

■ OAKES, CIRCUIT JUDGE (concurring)(with whom JUDGE FEINBERG joins):

I concur in Judge Kearse's opinion and her analysis of RICO's "pattern" requirement. I write separately because it is important to emphasize that Indelicato's "pattern" of racketeering activity did not consist solely of the three murders at Joe & Mary's Restaurant on July 12, 1979. Proof of these murders was necessary but not sufficient to prove a RICO pattern of racketeering activity. This is a case where evidence concerning the nature of the RICO enterprise also served to prove the existence of a pattern of racketeering activity. Facts external to the predicate acts—the three murders—were essential to prove relatedness and the threat of continuity.

This was the quintessential racketeering case. The indictment, the proof, and the trial judge's charge demonstrate that Indelicato was not an "independent contractor" called upon to commit an isolated crime. On the contrary, he was associated for some years with the ultimate criminal enterprise, the Commission of La Cosa Nostra. Indelicato committed murders which were critical to the enterprise's achieving its goal of resolving family leadership disputes; these were not "isolated acts of racketeering activity." Sedima, S.P.R.L. v. Imrex Co., 473 U.S. 479, 496 n. 14 (1985).

The indictment further charged that one of the purposes of the Commission enterprise was to "extend[ ] formal recognition to newly-elected bosses of La Cosa Nostra Families, and [to] resolv[e] leadership disputes within a family," as well as to "keep persons inside and outside La Cosa Nostra in fear of the Commission by identifying the Commission with threats, violence, and murder." Among the means used by the Commission to advance these general purposes was the resolution of "a leadership dispute within the Bonanno family ... by authorizing the murders of Carmine Galante, a/k/a 'Lilo,' who was boss of the Bonanno Family, and Leonard Coppola and Giuseppe Turano." Thus, the indictment charged that there was an important connection between Indelicato's conduct and the overall, common purposes of the racketeering enterprise. The murders were part of a larger plan, a reorganization or realignment of the Bonanno family by the Commission.

The evidence was that in 1979, Indelicato was a formally inducted soldier in the Bonanno family, a family that, because of its many factional disputes, was managed directly by the Commission. As a "made" member, Indelicato necessarily learned the Mafia rules set down by the Commission and took the oath to abide by those rules and to obey the Commission. Indelicato knew of the exclusively criminal purposes of the Commission and knew it had been engaging in, and that it would continue to engage in, racketeering activity.

Indelicato was chosen to carry out a murder plan so important that the Commission itself had the exclusive power to authorize it—namely, the assassination of the boss of a La Cosa Nostra family. Indelicato's conspiracy with the Commission to murder the three involved planning which continued over a significant time period, beginning in June 1979, when the getaway car eventually used in the killing was stolen. There was evidence that a few days before July 12, Louis Giongetti—an associate of Indelicato—was instructed to collect a cache of shotguns and handguns and place them in the trunk of a car, and to return with them to a bar where

Indelicato and another Mafioso were waiting. Indelicato was promoted to captain in the Bonanno family as a reward for the killings.

The district judge correctly instructed the jury on the elements of the RICO substantive offense[:]

> "Whether you are considering a pattern of loansharking, extortion, labor law violations or acts of murder, . . . when you are considering whether they form a pattern as to any defendant, you must find that the defendant's acts are not isolated or disconnected. You must find that they are related or connected by some common scheme, plan, or motive. Thus you must find that the acts constituted *part of a larger pattern of activity* that characterized the defendant's participation in the affairs of the enterprise and you must consider and find whether or not there is a continuity plus relationship in the acts as to the defendant you are considering." (Emphasis added.)

Thus, the jury was instructed that it could convict Indelicato only if it found his acts to be integrally related to the larger pattern of the enterprise's activities, and not merely isolated or sporadic. The criminal nature of the enterprise involved in this case provides the continuity or threat of continuity necessary to establish a pattern. I believe that this is implicit in the majority opinion; accordingly, I concur.

■ MAHONEY, CIRCUIT JUDGE (concurring):

I am in general agreement with Judge Kearse's excellent opinion, and write separately only to state my disagreement with its assertion that "the concepts of relatedness and continuity are attributes of activity, not of a RICO enterprise," a point reiterated in several variations in the majority opinion.

The Supreme Court stated in United States v. Turkette, 452 U.S. 576 (1981), that:

> "The [enterprise] is proved by evidence of an *ongoing organization*, formal or informal, and by evidence that the associates *function as a continuing unit*."

It would thus appear clear that continuity is an attribute of a RICO enterprise, as well as a RICO pattern. As to relatedness, there will presumably be a relationship (1) between the associates that function as a continuing unit, and (2) between the associates and the unit.

The majority's essential point is that the discussion of relatedness and continuity in *Sedima* footnote 14 refers to the RICO pattern rather than the RICO enterprise. I agree, and think that is what we should say.

NOTE ON *UNITED STATES v. INDELICATO*

The disposition in *Indelicato* was a remand to the panel for further proceedings consistent with the ruling of the en banc court. Several aspects of the panel's opinion on remand, reported as United States v.

Salerno, 868 F.2d 524 (2d Cir.1989), are worthy of note. The first is the court's more elaborate statement of the facts and legal proceedings surrounding the entire prosecution:

"Anthony Salerno, Carmine Persico, Gennaro Langella, Anthony Corallo, Salvatore Santoro, Ralph Scopo, Christopher Furnari and Anthony Indelicato appeal from judgments of conviction entered in the United States District Court for the Southern District of New York, Richard Owen, Judge, after an 11 week jury trial. All appellants were convicted of RICO conspiracy, 18 U.S.C. § 1962(d), and substantive RICO, 18 U.S.C. § 1962(c), violations. All appellants except Indelicato were convicted of conspiracy to commit extortion and 12 counts of extortion or attempted extortion, in violation of 18 U.S.C. § 1951(a). Scopo was convicted as a principal, and all other appellants except Indelicato were convicted as aiders and abettors, 18 U.S.C. § 2, of six labor bribery violations, 29 U.S.C. § 186(b)(1)(Supp. IV 1986). Corallo and Santoro were convicted of conspiracy to make extortionate extensions of credit in violation of 18 U.S.C. § 892. The non-RICO convictions correspond to the predicate acts of the two RICO counts. In addition, Indelicato was charged with three RICO predicate acts of murder, which the jury found he committed, for which there were no corresponding non-RICO counts in the indictment.

"Each defendant except Indelicato was sentenced to a total of 100 years imprisonment. Indelicato was sentenced to 40 years imprisonment for his two RICO violations. Corallo and Santoro were each sentenced to total fines of $250,000 and assessed costs of prosecution. All other appellants except Indelicato were each sentenced to total fines of $240,000 and assessed costs of prosecution. Indelicato was fined $50,000. In addition to challenging their convictions on numerous grounds, appellants also challenge the severity of these sentences.

"By order entered April 1, 1988, this court determined to hear the appeal of defendant Indelicato in banc, limited to the issue ... whether the simultaneous murders of Carmine Galante, Leonard Coppola and Giuseppe Turano constituted a 'pattern of racketeering activity' within the meaning of 18 U.S.C. § 1962(c). The in banc court thereafter decided that issue adversely to Indelicato and remanded the case to this panel for further proceedings consistent with the in banc ruling. See United States v. Indelicato, 865 F.2d 1370 (2d Cir.1989).

"We affirm the judgment of the district court, except that we reverse the conviction of Indelicato on the substantive RICO count.

"The RICO enterprise alleged in the indictment is an organization known as the 'Commission' of La Cosa Nostra, a nationwide criminal society which operates through local organizations known as 'families.' The indictment alleged, and substantial evidence at trial established, that the Commission has for some time acted as the ultimate ruling body over the five La Cosa Nostra families in New York City and affiliated families in other cities. The general purpose of the Commission is to regulate and facilitate the relationships between and among the several La Cosa Nostra families, and more specifically to promote and coordinate joint ventures of a criminal nature involving the families, to resolve disputes among the families, to extend formal recognition to 'bosses' of the families and on occasion resolve leadership disputes within a family, to approve the initiation or 'making' of new members of the families, and to establish rules governing the families, officers and members of La Cosa Nostra. There are five New York City families (i.e., the Genovese, Gambino, Colombo, Lucchese and Bonanno families). Since the late 1970s, the Commission was controlled by the bosses of four of those families, often acting through their deputies. Due to internal instability, the Bonanno family was denied a seat on the Commission during this period.

"The government established that from the late 1970s until 1985, Salerno was first acting boss and subsequently boss of the Genovese family; Corallo was boss of the Lucchese family, which Santoro served as 'underboss' and Furnari as 'consigliere' (the positions ranking immediately below the family boss); Persico was boss of the Colombo family, Langella its underboss and Scopo a member of that family and the president and business manager of the District Council of Cement and Concrete Workers, Laborers International Union of North America (the 'District Council'); and Indelicato was a member of the Bonanno family, who was approved by the Commission for promotion to the rank of 'capo' (i.e., leader of a subordinate group within the family) some time after his participation in the murder of Carmine Galante and two associates, at the direction of the Commission. Philip Rastelli, a rival to Galante for Bonanno family leadership, was originally named a defendant, but was severed from the trial of this case because he was on trial in the Eastern District of New York in another criminal case. Paul Castellano, boss of the Gambino family, was also named a defendant, but was murdered prior to trial.

"The indictment alleged racketeering acts related to three general Commission schemes.

"The first scheme, an extortion and labor bribery operation known as the 'Club,' involved all appellants except Indelicato. The Club was an arrangement between the Commission, several concrete construction companies working in New York City, and the District Council, a union headed by Scopo. The Club was a cooperative venture among the Families, and the Commission set rules and settled major disputes arising out of the scheme. The rules of the Club were: only such construction companies as the

Commission approved would be permitted to take concrete construction jobs worth more than two million dollars in New York City; any contractor taking a concrete job worth more than two million dollars would be required to pay the Commission two per cent of the construction contract price; the Commission would approve which construction companies in the Club would get which jobs and would rig the bids so that the designated company submitted the lowest bid; the Commission would guarantee 'labor peace' to the construction companies in exchange for compliance with the rules of the Club; and the Commission would enforce compliance by threatened or actual labor unrest or physical harm, even to the point of driving a company out of the concrete business. According to the government, seven concrete construction companies were participants in this extortionate scheme.

"The second scheme, a loansharking conspiracy, involved appellants Corallo and Santoro. Corallo's nephew, John DiLeo, had been running a loansharking operation on Staten Island, in Gambino family 'territory,' without the permission of the Gambino family. DiLeo's son-in-law, who was the son of a Gambino family member and was engaged in criminal activities with DiLeo, was then ordered to conduct those activities under the supervision of the Gambino family, and DiLeo complained to Corallo, the boss of the Lucchese family. Several recorded conversations show that DiLeo asked Corallo to intercede with Paul Castellano and the Gambino family to resolve this dispute. At Corallo's direction, Santoro and Salvatore Avellino, Corallo's driver, met with Paul Castellano and two other Gambino family members. As a result, the Lucchese and Gambino families reached an accord allowing DiLeo to continue his illegal activities on Staten Island as long as he was not doing so on his own; he was to report to Corallo, and the Gambino family was to be kept informed concerning DiLeo's activities. DiLeo was subsequently ordered by Corallo to continue reporting to him, and surveillance photographs show that DiLeo did in fact continue to meet with Avellino and Corallo after the accord was reached.

"The third scheme involved the murder of Carmine Galante and his associates, Giuseppe Turano and Leonard Coppola, on July 12, 1979, allegedly as part of a Commission plan to end the internal Bonanno family dispute between Galante and Philip Rastelli. Only Indelicato, the alleged hit man, was charged with the murders of Galante and his associates as predicate acts in the RICO counts. The three men were shot, allegedly by Indelicato and several accomplices, while they were sitting together on the terrace of Turano's restaurant in Brooklyn. A palmprint on the door handle of the getaway car, as well as eyewitness reports and expert testimony, tied Indelicato to the murders. The government introduced surveillance evidence showing that Indelicato, a Bonanno family member, reported to Gambino family underboss Aniello

Dellacroce and Bonanno family consigliere Stefano Canone approximately one-half hour after the killings. Dellacroce and Canone were originally named as defendants, but both died of natural causes in 1985. The murders were the only predicate acts with which Indelicato was charged."

The defendants urged numerous grounds for reversal, most of them having to do with matters not going to the substantive meaning of the RICO statute. For example, they raised claims of insufficiency of the evidence in various respects, claims as to the admission or the exclusion of evidence, a claim that the jury should have been sequestered for the entire trial, a claim that one of the attorneys had a conflict of interest, etc. Two of their arguments are worth attention here.

The first concerns the fate of Indelicato himself:

"Indelicato was indicted on RICO conspiracy and substantive RICO counts on November 19, 1985. All three of his alleged racketeering acts, however, occurred in 1979. Indelicato contends that his convictions on both the substantive RICO and RICO conspiracy counts are barred by the applicable five-year statute of limitations, 18 U.S.C. § 3282.[a] The jury was charged that in order to convict Indelicato on the RICO conspiracy count, it must find that the Commission enterprise continued to exist after November 19, 1980, and that Indelicato continued after that date to be a coconspirator or associate of that enterprise. It was charged that in order to convict him on the substantive RICO count, it must find that he continued to be an associate of the Commission enterprise after November 19, 1980, and that any one of the other defendants found to be guilty under the substantive RICO count committed a racketeering act after November 19, 1980.

"Subsequent to oral argument, this court decided in United States v. Persico, 832 F.2d 705 (2d Cir.1987), that a RICO conspiracy offense is complete, thus commencing the running of the five-year statute of limitations, only when the purposes of the conspiracy have either been accomplished or abandoned,[4] but that a substantive RICO charge is barred by limitations as to any defendant unless that defendant committed a predicate act within the five-year limitations period. We are, of course, bound by *Persico*, as by any Second Circuit panel decision unless it is overruled in banc or by the Supreme Court.

---

[a] Section 3282 provides:

"Except as otherwise expressly provided by law, no person shall be prosecuted, tried, or punished for any offense, not capital, unless the indictment is found or the information is instituted within five years next after such offense shall have been committed." [Footnote by eds.]

[4] Although the issue was not raised on the facts in *Persico*, it is clear that even when a RICO conspiracy continues into the limitations period, an individual conspirator can commence the running of the statute of limitations as to him by affirmatively withdrawing from the conspiracy. See In Re Corrugated Container Antitrust Litigation, 662 F.2d 875, 886 (D.C.Cir.1981).

"The jury here was properly charged that the conspiracy count against Indelicato must be dismissed on statute of limitations grounds unless they found that the Commission enterprise continued after November 19, 1980, and that Indelicato continued after that date as a co-conspirator or an associate of that enterprise. There was ample evidence to support its determinations adverse to Indelicato on those issues. Accordingly, and pursuant to the in banc determination of this court, Indelicato's conviction for violation of 18 U.S.C. § 1962(d)(RICO conspiracy) will be affirmed. On the other hand, since all predicate acts committed by Indelicato occurred prior to November 19, 1980, *Persico* requires reversal of his conviction for violation of 18 U.S.C. § 1962(c)(substantive RICO) on limitations grounds."

The second concerns the court's disposition of the argument by all of the defendants that their sentences were too long:

"All appellants, except Indelicato, received prison sentences of 100 years. Santoro, Persico, Langella, Furnari and Scopo each received consecutive 20-year sentences for Count I (RICO conspiracy), Count 2 (substantive RICO), Count 4 (extortion), Count 12 (extortion), and Count 14 (extortion).[b] Corallo and Santoro received consecutive 20-year sentences on Counts 1, 2, 4, 12 and 25 (loan sharking conspiracy).[c] If Judge Owen had not made the sentences on all other counts concurrent, however, these defendants could have received prison terms of over 300 years. Furthermore, although appellants received a number of consecutive sentences and maximum sentences on several counts, as was stated in Carmona v. Ward, 576 F.2d 405 (2d Cir.1978), '[l]ong periods of imprisonment resulting from consecutive sentences for multiple convictions have in the past been upheld as constitutional.'

"Appellants nonetheless claim that their sentences violate the eighth amendment. Furnari and Scopo specifically claim that their sentences are disproportionate to the gravity of their crimes. All appellants also claim that Judge Owen, in imposing identical 100-year sentences upon all defendants except Indelicato, engaged in impermissibly 'uniform' or 'mechanistic' sentencing.

"As we stated recently in United States v. Gaggi, 811 F.2d 47 (2d Cir.1987), '[t]he Supreme Court has warned that we should not substitute our judgment for that of the sentencing court, but when applying the eighth amendment to decide only whether the sentence is within constitutional limits; a review that rarely requires extended analysis.' Id., at 63 (citing Solem v. Helm, 463 U.S. 277, 290 n. 16 (1983)).

---

[b] The extortion charges were filed under 18 U.S.C. § 1951. [Footnote by eds.]

[c] The loansharking charges were based on 18 U.S.C. § 892(a). [Footnote by eds.]

"As to Furnari and Scopo's contention that their culpability was not as great as their codefendants', Judge Owen noted that although Furnari and Scopo were not 'bosses' or 'underbosses,' Furnari was 'consigliere of the Lucchese Family which [is] practically the equivalent of the underboss,' and that he had been involved in many of the recorded meetings where intimate knowledge of the Commission's violent business was evident. With respect to Scopo, Judge Owen noted his association with the Colombo family, his importance to the Commission bosses, and his inclusion in sensitive La Cosa Nostra discussions. The Judge also considered Scopo's own recorded words, which showed that for at least 15 years Scopo had been involved in corrupting organized labor and extorting construction contractors.

"Nor do we find the District Court's sentencing to be improperly mechanistic or uniform. The court articulated its consideration of individual factors in the sentencing of each defendant. While we admit that the 100–year sentences have a certain symbolic quality, we cannot say that Judge Owen relied so heavily on abstract considerations of deterrence and so little on considerations of individual circumstances as to amount to an abuse of his wide discretion in sentencing."

The court concluded that "[w]e reverse the conviction of Indelicato for violation of 18 U.S.C. § 1962(c) as time-barred, and affirm on all other counts with respect to all appellants."

Beauford v. Helmsley

United States Court of Appeals, Second Circuit, 1989.
865 F.2d 1386.

Before Oakes, Chief Judge, and Lumbard, Feinberg, Meskill, Newman, Kearse, Cardamone, Pierce, Winter, Pratt, Miner, Altimari and Mahoney, Circuit Judges, sitting en banc.

■ Kearse, Circuit Judge:

Plaintiffs ... appeal from a final judgment ... dismissing their amended complaint which sought damages from defendants for mailings of allegedly fraudulent materials relating to the sale of condominium apartments, in violation of [RICO]. The District Court dismissed the amended complaint on the ground, inter alia, that it failed to state a claim upon which relief can be granted under RICO because it failed to allege a sufficient "pattern of racketeering activity." A unanimous panel of this court affirmed ... but suggested that the appeal be "reheard en banc to clarify Second Circuit law." On rehearing, we conclude for the reasons stated below and in *United States v. Indelicato*, heard en banc in tandem with the present case and published simultaneously herewith, that the amended complaint sufficiently alleged a pattern of racketeering activity.

We therefore vacate the panel decision and the judgment of the District Court and remand . . . for further proceedings.

I. BACKGROUND

The present lawsuit, styled a class action, focuses on the conversion of a large Bronx, New York apartment complex known as "Parkchester" into condominiums. Parkchester comprises 51 buildings containing a total of 12,271 apartments; it is divided into the North, East, South, and West quadrants. It is principally the conversion of the East, West, and South quadrants ("EWS quadrants") that is at issue here.

Plaintiffs are one tenant of Parkchester who purchased his apartment and four tenants who did not. Defendants are the partners in Parkchester Apartments Co., which is the real estate partnership sponsoring the conversion, the sponsor's sales agent (all of the foregoing collectively referred to as the "sponsoring defendants"), and an engineering firm and an individual engineer (collectively the "engineering defendants") who supplied reports and studies as part of the conversion.

The amended complaint alleged that in connection with the offering plan for the conversion of the EWS quadrants, comprising 8,286 apartments, defendants made a number of material misrepresentations including the concealment of (a) serious structural defects in the buildings, (b) the presence of asbestos in their insulation, and (c) the need to replace their plumbing and electrical systems. The alleged means of concealment included material misstatements by the engineering defendants, failures to disclose by the sponsoring defendants, and absorption by the sponsoring defendants of certain repair costs in order to set forth artificially low maintenance levels for the apartments. Plaintiffs alleged that had they received accurate and complete information, their decisions whether or not to purchase condominiums would have been affected, and that defendants' frauds artificially inflated the purchase prices of the apartments.

In addition to alleging that defendants' conduct constituted common-law fraud, the amended complaint alleged that the frauds had been committed through the mailing of the conversion offering plans and plan amendments to tenants of all 8,286 apartments and to other potential buyers, in violation of 18 U.S.C. § 1341; that both the partnership itself and the defendants as a group constituted enterprises within the meaning of RICO; and that plaintiffs were entitled to recover under civil RICO.

[T]he District Court granted defendants' motion to dismiss the amended complaint for failure to state a federal claim on which relief could be granted because it failed to allege a pattern of racketeering activity. With respect to the RICO claim, the court stated as follows:

"Even assuming that plaintiffs have adequately alleged fraud, they have failed to adequately allege a 'pattern' of racketeering, despite their conclusory description of the fraud as 'several distinct schemes to defraud' both potential buyers and partners and investors. All alleged misrepresentations appear in one document, the offering plan for condominium conversion. Even under the most liberal reading of 'pattern,' the defrauding of potential buyers of condominium units by individually mailing them copies of a single fraudulent document and failing to remedy the fraud in subsequent amendments does not constitute a pattern of racketeering activity."

Having also dismissed plaintiffs' only other alleged basis for federal-question jurisdiction, and there being no claim of diversity of citizenship, the court also declined to entertain plaintiffs' pendent state-law claims.

The court denied plaintiffs' motion for leave to file a second amended complaint that would have added allegations that defendants had, inter alia, denied claims by tenants based on water damage; misallocated expenses from one quadrant to another; destroyed documents; lowered the levels of services in categories such as hot water, electricity, elevators, painting, landscaping, and central mall maintenance; failed to disclose purchases of supplies through a related company; and engaged in discriminatory enforcement of regulations against tenants. The court was unpersuaded that the proposed new allegations would cure the amended complaint's failure to allege a pattern of racketeering activity. Accordingly, judgment was entered dismissing the action.

On appeal, a panel of this court affirmed the judgment of dismissal. We noted that the pattern of this circuit's RICO precedents was somewhat confusing, in that it had imposed a continuity requirement on the enterprise element and had

"[found] insufficient evidence of continuity in a single criminal episode regardless of how many fraudulent acts it entails. In other words, a single criminal episode or scheme does not charge a claim under RICO because it lacks sufficient continuity to constitute an enterprise, even if its fraudulent acts constitute a pattern."

We concluded that given our precedents, the present case was properly dismissed for lack of a RICO enterprise, stating that "a single alleged scheme" to defraud tenants and other prospective buyers is not sufficient to permit a plaintiff to take advantage of RICO where the scheme, though "widespread," is "discrete," and, though "continuing," is "finite."

The panel recommended that the appeal be reheard en banc to clarify Second Circuit law, and this rehearing was joined with an en banc rehearing of an appeal from a judgment of conviction in *Indelicato*, which raises a similar issue with regard to the RICO requirement of a "pattern" of racketeering activity. For the reasons stated below and in *Indelicato*, we conclude that the amended complaint in the present case met the "pattern" requirement.

II. DISCUSSION

[O]ur current review of the language and legislative history of RICO has led us to the conclusion, inter alia, that proof of two acts of racketeering activity without more does not suffice to establish a RICO pattern. Since Congress's goal in fashioning its definition of "pattern of racketeering activity" was to exclude from the reach of RICO criminal acts that were merely "isolated" or "sporadic," we must determine whether two or more acts of racketeering activity have sufficient interrelationship and whether there is sufficient continuity or threat of continuity to constitute such a pattern. Accordingly, our analysis of relatedness and continuity has shifted from the enterprise element to the pattern element.

Within this framework, there is no question that the amended complaint in the present case adequately pleaded the RICO enterprise element. It alleged that there were two such enterprises: the partnership that sponsored the conversion, and all of the defendants in association with one another for the purpose of accomplishing the apartment sales. Each is within the statutory definition of enterprise. The more interesting question is whether the amended complaint adequately alleged a pattern of racketeering activity.

Our *Indelicato* analysis has persuaded us that a RICO pattern may be established without proof of multiple schemes, multiple episodes, or multiple transactions; and that acts that are not widely separated in time or space may nonetheless properly be viewed as separate acts of racketeering activity for purposes of establishing a RICO pattern. Thus, in *Indelicato*, we found that three acts of murder could constitute a RICO pattern even though there was proof of but one scheme, and even though the three murders, carried out virtually simultaneously, could not be viewed as separable episodes or transactions. This analysis is equally applicable to the present case, for since a RICO violation is an element to be proven in a civil RICO action, the substantive standards as to what must be proven in a criminal RICO prosecution also govern civil RICO actions. [W]e can no longer say, as we once did, that there is "insufficient evidence of continuity," or of pattern, "in a single criminal episode regardless of how many fraudulent acts it entails." 843 F.2d at 110. We impose no multiple episode requirement, and we conclude that for a determination of whether there is a RICO pattern, each individual racketeering act should be separately counted.

In the present case, we conclude also that a RICO pattern may be adequately pleaded without an allegation that the scheme pursuant to which the racketeering acts were performed is an ongoing scheme having no demonstrable ending point. We reach this conclusion because nothing in the statute or the legislative history reveals an intent to require such an open-ended scheme. What is required is that the complaint plead a basis from which it could be inferred that the acts of racketeering activity were neither isolated nor sporadic. In *Indelicato*, we found the threat of continuity inherent in the criminal nature of the enterprise at whose behest the three related murders were committed. Were the same type of enterprise alleged here, we would have no difficulty in finding a sufficient allegation of the threat of continuity needed to show a pattern. When, however, there is no indication that the enterprise whose affairs are said to be conducted through racketeering acts is associated with organized crime, the nature of the enterprise does not of itself suggest that racketeering acts will continue, and proof of continuity or the threat of continuity of racketeering activity must thus be found in some factor other than the enterprise itself. We conclude that the amended complaint alleged sufficient other factors with respect to continuity to avoid dismissal for failure to allege a RICO pattern.

The amended complaint alleged that the conversion of the apartments in the EWS quadrants in 1984 was commenced by means of an offering plan that was mailed to the tenants of 8,286 apartments as well as other potential buyers. The offering plan was alleged to have contained a number of material misrepresentations and omissions of material facts, concealing, inter alia, that the plumbing and electrical systems in all of the buildings needed to be replaced and that there were serious structural defects in some of the buildings. It was also alleged that since 1984 there had been several amendments to the offering plan which perpetuated the misrepresentations in the original offering plan, and that these amendments also were mailed to the tenants and potential buyers.

In assessing the sufficiency of these allegations to show a pattern, we note first that § 1961(1)(B) defines racketeering activity, in pertinent part, as "any act which is indictable under ... section 1341 (relating to mail fraud)," and that each act of fraudulent mailing is separately indictable, see Badders v. United States, 240 U.S. 391, 394 (1916)("each putting of a letter into the postoffice a separate offence" under predecessor of § 1341). Second, there can be no question that the thousands of alleged mail frauds here had the necessary interrelationship to be considered a pattern. All of the mailings were made to groups of persons related by either their tenancy in Parkchester apartments or their potential interest in purchasing such apartments. All of the frauds allegedly had the same goal, i.e., inflating the profits to be made by the defendants in the sale of the Parkchester apartments. See *Indelicato* ("the simultaneous commission of like acts for similar purposes against a number of victims" may constitute a pattern).

Further, assuming that one could ever characterize more than 8,000 mailings as "isolated" or "sporadic" as a matter of law, which we doubt Congress would have envisioned, we interpret the amended complaint as containing sufficient other allegations to reveal continuity or the threat of continuity. Thus, that pleading suggested that further amendments to the 1984 offering plan were likely since some 40 per cent of the EWS quadrant apartments remained unsold; as precedent, it alleged that although the conversion of the North quadrant was commenced in 1973, some 20 per cent of the apartments in that quadrant remained unsold and the North quadrant offering plan had been repeatedly updated by amendments, most recently in 1986.

In sum, read with ordinary charity, the amended complaint alleged that on each of several occasions defendants had mailed fraudulent documents to thousands of persons and that there was reason to believe that similarly fraudulent mailings would be made over an additional period of years. These allegations sufficed to set forth acts that cannot be deemed, as a matter of law, isolated or sporadic. We conclude that the relatedness and continuity factors have been adequately revealed in the pleading and that the amended complaint did not fail to satisfy the pattern requirement. . . . We of course express no view as to whether plaintiffs' allegations of a RICO pattern, which we think sufficient at the pleading stage, will be sufficiently supportable to withstand a motion for summary judgment or whether the evidence will suffice to persuade a jury that such a pattern is in fact established.

We recognize that our reframing today of the enterprise and pattern requirements, and particularly our rejection of any requirements that there be multiple schemes or long-term goals or temporal separation of racketeering acts, will open the door to far more civil RICO cases than have heretofore survived our scrutiny. This more liberal approach is, however, required by the statute[:]

> "RICO is to be read broadly. This is the lesson not only of Congress' self-consciously expansive language and overall approach, see United States v. Turkette, 452 U.S. 576, 586–87 (1981), but also of its express admonition that RICO is to 'be liberally construed to effectuate its remedial purposes,' Pub.L. 91–452, § 904(a), 84 Stat. 947. The statute's 'remedial purposes' are nowhere more evident than in the provision of a private action for those injured by racketeering activity." Sedima, 473 U.S. at 497–98.

And notwithstanding our own views that the RICO provisions cast too wide a net with respect to the civil actions that may be brought, see also id. at 499 ("[i]t is true that private civil actions under the statute are being brought almost solely against [respected and legitimate] defendants, rather than against the archetypal, intimidating mobster"), it is clear that Congress was aware that some persons having no association with organized crime would be ensnared by RICO. Thus, with respect to the list of criminal acts that could constitute predicate racketeering activities under RICO, Senator McClellan, sponsor of S.30, 91st Cong., 1st Sess., 115 Cong. Rec. 827 (1969)(bill containing RICO), noted that a committee of the Association of the Bar of the City of New York had "complain[ed] that the list is too inclusive, since it includes offenses which often are committed by persons not engaged in organized crime." 116 Cong. Rec. 18940 (1970). The Senator responded that it was simply not possible to draw the statute in such a way that it would be sure to reach the organized crime activities that were targeted yet not reach others:

> "The Senate report does not claim . . . that the listed offenses are committed primarily by members of organized crime, only that those offenses are characteristic of organized crime. The listed offenses lend themselves to organized commercial exploitation, unlike some other offenses such as rape, and experience has shown they are commonly committed by participants in organized crime. That is all the title IX list of offenses purports to be, that is all the Senate report claims it to be, and that is all it should be.

> "Members of La Cosa Nostra and smaller organized crime groups
> are sufficiently resourceful and enterprising that one constantly is
> surprised by the variety of offenses that they commit. *It is
> impossible to draw an effective statute which reaches most of the
> commercial activities of organized crime, yet does not include
> offenses commonly committed by persons outside organized crime
> as well.*" Id. (emphasis added).

Thus, Congress made the legislative judgment, as it was entitled to do and
which must be given deference, that in order to reach members of organized crime, it was worth reaching other offenders as well.

CONCLUSION

The decision of the panel is vacated; the judgment of the district court
is vacated, and the matter is remanded to the district court for further
proceedings not inconsistent with this opinion.

■ OAKES, CIRCUIT JUDGE (dissenting)(with whom JUDGES LUMBARD and
FEINBERG join):

I welcome the clarification of Second Circuit RICO law provided by
today's two opinions: "Continuity" and "relatedness" are aspects of a
"pattern of racketeering activity," and not of the "enterprise." However, I
must still dissent in this case, for the actions alleged here constitute a
single scheme that is discrete and finite. There is no continuity, or the
threat of continuity; hence, there is no *pattern* of racketeering activity.

I continue to agree with the District Court that since "[a]ll alleged
misrepresentations appear in one document, the offering plan for condominium conversion," there can be no "pattern." It does not matter how
many people received that document or how many amendments were
mailed without remedying the original fraud. The alleged scheme has a
discrete, finite nature even though it involved a very large condominium
conversion lasting over a long period of time.

Two additional factors distinguish this case from *United States v.
Indelicato.* The first is that the enterprises here, the sponsoring partnership and the individuals associating to sell the apartments, are not illegitimate enterprises such as the enterprise there, the Commission of La Cosa
Nostra. This does not exempt the enterprises here from RICO liability,
Sedima, S.P.R.L. v. Imrex Co., 473 U.S. 479, 499 (1985), but it does affect
the manner of proving the pattern of racketeering activity. In *Indelicato,*
evidence concerning the nature of the enterprise also proved the existence
of a pattern by showing relatedness and continuity. Here, however, that
sort of evidence is unavailable.

The second factor distinguishing this case from *Indelicato* is the
predicate acts involved—here alleged mail frauds, there murders to achieve
Commission goals. As pointed out by Judge Cudahy:

> "Mail fraud and wire fraud are perhaps unique among the various
> sorts of 'racketeering activity' possible under RICO in that the
> existence of a multiplicity of predicate acts (here, the mailings)

may be no indication of the requisite continuity of the underlying fraudulent activity. Thus, a multiplicity of mailings does not necessarily translate directly into a 'pattern' of racketeering activity." Lipin Enters Inc. v. Lee, 803 F.2d 322, 325 (7th Cir.1986)(concurring opinion)

In this case, the mailing of copies of a single document to many people, followed by amendments that did not correct the alleged misstatements, may yield many counts of mail fraud, but it does not suffice to show continuity.

To me, today's ruling pushes civil RICO to its logical extreme, a regrettable development. Any real estate conversion involving the mailing of an offering plan with one misrepresentation to apartment house tenants, coupled with the mailing of an amendment to the plan that fails to remedy the fraud, is now subject to civil RICO charges. This decision invites plaintiffs into federal court and arms them with a civil RICO that, for all practical purposes, is unlimited. In many cases, reliance on tort or contract law, or any resort to the state courts, will become unnecessary. The majority has declined to accept the Supreme Court's invitation to "develop a meaningful concept of 'pattern,'" Sedima, 473 U.S., at 500, and would instead, in its own words, "open the door to far more civil RICO cases than have heretofore survived our scrutiny." Accordingly, I dissent.

H.J. Inc. v. Northwestern Bell Telephone Company

Supreme Court of the United States, 1989.
492 U.S. 229.

■ JUSTICE BRENNAN delivered the opinion of the Court.

The Racketeer Influenced and Corrupt Organizations Act (RICO) imposes criminal and civil liability upon those who engage in certain "prohibited activities." Each prohibited activity is defined ... to include, as one necessary element, proof either of "a pattern of racketeering activity" or of "collection of an unlawful debt." "Racketeering activity" is defined in RICO to mean "any act or threat involving" specified state-law crimes, any "act" indictable under various specified federal statutes, and certain federal "offenses"; but of the term "pattern" the statute says only that it "requires at least two acts of racketeering activity" within a 10–year period. We are called upon in this civil case to consider what conduct meets RICO's pattern requirement.

I

RICO renders criminally and civilly liable "any person" who uses or invests income derived "from a pattern of racketeering activity" to acquire an interest in or to operate an enterprise engaged in interstate commerce; who acquires or maintains an interest in or control of such an enterprise "through a pattern of racketeering activity"; who, being employed by or associated with such an enterprise, conducts or participates in the conduct of its affairs "through a pattern of racketeering activity"; or, finally, who conspires to violate [one of these provisions]. RICO provides for drastic remedies: conviction for a violation of RICO carries severe criminal penalties and forfeiture of illegal proceeds; and a person found in a private civil action to have violated RICO is liable for treble damages, costs, and attorney's fees.

Petitioners, customers of respondent Northwestern Bell Telephone Co., filed this putative class action in 1986 in the District Court for the District of Minnesota. Petitioners alleged violations of 18 U.S.C. §§ 1962(a), (b), (c), and (d) by Northwestern Bell and the other respondents—some of the telephone company's officers and employees, various members of the Minnesota Public Utilities Commission (MPUC), and other unnamed individuals and corporations—and sought an injunction and treble damages under RICO's civil liability provisions, §§ 1964(a) and (c).

The MPUC is the state body responsible for determining the rates that Northwestern Bell may charge. Petitioners' five-count complaint alleged that between 1980 and 1986 Northwestern Bell sought to influence members of the MPUC in the performance of their duties—and in fact caused them to approve rates for the company in excess of a fair and reasonable amount—by making cash payments to commissioners, negotiating with them regarding future employment, and paying for parties and meals, for tickets to sporting events and the like, and for airline tickets. Based upon these factual allegations, petitioners alleged in their first count a pendent state-law claim, asserting that Northwestern Bell violated the Minnesota bribery statute, as well as state common law prohibiting bribery. They also raised four separate claims under § 1962 of RICO. Count II alleged that, in violation of § 1962(a), Northwestern Bell derived income from a pattern of racketeering activity involving predicate acts of bribery and used this income to engage in its business as an interstate "enterprise." Count III claimed a violation of § 1962(b), in that, through this same pattern of racketeering activity, respondents acquired an interest in or control of the MPUC, which was also an interstate "enterprise." In Count IV, petitioners asserted that respondents participated in the conduct and affairs of the MPUC through this pattern of racketeering activity, contrary to § 1962(c). Finally, Count V alleged that respondents conspired together to violate §§ 1962(a), (b), and (c), thereby contravening § 1962(d).

The District Court granted respondents' ... motion, dismissing the complaint for failure to state a claim upon which relief could be granted. The Court found that "[e]ach of the fraudulent facts alleged by [petitioners] was committed in furtherance of a single scheme to influence MPUC commissioners to the detriment of Northwestern Bell's ratepayers." It held that dismissal was therefore mandated by the Court of Appeals for the Eighth Circuit's decision in Superior Oil Co. v. Fulmer, 785 F.2d 252 (8th Cir.1986), which the District Court interpreted as adopting an "extremely restrictive" test for a pattern of racketeering activity that required proof of "multiple illegal schemes."[1] The Court of Appeals for the Eighth Circuit

---

[1] The District Court also held that, because the MPUC had conclusively determined that Northwestern Bell's allegedly excessive rates were reasonable, the "filed rate" doc-

affirmed the dismissal of petitioners' complaint, confirming that under Eighth Circuit precedent "[a] single fraudulent effort or scheme is insufficient" to establish a pattern of racketeering activity, and agreeing with the District Court that petitioners' complaint alleged only a single scheme. ... Most Courts of Appeals have rejected the Eighth Circuit's interpretation of RICO's pattern concept to require an allegation and proof of multiple schemes, and we granted certiorari to resolve this conflict. We now reverse.

II

In Sedima, S.P.R.L. v. Imrex Co., 473 U.S. 479 (1985), this Court rejected a restrictive interpretation of § 1964(c) that would have made it a condition for maintaining a civil RICO action both that the defendant had already been convicted of a predicate racketeering act or of a RICO violation, and that plaintiff show a special racketeering injury. In doing so, we acknowledged concern in some quarters over civil RICO's use against "legitimate" businesses, as well as "mobsters and organized criminals"—a concern that had frankly led to the Court of Appeals' interpretation of § 1964(c) in Sedima. But we suggested that RICO's expansive uses "appear to be primarily the result of the breadth of the predicate offenses, in particular the inclusion of wire, mail, and securities fraud, and the failure of Congress and the courts to develop a meaningful concept of 'pattern' "—both factors that apply to criminal as well as civil applications of the act. Congress has done nothing in the interim further to illuminate RICO's key requirement of a pattern of racketeering; and as the plethora of different views expressed by the Courts of Appeals since Sedima demonstrates, developing a meaningful concept of "pattern" within the existing statutory framework has proved to be no easy task.

It is, nevertheless, a task we must undertake in order to decide this case. Our guides in the endeavor must be the text of the statute and its legislative history. We find no support in those sources for the proposition, espoused by the Court of Appeals for the Eighth Circuit in this case, that predicate acts of racketeering may form a pattern only when they are part of separate illegal schemes. Nor can we agree with those courts that have suggested that a pattern is established merely by proving two predicate acts, see, e.g., United States v. Jennings, 842 F.2d 159, 163 (6th Cir.1988), or with amici in this case who argue that the word "pattern" refers only to predicates that are indicative of a perpetrator involved in organized crime or its functional equivalent. In our view, Congress had a more natural and

trine provided an independent ground for dismissal of the complaint. The Court of Appeals did not consider this issue, and we have no occasion to address it here. Nor do we express any opinion as to the District Court's view that Count II was defective because it failed to "allege the existence of an 'enterprise' separate and distinct from the 'person' identified," as the court held was required by § 1962(a).

[Note by eds.—The "filed-rate" doctrine holds that, in certain circumstances at least, invalid rates established by a regulatory commission can be remedied only in proceedings before the commission and not by private suit.]

commonsense approach to RICO's pattern element in mind, intending a more stringent requirement than proof simply of two predicates, but also envisioning a concept of sufficient breadth that it might encompass multiple predicates within a single scheme that were related and that amounted to, or threatened the likelihood of, continued criminal activity.

A

We begin, of course, with RICO's text, in which Congress followed a "pattern [of] utilizing terms and concepts of breadth." Russello v. United States, 464 U.S. 16, 21 (1983). As we remarked in [footnote 14 of] *Sedima*, the section of the statute headed "definitions" does not so much define a pattern of racketeering activity as state a minimum necessary condition for the existence of such a pattern. Unlike other provisions in § 1961 that tell us what various concepts used in the act "mean," § 1961(5) says of the phrase "pattern of racketeering activity" only that it "requires at least two acts of racketeering activity, one of which occurred after [October 15, 1970] and the last of which occurred within ten years (excluding any period of imprisonment) after the commission of a prior act of racketeering activity." It thus places an outer limit on the concept of a pattern of racketeering activity that is broad indeed.

Section 1961(5) does indicate that Congress envisioned circumstances in which no more than two predicates would be necessary to establish a pattern of racketeering—otherwise it would have drawn a narrower boundary to RICO liability, requiring proof of a greater number of predicates. But, at the same time, the statement that a pattern "requires at least" two predicates implies "that while two acts are necessary, they may not be sufficient." Section 1961(5) concerns only the minimum *number* of predicates necessary to establish a pattern; and it assumes that there is something to a RICO pattern *beyond* simply the number of predicate acts involved. The legislative history bears out this interpretation, for the principal sponsor of the Senate bill expressly indicated that "proof of two acts of racketeering activity, without more, does not establish a pattern." 116 Cong. Rec. 18940 (1970)(statement of Sen. McClellan). Section 1961(5) does not identify, though, these additional prerequisites for establishing the existence of a RICO pattern.

In addition to § 1961(5), there is the key phrase "pattern of racketeering activity" itself, from § 1962, and we must "start with the assumption that the legislative purpose is expressed by the ordinary meaning of the words used." Richards v. United States, 369 U.S. 1, 9 (1962). In normal usage, the word "pattern" here would be taken to require more than just a multiplicity of racketeering predicates. A "pattern" is an "arrangement or order of things or activity," 11 Oxford English Dictionary 357 (2d ed. 1989), and the mere fact that there are a number of predicates is no guarantee that they fall into any arrangement or order. It is not the number of predicates but the relationship that they bear to each other or to some external organizing principle that renders them "ordered" or "arranged." The text of RICO conspicuously fails anywhere to identify, however, forms of relationship or external principles to be used in determining whether racketeering activity falls into a pattern for purposes of the act.

It is reasonable to infer, from this absence of any textual identification of sorts of pattern that would satisfy § 1962's requirement, in combination with the very relaxed limits to the pattern concept fixed in § 1961(5), that Congress intended to take a flexible approach, and envisaged that a pattern might be demonstrated by reference to a range of different ordering principles or relationships between predicates, within the expansive bounds set. For any more specific guidance as to the meaning of "pattern," we must look past the text to RICO's legislative history, as we have done in prior cases construing the act.

The legislative history ... shows that Congress indeed had a fairly flexible concept of a pattern in mind. A pattern is not formed by "sporadic activity," S. Rep. No. 91–617, p. 158 (1969), and a person cannot "be subjected to the sanctions of title IX simply for committing two widely separated and isolated criminal offenses," 116 Cong. Rec. 18940 (1970)(Sen. McClellan). Instead, "[t]he term 'pattern' itself requires the showing of a relationship" between the predicates and of " 'the threat of continuing activity.' " "It is this factor of *continuity plus relationship* which combines to produce a pattern." RICO's legislative history reveals Congress' intent that to prove a pattern of racketeering activity a plaintiff or prosecutor must show that the racketeering predicates are related, *and* that they amount to or pose a threat of continued criminal activity.

B

For analytic purposes these two constituents of RICO's pattern requirement must be stated separately, though in practice their proof will often overlap. The element of relatedness is the easier to define, for we may take guidance from a provision elsewhere in the Organized Crime Control Act of 1970 (OCCA), of which RICO formed title IX. OCCA included as title X the Dangerous Special Offender Sentencing Act, 18 U.S.C. § 3575 et seq. (now partially repealed). Title X provided for enhanced sentences where, among other things, the defendant had committed a prior felony as part of a pattern of criminal conduct or in furtherance of a conspiracy to engage in a pattern of criminal conduct. As we noted in *Sedima*, n.14, Congress defined title X's pattern requirement solely in terms of the *relationship* of the defendant's criminal acts one to another: "criminal conduct forms a pattern if it embraces criminal acts that have the same or similar purposes, results, participants, victims, or methods of commission, or otherwise are interrelated by distinguishing characteristics and are not isolated events." 18 U.S.C. § 3575(e). We have no reason to suppose that Congress had in mind for RICO's pattern of racketeering component any more constrained a notion of the relationships between predicates that would suffice.

RICO's legislative history tells us, however, that the relatedness of racketeering activities is not alone enough to satisfy § 1962's pattern element. To establish a RICO pattern it must also be shown that the predicates themselves amount to, or that they otherwise constitute a threat of, *continuing* racketeering activity. As to this continuity requirement, § 3575(e) is of no assistance. It is this aspect of RICO's pattern element that has spawned the "multiple scheme" test adopted by some lower courts, including the Court of Appeals in this case. But although proof that a RICO defendant has been involved in multiple criminal schemes would certainly be highly relevant to the inquiry into the continuity of the defendant's racketeering activity, it is implausible to suppose that Congress thought continuity might be shown *only* by proof of multiple schemes. The Eighth Circuit's test brings a rigidity to the available methods of proving a pattern that simply is not present in the idea of "continuity" itself; and it does so, moreover, by introducing a concept—the "scheme"—that appears nowhere in the language or legislative history of the act.[3] We adopt a less inflexible approach that seems to us to derive from a common-sense, everyday understanding of RICO's language and Congress' gloss on it. What a plaintiff or prosecutor must prove is continuity of racketeering activity, or its threat, simpliciter. This may be done in a variety of ways, thus making it difficult to formulate in the abstract any general test for continuity. We can, however, begin to delineate the requirement.

"Continuity" is both a closed-and open-ended concept, referring either to a closed period of repeated conduct, or to past conduct that by its nature projects into the future with a threat of repetition. See Barticheck v. Fidelity Union Bank/First National State, 832 F.2d 36, 39 (3d Cir.1987). It is, in either case, centrally a temporal concept—and particularly so in the RICO context, where *what* must be continuous, RICO's predicate acts or offenses, and the *relationship* these predicates must bear one to another, are distinct requirements. A party alleging a RICO violation may demonstrate continuity over a closed period by proving a series of related predicates extending over a substantial period of time. Predicate acts extending over a few weeks or months and threatening no future criminal

[3] Nor does the multiple-scheme approach to identifying continuing criminal conduct have the advantage of lessening the uncertainty inherent in RICO's pattern component, for "'scheme' is hardly a self-defining term." Barticheck v. Fidelity Union Bank/First National State, 832 F.2d 36, 39 (3d Cir.1987). A "scheme" is in the eye of the beholder, since whether a scheme exists depends on the level of generality at which criminal activity is viewed. For example, petitioners' allegation that Northwestern Bell attempted to subvert public utility commissioners who would be voting on the company's rates might be described as a single scheme to obtain a favorable rate, or as multiple schemes to obtain favorable votes from individual commissioners on the ratemaking decision. Similarly, though interference with rate making spanning several ratemaking de-cisions might be thought of as a single scheme with advantageous rates as its objective, each ratemaking decision might equally plausibly be regarded as distinct and the object of its own "scheme." There is no obviously "correct" level of generality for courts to use in describing the criminal activity alleged in RICO litigation. Because of this problem of generalizability, the Eighth Circuit's "scheme" concept is highly elastic. Though the definitional problems that arise in interpreting RICO's pattern requirement inevitably lead to uncertainty regarding the statute's scope—whatever approach is adopted—we prefer to confront these problems directly, not "by introducing a new and perhaps more amorphous concept into the analysis" that has no basis in text or legislative history. Ibid.

conduct do not satisfy this requirement: Congress was concerned in RICO with long-term criminal conduct. Often a RICO action will be brought before continuity can be established in this way. In such cases, liability depends on whether the *threat* of continuity is demonstrated.

Whether the predicates proved establish a threat of continued racketeering activity depends on the specific facts of each case. Without making any claim to cover the field of possibilities—preferring to deal with this issue in the context of concrete factual situations presented for decision—we offer some examples of how this element might be satisfied. A RICO pattern may surely be established if the related predicates themselves involve a distinct threat of long-term racketeering activity, either implicit or explicit. Suppose a hoodlum were to sell "insurance" to a neighborhood's storekeepers to cover them against breakage of their windows, telling his victims he would be reappearing each month to collect the "premium" that would continue their "coverage." Though the number of related predicates involved may be small and they may occur close together in time, the racketeering acts themselves include a specific threat of repetition extending indefinitely into the future, and thus supply the requisite threat of continuity. In other cases, the threat of continuity may be established by showing that the predicate acts or offenses are part of an ongoing entity's regular way of doing business. Thus, the threat of continuity is sufficiently established where the predicates can be attributed to a defendant operating as part of a long-term association that exists for criminal purposes. Such associations include, but extend well beyond, those traditionally grouped under the phrase "organized crime." The continuity requirement is likewise satisfied where it is shown that the predicates are a regular way of conducting defendant's ongoing legitimate business (in the sense that it is not a business that exists for criminal purposes), or of conducting or participating in an ongoing and legitimate RICO "enterprise."[4]

The limits of the relationship and continuity concepts that combine to define a RICO pattern, and the precise methods by which relatedness and continuity or its threat may be proved, cannot be fixed in advance with such clarity that it will always be apparent whether in a particular case a "pattern of racketeering activity" exists. The development of these concepts must await future cases, absent a decision by Congress to revisit RICO to provide clearer guidance as to the act's intended scope.

III

Various amici urge that RICO's pattern element should be interpreted more narrowly than as requiring relationship and continuity in the senses

---

[4] Insofar as the concurrence seems to suggest that very short periods of criminal activity that do *not* in any way carry a threat of continued criminal activity constitute "obvious racketeer[ing]" to which Congress intended RICO, with its enhanced penalties, to apply, we have concluded that it is mistaken, and that when Congress said predicates must demonstrate "continuity" before they may form a RICO pattern, it expressed an intent that RICO reach activities that amount to or threaten long-term criminal activity.

outlined above, so that a defendant's racketeering activities form a pattern only if they are characteristic either of organized crime in the traditional sense, or of an organized-crime-type perpetrator, that is, of an association dedicated to the repeated commission of criminal offenses. Like the Court of Appeals' multiple scheme rule, however, the argument for reading an organized crime limitation into RICO's pattern concept, whatever the merits and demerits of such a limitation as an initial legislative matter, finds no support in the act's text, and is at odds with the tenor of its legislative history.

One evident textual problem with the suggestion that predicates form a RICO pattern only if they are indicative of an organized crime perpetrator—in either a traditional or functional sense—is that it would seem to require proof that the racketeering acts were the work of an association or group, rather than of an individual acting alone. RICO's language supplies no grounds to believe that Congress meant to impose such a limit on the act's scope. A second indication from the text that Congress intended no organized crime limitation is that no such restriction is explicitly stated. In those titles of OCCA where Congress did intend to limit the new law's application to the context of organized crime, it said so. Thus title V, authorizing the witness protection program, stated that the Attorney General may provide for the security of witnesses "in legal proceedings against any person alleged to have participated in an organized criminal activity." 84 Stat. 933, note preceding 18 U.S.C. § 3481 (since repealed). And title VI permitted the deposition of a witness to preserve testimony for a legal proceeding, upon motion by the Attorney General certifying that "the legal proceeding is against a person who is believed to have participated in an organized criminal activity." 18 U.S.C. § 3503(a). Moreover, Congress' approach in RICO can be contrasted with its decision to enact explicit limitations to organized crime in other statutes. E.g., Omnibus Crime Control and Safe Streets Act of 1968, § 601(b), Pub. L. 90–351, 82 Stat. 209 (defining "organized crime" as "the unlawful activities of the members of a highly organized, disciplined association engaged in supplying illegal goods and services, including but not limited to gambling, prostitution, loan sharking, narcotics, labor racketeering, and other unlawful activities of members of such organizations"). Congress' decision not explicitly to limit RICO's broad terms strongly implies that Congress had in mind no such narrow and fixed idea of what constitutes a pattern as that suggested by amici here.

It is argued, nonetheless, that Congress' purpose in enacting RICO, as revealed in the act's title, in OCCA's preamble, 84 Stat. 923 (Congress seeking "the eradication of organized crime in the United States"), and in the legislative history, was to combat organized crime; and that RICO's broad language should be read narrowly so that the act's scope is coextensive with this purpose. We cannot accept this argument for a narrowing construction of the act's expansive terms.

To be sure, Congress focused on, and the examples used in the debates and reports to illustrate the act's operation concern, the predations of mobsters. Organized crime was without a doubt Congress' major target, as we have recognized elsewhere. But the definition of a "pattern of criminal conduct" in title X of OCCA in terms only of the relationship between criminal acts shows that Congress was quite capable of conceiving of "pattern" as a flexible concept not dependent on tying predicates to the major objective of the law, which for title X as for title IX was the eradication of organized crime. Title X's definition of pattern should thus create a good deal of skepticism about any claim that, despite the capacious language it used, Congress must have intended the RICO pattern element to pick out only racketeering activities with an organized crime nexus. And, indeed, the legislative history shows that Congress knew what it was doing when it adopted commodious language capable of extending beyond organized crime.

Opponents criticized OCCA precisely because it failed to limit the statute's reach to organized crime. See, e.g., S. Rep. No. 91–617, at 215 (Sens. Hart and Kennedy complaining that the Organized Crime Control bill "goes beyond organized criminal activity"). In response, the statute's sponsors made evident that the omission of this limit was no accident, but a reflection of OCCA's intended breadth. Senator McClellan was most plain in this respect:

"The danger posed by organized crime-type offenses to our society has, of course, provided the occasion for our examination of the working of our system of criminal justice. But should it follow ... that any proposals for action stemming from that examination be limited to organized crime?

"[T]his line of analysis ... is seriously defective in several regards. Initially, it confuses the occasion for reexamining an aspect of our system of criminal justice with the proper scope of any new principle or lesson derived from that reexamination. ...

"In addition, the objection confuses the role of the Congress with the role of a court. Out of a proper sense of their limited lawmaking function, courts ought to confine their judgments to the facts of the cases before them. But the Congress in fulfilling its proper legislative role must examine not only individual instances, but whole problems. In that connection, it has a duty not to engage in piecemeal legislation. Whatever the limited occasion for the identification of a problem, the Congress has the duty of enacting a principled solution to the entire problem. Comprehensive solutions to identified problems must be translated into well integrated legislative programs.

"The objection, moreover, has practical as well as theoretical defects. Even as to the titles of [the Organized Crime Control bill] needed primarily in organized crime cases, there are very real limits on the degree to which such provisions can be strictly confined to organized crime cases. ... On the other hand, each title ... which is justified primarily in organized crime prosecutions has been confined to such cases to the maximum degree

> possible, while preserving the ability to administer the act and its effectiveness as a law enforcement tool." 116 Cong. Rec. 18913–14 (1970).

Representative Poff, another sponsor of the legislation, also answered critics who complained that a definition of organized crime was needed:

> "It is true that there is no organized crime definition in many parts of the bill. This is, in part, because it is probably impossible precisely and definitively to define organized crime. But if it were possible, I ask my friend, would he not be the first to object that in criminal law we establish procedures which would be applicable only to a certain type of defendant? " Id., at 35204.

See also id., at 35344 (Rep. Poff)("organized crime" simply "a shorthand method of referring to a large and varying group of individual criminal offenses committed in diverse circumstances," not a precise concept).

The thrust of these explanations seems to us reasonably clear. The occasion for Congress' action was the perceived need to combat organized crime. But Congress for cogent reasons chose to enact a more general statute, one which, although it had organized crime as its focus, was not limited in application to organized crime. In title IX, Congress picked out as key to RICO's application broad concepts that might fairly indicate an organized crime connection, but that it fully realized do not either individually or together provide anything approaching a perfect fit with "organized crime." See, e.g., id., at 18940 (Sen. McClellan)("It is impossible to draw an effective statute which reaches most of the commercial activities of organized crime, yet does not include offenses commonly committed by persons outside organized crime as well").

It seems, moreover, highly unlikely that Congress would have intended the pattern requirement to be interpreted by reference to a concept that it had itself rejected for inclusion in the text of RICO at least in part because "it is probably impossible precisely and definitively to define." Id., at 35204 (Rep. Poff). Congress realized that the stereotypical view of organized crime as consisting in a circumscribed set of illegal activities, such as gambling and prostitution—a view expressed in the definition included in the Omnibus Crime Control and Safe Streets Act, and repeated in the OCCA preamble—was no longer satisfactory because criminal activity had expanded into legitimate enterprises. Section 1961(1) of RICO, with its very generous definition of "racketeering activity," acknowledges the breakdown of the traditional conception of organized crime, and responds to a new situation in which persons engaged in long-term criminal activity often operate *wholly* within legitimate enterprises. Congress drafted RICO broadly enough to encompass a wide range of criminal activity, taking many different forms and likely to attract a broad array of perpetrators operating in many different ways. It would be counterproductive and a mismeasure of congressional intent now to adopt a narrow construction of the statute's pattern element that would require proof of an organized crime nexus.

As this Court stressed in *Sedima*, in rejecting a pinched construction of RICO's provision for a private civil action, adopted by a lower court because it perceived that RICO's use against non-organized crime defendants was an "abuse" of the act, "Congress wanted to reach both 'legitimate' and 'illegitimate' enterprises." Legitimate businesses "enjoy neither an inherent incapacity for criminal activity nor immunity from its consequences"; and, as a result, § 1964(c)'s use "against respected businesses allegedly engaged in a pattern of specifically identified criminal conduct is hardly a sufficient reason for assuming that the provision is being misconstrued." If plaintiffs' ability to use RICO against businesses engaged in a pattern of criminal acts is a defect, we said, it is one "inherent in the statute as written," and hence beyond our power to correct. RICO may be a poorly drafted statute; but rewriting it is a job for Congress, if it is so inclined, and not for this Court. There is no more room in RICO's "self-consciously expansive language and overall approach" for the imposition of an organized crime limitation than for the "amorphous 'racketeering injury' requirement" we rejected in *Sedima*. We thus decline the invitation to invent a rule that RICO's pattern of racketeering concept requires an allegation and proof of an organized crime nexus.

IV

We turn now to the application of our analysis of RICO's pattern requirement. Because respondents prevailed on a motion [to dismiss], we read the facts alleged in the complaint in the light most favorable to petitioners. And we may only affirm the dismissal of the complaint if "it is clear that no relief could be granted under any set of facts that could be proved consistent with the allegations." Hishon v. King & Spalding, 467 U.S. 69, 73 (1984).

Petitioners' complaint alleges that at different times over the course of at least a six-year period the noncommissioner respondents gave five members of the MPUC numerous bribes, in several different forms, with the objective—in which they were allegedly successful—of causing these Commissioners to approve unfair and unreasonable rates for Northwestern Bell. RICO defines bribery as a "racketeering activity," so petitioners have alleged multiple predicate acts.

Under the analysis we have set forth above, and consistent with the allegations in their complaint, petitioners may be able to prove that the multiple predicates alleged constitute "a pattern of racketeering activity," in that they satisfy the requirements of relationship and continuity. The acts of bribery alleged are said to be related by a common purpose, to influence Commissioners in carrying out their duties in order to win approval of unfairly and unreasonably high rates for Northwestern Bell. Furthermore, petitioners claim that the racketeering predicates occurred with some frequency over at least a six-year period, which may be sufficient to satisfy the continuity requirement. Alternatively, a threat of continuity of racketeering activity might be established at trial by showing that the alleged bribes were a regular way of conducting Northwestern Bell's ongoing business, or a regular way of conducting or participating in the conduct of the alleged and ongoing RICO enterprise, the MPUC.

The Court of Appeals thus erred in affirming the District Court's dismissal of petitioners' complaint for failure to plead "a pattern of racketeering activity." The judgment is reversed and the case is remanded for further proceedings consistent with this opinion.

It is so ordered.

■ JUSTICE SCALIA, with whom THE CHIEF JUSTICE, JUSTICE O'CONNOR, and JUSTICE KENNEDY join, concurring in the judgment.

Four Terms ago, in Sedima, S.P.R.L. v. Imrex Co., 473 U.S. 479, 496 n. 14 (1985), we gave lower courts the following four clues concerning the meaning of the enigmatic term "pattern of racketeering activity" in the Racketeer Influenced and Corrupt Organizations Act (RICO). First, we stated that the statutory definition of the term in 18 U.S.C. § 1961(5) implies "that while two acts are necessary, they may not be sufficient." Second, we pointed out that "two isolated acts of racketeering activity," "sporadic activity," and "proof of two acts of racketeering activity, without more" would not be enough to constitute a pattern. Third, we quoted a snippet from the legislative history stating "[i]t is this factor of *continuity plus relationship* which combines to produce a pattern." Finally, we directed lower courts' attention to 18 U.S.C. § 3575(e), which defined the term "pattern of conduct which was criminal" used in a different title of the same act, and instructed them that "[t]his language may be useful in interpreting other sections of the act." Thus enlightened, the district and circuit courts set out "to develop a meaningful concept of 'pattern,'" and promptly produced the widest and most persistent circuit split on an issue of federal law in recent memory. Today, four years and countless millions in damages and attorney's fees later (not to mention prison sentences under the criminal provisions of RICO), the Court does little more than repromulgate those hints as to what RICO means, though with the caveat that Congress intended that they be applied using a "flexible approach."

Elevating to the level of statutory text a phrase taken from the legislative history, the Court counsels the lower courts: "continuity plus relationship." This seems to me about as helpful to the conduct of their affairs as "life is a fountain." Of the two parts of this talismanic phrase, the relatedness requirement is said to be the "easier to define," yet here is the Court's definition, in toto: "[C]riminal conduct forms a pattern if it embraces criminal acts that have the same or similar purposes, results, participants, victims, or methods of commission, or otherwise are interrelated by distinguishing characteristics and are not isolated events." This definition has the feel of being solidly rooted in law, since it is a direct quotation of 18 U.S.C. § 3575(e). Unfortunately, if normal (and sensible) rules of statutory construction were followed, the existence of § 3575(e)— which is the definition contained in another title of the act that was explicitly *not* rendered applicable to RICO—suggests that *whatever* "pattern" might mean in RICO, it assuredly *does not* mean that. "[W]here Congress includes particular language in one section of a statute but omits it in another section of the same act, it is generally presumed that Congress acts intentionally and purposely in the disparate inclusion or exclusion." Russello v. United States, 464 U.S. 16, 23 (1983). But that does not really matter, since § 3575(e) is utterly uninformative anyway. It hardly closes in on the target to know that "relatedness" refers to acts that are related by "purposes, results, participants, victims, . . . methods of commission, *or* [just in case that is not vague enough] *otherwise*." Is the fact that the victims of both predicate acts were women enough? Or that both acts had the purpose of enriching the defendant? Or that the different coparticipants of the defendant in both acts were his co-employees? I doubt that the lower courts will find the Court's instructions much more helpful than telling them to look for a "pattern"—which is what the statute already says.

The Court finds "continuity" more difficult to define precisely. "Continuity," it says, "is both a closed-and open-ended concept, referring either to a closed period of repeated conduct, or to past conduct that by its nature projects into the future with a threat of repetition." I have no idea what this concept of a "closed period of repeated conduct" means. Virtually all allegations of racketeering activity, in both civil and criminal suits, will relate to past periods that are "closed" (unless one expects plaintiff or the prosecutor to establish that the defendant not only committed the crimes he did, but is still committing them), and all of them *must* relate to conduct that is "repeated," because of RICO's multiple-act requirement. I had thought, initially, that the Court was seeking to draw a distinction between, on the one hand, past repeated conduct (multiple racketeering acts) that is "closed-ended" in the sense that, in its totality, it constitutes only one criminal "scheme" or "episode"—which would not fall within RICO unless in its nature (for one or more of the reasons later described by the Court) it threatened future criminal endeavors as well; and, on the other hand, past repeated conduct (multiple racketeering acts) that constitutes several separate schemes—which is alone enough to invoke RICO. But of course that cannot be what it means, since the Court rejects the "multiple-schemes" concept, not merely as the *exclusive* touchstone of RICO liability, but in all its applications, since it "introduc[es] a concept . . . that appears nowhere in the language or legislative history of the act" and is so vague and "amorphous" as to exist only "in the eye of the beholder." Moreover, the Court tells us that predicate acts extending, not over a "substantial period of time," but only over a "few weeks or months and threatening no future criminal conduct" do not satisfy the continuity requirement. Since the Court has rejected the concept of separate criminal "schemes" or "episodes" as a criterion of "threatening future criminal conduct," I think it must be saying that at least a few months of racketeering activity (and who knows how much more?) is generally for free, as far as RICO is concerned. The "closed period" concept is a sort of safe harbor for racketeering activity that does not last *too* long, no matter how many different crimes and different schemes are involved, so long as it does not otherwise "establish a threat of continued racketeering activity." A gang of hoodlums that commits one act of extortion on Monday in New York, a second in Chicago on Tuesday, a third in San Francisco on Wednesday, and so on through an entire week, and then finally and completely disbands, cannot be reached under RICO. I am sure that is not what the statute intends, but I cannot imagine what else the Court's murky discussion can possibly mean.

Of course it cannot be said that the Court's opinion operates only in the direction of letting some obvious racketeers get out of RICO. It also makes it clear that a hitherto dubious category is included, by establishing the rule that the "multiple scheme" test applied by the Court of Appeals here is not only nonexclusive but indeed nonexistent. This is, as far as I can discern, the Court's only substantive contribution to our prior guidance—and it is a contribution that makes it *more* rather than *less* difficult for a potential defendant to know whether his conduct is covered by RICO. Even if he is only involved in a single scheme, he may still be covered if there is present whatever is needed to establish a "threat of continuity." The Court gives us a nonexclusive list of three things that do so. Two of those presumably polar examples seem to me extremely difficult to apply— whether "the predicates can be attributed to a defendant operating as part of a long-term association that exists for criminal purposes," and whether "the predicates are a regular way of conducting defendant's ongoing legitimate business." What is included beyond these examples is vaguer still.

It is, however, unfair to be so critical of the Court's effort, because I would be unable to provide an interpretation of RICO that gives significantly more guidance concerning its application. It is clear to me from the prologue of the statute, which describes a relatively narrow focus upon "organized crime," see Statement of Findings and Purpose, The Organized Crime Control Act of 1970, Pub. L. 91–452, 84 Stat. 922–23, that the word "pattern" in the phrase "pattern of racketeering activity" was meant to import some requirement beyond the mere existence of multiple predicate acts. Thus, when § 1961(5) says that a pattern "requires at least two acts of racketeering activity" it is describing what is needful but not sufficient. (If that were not the case, the concept of "pattern" would have been unnecessary, and the statute could simply have attached liability to "multiple acts of racketeering activity.") But what that something more is, is beyond me. As I have suggested, it is also beyond the Court. Today's opinion has added nothing to improve our prior guidance, which has created a kaleidoscope of circuit positions, except to clarify that RICO may in addition be violated when there is a "threat of continuity." It seems to me this increases rather than removes the vagueness. There is no reason to believe that the Courts of Appeals will be any more unified in the future, than they have in the past, regarding the content of this law.

That situation is bad enough with respect to any statute, but it is intolerable with respect to RICO. For it is not only true, as Justice Marshall commented in Sedima, S.P.R.L. v. Imrex Co., 473 U.S. 479, 501 (1985), that our interpretation of RICO has "quite simply revolutionize[d] private litigation" and "validate[d] the federalization of broad areas of state common law of frauds" so that clarity and predictability in RICO's civil applications are particularly important; but it is also true that RICO, since it has criminal applications as well, must, even in its civil applications, possess the degree of certainty required for criminal laws, FCC v. American Broadcasting Co., 347 U.S. 284, 296 (1954). No constitutional challenge to this law has been raised in the present case, and so that issue is not before us. That the highest Court in the land has been unable to derive from this statute anything more than today's meager guidance bodes ill for the day when that challenge is presented.

However unhelpful its guidance may be, however, I think, the Court is correct in saying that nothing in the statute supports the proposition that predicate acts constituting part of a single scheme (or single episode) can never support a cause of action under RICO. Since the Court of Appeals here rested its decision on the contrary proposition, I concur in the judgment of the Court reversing the decision below.

FURTHER NOTE ON *BEAUFORD v. HELMSLEY*

The *Beauford* case was remanded to the Second Circuit for reconsideration in light of *H.J. Inc.* In Beauford v. Helmsley, 893 F.2d 1433 (2d Cir.1989), that court issued a one-sentence order: "Upon further consideration in light of H.J. Inc. v. Northwestern Bell Telephone Co., 492 U.S. 229 (1989), we adhere to our en banc decision in this case, 865 F.2d 1386 (2d Cir.1989), and remand to the district court for further proceedings in accordance with the en banc decision."

SUBSECTION C: "PARTICIPATE IN THE CONDUCT OF AN ENTERPRISE'S AFFAIRS"

Reves v. Ernst & Young

Supreme Court of the United States, 1993.
507 U.S. 170.

■ JUSTICE BLACKMUN delivered the opinion of the Court.

This case requires us once again to interpret the provisions of the Racketeer Influenced and Corrupt Organizations (RICO) chapter of the Organized Crime Control Act of 1970, Pub.L. 91–452, Title IX, 84 Stat. 941, as amended, 18 U.S.C. §§ 1961–1968 (1988 ed. and Supp.II). Section 1962(c) makes it unlawful "for any person employed by or associated with any enterprise engaged in, or the activities of which affect, interstate or foreign commerce, to conduct or participate, directly or indirectly, in the conduct of such enterprise's affairs through a pattern of racketeering activity...." The question presented is whether one must participate in the operation or management of the enterprise itself to be subject to liability under this provision.

I

The Farmer's Cooperative of Arkansas and Oklahoma, Inc. (the Co–Op), began operating in western Arkansas and eastern Oklahoma in 1946. To raise money for operating expenses, the Co–Op sold promissory notes payable to the holder on demand. Each year, Co–Op members were elected to serve on its board. The board met monthly but delegated actual management of the Co–Op to a general manager. In 1952, the board appointed Jack White as general manager.

In January 1980, White began taking loans from the Co–Op to finance the construction of a gasohol plant by his company, White Flame Fuels, Inc. By the end of 1980, White's debts to the Co–Op totalled approximately $4 million. In September of that year, White and Gene Kuykendall, who served as the accountant for both the Co–Op and White Flame, were indicted for federal tax fraud. At a board meeting on November 12, 1980, White proposed that the Co–Op purchase White Flame. The board agreed. One month later, however, the Co–Op filed a declaratory action against White and White Flame in Arkansas state court alleging that White actually had sold White Flame to the Co–Op in February 1980. The complaint was drafted by White's attorneys and led to a consent decree relieving White of his debts and providing that the Co–Op had owned White Flame since February 15, 1980.

White and Kuykendall were convicted of tax fraud in January 1981. See United States v. White, 671 F.2d 1126 (8th Cir.1982)(affirming their convictions). Harry Erwin, the managing partner of Russell Brown and Company, an Arkansas accounting firm, testified for White, and shortly thereafter the Co–Op retained Russell Brown to perform its 1981 financial audit. Joe Drozal, a partner in the Brown firm, was put in charge of the audit and Joe Cabaniss was selected to assist him. On January 2, 1982, Russell Brown and Company merged with Arthur Young and Company, which later became respondent Ernst & Young.

One of Drozal's first tasks in the audit was to determine White Flame's fixed-asset value. After consulting with White and reviewing White Flame's books (which Kuykendall had prepared), Drozal concluded that the plant's value at the end of 1980 was $4,393,242.66, the figure Kuykendall had employed. Using this figure as a base, Drozal factored in the 1981 construction costs and capitalized expenses and concluded that White Flame's 1981 fixed-asset value was approximately $4.5 million. Drozal then had to determine how that value should be treated for accounting purposes. If the Co–Op had owned White Flame from the beginning of construction in 1979, White Flame's value for accounting purposes would be its fixed-asset value of $4.5 million. If, however, the Co–Op had purchased White Flame from White, White Flame would have to be given its fair market value at the time of purchase, which was somewhere between $444,000 and $1.5 million. If White Flame were valued at less than $1.5 million, the Co–Op was insolvent. Drozal concluded that the Co–Op had owned White Flame from the start and that the plant should be valued at $4.5 million on its books.

On April 22, 1982, Arthur Young presented its 1981 audit report to the Co–Op's board. In that audit's Note 9, Arthur Young expressed doubt whether the investment in White Flame could ever be recovered. Note 9 also observed that White Flame was sustaining operating losses averaging $100,000 per month. See Arthur Young & Co. v. Reves, 937 F.2d 1310, 1318 (8th Cir.1991). Arthur Young did not tell the board of its conclusion that the Co–Op always had owned White Flame or that without that conclusion the Co–Op was insolvent.

On May 27, the Co–Op held its 1982 annual meeting. At that meeting, the Co–Op, through Harry C. Erwin, a partner in Arthur Young, distributed to the members condensed financial statements. These included White Flame's $4.5 million asset value among its total assets but omitted the information contained in the audit's Note 9. Cabaniss was also present. Erwin saw the condensed financial statement for the first time when he arrived at the meeting. In a 5–minute presentation, he told his audience that the statements were condensed and that copies of the full audit were available at the Co–Op's office. In response to questions, Erwin explained that the Co–Op owned White Flame and that the plant had incurred approximately $1.2 million in losses but he revealed no other information relevant to the Co–Op's true financial health.

The Co–Op hired Arthur Young also to perform its 1982 audit. The 1982 report, presented to the board on March 7, 1983, was similar to the 1981 report and restated (this time in its Note 8) Arthur Young's doubt whether the investment in White Flame was recoverable. The gasohol plant again was valued at approximately $4.5 million and was responsible for the Co–Op's showing a positive net worth. The condensed financial statement distributed at the annual meeting on March 24, 1983, omitted the information in Note 8. This time, Arthur Young reviewed the condensed statement in advance but did not act to remove its name from the statement. Cabaniss, in a 3–minute presentation at the meeting, gave the financial report. He informed the members that the full audit was available at the Co–Op's office but did not tell them about Note 8 or that the Co–Op was in financial difficulty if White Flame were written down to its fair market value.

In February 1984, the Co–Op experienced a slight run on its demand notes. On February 23, when it was unable to secure further financing, the Co–Op filed for bankruptcy. As a result, the demand notes were frozen in the bankruptcy estate and were no longer redeemable at will by the noteholders.

II

On February 14, 1985, the trustee in bankruptcy filed suit [under both state and federal securities laws and RICO] against 40 individuals and entities, including Arthur Young, on behalf of the Co–Op and certain noteholders. The District Court certified a class of noteholders, petitioners here, consisting of persons who had purchased demand notes between February 15, 1980, and February 23, 1984. Petitioners settled with all defendants except Arthur Young. The District Court . . . granted summary judgment in favor of Arthur Young on the RICO claim. The District Court applied the test established by the Eighth Circuit in Bennett v. Berg, 710 F.2d 1361, 1364 (1983)(en banc), that § 1962(c) requires "some participation in the operation or management of the enterprise itself." The court ruled: "Plaintiffs have failed to show anything more than that the accountants reviewed a series of completed transactions, and certified the Co–Op's records as fairly portraying its financial status as of a date three or four months preceding the meetings of the directors and the shareholders at which they presented their reports. We do not hesitate to declare that such activities fail to satisfy the degree of management required by *Bennett v. Berg*."

The case went to trial on the state and federal securities fraud claims. The jury found that Arthur Young had committed both state and federal securities fraud and awarded approximately $6.1 million in damages. The Court of Appeals reversed, concluding that the demand notes were not securities under federal or state law. See Arthur Young & Co. v. Reves, 856 F.2d 52, 55 (1988). On writ of certiorari, this Court ruled that the notes were securities within the meaning of § 3(a)(10) of the Securities Exchange Act of 1934, 48 Stat. 882, as amended, 15 U.S.C. § 78c(a)(10). Reves v. Ernst & Young, 494 U.S. 56, 70 (1990).

On remand, the Court of Appeals affirmed the judgment of the District Court in all major respects except the damages award, which it reversed and remanded for a new trial. The only part of the Court of Appeals' decision that is at issue here is its affirmance of summary judgment in favor of Arthur Young on the RICO claim. Like the District Court, the Court of Appeals applied the "operation or management" test articulated in *Bennett v. Berg* and held that Arthur Young's conduct did not "rise to the level of participation in the management or operation of the Co-op." The Court of Appeals for the District of Columbia Circuit also has adopted an "operation or management" test. See Yellow Bus Lines, Inc. v. Drivers, Chauffeurs & Helpers Local Union 639, 913 F.2d 948, 954 (1990)(en banc). We granted certiorari to resolve the conflict between these cases and Bank of America National Trust & Savings Assn. v. Touche Ross & Co., 782 F.2d 966, 970 (11th Cir.1986)(rejecting requirement that a defendant participate in the operation or management of an enterprise).

III

"In determining the scope of a statute, we look first to its language. If the statutory language is unambiguous, in the absence of a clearly expressed legislative intent to the contrary, that language must ordinarily be regarded as conclusive." United States v. Turkette, 452 U.S. 576, 580 (1981). Section 1962(c) makes it unlawful "for any person employed by or associated with any enterprise . . . to conduct or participate, directly or indirectly, in the conduct of such enterprise's affairs through a pattern of racketeering activity. . . ."

The narrow question in this case is the meaning of the phrase "to conduct or participate, directly or indirectly, in the conduct of such enterprise's affairs." The word "conduct" is used twice, and it seems reasonable to give each use a similar construction. See Sorenson v. Secretary of the Treasury, 475 U.S. 851, 860 (1986). As a verb, "conduct" means to lead, run, manage, or direct. Webster's Third New International Dictionary 474 (1976). Petitioners urge us to read "conduct" as "carry on," so that almost any involvement in the affairs of an enterprise would satisfy the "conduct or participate" requirement. But context is important, and in the context of the phrase "to conduct ... [an] enterprise's affairs," the word indicates some degree of direction.[3]

The dissent agrees that, when "conduct" is used as a verb, "it is plausible to find in it a suggestion of control." The dissent prefers to focus on "conduct" as a noun, as in the phrase "participate, directly or indirectly, in the conduct of [an] enterprise's affairs." But unless one reads "conduct" to include an element of direction when used as a noun in this phrase, the word becomes superfluous. Congress could easily have written "participate, directly or indirectly, in [an] enterprise's affairs," but it chose to repeat the word "conduct." We conclude, therefore, that as both a noun and a verb in this subsection "conduct" requires an element of direction.

The more difficult question is what to make of the word "participate." This Court previously has characterized this word as a "ter[m] ... of breadth." Russello v. United States, 464 U.S. 16, 21–22 (1983). Petitioners argue that Congress used "participate" as a synonym for "aid and abet." That would be a term of breadth indeed, for "aid and abet" "comprehends all assistance rendered by words, acts, encouragement, support, or presence." Black's Law Dictionary 68 (6th ed. 1990). But within the context of § 1962(c), "participate" appears to have a narrower meaning. We may mark the limits of what the term might mean by looking again at what Congress did not say. On the one hand, "to participate ... in the conduct of ... affairs" must be broader than "to conduct affairs" or the "participate" phrase would be superfluous. On the other hand, as we already have noted, "to participate ... in the conduct of ... affairs" must be narrower than "to participate in affairs" or Congress' repetition of the word "conduct" would serve no purpose. It seems that Congress chose a middle ground, consistent with a common understanding of the word "participate"—"to take part in." Webster's Third New International Dictionary 1646 (1976).

Once we understand the word "conduct" to require some degree of direction and the word "participate" to require some part in that direction,

---

[3] The United States calls our attention to the use of the word "conduct" in 18 U.S.C. § 1955(a), which penalizes anyone who "conducts, finances, manages, supervises, directs, or owns all or part of an illegal gambling business." This Court previously has noted that the Courts of Appeals have interpreted this statute to proscribe "any degree of participation in an illegal gambling business, except participation as a mere bettor." Sanabria v. United States, 437 U.S. 54, 70–71, n. 26 (1978). We may assume, however, that "conducts" has been given a broad reading in this context to distinguish it from "manages, supervises, [or] directs."

the meaning of § 1962(c) comes into focus. In order to "participate, directly or indirectly, in the conduct of such enterprise's affairs," one must have some part in directing those affairs. Of course, the word "participate" makes clear that RICO liability is not limited to those with primary responsibility for the enterprise's affairs, just as the phrase "directly or indirectly" makes clear that RICO liability is not limited to those with a formal position in the enterprise,[4] but some part in directing the enterprise's affairs is required. The "operation or management" test expresses this requirement in a formulation that is easy to apply.

IV

A

This test finds further support in the legislative history of § 1962. The basic structure of § 1962 took shape in the spring of 1969. On March 20 of that year, Senator Hruska introduced S. 1623, 91st Cong., 1st Sess., which combined his previous legislative proposals. See Gerard E. Lynch, RICO: The Crime of Being a Criminal, Parts I & II, 87 Colum.L.Rev. 661, 676 (1987); G. Robert Blakey & Brian Gettings, Racketeer Influenced and Corrupt Organizations (RICO): Basic Concepts—Criminal and Civil Remedies, 53 Temp.L.Q. 1009, 1017 (1980). S. 1623 was titled the "Criminal Activities Profits Act" and was directed solely at the investment of proceeds derived from criminal activity.[5] It was § 2(a) of this bill that ultimately became § 1962(a).

On April 18, Senators McClellan and Hruska introduced S. 1861, 91st Cong., 1st Sess., which recast S. 1623 and added provisions that became §§ 1962(b) and (c).[6] See G. Robert Blakey, The RICO Civil Fraud Action

---

[4] For these reasons, we disagree with the suggestion of the Court of Appeals for the District of Columbia Circuit that § 1962(c) requires "significant control over or within an enterprise." Yellow Bus Lines, Inc. v. Drivers, Chauffeurs & Helpers Local Union 639, 913 F.2d 948, 954 (1990)(en banc).

[5] S. 1623 provided in relevant part: "SEC. 2. (a) Whoever, being a person who has received any income derived directly or indirectly from any criminal activity in which such person has participated as a principal within the meaning of § 2, title 18, United States Code applies any part of such income or the proceeds of any such income to the acquisition by or on behalf of such person of legal title to or any beneficial interest in any of the assets, liabilities, or capital of any business enterprise which is engaged in, or the activities of which affect, interstate or foreign commerce shall be guilty of a felony and shall be fined not more than $10,000, or imprisoned not more than ten years, or both."

[6] S. 1861 provided in relevant part: "§ 1962. Prohibited racketeering activities (a) It shall be unlawful for any person who has knowingly received any income derived, directly or indirectly, from a pattern by [sic] racketeering activity to use or invest, directly or indirectly, any part of such income, or the proceeds of such income, in acquisition of any interest in, or the establishment or operation of, any enterprise which is engaged in, or the activities of which affect, interstate or foreign commerce. (b) It shall be unlawful for any person to acquire or maintain, directly or indirectly, any interest in or control of any enterprise which is engaged in, or the activities of which affect, interstate or foreign commerce, through a pattern of racketeering activity or through collection of unlawful debt. (c) It shall be unlawful for any person employed by or associated with any enterprise engaged in, or the activities of which affect, interstate or foreign commerce, to conduct or participate, directly or indirectly, in the con-

in Context: Reflections on *Bennett v. Berg*, 58 Notre Dame L.Rev. 237, 264, n. 76 (1982). The first line of S. 1861 reflected its expanded purpose: "to prohibit the infiltration or management of legitimate organizations by racketeering activity or the proceeds of racketeering activity."

On June 3, Assistant Attorney General Will Wilson presented the views of the Department of Justice on a number of bills relating to organized crime, including S. 1623 and S. 1861, to the Subcommittee on Criminal Laws and Procedures of the Senate Committee on the Judiciary. Wilson criticized S. 1623 on the ground that "it is too narrow in that it merely prohibits the investment of prohibited funds in a business, but fails to prohibit the control or operation of such a business by means of prohibited racketeering activities." Measures Related to Organized Crime: Hearings before the Subcommittee on Criminal Laws and Procedures of the Senate Committee on the Judiciary, 91st Cong., 1st Sess., 387 (1969). He praised S. 1861 because the "criminal provisions of the bill contained in Section 1962 are broad enough to cover most of the methods by which ownership, control and operation of business concerns are acquired." Ibid. See Blakey, supra, at 258, n. 59.

With alterations not relevant here, S. 1861 became Title IX of S. 30. The House and Senate Reports that accompanied S. 30 described the three-part structure of § 1962: "(1) making unlawful the receipt or use of income from 'racketeering activity' or its proceeds by a principal in commission of the activity to acquire an interest in or establish an enterprise engaged in interstate commerce; (2) prohibiting the acquisition of any enterprise engaged in interstate commerce through a 'pattern' of 'racketeering activity;' and (3) proscribing the operation of any enterprise engaged in interstate commerce through a 'pattern' of 'racketeering activity.' " H.R.Rep. No. 91–1549, p. 35 (1970); S.Rep. No. 91–617, p. 34 (1969). In their comments on the floor, members of Congress consistently referred to subsection (c) as prohibiting the operation of an enterprise through a pattern of racketeering activity and to subsections (a) and (b) as prohibiting the acquisition of an enterprise.[7] Representative Cellar, who was Chairman of the House Judiciary Committee that voted RICO out in 1970, described § 1962(c) as proscribing the "conduct of the affairs of a business by a person acting in a managerial capacity, through racketeering activity." 116 Cong.Rec. 35196 (1970).

Of course, the fact that members of Congress understood § 1962(c) to prohibit the operation or management of an enterprise through a pattern of

---

duct of such enterprise's affairs through a pattern of racketeering activity."

[7] See, e.g., 116 Cong.Rec. 607 (1970)(remarks of Sen. Byrd of West Virginia)("to acquire an interest in businesses . . ., or to acquire or operate such businesses by racketeering methods"); id., at 36294 (remarks of Sen. McClellan)("to acquire an interest in a business . . ., to use racketeering activities as a means of acquiring such a business, or to operate such a business by racketeering methods"); id., at 36296 (remarks of Sen. Dole)("using the proceeds of racketeering activity to acquire an interest in businesses engaged in interstate commerce, or to acquire or operate such businesses by racketeering methods"); id., at 35227 (remarks of Rep. Steiger)("the use of specified racketeering methods to acquire or operate commercial organizations").

racketeering activity does not necessarily mean that they understood § 1962(c) to be limited to the operation or management of an enterprise. Cf. *Turkette*, 452 U.S., at 591 (references to the infiltration of legitimate organizations do not "requir[e] the negative inference that [RICO] did not reach the activities of enterprises organized and existing for criminal purposes"). It is clear from other remarks, however, that Congress did not intend RICO to extend beyond the acquisition or operation of an enterprise. While S. 30 was being considered, critics of the bill raised concerns that racketeering activity was defined so broadly that RICO would reach many crimes not necessarily typical of organized crime. See 116 Cong.Rec. 18912–14, 18939–40 (1970)(remarks of Sen. McClellan). Senator McClellan reassured the bill's critics that the critical limitation was not to be found in § 1961(1)'s list of predicate crimes but in the statute's other requirements, including those of § 1962: "The danger that commission of such offenses by other individuals would subject them to proceedings under title IX [RICO] is even smaller than any such danger under title III of the 1968 [Safe Streets] [A]ct, since commission of a crime listed under title IX provides only one element of title IX's prohibitions. Unless an individual not only commits such a crime but engages in a pattern of such violations, and uses that pattern to obtain or operate an interest in an interstate business, he is not made subject to proceedings under title IX." 116 Cong.Rec., at 18940.

Thus, the legislative history confirms what we have already deduced from the language of § 1962(c)—that one is not liable under that provision unless one has participated in the operation or management of the enterprise itself.

B

RICO's "liberal construction" clause does not require rejection of the "operation or management" test. Congress directed, by § 904(a) of Pub.L. 91–452, 84 Stat. 947, that the "provisions of this title shall be liberally construed to effectuate its remedial purposes." This clause obviously seeks to ensure that Congress' intent is not frustrated by an overly narrow reading of the statute, but it is not an invitation to apply RICO to new purposes that Congress never intended. Nor does the clause help us to determine what purposes Congress had in mind. Those must be gleaned from the statute through the normal means of interpretation. The clause " 'only serves as an aid for resolving an ambiguity; it is not to be used to beget one.' " Sedima, S.P.R.L. v. Imrex Co., 473 U.S. 479, 492, n. 10 (1985). In this case it is clear that Congress did not intend to extend RICO liability under § 1962(c) beyond those who participate in the operation or management of an enterprise through a pattern of racketeering activity.[8]

---

[8] Because the meaning of the statute is clear from its language and legislative history, we have no occasion to consider the application of the rule of lenity. We note, however, that the rule of lenity would also favor the narrower "operation or management" test that we adopt.

V

Petitioners argue that the "operation or management" test is flawed because liability under § 1962(c) is not limited to upper management but may extend to "any person employed by or associated with [the] enterprise." We agree that liability under § 1962(c) is not limited to upper management, but we disagree that the "operation or management" test is inconsistent with this proposition. An enterprise is "operated" not just by upper management but also by lower-rung participants in the enterprise who are under the direction of upper management.[9] An enterprise also might be "operated" or "managed" by others "associated with" the enterprise who exert control over it as, for example, by bribery.

The United States also argues that the "operation or management" test is not consistent with § 1962(c) because it limits the liability of "outsiders" who have no official position within the enterprise. The United States correctly points out that RICO's major purpose was to attack the "infiltration of organized crime and racketeering into legitimate organizations," S.Rep. No. 91–617, at 76, but its argument fails on several counts. First, it ignores the fact that § 1962 has four subsections. Infiltration of legitimate organizations by "outsiders" is clearly addressed in subsections (a) and (b), and the "operation or management" test that applies under subsection (c) in no way limits the application of subsections (a) and (b) to "outsiders."[10] Second, § 1962(c) is limited to persons "employed by or associated with" an enterprise, suggesting a more limited reach than subsections (a) and (b), which do not contain such a restriction. Third, § 1962(c) cannot be interpreted to reach complete "outsiders" because liability depends on showing that the defendants conducted or participated in the conduct of the "enterprise's affairs," not just their own affairs. Of course, "outsiders" may be liable under § 1962(c) if they are "associated with" an enterprise and participate in the conduct of its affairs—that is, participate in the operation or management of the enterprise itself—but it would be consistent with neither the language nor the legislative history of § 1962(c) to interpret it as broadly as petitioners and the United States urge.

In sum, we hold that "to conduct or participate, directly or indirectly, in the conduct of such enterprise's affairs," § 1962(c), one must participate in the operation or management of the enterprise itself.

VI

Both the District Court and the Court of Appeals applied the standard we adopt today to the facts of this case, and both found that respondent was entitled to summary judgment. Neither petitioners nor the United

---

[9] At oral argument, there was some discussion about whether low-level employees could be considered to have participated in the conduct of an enterprise's affairs. We need not decide in this case how far § 1962(c) extends down the ladder of operation because it is clear that Arthur Young was not acting under the direction of the Co–Op's officers or board.

[10] Subsection (d) makes it unlawful to conspire to violate any of the other three subsections.

States have argued that these courts misapplied the "operation or management" test. The dissent argues that by creating the Co–Op's financial statements Arthur Young participated in the management of the Co–Op because " 'financial statements are management's responsibility' " (quoting 1 CCH AICPA Professional Standards, SAS No. 1, § 110.02 (1982)). Although the professional standards adopted by the accounting profession may be relevant, they do not define what constitutes management of an enterprise for the purposes of § 1962(c).

In this case, it is undisputed that Arthur Young relied upon existing Co–Op records in preparing the 1981 and 1982 audit reports. The AICPA's professional standards state that an auditor may draft financial statements in whole or in part based on information from management's accounting system. See 1 CCH AICPA Professional Standards, SAS No. 1, § 110.02 (1982). It is also undisputed that Arthur Young's audit reports revealed to the Co–Op's board that the value of the gasohol plant had been calculated based on the Co–Op's investment in the plant. Thus, we only could conclude that Arthur Young participated in the operation or management of the Co–Op itself if Arthur Young's failure to tell the Co–Op's board that the plant should have been given its fair market value constituted such participation. We think that Arthur Young's failure in this respect is not sufficient to give rise to liability under § 1962(c).

The judgment of the Court of Appeals is affirmed.

It is so ordered.

■ JUSTICE SOUTER, with whom JUSTICE WHITE joins, dissenting.

In the word "conduct," the Court today finds a clear congressional mandate to limit RICO liability under 18 U.S.C. § 1962(c) to participants in the "operation or management" of a RICO enterprise. What strikes the Court as clear, however, looks at the very least hazy to me, and I accordingly find the statute's "liberal construction" provision not irrelevant, but dispositive. But even if I were to assume, with the majority, that the word "conduct" clearly imports some degree of direction or control into § 1962(c), I would have to say that the majority misapplies its own "operation or management" test to the facts presented here. I therefore respectfully dissent.

The word "conduct" occurs twice in § 1962(c), first as a verb, then as a noun. "It shall be unlawful for any person employed by or associated with any enterprise engaged in, or the activities of which affect, interstate or foreign commerce, to conduct or participate, directly or indirectly, in the conduct of such enterprise's affairs through a pattern of racketeering activity or collection of unlawful debt." 18 U.S.C. § 1962(c). Although the Court is surely correct that the cognates should receive consistent readings, and correct again that "context is important" in coming to understand the sense of the terms intended by Congress, the majority goes astray in quoting only the verb form of "conduct" in its statement of the context for divining a meaning that must fit the noun usage as well. Thus, the majority reaches its pivotal conclusion that "in the context of the phrase 'to conduct ... [an] enterprise's affairs,' the word indicates some degree of direction." To be sure, if the statutory setting is so abbreviated as to limit consideration to the word as a verb, it is plausible to find in it a suggestion of control, as in the phrase "to conduct an orchestra." (Even so, the suggestion is less than emphatic, since even when "conduct" is used as a verb, "[t]he notion of direction or leadership is often obscured or lost; e.g. an investigation is conducted by all those who take part in it." 3 Oxford English Dictionary 691 (2d ed. 1989).)

In any event, the context is not so limited, and several features of the full subsection at issue support a more inclusive construction of "conduct." The term, when used as a noun, is defined by the majority's chosen dictionary as, for example, "carrying forward" or "carrying out," Webster's Third New International Dictionary 473 (1976), phrases without any implication of direction or control. The suggestion of control is diminished further by the fact that § 1962(c) covers not just those "employed by" an enterprise, but those merely "associated with" it, as well. And associates (like employees) are prohibited not merely from conducting the affairs of an enterprise through a pattern of racketeering, not merely from participating directly in such unlawful conduct, but even from indirect participation in the conduct of an enterprise's affairs in such a manner. The very breadth of this prohibition renders the majority's reading of "conduct" rather awkward, for it is hard to imagine how the "operation or management" test would leave the statute with the capacity to reach the indirect participation of someone merely associated with an enterprise. I think, then, that this contextual examination shows "conduct" to have a long arm, unlimited by any requirement to prove that the activity includes an element of direction. But at the very least, the full context is enough to defeat the majority's conviction that the more restrictive interpretation of the word "conduct" is clearly the one intended.[1]

What, then, if we call it a tie on the contextual analysis? The answer is that Congress has given courts faced with uncertain meaning a clear tiebreaker in RICO's "liberal construction" clause, which directs that the "provisions of this title shall be liberally construed to effectuate its remedial purposes." Pub.L. 91–452, § 904(a), 84 Stat. 947. We have relied before on this "express admonition" to read RICO provisions broadly, see Sedima, S.P.R.L. v. Imrex Co., 473 U.S. 479, 497–98 (1985), and in this instance, the "liberal construction" clause plays its intended part, directing

---

[1] The Court attempts to shore up its interpretation with an examination of relevant legislative materials. The legislative history demonstrates only that when members of Congress needed a shorthand method of referring to § 1962(c), they spoke of prohibiting "the operation" of an enterprise through a pattern of racketeering activity. As Arthur Young points out, "operation" is essentially interchangeable with "conduct"; each term can include a sense of direction, but each is also definable as "carrying on" or "carrying out." There is no indication that the congressional shorthand was meant to attend to the statutory nuance at issue here. As the Court concedes, "[T]he fact that members of Congress understood § 1962(c) to prohibit the operation or management of an enterprise through a pattern of racketeering activity does not necessarily mean that they understood § 1962(c) to be limited to the operation or management of an enterprise."

us to recognize the more inclusive definition of the word "conduct," free of any restricting element of direction or control.[2] Because the Court of Appeals employed a narrower reading, I would reverse.

Even if I were to adopt the majority's view of § 1962(c), however, I still could not join the judgment, which seems to me unsupportable under the very "operation or management" test the Court announces. If Arthur Young had confined itself in this case to the role traditionally performed by an outside auditor, I could agree with the majority that Arthur Young took no part in the management or operation of the Co-op. But the record on summary judgment, viewed most favorably to Reves,[3] shows that Arthur Young created the very financial statements it was hired, and purported, to audit. Most importantly, Reves adduced evidence that Arthur Young took on management responsibilities by deciding, in the first instance, what value to assign to the Co-op's most important fixed asset, the White Flame gasohol plant, and Arthur Young itself conceded below that the alleged activity went beyond traditional auditing. Because I find, then, that even under the majority's "operation or management" test the Court of Appeals erroneously affirmed the summary judgment for Arthur Young, I would (again) reverse.

For our purposes, the line between managing and auditing is fairly clear. In describing the "respective responsibilities of management and auditor," Arthur Young points to the Code of Professional Conduct developed by the American Institute of Certified Public Accountants (AICPA). This auditors' code points up management's ultimate responsibility for the content of financial statements: "The financial statements are management's responsibility. The auditor's responsibility is to express an opinion on the financial statements. Management is responsible for adopting sound accounting policies and for establishing and maintaining an internal control structure that will, among other things, record, process, summarize, and report financial data that is consistent with management's assertions embodied in the financial statements.... The independent auditor may make suggestions about the form or content of the financial statements or draft them, in whole or in part, based on information from management's accounting system." 1 CCH AICPA Professional Standards, SAS No. 1, § 110.02 (1982). In short, management chooses the assertions to appear in financial statements; the auditor "simply expresses an opinion on the client's financial statements." Brief for Respondent 30. These standards leave no doubt that an accountant can in no sense independently audit financial records when he has selected their substance himself. See In re

[2] The majority claims that without an element of direction, the word "conduct," when it appears as a noun, becomes superfluous. Given the redundant language Congress has chosen for § 1962(c), however, any consistent reading of "conduct" will tend to make one of its two appearances superfluous.

[3] In ruling on a motion for summary judgment, "[t]he evidence of the nonmovant is to be believed, and all justifiable inferences are to be drawn in his favor." Anderson v. Liberty Lobby, Inc., 477 U.S. 242, 255 (1986). My description of the facts, based primarily on the District Court's view of the evidence at summary judgment, conforms to this standard.

Thomas P. Reynolds Securities, Ltd., Exchange Act Release No. 29689, 1991 SEC Lexis 1855, *6–*7 (Sept. 16, 1991)("A company may, of course, rely on an outside firm to prepare its books of account and financial statements. However, once an accounting firm performs those functions, it has become identified with management and may not perform an audit").

The evidence on summary judgment, read favorably to Reves, indicates that Arthur Young did indeed step out of its auditing shoes and into those of management, in creating the financial record on which the Co-op's solvency was erroneously predicated. The Co-op's 1980 financial statement gave no fixed asset value for the White Flame gasohol plant (although the statement did say that the Co-op had advanced the plant $4.1 million during 1980), and there is no indication that a valuation statement occurred anywhere else in the Co-op's records at that time. When Arthur Young accepted the job of preparing the Co-op's financial statement for 1981, the value to be given the plant was a matter of obvious moment. Instead of declaring the plant's valuation to be the Co-op's responsibility, and instead even of turning to management for more reliable information about the plant's value, Arthur Young basically set out to answer its own questions and to come up with its own figure for White Flame's fixed asset value. In doing so, it repeatedly made choices calling for the exercise of a judgment that belonged to the Co-op's management in the first instance.

Arthur Young realized it could not rely on White Flame's 1980 financial statement, which had been prepared by a convicted felon (who also happened to be the Co-op's former accountant),[4] see Arthur Young & Co. v. Reves, 937 F.2d 1310, 1316–17 (8th Cir.1991), and an internal memo that appears in the record shows that Arthur Young had a number of serious questions about White Flame's cost figures for the plant. See App. in No. 87–1726 (8th Cir.). Nonetheless, Arthur Young "essentially invented" a cost figure that matched, to the penny, the phoney figure that Kuykendall, White Flame's convicted accountant, had created. App. 138–140. With this "invented" cost figure in hand, Arthur Young then proceeded to decide, again without consulting management, when the Co-op had acquired White Flame. Although the Co-op's 1980 financial statement indicated an acquisition of White Flame in February 1980, as did a local court decree, Arthur Young "adopted a blatant fiction—that the Co-op [had] owned the entire plant at its inception in May, 1979—in order to justify carrying the asset on [the Co-op's] books at its total cost, as if the Co-op had built it from scratch." App. 137. Apparently, the idea that the Co-op had owned the gasohol plant since 1979 was reflected nowhere in the Co-op's books, and Arthur Young was solely responsible for the Co-op's

---

[4] Gene Kuykendall, the Co-op's previous "independent auditor," was involved in keeping the Co-op's books in addition to preparing and "auditing" financial statements for White Flame. See Arthur Young & Co. v. Reves, 937 F.2d 1310, 1316–17 (8th Cir. 1991); United States v. White, 671 F.2d 1126 (8th Cir.1982); Robertson v. White, 633 F.Supp. 954 (W.D.Ark.1986). Thus, the Co-

decision to treat the transaction in this manner.[5]

Relying on this fiction, the unreality of which it never shared with the Co-op's Board of Directors,[6] let alone the membership, Arthur Young prepared the Co-op's 1981 financial statement and listed a fixed asset value of more than $4.5 million for the gasohol plant. Arthur Young listed a similar value for White Flame in the Co-op's financial statement for 1982. By these actions, Arthur Young took on management responsibilities, for it thereby made assertions about the fixed asset value of White Flame that were derived, not from information or any figure provided by the Co-op's management, but from its own financial analysis.

Thus, the District Court, after reviewing this evidence, concluded that petitioners could show from the record that Arthur Young had "created the Co-op's financial statements." App. 199. The court also took note of evidence supporting petitioners' allegation that Arthur Young had "participated in the creation of condensed financial statements" that were handed out each year at the annual meeting of the Co-op. Ibid. Before the Court of Appeals, although Arthur Young disputed petitioners' claim that it had been functioning as the Co-op's de facto chief financial officer, it did not dispute the District Court's conclusion that Reves had presented evidence showing that Arthur Young had created the Co-op's financial statements and had participated in the creation of condensed financial statements.

---

op had a history of relying on "outside" auditors for such services.

[5] If Arthur Young had decided otherwise, the value of White Flame on the Co-op's books would have been its fair market value at the time of sale—three to four million dollars less. The "blatant fiction" created by Arthur Young maintained the Co-op's appearance of solvency and made Jack White's management "look better." App. 137–38. The District Court noted some plausible motives for Arthur Young's conduct, including a desire to keep the Co-op's business and the accountants' need "to cover themselves for having testified on behalf of White and Kuykendall in [their] 1981 criminal trial." App. 136. The majority asserts, as an "undisputed" fact, "that Arthur Young relied upon existing Co-op records in preparing the 1981 and 1982 audit reports." In fact, however, the District Court found that Reves had presented evidence sufficient to show that Arthur Young "essentially invented" a cost figure for White Flame (after examining White Flame records created by Kuykendall). See App. 138–40. Since the Co-op's 1980 financial statement indicated that the Co-op had advanced White Flame only $4.1 million through the end of 1980, Arthur Young could not have relied on the Co-op's records in

concluding that the plant's value was nearly $4.4 million at the end of 1980. See 937 F.2d, at 1317. The District Court also found sufficient evidence in the record to support the conclusion that Arthur Young had created the "blatant fiction" that the Co-op had owned White Flame from its inception, despite overwhelming evidence to the contrary in the Co-op's records. See App. 137–38; see also 937 F.2d, at 1317 ("In concluding that the Co-op had always owned White Flame, [Arthur Young] ignored a great deal of information suggesting exactly the opposite"). The evidence indicates that it was creative accounting, not reliance on the Co-op's books, that led Arthur Young to treat the Co-op as the plant's owner from the time of its construction in 1979 (a conclusion necessary to support Arthur Young's decision to value the plant at total cost). Not even the decree procured in the friendly lawsuit engineered by White and his lawyers treated the Co-op as building the plant, or as owning it before February 1980.

[6] See 937 F.2d, at 1318. In fact, Note 9 to the 1981 financial statement continued to indicate that the Co-op "acquired legal ownership" of White Flame in February 1980. App. in No. 87–1726 (8th Cir.).

Instead, Arthur Young argued that "[e]ven if, as here, the alleged activity goes beyond traditional auditing, it was neither an integral part of the management of the Co-op's affairs nor part of a dominant, active ownership or managerial role."

It was only by ignoring these crucial concessions, and the evidence that obviously prompted them, that the Court of Appeals could describe Arthur Young's involvement with the Co-op as "limited to the audits, meetings with the Board of Directors to explain the audits, and presentations at the annual meetings." 937 F.2d, at 1324. And only then could the court have ruled that, "as a matter of law, Arthur Young's involvement with the Co-op did not rise to the level required for a RICO violation," which it described (quoting Bennett v. Berg, 710 F.2d 1361 (8th Cir.1983)) as requiring only "some participation in the operation or management of the enterprise itself." Ibid. (internal quotes omitted).

But petitioners' evidence and respondent's concessions of activity going beyond outside auditing can neither be ignored nor declared irrelevant. As the Court explains today, " 'outsiders' may be liable under § 1962(c) if they are 'associated with' an enterprise and participate in the conduct of its affairs—that is, participate in the operation or management of the enterprise itself. . . ." Thus, the question here is whether Arthur Young, which was "associated with" the Co-op, "participated" in the Co-op's operation or management. As the Court has noted, "participate" should be read broadly in this context, Russello v. United States, 464 U.S. 16, 21–22 (1983), since Congress has provided that even "indirect" participation will suffice. Cf. Sedima, S.P.R.L. v. Imrex Co., 473 U.S., at 497–98 ("Congress' self-consciously expansive language" supports the conclusion that "RICO is to be read broadly").

The evidence petitioners presented in opposing the motion for summary judgment demonstrated Arthur Young's "participation" in this broad sense. By assuming the authority to make key decisions in stating the Co-op's own valuation of its major fixed asset, and by creating financial statements that were the responsibility of the Co-op's management, Arthur Young crossed the line separating "outside" auditors from "inside" financial managers. Because the majority, like the Court of Appeals, affirms the grant of summary judgment in spite of this evidence, I believe that it misapplies its own "operation or management" test, and I therefore respectfully dissent.

SUBSECTION D: PROXIMATE CAUSATION

Holmes v. Securities Investor Protection Corp.

Supreme Court of the United States, 1992.
503 U.S. 258.

■ JUSTICE SOUTER delivered the opinion of the Court.

Respondent Securities Investor Protection Corporation (SIPC) alleges that petitioner Robert G. Holmes, Jr., conspired in a stock-manipulation scheme that disabled two broker-dealers from meeting obligations to customers, thus triggering SIPC's statutory duty to advance funds to reimburse the customers. The issue is whether SIPC can recover from Holmes under the Racketeer Influenced and Corrupt Organizations Act (RICO), 84 Stat. 941, as amended, 18 U.S.C. §§ 1961–1968 (1988 ed. and Supp. I). We hold that it cannot.

I

A

In 1970, Congress enacted the Securities Investor Protection Act (SIPA), 84 Stat. 1636, as amended, 15 U.S.C. §§ 78aaa–78lll, which authorized the formation of SIPC, a private nonprofit corporation, § 78ccc(a)(1), of which most broker-dealers registered under § 15(b) of the Securities Exchange Act of 1934, § 78o(b), are required to be "members." § 78ccc(a)(2)(A). Whenever SIPC determines that a member "has failed or is in danger of failing to meet its obligations to customers," and finds certain other statutory conditions satisfied, it may ask for a "protective decree" in federal district court. § 78eee(a)(3). Once a court finds grounds for granting such a petition, § 78eee(b)(1), it must appoint a trustee charged with liquidating the member's business, § 78eee(b)(3).

After returning all securities registered in specific customers' names, §§ 78fff–2(c)(2); 78fff(a)(1)(A); 78lll (3), the trustee must pool securities not so registered together with cash found in customers' accounts and divide this pool ratably to satisfy customers' claims, § 78fff–2(b); § 78fff(a)(1)(B). To the extent the pool of customer property is inadequate, SIPC must advance up to $500,000 per customer to the trustee for use in satisfying those claims. § 78fff–3(a).[3]

B

On July 24, 1981, SIPC sought a decree from the United States District Court for the Southern District of Florida to protect the customers of First State Securities Corporation (FSSC), a broker-dealer and SIPC member. Three days later, it petitioned the United States District Court for the Central District of California, seeking to protect the customers of Joseph Sebag, Inc. (Sebag), also a broker-dealer and SIPC member. Each court issued the requested decree and appointed a trustee, who proceeded to liquidate the broker-dealer.

Two years later, SIPC and the two trustees brought this suit in the United States District Court for the Central District of California, accusing some 75 defendants of conspiracy in a fraudulent scheme leading to the demise of FSSC and Sebag. Insofar as they are relevant here, the allega-

---

[3] To cover these advances, SIPA provides for the establishment of a SIPC Fund. § 78ddd(a)(1). SIPC may replenish the fund from time to time by levying assessments, § 78ddd(c)(2), which members are legally obligated to pay, § 78jjj(a).

tions were that, from 1964 through July 1981, the defendants manipulated stock of six companies by making unduly optimistic statements about their prospects and by continually selling small numbers of shares to create the appearance of a liquid market; that the broker-dealers bought substantial amounts of the stock with their own funds; that the market's perception of the fraud in July 1981 sent the stocks plummeting; that this decline caused the broker-dealers' financial difficulties resulting in their eventual liquidation and SIPC's advance of nearly $13 million to cover their customers' claims.   The complaint described Holmes' participation in the scheme by alleging that he made false statements about the prospects of one of the six companies, Aero Systems, Inc., of which he was an officer, director, and major shareholder; and that over an extended period he sold small amounts of stock in one of the other six companies, the Bunnington Corporation, to simulate a liquid market.   The conspirators were said to have violated § 10(b) of the Securities Exchange Act of 1934, 15 U.S.C. § 78j(b), SEC Rule 10b–5, 17 CFR § 240.10b–5 (1991), and the mail and wire fraud statutes, 18 U.S.C. §§ 1341, 1343 (1988 ed., Supp. I).   Finally, the complaint concluded that their acts amounted to a "pattern of racketeering activity" within the meaning of the RICO statute, 18 U.S.C. §§ 1962, 1961(1) and (5)(1988 ed. and Supp. I), so as to entitle the plaintiffs to recover treble damages, § 1964(c).

After some five years of litigation over other issues, the District Court entered summary judgment for Holmes on the RICO claims, ruling that SIPC "does not meet the 'purchaser-seller' requirements for standing to assert RICO claims which are predicated upon violation of Section 10(b) and Rule 10b–5," and that neither SIPC nor the trustees had satisfied the "proximate cause requirement under RICO."   Although SIPC's claims against many other defendants remained pending, the District Court under Fed.Rule Civ.Proc. 54(b) entered a partial judgment for Holmes, immediately appealable.   SIPC and the trustees appealed.

The United States Court of Appeals for the Ninth Circuit reversed and remanded after rejecting both of the District Court's grounds.   Securities Investor Protection Corp. v. Vigman, 908 F.2d 1461 (9th Cir.1990)(*Vigman III*).   The Court of Appeals held first that, whereas a purchase or sale of a security is necessary for entitlement to sue on the implied right of action recognized under § 10(b) and Rule 10b–5, see Blue Chip Stamps v. Manor Drug Stores, 421 U.S. 723 (1975), the cause of action expressly provided by § 1964(c) of RICO imposes no such requirement limiting SIPC's standing. *Vigman III*, supra, at 1465–67.   Second, the appeals court held the finding of no proximate cause to be error, the result of a mistaken focus on the causal relation between SIPC's injury and the acts of Holmes alone; since Holmes could be held responsible for the acts of all his co-conspirators, the Court of Appeals explained, the District Court should have looked to the causal relation between SIPC's injury and the acts of all conspirators.   Id., at 1467–69.[6]

---

[6] For purposes of this decision, we will assume without deciding that the Court of Appeals correctly held that Holmes can be held responsible for the acts of his co-conspirators.

Holmes' ensuing petition to this Court for certiorari presented two issues, whether SIPC had a right to sue under RICO,[7] and whether Holmes could be held responsible for the actions of his co-conspirators. We granted the petition on the former issue alone, and now reverse.

II

A

RICO's provision for civil actions reads that "[a]ny person injured in his business or property by reason of a violation of section 1962 of this chapter may sue therefor in any appropriate United States district court and shall recover threefold the damages he sustains and the cost of the suit, including a reasonable attorney's fee." 18 U.S.C. § 1964(c).

This language can of course be read to mean that a plaintiff is injured "by reason of" a RICO violation, and therefore may recover, simply on showing that the defendant violated § 1962, the plaintiff was injured, and the defendant's violation was a "but for" cause of plaintiff's injury. Cf. Associated General Contractors of Cal., Inc. v. Carpenters, 459 U.S. 519, 529 (1983). This construction is hardly compelled, however, and the very unlikelihood that Congress meant to allow all factually injured plaintiffs to recover[10] persuades us that the Act should not get such an expansive reading. Not even SIPC seriously argues otherwise.

The key to the better interpretation lies in some statutory history. We have repeatedly observed, see Shearson/American Express Inc. v. McMahon, 482 U.S. 220, 241 (1987); Sedima, S.P.R.L. v. Imrex Co., 473 U.S. 479, 489 (1985), that Congress modeled § 1964(c) on the civil-action provision of the federal antitrust laws, § 4 of the Clayton Act, which reads in relevant part that "any person who shall be injured in his business or property by reason of anything forbidden in the antitrust laws may sue therefor ... and shall recover threefold the damages by him sustained, and the cost of suit, including a reasonable attorney's fee." 15 U.S.C. § 15.

---

[7] The petition phrased the question as follows: "Whether a party which was neither a purchaser nor a seller of securities, and for that reason lacked standing to sue under Section 10(b) of the Securities Exchange Act of 1934 and Rule 10b–5 thereunder, is free of that limitation on standing when presenting essentially the same claims under the Racketeer Influenced and Corrupt Organizations Act ("RICO")."

[10] "In a philosophical sense, the consequences of an act go forward to eternity, and the causes of an event go back to the dawn of human events, and beyond. But any attempt to impose responsibility upon such a basis would result in infinite liability for all wrongful acts, and would 'set society on edge and fill the courts with endless litigation.' " W. Keeton, D. Dobbs, R. Keeton, & D. Owen, Prosser and Keeton on Law of Torts § 41, p. 264 (5th ed. 1984)(quoting North v. Johnson, 58 Minn. 242, 59 N.W. 1012 (1894)). As we put it in the antitrust context, "[a]n antitrust violation may be expected to cause ripples of harm to flow through the Nation's economy; but despite the broad wording of § 4 [of the Clayton Act, 15 U.S.C. § 15,] there is a point beyond which the wrongdoer should not be held liable." Blue Shield of Virginia v. McCready, 457 U.S. 465, 476–77 (1982)(internal quotation marks and citation omitted).

In *Associated General Contractors*, supra, we discussed how Congress enacted § 4 in 1914 with language borrowed from § 7 of the Sherman Act, passed 24 years earlier.[13] Before 1914, lower federal courts had read § 7 to incorporate common-law principles of proximate causation, 459 U.S., at 533–34, and n. 29, and we reasoned, as many lower federal courts had done before us, that congressional use of the § 7 language in § 4 presumably carried the intention to adopt "the judicial gloss that avoided a simple literal interpretation," 459 U.S., at 534. Thus, we held that a plaintiff's right to sue under § 4 required a showing not only that the defendant's violation was a "but for" cause of his injury, but was the proximate cause as well.

The reasoning applies just as readily to § 1964(c). We may fairly credit the 91st Congress, which enacted RICO, with knowing the interpretation federal courts had given the words earlier Congresses had used first in § 7 of the Sherman Act, and later in the Clayton Act's § 4. See Cannon v. University of Chicago, 441 U.S. 677, 696–98 (1979). It used the same words, and we can only assume it intended them to have the same meaning that courts had already given them. Proximate cause is thus required.

B

Here we use "proximate cause" to label generically the judicial tools used to limit a person's responsibility for the consequences of that person's own acts. At bottom, the notion of proximate cause reflects "ideas of what justice demands, or of what is administratively possible and convenient." W. Keeton, D. Dobbs, R. Keeton, & D. Owen, Prosser and Keeton on Law of Torts § 41, p. 264 (5th ed. 1984). Accordingly, among the many shapes this concept took at common law was a demand for some direct relation between the injury asserted and the injurious conduct alleged. Thus, a plaintiff who complained of harm flowing merely from the misfortunes visited upon a third person by the defendant's acts was generally said to stand at too remote a distance to recover. See, e.g., 1 J. Sutherland, Law of Damages 55–56 (1882).

Although such directness of relationship is not the sole requirement of Clayton Act causation,[15] it has been one of its central elements, for a

---

[13] When Congress enacted § 4 of the Clayton Act, § 7 of the Sherman Act read in relevant part: "Any person who shall be injured in his business or property by any other person or corporation by reason of anything forbidden or declared to be unlawful by this act, may sue...." 26 Stat. 210 (1890).

[15] We have sometimes discussed the requirement that a § 4 plaintiff has suffered "antitrust injury" as a component of the proximate-cause enquiry. See Associated General Contractors of Cal., Inc. v. Carpenters, 459 U.S. 519, 538 (1983); Blue Shield of Virginia v. McCready, 457 U.S. 465, 481–84 (1982). We need not discuss it here, howev-

Low,Fed.Crim.Law —13

er, since "antitrust injury" has no analogue in the RICO setting. See Sedima, S.P.R.L. v. Imrex Co., 473 U.S. 479, 495–97 (1985). For the same reason, there is no merit in SIPC's reliance on legislative history to the effect that it would be inappropriate to have a "private litigant ... contend with a body of precedent—appropriate in a purely antitrust context—setting strict requirements on questions such as 'standing to sue' and 'proximate cause.'" 115 Cong.Rec. 6995 (1969)(ABA comments on S. 2048). That statement is rightly understood to refer only to the applicability of the concept of "antitrust injury" to RICO, which we rejected in *Sedima*, supra,

variety of reasons. First, the less direct an injury is, the more difficult it becomes to ascertain the amount of a plaintiff's damages attributable to the violation, as distinct from other, independent, factors. Second, quite apart from problems of proving factual causation, recognizing claims of the indirectly injured would force courts to adopt complicated rules apportioning damages among plaintiffs removed at different levels of injury from the violative acts, to obviate the risk of multiple recoveries. And, finally, the need to grapple with these problems is simply unjustified by the general interest in deterring injurious conduct, since directly injured victims can generally be counted on to vindicate the law as private attorneys general, without any of the problems attendant upon suits by plaintiffs injured more remotely. See *Associated General Contractors*, supra, 459 U.S., at 540–44.

We will point out in Part III–A below that the facts of the instant case show how these reasons apply with equal force to suits under § 1964(c).

III

As we understand SIPC's argument, it claims entitlement to recover, first, because it is subrogated to the rights of those customers of the broker-dealers who did not purchase manipulated securities, and, second, because a SIPA provision gives it an independent right to sue. The first claim fails because the conspirators' conduct did not proximately cause the nonpurchasing customers' injury, the second because the provision relied on gives SIPC no right to sue for damages.

A

As a threshold matter, SIPC's theory of subrogation is fraught with unanswered questions. In suing Holmes, SIPC does not rest its claimed subrogation to the rights of the broker-dealers' customers on any provision of SIPA. SIPC assumes that SIPA provides for subrogation to the customers' claims against the failed broker-dealers, see 15 U.S.C. §§ 78fff–3(a), 78fff–4(c); see also § 78fff–2(c)(1)(C), but not against third parties like Holmes. As against him, SIPC relies rather on "common law rights of subrogation" for what it describes as "its money paid to customers for customer claims against third parties." At oral argument in this Court, SIPC narrowed its subrogation argument to cover only the rights of customers who never purchased manipulated securities.[16] But SIPC stops there, leaving us to guess at the nature of the "common law rights of subrogation" that it claims, and failing to tell us whether they derive from federal or state common law, or, if the latter, from common law of which State. Nor does SIPC explain why it declines to assert the rights of

at 495–97. Besides, even if we were to read this statement to say what SIPC says it means, it would not amount to more than background noise drowned out by the statutory language.

[16] And, SIPC made no allegation that any of these customers failed to do so in

customers who bought manipulated securities.[18]

It is not these questions, however, that stymie SIPC's subrogation claim, for even assuming, arguendo, that it may stand in the shoes of nonpurchasing customers, the link is too remote between the stock manipulation alleged and the customers' harm, being purely contingent on the harm suffered by the broker-dealers. That is, the conspirators have allegedly injured these customers only insofar as the stock manipulation first injured the broker-dealers and left them without the wherewithal to pay customers' claims. Although the customers' claims are senior (in recourse to "customer property") to those of the broker-dealers' general creditors, see § 78fff–2(c)(1), the causes of their respective injuries are the same: The broker-dealers simply cannot pay their bills, and only that intervening insolvency connects the conspirators' acts to the losses suffered by the nonpurchasing customers and general creditors.

As we said, however, in *Associated General Contractors*, quoting Justice Holmes, " 'The general tendency of the law, in regard to damages at least, is not to go beyond the first step.' " 459 U.S., at 534 (quoting Southern Pacific Co. v. Darnell–Taenzer Lumber Co., 245 U.S. 531, 533 (1918)),[19] and the reasons that supported conforming Clayton Act causation to the general tendency apply just as readily to the present facts, underscoring the obvious congressional adoption of the Clayton Act direct-injury limitation among the requirements of § 1964(c).[20] If the nonpurchasing customers

reliance on acts or omissions of the conspirators.

[18] The record reveals that those customers have brought their own suit against the conspirators.

[19] SIPC tries to avoid foundering on the rule that creditors generally may not sue for injury affecting their debtors' solvency by arguing that those customers that owned manipulated securities themselves were victims of Holmes' fraud. While that may well be true, since SIPC does not claim subrogation to the rights of the customers that purchased manipulated securities, it gains nothing by the point. We further note that SIPC alleged in the courts below that, in late May 1981, Joseph Lugo, an officer of FSSC and one of the alleged conspirators, parked manipulated stock in the accounts of customers, among them Holmes, who actively participated in the parking transaction involving his account. Lugo "sold" securities owned by FSSC to customers at market price, and "bought" back the same securities some days later at the same price plus interest. Under applicable regulations, a broker-dealer must discount the stock it holds in its own account, see 17 CFR § 240.15c3–1(c)(2)(iv)(F)(1)(vi)(1991), and the sham transactions allowed FSSC to avoid the discount. But for the parking transactions, FSSC would allegedly have failed capital requirements sooner; would have been shut down by regulators; and would not have dragged Sebag with it in its demise. Thus, their customers would have been injured to a lesser extent. We do not rule out that, if, by engaging in the parking transactions, the conspirators committed mail fraud, wire fraud, or "fraud in the sale of securities," see 18 U.S.C. §§ 1961(1)(B) and (D)(1988 ed., Supp. I), the broker-dealers' customers might be proximately injured by these offenses. See, e.g., Taffet v. Southern Co., 930 F.2d 847, 856–57 (11th Cir.1991); County of Suffolk v. Long Island Lighting Co., 907 F.2d 1295, 1311–12 (2d Cir.1990). However this may be, SIPC in its brief on the merits places exclusive reliance on a manipulation theory, and is completely silent about the alleged parking scheme.

[20] As we said in *Associated General Contractors*, "the infinite variety of claims that may arise make it virtually impossible to announce a black-letter rule that will dictate the result in every case." 459 U.S., at 536 (footnote omitted). Thus, our use of the

were allowed to sue, the district court would first need to determine the extent to which their inability to collect from the broker-dealers was the result of the alleged conspiracy to manipulate, as opposed to, say, the broker-dealers' poor business practices or their failures to anticipate developments in the financial markets. Assuming that an appropriate assessment of factual causation could be made out, the district court would then have to find some way to apportion the possible respective recoveries by the broker-dealers and the customers, who would otherwise each be entitled to recover the full treble damages. Finally, the law would be shouldering these difficulties despite the fact that those directly injured, the broker-dealers, could be counted on to bring suit for the law's vindication. As noted above, the broker-dealers have in fact sued in this case, in the persons of their SIPA trustees appointed on account of their insolvency. Indeed, the insolvency of the victim directly injured adds a further concern to those already expressed, since a suit by an indirectly injured victim could be an attempt to circumvent the relative priority its claim would have in the directly injured victim's liquidation proceedings.

As against the force of these considerations of history and policy, SIPC's reliance on the congressional admonition that RICO be "liberally construed to effectuate its remedial purposes," § 904(a), 84 Stat. 947, does not deflect our analysis. There is, for that matter, nothing illiberal in our construction: We hold not that RICO cannot serve to right the conspirators' wrongs, but merely that the nonpurchasing customers, or SIPC in their stead, are not proper plaintiffs. Indeed, we fear that RICO's remedial purposes would more probably be hobbled than helped by SIPC's version of liberal construction: Allowing suits by those injured only indirectly would open the door to "massive and complex damages litigation[, which would] not only burde[n] the courts, but also undermin[e] the effectiveness of treble-damages suits." *Associated General Contractors*, 459 U.S., at 545.

In sum, subrogation to the rights of the manipulation conspiracy's secondary victims does, and should, run afoul of proximate-causation standards, and SIPC must wait on the outcome of the trustees' suit. If they recover from Holmes, SIPC may share according to the priority SIPA gives its claim. See 15 U.S.C. § 78fff–2(c).

B

SIPC also claims a statutory entitlement to pursue Holmes for funds advanced to the trustees for administering the liquidation proceedings. Its theory here apparently is not one of subrogation, to which the statute makes no reference in connection with SIPC's obligation to make such advances. See 15 U.S.C. § 78fff–3(b)(2). SIPC relies instead on this SIPA provision:

term "direct" should merely be understood as a reference to the proximate-cause enquiry that is informed by the concerns set out in the text. We do not necessarily use it in the same sense as courts before us have, and intimate no opinion on results they reached. See, e.g., *Sedima*, 473 U.S., at 497, n. 15 (Marshall, J., dissenting).

"SIPC participation—SIPC shall be deemed to be a party in interest as to all matters arising in a liquidation proceeding, with the right to be heard on all such matters, and shall be deemed to have intervened with respect to all such matters with the same force and effect as if a petition for such purpose had been allowed by the court." 15 U.S.C. § 78eee(d).

The language is inapposite to the issue here, however. On its face, it simply qualifies SIPC as a proper party in interest in any "matter arising in a liquidation proceeding" as to which it "shall be deemed to have intervened." By extending a right to be heard in a "matter" pending between other parties, however, the statute says nothing about the conditions necessary for SIPC's recovery as a plaintiff. How the provision could be read, either alone or with § 1964(c), to give SIPC a right to sue Holmes for money damages simply eludes us.

IV

Petitioner urges us to go further and decide whether every RICO plaintiff who sues under § 1964(c) and claims securities fraud as a predicate offense must have purchased or sold a security, an issue on which the Circuits appear divided.[23] We decline to do so. Given what we have said in Parts II and III, our discussion of the issue would be unnecessary to the resolution of this case. Nor do we think that leaving this question unanswered will deprive the lower courts of much-needed guidance. A review of the conflicting cases shows that all could have been resolved on proximate-causation grounds, and that none involved litigants like those in Blue Chip Stamps v. Manor Drug Stores, 421 U.S. 723 (1975), persons who had decided to forgo securities transactions in reliance on misrepresentations. Thus, we think it inopportune to resolve the issue today.

V

We hold that, because the alleged conspiracy to manipulate did not proximately cause the injury claimed, SIPC's allegations and the record before us fail to make out a right to sue petitioner under § 1964(c). We reverse the judgment of the Court of Appeals and remand the case for further proceedings consistent with this opinion.

It is so ordered.

■ JUSTICE O'CONNOR, with whom JUSTICE WHITE and JUSTICE STEVENS join, concurring in part and concurring in the judgment.

I agree with the Court that the civil action provisions of the Racketeer Influenced and Corrupt Organizations Act (RICO), 84 Stat. 941, as amended, 18 U.S.C. §§ 1961–1968 (1988 ed. and Supp. I), have a proximate cause

---

[23] Compare *Vigman III*, 908 F.2d 1461, 1465–67 (9th Cir.1990)(no purchaser-seller rule under RICO); Warner v. Alexander Grant & Co., 828 F.2d 1528, 1530 (11th Cir. 1987)(same), with International Data Bank, Ltd. v. Zepkin, 812 F.2d 149, 151–54 (4th Cir.1987)(RICO plaintiff relying on securities fraud as predicate offense must have been purchaser or seller); Brannan v. Eisenstein, 804 F.2d 1041, 1046 (8th Cir.1986)(same).

element, and I can even be persuaded that the proximate-cause issue is "fairly included" in the question on which we granted certiorari. In my view, however, before deciding whether the Securities Investor Protection Corporation (SIPC) was proximately injured by petitioner's alleged activities, we should first consider the standing question that was decided below, and briefed and argued here, and which was the only clearly articulated question on which we granted certiorari. In resolving that question, I would hold that a plaintiff need not be a purchaser or a seller to assert RICO claims predicated on violations of fraud in the sale of securities.

Section 10(b) of the Securities Exchange Act of 1934 (1934 Act) makes it unlawful for any person to use, "in connection with the purchase or sale of any security," any "manipulative or deceptive device or contrivance" in contravention of rules or regulations that the Securities and Exchange Commission (SEC) may prescribe. 15 U.S.C. § 78j(b). Pursuant to its authority under § 10(b), the SEC has adopted Rule 10b–5, which prohibits manipulative or deceptive acts "in connection with the purchase or sale of any security." 17 CFR § 240.10b–5 (1991). In 1971, we ratified without discussion the "established" view that § 10(b) and Rule 10b–5 created an implied right of action. *Superintendent of Insurance v. Bankers Life & Cas. Co.*, 404 U.S. 6, 13, n. 9. Four years later, in Blue Chip Stamps v. Manor Drug Stores, 421 U.S. 723 (1975), we confirmed the federal courts' "longstanding acceptance" of the rule that a plaintiff must have actually purchased or sold the securities at issue in order to bring a Rule 10b–5 private damages action.

In this case, the District Court held that SIPC, which was neither a purchaser nor a seller of the allegedly manipulated securities, lacked standing to assert RICO claims predicated on alleged violations of § 10(b) and Rule 10b–5. The Court of Appeals reversed and held that *Blue Chip Stamps'* purchaser/seller limitation does not apply to suits brought under RICO. Securities Investor Protection Corp. v. Vigman, 908 F.2d 1461 (9th Cir.1990). An examination of the text of RICO, and a comparison with the situation the Court confronted in *Blue Chip Stamps*, persuades me that the Court of Appeals' determination was correct. Because the Court's decision today leaves intact a division among the Circuits on whether *Blue Chip Stamps'* standing requirement applies in RICO suits, I would affirm this portion of the decision below, even though we go on to hold that the alleged RICO violation did not proximately cause SIPC's injuries.

Our obvious starting point is the text of the statute under which SIPC sued. RICO makes it unlawful for any person who has engaged in a "pattern of racketeering activity" to invest, maintain an interest, or participate in an enterprise that is engaged in interstate or foreign commerce. 18 U.S.C. § 1962. "[R]acketeering activity" is defined to include a number of state and federal offenses, including any act indictable under 18 U.S.C. § 1341 (mail fraud) or § 1343 (wire fraud), and "any offense involving . . . fraud in the sale of securities . . . punishable under any law of the United States." § 1961(1). RICO authorizes "[a]ny person injured in his business or property by reason of a violation of section 1962" to sue for treble damages in federal court. 18 U.S.C. § 1964(c).

RICO's civil suit provision, considered on its face, has no purchaser/seller standing requirement. The statute sweeps broadly, authorizing "[a]ny person" who is injured by reason of a RICO violation to sue. "[P]erson" is defined to include "any individual or entity capable of holding a legal or beneficial interest in property." § 1961(3). "Insofar as 'any' encompasses 'all'," Mobil Oil Exploration & Producing Southeast, Inc. v. United Distribution Cos., 498 U.S. 211, 223, (1991), the words "any person" cannot reasonably be read to mean only purchasers and sellers of securities. As we have explained in rejecting previous efforts to narrow the scope of civil RICO: "If the defendant engages in a pattern of racketeering activity in a manner forbidden by [§ 1962's] provisions, and the racketeering activities injure the plaintiff in his business or property, the plaintiff has a claim under § 1964(c). There is no room in the statutory language for an additional ... requirement." Sedima, S.P.R.L. v. Imrex Co., 473 U.S. 479, 495 (1985).

Of course, a RICO plaintiff "only has standing if, and can only recover to the extent that, he has been injured in his business or property by [reason of] the conduct constituting the violation." Id., at 496. We have already remarked that the requirement of injury in one's "business or property" limits the availability of RICO's civil remedies to those who have suffered injury-in-fact. Id., at 497 (citing Haroco, Inc. v. American National Bank & Trust Co. of Chicago, 747 F.2d 384, 398 (7th Cir.1984)). Today, the Court sensibly holds that the statutory words "by reason of" operate, as they do in the antitrust laws, to confine RICO's civil remedies to those whom the defendant has truly injured in some meaningful sense. Requiring a proximate relationship between the defendant's actions and the plaintiff's harm, however, cannot itself preclude a nonpurchaser or nonseller of securities, alleging predicate acts of fraud in the sale of securities, from bringing suit under § 1964(c). Although the words "injury in [one's] business or property" and "by reason of" are words of limitation, they do not categorically exclude nonpurchasers and nonsellers of securities from the universe of RICO plaintiffs.

Petitioner argues that the civil suit provisions of § 1964(c) are not as sweeping as they appear because § 1964(c) incorporates the standing requirements of the predicate acts alleged. But § 1964(c) focuses on the "injur[y]" of any "person," not the legal right to sue of any proper plaintiff for a predicate act. If standing were to be determined by reference to the predicate offenses, a private RICO plaintiff could not allege as predicates many of the acts that constitute the definition of racketeering activity. The great majority of acts listed in § 1961(1) are criminal offenses for which only a State or the Federal Government is the proper party to bring suit. In light of § 1964(c)'s provision that "any person" injured by reason of a RICO violation may sue, I would not accept that this same section envisions an overlay of standing requirements from the predicate acts, with the result that many RICO suits could be brought only by government entities.

Nor can I accept the contention that, even if § 1964(c) does not normally incorporate the standing requirements of the predicate acts, an exception should be made for "fraud in the sale of securities" simply because it is well established that a plaintiff in a civil action under § 10(b) and Rule 10b–5 must be either a purchaser or seller of securities. A careful reading of § 1961(1) reveals the flaw in this argument. The relevant predicate offense is "any offense involving . . . fraud in the sale of securities . . . punishable under any law of the United States." The embracing words "offense . . . punishable under any law of the United States" plainly signify the elements necessary to bring a criminal prosecution. To the extent that RICO's reference to an "offense involving fraud in the sale of securities" encompasses conduct that violates § 10(b), the relevant predicate is defined not by § 10(b) itself, but rather by § 32(a) of the 1934 Act, 15 U.S.C. § 78ff(a), which authorizes criminal sanctions against any person who willfully violates the Act or rules promulgated thereunder. As we have previously made clear, the purchaser/seller standing requirement for private civil actions under § 10(b) and Rule 10b–5 is of no import in criminal prosecutions for willful violations of those provisions. United States v. Naftalin, 441 U.S. 768, 774, n. 6 (1979); SEC v. National Securities, Inc., 393 U.S. 453, 467, n. 9 (1969). Thus, even if Congress intended RICO's civil suit provision to subsume established civil standing requirements for predicate offenses, that situation is not presented here.

Although the civil suit provisions of § 1964(c) lack a purchaser/seller requirement, it is still possible that one lurks in § 1961(1)'s catalog of predicate acts; i.e., it is possible that § 1961(1) of its own force limits RICO standing to the actual parties to a sale. As noted above, the statute defines "racketeering activity" to include "any offense involving . . . fraud in the sale of securities . . . punishable under any law of the United States." Unfortunately, the term "fraud in the sale of securities" is not further defined. "[A]ny offense . . . punishable under any law of the United States" presumably means that Congress intended to refer to the federal securities laws and not common-law tort actions for fraud. Unlike most of the predicate offenses listed in § 1961(1), however, there is no cross-reference to any specific sections of the United States Code. Nor is resort to the legislative history helpful in clarifying what kinds of securities violations Congress contemplated would be covered. See generally Andrew P. Bridges, Private RICO Litigation Based Upon "Fraud in the Sale of Securities," 18 Ga.L.Rev. 43, 58–59 (1983)(discussing paucity of legislative history); Note, RICO and Securities Fraud: A Workable Limitation, 83 Colum.L.Rev. 1513, 1536–1539 (1983)(reviewing testimony before Senate Judiciary Committee).

Which violations of the federal securities laws, if any, constitute a "fraud in the sale of securities" within the meaning of § 1961(1) is a question that has generated much ink and little agreement among courts or commentators, and one which we need not definitively resolve here. The statute unmistakably requires that there be fraud, sufficiently willful to constitute a criminal violation, and that there be a sale of securities. At the same time, however, I am persuaded that Congress' use of the word "sale" in defining the predicate offense does not necessarily dictate that a RICO plaintiff have been a party to an executed sale.

Section 1961(1)'s list of racketeering offenses provides the RICO predicates for both criminal prosecutions and civil actions. Obviously there is no requirement that the Government be party to a sale before it can bring a RICO prosecution predicated on "fraud in the sale of securities." Accordingly, any argument that the offense itself embodies a standing requirement must apply only to private actions. That distinction is not tenable, however. By including a private right of action in RICO, Congress intended to bring "the pressure of 'private attorneys general' on a serious national problem for which public prosecutorial resources [were] deemed inadequate." Agency Holding Corp. v. Malley–Duff & Assocs., 483 U.S. 143, 151 (1987). Although not everyone can qualify as an appropriate "private attorney general," the prerequisites to the role are articulated, not in the definition of the predicate act, but in the civil action provisions of § 1964(c)—a plaintiff must allege "injur[y] in his business or property by reason of" a RICO violation.

Construing RICO's reference to "fraud in the sale of securities" to limit standing to purchasers and sellers would be in tension with our reasoning in *Blue Chip Stamps*. In that case, the Court admitted that it was not "able to divine from the language of § 10(b) the express 'intent of Congress' as to the contours of a private cause of action under Rule 10b–5." 421 U.S., at 737. The purchaser/seller standing limitation in Rule 10b–5 damages actions thus does not stem from a construction of the phrase "in connection with the purchase or sale of any security." Rather, it rests on the relationship between § 10(b) and other provisions of the securities laws, id., at 733–36, and the practical difficulties in granting standing in the absence of an executed transaction, id., at 737–49, neither of which are relevant in the RICO context.

Arguably, even if § 10(b)'s reference to fraud "in connection with "the sale of a security is insufficient to limit the plaintiff class to purchasers and sellers, § 1961(1)'s reference to fraud "in" the sale of a security performs just such a narrowing function. But we have previously had occasion to express reservations on the validity of that distinction. In United States v. Naftalin, 441 U.S. 768 (1979), we reinstated the conviction of a professional investor who engaged in fraudulent "short selling" by placing orders with brokers to sell shares of stock which he falsely represented that he owned. This Court agreed with the District Court that Naftalin was guilty of fraud "in" the "offer" or "sale" of securities in violation of § 17(a)(1) of the Securities Act of 1933, 15 U.S.C. § 77q(a)(1), even though the fraud was perpetrated on the brokers, not their purchasing clients. The Court noted: "[Naftalin] contends that the requirement that the fraud be 'in' the offer or sale connotes a narrower range of activities than does the phrase 'in connection with,' which is found in § 10(b).... First, we are not necessarily persuaded that 'in' is narrower than 'in connection with.' Both Congress, see H.R.Rep. No. 85, 73d Cong., 1st Sess., 6 (1933), and this Court, see Superintendent of Insurance v. Bankers Life & Cas. Co., 404 U.S. 6, 10 (1971), have on occasion used the terms interchangeably. But even if 'in' were meant to connote a narrower group of transactions than 'in connection with,' there is nothing to indicate that 'in' is narrower in the sense insisted upon by Naftalin." 441 U.S., at 773, n. 4.

So also in today's case. To the extent that there is a meaningful difference between Congress' choice of "in" as opposed to "in connection with," I do not view it as limiting the class of RICO plaintiffs to those who were parties to a sale. Rather, consistent with today's decision, I view it as confining the class of defendants to those proximately responsible for the plaintiff's injury and excluding those only tangentially "connect[ed] with" it.

In *Blue Chip Stamps*, we adopted the purchaser/seller standing limitation in § 10(b) cases as a prudential means of avoiding the problems of proof when no security was traded and the nuisance potential of vexatious litigation. 421 U.S., at 738–39. In that case, however, we were confronted with limiting access to a private cause of action that was judicially implied. We expressly acknowledged that "if Congress had legislated the elements of a private cause of action for damages, the duty of the Judicial Branch would be to administer the law which Congress enacted; the Judiciary may not circumscribe a right which Congress has conferred because of any disagreement it might have with Congress about the wisdom of creating so expansive a liability." Id., at 748. To be sure, the problems of expansive standing identified in *Blue Chip Stamps* are exacerbated in RICO. In addition to the threat of treble damages, a defendant faces the stigma of being labeled a "racketeer." Nonetheless, Congress has legislated the elements of a private cause of action under RICO. Specifically, Congress has authorized "[a]ny person injured in his business or property by reason of" a RICO violation to bring suit under section 1964(c). Despite the very real specter of vexatious litigation based on speculative damages, it is within Congress' power to create a private right of action for plaintiffs who have neither bought nor sold securities. For the reasons stated above, I think Congress has done so. "That being the case, the courts are without authority to restrict the application of the statute." United States v. Turkette, 452 U.S. 576, 587 (1981).

In sum, we granted certiorari to resolve a split among the Circuits as to whether a nonpurchaser or nonseller of securities could assert RICO claims predicated on violations of § 10(b) and Rule 10b–5. I recognize that, like the case below, some of those decisions might have been more appropriately cast in terms of proximate causation. That we have now more clearly articulated the causation element of a civil RICO action does not change the fact that the governing precedent in several Circuits is in disagreement as to *Blue Chip Stamps'* applicability in the RICO context. Because that issue was decided below and fully addressed here, we should resolve it today. I would sustain the Court of Appeals' determination that

RICO plaintiffs alleging predicate acts of fraud in the sale of securities need not be actual purchasers or sellers of the securities at issue. Accordingly, I join all of the Court's opinion except Part IV.

■ JUSTICE SCALIA, concurring in the judgment.

I agree with Justice O'Connor that in deciding this case we ought to reach rather than avoid the question on which we granted certiorari. I also agree with her on the answer to that question: that the purchaser-seller rule does not apply in civil RICO cases alleging as predicate acts violations of Securities and Exchange Commission Rule 10b–5, 17 CFR § 240.10b–5 (1991). My reasons for that conclusion, however, are somewhat different from hers.

The ultimate question here is statutory standing: whether the so-called nexus (mandatory legalese for "connection") between the harm of which this plaintiff complains and the defendant's so-called predicate acts is of the sort that will support an action under civil RICO. See Sedima S.P.R.L. v. Imrex Co., Inc., 473 U.S. 479, 497 (1985). One of the usual elements of statutory standing is proximate causality. It is required in RICO not so much because RICO has language similar to that of the Clayton Act, which in turn has language similar to that of the Sherman Act, which, by the time the Clayton Act had been passed, had been interpreted to include a proximate-cause requirement; but rather, I think, because it has always been the practice of common-law courts (and probably of all courts, under all legal systems) to require as a condition of recovery, unless the legislature specifically prescribes otherwise, that the injury have been proximately caused by the offending conduct. Life is too short to pursue every human act to its most remote consequences; "for want of a nail, a kingdom was lost" is a commentary on fate, not the statement of a major cause of action against a blacksmith. See Associated General Contractors of Cal., Inc. v. Carpenters, 459 U.S. 519, 536 (1983).

Yet another element of statutory standing is compliance with what I shall call the "zone of interests" test, which seeks to determine whether, apart from the directness of the injury, the plaintiff is within the class of persons sought to be benefitted by the provision at issue.[1] Judicial inference of a zone-of-interests requirement, like judicial inference of a proximate-cause requirement, is a background practice against which Congress legislates. See Block v. Community Nutrition Institute, 467 U.S. 340, 345–48 (1984). Sometimes considerable limitations upon the zone of interests are set forth explicitly in the statute itself—but rarely, if ever, are those limitations so complete that they are deemed to preclude the judicial inference of others. If, for example, a securities fraud statute specifically conferred a cause of action upon "all purchasers, sellers, or owners of stock injured by securities fraud," I doubt whether a stockholder who suffered a

---

[1] My terminology may not be entirely orthodox. It may be that proximate causality is itself an element of the zone of interests test as that phrase has ordinarily been used, see, e.g., Wyoming v. Oklahoma, 502 U.S. 437, 468–73 (1992)(Scalia, J., dissenting), but that usage would leave us bereft of terminology to connote those aspects of the "violation-injury connection" aspect of standing that are distinct from proximate causality.

heart attack upon reading a false earnings report could recover his medical expenses. So also here. The phrase "any person injured in his business or property by reason of" the unlawful activities makes clear that the zone of interests does not extend beyond those injured in that respect—but does not necessarily mean that it includes all those injured in that respect. Just as the phrase does not exclude normal judicial inference of proximate cause, so also it does not exclude normal judicial inference of zone of interests.

It seems to me obvious that the proximate-cause test and the zone-of-interests test that will be applied to the various causes of action created by 18 U.S.C. § 1964 are not uniform, but vary according to the nature of the criminal offenses upon which those causes of action are based. The degree of proximate causality required to recover damages caused by predicate acts of sports bribery, for example, see 18 U.S.C. § 224, will be quite different from the degree required for damages caused by predicate acts of transporting stolen property, see 18 U.S.C. §§ 2314–15. And so also with the applicable zone-of-interests test: It will vary with the underlying violation. (Where the predicate acts consist of different criminal offenses, presumably the plaintiff would have to be within the degree of proximate causality and within the zone of interests as to all of them.)

It also seems to me obvious that unless some reason for making a distinction exists, the background zone-of-interests test applied to one cause of action for harm caused by violation of a particular criminal provision should be the same as the test applied to another cause of action for harm caused by violation of the same provision. It is principally in this respect that I differ from Justice O'Connor's analysis. If, for example, one statute gives persons injured by a particular criminal violation a cause of action for damages, and another statute gives them a cause of action for equitable relief, the persons coming within the zone of interests of those two statutes would be identical. Hence the relevance to this case of our decision in Blue Chip Stamps v. Manor Drug Stores, 421 U.S. 723 (1975). The predicate acts of securities fraud alleged here are violations of Rule 10b–5; and we held in *Blue Chip Stamps* that the zone of interests for civil damages attributable to violation of that provision does not include persons who are not purchasers or sellers. As I have described above, just as RICO's statutory phrase "injured in his business or property by reason of" does not extend the rule of proximate causation otherwise applied to congressionally created causes of action, so also it should not extend the otherwise applicable rule of zone of interests.

What prevents that proposition from being determinative here, however, is the fact that *Blue Chip Stamps* did not involve application of the background zone-of-interests rule to a congressionally created Rule 10b–5 action, but rather specification of the contours of a Rule 10b–5 action "implied" (i.e., created) by the Court itself—a practice we have since happily abandoned, see, e.g., Touche Ross & Co. v. Redington, 442 U.S. 560, 568–71, 575–76 (1979). The policies that we identified in *Blue Chip Stamps*, supra, as supporting the purchaser-seller limitation (namely, the difficulty of assessing the truth of others' claims, see id., 421 U.S., at 743–

47, and the high threat of "strike" or nuisance suits in securities litigation, see id., at 740–41) are perhaps among the factors properly taken into account in determining the zone of interests covered by a statute, but they are surely not alone enough to restrict standing to purchasers or sellers under a text that contains no hint of such a limitation. I think, in other words, that the limitation we approved in *Blue Chip Stamps* was essentially a legislative judgment rather than an interpretive one. Cf. Franklin v. Gwinnett County Public Schools, 503 U.S. 60, 76 (1992)(Scalia, J., concurring in judgment). It goes beyond the customary leeway that the zone-of-interests test leaves to courts in the construction of statutory texts.

In my view, therefore, the Court of Appeals correctly rejected the assertion that SIPC had no standing because it was not a purchaser or seller of the securities in question. A proximate-cause requirement also applied, however, and I agree with the Court that that was not met. For these reasons, I concur in the judgment.

SECTION 3: ENTERPRISE CRIMINALITY AND DOUBLE JEOPARDY

Since the enactment of RICO and CCE, the courts have struggled to apply traditional doctrines of double jeopardy law to the new concept of "enterprise criminality." Traditional double jeopardy doctrines were developed for traditional crimes, which generally address a specific act or series of acts committed at one or more discrete moments in time. Statutes like RICO and CCE, on the other hand, criminalize something more like an ongoing "status," which creates special double jeopardy problems. The cases in this section present some of those special problems.

The double jeopardy clause of the fifth amendment provides: "nor shall any person be subject for the same offense to be twice put in jeopardy of life or limb." This prohibition has been held to include three separate guarantees: "It protects against a second prosecution for the same offense after acquittal. It protects against a second prosecution for the same offense after conviction. And it protects against multiple punishments for the same offense." North Carolina v. Pearce, 395 U.S. 711, 717 (1969). The first two of these are usually said to raise "successive prosecution" or "multiple prosecution" issues, while the third raises "multiple punishment" issues.

One common kind of double jeopardy issue involves the following question: When are two distinct statutory crimes (charged with respect to the same conduct) considered to be "the same offense" within the meaning of the double jeopardy clause? The Supreme Court provided a general answer to this question in Blockburger v. United States, 284 U.S. 299 (1932):

> "The applicable rule is that where the same act or transaction constitutes a violation of two distinct statutory provisions, the test to be applied to determine whether there are two offenses or only one, is whether each provision requires proof of a fact which the other does not...." 284 U.S., at 304.

In later cases, the Court explained that the *Blockburger* test focuses on the elements of the two statutory crimes, not the evidence presented in support of the charges. "If each [statute] requires proof that the other does not, the *Blockburger* test would be satisfied, notwithstanding a substantial overlap in the proof offered to establish the crimes...." Iannelli v. United States, 420 U.S. 770, 785 n. 17 (1975).

To take a relatively simple example, if crime X involves the statutory elements (A + B + C) and crime Y involves the statutory elements (B + C + D), then the *Blockburger* test would be satisfied; crime X and crime Y would be treated as separate offenses for double jeopardy purposes. A defendant could be prosecuted for *both* crime X *and* crime Y, based on the same conduct, in successive prosecutions, without violating the double jeopardy clause.

On the other hand, if crime Z involves the statutory elements (A + B + C + E), then the *Blockburger* test would treat crime X and crime Z as "the same offense" for double jeopardy purposes. (In this situation, where crime Z includes all of the statutory elements of crime X, plus additional elements, crime X would be called a "lesser included offense" of crime Z.) After a prosecution for *either* crime X *or* crime Z, the double jeopardy clause would prohibit a successive prosecution for the *other* crime, based on the same conduct. See Brown v. Ohio, 432 U.S. 161 (1977). Note that, given the first two of the aforementioned three separate interests served by the double jeopardy clause, this prohibition applies without regard to the outcome of the first prosecution.

With respect to the prohibition of multiple punishments for the same offense, the Court has taken a different approach. Unlike in the successive prosecution context (where the *Blockburger* test defines the scope of constitutional double jeopardy protection), in the multiple punishment context the Court has declared that *Blockburger* is merely a tool for statutory construction. The legislature retains the constitutional power to provide multiple punishments for the same offense, so long as this legislative intent is made clear. See Missouri v. Hunter, 459 U.S. 359 (1983). Of course, if two separate statutory crimes are indeed "the same offense" for double jeopardy purposes, then multiple punishments (even assuming legislative intent to so authorize is clear) may be imposed only in a single, joint trial; otherwise, the successive prosecution bar will be violated.

These general principles should be kept in mind when reading the following cases, which involve the application of double jeopardy doctrines to enterprise criminality.

Jeffers v. United States

Supreme Court of the United States, 1977.
432 U.S. 137.

◼ JUSTICE BLACKMUN announced the judgment of the Court and issued an opinion in which THE CHIEF JUSTICE, JUSTICE POWELL, and JUSTICE REHNQUIST joined.

This case involves the extent of the protection against multiple prosecutions afforded by the Double Jeopardy Clause of the Fifth Amendment, under circumstances in which the defendant opposes the Government's efforts to try charges under 21 U.S.C. §§ 846 and 848 in one proceeding. It also raises the question whether § 846 is a lesser included offense of § 848. Finally, it requires further explication of the Court's decision in Iannelli v. United States, 420 U.S. 770 (1975).

I

A.

According to evidence presented at trial, petitioner Garland Jeffers was the head of a highly sophisticated narcotics distribution network that operated in Gary, Ind., from January 1972 to March 1974. The "Family," as the organization was known, originally was formed by Jeffers and five others and was designed to control the local drug traffic in the city of Gary. Petitioner soon became the dominant figure in the organization. He exercised ultimate authority over the substantial revenues derived from the Family's drug sales, extortionate practices, and robberies. He disbursed funds to pay salaries of Family members, commissions of street workers, and incidental expenditures for items such as apartment rental fees, bail bond fees, and automobiles for certain members. Finally, he maintained a strict and ruthless discipline within the group, beating and shooting members on occasion. The Family typically distributed daily between 1,000 and 2,000 capsules of heroin. This resulted in net daily receipts of about $5,000, exclusive of street commissions. According to what the Court of Appeals stated was "an extremely conservative estimate," petitioner's personal share from the operations exceeded a million dollars over the two-year period.

On March 18, 1974, a federal grand jury for the Northern District of Indiana returned two indictments against petitioner in connection with his role in the Family's operations. The first charged petitioner and nine others with an offense under 21 U.S.C. § 846[2] by conspiring to distribute both heroin and cocaine during the period between November 1, 1971, and the date of the indictment, in violation of 21 U.S.C. § 841(a)(1).[3] The indictment specified, among other things, that the conspiracy was to be accomplished by petitioner's assumption of leadership of the Family organization, by distribution of controlled substances, and by acquisition of

[2] Section 846 provides: "Any person who attempts or conspires to commit any offense defined in this subchapter (Control and Enforcement) is punishable by imprisonment or fine or both which may not exceed the maximum punishment prescribed for the offense, the commission of which was the object of the attempt or conspiracy."

[3] Section 841(a)(1) provides: "(a) ... Except as authorized by this subchapter, it shall be unlawful for any person knowingly or intentionally (1) to manufacture, distribute, or dispense, or possess with intent to manufacture, distribute, or dispense, a controlled substance." Heroin is classified as a Schedule I narcotic drug controlled substance. 21 U.S.C. § 812(c)(Sch. I)(b)(10); 21 CFR § 1308.11(c)(11)(1976). Cocaine is a Schedule II narcotic drug controlled substance. 21 U.S.C. § 812(c)(Sch. II)(a)(4); 21 CFR § 1308.12(b)(4)(1976).

substantial sums of money through the distribution of the controlled substances. The second indictment charged petitioner alone with a violation of 21 U.S.C. § 848, which prohibits conducting a continuing criminal enterprise to violate the drug laws.[4] Like the first, or conspiracy, indictment, this second indictment charged that petitioner had distributed and possessed with intent to distribute both heroin and cocaine, in violation of § 841(a)(1), again between November 1, 1971, and the date of the indictment. As required by the statute, the indictment alleged that petitioner had undertaken the distribution "in concert with five or more other people with respect to whom he occupied a position of organizer, supervisor and manager," and that as a result of the distribution and other activity he had obtained substantial income.

Shortly after the indictments were returned, the Government filed a motion for trial together, requesting that the continuing-criminal-enterprise charge be tried with the general conspiracy charges against petitioner and his nine codefendants. The motion alleged that joinder would be proper under Fed. Rule Crim. Proc. 8, since the offenses charged were of the same or similar character and they were based on the same acts or transactions constituting parts of a common scheme or plan. It also represented that much of the evidence planned for the § 848 trial was based on the same transactions as those involved in the § 846 case. Consequently, it argued that joinder was appropriate and within the court's power pursuant to Fed. Rule Crim. Proc. 13.

The defendants in the § 846 case filed a joint objection to the Government's motion. Petitioner and his nine codefendants argued generally that joinder would be improper under Fed. Rules Crim. Proc. 8 and 14, since neither the parties nor the charges were the same. The codefendants were particularly concerned about the probable effect of the evidence that would be introduced to support the continuing-criminal-enterprise charge and about the jury's ability to avoid confusing the two cases. Another argu-

---

[4] Section 848 provides, in relevant part: "(a) ... (1) Any person who engages in a continuing criminal enterprise shall be sentenced to a term of imprisonment which may not be less than 10 years and which may be up to life imprisonment, to a fine of not more than $100,000, and to the forfeiture prescribed in paragraph (2).... (2) Any person who is convicted under paragraph (1) of engaging in a continuing criminal enterprise shall forfeit to the United States (A) the profits obtained by him in such enterprise, and (B) any of his interest in, claim against, or property or contractual rights of any kind affording a source of influence over, such enterprise.

"(b) ... For purposes of subsection (a) of this section, a person is engaged in a continuing criminal enterprise if (1) he violates any provision of this subchapter or subchapter II of this chapter (Import and Export) the punishment for which is a felony, and (2) such violation is a part of a continuing series of violations of this subchapter or subchapter II of this chapter (A) which are undertaken by such person in concert with five or more other persons with respect to whom such person occupies a position of organizer, a supervisory position, or any other position of management, and, (B) from which such person obtains substantial income or resources.

"(c) ... In the case of any sentence imposed under this section, imposition or execution of such sentence shall not be suspended, probation shall not be granted, and section 4202 of Title 18 (repealed March 15, 1976, by Pub.L. 94–233, 90 Stat. 219, and replaced by a new § 4205, each relating to eligibility of prisoners for parole) ... shall not apply."

ment in the objection focused directly on petitioner. It noted that the § 846 indictment charged 17 overt acts, but that petitioner was named in only ten of them, and was alleged to have participated actively in only nine. Thus, the argument went, it was likely that much of the evidence in the conspiracy trial would not inculpate petitioner and would therefore be inadmissible against him in the continuing-criminal-enterprise trial. Although a severance of the conspiracy charges against petitioner from those against the nine codefendants might have alleviated this problem, petitioner never made such a motion under Rule 14. On May 7, the court denied the Government's motion for trial together and thereby set the stage for petitioner's first trial on the conspiracy charges.

B.

The trial on the § 846 indictment took place in June 1974. A jury found petitioner and six of his codefendants guilty. Petitioner received the maximum punishment applicable to him under the statute 15 years in prison, a fine of $25,000, and a 3–year special parole term. The Court of Appeals affirmed the conviction, and this Court denied certiorari.

While the conspiracy trial and appeal were proceeding, petitioner was filing a series of pretrial motions in the pending criminal-enterprise case. When it appeared that trial was imminent, petitioner filed a motion to dismiss the indictment on the ground that in the conspiracy trial he already had been placed in jeopardy once for the same offense. He argued both that the two indictments arose out of the same transaction, and therefore the second trial should be barred under that theory of double jeopardy, and that the "same evidence" rule of Blockburger v. United States, 284 U.S. 299 (1932), should bar the second prosecution, since a § 846 conspiracy was a lesser included offense of a § 848 continuing criminal enterprise.[8] To forestall the Government's anticipated waiver argument, petitioner asserted that waiver was impossible, since his objection to trying the two counts together was based on his Sixth Amendment right to a fair trial, and his opposition to the § 848 trial was based on his Fifth Amendment double jeopardy right. A finding of waiver, according to his argument, would amount to penalizing the exercise of one constitutional right by denying another.

The Government, in its response to the motion to dismiss, asserted that §§ 846 and 848 were separate offenses, and for this reason petitioner would not be placed twice in jeopardy by the second trial. The District Court agreed with this analysis and denied petitioner's motion shortly before the second trial began.

At the second trial, the jury found petitioner guilty of engaging in a continuing criminal enterprise. Again, he received the maximum sentence for a first offender: life imprisonment and a fine of $100,000. See n. 4,

---

[8] In his opposition to the Government's motion for trial together, however, when he joined the argument that the jury would be confused by consolidation, petitioner apparently had argued in favor of construing the statutes to create separate offenses. He also joined the argument that "identity of charges" was lacking.

supra. The judgment specified that the prison sentence and the fine were "to run consecutive with sentence imposed in [the conspiracy case]." Thus, at the conclusion of the second trial, petitioner found himself with a life sentence without possibility of probation, parole, or suspension of sentence, and with fines totaling $125,000.

On appeal, the conviction and sentence were upheld. The Court of Appeals concluded that § 846 was a lesser included offense of § 848, since the continuing criminal enterprise statute expressly required proof that the accused had acted in concert with five or more other persons. In the court's view, this requirement was tantamount to a proof of conspiracy requirement.[11] Construing § 848 to require proof of agreement meant that all the elements of the § 846 offense had to be proved for § 848, in addition to the elements of a supervisory position and the obtaining of substantial income or resources; thus, §§ 846 and 848 satisfied the general test for lesser included offenses. Although the court stated that ordinarily conviction of a lesser included offense would bar a subsequent prosecution for the greater offense, relying on Gavieres v. United States, 220 U.S. 338 (1911); *Blockburger v. United States*, supra; and Waller v. Florida, 397 U.S. 387 (1970), it read Iannelli v. United States, 420 U.S. 770 (1975), to create a new double jeopardy rule applicable only to complex statutory crimes.

The two statutes at issue in *Iannelli* were 18 U.S.C. § 371, the general federal conspiracy statute, and 18 U.S.C. § 1955, the statute prohibiting illegal gambling businesses involving five or more persons. Despite language in *Iannelli* seemingly to the contrary, the Court of Appeals stated that § 371 is a lesser included offense of § 1955. The court attached no significance to the fact that § 1955 contains no requirement of action "in concert." It believed that *Iannelli* held that greater and lesser offenses could be punished separately if Congress so intended, and it adopted the same approach to the multiple-prosecution question before it. Finding that Congress, in enacting § 848, was interested in punishing severely those who made a substantial living from drug dealing, and that Congress intended to make § 848 an independent crime, the court concluded that §§ 846 and 848 were not the "same offense" for double jeopardy purposes. It therefore held that the conviction on the first indictment did not bar the prosecution on the second.

In his petition for certiorari, petitioner challenged the Court of Appeals' reading of *Iannelli* and suggested again that § 846 was a lesser included offense of § 848. He also contended that the Double Jeopardy Clause was violated by the prosecution on the greater offense after conviction for the lesser. Finally, he argued that he had not waived the double

---

[11] The District Court actually instructed the jury that the Government might prove that the object of the continuing criminal enterprise was to commit a violation under § 846, the conspiracy statute, rather than to violate § 841(a)(1). The court therefore gave a complete conspiracy charge to the jury. The Government argues that this instruction was erroneous. Without resolving that issue or exploring the implications of the Government's position, we merely note that the District Court's decision to give the instruction reflects the conceptual closeness of the two statutes.

jeopardy issue. In addition to these issues, it appears that cumulative fines were imposed on petitioner, which creates a multiple-punishment problem. We granted certiorari. We consider first the multiple prosecution, lesser included offense, and waiver points, and then we address the multiple-punishment problem.

II

A.

The Government's principal argument for affirming the judgment of the Court of Appeals is that *Iannelli* controls this case. Like the conspiracy and gambling statutes at issue in *Iannelli*, the conspiracy and continuing-criminal-enterprise statutes at issue here, in the Government's view, create two separate offenses under the "same evidence" test of *Blockburger*. The Government's position is premised on its contention that agreement is not an essential element of the § 848 offense, despite the presence in § 848(b)(2)(A) of the phrase "in concert with." If five "innocent dupes" each separately acted "in concert with" the ringleader of the continuing criminal enterprise, the Government asserts, the statutory requirement would be satisfied.

If the Government's position were right, this would be a simple case. In our opinion, however, it is not so easy to transfer the *Iannelli* result, reached in the context of two other and different statutes, to this case. In *Iannelli*, the Court specifically noted: "Wharton's Rule applies only to offenses that require concerted criminal activity, a plurality of criminal agents." 420 U.S., at 785. Elaborating on that point, the Court stated: "The essence of the crime of conspiracy is agreement, ... an element not contained in the statutory definition of the § 1955 offense." Id., at 785 n. 17. Because of the silence of § 1955 with regard to the necessity of concerted activity, the Court felt constrained to construe the statute to permit the possibility that the five persons "involved" in the gambling operation might not be acting together. See also Pinkerton v. United States, 328 U.S. 640, 643 (1946).

The same flexibility does not exist with respect to the continuing-criminal-enterprise statute. Section 848(b)(2)(A) restricts the definition of the crime to a continuing series of violations undertaken by the accused "in concert with five or more other persons." Clearly, then, a conviction would be impossible unless concerted activity were present. The express "in concert" language in the statutory definition quite plausibly may be read to provide the necessary element of "agreement" found wanting in § 1955. Even if § 848 were read to require individual agreements between the leader of the enterprise and each of the other five necessary participants, enough would be shown to prove a conspiracy. It would be unreasonable to assume that Congress did not mean anything at all when it inserted these critical words in § 848.[14] In the absence of any indication from the

---

[14] The legislative history, the use that Congress has made of the phrase "in con-cert" in other statutes, and the plain meaning of that term all support the interpreta-

legislative history or elsewhere to the contrary, the far more likely explanation is that Congress intended the word "concert" to have its common meaning of agreement in a design or plan. For the purposes of this case, therefore, we assume, arguendo, that § 848 does require proof of an agreement among the persons involved in the continuing criminal enterprise.[15] So construed, § 846 is a lesser included offense of § 848, because

tion suggested for § 848. The House Report on H.R. 18583, which eventually became Pub.L. 91–513, the Comprehensive Drug Abuse Prevention and Control Act of 1970, assumed that the meaning of "in concert" was clear, since it never defined the phrase further. See, e. g., H.R.Rep.No.91–1444, Pt. 1, p. 50 (1970). Even the writers of additional views did not include an objection to the nondefinition of the term in their criticisms of other aspects of the continuing-criminal-enterprise section of the law. The Senate Report on S. 3246, the Senate version of the same law, did shed some light on the problem. See S.Rep.No.91–613 (1969). In the Section-by-Section Analysis of the bill, the report states: "Subsection (f) of this section sets out the criteria which must be met before a defendant can be deemed involved in a continuing criminal enterprise. The court must find by a preponderance of evidence that the defendant acted in concert with or conspired with at least five other persons engaged in a continuing criminal enterprise involving violations of the act." Id., at 28. The actual language of the bill, however, used the words "in concert with" to cover both concerted action and conspiracy. Id., at 121. Thus, it is apparent that the Senate understood the term "in concert" to encompass the concept of agreement. The debates reveal that Congress was concerned with providing severe penalties for professional criminals when it included the continuing-criminal-enterprise section in the statute. See, e. g., 116 Cong.Rec. 995 (1970)(remarks of Sen. Dodd); id., at 1181 (remarks of Sen. Thurmond); id., at 33631 (remarks of Cong. Weicker); id., at 33314 (remarks of Cong. Bush). This concern undercuts the Government's argument that one professional criminal might have "conned" five innocent dupes into working for him, all of them being unaware that the purpose of the work was to conduct an illegal drug business, and none agreeing to do so. When the phrase "in concert" has been used in other statutes, it has generally connoted cooperative action and agreement. See, e. g., 2 U.S.C.

§§ 434(b)(13), 441a(a)(7)(B)(i)(1976 ed.)(Federal Election Campaign Act Amendments of 1976); 7 U.S.C. § 13c(a)(1970 ed., Supp. V)(Commodity Futures Trading Commission Act of 1974 liability as principal); 10 U.S.C. § 894(a)(Code of Military Justice mutiny or sedition); 29 U.S.C. §§ 52, 104, 105 (Norris–LaGuardia Act); 46 U.S.C. § 1227 (Merchant Marine Act agreements with other carriers forbidden); 49 U.S.C.§ 322(b)(1)(Interstate Commerce Act, Part II unlawful operation of motor carriers). This suggests that Congress intended the same words to have the same meaning in § 848. Even *Iannelli* did not require the word "conspiracy" to be spelled out in the statutory definition, as long as the concept of agreement was included therein. 420 U.S., at 785 n. 17. Since the word "concert" commonly signifies agreement of two or more persons in a common plan or enterprise, a clearly articulated statement from Congress to the contrary would be necessary before that meaning should be abandoned.

[15] In connection with this assumption, we note that until the Court of Appeals in this case found that § 846 was a lesser included offense of § 848, no other appellate court had considered the issue. Indeed, after *Iannelli* it would have been fair to assume that the question was open. The dissenting opinion here is based on the premise that it was beyond dispute that §§ 846 and 848 were so related. From there, it is easy to reason that the prosecutor should be held accountable for the presumed error that occurred. Because the premise fails, however, this case cannot be fit so neatly into the niche that would be fashioned by the dissent. Unless it is plain that two offenses are "the same" for double jeopardy purposes, the parties and the court should be entitled to assume that successive prosecutions are an available option. This assumption would only be reinforced if the defendant affirmatively asked the court to require two proceedings, and in connection with his request he actively sought postponement of the second trial, as Jeffers did. Under the circumstances, it is hardly accurate to say, as the dissent does, that Jeffers was

§ 848 requires proof of every fact necessary to show a violation under § 846 as well as proof of several additional elements[16]

B.

Brown v. Ohio, 432 U.S. 161 (1977), decided today, establishes the general rule that the Double Jeopardy Clause prohibits a State or the Federal Government from trying a defendant for a greater offense after it has convicted him of a lesser included offense. What lies at the heart of the Double Jeopardy Clause is the prohibition against multiple prosecutions for "the same offense." See United States v. Wilson, 420 U.S. 332, 343 (1975). *Brown* reaffirms the rule that one convicted of the greater offense may not be subjected to a second prosecution on the lesser offense, since that would be the equivalent of two trials for "the same offense." Because two offenses are "the same" for double jeopardy purposes unless each requires proof of an additional fact that the other does not, it follows that the sequence of the two trials for the greater and the lesser offense is immaterial, and trial on a greater offense after conviction on a lesser ordinarily is just as objectionable under the Double Jeopardy Clause as the reverse order of proceeding. Contrary to the suggestion of the Court of Appeals, *Iannelli* created no exception to these general jeopardy principles for complex statutory crimes.

The rule established in *Brown*, however, does have some exceptions. One commonly recognized exception is when all the events necessary to the greater crime have not taken place at the time the prosecution for the lesser is begun. See *Brown v. Ohio*, 432 U.S., at 169 n. 7. See also Ashe v. Swenson, 397 U.S. 436, 453 n. 7 (1970)(Brennan, J., concurring). This exception may also apply when the facts necessary to the greater were not discovered despite the exercise of due diligence before the first trial. Ibid.

If the defendant expressly asks for separate trials on the greater and the lesser offenses, or, in connection with his opposition to trial together, fails to raise the issue that one offense might be a lesser included offense of the other, another exception to the *Brown* rule emerges. This situation is no different from others in which a defendant enjoys protection under the Double Jeopardy Clause, but for one reason or another retrial is not barred. Thus, for example, in the case of a retrial after a successful appeal from a conviction, the concept of continuing jeopardy on the offense for which the defendant was convicted applies, thereby making retrial on that offense permissible. See Price v. Georgia, 398 U.S. 323 (1970); Green v. United States, 355 U.S. 184 (1957); United States v. Ball, 163 U.S. 662 (1896). In a slightly different context, the defendant's right to have the need for a

being required to give legal advice to the prosecution. On the contrary, he was simply under an obligation to preserve his double jeopardy point properly, by alerting both court and prosecution to the existence of a complex, unsettled issue.

[16] The two indictments in this case are remarkably similar in detail. It is clear that the identical agreement and transactions over the identical time period were involved in the two cases. It is also quite clear that none of the participants were "innocent dupes."

retrial measured by the strict "manifest necessity" standard of United States v. Perez, 22 U.S. (9 Wheat.) 579 (1824), does not exist if the mistrial was granted at the defendant's request. United States v. Dinitz, 424 U.S. 600 (1976). Both the trial after the appeal and the trial after the mistrial are, in a sense, a second prosecution for the same offense, but, in both situations, the policy behind the Double Jeopardy Clause does not require prohibition of the second trial. Similarly, although a defendant is normally entitled to have charges on a greater and a lesser offense resolved in one proceeding, there is no violation of the Double Jeopardy Clause when he elects to have the two offenses tried separately and persuades the trial court to honor his election.[20]

C.

In this case, trial together of the conspiracy and continuing-criminal-enterprise charges could have taken place without undue prejudice to petitioner's Sixth Amendment right to a fair trial. If the two charges had been tried in one proceeding, it appears that petitioner would have been entitled to a lesser included-offense-instruction. See Fed. Rule Crim. Proc. 31(c); Keeble v. United States, 412 U.S. 205 (1973). If such an instruction had been denied on the ground that § 846 was not a lesser included offense of § 848, petitioner could have preserved his point by proper objection. Nevertheless, petitioner did not adopt that course. Instead, he was solely responsible for the successive prosecutions for the conspiracy offense and the continuing-criminal-enterprise offense. Under the circumstances, we hold that his action deprived him of any right that he might have had against consecutive trials. It follows, therefore, that the Government was entitled to prosecute petitioner for the § 848 offense, and the only issue remaining is that of cumulative punishments upon such prosecution and conviction.

III

Although both parties, throughout the proceedings, appear to have assumed that no cumulative-punishment problem is present in this case, the imposition of the separate fines seems squarely to contradict that assumption. Fines, of course, are treated in the same way as prison sentences for purposes of double jeopardy and multiple punishment analysis. See North Carolina v. Pearce, 395 U.S. 711, 718 n. 12 (1969). In this case, since petitioner received the maximum fine applicable to him under

---

[20] The considerations relating to the propriety of a second trial obviously would be much different if any action by the Government contributed to the separate prosecutions on the lesser and greater charges. No hint of that is present in the case before us, since the Government affirmatively sought trial on the two indictments together.

Unlike the dissenters, we are unwilling to attach any significance to the fact that the grand jury elected to return two indictments against petitioner for the two statutory offenses. As the Court of Appeals' opinion made clear, before this case it was by no means settled law that § 846 was a lesser included offense of § 848. Even now, it has not been necessary to settle that issue definitively. . . .

§ 848, it is necessary to decide whether cumulative punishments are permissible for violations of §§ 846 and 848.

The critical inquiry is whether Congress intended to punish each statutory violation separately. See, e. g., *Callanan v. United States*, 364 U.S. 587, 594 (1961). In *Iannelli v. United States*, the Court concluded that Congress did intend to punish violations of § 1955 separately from § 371 conspiracy violations. Since the two offenses were different, there was no need to go further. If some possibility exists that the two statutory offenses are the "same offense" for double jeopardy purposes, however, it is necessary to examine the problem closely, in order to avoid constitutional multiple-punishment difficulties. See *North Carolina v. Pearce*, 395 U.S., at 717.

As petitioner concedes, the first issue to be considered is whether Congress intended to allow cumulative punishment for violations of §§ 846 and 848. We have concluded that it did not, and this again makes it unnecessary to reach the lesser-included-offense issue.

Section 848 itself reflects a comprehensive penalty structure that leaves little opportunity for pyramiding of penalties from other sections of the Comprehensive Drug Abuse Prevention and Control Act of 1970. Even for a first offender, the statute authorizes a maximum prison sentence of life, a fine of $100,000, and a forfeiture of all profits obtained in the enterprise and of any interest in, claim against, or property or contractual rights of any kind affording a source of influence over, the enterprise. §§ 848(a)(1), (2). The statute forbids suspension of the imposition or execution of any sentence imposed, the granting of probation, and eligibility for parole. § 848(c). In addition, § 848 is the only section in the statutes controlling drug abuse that provides for a mandatory minimum sentence. For a first offender, that minimum is 10 years. § 848(a)(1). A second or subsequent offender must receive a minimum sentence of 20 years, and he is subject to a fine of up to $200,000, as well as the forfeiture described above and the maximum of lifetime imprisonment. Ibid. Since every § 848 violation by definition also will involve a series of other felony violations of the Act, see §§ 848(b)(1), (2), there would have been no point in specifying maximum fines for the § 848 violation if cumulative punishment was to be permitted.

The legislative history of § 848 is inconclusive on the question of cumulative punishment. The policy reasons usually offered to justify separate punishment of conspiracies and underlying substantive offenses, however, are inapplicable to §§ 846 and 848. In *Callanan v. United States*, 364 U.S., at 593–94, the Court summarized these reasons:

> "(C)ollective criminal agreement partnership in crime presents a greater potential threat to the public than individual delicts. Concerted action both increases the likelihood that the criminal object will be successfully attained and decreases the probability that the individuals involved will depart from their path of criminality. Group association for criminal purposes often, if not normally, makes possible the attainment of ends more complex

than those which one criminal could accomplish. Nor is the danger of a conspiratorial group limited to the particular end toward which it has embarked. Combination in crime makes more likely the commission of crimes unrelated to the original purpose for which the group was formed. In sum, the danger which a conspiracy generates is not confined to the substantive offense which is the immediate aim of the enterprise."

As this discussion makes clear, the reason for separate penalties for conspiracies lies in the additional dangers posed by concerted activity. Section 848, however, already expressly prohibits this kind of conduct. Thus, there is little legislative need to further this admittedly important interest by authorizing consecutive penalties from the conspiracy statute.

Our conclusion that Congress did not intend to impose cumulative penalties under §§ 846 and 848 is of minor significance in this particular case. Since the Government had the right to try petitioner on the § 848 indictment, the court had the power to sentence him to whatever penalty was authorized by that statute. It had no power, however, to impose on him a fine greater than the maximum permitted by § 848. Thus, if petitioner received a total of $125,000 in fines on the two convictions, as the record indicates, he is entitled to have the fine imposed at the second trial reduced so that the two fines together do not exceed $100,000.

The judgment of the Court of Appeals, accordingly, is affirmed in part and vacated in part, and the case is remanded for further proceedings consistent with this opinion.

It is so ordered.

■ JUSTICE WHITE, concurring in the judgment in part and dissenting in part.

Because I agree with the United States that Iannelli v. United States, 420 U.S. 770 (1975), controls this case, I for that reason concur in the judgment of the Court with respect to petitioner's conviction. For the same reason and because the conspiracy proved was not used to establish the continuing criminal enterprise charged, I dissent from the Court's judgment with respect to the fines and from Part III of the plurality's opinion.

■ JUSTICE STEVENS, with whom JUSTICE BRENNAN, JUSTICE STEWART, and JUSTICE MARSHALL join, dissenting in part, and concurring in the judgment in part.

There is nothing novel about the rule that a defendant may not be tried for a greater offense after conviction of a lesser included offense. It can be traced back to Blackstone, and "has been this Court's understanding of the Double Jeopardy Clause at least since In re Nielsen, 131 U.S. 176 (1889), was decided," *Brown v. Ohio*, 432 U.S., at 168. I would not permit the prosecutor to claim ignorance of this ancient rule, or to evade it by arguing that the defendant failed to advise him of its existence or its applicability.

The defendant surely cannot be held responsible for the fact that two separate indictments were returned, or for the fact that other defendants were named in the earlier indictment, or for the fact that the Government elected to proceed to trial first on the lesser charge.[3] The other defendants had valid objections to the Government's motion to consolidate the two cases for trial. Most trial lawyers will be startled to learn that a rather routine joint opposition to that motion to consolidate has resulted in the loss of what this Court used to regard as "a vital safeguard in our society, one that was dearly won and one that should continue to be highly valued," Green v. United States, 355 U.S. 184, 198 (1957).[6]

It is ironic that, while the State's duty to give advice to an accused is contracting, see, e.g., Oregon v. Mathiason, 429 U.S. 492 (1977), a new requirement is emerging that the accused, in order to preserve a constitutional right, must inform the prosecution about the legal consequences of its acts. Even the desirability of extending Mr. Jeffers' incarceration does not justify this unique decision.

While I concur in the judgment to the extent that it vacates the cumulative fines, I respectfully dissent from the affirmance of the conviction.

NOTE ON *RUTLEDGE v. UNITED STATES*

Justice Blackmun's plurality opinion in *Jeffers* assumes, "arguendo," that 21 U.S.C. § 846 (conspiracy to distribute drugs) is a "lesser included offense" of 21 U.S.C. § 848 (conducting a continuing criminal enterprise to violate drug laws). Given what the plurality opinion says about the "concert" requirement of § 848, however, is there any possibility that § 846 and § 848 might satisfy the *Blockburger* test and be treated as separate offenses for double jeopardy purposes? Why, then, does the plurality hesitate to "settle that issue definitively"? See *Jeffers*, supra, fn. 20.

In Rutledge v. United States, ___ U.S. ___, 116 S.Ct. 1241(1996), the Court finally returned to the "lesser included offense" issue that had been left unsettled in *Jeffers*. Justice Stevens, writing for a unanimous Court, explained:

> "In the years since *Jeffers* was decided, the Courts of Appeals ... have concluded, without exception, that conspiracy is a lesser included offense of CCE. We think it is appropriate now to resolve the point definitively: For the reasons set forth in *Jeffers*, and

[3] The Government retained the alternative of trying petitioner on both charges at once, while trying the other defendants separately for conspiracy. The prosecutor never attempted this course, and defense counsel not having had an opportunity to read today's plurality opinion had no reason to believe he had a duty to suggest it. Until today it has never been the function of the defense to give legal advice to the prosecutor.

[6] The following sentence by Mr. Justice Black is also worth remembering: "If such great constitutional protections are given a narrow, grudging application, they are deprived of much of their significance." *Green*, 355 U.S., at 198.

particularly because the plain meaning of the phrase 'in concert' signifies mutual agreement in a common plan or enterprise, we hold that the element of the CCE offense requires proof of a conspiracy that would also violate § 846. Because § 846 does not require proof of any fact that is not also a part of the CCE offense, a straightforward application of the *Blockburger* test leads to the conclusion that conspiracy as defined in § 846 does not define a different offense from the CCE offense defined in § 848. Furthermore, since the latter offense is the more serious of the two, and because only one of its elements is necessary to prove a § 846 conspiracy, it is appropriate to characterize § 846 as a lesser included offense of § 848.''

Garrett v. United States

Supreme Court of the United States, 1985.
471 U.S. 773.

■ JUSTICE REHNQUIST delivered the opinion of the Court.

This case requires us to examine the double jeopardy implications of a prosecution for engaging in a "continuing criminal enterprise" (CCE), in violation of the Comprehensive Drug Abuse Prevention and Control Act of 1970, 21 U.S.C. § 848, when facts underlying a prior conviction are offered to prove one of three predicate offenses that must be shown to make out a CCE violation. Petitioner Jonathan Garrett contends that his prior conviction is a lesser included offense of the CCE charge, and, therefore, that the CCE prosecution is barred under Brown v. Ohio, 432 U.S. 161 (1977).

Between 1976 and 1981, Garrett directed an extensive marihuana importation and distribution operation involving off-loading, transporting, and storing boatloads of marihuana. These activities and related meetings and telephone calls occurred in several States, including Arkansas, Florida, Georgia, Louisiana, Massachusetts, Michigan, Texas, and Washington.

In March 1981, Garrett was charged in three substantive counts of an indictment in the Western District of Washington for his role in the off-loading and landing of approximately 12,000 pounds of marihuana from a "mother ship" at Neah Bay, Washington. He was named as a co-conspirator, but not indicted, in a fourth count charging conspiracy to import marihuana. Having learned that he was being investigated on CCE charges in Florida, Garrett moved to consolidate in the Washington proceedings "all charges anticipated, investigated and currently pending against [him]." The Government opposed the motion on the ground that no other charges had then been filed against Garrett, and the District Court denied it.

Garrett pleaded guilty to one count of importation of marihuana in violation of 21 U.S.C. §§ 952, 960(a)(1), 960(b)(2) and 18 U.S.C. § 2. He was sentenced to five years' imprisonment and a $15,000 fine; and the remaining counts against him, including possession of marihuana with intent to distribute, were dismissed without prejudice to the Government's right to prosecute him on any other offenses he may have committed.

Approximately two months after his guilty plea in Washington, Garrett was indicted in the Northern District of Florida for conspiring to import marihuana, 21 U.S.C. §§ 952, 960, 963, conspiring to possess marihuana with intent to distribute, 21 U.S.C. §§ 841, 846, using a telephone to facilitate illegal drug activities, 21 U.S.C. §§ 963, 846, 843(b), and engaging in a continuing criminal enterprise, 21 U.S.C. § 848. The District Court denied Garrett's pretrial motion to dismiss the CCE charge, made on the ground that it encompassed the Washington importation operation in violation of the Double Jeopardy Clause.

In the Florida trial, the Government introduced extensive evidence of Garrett's ongoing and widespread drug activities, including proof of the marihuana smuggling operation at Neah Bay, Washington. The court instructed the jury on the CCE count that it had to find beyond a reasonable doubt that Garrett had committed "a felony under Title 21 of the United States Code" that "was a part of a continuing series of violations," defined to be "three or more successive violations of Title 21 over a definite period of time with a single or substantially similar purpose." The court further instructed the jury that it had to find that Garrett acted "in concert with five or more other persons," that with respect to them Garrett occupied "a position of organizer, supervisor, or any position of management," and that he "received substantial income from this operation." As to the predicate violations making up the "series," the court instructed the jury that in addition to the offenses charged as substantive counts in the Florida indictment, the felony offenses of possession of marihuana with intent to distribute it, distribution of marihuana, and importation of marihuana would qualify as predicate offenses. The Washington evidence, as well as other evidence introduced in the Florida trial, tended to prove these latter three offenses.

The jury convicted Garrett on the CCE count, the two conspiracy counts, and the telephone facilitation count. He received consecutive prison terms totaling 14 years and a $45,000 fine on the latter three counts, and 40 years' imprisonment and a $100,000 fine on the CCE count. The CCE prison term was made concurrent with the prison terms on the other counts, but consecutive to the prison term from the Washington conviction. The CCE fine was in addition to the fine on the other counts and the Washington fine.

On appeal, the Court of Appeals for the Eleventh Circuit rejected Garrett's contention that his conviction in Washington for importing marihuana barred the subsequent prosecution in Florida for engaging in a continuing criminal enterprise. The court held that the Washington importation offense and the CCE offense were not the same under the Double Jeopardy Clause; hence successive prosecutions and cumulative sentences for these offenses were permissible. We granted certiorari to consider this question.

I

This case presents two of the three aspects of the Double Jeopardy Clause identified in North Carolina v. Pearce, 395 U.S. 711, 717 (1969): protection against a second prosecution for the Washington importation conviction; and protection against multiple punishments for that conviction. Garrett focuses primarily on the former protection, which we address first.

The heart of Garrett's argument entails two steps: First, notwithstanding Jeffers v. United States, 432 U.S. 137 (1977)(plurality opinion), CCE is a separate substantive offense and not a conspiracy offense because it requires completion of the criminal objective and not merely an agreement. Thus CCE is not distinct from its underlying predicates in the way that conspiracy is a distinct offense from the completed object of the conspiracy. Cf. Pinkerton v. United States, 328 U.S. 640, 643 (1946). Second, applying the test of Blockburger v. United States, 284 U.S. 299 (1932), each of the predicate offenses is the "same" for double jeopardy purposes as the CCE offense because the predicate offense does not require proof of any fact not necessary to the CCE offense. Because the latter requires proof of additional facts, including concerted activity with five other persons, a supervisory role, and substantial income, the predicates are lesser included offenses of the CCE provision. The relationship is the same, Garrett argues, as the relationship between the joyriding and auto theft statutes involved in *Brown v. Ohio*, supra, and thus a subsequent prosecution for the greater CCE offense is barred by the earlier conviction of the lesser marihuana importation offense.

Where the same conduct violates two statutory provisions, the first step in the double jeopardy analysis is to determine whether the legislature—in this case Congress—intended that each violation be a separate offense. If Congress intended that there be only one offense—that is, a defendant could be convicted under either statutory provision for a single act, but not under both—there would be no statutory authorization for a subsequent prosecution after conviction of one of the two provisions, and that would end the double jeopardy analysis. Cf. Albrecht v. United States, 273 U.S. 1, 11 (1927).

This question of legislative intent arose in *Blockburger* in the context of multiple punishments imposed in a single prosecution. Based on one drug sale, *Blockburger* was convicted of both selling a drug not in the original stamped package and selling it not in pursuance of a written order of the purchaser. The sale violated two separate statutory provisions, and the question was whether "the accused committed two offenses or only one." 284 U.S., at 303–04. The rule stated in *Blockburger* was applied as a rule of statutory construction to help determine legislative intent. Significantly, after setting out the rule, the Court cited a paragraph in *Albrecht*, supra, 273 U.S., at 11, which included the following statement: "There is nothing in the Constitution which prevents Congress from punishing separately each step leading to the consummation of a transaction which it has power to prohibit and punishing also the completed transaction." We have recently indicated that the *Blockburger* rule is not controlling when the legislative intent is clear from the face of the statute or the legislative history. Missouri v. Hunter, 459 U.S. 359, 368 (1983). Indeed, it would be difficult to contend otherwise without converting what is essentially a factual inquiry as to legislative intent into a conclusive presumption of law.

In the present case the application of the *Blockburger* rule as a conclusive determinant of legislative intent, rather than as a useful canon of statutory construction, would lead to the conclusion urged by Garrett: that Congress intended the conduct at issue to be punishable either as a predicate offense, or as a CCE offense, but not both. The language, structure, and legislative history of the Comprehensive Drug Abuse, Prevention and Control Act of 1970, however, show in the plainest way that Congress intended the CCE provision to be a separate criminal offense which was punishable in addition to, and not as a substitute for, the predicate offenses. Insofar as the question is one of legislative intent, the *Blockburger* presumption must of course yield to a plainly expressed contrary view on the part of Congress.

The language of 21 U.S.C. § 848 affirmatively states an offense for which punishment will be imposed. It begins: "Any person who engages in a continuing criminal enterprise shall be sentenced to a term of imprisonment which may not be less than 10 years and which may be up to life imprisonment, to a fine of not more than $100,000, and to the forfeiture prescribed in paragraph (2)." § 848(a)(1). At this point there is no reference to other statutory offenses, and a separate penalty is set out, rather than a multiplier of the penalty established for some other offense. This same paragraph then incorporates its own recidivist provision, providing for twice the penalty for repeat violators of this section. Significantly the language expressly refers to "one or more prior convictions ... under this section." Next, subparagraph (2), which sets out various forfeiture provisions, also refers to any person "who is convicted under paragraph (1) of engaging in a continuing criminal enterprise," again suggesting that § 848 is a distinct offense for which one is separately convicted.

Subsection (b) of § 848 defines the conduct that constitutes being "engaged in a continuing criminal enterprise": "(1) he violates any provision of this subchapter or subchapter II of this chapter [establishing various drug offenses] the punishment for which is a felony, and (2) such violation is a part of a continuing series of violations of this subchapter or subchapter II of this chapter—(A) which are undertaken by such person in concert with five or more other persons with respect to whom such person occupies a position of organizer, a supervisory position, or any other position of management, and (B) from which such person obtains substantial income or resources." A common-sense reading of this definition reveals a carefully crafted prohibition aimed at a special problem. This language is designed to reach the "top brass" in the drug rings, not the lieutenants and foot soldiers.

The definition of a continuing criminal enterprise is not drafted in the way that a recidivist provision would be drafted. Indeed § 848(a)(1), as already noted, contains language that is typical of that sort of provision. Moreover, the very next section of the statute entitled "Dangerous Special Drug Offender Sentencing" is a recidivist provision. It is drafted in starkly contrasting language which plainly is not intended to create a separate offense. For example, it provides for a special hearing before the court sitting without a jury to consider the evidence of prior offenses, and the determination that a defendant is a dangerous special drug offender is made on a preponderance of the information by the court. See 21 U.S.C. § 849.

This conclusion as to Congress' intent is fortified by the legislative history. H.R. 18583 is the bill that was enacted to become the Comprehensive Drug Abuse Prevention and Control Act of 1970. In its section-by-section analysis, the House Committee Report states: "Section 408(a) [21 U.S.C. § 848(a)] provides that any person who engages in a continuing criminal enterprise shall upon conviction for that offense be sentenced to a term of imprisonment for not less than 10 years and up to life.... If the person engages in this activity subsequent to one or more convictions under this section, he shall receive a penalty of not less than 20 years' imprisonment...." H.R.Rep. No. 91–1444, pt. 1, p. 50 (1970). The intent to create a separate offense could hardly be clearer.

As originally introduced in the House, H.R. 18583 had a section entitled "Continuing Criminal Enterprises" which in reality was a recidivist provision, like the current 21 U.S.C. § 849, that provided for enhanced sentences for "a special offender," who "committed [a drug] felony as part of a pattern of conduct which was criminal under applicable laws of any jurisdiction, which constituted a substantial source of his income, and in which he manifested special skill or expertise." The House Committee substituted for this provision an amendment offered by Representative Dingell that ultimately became the current § 848. "Instead of providing a post-conviction-presentencing procedure, [the Dingell amendment] made engagement in a continuing criminal enterprise a new and distinct offense with all its elements triable in court." H.R.Rep. No. 91–1444, pt. 1, pp. 83–84 (1970); see 116 Cong.Rec. 33302 (1970)(remarks of Rep. Eckhardt).

During consideration of the bill by the full House, Representative Poff offered an amendment which would restore the recidivist provision to the bill in addition to the Dingell provision. Explaining the differences between the two approaches, Representative Eckhardt stated: "[T]he Dingell amendment created a new offense which would have to be triable in all its parts by admissible evidence brought before the court, whereas the post-conviction presentence [procedure] of the original bill similar to the Poff provisions provided that some report upon which sentence would be based would be available to the judge, cross-examination would be available of those who presented the report, but not of those who may have contributed to it." Ibid. Later in the debate, Representative Poff explained his proposed amendment further: "Mr. Chairman, the most dangerous criminal in the criminal drug field is the organized crime offender, the habitual offender, the professional criminal." "Mr. Chairman, we need special penalties in my opinion for these special criminals. Constitutional scholars have suggested two approaches to deal with such offenders. The first is the creation of a separate crime with separate penalties. The second approach is the imposition of longer sentences upon those convicted first of the basic crime and then shown to be dangerous offenders." "Mr. Chairman, the first approach, the separate crime approach, is the approach taken by section 408 of the Committee bill [21 U.S.C. § 848]. The second is found in the amendment which I have just offered which adds two new sections to the bill, sections 409 and 410 [21 U.S.C. §§ 849 and 850]." Id., at 33630. The distinction between the two approaches was emphasized in the continuing debate. For example, Representative Eckhardt stated: "Under the Dingell amendment, if you are going to prove a man guilty, you have to come into court and prove every element of the continuing criminal offense." Representative Poff concurred in this characterization of the CCE provision "which embodies a new separate criminal offense with a separate criminal penalty." Representative Poff distinguished this approach from his proposed amendment which "authorizes the judge to impose the extended sentence upon the defendant in the dock who has already been found guilty by the jury of the basic charge." Id., at 33631. The Poff amendment was adopted, id., at 33634, and both approaches are contained in the statute, 21 U.S.C. §§ 848, 849, and 850.

In view of this legislative history, it is indisputable that Congress intended to create a separate CCE offense. One could still argue, however, that having created the separate offense, Congress intended it, where applicable, to be a substitute for the predicate offenses. Nowhere in the legislative history is it stated that a big-time drug operator could be prosecuted and convicted for the separate predicate offenses as well as the CCE offense. The absence of such a statement, however, is not surprising; given the motivation behind the legislation and the temper of the debate, such a statement would merely have stated the obvious. Congress was seeking to add a new enforcement tool to the substantive drug offenses already available to prosecutors. During the debate on the Poff amendment, for example, Representative Fascell stated: "I see no reason to treat a drug trafficker any less harshly than an organized crime racketeer. Their acts are equally heinous, the consequences equally severe, and their punishment equally justified." Representative Weicker stated: "The penalty structure has been designed to accommodate all types of drug offenders, from the casual drug user and experimenter to the organized crime syndicates engaged in unlawful transportation and distribution of illicit drugs." He continued, "This bill goes further in providing those persons charged with enforcing it a wide variety of enforcement tools which will enable them to more effectively combat the illicit drug trafficker and meet the increased demands we have imposed on them." Representative Taft stated: "[T]his amendment will do much at least to help a coordinated attack on the organized crime problem within the purview of this legislation.... Hopefully, we will see other legislation coming along broadening the attack on the crime syndicates even further." 116 Cong.Rec. 33630–31 (1970). It runs counter to common sense to infer from comments such as these, which pervade the entire debate and which stand unrebutted, that Congress intended to substitute the CCE offense for the underlying predicate offenses in the case of a big-time drug dealer rather than to permit prosecution for CCE in addition to prosecution for the predicate offenses.

Finally, it would be illogical for Congress to intend that a choice be made between the predicate offenses and the CCE offense in pursuing major drug dealers. While in the instant case Garrett claims that the Government was aware of the possibility of bringing the CCE charge before he was indicted on the Washington offenses, in many cases the Government would catch a drug dealer for one offense before it was aware of or had the evidence to make a case for other drug offenses he had committed or in the future would commit. The Government would then be forced to choose between prosecuting the dealer on the offense of which it could prove him guilty or releasing him with the idea that he would continue his drug-dealing activities so that the Government might catch him twice more and then be able to prosecute him on the CCE offense. Such a situation is absurd and clearly not what Congress intended.

II

Having determined that Congress intended CCE to be a separate offense and that it intended to permit prosecution for both the predicate offenses and the CCE offense, we must now determine whether prosecution for a CCE offense after an earlier prosecution for a predicate offense is constitutional under the Double Jeopardy Clause of the Fifth Amendment. The Double Jeopardy Clause provides: "[N]or shall any person be subject for the same offence to be twice put in jeopardy of life or limb." The critical inquiry is whether a CCE offense is considered the "same offense" as one or more of its predicate offenses within the meaning of the Double Jeopardy Clause.

Quite obviously the CCE offense is not, in any commonsense or literal meaning of the term, the "same" offense as one of the predicate offenses. The CCE offense requires the jury to find that the defendant committed a predicate offense, and in addition that the predicate offense was part of a continuing series of predicate offenses undertaken by the defendant in concert with five or more other persons, that the defendant occupied the position of an organizer or manager, and that the defendant obtained substantial income or resources from the continuing series of violations.

In order to properly analyze the successive prosecution issue, we must examine not only the statute which Congress has enacted, but also the charges which form the basis of the Government's prosecution here. Petitioner pleaded guilty in the Western District of Washington in May 1981 to a count charging importation of 12,000 pounds of marihuana at Neah Bay, Washington, on August 26, 1980. He was indicted in the Northern District of Florida in July 1981, on charges of conspiring to import "multi-ton quantities of marihuana and marihuana 'Thai sticks'" from January 1976 to July 16, 1981; of conspiring to possess with intent to distribute marihuana over the same period of time; and of engaging in a continuing criminal enterprise over the same period of time. Thus at the very moment he made his motion to require "consolidation" of all the charges against him in the Western District of Washington, he was engaging in criminal conduct of which he was later found guilty by a jury in the Northern District of Florida.

Petitioner contends that the marihuana importation charge to which he pleaded guilty in Washington was a "lesser included offense" of the CCE offense of which he was convicted in Florida. He points out that evidence of the Washington offense was introduced at the Florida trial, and that the jury was permitted to find that the Washington violation was one of the "predicate offenses" for the CCE charge in Florida. He relies on Brown v. Ohio, 432 U.S. 161 (1977), for his conclusion that the use of the Washington offense as an element of the Florida charge placed him twice in jeopardy in violation of the Fifth Amendment to the United States Constitution.

Brown v. Ohio held that, where the misdemeanor of joyriding was a lesser included offense in the felony of auto theft, a prosecution for the misdemeanor barred a second prosecution for the felony. We think there is a good deal of difference between the classic relation of the "lesser included offense" to the greater offense presented in *Brown*, on the one hand, and the relationship between the Washington marihuana offense and the CCE charge involved in this case, on the other. The defendant in *Brown* had stolen an automobile and driven it for several days. He had engaged in a single course of conduct—driving a stolen car. The very same conduct would support a misdemeanor prosecution for joyriding or a felony prosecution for auto theft, depending only on the defendant's state of mind while he engaged in the conduct in question. Every moment of his conduct was as relevant to the joyriding charge as it was to the auto theft charge.

In the case before us the situation is quite different. The count in the Washington indictment to which Garrett pleaded guilty charged importation of 12,000 pounds of marihuana at Neah Bay on August 26, 1980. The Washington indictment was returned on March 17, 1981, and a guilty plea entered on May 18, 1981. Two other counts of the indictment, including causing interstate travel to facilitate importation of marihuana on or about October 24, 1979, were dismissed without prejudice to the Government's right subsequently to prosecute any other offense Garrett may have committed.

The CCE indictment returned against Garrett in Florida was returned on July 16, 1981. It charged that he had, from January 1976, "up to and including [July 16, 1981]," conspired in that district and "divers other districts" to import multi-ton quantities of marihuana and marihuana "Thai sticks" in violation of applicable federal law. Another count charged conspiracy to possess with intent to distribute marihuana over the same period of more than five years. A third count of the Florida indictment charged that Garrett had engaged in the Northern District of Florida and in "divers other districts" in a continuing criminal enterprise over the same 5½-year period.

Obviously the conduct in which Garrett was charged with engaging in the Florida indictment, when compared with that with which he was charged in the Washington indictment, does not lend itself to the simple analogy of a single course of conduct—stealing a car—comprising a lesser included misdemeanor within a felony. Here the continuing criminal enterprise was alleged to have spanned more than five years; the acts charged in the Washington indictment were alleged to have occurred on single days in 1979 and 1980, respectively. Whenever it was during the 5½-year period alleged in the indictment that Garrett committed the first of the three predicate offenses required to form the basis for a CCE prosecution, it could not then have been said with any certainty that he would necessarily go ahead and commit the other violations required to render him liable on a CCE charge. Every minute that Nathaniel Brown drove or possessed the stolen automobile he was simultaneously committing both the lesser included misdemeanor and the greater felony, but the same simply is not true of Garrett. His various boatload smuggling operations in Louisiana, for example, obviously involved incidents of conduct wholly separate from his "mother boat" operations in Washington. These significant differences caution against ready transposition of the "lesser included offense" principles of double jeopardy from the classically simple situation presented in *Brown* to the multilayered conduct, both as to time and to place, involved in this case.

Were we to sustain Garrett's claim, the Government would have been able to proceed against him in either one of only two ways. It would have to have withheld the Washington charges, alleging crimes committed in October 1979 and August 1980, from the grand jury which indicted Garrett in March 1981, until it was prepared to present to a grand jury the CCE charge which was alleged to have been, and found by a jury to be, continuing on each of those dates; or it would have to have submitted the CCE charge to the Washington grand jury in March 1981, even though the indictment ultimately returned against Garrett on that charge alleged that the enterprise had continued until July 1981.[2] We do not think that the

---

[2] Justice Stevens in dissent argues that, although the Neah Bay prosecution in Washington does not bar Garrett's later prosecution for a CCE that ended before the Neah Bay importation took place, none of the evidence pertaining to the latter crime could be used consistently with the Double Jeopardy Clause to show a CCE. While it may be true that with the benefit of hindsight the Government could have indicted and the jury convicted for a CCE that began in December 1976, and continued until October 1979, that is not the crime which the indictment charged nor for which the jury convicted. The Government indicted for a CCE beginning in 1976 and continuing through July 1981, months after the Neah Bay indictment had been returned. Nothing in the record indicates that the Government's inclusion of the months following the Neah Bay indictment within the time of the CCE charge was unsupported by the evidence which would be adduced, and therefore merely an artificial attempt by the Government to extend the time period covered by the indictment to avoid a double jeopardy claim. The Government, and not the courts, is responsible for initiating a criminal prosecution, and subject to applicable constitutional limitations it is entitled to choose those offenses for which it wishes to indict and the evidence upon which it wishes to base the prosecution. Whether or not Justice Stevens is correct in asserting that the Neah Bay charge was not necessary to establish one of the three predicate of-

Double Jeopardy Clause may be employed to force the Government's hand in this manner, however we were to resolve Garrett's lesser-included-offense argument. One who insists that the music stop and the piper be paid at a particular point must at least have stopped dancing himself before he may seek such an accounting.

Petitioner urges that "[w]here the charges arise from a single criminal act, occurrence, episode, or transaction, they must be tried in a single proceeding. *Brown v. Ohio*, 432 U.S., at 170 (Brennan, J., concurring)." We have steadfastly refused to adopt the "single transaction" view of the Double Jeopardy Clause. But it would seem to strain even that doctrine to describe Garrett's multifarious multistate activities as a "single transaction." For the reasons previously stated, we also have serious doubts as to whether the offense to which Garrett pleaded guilty in Washington was a "lesser included offense" within the CCE charge so that the prosecution of the former would bar a prosecution of the latter. But we may assume, for purposes of decision here, that the Washington offense was a lesser included offense, because in our view Garrett's claim of double jeopardy would still not be sustainable.

In Diaz v. United States, 223 U.S. 442 (1912), the Court had before it an initial prosecution for assault and battery, followed by a prosecution for homicide when the victim eventually died from injuries inflicted in the course of the assault. The Court rejected the defendant's claim of double jeopardy, holding that the two were not the "same offense": "The homicide charged against the accused in the Court of First Instance and the assault and battery for which he was tried before the justice of the peace, although identical in some of their elements, were distinct offenses both in law and in fact. The death of the injured person was the principal element of the homicide, but was no part of the assault and battery. At the time of the trial for the latter the death had not ensued, and not until it did ensue was the homicide committed. Then, and not before, was it possible to put the accused in jeopardy for that offense." Id., at 448-49.

In the present case, as in *Diaz*, the continuing criminal enterprise charged against Garrett in Florida had not been completed at the time that he was indicted in Washington. The latter event took place in March 1981, whereas the continuing criminal enterprise charged in the Florida indictment and found by the trial jury extended from January 1976 to July 1981. The evidence at trial showed, for example, that Garrett was arrested for traffic offenses and other violations on July 23, 1981, while out on bail pending sentencing for the Washington conviction. He told the arresting officer that the officer had caught "somebody big" and that he was a "smuggler." At the time of the arrest, Garrett was carrying $6,253 in cash. About $30 of this was in quarters. He explained that he needed them to make long-distance phone calls, on which he sometimes spent $25

fenses for a CCE charge, the Government obviously viewed the matter differently. We think that for the reasons stated in the text the Double Jeopardy Clause does not require the Government to dispense with the use of the Neah Bay operation as a predicate offense in the CCE prosecution in Florida.

to $50 a day. He also told the arresting officer and a federal agent who interviewed him the next morning that he had just bought the truck he had been driving for $13,000 cash and that he used it for smuggling. He further stated that he had a yacht in Hawaii which he had purchased for $160,000 cash. This evidence is consistent with the jury's verdict that Garrett continued his CCE activities into July 1981.

We think this evidence not only permits but requires the conclusion that the CCE charged in Florida, alleged to have begun in January 1976, and continued up to mid-July 1981, was under *Diaz* a different offense from that charged in the Washington indictment. We cannot tell, without considerable sifting of the evidence and speculating as to what juries might do, whether the Government could in March 1981 have successfully indicted and prosecuted Garrett for a different continuing criminal enterprise—one ending in March 1981. But we do not think any such sifting or speculation is required at the behest of one who at the time the first indictment is returned is continuing to engage in other conduct found criminal by the jury which tried the second indictment.

It may well be, as Justice Stevens suggests in his dissenting opinion, that the Florida indictment did not by its terms indicate that the Neah Bay importation would be used as evidence to support it, and therefore at the time the pretrial motion to dismiss on double jeopardy grounds was made the District Court in Florida could not have rendered an informed decision on petitioner's motion. But there can be no doubt that by the time the evidence had all been presented in the Florida trial, and the jury was charged, only one reasonable conclusion could be drawn by the District Court: the Government's evidence with respect to the CCE charge included acts which took place after March 1981, the date of the Washington indictment, and up to and including July 1981. Therefore, the continuing criminal enterprise charged by the Government had not been completed at the time the Washington indictment was returned, and under the *Diaz* rule evidence of the Neah Bay importation might be used to show one of the predicate offenses.

Having concluded that Congress intended CCE to be a separate offense and that it does not violate the Double Jeopardy Clause under the facts of this case to prosecute the CCE offense after a prior conviction for one of the predicate offenses, the only remaining issue is whether the Double Jeopardy Clause bars cumulative punishments. Garrett's sentence on the CCE conviction was consecutive to his sentence on the Washington conviction. In this connection, "the Double Jeopardy Clause does no more than prevent the sentencing court from prescribing greater punishment than the legislature intended." *Missouri v. Hunter*, 459 U.S., at 366. As discussed above, Congress intended to create a separate offense. The presumption when Congress creates two distinct offenses is that it intends to permit cumulative sentences, and legislative silence on this specific issue does not establish an ambiguity or rebut this presumption: "[The defendants] read much into nothing. Congress cannot be expected to specifically address each issue of statutory construction which may arise. But, as we have previously noted, Congress is 'predominantly a lawyer's body,' ... and it is appropriate for us 'to assume that our elected representatives ... know the law.' ... As a result if anything is to be assumed from the congressional silence on this point, it is that Congress was aware of the *Blockburger* rule and legislated with it in mind. It is not a function of this Court to presume that 'Congress was unaware of what it accomplished.' " Id., 450 U.S., at 341–42. Here, of course, Congress was not silent as to its intent to create separate offenses notwithstanding *Blockburger*, and we can assume it was aware that doing so would authorize cumulative punishments absent some indication of contrary intent.

Moreover, disallowing cumulative sentences would have the anomalous effect in many cases of converting the large fines provided by § 848 into ceilings. Congress established the large fines in § 848 in an effort to deprive big-time drug dealers of some of their enormous profits, which often cannot be traced directly to their crimes for forfeiture purposes. The fines for a three-time offender who has been previously convicted of a drug felony could amount to $150,000 for the predicate offenses standing alone—an amount that exceeds the ceiling for a first-time CCE fine. Compare § 841(b)(1)(A) with § 848(a)(1). Congress was bent on depriving the big-time drug dealer of his profits; it is doubtful that Congress intended to force an election of a lower maximum fine in such a situation in order to attempt to obtain the life imprisonment penalty available under the CCE provision.

In *Jeffers v. United States*, 432 U.S., at 156–57, a plurality of this Court stated that § 848 "reflects a comprehensive penalty structure that leaves little opportunity for pyramiding of penalties from other sections of the Comprehensive Drug Abuse Prevention and Control Act of 1970." The focus of the analysis in *Jeffers* was the permissibility of cumulative punishments for conspiracy under § 846 and for CCE under § 848, and the plurality reasonably concluded that the dangers posed by a conspiracy and a CCE were similar and thus there would be little purpose in cumulating the penalties. The same is not true of the substantive offenses created by the Act and conspiracy, and by the same logic, it is not true of the substantive offenses and CCE. We have been required in the present case, as we were not in *Jeffers*, to consider the relationship between substantive predicate offenses and a CCE. We think here logic supports the conclusion, also indicated by the legislative history, that Congress intended separate punishments for the underlying substantive predicates and for the CCE offense. Congress may, of course, so provide if it wishes.

The judgment of the Court of Appeals is affirmed.

It is so ordered.

■ JUSTICE POWELL took no part in the decision of this case.

■ JUSTICE O'CONNOR, concurring.

I agree that, on the facts of this case, the Double Jeopardy Clause does not bar prosecution and sentencing under 21 U.S.C. § 848 for engaging in a continuing criminal enterprise even though Garrett pleaded guilty to one of the predicate offenses in an earlier prosecution. This conclusion is admittedly in tension with certain language in prior opinions of the Court. E.g., Brown v. Ohio, 432 U.S. 161, 166 (1977). I write separately to explain why I believe that today's holding comports with the fundamental purpose of the Double Jeopardy Clause and with the method of analysis used in our more recent decisions.

The Double Jeopardy Clause declares: "[N]or shall any person be subject for the same offense to be twice put in jeopardy of life or limb...." This constitutional proscription serves primarily to preserve the finality of judgments in criminal prosecutions and to protect the defendant from prosecutorial overreaching. See, e.g., Ohio v. Johnson, 467 U.S. 493, 498–99 (1984). In Green v. United States, 355 U.S. 184 (1957), the Court explained: "The underlying idea, one that is deeply ingrained in at least the Anglo-American system of jurisprudence, is that the State with all its resources and power should not be allowed to make repeated attempts to convict an individual for an alleged offense, thereby subjecting him to embarrassment, expense and ordeal and compelling him to live in a continuing state of anxiety and insecurity, as well as enhancing the possibility that even though innocent he may be found guilty." Id., at 187–88.

Decisions by this Court have consistently recognized that the finality guaranteed by the Double Jeopardy Clause is not absolute, but instead must accommodate the societal interest in prosecuting and convicting those who violate the law. The Court accordingly has held that a defendant who successfully appeals a conviction generally is subject to retrial. Similarly, double jeopardy poses no bar to another trial where a judge declares a mistrial because of "manifest necessity." Illinois v. Somerville, 410 U.S. 458 (1973). Such decisions indicate that absent "governmental oppression of the sort against which the Double Jeopardy Clause was intended to protect," United States v. Scott, 437 U.S. 82, 91 (1978), the compelling public interest in punishing crimes can outweigh the interest of the defendant in having his culpability conclusively resolved in one proceeding.

Brown v. Ohio, supra, held that the Double Jeopardy Clause prohibits prosecution of a defendant for a greater offense when he has already been tried and acquitted or convicted on a lesser included offense. The concerns for finality that support this conclusion, however, are no more absolute than those involved in other contexts. See Jeffers v. United States, 432 U.S. 137, 152 (1977)(plurality opinion). Instead, successive prosecution on a greater offense may be permitted where justified by the public interest in law enforcement and the absence of prosecutorial overreaching. For example, in Diaz v. United States, 223 U.S. 442, 449 (1912), the Court found no double jeopardy bar to a prosecution for murder where the victim of an assault died after the defendant's trial for assault and battery. *Diaz* implies that prosecution for a lesser offense does not prevent subsequent prosecution for a greater offense where the latter depends on facts occurring after the first trial. Dicta in *Brown v. Ohio* suggested that the same conclusion would apply where the later prosecution rests on facts that the government could not have discovered earlier through due diligence.

Application of the rule of *Brown v. Ohio* is also affected by the actions of the defendant himself. In *Jeffers v. United States,* supra, the plurality opinion rejected a claim of double jeopardy where prosecution for a greater offense followed a guilty verdict for a lesser offense, and the successive prosecution resulted from the defendant's opposition to consolidated trials. Last Term, the Court relied on *Jeffers* to hold that where a court accepts, over the prosecution's objection, a defendant's guilty plea to lesser included offenses, double jeopardy does not prevent further prosecution on remaining, greater offenses. *Ohio v. Johnson*, supra, 467 U.S. at 501–02. After noting the State's interest in convicting those who have violated its laws and the absence of governmental overreaching, *Johnson* observed that the defendant "should not be entitled to use the Double Jeopardy Clause as a sword to prevent the State from completing its prosecution on the remaining charges."

Turning to the circumstances of this case, I conclude that Garrett cannot validly argue that the Government is prevented from using evidence relating to his May 1981 conviction to prove his participation in a continuing criminal enterprise from January 1976 through July 1981. I am willing to assume, arguendo, that the 1981 conviction for importation of marihuana is a lesser included offense of the charges for violating 18 U.S.C. § 848. As noted ante, the Government both alleged and presented evidence that Garrett's violation of § 848 continued after the conviction on the lesser included offense. Although the Government alleged participation in the unlawful continuing enterprise through July 1981, none of the events occurring after the date of the earlier prosecution were essential elements to prove a violation of § 848. Thus, this case falls somewhere between *Diaz* and *Brown v. Ohio*. The dissent reads the latter decision as limiting application of *Diaz* to circumstances where the facts necessary to the greater offense occur or are discovered after the first prosecution. Although I find merit to this position, I reach a different conclusion upon balancing the interests protected by the Double Jeopardy Clause.

The approach advocated by the dissent would effectively force the Government's hand with respect to prosecution under § 848. Under that approach, once the Government believes that facts sufficient to prove a continuing criminal enterprise exist, it can either bring charges under § 848 or seek conviction only for a predicate offense while forgoing its later use to prove a continuing violation of § 848. The decision to bring charges under § 848, however, will necessarily and appropriately depend on prosecutorial judgments concerning the adequacy of the evidence, the efficient allocation of enforcement resources, and the desirability of seeking the statute's severe sanctions. These considerations may be affected by events occurring after the last necessary predicate offense. Where the defendant continues unlawful conduct after the time the Government prosecutes him for a predicate offense, I do not think he can later contend that the Government is foreclosed from using that offense in another prosecution to prove the continuing violation of § 848. Cf. *Jeffers, supra,* 432 U.S. at 154. As the Court noted in another context, "the Double Jeopardy Clause, which guards against Government oppression, does not relieve a defendant from the consequences of his voluntary choice." *United States v. Scott, supra,* 437 U.S., at 99.

The Court's holding does not leave the defendant unduly exposed to oppressive tactics by the Government. Any acquittal on a predicate offense would of course bar the Government from later attempting to relitigate issues in a prosecution under § 848. Ashe v. Swenson, 397 U.S. 436 (1970). This fact will prevent the Government from "treat[ing] the first trial as no more than a dry run for the second prosecution," id., at 447. Moreover, I note that we do not decide in this case whether a defendant would have a valid double jeopardy claim if the Government failed in a later prosecution to allege and to present evidence of a continuing violation of § 848 after an earlier conviction for a predicate offense. Certainly the defendant's interest in finality would be more compelling where there is no indication of continuing wrongdoing after the first prosecution.

For the reasons stated, I agree that under the circumstances of this case the Double Jeopardy Clause does not bar Garrett's prosecution under § 848. Because I also agree that Congress intended to authorize separate punishment for the underlying predicate offenses and the violation of § 848, I join the opinion of the Court.

■ JUSTICE STEVENS, with whom JUSTICE BRENNAN and JUSTICE MARSHALL join, dissenting.

While I agree with the Court that petitioner's conviction for importing 12,000 pounds of marihuana into Neah Bay, Washington, on August 26, 1980, does not bar his prosecution for a continuing criminal enterprise that began in December 1976, and continued into October 1979, I do not agree with the Court's analysis of the double jeopardy implications of the first conviction or with its decision to affirm the judgment of the Court of Appeals. In my opinion, the separate indictment, conviction, and sentencing for the Neah Bay transaction make it constitutionally impermissible to use that transaction as one of the predicate offenses needed to establish a continuing criminal enterprise in a subsequent prosecution under 21 U.S.C. § 848.

In order to explain my position, I shall first emphasize the difference between the Washington and the Florida proceedings and the limited extent of their overlap, then identify the relevant constraint that is imposed by the Double Jeopardy Clause, and finally note the flaw in the Court's analysis.

I

The Washington and Florida indictments were returned within three months of each other; they focus on two sets of transactions that occurred in almost mutually exclusive time periods. The fact that the later Florida indictment deals with the earlier series of events is a source of some confusion that, I believe, can be put to one side if we begin by describing the Florida indictment—the one that gave rise to the case we are now reviewing.

The Florida Indictment

On July 16, 1981, a grand jury in the Northern District of Florida returned an 11–count indictment against petitioner and five other defendants. Petitioner was named as a defendant in seven counts, four of which refer to the use of a telephone on a specific date in 1978 or 1979. The three counts relevant to the present issue charged petitioner with conspiracy to import marihuana (Counts I and II) and with conducting a continuing criminal enterprise (Count XI) in violation of 21 U.S.C. § 848.

The contours of the prosecution's case are suggested by the 34 overt acts alleged in Count I as having been performed by the six defendants and five named co-conspirators. Each of the first 33 overt acts was alleged to have occurred in the period between December 1976 and August 1979; the 34th occurred on October 25, 1979. The three principal transactions involved (1) the unloading of about 30,000 pounds of marihuana from the vessel Buck Lee at Fourchan Landing, Louisiana, in December 1976; (2) the arrival of the vessel Mr. Frank with a multi-ton load of marihuana at a boatyard near Crown Point, Louisiana, in June 1977; and (3) the voyage of the vessel Morning Star from Mobile, Alabama, to Santa Marta, Colombia, to pick up 28,145 pounds of marihuana in June 1979. Notably, although each of the three principal transactions would obviously have supported a substantive charge of importation in violation of 21 U.S.C. § 812 and § 952, no such charge was made against petitioner. Instead, Count XI charged that he had engaged in a continuing criminal enterprise (CCE) in violation of 21 U.S.C. § 848 "from in or about the month of January, 1976, and continuing thereafter up to and including the date of the filing of this indictment."

The Washington Indictment

On March 17, 1981, a grand jury in the Western District of Washington returned a four-count indictment against petitioner and three other defendants. None of these co-defendants was named as a defendant in the Florida indictment. Count I alleged a conspiracy beginning in or about September 1979 and continuing through August 26, 1980, to import 12,000 pounds of marihuana. The 15 alleged overt acts all occurred between September 1979 and October 1980, and all related to the unloading of 12,000 pounds of marihuana from a "mother ship" to fishing vessels in Neah Bay, Washington. In addition to the conspiracy count, the indictment also contained three substantive counts, but it did not make a CCE charge.

There is some overlap between the Florida and the Washington indictments. The 34th overt act alleged in the Florida indictment was a meeting in Bellevue, Washington, on October 25, 1979, to discuss plans to import a shipload of marihuana. The first three overt acts in the Washington indictment refer to activities in Bellevue, Washington, in September and October 1979, which apparently related to the Neah Bay landing in August of the following year. Moreover, the final allegation in Count XI of the Florida indictment refers to the yacht Sun Chaser III, which apparently was the "mother ship" in the Neah Bay incident.

Thus, the two indictments appear to identify a series of four major importations in four different vessels over a 4–year period. The first three, together with the initial planning of the fourth, are plainly adequate to constitute a CCE. The question in the case, therefore, is whether the conviction on the fourth transaction, at Neah Bay—which occurred before the Florida case went to trial—makes it impermissible to use that transaction as a predicate offense to establish the CCE violation in the later prosecution.

II

Proper analysis of the double jeopardy implications of petitioner's conviction for importing marihuana into Neah Bay, Washington, in August 1980 requires consideration not only of the general rule prohibiting successive prosecutions for greater and lesser offenses but also of an exception that may apply when the lesser offense is first prosecuted. The general rule is easily stated. The "Double Jeopardy Clause prohibits a State or the Federal Government from trying a defendant for a greater offense after it has convicted him of a lesser included offense." This rule applies to "complex statutory crimes." The CCE offense proscribed by § 848 is clearly such a crime.

In Brown v. Ohio, 432 U.S. 161 (1977), after making a full statement of the general rule,[15] we noted the exception that may preserve the government's right to prosecute for a greater offense after a prosecution for a lesser offense. We stated:

> "An exception may exist where the State is unable to proceed on the more serious charge at the outset because the additional facts necessary to sustain that charge have not occurred or have not been discovered despite the exercise of due diligence. See Diaz v. United States, 223 U.S. 442, 448–49 (1912); *Ashe v. Swenson*, [397 U.S.], at 453 n. 7 (Brennan, J., concurring)."

The fact that the general rule and the exception may be easily stated does not mean that either may be easily applied to this case. The problem may, however, be clarified by a somewhat oversimplified statement of the elements of the CCE offense. It, of course, requires that the defendant be a manager, organizer, or supervisor of the enterprise, that he act in concert with at least five other persons, and that he obtain substantial income from it. The most important requirement for present purposes, however, is that he must commit a felony as "a part of a continuing series of violations of this subchapter...." I assume that the words "continuing series" con-

---

[15] The Court wrote: "The greater offense is therefore by definition the 'same' for purposes of double jeopardy as any lesser offense included in it."

template at least three successive felony violations, but of course the series could involve more.

Thus, if we view the entire course of petitioner's conduct as alleged in both indictments, it would appear that the Government could have alleged that all four importations constituted proof of a single CCE. Moreover, even though the prosecutor was clearly aware of the fourth importation when the Florida indictment was returned, I see no reason why he could not properly establish a CCE violation based on only the first three importations.[20] As written, the Florida indictment did not raise any double jeopardy problem because it did not rely on the Neah Bay importation and, indeed, did not separately charge any of the three earlier importations as substantive violations. Evidence of those felonies was offered to establish the greater CCE offense rather than separate, lesser offenses.

A double jeopardy issue was, however, created because the Government did not limit its proof to the three earlier importations. Instead, it offered extensive and dramatic evidence concerning the Neah Bay importation. Moreover, the jury was expressly instructed that the evidence concerning the Sun Chaser III "can only be considered by you in your deliberations concerning Count 11 of the indictment, which is the so called continuing criminal enterprise count, that's the allegation that Jonathan Garrett was engaged in, a continuing criminal enterprise."

It therefore seems clear to me that even though the indictment properly alleged a CCE violation predicated only on the three earlier importations, as the case was actually tried, and as the jury was instructed, it is highly likely that the CCE conviction rested on the Neah Bay evidence and not merely on the earlier transactions. The error, in my opinion, does not bar a retrial on the CCE count. But I think that it is perfectly clear that the CCE conviction cannot stand because the instructions on the CCE count did not inform the jury that the Neah Bay incident could not constitute a predicate felony to the CCE charge.

It is also clear that the exception identified in Brown v. Ohio, 432 U.S. 161 (1977), is not applicable to this case. All of the facts necessary to sustain the CCE charge in the Florida indictment occurred before the Washington indictment was returned. Moreover, the Government has not claimed that the evidence necessary to sustain the CCE charge in the Florida indictment was not discovered until after the Washington conviction. Indeed, if one compares the indictments, and if one assumes that the

[20] In fact, the United States plainly concedes as much: "Petitioner does not dispute that the CCE prosecution could be maintained if predicated on a series of Title 21 violations for which he had not previously been prosecuted, and the proof at trial showed many such violations. The Washington offense was therefore by no means indispensable to establishment of the CCE offense...." Brief for United States 5. Moreover, the United States later states that "the substantive Washington offense was not an essential part of the government's proof on the CCE count" and that "in this case the Washington offense is not a necessary predicate for the CCE violation." Id., at 10, n. 3. I also note that the fact that the Government might have proved a CCE by relying on felonies A, B, C, and D, or perhaps B, C, and D, would not prevent it from relying just on A, B, and C.

Government was prepared to prove what it alleged in the Florida indictment, the Neah Bay evidence was not needed in order to sustain the CCE charge. The record discloses no basis for applying the exception identified in *Brown* to this case.

III

The Court's reasons for not applying the general rule to this case are somewhat unclear. It seems to place its entire reliance on the fact that the CCE charge alleges that the enterprise continued to the date of the Florida indictment on July 16, 1981, together with the fact that when petitioner was arrested a week later, he made some damaging admissions. Neither of these considerations has any constitutional significance that I can discern. Further, although I did not subscribe to the analysis in the plurality opinion in Jeffers v. United States, 432 U.S. 137 (1977), I had thought every Member of the Court endorsed this proposition: "What lies at the heart of the Double Jeopardy Clause is the prohibition against multiple prosecutions for 'the same offense.' See United States v. Wilson, 420 U.S. 332, 343 (1975)." In my opinion it is far more important to vindicate that constitutional principle than to create a new doctrine in order to avoid the risk that a retrial may result in freeing this petitioner after only 19 years of imprisonment.

I respectfully dissent.

NOTES ON LESSER INCLUDED OFFENSES

1. Enterprise Criminality and Lesser Included Offenses. In contrast to *Jeffers*, which involved the relationship (within the double jeopardy context) between what might be described as "parallel" statutory crimes—namely, CCE (§ 848) and the general drug conspiracy crime (§ 846)—*Garrett* deals with what might be described as the "vertical" relationship between CCE and the specific substantive drug crimes that the defendant's "continuing criminal enterprise" allegedly committed. This kind of relationship, between an enterprise crime and the substantive crimes committed by the enterprise, presents a particularly difficult double jeopardy problem. In *Garrett*, however—because the defendant had not "stopped dancing" before he "insist[ed] that the music stop and the piper be paid"—the Court was able to finesse the problem and rest its decision on something like an "implied waiver" theory.

How should the Court apply the double jeopardy clause to the relationship between enterprise crimes and their constituent substantive offenses? Think back to the algebraic model that was used at the beginning of this Section to help explain the *Blockburger* test. Can the same algebraic model be used to describe CCE and the specific substantive drug crimes—identified in § 848 (c)—that are necessary to establish the existence of a "continuing criminal enterprise"? Does the algebraic model reveal a possible defect in the *Blockburger* test, as applied to enterprise crimes like CCE?

What about RICO? Can the same algebraic model be used to describe RICO and the so-called "predicate offenses" that are defined as "racketeering activity" under 18 U.S.C. § 1961? Once again, does the algebraic model reveal a possible defect in the *Blockburger* test?

2. *Harris v. Oklahoma, Illinois v. Vitale, Grady v. Corbin*, and *United States v. Dixon*. Although the Supreme Court has never directly confronted the problem discussed above in the specific context of enterprise criminality, it has addressed similar problems concerning the application of the *Blockburger* test. In a series of decisions, the Court has considered whether *Blockburger* might require modification to deal with statutory crimes that contain an element that may be satisfied in more than one way.

In Harris v. Oklahoma, 433 U.S. 682 (1977), the defendant was initially convicted of felony murder based on a killing (by his accomplice) during the course of an armed robbery. He was then charged in a separate proceeding with the same armed robbery that had supported the felony murder conviction. The prosecution conceded that "it was necessary for all of the ingredients of the underlying felony ... to be proved" during the felony murder trial. The Supreme Court unanimously held that the armed robbery prosecution was a violation of the double jeopardy clause.

In Illinois v. Vitale, 447 U.S. 410 (1980), the defendant was initially convicted, in connection with a fatal auto accident, of "failing to reduce speed to avoid an accident" (a crime of negligence). Later, he was charged—in connection with the same accident—with "involuntary manslaughter" (a crime of recklessness). In a pre-trial motion to dismiss the involuntary manslaughter charge, Vitale argued that "failing to reduce speed" was a lesser included offense of "involuntary manslaughter," because proving "involuntary manslaughter" by showing that he recklessly failed to reduce his speed to avoid the accident would also necessarily prove his guilt for negligently "failing to reduce speed." The prosecution countered, however, that the Illinois involuntary manslaughter statute provided for many alternative ways of proving Vitale guilty of "involuntary manslaughter"—the statute was not limited to cases of "failing to reduce speed."

The Supreme Court, in a 5–4 decision per Justice White, noted that the two statutes satisfied a strict application of the *Blockburger* test. Obviously, "involuntary manslaughter" requires proof of a fact—a death—that is not required for "failing to reduce speed." But "failing to reduce speed" also requires proof of a fact—a duty to reduce speed—that is not *required* for "involuntary manslaughter" (because there are many other ways to satisfy the recklessness element of "involuntary manslaughter"). Nevertheless, according to the *Vitale* Court, "if in the pending manslaughter prosecution Illinois relies on and proves a failure to slow to avoid an accident as the reckless act necessary to prove manslaughter, Vitale would have a substantial claim of double jeopardy...." 447 U.S., at 421. The Court remanded the case for further proceedings.

Ten years later, in Grady v. Corbin, 495 U.S. 508 (1990), the Court revisited the *Vitale* issue on nearly identical facts. In *Corbin*, a New York case involving another fatal auto accident, the defendant pled guilty to misdemeanor charges of "driving while intoxicated" and "failing to keep right of the median." He was then indicted and charged with "reckless manslaughter," "second-degree vehicular manslaughter," "criminally negligent homicide," "third-degree reckless assault," and "driving while intoxicated," based on the same accident. The prosecution filed a bill of particulars indicating that it would rely on three acts to prove the homicide and assault charges: driving while intoxicated, failing to keep right of the median, and driving 45 to 50 miles per hour in a heavy rain.

The Supreme Court, in another 5–4 decision (this time authored by Justice Brennan, who had dissented in *Illinois v. Vitale*), held that "the Double Jeopardy Clause bars a subsequent prosecution if, to establish an essential element of an offense charged in that prosecution, the government will prove conduct that constitutes and offense for which the defendant has already been prosecuted." 495 U.S., at 510. Based on the bill of particulars, the *Corbin* Court concluded that the prosecution "will prove the entirety of the conduct for which Corbin was convicted ... to establish essential elements of the homicide and assault offenses. Therefore, the Double Jeopardy Clause bars this successive prosecution...." 495 U.S., at 523.

Finally, United States v. Dixon, 509 U.S. 688 (1993), involved two consolidated cases. In the first case, defendant Dixon was convicted of criminal contempt for possessing cocaine with intent to distribute, in violation of a judicial order, while awaiting trial on another charge. He was then charged with the cocaine-possession offense. In the second case, defendant Foster was convicted of four counts of criminal contempt for violating a Civil Protection Order by assaulting his wife. He was then charged with simple assault, threatening to injure another, and assault with intent to kill, based on the same conduct. In Dixon's case, a majority of the Supreme Court ruled that the successive prosecution violated the double jeopardy clause. In Foster's case, however, the Court barred only the simple assault charge, and allowed the remaining charges to proceed to trial.

Justice Scalia (who had dissented in *Grady v. Corbin*) wrote the lead opinion in *United States v. Dixon*, but only part of his lead opinion was joined by a majority of the Court. One part of Justice Scalia's opinion that received majority support was the part that overruled *Grady v. Corbin*. See 113 S.Ct., at 2859–60. But Justice Scalia failed to obtain a majority for another part of his opinion that explained his view about how best to apply the *Blockburger* test to the facts of the two cases before the Court. According to Justice Scalia, the *Blockburger* test should be interpreted more broadly to bar successive prosecution whenever a judge's order (on which a criminal contempt charge is based) effectively "incorporates" the elements of an underlying substantive criminal offense. See 113 S.Ct., at 2857. This was true in Dixon's case, but it was true only for the simple assault charge in Foster's case.

Only Justice Kennedy joined the part of Justice Scalia's opinion explaining his view of the *Blockburger* test. Chief Justice Rehnquist wrote separately, joined by Justices O'Connor and Thomas, to say that *Blockburger* should be applied traditionally and strictly (thus allowing the successive prosecutions to proceed against both Dixon and Foster). Justice White also wrote separately, joined by Justices Stevens, Blackmun, and Souter, to say that *Grady v. Corbin* should be retained (thus barring the successive prosecutions against both Dixon and Foster).

Based on the fragmented opinions in *United States v. Dixon*, it can be concluded that *Grady v. Corbin* is dead, and that the *Blockburger* test remains the appropriate method for determining whether two offenses are "the same offense" for double jeopardy purposes. However, it is an understatement to say that the Court has failed to provide clear guidance concerning the proper double jeopardy approach under *Blockburger* in complex situations like those presented in *Harris*, *Vitale*, *Corbin*, and *Dixon*, and more importantly for present purposes, CCE and RICO.

United States v. Ruggiero

United States Court of Appeals, Eleventh Circuit, 1985.
754 F.2d 927.

Before KRAVITCH and HENDERSON, CIRCUIT JUDGES, and ATKINS, DISTRICT JUDGE.

■ KRAVITCH, CIRCUIT JUDGE:

In late 1982, appellants Benjamin Ruggiero and John Cerasani were prosecuted in the United States District Court for the Southern District of New York for substantive and conspiracy violations of the Racketeer Influenced and Corrupt Organizations Act (RICO), 18 U.S.C. §§ 1962(c) and (d). Ruggiero was convicted of conspiring to violate RICO, but was acquitted of the substantive RICO count. He was sentenced to fifteen years in prison. Cerasani was acquitted on both counts.

In early 1983, the indictment in the instant case was returned in the United States District Court for the Middle District of Florida, and the appellants again were charged with substantive and conspiracy RICO violations. The appellants moved to dismiss the Florida indictment on the grounds of double jeopardy. Their motion was denied, and this appeal ensued.

The appeal presents an issue of first impression in this circuit: How to define the scope of a RICO violation for double jeopardy purposes. We conclude that the substantive and conspiracy RICO violations charged in the Florida indictment are distinct from those for which the appellants previously were prosecuted in New York, and therefore hold that the appellants are not entitled to a dismissal of the Florida indictment on the grounds of double jeopardy. We also hold that the doctrine of collateral estoppel does not require the dismissal of the charges against Cerasani in the Florida indictment.

I. BACKGROUND

A. The New York Indictment

The New York indictment, which was returned on July 7, 1982, charged the appellants and eight others with conspiring to violate RICO, and the appellants and seven others with substantive violations of RICO, in connection with the activities of the so-called "Bonnano Family" of La Cosa Nostra, also known as the Mafia. The indictment alleged the occurrence of numerous illegal activities between 1974 and July, 1982, including: (1) the murders of Alphonse Indelicato, Philip Giaccone, and Dominick Trinchera, three "captains" of the Bonnano Family who were seeking to wrest control of the family away from two other "captains," Dominick Napolitano and Joseph Messina;[3] (2) a conspiracy to murder Anthony "Bruno" Indelicato, Alphonse's son; (3) the receipt, storage, and resale of a truckload of stolen tuna fish; (4) the theft of a tractor-trailer containing clothing and other freight; (5) the attempted robbery of the occupants of an apartment belonging to the sister of the Shah of Iran; (6) a conspiracy to rob the Landmark Union Trust Bank in St. Petersburg, Florida; (7) a conspiracy to rob the Pan Am Credit Union in Rockleigh, New Jersey; (8) a conspiracy to rob the occupants of the Galerie Des Monies in New York; (9) the possession and distribution of methaqualone in the Eastern and Southern Districts of New York; and (10) the operation of an illegal sports and numbers gambling business.

The indictment alleged that Ruggiero conspired to commit the four murders and to distribute methaqualone in the Eastern District of New York, and that he actually participated in the murders of Alphonse Indelicato, Giaccone, and Trinchera. Cerasani was named as a conspirator in the two truck thefts and all of the robberies except the robbery of the Landmark Union Trust Bank, the distribution of methaqualone in the Eastern District of New York, and the operation of the illegal gambling business, and as an actual participant in the two truck thefts, the attempted robbery of the apartment belonging to the sister of the Shah of Iran, the distribution of methaqualone in the Eastern District of New York, and the operation of the illegal gambling business.

Ruggiero was convicted of conspiring to violate RICO, but was acquitted on the substantive RICO count. He was sentenced to fifteen years in prison. His RICO conspiracy conviction was affirmed on appeal. See United States v. Ruggiero, 726 F.2d 913 (2d Cir.1984). Cerasani was acquitted on both counts.

B. The Florida Indictment

The Florida indictment, which was returned on March 31, 1983, charged the appellants and ten others with conspiring to violate RICO, and the appellants and nine others with substantive violations of RICO, in

---

[3] The evidence at trial revealed that Ruggiero was a member of the "crew" captained by Napolitano. Neither Napolitano nor Messina appeared for trial, and Napolitano later was found murdered.

connection with the activities of a loose-knit enterprise composed of members of several La Cosa Nostra "families." The enterprise included members of the "Trafficante Family," the "Luchese Family," the "Gambino Family," the "Chicago Outfit," and the "Bonnano Family."[4] The indictment alleged the occurrence of numerous illegal activities between March, 1979, and November, 1981, including: (1) the operation of an illegal gambling business at an apartment in Port Richey, Florida; (2) the operation of an illegal gambling business at the Kings Court Club in Holiday, Florida; (3) a conspiracy to operate an illegal gambling business at the Ridgerunner Club in Port Richey, Florida; (4) a conspiracy to maintain an illegal gambling facility in the Middle District of Florida; (5) the operation of an illegal sports bookmaking business; (6) travelling in interstate commerce to facilitate the operation of an illegal gambling business; (7) the extortion of money from one Sylvester Hutchins; (8) a conspiracy to interfere with commerce by extorting money from persons and organizations engaged in the private sanitation industry on the west coast of Florida; (9) a conspiracy to collect debts by violent means and by threats of violence; (10) a conspiracy to obtain through bribery a license to operate a parimutuel dog track in Pasco County, Florida; (11) a conspiracy to rob the Landmark Union Trust Bank in St. Petersburg, Florida; (12) a conspiracy to possess, sell, and distribute marihuana, cocaine, and heroin; (13) a conspiracy to obstruct justice by paying bribes to the captain of the Pasco County, Florida, Sheriff's Office; and (14) the obstruction of justice by giving false testimony before a federal grand jury.

The indictment alleged that Ruggiero conspired to operate the illegal gambling business at the Kings Court Club, to operate the illegal sports bookmaking business, to maintain the illegal gambling facility in the Middle District of Florida, to travel in interstate commerce to facilitate the operation of an illegal gambling business, to obtain through bribery the license to operate the parimutuel dog track in Pasco County, to rob the Landmark Union Trust Bank, and to possess, sell, and distribute marihuana, cocaine, and heroin, and that he actually travelled in interstate commerce to facilitate an illegal gambling business and participated in the operation of the illegal gambling business at the Kings Court Club. Cerasani allegedly conspired to rob the Landmark Union Trust Bank and to possess, sell, and distribute marihuana, cocaine, and heroin....

II.   RICO AND DOUBLE JEOPARDY

The Double Jeopardy Clause of the Fifth Amendment provides: "[N]or shall any person be subject for the same offense to be twice put in jeopardy of life or limb...." The Supreme Court has emphasized that the Double Jeopardy Clause protects a person not only against being twice convicted of the same offense, but also against being twice put to trial for the same

---

[4] The indictment alleged that Santo Trafficante, Jr., the head of the "Trafficante Family," agreed to permit the members of the other families to engage in criminal activities on the west coast of Florida in return for a percentage of the profits derived from those activities.

offense. See Abney v. United States, 431 U.S. 651, 660–61 (1977). Therefore, we must dismiss the Florida indictment if we find that the indictment charges the appellants with the same offenses for which they previously were prosecuted in New York.

Our task is made more difficult by the peculiar nature of the RICO statute. The subsection of RICO that the appellants are charged with violating and conspiring to violate, 18 U.S.C. § 1962(c), provides:

> "(c) It shall be unlawful for any person employed by or associated with any enterprise engaged in, or the activities of which affect, interstate or foreign commerce, to conduct or participate, directly or indirectly, in the conduct of such enterprise's affairs through a pattern of racketeering activity or collection of unlawful debt."

Unlike most criminal statutes, subsection 1962(c) deals not with clearly distinguishable discrete acts, but with ongoing criminal activity. At the same time, subsection 1962(c) differs from most other criminal statutes dealing with ongoing criminal activity. Such statutes generally prohibit participation in a particular kind of criminal venture. See, e.g., 18 U.S.C. § 1955 ("Whoever conducts, finances, manages, supervises, directs, or owns all or part of an illegal gambling business shall be fined not more than $20,000 or imprisoned not more than five years, or both."); 21 U.S.C. § 848 ("Any person who engages in a continuing criminal enterprise shall be sentenced to a term of imprisonment which may not be less than 10 years and which may be up to life imprisonment. . . ."). Thus, under such statutes, a potential double jeopardy problem arises whenever a defendant is charged twice with participating in the same criminal venture during the same period of time. See Sanabria v. United States, 437 U.S. 54, 69–74 (1978)(defendant may be prosecuted only once under 18 U.S.C. § 1955 for participating in an illegal gambling business during given period of time, even if the illegal gambling business violated more than one criminal statute).

Subsection 1962(c), on the other hand, prohibits participation in an enterprise "through a pattern of racketeering activity." The "pattern of racketeering activity" is a separate element of the RICO offense, distinct from both the existence of the enterprise and the participation of the individual in the enterprise. See United States v. Phillips, 664 F.2d 971, 1011 (5th Cir. Unit B 1981). Because of this separate element, an individual may be prosecuted for more than one violation of subsection 1962(c) in connection with the same enterprise, so long as each violation involved a different "pattern of racketeering activity." See United States v. Russotti, 717 F.2d 27, 33 (2d Cir.1983); United States v. Dean, 647 F.2d 779, 787 (8th Cir.1981).

The crucial inquiry in this case, therefore, is whether the activities set out in the New York and Florida indictments constitute one "pattern of racketeering activity" or two different "pattern[s]." Although we have not conducted this kind of inquiry before, we do not write on an entirely clean slate. Both the Eighth Circuit, in *Dean*, and the Second Circuit, in *Russotti*, addressed double jeopardy claims raised by defendants who had been charged with multiple RICO violations.[10] The *Dean* and *Russotti* courts considered the following five factors in determining whether the indictments charged the existence of one "pattern of racketeering activity" or two different "pattern[s]": (1) whether the activities that allegedly constituted two different RICO "pattern[s]" occurred during the same time periods; (2) whether the activities occurred in the same places; (3) whether the activities involved the same persons; (4) whether the two indictments alleged violations of the same criminal statutes; and (5) whether the overall nature and scope of the activities set out in the two indictments were the same. See *Russotti*, 717 F.2d at 33; *Dean*, 647 F.2d at 788. These five factors are modified versions of the factors long used to determine whether multiple indictments charge the existence of one or several conspiracies.[11]

We are persuaded that these five factors constitute an appropriate method for determining whether multiple RICO indictments allege the existence of one "pattern of racketeering activity" or several "pattern[s]." In this regard, we agree with the following observations of the *Dean* court:

> "A RICO charge focusses upon the 'pattern' formed by a number of unlawful acts, while a conspiracy charge focusses upon the agreement formed by persons to do unlawful acts. Thus, a RICO charge, like a conspiracy charge, focusses upon a relation between various elements of criminal activity rather than a single criminal act. Determination in a given case of the number of patterns or agreements requires examination of the four corners of the charges. The cases have employed five factors to make this

[10] In *Dean*, the defendant, an Arkansas county judge, was charged in two indictments with two substantive RICO violations, 18 U.S.C. § 1962(c), and thirty-six violations of the Travel Act, 18 U.S.C. § 1952. The first RICO violation involved actual and fictitious county purchases of corrugated metal culverts and other items from a supplier who paid kickbacks to the defendant. The second RICO violation involved county purchases of diesel fuel additives, gasoline additives, motor oil, and other automotive products from a different supplier who also paid kickbacks to the defendant. The defendant was tried and convicted on all counts. On appeal, the Eighth Circuit reversed and remanded the case for a new trial because one of the jurors was biased against the defendant. *Dean*, 647 F.2d at 785. The court also, however, rejected the defendant's contention that his conviction on both RICO counts violated the Double Jeopardy Clause. Id. at 785–89. On rehearing, the en banc court held that the defendant had waived the issue of juror bias, and affirmed the convictions. *Dean*, 667 F.2d at 734.

In *Russotti*, four defendants were indicted for substantive and conspiracy RICO offenses, 18 U.S.C. §§ 1962(c) and (d). Two of the defendants had been tried and acquitted of substantive and conspiracy RICO charges some five years earlier. The two defendants filed motions to dismiss the indictment based on, inter alia, the Double Jeopardy Clause and the doctrine of collateral estoppel. The District Court denied the motions to dismiss, and the Second Circuit affirmed. *Russotti*, 717 F.2d at 35.

[11] The five factors, as applied to multiple conspiracy indictments, include: (1) the time periods during which the events alleged to be part of the conspiracies occurred; (2) the places where the events occurred; (3) the persons acting as coconspirators; (4) the statutory offenses charged in the indictments; and (5) the overt acts or any other description of the offense charged that indicates the nature and scope of the activity that the government sought to punish in each case. See United States v. Marable, 578 F.2d 151, 154 (5th Cir.1978).

determination in conspiracy cases, and similar factors appear to us relevant in the RICO context...."

647 F.2d at 788; see Barry Tarlow, RICO: The New Darling of the Prosecutor's Nursery, 49 Fordham L.Rev. 165, 257–59 (1980)("The practical approach to multiple conspiracy indictments should affect cases involving separate section 1962(c) indictments.").[12]   We also agree with the *Russotti* court that the fifth factor, which involves a comparison of the overall nature and scope of the activities set out in the two indictments, is the most important factor.   See *Russotti*, 717 F.2d at 34.   We therefore proceed to apply the five factors to the indictments involved in this case.

Applying the first factor, we find a significant overlap in the time periods covered by the two indictments.   The New York indictment included activities that occurred between 1974 and July, 1982, and the Florida indictment included activities that occurred between March, 1979, and November, 1981.   Thus, the time period covered by the Florida indictment fits completely within the time period covered by the New York indictment.

The second and third factors, however, involve only minor overlaps. The activities set out in the two indictments generally occurred in different places.   The activities in the New York indictment primarily occurred in New York and New Jersey, and the activities in the Florida indictment primarily occurred in Florida.   The only geographic overlap is created by the reference in both indictments to the conspiracy to rob the Landmark Union Trust Bank in St. Petersburg, Florida.   The activities set out in the two indictments also generally involved different persons.   In fact, the only persons named in both indictments are the appellants.

The fourth factor also involves only a minor overlap in the two indictments. The New York indictment involved the underlying statutory crimes of murder (New York law), theft (18 U.S.C. §§ 2315 and 659), robbery (New York, New Jersey, and Florida law), possession and distribution of methaqualone (21 U.S.C. §§ 812, 841(a)(1), and 841(b)(1)(A)), and gambling (New York law and 18 U.S.C. § 1955).   The Florida indictment involved the underlying statutory crimes of gambling (Florida law and 18 U.S.C. § 1955), bribery (Florida law), obstruction of law enforcement (18 U.S.C. § 1511), interference with commerce (18 U.S.C. § 1951), interstate travel in aid of a racketeering enterprise (18 U.S.C. § 1952), extortion (18

---

[12] Although subsection 1962(c) is not a conspiracy statute, we find it to be sufficiently similar to allow the use of the same five factors for double jeopardy analysis.   In particular, although the search for one or more conspiratorial "agreements" may differ in some respects from the search for one or more RICO "pattern[s]," this court's predecessor has discussed the multiple conspiracy issue in terms perfectly applicable to RICO:

"The evidence discloses that the unlawful agreement pursuant to which the conspirators acted was but a single agreement to deal in drugs.   It cannot be separated into dual conspiracies under Section 846 to distribute cocaine and heroin without offending the Double Jeopardy Clause.   When the events of the alleged heroin conspiracy are overlaid with those of the cocaine conspiracy, there emerges not two discrete patterns of activity but a single design with the events most important in each case appearing at crucial and common junctures."   *Marable*, 578 F.2d at 155–56.

U.S.C. § 894), obstruction of justice (18 U.S.C. § 1503), robbery (Florida law), and possession and distribution of controlled substances (21 U.S.C. §§ 841(a)(1) and 846). Thus, the two indictments overlap only in their references to the federal drug statutes, 21 U.S.C. §§ 841 and 846, the federal gambling statute, 18 U.S.C. § 1955, and the Florida robbery statute.

Finally, we find no overlap in the fifth and most important factor. The New York indictment, viewed in its totality, involved the efforts of the "Bonnano Family" to establish and maintain a criminal empire in the New York/New Jersey area. The Florida indictment, on the other hand, involved a "joint venture" by members of several La Cosa Nostra families to conduct various criminal activities on the west coast of Florida. We find this distinction in the overall nature and scope of the activities set out in the indictments more than sufficient, in this case, to outweigh the overlaps in connection with the other factors.

On balance, then, we conclude that the New York and Florida indictments charged the existence of two different "pattern[s] of racketeering activity." In view of this conclusion, the presence of one particular "racketeering act" in both indictments, namely, the conspiracy to rob the Landmark Union Trust Bank in St. Petersburg, Florida, is not significant. We see no reason why one "racketeering act" may not be a part of two different "pattern[s] of racketeering activity."[13] The Double Jeopardy Clause protects a person against successive prosecutions for the same crime, not against successive prosecutions for two different crimes that happen to include the same underlying act.[14]

Like the *Dean* and *Russotti* courts, we are mindful of the Supreme Court's admonition that "[t]he Double Jeopardy Clause is not such a fragile guarantee that prosecutors can avoid its limitations by the simple expedient of dividing a single crime into a series of temporal and spatial units."

---

[13] By way of comparison, we note that one "overt act" can be in furtherance of two different conspiracies. For example, A might purchase a gun for the dual purposes of (1) committing a bank robbery pursuant to a conspiracy with B and C, and (2) committing a murder pursuant to a different conspiracy with X and Y. The presence of the same overt act, the purchase of the gun, in separate indictments for the two conspiracies certainly would not create a double jeopardy problem.

[14] For similar reasons, we reject the appellants' contention that the Double Jeopardy Clause was offended by the introduction, at the New York trial, of evidence relating to some of the activities later set out in the Florida indictment. This contention would have merit only if the evidence at the New York trial revealed that the "pattern of rack-

eteering activity" was broader in scope than alleged in the indictment. Upon reviewing the excerpts from the New York trial contained in the record on appeal in this case, we conclude that the challenged evidence primarily was offered to explain how the government's witnesses, who had infiltrated the criminal enterprise in Florida, had obtained their information. We find no indication, either in the trial excerpts or in the Second Circuit's opinion on appeal, that the "pattern of racketeering activity" was broadened at trial to include the activities set out in the Florida indictment. In fact, the one "racketeering act" contained in both indictments, the conspiracy to rob the Landmark Union Trust Bank in St. Petersburg, Florida, was not even submitted to the jury at the New York trial.

Brown v. Ohio, 432 U.S. 161, 169 (1977). We also recognize that the RICO statute is susceptible to abuse in the hands of overzealous prosecutors. See *Russotti*, 717 F.2d at 34 & n. 4; Barry Tarlow, RICO: The New Darling of the Prosecutor's Nursery, 49 Fordham L.Rev. 165, 259 n. 505 (1980). Nevertheless, we perceive no such abuse in this case. Here, the appellants engaged in two fundamentally different "pattern[s]" of criminal conduct. Hence, the Florida indictment did not charge the appellants with the same offenses for which they previously were prosecuted in New York, and the appellants' motion to dismiss properly was denied.[15]

III. COLLATERAL ESTOPPEL

Appellant Cerasani also contends that the doctrine of collateral estoppel requires the dismissal of the charges against him in the Florida indictment. It is true that, in criminal cases, the doctrine of collateral estoppel is a corollary of the Double Jeopardy Clause. See Ashe v. Swenson, 397 U.S. 436, 445–46 (1970). The doctrine, however, requires the dismissal of charges against an individual only if, in order to prove those charges, the government must relitigate an issue of ultimate fact that necessarily was resolved in favor of the individual in a previous trial. See *Russotti*, 717 F.2d at 35. The crucial issue is "whether a rational jury could have grounded its verdict upon an issue other than that which the defendant seeks to foreclose from consideration." *Ashe*, 397 U.S. at 444. . . .

The doctrine does not apply to the instant case because there is no issue of ultimate fact raised by the Florida indictment that necessarily was resolved in favor of Cerasani in the New York trial. Cerasani's previous acquittal could have been based on the jury's conclusion that, although Cerasani was an active member of the "Bonnano Family," he did not

---

[15] The government also contends that the New York and Florida indictments involved two different RICO "enterprises." According to the government, the New York indictment involved a group of persons affiliated with the "Bonnano Family," and the Florida indictment involved a basically different group of persons affiliated with several La Cosa Nostra families. It is true that Congress gave the term "enterprise" under the RICO statute an extremely broad definition, see United States v. Thevis, 665 F.2d 616, 625 (5th Cir.1982), and that "any union or group of individuals associated in fact," whether legitimate or illegitimate, can constitute a RICO "enterprise," see United States v. Turkette, 452 U.S. 576, 580–81 (1981). Furthermore, multiple RICO indictments involving truly different "enterprises" pose no double jeopardy problem, even assuming that the indictments allege only one "pattern of racketeering activity." See *Russotti*, 717 F.2d at 33 ("[I]n order for the present indictment to give rise to a valid claim of double jeopardy, both the enterprise and the pattern of activity alleged in the [previous] indictment must be the same as those alleged in the [present] indictment."). The problem is in determining whether two RICO "enterprises" are truly different for double jeopardy purposes. See Barry Tarlow, RICO: The New Darling of the Prosecutor's Nursery, 49 Fordham L. Rev. 165, 258–59 & n. 505 (1980). Eventually, courts may find it necessary to devise a method, perhaps similar to the one we employ today to compare RICO "pattern[s]," for determining whether two RICO "enterprises" are the same or different. We need not address the issue here, however. Because we find that the New York and Florida indictments charged the existence of two different "pattern[s] of racketeering activity," it is immaterial whether the indictments also alleged the existence of two different RICO "enterprises."

participate in the particular "pattern of racketeering activity" set out in the New York indictment. The Florida indictment, on the other hand, charges the existence of a different "pattern of racketeering activity." Thus, in the words of the *Russotti* court, "at this stage of the proceedings, we fail to see any indication of an attempt by the government 'to persuade a second jury of the same fact already litigated' in defendants' favor." 717 F.2d at 35 (quoting United States v. Mespoulede, 597 F.2d 329, 335 (2d Cir.1979)); see also United States v. Boffa, 513 F.Supp. 444, 483 (D.Del. 1980)("A fortiori the jury could have reached its decision to acquit without resolving any of the present issues in favor of the defendant. Consequently, the doctrine of collateral estoppel does not require dismissal of any portion of the present Indictment."). We hold that Cerasani is not entitled to a dismissal of the charges against him in the Florida indictment under the doctrine of collateral estoppel.

IV. CONCLUSION

For the foregoing reasons, the order of the district court denying the appellants' motion to dismiss the indictment is affirmed.

NOTE ON *UNITED STATES v. FELIX*

In United States v. Felix, 503 U.S. 378 (1992), the Supreme Court dealt with the question whether double jeopardy prohibits the government, in a conspiracy prosecution, from relying on "overt acts" that were previously prosecuted as separate substantive crimes. The Court held that such reliance did not violate double jeopardy. In the course of reaching its conclusion, the Court, per Chief Justice Rehnquist, noted the longstanding rule that "a substantive crime, and a conspiracy to commit that crime, are not the 'same offense' for double jeopardy purposes," 503 U.S., at 389:

> "For example, in United States v. Bayer, 331 U.S. 532 (1947), a military officer had been convicted in court-martial proceedings of discrediting the military service by accepting payments in return for transferring soldiers to noncombat units. We held that his subsequent prosecution in federal court on charges of conspiring to defraud the government of his faithful services was not barred by the Double Jeopardy Clause, despite the fact that it was based on the same underlying incidents, because the 'essence' of a conspiracy offense 'is in the agreement or confederation to commit a crime.' Id., at 542. In language applicable here, we pointedly stated that 'the same overt acts charged in a conspiracy count may also be charged and proved as substantive offenses, for the agreement to do the act is distinct from the act itself.' Ibid.; see also Pinkerton v. United States, 328 U.S. 640, 643 (1946)('[T]he commission of the substantive offense and a conspiracy to commit it are separate and distinct offenses ... [a]nd the plea of double jeopardy is no defense to a conviction for both offenses'). We have continued to recognize this principle over the years. See Iannelli v. United States, 420 U.S. 770, 777–79 (1975); Garrett v. United

States, 471 U.S. 773, 778 (1985)('[C]onspiracy is a distinct offense from the completed object of the conspiracy'); cf. id., at 793 ('[I]t does not violate the Double Jeopardy Clause ... to prosecute [a continuing criminal enterprise] offense after a prior conviction for one of the predicate offenses').

"In a related context, we recently cautioned against 'ready transposition of the "lesser included offense" principles of double jeopardy from the classically simple situation presented in *Brown v. Ohio* to the multilayered conduct, both as to time and to place, involved in [continuing criminal enterprise (CCE) prosecutions].' Id., at 789. The great majority of conspiracy prosecutions involve similar allegations of multilayered conduct as to time and place; the conspiracy charge against Felix is a perfect example. Reliance on the lesser included offense analysis, however useful in the context of a 'single course of conduct,' is therefore much less helpful in analyzing subsequent conspiracy prosecutions that are supported by previously prosecuted overt acts, just as it falls short in examining CCE offenses that are based on previously prosecuted predicate acts. Id., at 788–89." 503 U.S., at 389–90.

What did Chief Justice Rehnquist mean when, in *Felix*, he "cautioned against 'ready transposition of the "lesser included offense" principles of double jeopardy'" to such "multilayered conduct" as is typically found in CCE prosecutions? Did he mean that the courts need no longer review cases arising under "enterprise crime" statutes like RICO and CCE for possible double jeopardy problems? Or did he mean that the courts should begin to develop new ways of thinking about double jeopardy, designed specifically for the concept of "enterprise criminality"? What might such a new approach entail?

SECTION 4: ENTERPRISE CRIMINALITY AND "AIDER AND ABETTOR" LIABILITY

Another set of special problems that has arisen under RICO and CCE involves accomplice, or "aider and abettor," liability. What does it mean to say that a defendant has "aided and abetted" another defendant in the commission of a RICO or CCE violation? How does one "aid and abet" another in being a drug kingpin? Or in being a racketeer?

United States v. Pino–Perez

United States Court of Appeals, Seventh Circuit, 1989.
870 F.2d 1230.

Before BAUER, CHIEF JUDGE, CUMMINGS, WOOD, JR., CUDAHY, POSNER, FLAUM, COFFEY, EASTERBROOK, RIPPLE, MANION, and KANNE, CIRCUIT JUDGES, and ESCHBACH, SENIOR CIRCUIT JUDGE, sitting en banc.

■ POSNER, CIRCUIT JUDGE:

We decided to hear this case en banc, pursuant to Circuit Rule 40(f), in order to decide whether violation of the federal "kingpin" statute, 21

U.S.C. § 848 (Continuing Criminal Enterprises, Title II, § 408, of the Organized Crime Control Act of 1970), is "an offense against the United States" within the meaning of the federal aider and abettor statute, 18 U.S.C. § 2(a). That statute provides: "Whoever commits an offense against the United States or aids, abets, counsels, commands, induces or procures its commission, is punishable as a principal." A panel of this court had answered the question "yes" in United States v. Ambrose, 740 F.2d 505, 507–08 (7th Cir.1984), followed by a district judge in United States v. Vasta, 649 F.Supp. 974, 982 (S.D.N.Y.1986). Subsequently the Second Circuit, emphasizing legislative history not discussed in *Ambrose*, answered "no" in United States v. Amen, 831 F.2d 373, 381–82 (2d Cir.1987), followed in United States v. Benevento, 836 F.2d 60, 71–72 (2d Cir.1987). Oddly—when one considers that the kingpin statute has been on the books for almost twenty years—no other court has decided whether there can be liability for aiding and abetting a drug kingpin.

A court of appeals has a responsibility to reexamine its decisions in light of new arguments, new evidence, new experience, especially when by doing so it may be able to eliminate a conflict between circuits and thereby lighten the Supreme Court's burden of resolving such conflicts. In that spirit we have undertaken to reexamine *Ambrose*, but having done so we adhere to our view that there is aider and abettor liability for assisting a kingpin.

The kingpin statute imposes heavy penalties for the commission of a felony narcotics violation as part of a continuing series of violations from which the perpetrator obtains substantial income or resources and which he conducts in concert with five or more persons with respect to whom he "occupies a position of organizer, a supervisory position, or any other position of management." 21 U.S.C. § 848(b)(2). (This section was renumbered to (d)(2)(A) pursuant to amendments made to the kingpin statute in 1986, but Pino–Perez was convicted under the original statute.) The minimum penalty is ten years in prison and the maximum is life in prison plus a $100,000 fine (raised to $2 million in 1986). 21 U.S.C. § 848(a)(1). There is no parole, see § 848(c), although time off for good behavior and work in an industry or camp can cut the kingpin's sentence by more than a third. See 18 U.S.C. §§ 4161, 4162. The new federal sentencing statute enacted in 1986 abolishes parole for all federal crimes committed after its effective date (and time off for good behavior has also been trimmed), but when the kingpin statute was originally enacted its provision disallowing parole was unusual. Suspension and probation are also disallowed. See 21 U.S.C. § 848(c). Congress imposed a stiff minimum mandatory prison sentence—and meant it.

As the government has rightly conceded in these cases, the persons supervised by the kingpin cannot be punished as aiders and abettors. See *United States v. Ambrose*, supra, 740 F.2d at 507–08; *United States v. Amen*, supra, 831 F.2d at 381–82. When a "crime is so defined that

participation by another is necessary to its commission," that other participant is not an aider and abettor. United States v. Southard, 700 F.2d 1, 20
(1st Cir.1983). "[B]y specifying the kind of individual who is to be found
guilty when participating in a transaction necessarily involving one or more
other persons, [the legislature] must not have intended to include the
participation by others in the offense as a crime. This exception applies
even though the statute was not intended to protect the other participants." Id. The exception covers persons whom a kingpin supervises. If
they were chargeable as his aiders and abettors, the purpose of the kingpin
statute—to punish the kingpin more severely than other drug offenders—
would be thwarted. Since the lowliest mixer, if punishable as an aider and
abettor, would be subject to the same ten-year minimum as the kingpin
himself, there would be no incremental deterrence of the kingpin in cases
where the sentencing judge thought the statutory minimum adequate for
the kingpin.

Southard describes two other exceptions to aider and abettor liability
(see 700 F.2d at 19–20). The first concerns the victim of the crime. Even
if, as in such crimes as extortion, blackmail, and bribery, his conduct
significantly assisted in the commission of the crime, he cannot be charged
as an aider and abettor. The second exception concerns members of a
group that the criminal statute seeks to protect: a woman who is transported willingly across state lines for the purpose of prostitution cannot be
charged as an aider and abettor of the transporter's Mann Act violation.
Gebardi v. United States, 287 U.S. 112, 123 (1932).

Persons who assist a kingpin but are not supervised, managed, or
organized by him do not fit any of these three exceptions, and we are
reluctant to create a fourth. In *Ambrose*, the kingpin's aiders and abettors
were police officers who protected the kingpin's operation. The role of the
aider and abettor in *Amen*, Paradiso, is unclear from the Second Circuit's
opinion; since the Second Circuit rejected aider and abettor liability, it had
no reason to particularize Paradiso's activities. The government's brief in
Amen describes Paradiso as "Abbamonte's [the kingpin's] trusted friend
who assisted him in directing his distribution network from prison by
arranging to punish one of his workers and by arranging for the acquisition
of heroin. Without in any sense being employed or supervised by Abbamonte, Paradiso provided valuable assistance to the head of the network
and his underlings." Brief for the United States of America in Nos. 87–
1028 et al. (*United States v. Amen*), at p. 42. And *United States v. Vasta*,
supra, a decision on pretrial motions in the same prosecution, reports the
government's contention that the assistance of Paradiso and another alleged aider and abettor, Squitieri, "was of critical importance in keeping
Abbamonte's operation alive." 649 F.Supp. at 982. Ernest A. Benevento,
the person charged with aiding and abetting a kingpin in *United States v.
Benevento*, supra, "engaged in managerial functions throughout J.E.M.'s
drug operations [J.E.M. was an international criminal enterprise engaged
in the manufacture and distribution of heroin] and provided substantial
assistance to Ernesto J. Benevento [the kingpin. Ernest] ... provided
J.E.M. with the use of his Arizona home for the drug manufacturing

laboratory, maintained detailed financial records for the enterprise on his computer at home, contributed substantial amounts of capital to fund the second drug venture and attempted to smuggle currency out of the United States for J.E.M." 836 F.2d at 71.

The aider and abettor in the present case, Pino–Perez, supplied cocaine to a drug ring in southern Wisconsin headed by Harold Nichols. Pino–Perez was the supplier to Nichols's enterprise, and the quantities supplied were impressive. Pino–Perez once received $30,000 in cash for two kilograms of cocaine that he sold to the Nichols enterprise. He sold the enterprise as much as five kilograms at a time, and planned a final sale of 20 kilograms to it. His sales were frequent, and they continued for a long time. He claimed to know all or at least most of the big cocaine dealers in the country. This may have been braggadoccio, but there is no question that he was a big dealer—much bigger than Nichols, the kingpin.

The judge sentenced Pino–Perez to 40 years in prison under the kingpin statute for aiding and abetting Nichols's enterprise. Besides asking us to overrule *Ambrose*, Pino–Perez contends that the trial demonstrated either a fatal variance between the indictment and the proof or a "constructive" amendment of the indictment. This contention has no possible merit and requires no discussion. His remaining contentions are equally meritless, so we may turn to the issue of aider and abettor liability.

What is now § 2(a) of the federal criminal code dates back to 1909. See Act of March 4, 1909, ch. 321, § 332, 35 Stat. 1152; Standefer v. United States, 447 U.S. 10, 15–20 (1980). Ever since then, every time Congress has passed a new criminal statute the aider and abettor provision has automatically kicked in and made the aiders and abettors of violations of the new statute punishable as principals. "With the enactment of that section [the 1909 predecessor to § 2(a)], all participants in conduct violating a federal statute are 'principals.' " Id. at 20 (dictum). "The aiding and abetting provision [§ 2(a)] . . . is applicable to the entire criminal code." United States v. Jones, 678 F.2d 102, 105 (9th Cir.1982). No cases other than *Amen* and *Benevento* hold § 2(a) totally inapplicable to a federal criminal statute. Not every accomplice in the commission of a federal criminal offense is an aider and abettor, but until *Amen* every aider and abettor of a federal criminal offense had been thought punishable for the offense as a principal by virtue of § 2(a). The prostitute transported across state lines is not an aider and abettor of a Mann Act violation, but a supplier of prostitutes to the transporter may be (depending on what he knows—more on this shortly), and he is therefore punishable by virtue of § 2(a) as a principal violator of the Mann Act. United States v. Simmons, 610 F.Supp. 295, 304 (M.D.Tenn.1984). The kingpin's employees are not aiders and abettors, but—one might have thought—the supplier of the kingpin's drugs may be.

In reaching a contrary conclusion, *Amen* relied primarily on the legislative history of the kingpin statute. Early versions of the bill that became § 848 were sentence-enhancement provisions under which if a defendant was convicted of a drug offense (such as manufacture, distribution, or possession with intent to distribute, see 18 U.S.C. § 841(a)(1)), the prosecutor would have been allowed to argue to the sentencing judge that the defendant should be punished more heavily than usual because he was a drug kingpin.   See H.R.Rep. No. 1444, 91st Cong., 2d Sess. 80–84 (1970)(additional views of four Congressmen).   If the sentence-enhancement format had been retained in § 848 as enacted, there would have been no aider and abettor liability for assisting a kingpin, because there would have been no kingpin offense; there would just have been kingpin offenders against other criminal statutes.   But it was not retained.   In response to objections that in a sentencing hearing the defendant would not be able to cross-examine those who had accused him of being a kingpin, the bill was amended to make "engagement in a continuing criminal enterprise a new and distinct offense with all its elements triable in court."   Id. at 84. From this history the Second Circuit concluded in *Amen* that "while the legislative history makes no mention of aiders and abettors, it makes it clear that the purpose of making CCE [Continuing Criminal Enterprises— the official name of the kingpin statute] a new offense rather than leaving it as sentence enhancement was not to catch in the CCE net those who aided and abetted the supervisors' activities, but to correct its possible constitutional defects by making the elements of the CCE triable before a jury."   831 F.2d at 382.   To this we cannot say "amen."   True, it was not Congress's purpose in making the operation of a continuing criminal enterprise a separate offense to bring § 2(a) into play.   But such is never Congress's purpose in creating a new offense.   Congress doesn't have to think about aider and abettor liability when it passes a new criminal statute, because § 2(a) attaches automatically.   The question is not whether § 2(a) is applicable—it always is.   The question is whether a given accomplice is an aider and abettor.   The statute, here the kingpin statute, is used to determine who counts as an aider and abettor, for the term is not defined by § 2(a).   But once that determination is made, liability is automatic by virtue of § 2(a).

It would introduce great uncertainty into federal criminal law if the liability of a conceded aider and abettor depended on the results of an inquiry into Congress's intent concerning such liability in creating the offense that the defendant aided and abetted.   Yet that is the inquiry required by *Amen*.   The passage we have quoted could even be interpreted to mean that unless a specific intent to punish aiders and abettors appears in the legislative history of a criminal statute, § 2(a) does not apply to that statute; aiding and abetting violations of the statute is not a crime.   That approach would essentially abolish federal aider and abettor liability.   A more modest version of the approach would require the kind of inquiry that the Supreme Court uses to decide whether a regulatory statute that is silent on private rights of action can be enforced by them: it asks "whether Congress, either expressly or by implication, intended to create a private right of action."   Touche Ross & Co. v. Redington, 442 U.S. 560, 576 (1979).   Until *Amen* the presumption with regard to aiding and abetting had been different.   There had to be " 'an affirmative legislative policy' to create an exemption from the ordinary rules of accessorial liability."

United States v. Falletta, 523 F.2d 1198, 1200 (5th Cir.1975), quoting *Gebardi v. United States*, supra, 287 U.S. at 123.   Doubt about Congress's intentions was resolved in favor of aider and abettor liability.

The opinion in *Amen* gives the impression that the conversion of the kingpin statute from a sentence-enhancement provision to a provision creating a new and distinct offense was an unconsidered last-minute switch.   That is not correct.   The Dingell Amendment (which brought about the switch) was debated extensively; what is more, the sentence-enhancement provision was ultimately restored to another provision of Title II of the omnibus act.   See 21 U.S.C. § 849 (dangerous special drug offender sentencing).   The full story is told in Garrett v. United States, 471 U.S. 773, 780–85 (1985).   The new and distinct offense created by § 848 was more fully debated than most federal criminal statutes, and there is no more reason to infer from its legislative history an intent to preclude aider and abettor liability than there would be to draw such an inference from the legislative history of any other federal criminal statute.   The three exceptions recognized in *Southard* exhaust the cases in which an inference can confidently be drawn that Congress in enacting a criminal statute meant to protect a class of accomplices from being charged as aiders and abettors.

Besides legislative history, *Amen* emphasizes practical objections to aider and abettor liability in kingpin cases.   "How does one determine whether a person is an employee [of the kingpin, and hence not an aider and abettor] or third party?   What of the businessman who leases a boat to a CCE engaged in importation?   What about the kingpin's bodyguard?   Or his lawyer? "   831 F.2d at 382.   These are legitimate rhetorical questions, and they can be multiplied.   If there is aider and abettor liability in kingpin cases, could not assistants outside the organization be deemed aiders and abettors and be punished more severely than important operatives within the organization?   And would not assistants with roles in two or more organizations be simultaneously covered and excluded?   Suppose the main supplier to a distribution network in Wisconsin was the henchman of a larger network in Colombia that had subsidiaries in Florida.   If the government prosecuted the Colombia or Florida operations, their operatives could not be convicted as aiders and abettors, because they would be subordinates; but if the government prosecuted only the Wisconsin operation, a member of the Florida organization could be convicted because he was not a subordinate of the Wisconsin kingpin.   Indeed, someone charged as an aider and abettor of a kingpin might feel impelled to show that he was really one of the kingpin's employees—which would get him out of the § 848 frying pan but land him in a § 841 fire.   And the supplier of a small quantity of drugs to a kingpin—a quantity too small to permit severe punishment under § 841—would, if liable as an aider and abettor of the kingpin, be severely punishable under § 848.   See 21 U.S.C. § 841(b).

These rhetorical questions and classroom-type hypotheticals sound more ominous than they are.   (The absence of any litigation over the issue of which accomplices of a drug kingpin are aiders and abettors provides some reassurance on this score.) Let us consider each of them. The lessor of the boat would be an aider and abettor of the kingpin—provided he met the requirements for an aider and abettor. This is an important qualification and it undercuts *Amen*'s position. We and other courts have endorsed Judge Learned Hand's definition of aiding and abetting, which requires that the alleged aider and abettor "in some sort associate himself with the venture, that he participate in it as in something that he wishes to bring about, that he seek by his action to make it succeed." United States v. Peoni, 100 F.2d 401, 402 (2d Cir.1938); *United States v. Ambrose*, supra, 740 F.2d at 509, and cases cited there. The venture in a kingpin case is, of course, the continuing criminal enterprise. It is that enterprise which the boat lessor in *Amen*'s example would have to be found to have associated with, participated in, and sought by his action to make succeed, in order to be punishable as an aider and abettor. The mere fact of leasing a boat to a person known to be a drug trafficker would not be enough to make him guilty of aiding and abetting a drug kingpin. And so with the last hypothetical as well. One who sells a small—or for that matter a large— quantity of drugs to a kingpin is not by virtue of the sale alone an aider and abettor. It depends on what he knows and what he wants: Does he want the kingpin's enterprise to succeed or is the kingpin just another customer? If he does want the enterprise to succeed, there is no anomaly in holding him liable as an aider and abettor. Instead of buying from one large supplier (Pino–Perez), kingpin Nichols might have decided to buy from a host of small suppliers. If they knew he was a kingpin, associated themselves with his enterprise, participated in it as something they wanted to see succeed, and by their action sought to make it succeed, then they would indeed be punishable as aiders and abettors—and rightly so. The application of the *Peoni* test will sometimes require difficult factual appraisals, but the paucity of reported cases suggests that the factfinding task is a manageable one.

The bodyguard mentioned in *Amen* would presumably be a person supervised by the kingpin, hence not an aider and abettor. A lawyer is of course not an aider and abettor of his clients, whether or not he fits the *Peoni* definition; this is merely a commentary on the limitations of definition. A drug dealer could be both the underling of one kingpin and the aider and abettor of another. So much the worse for him; he need not be the top man to be convicted of the kingpin offense. We so held in United States v. Moya–Gomez, 860 F.2d 706, 745–49 (7th Cir.1988); see also other decisions cited in *Moya-Gomez*, supra, at 746. For all we know, Pino–Perez is the employee of some superkingpin. He could not be convicted of aiding and abetting that kingpin, but so what? Granted, it may sometimes be to the advantage of one accused of being a kingpin's aider and abettor to inculpate himself as an underling; but nothing is more common than for a criminal defendant to seek to exculpate himself of a major offense by accusing himself of a lesser one.

Finally, it is unlikely that important operatives of a drug kingpin would be punished less severely than less important aiders and abettors. Kingpins are not limited to heads of organizations; a kingpin is anyone who has supervisory or managerial responsibility with regard to five or more members of the organization. A large organization will contain more than one person with such supervisory responsibilities. In United States v. Rosenthal, 793 F.2d 1214, 1225–26 (11th Cir.1986), both the boss of the enterprise and one of his foremen were convicted of the kingpin offense. Even Nichols's relatively modest enterprise had two "managers," besides himself. Moreover, drug underlings are subject to punishment under § 841, which has its own severe minimum penalties. And, on the other hand, not every accessory is an aider and abettor; as Judge Hand's definition and the history of § 2(a) show, an accessory after the fact is not an aider and abettor. See, e.g., Bollenbach v. United States, 326 U.S. 607, 611 (1946).... S.Rep. No. 10, 60th Cong., 1st Sess. 13 (1908). This is another reason to believe that aider and abettor liability will not create an anomalous pattern in which the more culpable are let off more lightly than the less culpable.

The remaining objection to aider and abettor liability in kingpin cases (surprisingly not mentioned in *Amen* even though it had greatly troubled this court in *Ambrose*) arises from the heavy minimum penalty that the kingpin statute imposes. The least culpable kingpin is to be punished by at least ten years in prison with no possibility of parole. Since an aider and abettor is punishable as a principal—that is, punishable under the statute creating the offense that he was found to have aided and abetted—the least culpable aider and abettor of a kingpin must likewise be punished by no less than ten years in prison with no possibility of parole. This is a harsh result, and while it did not persuade us in *Ambrose* that there is no aider and abettor liability in kingpin cases, it did persuade us that § 2(a) authorizes the sentencing judge to disregard the minimum penalty in § 848. 740 F.2d at 508–10. We pointed out that the concept of aiding and abetting had come into the law at a time when all felonies carried the death penalty, and had been welcomed as a device for enabling the lesser participants in a felony to be punished more leniently than by death. See 4 Blackstone, Commentaries on the Laws of England 39 (1769); Rollin M. Perkins, Parties to Crimes, 89 U.Pa.L.Rev. 581, 613–15 (1941). As judges acquired more and more sentencing discretion, the felt need to distinguish between principals on the one hand and aiders and abettors on the other in order to mitigate the severity of criminal punishment diminished, and the distinction was eventually discarded, as in § 2(a).

The historic purpose of aiding and abetting liability coexists uneasily with criminal offenses that carry mandatory minimum penalties, such as the kingpin statute. We said in *Ambrose* that "a policeman who took an isolated bribe from a kingpin but did not engage in a prolonged and systematic protection racket, as these defendants did, would still be an aider and abettor of the kingpin, and therefore under the view that the aiding and abetting statute mechanically incorporates the whole punishment schedule of § 848 would have to be sentenced to a minimum of 10 years in prison without possibility of parole. Yet if there were no minimum the judge might sentence the policeman to only two or three years in prison and the policeman would be eligible for parole after serving a third of that time." 740 F.2d at 509. We therefore held that in sentencing a kingpin's aider and abettor the judge was not bound by the minimum penalty provisions of the kingpin statute. Judge Wood dissented from this holding. See id. at 513–16.

Further reflection has convinced us that Judge Wood's position is correct. Three reasons are decisive. First, § 2(a) does not contain its own schedule of punishments but instead makes the aider and abettor punishable as a principal for the offense that he aided and abetted. That is, punishment is imposed under the statute creating that offense. Here that is the kingpin statute, which imposes a minimum penalty applicable to everyone punishable under the statute—and an aider and abettor is punishable under the statute creating the offense he has aided and abetted and under no other statute. We recognize, not disapprovingly, that judges engage in a certain amount of statutory revision, especially when dealing with two statutes that were passed at different times without explicit reference to each other and that don't fit together nicely. But simply lopping off a minimum statutory penalty for one class of violators (aiders and abettors) now strikes us, as it did Judge Wood back in 1984, as exceeding the prudent bounds of judicial creativity.

Second, while endorsing Judge Hand's definition of aider and abettor *Ambrose* paid insufficient heed to the limitations built into it. "A policeman who took an isolated bribe from a kingpin" would not be likely to be convicted of aiding and abetting the kingpin's violations—would not be likely even to know he was dealing with a kingpin. Aiding and abetting implies a fuller engagement with the kingpin's activities. Third, and related, in no reported case has the participation of the aider and abettor been so meager relative to the kingpin's that subjecting him to the minimum penalty in the kingpin statute would be savage or incongruous. The "Marquette 10"—the corrupt policemen who protected the kingpin in *Ambrose*—were not small fry, and of course neither is Pino–Perez—he was a bigger drug dealer than Nichols, the kingpin, whom he supplied. Paradiso, the aider and abettor in *Amen*, was not a small fry either; we know because he was sentenced not to the statutory minimum but to 40 years, of which 20 were for aiding and abetting the kingpin. Squitieri's role was apparently a large one too, as was Ernest A. Benevento's role in assisting the kingpin in *United States v. Benevento*. Experience since *Ambrose* teaches that the danger which concerned us in that case—the danger that ferocious mandatory minimum sentences might be meted out to minor accomplices—is, as a practical matter, insufficiently serious to warrant so athletic an exercise in interpretive creativity as attempted in that case, let alone the casting of a cloud of uncertainty over all federal aider and abettor liability, as in *Amen*.

Congress may want to give attention to the problem of subjecting aiders and abettors to stiff mandatory minimum criminal penalties, although we recognize both that lenity for drug offenders is not high on the current list of national priorities and that, as illustrated by United States v. Martinez–Zayas, 857 F.2d 122, 131–33 (3d Cir.1988), a drug dealer who might be convicted as a kingpin's aider and abettor is quite likely to be punishable in any event under provisions of § 841 that themselves carry heavy mandatory minimum penalties. (Not all aiders and abettors of drug kingpins are themselves drug dealers, however, as illustrated by *Ambrose*.) But we think that both the aider and abettor statute and the kingpin statute mean what they say. If the mesh between them is imperfect— which it is—still the judicial cure that we attempted in *Ambrose*, and the even more drastic cure that our respected colleagues in the Second Circuit attempted in *Amen*, are, we believe, even worse than the disease.

Affirmed.

■ EASTERBROOK, CIRCUIT JUDGE, with whom CUDAHY and MANION, CIRCUIT JUDGES, join, dissenting with respect to the aiding and abetting conviction but otherwise concurring.

We held in United States v. Ambrose, 740 F.2d 505 (7th Cir.1984), that a person who aids and abets a criminal "kingpin" may be punished under the Continuing Criminal Enterprise ("CCE") statute, 21 U.S.C. § 848. The argument for this conclusion is simple. "Whoever commits an offense against the United States or aids, abets, counsels, commands, induces or procures its commission, is punishable as a principal." 18 U.S.C. § 2(a). The CCE statute establishes "an offense against the United States", and Pino–Perez aided and abetted the commission of that offense. He is therefore "punishable as a principal." Aides do not satisfy the five-supervised-persons requirement of the CCE statute, but § 2(a) may apply even when the assistant could not have committed the principal offense. E.g., Standefer v. United States, 447 U.S. 10 (1980)(a private person may be convicted under § 2(a) for abetting a violation of 26 U.S.C. § 7214(a)(2), which makes it a crime for an officer of the United States to take a bribe in the course of executing the revenue laws).

The task of interpretation is not quite so straightforward, though, for several reasons. Section 848 imposes a minimum term of ten years' imprisonment and a maximum of life, all without possibility of parole. The term was set so high because the statute condemns only managers who supervise at least five others for extended periods. Liability for aiding and abetting sweeps up persons who supervise no one. This led us to hold in *Ambrose* that the judge need not adhere to the minimum-sentence provisions of § 848 when sentencing aiders and abettors. 740 F.2d at 508–10. The court abandons that limitation today as unsupportable, with the result that the aider and abettor faces the kingpin's minimum term although his role may be far less significant than the kingpin's. Suppliers, such as Pino–Perez, are among the enterprise's aiders and abettors. Section 841 addresses suppliers in detail. If the defendant sells five or more kilograms of cocaine, then the penalties under §§ 841 and 846 are the same as those under the CCE statute, see 21 U.S.C. § 841(b)(1)(A)(ii). If the defendant sells between 0.5 and 5.0 kilograms, the penalties are lower, § 841(b)(1)(B)(ii). Smaller amounts yield still smaller sanctions, § 841(b)(1)(C). See United States v. Martinez–Zayas, 857 F.2d 122, 127–32 (3d Cir.1988). To treat an aider and abettor as a kingpin on the authority of § 2(a) is to demolish the graduated structure of penalties under § 841. Employees of an organization aid and abet their boss. The CCE statute authorizes higher punishment for higher-ups. Only a person who supervises five or more others is a kingpin. It would be absurd to treat lords and vassals identically under the CCE law on the ground that vassals lend aid and assistance; the structure of the CCE statute is set against it. *Ambrose* therefore added an element, which the court today reaffirms: "[T]he persons supervised by the kingpin cannot be punished as aiders and abettors." The addition of this extra-statutory element has the potential to create a crazy-quilt pattern of liability. Assistants outside the organization may be called aiders and abettors, receiving higher punishment than more important operatives within the organization. Assistants with roles in two or more organizations may be both covered and excluded. Pino–Perez undoubtedly is such a person. (No one supposes that he tended and harvested the plants, refined the cocaine, smuggled and transported the drug himself.) The extra element could put the defendant in a pickle if he really is a subordinate of the kingpin, but the prosecutor omits him from the list of those the kingpin is charged with supervising. The only defense to the charge of aiding and abetting the CCE offense might be to paint oneself as a henchman of the person charged as the kingpin, which greatly enhances the possibility of conviction on other charges. Anyway, why should liability depend on whether the prosecutor claims that the aider and abettor is not in the chain of command of the criminal organization? Are all but five of the criminal enterprise's couriers to be convicted as aiders and abettors and sentenced under the CCE statute? These difficulties show that statutory texts cannot dispose of the case. To follow the language of 18 U.S.C. § 2(a) is to require at least one addition to the equally plain language of 21 U.S.C. § 848 and to do substantial damage to the exquisitely clear language of 21 U.S.C. § 841 establishing a scale of punishment graduated by amounts sold.

If § 2(a) traditionally were read woodenly, that would be that, for the CCE statute must be understood against the interpretation § 2(a) had when Congress acted. But § 2(a) has never been applied mechanically; its scope depends on the structure and functions of the substantive statute. See United States v. Farrar, 281 U.S. 624 (1930), implying that purchasers of liquor from a bootlegger are not liable as aiders and abettors because Congress meant to limit liability to sellers, and Gebardi v. United States, 287 U.S. 112 (1932), holding that prostitutes may not be convicted as aiders and abettors of the Mann Act offense, because that law requires the prosecutor to show that the defendant transported prostitutes across state lines, implicitly establishing a difference in culpability between the organizer and the prostitute. When the structure of the main offense speaks to the scope of accessorial liability, *Gebardi* tells us, § 2(a) ought not be taken literally. Indeed, the court today refuses to take § 2(a) literally, for it says that the kingpin's subordinates may not be convicted as aiders and abettors. To curb the worst effects of punishing casual hangers-on and minor assistants under the draconian terms of § 848, the court adds that a person may be convicted under § 2(a) only if he "want[s] the kingpin's enterprise to succeed", a novel mental element that can't be located in the text or history of either § 2(a) or § 848.   So the only question is the extent to which we must depart from literal implementation to make the statutes work together.   On this question, the legislative history is suggestive.

The legislative proposals that led to § 848 did not start with suggestions for a new criminal law.   Congress was dissatisfied with the penalties being imposed on higher-ups in drug-peddling organizations.   This led to proposals to enhance the sentences of those so convicted.   The first versions of what became § 848 were sentence-enhancement provisions.   If the defendant were convicted of a drug offense, the prosecutor would be allowed to argue to the sentencing judge that the defendant was a kingpin (a perpetrator of a "pattern of conduct"), authorizing extra punishment. United States v. Amen, 831 F.2d 373, 381–82 (2d Cir.1987), reports what happened next: The Association of the Bar of the City of New York and others objected that these provisions allowed sentencing to be imposed without providing a defendant with an opportunity to cross-examine persons providing information as to the continuing criminal offense. [H.R.Rep. 91–1444, 91st Cong., 2d Sess. (1970).]   An amendment offered by Representative John D. Dingel and adopted by the Interstate and Foreign Commerce Committee corrected the defects in the original sentencing bill. "Instead of providing a post-conviction-presentencing procedure, it made engagement in a continuing criminal enterprise a new and distinct offense with all its elements triable in court."   Id.   While the legislative history makes no mention of aiders and abettors, it makes it clear that the purpose of making CCE a new offense rather than leaving it as sentence enhancement was not to catch in the CCE net those who aided and abetted the supervisors' activities, but to correct its possible constitutional defects by making the elements of the CCE triable before a jury.   *Amen* presents the history of the bill in the House.   The Conference Committee accepted the House version of the CCE provision with only technical changes, so that the history in the House turns out to be the only important history.   See H.R.Conf.Rep. No. 91–1603, 91st Cong., 2d Sess. (1970).   On the other side one might point to a comment in the Senate Report that to be culpable under the CCE statute the "defendant must have occupied a position of organizer or assumed a management role such as a hit man", S.Rep. 91–613, 91st Cong., 1st Sess. 28 (1969), which suggests that important operatives of the venture may be convicted.   But the Senate Report does not tie this comment to the language of the statute, which requires supervision, and as we have emphasized the transformation in the House is what matters, given that the Conference Committee adopted the House's language.

Section 848 became a substantive statute only in order to afford defendants greater procedural rights than a sentence-enhancement statute would have done.   Nothing in the debates leading to this conversion suggests that any Member of Congress wanted to enlarge the liability of hired hands, suppliers, or other aiders and abettors, or contemplated that § 848 would produce this result.

Legislative contemplation is of course not a condition to the application of § 2(a), which comes into play whenever Congress defines a substantive crime. "It is not the law that a statute can have no effects which are not explicitly mentioned in its legislative history." Pittston Coal Group v. Sebben, 488 U.S. 105 (1988). So if we were prepared to hold that § 2(a) applies to § 848 in the way it applies to any other crime, then we might dismiss the evolution of § 848 as irrelevant. Yet it is common ground among members of the court that the structure and function of § 848 matter—that is why the majority holds that the kingpin's subordinates cannot be aiders and abettors, why it emphasizes that only those who "want the kingpin's enterprise to succeed," may be convicted under § 2(a). The majority's slippery slope argument—that once we start looking at the structure and history of the CCE statute, certainty is lost—does not carry the day when the majority does what it decries: it uses the structure of § 848, and the purposes ascribed to Congress, to cut back on the scope of § 2(a). Once we enter the business of reading the structure and functions of § 848, how § 848 came to its current form and how aiding-and-abetting liability undercuts the limitations of § 841 become important. The debates show Congress in a savage mood, no doubt, but its wrath had a specific object. See also Garrett v. United States, 471 U.S. 773, 781 (1985)(the CCE statute is "a carefully crafted prohibition aimed at a special problem. [It] is designed to reach the 'top brass' in the drug rings, not the lieutenants and foot soldiers"). The concern of the legislature lay in its desire to create mandatory minimum (and life maximum) penalties for the doyens of drugs, not in achieving increases in the sentences of aides-de-camp.

My colleagues imply that they have not really cut back on the scope of § 2(a) by preventing its application to a kingpin's subordinates. They treat *Gebardi* as holding that when an accomplice's action is part of the definition of the offense, he is not an aider and abettor, see United States v. Southard, 700 F.2d 1, 20 (1st Cir.1983), and say that they have enforced the full scope of § 2(a) as so read. That interpretation cannot account for *Standefer*, which holds that the payor of a bribe may be convicted of aiding and abetting the receipt of that bribe, although the payor's role is an essential element of the recipient's crime. As for the Mann Act: interstate transportation of prostitutes is unlawful, and *Gebardi*, treating prostitutes as victims, holds that they may not be convicted of aiding or abetting their own transportation. The kingpin's subordinates are not victims; section 848 was not enacted for their protection. The court excludes the subordinates not because *Gebardi* compels this but because it believes that otherwise "the purpose of the kingpin statute—to punish the kingpin more severely than other drug offenders—would be thwarted." Decisions based on structure and purpose ought to be based on the whole structure and all of the purposes.

Forced to choose between damage to the language of § 2(a)(by having no aiding and abetting liability) and damage to the language and structure of both § 848 (by adding new elements for aiders and abettors) and § 841 (by eliminating the gradation of penalty by the amount of drugs supplied), we should preserve as much as possible of §§ 841 and 848. Suppliers come within 21 U.S.C. §§ 841 and 846, which read directly on their conduct and are no more lenient for big sellers than § 848 is for big cheeses. Pino–Perez, a wholesaler, was sentenced to 40 years' imprisonment without parole under § 846 and § 841, concurrent with the CCE sentence except for a $50 special assessment. When the supplier runs a delivery organization of his own, then he too faces prosecution under the CCE statute. See United States v. Bond, 847 F.2d 1233 (7th Cir.1988)(CCE conviction, as a principal, of one situated similarly to Pino–Perez). A prosecutor need not choose whichever statute is most favorable to the accused. United States v. Batchelder, 442 U.S. 114 (1979). But the prosecutor must find a statute that is applicable, and the interplay among provisions helps us to know a statute's domain. The CCE statute covers suppliers only if they have organizations over which to reign. A prosecutor who wants a mandatory minimum sentence or a life maximum should not be allowed to evade the need to prove the defendant's supervisory role under § 848 or the quantity of drugs involved under § 841.

■ CUDAHY, CIRCUIT JUDGE, dissenting in part:

I join fully in the dissenting opinion of Judge Easterbrook as to the inapplicability of § 2(a) in this case. The Continuing Criminal Enterprise statute, 21 U.S.C. § 848, is aimed at defendants occupying a particular status, that of "kingpin," and application of the aiding and abetting provision makes little sense in this setting.

I write separately to address the problem that occupied most of the defendant's brief, and which has been dealt with summarily by the majority: whether changes between the indictment and the proof at trial varied or amended the indictment in this case. This court addresses many claims that we conclude to be without merit; it has been our custom to state some reason for our conclusions, even if the reasoning can be summarized in a sentence or two. This procedure seems basic in most cases to the legitimacy of the system.

In this case Pino–Perez complains that because a key government witness became unavailable, the government's proof at trial on two of the counts of the indictment pertained to completely different transactions than those forming the original basis for these counts as brought in by the grand jury.[2] This presents a somewhat different situation from the more usual variance problem, in which the incident alleged in the indictment and proved at trial are the same, but the original date alleged in the indictment was incorrect. See U.S. v. Leibowitz, 857 F.2d 373 (7th Cir.1988). While some inaccuracy as to dates is clearly permissible, Ledbetter v. United States, 170 U.S. 606 (1898), the government is not permitted to generate

---

[2] Specifically, Count XI was apparently based on an incident, involving only Pino–Perez and Nichols, that Nichols reported as having occurred on or about November 17. Count IX had apparently been based upon an incident involving a witness, Janet Rains, who testified only that the transaction had occurred "in the winter months." At trial the government used the Rains transaction as proof of Count XI, and introduced a wholly new incident not mentioned in Nichols' original report (a transaction involving witness Larry Chapel) as proof on Count IX.

new grounds for counts of an indictment when witnesses become unavailable or new crimes come to light. See Stirone v. United States, 361 U.S. 212 (1960). However, in this case, we cannot say with certainty that this is what has happened because there was no bill of particulars from which to ascertain exactly which incidents are alleged in each count of the indictment. The proof at trial seems adequate under the language of the grand jury indictments, although the circumstances strongly suggest that the defendant's argument is not frivolous.

NOTES ON "AIDER AND ABETTOR" LIABILITY

1. The Model Penal Code Complicity Provision. Perhaps the best-known and most widely accepted definition of "aider and abettor" liability is the one set out by Judge Learned Hand in United States v. Peoni, 100 F.2d 401 (2d Cir.1938). Under this definition, cited and discussed by the *Pino-Perez* court, the prosecution must prove that an alleged aider and abettor "in some sort associate himself with the venture, that he participate in it as in something that he wishes to bring about, that he seek by his action to make it succeed." Id., at 402.

Another classic statement of the scope of "aider and abettor" liability is the one contained in the Model Penal Code:

"Section 2.06. Liability for Conduct of Another; Complicity.

"(1) A person is guilty of an offense if it is committed by his own conduct or by the conduct of another person for which he is legally accountable, or both.

"(2) A person is legally accountable for the conduct of another person when:

"(a) acting with the kind of culpability that is sufficient for the commission of the offense, he causes an innocent or irresponsible person to engage in such conduct; or

"(b) he is made accountable for the conduct of such other person by the Code or by the law defining the offense; or

"(c) he is an accomplice of such other person in the commission of the offense.

"(3) A person is an accomplice of another person in the commission of an offense if:

"(a) with the purpose of promoting or facilitating the commission of the offense, he

"(i) solicits such other person to commit it, or

"(ii) aids or agrees or attempts to aid such other person in planning or committing it, or

"(iii) having a legal duty to prevent the commission of the offense, fails to make proper effort so to do; or "(b) his conduct is expressly declared by law to establish his complicity.

"(4) When causing a particular result is an element of an offense, an accomplice in the conduct causing such result is an accomplice in the commission of that offense if he acts with the kind of culpability, if any, with respect to that result that is sufficient for the commission of the offense.

"(5) A person who is legally incapable of committing a particular offense himself may be guilty thereof if it is committed by the conduct of another person for which he is legally accountable, unless such liability is inconsistent with the purpose of the provision establishing his incapacity.

"(6) Unless otherwise provided by the Code or by the law defining the offense, a person is not an accomplice in an offense committed by another person if:

"(a) he is a victim of that offense; or

"(b) the offense is so defined that his conduct is inevitably incident to its commission; or

"(c) he terminates his complicity prior to the commission of the offense and

"(i) wholly deprives it of effectiveness in the commission of the offense; or

"(ii) gives timely warning to the law enforcement authorities or otherwise makes proper effort to prevent the commission of the offense.

"(7) An accomplice may be convicted on proof of the commission of the offense and of his complicity therein, though the person claimed to have committed the offense has not been prosecuted or convicted or has been convicted of a different offense or degree of offense or has an immunity to prosecution or conviction or has been acquitted."

How would the Model Penal Code's definition of "aider and abettor" liability under § 2.06 apply to the various situations discussed in the *Pino-Perez* case?   In particular, does § 2.06(5) make both employees *and* suppliers of drug kingpins liable as "aiders and abettors"?   Or does § 2.06(6)(b) suggest the opposite conclusion, at least with respect to employees?

2. *Petro-Tech, Inc. v. The Western Company of North America.* In Petro–Tech, Inc. v. The Western Company of North America, 824 F.2d 1349 (3d Cir.1987), the Third Circuit, per Circuit Judge Becker, dealt with a defendant's claim that RICO civil liability could not be predicated on an "aider and abettor" theory:

"Western contends that the complaint impermissibly alleges it to be both an enterprise and a person for RICO purposes when in fact, Western argues, a defendant may fit into one or another of those legal categories but not both at the same time. Specifically, Western attacks Counts XI and XII of the complaint, which allege that it is liable on the basis of the doctrine of respondeat superior or as an aider and abettor for all of the wrongs alleged in Counts I through X of the complaint. Western contends that imposing liability under either of these theories would enable plaintiffs to circumvent what it contends is the rule preventing an enterprise from being liable to the (other) victims of racketeering activity.

"Since there is no federal general common law, Erie Railroad v. Tompkins, 304 U.S. 64, 78 (1938), the applicability of common law doctrines in litigation under federal statutes depends on whether those principles advance the goals of the particular federal statute which plaintiffs allege has been violated. American Society of Mechanical Engineers v. Hydrolevel Corp., 456 U.S. 556, 570 (1982)(applying common law principle of apparent authority in antitrust context because the doctrine 'is consistent with the congressional intent to encourage competition' which animates the antitrust laws).

"This Court has already held that one can violate RICO criminally by aiding and abetting the commission of two predicate acts, provided that all of RICO's other requirements are also satisfied. United States v. Local 560, 780 F.2d 267, 288 n. 25 (3d Cir.1985). We have not yet addressed the question of civil RICO liability for aiding and abetting. But the Fifth Circuit has declared its willingness to find civil RICO violated by an aider and abettor, Armco Indus. Credit Corp. v. SLT Warehouse Co., 782 F.2d 475, 485–86 (5th Cir.1986), as has one judge in the Southern District of New York. Laterza v. American Broadcasting Co., 581 F.Supp. 408, 412 (S.D.N.Y.1984). We now join those courts, and hold that, if all of RICO's other requirements are met, an aider and abettor of two predicate acts can be civilly liable under RICO.

"We begin our explanation of this conclusion by observing that aiding and abetting is most commonly used as a theory of criminal, rather than civil liability. It is generally said to be defined in American law by several well known criminal law cases, see Pinkerton v. United States, 328 U.S. 640 (1946); Nye & Nissen v. United States, 336 U.S. 613 (1949); United States v. Peoni, 100 F.2d 401 (2d Cir.1938), and is now a basis of federal criminal liability by operation of 18 U.S.C. § 2. Through the criminal law, however, aiding and abetting has also become a basis for civil liability under the federal securities laws. See David S. Ruder, Multiple Defendants in Securities Law Fraud Cases: Aiding and Abetting, Conspiracy, In Pari Delicto, Indemnification and Contribution, 120 U.Pa.L.Rev. 597, 620–28 (1972). While the Supreme Court has reserved the issue, Ernst & Ernst v. Hochfelder, 425 U.S. 185, 190–91 n. 7 (1976), every circuit court to have addressed the question has held that there can be civil liability for aiders and abettors of securities law violations. See Monsen v. Consolidated Dressed Beef Co., 579 F.2d 793 (3d Cir.1978)(imposing aiding and abetting liability under § 10b of the Securities and Exchange Act of 1934); Thomas Lee Hazen, Securities Regulation § 7.8 at 208–09 & n. 4 (1985)(collecting cases).

"The doctrine also has a civil common law application. The Restatement (Second) of Torts § 876(b) holds that liability '[f]or harm resulting to a third person from the tortious conduct of another . . . [can be imposed upon a party who] (b) knows that the other's conduct constitutes a breach of duty and gives substantial assistance or encouragement to the other so to conduct himself.' That Restatement provision has been applied by a number of state and federal courts in civil litigation. See the scholarly discussion of civil aiding and abetting by Judge Wald in Halberstam v. Welch, 705 F.2d 472, 481–86 (D.C.Cir.1983), which reviews in detail the nature and scope of civil liability for aiding and abetting tortious conduct.

"Applying the teaching of *Mechanical Engineers* in the aiding and abetting context, we note that one important purpose of RICO's civil provisions is to permit recovery by the victims of racketeering activity. One who has aided and abetted the commission of two predicate offenses is guilty of those offenses. Standefer v. United States, 447 U.S. 10 (1980); United States v. Kegler, 724 F.2d 190, 201 (D.C.Cir.1984)('[a]n individual can be indicted as a principal for commission of a substantive crime and convicted by proof showing him to be an aider and abettor'). The doctrine of aiding and abetting is simply one way that an individual can violate the substantive criminal laws. See 18 U.S.C. § 2 ('[w]hoever commits an offense against the United States or aids, abets, counsels, commands, induces or procures its commission, is punishable as a principal'); *Kegler*, 724 F.2d at 200 ('aiding and abetting . . . is not an independent crime under 18 U.S.C. § 2'). So long as all of RICO's other requirements are met, we can see no reason why victims should not be able to recover from anyone who has committed the predicate offenses RICO enumerates, regardless of how he committed them. As a general matter, therefore, civil RICO liability for aiding and abetting will advance RICO's goals, and *Mechanical Engineers* instructs us that the doctrine should therefore be applied in this context.

"While many commentators have noted the difficulty of explaining the goals of the doctrine of respondeat superior, see W. Page Keeton, et al., Prosser & Keeton on Torts § 69 (5th ed. 1984), the doctrine can probably be best explained as an outgrowth of the sentiment that 'it would be unjust to permit an employer to gain from the intelligent cooperation of others without being responsible for the mistakes, the errors of judgment and the frailties of those working under his direction and for his benefit.'

Restatement (Second) of Agency § 219, comment a on subsection (1). Here too the goals of the common law doctrine are entirely consistent with RICO's goal to facilitate recovery by the victims of racketeering activity. We therefore hold that the doctrine of respondeat superior may be applied under RICO where the structure of the statute does not otherwise forbid it.

"As the foregoing qualification suggests, however, there are some circumstances in which both theories of liability are inconsistent with RICO's goals and operation. In particular, this and most other courts have held that for purposes of § 1962(c) an enterprise may not be held liable under RICO. Hirsch v. Enright Refining Co., 751 F.2d 628 (3d Cir.1984); Haroco, Inc. v. American National Bank & Trust Co., 747 F.2d 384, 401–02 (7th Cir.1984); see Schreiber Distributing Co. v. Serv–Well Furniture Co., 806 F.2d 1393, 1396 n. 2 (9th Cir.1986)(collecting cases). The contrary rule has been adopted only by the Eleventh Circuit, in United States v. Hartley, 678 F.2d 961 (11th Cir.1982).

"If the enterprise in a particular RICO case is also the employer of the RICO persons, respondeat superior liability may be inconsistent with the rule in *Enright*. That case would also suggest that a 1962(c) enterprise cannot have aided and abetted the RICO persons. Because the rule in *Enright* pertains only to § 1962(c), however, the applicability of this argument to the complaint before us depends on which subsection of RICO each individual Count is brought under; whether that Count is brought against Western as a defendant, and whether or not Western is alleged to be an "enterprise" for purposes of that Count. Application of the rule in *Mechanical Engineers*—that common law doctrines will be applied in federal litigation to the extent that they advance the goals of the statutes sued under—will therefore require a detailed inspection of the bases on which each count of the complaint seeks to hold Western liable."

The Third Circuit went on to hold that Western could not be held liable, on either a respondeat superior or an "aider and abettor" theory, under § 1962(c) so long as it also was alleged to be the "enterprise"; but that a corporation, like Western, could be held liable on both theories under § 1962(a) "when the corporation is actually the direct or indirect beneficiary of the pattern of racketeering activity" rather than "when it is merely the victim, prize, or passive instrument of racketeering."

SECTION 5: ENTERPRISE CRIMINALITY AND FORFEITURE

Statutes aimed at "organized crime," like RICO and CCE (as well as other federal drug crimes), commonly provide for a special kind of sanction or remedy—the forfeiture of the assets of the criminal "enterprise." As prosecutors have pursued forfeiture more and more vigorously, the courts have been required to address claims that forfeiture has gone "too far"—in violation of the relevant statute, the Eighth Amendment's prohibition of "excessive fines," and/or other constitutional provisions.

In the materials that follow, various challenges brought by defendants in connection with forfeiture under RICO, CCE, and similar state and federal statutes will be examined. Although the forfeiture provisions of these statutes vary, the primary focus of this Chapter will be on general principles of law that apply to all forfeiture actions.

SUBSECTION A: LIMITS ON THE SCOPE OF FORFEITURE

Russello v. United States

Supreme Court of the United States, 1983.
464 U.S. 16.

■ JUSTICE BLACKMUN delivered the opinion of the Court.

This is yet another case concerning the Racketeer Influenced and Corrupt Organizations (RICO) chapter of the Organized Crime Control Act of 1970. At issue here is the interpretation of the chapter's forfeiture provision, 18 U.S.C. § 1963(a)(1), and, specifically, the meaning of the words "any interest [the defendant] has acquired ... in violation of section 1962."

I

On June 8, 1977, petitioner Joseph C. Russello and others were indicted for racketeering, conspiracy, and mail fraud, in violation of 18 U.S.C. §§ 1341, 1962(c) and (d), and 2.

After a jury trial in the United States District Court for the Middle District of Florida, petitioner was convicted as charged in four counts of the indictment. The jury then returned special verdicts for the forfeiture to the United States, under 18 U.S.C. § 1963(a), of four payments, aggregating $340,043.09, made to petitioner by a fire insurance company. These verdicts related to the racketeering activities charged in the second count of the indictment under which petitioner had been convicted. The District Court, accordingly, entered a judgment of forfeiture against petitioner in that amount.

Petitioner took an appeal to the former United States Court of Appeals for the Fifth Circuit. A panel of that court affirmed petitioner's criminal conviction, and this Court denied certiorari as to that aspect of the case. The panel, however, reversed the judgment of forfeiture. The full court granted rehearing en banc on the forfeiture issue and, by a vote of 16–7, vacated that portion of the panel opinion, and then affirmed the forfeiture judgment entered by the District Court. Because of this significant division among the judges of the Court of Appeals, and because the Fifth Circuit majority stated that its holding "squarely conflict[ed]" with [a] Ninth Circuit [case], we granted certiorari. ...

II

So far as the case in its present posture is concerned, the basic facts are not in dispute. The majority opinion of the en banc court described them succinctly:

"Briefly, the evidence showed that a group of individuals associated for the purpose of committing arson with the intent to defraud insurance companies. This association in fact enterprise, composed of an insurance adjuster, homeowners, promoters, investors, and arsonists, operated to destroy at least eighteen residential and commercial properties in Tampa and Miami, Florida between July 1973 and April 1976. The panel summarized the ring's operations as follows:

" 'At first the arsonists only burned buildings already owned by those associated with the ring. Following a burning, the building owner filed an inflated proof of loss statement and collected the insurance proceeds from which his co-conspirators were paid. Later, ring members bought buildings suitable for burning, secured insurance in excess of value and, after a burning, made claims for the loss and divided the proceeds.' "

Specifically, petitioner was the owner of the Central Professional Building in Tampa. This structure had two parts, an original smaller section in front and a newer addition at the rear. The latter contained apartments, offices, and parking facilities. Petitioner arranged for arsonists to set fire to the front portion. He intended to use the insurance proceeds to rebuild that section. The fire, however, spread to the rear. Joseph Carter, another member of the arson ring, was the adjuster for petitioner's insurance claim and helped him to obtain the highest payments possible. The resulting payments made up the aggregate sum of $340,043.09 mentioned above. From those proceeds, petitioner paid Carter $30,000 for his assistance.

III

Title 18 U.S.C. § 1962(c) states that it shall be unlawful "for any person employed by or associated with any enterprise engaged in, or the activities of which affect, interstate ... commerce, to conduct or participate, directly or indirectly, in the conduct of such enterprise's affairs through a pattern of racketeering activity or collection of unlawful debt." Section 1962(d) makes it unlawful to conspire to violate § 1962(c). Section 1963(a)(1) provides that a person convicted under § 1962 shall forfeit to the United States "any interest he has acquired or maintained in violation of section 1962."

The sole issue in this case is whether profits and proceeds derived from racketeering constitute an "interest" within the meaning of this statute and are therefore subject to forfeiture. Petitioner contends that § 1963(a)(1) reaches only "interests in an enterprise" and does not authorize the forfeiture of mere "profits and proceeds." He rests his argument upon the propositions that criminal forfeitures are disfavored in law and that forfeiture statutes, as a consequence, must be strictly construed.

In a RICO case recently decided, this Court observed: "In determining the scope of a statute, we look first to its language. If the statutory language is unambiguous, in the absence of 'a clearly expressed legislative intent to the contrary, that language must ordinarily be regarded as conclusive.' " United States v. Turkette, 452 U.S. 576, 580 (1981).

Here, 18 U.S.C. § 1963(a)(1) calls for the forfeiture to the United States of "any interest ... acquired ... in violation of section 1962." There is no question that petitioner Russello acquired the insurance proceeds at issue in violation of § 1962(c); that much has been definitely and finally settled. Accordingly, if those proceeds qualify as an "interest," they are forfeitable.

The term "interest" is not specifically defined in the RICO statute. This silence compels us to "Start with the assumption that the legislative purpose is expressed by the ordinary meaning of the words used." Richards v. United States, 369 U.S. 1, 9 (1962). The ordinary meaning of "interest" surely encompasses a right to profits or proceeds. See Webster's Third New International Dictionary 1178 (1976), broadly defining "interest," among other things, as a "good," "benefit," or "profit." Random House Dictionary of the English Language 741 (1979) defines interest to include "benefit." Black's Law Dictionary 729 (5th ed., 1979) provides a significant definition of "interest": "The most general term that can be employed to denote a right, claim, title, or legal share in something." It is thus apparent that the term "interest" comprehends all forms of real and personal property, including profits and proceeds.

This Court repeatedly has relied upon the term "interest" in defining the meaning of "property" in the due process clause of the 14th amendment of the Constitution. See Perry v. Sindermann, 408 U.S. 593, 601 (1972)("'property' denotes a broad range of interests"). It undoubtedly was because Congress did not wish the forfeiture provision of § 1963(a) to be limited by rigid and technical definitions drawn from other areas of the law that it selected the broad term "interest" to describe those things that are subject to forfeiture under the statute. Congress selected this general term apparently because it was fully consistent with pattern of the RICO statute in utilizing terms and concepts of breadth. Among these are "enterprise" in § 1961(4); "racketeering activity" in § 1961(1)(1982 ed.); and "participate" in § 1962(c).

Petitioner himself has not attempted to define the term "interest" as used in § 1963(a)(1). He insists, however, that the term does not reach money or profits because, he says: " 'Interest,' by definition, includes of necessity an interest in something." Petitioner then asserts that the "something" emerges from the wording of § 1963(a)(1) itself, that is, an interest "acquired ... in violation of section 1962," and thus derives its meaning from the very activities barred by the statute. In other words, a direct relationship exists between that which is subject to forfeiture as a result of racketeering activity and that which constitutes racketeering. This relationship, it is said, means that forfeiture is confined to an interest in an "enterprise" itself. . . .

We do not agree. Every property interest, including a right to profits or proceeds, may be described as an interest in something. Before profits of an illegal enterprise are divided, each participant may be said to own an "interest" in the ill-gotten gains. After distribution, each will have a possessory interest in currency or other items so distributed. We therefore conclude that the language of the statute plainly covers the insurance proceeds petitioner received as a result of his arson activities.

IV

We are fortified in this conclusion by our examination of the structure of the RICO statute. We disagree with those courts that have felt that a broad construction of the word "interest" is necessarily undermined by the statute's other forfeiture provisions. The argument for a narrow construction of § 1963(a)(1) is refuted by the language of the succeeding subsection (a)(2). The former speaks broadly of "any interest . . . acquired," while the latter reaches only "any interest in . . . any enterprise which [the defendant] has established[,] operated, controlled, conducted, or participated in the conduct of, in violation of section 1962." Similar less expansive language appears in §§ 1962(b) and 1964(a). . . . Had Congress intended to restrict § 1963(a)(1) to an interest in an enterprise, it presumably would have done so expressly as it did in the immediately following subsection (a)(2). . . . We refrain from concluding here that the differing language in the two subsections has the same meaning in each. We would not presume to ascribe this difference to a simple mistake in draftsmanship.

The evolution of these statutory provisions supplies further evidence that Congress intended § 1963(a)(1) to extend beyond an interest in an enterprise. An early proposed version of RICO, S.1861, 91st Cong., 1st Sess. (1969), has a single forfeiture provision for § 1963(a) that was limited to "all interest in the enterprise." This provision, however, later was divided into the present two subsections and the phrase "in the enterprise" was excluded from the first. Where Congress includes limiting language in an earlier version of a bill but deletes it prior to enactment, it may be presumed that the limitation was not intended. See Edward C. Weiner, Crime Must Not Pay: RICO Criminal Forfeiture in Perspective, 1981 N. Ill. U. L. Rev. 225, 238, and n. 49. It is no answer to say, as petitioner does, that if the term "interest" were as all-encompassing as suggested by the majority opinion of the Court of Appeals, § 1963(a)(2) would have no meaning independent of § 1963(a)(1), and would be mere surplusage. This argument is plainly incorrect. Subsection (a)(2), on the other hand, is restricted to an interest in an enterprise, but that interest itself need not have been illegally acquired. Thus, there are things forfeitable under one, but not the other, of each of the subsections.[2]

---

[2] There may well be factual situations to which both subsections apply. The subsec- tions, however, are clearly not wholly redun- dant.

We note that the RICO statute's definition of the term "enterprise" in § 1961(4) encompasses both legal entities and illegitimate associations-in-fact. See *United States v. Turkette*, 452 U.S., at 580–93. Forfeiture of an interest in an illegitimate association-in-fact ordinarily would be little use because an association of that kind rarely has identifiable assets; instead, proceeds or profits usually are distributed immediately. Thus, construing § 1963(a)(1) to reach only interests in an enterprise would blunt the effectiveness of the provision in combating illegitimate enterprises, and would mean that "[w]hole areas of organized criminal activity would be placed beyond" the reach of the statute. *United States v. Turkette*, 452 U.S., at 589.

Petitioner stresses that 21 U.S.C. § 848(a)(2), contained in the Controlled Substances Act [enacted within the same month as RICO], specifically authorizes the forfeiture of "profits" obtained in a continuing criminal enterprise engaged in certain drug offenses. ... We feel, however, that the specific mention of "profits" in the Controlled Substances Act cannot be accepted as an indication that the broader language of § 1963(a)(1) was not meant to reach profits as well as other types of property interests. Language in one statute usually sheds little light upon the meaning of different language in another statute, even when the two are enacted at or about the same time. The term "profits" is specific; the term "interest" is general. The use of the specific in the one statute cannot fairly be read as imposing a limitation upon the general provision in the other statute. In addition, the RICO statute was aimed at organized crime's economic power in all its forms, and it was natural to use the broad term "interest" to fulfill that aim. In contrast, the narcotics activity proscribed by § 848 usually generates only monetary profits, a fact which would explain the use of the narrower term in § 848(a)(2).

Petitioner, of course, correctly suggests that members of Congress who voted for the RICO statute were aware of the Controlled Substances Act. It is most unlikely, however, that without explanation a potent forfeiture weapon was withheld from the RICO statute, intended for use in a broad assault on organized crime, while the same weapon was included in the Controlled Substances Act, meant for use in only one part of the same struggle. If this was Congress' intent, one would expect it to have said so in clear and understandable terms.

Petitioner also suggests that subsequent proposed legislation demonstrates that the RICO forfeiture provision of 1970 excludes profits. The bills to which petitioner refers, however, were introduced in order to overcome [narrow Circuit Court decisions]. The introduction of these bills hardly suggests that their sponsors viewed those decisions as correct interpretations of § 1963(a)(1). In any event, it is well settled that " 'the views of a subsequent Congress form a hazardous basis for inferring the intent of an earlier one.' " Jefferson County Pharmaceutical Assn. v.

Abbott Laboratories, 460 U.S. 150, 165, n. 27 (1983), quoting from United States v. Price, 361 U.S. 304, 313 (1960).

Neither are we persuaded by petitioner's argument that his position is supported by the fact that certain state racketeering statutes expressly provide for the forfeiture of "profits," "money," "interest or property," or "all property, real or personal," acquired from racketeering. ...

V

If it is necessary to turn to the legislation history of the RICO statute, one finds that that history does not reveal, as petitioner would have us hold, a limited congressional intent.

The legislative history clearly demonstrates that the RICO statute was intended to provide new weapons of unprecedented scope for an assault upon organized crime and its economic roots. Congress' statement of findings and purpose in enacting [RICO], is set forth in its § 1. This statement dramatically describes the problem presented by organized crime. Congress declared: "It is the purpose of this act to seek the eradication of organized crime in the United States ... by providing enhanced sanctions and new remedies to deal with the unlawful activities of those engaged in organized crime." This Court has recognized the significance of this statement of findings and purpose. *United States v. Turkette*, 452 U.S., at 588–89. Further, Congress directed, by § 904(a): "The provisions of this title shall be liberally construed to effectuate its remedial purposes." So far as we have been made aware, this is the only substantive federal criminal statute that contains such a directive....

Congress emphasized the need to fashion new remedies in order to achieve its far-reaching objectives.

> "What is needed here ... are new approaches that will deal not only with individuals, but also with the economic base through which those individuals constitute such a serious threat to the economic well-being of the Nation. In short, an attack must be made on their source of economic power itself, and the attack must take place on all available fronts."

Senator Scott spoke of "new legal weapons," 116 Cong. Rec. 819 (1970), and Senator McClellan stressed the need for new penal remedies. Id., at 591–92. Representative Poff, floor manager of the bill in the House, made similar observations. Id., at 35193. Representative Rodino observed that "[d]rastic methods ... are essential, and we must develop law enforcement measures at least as efficient as those of organized crime." Id., at 35199. The RICO statute was viewed as one such "extraordinary" weapon. Id., at 602 (remarks of Sen. Hruska). And the forfeiture provision was intended to serve all the aims of the RICO statute, namely, to "punish, deter, incapacitate, and ... directly to remove the corrupting influence from the channels of commerce." Id., at 18955 (remarks of Sen. McClellan).

The legislative history leaves no doubt that, in the view of Congress, the economic power of organized crime derived from its huge illegal profits.

See G. Robert Blakey, The RICO Civil Fraud Action in Context: Reflections on *Bennett v. Berg*, 58 Notre Dame L. Rev. 237, 249–56 (1982). Congress could not have hoped successfully to attack organized crime's economic roots without reaching racketeering profits. During the congressional debates, the sources and magnitude of organized crime's income were emphasized repeatedly. From all this, the intent to authorize forfeiture of racketeering profits seems obvious. H.R. Rep. No. 91–1549, p. 57 (1970), recites that the forfeiture provision extends to "all property and interests, as broadly defined, which are related to the violations."

It is true that Congress viewed the RICO statute in large part as a response to organized crime's infiltration of legitimate enterprises. *United States v. Turkette*, 452 U.S., at 591. But Congress' concerns were not limited to infiltration. The broader goal was to remove the profit from organized crime by separating the racketeer from his dishonest gains. Forfeiture of interest in an enterprise often would do little to deter; indeed, it might only encourage the speedy looting of an infiltrated company. It is unlikely that Congress intended to enact a forfeiture provision that provided an incentive for activity of this kind while authorizing forfeiture of an interest of little worth in a bankrupt shell.

We are not persuaded otherwise by the presence of a 1969 letter from the then Deputy Attorney General to Senator McClellan. See Measures Relating to Organized Crime: Hearings before the Subcommittee on Criminal Laws and Procedures of the Senate Committee on the Judiciary, 91st Cong. 1st Sess., 407 (1969). That letter, with its reference to "one's interest in the enterprise" does not indicate, for us, any congressional intent to preclude forfeiture of racketeering profits. The reference, indeed, is not to § 1963(a) as finally enacted but to an earlier version in which forfeiture was to be expressly limited to an interest in an enterprise. The letter was merely following the language of the then pending bill. Furthermore, the real purpose of the sentence was not to explain what the statutory provision meant, but to explain why the Department of Justice believed it was constitutional.

The rule of lenity, which this Court has recognized in certain situations of statutory ambiguity, see *United States v. Turkette*, 452 U.S., at 587, n.10, has no application here. That rule "comes into operation at the end of the process of construing what Congress has expressed, not at the beginning as an overriding consideration of being lenient to wrongdoers." Callanan v. United States, 364 U.S. 587, 596 (1961). Here, the language of the RICO forfeiture provision is clear, and "the rule of lenity does not come into play." *United States v. Turkette*, 452 U.S., at 588, n.10.

We therefore ... affirm the judgment of the United States Court of Appeals for the Fifth Circuit.[3]

[3] In our ruling today, we recognize that we have not resolved any ambiguity that might be inherent in the terms "profits" and "proceeds." Our use of those terms is not intended to suggest a particular means of calculating the precise amount that is subject to RICO forfeiture in any given case. We hold simply that the "interests" subject to

It is so ordered.

NOTE ON FORFEITURE AND THE EIGHTH AMENDMENT

In Austin v. United States, 509 U.S. 602 (1993), the Supreme Court was asked to decide whether the Excessive Fines Clause of the Eighth Amendment applies to civil forfeitures of property pursuant to two federal drug statutes, 21 U.S.C. §§ 881(a)(4) and (a)(7). The Court, per Justice Blackmun, held that it did:

"The purpose of the Eighth Amendment, putting the Bail Clause to one side, was to limit the government's power to punish. See Browning-Ferris Ind. of Vermont, Inc. v. Kelco Disposal, Inc., 492 U.S. 257, 266–67, 275 (1989). The Cruel and Unusual Punishments Clause is self-evidently concerned with punishment. The Excessive Fines Clause limits the Government's power to extract payments, whether in cash or in kind, 'as punishment for some offense.' Id., at 265. 'The notion of punishment, as we commonly understand it, cuts across the division between the civil and the criminal law.' United States v. Halper, 490 U.S. 435, 447–48 (1989). 'It is commonly understood that civil proceedings may advance punitive and remedial goals, and, conversely, that both punitive and remedial goals may be served by criminal penalties.' Id., at 447. See also United States ex rel. Marcus v. Hess, 317 U.S. 537, 554 (1943)(Frankfurter, J., concurring). Thus, the question is not, as the United States would have it, whether forfeiture under §§ 881(a)(4) and (a)(7) is civil or criminal, but rather whether it is punishment.

" '[T]his Court ... consistently has recognized that forfeiture serves, at least in part, to punish the owner.' See Dobbins's Distillery v. United States, 96 U.S. 395, 404 (1878)('the acts of violation as to the penal consequences to the property are to be considered just the same as if they were the acts of the owner'). More recently, we have noted that forfeiture serves 'punitive and deterrent purposes,' Calero–Toledo v. Pearson Yacht Leasing Co., 416 U.S. 663, 686 (1974), and 'impos[es] an economic penalty,' id., at 687. We conclude, therefore, that forfeiture generally and statutory in rem forfeiture in particular historically have been understood, at least in part, as punishment.

"We turn next to consider whether forfeitures under 21 U.S.C. §§ 881(a)(4) and (a)(7) are properly considered punishment today. We find nothing in these provisions or their legislative history to contradict the historical understanding of forfeiture as punishment. Unlike traditional forfeiture statutes, §§ 881(a)(4) and (a)(7) expressly provide an 'innocent owner' defense. See § 881(a)(4)(C)('no conveyance shall be forfeited under this para-

forfeiture under § 1963(a)(1) are not limited
to interests in an enterprise.

graph to the extent of an interest of an owner, by reason of any act or omission established by that owner to have been committed or omitted without the knowledge, consent, or willful blindness of the owner'); § 881(a)(7)('no property shall be forfeited under this paragraph, to the extent of an interest of an owner, by reason of any act or omission established by that owner to have been committed or omitted without the knowledge or consent of that owner'); see also United States v. 92 Buena Vista Avenue, Rumson, 507 U.S. 111(1993)(plurality opinion)(noting difference from traditional forfeiture statutes). These exemptions serve to focus the provisions on the culpability of the owner in a way that makes them look more like punishment, not less. In United States v. United States Coin & Currency, 401 U.S. 715 (1971), we reasoned that 19 U.S.C. § 1618, which provides that the Secretary of the Treasury is to return the property of those who do not intend to violate the law, demonstrated Congress' intent 'to impose a penalty only upon those who are significantly involved in a criminal enterprise.' 401 U.S., at 721–22. The inclusion of innocent-owner defenses in §§ 881(a)(4) and (a)(7) reveals a similar congressional intent to punish only those involved in drug trafficking.

"Furthermore, Congress has chosen to tie forfeiture directly to the commission of drug offenses. Thus, under § 881(a)(4), a conveyance is forfeitable if it is used or intended for use to facilitate the transportation of controlled substances, their raw materials, or the equipment used to manufacture or distribute them. Under § 881(a)(7), real property is forfeitable if it is used or intended for use to facilitate the commission of a drug-related crime punishable by more than one year's imprisonment.

"The legislative history of § 881 confirms the punitive nature of these provisions. When it added subsection (a)(7) to § 881 in 1984, Congress recognized 'that the traditional criminal sanctions of fine and imprisonment are inadequate to deter or punish the enormously profitable trade in dangerous drugs.' S.Rep. No. 98–225, p. 191 (1983). It characterized the forfeiture of real property as 'a powerful deterrent.' Id., at 195. See also Joint House–Senate Explanation of Senate Amendment to Titles II and III of the Psychotropic Substances Act of 1978, 124 Cong.Rec. 34671 (1978)(noting 'the penal nature of forfeiture statutes'). . . .

"Fundamentally, even assuming that §§ 881(a)(4) and (a)(7) serve some remedial purpose, the Government's argument must fail. '[A] civil sanction that cannot fairly be said solely to serve a remedial purpose, but rather can only be explained as also serving either retributive or deterrent purposes, is punishment, as we have come to understand the term.' *Halper*, 490 U.S., at 448. In light of the historical understanding of forfeiture as punishment, the clear focus of §§ 881(a)(4) and (a)(7) on the culpability of the owner, and the evidence that Congress understood those provisions as serving to deter and to punish, we cannot conclude that forfeiture under §§ 881(a)(4) and (a)(7) serves solely a remedial purpose. We therefore conclude that forfeiture under these provisions constitutes 'payment to a sovereign as punishment for some offense,' *Browning-Ferris*, 492 U.S., at 265, and, as such, is subject to the limitations of the Eighth Amendment's Excessive Fines Clause.''

The Court remanded the case to the Eighth Circuit to determine, in the first instance, whether or not the relevant forfeiture violated the Eighth Amendment's prohibition of excessive fines.

NOTE ON FORFEITURE AND THE DOUBLE JEOPARDY CLAUSE

In United States v. $405,089.23 U.S. Currency, 33 F.3d 1210 (9th Cir.1994), *en banc rehearing denied,* 56 F.3d 41 (9th Cir.1995), a unanimous panel of the Ninth Circuit ruled that civil forfeiture under 18 U.S.C. § 981(a)(1)(A) and 21 U.S.C. § 881(a)(6) constitutes "punishment," and that it is a violation of the double jeopardy clause for the government to pursue such forfeiture after a defendant has already been prosecuted for the underlying drug crime. The Ninth Circuit relied on United States v. Halper, 490 U.S. 435 (1989), and Austin v. United States, 509 U.S. 602 (1993), concluding that those two decisions reflected a change in the Supreme Court's traditional view that civil forfeiture was not a proceeding governed by double jeopardy. According to the Ninth Circuit:

"There can be little doubt that this case implicates the core Double Jeopardy protection. Over a year after the claimants' criminal convictions, a different district judge in a different proceeding awarded the government title to nearly all of the claimants' property, because of its connection with the very offenses that resulted in criminal punishment. The forfeiture complaint in this case was based on precisely the same conduct addressed in the claimants' criminal case, and it sought to forfeit title to the claimants' property on the basis of precisely the same violations of the same statutes. In short, this civil forfeiture action and the claimants' criminal prosecution addressed the identical violations of the identical laws; the only difference between the two proceedings was the remedy sought by the government. Yet the government could have sought both remedies without subjecting [the defendants] to multiple and successive proceedings. It could have included a criminal forfeiture count in the indictment which led to the claimants' convictions. However, it did not choose to follow that course. Rather, it elected to pursue its forfeiture action in a separate and parallel proceeding, which was decided after the criminal trial. By doing so, the government prevented [the defendants] from 'being able, once and for all, to conclude [their] confrontation with society' at the time of the jury's verdict. United States v. Jorn, 400 U.S. 470, 486 (1971)(opinion of Harlan, J.).

"The government's actions in this case clearly raise substantial double jeopardy concerns. However, to determine whether these actions violate the Fifth Amendment, we must consider two questions: whether the civil forfeiture action and the claimants' criminal prosecution constituted separate 'proceedings,' and whether civil forfeiture under 21 U.S.C. § 881(a)(6) and 18 U.S.C.§ 981(a)(1)(A) constitutes 'punishment.' If the answer to both of these questions is yes, then the government's actions constituted a successive attempt to impose punishment, in violation of the Double Jeopardy Clause.

.   .   .

"We fail to see how two separate actions, one civil and one criminal, instituted at different times, tried at different times before different factfinders, presided over by different district judges, and resolved by separate judgments, constitute the same 'proceeding.' In ordinary legal parlance, such actions are often characterized as 'parallel proceedings,' but not as the 'same proceeding.' A forfeiture case and a criminal prosecution would constitute the same proceeding only if they were brought in the same indictment and tried at the same time. The government could have sought criminal forfeiture in this case pursuant to 18 U.S.C. §§ 982, 3554 and 21 U.S.C. § 853. If it had done so and included the forfeiture count in the same indictment as the other criminal counts and then proceeded to trial against the defendants on all counts, the forfeiture case and the criminal prosecution would have constituted the 'same proceeding.'

"However, the government chose to proceed against the claimants on two separate fronts—in two separate, parallel proceedings. Because the district court followed the customary practice and held the civil action in abeyance pending the outcome of the criminal prosecution, the government obtained a significant advantage: if it succeeded in the criminal case it could obtain summary judgment based on the conviction (assuming of course that it had probable cause at the time it instituted the forfeiture action), while if it lost it could still seek forfeiture and urge that the more lenient standards applicable in civil proceedings applied. See 1 David B. Smith, Prosecution and Defense of Forfeiture Cases, Par. 10.01, at 10–4 to 10–5 (1993)(noting that it is to the government's advantage to have the civil forfeiture action heard after the criminal case). We believe that such a coordinated, manipulative prosecution strategy heightens, rather than diminishes, the concern that the government is forcing an individual to 'run the gantlet' more than once. *Green*, 355 U.S. at 190. We are not willing to whitewash the double jeopardy violation in this case by affording constitutional significance to the label of 'single, coordinated prosecution.'

.   .   .

"As the government notes, the specific holding in *Austin* was that the Eighth Amendment's Excessive Fines Clause applies to civil forfeiture actions.   However, in determining whether the Excessive Fines Clause applied, the Court found it necessary to determine, as we are required to determine here, whether the forfeiture statutes at issue constituted 'punishment.'   It employed the *Halper* test—the same test it had used to decide whether a civil monetary penalty constituted 'punishment' for purposes of the Double Jeopardy Clause—in making that determination.   We believe that the only fair reading of the Court's decision in *Austin* is that it resolves the 'punishment' issue with respect to forfeiture cases for purposes of the Double Jeopardy Clause as well as the Excessive Fines Clause.   In short, if a forfeiture constitutes punishment under the *Halper* criteria, it constitutes 'punishment' for purposes of both clauses.   See Smith, supra, Par. 12.10[2], at 12–131 ("The Supreme Court's decision in *Austin v. United States*, makes it clear that *Halper*'s double jeopardy protections do apply to the vast majority of civil forfeiture cases.").   In light of the decision in *Austin*, and applying the *Halper* test here, we find the conclusion inescapable that civil forfeiture under 18 U.S.C. § 981(a)(1)(A) and 21 U.S.C. § 881(a)(6) constitutes 'punishment' which triggers the protections of the Double Jeopardy Clause.

. . .

For a similar view, see United States v. Ursery, 59 F.3d 568 (6th Cir.1995), where the Sixth Circuit held that an in rem civil forfeiture proceeding under 21 U.S.C. § 881(7) constituted "punishment" for purposes of double jeopardy, necessitating reversal of a subsequently obtained criminal conviction relating to the same drug offense.

In June, 1996, however, the Supreme Court overturned the rulings of both the Ninth and Sixth Circuits.   In United States v. Ursery, ___ U.S. ___, 116 S.Ct. 2135 (1996), decided together with the *$405,089.23 in U.S. Currency* case, the Court adhered to its "traditional understanding that civil forfeiture does not constitute punishment for the purpose of the Double Jeopardy Clause."   The Court rejected the claim that, under *Halper* and *Austin,* "remedial civil sanction[s]" such as in rem civil forfeiture must be analyzed using the same double-jeopardy approach as would apply to "potentially punitive in personam civil penalties such as fines":

"It is difficult to see how the rule of *Halper* could be applied to a civil forfeiture.   Civil penalties are designed as a rough form of 'liquidated damages' for the harms suffered by the Government as a result of the defendant's conduct.   ...   Civil forfeitures, in contrast to civil penalties, ... serve a variety of purposes, but are designed primarily to confiscate property used in violation of the law, and to require disgorgement of the fruits of illegal conduct. Though it may be possible to quantify the value of the property forfeited, it is virtually impossible to quantify, even approximately, the nonpunitive purposes served by a particular civil forfeiture. Hence, it is practically difficult to determine whether a particular forfeiture bears no rational relationship to the nonpunitive purposes of that forfeiture. Quite simply, the case-by-case balancing test set forth in *Halper,* in which a court must compare the harm suffered by the Government against the size of the penalty imposed, is inapplicable to civil forfeiture.

. . .

"In the cases that we review, the Courts of Appeals did not find *Halper* difficult to apply to civil forfeiture because they concluded that its case-by-case balancing approach had been supplanted in *Austin* by a categorical approach that found a civil sanction to be punitive if it could not 'fairly be said solely to serve a remedial purpose.' ... But *Austin,* it must be remembered, did not involve the Double Jeopardy Clause at all. ... The holding of *Austin* was limited to the Excessive Fines Clause of the Eighth Amendment, and we decline to import the analysis of *Austin* into our double jeopardy jurisprudence."

The Court added in a footnote:

"We do not hold that in rem civil forfeiture is per se exempt from the scope of the Double Jeopardy Clause. Similarly, we do not rest our conclusion in this case upon the long-recognized fiction that a forfeiture in rem punishes only the malfeasant property rather than a particular person. That a forfeiture is designated as civil by Congress and proceeds in rem establishes a presumption that it is not subject to double jeopardy. See, e.g., United States v. One Assortment of 89 Firearms, 465 U.S. 354, 363 (1984). Nevertheless, where the 'clearest proof' indicates that an in rem civil forfeiture is 'so punitive either in purpose or effect' as to be equivalent to a criminal proceeding, that forfeiture may be subject to the Double Jeopardy Clause."

SUBSECTION B: PROTECTION FOR "INNOCENT OWNERS"

United States v. A Parcel of Land, Buildings, Appurtenances and Improvements, Known as 92 Buena Vista Avenue, Rumson, New Jersey

Supreme Court of the United States, 1993.
507 U.S. 111.

■ STEVENS, J., announced the judgment of the Court and delivered an opinion, in which BLACKMUN, O'CONNOR, AND SOUTER, JJ., joined.

The question presented is whether an owner's lack of knowledge of the fact that her home had been purchased with the proceeds of illegal drug transactions constitutes a defense to a forfeiture proceeding under The

Comprehensive Drug Abuse Prevention and Control Act of 1970, § 511(a), 84 Stat. 1276, as amended, 21 U.S.C.§ 881(a)(6).[1]

1

On April 3, 1989, the Government filed an in rem action against the parcel of land in Rumson, New Jersey, on which respondent's home is located. The verified complaint alleged that the property had been purchased in 1982 by respondent with funds provided by Joseph Brenna that were "the proceeds traceable to an [unlawful] exchange for a controlled substance," App. 13, and that the property was therefore subject to seizure and forfeiture under § 881(a)(6).

On April 12, 1989, in an ex parte proceeding, the District Court determined that there was probable cause to believe the premises were subject to forfeiture, and issued a summons and warrant for arrest authorizing the United States Marshal to take possession of the premises. Respondent thereafter asserted a claim to the property, was granted the right to defend the action, and filed a motion for summary judgment.

During pretrial proceedings, the following facts were established. In 1982, Joseph Brenna gave respondent approximately $240,000 to purchase the home that she and her three children have occupied ever since. Respondent is the sole owner of the property. From 1981 until their separation in 1987, she maintained an intimate personal relationship with Brenna. There is probable cause to believe that the funds used to buy the house were proceeds of illegal drug trafficking, but respondent swears that she had no knowledge of its origins.

Among the grounds advanced in support of her motion for summary judgment was the claim that she was an "innocent owner" within the meaning of § 881(a)(6). The District Court rejected this defense for two reasons: First it ruled that "the innocent owner defense may only be invoked by those who can demonstrate that they are bona fide purchasers for value." Second, the court read the statute to offer the innocent owner defense only to persons who acquired an interest in the property before the acts giving rise to the forfeiture took place.

Respondent was allowed to take an interlocutory appeal pursuant to 28 U.S.C.§ 1292(b). One of the controlling questions of law presented to the Court of Appeals was: "Whether an innocent owner defense may be asserted by a person who is not a bona fide purchaser for value concerning

---

[1] The statute provides: "The following shall be subject to forfeiture to the United States and no property right shall exist in them:

. . .

"(6) All moneys, negotiable instruments, securities, or other things of value furnished or intended to be furnished by any person in exchange for a controlled substance in violation of [21 U.S.C. §§ 801–904], all proceeds traceable to such an exchange, and all moneys, negotiable instruments, and securities used or intended to be used to facilitate any violation of this subchapter, except that no property shall be forfeited under this paragraph, to the extent of the interest of an owner, by reason of any act or omission established by that owner to have been committed or omitted without the knowledge or consent of that owner."

a parcel of land where the government has established probable cause to believe that the parcel of land was purchased with monies traceable to drug proceeds." 742 F.Supp. 189, 192 (D.N.J.1990).

Answering that question in the affirmative, the Court of Appeals remanded the case to the District Court to determine whether respondent was, in fact, an innocent owner. The Court of Appeals refused to limit the innocent owner defense to bona fide purchasers for value because the plain language of the statute contains no such limitation, because it read the legislative history as indicating that the term "owner" should be broadly construed, and because the difference between the text of § 881(a)(6) and the text of the criminal forfeiture statute evidenced congressional intent not to restrict the civil section in the same way.

The Court of Appeals also rejected the argument that respondent could not be an innocent owner unless she acquired the property before the drug transaction occurred. In advancing that argument the Government had relied on the "relation back" doctrine embodied in § 881(h), which provides that "[a]ll right, title and interest in property described in subsection (a) of this section shall vest in the United States upon commission of the act giving rise to forfeiture under this section." The court held that the relation back doctrine applied only to "property described in subsection (a)" and that the property at issue would not fit that description if respondent could establish her innocent owner defense. The court concluded that the Government's interpretation of § 881(h) "would essentially serve to emasculate the innocent owner defense provided for in § 881(a)(6). No one obtaining property after the occurrence of the drug transaction—including a bona fide purchaser for value—would be eligible to offer an innocent owner defense on his behalf." 937 F.2d 98, 102 (3d Cir.1991) at 9a.

The conflict between the decision of the Court of Appeals and decisions of the Fourth and Tenth Circuits, see In re One 1985 Nissan, 889 F.2d 1317 (4th Cir.1989); Eggleston v. Colorado, 873 F.2d 242, 245–48 (10th Cir.1989), led us to grant certiorari. We now affirm.

II

Laws providing for the official seizure and forfeiture of tangible property used in criminal activity have played an important role in the history of our country. Colonial courts regularly exercised jurisdiction to enforce English and local statutes authorizing the seizure of ships and goods used in violation of customs and revenue laws. Indeed, the misuse of the hated general warrant is often cited as an important cause of the American Revolution.

The First Congress enacted legislation authorizing the seizure and forfeiture of ships and cargos involved in customs offenses. Other statutes authorized the seizure of ships engaged in piracy. When a ship was engaged in acts of "piratical aggression," it was subject to confiscation notwithstanding the innocence of the owner of the vessel.[13] Later statutes involved the seizure and forfeiture of distilleries and other property used to defraud the United States of tax revenues from the sale of alcoholic beverages. See, e.g., United States v. Stowell, 133 U.S. 1, 11–12 (1890). In these cases, as in the piracy cases, the innocence of the owner of premises leased to a distiller would not defeat a decree of condemnation based on the fraudulent conduct of the lessee.[14]

In all of these early cases the Government's right to take possession of property stemmed from the misuse of the property itself. Indeed, until our decision in Warden v. Hayden, 387 U.S. 294 (1967), the Government had power to seize only property that " 'the private citizen was not permitted to possess.' " The holding in that case that the Fourth Amendment did not prohibit the seizure of "mere evidence" marked an important expansion of governmental power. See Zurcher v. Stanford Daily, 436 U.S. 547, 577–80 (1978)(Stevens, J., dissenting).

The decision by Congress in 1978 to amend the Comprehensive Drug Abuse Prevention and Control Act of 1970, 84 Stat. 1236, to authorize the seizure and forfeiture of proceeds of illegal drug transactions, see 92 Stat.

[13] "The next question is, whether the innocence of the owners can withdraw the ship from the penalty of confiscation under the act of Congress. Here, again, it may be remarked that the act makes no exception whatsoever, whether the aggression be with or without the cooperation of the owners. The vessel which commits the aggression is treated as the offender, as the guilty instrument or thing to which the forfeiture attaches, without any reference whatsoever to the character or conduct of the owner. The vessel or boat (says the act of Congress) from which such piratical aggression, & c., shall have been first attempted or made shall be condemned. Nor is there any thing new in a provision of this sort. It is not an uncommon course in the admiralty, acting under the law of nations, to treat the vessel in which or by which, or by the master or crew thereof, a wrong or offense has been done as the offender, without any regard whatsoever to the personal misconduct or responsibility of the owner thereof. And this is done from the necessity of the case, as the only adequate means of suppressing the offense or wrong, or insuring an indemnity to the injured party. The doctrine also is familiarly applied to cases of smuggling and other misconduct under our revenue laws; and has been applied to other kindred cases, such as cases arising on embargo and non-intercourse acts. In short, the acts of the master and crew, in cases of this sort, bind the interest of the owner of the ship, whether he be innocent or guilty; and he impliedly submits to whatever the law denounces as a forfeiture attached to the ship by reason of their unlawful or wanton wrongs." United States v. Brig Malek Adhel, 43 U.S. (2 How.) 210, 233–34.

[14] "Beyond controversy, the title of the premises and property was in the claimant; and it is equally certain that he leased the same to the lessee for the purposes of a distillery, and with the knowledge that the lessee intended to use the premises to carry on that business, and that he did use the same for that purpose. 'Fraud is not imputed to the owner of the premises; but the evidence and the verdict of the jury warrant the conclusion that the frauds charged in the information were satisfactorily proved, from which it follows that the decree of condemnation is correct, if it be true, as heretofore explained, that it was the property and not the claimant that was put to trial under the pleadings; and we are also of the opinion that the theory adopted by the court below, that, if the lessee of the premises and the operator of the distillery committed the alleged frauds, the government was entitled to a verdict, even though the jury were of the opinion that the claimant was ignorant of the fraudulent acts or omissions of the distiller.' " Dobbins's Distillery v. United States, 96 U.S. 395, 403–04 (1878).

3777, also marked an important expansion of governmental power.[16] Before that amendment, the statute had authorized forfeiture of only the illegal substances themselves and the instruments by which they were manufactured and distributed. The original forfeiture provisions of the 1970 statute had closely paralleled the early statutes used to enforce the customs laws, the piracy laws, and the revenue laws: They generally authorized the forfeiture of property used in the commission of criminal activity, and they contained no innocent owner defense. They applied to stolen goods, but they did not apply to proceeds from the sale of stolen goods. Because the statute, after its 1978 amendment, does authorize the forfeiture of such proceeds and also contains an express and novel protection for innocent owners, we approach the task of construing it with caution.

III

The Court of Appeals correctly concluded that the protection afforded to innocent owners is not limited to bona fide purchasers. The text of the statute is the strongest support for this conclusion. The statute authorizes the forfeiture of moneys exchanged for a controlled substance, and "all proceeds traceable to such an exchange," with one unequivocal exception: "[N]o property shall be forfeited under this paragraph, to the extent of the interest of an owner, by reason of any act or omission established by that owner to have been committed or omitted without the knowledge or consent of that owner." 21 U.S.C. § 881(a)(6). The term "owner" is used three times and each time it is unqualified. Such language is sufficiently unambiguous to foreclose any contention that it applies only to bona fide purchasers. Presumably that explains why the Government does not now challenge this aspect of the Court of Appeals' ruling.

That the funds respondent used to purchase her home were a gift does not, therefore, disqualify respondent from claiming that she is an owner who had no knowledge of the alleged fact that those funds were "proceeds traceable" to illegal sales of controlled substances. Under the terms of the statute, her status would be precisely the same if, instead of having received a gift of $240,000 from Brenna, she had sold him a house for that price and used the proceeds to buy the property at issue.

IV

Although the Government does not challenge our interpretation of the statutory term "owner", it insists that respondent is not the "owner" of a house she bought in 1982 and has lived in ever since. Indeed, it contends that she never has been the owner of this parcel of land because the statute vested ownership in the United States at the moment when the proceeds of

---

[16] A precedent for this expansion had been established in 1970 by the Racketeer Influenced and Corrupt Organizations Act (RICO), see 18 U.S.C. section 1963(a). Even RICO, however, did not specifically provide for the forfeiture of "proceeds" until 1984, when Congress added section 1963(a)(3) to resolve any doubt whether it intended the statute to reach so far. See S.Rep. No. 98-225, pp. 191–200 (1983); Russello v. United States, 464 U.S. 16 (1983).

an illegal drug transaction were used to pay the purchase price. In support of its position, the Government relies on both the text of the 1984 amendment to the statute and the common-law relation back doctrine. We conclude, however, that neither the amendment nor the common-law rule makes the Government an owner of property before forfeiture has been decreed.

In analyzing the Government's relation back argument, it is important to remember that respondent invokes the innocent owner defense against a claim that proceeds traceable to an illegal transaction are forfeitable. The Government contends that the money that Brenna received in exchange for narcotics became Government property at the moment Brenna received it and that respondent's house became Government property when that tainted money was used in its purchase. Because neither the money nor the house could have constituted forfeitable proceeds until after an illegal transaction occurred, the Government's submission would effectively eliminate the innocent owner defense in almost every imaginable case in which proceeds could be forfeited. It seems unlikely that Congress would create a meaningless defense. Moreover, considering that a logical application of the Government's submission would result in the forfeiture of property innocently acquired by persons who had been paid with illegal proceeds for providing goods or services to drug traffickers,[18] the burden of persuading us that Congress intended such an inequitable result is especially heavy.

The Government recognizes that the 1984 amendment did not go into effect until two years after respondent acquired the property at issue in this case. It therefore relies heavily on the common-law relation back doctrine applied to in rem forfeitures. That doctrine applied the fiction that property used in violation of law was itself the wrongdoer that must be held to account for the harms it had caused. Because the property, or "res", was treated as the wrongdoer, it was appropriate to regard it as the actual party to the in rem forfeiture proceeding. Under the relation back doctrine, a decree of forfeiture had the effect of vesting title to the offending res in the Government as of the date of its offending conduct. Because we are not aware of any common-law precedent for treating proceeds traceable to an unlawful exchange as a fictional wrongdoer subject to forfeiture, it is not entirely clear that the common-law relation back doctrine is applicable. Assuming that the doctrine does apply, however, it is nevertheless clear that under the common-law rule the fictional and retroactive vesting was not self-executing.

Chief Justice Marshall explained that forfeiture does not automatically vest title to property in the Government: "It has been proved, that in all forfeitures accruing at common law, nothing vests in the government until some legal step shall be taken for the assertion of its right, after which, for

[18] At oral argument the Government suggested that a narrow interpretation of the word "proceeds" would "probably" prevent this absurdity, see Tr. of Oral Arg. 27. The Government's brief, however, took the un- equivocal position that the statute withholds the innocent owner defense from anyone who acquires proceeds after the illegal transaction took place.

many purposes, the doctrine of relation carries back the title to the commission of the offence." United States v. Grundy, 7 U.S. (3 Cranch) 337, 350–51 (1806).[20]

The same rule applied when a statute (a statute that contained no specific relation back provision) authorized the forfeiture. In a passage to which the Government has referred us, we stated our understanding of how the Government's title to forfeited property relates back to the moment of forfeitability:

> "By the settled doctrine of this court, whenever a statute enacts that upon the commission of a certain act specific property used in or connected with that act shall be forfeited, the forfeiture takes effect immediately upon the commission of the act; the right to the property then vests in the United States, although their title is not perfected until judicial condemnation; the forfeiture constitutes a statutory transfer of the right to the United States at the time the offence is committed; and the condemnation, when obtained, relates back to that time, and avoids all intermediate sales and alienations, even to purchasers in good faith." *United States v. Stowell*, 133 U.S., at 16–17.

If the Government wins a judgment of forfeiture under the common-law rule—which applied to common-law forfeitures and to forfeitures under statutes without specific relation back provisions—the vesting of its title in the property relates back to the moment when the property became forfeitable. Until the Government does win such a judgment, however, someone else owns the property. That person may therefore invoke any

---

[20] In his dissent, Justice Kennedy advocates the adoption of a new common-law rule that would avoid the need to construe the terms of the statute that created the Government's right to forfeit proceeds of drug transactions. Under his suggested self-executing rule, patterned after an amalgam of the law of trusts and the law of secured transactions, the Government would be treated as the owner of a secured or beneficial interest in forfeitable proceeds even before a decree of forfeiture is entered. The various authorities that he cites support the proposition that if such an interest exists, it may be extinguished by a sale to a bona fide purchaser; they provide no support for the assumption that such an interest springs into existence independently. As a matter of common law, his proposal is inconsistent with Chief Justice Marshall's statement that "nothing vests in the government until some legal step shall be taken," and with the cases cited by Justice Scalia. As a matter of statutory law, it is improper to rely on § 881(a) as the source of the Government's interest in proceeds without also giving effect to the statutory language defining the scope of that interest. That a statutory provision contains "puzzling" language, or seems unwise, is not an appropriate reason for simply ignoring its text. Justice Kennedy's dramatic suggestion that our construction of the 1984 amendment "rips out" the "centerpiece of the nation's drug enforcement laws" rests on what he characterizes as the "safe" assumption that the innocent owner defense would be available to "an associate" of a criminal who could "shelter the proceeds from forfeiture, to be reacquired once he is clear from law enforcement authorities." As a matter of fact, forfeitable proceeds are much more likely to be possessed by drug dealers themselves than by transferees sufficiently remote to qualify as innocent owners; as a matter of law, it is quite clear that neither an "associate" in the criminal enterprise nor a temporary custodian of drug proceeds would qualify as an innocent owner; indeed, neither would a sham bona fide purchaser.

defense available to the owner of the property before the forfeiture is decreed.

In this case a statute allows respondent to prove that she is an innocent owner. And, as the Chief Justice further explained in *Grundy*, if a forfeiture is authorized by statute, "the rules of the common law may be dispensed with," 7 U.S., at 351. Congress had the opportunity to dispense with the common-law doctrine when it enacted § 881(h); as we read that subsection, however, Congress merely codified the common-law rule. Because that rule was never applied to the forfeiture of proceeds, and because the statute now contains an innocent owner defense, it may not be immediately clear that they lead to the same result.

The 1984 amendment provides: "All right, title, and interest in property described in subsection (a) of this section shall vest in the United States upon commission of the act giving rise to forfeiture under this section." 21 U.S.C. § 881(h). Because proceeds traceable to illegal drug transactions are a species of "property described in subsection (a)," the Government argues that this provision has the effect of preventing such proceeds from becoming the property of anyone other than the United States. The argument fails.

Although proceeds subject to § 881(h) are "described" in the first part of subsection (a)(6), the last clause of that subsection exempts certain proceeds—proceeds owned by one unaware of their criminal source—from forfeiture. As the Senate Report on the 1984 amendment correctly observed, the amendment applies only to "property which is subject to civil forfeiture under § 881(a)." Under § 881(a)(6), the property of one who can satisfy the innocent owner defense is not subject to civil forfeiture. Because the success of any defense available under § 881(a) will necessarily determine whether § 881(h) applies, § 881(a)(6) must allow an assertion of the defense before § 881(h) applies.

Therefore, when Congress enacted this innocent owner defense, and then specifically inserted this relation back provision into the statute, it did not disturb the common-law rights of either owners of forfeitable property or the Government. The common-law rule had always allowed owners to invoke defenses made available to them before the Government's title vested, and after title did vest, the common-law rule had always related that title back to the date of the commission of the act that made the specific property forfeitable. Our decision denies the Government no benefits of the relation back doctrine. The Government cannot profit from the common-law doctrine of relation back until it has obtained a judgment of forfeiture. And it cannot profit from the statutory version of that doctrine in § 881(h) until respondent has had the chance to invoke and offer evidence to support the innocent owner defense under § 881(a)(6).[23]

---

[23] The logic of the Government's argument would apparently apply as well to the innocent owner defense added to the statute in 1988. That amendment provides, in part:

"[N]o conveyance shall be forfeited under this paragraph to the extent of an interest of an owner, by reason of any act or omission established by that owner to have been com-

V

As a postscript we identify two issues that the parties have addressed, but that need not be decided.

The Government has argued that the Court of Appeals' construction of the statute is highly implausible because it would enable a transferee of the proceeds of an illegal exchange to qualify as an innocent owner if she was unaware of the illegal transaction when it occurred but learned about it before she accepted the forfeitable proceeds. Respondent disputes this reading of the statute and argues that both legislative history and common sense suggest that the transferee's lack of knowledge must be established as of the time the proceeds at issue are transferred. Moreover, whether or not the text of the statute is sufficiently ambiguous to justify resort to the legislative history, equitable doctrines may foreclose the assertion of an innocent owner defense by a party with guilty knowledge of the tainted character of the property. In all events, we need not resolve this issue in this case; respondent has assumed the burden of convincing the trier of fact that she had no knowledge of the alleged source of Brenna's gift in 1982, when she received it. In its order denying respondent's motion for summary judgment, the District Court assumed that respondent could prove what she had alleged, as did the Court of Appeals in allowing the interlocutory appeal from that order. We merely decide, as did both of those courts, whether her asserted defense was insufficient as a matter of law.[26]

At oral argument, the Government also suggested that the statutory reference to "all proceeds traceable to such an exchange" is subject to a narrowing construction that might avoid some of the harsh consequences suggested in the various amici briefs expressing concerns about the impact of the statute on real estate titles. See Tr. of Oral Arg. 5–10, 19–25. If a house were received in exchange for a quantity of illegal substances and that house were in turn exchanged for another house, would the traceable proceeds consist of the first house, the second house, or both, with the

mitted or omitted without the knowledge, consent, or willful blindness of the owner." § 6075(3)(C), 102 Stat. 4324. That amendment presumably was enacted to protect lessors like the owner whose yacht was forfeited in a proceeding that led this Court to observe:

"It therefore has been implied that it would be difficult to reject the constitutional claim of an owner whose property subjected to forfeiture had been taken from him without his privity or consent. See Goldsmith, Jr.,Grant Co. v. United States, 254 U.S. 505, 512 (1921); United States v. One Ford Coupe' Automobile, 272 U.S. 321, 333 (1926); Van Oster v. Kansas, 272 U.S. 465, 467 (1926). Similarly, the same might be said of an owner

who proved not only that he was uninvolved in and unaware of the wrongful activity, but also that he had done all that reasonably could be expected to prevent the proscribed use of his property; for, in that circumstance, it would be difficult to conclude that forfeiture served legitimate purposes and was not unduly oppressive."

Calero–Toledo v. Pearson Yacht Leasing Co., 416 U.S. 663, 689–90 (1974).

[26] If she can show that she was unaware of the illegal source of the funds at the time Brenna transferred them to her, then she was necessarily unaware that they were the profits of an illegal transaction at the time of the transaction itself.

Government having an election between the two? Questions of this character are not embraced within the issues that we granted certiorari to resolve, however, and for that reason, see Yee v. Escondido, 503 U.S. 519 (1992), we express no opinion concerning the proper construction of that statutory term.

The judgment of the Court of Appeals is affirmed.

It is so ordered.

■ JUSTICE SCALIA, with whom JUSTICE THOMAS joins, concurring in the judgment.

I am in accord with much of the plurality's reasoning, but cannot join its opinion for two reasons. First, while I agree that the "innocent owner" exception in this case produces the same result as would an "innocent owner" exception to traditional common-law forfeiture (with its relation-back principle), I do not reach that conclusion through the plurality's reading of the phrase "property described in subsection (a)," which seems to me implausible. Secondly, I see no proper basis for the plurality's concluding that "respondent has assumed the burden of convincing the trier of fact that she had no knowledge of the alleged source of Brenna's gift in 1982, when she received it."

I

The Government's argument in this case has rested on the fundamental misconception that, under the common-law relation-back doctrine, all rights and legal title to the property pass to the United States "at the moment of illegal use." Brief for United States 16. Because the Government believes that the doctrine operates at the time of the illegal act, it finds the term "relation back" to be "something of a misnomer." Ibid. But the name of the doctrine is not wrong; the Government's understanding of it is. It is a doctrine of retroactive vesting of title that operates only upon entry of the judicial order of forfeiture or condemnation: "[T]he decree of condemnation when entered relates back to the time of the commission of the wrongful acts, and takes date from the wrongful acts and not from the date of the sentence or decree." Henderson's Distilled Spirits, 81 U.S. (14 Wall.) 44, 56 (1871). "While, under the statute in question, a judgment of forfeiture relates back to the date of the offense as proved, that result follows only from an effective judgment of condemnation." Motlow v. State ex rel. Koeln, 295 U.S. 97, 99 (1935). The relation-back rule applies only "in cases where the [Government's] title ha[s] been consummated by seizure, suit, and judgment, or decree of condemnation," Confiscation Cases, 74 U.S. (7 Wall.) 454, 460 (1869), whereupon "the doctrine of relation carries back the title to the commission of the offense," United States v. Grundy, 7 U.S. (3 Cranch) 337, 350–51 (1806)(Marshall, C.J.). See also United States v. Stowell, 133 U.S. 1, 16–17 (1890).

Though I disagree with the Government as to the meaning of the common-law doctrine, I agree with the Government that the doctrine is embodied in the statute at issue here. The plurality, if I understand it correctly, does not say that, but merely asserts that in the present case the consequence of applying the statutory language is to produce the same result that an "innocent owner" exception under the common-law rule would produce. Title 21 U.S.C. § 881(h) provides: "All right, title, and interest in property described in subsection (a) of this section shall vest in the United States upon commission of the act giving rise to forfeiture under this section." The plurality would read the phrase "property described in subsection (a)" as not encompassing any property that is protected from forfeiture by the "innocent owner" provision of § 881(a)(6). It proceeds to reason that since, therefore, the application of (a)(6) must be determined before (h) can be fully applied, respondent must be considered an "owner" under that provision—just as she would have been considered an "owner" (prior to decree of forfeiture) at common law.

I would not agree with the plurality's conclusion, even if I agreed with the premises upon which it is based. The fact that application of (a)(6) must be determined before (h) can be fully applied simply does not establish that the word "owner" in (a)(6) must be deemed to include (as it would at common law) anyone who held title prior to the actual decree of forfeiture. To assume that is simply to beg the question. Besides the fact that its conclusion is a non sequitur, the plurality's premises are mistaken. To begin with, the innocent-owner provision in (a)(6) does not insulate any "property described" in (a)(6) from forfeiture; it protects only the "interest" of certain owners in any of the described property. But even if it could be regarded as insulating some "property described" from forfeiture, that property would still be covered by subsection (h), which refers to "property described," not "property forfeited." In sum, I do not see how the plurality can, solely by focusing on the phrase "property described in subsection (a)," establish that the word "owner" in subsection (a) includes persons holding title after the forfeiture-producing offense.

The Government agrees with me that § 881(h) "covers all 'property described in subsection (a),' including property so described that is nonetheless exempted from forfeiture because of the innocent owner defense." Brief for United States 29. That position is quite incompatible, however, with the Government's contention that § 881(h) operates at the time of the wrongful act, since if both were true no one would be protected under the plain language of the innocent-owner provision. In the Government's view, the term "owner" in § 881(a)(6) refers to individuals "who owned the seized assets before those assets were ever tainted by involvement in drug transactions." But if § 881(h) operates immediately to vest in the Government legal title to all property described in § 881(a), even that class of "owners" would be immediately divested of their property interests and would be at most "former owners" at the time of forfeiture proceedings. Because of this difficulty, the Government is forced to argue that the word "owner" in § 881(a)(6) should be interpreted to mean "former owner." Thus, if § 881(h) operates at the time of the illegal transaction as the Government contends, either the plain language of the innocent-owner provision must be slighted or the provision must be deprived of all effect.

This problem does not exist if § 881(h) is read to be, not an unheard-of provision for immediate, undecreed, secret vesting of title in the United States, but rather an expression of the traditional relation-back doctrine—stating when title shall vest if forfeiture is decreed. On that hypothesis, the person holding legal title is genuinely the "owner" at the time (prior to the decree of forfeiture) that the court applies § 881(a)(6)'s innocent-owner provision.

I acknowledge that there is some textual difficulty with the interpretation I propose as well: § 881(h) says that title "shall vest in the United States upon commission of the act giving rise to forfeiture," and I am reading it to say that title "shall vest in the United States upon forfeiture, effective as of commission of the act giving rise to forfeiture." The former is certainly an imprecise way of saying the latter. But it is, I think, an imprecision one might expect in a legal culture familiar with retroactive forfeiture, and less of an imprecision than any of the other suggested interpretations require. Moreover, this interpretation locates the imprecision within a phrase where clear evidence of imprecision exists, since § 881(h)'s statement that "all right ... shall vest in the United States" flatly contradicts the statement in § 881(a) that "[t]he following shall be subject to forfeiture to the United States." What the United States already owns cannot be forfeited to it.

This interpretation of § 881(h) is the only one that makes sense within the structure of the statutory forfeiture procedures. Subsection 881(d) provides that forfeitures under § 881 are governed by the procedures applicable to "summary and judicial forfeiture, and condemnation of property for violation of the customs laws," set forth in 19 U.S.C. § 1602 et seq. It is clear from these procedures that the Government does not gain title to the property until there is a decree of forfeiture. Section 1604, for example, requires the Attorney General to commence proceedings in district court where such proceedings are "necessary" "for the recovery" of a forfeiture. See United States v. $8,850, 461 U.S. 555, 557–58, and n. 2 (1983)(detailing circumstances requiring judicial forfeiture proceedings). If, however, legal title to the property actually vested in the United States at the time of the illegal act, judicial forfeiture proceedings would never be "necessary." Under the customs forfeiture procedures the United States can, in certain limited circumstances, obtain title to property by an executive declaration of forfeiture. The statute provides that such an executive "declaration of forfeiture ... shall have the same force and effect as a final decree and order of forfeiture in a judicial forfeiture proceeding in a district court of the United States," and then specifies what that effect is: "Title shall be deemed to vest in the United States ... from the date of the act for which the forfeiture was incurred." 19 U.S.C. § 1609(b)(emphasis added). Finally, if the Government's construction of § 881(h) were correct, the statute-of-limitations provision, 19 U.S.C. § 1621, would need to state that title reverts to the former owners of the property, rather than (as it does) simply limit the right of the United States to institute an "action to recover" a forfeiture.

The traditional operation of the relation-back doctrine also explains the textual difference between § 881(a)(6)'s innocent-"owner" and § 853's innocent-"transferee" provisions—a difference on which the Government relies heavily. See Brief for United States 31–35; Reply Brief for United States 10–11. Section 853, which provides for forfeiture of drug-related assets in connection with criminal convictions, uses the term "transferee"—not "owner"—to protect the interests of persons who acquire property after the illegal act has occurred.[3] The Government contends that the reason for this variance is that the term "owner" simply does not cover persons acquiring interests after the illegal act. That explanation arrives under a cloud of suspicion, since it is impossible to imagine (and the Government was unable to suggest) why Congress would provide greater protection for postoffense owners (or "transferees") in the context of criminal forfeitures. The real explanation, I think, is that the term "owner" could not accurately be used in the context of § 853 because third parties can assert their property rights under that section only "[f]ollowing the entry of an order of forfeiture." 21 U.S.C. § 853(n). See also § 853(k)(prohibiting third parties from intervening to vindicate their property interests except as provided in subsection (n)). Thus, at the time the third-party interests are being adjudicated, the relation-back doctrine has already operated to carry back the title of the United States to the time of the act giving rise to the forfeiture, and the third parties have been divested of their property interests. See § 853(c)(codifying the relation-back principle for criminal forfeiture). Indeed, if the court finds that the transferee has a valid claim under the statute, it must "amend the order of forfeiture." § 853(n)(6).

The owner/transferee distinction is found in other provisions throughout the United States Code, and the traditional relation-back doctrine provides the only explanation for it. While Congress has provided for the protection of "owners" in many other forfeiture statutes, see, e.g., 15 U.S.C. § 715f(a)(allowing court to order the return of oil subject to forfeiture "to the owner thereof"); 16 U.S.C. § 2409(c)(permitting the "owner" of property seized for forfeiture to recover it, pendente lite, by posting bond); § 2439(c)(same); 18 U.S.C. § 512(a)(permitting the "owner" of motor vehicle with altered identification number to avoid forfeiture by proving lack of knowledge), it consistently protects "transferees" in criminal forfeiture statutes that follow the procedure set forth in § 853: forfeiture first, claims of third parties second. See 18 U.S.C. § 1467 (criminal

[3] Title 21 U.S.C. § 853(c) provides: "All right, title, and interest in property described in subsection (a) of this section vests in the United States upon the commission of the act giving rise to forfeiture under this section. Any such property that is subsequently transferred to a person other than the defendant may be the subject of a special verdict of forfeiture and thereafter shall be ordered forfeited to the United States, unless the transferee establishes in a hearing pursuant to subsection (n) of this section that he is a bona fide purchaser for value of such property who at the time of purchase was reasonably without cause to believe that the property was subject to forfeiture under this section."

forfeitures for obscenity); 18 U.S.C. § 1963 (criminal RICO forfeitures); 18 U.S.C. § 2253 (criminal forfeitures for sexual exploitation of children).[4]

I think the result reached today is correct because the relation-back principle recited in § 881(h) is the familiar, traditional one, and the term "owner" in § 881(a)(6) bears its ordinary meaning.

II

I cannot join the plurality's conclusion that respondent has assumed the burden of proving that "she had no knowledge of the alleged source of Brenna's gift in 1982, when she received it." To support this, the plurality cites a passage from respondent's brief taking the position that the owner's lack of knowledge of the criminal activity should be tested "at the time of the transfer," Brief for Respondent 37–38. The fact of the matter is that both parties took positions before this Court that may be against their interests on remand. The Government may find inconvenient its contention that "the statutory test for innocence ... looks to the claimant's awareness of the illegal acts giving rise to forfeiture at the time they occur." Reply Brief for United States 8. Which, if either, party will be estopped from changing position is an issue that we should not address for two simple reasons: (1) Neither party has yet attempted to change position. (2) The issue is not fairly included within the question on which the Court granted certiorari. (That question was, "Whether a person who receives a gift of money derived from drug trafficking and uses that money to purchase real property is entitled to assert an 'innocent owner' defense in an action seeking civil forfeiture of the real property." The plurality's reformulation of the question in the first sentence of the opinion is inexplicable.)

This question of the relevant time for purposes of determining knowledge was not a separate issue in the case, but arose indirectly, by way of argumentation on the relation-back point. The Government argued that since (as it believed) knowledge had to be measured at the time of the illegal act, § 881(h) must be interpreted to vest title in the United States immediately, because otherwise the statute would produce the following "untenable result": A subsequent owner who knew of the illegal act at the time he acquired the property, but did not know of it at the time the act was committed, would be entitled to the innocent-owner defense. Brief for United States 25. That argument can be rejected by deciding either that

---

[4] It is worth observing that, if the Government's view of the relation-back principle were correct, the protection provided for transferees in the last-mentioned statute would be utterly illusory. The property subject to forfeiture under 18 U.S.C. § 2253 is also covered by a parallel civil forfeiture statute that follows the pattern of § 881: It protects only the rights of "owners," and has an express relation-back provision. See 18 U.S.C. §§ 2254(a), 2254(g). Under the Government's view, whenever the United States would be unable to obtain property through the criminal forfeiture mechanism because of the innocent—"transferee" defense, it could simply move against the same property in a civil forfeiture proceeding, which gives a defense only to "owners." See also 18 U.S.C. § 981 (civil forfeiture provision), 18 U.S.C. § 982 (parallel criminal forfeiture statute incorporating by reference the procedures in 21 U.S.C. § 853).

the Government's view of the timing of knowledge is wrong, or that, even if it may be right, the problem it creates is not so severe as to compel a ruling for the Government on the relation-back issue. (I take the latter course: I do not find inconceivable the possibility that post-illegal-act transferees with post-illegal-act knowledge of the earlier illegality are provided a defense against forfeiture. The Government would still be entitled to the property held by the drug dealer and by close friends and relatives who are unable to meet their burden of proof as to ignorance of the illegal act when it occurred.) But it entirely escapes me how the Government's argument, an argument in principle, can be answered by simply saying that, in the present case, respondent has committed herself to prove that she had no knowledge of the source of the funds at the time she received them.

For the reasons stated, I concur in the judgment.

■ Justice Kennedy, with whom The Chief Justice and Justice White join, dissenting.

Once this case left the District Court, the appellate courts and all counsel began to grapple with the wrong issue, one that need not be addressed. The right question, I submit, is not whether the donee's ownership meets the statutory test of innocence. 21 U.S.C. § 881(a)(6). Instead, the threshold and dispositive inquiry is whether the donee had any ownership rights that required a separate forfeiture, given that her title was defective and subject to the Government's claim from the outset. We must ask whether a wrongdoer holding a forfeitable asset, property in which the United States has an undoubted superior claim, can defeat that claim by a transfer for no value. Under settled principles of property transfers, trusts and commercial transactions, the answer is no. We need not address the donee's position except to acknowledge that she has whatever right the donor had, a right which falls before the Government's superior claim. In this case, forfeiture is determined by the title and ownership of the asset in the hands of the donor, not the donee. The position of respondent as the present holder of the asset and her knowledge, or lack of knowledge, regarding any drug offenses are, under these facts, but abstract inquiries, unnecessary to the resolution of the case.

I

We can begin with the state of affairs when the alleged drug dealer held the funds he was later to transfer to respondent. Those moneys were proceeds of unlawful drug transactions and in the dealer's hands were, without question, subject to forfeiture under § 881(a)(6). The dealer did not just know of the illegal acts; he performed them. As the case is presented to us, any defense of his based on lack of knowledge is not a possibility. As long as the dealer held the illegal asset, it was subject to forfeiture and to the claim of the United States, which had a superior interest in the property.

Suppose the drug dealer with unlawful proceeds had encountered a swindler who, knowing nothing of the dealer's drug offenses, defrauded him of the forfeitable property. In an action by the Government against the property, it need not seek to forfeit any ownership interest of the swindler. In the in rem proceeding the Government would need to establish only the forfeitable character of the property in the hands of the dealer and then trace the property to the swindler who, having no higher or better title to interpose, must yield to the Government's interest. In this context we would not entertain an argument that the swindler could keep the property because he had no knowledge of the illegal drug transaction. The defect in title arose in the hands of the first holder and was not eliminated by the transfer procured through fraud. Thus the only possible "interest of an owner," § 881(a)(6), that the swindler could hold was one inferior to the interest of the United States.

Here, of course, the holder is a donee, not a swindler, but the result is the same. As against a claimant with a superior right enforceable against the donor, a donee has no defense save as might exist, say, under a statute of limitations. The case would be different, of course, if the donee had in turn transferred the property to a bona fide purchaser for full consideration. The voidable title in the asset at that point would become unassailable in the purchaser, subject to any heightened rules of innocence the Government might lawfully impose under the forfeiture laws. But there is no bona fide purchaser here.

The matter not having been argued before us in these terms, perhaps it is premature to say whether the controlling law for transferring and tracing property rights of the United States under § 881 is federal common law, see Boyle v. United Technologies Corp., 487 U.S. 500 (1988); Clearfield Trust Co. v. United States, 318 U.S. 363 (1943), or the law of the State governing the transfer under normal conflict-of-law rules, which here appears to be New Jersey. That matter could be explored on remand if the parties thought anything turned upon it, though the result likely would be the same under either source of law because the controlling principles are so well settled.

The controlling principles are established by the law of voidable title, a centuries-old concept now codified in 49 States as part of their adoption of the Uniform Commercial Code. 1 J. White & R. Summers, Uniform Commercial Code 1, 186–191 (3d ed. 1988). These principles should control the inquiry into whether property once "subject to forfeiture to the United States," § 881(a), remains so after subsequent transactions. Cf. R. Brown, Personal Property section 70, pp. 237–38 (2d ed. 1955); Restatement (Second) of Trusts §§ 284, 287, 289, pp. 47–48, 54–56 (1959); Restatement (Second) of Property section 34.9, p. 338 (1992). The primary rules of voidable title are manageable and few in number. The first is that one who purchases property in good faith and for value from the holder of voidable title obtains good title. The second rule, reciprocal to the first, is that one who acquires property from a holder of voidable title other than by a good faith purchase for value obtains nothing beyond what the transferor held. The third rule is that a transferee who acquires property from a good faith purchaser for value or one of his lawful successors obtains good title, even if the transferee did not pay value or act in good faith. See J.B.

Ames, Purchase for Value Without Notice, 1 Harv.L.Rev. 1 (1887); Uniform Commercial Code § 2–403(1)(Official Draft 1978); Uniform Commercial Code § 2–403(1) (Official Draft 1957); Uniform Commercial Code § 2–403(1)(Official Draft 1952). See also 4 A. Scott & W. Fratcher, Law of Trusts §§ 284–289, pp. 35–70 (4th ed. 1989); W.A. Searey, Purchase for Value Without Notice, 23 Yale L.J. 447 (1914).

Applying these rules to a transferee of proceeds from a drug sale, it follows that the transferee must be, or take from, a bona fide purchaser for value to assert an innocent owner defense under § 881(a)(6). Bona fide purchasers for value or their lawful successors, having engaged in or benefited from a transaction that the law accepts as capable of creating property rights instead of merely transferring possession, are entitled to test their claim of ownership under § 881(a)(6) against what the Government alleges to be its own superior right. The outcome, that one who had defective title can create good title in the new holder by transfer for value, is not to be condemned as some bizarre surprise. This is not alchemy. It is the common law. See Independent Coal & Coke Co. v. United States, 274 U.S. 640, 647 (1927); United States v. Chase National Bank, 252 U.S. 485, 494 (1920); Wright–Blodgett Co. v. United States, 236 U.S. 397, 403 (1915). By contrast, the donee of drug trafficking proceeds has no valid claim to the proceeds, not because she has done anything wrong but because she stands in the shoes of one who has. It is the nature of the donor's interest, which the donee has assumed, that renders the property subject to forfeiture. Cf. Otis v. Otis, 167 Mass. 245, 246, 45 N.E. 737 (1897)(Holmes, J.)("A person to whose hands a trust fund comes by conveyance from the original trustee is chargeable as a trustee in his turn, if he takes it without consideration, whether he has notice of the trust or not. This has been settled for three hundred years, since the time of uses").

When the Government seeks forfeiture of an asset in the hands of a donee, its forfeiture claim rests on defects in the title of the asset in the hands of the donor. The transferee has no ownership superior to the transferor's which must be forfeited, so her knowledge of the drug transaction, or lack thereof, is quite irrelevant, as are the arcane questions concerning the textual application of § 881(a) to someone in a donee's position. The so-called innocent owner provisions of § 881(a)(6) have ample scope in other instances, say where a holder who once had valid ownership in property is alleged to have consented to its use to facilitate a drug transaction. Furthermore, whether respondent's marital rights were present value or an antecedent debt and whether either could provide the necessary consideration for a bona fide purchase are questions that could be explored on remand, were my theory of the case to control.

II

As my opening premise is so different from the one the plurality adopts, I do not address the difficult, and quite unnecessary, puzzles encountered in its opinion and in the concurring opinion of Justice Scalia.

It is my obligation to say, however, that the plurality's opinion leaves the forfeiture scheme that is the centerpiece of the Nation's drug enforcement laws in quite a mess.

The practical difficulties created by the plurality's interpretation of § 881 are immense, and we should not assume Congress intended such results when it enacted § 881(a)(6). To start, the plurality's interpretation of § 881(a)(6) conflicts with the principal purpose we have identified for forfeiture under the Continuing Criminal Enterprise Act, which is "the desire to lessen the economic power of ... drug enterprises." Caplin & Drysdale v. United States, 491 U.S. 617, 630 (1989). When a criminal transfers drug transaction proceeds to a good faith purchaser for value, one would presume he does so because he considers what he receives from the purchaser to be of equal or greater value than what he gives to the purchaser, or because he is attempting to launder the proceeds by exchanging them for other property of near equal value. In either case, the criminal's economic power is diminished by seizing from him whatever he received in the exchange with the good faith purchaser. On the other hand, when a criminal transfers drug transaction proceeds to another without receiving value in return, he does so, it is safe to assume, either to use his new-found, albeit illegal, wealth to benefit an associate or to shelter the proceeds from forfeiture, to be reacquired once he is clear from law enforcement authorities. In these cases, the criminal's economic power cannot be diminished by seizing what he received in the donative exchange, for he received no tangible value. If the Government is to drain the criminal's economic power, it must be able to pierce donative transfers and recapture the property given in the exchange. It is serious and surprising that the plurality today denies the Government the right to pursue the same ownership claims that under traditional and well-settled principles any other claimant or trust beneficiary or rightful owner could assert against a possessor who took for no value and who has no title or interest greater than that of the transferor.

Another oddity now given to us by the plurality's interpretation is that a gratuitous transferee must forfeit the proceeds of a drug deal if she knew of the drug deal before she received the proceeds but not if she discovered it a moment after. Yet in the latter instance, the donee, having given no value, is in no different position from the donee who had knowledge all along, save perhaps that she might have had a brief expectation the gift was clean. By contrast, the good faith purchaser for value who, after an exchange of assets, finds out about his trading partner's illegal conduct has undergone a significant change in circumstances: He has paid fair value for those proceeds in a transaction which, as a practical matter in most cases, he cannot reverse.

III

The statutory puzzle the plurality and concurrence find so engaging is created because of a false premise, the premise that the possessor of an asset subject to forfeiture does not stand in the position of the transferor but must be charged with some guilty knowledge of her own. Forfeiture proceedings, though, are directed at an asset, and a donee in general has no more than the ownership rights of the donor. By denying this simple principle, the plurality rips out the most effective enforcement provisions in all of the drug forfeiture laws. I would reverse the judgment of the Court of Appeals, and with all due respect, I dissent from the judgment of the Court.

NOTE ON *BENNIS v. MICHIGAN*

In Bennis v. Michigan, __ U.S. __, 116 S.Ct. 994 (1996), the Supreme Court, by a 5–4 decision, rejected a claim by an "innocent owner" that she was entitled to some kind of compensation, under the due process clause and/or the takings clause, where a state nuisance-abatement law was used to forfeit a car that belonged jointly to the claimant and her husband. The forfeiture was premised on the husband's use of the car in connection with sexual activity with a prostitute. Chief Justice Rehnquist, writing for the majority, assumed that the claimant had no knowledge of her husband's illegal activities, but refused to find any constitutional right to compensation based on her partial interest in the forfeited car:

"[A] long and unbroken line of [due process] cases holds that an owner's interest in property may be forfeited by reason of the use to which the property is put even though the owner did not know that it was to be put to such use. . . .

"Petitioner relies on a passage from Calero–Toledo v. Pearson Yacht Leasing Co., 416 U.S. 663 (1974), that 'it would be difficult to reject the constitutional claim of . . . an owner who proved not only that he was uninvolved in and unaware of the wrongful activity, but also that he had done all that reasonably could be expected to prevent the proscribed use of his property.' 416 U.S., at 689. But she concedes that this comment was obiter dictum. . . .

"[F]orfeiture . . . serves a deterrent purpose distinct from any punitive purpose. Forfeiture of property prevents illegal uses 'both by preventing further illicit use of the [property] and by imposing an economic penalty, thereby rendering illegal behavior unprofitable.' *Calero-Toledo*, supra, at 687. This deterrent mechanism is hardly unique to forfeiture. For instance, because Michigan also deters dangerous driving by making a motor vehicle owner liable for the negligent operation of the vehicle by a driver who had the owner's consent to use it, petitioner was also potentially liable for her husband's use of the car in violation of Michigan negligence law. . . .

"Petitioner also claims that the forfeiture in this case was a taking of private property for public use in violation of the Takings Clause of the Fifth Amendment, made applicable to the States by the Fourteenth Amendment. But if the forfeiture proceeding here in question did not violate the Fourteenth Amendment, the property in the automobile was transferred by virtue of that proceeding from petitioner to the State. The government may not be required to compensate an owner for property which it has already lawfully acquired under the exercise of governmental authority other than the power of eminent domain. United States v. Fuller, 409 U.S. 488, 492 (1973).

"At bottom, petitioner's claims depend on an argument that the Michigan forfeiture statute is unfair because it relieves prosecutors from the burden of separating co-owners who are complicit in the wrongful use of property from innocent co-owners. This argument, in the abstract, has considerable appeal.... Its force is reduced in the instant case, however, by the Michigan Supreme Court's confirmation of the trial court's remedial discretion ... and petitioner's recognition that Michigan may forfeit her and her husband's car whether or not she is entitled to an offset for her interest in it.

"We conclude today, as we concluded 75 years ago, that the cases authorizing actions of the kind at issue are 'too firmly fixed in the punitive and remedial jurisprudence of this country to be now displaced.' J.W. Goldsmith, Jr.-Grant Co. v. United States, 254 U.S. 505, 511 (1921)."

SUBSECTION C: FORFEITURE AND THE RIGHT TO COUNSEL

United States v. Monsanto

Supreme Court of the United States, 1989.
491 U.S. 600.

■ JUSTICE WHITE delivered the opinion of the Court.

The questions presented here are whether the federal drug forfeiture statute authorizes a District Court to enter a pretrial order freezing assets in a defendant's possession, even where the defendant seeks to use those assets to pay an attorney; if so, we must decide whether such an order is permissible under the Constitution. We answer both of these questions in the affirmative.

I

In July 1987, an indictment was entered, alleging that respondent had directed a large-scale heroin distribution enterprise. The multicount indictment alleged violations of racketeering laws, creation of a continuing criminal enterprise (CCE), and tax and firearm offenses. The indictment also alleged that three specific assets—a home, an apartment, and $35,000 in cash—had been accumulated by respondent as a result of his narcotics trafficking. These assets, the indictment alleged, were subject to forfeiture under the Comprehensive Forfeiture Act of 1984, 21 U.S.C. § 853(a)(1982 ed., Supp. V), because they were "property constituting, or derived from ... proceeds ... obtained" from drug-law violations.[1]

On the same day that the indictment was unsealed, the District Court granted the government's ex parte motion, pursuant to 21 U.S.C. § 853(e)(1)(A)(1982 ed., Supp. V),[2] for a restraining order freezing the above-mentioned assets pending trial. Shortly thereafter, respondent moved to vacate this restraining order, to permit him to use the frozen assets to retain an attorney. Respondent's motion further sought a declaration that if these assets were used to pay an attorney's fees, § 853(c)'s third-party transfer provision would not subsequently be used to reclaim such payments if respondent was convicted, and his assets forfeited.[3]

[1] The Comprehensive Forfeiture Act of 1984 (CFA) added or amended forfeiture provisions for two classes of violations under federal law, racketeering (RICO) offenses and continuing criminal enterprise (CCE) offenses. The CCE forfeiture statute at issue here, now provides:

"§ 853. Criminal forfeitures

"(a) Property subject to criminal forfeiture

"Any person convicted of a violation of this subchapter or subchapter II of this chapter punishable by imprisonment for more than one year shall forfeit to the United States, irrespective of any provision of State law—

"(1) any property constituting, or derived from, any proceeds the person obtained, directly or indirectly, as the result of such violation;

"(2) any of the person's property used, or intended to be used, in any manner or part, to commit or to facilitate the commission of, such violation; and

"(3) in the case of a person convicted of engaging in a continuing criminal enterprise in violation of section 848 of this title, the person shall forfeit, in addition to any property described in paragraph (1) or (2), any of his interest in, claims against, and property or contractual rights affording a source of control over, the continuing criminal enterprise.

"The Court, in imposing sentence on such person, shall order, in addition to any other sentence imposed pursuant to this subchapter or subchapter II of this chapter, that the person forfeit to the United States all property described in this subsection. In lieu of a fine otherwise authorized by this part, a defendant

who derives profits or other proceeds from an offense may be fined not more than twice the gross profits or other proceeds." 21 U.S.C. § 853 (1982 ed., Supp. IV).

[2] This statutory provision, the principal focus of this petition, says that:

"Upon application of the United States, the court may enter a restraining order or injunction ... or take any other action to preserve the availability of property described in subsection (a) of [§ 853] for forfeiture under this section—

"(A) upon the filing of an indictment or information charging a violation ... for which criminal forfeiture may be ordered under [§ 853] and alleging that the property with respect to which the order is sought would, in the event of conviction, be subject to forfeiture under this section." 21 U.S.C. § 853(e)(1)(1982 ed., Supp. V).

[3] Section 853(c), the third-party transfer provision, states that:

"All right, title, and interest in property described in [§ 853] vests in the United States upon the commission of the act giving rise to forfeiture under this section. Any such property that is subsequently transferred to a person other than the defendant may be the subject of a special verdict of forfeiture and thereafter shall be ordered forfeited to the United States, unless the transferee [establishes his entitlement to such property pursuant to § 853(n).]" 21 U.S.C. § 853(c)(1982 ed., Supp. V).

As noted in the quotation of § 853(c), a person making a claim for forfeited assets

Respondent raised various statutory challenges to the restraining order, and claimed that it interfered with his sixth amendment right to counsel of choice. The District Court denied the motion to vacate.

On appeal, the Second Circuit concluded that respondent's statutory and sixth amendment challenges were lacking, but remanded the case to the District Court for an adversarial hearing "at which the government ha[d] the burden to demonstrate the likelihood that the assets are forfeitable;" if the government failed its burden at such a hearing, the Court of Appeals held, any fees paid to an attorney would be exempt from forfeiture irrespective of the final outcome at respondent's trial. Pursuant to this mandate, on remand, the District Court held a four-day hearing on whether continuing the restraining order was proper. At the end of the hearing, the District Court ruled that it would continue the restraining order because the government had "overwhelmingly established a likelihood" that the property in question would be forfeited at the end of trial. Ultimately, respondent's criminal case proceeded to trial, where he was represented by a Criminal Justice Act-appointed attorney.[4]

In the meantime, the Second Circuit vacated its earlier opinion, and heard respondent's appeal en banc.[5] The en banc court, by an 8–4 vote,

---

must file a petition with the court pursuant to § 853(n):

> "If, after [a] hearing [on the petition], the court determines that the petitioner has established . . . that—
>
> "(A) the petitioner has a legal right, title, or interest in the property . . . [that predates] commission of the acts which give rise to the forfeiture of the property under [§ 853]; or
>
> "(B) the petitioner is a bona fide purchaser for value of the . . . property and was at the time of purchase reasonably without cause to believe that the property was subject to forfeiture under this section;
>
> "the court shall amend the order of forfeiture in accordance with its determination." 21 U.S.C. § 853(n)(6)(1982 ed., Supp. V).

An attorney seeking a payment of fees from forfeited assets under § 853(n)(6) would presumably rest his petition on subsection (B) quoted above, though (for reasons we explain in Caplin & Drysdale, Chartered v. United States, 491 U.S. 617 (1989)), it is highly doubtful that one who defends a client in a criminal case that results in forfeiture could prove that he was "without cause to believe that the property was subject to forfeiture."

[4] At the end of the trial, respondent was convicted of the charges against him, and the jury returned a special verdict finding the assets in question to be forfeitable beyond a reasonable doubt. Accordingly, the District Court entered a judgment of conviction, and declared the assets forfeited.

We do not believe that these subsequent proceedings render the dispute over the pretrial restraining order moot. The restraining order remains in effect pending the appeal of respondent's conviction, which has not yet been decided. Consequently, the dispute before us concerning the District Court's order remains a live one.

[5] Respondent's trial had commenced on February 16, 1988, after the Court of Appeals had agreed to hear the case en banc, but before it rendered its ruling. Consequently, respondent's assets remained frozen, and respondent was defended by appointed counsel.

In the midst of respondent's trial—on July 1, 1988—the en banc Court of Appeals rendered its decision for respondent. At a hearing held four days later, the District Court offered to permit respondent to use the frozen assets to hire private counsel. Respondent rejected this offer, coming as summations were about to get underway at the end of a four-and-a-half-month trial, and instead continued with his appointed attorney.

ordered that the District Court's restraining order be modified to permit the restrained assets to be used to pay attorney's fees. The Court was sharply divided as to its rationale. Three of the judges found that the order violated the sixth amendment, while three others questioned it on statutory grounds; two judges found § 853 suspect under the due process clause for its failure to include a statutory provision requiring the sort of hearing that the panel had ordered in the first place. The four dissenting judges would have upheld in the first place. The four dissenting judges would have upheld the restraining order.

We granted certiorari because the Second Circuit's decision created a conflict among the Courts of Appeals over the statutory and constitutional questions presented. We now reverse.

II

We first must address the question whether § 853 requires, upon conviction, forfeiture of assets that an accused intends to use to pay his attorneys.

A

"In determining the scope of a statute, we look first to its language." United States v. Turkette, 452 U.S. 576, 580 (1981). In the case before us, the language of § 853 is plain and unambiguous: all assets falling within its scope are to be forfeited upon conviction, with no exception existing for the assets used to pay attorney's fees—or anything else, for that matter.

As observed above, § 853(a) provides that a person convicted of the offenses charged in respondent's indictment "shall forfeit ... any property" that was derived from the commission of these offenses. After setting out this rule, § 853(a) repeats later in its text that upon conviction a sentencing court "shall order" forfeiture of *all* property described in § 853(a). Congress could not have chosen stronger words to express its intent that forfeiture be mandatory in cases where the statute applied, or broader words to define the scope of what was to be forfeited. Likewise, the statute provides a broad definition of "property," when describing what types of assets are within the section's scope "real property ... tangible and intangible personal property, including rights, privileges, interests, claims, and securities." 21 U.S.C. § 853(b)(1982 ed., Supp. V). Nothing in this all-inclusive listing even hints at the idea that assets to be used to pay an attorney are not "property" within the statute's meaning.

Nor are we alone in concluding that the statute is unambiguous in failing to exclude assets that could be used to pay an attorney from its definition of forfeitable property. This argument, advanced by respondent here, has been unanimously rejected by every Court of Appeals that has finally passed on it, as it was by the Second Circuit panel below; even the judges who concurred on statutory grounds in the en banc decision did not accept this position. We note also that the Brief for American Bar

Three weeks later, on July 25, 1988, the jury returned a guilty verdict.

Association as Amicus Curiae frankly admits that the statute "on [its] face, broadly cover[s] no specific exemption for property used to pay bona fide attorneys' fees."

Respondent urges us, nonetheless, to interpret the statute to exclude such property for several reasons. Principally, respondent contends that we should create such an exemption because the statute does not expressly include property to be used for attorneys' fees, and/or because Congress simply did not consider the prospect that forfeiture would reach assets that could be used to pay for an attorney. In support, respondent observes that the legislative history is "silent" on this question, and that the House and Senate debates fail to discuss this prospect.[8] But this proves nothing: the legislative history and congressional debates are similarly silent on the use of forfeitable assets to pay stock-broker's fees, laundry bills, or country club memberships; no one could credibly argue that, as a result, assets to be used for these purposes are similarly exempt from the statute's definition

---

[8] Respondent is correct that, by and large, the relevant House and Senate Reports make no mention of the attorney's fees question. However, in discussing the background motivating the adoption of the CFA, the House Judiciary Committee discussed the failure of previous, more lax forfeiture statutes:

> "One highly publicized case ... is illustrative of the problem. That case was *United States v. Meinster* .... In this prosecution ... a Florida based criminal organization had ... grossed about $300 million over a 16-month period. The federal government completed a successful prosecution in which the three primary defendants were convicted and this major drug operation was aborted. However, forfeiture was attempted on only two [residences] worth $750,000....
>
> "Of the $750,000 for the residences, $175,000 was returned to the wife of one of the defendants, *and $559,000 was used to pay the defendant's attorneys.* ...
>
> "The Government wound up with $16,000. ...
>
> "It is against this background that present federal forfeiture procedures are tested and found waiting." H.R. Rep. No. 98–845, pt. 1, p. 3 (1984)(emphasis added).

This passage suggests, at the very least, congressional frustration with the diversion of large amounts of forfeitable assets to pay attorney's fees. It certainly does not suggest an intent on Congress' part to exempt from forfeiture such fees.

Respondent claims support from only one piece of pre-enactment legislative history: a footnote in the same House Report quoted above, which discussed the newly proposed provision for pretrial restraint on forfeitable assets. The footnote stated that:

> "Nothing in this section is intended to interfere with a person's sixth amendment right to counsel. The Committee, therefore, does not resolve the conflict in District Court opinions on the use of restraining orders that impinge on a person's right to retain counsel in a criminal case." Id., at 19, n.1.

Respondent argues that the Committee's disclaimer of any interest in resolving the conflict among the district courts indicates the Committee's understanding that the statute would not be employed to freeze assets that might be used to pay legitimate attorney's fees.

This ambiguous passage however, can be read for the opposite proposition as well, as the Report expressly refrained from disapproving of cases where pretrial restraining orders similar to the one issued here were imposed. See H.R. Rep. No. 98–845, supra, at 19, n. 1. (citing United States v. Bello, 470 F.Supp. 723, 724–25 (S.D.Cal.1979)). Moreover, the Committee's statement that the statute should not be applied in a manner contrary to the sixth amendment appears to be nothing more than an exhortation for the courts to tread carefully in this delicate area.

of forfeitable property. The fact that the forfeiture provision reaches assets that could be used to pay attorney's fees, even though it contains no express provisions to this effect," 'does not demonstrate ambiguity' " in the statute: " 'It demonstrates breadth.' " Sedima, S.P.R.L. v. Imrex Co., 473 U.S. 479, 499 (1985). The statutory provision at issue here is broad and unambiguous, and Congress' failure to supplement § 853(a)'s comprehensive phrase—"*any* property"—with an exclamatory "and we even mean assets to be used to pay an attorney" does not lessen the force of the statute's plain language.

We also find unavailing respondent's reliance on the comments of several legislators—made following enactment—to the effect that Congress did not anticipate the use of the forfeiture law to seize assets that would be used to pay attorneys. As we have noted before, such postenactment views "form a hazardous basis for inferring the intent" behind a statute, United States v. Price, 361 U.S. 304, 313 (1960); instead, Congress' intent is "best determined by [looking to] the statutory language that it chooses," *Sedima, S.P.R.L.*, supra, at 495, n. 13. Moreover, we observe that these comments are further subject to question because Congress has refused to act on repeated suggestions by the defense bar for the sort of exemption respondent urges here,[9] even though it has amended § 853 in other respects since these entreaties were first heard. See Pub. L. 99–570, §§ 1153(b), 1864, 100 Stat. 3207–13, 3207–54.

In addition, we observe that in the very same law by which Congress adopted the CFA Congress also adopted a provision for the special forfeiture of collateral profits (e.g., profits from books, movies, etc.) that a convicted defendant derives from his crime. See Victims of Crime Act of 1984, (now codified at 18 U.S.C. §§ 3681–3682 (1982 ed., Supp. V)). That forfeiture provision expressly exempts "pay[ments] for legal representation of the defendant in matters arising from the offense for which such defendant has been convicted, but no more than 20 percent of the total [forfeited collateral profits] may be used." 18 U.S.C. § 3681(c)(1)(B)(ii)(1982 ed., Supp. V). Thus, Congress adopted *expressly*—in a statute enacted *simultaneously* with the one under review in this case—the *precise* exemption from forfeiture which respondent asks us to imply into § 853. The express exemption from forfeiture of assets that could be used to pay attorney's fees in chapter XIV, indicates to us that Congress understood what it was doing in omitting such an exemption from Chapter III of that enactment.

Finally, respondent urges us to invoke a variety of general canons of statutory construction, as well as several prudential doctrines of this Court, to create the statutory exemption he advances; among these doctrines is our admonition that courts should construe statutes to avoid decision as to their constitutionality. We respect these canons, and they are quite often

[9] See, e.g., Attorneys' Fees Forfeiture: Hearing before the Senate Committee on the Judiciary, 99th Cong., 2d Sess., 148–213 (1986); Forfeiture Issues: Hearing Before the Subcommittee on Crime of the House Committee on the Judiciary, 99th Cong., 1st Sess., 187–242 (1985).

useful in close cases, or when statutory language is ambiguous. But we have observed before that such "interpretative canon[s are] not a license for the judiciary to rewrite language enacted by the legislature." United States v. Albertini, 472 U.S. 675, 680 (1985). Here, the language is clear and the statute comprehensive: § 853 does not exempt assets to be used for attorney's fees from its forfeiture provisions.

In sum, whatever force there *might* be to respondent's claim for an exemption from forfeiture under § 853(a) of assets necessary to pay attorney's fees—based on his theories about the statute's purpose, or the implications of interpretative canons, or the understanding of individual members of Congress about the statute's scope—"[t]he short answer is that Congress did not write the statute that way." United States v. Naftalin, 441 U.S. 768, 773 (1979).

B

Although § 853(a) recognizes no general exception for assets used to pay an attorney, we are urged that the provision in § 853(e)(1)(A) for pretrial restraining orders on assets in a defendant's possession should be interpreted to include such an exemption. It was on this ground that Judge Winter concurred below.

The restraining order subsection provides that, on the government's application, a district court "may enter a restraining order or injunction ... or take any other action to preserve the availability of property ... for forfeiture under this section." 21 U.S.C. § 853(e)(1)(1982 ed., Supp. V). Judge Winter read the permissive quality of the subsection (i.e., "may enter") to authorize a district court to employ "traditional principles of equity" before restraining a defendant's use of forfeitable assets; a balancing of hardships, he concluded, generally weighed against restraining a defendant's use of forfeitable assets to pay for an attorney. Judge Winter further concluded that assets not subjected to pre-trial restraint under § 853(e), if used to pay an attorney, may not be subsequently seized for forfeiture to the government, notwithstanding the authorization found in § 853(c) for recoupment of forfeitable assets transferred to third parties.

This reading seriously misapprehends the nature of the provisions in question. As we have said, § 853(a) is categorical: it contains no reference at all to §§ 853(e) or 853(c), let alone any reference indicating that its reach is limited by those sections. Perhaps some limit could be implied if these provisions were necessarily inconsistent with § 853(a). But that is not the case. Under § 853(e), the trial court "may" enter a restraining order if the United States requests it, but not otherwise, and it is not required to enter such an order if a bond or some other means to "preserve the availability of property described in subsection (a) of this section for forfeiture" is employed. 21 U.S.C. § 853(e)(1). (1982 ed., Supp. V). Thus, § 853(e)(1)(A) is plainly aimed at implementing the commands of § 853(a) and cannot sensibly be construed to give the District Court discretion to permit the dissipation of the very property that § 853(a) requires be forfeited upon conviction.

We note that the "equitable discretion" that is given to the judge under § 853(e)(1)(A) turns out to be no discretion at all as far as the issue before us here is concerned: Judge Winter concludes that assets necessary to pay attorney's fees *must* be excluded from any restraining order. For that purpose, the word "may" becomes "may not." The discretion found in § 853(e) becomes a command to use that subsection (and § 853(c)) to frustrate the attainment of § 853(c), that discretion must be cabined by the purposes for which Congress created it: "to preserve the availability of property . . . for forfeiture." We cannot believe that Congress intended to permit the effectiveness of the powerful "relation-back" provision of § 853(c) and the comprehensive "any property . . . any proceeds" language of § 853(a), to be nullified by any other construction of the statute.

This result may seem harsh, but we have little doubt that it is the one that the statute mandates. Section 853(c) states that "[a]ll right, title, and interest in [forfeitable] property . . . vests in the United States upon the commission of the act giving rise to forfeiture." 21 U.S.C. § 853(c)(1982 ed., Supp. V). Permitting a defendant to use assets for his private purposes that, under this provision, will become the property of the United States if a conviction occurs, cannot be sanctioned. Moreover, this view is supported by the relevant legislative history, which states that "[t]he sole purpose of [§ 853's] restraining order provision . . . is to preserve the status quo, i.e., to assure the availability of the property pending disposition of the criminal case." S. Rep. No. 98–225, p. 204 (1983). If, instead, the statutory interpretation adopted by Judge Winter's concurrence were applied, this purpose would not be achieved.

We conclude that there is no exemption from § 853's forfeiture or pretrial restraining order provisions for assets which a defendant wishes to use to retain an attorney. In enacting § 853, Congress decided to give force to the old adage that "crime does not pay." We find no evidence that Congress intended to modify that nostrum to read, "crime does not pay, except for attorney's fees." If, as respondent and supporting amici so vigorously assert, we are mistaken as to Congress' intent, that body can amend this statute to otherwise provide. But the statute, as presently written, cannot be read any other way.

III

Having concluded that the statute authorized the restraining order entered by the District Court, we reach the question whether the order violated respondent's right to counsel of choice as protected by the sixth amendment or the due process clause of the fifth amendment.

A

Respondent's most sweeping constitutional claims are that, as a general matter, operation of the forfeiture statute interferes with a defendant's sixth amendment right to counsel of choice, and the guarantee afforded by the fifth amendment's due process clause of a "balance of forces" between the accused and the government. In this regard, respondent contends, the mere prospect of post-trial forfeiture is enough to deter a defendant's counsel of choice from representing him.

In another decision we announce today, Caplin & Drysdale, Chartered v. United States, 491 U.S. 617 (1989), we hold that neither of the fifth or sixth amendments to the Constitution requires Congress to permit a defendant to use assets adjudged to be forfeitable to pay that defendant's legal fees. We rely on our conclusion in that case to dispose of the similar constitutional claims raised by respondent here.

B

In addition to the constitutional issues raised in *Caplin & Drysdale*, respondent contends that freezing the assets in question before he is convicted—and before they are finally adjudged to be forfeitable—raises distinct constitutional concerns. We conclude, however, that assets in a defendant's possession may be restrained in the way they were here based on a finding of probable cause to believe that the assets are forfeitable.[10]

We have previously permitted the government to seize property based on a finding of probable cause to believe that the property will ultimately be proven forfeitable. See, e.g., United States v. $8,850, 461 U.S. 555 (1983); Calero–Toledo v. Pearson Yacht Leasing Co., 416 U.S. 663 (1974). Here, where respondent was not ousted form his property, but merely restrained from disposing of it, the governmental intrusion was even less severe than those permitted by our prior decisions.

Indeed, it would be odd to conclude that the government may not restrain property, such as the home and apartment in respondent's possession, based on a finding of probable cause, when we have held that (under appropriate circumstances), the Government may restrain *persons* where there is a finding of probable cause to believe that the accused has committed a serious offense. See United States v. Salerno, 481 U.S. 739 (1987). Given the gravity of the offenses charged in the indictment, respondent himself could have been subjected to pretrial restraint if deemed necessary to "reasonably assure [his] appearance [at trial] and the safety of . . . the community," 18 U.S.C. § 3142(e)(1982 ed., Supp. V); we find no constitutional infirmity in § 853(e)'s authorization of a similar restraint on respondent's property to protect its "appearance" at trial, and protect the community's interest in full recovery of any ill-gotten gains.

---

[10] We do not consider today, however, whether the due process clause requires a hearing before a pretrial restraining order can be imposed. As noted above, in its initial consideration of this case, a panel of the Second Circuit ordered that such a hearing be held before permitting the entry of a restraining order; on remand, the District Court held an extensive, four-day hearing on the question of probable cause.

Though the Solicitor General petitioned for review of the Second Circuit's holding that such a hearing was required, given that the government prevailed in the District Court notwithstanding the hearing, it would be pointless for us now to consider whether a hearing was required by the due process clause. Furthermore, because the Court of Appeals, in its en banc decision, did not address the procedural due process issue, we also do not inquire whether the hearing—if a hearing was required at all—was an adequate one.

Respondent contends that both the nature of the government's property right in forfeitable assets, and the nature of the use to which he would have put these assets (i.e., retaining an attorney), require some departure from our established rule of permitting pretrial restraint of assets based on probable cause. We disagree. In *Caplin & Drysdale*, we conclude that a weighing of these very interests suggests that the government may—without offending the fifth or sixth amendments—obtain forfeiture of property that a defendant might have wished to use to pay his attorney. Given this holding, we find that a pretrial restraining order does not "arbitrarily" interfere with defendant's "fair opportunity" to retain counsel. Cf. Powell v. Alabama, 287 U.S. 45, 69, 53 (1932). Put another way: if the government may, post-trial, forbid the use of forfeited assets to pay an attorney, then surely no constitutional violation occurs when, after probable cause is adequately established, the government obtains an order barring a defendant from frustrating that end by dissipating his assets prior to trial.

IV

For the reasons given above, the judgment of the Second Circuit is reversed, and the case remanded for further proceedings.

It is so ordered.

■ JUSTICE BLACKMUN, with whom JUSTICE BRENNAN, JUSTICE MARSHALL, and JUSTICE STEVENS join, dissenting.

Those jurists who have held forth against the result the majority reaches in these cases have been guided by one core insight: that it is unseemly and unjust for the government to beggar those it prosecutes in order to disable their defense at trial. The majority trivializes "the burden the forfeiture law imposes on a criminal defendant." Caplin & Drysdale v. United States, 491 U.S. 617 (1989). Instead, it should heed the warnings of our district court judges, whose day-to-day exposure to the criminal-trial process enables them to understand, perhaps far better than we, the devastating consequences of attorney's fee forfeiture for the integrity of our adversarial system of justice.[1]

The criminal-forfeiture statute we consider today could have been interpreted to avoid depriving defendants of the ability to retain private counsel—and should have been so interpreted, given the grave "constitutional and ethical problems" raised by the forfeiture of funds used to pay legitimate counsel fees. But even if Congress in fact required this substantial incursion on the defendant's choice of counsel, the Court should have recognized that the Framers stripped Congress of the power to do so when they added the sixth amendment to our Constitution.

I

The majority acknowledges, as it must, that *no* language in the Comprehensive Forfeiture Act of 1984 expressly provides for the forfeiture

---

[1] [Citation to six District Court opinions omitted.]

of attorney's fees, and that the legislative history contains no substantive discussion of the question.[2] The fact that "the legislative history and congressional debates are similarly silent on the use of forfeitable assets to pay stock-broker's fees, laundry bills, or country club memberships" means nothing, for one cannot believe that Congress was unaware that interference with the payment of attorney's fees, unlike interference with these other expenditures would raise sixth amendment concerns.

Despite the absence of any indication that Congress intended to use the forfeiture weapon against legitimate attorney's fees, the majority—all the while purporting to "respect" the established practice of construing a statute to avoid constitutional problems—contends that it is constrained to conclude that the act reaches attorney's fees. The Court cannot follow its usual practice here, we are told, because this is not a "close cas[e]" in which "statutory language is ambiguous." The majority finds unambiguous language in § 853(a) of the Act, which provides that when a defendant is convicted of certain crimes, the defendant "shall forfeit to the United States" any property derived from proceeds of the crime or used to facilitate the crime. I agree that § 853(a) is broad in language and is cast in mandatory terms. But I do not agree with the majority's conclusion that the lack of an express exemption for attorney's fees in § 853(a) makes the act *as a whole* unambiguous.

The majority succeeds in portraying the act as "unambiguous" by making light of its most relevant provisions. As Judge Winter observed, the broad mandatory language of § 853(a) applies by its terms only to " 'any person convicted' of the referenced crimes." United States v. Monsanto, 852 F.2d 1400, 1410 (2d Cir.1988). Because third parties to whom assets have been transferred in return for services rendered are not "persons convicted," however, forfeiture of property in *their* possession is controlled by § 853(c) rather than by § 853(a). Section 853(c) provides: "Any such property that is subsequently transferred to a person other than the defendant *may be the subject of a special verdict of forfeiture* and thereafter shall be ordered forfeited to the United States" (emphasis added) if the third party fails to satisfy certain requirements for exemption. Thus, § 853(c) does not, like § 853(a), provide that all property defined as forfeitable under § 853 "must" or "shall" be forfeited:[4] forfeitable proper-

---

[2] Indeed, the strongest statement on the question is the comment in the House Report: "Nothing in this section is intended to interfere with a person's sixth amendment right to counsel." H.R. Rep. No. 98–845, pt. 1, p. 19, n. 1 (1984). Even if the majority were correct that this statement is "nothing more than an exhortation for the courts to tread carefully in this delicate area," the majority does not explain why it proceeds to ignore Congress' exhortation to construe the statute to avoid implicating sixth amendment concerns.

[4] This language differs from the language in Federal Rule of Criminal Procedure 31(e), which was promulgated in 1972 to provide procedural rules for Congress' earlier forays into criminal forfeiture. The Rule provides: "If the indictment or the information alleges that an interest or property is subject to criminal forfeiture, a special verdict *shall* be returned as to the extent of the interest or property subject to forfeiture, if any" (emphasis added). Congress' decision to depart from mandatory language in § 853(c), where it fashioned a special verdict provision for

ty held by a third party presumptively "shall be ordered forfeited" only if it is included in the special verdict, and its inclusion in the verdict is discretionary.[5]

There is also considerable room for discretion in the language of § 853(e)(1), which controls the government's use of post-indictment protective orders to prevent the pre-conviction transfer of potentially forfeitable assets to third-parties. That section provides:

> "Upon application of the United States, the court *may enter a restraining order or injunction* . . . or take any other action to preserve the availability of property . . . for forfeiture under this section . . . upon the filing of an indictment or information charging a violation . . . for which criminal forfeiture may be ordered . . . and alleging the property with respect to which the order is sought would, in the event of conviction, be subject to forfeiture under this section" (emphasis added).

The Senate Report makes clear that a district court may hold a hearing to "consider factors bearing on the reasonableness of the order sought." S. Rep. No. 98–225, p. 202 (1983). Even if the court chooses to enter an order ex parte at the government's request, it may "modify the order" if it later proves to be unreasonable. In the course of this process, the court may also consider the circumstances of any third party whose interests are implicated by the restraining order. Thus, the government does not have an absolute right to an order preserving the availability of property by barring its transfer to third parties. Pre-conviction injunctive relief is available, but at the discretion of the district court.

The majority does not deny that §§ 853(c) and 853(e)(1) contain discretionary language. It argues, however, that the exercise of discretion must be "cabined by the purposes" of the act. That proposition, of course, is unassailable: I agree that discretion created by the act cannot be used to defeat the purposes of the act. The majority errs, however, in taking an overly broad view of the act's purposes.

Under the majority's view, the act aims to preserve the availability of *all* potentially forfeitable property during the pre-conviction period, and to

---

assets transferred to third parties, is significant.

[5] That the act is mandatory in its treatment of forfeiture of property in the defendant's hands, but not in its treatment of property transferred to third parties, is consistent with the distinction between civil forfeiture and criminal forfeiture. The theory (or, more properly, the fiction) underlying civil forfeiture is that the property subject to forfeiture is itself tainted by having been used in an unlawful manner. The right of the government to take possession does not depend on the government's ultimately convicting the person who used the property in

an unlawful way, nor is it diminished by the innocence or bona fides of the party into whose hands the property falls. Criminal forfeiture, in contrast, is penal in nature: it is predicated on the adjudicated guilt of the defendant, and has punishment of the defendant as its express purpose. See generally Morgan Cloud, Forfeiting Defense Attorneys' Fees: Applying an Institutional Role Theory to Define Individual Constitutional Rights, 1987 Wis. L. Rev. 1, 18–19 (Forfeiting Fees). Where the purpose of forfeiture is to punish the defendant, the government's penal interests are weakest when the punishment also burdens third parties.

achieve the forfeiture of *all* such property upon conviction. This view of the act's purposes effectively writes all discretion out of §§ 853(c) and 853(e)(1), because any exercise of discretion will diminish the government's post-conviction "take." But a review of the legislative history of the act demonstrates that the act does not seek forfeiture of property for its own sake merely to maximize the amount of money the government collects.[6] The central purposes of the act, properly understood, are fully served by an approach to forfeiture that leaves ample room for the exercise of statutory discretion.

Congress' most systemic goal for criminal forfeiture was to prevent the profits of criminal activity from being poured into future such activity, for "it is through economic power that [criminal activity] is sustained and grows." Senate Report, at 191. "Congress recognized in its enactment of statutes specifically addressing organized crime and illegal drugs that the conviction of individual racketeers and drug dealers would be of only limited effectiveness if the economic power bases of criminal organizations or enterprises were left intact, and so included forfeiture authority designed to strip these offenders and organization of their economic power." Ibid.; see also H.R. Rep. No. 98–845, pt. 1, p. 6 (1984)(criminal forfeiture statutes are "a bold attempt to attack the economic base of the criminal activity").[7]

Congress also had a more traditional punitive goal in mind: to strip convicted criminals of all assets purchased with the proceeds of their criminal activities. Particularly in the area of drug trafficking, Congress concluded that crime had become too lucrative for criminals to be deterred by conventional punishments. "Drug dealers have been able to accumulate huge fortunes as a result of their illegal activities. The sad truth is that

---

[6] In adopting this view of the Act, the majority ignores the government's concession at oral argument before the en banc Second Circuit Court of Appeals that the act was not enacted as a revenue-raising measure. Thus, although the government's interest in "using the profits of crime to fund [law-enforcement] activities" should perhaps not be "discounted," *Caplin & Drysdale*, it is not dispositive. Nor does Congress' willingness to return forfeited funds to victims of crime instead of using them for law-enforcement purposes indicate that restitution is a primary goal of the act. Restitution, in any event, is not a likely result in the typical case for which the act was designed: one in which the property forfeited consists of derivative proceeds of illegal activity, rather than of stolen property that is readily traceable to a particular victim. See Forfeiting Fees, 1987 Wis. L. Rev., at 20.

[7] The majority contends that "the desire to lessen the economic power of organized crime and drug-enterprises. ... includes the use of such economic power to retain private counsel." *Caplin & Drysdale*. "The notion that the government has a legitimate interest in depriving criminals"—*before they are convicted*—"of economic power, even in so far as that power is used to retain counsel of choice" is more than just "somewhat unsettling," as the majority suggests. Ibid. That notion is constitutionally suspect, and—equally important for present purposes—completely foreign to Congress' stated goals. The purpose of the relation-back provision is to assure that assets *proved at trial* to be the product of criminal activity cannot be channeled into further criminal activity—not to strip defendants of their assets on no more than a showing of probable cause that they are "tainted." See Comment, 61 N.Y.U. L. Rev. 124, 139 (1986). For its contrary view, the majority relies on nothing more than the rhetoric of the en banc Court of Appeals' majority opinion in *Caplin & Drysdale*.

the financial penalties for drug dealing are frequently only seen by dealers as a cost of doing business." House Report, at 2. The image of convicted drug dealers returning home from their prison terms to all the comforts their criminal activity can buy is one Congress could not abide.[8]

Finally, Congress was acutely aware that defendants, if unhindered, routinely would defeat the purposes of the act by sheltering their assets in order to preserve them for their own future use and for the continued use of their criminal organizations. The purpose of § 853(c) is to "to permit the voiding of certain pre-conviction transfers and so close a potential loophole in current law whereby the criminal forfeiture sanction could be avoided by transfers that were not 'arms' length' transactions." Senate Report, at 200–01.

With these purposes in mind, it becomes clear that a district court acts within the bounds of its statutory discretion when it exempts from pre-conviction restraint and post-conviction forfeiture those assets a defendant needs to retain private counsel for his criminal trial. Assets used to retain counsel by definition will be unavailable to the defendant or his criminal organization after trial, even if the defendant is eventually acquitted. See Morgan Cloud, Government Intrusions Into the Attorney–Client Relationship: The Impact of Fee Forfeitures on the Balance of Power in the Adversary System of Criminal Justice, 36 Emory L.J. 817, 832 (1987)(Intrusions). Thus, no important and legitimate purpose is served by employing § 853(c) to require post-conviction forfeiture of funds used for legitimate attorney's fees, or by employing § 853(e)(1) to bar pre-conviction payment of fees. The government's interests are adequately protected so long as the district court supervises transfers to the attorney to make sure they are made in good faith.[9] See Comment, 61 N.Y.U. L. Rev. 124, 138–39 (1986). All that is lost is the government's power to punish the defendant before he is convicted. That power is not one the act intended to grant.[10]

[8] Congress' desire to maximize punishment, however, cannot be viewed as a blanket authorization of government action that punishes the defendant before he is proved guilty.

[9] Judge Winter noted that the same logic suggests that the forfeiture of assets the defendant uses to support himself and his family is unduly harsh and is not necessary to achieve the goals of the act. *United States v. Monsanto*, 852 F.2d, at 1405. The majority chides Judge Winter for suggesting that, once it is established that there is discretion to exclude assets used to pay attorney's fees and normal living expenses from forfeiture, the necessary result is that such assets *must* be excluded. I find it exceedingly unlikely that a district court, instructed that it had the discretion to permit a defendant to retain counsel, would ever choose not to do so. Normal equitable considerations, combined with a proper regard for sixth amendment interests, would weigh so strongly in favor of that result that any "slippage" from permissive to mandatory language on Judge Winter's part seems to me entirely accurate as a predictive matter.

[10] The majority states that another forfeiture statute contemporaneous with the Act contains "the *precise* exemption from forfeiture which respondent asks us to imply into § 853," and suggests that this is evidence that "Congress understood what it was doing in omitting such an exemption" from the act. This argument is makeweight. The express exemption to which the majority refers involves the use of proceeds from publications and other accounts of a crime to:

"(i) satisfy a money judgment rendered in any court in favor of a victim of any offense for which such defendant has

A careful analysis of the language of the act and its legislative history thus proves that "a construction of the statute is fairly possible by which the [constitutional] question may be avoided." Crowell v. Benson, 285 U.S. 22, 62 (1932). Indeed, the prudentially preferable construction is also the only one that gives full effect to the discretionary language in §§ 853(c) and 853(e)(1). Thus, "if anything remains of the canon that statutes capable of differing interpretations should be construed to avoid constitutional issues . . . it surely applies here." *United States v. Monsanto*, 852 F.2d, at 1409.

II

The majority has decided otherwise, however, and for that reason is compelled to reach the constitutional issue it could have avoided. But the majority pauses hardly long enough to acknowledge "the sixth amendment's protection of one's right to retain counsel of his choosing," let alone to explore its "full extent." *Caplin & Drysdale.* Instead, it moves rapidly from the observation that "a defendant may not insist on representation by an attorney he cannot afford," Wheat v. United States, 486 U.S. 153, 161 (1988), to the conclusion that the government is free to deem the defendant indigent by declaring his assets "tainted" by criminal activity the government has yet to prove. That the majority implicitly finds the sixth amendment right to counsel of choice so insubstantial that it can be outweighed by a legal fiction demonstrates, still once again, its " 'apparent unawareness of the function of the independent lawyer as a guardian of our freedom.' " See Walters v. National Assn. of Radiation Survivors, 473 U.S. 305, 371 (1985)(Stevens, J., dissenting).

A

Over 50 years ago, this Court observed: "It is hardly necessary to say that the right to counsel being conceded, a defendant should be afforded a fair opportunity to secure counsel of his own choice." Powell v. Alabama, 287 U.S. 45, 53 (1932). For years, that proposition was settled; the controversial question was whether the defendant's right to use his own funds to retain his chosen counsel was the outer limit of the right protected by the sixth amendment. See e.g., Chandler v. Fretag, 348 U.S. 3, 9 (1954). The Court's subsequent decisions have made clear that an indigent defendant has the right to appointed counsel, see, e.g. Gideon v. Wainwright, 372

---

been convicted, or a legal representative of such victim; and

(ii) pay for legal representation of the defendant in matters *arising from the offense for which such defendant has been convicted,* but no more than 20 percent of the total proceeds may be so used." 18 U.S.C. § 3681 (1982 ed., Supp. V)(emphasis added).

When this provision is read in context, it is clear that it concerns payment of attorney's fees related to post-conviction civil suits brought against convicted defendants by their victims. It does not, therefore, constitute the "*precise* exemption" sought in these cases. Indeed, the provision cuts against the result the majority reaches. In light of Congress' decision to permit a convicted criminal to use wealth he has obtained by publicizing his crime to hire counsel to resist his victim's damages claims, it would be bizarre to think that Congress intended to be *more* punitive when it comes to a defendant's need for counsel prior to conviction, when the defendant's own liberty is at stake.

U.S. 335 (1963), and that the sixth amendment guarantees at least minimally effective assistance of counsel, see e.g., Strickland v. Washington, 466 U.S. 668 (1984). But while court appointment of effective counsel plays a crucial role in safeguarding the fairness of criminal trials, it has never defined the outer limits of the sixth amendment's demands. The majority's decision in this case reveals that it has lost track of the distinct role of the right to counsel of choice in protecting the integrity of the judicial process, a role that makes "the right to be represented by privately retained counsel ... the primary, preferred component of the basic right" protected by the sixth amendment. United States v. Harvey, 814 F.2d 905, 923 (4th Cir.1987).

The right to retain private counsel serves to foster the trust between attorney and client that is necessary for the attorney to be a truly effective advocate. See ABA Standards for Criminal Justice 4–3.1, p. 4–29 (commentary 2d ed. 1980). Not only are decisions crucial to the defendant's liberty placed in counsel's hands, but the defendant's perception of the fairness of the process, and his willingness to acquiesce in its results, depend upon his confidence in his counsel's dedication, loyalty, and ability. When the government insists upon the right to choose the defendant's counsel for him, that relationship of trust is undermined: counsel is too readily perceived as the government's agent rather than his own. Indeed, when the Court in Faretta v. California, 422 U.S. 806, 834 (1975), held that the sixth amendment prohibits a court from imposing appointed counsel on a defendant who prefers to represent himself, its decision was predicated on the insight that "[t]o force a lawyer on a defendant can only lead him to believe that the law contrives against him."

The right to retain private counsel also serves to assure some modicum of equality between the government and those it chooses to prosecute. The government can be expected to "spend vast sums of money ... to try defendants accused of crime," *Gideon v. Wainwright*, 372 U.S., at 344, and of course will devote greater resources to complex cases in which the punitive stakes are high. Precisely for this reason, "there are few defendants charged with crime, few indeed, who fail to hire the best lawyers they can get to prepare and present their defenses." Ibid. But when the government provides for appointed counsel, there is no guarantee that levels of compensation and staffing will be even average.[12] Where cases are complex, trials long, and stakes high, that problem is exacerbated. "Despite the legal profession's commitment to pro bono work," United States

---

[12] "Even in the federal courts under the Criminal Justice Act of 1964, 18 U.S.C. § 3006A, which provides one of the most generous compensation plans, the rates for appointed counsel ... are low by American standards. Consequently, the majority of persons willing to accept appointments are the young and inexperienced." Argersinger v. Hamlin, 407 U.S. 25, 57, n. 21 (1972)(Powell, J., concurring in result). Indeed, there is evidence that "Congress did not design [the Criminal Justice Act] to be compensatory, but merely to reduce financial burdens on assigned counsel." See Bruce J. Winick, Forfeiture of Attorneys' Fees under RICO and CCE and the Right to Counsel of Choice: The Constitutional Dilemma and How to Avoid It, 43 U. Miami L. Rev. 765, 773 and n. 40 (1989).

v. Bassett, 632 F.Supp. 1308, 1316 (D.Md.1986), even the best-intentioned of attorneys may have no choice but to decline the task of representing defendants in cases for which they will not receive adequate compensation. Over the long haul, the result of lowered compensation levels will be that talented attorneys will "decline to enter criminal practice ... This exodus of talented attorneys could devastate the criminal defense bar." Bruce J. Winick, Forfeiture of Attorneys' Fees under RICO and CCE and the Right to Counsel of Choice: The Constitutional Dilemma and How to Avoid It, 43 U. Miami L. Rev. 765, 781 (1989). Without the defendant's right to retain private counsel, the government too readily could defeat its adversaries simply by outspending them.[13]

The right to privately chosen and compensated counsel also serves broader institutional interests. The "virtual socialization of criminal defense work in this country" that would be the result of a widespread abandonment of the right to retain chosen counsel, Brief for Committees on Criminal Advocacy and Criminal Law of the Association of the Bar of the City of New York, et al., as Amici Curiae, too readily would standardize the provision of criminal-defense services and diminish defense counsel's independence. There is a place in our system of criminal justice for the maverick and the risk-taker, for approaches that might not fit into the structured environment of a public defender's office, or that might displease a judge whose preference for nonconfrontational styles of advocacy might influence the judge's appointment decisions. See David Bazelon, The Defective Assistance of Counsel, 42 U. Cin. L. Rev. 1, 6–7 (1973); S. Kadish, S. Schulhofer and M. Paulsen, Criminal Law and its Processes 32 (4th ed. 1983); cf. Sacher v. United States, 343 U.S. 1, 8–9 (1952)("The nature of the proceedings presupposes, or at least stimulates, zeal in the opposing lawyers"). There is also a place for the employment of "specialized defense counsel" for technical and complex cases, see United States v. Thier, 801 F.2d 1463, 1476 (5th Cir.1986)(concurring opinion). The choice of counsel is the primary means for the defendant to establish the kind of defense he will put forward. Only a healthy, independent defense bar can be expected to meet the demands of the varied circumstances faced by criminal defendants, and assure that the interests of the individual defendant are not unduly "subordinat[ed] ... to the needs of the system." Bazelon, supra, at 7.

In sum, our chosen system of criminal justice is built upon a truly equal and adversarial presentation of the case, and upon the trust that can exist only when counsel is independent of the government. Without the right, reasonably exercised, to counsel of choice, the effectiveness of that system is imperilled.

B

Had it been Congress' express aim to undermine the adversary system as we know it, it could hardly have found a better engine of destruction

---

[13] That the government has this power when the defendant is indigent is unfortunate, but "[i]t is an irrelevancy once recognized." *United States v. Harvey*, 814 F.2d, at 923.

than attorney's-fee forfeiture. The main effect of forfeitures under the act, of course, will be to deny the defendant the right to retain counsel, and therefore the right to have his defense designed and presented by an attorney he has chosen and trusts.[14] If the government restrains the defendant's assets before trial, private counsel will be unwilling to continue or to take on the defense. Even if no restraining order is entered, the possibility of forfeiture after conviction will itself substantially diminish the likelihood that private counsel will agree to take the case. The "message [to private counsel] is 'Do not represent this defendant or you will lose your fee.' That being the kind of message lawyers are likely to take seriously, the defendant will find it difficult or impossible to secure representation." United States v. Badalamenti, 614 F.Supp. 194, 196 (S.D.N.Y.1985).

The resulting relationship between the defendant and his court-appointed counsel will likely begin in distrust, and be exacerbated to the extent that the defendant perceives his new-found "indigency" as a form of punishment imposed by the government in order to weaken his defense. If the defendant had been represented by private counsel earlier in the proceedings, the defendant's sense that the government has stripped him of his defenses will be sharpened by the concreteness of his loss. Appointed counsel may be inexperienced and undercompensated and, for that reason, may not have adequate opportunity or resources to deal with the special problems presented by what is likely to be a complex trial. The already scarce resources of a public defender's office will be stretched to the limit. Facing a lengthy trial against a better-armed adversary, the temptation to recommend a guilty plea will be great. The result, if the defendant is convicted, will be a sense, often well grounded, that justice was not done.

Even if the defendant finds a private attorney who is "so foolish, ignorant, beholden or idealistic as to take the business," id., at 196, the attorney-client relationship will be undermined by the forfeiture statute. Perhaps the attorney will be willing to violate ethical norms by working on a contingent fee basis in a criminal cas. See *Caplin & Drysdale*, n.10. But if he is not—and we should question the integrity of any criminal-defense attorney who would violate the ethical norms of the profession by doing so—the attorney's own interests will dictate that he remain ignorant of the source of the assets from which he is paid. Under § 853(c), a third-party transferee may keep assets if "the transferee establishes ... that he is a bona fide purchaser for value of such property who at the time of purchase was reasonably without cause to believe that the property was subject to

---

[14] There is reason to fear that, in addition to depriving a defendant of counsel of choice, there will be circumstances in which the threat of forfeiture will deprive the defendant of *any* counsel. If the government chooses not to restrain transfers by employing § 853(e)(1), it is likely that the defendant will not qualify as "indigent" under the Criminal Justice Act. Potential private counsel will be aware of the threat of forfeiture, and, as a result, will likely refuse to take the case. Although it is to be hoped that a solution will be developed for a defendant who "falls between the cracks" in this manner, there is no guarantee that accommodation will be made in an orderly fashion, and that trial preparation will not be substantially delayed because of the difficulties in securing counsel.

forfeiture under this section." The less an attorney knows, the greater the likelihood that he can claim to have been an "innocent" third party. The attorney's interest in knowing nothing is directly adverse to his client's interest in full disclosure. The result of the conflict may be a less vigorous investigation of the defendant's circumstances, leading in turn to a failure to recognize or pursue avenues of inquiry necessary to the defense. Other conflicts of interest are also likely to develop. The attorney who fears for his fee will be tempted to make the government's waiver of fee-forfeiture the sine qua non for any plea agreement, a position which conflicts with his client's best interests.

Perhaps most troubling is the fact that forfeiture statutes place the government in the position to exercise an intolerable degree of power over any private attorney who takes on the task of representing a defendant in a forfeiture case. The decision whether to seek a restraining order rests with the prosecution, as does the decision whether to waive forfeiture upon a plea of guilty or a conviction at trial. The government will be ever tempted to use the forfeiture weapon against a defense attorney who is particularly talented or aggressive on the client's behalf—the attorney who is better than what, in the government's view, the defendant deserves. The spectre of the government's selectively excluding only the most talented defense counsel is a serious threat to the equality of forces necessary for the adversarial system to perform at its best. An attorney whose fees are potentially subject to forfeiture will be forced to operate in an environment in which the government is not only the defendant's adversary, but also his own.

The long-term effects of the fee-forfeiture practice will be to decimate the private criminal-defense bar. As the use of the forfeiture mechanism expands to new categories of federal crimes and spreads to the states, only one class of defendants will be free routinely to retain private counsel: the affluent defendant accused of a crime that generates no economic gain. As the number of private clients diminishes, only the most idealistic and the least skilled of young lawyers will be attracted to the field, while the remainder seek greener pastures elsewhere. See Winick, 43 U. Miami L. Rev., at 781–82.

In short, attorney's-fee forfeiture substantially undermines every interest served by the sixth amendment right to chosen counsel, on the individual and institutional levels, over the short term and the long haul.

C

We have recognized that although there is a "presumption in favor of [the defendant's] counsel of choice," *Wheat v. United States*, 486 U.S., at 158, 162, the right to counsel of choice is not absolute. Some substantial and legitimate governmental interests may require the courts to disturb the defendant's choice of counsel, as "[w]hen a defendant's selection of counsel, under the particular facts and circumstances of a case, gravely imperils the prospect of a fair trial," id., at 166 (Marshall, J., dissenting), or threatens to undermine the orderly disposition of the case, see Ungar v.

Sarafite, 376 U.S. 575, 589 (1964). But never before today has the Court suggested that the government's naked desire to deprive a defendant of "the best counsel money can buy," *Caplin & Drysdale*, is itself a legitimate government interest that can justify the government's interference with the defendant's right to chosen counsel—and for good reason. "[W]eakening the ability of an accused to defend himself at trial is an advantage for the government. But it is not a legitimate government interest that can be used to justify invasion of a constitutional right." *United States v. Monsanto*, 852 F.2d, at 1403 (Feinberg, C.J., concurring). And the *legitimate* interests the government asserts are extremely weak, far too weak to justify the act's substantial erosion of the defendant's sixth amendment rights.

The government claims a property interest in forfeitable assets, predicated on the relation-back provision, § 853(c), which employs a legal fiction to grant the government title in all forfeitable property as of the date of the crime. The majority states: "Permitting a defendant to use assets for his private purposes that, under this provision, will become the property of the United States if conviction occurs, cannot be sanctioned." But the government's insistence that it has a paramount interest in the defendant's resources "simply begs the constitutional question rather than answering it. Indeed, the ultimate constitutional issue might well be framed precisely as whether Congress may use this wholly fictive device of property law to cut off this fundamental right of the accused in a criminal case. If the right must yield here to countervailing governmental interests, the relation-back device undoubtedly could be used to implement the governmental interests, but surely it cannot serve as a substitute for them." In re Forfeiture Hearing as to Caplin & Drysdale, 837 F.2d 637, 652 (4th Cir.1988)(en banc)(dissenting opinion).

Furthermore, the relation-back fiction gives the government no property interest whatsoever in the defendant's assets before the defendant is convicted. In most instances, the assets the government attempts to reach by using the forfeiture provisions of the act are derivative proceeds of crime, property that was not itself acquired illegally, but was purchased with the profits of criminal activity. Prior to conviction, sole title to such asset—not merely possession, as is the case in the majority's bank robbery example, *Caplin & Drysdale*—rests in the defendant; no other party has any present legal claim to them.[15] Yet it is in the preconviction period that

---

[15] Other analogies the majority and the government have drawn are also inapt. We do not deal with contraband, which the government is free to seize because the law recognizes no right to possess it. Nor do we deal with instrumentalities of crime, which may have evidentiary value, and may also traditionally be seized by the government and retained even if the defendant is not proved guilty, unless a party with a rightful claim to the property comes forward to refute the government's contention that the property was put to an unlawful use. Comment, 48 U. Chi. L. Rev. 960, 963–64 (1981). As to the analogy to "jeopardy assessments" under the Internal Revenue Code, the IRS in that situation has a legal claim to the sums at issue at the time of the assessment, based upon substantive provisions of the Code. Here, in contrast, the government's claim will not arise until after conviction. In addition, even if a jeopardy assessment were to deprive a

the forfeiture threat (or the force of a § 853(e)(1) restraining order) deprives the defendant of use of the assets to retain counsel. The government's interest in the assets at the time of their restraint is no more than an interest in safeguarding fictive property rights, one which hardly weighs at all against the defendant's formidable sixth amendment right to retain counsel for his defense.

The majority contends, of course, that assets are only restrained upon a finding of probable cause to believe that the property ultimately will be proved forfeitable, and that because "the government may restrain *persons* where there is a finding of probable cause that the accused has committed a serious offense," the government necessarily has the right to restrain property the defendant seeks to use to retain counsel on a showing of probable cause as well. Neither the majority's premise nor its conclusion is well founded.

Although obtaining a restraining order requires a showing of probable cause, the practical effects of the threat of forfeiture are felt long before the indictment stage. Any attorney who is asked to represent the target of a drug or RICO investigation—or even a routine tax investigation, as the facts of *Caplin & Drysdale* demonstrate—must think ahead to the possibility that the defendant's assets will turn out to be forfeitable. While the defendant is not formally restrained from using his assets to pay counsel during this period, the reluctance of any attorney to represent the defendant in the face of the forfeiture threat effectively strips the defendant of the right to retain counsel. The threat of forfeiture does its damage long before the government must come forward with a showing of probable cause.

But even if the majority were correct that no defendant is ever deprived of the right to retain counsel without a showing of probable cause, the majority's analogy to permissible pretrial restraints would fail. The act gives the government the right to seek a restraining order solely on the basis of the indictment, which signifies that there has been a finding of probable cause to believe that the assets are tainted. When a defendant otherwise is incarcerated before trial, in contrast, the restraint cannot be justified by the fact of the indictment alone. In addition, there must be a showing that other alternatives will not "reasonably assure the appearance of the person [for trial] and the safety of any other person and the community." 18 U.S.C. § 3142(e)(1982 ed., Supp. V). No equivalent individualized showing that the defendant will likely dissipate his assets or fraudulently transfer them to third parties is necessary under the majority's reading of § 853(e)(1). Furthermore, the potential danger resulting from the failure to restrain assets differs in kind and severity from the

taxpayer of the funds necessary to file a challenge to the assessment in the Tax Court, the proceeding in that court is civil, and the sixth amendment therefore does not apply. I agree with Judge Phillips when he observes that the constitutionality of a jeopardy assessment that deprived the defendant of the funds necessary to hire counsel to ward off a criminal challenge is not to be assumed. See *United States v. Harvey*, 814 F.2d, at 926.

danger faced by the public when a defendant who is believed to be violent remains at large before trial.

Finally, even if the government's asserted interests were entitled to some weight, the manner in which the government has chosen to protect them undercuts its position. Under § 853(c), a third-party transferee may keep assets if he was "reasonably without cause to believe that the property was subject to forfeiture." Most legitimate providers of services will meet the requirements for this statutory exemption. The exception is the defendant's attorney, who cannot do his job (or at least cannot do his job well) without asking questions that will reveal the source of the defendant's assets. It is difficult to put great weight on the government's interest in increasing the amount of property available for forfeiture when the means chosen are so starkly underinclusive, and the burdens fall almost exclusively upon the exercise of a constitutional right.[16]

Interests are ephemeral as these should not be permitted to defeat the defendant's right to the assistance of his chosen counsel.

III

In my view, the act as interpreted by the majority is inconsistent with the intent of Congress, and seriously undermines the basic fairness of our criminal-justice system. That a majority of this Court has upheld the constitutionality of the act as so interpreted will not deter Congress, I hope, from amending the act to make clear that Congress did not intend this result. This Court has the power to declare the act constitutional, but it cannot thereby make it wise.

I dissent.

Caplin & Drysdale, Chartered v. United States

Supreme Court of the United States, 1989.
491 U.S. 617.

■ JUSTICE WHITE delivered the opinion of the Court.

We are called on to determine whether the federal drug forfeiture statute includes an exemption for assets that a defendant wishes to use to pay an attorney who conducted his defense in the criminal case where forfeiture was sought. Because we determine that no such exemption

---

[16] Certainly criminal defendants "are not exempted from federal, state, and local taxation simply because these financial levies may deprive them of resources that could be used to hire an attorney." *Caplin & Drysdale.* The government's interest in raising revenue need not stand aside merely because the individual being taxed would rather spend the money by participating in a constitutionally protected activity. But I doubt that we would hesitate to reject as an undue burden on the exercise of a constitutional right a system that generally exempted personal-service transactions from taxation, but taxed payments to criminal-defense attorneys. In such circumstances, a clear-headed analysis of the government's action would likely reveal that burdening the exercise of the defendant's sixth amendment right was not the unfortunate consequence of the government's action, but its very purpose.

exists, we must decide whether that statute, so interpreted, is consistent with the fifth and sixth amendments. We hold that it is.

I

In January 1985, Christopher Reckmeyer was charged in a multicount indictment with running a massive drug importation and distribution scheme. The scheme was alleged to be a continuing criminal enterprise (CCE), in violation of 21 U.S.C. § 848 (1982 ed., Supp. V). Relying on a portion of the CCE statute that authorizes forfeiture to the government of "property constituting, or derived from ... proceeds ... obtained" from drug-law violations, 21 U.S.C. § 853(a)(1982 ed., Supp. V),[1] the indictment sought forfeiture of specified assets in Reckmeyer's possession. At this time, the District Court, acting pursuant to 21 U.S.C. § 853(e)(1)(A),[2] entered a restraining order forbidding Reckmeyer to transfer any of the listed assets that were potentially forfeitable.

Sometime earlier, Reckmeyer had retained petitioner, a law firm, to represent him in the ongoing grand jury investigation which resulted in the January 1985 indictments. Notwithstanding the restraining order, Reckmeyer paid the firm $25,000 for preindictment legal services a few days after the indictment was handed down; this sum was placed by petitioner in an escrow account. Petitioner continued to represent Reckmeyer following the indictment.

On March 7, 1985, Reckmeyer moved to modify the District Court's earlier restraining order to permit him to use some of the restrained assets to pay petitioner's fees; Reckmeyer also sought to exempt from any postconviction forfeiture order the assets that he intended to use to pay petitioner. However, one week later, before the District Court could conduct a hearing on this motion, Reckmeyer entered a plea agreement with the government. Under the agreement, Reckmeyer pleaded guilty to the drug-related CCE charge, and agreed to forfeit all of the specified assets listed in the indictment. The day after the Reckmeyer's plea was entered, the District Court denied his earlier motion to modify the restraining order,

---

[1] The forfeiture statute provides, in relevant part, that any person convicted of a particular class of criminal offenses:

"shall forfeit to the United States, irrespective of any provision of State law—

"(1) any property constituting, or derived from, any proceeds the person obtained, directly or indirectly, as the result of such violation;

"The court, in imposing sentence on such person, shall order, in addition to any other sentence imposed ... that the person forfeit to the United States all property described in this subsection." 21 U.S.C. § 853 (1982 ed. Supp. V).

There is no question here that the offenses respondent was accused of in the indictment fell within the class of crimes triggering this forfeiture provision.

[2] The pretrial restraining order provision states that

"[U]pon application of the United States, the court may enter a restraining order or injunction ... or take any other action to preserve the availability of property described in subsection (a) of [§ 853] and alleging that the property with respect to which the order is sought would, in the event of conviction, be subject to forfeiture under this section." 21 U.S.C. § 853(e)(1)(1982 ed., Supp. V).

concluding that the plea and forfeiture agreement rendered irrelevant any further consideration of the propriety of the court's pretrial restraints. Subsequently, an order forfeiting virtually all of the assets in Reckmeyer's possession was entered by the District Court in conjunction with his sentencing.

After this order was entered, petitioner filed a petition under 21 U.S.C. § 853(n)(1982 ed., Supp. V), which permits third parties with an interest in forfeited property to ask the sentencing court for an adjudication of their rights to that property; specifically, § 853(n)(6)(B) gives a third party who entered into a bona fide transaction with a defendant a right to make claims against forfeited property, if that third party was "at the time of [the transaction] reasonably without cause to believe that the [defendant's assets were] subject to forfeiture." See Also 21 U.S.C. § 853(c)(1982 ed., Supp. V). Petitioner claimed an interest in $170,000 of Reckmeyer's assets, for services it had provided Reckmeyer in conducting his defense; petitioner also sought the $25,000 being held in the escrow account, as payment for preindictment legal services. Petitioner argued alternatively that assets used to pay an attorney were exempt from forfeiture under § 853, and if not, the failure of the statute to provide such an exemption rendered it unconstitutional. The District Court granted petitioner's claim for a share of the forfeited assets.

A panel of the Fourth Circuit affirmed, finding that—while § 853 contained no statutory provision authorizing the payment of attorney's fees out of forfeited assets—the statute's failure to do so impermissibly infringed a defendant's sixth amendment right to the counsel of his choice. The Court of Appeals agreed to hear the case en banc, and reversed. All the judges of the Fourth Circuit agreed that the language of the CCE statute acknowledged no exception to its forfeiture requirement that would recognize petitioner's claim to the forfeited assets. A majority found this statutory scheme constitutional; four dissenting judges, however, agreed with the panel's view that the statute so-construed violated the sixth amendment.

Petitioner sought review of the statutory and constitutional issues raised by the Court of Appeals' holding. We granted certiorari and now affirm.

II

Petitioner's first submission is that the statutory provision that authorizes pretrial restraining orders on potentially forfeitable assets in a defendant's possession, 21 U.S.C. § 853(e), grants district courts equitable discretion to determine when such orders should be imposed. This discretion should be exercised under "traditional equitable standards," petitioner urges, including a "weigh[ing] of the equities and competing hardships on the parties"; under this approach, a court "must invariably strike the balance so as to allow a defendant [to pay] ... for bona fide attorneys fees," petitioner argues. Petitioner further submits that once a district court so exercises its discretion, and fails to freeze assets that a defendant then uses to pay an attorney, the statute's provision for recapture of forfeitable assets transferred to third parties, 21 U.S.C. § 853(c), may not operate on such sums.

Petitioner's argument, as it acknowledges, is based on the view of the statute expounded by Judge Winter of the Second Circuit in his concurring opinion in that Court of Appeals' en banc decision, United States v. Monsanto, 852 F.2d 1400, 1405–11 (1988). We reject this interpretation of the statute today in our decision in *United States v. Monsanto*, which reverses the Second Circuit's holding in that case. As we explain in our *Monsanto* decision, whatever discretion § 853(e) provides district court judges to refuse to enter pretrial restraining orders, it does not extend as far as petitioner urges—nor does the exercise of that discretion "immunize" nonrestrained assets from subsequent forfeiture under § 853(c), if they are transferred to an attorney to pay legal fees. Thus, for the reasons provided in our opinion in *Monsanto*, we reject petitioner's statutory claim.

III

We therefore address petitioner's constitutional challenges to the forfeiture law.[3] Petitioner contends that the statute infringes on criminal defendants' sixth amendment right to counsel of choice, and upsets the "balance of power" between the government and the accused in a manner contrary to the due process clause of the fifth amendment. We consider these contentions in turn.

A

Petitioner's first claim is that the forfeiture law makes impossible, or at least impermissibly burdens, a defendant's right "to select and be

[3] The Solicitor General argues that petitioner lacks jus tertii standing to advance Reckmeyer's sixth amendment rights. Though the argument is not without force, we conclude that petitioner has the requisite standing.

When a person or entity seeks standing to advance the constitutional rights of others, we ask two questions: first, has the litigant suffered some injury in fact, adequate to satisfy article III's case-or-controversy requirement; and second, do prudential considerations which we have identified in our prior cases point to permitting the litigant to advance the claim? See Singleton v. Wulff, 428 U.S. 106, 112 (1976). As to the first inquiry, there can be little doubt that petitioner's stake in $170,000 of the forfeited assets—which it would almost certainly receive if the sixth amendment claim it advances here were vindicated—is adequate injury-in-fact to meet the constitutional minimum of article III standing.

The second inquiry—the prudential one—is more difficult. To answer this question, our cases have looked at three factors: the relationship of the litigant to the person whose rights are being asserted; the ability of the person to advance his own rights; and the impact of the litigation on third-party interests. See, e.g., Craig v. Boren, 429 U.S. 190, 196 (1976); *Singleton v. Wulff*, supra, at 113–18; Eisenstadt v. Baird, 405 U.S. 438, 443–46 (1972). The second of these factors counsels against review here: as *Monsanto* illustrates, a criminal defendant suffers none of the obstacles discussed in *Wulff*, supra, at 116–17, to advancing his own constitutional claim. We think that the first and third factors, however, clearly weigh in petitioner's favor. The attorney-client relationship between petitioner and Reckmeyer, like the doctor-patient relationship in *Baird* is one of special consequence; and like *Baird*, it is credibly alleged that the statute at issue here may "materially impair the ability of" third persons in Reckmeyer's position to exercise their constitutional rights. Petitioner therefore satisfies our requirements for jus tertii standing.

represented by one's preferred attorney." Wheat v. United States, 486 U.S. 153, 159 (1988). Petitioner does not, nor could it defensibly do so, assert that impecunious defendants have a sixth amendment right to choose their counsel. The amendment guarantees defendants in criminal cases the right to adequate representation, but those who do not have the means to hire their own lawyers have no cognizable complaint so long as they are adequately represented by attorneys appointed by the courts. "[A] defendant may not insist on representation by an attorney he cannot afford." *Wheat*, supra, at 159. Petitioner does not dispute these propositions. Nor does the government deny that the sixth amendment guarantees a defendant the right to be represented by an otherwise qualified attorney whom that defendant can afford to hire, or who is willing to represent the defendant even though he is without funds. Applying these principles to the statute in question here, we observe that nothing in § 853 prevents a defendant from hiring the attorney of his choice, or disqualifies any attorney from serving as a defendant's counsel. Thus, unlike *Wheat* this case does not involve a situation where the government has asked a court to prevent a defendant's chosen counsel from representing the accused. Instead, petitioner urges that a violation of the sixth amendment arises here because of the forfeiture, at the instance of the government, of assets that defendants intend to use to pay their attorneys.

Even in this sense, of course, the burden the forfeiture law imposes on a criminal defendant is limited. The forfeiture statute does not prevent a defendant who has nonforfeitable assets from retaining any attorney of his choosing. Nor is it necessarily the case that a defendant who possess nothing but assets the government seeks to have forfeited will be prevented from retaining counsel of choice. Defendants like Reckmeyer may be able to find lawyers willing to represent them, hoping that their fees will be paid in the event of acquittal, or via some other means that a defendant might come by in the future. The burden placed on defendants by the forfeiture law is therefore a limited one.

Nonetheless, there will be cases where a defendant will be unable to retain the attorney of his choice, when that defendant would have been able to hire that lawyer if he had access to forfeitable assets, and if there was no risk that fees paid by the defendant to his counsel would later be recouped under § 853(c).[4] It is in these cases, petitioner argues, that the sixth amendment puts limits on the forfeiture statute.

This submission is untenable. Whatever the full extent of the sixth amendment's protection of one's right to retain counsel of his choosing,

---

[4] That section of the statute, which includes the co-called "relation back" provision, states:

"All right, title, and interest in property described in [§ 853] vests in the United States upon the commission of the act giving rise to forfeiture under this section. Any such property that is subsequently transferred to a person other than the defendant may be the subject of a special verdict of forfeiture and thereafter shall be forfeited to the United States, unless the transferee [establishes his entitlement to such property pursuant to § 853(n)(discussed supra)]." 21 U.S.C. § 853(c)(1982 ed., Supp. V).

that protection does not go beyond "the individual's right to spend his own money to obtain the advice and assistance of . . . counsel." Cf. Walters v. National Assn. of Radiation Survivors, 473 U.S. 305, 370 (1985)(Stevens, J., dissenting). A defendant has no sixth amendment right to spend another person's money for services rendered by an attorney, even if those funds are the only way that that defendant will be able to retain the attorney of his choice. A robbery suspect, for example, has no sixth amendment right to use funds he has stolen from a bank to retain an attorney to defend him if he is apprehended. The money, though in his possession, is not rightfully his; the government does not violate the sixth amendment if it seizes the robbery proceeds, and refuses to permit the defendant to use them to pay for his defense. "[N]o lawyer, in any case, . . . has the right to accept stolen property, or . . . ransom money, in payment of a fee . . . The privilege to practice law is not a license to steal." Laska v. United States, 82 F.2d 672, 677 (10th Cir.1936). Petitioner appears to concede as much, as respondent in *Monsanto* clearly does.

Petitioner seeks to distinguish such cases for sixth amendment purposes by arguing that the bank's claim to robbery proceeds rests on "pre-existing property rights," while the government's claim to forfeitable assets rests on a "penal statute" which embodies the "fictive property-law concept of . . . relation-back" and is merely "a mechanism for preventing fraudulent conveyances of the defendant's assets, not . . . a device for determining true title to property." In light of this, petitioner contends, the burden placed on defendant's sixth amendment rights by the forfeiture statute outweighs the government's interest in forfeiture.

The premises of petitioner's constitutional analysis are unsound in several respects. First, the property rights given the Government by virtue of the forfeiture statute are more substantial than petitioner acknowledges. In § 853(c), the so-called "relation-back" provision, Congress dictated that "[a]ll right, title and interest in property" obtained by criminals via the illicit means described in the statute "vests in the United States upon the commission of the act giving rise to forfeiture." 21 U.S.C. § 853(c)(1982 ed., Supp. V). As Congress observed when the provision was adopted, this approach, known as the "taint theory," is one that "has long been recognized in forfeiture cases," including the decision in United States v. Stowell, 133 U.S. 1 (1890). See S. Rep. No. 98–225, p. 200, and n. 27 (1983). In *Stowell*, the Court explained the operation of a similar forfeiture provision (for violations of the Internal Revenue Code) as follows:

> "As soon [the possessor of the forfeitable asset committed the violation] of the internal revenue laws, the forfeiture under those laws took effect, and (though needing judicial condemnation to perfect it) operated from that time as a statutory conveyance to the United States of all the right, title, and interest then remaining in the [possessor]; and was as valid and effectual, against all the world, as a recorded deed. The right so vested in the United States could not be defeated or impaired by any subsequent dealings of the . . . [possessor]."

In sum, § 853(c) reflects the application of the long-recognized and lawful practice of vesting title to any forfeitable assets, in the United States, at the time of the criminal act giving rise to forfeiture. Concluding that Reckmeyer cannot give good title to such property to petitioner because he did not hold good title is neither extraordinary or novel. Nor does petitioner claim, as a general proposition that the relation-back provision is unconstitutional, or that Congress cannot, as a general matter, vest title to assets derived from the crime in the government, as of the date of the criminal act in question. Petitioner's claim is that whatever part of the assets that is necessary to pay attorney's fees cannot be subjected to forfeiture. But given the government's title to Reckmeyer's assets upon conviction, to hold that the sixth amendment creates some right in Reckmeyer to alienate such assets, or creates a right on petitioner's part to receive these assets, would be peculiar.

There is no constitutional principle that gives one person the right to give another's property to a third party, even where the person seeking to complete the exchange wishes to do so in order to exercise a constitutionally protected right. While petitioner and its supporting amici attempt to distinguish between the expenditure of forfeitable assets to exercise one's sixth amendment rights, and expenditures in the pursuit of other constitutionally protected freedoms, there is no such distinction between, or hierarchy among, constitutional rights. If defendants have a right to spend forfeitable assets on attorney's fees, why not on exercises of the right to speak, practice one's religion, or travel? The full exercise of these rights, too, depends in part on one's financial wherewithal; and forfeiture, or even the threat of forfeiture, may similarly prevent a defendant from enjoying these rights as fully as he might otherwise. Nonetheless, we are not about to recognize an antiforfeiture exception for the exercise of each such right; nor does one exist for the exercise of sixth amendment rights, either.[5]

Petitioner's "balancing analysis" to the contrary rests substantially on the view that the government has only a modest interest in forfeitable assets that may be used to retain an attorney. Petitioner takes the position that, in large part, once assets have been paid over from client to attorney, the principal ends of forfeiture have been achieved: dispossessing a drug dealer or racketeer of the proceeds of his wrong-doing. We think that this view misses the mark for three reasons.

First, the government has a pecuniary interest in forfeiture that goes beyond merely separating a criminal from his ill-gotten gains; that legitimate interest extends to recovering *all* forfeitable assets, for such assets are deposited in a fund that supports law-enforcement efforts in a variety of important and useful ways. See 28 U.S.C. § 524(c), which establishes the

[5] It would be particularly odd to recognize the sixth amendment as a defense to forfeiture, because forfeiture is a substantive charge in the indictment against a defendant. Thus, petitioner asks us to take the sixth amendment's guarantee of counsel "for his defense," and make that guarantee *petition-er's defense* to the indictment. We doubt that the amendment's guarantees, which are procedural in nature, cf. Faretta v. California, 422 U.S. 806, 818 (1975), provide such a substantive defense to charges against an accused.

Department of Justice Assets Forfeiture Fund. The sums of money that can be raised for law-enforcement activities this way are substantial,[6] and the government's interest in using the profits of crime to fund these activities should not be discounted.

Second, the statute permits "rightful owners" of forfeited assets to make claims for forfeited assets before they are retained by the government. See 21 U.S.C. § 853(n)(6)(A). The government's interest in winning undiminished forfeiture thus includes the objective of returning property, in full, to those wrongfully deprived or defrauded of it. Where the government pursues this restitutionary end, the government's interest in forfeiture is virtually indistinguishable from its interest in returning to a bank the proceeds of a bank robbery; and a forfeiture-defendant's claim of right to use such assets to hire an attorney, instead of having them returned to their rightful owners, is no more persuasive than a bank robber's similar claim.

Finally, as we have recognized previously, a major purpose motivating congressional adoption and continued refinement of the RICO and CCE forfeiture provisions has been the desire to lessen the economic power of organized crime and drug enterprises. See Russello v. United States, 464 U.S. 16, 27–28 (1983). This includes the use of such economic power to retain private counsel. As the Court of Appeals put it: "Congress has already underscored the compelling public interest in stripping criminals such as Reckmeyer of their undeserved economic power, and part of that undeserved power may be the ability to command high-priced legal talent." The notion that the government has a legitimate interest in depriving criminals of economic power, even in so far as that power is used to retain counsel of choice, may be somewhat unsettling. But when a defendant claims that he has suffered some substantial impairment of his sixth amendment rights by virtue of the seizure or forfeiture of assets in his possession, such a complaint is no more than the reflection of "the harsh reality that the quality of a criminal defendant's representation frequently may turn on his ability to retain the best counsel money can buy." Morris v. Slappy, 461 U.S. 1, 23 (1983)(Brennan, J., concurring in result). Again, the Court of Appeals put it aptly: "The modern day Jean Valjean must be satisfied with appointed counsel. Yet the drug merchant claims that his possession of huge sums of money ... entitles him to something more. We reject this contention, and any notion of a constitutional right to use the proceeds of crime to finance an expensive defense."[7]

It is our view that there is a strong governmental interest in obtaining full recovery of all forfeitable assets, an interest that overrides any sixth

---

[6] For example, just one of the assets which Reckmeyer agreed to forfeit, a parcel of land known as "Shelburne Glebe," was recently sold by federal authorities for $5.3 million. Washington Post, May 10, 1989, p. D1, cols. 1–4. The proceeds of the sale will fund federal, state, and local law enforcement activities.

[7] We also reject the contention, advanced by amici that a type of "per se" ineffective assistance of counsel results—due to the particular complexity of RICO or drug-enterprise cases—when a defendant is not permitted to use assets in his possession to retain counsel of choice, and instead must rely on appointed counsel. If such an argument were accepted,

amendment interest in permitting criminals to use assets adjudged forfeitable to pay for their defense. Otherwise, there would be an interference with a defendant's sixth amendment rights whenever the government freezes or takes some property in a defendant's possession before, during or after a criminal trial. So-called "jeopardy assessments"—IRS seizures of assets to secure potential tax liabilities, see 26 U.S.C. § 6861—may impair a defendant's ability to retain counsel in a way similar to that complained of here. Yet these assessments have been upheld against constitutional attack, and we note that the respondent in *Monsanto* concedes their constitutionality. Moreover, petitioner's claim to a share of the forfeited assets postconviction would suggest that the government could never impose a burden on assets within a defendant's control that could be used to pay a lawyer.[9] Criminal defendants, however, are not exempted from federal, state, and local taxation simply because these financial levies may deprive them of resources that could be used to hire an attorney.

We therefore reject petitioner's claim of a sixth amendment right of criminal defendants to use assets that are the government's—assets adjudged forfeitable, as Reckmeyer's were—to pay attorneys' fees, merely because those assets are in their possession.[10] See also *Monsanto*, which rejects a similar claim with respect to pretrial orders and assets not yet judged forfeitable.

---

it would bar the trial of indigents charged with such offenses, because those persons would have to rely on appointed counsel—which this view considers per se ineffective.

If appointed counsel is ineffective in a particular case, a defendant has resort to the remedies discussed in Strickland v. Washington, 466 U.S. 668 (1984). But we cannot say that the sixth amendment's guarantee of effective assistance of counsel is a guarantee of a privately-retained counsel in every complex case, irrespective of a defendant's ability to pay.

[9] A myriad of other law-enforcement mechanisms operate in a manner similar to IRS jeopardy assessments, and might also be subjected to sixth amendment invalidation if petitioner's claim were accepted. See Kathleen F. Brickey, Attorneys' Fee Forfeitures, 36 Emory L. J. 761, 770–72 (1987).

[10] Petitioner advances three additional reasons for invalidating the forfeiture statute, all of which concern possible ethical conflicts created for lawyers defending persons facing forfeiture of assets in their possession.

Petitioner first notes the statute's exemption from forfeiture of property transferred to a bona fide purchaser who was "reasonably without cause to believe that the property was subject to forfeiture." 21

U.S.C. § 853(n)(6)(B). This provision, it is said, might give an attorney an incentive not to investigate a defendant's case as fully as possible, so that the lawyer can invoke it to protect from forfeiture any fees he has received. Yet given the requirement that any assets which the government wishes to have forfeited must be specified in the indictment, see Fed. Rule Crim. Proc. 7(c)(2), the only way a lawyer could be a beneficiary of § 853(n)(6)(B) would be to fail to read the indictment of his client. In this light, the prospect that a lawyer might find himself in conflict with his client, by seeking to take advantage of § 853(n)(6)(B), amounts to very little. Petitioner itself concedes that such a conflict will, as a practical matter, never arise: a defendant's "lawyer ... could not demonstrate that he was 'reasonably without cause to believe that the property was subject to forfeiture,'" petitioner concludes at one point.

The second possible conflict arises in plea bargaining: petitioner posits that a lawyer may advise a client to accept an agreement entailing a mere harsh prison sentence but no forfeiture—even where contrary to the client's interests—in an effort to preserve the lawyer's fee. Following such a strategy, however, would surely constitute ineffective assis-

B

Petitioner's second constitutional claim is that the forfeiture statute is invalid under the due process clause of the fifth amendment because it permits the government to upset the "balance of forces between the accused and his accuser." Wardius v. Oregon, 412 U.S. 470, 474 (1973). We are not sure that this contention adds anything to petitioner's sixth amendment claim, because, while "[t]he Constitution guarantees a fair trial through the due process clauses . . . it defines the basic elements of a fair trial largely through the several provisions of the sixth amendment," Strickland v. Washington, 466 U.S. 668, 684–85 (1984). We have concluded above that the sixth amendment is not offended by the forfeiture provisions at issue here. Even if, however, the fifth amendment provides some added protection not encompassed in the sixth amendment's more specific provisions, we find petitioner's claim based on the fifth amendment unavailing.

Forfeiture provisions are powerful weapons in the war crime; like any such weapons, their impact can be devastating when used unjustly. But due process claims alleging such abuses are cognizable only in specific cases of prosecutorial misconduct (and petitioner has made no such allegation here) or when directed to a rule that is inherently unconstitutional. "The fact that the . . . act might operate unconstitutionally under some conceivable set of circumstances is insufficient to render it . . . invalid," United States v. Salerno, 481 U.S. 739, 745 (1987). Petitioner's claim—that the power available to prosecutors under the statute *could* be abused—proves too much, for many tools available to prosecutors can be misused in a way that violates the rights of innocent persons. As the Court of Appeals put it, in rejecting this claim when advanced below: "Every criminal law carries with it the potential for abuse, but a potential for abuse does not require a finding of facial invalidity."

We rejected a claim similar to petitioner's last Term, in Wheat v. United States, 486 U.S. 153 (1988). In *Wheat*, the petitioner argued that permitting a court to disqualify a defendant's chosen counsel because of

---

tance of counsel. We see no reason why our cases such as Strickland v. Washington, 466 U.S. 668 (1984), are inadequate to deal with any such ineffectiveness where it arises. In any event, there is no claim that such conduct occurred here, nor could there be, as Reckmeyer's plea agreement included forfeiture of virtually every asset in his possession. Moreover, we rejected a claim similar to this one in Evans v. Jeff D., 475 U.S. 717, 727–28 (1986).

Finally, petitioner argues that the forfeiture statute, in operation, will create a system akin to "contingency fees" for defense lawyers: only a defense lawyer who wins acquittal for his client will be able to collect his fees, and contingent fees in criminal cases are generally considered unethical. See ABA Model Rules of Professional Conduct, Rule 1.5(d)(2) (1983); ABA Model Code of Professional Responsibility DR 2–106(C)(1979). But there is no indication here that petitioner, or any other firm, has actually sought to charge a defendant on a contingency basis; rather the claim is that a law firm's prospect of collecting its fee may turn on the outcome at trial. This, however, may often be the case in criminal defense work. Nor is it clear why permitting contingent fees in criminal cases—if that is what the forfeiture statute does—violates a criminal defendant's sixth amendment rights. The fact that a federal statutory scheme authorizing contingency fees—again, if that is what Congress has created in § 853 (a premise we doubt)—is at odds with model disciplinary rules or state disciplinary codes hardly renders the federal statute invalid.

conflicts of interest—over that defendant's objection to the disqualification—would encourage the government to "manufacture" such conflicts to deprive a defendant of his chosen attorney. While acknowledging that this was possible, we declined to fashion the per se constitutional rule petitioner sought in *Wheat*, instead observing that "trial courts are undoubtedly aware of [the] possibility" of abuse, and would have to "take it into consideration," when dealing with disqualification motions.

A similar approach should be taken here. The Constitution does not forbid the imposition of an otherwise permissible criminal sanction, such as forfeiture, merely because in some cases prosecutors may abuse the processes available to them, e.g., by attempting to impose them on persons who should not be subjected to that punishment. Cases involving particular abuses can be dealt with individually by the lower courts, when (and if) any such cases arise.

IV

For the reasons given above, we find that petitioner's statutory and constitutional challenges to the forfeiture imposed here are without merit. The judgment of the Court of Appeals is therefore

Affirmed.

■ JUSTICE BLACKMUN, with whom JUSTICE BRENNAN, JUSTICE MARSHALL, and JUSTICE STEVENS join, dissenting.

[Justice Blackmun's dissent in *Monsanto*, supra, is also applicable to *Caplin & Drysdale*.]

NOTE ON FORFEITURE AND THE RIGHT TO COUNSEL

What did Justice Blackmun mean when, in footnote 13 of his *Monsanto* dissent, he wrote, in connection with his argument that the government should not be allowed to "outspend" its adversaries: "That the government has this power when the defendant is indigent is unfortunate, but '[i]t is an irrelevancy once recognized'"? Is there any merit to the majority's view that it cannot possibly violate the sixth amendment for the government to reduce non-indigent defendants whose assets are subject to forfeiture to the same status, with respect to their enjoyment of the right to counsel, as indigent defendants? In other words, if it does not violate the sixth amendment rights of indigent defendants to require them to accept appointed counsel, then how can it violate the sixth amendment rights of the defendants in *Monsanto* and *Caplin & Drysdale* for the government to force them to suffer the same fate?

SUBSECTION D: FORFEITURE AND THE FIRST AMENDMENT

Fort Wayne Books, Inc. v. Indiana

Supreme Court of the United States, 1989.
489 U.S. 46.

■ JUSTICE WHITE delivered the opinion of the Court.

We have before us two decisions of the Indiana courts, involving the applications of that State's Racketeer Influenced and Corrupt Organizations (RICO) and Civil Remedies for Racketeering (CRRA) Acts to cases involving bookstores containing allegedly obscene materials.

I

The two causes before us arise from wholly unrelated incidents.

A

Petitioner in No. 87–470, Fort Wayne Books, Inc., and two other corporations[1] each operated an "adult bookstore" in Fort Wayne, Indiana. On March 19, 1984, the state of Indiana and a local prosecutor, respondents here, filed a civil action against the three corporations and certain of their employees alleging that defendants had engaged in a pattern of racketeering activity by repeatedly violating the state laws barring the distribution of obscene books and films, thereby violating the state's RICO law.[2] The complaint recited 39 criminal convictions for selling obscene publications from the three stores. It was also alleged that there were currently other obscene materials available for sale in the stores. The proceeds from the sales of obscene materials, it was alleged, were being used to operate and maintain the bookstores. Respondents sought civil injunctive relief to bar further racketeering violations, invoking the State's Civil Remedies for Racketeering Activity (CRRA) statute, Ind. Code. § 34–430.5–1 et. seq. (1982 and Supp. 1987). Among the remedies requested in the complaint was forfeiture of all Fort Wayne Books' property, real and personal, that "was used in the course of, intended for use in the course of, derived from, or realized through" petitioner's "racketeering activity." Such forfeiture is authorized by the CRRA. Ind. Code. § 34–4–30.5–3(a)(1982).

Respondents also moved, in a separate "Verified Petition for Seizure of Property Subject to Forfeiture," for the particular judicial order that is the subject of our consideration here. Specifically, respondents asked the Allen County Circuit Court "to immediately seize ... all property 'subject to forfeiture' as set forth in [the CRRA] complaint." Such pretrial seizures are authorized under Ind. Code. § 34–4–30.5–3(b)(1982), which empowers prosecutors bringing CRRA actions to move for immediate seizure of the property subject to forfeiture, and permits courts to issue seizure orders "upon a showing of probable cause to believe that a violation of [the State's RICO law] involving the property in question has occurred." The seizure petition was supported by an affidavit executed by a local police officer,

---

[1] In addition to petitioner Fort Wayne Books, Inc., the Fort Wayne proceedings involved two other corporations: Cinema Blue of Fort Wayne, Inc., and Erotica House Bookstore, Inc.

These other entities did not seek certiorari or enter an appearance in this Court.

We therefore deal only with the claims and issues raised by Fort Wayne Books, Inc.

[2] A 1984 amendment to the state RICO law had added obscenity violations to the list of predicate offenses deemed to constitute "racketeering activity" under Indiana law. See Ind. Code § 35–45–6–1 (Supp. 1987).

recounting the 39 criminal convictions involving the defendants, further describing various other books and films available for sale at petitioner's bookstores and believed by affiant to be obscene, and alleging a conspiracy among several of petitioner's employees and officers who had previous convictions for obscenity offenses.

The trial court, ex parte, heard testimony in support of the petition and had supporting exhibits before it. On the same day, the court entered an order finding that probable cause existed to conclude that Fort Wayne Books was violating the State RICO law, and directing the immediate seizure of the real estate, publications and other personal property comprising each of the three bookstores operated by the corporate defendants. The court's order authorized the County Sheriff to padlock the stores. This was done, and a few days later, the contents of the stores were hauled away by law enforcement officials. No trial date on the CRRA complaint was ever set.

Following the March 1984 seizure of the bookstores, Fort Wayne Books sought to vacate the ex parte seizure order. An adversarial hearing on a motion to vacate the order based on federal constitutional grounds failed to yield relief. Other efforts to obtain some measure of relief also failed. The trial court did, however, certify the constitutional issues to the Indiana Court of Appeals. In June 1985, that court held that the relevant RICO/ CRRA provisions were violative of the U.S. Constitution. The Indiana Supreme Court reversed, upholding the constitutionality of the CRRA statute as a general proposition and the pretrial seizure of Fort Wayne Books' stores as a specific matter.

We granted Fort Wayne's petition for certiorari for the purpose of considering the substantial constitutional issues raised by the pretrial seizure.

B

In No. 87–614, an investigation of adult bookstores in Howard County, Indiana, led prosecutors there, in April 1985, to charge petitioner Sappenfield with six counts of distribution of obscene matter, in violation of Ind. Code § 35–49–3–1 (Supp. 1987). In addition, employing the 1984 amendments to the Indiana RICO statute discussed above, prosecutors used these alleged predicate acts of obscenity as a basis for filing two charges of RICO violations against petitioner. The obscenity charges were Class A Misdemeanors under Indiana law, the racketeering offenses Class C felonies.

The trial court dismissed the two RICO counts on the ground that the RICO statute was unconstitutionally vague as applied to obscenity predicate offenses. The Indiana Court of Appeals reversed, and reinstated the charges against petitioner. Relying on the Indiana Supreme Court's opinion under review here in No. 87–470, the Court of Appeals held that "Indiana's RICO statute is not unconstitutional as applied to the state's obscenity statute." The Indiana Supreme Court declined to review this holding of the Indiana Court of Appeals.

We granted certiorari and consolidated this case with No. 87–470, to consider the common and separate issues presented by both cases.

II

Since it involves challenges to the constitutionality of the Indiana RICO statute, we deal first with No. 87–614.

As noted above, petitioner was charged with six substantive obscenity violations and two RICO offenses. Petitioner challenged only the latter charges, raising no objection to the obscenity indictments. He makes no claim here that the Constitution bars a criminal prosecution for distributing obscene materials.[4] Rather, petitioner's claim is that certain particulars of the Indiana RICO law render the prosecution of petitioner under *that* statute unconstitutional. Petitioner advances several specific attacks on the RICO statute.

A

Before we address the merits of petitioner's claims we must first consider our jurisdiction to hear this case. . . .

[The Court upheld its jurisdiction. The problem was the limitation in 28 U.S.C. § 1257 of Supreme Court review of state court decisions to "[f]inal judgments or decrees" by the highest court of the state eligible to hear the case. "The general rule," the Court said, "is that finality in the context of a criminal prosecution is defined by a judgment of conviction and the imposition of a sentence." Since neither was present in this case, the normal assumption would be that the case was unreviewable at this stage. But it fit within an exception, one of four articulated in Cox Broadcasting Corp. v. Cohn, 420 U.S. 469, 482–83 (1975):

> "[W]here the federal issue has been finally decided in the state courts with further proceedings pending in which the party seeking review here might prevail on the merits on nonfederal grounds, thus rendering unnecessary review of the federal issue by this Court, and where reversal of the state court on the federal issue would be preclusive of any further litigation on the relevant cause of action . . . in the state court proceedings still to come. In these circumstances, if a refusal immediately to review the state-court decision might seriously erode federal policy, the Court has entertained and decided the federal issue, which itself has been finally determined by the state courts for the purposes of the state litigation."

The Court said that "[a]djudicating the proper scope of first amendment protections has often been recognized by this Court as a 'federal policy'

---

[4] The constitutionality of criminal sanctions against those who distribute obscene materials is well established by our prior cases. See, e.g., Pinkus v. United States, 436 U.S. 293, 303–04 (1978); Splawn v. Califor-nia, 431 U.S. 595, 597–99 (1977); Miller v. California, 413 U.S. 15, 23–26 (1973); Kingsley Books, Inc. v. Brown, 354 U.S. 436, 441 (1957).

that merits application of an exception to the general finality rule." Since the petitioner's "challenge to the constitutionality of the use of RICO statutes to criminalize patterns of obscenity offenses calls into question the legitimacy of the law enforcement practices of several states, as well as the federal government", "[r]esolution of this important issue of the possible limits the first amendment places on state and federal efforts to control organized crime should not remain in doubt." The Court added in a footnote that the "federal RICO statute also permits prosecutions for a pattern of obscenity violations" and that the outcome of the case thus could determine the constitutionality of future federal prosecutions.]

B

Petitioner's broadest contention is that the Constitution forbids the use of obscenity violations as predicate acts for a RICO conviction. Petitioner's argument in this regard is twofold: first, that the Indiana RICO law, as applied to an "enterprise" that has allegedly distributed obscene materials, is unconstitutionally vague: and second, that the potential punishments available under the RICO law are so severe that the statute lacks a "necessary sensitivity to first amendment rights." We consider each of these arguments in turn.

(1)

The "racketeering activities" forbidden by the Indiana RICO law are a "pattern" of multiple violations of certain substantive crimes, of which distributing obscenity is one. Thus, the RICO statute at issue wholly incorporates the state obscenity law by reference.

Petitioner argues that the "inherent vagueness" of the standards established by Miller v. California, 413 U.S. 15 (1973), are at the root of his objection to any RICO prosecution based on predicate acts of obscenity. Yet, this nothing less than an invitation to overturn *Miller*—an invitation that we reject. And we note that the Indiana obscenity statute, Ind. Code § 35–49–1–1 et seq. (Supp. 1987), is closely tailored to conform to the *Miller* standards. Moreover, petitioner's motion to dismiss the RICO charges in the trial court rested on the alleged vagueness of *that* statute, and not any alleged defect in the underlying obscenity law.

We find no merit in petitioner's claim that the Indiana RICO law is unconstitutionally vague as applied to obscenity predicate offenses. Given that the RICO statute totally encompasses the obscenity law, if the latter is not unconstitutionally vague, the former cannot be vague either. At petitioner's forthcoming trial, the prosecution will have to prove beyond a reasonable doubt each element of the alleged RICO offense, including the allegation that petitioner violated (or attempted or conspired to violate) the Indiana obscenity law. Thus, petitioner cannot be convicted of violating the RICO law without first being "found guilty" of two counts of distributing (or attempting to, or conspiring to, distribute) obscene materials.

It is true, as petitioner argues, that the punishments available in a RICO prosecution are different from those for obscenity violations. But we fail to see how this difference renders the RICO statute void for *vagueness*.[7]

(2)

Petitioner's next contention rests on the difference between the sanctions imposed on obscenity law violators and those imposed on convicted "racketeers": the sanctions imposed on RICO violators are so "draconian," that they have an improper chilling effect on First Amendment freedoms, petitioner contends. The use of such "heavy artillery" from the "war on crime" against obscenity is improper, petitioner argues, and therefore, obscenity offenses should not be permitted to be used as predicate acts for RICO purposes.

It is true that the criminal penalties for a RICO violation under Indiana law, a Class C felony, are more severe than those authorized for an obscenity offense, a Class A misdemeanor. Specifically, if petitioner is found guilty of the two RICO counts against him, he faces a maximum sentence of 10 years in prison and a $20,000 fine; if petitioner were convicted instead of only the six predicate obscenity offenses charged in the indictments, the maximum punishment he could face would be six years in jail and $30,000 in fines. While the RICO punishment is obviously greater than that for obscenity violations, we do not perceive any constitutionally significant difference between the two potential punishments.[8] Indeed, the Indiana RICO provisions in this respect function quite similarly to an enhanced sentencing scheme for multiple obscenity violations. As such, "[i]t is not for this Court . . . to limit the state in resorting to various weapons in the armory of the law." Kingsley Books, Inc. v. Brown, 354 U.S. 436, 441 (1957).

It may be true that the stiffer RICO penalties will provide an additional deterrent to those who might otherwise sell obscene materials; perhaps this means—as petitioner suggests—that some cautious booksellers will practice self-censorship and remove first amendment protected materials from their shelves. But deterrence of the sale of obscene materials is a legitimate end of state anti-obscenity laws, and our cases have long recognized the practical reality that "any form of criminal obscenity statute applicable to a bookseller will induce some tendency to self-censorship and have some inhibitory effect on the dissemination of material not obscene."

---

[7] Indeed, because the scope of the Indiana RICO law is more limited than the scope of the state's obscenity statute—with obscenity-related RICO prosecutions possible only where one is guilty of a "pattern" of obscenity violation—it would seem that the RICO statute is inherently *less* vague than any state obscenity law: a prosecution under the RICO law will be possible only where all the elements of an obscenity offense are present, and then some.

[8] We have in the past upheld the constitutionality of statutes that provide criminal penalties for obscenity offenses that are not significantly different from those provided in the Indiana RICO law. See, e.g., Smith v. United States, 431 U.S. 291, 296, n. 3 (1977)(5–year prison term and $5,000 fine for first offense; 10–year term and $10,000 fine for each subsequent violation); Ginzburg v. United States, 383 U.S. 463, 464–65, n. 2 (1966)(5–year prison term and $5,000 fine).

Smith v. California, 361 U.S. 147, 154–55 (1959). The mere assertion of some possible self-censorship resulting from a statute is not enough to render an anti-obscenity law unconstitutional under our precedents.

Petitioner further raises the question of whether the civil sanctions available against RICO violations—under the CRRA—are so severe as to render the RICO statute itself unconstitutional. However, this contention is not ripe, since the state has not sought any civil penalties in this case. These claims can only be reviewed when (or if) such remedies are enforced against petitioner.

Consequently, we find no constitutional bar to the state's inclusion of substantive obscenity violations among the predicate offenses under its RICO statute.

C

Finally, petitioner advances two narrower objections to the application of the Indiana RICO statute in obscenity-related prosecutions.

(1)

First, petitioner contends that even if the statute is constitutional on its face, "the first amendment ... requires that predicate obscenity offenses must be affirmed convictions on successive dates ... in the same jurisdiction as that where the RICO charge is brought."

We find no constitutional basis for the claim that the alleged predicate acts used in a RICO/obscenity prosecution must be "affirmed convictions." We rejected a like contention, albeit in dicta, when considering a case under the federal RICO statute. See Sedima, S.P.R.L. v. Imrex Co., 473 U.S. 479, 488 (1985). We see no reason for a different rule where the alleged predicate acts are obscenity. As long as the standard of proof is the proper one with respect to all of the elements of the RICO allegation—including proof, beyond a reasonable doubt, of the requisite number of constitutionally-proscribable predicate acts—all of the relevant constitutional requirements have been met. The analogy suggested by the Solicitor General in his amicus brief is apt: "This Court has never required a state to fire warning shots, in the form of misdemeanor prosecutions, before it may bring felony charges for distributing obscene materials." We likewise decline to impose such a "warning shot" requirement here.

The second aspect of this claim—that all of the predicate offenses charged must have occurred in the jurisdiction where the RICO indictment is brought—also lacks merit. This contention must be rejected in this case, if for no other reason than the fact that all of petitioner's alleged predicate acts of distributing obscenity *did* take place in the same jurisdiction (Howard County) where the RICO prosecution was initiated; petitioner lacks standing to advance this claim on these facts. More significantly, petitioner's suggestion fails because such a rule would essentially turn the RICO statute on its head: barring RICO prosecutions of large national enterprises that commit single predicate offenses in numerous jurisdictions, for example.

Of course, petitioner is correct when he argues that "community standards" may vary from jurisdiction to jurisdiction where different predicate obscenity offenses allegedly were committed. But as long as, for example, each previous obscenity conviction was measured by the appropriate community's standard, we see no reason why the RICO prosecution—alleging a pattern of such violations—may take place only in a jurisdiction where two or more such offenses have occurred.

(2)

Second, petitioner contends that he should have been provided with a prompt adversarial hearing, shortly after his arrest, on the question of the obscenity of the materials he allegedly distributed.

This contention lacks merit for several reasons. First, it does not appear that petitioner requested such a hearing below. Second, unlike No. 87–470, in this case, there was no seizure of any books or films owned by petitioner. The only expressive materials "seized" by Howard County officials in this case were a few items purchased by police officers in connection with their investigation of petitioner's stores. We have previously rejected the argument that such purchases trigger constitutional concerns. See Maryland v. Macon, 472 U.S. 463, 468–71 (1985).

We consequently affirm the judgment in No. 87–614.

III

We reverse, however, the judgment in No. 87–470 sustaining the pretrial seizure order.

In a line of cases dating back to Marcus v. Search Warrant, 367 U.S. 717 (1961), this Court has repeatedly held that rigorous procedural safeguards must be employed before expressive materials can be seized as "obscene." In *Marcus*, and again in A Quantity of Books v. Kansas, 378 U.S. 205 (1964), the Court invalidated large-scale confiscations of books and films, where numerous copies of selected books were seized without a prior adversarial hearing on their obscenity. In those cases, and the ones that immediately came after them, the Court established that pretrial seizures of expressive materials could only be undertaken pursuant to a "procedure 'designed to focus searchingly on the question of obscenity.' "

We refined that approach further in our subsequent decisions. Most importantly, in Heller v. New York, 413 U.S. 483, 492 (1973), the Court noted that "seizing films to destroy them or to block their distribution or exhibition is a very different matter from seizing a single copy of a film for the bona fide purpose of preserving it as evidence in a criminal proceeding." As a result, we concluded that until there was a "judicial determination of the obscenity issue in an adversary proceeding," exhibition of a film could not be restrained by seizing all the available copies of it. The same is obviously true for books or any other expressive materials. While a single copy of a book or film may be seized and retained for evidentiary purposes based on a finding of probable cause, the publication may not be taken out of circulation completely until there has been a determination of obscenity after an adversary hearing.

Thus, while the general rule under the fourth amendment is that any and all contraband, instrumentalities, and evidence of crimes may be seized on probable cause (and even without a warrant in various circumstances), it is otherwise when materials presumptively protected by the first amendment are involved. It is "[t]he risk of prior restraint, which is the underlying basis for the special fourth amendment protections accorded searches for and seizure of first amendment materials" that motivates this rule. *Maryland v. Macon*, supra, at 470. These same concerns render invalid the pre-trial seizure at issue here.[9]

In its decision below, the Indiana Supreme Court did not challenge our precedents, or the limitations on seizures that our decisions in this area have established. Rather, the court found those rules largely inapplicable in this case. The court noted that the alleged predicate offenses included 39 convictions for violating the state's obscenity laws[10] and observed that the pretrial seizures (which were made in strict accordance with Indiana law), were not based on the nature or suspected obscenity of the contents of the items seized, but upon the neutral ground that the sequestered property represented assets used and acquired in the course of racketeering activity. The remedy of forfeiture is intended not to restrain the future distribution of presumptively protected speech but rather to disgorge assets acquired through racketeering activity. Stated simply, it is "irrelevant whether assets derived from an alleged violation of the RICO statute are or are not obscene." The court also specifically rejected petitioner's claim that the legislative inclusion of violations of obscenity laws as a form of racketeering activity was "merely a semantic device intended to circumvent well-established first amendment doctrine." The assets seized were subject to forfeiture "if the elements of a pattern of racketeering activity are shown;" there being probable cause to believe this was the case here, the pretrial seizure was permissible, the Indiana Supreme Court concluded.

We do not question the holding of the court below that adding obscenity-law violations to the list of RICO predicate crimes was not a mere ruse to sidestep the first amendment. And for the purpose of disposing of this case, we assume without deciding that bookstores and their contents are forfeitable (like other property such as a bank account or a yacht) where it is proved that these items are property actually used in, or derived

---

[9] ... Because we dispose of petitioner's claims on first amendment grounds, we need not reach any due process questions that may be involved in this case.

[10] Respondent suggested at argument that the fact that petitioner (and/or those employed by petitioner) had numerous prior *convictions* for obscenity offenses sufficed to justify this pretrial seizure even if it were otherwise impermissible. But the state trial court did not purport to impose the seizure as a punishment for the past criminal acts (even if such a punishment were permissible under the first amendment). Instead, as noted above, the seizure was undertaken to prevent future violations of Indiana's RICO laws; as a prospective, pretrial seizure, it was required to comply with the *Marcus* line of cases, which (as we explain below) it did not.

from, a pattern of violations of the state's obscenity laws.[11] Even with these assumptions, though, we find the seizure at issue here unconstitutional. It is incontestable that these proceedings were begun to put an end to the sale of obscenity at the three bookstores named in the complaint, and hence we are quite sure that the special rules applicable to removing first amendment materials from circulation are relevant here. This includes specifically the admonition that probable cause to believe that there are valid grounds for seizure is insufficient to interrupt the sale of presumptively protected books and films.

Here there was not—and has not been—any determination that the seized items were "obscene" or that a RICO violation *has occurred*. True, the predicate crimes on which the seizure order was based had been adjudicated and are unchallenged. But the petition for seizure and the hearing thereon were aimed at establishing no more than *probable cause to believe* that a RICO violation had occurred, and the order for seizure recited no more than probable cause in that respect. As noted above, our cases firmly hold that mere probable cause to believe a legal violation has transpired is not adequate to remove books or films from circulation. The elements of a RICO violation other than the predicate crimes remain to be established in this case; e.g., whether the obscenity violations by the three corporations or their employees established a pattern of racketeering activity, and whether the assets seized were forfeitable under the State's CRRA statute. Therefore, the pretrial seizure at issue here was improper.

The fact that the respondent's motion for seizure was couched as one under the Indiana RICO law—instead of being brought under the substantive obscenity statute—is unavailing. As far back as the decision in Near v. Minnesota, 283 U.S. 697, 720–21 (1931), this Court has recognized that the way in which a restraint on speech is "characterized" under state law is of little consequence. ... While we accept the Indiana Supreme Court's finding that Indiana's RICO law is not "pretextual" as applied to obscenity offenses; it is true that the state cannot escape the constitutional safeguards of our prior cases by merely recategorizing a pattern of obscenity violations as "racketeering."

At least where the RICO violation claimed is a pattern of racketeering that can be established only by rebutting the presumption that expressive materials are protected by the first amendment,[12] that presumption is not rebutted until the claimed justification for seizing books or other publications is properly established in an adversary proceeding. Here, literally thousands of books and films were carried away and taken out of circula-

---

[11] Contrary to petitioner's urging, we do not reach the question of the constitutionality of post-trial forfeiture—or any other civil post-trial sanction authorized by the Indiana RICO/CRRA laws—in this context. None of the cases before us involves such a forfeiture, and we see no reason to depart from our usual practice of deciding only "concrete legal issues, presented in actual cases...." See Public Workers v. Mitchell, 330 U.S. 75, 89 (1947).

[12] We do not hold today that the pretrial seizure of petitioner's nonexpressive property was invalid. Petitioner did not challenge this aspect of the seizure here.

tion by the pretrial order. Yet it remained to be proved whether the seizure was actually warranted under the Indiana CRRA and RICO statutes. If we are to maintain the regard for first amendment values expressed in our prior decisions dealing with interrupting the flow of expressive materials, the judgment of the Indiana Court must be reversed.[13]

IV

For the reason given above, the judgment in No. 87–470 is reversed, and the case is remanded for further proceedings. The judgment in No. 87–614 is affirmed, and it too is remanded for further proceedings.

It is so ordered.

■ JUSTICE BLACKMUN, concurring in part and concurring in the judgment.

Although I agree with Justice O'Connor in her conclusion that the *Sappenfield* case, No. 87–614, is not properly here under 28 U.S.C. § 1257, a majority of the Court has decided otherwise. This majority on the jurisdictional issue, however, is divided 4 to 3 on the merits of the question presented in *Sappenfield*: whether the distribution of constitutionally obscene materials may be punished as predicate acts of a racketeering offense. Disposition of the case deserves—if not requires—a majority of participating Justices.

Thus, notwithstanding my dissenting jurisdictional view, I feel obligated to reach the merits in *Sappenfield*. Because I agree that what may be punished under Miller v. California, 413 U.S. 15 (1973), may form the basis of a racketeering conviction, I join Justice White's opinion (except for Part II–A) and the judgment of the Court.

■ JUSTICE O'CONNOR, concurring in part and dissenting in part.

Because I believe that this Court does not have jurisdiction to hear the petition in Sappenfield v. Indiana, No. 87–614 (*Sappenfield*), I dissent from the Court's disposition of Fort Wayne Books, Inc. v. Indiana, No. 87–470 (*Fort Wayne Books*), which presents, among others, the same question as presented in *Sappenfield*.

Petitioners Sappenfield and his bookstore corporations, Fantasy One, Inc. and Fantasy Two, Inc., have yet to be tried or convicted on the Racketeer Influenced and Corrupt Organizations (RICO) counts brought them by the state of Indiana. Petitioners' motion to dismiss the RICO counts and the state's subsequent appeal were, therefore, interlocutory. Except in limited circumstances, this Court has jurisdiction only to review final judgments rendered by the highest court of the state in which decision may be had. [Justice O'Connor's reasons for finding none of the exceptions to the finality requirement applicable are omitted. She concluded

---

[13] Although it is of no direct significance, we note that the federal government—which has a RICO statute similar to Indiana's, 18 U.S.C. § 1961 et seq.—does not pursue pre-trial seizure of expressive materials in its RICO actions against "adult bookstores" or like operations. See Brief for United States as Amicus Curiae 15, n.12.

that she] would dismiss the writ of certiorari in *Sappenfield* for want of jurisdiction.

The petition in *Fort Wayne Books* is also from an interlocutory appeal to the Indiana appellate courts. In this case, however, pre-trial sanctions have already been imposed on petitioners. Where first amendment interests are actually affected, we have held that such interlocutory orders are immediately reviewable by this Court. National Socialist Party of America v. Skokie, 432 U.S. 43 (1977)(per curiam). Although *Fort Wayne Books* is a civil action brought under Indiana's Civil Remedies for Racketeering Activity statute, such civil actions depend on pre-existing violations of the State's criminal RICO statute. Consequently, the question presented in *Sappenfield*—whether violations of Indiana's obscenity statute may be predicate acts for charges brought under the state's criminal RICO statute—is also presented in *Fort Wayne Books*. Were it unconstitutional for Indiana to include obscenity violations among possible predicate acts for RICO violations, the civil remedies sought in *Fort Wayne Books* would be equally invalid. I fully agree with the Court's disposition of this question as it applies to *Fort Wayne Books*. There is "no constitutional bar to the state's inclusion of substantive obscenity violations among the predicate offenses under its RICO statute." I also agree and concur with the Court's statement of the cases in Part I and its disposition in part III of the separate questions presented in *Fort Wayne Books*.

■ JUSTICE STEVENS, with whom JUSTICE BRENNAN and JUSTICE MARSHALL join, dissenting in No. 87–614, and concurring in part and dissenting in part in No. 87–470.

The Court correctly decides that we have jurisdiction and that the pretrial seizures to which petitioners in No. 87–470 were subjected are unconstitutional. But by refusing to evaluate Indiana's Racketeer Influenced and Corrupt Organizations (RICO) and Civil Remedies for Racketeering Activity (CRRA) statutes as an interlinked whole, the Court otherwise reaches the wrong result.

It is true that a bare majority of the Court has concluded that delivery of obscene messages to consenting adults may be prosecuted as a crime.[1]

[1] Each of the cases the Court cites to demonstrate that this proposition is "well established," ante, at n.4, was decided by a 5–4 vote. ...In Splawn v. California, 431 U.S. 595 (1977), and Pinkus v. United States, 436 U.S. 293 (1978), Justices Brennan, Stewart, Marshall, and Stevens expressed the opinion that criminal prosecution for obscenity-related offenses violates the first amendment.

In 1970, moreover, the President's Commission on Obscenity and Pornography advocated that laws regulating adults' access to sexually explicit materials be repealed. Report of The Commission on Obscenity and

Pornography 51–56 (1970). The most recent federal pornography commission disagreed with this conclusion yet acknowledged that scholarly comment generally agrees with the dissenters:

"Numerous people, in both oral and written evidence, have urged upon us the view that the Supreme Court's approach is a mistaken interpretation of the first amendment. They have argued that we should conclude that any criminal prosecution based on the distribution to consenting adults of sexually explicit material, no matter how offensive to some, and no matter how hardcore, and no matter how devoid of literary,

The Indiana Legislature has done far more than that: by injecting offenses into a statutory scheme designed to curtail an entirely different kind of antisocial conduct, it has not only enhanced criminal penalties, but also authorized wide-ranging civil sanctions against both protected and unprotected speech. In my judgment there is a vast difference between the conclusion that a state may proscribe the distribution of obscene materials and the notion that this legislation can survive constitutional scrutiny.

I

At the outset it is important to identify the limited nature of the "racketeering activity" alleged in No. 87–614. Petitioners are accused of selling to the same willing purchaser three obscene magazines in each of two stores. There is no charge that anyone engaged in any sexual misconduct on petitioners' premises, that petitioners displayed or advertised their inventory in an offensive way, that children were given access to any of their publications or films, or that they foisted any obscene messages upon unwilling recipients. There is no claim that petitioners' bookstores are public nuisances operating in inappropriate places, manners, or times.

In Indiana, the sale of an obscene magazine is a misdemeanor. A person who commits two such misdemeanors, however, engages in a "pattern of racketeering activity" as defined in the State's RICO statute.[8] If by means of that pattern the person acquires, maintains, or otherwise operates an "enterprise,"[9] he or she commits the Indiana felony of "cor-

artistic, political, or scientific value, is impermissible under the first amendment.

"We have taken these arguments seriously. In light of the facts that the Supreme Court did not in Roth [v. United States, 354 U.S. 476 (1957)] or since unanimously conclude that obscenity is outside of the coverage of the first amendment, and that its 1973 rulings were all decided by a scant 5–4 majority on this issue, there is no doubt that the issue was debatable within the Supreme Court, and thus could hardly be without difficulty. Moreover, we recognize that the bulk of scholarly commentary is of the opinion that the Supreme Court's resolution of and basic approach to the first amendment issues is incorrect." 1 Attorney General's Commission on Pornography, Final Report 260–61 (July 1986)(hereinafter Report).

[8] Indiana Code § 35–45–6–1, entitled "Racketeer Influenced and Corrupt Organizations," provides in part:

" 'Pattern of racketeering activity' means engaging in at least two (2) incidents of racketeering activity that have the same or similar intent, result, accomplice, victim, or method of commission, or that otherwise interrelated by distin-

guishing characteristics that are not isolated incidents. . . .

" 'Racketeering activity' means to commit, to attempt to commit, or to conspire to commit . . . a violation of IC 35–49–3; murder (IC 35–42–1–1); battery as a Class C felony (IC 35–42–2–1); kidnapping (IC 35–42–3–2); child exploitation (IC 35–42–4–4); robbery (IC 35–42–5–1); arson (IC 35–43–1–1); burglary (IC 35–43–2–1); theft (IC 35–43–4–2); receiving stolen property (IC 35–43–4–2). . . ."

This enumeration of predicate offenses inexplicably omits a parenthetical description of Ind. Code § 35–49–3. That latter statute is Indiana's current obscenity law, which makes it a misdemeanor to disseminate or distribute matter that is obscene or harmful to minors, or to present a performance that is obscene or harmful to minors.

[9] The term "enterprise" is defined in both the Racketeer Influenced and Corrupt Organizations (RICO) Act and the Civil Remedies for Racketeering Activity (CRRA) Act to include a sole proprietorship and a corporation. Thus, each of the stores at which obscenity offenses allegedly occurred is an enterprise within the meaning of Indiana RICO.

rupt business influence."[10]   Thus does Indiana's RICO act transform two obscenity misdemeanors into a felony punishable by up to eight years of imprisonment.[11]

Proof of a RICO violation further exposes a defendant to the civil sanctions prescribed in the CRRA Act, including an order dissolving the enterprise, forfeiting its property to the state, and enjoining the defendant from engaging in the same type of business in the future.   Ind. Code §§ 34–4–30.5–2 to 34–4–30.5–4 (1982).   Thus, even if only a small fraction of the activities of the enterprise is unlawful, the state may close the entire business, seize its inventory, and bar its owner from engaging in his or her chosen line of work.

In its decision upholding the constitutionality of the Indiana RICO/ CRRA scheme, the Indiana Supreme Court expressly approved the civil remedies as well as the criminal sanctions, and unequivocally rejected the suggestion that the nature of a business or of its assets should affect a court's remedial powers.   It categorically stated that if the elements of a pattern of racketeering activity have been proved, all of a bookstore's expressive materials, obscene or not, are subject to forfeiture.[13]

[10] Indiana Code § 35–45–6–2(a)(1982) provides that a "person":

"(1) who has knowingly or intentionally received any proceeds directly or indirectly derived from a pattern of racketeering activity, and who uses or invests those proceeds or the proceeds derived from them to acquire an interest in real property or to establish or to operate an enterprise;

"(2) who through a pattern of racketeering activity, knowingly or intentionally acquires or maintains, either directly or indirectly, an interest in or control of real property or an enterprise; or

"(3) who is employed by or associated with an enterprise, and who knowingly or intentionally conducts or otherwise participates in the activities of that enterprise through a pattern of racketeering activity;

"commits corrupt business influence, a Class C felony."

[11] Under Indiana law, a person convicted of a Class C felony such as this is subject to a $10,000 fine and to a term of five years, which may be increased to eight or reduced to two years.   Ind. Code § 35–50–2–6 (1982).

[13] The Indiana Supreme Court explained:

"We believe the overall purpose of the RICO statute is as applicable to obscenity violations as it is to the other enumerated predicate offenses which have no conceivable first amendment ramifications.   Thus we can not agree with either appellants or the Court of Appeals that the purpose of the Indiana RICO/CRRA scheme, as it pertains to the predicate offense of obscenity, is to restrain the sale or distribution of expressive materials.   It is irrelevant whether assets acquired through racketeering activity are obscene or not.   They are subject to forfeiture if the elements of a pattern of racketeering activity are shown.   The other CRRA remedies, such as license revocation, are also available regardless of the nature of the racketeering enterprise. . . .

"[T]he purpose of the forfeiture provisions is totally unrelated to the nature of the assets in question.   The overall purpose of the anti-racketeering laws is unequivocal, even where the predicate offense alleged is a violation of the obscenity statute.   The remedy of forfeiture is intended not to restrain the future distribution of presumptively protected speech but rather to disgorge assets acquired through racketeering activity.   Stated simply, it is irrelevant whether assets derived from an alleged violation of the RICO statute are or are not obscene. . . .

"In sum, these actions seeking various CRRA remedies were instituted in an

II

This Court finds no merit in the claim that Indiana's RICO law is unconstitutionally vague as applied to obscenity predicate offenses. Since Indiana's obscenity law satisfies the strictures set out in Miller v. California, 413 U.S. 15 (1973), the Court reasons, the predicate offense is not too vague; necessarily, a "pattern" of such offenses is even less vague. This is a non sequitur. Reference to a "pattern" of at least two violations only compounds the intractable vagueness of the obscenity concept itself.[14] The Court's contrary view rests on a construction of the RICO statute that requires nothing more than proof that a defendant sold or exhibited to a willing reader two obscene magazines—or perhaps just two copies of one such magazine. I would find the statute unconstitutional even without the special threat to first amendment interests posed by the CRRA remedies.[15] Instead of reiterating what I have already written, however, I shall limit this opinion to a discussion of the significance of the civil remedies.

I disagree with the Court's view that questions relating to the severity of the civil sanctions that may follow a RICO conviction are not ripe for review. For the Indiana Supreme Court's opinion ... makes it perfectly clear that the RICO and CRRA Acts, enacted at the same time and targeting precisely the same subject matter, are parts of a single statutory scheme. It is also obvious that the principal purpose of proving a pattern of racketeering activity is to enable the prosecutor to supplement criminal penalties with unusually severe civil sanctions. The Indiana court's descriptions of the "overall purpose of the anti-racketeering laws" and specifically of "the purpose of the Indiana RICO/CRRA scheme as it pertains to the predicate offense of obscenity" confirm what is in any event an obvious reading of this legislation. The significance of making obscenity a predicate offense comparable to murder, kidnapping, extortion, or arson cannot be evaluated fairly if the CRRA portion of the RICO/CRRA scheme is ignored.

III

Recurrent in the history of obscenity regulation is an abiding concern about media that have a "tendency to deprave or corrupt" those who view them, "to stir sexual impulses and lead to sexually impure thoughts," or to "appeal ... to prurient interest." See Alberts v. California (decided with

---

attempt to compel the forfeiture of the proceeds of alleged racketeering activity and not to restrain the future distribution of expressive materials. We hold that the RICO/CRRA statutes as they pertain to the predicate offense of obscenity do not violate the first and 14th amendments of the United States Constitution."

[14] ... Ironically, the legal test for determining the existence of a pattern of racketeering activity has been likened to "Justice Stewart's famous test for obscenity—'I know

it when I see it'—set forth in his concurrence in Jacobellis v. Ohio, 378 U.S. 184, 197 (1964)." Morgan v. Bank of Waukegan, 804 F.2d 970, 977 (7th Cir.1986).

[15] It long has been "my conviction that government may not constitutionally criminalize mere possession or sale of obscene literature, absent some connection to minors or obtrusive display to unconsenting adults." Pope v. Illinois, 481 U.S. 497, 513 (1987)(Stevens, J., dissenting).

Roth v. United States), 354 U.S. 476, 498–99 (1957)(Harlan, J., concurring in result).   Antecedents of the statutory scheme under review in these cases plainly reflect this concern.   Early Indiana statutes classified as crimes "Against Public Morals" or "Against Chastity and Morality" the distribution not only of "obscene" materials, but also of materials that were "lewd," "indecent," or "lascivious" or that described or depicted "criminal, desperadoes, or . . . men or women in lewd and unbecoming positions or improper dress."   Prohibited in the same category were profane cursing, advertising drugs for female use, Sunday baseball, and letting stallions in public.   Indiana's regulation of morals offenses paralleled efforts elsewhere in the United States and in Great Britain.   Quite simply, the longstanding justification for suppressing obscene materials has been to prevent people from having immoral thoughts.[18] The failure to do so, it is argued, threatens the moral fabric of our society.[19]

Limiting society's expression of that concern is the federal Constitution.   The first amendment presumptively protects communicative materials.   Because the line between protected pornographic speech and obscenity is "dim and uncertain," Bantam Books, Inc. v. Sullivan, 372 U.S. 58, 66 (1963), "a state is not free to adopt whatever procedures it pleases for dealing with obscenity," Marcus v. Search Warrant, 367 U.S. 717, 731 (1961), but must employ careful procedural safeguards to assure that only those materials adjudged obscene are withdrawn from public commerce. Freedman v. Maryland, 380 U.S. 51 (1965); see *Miller v. California,* 413

[18] As Professor Henkin explained, American obscenity laws are "rooted in this country's religious antecedents, of governmental responsibility for communal and individual 'decency' and 'morality.'" Louis Henkin, Morals and the Constitution: The Sin of Obscenity, 63 Colum. L. Rev. 391 (1963).   He continued:

"Communities believe, and act on the belief, that obscenity is immoral, is wrong for the individual, and has no place in a decent society.   They believe, too, that adults as well as children are corruptible in morals and character, and that obscenity is a source of corruption that should be eliminated.   Obscenity is not suppressed for the purity of the community and for the salvation and welfare of the 'consumer.'   Obscenity, at bottom, is not crime.   Obscenity is sin." Id., at 395.

[19] In proposing the addition of state and federal obscenity violations as predicate offenses under Federal RICO, Senator Helms stated:

"[W]e are experiencing an explosion in the volume and availability of pornography in our society.   Today it is almost

impossible to open mail, turn on the television, or walk in the downtown areas of our cities, or even in some suburban areas, without being accosted by pornographic materials.   The sheer volume and pervasiveness of pornography in our society tends to make adults less sensitive to the traditional value of chaste conduct and leads children to abandon the moral values their parents have tried so hard to instill in them.

" . . . Surely it is not just coincidential [sic] that, as [sic] a time in our history when pornography and obscene materials are rampant, we are also experiencing record levels of promiscuity, veneral [sic] disease, herpes, acquired immune deficiency syndrome (AIDS), abortion, divorce, family breakdown, and related problems.   At a minimum, pornography lowers the general moral tone of society and contributes to social problems that were minimal or nonexistent in earlier periods of our history."   130 Cong. Rec. 844 (1984).

The amendment was enacted in the Act of Oct. 12, 1984, Pub. L. 98–473, 98 Stat. 2143, codified at 18 U.S.C. § 1961(1).

U.S., at 23–24.[20] The Constitution confers a right to possess even materials that are legally obscene. Stanley v. Georgia, 394 U.S. 557 (1969). Moreover, public interest in access to sexually explicit materials remains strong despite continuing efforts to stifle distribution.[21]

Whatever harm society incurs from the sale of a few obscene magazines to consenting adults is indistinguishable from the harm caused by the distribution of a great volume of pornographic material that is protected by the first amendment.[22] Elimination of a few obscene volumes or videotapes

[20] "To the extent, therefore, that regulation of pornography constitutes an abridgment of the freedom of speech, or an abridgment of the freedom of the press, it is at least presumptively unconstitutional. And even if some or all forms of regulation of pornography are seen ultimately not to constitute abridgments of the freedom of speech or the freedom of the press, the fact remains that the Constitution treats speaking and printing as special, and thus the regulation of anything spoken or printed must be examined with extraordinary care. For even when some forms of regulation of what is spoken or printed are not abridgments of the freedom of speech, or abridgments of freedom of the press, such regulations are closer to constituting abridgments than other forms of governmental action. If nothing else, the barriers between permissible restrictions on what is said or printed and unconstitutional abridgments must be scrupulously guarded." 1 Report, at 249–50.

[21] The videotape dealers' association, for example, reports that in the "three-quarters of the nation's video stores carry[ing] adult titles," that material, often to be viewed by private individuals on their own video cassette recorders, "accounts for about 13% of their business, valued at $250 million annually." Karl A. Groskaufmanis, What Films We May Watch: Videotape Distribution and the First Amendment, 136 U. Pa. L. Rev. 1263, 1273, n.75 (1988).

The Attorney's General's Commission on Pornography quotes Geoffrey R. Stone, now dean of the University of Chicago Law School, as follows:

" '[T]he very fact . . . that there is a vast market in our society for sexually explicit expression suggests that for many people, this type of speech serves what they believe to be, it may be amusement, it m[a]y be containment, it may be sexual stimulation, it may be fantasy, whatever

it is, many of us believe that this expression is to our own lives, in some way, valuable. That value should not be overlooked.' "

2 Report, at 1269. See also *Marks v. United States*, 430 U.S., at 198 (Stevens, J., concurring in part and dissenting in part)("However distasteful these materials are to some of us, they are nevertheless a form of communication and entertainment acceptable to a substantial segment of society; otherwise, they would have no value in the marketplace.").

[22] The Attorney General's Commission on Pornography highlighted this fact as follows:

"A central part of our mission has been to examine the question whether pornography is harmful. In attempting to answer this question, we have made a conscious decision not to allow our examination of the harm question to be constricted by the existing legal/constitutional definition of the legally obscene.

. . .

"A result, our inquiry into harm encompasses much material that may not be legally obscene, and also encompasses much material that would not generally be considered 'pornographic' as we use that term here. . . .

"To a number of us, the most important harms must be seen in moral terms, and the act of moral condemnation of that which is immoral is not merely important but essential. From this perspective there are acts that need be seen not only as causes of immorality but as manifestations of it. Issues of human dignity and human decency, no less real for their lack of scientific measurability, are for many of us central to thinking about the question of harm. And when we think about harm in this way, there are acts that must be condemned not

from an adult bookstore's shelves thus scarcely serves the state's purpose of controlling public morality. But the state's RICO/CRRA scheme, like the Federal RICO law after which it was patterned, furnishes prosecutors with "drastic methods" for curtailing undesired activity.[23] The Indiana RICO/CRRA statutes allow prosecutors to cast wide nets[24] and seize, upon a showing that two obscene materials have been sold, or even just exhibited, all a store's books, magazines, films, and videotapes—the obscene, those nonobscene yet sexually explicit, even those devoid of sexual reference.[25] Reported decisions indicate that the enforcement of Indiana's RICO/CRRA statutes has been primarily directed at adult bookstores.[26] Patently, successful prosecutions would advance significantly the State's efforts to silence immoral speech and repress immoral thoughts.

In my opinion it is fair to identify the effect of Indiana's RICO/CRRA

because the evils of the world will thereby be eliminated, but because conscience demands it." 1 Report at 299, 302, 303.

[23] "Drastic methods to combat [organized crime] are essential, and we must develop law enforcement measures at least as efficient as those of organized crime." 116 Cong. Rec. 35199 (1970)(remarks of Rep. Rodino). See also Russello v. United States, 464 U.S. 16, 26–29 (1983); United States v. Turkette, 452 U.S. 576, 586–93 (1981).

[24] Cf. United States v. Elliott, 571 F.2d 880, 903 (5th Cir.1978)("the [Federal] RICO net is woven tightly to trap even the smallest fish").

[25] The Court of Appeals of Indiana made this observation:

"[T]he state concedes that the obscenity of the seized inventories of books, magazines, and films is irrelevant and need not even be alleged. This argument reflects an accurate reading of the statutes but also reveals the deeply-flawed nature of the regulatory scheme as a response to obscenity. May avant-garde booksellers and theaters be padlocked and forfeited to the state upon a showing that alongside literary, political, and cinematic classics, they have twice disseminated controversial works subsequently adjudged to be obscene? [T]he guarantees of the first amendment mean nothing if the state may arrogate such discretion over the continued existence of bookstores and theaters."

The state Supreme Court did not deny that the RICO/CRRA Acts permitted that result, but rather professed faith that prosecutors

would not abuse the power given them under the statutes.

Even the suppression only of sex-oriented materials on the borderline between protected and unprotected speech might remove a vast number of materials from circulation. See Park E. Dietz & Alan E. Sears, Pornography and Obscenity Sold in "Adult Bookstores": A Survey of 5132 Books, Magazines, and Films in Four American Cities, 21 U. Mich. J.L. Ref. 7, 42 (1987–1988)(36% of materials in adult bookstores surveyed would be obscene "in the eyes of a juror with sexually liberal attitudes and values," while 100% would be obscene "in the eyes of those with sexually traditional attitudes and values").

[26] In five of the eight reported opinions reviewing prosecutions pursuant to Indiana's RICO/CRRA statutes, the predicate offenses are obscenity violations. ...

The first Federal RICO prosecution based on obscenity violations occurred in United States v. Pryba, Crim. No. 87–00208–A (E.D. Va. Nov. 10, 1987). After the District Court had rejected constitutional challenges to the inclusion of obscenity offenses in the Federal RICO statute, 674 F.Supp. 1504 (E.D.Va.1987), a jury found defendants " 'guilty of interstate distribution of $105.30 worth of obscene material and decided that Dennis Pryba's three Washington, D.C., area hardcore bookstores and eight videotape clubs [valued at $1 million] were forfeitable under the terms of the RICO statute.' " Tod R. Eggenberger, RICO vs. Dealers in Obscene Matter: The First Amendment Battle, 22 Colum. J.L. & Soc. Probs. 71 (1988)(quoting Arthur Hayes, A Jury Wrestles with Pornography, American Lawyer 96, 97 (Mar. 1988)).

acts as the specific purpose of the legislation.[27] The most realistic interpretation of the Indiana Legislature's intent in making obscenity a RICO predicate offense is to expand beyond traditional prosecution of legally obscene materials into restriction of materials that, though constitutionally protected, have the same undesired effect on the community's morals as those that are actually obscene.[28] Fulfillment of that intent surely would overflow the boundaries imposed by the Constitution.

The Court properly holds today that when the predicate offenses are obscenity violations, the state may not undertake the pretrial seizures of expressive materials that Indiana's RICO/CRRA legislation authorizes. Yet it does so only after excluding from its holding pretrial seizures of "nonexpressive property" and "assum[ing] without deciding that bookstores and their contents are forfeitable" and otherwise subject to CRRA's post-trial civil sanctions. I would extend the Court's holding to prohibit the seizure of these stores' inventories, even after trial, based on nothing more than "a pattern" of obscenity misdemeanors.

For there is a difference of constitutional dimension between an enterprise that is engaged in the business of selling and exhibiting books, magazines, and videotapes and one that is engaged in another commercial activity, lawful or unlawful. A bookstore receiving revenue from sales of obscene books is not the same as a hardware store or pizza parlor funded by loan-sharking proceeds. The presumptive first amendment protection accorded the former does not apply either to the predicate offense or to the business use in the latter. Seldom will first amendment protections have any relevance to the sanctions that might be invoked against an ordinary commercial establishment. Nor will use of RICO/CRRA sanctions to rid

[27] "Frequently the most probative evidence of intent will be objective evidence of what actually happened rather than evidence describing the subjective state of mind of the actor. For normally the actor is presumed to have intended the natural consequences of his deeds. This is particularly true in the case of governmental action which is frequently the product of compromise, of collective decisionmaking, and of mixed motivation." Washington v. Davis, 426 U.S. 229, 253 (1976)(Stevens, J., concurring). See also Near v. Minnesota, 283 U.S. 697, 708 (1931)("in passing upon constitutional questions . . ., the statute must be tested by its operation and effect").

[28] Indiana is far from the only governmental entity to have moved against undesirable, sexually explicit materials in this manner. Of 26 States besides Indiana that have passed laws patterned after the federal RICO statute, 14 include violations of obscenity laws as predicate offenses upon which a RICO-type prosecution may be based.

The trend toward using RICO statutes to enforce obscenity laws comports with the urgings of the Attorney General's Commission on Pornography. 1 Report at 435 (Recommendation "10. STATE LEGISLATURES SHOULD ENACT A RACKETEER INFLUENCE CORRUPT ORGANIZATIONS (RICO) STATUTE WHICH HAS OBSCENITY AS A PREDICATE ACT"); id., at 437 (Recommendation "15. THE DEPARTMENT OF JUSTICE AND UNITED STATES ATTORNEYS SHOULD USE THE RACKETEER INFLUENCED CORRUPT ORGANIZATION ACT (RICO) AS A MEANS OF PROSECUTING MAJOR PRODUCERS AND DISTRIBUTORS OF OBSCENE MATERIAL"); id., at 464, 498, 515. Cf. id., at 433, 465, 472, 497 (recommending that federal and state governments enact statutes authorizing forfeitures even if two predicate offenses cannot be proved, barring a RICO prosecution).

that type of enterprise of illegal influence, even by closing it, engender suspicion of censorial motive. Prosecutors in such cases desire only to purge the organized-crime taint; they have no interest in deterring the sale of pizzas or hardware. Sexually explicit books and movies, however, are commodities the state does want to exterminate. The RICO/CRRA scheme promotes such extermination through elimination of the very establishments where sexually explicit speech is disseminated.

Perhaps all, or virtually all, of the protected films and publications that petitioners offer for sale are so objectionable that their sales should only be permitted in secluded areas. Cf. Young v. American Mini Theatres, Inc., 427 U.S. 50 (1976). Many sexually explicit materials are little more than noxious appendages to a sprawling media industry. It is nevertheless true that a host of citizens desires them, that at best remote and indirect injury to third parties flows from them, and that purchasers have a constitutional right to possess them. The first amendment thus requires the use of "sensitive tools" to regulate them. Speiser v. Randall, 357 U.S. 513, 525 (1958). Indiana's RICO/CRRA statutes arm prosecutors not with scalpels to excise obscene portions of an adult bookstore's inventory but with sickles to mow down the entire undesired use. This the first amendment will not tolerate. " '[I]t is better to leave a few … noxious branches to their luxuriant growth, than, by pruning them away, to injure the vigour of those yielding the proper fruits,' "[29] for the "right to receive information and ideas, regardless of their social worth, is fundamental to our free society."[30]

Accordingly, I would reverse the decision in No. 87–614. In No. 87–470, I would not only invalidate the pretrial seizures but would also direct that the complaint be dismissed.

Alexander v. United States

Supreme Court of the United States, 1993.
509 U.S. 544.

■ CHIEF JUSTICE REHNQUIST delivered the opinion of the Court.

After a full criminal trial, petitioner Ferris J. Alexander, owner of more than a dozen stores and theaters dealing in sexually explicit materials, was convicted on, inter alia, 17 obscenity counts and 3 counts of violating the Racketeer Influenced and Corrupt Organizations Act (RICO). The obscenity convictions, based on the jury's findings that four magazines and three videotapes sold at several of petitioner's stores were obscene, served as the predicates for his three RICO convictions. In addition to imposing a prison term and fine, the District Court ordered petitioner to forfeit, pursuant to 18 U.S.C. § 1963 (1988 ed. and Supp. III), certain assets that were directly related to his racketeering activity as punishment for his RICO violations.

---

[29] Near v. Minnesota, 283 U.S., at 718 (Hughes, C.J.)(quoting 4 Writings of James Madison 544 (1865)).

[30] Stanley v. Georgia, 394 U.S. 557, 564 (1969).

Petitioner argues that this forfeiture violated the First and Eighth Amendments to the Constitution. We reject petitioner's claims under the First Amendment but remand for reconsideration of his Eighth Amendment challenge.

Petitioner was in the so-called "adult entertainment" business for more than 30 years, selling pornographic magazines and sexual paraphernalia, showing sexually explicit movies, and eventually selling and renting videotapes of a similar nature. He received shipments of these materials at a warehouse in Minneapolis, Minnesota, where they were wrapped in plastic, priced, and boxed. He then sold his products through some 13 retail stores in several different Minnesota cities, generating millions of dollars in annual revenues. In 1989, federal authorities filed a 41–count indictment against petitioner and others, alleging, inter alia, operation of a racketeering enterprise in violation of RICO. The indictment charged 34 obscenity counts and 3 RICO counts, the racketeering counts being predicated on the obscenity charges. The indictment also charged numerous counts of tax evasion and related offenses that are not relevant to the questions before us.

Following a four-month jury trial in the United States District Court for the District of Minnesota, petitioner was convicted of 17 substantive obscenity offenses: 12 counts of transporting obscene material in interstate commerce for the purpose of sale or distribution, in violation of 18 U.S.C. § 1465; and five counts of engaging in the business of selling obscene material, in violation of 18 U.S.C. § 1466 (1988 ed. and Supp. III). He also was convicted of three RICO offenses which were predicated on the obscenity convictions: one count of receiving and using income derived from a pattern of racketeering activity, in violation of 18 U.S.C. § 1962(a); one count of conducting a RICO enterprise, in violation of § 1962(c); and one count of conspiring to conduct a RICO enterprise, in violation of § 1962(d). As a basis for the obscenity and RICO convictions, the jury determined that four magazines and three videotapes were obscene. Multiple copies of these magazines and videos, which graphically depicted a variety of "hard core" sexual acts, were distributed throughout petitioner's adult entertainment empire.

Petitioner was sentenced to a total of six years in prison, fined $100,000, and ordered to pay the cost of prosecution, incarceration, and supervised release. In addition to these punishments, the District Court reconvened the same jury and conducted a forfeiture proceeding pursuant to § 1963(a)(2). At this proceeding, the Government sought forfeiture of the businesses and real estate that represented petitioner's interest in the racketeering enterprise, § 1963(a)(2)(A), the property that afforded petitioner influence over that enterprise, § 1963(a)(2)(D), and the assets and proceeds petitioner had obtained from his racketeering offenses, §§ 1963(a)(1), (3). The jury found that petitioner had an interest in ten pieces of commercial real estate and 31 current or former businesses, all of which had been used to conduct his racketeering enterprise. Sitting without the jury, the District Court then found that petitioner had acquired a variety of assets as a result of his racketeering activities. The court ultimately ordered petitioner to forfeit his wholesale and retail businesses (including all the assets of those businesses) and almost $9 million in moneys acquired through racketeering activity.[1]

The Court of Appeals affirmed the District Court's forfeiture order. Alexander v. Thornburgh, 943 F.2d 825 (8th Cir.1991). It rejected petitioner's argument that the application of RICO's forfeiture provisions constituted a prior restraint on speech and hence violated the First Amendment. Recognizing the well-established distinction between prior restraints and subsequent criminal punishments, the Court of Appeals found that the forfeiture here was "a criminal penalty imposed following a conviction for conducting an enterprise engaged in racketeering activities," and not a prior restraint on speech. Id., at 834. The court also rejected petitioner's claim that RICO's forfeiture provisions are constitutionally overbroad, pointing out that the forfeiture order was properly limited to assets linked to petitioner's past racketeering offenses. Id., at 835. Lastly, the Court of Appeals concluded that the forfeiture order does not violate the Eighth Amendment's prohibition against "cruel and unusual punishments" and "excessive fines." In so ruling, however, the court did not consider whether the forfeiture in this case was grossly disproportionate or excessive, believing that the Eighth Amendment " 'does not require a proportionality review of any sentence less than life imprisonment without the possibility of parole.' " Id., at 836 (quoting United States v. Pryba, 900 F.2d 748, 757 (4th Cir.1990)). We granted certiorari.

Petitioner first contends that the forfeiture in this case, which effectively shut down his adult entertainment business, constituted an unconstitutional prior restraint on speech, rather than a permissible criminal punishment. According to petitioner, forfeiture of expressive materials and the assets of businesses engaged in expressive activity, when predicated solely upon previous obscenity violations, operates as a prior restraint because it prohibits future presumptively protected expression in retaliation for prior unprotected speech. Practically speaking, petitioner argues, the effect of the RICO forfeiture order here was no different from the injunction prohibiting the publication of expressive material found to be a prior restraint in Near v. Minnesota ex rel. Olson, 283 U.S. 697 (1931). As petitioner puts it, the forfeiture order imposed a complete ban on his future expression because of previous unprotected speech. We disagree. By lumping the forfeiture imposed in this case after a full criminal trial with an injunction enjoining future speech, petitioner stretches the term "prior restraint" well beyond the limits established by our cases. To accept petitioner's argument would virtually obliterate the distinction, solidly grounded in our cases, between prior restraints and subsequent punishments.

---

[1] Not wishing to go into the business of selling pornographic materials—regardless of whether they were legally obscene—the Government decided that it would be better to destroy the forfeited expressive materials than sell them to members of the public. See Brief for United States 26–27, n. 11.

The term prior restraint is used "to describe administrative and judicial orders forbidding certain communications when issued in advance of the time that such communications are to occur." M. Nimmer, Nimmer on Freedom of Speech § 4.03, p. 4–14 (1984). Temporary restraining orders and permanent injunctions—i.e., court orders that actually forbid speech activities—are classic examples of prior restraints. See id., § 4.03, at 4–16. This understanding of what constitutes a prior restraint is borne out by our cases, even those on which petitioner relies. In *Near v. Minnesota ex rel. Olson*, supra, we invalidated a court order that perpetually enjoined the named party, who had published a newspaper containing articles found to violate a state nuisance statute, from producing any future "malicious, scandalous and defamatory" publication. *Near*, therefore, involved a true restraint on future speech—a permanent injunction. So, too, did Organization for a Better Austin v. Keefe, 402 U.S. 415 (1971), and Vance v. Universal Amusement Co., 445 U.S. 308 (1980)(per curiam), two other cases cited by petitioner. In *Keefe*, we vacated an order "enjoining petitioners from distributing leaflets anywhere in the town of Westchester, Illinois." 402 U.S., at 415. And in *Vance*, we struck down a Texas statute that authorized courts, upon a showing that obscene films had been shown in the past, to issue an injunction of indefinite duration prohibiting the future exhibition of films that have not yet been found to be obscene. 445 U.S., at 311. See also New York Times Co. v. United States, 403 U.S. 713, 714 (1971)(per curiam)(Government sought to enjoin publication of the Pentagon Papers).

By contrast, the RICO forfeiture order in this case does not forbid petitioner from engaging in any expressive activities in the future, nor does it require him to obtain prior approval for any expressive activities. It only deprives him of specific assets that were found to be related to his previous racketeering violations. Assuming, of course, that he has sufficient untainted assets to open new stores, restock his inventory, and hire staff, petitioner can go back into the adult entertainment business tomorrow, and sell as many sexually explicit magazines and videotapes as he likes, without any risk of being held in contempt for violating a court order. Unlike the injunctions in *Near*, *Keefe*, and *Vance*, the forfeiture order in this case imposes no legal impediment to—no prior restraint on—petitioner's ability to engage in any expressive activity he chooses. He is perfectly free to open an adult bookstore or otherwise engage in the production and distribution of erotic materials; he just cannot finance these enterprises with assets derived from his prior racketeering offenses.

The constitutional infirmity in nearly all of our prior restraint cases involving obscene material, including those on which petitioner and the dissent rely, was that Government had seized or otherwise retrained materials suspected of being obscene without a prior judicial determination that they were in fact so. See, e.g., Marcus v. Search Warrant, 367 U.S. 717 (1961); Bantam Books, Inc. v. Sullivan, 372 U.S. 58 (1963); A Quantity of Copies of Books v. Kansas, 378 U.S. 205 (1964); Roaden v. Kentucky, 413 U.S. 496 (1973); *Vance*, supra. In this case, however, the assets in question were not ordered forfeited because they were believed to be obscene, but because they were directly related to petitioner's past racketeering violations. The RICO forfeiture statute calls for the forfeiture of assets because of the financial role they play in the operation of the racketeering enterprise. The statute is oblivious to the expressive or nonexpressive nature of the assets forfeited; books, sports cars, narcotics, and cash are all forfeitable alike under RICO. Indeed, a contrary scheme would be disastrous from a policy standpoint, enabling racketeers to evade forfeiture by investing the proceeds of their crimes in businesses engaging in expressive activity.

Nor were the assets in question ordered forfeited without according petitioner the requisite procedural safeguards, another recurring theme in our prior restraint cases. Contrasting this case with Fort Wayne Books, Inc. v. Indiana, 489 U.S. 46 (1989), aptly illustrates this point. In *Fort Wayne Books*, we rejected on constitutional grounds the pretrial seizure of certain expressive material that was based upon a finding of "no more than probable cause to believe that a RICO violation had occurred." Id., at 66. In so holding, we emphasized that there had been no prior judicial "determination that the seized items were 'obscene' or that a RICO violation ha[d] occurred." Ibid. "[M]ere probable cause to believe a legal violation ha[d] transpired," we said, "is not adequate to remove books or films from circulation." Ibid. Here, by contrast, the seizure was not premature, because the Government established beyond a reasonable doubt the basis for the forfeiture. Petitioner had a full criminal trial on the merits of the obscenity and RICO charges during which the Government proved that four magazines and three videotapes were obscene and that the other forfeited assets were directly linked to petitioner's commission of racketeering offenses.

Petitioner's claim that the RICO forfeiture statute operated as an unconstitutional prior restraint in this case is also inconsistent with our decision in Arcara v. Cloud Books, Inc., 478 U.S. 697 (1986). In that case, we sustained a court order, issued under a general nuisance statute, that closed down an adult bookstore that was being used as a place of prostitution and lewdness. In rejecting out-of-hand a claim that the closure order amounted to an improper prior restraint on speech, we stated: "The closure order sought in this case differs from a prior restraint in two significant respects. First, the order would impose no restraint at all on the dissemination of particular materials, since respondents are free to carry on their bookselling business at another location, even if such locations are difficult to find. Second, the closure order sought would not be imposed on the basis of an advance determination that the distribution of particular materials is prohibited—indeed, the imposition of the closure order has nothing to do with any expressive conduct at all." Id., at 705–06, n. 2. This reasoning applies with equal force to this case, and thus confirms that the RICO forfeiture order was not a prior restraint on speech, but a punishment for past criminal conduct. Petitioner attempts to distinguish *Arcara* on the ground that obscenity, unlike prostitution or lewdness, has " 'a significant expressive element.' " Brief for Petitioner 16 (quoting *Arcara*, supra, 478 U.S., at 706). But that distinction has no bearing on the question whether the forfeiture order in this case was an impermissible prior restraint.

Finally, petitioner's proposed definition of the term "prior restraint" would undermine the time-honored distinction between barring speech in the future and penalizing past speech. The doctrine of prior restraint originated in the common law of England, where prior restraints of the press were not permitted, but punishment after publication was. This very limited application of the principle of freedom of speech was held inconsistent with our First Amendment as long ago as Grosjean v. American Press Co., 297 U.S. 233, 246 (1936). While we may have given a broader definition to the term "prior restraint" than was given to it in English common law,[2] our decisions have steadfastly preserved the distinction between prior restraints and subsequent punishments. Though petitioner tries to dismiss this distinction as "neither meaningful nor useful," Brief for Petitioner 29, we think it is critical to our First Amendment jurisprudence. Because we have interpreted the First Amendment as providing greater protection from prior restraints than from subsequent punishments, see Southeastern Promotions, Ltd. v. Conrad, 420 U.S. 546, 558–59 (1975), it is important for us to delineate with some precision the defining characteristics of a prior restraint. To hold that the forfeiture order in this case constituted a prior restraint would have the exact opposite effect: it would blur the line separating prior restraints from subsequent punishments to such a degree that it would be impossible to determine with any certainty whether a particular measure is a prior restraint or not.

In sum, we think that fidelity to our cases requires us to analyze the forfeiture here not as a prior restraint, but under normal First Amendment standards. So analyzing it, we find that petitioner's claim falls well short of the mark. He does not challenge either his six-year jail sentence or his $100,000 fine as violative of the First Amendment. The first inquiry that comes to mind, then, is why, if incarceration for six years and a fine of $100,000 are permissible forms of punishment under the RICO statute, the challenged forfeiture of certain assets directly related to petitioner's racketeering activity is not. Our cases support the instinct from which this question arises; they establish quite clearly that the First Amendment does not prohibit either stringent criminal sanctions for obscenity offenses or forfeiture of expressive materials as punishment for criminal conduct.

---

[2] The doctrine of prior restraint has its roots in the 16th- and 17th-century English system of censorship. Under that system, all printing presses and printers were licensed by the government, and nothing could lawfully be published without the prior approval of a government or church censor. See generally T. Emerson, System of Freedom of Expression 504 (1970). Beginning with Near v. Minnesota ex rel. Olson, 283 U.S. 697 (1931), we expanded this doctrine to include not only licensing schemes requiring speech to be submitted to an administrative censor for prepublication review, but also injunctions against future speech issued by judges. See Pittsburgh Press Co. v. Pittsburgh Comm'n on Human Relations, 413 U.S. 376, 389–390 (1973)("[T]he protection against prior restraint at common law barred only a system of administrative censorship.... [T]he Court boldly stepped beyond this narrow doctrine in *Near*"). Quite obviously, however, we have never before countenanced the essentially limitless expansion of the term that petitioner proposes.

We have in the past rejected First Amendment challenges to statutes that impose severe prison sentences and fines as punishment for obscenity offenses. See, e.g., Ginzburg v. United States, 383 U.S. 463, 464–65, n. 2 (1966); Smith v. United States, 431 U.S. 291, 296, n. 3 (1977); *Fort Wayne Books*, 489 U.S., at 59, n. 8. Petitioner does not question the holding of those cases; he instead argues that RICO's forfeiture provisions are constitutionally overbroad, because they are not limited solely to obscene materials and the proceeds from the sale of such materials. Petitioner acknowledges that this is an unprecedented use of the overbreadth principle. The "overbreadth" doctrine, which is a departure from traditional rules of standing, permits a defendant to make a facial challenge to an overly broad statute restricting speech, even if he himself has engaged in speech that could be regulated under a more narrowly drawn statute. See, e.g., Broadrick v. Oklahoma, 413 U.S. 601, 612–13 (1973); City Council of Los Angeles v. Taxpayers for Vincent, 466 U.S. 789, 798–801 (1984). But the RICO statute does not criminalize constitutionally protected speech and therefore is materially different from the statutes at issue in our overbreadth cases. Cf., e.g., Board of Airport Comm'rs of Los Angeles v. Jews for Jesus, Inc., 482 U.S. 569, 574–75 (1987).

Petitioner's real complaint is not that the RICO statute is overbroad, but that applying RICO's forfeiture provisions to businesses dealing in expressive materials may have an improper "chilling" effect on free expression by deterring others from engaging in protected speech. No doubt the monetarily large forfeiture in this case may induce cautious booksellers to practice self-censorship and remove marginally protected materials from their shelves out of fear that those materials could be found obscene and thus subject them to forfeiture. But the defendant in *Fort Wayne Books* made a similar argument, which was rejected by the Court in this language: "[D]eterence of the sale of obscene materials is a legitimate end of state antiobscenity laws, and our cases have long recognized the practical reality that 'any form of criminal obscenity statute applicable to a bookseller will induce some tendency to self-censorship and have some inhibitory effect on the dissemination of material not obscene.'" 489 U.S., at 60 (quoting Smith v. California, 361 U.S. 147, 154–55 (1959)).

Fort Wayne Books is dispositive of any chilling argument here, since the threat of forfeiture has no more of a chilling effect on free expression than the threat of a prison term or a large fine. Each racketeering charge exposes a defendant to a maximum penalty of 20 years' imprisonment and a fine of up to $250,000. 18 U.S.C. § 1963(a)(1988 ed. and Supp. III). Needless to say, the prospect of such a lengthy prison sentence would have a far more powerful deterrent effect on protected speech than the prospect of any sort of forfeiture. Cf. Blanton v. North Las Vegas, 489 U.S. 538, 542 (1989)(loss of liberty is a more severe form of punishment than any monetary sanction). Similarly, a fine of several hundred thousand dollars would certainly be just as fatal to most businesses—and, as such, would result in the same degree of self-censorship—as a forfeiture of assets. Yet these penalties are clearly constitutional under *Fort Wayne Books*.

We also have rejected a First Amendment challenge to a court order closing down an entire business that was engaged in expressive activity as punishment for criminal conduct. See *Arcara*, 478 U.S., at 707. Once again, petitioner does not question the holding of that case; in fact, he concedes that expressive businesses and assets can be forfeited under RICO as punishment for, say, narcotic offenses. See Brief for Petitioner 11 ("forfeiture of a media business purchased by a drug cartel would be constitutionally permissible"). Petitioner instead insists that the result here should be different because the RICO predicate acts were obscenity offenses. In *Arcara*, we held that criminal and civil sanctions having some incidental effect on First Amendment activities are subject to First Amendment scrutiny "only where it was conduct with a significant expressive element that drew the legal remedy in the first place, as in United States v. O'Brien, 391 U.S. 367 (1968), or where a statute based on a nonexpressive activity has the inevitable effect of singling out those engaged in expressive activity, as in Minneapolis Star & Tribune Co. v. Minnesota Comm'r of Revenue, 460 U.S. 575 (1983)." 478 U.S., at 706–07. Applying that standard, we held that prostitution and lewdness, the criminal conduct at issue in *Arcara*, involve neither situation, and thus concluded that the First Amendment was not implicated by the enforcement of a general health regulation resulting in the closure of an adult bookstore. Id., at 707. Under our analysis in *Arcara*, the forfeiture in this case cannot be said to offend the First Amendment. To be sure, the conduct that "drew the legal remedy" here—racketeering committed through obscenity violations—may be "expressive," see R.A.V. v. St. Paul, 505 U.S. 377, 384–85 (1992), but our cases clearly hold that "obscenity" can be regulated or actually proscribed consistent with the First Amendment, see, e.g., Roth v. United States, 354 U.S. 476, 485 (1957); Miller v. California, 413 U.S. 15, 23 (1973).

Confronted with our decisions in *Fort Wayne Books* and *Arcara*— neither of which he challenges—petitioner's position boils down to this: stiff criminal penalties for obscenity offenses are consistent with the First Amendment; so is the forfeiture of expressive materials as punishment for criminal conduct; but the combination of the two somehow results in a violation of the First Amendment. We reject this counter-intuitive conclusion, which in effect would say that the whole is greater than the sum of the parts.

Petitioner also argues that the forfeiture order in this case—considered atop his six-year prison term and $100,000 fine—is disproportionate to the gravity of his offenses and therefore violates the Eighth Amendment, either as a "cruel and unusual punishment" or as an "excessive fine." The Court of Appeals, though, failed to distinguish between these two components of petitioner's Eighth Amendment challenge. Instead, the court lumped the two together, disposing of them both with the general statement that the Eighth Amendment does not require any proportionality review of a sentence less than life imprisonment without the possibility of parole. But that statement has relevance only to the Eighth Amendment's prohibition against cruel and unusual punishments. Unlike the Cruel and Unusual

Punishments Clause, which is concerned with matters such as the duration or conditions of confinement, "[t]he Excessive Fines Clause limits the Government's power to extract payments, whether in cash or in kind, as punishment for some offense." Austin v. United States, 509 U.S. 602, 609 (1993); accord, Browning–Ferris Industries of Vermont, Inc. v. Kelco Disposal, Inc., 492 U.S. 257, 265 (1989)("[A]t the time of the drafting and ratification of the [Eighth] Amendment, the word 'fine' was understood to mean a payment to a sovereign as punishment for some offense"); id., at 265, n. 6. The in personam criminal forfeiture at issue here is clearly a form of monetary punishment no different, for Eighth Amendment purposes, from a traditional "fine." Accordingly, the forfeiture in this case should be analyzed under the Excessive Fines Clause.

Petitioner contends that forfeiture of his entire business was an "excessive" penalty for the Government to exact "[o]n the basis of a few materials the jury ultimately decided were obscene." Brief for Petitioner 40. It is somewhat misleading, we think, to characterize the racketeering crimes for which petitioner was convicted as involving just a few materials ultimately found to be obscene. Petitioner was convicted of creating and managing what the District Court described as "an enormous racketeering enterprise." It is in the light of the extensive criminal activities which petitioner apparently conducted through this racketeering enterprise over a substantial period of time that the question of whether or not the forfeiture was "excessive" must be considered. We think it preferable that this question be addressed by the Court of Appeals in the first instance.

For these reasons, we hold that RICO's forfeiture provisions, as applied in this case, did not violate the First Amendment, but that the Court of Appeals should have considered whether they resulted in an "excessive" penalty within the meaning of the Eighth Amendment's Excessive Fines Clause. Accordingly, we vacate the judgment of the Court of Appeals and remand the case for further proceedings consistent with this opinion.

It is so ordered.

■ JUSTICE SOUTER, concurring in the judgment in part and dissenting in part.

I agree with the Court that petitioner has not demonstrated that the forfeiture at issue here qualifies as a prior restraint as we have traditionally understood that term. I also agree with the Court that the case should be remanded for a determination whether the forfeiture violated the Excessive Fines Clause of the Eighth Amendment. Nonetheless, I agree with Justice Kennedy that the First Amendment forbids the forfeiture of petitioner's expressive material in the absence of an adjudication that it is obscene or otherwise of unprotected character, and therefore I join Part II of his dissenting opinion.

■ JUSTICE KENNEDY, with whom JUSTICE BLACKMUN and JUSTICE STEVENS join, and with whom JUSTICE SOUTER joins as to Part II, dissenting.

The Court today embraces a rule that would find no affront to the First Amendment in the Government's destruction of a book and film business and its entire inventory of legitimate expression as punishment for a single past speech offense. Until now I had thought one could browse through any book or film store in the United States without fear that the proprietor had chosen each item to avoid risk to the whole inventory and indeed to the business itself. This ominous, onerous threat undermines free speech and press principles essential to our personal freedom.

Obscenity laws would not work unless an offender could be arrested and imprisoned despite the resulting chill on his own further speech. But, at least before today, we have understood state action directed at protected books or other expressive works themselves to raise distinct constitutional concerns. The Court's decision is a grave repudiation of First Amendment principles, and with respect I dissent.

I

A

The majority believes our cases "establish quite clearly that the First Amendment does not prohibit either stringent criminal sanctions for obscenity offenses or forfeiture of expressive materials as punishment for criminal conduct." True, we have held that obscenity is expression which can be regulated and punished, within proper limitations, without violating the First Amendment. See, e.g., New York v. Ferber, 458 U.S. 747 (1982); Miller v. California, 413 U.S. 15 (1973); Paris Adult Theatre I v. Slaton, 413 U.S. 49, 57–58 (1973); Roth v. United States, 354 U.S. 476 (1957). And the majority is correct to note that we have upheld stringent fines and jail terms as punishments for violations of the federal obscenity laws. See Fort Wayne Books, Inc. v. Indiana, 489 U.S. 46, 60 (1989); Ginzburg v. United States, 383 U.S. 463, 464–65, n. 2 (1966). But that has little to do with the destruction of protected titles and the facilities for their distribution or publication. None of our cases address that matter, or it would have been unnecessary for us to reserve the specific question four Terms ago in *Fort Wayne Books, Inc. v. Indiana*, supra, 489 U.S., at 60, 65.

The fundamental defect in the majority's reasoning is a failure to recognize that the forfeiture here cannot be equated with traditional punishments such as fines and jail terms. Noting that petitioner does not challenge either the six-year jail sentence or the $100,000 fine imposed against him as punishment for his RICO convictions, the majority ponders why RICO's forfeiture penalty should be any different. The answer is that RICO's forfeiture penalties are different from traditional punishments by Congress' own design as well as in their First Amendment consequences.

The federal Racketeer Influenced and Corrupt Organizations Act (RICO) statute was passed to eradicate the infiltration of legitimate business by organized crime. Pub.L. 91–452, Title IX, 84 Stat. 941, as amended, 18 U.S.C. §§ 1961–1968 (1988 ed. and Supp. III). Earlier steps to combat organized crime were not successful, in large part because traditional penalties targeted individuals engaged in racketeering activity rather than the criminal enterprise itself. Punishing racketeers with fines and jail terms failed to break the cycle of racketeering activity because the criminal enterprises had the resources to replace convicted racketeers with new recruits. In passing RICO, Congress adopted a new approach aimed at the economic roots of organized crime: "What is needed here ... are new approaches that will deal not only with individuals, but also with the economic base through which those individuals constitute such a serious threat to the economic well-being of the Nation. In short, an attack must be made on their source of economic power itself, and the attack must take place on all available fronts." S.Rep. No. 91–617, p. 79 (1969).

Criminal liability under RICO is premised on the commission of a "pattern of racketeering activity," defined by the statute as engaging in two or more related predicate acts of racketeering within a 10–year period. 18 U.S.C. § 1961(5). A RICO conviction subjects the violator not only to traditional, though stringent, criminal fines and prison terms, but also mandatory forfeiture under § 1963.[1] It is the mandatory forfeiture penalty that is at issue here.

While forfeiture remedies have been employed with increasing frequency in civil proceedings, forfeiture remedies and penalties are the subject of historic disfavor in our country. Although in personam forfeiture statutes were well grounded in the English common law, see Calero–Toledo v. Pearson Yacht Leasing Co., 416 U.S. 663, 682–83 (1974), in personam criminal forfeiture penalties like those authorized under § 1963 were unknown in the federal system until the enactment of RICO in 1970. See 1 C. Wright, Federal Practice and Procedure § 125.1, p. 389 (2d ed. 1982). Section 1963's forfeiture penalties are novel for their punitive character as well as for their unprecedented sweep. Civil in rem forfeiture is limited in application to contraband and articles put to unlawful use, or in its broadest reach, to proceeds traceable to unlawful activity. See United States v. Parcel of Land, 92 Buena Vista Ave., Rumson, 507 U.S. 111 (1993); The Palmyra, 25 U.S. (12 Wheat.) 1, 14–15 (1827). Extending beyond contraband or its traceable proceeds, RICO mandates the forfeiture of property constituting the defendant's "interest in the racketeering enterprise" and property affording the violator a "source of influence" over the RICO enterprise. 18 U.S.C. § 1963(a). In a previous decision, we acknowledged the novelty of RICO's penalty scheme, stating that Congress

[1] Section 1963(a) provides that in imposing sentence on one convicted of racketeering offenses under § 1962, the district court shall order forfeiture of three classes of assets:

"(1) any interest the person has acquired or maintained in violation of section 1962;

"(2) any—

"(A) interest in;

"(B) security of;

"(C) claim against;

"or (D) property or contractual right of any kind affording a source of influence over; any enterprise which the person has established, operated, controlled, conducted, or participated in the conduct of, in violation of section 1962; and

"(3) any property constituting, or derived from, any proceeds which the person obtained, directly or indirectly, from racketeering activity or unlawful debt collection in violation of section 1962."

18 U.S.C. § 1963(a)(1)-(3).

passed RICO to provide "new weapons of unprecedented scope for an assault upon organized crime and its economic roots." Russello v. United States, 464 U.S. 16, 26 (1983).

As enacted in 1970, RICO targeted offenses then thought endemic to organized crime. 18 U.S.C. § 1961(1). When RICO was amended in 1984 to include obscenity as a predicate offense, there was no comment or debate in Congress on the First Amendment implications of the change. Act of Oct. 12, 1984, Pub.L. 98–473, 98 Stat. 2143. The consequence of adding a speech offense to a statutory scheme designed to curtail a different kind of criminal conduct went far beyond the imposition of severe penalties for obscenity offenses. The result was to render vulnerable to government destruction any business daring to deal in sexually explicit materials. The unrestrained power of the forfeiture weapon was not lost on the Executive Branch, which was quick to see in the amended statute the means and opportunity to move against certain types of disfavored speech. The Attorney General's Commission on Pornography soon advocated the use of RICO and similar state statutes to "substantially handicap" or "eliminate" pornography businesses. 1 United States Dept. of Justice, Attorney General's Commission on Pornography, Final Report 498 (1986). As these comments illustrate, the constitutional concerns raised by a penalty of this destructive capacity are distinct from the concerns raised by traditional methods of punishment.

The Court says that, taken together, our decisions in *Fort Wayne Books* and Arcara v. Cloud Books, Inc., 478 U.S. 697 (1986) dispose of petitioner's First Amendment argument. But while instructive, neither case is dispositive. In *Fort Wayne Books* we considered a state law patterned on the federal RICO statute, and upheld its scheme of using obscenity offenses as the predicate acts resulting in fines and jail terms of great severity. We recognized that the fear of severe penalties may result in some self-censorship by cautious booksellers, but concluded that this is a necessary consequence of conventional obscenity prohibitions. In rejecting the argument that the fines and jail terms in *Fort Wayne Books* infringed upon First Amendment principles, we regarded the penalties as equivalent to a sentence enhancement for multiple obscenity violations, a remedy of accepted constitutional legitimacy. We did not consider in *Fort Wayne Books* the First Amendment implications of extensive penal forfeitures, including the official destruction of protected expression. Further, while *Fort Wayne Books* acknowledges that some degree of self-censorship may be unavoidable in obscenity regulation, the alarming element of the forfeiture scheme here is the pervasive danger of government censorship, an issue, I submit, the Court does not confront.

In *Arcara*, we upheld against First Amendment challenge a criminal law requiring the temporary closure of an adult book store as a penal sanction for acts of prostitution occurring on the premises. We did not subject the closure penalty to First Amendment scrutiny even though the collateral consequence of its imposition would be to affect interests of traditional First Amendment concern. We said that such scrutiny was not required when a criminal penalty followed conduct "manifest[ing] absolutely no element of protected expression." 478 U.S., at 705. That the RICO prosecution of Alexander involved the targeting of a particular class of unlawful speech itself suffices to distinguish the instant case from *Arcara*. There can be little doubt that regulation and punishment of certain classes of unprotected speech has implications for other speech which is close to the proscribed line, speech which is entitled to the protections of the First Amendment. See Speiser v. Randall, 357 U.S. 513, 525 (1958). Further, a sanction requiring the temporary closure of a book store cannot be equated, as it is under the Court's unfortunate analysis, with a forfeiture punishment mandating its permanent destruction.

B

The majority tries to occupy the high ground by assuming the role of the defender of the doctrine of prior restraint. It warns that we disparage the doctrine if we reason from it. But as an analysis of our prior restraint cases reveals, our application of the First Amendment has adjusted to meet new threats to speech. The First Amendment is a rule of substantive protection, not an artifice of categories. The admitted design and the overt purpose of the forfeiture in this case are to destroy an entire speech business and all its protected titles, thus depriving the public of access to lawful expression. This is restraint in more than theory. It is censorship all too real.

Relying on the distinction between prior restraints and subsequent punishments, the majority labels the forfeiture imposed here a punishment and dismisses any further debate over the constitutionality of the forfeiture penalty under the First Amendment. Our cases do recognize a distinction between prior restraints and subsequent punishments, but that distinction is neither so rigid nor so precise that it can bear the weight the Court places upon it to sustain the destruction of a speech business and its inventory as a punishment for past expression.

In its simple, most blatant form, a prior restraint is a law which requires submission of speech to an official who may grant or deny permission to utter or publish it based upon its contents. See Staub v. City of Baxley, 355 U.S. 313, 322 (1958); Joseph Burstyn, Inc. v. Wilson, 343 U.S. 495, 503 (1952); A Quantity of Copies of Books v. Kansas, 378 U.S. 205, 222 (1964)(Harlan, J., dissenting); see also M. Nimmer, Nimmer on Freedom of Speech § 4.03, pp. 4–14 (1984). In contrast are laws which punish speech or expression only after it has occurred and been found unlawful. See Kingsley Books, Inc. v. Brown, 354 U.S. 436, 440–42 (1957). While each mechanism, once imposed, may abridge speech in a direct way by suppressing it, or in an indirect way by chilling its dissemination, we have interpreted the First Amendment as providing greater protection from prior restraints than from subsequent punishments. See, e.g., *Arcara v. Cloud Books, Inc.*, supra, 478 U.S., at 705–06; Southeastern Promotions, Ltd. v. Conrad, 420 U.S. 546, 558–59 (1975); *Kingsley Books, Inc. v. Brown*, supra, 354 U.S., at 440–42. In *Southeastern Promotions, Ltd. v. Conrad*, we explained that "[b]ehind the distinction is a theory deeply etched in our law: a free society prefers to punish the few who abuse rights of speech after they break the law than to throttle them and all others beforehand." 420 U.S., at 559.

It has been suggested that the distinction between prior restraints and subsequent punishments may have slight utility, see M. Nimmer, supra, at § 4.04, pp. 4–18 to 4–25, for in a certain sense every criminal obscenity statute is a prior restraint because of the caution a speaker or bookseller must exercise to avoid its imposition. See Vance v. Universal Amusement Co., 445 U.S. 308, 324 (1980)(White, J., dissenting, joined by Rehnquist, J.); also John C. Jeffries, Jr., Rethinking Prior Restraint, 92 Yale L.J. 409, 437 (1982). To be sure, the term prior restraint is not self-defining. One problem, of course, is that some governmental actions may have the characteristics both of punishment and prior restraint. A historical example is the sentence imposed on Hugh Singleton in 1579 after he had enraged Elizabeth I by printing a certain tract. See F. Siebert, Freedom of the Press in England, 1476–1776, pp. 91–92 (1952). Singleton was condemned to lose his right hand, thus visiting upon him both a punishment and a disability encumbering all further printing. Though the sentence appears not to have been carried out, it illustrates that a prior restraint and a subsequent punishment may occur together. Despite the concurrent operation of the two kinds of prohibitions in some cases, the distinction between them persists in our law, and it is instructive here to inquire why this is so.

Early in our legal tradition the source of the distinction was the English common law, in particular the oft cited passage from William Blackstone's 18th-century Commentaries on the Laws of England. He observed as follows: "The liberty of the press is indeed essential to the nature of a free state; but this consists in laying no previous restraints upon publications, and not in freedom from censure for criminal matter when published. Every freeman has an undoubted right to lay what sentiments he pleases before the public: to forbid this, is to destroy the freedom of the press: but if he publishes what is improper, mischievous, or illegal, he must take the consequence of his own temerity." 4 W. Blackstone, Commentaries. The English law which Blackstone was compiling had come to distrust prior restraints, but with little accompanying condemnation of subsequent punishments. Part of the explanation for this lies in the circumstance that, in the centuries before Blackstone wrote, prior censorship, including licensing, was the means by which the Crown and the Parliament controlled speech and press. See F. Siebert, Freedom of the Press in England, 1476–1776, pp. 56–63, 68–74 (1952). As those methods were the principal means used by government to control speech and press, it follows that an unyielding populace would devote its first efforts to avoiding or repealing restrictions in that form.

Even as Blackstone wrote, however, subsequent punishments were replacing the earlier censorship schemes as the mechanism for government control over disfavored speech in England. Whether Blackstone's apparent tolerance of subsequent punishments resulted from his acceptance of the English law as it then existed or his failure to grasp the potential threat these measures posed to liberty, or both, subsequent punishment in the broad sweep that he commented upon would be in flagrant violation of the principles of free speech and press that we have come to know and understand as being fundamental to our First Amendment freedoms. Indeed, in the beginning of our Republic, James Madison argued against the adoption of Blackstone's definition of free speech under the First Amendment. Said Madison: "this idea of the freedom of the press can never be admitted to be the American idea of it" because a law inflicting penalties would have the same effect as a law authorizing a prior restraint. 6 Writings of James Madison 386 (G. Hunt 1906).

The enactment of the alien and sedition laws early in our own history is an unhappy testament to the allure that restrictive measures have for governments tempted to control the speech and publications of their people. And our earliest cases tended to repeat the suggestion by Blackstone that prior restraints were the sole concern of First Amendment protections. See Patterson v. Colorado ex rel. Attorney General of Colorado, 205 U.S. 454, 462 (1907); Robertson v. Baldwin, 165 U.S. 275, 281 (1897). In time, however, the Court rejected the notion that First Amendment freedoms under our Constitution are coextensive with liberties available under the common law of England. See Grosjean v. American Press Co., 297 U.S. 233, 248–49 (1936). From this came the conclusion that "[t]he protection of the First Amendment ... is not limited to the Blackstonian idea that freedom of the press means only freedom from restraint prior to publication." Chaplinsky v. New Hampshire, 315 U.S. 568, 572, n. 3 (1942).

As our First Amendment law has developed, we have not confined the application of the prior restraint doctrine to its simpler forms, outright licensing or censorship before speech takes place. In considering governmental measures deviating from the classic form of a prior restraint yet posing many of the same dangers to First Amendment freedoms, we have extended prior restraint protection with some latitude, toward the end of declaring certain governmental actions to fall within the presumption of invalidity. This approach is evident in Near v. Minnesota ex rel. Olson, 283 U.S. 697 (1931), the leading case in which we invoked the prior restraint doctrine to invalidate a state injunctive decree.

In *Near* a Minnesota statute authorized judicial proceedings to abate as a nuisance a " 'malicious, scandalous and defamatory newspaper, magazine or other periodical.' " In a suit brought by the attorney for Hennepin County it was established that *Near* had published articles in various editions of The Saturday Press in violation of the statutory standard. Citing the instance of these past unlawful publications, the court enjoined any future violations of the state statute. In one sense the injunctive order, which paralleled the nuisance statute, did nothing more than announce the conditions under which some later punishment might be imposed, for one presumes that contempt could not be found until there was a further violation in contravention of the order. But in *Near* the publisher, because of past wrongs, was subjected to active state intervention for the control of future speech. We found that the scheme was a prior restraint because it embodied "the essence of censorship." This understanding is confirmed by our later decision in *Kingsley Books v. Brown*, where we said that it had been enough to condemn the injunction in *Near* that Minnesota had "empowered its courts to enjoin the dissemination of future issues of a publication because its past issues had been found offensive." 354 U.S., at 445.

Indeed the Court has been consistent in adopting a speech-protective definition of prior restraint when the state attempts to attack future speech in retribution for a speaker's past transgressions. See Vance v. Universal Amusement Co., 445 U.S. 308 (1980)(per curiam)(invalidating as a prior restraint procedure authorizing state courts to abate as a nuisance an adult theater which had exhibited obscene films in the past because the effect of the procedure was to prevent future exhibitions of pictures not yet found to be obscene). It is a flat misreading of our precedents to declare as the majority does that the definition of a prior restraint includes only those measures which impose a "legal impediment,"on a speaker's ability to engage in future expressive activity. Bantam Books, Inc. v. Sullivan, 372 U.S. 58, 70 (1963), best illustrates the point. There a state commission did nothing more than warn book sellers that certain titles could be obscene, implying that criminal prosecutions could follow if their warnings were not heeded. The commission had no formal enforcement powers and failure to heed its warnings was not a criminal offense. Although the commission could impose no legal impediment on a speaker's ability to engage in future expressive activity, we held that scheme was an impermissible "system of prior administrative restraints." There we said: "We are not the first court to look through forms to the substance and recognize that informal censorship may sufficiently inhibit the circulation of publications to warrant injunctive relief." If mere warning against sale of certain materials was a prior restraint, I fail to see why the physical destruction of a speech enterprise and its protected inventory is not condemned by the same doctrinal principles.

One wonders what today's majority would have done if faced in *Near* with a novel argument to extend the traditional conception of the prior restraint doctrine. In view of the formalistic approach the Court advances today, the Court likely would have rejected *Near*'s pleas on the theory that to accept his argument would be to "blur the line separating prior restraints from subsequent punishments to such a degree that it would be impossible to determine with any certainty whether a particular measure is a prior restraint or not." In so holding the Court would have ignored, as the Court does today, that the applicability of First Amendment analysis to a governmental action depends not alone upon the name by which the action is called, but upon its operation and effect on the suppression of speech. *Near*, supra, 283 U.S., at 708 ("the court has regard to substance and not to mere matters of form, and ... in accordance with familiar principles ... statute[s] must be tested by [their] operation and effect").

See also Smith v. Daily Mail Publishing Co., 443 U.S. 97, 101 (1979)(the First Amendment's application to a civil or criminal sanction is not determined solely by whether that action is viewed "as a prior restraint or as a penal sanction"); *Southeastern Promotions, Ltd. v. Conrad*, 420 U.S., at 552–53 (challenged action is "indistinguishable in its censoring effect" from official actions consistently identified as prior restraints); Schneider v. State (Town of Irvington), 308 U.S. 147, 161 (1939)("In every case, therefore, where legislative abridgement of [First Amendment] rights is asserted, the courts should be astute to examine the effect of the challenged legislation").

The cited cases identify a progression in our First Amendment jurisprudence which results from a more fundamental principle. As governments try new ways to subvert essential freedoms, legal and constitutional systems respond by making more explicit the nature and the extent of the liberty in question. First in *Near*, and later in *Bantam Books* and *Vance*, we were faced with official action which did not fall within the traditional meaning of the term prior restraint, yet posed many of the same censorship dangers. Our response was to hold that the doctrine not only includes licensing schemes requiring speech to be submitted to a censor for review prior to dissemination, but also encompasses injunctive systems which threaten or bar future speech based on some past infraction.

Although we consider today a new method of government control with unmistakable dangers of official censorship, the majority concludes that First Amendment freedoms are not endangered because forfeiture follows a lawful conviction for obscenity offenses. But this explanation does not suffice. The rights of free speech and press in their broad and legitimate sphere cannot be defeated by the simple expedient of punishing after in lieu of censoring before. See *Smith v. Daily Mail Publishing Co.*, supra, 443 U.S., at 101–02; Thornhill v. Alabama, 310 U.S. 88, 101–02 (1940). This is so because in some instances the operation and effect of a particular enforcement scheme, though not in the form of a traditional prior restraint, may be to raise the same concerns which inform all of our prior restraint cases: the evils of state censorship and the unacceptable chilling of protected speech.

The operation and effect of RICO's forfeiture remedies is different from a heavy fine or a severe jail sentence because RICO's forfeiture provisions are different in purpose and kind from ordinary criminal sanctions. The government's stated purpose under RICO, to destroy or incapacitate the offending enterprise, bears a striking resemblance to the motivation for the state nuisance statute the Court struck down as an impermissible prior restraint in *Near*. The purpose of the state statute in *Near* was "not punishment, in the ordinary sense, but suppression of the offending newspaper or periodical." 283 U.S., at 711. In the context of the First Amendment, it is quite odd indeed to apply a measure implemented not only to deter unlawful conduct by imposing punishment after violations, but to " 'incapacitate, and . . . directly to remove the corrupting influence from the channels of commerce.' " *Russello v. United States*, 464

U.S., at 28, quoting 116 Cong.Rec. 18955 (1970)(remarks of sponsor Sen. McClellan). The particular nature of Ferris Alexander's activities ought not blind the Court to what is at stake here. Under the principle the Court adopts, any bookstore or press enterprise could be forfeited as punishment for even a single obscenity conviction.

Assuming the constitutionality of the mandatory forfeiture under § 1963 when applied to nonspeech-related conduct, the constitutional analysis must be different when that remedy is imposed for violations of the federal obscenity laws. "Our decisions furnish examples of legal devices and doctrines, in most applications consistent with the Constitution, which cannot be applied in settings where they have the collateral effect of inhibiting the freedom of expression[.]" Smith v. California, 361 U.S. 147, 150–51 (1959). The regulation of obscenity, often separated from protected expression only by a "dim and uncertain line," must be accomplished through "procedures that will ensure against the curtailment of constitutionally protected expression." *Bantam Books v. Sullivan*, 372 U.S., at 66. Because freedoms of expression are "vulnerable to gravely damaging yet barely visible encroachments," ibid., the Government must use measures that are sensitive to First Amendment concerns in its task of regulating or punishing speech. *Speiser v. Randall*, 357 U.S., at 525.

Whatever one might label the RICO forfeiture provisions at issue in this case, be it effective, innovative, or draconian, § 1963 was not designed for sensitive and exacting application. What is happening here is simple: Books and films are condemned and destroyed not for their own content but for the content of their owner's prior speech. Our law does not permit the government to burden future speech for this sort of taint. Section 1963 requires trial courts to forfeit not only the unlawful items and any proceeds from their sale, but also the defendant's entire interest in the enterprise involved in the RICO violations and any assets affording the defendant a source of influence over the enterprise. 18 U.S.C. §§ 1963(a)(1)-(3). A defendant's exposure to this massive penalty is grounded on the commission of just two or more related obscenity offenses committed within a ten-year period. Aptly described, RICO's forfeiture provisions "arm prosecutors not with scalpels to excise obscene portions of an adult bookstore's inventory but with sickles to mow down the entire undesired use." *Fort Wayne Books*, 489 U.S., at 85 (Stevens, J., concurring in part and dissenting in part).

What is at work in this case is not the power to punish an individual for his past transgressions but the authority to suppress a particular class of disfavored speech. The forfeiture provisions accomplish this in a direct way by seizing speech presumed to be protected along with the instruments of its dissemination, and in an indirect way by threatening all who engage in the business of distributing adult or sexually explicit materials with the same disabling measures. Cf. Pittsburgh Press Co. v. Pittsburgh Comm'n on Human Relations, 413 U.S. 376, 390 (1973)(the special vice of the prior restraint is suppression of speech, either directly or by inducing caution in the speaker, prior to a determination that the targeted speech is unprotected by the First Amendment).

In a society committed to freedom of thought, inquiry, and discussion without interference or guidance from the state, public confidence in the institutions devoted to the dissemination of written matter and films is essential. That confidence erodes if it is perceived that speakers and the press are vulnerable for all of their expression based on some errant expression in the past. Independence of speech and press can be just as compromised by the threat of official intervention as by the fact of it. See *Bantam Books, Inc. v. Sullivan*, supra, 372 U.S., at 70. Though perhaps not in the form of a classic prior restraint, the application of the forfeiture statute here bears its censorial cast.

Arcara recognized, as the Court today does not, the vital difference between a punishment imposed for a speech offense and a punishment imposed for some other crime. Where the government seeks forfeiture of a bookstore because of its owner's drug offenses, there is little reason to surmise, absent evidence of selective prosecution, that abolishing the bookstore is related to the government's disfavor of the publication outlet or its activities. Where, however, RICO forfeiture stems from a previous speech offense, the punishment serves not only the government's interest in purging organized-crime taint, but also its interest in deterring the activities of the speech-related business itself. The threat of a censorial motive and of on going speech supervision by the state justifies the imposition of First Amendment protection. Free speech principles, well established by our cases, require in this case that the forfeiture of the inventory and of the speech distribution facilities be held invalid.

The distinct concern raised by § 1963 forfeiture penalties is not a proportionality concern; all punishments are subject to analysis for proportionality and this concern should be addressed under the Eighth Amendment. See Austin v. United States, 509 U.S. 602 (1993). Here, the question is whether, when imposed as punishment for violation of the federal obscenity laws, the operation of RICO's forfeiture provisions is an exercise of government censorship and control over protected speech as condemned in our prior restraint cases. In my view the effect is just that. For this reason I would invalidate those portions of the judgment which mandated the forfeiture of petitioner's business enterprise and inventory, as well as all property affording him a source of influence over that enterprise.

II

Quite apart from the direct bearing that our prior restraint cases have on the entire forfeiture that was ordered in this case, the destruction of books and films that were not obscene and not adjudged to be so is a remedy with no parallel in our cases. The majority says that our cases "establish quite clearly that the First Amendment does not prohibit ... forfeiture of expressive materials as punishment for criminal conduct." But the single case cited in support of this stark new threat to all speech enterprises is *Arcara v. Cloud Books*. *Arcara*, as discussed above, is quite inapposite.   There we found unconvincing the argument that protected bookselling activities were burdened by the closure, saying that the owners "remain free to sell [and the public remains free to acquire] the same materials at another location." 478 U.S., at 705. Alexander and the public do not have those choices here for a simple reason: The Government has destroyed the inventory. Further, the sanction in *Arcara* did not involve a complete confiscation or destruction of protected expression as did the forfeiture in this case. Here the inventory forfeited consisted of hundreds of original titles and thousands of copies, all of which are presumed to be protected speech. In fact, some of the materials seized were the very ones the jury here determined not to be obscene. Even so, all of the inventory was seized and destroyed.

Even when interim pretrial seizures are used, we have been careful to say that First Amendment materials cannot be taken out of circulation until they have been determined to be unlawful. "[W]hile the general rule under the Fourth Amendment is that any and all contraband, instrumentalities, and evidence of crimes may be seized on probable cause . . ., it is otherwise when materials presumptively protected by the First Amendment are involved." *Fort Wayne Books*, supra, 489 U.S., at 63. See id., at 65–66; Lo–Ji Sales, Inc. v. New York, 442 U.S. 319, 326, n. 5 (1979)(the First Amendment imposes special constraints on searches for and seizures of presumptively protected materials).

In Marcus v. Search Warrant, 367 U.S. 717, 731–33 (1961), we invalidated a mass pretrial seizure of allegedly obscene publications achieved through a warrant that was vague and unspecific. The constitutional defect there was that the seizure was imposed without safeguards necessary to assure nonobscene material the constitutional protection to which it is entitled. In similar fashion we invalidated in *A Quantity of Copies of Books v. Kansas*, 378 U.S., at 211–13, a state procedure authorizing seizure of books alleged to be obscene prior to hearing, even though the system involved judicial examination of some of the seized titles. While the force behind the special protection accorded searches for and seizures of First Amendment materials is the risk of prior restraint, see Maryland v. Macon, 472 U.S. 463, 470 (1985), in substance the rule prevents seizure and destruction of expressive materials in circumstances such as are presented in this case without an adjudication of their unlawful character.

It follows from the search cases in which the First Amendment required exacting protection, that one title does not become seizable or tainted because of its proximity on the shelf to another. And if that is the rule for interim seizures, it follows with even greater force that protected materials cannot be destroyed altogether for some alleged taint from an owner who committed a speech violation. In attempting to distinguish the holdings of *Marcus* and *A Quantity of Books*, the Court describes the constitutional infirmity in those cases as follows: "the Government had seized or otherwise restrained materials suspected of being obscene without a prior judicial determination that they were in fact so." But the same constitutional defect is present in the case before us today and the Court fails to explain why it is not fatal to the forfeiture punishment here under review. Thus, while in the past we invalidated seizures which resulted in a temporary removal of presumptively protected materials from circulation, today the Court approves of government measures having the same permanent effect. In my view, the forfeiture of expressive material here that had not been adjudged to be obscene, or otherwise without the protection of the First Amendment, was unconstitutional.

. . .

Given the Court's principal holding, I can interpose no objection to remanding the case for further consideration under the Eighth Amendment. But it is unnecessary to reach the Eighth Amendment question. The Court's failure to reverse this flagrant violation of the right of free speech and expression is a deplorable abandonment of fundamental First Amendment principles. I dissent from the judgment and from the opinion of the Court.

CONCLUDING NOTE ON ENTERPRISE CRIMINALITY AND FORFEITURE

Beyond the issues that have already been discussed in this Chapter, several additional legal bases for challenging forfeitures deserve at least passing mention. In United States v. James Daniel Good Real Property, 510 U.S. 43 (1993), the Supreme Court held that "absent exigent circumstances, the Due Process Clause requires the Government to afford notice and an opportunity to be heard before seizing real property subject to civil forfeiture." And in Republic Nat'l Bank v. United States, 506 U.S. 80 (1992), the Court ruled that the government cannot transfer the proceeds derived from seized property out of the judicial district in order to deprive the appellate court of jurisdiction.

In United States v. Lot 5, Fox Grove, 23 F.3d 359 (11th Cir.1994), the Eleventh Circuit became the first Court of Appeals to address the interaction between state constitutional homestead provisions and federal civil forfeiture statutes; not surprisingly, the court held that the federal statutes pre-empt such state constitutional laws. See also United States v. Curtis, 965 F.2d 610 (8th Cir.1992)(reaching same result with respect to state homestead statutes).

Nancy J. King has recently articulated an interesting new theory of "cumulative excessiveness," derived from the fifth and eighth amendments, that would permit legislatures to impose multiple penalties—including civil and criminal forfeitures—for the same conduct, but that would also empower courts to impose limits on the total amount of punishment that could be "piled up" on an offender in this way. King's theory would, she contends, relieve some of the pressure that may be distorting the Supreme Court's double-jeopardy jurisprudence. See Nancy J. King, Portioning Punishment: Constitutional Limits on Successive and Excessive Penalties, 144 U. Pa. L. Rev. 101 (1995).

Finally, other recent and useful academic commentaries on forfeiture law include Sarah N. Welling & Medrith Lee Hager, Defining Excessiveness: Applying the Eighth Amendment to Forfeiture After *Austin v. United States*, 83 Ky. L.J. 835 (1995); Sandra Guerra, Reconciling Federal Asset Forfeitures and Drug Offense Sentencing, 78 Minn. L. Rev. 805 (1994); and the various articles contained in a special symposium issue on civil forfeiture laws, beginning at 39 New York Law School L. Rev. 1 (1994).

CHAPTER V

SENTENCING FOR FEDERAL CRIMES

In the federal system, sentencing is governed primarily by the Sentencing Reform Act of 1984 and the Federal Sentencing Guidelines promulgated thereunder. In many ways, the Federal Sentencing Guidelines—which severely restrict the traditional sentencing discretion of judges in favor of so-called "determinate sentencing"—resemble the sentencing guidelines presently in effect in several states. But some aspects of federal sentencing, including the overall severity of many sentences (especially for drug-related crimes), the widespread use of "real offense" factors (i.e., sentencing based on a defendant's entire course of conduct, not just the offense of conviction), and the power given to judges to depart entirely from the Guidelines if the prosecutor certifies that a defendant has rendered "substantial assistance," give federal prosecutors much more leverage than their state counterparts in dealing with members of criminal organizations.

This chapter begins with an introduction to the structure and operation of the Federal Sentencing Guidelines. It then examines several aspects of federal sentencing that seem tailor-made for combatting organized crime. It closes with a brief look at the federal death penalty, a specific sentence that—at least in terms of its potential application—has been substantially expanded by the Violent Crime Control and Law Enforcement Assistance Act of 1994.

SECTION 1: INTRODUCTION TO THE FEDERAL SENTENCING GUIDELINES

Mistretta v. United States
Supreme Court of the United States, 1989.
488 U.S. 361.

■ JUSTICE BLACKMUN delivered the opinion of the Court.

In this litigation, we granted certiorari before judgment in the United States Court of Appeals for the Eighth Circuit in order to consider the constitutionality of the Sentencing Guidelines promulgated by the United States Sentencing Commission. The Commission is a body created under the Sentencing Reform Act of 1984 (Act), as amended, 18 U.S.C. § 3551 et seq., and 28 U.S.C. §§ 991–998.[1] The United States District Court for the

---

[1] Hereinafter, for simplicity in citation, each reference to the Act is directed to Supplement IV to the 1982 edition of the United States Code.

Western District of Missouri ruled that the Guidelines were constitutional. United States v. Johnson, 682 F.Supp. 1033 (W.D.Mo.1988).

I

A

Background

For almost a century, the Federal Government employed in criminal cases a system of indeterminate sentencing. Statutes specified the penalties for crimes but nearly always gave the sentencing judge wide discretion to decide whether the offender should be incarcerated and for how long, whether he should be fined and how much, and whether some lesser restraint, such as probation, should be imposed instead of imprisonment or fine. This indeterminate-sentencing system was supplemented by the utilization of parole, by which an offender was returned to society under the "guidance and control" of a parole officer. See Zerbst v. Kidwell, 304 U.S. 359, 363 (1938).

Both indeterminate sentencing and parole were based on concepts of the offender's possible, indeed probable, rehabilitation, a view that it was realistic to attempt to rehabilitate the inmate and thereby to minimize the risk that he would resume criminal activity upon his return to society. It obviously required the judge and the parole officer to make their respective sentencing and release decisions upon their own assessments of the offender's amenability to rehabilitation. As a result, the court and the officer were in positions to exercise, and usually did exercise, very broad discretion. See Sanford H. Kadish, The Advocate and the Expert—Counsel in the Peno–Correctional Process, 45 Minn.L.Rev. 803, 812–13 (1961). This led almost inevitably to the conclusion on the part of a reviewing court that the sentencing judge "sees more and senses more" than the appellate court; thus, the judge enjoyed the "superiority of his nether position," for that court's determination as to what sentence was appropriate met with virtually unconditional deference on appeal. See Maurice Rosenberg, Judicial Discretion of the Trial Court, Viewed From Above, 22 Syracuse L.Rev. 635, 663 (1971). See Dorszynski v. United States, 418 U.S. 424, 431 (1974). The decision whether to parole was also "predictive and discretionary." Morrissey v. Brewer, 408 U.S. 471, 480 (1972). The correction official possessed almost absolute discretion over the parole decision.

Historically, federal sentencing—the function of determining the scope and extent of punishment—never has been thought to be assigned by the Constitution to the exclusive jurisdiction of any one of the three Branches of Government. Congress, of course, has the power to fix the sentence for a federal crime, United States v. Wiltberger, 18 U.S. (5 Wheat.) 76 (1820), and the scope of judicial discretion with respect to a sentence is subject to congressional control. Ex parte United States, 242 U.S. 27 (1916). Congress early abandoned fixed-sentence rigidity, however, and put in place a system of ranges within which the sentencer could choose the precise punishment. See United States v. Grayson, 438 U.S. 41, 45–46 (1978). Congress delegated almost unfettered discretion to the sentencing judge to determine what the sentence should be within the customarily wide range so selected. This broad discretion was further enhanced by the power later granted the judge to suspend the sentence and by the resulting growth of an elaborate probation system. Also, with the advent of parole, Congress moved toward a "three-way sharing" of sentencing responsibility by granting corrections personnel in the Executive Branch the discretion to release a prisoner before the expiration of the sentence imposed by the judge. Thus, under the indeterminate-sentence system, Congress defined the maximum, the judge imposed a sentence within the statutory range (which he usually could replace with probation), and the Executive Branch's parole official eventually determined the actual duration of imprisonment. See Williams v. New York, 337 U.S. 241, 248 (1949). See also United States v. Brown, 381 U.S. 437, 443 (1965)("[I]f a given policy can be implemented only by a combination of legislative enactment, judicial application, and executive implementation, no man or group of men will be able to impose its unchecked will").

Serious disparities in sentences, however, were common. Rehabilitation as a sound penological theory came to be questioned and, in any event, was regarded by some as an unattainable goal for most cases. See Norval Morris, The Future of Imprisonment 24–43 (1974); Frank Allen, The Decline of the Rehabilitative Ideal (1981). In 1958, Congress authorized the creation of judicial sentencing institutes and joint councils, see 28 U.S.C. § 334, to formulate standards and criteria for sentencing. In 1973, the United States Parole Board adopted guidelines that established a "customary range" of confinement. See United States Parole Comm'n v. Geraghty, 445 U.S. 388, 391 (1980). Congress in 1976 endorsed this initiative through the Parole Commission and Reorganization Act, 18 U.S.C. §§ 4201–4218, an attempt to envision for the Parole Commission a role, at least in part, "to moderate the disparities in the sentencing practices of individual judges." United States v. Addonizio, 442 U.S. 178, 189 (1979). That Act, however, did not disturb the division of sentencing responsibility among the three Branches. The judge continued to exercise discretion and to set the sentence within the statutory range fixed by Congress, while the prisoner's actual release date generally was set by the Parole Commission.

This proved to be no more than a way station. Fundamental and widespread dissatisfaction with the uncertainties and the disparities continued to be expressed. Congress had wrestled with the problem for more than a decade when, in 1984, it enacted the sweeping reforms that are at issue here.

Helpful in our consideration and analysis of the statute is the Senate Report on the 1984 legislation, S.Rep. No. 98–225 (1983). The Report referred to the "outmoded rehabilitation model" for federal criminal sentencing, and recognized that the efforts of the criminal justice system to achieve rehabilitation of offenders had failed. Id., at 38. It observed that the indeterminate-sentencing system had two "unjustifi[ed]" and "shameful" consequences. Id., at 38, 65. The first was the great variation among sentences imposed by different judges upon similarly situated offenders. The second was the uncertainty as to the time the offender would spend in prison. Each was a serious impediment to an evenhanded and effective operation of the criminal justice system. The Report went on to note that parole was an inadequate device for overcoming these undesirable consequences. This was due to the division of authority between the sentencing judge and the parole officer who often worked at cross purposes; to the fact that the Parole Commission's own guidelines did not take into account factors Congress regarded as important in sentencing, such as the sophistication of the offender and the role the offender played in an offense committed with others; and to the fact that the Parole Commission had only limited power to adjust a sentence imposed by the court.

Before settling on a mandatory-guideline system, Congress considered other competing proposals for sentencing reform. It rejected strict determinate sentencing because it concluded that a guideline system would be successful in reducing sentence disparities while retaining the flexibility needed to adjust for unanticipated factors arising in a particular case. The Judiciary Committee rejected a proposal that would have made the sentencing guidelines only advisory.

B

The Act

The Act, as adopted, revises the old sentencing process in several ways:

1. It rejects imprisonment as a means of promoting rehabilitation, 28 U.S.C. § 994(k), and it states that punishment should serve retributive, educational, deterrent, and incapacitative goals, 18 U.S.C. § 3553(a)(2).

2. It consolidates the power that had been exercised by the sentencing judge and the Parole Commission to decide what punishment an offender should suffer. This is done by creating the United States Sentencing Commission, directing that Commission to devise guidelines to be used for sentencing, and prospectively abolishing the Parole Commission. 28 U.S.C. §§ 991, 994, and 995(a)(1).

3. It makes all sentences basically determinate. A prisoner is to be released at the completion of his sentence reduced only by any credit earned by good behavior while in custody. 18 U.S.C. §§ 3624(a) and (b).

4. It makes the Sentencing Commission's guidelines binding on the courts, although it preserves for the judge the discretion to depart from the guideline applicable to a particular case if the judge finds an aggravating or mitigating factor present that the Commission did not adequately consider when formulating guidelines. §§ 3553(a) and (b). The Act also requires the court to state its reasons for the sentence imposed and to give "the specific reason" for imposing a sentence different from that described in the guideline. § 3553(c).

5. It authorizes limited appellate review of the sentence. It permits a defendant to appeal a sentence that is above the defined range, and it permits the Government to appeal a sentence that is below that range. It also permits either side to appeal an incorrect application of the guideline. §§ 3742(a) and (b).

Thus, guidelines were meant to establish a range of determinate sentences for categories of offenses and defendants according to various specified factors, "among others." 28 U.S.C. §§ 994(b), (c), and (d). The maximum of the range ordinarily may not exceed the minimum by more than the greater of 25% or six months, and each sentence is to be within the limit provided by existing law. §§ 994(a) and (b)(2).

C

The Sentencing Commission

The Commission is established "as an independent commission in the judicial branch of the United States." § 991(a). It has seven voting members (one of whom is the Chairman) appointed by the President "by and with the advice and consent of the Senate." "At least three of the members shall be Federal judges selected after considering a list of six judges recommended to the President by the Judicial Conference of the United States." Ibid. No more than four members of the Commission shall be members of the same political party. The Attorney General, or his designee, is an ex officio non-voting member. The Chairman and other members of the Commission are subject to removal by the President "only for neglect of duty or malfeasance in office or for other good cause shown." Ibid. Except for initial staggering of terms, a voting member serves for six years and may not serve more than two full terms. §§ 992(a) and (b).

D

The Responsibilities of the Commission

In addition to the duty the Commission has to promulgate determinative-sentence guidelines, it is under an obligation periodically to "review and revise" the guidelines. § 994(*o*). It is to "consult with authorities on, and individual and institutional representatives of, various aspects of the Federal criminal justice system." Ibid. It must report to Congress "any amendments of the guidelines." § 994(p). It is to make recommendations to Congress whether the grades or maximum penalties should be modified. § 994(r). It must submit to Congress at least annually an analysis of the operation of the guidelines. § 994(w). It is to issue "general policy statements" regarding their application. § 994(a)(2). And it has the power to "establish general policies . . . as are necessary to carry out the purposes" of the legislation, § 995(a)(1); to "monitor the performance of probation officers" with respect to the guidelines, § 995(a)(9); to "devise and conduct periodic training programs of instruction in sentencing techniques for judicial and probation personnel" and others, § 995(a)(18); and to "perform such other functions as are required to permit Federal courts to meet their responsibilities" as to sentencing, § 995(a)(22).

We note, in passing, that the monitoring function is not without its burden. Every year, with respect to each of more than 40,000 sentences, the federal courts must forward, and the Commission must review, the presentence report, the guideline worksheets, the tribunal's sentencing statement, and any written plea agreement.

II

This Litigation

On December 10, 1987, John M. Mistretta (petitioner) and another were indicted in the United States District Court for the Western District of Missouri on three counts centering in a cocaine sale. Mistretta moved to have the promulgated Guidelines ruled unconstitutional on the grounds that the Sentencing Commission was constituted in violation of the established doctrine of separation of powers, and that Congress delegated excessive authority to the Commission to structure the Guidelines. As has been noted, the District Court was not persuaded by these contentions.

The District Court rejected petitioner's delegation argument on the ground that, despite the language of the statute, the Sentencing Commission "should be judicially characterized as having Executive Branch status," and that the Guidelines are similar to substantive rules promulgated by other agencies. The court also rejected petitioner's claim that the Act is unconstitutional because it requires Article III federal judges to serve on the Commission. The court stated, however, that its opinion "does not imply that I have no serious doubts about some parts of the Sentencing Guidelines and the legality of their anticipated operation."

Petitioner had pleaded guilty to the first count of his indictment (conspiracy and agreement to distribute cocaine, in violation of 21 U.S.C. §§ 846 and 841(b)(1)(B)). The Government thereupon moved to dismiss the remaining counts. That motion was granted. Petitioner was sentenced under the Guidelines to 18 months' imprisonment, to be followed by a 3-year term of supervised release. The court also imposed a $1,000 fine and a $50 special assessment.

Petitioner filed a notice of appeal to the Eighth Circuit, but both petitioner and the United States, pursuant to this Court's Rule 18, petitioned for certiorari before judgment. Because of the "imperative public importance" of the issue, as prescribed by the Rule, and because of the disarray among the Federal District Courts, we granted those petitions.

III

Delegation of Power

Petitioner argues that in delegating the power to promulgate sentencing guidelines for every federal criminal offense to an independent Sentencing Commission, Congress has granted the Commission excessive legislative discretion in violation of the constitutionally based nondelegation doctrine. We do not agree.

The nondelegation doctrine is rooted in the principle of separation of powers that underlies our tripartite system of Government. The Constitution provides that "[a]ll legislative Powers herein granted shall be vested in a Congress of the United States," U.S. Const., Art. I, § 1, and we long have insisted that "the integrity and maintenance of the system of government ordained by the Constitution" mandate that Congress generally cannot delegate its legislative power to another Branch. Field v. Clark, 143 U.S. 649, 692 (1892). We also have recognized, however, that the separation-of-powers principle, and the nondelegation doctrine in particular, do not prevent Congress from obtaining the assistance of its coordinate Branches. In a passage now enshrined in our jurisprudence, Chief Justice Taft, writing for the Court, explained our approach to such cooperative ventures: "In determining what [Congress] may do in seeking assistance from another branch, the extent and character of that assistance must be fixed according to common sense and the inherent necessities of the government co-ordination." J.W. Hampton, Jr., & Co. v. United States, 276 U.S. 394, 406 (1928). So long as Congress "shall lay down by legislative act an intelligible principle to which the person or body authorized to [exercise the delegated authority] is directed to conform, such legislative action is not a forbidden delegation of legislative power." Id., at 409.

Applying this "intelligible principle" test to congressional delegations, our jurisprudence has been driven by a practical understanding that in our increasingly complex society, replete with ever changing and more technical problems, Congress simply cannot do its job absent an ability to delegate power under broad general directives. See Opp Cotton Mills, Inc. v. Administrator, Wage and Hour Div. of Dept. of Labor, 312 U.S. 126, 145 (1941)("In an increasingly complex society Congress obviously could not perform its functions if it were obliged to find all the facts subsidiary to the basic conclusions which support the defined legislative policy"). "The Constitution has never been regarded as denying to the Congress the necessary resources of flexibility and practicality, which will enable it to perform its function." Panama Refining Co. v. Ryan, 293 U.S. 388, 421 (1935). Accordingly, this Court has deemed it "constitutionally sufficient if Congress clearly delineates the general policy, the public agency which is to apply it, and the boundaries of this delegated authority." American Power & Light Co. v. SEC, 329 U.S. 90, 105 (1946).

Until 1935, this Court never struck down a challenged statute on delegation grounds. See Synar v. United States, 626 F.Supp. 1374, 1383 (D.C.)(three-judge court), aff'd sub nom. Bowsher v. Synar, 478 U.S. 714 (1986). After invalidating in 1935 two statutes as excessive delegations, see A.L.A. Schechter Poultry Corp. v. United States, 295 U.S. 495 (1935), and *Panama Refining Co. v. Ryan*, supra, we have upheld, again without deviation, Congress' ability to delegate power under broad standards.[7] See,

---

[7] In *Schechter* and *Panama Refining* the Court concluded that Congress had failed to articulate any policy or standard that would serve to confine the discretion of the authori-ties to whom Congress had delegated power. No delegation of the kind at issue in those cases is present here. The Act does not make crimes of acts never before criminal-

e.g., Lichter v. United States, 334 U.S. 742, 785–86 (1948)(upholding delegation of authority to determine excessive profits); *American Power & Light Co. v. SEC*, 329 U.S., at 105 (upholding delegation of authority to Securities and Exchange Commission to prevent unfair or inequitable distribution of voting power among security holders); Yakus v. United States, 321 U.S. 414, 426 (1944)(upholding delegation to Price Administrator to fix commodity prices that would be fair and equitable, and would effectuate purposes of Emergency Price Control Act of 1942); FPC v. Hope Natural Gas Co., 320 U.S. 591, 600 (1944)(upholding delegation to Federal Power Commission to determine just and reasonable rates); National Broadcasting Co. v. United States, 319 U.S. 190, 225–26 (1943)(upholding delegation to Federal Communications Commission to regulate broadcast licensing "as public interest, convenience, or necessity" require).

In light of our approval of these broad delegations, we harbor no doubt that Congress' delegation of authority to the Sentencing Commission is sufficiently specific and detailed to meet constitutional requirements. Congress charged the Commission with three goals: to "assure the meeting of the purposes of sentencing as set forth" in the Act; to "provide certainty and fairness in meeting the purposes of sentencing, avoiding unwarranted sentencing disparities among defendants with similar records ... while maintaining sufficient flexibility to permit individualized sentences," where appropriate; and to "reflect, to the extent practicable, advancement in knowledge of human behavior as it relates to the criminal justice process." 28 U.S.C. § 991(b)(1). Congress further specified four "purposes" of sentencing that the Commission must pursue in carrying out its mandate: "to reflect the seriousness of the offense, to promote respect for the law, and to provide just punishment for the offense"; "to afford adequate deterrence to criminal conduct"; "to protect the public from further crimes of the defendant"; and "to provide the defendant with needed ... correctional treatment." 18 U.S.C. § 3553(a)(2).

In addition, Congress prescribed the specific tool—the guidelines system—for the Commission to use in regulating sentencing. More particularly, Congress directed the Commission to develop a system of "sentencing ranges" applicable "for each category of offense involving each category of defendant." 28 U.S.C. § 994(b).[8] Congress instructed the Commission

---

ized, see Fahey v. Mallonee, 332 U.S. 245, 249 (1947)(analyzing *Panama Refining*), or delegate regulatory power to private individuals, see Yakus v. United States, 321 U.S. 414, 424 (1944)(analyzing *Schechter*). In recent years, our application of the nondelegation doctrine principally has been limited to the interpretation of statutory texts, and, more particularly, to giving narrow constructions to statutory delegations that might otherwise be thought to be unconstitutional. See, e.g., Industrial Union Dept. v. American Petroleum Institute, 448 U.S. 607, 646 (1980); Na-

tional Cable Television Assn. v. United States, 415 U.S. 336, 342 (1974).

[8] Congress mandated that the guidelines include:

"(A) a determination whether to impose a sentence to probation, a fine, or a term of imprisonment;

"(B) a determination as to the appropriate amount of a fine or the appropriate length of a term of probation or a term of imprisonment;

"(C) a determination whether a sentence to a term of imprisonment should in-that these sentencing ranges must be consistent with pertinent provisions of Title 18 of the United States Code and could not include sentences in excess of the statutory maxima. Congress also required that for sentences of imprisonment, "the maximum of the range established for such a term shall not exceed the minimum of that range by more than the greater of 25 percent or 6 months, except that, if the minimum term of the range is 30 years or more, the maximum may be life imprisonment." § 994(b)(2). Moreover, Congress directed the Commission to use current average sentences "as a starting point" for its structuring of the sentencing ranges. § 994(m).

To guide the Commission in its formulation of offense categories, Congress directed it to consider seven factors: the grade of the offense; the aggravating and mitigating circumstances of the crime; the nature and degree of the harm caused by the crime; the community view of the gravity of the offense; the public concern generated by the crime; the deterrent effect that a particular sentence may have on others; and the current incidence of the offense. §§ 994(c)(1)-(7).[9] Congress set forth 11 factors for the Commission to consider in establishing categories of defendants. These include the offender's age, education, vocational skills, mental and emotional condition, physical condition (including drug dependence), previous employment record, family ties and responsibilities, community ties, role in the offense, criminal history, and degree of dependence upon crime for a livelihood. § 994(d)(1)-(11).[10] Congress also prohibited the Commission from considering the "race, sex, national origin, creed, and socioeconomic status of offenders," § 994(d), and instructed that the guidelines should reflect the "general inappropriateness" of considering certain other

clude a requirement that the defendant be placed on a term of supervised release after imprisonment, and, if so, the appropriate length of such a term; and

"(D) a determination whether multiple sentences to terms of imprisonment should be ordered to run concurrently or consecutively." 28 U.S.C. § 994(a)(1).

[9] The Senate Report on the legislation elaborated on the purpose to be served by each factor. The Report noted, for example, that the reference to the community view of the gravity of an offense was "not intended to mean that a sentence might be enhanced because of public outcry about a single offense," but "to suggest that changed community norms concerning particular certain criminal behavior might be justification for increasing or decreasing the recommended penalties for the offense." Report, at 170. The Report, moreover, gave specific examples of areas in which prevailing sentences might be too lenient, including the treatment of major white-collar criminals. Id., at 177.

[10] Again, the legislative history provides additional guidance for the Commission's consideration of the statutory factors. For example, the history indicates Congress' intent that the "criminal history ... factor includes not only the number of prior criminal acts—whether or not they resulted in convictions—the defendant has engaged in, but their seriousness, their recentness or remoteness, and their indication whether the defendant is a 'career criminal' or a manager of a criminal enterprise." Report, at 174. This legislative history, together with Congress' directive that the Commission begin its consideration of the sentencing ranges by ascertaining the average sentence imposed in each category in the past, and Congress' explicit requirement that the Commission consult with authorities in the field of criminal sentencing provide a factual background and statutory context that give content to the mandate of the Commission. See American Power & Light Co. v. SEC, 329 U.S. 90, 104–05 (1946).

factors, such as current unemployment, that might serve as proxies for forbidden factors, § 994(e).

In addition to these overarching constraints, Congress provided even more detailed guidance to the Commission about categories of offenses and offender characteristics. Congress directed that guidelines require a term of confinement at or near the statutory maximum for certain crimes of violence and for drug offenses, particularly when committed by recidivists. § 994(h). Congress further directed that the Commission assure a substantial term of imprisonment for an offense constituting a third felony conviction, for a career felon, for one convicted of a managerial role in a racketeering enterprise, for a crime of violence by an offender on release from a prior felony conviction, and for an offense involving a substantial quantity of narcotics. § 994(i). Congress also instructed "that the guidelines reflect . . . the general appropriateness of imposing a term of imprisonment" for a crime of violence that resulted in serious bodily injury. On the other hand, Congress directed that guidelines reflect the general inappropriateness of imposing a sentence of imprisonment "in cases in which the defendant is a first offender who has not been convicted of a crime of violence or an otherwise serious offense." § 994(j). Congress also enumerated various aggravating and mitigating circumstances, such as, respectively, multiple offenses or substantial assistance to the Government, to be reflected in the guidelines. §§ 994(*l*) and (n). In other words, although Congress granted the Commission substantial discretion in formulating guidelines, in actuality it legislated a full hierarchy of punishment—from near maximum imprisonment, to substantial imprisonment, to some imprisonment, to alternatives—and stipulated the most important offense and offender characteristics to place defendants within these categories.

We cannot dispute petitioner's contention that the Commission enjoys significant discretion in formulating guidelines. The Commission does have discretionary authority to determine the relative severity of federal crimes and to assess the relative weight of the offender characteristics that Congress listed for the Commission to consider. See §§ 994(c) and (d)(Commission instructed to consider enumerated factors as it deems them to be relevant). The Commission also has significant discretion to determine which crimes have been punished too leniently, and which too severely. § 994(m). Congress has called upon the Commission to exercise its judgment about which types of crimes and which types of criminals are to be considered similar for the purposes of sentencing.

But our cases do not at all suggest that delegations of this type may not carry with them the need to exercise judgment on matters of policy. In Yakus v. United States, 321 U.S. 414 (1944), the Court upheld a delegation to the Price Administrator to fix commodity prices that "in his judgment will be generally fair and equitable and will effectuate the purposes of this Act" to stabilize prices and avert speculation. See id., at 420. In National Broadcasting Co. v. United States, 319 U.S. 190 (1943), we upheld a delegation to the Federal Communications Commission granting it the authority to promulgate regulations in accordance with its view of the "public interest." In *Yakus*, the Court laid down the applicable principle:

> "It is no objection that the determination of facts and the inferences to be drawn from them in the light of the statutory standards and declaration of policy call for the exercise of judgment, and for the formulation of subsidiary administrative policy within the prescribed statutory framework....

> " ... Only if we could say that that there is an absence of standards for the guidance of the Administrator's action, so that it would be impossible in a proper proceeding to ascertain whether the will of Congress has been obeyed, would we be justified in overriding its choice of means for effecting its declared purpose...." 321 U.S., at 425–26.

Congress has met that standard here. The Act sets forth more than merely an "intelligible principle" or minimal standards. One court has aptly put it: "The statute outlines the policies which prompted establishment of the Commission, explains what the Commission should do and how it should do it, and sets out specific directives to govern particular situations." United States v. Chambless, 680 F.Supp. 793, 796 (E.D.La.1988).

Developing proportionate penalties for hundreds of different crimes by a virtually limitless array of offenders is precisely the sort of intricate, labor-intensive task for which delegation to an expert body is especially appropriate. Although Congress has delegated significant discretion to the Commission to draw judgments from its analysis of existing sentencing practice and alternative sentencing models, "Congress is not confined to that method of executing its policy which involves the least possible delegation of discretion to administrative officers." *Yakus v. United States*, 321 U.S., at 425–26. We have no doubt that in the hands of the Commission "the criteria which Congress has supplied are wholly adequate for carrying out the general policy and purpose" of the Act. Sunshine Coal Co. v. Adkins, 310 U.S. 381, 398 (1940).

IV

Separation of Powers

Having determined that Congress has set forth sufficient standards for the exercise of the Commission's delegated authority, we turn to Mistretta's claim that the Act violates the constitutional principle of separation of powers.

This Court consistently has given voice to, and has reaffirmed, the central judgment of the Framers of the Constitution that, within our political scheme, the separation of governmental powers into three coordinate Branches is essential to the preservation of liberty. See, e.g., Morrison v. Olson, 487 U.S. 654, 685–696 (1988); *Bowsher v. Synar*, 478 U.S., at 725. Madison, in writing about the principle of separated powers, said: "No political truth is certainly of greater intrinsic value or is stamped with the authority of more-enlightened patrons of liberty." The Federalist No. 47, p. 324 (J. Cooke ed. 1961).

In applying the principle of separated powers in our jurisprudence, we have sought to give life to Madison's view of the appropriate relationship among the three coequal Branches. Accordingly, we have recognized, as Madison admonished at the founding, that while our Constitution mandates that "each of the three general departments of government [must remain] entirely free from the control or coercive influence, direct or indirect, of either of the others," Humphrey's Executor v. United States, 295 U.S. 602, 629 (1935), the Framers did not require—and indeed rejected—the notion that the three Branches must be entirely separate and distinct. See, e.g., Nixon v. Administrator of General Services, 433 U.S. 425, 443 (1977)(rejecting as archaic complete division of authority among the three Branches); United States v. Nixon, 418 U.S. 683 (1974)(affirming Madison's flexible approach to separation of powers). Madison, defending the Constitution against charges that it established insufficiently separate Branches, addressed the point directly. Separation of powers, he wrote, "d[oes] not mean that these [three] departments ought to have no partial agency in, or no controul over the acts of each other," but rather "that where the whole power of one department is exercised by the same hands which possess the whole power of another department, the fundamental principles of a free constitution, are subverted." The Federalist No. 47, pp. 325–26 (J. Cooke ed. 1961). See *Nixon v. Administrator of General Services*, 433 U.S., at 442, n. 5. Madison recognized that our constitutional system imposes upon the Branches a degree of overlapping responsibility, a duty of interdependence as well as independence the absence of which "would preclude the establishment of a Nation capable of governing itself effectively." Buckley v. Valeo, 424 U.S. 1, 121 (1976). In a passage now commonplace in our cases, Justice Jackson summarized the pragmatic, flexible view of differentiated governmental power to which we are heir: "While the Constitution diffuses power the better to secure liberty, it also contemplates that practice will integrate the dispersed powers into a workable government. It enjoins upon its branches separateness but interdependence, autonomy but reciprocity." Youngstown Sheet & Tube Co. v. Sawyer, 343 U.S. 579, 635 (1952)(concurring opinion).

In adopting this flexible understanding of separation of powers, we simply have recognized Madison's teaching that the greatest security against tyranny—the accumulation of excessive authority in a single Branch—lies not in a hermetic division among the Branches, but in a carefully crafted system of checked and balanced power within each Branch. "[T]he greatest security," wrote Madison, "against a gradual concentration of the several powers in the same department, consists in giving to those who administer each department, the necessary constitutional means, and personal motives, to resist encroachments of the others." The Federalist No. 51, p. 349 (J. Cooke ed. 1961). Accordingly, as we have noted many times, the Framers "built into the tripartite Federal Government ... a self-executing safeguard against the encroachment or aggrandizement of one branch at the expense of the other." *Buckley v. Valeo*, 424 U.S., at 122. See also INS v. Chadha, 462 U.S. 919, 951 (1983).

It is this concern of encroachment and aggrandizement that has animated our separation-of-powers jurisprudence and aroused our vigilance against the "hydraulic pressure inherent within each of the separate Branches to exceed the outer limits of its power." Ibid. Accordingly, we have not hesitated to strike down provisions of law that either accrete to a single Branch powers more appropriately diffused among separate Branches or that undermine the authority and independence of one or another coordinate Branch. For example, just as the Framers recognized the particular danger of the Legislative Branch's accreting to itself judicial or executive power, so too have we invalidated attempts by Congress to exercise the responsibilities of other Branches or to reassign powers vested by the Constitution in either the Judicial Branch or the Executive Branch. Bowsher v. Synar, 478 U.S. 714 (1986)(Congress may not exercise removal power over officer performing executive functions); *INS v. Chadha*, supra (Congress may not control execution of laws except through Art. I procedures); Northern Pipeline Construction Co. v. Marathon Pipe Line Co., 458 U.S. 50 (1982)(Congress may not confer Art. III power on Art. I judge). By the same token, we have upheld statutory provisions that to some degree commingle the functions of the Branches, but that pose no danger of either aggrandizement or encroachment. Morrison v. Olson, 487 U.S. 654 (1988)(upholding judicial appointment of independent counsel); Commodity Futures Trading Comm'n v. Schor, 478 U.S. 833 (1986)(upholding agency's assumption of jurisdiction over state-law counterclaims).

In *Nixon v. Administrator of General Services*, supra, upholding, against a separation-of-powers challenge, legislation providing for the General Services Administration to control Presidential papers after resignation, we described our separation-of-powers inquiry as focusing "on the extent to which [a provision of law] prevents the Executive Branch from accomplishing its constitutionally assigned functions." 433 U.S., at 443 (citing *United States v. Nixon*, 418 U.S., at 711–12).[13] In cases specifically involving the Judicial Branch, we have expressed our vigilance against two dangers: first, that the Judicial Branch neither be assigned nor allowed "tasks that are more properly accomplished by [other] branches," *Morrison v. Olson*, 487 U.S., at 680–81, and, second, that no provision of law "impermissibly threatens the institutional integrity of the Judicial Branch." *Commodity Futures Trading Comm'n v. Schor*, 478 U.S., at 851.

Mistretta argues that the Act suffers from each of these constitutional infirmities. He argues that Congress, in constituting the Commission as it did, effected an unconstitutional accumulation of power within the Judicial Branch while at the same time undermining the Judiciary's independence and integrity. Specifically, petitioner claims that in delegating to an independent agency within the Judicial Branch the power to promulgate

[13] If the potential for disruption is present, we then determine "whether that impact is justified by an overriding need to promote objectives within the constitutional authority of Congress." *Nixon v. Administrator of General Services*, 433 U.S., at 443.

sentencing guidelines, Congress unconstitutionally has required the Branch, and individual Article III judges, to exercise not only their judicial authority, but legislative authority—the making of sentencing policy—as well. Such rulemaking authority, petitioner contends, may be exercised by Congress, or delegated by Congress to the Executive, but may not be delegated to or exercised by the Judiciary.

At the same time, petitioner asserts, Congress unconstitutionally eroded the integrity and independence of the Judiciary by requiring Article III judges to sit on the Commission, by requiring that those judges share their rulemaking authority with nonjudges, and by subjecting the Commission's members to appointment and removal by the President. According to petitioner, Congress, consistent with the separation of powers, may not upset the balance among the Branches by co-opting federal judges into the quintessentially political work of establishing sentencing guidelines, by subjecting those judges to the political whims of the Chief Executive, and by forcing judges to share their power with nonjudges.

"When this Court is asked to invalidate a statutory provision that has been approved by both Houses of the Congress and signed by the President, particularly an Act of Congress that confronts a deeply vexing national problem, it should only do so for the most compelling constitutional reasons." *Bowsher v. Synar*, 478 U.S., at 736 (opinion concurring in judgment). Although the unique composition and responsibilities of the Sentencing Commission give rise to serious concerns about a disruption of the appropriate balance of governmental power among the coordinate Branches, we conclude, upon close inspection, that petitioner's fears for the fundamental structural protections of the Constitution prove, at least in this case, to be "more smoke than fire," and do not compel us to invalidate Congress' considered scheme for resolving the seemingly intractable dilemma of excessive disparity in criminal sentencing.

A

Location of the Commission

The Sentencing Commission unquestionably is a peculiar institution within the framework of our Government. Although placed by the Act in the Judicial Branch, it is not a court and does not exercise judicial power. Rather, the Commission is an "independent" body comprised of seven voting members including at least three federal judges, entrusted by Congress with the primary task of promulgating sentencing guidelines. 28 U.S.C. § 991(a). Our constitutional principles of separated powers are not violated, however, by mere anomaly or innovation. Setting to one side, for the moment, the question whether the composition of the Sentencing Commission violates the separation of powers, we observe that Congress' decision to create an independent rulemaking body to promulgate sentencing guidelines and to locate that body within the Judicial Branch is not unconstitutional unless Congress has vested in the Commission powers that are more appropriately performed by the other Branches or that undermine the integrity of the Judiciary.

According to express provision of Article III, the judicial power of the United States is limited to "Cases" and "Controversies." See Muskrat v. United States, 219 U.S. 346, 356 (1911). In implementing this limited grant of power, we have refused to issue advisory opinions or to resolve disputes that are not justiciable. See, e.g., Flast v. Cohen, 392 U.S. 83 (1968); United States v. Ferreira, 54 U.S. (13 How.) 40 (1852). These doctrines help to ensure the independence of the Judicial Branch by precluding debilitating entanglements between the Judiciary and the two political Branches, and prevent the Judiciary from encroaching into areas reserved for the other Branches by extending judicial power to matters beyond those disputes "traditionally thought to be capable of resolution through the judicial process." *Flast v. Cohen*, 392 U.S., at 97; see also *United States Parole Comm'n v. Geraghty*, 445 U.S., at 396. As a general principle, we stated as recently as last Term that " 'executive or administrative duties of a nonjudicial nature may not be imposed on judges holding office under Art. III of the Constitution.' " *Morrison v. Olson*, 487 U.S., at 677, quoting *Buckley v. Valeo*, 424 U.S., at 123, citing in turn *United States v. Ferreira*, supra, and Hayburn's Case, 2 U.S. (2 Dall.) 409 (1792).

Nonetheless, we have recognized significant exceptions to this general rule and have approved the assumption of some nonadjudicatory activities by the Judicial Branch. In keeping with Justice Jackson's *Youngstown* admonition that the separation of powers contemplates the integration of dispersed powers into a workable Government, we have recognized the constitutionality of a "twilight area" in which the activities of the separate Branches merge. In his dissent in Myers v. United States, 272 U.S. 52 (1926), Justice Brandeis explained that the separation of powers "left to each [Branch] power to exercise, in some respects, functions in their nature executive, legislative and judicial."

That judicial rulemaking, at least with respect to some subjects, falls within this twilight area is no longer an issue for dispute. None of our cases indicate that rulemaking per se is a function that may not be performed by an entity within the Judicial Branch, either because rulemaking is inherently nonjudicial or because it is a function exclusively committed to the Executive Branch.[14] On the contrary, we specifically have held

---

[14] Our recent cases cast no doubt on the continuing vitality of the view that rulemaking is not a function exclusively committed to the Executive Branch. Although in INS v. Chadha, 462 U.S. 919 (1983), we characterized rulemaking as "Executive action" not governed by the Presentment Clauses, we did so as part of our effort to distinguish the rulemaking of administrative agencies from "lawmaking" by Congress which is subject to the presentment requirements of Article I. Id., at 953, n. 16. Plainly, this reference to rulemaking as an executive function was not intended to undermine our recognition in previous cases and in over 150 years of practice that rulemaking pursuant to a legislative delegation is not the exclusive prerogative of the Executive. See, e.g., Buckley v. Valeo, 424 U.S. 1, 138 (1976)(distinguishing between Federal Election Commission's exclusively executive enforcement power and its other powers, including rulemaking); see also Humphrey's Executor v. United States, 295 U.S. 602, 617 (1935). On the contrary, rulemaking power originates in the Legislative Branch and becomes an executive function only when delegated by the Legislature to the Executive Branch.

that Congress, in some circumstances, may confer rulemaking authority on the Judicial Branch. In Sibbach v. Wilson & Co., 312 U.S. 1 (1941), we upheld a challenge to certain rules promulgated under the Rules Enabling Act of 1934, which conferred upon the Judiciary the power to promulgate federal rules of civil procedure. See 28 U.S.C. § 2072. We observed: "Congress has undoubted power to regulate the practice and procedure of federal courts, and may exercise that power by delegating to this or other federal courts authority to make rules not inconsistent with the statutes or constitution of the United States." 312 U.S., at 9–10. This passage in *Sibbach* simply echoed what had been our view since Wayman v. Southard, 23 U.S. (10 Wheat.) 1, 43 (1825), decided more than a century earlier, where Chief Justice Marshall wrote for the Court that rulemaking power pertaining to the Judicial Branch may be "conferred on the judicial department." Discussing this delegation of rulemaking power, the Court found Congress authorized

> "to make all laws which shall be necessary and proper for carrying into execution the foregoing powers, and all other powers vested by this constitution in the government of the United States, or in any department or officer thereof. The judicial department is invested with jurisdiction in certain specified cases, in all which it has power to render judgment. 'That a power to make laws for carrying into execution all the judgments which the judicial department has power to pronounce, is expressly conferred by this clause, seems to be one of those plain propositions which reasoning cannot render plainer.' " Id., at 22.

See also Hanna v. Plumer, 380 U.S. 460 (1965). Pursuant to this power to delegate rulemaking authority to the Judicial Branch, Congress expressly has authorized this Court to establish rules for the conduct of its own business and to prescribe rules of procedure for lower federal courts in bankruptcy cases, in other civil cases, and in criminal cases, and to revise the Federal Rules of Evidence. See generally J. Weinstein, Reform of Court Rule–Making Procedures (1977).

Our approach to other nonadjudicatory activities that Congress has vested either in federal courts or in auxiliary bodies within the Judicial Branch has been identical to our approach to judicial rulemaking: consistent with the separation of powers, Congress may delegate to the Judicial Branch nonadjudicatory functions that do not trench upon the prerogatives of another Branch and that are appropriate to the central mission of the

---

More generally, it hardly can be argued in this case that Congress has impaired the functioning of the Executive Branch. In the field of sentencing, the Executive Branch never has exercised the kind of authority that Congress has vested in the Commission. Moreover, since Congress has empowered the President to appoint and remove Commission members, the President's relationship to the Commission is functionally no different from what it would have been had Congress not located the Commission in the Judicial Branch. Indeed, since the Act grants ex officio membership on the Commission to the Attorney General or his designee, 28 U.S.C. § 991(a), the Executive Branch's involvement in the Commission is greater than in other independent agencies, such as the Securities and Exchange Commission, not located in the Judicial Branch.

Judiciary. Following this approach, we specifically have upheld not only Congress' power to confer on the Judicial Branch the rulemaking authority contemplated in the various enabling Acts, but also to vest in judicial councils authority to "make 'all necessary orders for the effective and expeditious administration of the business of the courts.' " Chandler v. Judicial Council, 398 U.S. 74, 86, n. 7 (1970), quoting 28 U.S.C. § 332 (1970 ed.). Though not the subject of constitutional challenge, by established practice we have recognized Congress' power to create the Judicial Conference of the United States, the Rules Advisory Committees that it oversees, and the Administrative Office of the United States Courts whose myriad responsibilities include the administration of the entire probation service. These entities, some of which are comprised of judges, others of judges and nonjudges, still others of nonjudges only, do not exercise judicial power in the constitutional sense of deciding cases and controversies, but they share the common purpose of providing for the fair and efficient fulfillment of responsibilities that are properly the province of the Judiciary. Thus, although the judicial power of the United States is limited by express provision of Article III to "Cases" and "Controversies," we have never held, and have clearly disavowed in practice, that the Constitution prohibits Congress from assigning to courts or auxiliary bodies within the Judicial Branch administrative or rulemaking duties that, in the words of Chief Justice Marshall, are "necessary and proper ... for carrying into execution all the judgments which the judicial department has power to pronounce." *Wayman v. Southard*, 23 U.S. (10 Wheat.), at 22.[16] Because of their close relation to the central mission of the Judicial Branch, such extrajudicial activities are consonant with the integrity of the Branch and are not more appropriate for another Branch.

In light of this precedent and practice, we can discern no separation-of-powers impediment to the placement of the Sentencing Commission within the Judicial Branch. As we described at the outset, the sentencing function long has been a peculiarly shared responsibility among the Branches of Government and has never been thought of as the exclusive constitutional province of any one Branch. See, e.g., *United States v. Addonizio*, 442 U.S., at 188–89. For more than a century, federal judges have enjoyed

[16] We also have upheld Congress' power under the Appointments Clause to vest appointment power in the Judicial Branch, concluding that the power of appointment, though not judicial, was not "inconsistent as a functional matter with the courts' exercise of their Article III powers." Morrison v. Olson, 487 U.S. 654, 679, n. 16 (1988). See also Ex parte Siebold, 100 U.S. 371 (1880)(appointment power not incongruous to Judiciary). In *Morrison*, we noted that Article III courts perform a variety of functions not necessarily or directly connected to adversarial proceedings in a trial or appellate court. Federal courts supervise grand juries and compel the testimony of witnesses before those juries, see Brown v. United States, 359 U.S. 41, 49 (1959), participate in the issuance of search warrants, see Fed.R.Crim.P. 41, and review wiretap applications, see 18 U.S.C. §§ 2516, 2518 (1982 ed. and Supp. IV). In the interest of effectuating their judgments, federal courts also possess inherent authority to initiate a contempt proceeding and to appoint a private attorney to prosecute the contempt. Young v. United States ex rel. Vuitton et Fils S.A., 481 U.S. 787 (1987). See also In re Certain Complaints Under Investigation, 783 F.2d 1488, 1505 (11th Cir.1986)(upholding statute authorizing judicial council to investigate improper conduct by federal judge).

wide discretion to determine the appropriate sentence in individual cases and have exercised special authority to determine the sentencing factors to be applied in any given case. Indeed, the legislative history of the Act makes clear that Congress' decision to place the Commission within the Judicial Branch reflected Congress' "strong feeling" that sentencing has been and should remain "primarily a judicial function." Report, at 159. That Congress should vest such rulemaking in the Judicial Branch, far from being "incongruous" or vesting within the Judiciary responsibilities that more appropriately belong to another Branch, simply acknowledges the role that the Judiciary always has played, and continues to play, in sentencing.[17]

Given the consistent responsibility of federal judges to pronounce sentence within the statutory range established by Congress, we find that the role of the Commission in promulgating guidelines for the exercise of that judicial function bears considerable similarity to the role of this Court in establishing rules of procedure under the various enabling Acts. Such guidelines, like the Federal Rules of Criminal and Civil Procedure, are court rules—rules, to paraphrase Chief Justice Marshall's language in *Wayman*, for carrying into execution judgments that the Judiciary has the power to pronounce. Just as the rules of procedure bind judges and courts in the proper management of the cases before them, so the Guidelines bind judges and courts in the exercise of their uncontested responsibility to pass sentence in criminal cases. In other words, the Commission's functions, like this Court's function in promulgating procedural rules, are clearly attendant to a central element of the historically acknowledged mission of the Judicial Branch.

Petitioner nonetheless objects that the analogy between the Guidelines and the rules of procedure is flawed: Although the Judicial Branch may participate in rulemaking and administrative work that is "procedural" in nature, it may not assume, it is said, the "substantive" authority over sentencing policy that Congress has delegated to the Commission. Such substantive decisionmaking, petitioner contends, entangles the Judicial Branch in essentially political work of the other Branches and unites both judicial and legislative power in the Judicial Branch.

We agree with petitioner that the nature of the Commission's rulemaking power is not strictly analogous to this Court's rulemaking power under the enabling Acts. Although we are loath to enter the logical morass of distinguishing between substantive and procedural rules, see Sun Oil Co. v.

---

[17] Indeed, had Congress decided to confer responsibility for promulgating sentencing guidelines on the Executive Branch, we might face the constitutional questions whether Congress unconstitutionally had assigned judicial responsibilities to the Executive or unconstitutionally had united the power to prosecute and the power to sentence within one Branch. Ronald L. Gainer, Acting Deputy Assistant Attorney General, Department of Justice, testified before the Senate to this very effect: "If guidelines were to be promulgated by an agency outside the judicial branch, it might be viewed as an encroachment on a judicial function...." Reform of the Federal Criminal Laws, hearing on S. 1437 et al. before the Subcommittee on Criminal Laws and Procedure of the Senate Committee on the Judiciary, 95th Cong., 1st Sess., pt. 13, p. 9005 (1977).

Wortman, 486 U.S. 717 (1988)(distinction between substance and procedure depends on context), and although we have recognized that the Federal Rules of Civil Procedure regulate matters "falling within the uncertain area between substance and procedure, [and] are rationally capable of classification as either," *Hanna v. Plumer*, 380 U.S., at 472, we recognize that the task of promulgating rules regulating practice and pleading before federal courts does not involve the degree of political judgment integral to the Commission's formulation of sentencing guidelines.[18] To be sure, all rulemaking is nonjudicial in the sense that rules impose standards of general application divorced from the individual fact situation which ordinarily forms the predicate for judicial action. Also, this Court's rulemaking under the enabling Acts has been substantive and political in the sense that the rules of procedure have important effects on the substantive rights of litigants.[19] Nonetheless, the degree of political judgment about crime and criminality exercised by the Commission and the scope of the substantive effects of its work does to some extent set its rulemaking powers apart from prior judicial rulemaking. Cf. *Miller v. Florida*, 482 U.S. 423 (1987)(state sentencing guidelines not procedural).

We do not believe, however, that the significantly political nature of the Commission's work renders unconstitutional its placement within the Judicial Branch. Our separation-of-powers analysis does not turn on the labeling of an activity as "substantive" as opposed to "procedural," or "political" as opposed to "judicial." See *Bowsher v. Synar*, 478 U.S., at 749 ("[G]overnmental power cannot always be readily characterized with only one ... labe[l]")(opinion concurring in judgment). Rather, our inquiry is focused on the "unique aspects of the congressional plan at issue and its practical consequences in light of the larger concerns that underlie Article III." *Commodity Futures Trading Comm'n v. Schor*, 478 U.S., at 857. In this case, the "practical consequences" of locating the Commission within the Judicial Branch pose no threat of undermining the integrity of the Judicial Branch or of expanding the powers of the Judiciary beyond constitutional bounds by uniting within the Branch the political or quasi-legislative power of the Commission with the judicial power of the courts.

First, although the Commission is located in the Judicial Branch, its powers are not united with the powers of the Judiciary in a way that has meaning for separation-of-powers analysis. Whatever constitutional problems might arise if the powers of the Commission were vested in a court, the Commission is not a court, does not exercise judicial power, and is not controlled by or accountable to members of the Judicial Branch. The

---

[18] Under its mandate, the Commission must make judgments about the relative importance of such considerations as the "circumstances under which the offense was committed," the "community view of the gravity of the offense," and the "deterrent effect a particular sentence may have on the commission of the offense by others." 28 U.S.C. §§ 994(c)(2), (4), (6).

[19] Rule 23 of the Federal Rules of Civil Procedure, for example, has inspired a controversy over the philosophical, social, and economic merits and demerits of class actions. See Arthur R. Miller, Of Frankenstein Monsters and Shining Knights: Myth, Reality, and the "Class Action Problem," 92 Harv. L.Rev. 664 (1979).

Commission, on which members of the Judiciary may be a minority, is an independent agency in every relevant sense. In contrast to a court's exercising judicial power, the Commission is fully accountable to Congress, which can revoke or amend any or all of the Guidelines as it sees fit either within the 180–day waiting period, see § 235(a)(1)(B)(ii)(III) of the Act, 98 Stat. 2032, or at any time. In contrast to a court, the Commission's members are subject to the President's limited powers of removal. In contrast to a court, its rulemaking is subject to the notice and comment requirements of the Administrative Procedure Act, 28 U.S.C. § 994(x). While we recognize the continuing vitality of Montesquieu's admonition: " 'Were the power of judging joined with the legislative, the life and liberty of the subject would be exposed to arbitrary controul,' " The Federalist No. 47, p. 326 (J. Cooke ed. 1961)(Madison), quoting Montesquieu, because Congress vested the power to promulgate sentencing guidelines in an independent agency, not a court, there can be no serious argument that Congress combined legislative and judicial power within the Judicial Branch.[20]

Second, although the Commission wields rulemaking power and not the adjudicatory power exercised by individual judges when passing sentence, the placement of the Sentencing Commission in the Judicial Branch has not increased the Branch's authority. Prior to the passage of the Act, the Judicial Branch, as an aggregate, decided precisely the questions assigned to the Commission: what sentence is appropriate to what criminal conduct under what circumstances. It was the everyday business of judges, taken collectively, to evaluate and weigh the various aims of sentencing and to apply those aims to the individual cases that came before them. The Sentencing Commission does no more than this, albeit basically through the methodology of sentencing guidelines, rather than entirely individualized sentencing determinations. Accordingly, in placing the Commission in

[20] We express no opinion about whether, under the principles of separation of powers, Congress may confer on a court rulemaking authority such as that exercised by the Sentencing Commission. Our precedents and customs draw no clear distinction between nonadjudicatory activity that may be undertaken by auxiliary bodies within the Judicial Branch, but not by courts. We note, however, that the constitutional calculus is different for considering nonadjudicatory activities performed by bodies that exercise judicial power and enjoy the constitutionally mandated autonomy of courts from what it is for considering the nonadjudicatory activities of independent nonadjudicatory agencies that Congress merely has located within the Judicial Branch pursuant to its powers under the Necessary and Proper Clause. We make no attempt here to define the nonadjudicatory duties that are appropriate for auxiliary bodies within the Judicial Branch, but not for courts. Nonetheless, it is clear to us that an independent agency located within the Judicial Branch may undertake without constitutional consequences policy judgments pursuant to a legitimate congressional delegation of authority that, if undertaken by a court, might be incongruous to or destructive of the central adjudicatory mission of the Branch. See United States v. Ferreira, 54 U.S. (13 How.) 40 (1852). In this sense, the issue we face here is different from the issue we faced in Morrison v. Olson, 487 U.S. 654 (1988), where we considered the constitutionality of the nonadjudicatory functions assigned to the "Special Division" court created by the Ethics in Government Act of 1978, 28 U.S.C. §§ 49, 591 et seq. (1982 ed. and Supp. IV), or the issue we faced in Hayburn's Case, 2 U.S. (2 Dall.) 409 (1792), and in *Ferreira*, in which Article III courts were asked to render judgments that were reviewable by an executive officer.

the Judicial Branch, Congress cannot be said to have aggrandized the authority of that Branch or to have deprived the Executive Branch of a power it once possessed. Indeed, because the Guidelines have the effect of promoting sentencing within a narrower range than was previously applied, the power of the Judicial Branch is, if anything, somewhat diminished by the Act. And, since Congress did not unconstitutionally delegate its own authority, the Act does not unconstitutionally diminish Congress' authority. Thus, although Congress has authorized the Commission to exercise a greater degree of political judgment than has been exercised in the past by any one entity within the Judicial Branch, in the unique context of sentencing, this authorization does nothing to upset the balance of power among the Branches.

What Mistretta's argument comes down to, then, is not that the substantive responsibilities of the Commission aggrandize the Judicial Branch, but that that Branch is inevitably weakened by its participation in policymaking. We do not believe, however, that the placement within the Judicial Branch of an independent agency charged with the promulgation of sentencing guidelines can possibly be construed as preventing the Judicial Branch "from accomplishing its constitutionally assigned functions." *Nixon v. Administrator of General Services*, 433 U.S., at 443. Despite the substantive nature of its work, the Commission is not incongruous or inappropriate to the Branch. As already noted, sentencing is a field in which the Judicial Branch long has exercised substantive or political judgment. What we said in *Morrison* when upholding the power of the Special Division to appoint independent counsel applies with even greater force here: "This is not a case in which judges are given power ... in an area in which they have no special knowledge or expertise." 487 U.S., at 676, n. 13. On the contrary, Congress placed the Commission in the Judicial Branch precisely because of the Judiciary's special knowledge and expertise.

Nor do the Guidelines, though substantive, involve a degree of political authority inappropriate for a nonpolitical Branch. Although the Guidelines are intended to have substantive effects on public behavior (as do the rules of procedure), they do not bind or regulate the primary conduct of the public or vest in the Judicial Branch the legislative responsibility for establishing minimum and maximum penalties for every crime. They do no more than fetter the discretion of sentencing judges to do what they have done for generations—impose sentences within the broad limits established by Congress. Given their limited reach, the special role of the Judicial Branch in the field of sentencing, and the fact that the Guidelines are promulgated by an independent agency and not a court, it follows that as a matter of "practical consequences" the location of the Sentencing Commission within the Judicial Branch simply leaves with the Judiciary what long has belonged to it.

In sum, since substantive judgment in the field of sentencing has been and remains appropriate to the Judicial Branch, and the methodology of rulemaking has been and remains appropriate to that Branch, Congress' considered decision to combine these functions in an independent Sentencing Commission and to locate that Commission within the Judicial Branch does not violate the principle of separation of powers.

B

Composition of the Commission

[The Court here considered, and rejected, petitioner's claim that Congress's decision to require at least three federal judges to serve on the Commission and to require those judges to share their authority with nonjudges impermissibly undermines the integrity of the Judicial Branch. The Court noted the absence of any explicit constitutional restriction on federal judges serving in other official capacities, and listed numerous prior examples of such service, including Justice Jackson's serving as one of the prosecutors at the Nuremberg trials and Chief Justice Warren's presiding over the commission that investigated the assassination of President Kennedy. The Court emphasized that service on the Sentencing Commission is voluntary, not compulsory, and that such service would not necessarily require a judge to recuse herself from reviewing the validity of the Guidelines or participating in individual sentencing decisions. The Court also disagreed with petitioner's contention that Congress was improperly seeking to "cloak" the fundamentally political work of the Commission in the integrity of the judiciary. According to the Court, the Commission "is devoted exclusively to the development of rules to rationalize a process that has been and will continue to be performed exclusively by the Judicial Branch." Thus, its work is "essentially neutral" rather than legislative (as in enacting criminal statutes) or executive (as in enforcing those statutes) in nature. Judicial participation in such an endeavor ensures that the Commission will benefit from the real-world sentencing experience of judges. At the same time, because the Commission exercises no judicial powers, it is also appropriate for nonjudges to serve on the Commission.]

C

Presidential Control

[The Court also considered, and rejected, petitioner's argument that the President's power to appoint Commission members (with the advice and consent of the Senate) and remove them for "neglect of duty or malfeasance in office or for other good cause shown," 28 U.S.C. § 991(a), impermissibly infringes on the independence of the Judicial Branch. The Court found "fanciful" the contention that federal judges might alter their behavior in order to curry favor with the President in hopes of being appointed to the Commission. And it noted that removal from the Commission by the President would not in any way affect a federal judge's Article III-protected life tenure or judicial salary.]

V

We conclude that in creating the Sentencing Commission—an unusual hybrid in structure and authority—Congress neither delegated excessive legislative power nor upset the constitutionally mandated balance of powers among the coordinate Branches. The Constitution's structural protections do not prohibit Congress from delegating to an expert body located within the Judicial Branch the intricate task of formulating sentencing guidelines consistent with such significant statutory direction as is present here. Nor does our system of checked and balanced authority prohibit Congress from calling upon the accumulated wisdom and experience of the Judicial Branch in creating policy on a matter uniquely within the ken of judges. Accordingly, we hold that the Act is constitutional.

The judgment of United States District Court for the Western District of Missouri is affirmed.

It is so ordered.

■ JUSTICE SCALIA, dissenting.

While the products of the Sentencing Commission's labors have been given the modest name "Guidelines," see 28 U.S.C. § 994(a)(1); United States Sentencing Commission Guidelines Manual (June 15, 1988), they have the force and effect of laws, prescribing the sentences criminal defendants are to receive. A judge who disregards them will be reversed, 18 U.S.C. § 3742. I dissent from today's decision because I can find no place within our constitutional system for an agency created by Congress to exercise no governmental power other than the making of laws.

I

There is no doubt that the Sentencing Commission has established significant, legally binding prescriptions governing application of governmental power against private individuals—indeed, application of the ultimate governmental power, short of capital punishment. Statutorily permissible sentences for particular crimes cover as broad a range as zero years to life, see, e.g., 18 U.S.C. § 1201 (kidnaping), and within those ranges the Commission was given broad discretion to prescribe the "correct" sentence, 28 U.S.C. § 994(b)(2). Average prior sentences were to be a starting point for the Commission's inquiry, § 994(m), but it could and regularly did deviate from those averages as it thought appropriate. It chose, for example, to prescribe substantial increases over average prior sentences for white-collar crimes such as public corruption, antitrust violations, and tax evasion. Guidelines, at 2.31, 2.133, 2.140. For antitrust violations, before the Guidelines only 39% of those convicted served any imprisonment, and the average imprisonment was only 45 days, id., at 2.133, whereas the Guidelines prescribe base sentences (for defendants with no prior criminal conviction) ranging from 2-to-8 months to 10-to-16 months, depending upon the volume of commerce involved. See id., at 2.131, 5.2.

The Commission also determined when probation was permissible, imposing a strict system of controls because of its judgment that probation had been used for an "inappropriately high percentage of offenders guilty of certain economic crimes." Id., at 1.8. Moreover, the Commission had free rein in determining whether statutorily authorized fines should be imposed in addition to imprisonment, and if so, in what amounts. It ultimately decided that every nonindigent offender should pay a fine according to a schedule devised by the Commission. Id., at 5.18. Congress also gave the Commission discretion to determine whether 7 specified characteristics of offenses, and 11 specified characteristics of offenders, "have any relevance," and should be included among the factors varying the sentence. 28 U.S.C. §§ 994(c), (d). Of the latter, it included only three among the factors required to be considered, and declared the remainder not ordinarily relevant. Guidelines, at 5.29–5.31.

It should be apparent from the above that the decisions made by the Commission are far from technical, but are heavily laden (or ought to be) with value judgments and policy assessments. This fact is sharply reflected in the Commission's product, as described by the dissenting Commissioner: "Under the guidelines, the judge could give the same sentence for abusive sexual contact that puts the child in fear as for unlawfully entering or remaining in the United States. Similarly, the guidelines permit equivalent sentences for the following pairs of offenses: drug trafficking and a violation of the Wild Free–Roaming Horses and Burros Act; arson with a destructive device and failure to surrender a cancelled naturalization certificate; operation of a common carrier under the influence of drugs that causes injury and alteration of one motor vehicle identification number; illegal trafficking in explosives and trespass; interference with a flight attendant and unlawful conduct relating to contraband cigarettes; aggravated assault and smuggling $11,000 worth of fish." Dissenting View of Commissioner Paul H. Robinson on the Promulgation of the Sentencing Guidelines by the United States Sentencing Commission 6–7 (May 1, 1987).

Petitioner's most fundamental and far-reaching challenge to the Commission is that Congress' commitment of such broad policy responsibility to any institution is an unconstitutional delegation of legislative power. It is difficult to imagine a principle more essential to democratic government than that upon which the doctrine of unconstitutional delegation is founded: Except in a few areas constitutionally committed to the Executive Branch, the basic policy decisions governing society are to be made by the Legislature. Our Members of Congress could not, even if they wished, vote all power to the President and adjourn sine die.

But while the doctrine of unconstitutional delegation is unquestionably a fundamental element of our constitutional system, it is not an element readily enforceable by the courts. Once it is conceded, as it must be, that no statute can be entirely precise, and that some judgments, even some judgments involving policy considerations, must be left to the officers executing the law and to the judges applying it, the debate over unconstitutional delegation becomes a debate not over a point of principle but over a question of degree. As Chief Justice Taft expressed the point for the Court in the landmark case of J.W. Hampton, Jr., & Co. v. United States, 276 U.S. 394, 406 (1928), the limits of delegation "must be fixed according to common sense and the inherent necessities of the governmental co-ordination." Since Congress is no less endowed with common sense than we are, and better equipped to inform itself of the "necessities" of government; and since the factors bearing upon those necessities are both multifarious and (in the nonpartisan sense) highly political—including, for example, whether the Nation is at war, see Yakus v. United States, 321 U.S. 414 (1944), or whether for other reasons "emergency is instinct in the situation," Amalgamated Meat Cutters and Butcher Workmen of North America v. Connally, 337 F.Supp. 737, 752 (D.C. 1971)(three-judge court)—it is small wonder that we have almost never felt qualified to second-guess Congress regarding the permissible degree of policy judgment that can be left to those executing or applying the law. As the Court points out, we have invoked the doctrine of unconstitutional delegation to invalidate a law only twice in our history, over half a century ago. See Panama Refining Co. v. Ryan, 293 U.S. 388 (1935); A.L.A. Schechter Poultry Corp. v. United States, 295 U.S. 495 (1935). What legislated standard, one must wonder, can possibly be too vague to survive judicial scrutiny, when we have repeatedly upheld, in various contexts, a "public interest" standard?

In short, I fully agree with the Court's rejection of petitioner's contention that the doctrine of unconstitutional delegation of legislative authority has been violated because of the lack of intelligible, congressionally prescribed standards to guide the Commission.

II

Precisely because the scope of delegation is largely uncontrollable by the courts, we must be particularly rigorous in preserving the Constitution's structural restrictions that deter excessive delegation. The major one, it seems to me, is that the power to make law cannot be exercised by anyone other than Congress, except in conjunction with the lawful exercise of executive or judicial power.

The whole theory of lawful congressional "delegation" is not that Congress is sometimes too busy or too divided and can therefore assign its responsibility of making law to someone else; but rather that a certain degree of discretion, and thus of lawmaking, inheres in most executive or judicial action, and it is up to Congress, by the relative specificity or generality of its statutory commands, to determine—up to a point—how small or how large that degree shall be. Thus, the courts could be given the power to say precisely what constitutes a "restraint of trade," see Standard Oil Co. of New Jersey v. United States, 221 U.S. 1 (1911), or to adopt rules of procedure, see Sibbach v. Wilson & Co., 312 U.S. 1 (1941), or to prescribe by rule the manner in which their officers shall execute their judgments, Wayman v. Southard, 23 U.S. (10 Wheat.) 1, 45 (1825), because that "lawmaking" was ancillary to their exercise of judicial powers. And the Executive could be given the power to adopt policies and rules specifying in detail what radio and television licenses will be in the "public interest, convenience or necessity," because that was ancillary to the exercise of its executive powers in granting and policing licenses and making a "fair and equitable allocation" of the electromagnetic spectrum.

See Federal Radio Comm'n v. Nelson Brothers Bond & Mortgage Co., 289 U.S. 266, 285 (1933).[2] Or to take examples closer to the case before us: Trial judges could be given the power to determine what factors justify a greater or lesser sentence within the statutorily prescribed limits because that was ancillary to their exercise of the judicial power of pronouncing sentence upon individual defendants. And the President, through the Parole Commission subject to his appointment and removal, could be given the power to issue Guidelines specifying when parole would be available, because that was ancillary to the President's exercise of the executive power to hold and release federal prisoners. See 18 U.S.C. §§ 4203(a)(1) and (b); 28 CFR § 2.20 (1988).

As Justice Harlan wrote for the Court in Field v. Clark, 143 U.S. 649 (1892): " 'The true distinction ... is between the delegation of power to make the law, which necessarily involves a discretion as to what it shall be, and conferring authority or discretion as to its execution, to be exercised under and in pursuance of the law. The first cannot be done; to the latter no valid objection can be made.' " Id., at 693–94, quoting Cincinnati, W. & Z.R. Co. v. Commissioners of Clinton County, 1 Ohio St. 77, 88–89 (1852). " 'Half the statutes on our books are in the alternative, depending on the discretion of some person or persons to whom is confided the duty of determining whether the proper occasion exists for executing them. But it cannot be said that the exercise of such discretion is the making of the law.' " Id., at 694, quoting Moers v. Reading, 21 Pa. 188, 202 (1853). In United States v. Grimaud, 220 U.S. 506, 517 (1911), which upheld a statutory grant of authority to the Secretary of Agriculture to make rules and regulations governing use of the public forests he was charged with managing, the Court said: "From the beginning of the Government various acts have been passed conferring upon executive officers power to make rules and regulations—not for the government of their departments, but for administering the laws which did govern. None of these statutes could confer legislative power." Or, finally, as Chief Justice Taft described it in *Hampton & Co.*, 276 U.S., at 406: "The field of Congress involves all and many varieties of legislative action, and Congress has found it frequently necessary to use officers of the Executive Branch, within defined limits, to secure the exact effect intended by its acts of legislation, by vesting discretion in such officers to make public regulations interpreting a statute and directing the details of its execution, even to the extent of providing for penalizing a breach of such regulations."

The focus of controversy, in the long line of our so-called excessive delegation cases, has been whether the degree of generality contained in the authorization for exercise of executive or judicial powers in a particular field is so unacceptably high as to amount to a delegation of legislative powers. I say "so-called excessive delegation" because although that

---

[2] An executive agency can, of course, be created with no power other than the making of rules, as long as that agency is subject to the control of the President and the President has executive authority related to the rulemaking. In such circumstances, the rulemaking is ultimately ancillary to the President's executive powers.

convenient terminology is often used, what is really at issue is whether there has been any delegation of legislative power, which occurs (rarely) when Congress authorizes the exercise of executive or judicial power without adequate standards. Strictly speaking, there is no acceptable delegation of legislative power. As John Locke put it almost 300 years ago, "[t]he power of the legislative being derived from the people by a positive voluntary grant and institution, can be no other, than what the positive grant conveyed, which being only to make laws, and not to make legislators, the legislative can have no power to transfer their authority of making laws, and place it in other hands." J. Locke, Second Treatise of Government 87 (R. Cox ed. 1982). Or as we have less epigrammatically said: "That Congress cannot delegate legislative power to the President is a principle universally recognized as vital to the integrity and maintenance of the system of government ordained by the Constitution." *Field v. Clark*, 143 U.S. at 692. In the present case, however, a pure delegation of legislative power is precisely what we have before us. It is irrelevant whether the standards are adequate, because they are not standards related to the exercise of executive or judicial powers; they are, plainly and simply, standards for further legislation.

The lawmaking function of the Sentencing Commission is completely divorced from any responsibility for execution of the law or adjudication of private rights under the law. It is divorced from responsibility for execution of the law not only because the Commission is not said to be "located in the Executive Branch" (as I shall discuss presently, I doubt whether Congress can "locate" an entity within one Branch or another for constitutional purposes by merely saying so); but, more importantly, because the Commission neither exercises any executive power on its own, nor is subject to the control of the President who does. The only functions it performs, apart from prescribing the law, 28 U.S.C. §§ 994(a)(1), (3), conducting the investigations useful and necessary for prescribing the law, e.g., §§ 995(a)(13), (15), (16), (21), and clarifying the intended application of the law that it prescribes, e.g., §§ 994(a)(2), 995(a)(10), are data collection and intragovernmental advice giving and education, e.g., §§ 995(a)(8), (9), (12), (17), (18), (20). These latter activities—similar to functions performed by congressional agencies and even congressional staff—neither determine nor affect private rights, and do not constitute an exercise of governmental power. See Humphrey's Executor v. United States, 295 U.S. 602, 628 (1935). And the Commission's lawmaking is completely divorced from the exercise of judicial powers since, not being a court, it has no judicial powers itself, nor is it subject to the control of any other body with judicial powers. The power to make law at issue here, in other words, is not ancillary but quite naked. The situation is no different in principle from what would exist if Congress gave the same power of writing sentencing laws to a congressional agency such as the General Accounting Office, or to members of its staff.

The delegation of lawmaking authority to the Commission is, in short, unsupported by any legitimating theory to explain why it is not a delegation of legislative power. To disregard structural legitimacy is wrong in itself—but since structure has purpose, the disregard also has adverse practical consequences. In this case, as suggested earlier, the consequence is to facilitate and encourage judicially uncontrollable delegation. Until our decision last Term in Morrison v. Olson, 487 U.S. 654 (1988), it could have been said that Congress could delegate lawmaking authority only at the expense of increasing the power of either the President or the courts. Most often, as a practical matter, it would be the President, since the judicial process is unable to conduct the investigations and make the political assessments essential for most policymaking. Thus, the need for delegation would have to be important enough to induce Congress to aggrandize its primary competitor for political power, and the recipient of the policymaking authority, while not Congress itself, would at least be politically accountable. But even after it has been accepted, pursuant to Morrison, that those exercising executive power need not be subject to the control of the President, Congress would still be more reluctant to augment the power of even an independent executive agency than to create an otherwise powerless repository for its delegation. Moreover, assembling the full-time senior personnel for an agency exercising executive powers is more difficult than borrowing other officials (or employing new officers on a short-term basis) to head an organization such as the Sentencing Commission.

By reason of today's decision, I anticipate that Congress will find delegation of its lawmaking powers much more attractive in the future. If rulemaking can be entirely unrelated to the exercise of judicial or executive powers, I foresee all manner of "expert" bodies, insulated from the political process, to which Congress will delegate various portions of its lawmaking responsibility. How tempting to create an expert Medical Commission (mostly M.D.'s, with perhaps a few Ph.D.'s in moral philosophy) to dispose of such thorny, "no-win" political issues as the withholding of life-support systems in federally funded hospitals, or the use of fetal tissue for research. This is an undemocratic precedent that we set—not because of the scope of the delegated power, but because its recipient is not one of the three Branches of Government. The only governmental power the Commission possesses is the power to make law; and it is not the Congress.

III

The strange character of the body that the Court today approves, and its incompatibility with our constitutional institutions, is apparent from that portion of the Court's opinion entitled "Location of the Commission." This accepts at the outset that the Commission is a "body within the Judicial Branch," and rests some of its analysis upon that asserted reality. Separation-of-powers problems are dismissed, however, on the ground that "[the Commission's] powers are not united with the powers of the Judiciary in a way that has meaning for separation-of-powers analysis," since the Commission "is not a court, does not exercise judicial power, and is not controlled by or accountable to members of the Judicial Branch." In light of the latter concession, I am at a loss to understand why the Commission is "within the Judicial Branch" in any sense that has relevance to today's discussion. I am sure that Congress can divide up the Government any way it wishes, and employ whatever terminology it desires, for non constitutional purposes—for example, perhaps the statutory designation that the Commission is "within the Judicial Branch" places it outside the coverage of certain laws which say they are inapplicable to that Branch, such as the Freedom of Information Act, see 5 U.S.C. § 552(f)(1982 ed., Supp. IV). For such statutory purposes, Congress can define the term as it pleases. But since our subject here is the Constitution, to admit that that congressional designation "has [no] meaning for separation-of-powers analysis" is to admit that the Court must therefore decide for itself where the Commission is located for purposes of separation-of-powers analysis.

It would seem logical to decide the question of which Branch an agency belongs to on the basis of who controls its actions: If Congress, the Legislative Branch; if the President, the Executive Branch; if the courts (or perhaps the judges), the Judicial Branch. See, e.g., Bowsher v. Synar, 478 U.S. 714, 727–32 (1986). In Humphrey's Executor v. United States, 295 U.S. 602 (1935), we approved the concept of an agency that was controlled by (and thus within) none of the Branches. We seem to have assumed, however, that that agency (the old Federal Trade Commission, before it acquired many of its current functions) exercised no governmental power whatever, but merely assisted Congress and the courts in the performance of their functions. See Id., at 628. Where no governmental power is at issue, there is no strict constitutional impediment to a "branchless" agency, since it is only "[a]ll legislative Powers," Art. I, § 1, "[t]he executive Power," Art. II, § 1, and "[t]he judicial Power," Art. III, § 1, which the Constitution divides into three departments. (As an example of a "branchless" agency exercising no governmental powers, one can conceive of an Advisory Commission charged with reporting to all three Branches, whose members are removable only for cause and are thus subject to the control of none of the Branches.) Over the years, however, *Humphrey's Executor* has come in general contemplation to stand for something quite different—not an "independent agency" in the sense of an agency independent of all three Branches, but an "independent agency" in the sense of an agency within the Executive Branch (and thus authorized to exercise executive powers) independent of the control of the President.

We approved that concept last Term in *Morrison*. See 487 U.S., at 688–91. I dissented in that case, essentially because I thought that concept illogical and destructive of the structure of the Constitution. I must admit, however, that today's next step—recognition of an independent agency in the Judicial Branch—makes *Morrison* seem, by comparison, rigorously logical. "The Commission," we are told, "is an independent agency in every relevant sense." There are several problems with this. First, once it is acknowledged that an "independent agency" may be within any of the three Branches, and not merely within the Executive, then there really is no basis for determining what Branch such an agency belongs to, and thus what governmental powers it may constitutionally be given, except (what the Court today uses) Congress' say-so. More importantly, however, the concept of an "independent agency" simply does not translate into the legislative or judicial spheres. Although the Constitution says that "[t]he executive Power shall be vested in a President of the United States of America," Art. II, § 1, it was never thought that the President would have to exercise that power personally. He may generally authorize others to exercise executive powers, with full effect of law, in his place. See, e.g., Wolsey v. Chapman, 101 U.S. 755 (1880). It is already a leap from the proposition that a person who is not the President may exercise executive powers to the proposition we accepted in *Morrison* that a person who is neither the President nor subject to the President's control may exercise executive powers. But with respect to the exercise of judicial powers (the business of the Judicial Branch) the platform for such a leap does not even exist. For unlike executive power, judicial and legislative powers have never been thought delegable. A judge may not leave the decision to his law clerk, or to a master. See United States v. Raddatz, 447 U.S. 667, 683 (1980). Senators and Members of the House may not send delegates to consider and vote upon bills in their place. See Rules of the House of Representatives, Rule VIII(3); Standing Rules of the United States Senate, Rule XII. Thus, however well established may be the "independent agencies" of the Executive Branch, here we have an anomaly beyond equal: an independent agency exercising governmental power on behalf of a Branch where all governmental power is supposed to be exercised personally by the judges of courts.[3]

Today's decision may aptly be described as the *Humphrey's Executor* of the Judicial Branch, and I think we will live to regret it. Henceforth there may be agencies "within the Judicial Branch" (whatever that means), exercising governmental powers, that are neither courts nor controlled by courts, nor even controlled by judges. If an "independent agency" such as this can be given the power to fix sentences previously exercised by district courts, I must assume that a similar agency can be given the powers to adopt rules of procedure and rules of evidence previously exercised by this Court. The bases for distinction would be thin indeed.

Today's decision follows the regrettable tendency of our recent separation-of-powers jurisprudence, see *Morrison*, supra; Young v. United States ex rel. Vuitton et Fils S.A., 481 U.S. 787 (1987), to treat the Constitution as though it were no more than a generalized prescription that the functions of the Branches should not be commingled too much—how much is too much to be determined, case-by-case, by this Court. The Constitution is not that. Rather, as its name suggests, it is a prescribed structure, a framework, for the conduct of government. In designing that structure,

---

[3] There are of course agencies within the Judicial Branch (because they operate under the control of courts or judges) which are not themselves courts, see, e.g., 28 U.S.C. § 601 et seq. (Administrative Office of the United States Courts), just as there are agencies within the Legislative Branch (because they operate under the control of Congress) which are not themselves Senators or Representa-tives, see, e.g., 31 U.S.C. § 701 et seq. (General Accounting Office). But these agencies, unlike the Sentencing Commission, exercise no governmental powers, that is, they establish and determine neither private rights nor the prerogatives of the other Branches. They merely assist the courts and the Congress in their exercise of judicial and legislative powers.

the Framers themselves considered how much commingling was, in the generality of things, acceptable, and set forth their conclusions in the document. That is the meaning of the statements concerning acceptable commingling made by Madison in defense of the proposed Constitution, and now routinely used as an excuse for disregarding it. When he said, as the Court correctly quotes, that separation of powers " 'd[oes] not mean that these [three] departments ought to have no partial agency in, or no controul over the acts of each other,' " quoting The Federalist No. 47, pp. 325–26 (J. Cooke ed.1961), his point was that the commingling specifically provided for in the structure that he and his colleagues had designed—the Presidential veto over legislation, the Senate's confirmation of executive and judicial officers, the Senate's ratification of treaties, the Congress' power to impeach and remove executive and judicial officers—did not violate a proper understanding of separation of powers. He would be aghast, I think, to hear those words used as justification for ignoring that carefully designed structure so long as, in the changing view of the Supreme Court from time to time, "too much commingling" does not occur. Consideration of the degree of commingling that a particular disposition produces may be appropriate at the margins, where the outline of the framework itself is not clear; but it seems to me far from a marginal question whether our constitutional structure allows for a body which is not the Congress, and yet exercises no governmental powers except the making of rules that have the effect of laws.

I think the Court errs, in other words, not so much because it mistakes the degree of commingling, but because it fails to recognize that this case is not about commingling, but about the creation of a new Branch altogether, a sort of junior-varsity Congress. It may well be that in some circumstances such a Branch would be desirable; perhaps the agency before us here will prove to be so. But there are many desirable dispositions that do not accord with the constitutional structure we live under. And in the long run the improvisation of a constitutional structure on the basis of currently perceived utility will be disastrous.

I respectfully dissent from the Court's decision, and would reverse the judgment of the District Court.

NOTES ON *MISTRETTA* AND THE FEDERAL SENTENCING GUIDELINES

1. Discretion versus Rules in Sentencing. The dispute over the Federal Sentencing Guidelines—although played out in *Mistretta* in the context of the hoary constitutional principle of separation of powers—often involves a deep-seated disagreement about the relative desirability of individualized discretion (exercised, traditionally, by trial judges) versus generally applicable rules and standards in sentencing for federal crimes. As noted by the *Mistretta* Court, sentencing in the United States has traditionally been a matter of sound judicial discretion (within, of course, the upper and lower limits set by the relevant criminal statutes). In the area of sentencing, trial judges have historically been allowed to operate in a "black box"—unfettered by the rules of evidence (except for broad principles of relevancy), and without any obligation to justify, or even to explain, their individual sentencing decisions.

As recently as the late 1960's, most commentators clearly favored this discretionary approach. For example, the American Bar Association's Project on Minimum Standards for Criminal Justice proposed in September, 1968:

> "The sentencing court should be provided in all cases with a wide range of alternatives, with gradations of supervisory, supportive and custodial facilities at its disposal so as to permit a sentence appropriate for each individual case." Standards, at § 2.1(b).

In the commentaries, the Special Committee on Minimum Standards for the Administration of Criminal Justice (with the concurrence of the Advisory Committee on Sentencing and Review) explained:

> "[L]egislative attempts to particularize dispositions in advance and in the abstract cannot adequately account for the variations which will occur. There are inevitably going to be instances where a rigid sentencing structure, rigid with respect to a particular offense or to an entire punishment category, will require a disposition which even the strongest proponents of sentencing severity would disdain. The result in practice will be nullification of the statute or injustice to the individual, in neither case a desirable objective....

> "The principle which the Advisory Committee endorses ... is that the legislature serves its function best by arming the system with the power to deal individually with individuals. The legislature can create institutions and programs, can provide the system with funds and facilities, can isolate goals and objectives—but it cannot prescribe a proper sentence in advance of the event. [I]t should be a part of the legislative function to assess the outer limits of the punishment which society can appropriately demand in exchange for the violation of its laws. But within these limits, restrictions on the flexibility of the agencies charged with measuring and molding the individual will inevitably produce a case which does not fit the restrictions.... Neither offenses nor offenders are fungible." Standards with Commentary, at § 2.1(d).

2. Sentencing Commissions and the Rise of Determinate Sentencing. In the early 1970's, Judge Marvin E. Frankel first proposed—contrary to the long-standing tradition of judicial sentencing discretion—that criminal sentencing be made subject to a set of "sentencing guidelines," promulgated by a "Commission on Sentencing." See Marvin E. Frankel, Criminal Sentences: Law Without Order (New York: Hill & Wang, 1973); Marvin E. Frankel, Lawlessness in Sentencing, 47 U. Cin. L. Rev. 1 (1972). Judge Frankel wrote that unfettered judicial sentencing discretion led to inconsistent and sometimes absurd sentences, and he suggested that a system based on sentencing guidelines would lead to greater uniformity and fairness.

By the late 1970's, public dissatisfaction with seemingly unjustified sentencing disparities, along with growing public disdain for "soft" judges, psychiatric experts, and parole boards, led a number of American jurisdictions to move in the direction proposed by Judge Frankel. These jurisdictions, led by Minnesota, Pennsylvania, and Washington, shifted from discretionary sentencing to one form or another of "determinate sentencing," or sentencing governed by rules and standards established by a "sentencing commission" of the kind discussed in *Mistretta*. Often (although not always) this shift to determinate sentencing was accompanied by the abolition of parole, thus requiring a convicted criminal to serve his or her entire sentence, minus any possible "good time" credits. In some states, the combination of determinate sentencing and abolition of parole came to be known by the politically popular label, "truth in sentencing."

The trend toward determinate sentencing also received a strong boost from the revival of Kantian retributivism as a justification for criminal punishment. Beginning in 1976 with the influential book, "Doing Justice," authored by Andrew Von Hirsch on behalf of the Committee for the Study of Incarceration (sponsored by the Field and New World Foundations), many commentators began to argue that the severity and duration of criminal punishment should be based on what the criminal deserves—a matter at least theoretically susceptible to rational and predictable determination from the facts of the crime and the criminal's background—rather than on ad hoc predictions of future dangerousness, or findings by so-called "experts" about when a particular criminal has been adequately "rehabilitated."

Through the 1980's and early 1990's, the determinate sentencing movement continued to spread across the United States. By late 1995, almost half of the states had adopted some form of determinate sentencing; about 80% of these systems were based on sentencing guidelines issued by a sentencing commission, while the remainder were based on statutory sentencing ranges. See Kevin R. Reitz, The Cutting Edge of Sentencing Reform, 8 Fed. Sent. R. 64 (1995).

3. The Sentencing Reform Act of 1984. In 1984, Congress joined the trend toward determinate sentencing. As noted in *Mistretta*, in the Sentencing Reform Act of 1984, Congress created the United States Sentencing Commission and charged the Commission (at 28 U.S.C. § 991(b)) to pursue the following goals:

"(1) establish sentencing policies and practices for the Federal criminal justice system that—

"(A) assure the meeting of the purposes of sentencing as set forth in section 3553(a)(2) of title 18, United States Code;

"(B) provide certainty and fairness in meeting the purposes of sentencing, avoiding unwarranted sentencing disparities among defendants with similar records who have been found guilty of similar criminal conduct while maintaining sufficient flexibility to permit individualized sentences when warranted by mitigating or aggravating factors not taken into account in the establishment of general sentencing practices; and

"(C) reflect, to the extent practicable, advancement in knowledge of human behavior as it relates to the criminal justice process; and

"(2) develop means of measuring the degree to which the sentencing, penal, and correctional practices are effective in meeting the purposes of sentencing as set forth in section 3553(a)(2) of title 18, United States Code."

At 28 U.S.C. § 994, as part of a lengthy and complex statutory provision defining the "duties" of the Sentencing Commission, Congress identified some of the factors that it believed should (and should not) count in determining Guideline sentencing ranges and categories of defendants:

"(c) The Commission, in establishing categories of offenses for use in the guidelines and policy statements governing the imposition of sentences of probation, a fine, or imprisonment, governing the imposition of other authorized sanctions, governing the size of a fine or the length of a term of probation, imprisonment, or supervised release, and governing the conditions of probation, supervised release, or imprisonment, shall consider whether the following matters, among others, have any relevance to the nature, extent, place of service, or other incidents [sic] of an appropriate sentence, and shall take them into account only to the extent that they do have relevance—

"(1) the grade of the offense;

"(2) the circumstances under which the offense was committed which mitigate or aggravate the seriousness of the offense;

"(3) the nature and degree of the harm caused by the offense, including whether it involved property, irreplaceable property, a person, a number of persons, or a breach of public trust;

"(4) the community view of the gravity of the offense;

"(5) the public concern generated by the offense;

"(6) the deterrent effect a particular sentence may have on the commission of the offense by others; and

"(7) the current incidence of the offense in the community and in the Nation as a whole.

"(d) The Commission in establishing categories of defendants for use in the guidelines and policy statements governing the imposition of sentences of probation, a fine, or imprisonment, governing the imposition of other authorized sanctions, governing the size of a fine or the length of a term of probation, imprisonment, or supervised release, and governing the conditions of probation, supervised release, or imprisonment, shall consider whether the following matters, among others, with respect to a defendant, have any relevance to the nature, extent, place of service, or other incidents [sic] of an appropriate sentence, and shall take them into account only to the extent that they do have relevance—

"(1) age;

"(2) education;

"(3) vocational skills;

"(4) mental and emotional condition to the extent that such condition mitigates the defendant's culpability or to the extent that such condition is otherwise plainly relevant;

"(5) physical condition, including drug dependence;

"(6) previous employment record;

"(7) family ties and responsibilities;

"(8) community ties;

"(9) role in the offense;

"(10) criminal history; and

"(11) degree of dependence upon criminal activity for a livelihood.

"The Commission shall assure that the guidelines and policy statements are entirely neutral as to the race, sex, national origin, creed, and socioeconomic status of offenders."

Finally, at 18 U.S.C. § 3553, Congress listed the factors that should be considered by a judge in choosing a sentence for an individual defendant:

"(a) Factors to be considered in imposing a sentence.—The court shall impose a sentence sufficient, but not greater than necessary, to comply with the purposes set forth in paragraph (2) of this subsection. The court, in determining the particular sentence to be imposed, shall consider—

"(1) the nature and circumstances of the offense and the history and characteristics of the defendant;

"(2) the need for the sentence imposed—

"(A) to reflect the seriousness of the offense, to promote respect for the law, and to provide just punishment for the offense;

"(B) to afford adequate deterrence to criminal conduct;

"(C) to protect the public from further crimes of the defendant; and

"(D) to provide the defendant with needed educational or vocational training, medical care, or other correctional treatment in the most effective manner;

"(3) the kinds of sentences available;

"(4) the kinds of sentence and the sentencing range established for—

"(A) the applicable category of offense committed by the applicable category of defendant as set forth in the guidelines issued by the Sentencing Commission pursuant to section 994(a)(1) of title 28, United States Code, and that are in effect on the date the defendant is sentenced; or

"(B) in the case of a violation of probation or supervised release, the applicable guidelines or policy statements issued by the Sentencing Commission pursuant to section 994(a)(3) of title 28, United States Code;

"(5) any pertinent policy statement issued by the Sentencing Commission pursuant to 28 U.S.C. [§] 994(a)(2) that is in effect on the date the defendant is sentenced;

"(6) the need to avoid unwarranted sentence disparities among defendants with similar records who have been found guilty of similar conduct; and

"(7) the need to provide restitution to any victims of the offense.

"(b) Application of guidelines in imposing a sentence.—The court shall impose a sentence of the kind, and within the range, referred to in subsection (a)(4) unless the court finds that there exists an aggravating or mitigating circumstance of a kind, or to a degree, not adequately taken into consideration by the Sentencing Commission in formulating the guidelines that should result in a sentence different from that described. In determining whether a circumstance was adequately taken into consideration, the court shall consider only the sentencing guidelines, policy statements, and official commentary of the Sentencing Commission. In the absence of an applicable sentencing guideline, the court shall impose an appropriate sentence, having due regard for the purposes set forth in subsection (a)(2). In the absence of an applicable sentencing guideline in the case of an offense other than a petty offense, the court shall also have due regard for the relationship of the sentence imposed to sentences prescribed by guidelines applicable to similar offenses and offenders, and to the applicable policy statements of the Sentencing Commission."

Acting pursuant to the Sentencing Reform Act, the United States Sentencing Commission promulgated the initial version of the United States Sentencing Guidelines, which became effective on November 1, 1987.

NOTES ON APPLICATION OF THE FEDERAL SENTENCING GUIDELINES

1. An Overview. The United States Sentencing Guidelines (USSG) comprise an extremely complex patchwork-quilt of regulations, designed to take subtle and highly fact-specific sentencing decisions (previously committed to the discretion of trial judges) and largely reduce them to a series of numerical calculations. The magnitude of the undertaking is almost overwhelming; in one recently published compilation, the Guidelines, including Commentaries and Application Notes (but excluding Appendices), covered more than 350 pages of small print. Confusion and controversy abounds. The Commission's published handbook of the "Questions Most Frequently Asked About the Sentencing Guidelines" now contains more than 160 questions, and the Commission has recently found it necessary to develop a computer program, ASSYST, to help lawyers calculate sentences under the Guidelines. Nor is stability a hallmark of the Guidelines— between November 1, 1987 (the effective date of the original Guidelines) and the end of 1995, some 536 amendments were made to the Guidelines. At least one life-tenured federal district judge has resigned in protest over the changes brought about by the Guidelines.[a]

Although a comprehensive account of the complicated sentencing scheme created by the Guidelines would be well beyond the scope of this book, the scheme can be summarized in the following ten steps:

(1) *Determine the applicable offense guideline.* This generally involves looking in Chapter Two to find the guideline applicable to the defendant's most serious offense of conviction. See USSG § 1B1.2(a). But if the defendant pled guilty, and the plea agreement contained a stipulation that "specifically establishes a more serious offense than the offense of conviction," then the guideline applicable to the more serious stipulated offense is used. See id. The defendant's actual sentence, however, can never exceed the statutory maximum for the offense of conviction. See USSG § 5G1.1. If "no guideline expressly has been promulgated" for a particular offense, then "apply the most analogous offense guideline." See USSG § 2X5.1.

(2) *Determine the defendant's relevant conduct.* For the purpose of Guideline sentencing, a defendant is generally held accountable for all relevant conduct, which can extend far beyond the defendant's offense of conviction. For example, relevant conduct includes all acts or omissions "committed, aided, abetted, counseled, commanded, induced, procured, or willfully caused" by the defendant, as well as all "reasonably foreseeable acts and omissions of others" in furtherance of "jointly undertaken criminal activity," whether or not the defendant was charged with conspiracy. See USSG § 1B1.3(a)(1). If the defendant's offenses would be subject to "grouping" under USSG § 3D1.2 of the Guidelines (i.e., multiple offenses involving substantially the same harm, such as multiple counts of unlawful possession with intent to distribute a controlled substance), then the defendant is also held accountable for all such acts or omissions that were "part of the same course of conduct or common scheme or plan" as the offense of conviction. See USSG § 1B1.3(a)(2).

(3) *Determine the defendant's base offense level.* Using the offense of conviction and any relevant conduct, look in the applicable offense guide-

---

[a] See L.A. Times, A1 Sept. 27, 1990, reporting the resignation of Judge J. Lawrence Irving of the U.S. District Court for the Southern District of California.

line for the base offense level. This will produce a number somewhere between 3 (e.g., minor assault not involving physical conduct or possession and threatened use of a dangerous weapon, USSG § 2A2.3(a)(2)) and 43 (e.g., first degree murder, USSG § 2A1.1(a)).

(4) *Apply any specific offense characteristics (i.e., enhancements or reductions) and cross references in the applicable guideline.* Pursuant to the particular offense guideline, certain factors may require an enhancement or a reduction in the defendant's base offense level, or may require that another cross referenced guideline be used to determine the base offense level. For example, pursuant to the guideline for kidnapping, USSG § 2A4.1, the base offense level is increased by six levels if "a ransom demand or a demand upon government was made," see USSG § 2A4.1(b)(1), but is decreased by one level if "the victim was released before twenty-four hours had elapsed," see USSG § 2A4.1(b)(4)(C). In addition, if the kidnapping victim was killed "under circumstances that would constitute murder ... had such killing taken place within the territorial or maritime jurisdiction of the United States," then the base offense level for the kidnapping is determined by applying the cross referenced guideline for first degree murder, see USSG § 2A4.1(c)(1).

(5) *Apply any adjustments related to victim, role, and obstruction of justice.* Pursuant to Chapter Three, Parts A, B, and C, various upward and/or downward adjustments to the base offense level are made for such factors as the vulnerability or official status of the victim, see USSG § 3A, the defendant's aggravating or mitigating role in the offense, see USSG § 3B, and/or the defendant's attempts to obstruct the administration of justice, see USSG § 3C.

(6) *If there are multiple counts of conviction, apply the rules in Chapter Three, Part D.* Pursuant to Chapter Three, Part D, in cases involving multiple counts, one of three alternative procedures will be used. First, where the applicable guideline is based primarily on the amount of money or quantity of substance involved, or involves repetitive conduct, the quantities are added together and the guideline is applied to the total. Second, where the counts are closely interrelated, they are grouped together and the most serious remaining count is used to determine the base offense level. Third, in all other cases, the most serious count is used as a starting point for the base offense level, with increases for the additional unrelated counts. See USSG § 3D.

(7) *Apply any downward adjustments for acceptance of responsibility.* Pursuant to Chapter Three, Part E, the defendant receives a decrease of two levels for "clearly demonstrat[ing] acceptance of responsibility for the offense." See USSG § 3E1.1(a). If the base offense level is 16 or greater, and certain conditions involving timely cooperation with the authorities are met, an additional one-level decrease is dictated. See USSG § 3E1.1(b). These adjustments do not require the defendant to admit relevant conduct beyond the offense of conviction, although the adjustments may be refused if such relevant conduct has been falsely denied. See USSG § 3E1.1, comment. (n.1.(a)). A defendant's assertion of the right to a trial does not

necessarily preclude an adjustment for acceptance of responsibility, see USSG § 3E1.1, comment. (n.2); conversely, the entry of a guilty plea does not necessarily establish acceptance of responsibility, see USSG § 3E1.1, comment. (n.3)

(8) *Determine the defendant's criminal history category.* Pursuant to Chapter Four, a defendant's prior criminal history is examined to produce a criminal history score. Subject to certain time limits and other rules, a defendant generally receives three points for each prior sentence of imprisonment exceeding one year, see USSG § 4A1.1(a), two points for each prior sentence of imprisonment between sixty days and one year, see USSG § 4A1.1(b), and one point for each prior sentence less than or equal to sixty days (up to a total of four points), see USSG § 4A1.1(c). The defendant is then placed in a criminal history category on the basis of his criminal history score; the categories range from Category I (0 or 1 point) to Category VI (13 or more points). Career offenders, armed career criminals, and those who engage in criminal conduct as a livelihood are subject to special rules enhancing the offense levels for their crimes, see USSG § 4B.

(9) *Determine the appropriate guideline range corresponding to the defendant's offense level and criminal history category.* Based on the defendant's offense level (as adjusted) and criminal history category, the Sentencing Table contained in Chapter Five, Part A, identifies the range of prison sentences (in months) that may be imposed against the defendant. In addition, Parts B through G of Chapter Five set forth various sentencing requirements and options related to probation, imprisonment, supervision conditions, fines, and restitution. Subject to the rules contained in Chapter Five, a judge may sentence a defendant to any prison term that is both within the appropriate guideline range and falls between the maximum and minimum sentence authorized by the statute applicable to the offense of conviction. See USSG § 5G1.1. Of course, because the Sentencing Guidelines cannot "trump" the applicable statute, special attention must be paid to those crimes for which Congress has provided a so-called "mandatory minimum" sentence. For example, under 21 U.S.C. § 841(a)(1)(A), distributing (or conspiring to distribute) more than 500 grams of cocaine carries a "mandatory minimum" sentence of at least five years in prison. Regardless of the guideline range otherwise applicable to such a crime, the defendant must always be sentenced according to the relevant statute. See USSG § 5G1.1(b)(where statutorily required minimum sentence is greater than maximum of guideline range, statutory minimum sentence "shall be the guideline sentence").

(10) *Consider any possible grounds for departure from the guideline range.* Chapter Five, Parts H and K, along with several other provisions scattered throughout the Guidelines, address the circumstances under which a judge may depart from the appropriate guideline range. Chapter Five, Part H, addresses various characteristics of the defendant, such as age, education, vocational skills, mental and emotional conditions, physical conditions, employment record, family ties, military service, and lack of guidance as a youth; in general, the Guidelines reject the use of these

characteristics as grounds for departure. The most important ground for departure authorized by the Guidelines is contained in Chapter Five, Part K, which permits departure based on a motion by the government stating that the defendant "has provided substantial assistance in the investigation or prosecution of another person who has committed an offense," see USSG § 5K1.1. In addition, departure may be appropriate in certain rare instances where "there exists an aggravating or mitigating circumstance of a kind, or to a degree, not adequately taken into consideration by the Sentencing Commission in formulating the guidelines," see USSG § 5K2.0. Such departures, of course, cannot take the defendant's sentence outside of the range specified in the relevant statute.

As a procedural matter, this ten-step process for determining a defendant's sentence is generally undertaken, in the first instance, by officials of the United States Probation Office. Prior to the sentencing of a convicted defendant, the Probation Office prepares a presentence investigation report. This report, which incorporates all relevant sentencing information provided by the prosecution and defense as well as that produced by independent investigation, details the instant offense and the background and characteristics of the defendant. At the conclusion of the report, the Probation Office makes a sentencing recommendation to the trial judge. Based on this report, along with any additional information presented at the sentencing hearing by the prosecution and defense, the judge determines the defendant's sentence.[a]

2. An Example. Consider the following hypothetical defendant, as described in a mock presentence investigation report prepared with the assistance of the United States Probation Office for the Southern District of Indiana:

* * *

IN THE UNITED STATES DISTRICT COURT
FOR THE SOUTHERN DISTRICT OF INDIANA

UNITED STATES OF AMERICA vs. FRANK S. MOPE

Presentence Investigation Report
Docket No. IN 95–2023–CR–01

Offense: Count 1: Conspiracy to Possess with Intent to Distribute and to Distribute Cocaine, a Schedule II Narcot-

---

[a] Under the Sentencing Reform Act of 1984, the relevant federal criminal statutes, and the Sentencing Guidelines, a defendant's sentence may consist of one or more of the following: imprisonment, probation (which is now authorized as a specific sentence to be imposed by the trial judge, see 18 U.S.C. § 3561), supervised release (which is generally required, under the Guidelines, following imprisonment of more than one year), restitution, fines (mandatory in most cases), special assessments (also mandatory; the proceeds are used for victim assistance and compensation programs), and forfeitures. The statutes and Guidelines also authorize trial judges to use several other creative sentencing options, including community confinement, home detention, and community service.

ic Controlled Substance in a Quantity Greater than 500 Grams (21 U.S.C. §§ 841(a)(1) and 846)

Possible range of sentence: 5 to 40 years in prison

Count 2: Using or Carrying a Firearm During and in Relation to a Drug Trafficking Crime (18 U.S.C. § 924(c)(1))

Possible range of sentence: 5 years in prison, consecutive to Count 1

Codefendants: None
Related Cases: Marcus D. Cornwall, IN 95–2024–CR–01
Joseph P. Moster, IN 95–2024–CR–02
Frankie Steven Drake, IN 95–2024–CR–03
Thomass Donnie Friday, IN 95–2022–CR–01
Michael F. Beachbum, IN 95–0567M–05

Date Report Prepared: March 9, 1996

Defendant: Frank S. Mope

Identifying Data:

Date of Birth:	1–7–46
Age:	50
Race:	White
Sex:	Male
SSN No:	123–45–6789
Education:	High School Diploma
Dependents:	None
Citizenship:	U.S.A.
Legal Address:	1996 Mopehead Drive
	Indianapolis, IN 46226

PART A. THE OFFENSE

Charge(s) and Conviction(s)

i. Frank S. Mope, was charged by Criminal Complaint with Conspiracy to Possess with Intent to Distribute and Distribution of Cocaine, in violation of 21 U.S.C. §§ 841(a)(1) and 846, as well as Possession of a Firearm During a Drug Trafficking Offense, in violation of 18 U.S.C. § 924(c). The complaint was filed on January 20, 1996, under docket number IN 93–9042M–01. On February 22, 1996, Frank S. Mope was recharged in a two-count Information with Conspiracy to Possess with Intent to Distribute and to Distribute Cocaine, and Using or Carrying a Firearm during a Crime of Drug Trafficking. On the same date, the defendant filed a Final Plea Agreement and a petition to enter a plea of guilty to Count 1 of the two-count Information.

ii. Pursuant to the agreement, the defendant will waive indictment and will plead guilty to Count 1 of the two-count Information. Further, he agrees to cooperate fully with the United States. In exchange, the United States agrees to dismiss Count 2 of the two-count Information.

iii. The parties have entered into the following stipulations concerning the application of the Sentencing Guidelines: It is agreed by and between the parties that Frank S. Mope conspired to possess with intent to distribute 1.9 kilograms of cocaine; it is further agreed that in the event the Court accepts the plea agreement for this case and ultimately sentences the defendant to a term of imprisonment within the guideline range, then the defendant hereby expressly waives the right to appeal the conviction and sentence imposed on this case on any grounds except for errors of law.

iv. In related cases, on December 22, 1995, Thomass Donnie Friday was recharged via Information with Laundering a Monetary Instrument in violation of 18 U.S.C. § 1956(a)(1)(A)(i). On the same date Mr. Friday filed a petition to enter a plea of guilty and a final plea agreement pleading guilty to the one count Information. Sentencing is scheduled for April 1, 1996.

v. Joseph P. Moster filed a petition to plead guilty and a plea agreement in IN 95–2024–CR–02 on February 7, 1996. Sentencing is scheduled for May 16, 1996.

vi. Marcus D. Cornwall and Frankie Steven Drake are scheduled for jury trial in December of 1996.

vii. Charges against Michael F. Beachbum were dismissed.

The Offense Conduct

viii. Beginning in early 1995, agents of the Drug Enforcement Administration and the Internal Revenue Service, along with officers of the Indianapolis Police Department Narcotics Division, conducted an investigation of an organization smuggling cocaine and marijuana into the United States from the Caribbean area. A confidential informant (CI), who knows some of the individuals involved, assisted in the investigation.

ix. In July and August 1995, a series of consensually monitored recorded telephone conversations occurred between the CI and certain members of the drug smuggling organizations. During these conversations, the CI was provided with the telephone number of someone identified as ''Moe'' from Atlanta, Georgia. The CI was advised he should contact Moe for future drug dealings.

x. The CI gave Moe's telephone number to the U.S. Customs Service. A subscriber information check revealed the number belonged to Marcus D. Cornwall (Cornwall), residing at 107 Maple Dr., Atlanta, Georgia. After Cornwall was identified, he and the CI spoke via telephone several times. During these conversations, which were monitored, Cornwall acknowledged his drug trafficking relationship with the Caribbean smuggling organization. The CI and Cornwall agreed to maintain contact with one another for the purpose of negotiating future drug transactions.

xi. During one conversation in September 1995, Cornwall told the CI he had sent an associate to Jamaica to purchase and smuggle marijuana into the United States. When Cornwall's courier returned to the U.S., the courier was arrested. This eventually led to Cornwall being arrested.

xii. In late October and early November 1995, the CI and Cornwall negotiated Cornwall's purchase of several kilograms of cocaine from the CI. Cornwall said he represented two investors for the cocaine. One investor lived in Atlanta, and the other lived in Indianapolis, Indiana. Cornwall claimed he would be able to arrange the purchase of six kilograms of cocaine. The CI told Cornwall the cocaine would cost $17,000.00 per kilogram. Cornwall agreed to the price and also negotiated with the CI concerning the possible sale of an alleged stolen 1995 BMW automobile as part of the transaction. The CI agreed to accept the car but stipulated it must be delivered to Indianapolis in exchange for one or two kilograms of cocaine.

xiii. On November 18, 1995, Cornwall told the CI he and an unidentified person from Indianapolis would be flying to Indianapolis from Atlanta that day. Cornwall later said he had rented a burgundy Dodge automobile and would be driving to Indianapolis rather than flying. The next day, when the CI had not heard from Cornwall, the CI called Cornwall's residence and learned Cornwall was staying in Room 106 of the Motel Thirteen in Indianapolis. The CI called Cornwall and later went to the motel to meet with him. Law enforcement authorities conducted surveillance of the meeting from outside the motel. (Details not observed by surveillance were supplied later by the CI.)

xiv. When Cornwall answered the door, the CI saw another black male inside the room, using the telephone. A short time later, Cornwall left the room and accompanied the CI to the CI's car. Later, Cornwall returned to the room. The CI said he and Cornwall again discussed the cocaine transaction. Afterward, Cornwall and another person were seen driving away in a burgundy Dodge Spirit bearing Georgia license plate number MAP787.

xv. Later that day, Cornwall and the CI spoke several times via telephone. Cornwall tried to persuade the CI to break up their transaction into three separate cocaine sales, involving various amounts of money and cocaine. The purported reason for this was to keep the three distribution organizations separate in order to protect the identity of their respective customers. The CI and Cornwall, after several monitored conversations, agreed to meet again at the Motel Thirteen. During that meeting, Cornwall told the CI that his investors wanted to follow Cornwall and the CI to the location where the cocaine was to be purchased.

xvi.   At about 8:00 p.m., agents saw additional cars arriving at the Motel Thirteen. The CI met Joseph P. Moster and watched him leave the motel room and enter one of the cars which had just arrived at the motel. Three vehicles then left the area. The first contained Cornwall and the CI. Surveillance agents noted one of the vehicles was a 1982 blue Oldsmobile, bearing Indiana license plate number 101J1234; four males were in the car. The driver was later identified as Frank S. Mope. The third car was a 1986 silver Pontiac, bearing Indiana license plate number 101W5678. The driver, later identified as Michael F. Beachbum, was alone. Agents followed the three cars to the Holiday Hotel, located at the Indianapolis International Airport.

xvii.   Upon arrival, Cornwall went to Mope's car. When he returned, Cornwall told the CI the investors did not want to show the money prior to seeing the cocaine. Cornwall and the CI then entered Room 348 of the Holiday Hotel, which contained hidden electronic audio and visual recording equipment. Mope entered the room, bringing with him money to be used to purchase cocaine. The CI requested more money be brought to the room prior to the delivery of the cocaine. Mope and Cornwall arranged for the money to be brought to the room. Mope said there was an additional $12,000.

xviii.   When Mope first entered the room, the CI asked whether he or Cornwall had any weapons on them. Cornwall stated that Mope was carrying a gun. However, Mope never displayed a gun, and it does not appear by a preponderance of the evidence that Mope carried or used a gun in committing the offense.

xix.   After counting the money which had been brought to the room, the CI called Special Agent Frank Kleire of the U.S. Customs Service to arrange for a sample of the cocaine to be brought to the room. The agent brought 1.9 kilograms of cocaine to the room and showed it to Cornwall and Mope. Cornwall and Mope were then placed under arrest.

xx.   After this, the other occupants of the blue Oldsmobile and the silver Pontiac were arrested. They were identified as Moster, Frankie Steven Drake, and Thomass Donnie Friday, as well as Beachbum.

xxi.   It was later determined that approximately $32,860 had been brought to the hotel room to be applied toward the purchase of the cocaine. After Beachbum was arrested, approximately $11,400 was found inside a sock under the front passenger seat of the Pontiac.

xxii.   After he was arrested and advised of his rights, Cornwall admitted he and Moster had travelled together from Atlanta,

Georgia, to arrange the cocaine purchase. He said Moster was the person who had the connections in Indianapolis to purchase cocaine. Moster had arranged for Mope to purchase part of the cocaine.

Victim Impact

xxiii.   There are no identifiable victims of the offense.

Adjustment for Obstruction of Justice

xxiv.   The probation officer has no information suggesting the defendant impeded or obstructed justice.

Adjustment for Acceptance of Responsibility

xxv.   Mr. Mope is remorseful for his actions and indicates he would not do this again if given the opportunity. He has accepted responsibility for his actions in this offense. Further he has timely entered a plea of guilty, thereby permitting the government to avoid preparing for trial and permitting the Court to allocate its resources efficiently.

PART B.   DEFENDANT'S CRIMINAL HISTORY

Juvenile Adjudication(s)

xxvi.   None.

Adult Criminal Conviction(s)

xxvii.   On two previous occasions since 1994, the defendant was convicted of Battery, a Class A misdemeanor. On each of these two occasions, the defendant received a sentence of sixty days' imprisonment.

Other Criminal Conduct

xxviii.   The defendant related he had been involved in selling drugs for approximately the last one and a half to two years prior to his arrest.

Pending Charges

xxix.   None.

PART C.   OFFENDER CHARACTERISTICS

Personal and Family Data

xxx.   Johnny Mope was born on January 7, 1946, in Indianapolis, Indiana, to John Mope and Wanda Rainier. His parents were never married and did not live together. He indicated he was close to his mother and would see his father approximately four or five times a year. To make up for this lost adult male role model, the defendant indicates he was close to an uncle and his basketball coaches. Mr. Mope reports when he was in the fifth grade his mother lost her job and they had to move in with his aunt until the eighth grade. His mother then obtained employment sufficient enough to allow her and her children to move out on their own again. Mr. Mope reports his mother received child support until the death of his father in 1986. After that time, the defendant reports receiving a social security benefit. The defendant's mother, age 68, is employed as a factory worker in Indianapolis, Indiana. Mr. Mope's father died at the age of 52 as a result of suicide. Mr. Mope's occupation was a mechanic. The defendant has one half-sister, Theresa Boat, age 46.

xxxi. Mr. Mope reports he was not a problem child growing up and involved himself heavily in sports. He did not become involved in illegal activities until his return from Jr. College approximately two years ago.

xxxii. The defendant has never been married, but does have four children. They are: Jason Mope, age 3, residing with his mother Vickey Doe in Indianapolis, Indiana; Jerome Jones, age 1½, resides with his mother Cindy Jones in Indianapolis, Indiana; Franklin Mope, age 1, resides with his mother Juanita Sells in Indianapolis, Indiana; and Lisa Mope, 1½ years old, resides with her mother Wanda Bradford. Mr. Mope was ordered to pay $45.00 a week for Lisa in child support. He has been unable to pay since arrested. Prior to his arrest, he remained mostly current on payments.

Physical Condition

xxxiii. The defendant is 5'9" tall and weighs 175 pounds. He has brown eyes and black hair. Mr. Mope has no identifiable scars, tattoos, or birthmarks. He is not currently under a doctor's care and is not currently taking any medication. He related his only medical problem as occasional high blood pressure.

Mental and Emotional Health

xxxiv. Mr. Mope reports never having received counseling or treatment for mental or emotional health. He believes he has no need for it at this time.

Substance Abuse

xxxv. The defendant reports his first use of alcohol at the age of nineteen. He indicates he started drinking to gain weight for basketball and would drink mainly on the weekends or when going out for a special occasion.

xxxvi. The defendant's first use of illegal drugs was when he was twenty years old. He tried marijuana over the last six months prior to his arrest. He indicated he would smoke marijuana two to three times a week. Mr. Mope has not received any treatment for alcohol or drug abuse and does not believe he is in need of any kind of treatment.

Education and Vocational Skills

xxxvii. The defendant graduated from high school in Indianapolis, Indiana, in the spring of 1964. He was an average student and was involved in basketball for all four years. Mr. Mope then attended a Jr. College commuter school in Illinois. He attended there for two semesters before leaving due to financial difficulties. His first semester he was a C average student, and his grades started to slip the second semester before leaving. He also was involved on the basketball team.

Employment Record

xxxviii. For approximately the last 1½ to two years the defendant has been self-employed in various jobs supporting himself and his children. He has been a mechanic and has also lived on the proceeds of illegal drug sales.

xxxix. Mr. Mope indicated he was hoping to leave Indianapolis and get a fresh start prior to this arrest. The defendant started working in June 1991 in Indianapolis, Indiana, as an order processor. He earned minimum wage, working full time for approximately three weeks. After becoming sick one day at work the defendant went home and never returned.

xxxx. Between his sophomore and junior years of high school the defendant was employed at a fast food restaurant. He worked approximately 20 hours a week. In between high school and 1991, the defendant was a self-employed mechanic.

* * *

Given that the relevant statutes, 21 U.S.C. §§ 841(a)(1) and 846, authorize a prison sentence of between 5 and 40 years in prison on Count 1, what prison sentence should Mope receive?

Under the United States Sentencing Guidelines, Mope's sentence would be determined as follows:

(1) Applicable Offense Guideline: The United States Sentencing Commission Guideline for violation of 21 U.S.C. §§ 841(a)(1) and 846, Conspiracy to Possess with Intent to Distribute and to Distribute Cocaine, is USSG § 2D1.1;

(2) Relevant Conduct: No relevant conduct beyond the offense of conviction;

(3) Base Offense Level: Apply USSG § 2D1.1(a)(3) and USSG § 2D1.1(c)(7),[b] for a base offense level of 26;

---

[b] "§ 2D1.1. Unlawful Manufacturing, Importing, Exporting, or Trafficking (Including Possession with Intent to Commit These Offenses); Attempt or Conspiracy

"(a) Base Offense Level . . .

(3) the offense level specified in the Drug Quantity Table set forth in subsection (c) below.

. . .

(4) Specific Offense Characteristics and/or Cross References: None applicable;

(5) Adjustments for Victim, Role, and Obstruction of Justice: None applicable;

(6) Multiple Counts of Conviction: None applicable;

(7) Downward Adjustments for Acceptance of Responsibility: Apply USSG § 3E1.1,[c] for a reduction in the offense level from 26 to 23;

(8) Criminal History Category: Apply USSG § 4A1.1,[d] for a criminal history score of four;

(9) Appropriate Guideline Range: Look at Sentencing Table, USSG Chapter 5, Part A:

Criminal History Category (Criminal History Points)

Offense Level	I (0–1)	II (2–3)	III (4–6)	IV (7–9)	V (10–12)	VI (13+)
22	41–51	46–57	51–63	63–78	77–96	84–105
23	46–57	51–63	57–71	70–87	84–105	92–115
24	51–63	57–71	63–78	77–96	92–115	100–125
25	57–71	63–78	70–87	84–105	100–125	120–150

Using an adjusted offense level of 23, and criminal history category of III (based on a criminal history score of 4–6 points), the Sentencing Table establishes a guideline range of 57–71 months' imprisonment. Because

"(c) Drug Quantity Table
Controlled Substances and Quantity   Base Offense Level

. . .   . . .
(6) At least 2 KG but less than 3.5 KG of Cocaine . . .   Level 28
(7) At least 500 G but less than 2 KG of Cocaine . . .   Level 26
(8) At least 400 G but less than 500 G of Cocaine . . .   Level 24"

[c] "§ 3E1.1. Acceptance of Responsibility

"(a) If the defendant clearly demonstrates acceptance of responsibility for his offense, decrease the offense level by 2 levels.

"(b) If the defendant qualifies for a decrease under subsection (a), the offense level determined prior to the operation of subsection (a) is level 16 or greater, and the defendant has assisted authorities in the investigation or prosecution of his own misconduct by taking one or more of the following steps:

(1) timely providing complete information to the government concerning his own involvement in the offense; or

(2) timely notifying authorities of his intention to enter a plea of guilty, thereby permitting the government to avoid preparing for trial and permitting the court to allocate its resources efficiently,

decrease the offense level by 1 additional level."

[d] "§ 4A1.1. Criminal History Category

"The total points from items (a) through (f) determine the criminal history category in the Sentencing Table in Chapter Five, Part A.

"(a) Add 3 points for each prior sentence of imprisonment exceeding one year and one month.

"(b) Add 2 points for each prior sentence of imprisonment of at least sixty days not counted in (a).

"(c) Add 1 point for each prior sentence not counted in (a) or (b), up to a total of 4 points for this item . . . ."

violations of 21 U.S.C. §§ 841(a)(1) carry a "mandatory minimum" sentence of at least five years' imprisonment, however, this guideline range must be modified to 60–71 months' imprisonment.

(10) Grounds for Departure: None applicable.

CONCLUSION: Mope therefore can be given a prison sentence, under the Sentencing Guidelines, of between 60 and 71 months' imprisonment.

What effect, if any, does Mope's life history have on the sentence he can receive under the Sentencing Guidelines? Should the defendant's life history, including such matters as family ties, employment record, educational background, and other individual characteristics, be given greater weight?

Now consider the following factual variations; how would these affect Mope's sentence under the Sentencing Guidelines?

(A) In addition to the 1.9 kilograms of cocaine stipulated in connection with the plea agreement, the Probation Officer and trial judge find (as uncharged, "relevant conduct") that Mope also conspired to possess, with intent to distribute, an additional 0.11 kilograms of cocaine at the time of the instant offense.[e]

(B) The Probation Officer and trial judge find that, in an effort to act like a "tough guy," Mope brandished a small pocketknife during the commission of the instant offense.[f]

(C) Despite Mope's guilty plea, the Probation Officer and trial judge find that Mope is not sincerely remorseful, has not fully admitted the scope of his guilt, and therefore has not clearly demonstrated acceptance of responsibility for his offense.[g]

(D) Mope's two previous convictions for Battery resulted in sentences of fifty-nine days' imprisonment each, rather than sixty days' imprisonment each.[h]

(E) The U.S. Attorney files a motion pursuant to USSG § 5K1.1 and 18 U.S.C. § 3553(e), stating that Mope provided substantial assistance in

[e] See USSG § 2D1.1(c), supra note b.

[f] See USSG § 2D1.1(b)—Specific Offense Characteristics:

"(1) If a dangerous weapon (including a firearm) was possessed, increase by 2 levels...."

[g] See USSG § 3E1.1, comment. (n.3):

"Entry of a plea of guilty prior to the commencement of trial combined with truthfully admitting the conduct comprising the offense of conviction, and truthfully admitting or not falsely denying any additional relevant conduct for which he is accountable ... will constitute significant evidence of acceptance of responsibility.... However, this evidence may be outweighed by conduct of the defendant that is inconsistent with such acceptance of responsibility. A defendant who enters a guilty plea is not entitled to an adjustment under this section as a matter of right."

See also USSG § 3E1.1, comment. (n.5):

"The sentencing judge is in a unique position to evaluate a defendant's acceptance of responsibility. For this reason, the determination of the sentencing judge is entitled to great deference on review."

[h] See USSG § 4A1.1, supra note d.

the investigation and prosecution of Marcus D. Cornwall.[i]

3. The Practical Consequences of the Sentencing Reform Act of 1984. The Sentencing Reform Act of 1984, and the Sentencing Guidelines promulgated thereunder, may already have contributed to some rather startling changes in the federal criminal justice system. For example, the total number of federal prisoners jumped from less than 40,000 in 1987 (the year the Guidelines took effect) to more than 65,000 in 1990. From 1990 to 1995, a period during which many Guideline sentences—especially in drug-related cases—became increasingly severe, the federal prison population is estimated to have almost doubled. See 1992 Statistical Abstract of the United States, No. 343, at 210; U.S. Department of Justice, Bureau of Justice Statistics, Sourcebook of Criminal Justice Statistics, 1993, at 628, table 6.64; Kathleen F. Brickey, Criminal Mischief: The Federalization of American Criminal Law, 46 Hastings L.J. 1135, 1157–58 (1995).

Another predictable practical consequence of the Guidelines has been the growing burden of sentencing appeals on the federal appellate courts. The Sentencing Reform Act of 1984, which took sentencing out of its traditional "black box" and exposed it to the harsh light of day, created opportunities for both the defendant and the prosecutor to litigate on appeal such issues as Guideline applicability, eligibility for Guideline departures, and calculation of base offense levels and Guideline ranges. Before the Sentencing Guidelines went into effect, there were few federal sentencing appeals. In 1988 (the first year after the Guidelines took effect), only 225 sentencing appeals involving the Guidelines were filed. But the number shot up to over 7,000 Guideline appeals filed during 1990. See Administrative Office of the U.S. Courts, Annual Report of the Director, 1988, 1990. During fiscal 1994, 59.5% of *all* federal criminal appeals involved the Sentencing Guidelines, and 33.6% of all federal criminal appeals involved *solely* Guideline issues. See United States Sentencing Commission, 1994 Annual Report 135 (1995). Nor does it appear that the number of Guideline appeals is diminishing as the federal courts resolve more Guideline issues; if anything, the number of Guideline appeals appears to be going up with each succeeding year. See Steven L. Chanenson, Consistently Inconsistent: Circuit Rulings on the Guidelines in 1994, 7 Fed. Sent. Rep. 224, 225 (1995).

---

[i] See USSG § 5K1.1—Substantial Assistance to Authorities:

"Upon motion of the government stating that the defendant has provided substantial assistance in the investigation or prosecution of another person who has committed an offense, the court may depart from the guidelines...."

See also 18 U.S.C. § 3553(e), which provides, with respect to statutory "mandatory minimum" sentences such as the one mandated by 21 U.S.C. § 841(a)(1):

"(e) Limited authority to impose a sentence below a statutory minimum.—Upon motion of the Government, the court shall have the authority to impose a sentence below a level established by statute as a minimum sentence so as to reflect a defendant's substantial assistance in the investigation or prosecution of another person who has committed an offense. ...."

4. Questions. Many of the cases in the next two sections of this chapter raise the following fundamental questions: To what extent have the Federal Sentencing Guidelines succeeded in carrying out the Congressional intent behind the Sentencing Reform Act of 1984? To what extent *can* they succeed? Can *any* system of determinate sentencing ever eliminate (or even reduce substantially) "unwarranted sentencing disparities," while still maintaining "sufficient flexibility" to deal fairly with individual cases?

SECTION 2: "REAL OFFENSE" FACTORS UNDER THE GUIDELINES

United States v. Castellanos

United States Court of Appeals, Eleventh Circuit, 1990.
904 F.2d 1490.

Before TJOFLAT, CHIEF JUDGE, VANCE,[a] CIRCUIT JUDGE, and PITTMAN, SENIOR DISTRICT JUDGE.

■ TJOFLAT, CHIEF JUDGE:

I.

On January 5, 1988, a federal grand jury handed down a two-count indictment against appellant Alejandro Castellanos and others, charging them with (1) conspiracy to possess more than 500 grams of cocaine with intent to distribute it in violation of 21 U.S.C. §§ 841(a)(1), 846 (1988), and (2) possession of an unspecified quantity of cocaine in violation of 21 U.S.C. § 841(a)(1) and 18 U.S.C. § 2 (1988). On March 10, 1988, Castellanos reached a plea agreement with the Government pursuant to which he pled guilty to count two of his indictment. Castellanos' plea agreement stipulated the following facts:

> "On December 3, 1987, pursuant to discussions between co-conspirators and co-defendants Allessandro Ippolito, Marcia Usan, Alejandro Castellanos, Danny Rio and Carlos Carrasco, defendant Alejandro Castellanos and Marcia Usan traveled from Miami to Tampa in an automobile carrying approximately nine ounces [255 grams] of cocaine. Surveillance agents observed Allessandro Ippolito meet Castellanos and Usan at a restaurant in Tampa. A surveillance agent saw Usan remove a white package from the trunk of defendant's automobile and place it in the trunk of Ippolito's automobile. Castellanos was present during this exchange between Ippolito and Usan. Shortly thereafter, Ippolito delivered the cocaine to an undercover Drug Enforcement Agent.

[a] Judge Robert S. Vance was a member of the panel that heard oral arguments in *Castellanos*, but he was murdered on December 16, 1989, and did not participate in the final decision. The case was decided by a quorum of two judges. [Footnote by eds.]

Castellanos, Usan, and Ippolito were then arrested. A later chemical analysis of the substance prov[ed] positive for cocaine."

On April 10, 1989, Castellanos went before the district court for sentencing. Since Castellanos' offense occurred after November 1, 1987, his sentence was controlled by the sentencing guidelines promulgated by the United States Sentencing Commission.

The district court properly determined that Sentencing Guidelines § 2D1.1 (1989)("Unlawful Manufacturing, Importing, Exporting, or Trafficking (Including Possession with Intent to Commit These Offenses)") was applicable to Castellanos' offense.[4] Section 2D1.1 provides that the base offense level should vary depending on the type and quantity of narcotics involved in the offense. See id. at § 2D1.1(a)(3). In the presentence investigation report submitted to the court, the probation officer had found that Castellanos' offense involved over five kilograms of cocaine. Objecting to that finding in the addendum to the report, Castellanos contended that his offense involved only 255 grams as stipulated in his plea agreement. The Government also objected to the probation officer's finding; it contended that the offense involved slightly more than 500 grams of cocaine as charged in the dismissed conspiracy count and as proven through Castellanos' own testimony at the trial of his co-defendant.[5] Thus, the amount of cocaine involved in the offense of conviction became a disputed fact that the district court had to resolve at the sentencing hearing.

The district court, which had presided at the trial of Castellanos' co-defendant and had heard Castellanos' testimony there, adopted the Government's position that over 500 grams of cocaine were involved. Accordingly, the court determined Castellanos' base offense level to be 26. See id. § 2D1.1 drug quantity tbl. After factoring in other adjustments for a total offense level of 21, the court placed appellant in Criminal History Category I. The applicable sentencing range for the offense was thus from thirty-

---

[4] In this opinion, for convenience, we routinely cite the most recent (1989) version of the Sentencing Guidelines. If a particular guideline was amended in any significant way since the time of Castellanos' offense, however, we note that fact and cite the version then in effect.

[5] At the trial of co-defendant Marcia Usan, Castellanos testified about the cocaine transaction as follows:

A. He [the buyer] say, "Okay. First of all, we are going to do the nine ounces," ... and I say, "If you want some more, we go back to Miami. Okay?" He say, "How soon you come back to Miami?" I say, "Tomorrow, and I come back in the same day and bring it back to you nine more ounces cocaine.... [H]e told me, okay, do you think [we could] get more than nine ounces?"

Q. Hold it. Do you think you could get more than what?

A. Nine ounces.

Q. All right.

A. I say, "If we have cash money, we can give you anything you want. But it has to be cash money." And then he asks me, "What about a half kilo?" See, I have got to explain to Marcia, and she told me, "Maybe."

Q. So, in other words, do this nine-ounce deal. If everything went well, do nine ounces the next day?

A. Yes, sir.

Q. And then if things went well, possibly get into half kilograms?

A. Yes, sir.

seven to forty-six months of incarceration, see id. Ch. 5 Pt. A. Declining to grant the Government's motion for a downward departure for substantial assistance rendered to the Government, the district court sentenced Castellanos to a thirty-seven-month term of incarceration to be followed by a three-year term of supervised release. The court explained that it chose the lowest possible end of the sentencing range because of Castellanos' substantial assistance to the Government.

Castellanos now challenges his sentence. He contends that the district court erred in basing his offense level on the total amount of cocaine involved in the two offenses with which he was originally charged rather than on the lesser amount involved in the offense for which he was convicted. According to Castellanos, Sentencing Guidelines § 1B1.3 (1987), which permits consideration of conduct extrinsic to the offense of conviction, denies a criminal defendant the due process of law. Castellanos also contends that the district court erred in refusing to grant the Government's motion for a downward departure. We discuss each contention in turn.[6]

II.

A. The Challenge to Section 1B1.3

Under the guidelines, determination of the appropriate offense level is a two-step process: the court first determines which guideline section covers the offense of conviction, see Sentencing Guidelines § 1B1.2(a), then determines the applicable offense level in accordance with the "relevant conduct" section—1B1.3, see id. § 1B1.2(b). At the time of Castellanos' offense, section 1B1.3(a) instructed a court to consider all "acts and omissions committed or aided and abetted by the defendant . . . that (1) are part of the same course of conduct, or a common scheme or plan, as the offense of conviction" in determining the offense level.[7]

[6] Additionally, Castellanos submits that section 1B1.3 is impermissibly vague and that it denies equal protection of the laws to defendants charged with narcotics offenses. We have considered both contentions and find them to be without merit.

[7] The complete version of section 1B1.3 in force at the time of Castellanos' offense is set out below:

"Relevant Conduct. To determine the seriousness of the offense conduct, all conduct, circumstances, and injuries relevant to the offense of conviction shall be taken into account.

"(a) Unless otherwise specified under the guidelines, conduct and circumstances relevant to the offense of conviction means: acts or omissions committed or aided and abetted by the defendant, or by a person for whose conduct the defendant is legally accountable, that

"(1) are part of the same course of conduct, or a common scheme or plan, as the offense of conviction, or

"(2) are relevant to the defendant's state of mind or motive in committing the offense of conviction, or

"(3) indicate the defendant's degree of dependence upon criminal activity for a livelihood.

"(b) Injury relevant to the offense of conviction means harm which is caused intentionally, recklessly or by criminal negligence in the course of conduct relevant to the offense of conviction."

Castellanos' due process challenge to section 1B1.3 is essentially three-fold. He first argues that section 1B1.3(a) is facially invalid in that it allows a defendant to be sentenced not only for the offense of conviction but also for offenses that did not produce a conviction. According to Castellanos, there results a "distinction without a difference" between conviction and sentence, whereby a defendant may be convicted of a lesser offense under the stringent "beyond a reasonable doubt" standard of proof but sentenced for a more serious offense without the safeguard of the higher burden of proof. While acknowledging that pre-guideline jurisprudence established less rigorous due process requirements for sentencing proceedings than for trial of guilt or innocence, Castellanos asserts that the guidelines require new, more stringent standards.

We disagree. The pre-guideline sentencing model was based on "real offense" sentencing: federal courts considered the actual conduct in which a defendant was engaged and not solely that with which he was charged. This model placed few limits on the scope of the evidence that a court could consider. See United States v. Tucker, 404 U.S. 443, 446 (1972)("[A] judge may appropriately conduct an inquiry broad in scope, largely unlimited either as to the kind of information he may consider, or the source from which it may come."). Although the guidelines adopted something akin to a "charge offense" system, the Sentencing Commission that promulgated them cautions us that the guidelines do not install a pure charge offense system but, rather, one that contains a large number of real offense elements. Sentencing Guidelines Ch. 1, Pt. A introduction 4(a). Indeed, the guidelines explicitly state that extrinsic ("real offense") conduct remains relevant to sentencing, see id. § 1B1.2(b).

Under pre-guidelines sentencing law, due process demands were deemed satisfied if the relevant factors were established by a preponderance of the evidence. McMillan v. Pennsylvania, 477 U.S. 79, 91–93 (1986). In contrast to the elements that establish a defendant's guilt, which must be proved beyond a reasonable doubt, the extrinsic-conduct factors relevant to sentencing come into play "only after a defendant has been adjudged guilty beyond a reasonable doubt." See id. at 92 n. 8. Although the guidelines themselves do not identify the standard of proof required for relevant conduct, neither do they suggest "any reason why we must now change the due process calculus simply because the Congress has decided to provide federal sentencing courts with additional guidance." United States v. Guerra, 888 F.2d 247, 250–51 (2d Cir.1989). This court is one among

The more detailed version of section 1B1.3 now in force does not reflect a change in the substance of the section but was designed to clarify and to restate the intent of the original. See Amendments to the Sentencing Guidelines Manual of October 1987 § 1B1.3 commentary (Jan. 1988), reprinted in Federal Sentencing Guidelines Manual App. C, at 357, 362–63 (1990). Prior to the amendment, as now, the commentary to section 1B1.3 made clear that " '[n]o limitation [would] be placed on the information concerning the background, character, and conduct of a person convicted of an offense ... for the purpose of imposing an appropriate sentence,' 18 U.S.C. § 3577, so long as the information 'has sufficient indicia of reliability to support its probable accuracy.' " See Sentencing Guidelines § 1B1.3 commentary (1987).

many to have concluded that the calculus need not be changed. See, e.g., United States v. Alston, 895 F.2d 1362, 1373 (11th Cir.1990); United States v. Blanco, 888 F.2d 907, 909 (1st Cir.1989); *Guerra*, 888 F.2d at 250; United States v. Harris, 882 F.2d 902, 906–07 (4th Cir.1989). We therefore reject Castellanos' argument that section 1B1.3, on its face, denies a criminal defendant his or her right to due process in sentencing.

Second, Castellanos argues that the district court's application of section 1B1.3 violated his right to due process of law. Due process in sentencing demands, of course, that the relevant conduct considered by a court in any given case be supported by an "evidentiary basis beyond mere allegation in an indictment," United States v. Smith, 887 F.2d 104, 108 (6th Cir.1989), and that the defendant be given an opportunity to rebut factors that might enhance a sentence, see *Guerra*, 888 F.2d at 251. The guidelines accommodate these demands by establishing an adversarial factfinding process, during which a court may consider any information, including reliable hearsay, regardless of the information's admissibility at trial, provided that there are sufficient indicia of reliability to support its probable accuracy. See Sentencing Guidelines § 6A1.3 & commentary. A presentence report prepared by a United States probation officer initiates the process, see Sentencing Guidelines § 6A1.1, which we explained fully in United States v. Wise, 881 F.2d 970, 972 (11th Cir.1989):

> "Once the report is prepared, counsel for both the prosecution and the defense have the opportunity to review it and make objections to any guideline applications that they believe to be erroneous. See Committee on the Administration of the Probation System, Judicial Conference of the United States, Model Local Rule for Guideline Sentencing (1987). The probation officer considers these objections, makes any amendments to the report that may be required, and sets forth in an addendum to the report the objections that remain unresolved. See Probation Officer's Manual at 52. Prior to the sentencing hearing, the report and addendum, together with the probation officer's sentencing recommendation, are submitted to the court. Id. The presentence report and addendum thus serve the same purpose as a pretrial stipulation in a civil bench trial, the report establishing the factual and legal backdrop for the sentencing hearing and the addendum enumerating the disputed factual and legal issues that the court must resolve. The final step in the guideline sentencing process is the sentencing hearing. At this hearing, the court engages in a colloquy with both the prosecution and the defense concerning how the guidelines should be applied to the facts of the particular case before the court. In so doing, the court must resolve all factual and legal disputes raised in the addendum to the presentence report—as well as any other objections raised by the parties during the course of the hearing. The court performs this task by making findings of fact and conclusions of law."

This procedure was followed in the current case. Both the Government and Castellanos submitted their written objections to the probation officer's findings concerning the amount of cocaine involved in the total offense. Both parties had—and exercised—the opportunity to argue their objections at the sentencing hearing. The district court resolved the dispute in favor of the Government based on Castellanos' own testimony at his co-defendant's trial, see supra note 5. That testimony certainly provided a reliable evidentiary basis to support the district court's finding that over 500 grams of cocaine were involved in the total offense.[8] Thus, the district court's application of section 1B1.3 to Castellanos' case did not deprive him of due process.

[In a previous opinion issued by this panel in Castellanos' case,] we stated that evidence presented at the trial of a third party (other than admissions by the defendant himself) may not be used to fashion a defendant's sentence. We contrasted evidence from the trial of another with evidence presented at the defendant's own trial, pointing out that a sentencing court's reliance on the latter is entirely proper: the defendant, who has had the opportunity to cross-examine witnesses and make objections to evidence, cannot object to the court's considering the trial record when fashioning sentence. We now make explicit the intended implication of our previous statement: evidence presented at the trial of another may not—without more—be used to fashion a defendant's sentence if the defendant objects. In such a case, where the defendant has not had the opportunity to rebut the evidence or generally to cast doubt upon its reliability, he must be afforded that opportunity. It was never the position of this panel that a sentencing court may not consider testimony from the trial of a third party as a matter of law; rather, we were of the view that a sentencing court must follow the procedural safeguards incorporated in section 6A1.3 of the guidelines—safeguards designed to protect the defendant's right to respond to information offered against him and to ensure reliability of the information under consideration.

Finally, in this appeal Castellanos argues that the district court, after accepting his plea agreement, could no longer consider, without violating his right to due process of law, conduct other than that to which he stipulated in the agreement. We recognize that the breach of a plea agreement raises serious due process concerns. See Santobello v. New York, 404 U.S. 257, 262 (1971)("when a plea rests in any significant degree on a promise or agreement of the prosecutor, so that it can be said to be part of the inducement or consideration, such promise must be fulfilled"); United States v. Pelletier, 898 F.2d 297, 302 (2d Cir.1990)(due process requires government to adhere to terms of plea agreement); United States v. Harvey, 869 F.2d 1439, 1443–44 (11th Cir.1989)(court will enforce agreement when defendant or witness has kept his part of bargain).

---

[8] We note further that, even though admissibility at trial is not required before the court may consider information for sentencing purposes, this evidence would no doubt be admissible under the party-admission exception to the hearsay rule. See Fed.R.Evid. 801(d)(2).

In Castellanos' case, however, the Government did not breach the plea agreement, nor, after accepting the agreement, did the court: Count One of the indictment was dropped; the Government informed the court of Castellanos' cooperation and moved for a downward departure; the agreement recited Castellanos' understanding that the count to which he was pleading guilty carried a maximum statutory penalty of twenty years imprisonment, and Castellanos' sentence was well under the statutory maximum. This court has already considered and rejected the argument that, under such circumstances, a sentencing court's consideration of conduct extrinsic to the plea agreement is unfair or inequitable. See United States v. Scroggins, 880 F.2d 1204, 1212–13 (11th Cir.1989). We said in *Scroggins*:

> "The guidelines clearly indicate that such conduct is relevant to sentencing; thus, appellant by no means received a sentence that he could not have anticipated—to the contrary, appellant could have predicted that the court would so act. Nor did the Government's agreement to drop count one of appellant's indictment somehow impliedly preclude the district court from considering evidence of appellant's other thefts—under guideline sentencing, counsel cannot bind the sentencing discretion of the district judge or cloak the facts to reach a result contrary to the guidelines' mandate." Id. at 1214.

We therefore reject Castellanos' contention that the district court's consideration of conduct other than that to which Castellanos stipulated in his plea agreement deprived him of the due process of law.

B. The Refusal to Make a Downward Departure

Castellanos challenges the district court's denial of the Government's motion, pursuant to section 5K1.1, for a downward departure based on Castellanos' substantial assistance to the Government. This court has held that, pursuant to 18 U.S.C. § 3742(a), a defendant may not appeal a court's refusal to make a downward departure. See United States v. Fossett, 881 F.2d 976, 979 (11th Cir.1989)(defendant may appeal only upward departure, not refusal to depart downward). In *Fossett*, however, we permitted the appeal because the appellant argued that the district court was not aware of its authority to depart from the guideline sentencing range. We agreed that such a challenge presented a appealable claim. Id.; see 18 U.S.C. § 3742(a)(1), (2)(defendant may appeal if sentence was imposed in violation of law or as result of incorrect application of guidelines).

In the current case, Castellanos' challenge is based largely on the merits of the district court's refusal to depart and, as such, would not be appealable. He also points, however, to Sentencing Guidelines § 1B1.7, which states that "[f]ailure to follow [the guidelines'] commentary could constitute an incorrect application of the guidelines, subjecting the sentence to possible reversal on appeal," see also 18 U.S.C. § 3742(a)(2), and asserts that the district court erred in ignoring the commentary to section

5K1.1. We therefore entertain Castellanos' claim only to the extent that it involves a possible misapplication of the guidelines.

Sentencing Guidelines § 5K1.1, as it read prior to a 1989 amendment,[9] provided that "[u]pon motion of the government stating that the defendant has made a good faith effort to provide substantial assistance in the investigation of another person who has committed an offense, the court *may* depart from the guidelines" (emphasis added). The guideline implements the intent of Congress, expressed in the Sentencing Reform Act, that under guideline sentencing a court would still be permitted to impose a sentence below the statutory minimum. See 18 U.S.C. § 3553(e)("Upon motion of the Government, the court *shall have the authority* to impose a sentence below a level established by statute so as to reflect a defendant's substantial assistance in the investigation or prosecution of another person who has committed an offense." (emphasis added)). Thus, under both the guidelines and the statute, the district court's decision to grant a prosecutor's motion for downward departure is clearly discretionary.

The commentary accompanying section 5K1.1 states that "substantial weight should be given to the government's evaluation of the extent of the defendant's assistance, particularly where the extent and value of the assistance are difficult to ascertain." This instruction does not nullify the discretion expressly given to the district court by the text of the guideline itself; if it did nullify the court's discretion, the permissive wording of the text would be meaningless and a court would have to depart whenever the government so moved. This would be inconsistent, not only with the guideline text and with the permissive language of 18 U.S.C. § 3553(e), but also with other sections of the same commentary, where we read that a defendant's assistance may fall within "a broad spectrum of conduct that must be evaluated by the court on an individual basis "and (2) "[l]atitude is ... afforded the sentencing judge to reduce a sentence...." Sentencing Guidelines § 5K1.1 commentary. Thus, despite the commentary's instruction to give weight to the government's assessment, the district court's discretion remains intact. We conclude, therefore, that the court's refusal to grant the Government's motion does not establish that the district court ignored the commentary and, in so doing, misapplied the guidelines' directive to give substantial weight to the Government's motion.

Furthermore, we note that the commentary emphasizes that the government's position is to be accorded substantial weight "where the extent and value of the assistance are difficult to ascertain." Id. Such is not the case here, where the district court presided over the trial of the co-defendant against whom Castellanos testified and could judge for itself the extent and value of his assistance.

Our review of the transcript of Castellanos' sentencing hearing indicates that the district court considered the Government's motion, correctly

[9] In 1989, Sentencing Guidelines § 5K1.1 was amended by substituting "provided" for "made a good faith effort to provide." See Amendments to the Sentencing Guidelines Manual of October 1987 § 5K1.1 (Nov. 1989), reprinted in Federal Sentencing Guidelines Manual App. C, at 357, 506 (1990).

understood that it had discretion to depart or not to depart, and simply chose not to do so. Castellanos' challenge is reduced to a claim that the court erred in exercising its discretion not to make a downward departure, and such a claim is not appealable. *Fossett*, 881 F.2d at 979; see United States v. Evidente, 894 F.2d 1000, 1004–05 (8th Cir.1990)(citing *Fossett* and cases from six other circuits).

III.

For the foregoing reasons, the sentence imposed by the district court is affirmed.

NOTES ON *CASTELLANOS* AND "RELEVANT CONDUCT"

1. "Relevant Conduct," "Cross References," and Departures. As *Castellanos* demonstrates, the Sentencing Guidelines—although largely based on "charge offense" principles—also include a heavy dose of "real offense" sentencing. The Guidelines accomplish this in three primary ways. First, under § 1B1.3, the Guidelines provide that certain "real offense" factors (in the language in the 1989 version of the Guidelines, "all conduct, circumstances, and injuries *relevant to the offense of conviction*" (emphasis added)) are used to determine the "seriousness of the offense conduct." In other words, such "real offense" factors as the total amount of drugs sold or possessed by the defendant—regardless of the amount for which the defendant was actually convicted—are used to decide where, within the range of offense levels in the Sentencing Table, a particular defendant will be placed. The post-*Castellanos* amendments to § 1B1.3, effective November 1, 1992, include the following within the broad scope of "relevant conduct":

"(1)(A) all acts and omissions committed, aided, abetted, counseled, commanded, induced, procured, or willfully caused by the defendant; and

"(B) in the case of a jointly undertaken criminal activity (a criminal plan, scheme, endeavor, or enterprise undertaken by the defendant in concert with others, whether or not charged as a conspiracy), all reasonably foreseeable acts and omissions of others in furtherance of the jointly undertaken criminal activity, that occurred during the commission of the offense of conviction, in preparation for that offense, or in the course of attempting to avoid detection or responsibility for that offense...." U.S.S.G. § 1B1.3(a)(1).

The second primary means for accomplishing "real offense" sentencing is the inclusion, in Chapter Two of the Guidelines, of a series of "cross references," or provisions requiring that a defendant in certain cases be sentenced according to the Guideline applicable to his "real offense," rather than to his "charged offense"—subject, of course, to any maximum sentence that might be contained in the governing statute for the "charged offense." See § 2X1.1, which provides that in such "cross reference" cases a defendant's base offense level shall be set at "[t]he base offense level from the guideline for the object offense...." For example, in RICO conspiracy cases, defendants must be sentenced (within the RICO statutory maximum) according to "the offense level applicable to the *underlying racketeering activity*" (emphasis added), see § 2E1.1(a).

The third primary method is the limited authority of the district court to depart from the Guideline sentence—upward or downward—based on circumstances in a particular case that are so atypical as to lie totally outside the "heartland" of cases contemplated by the Sentencing Commission. See § 5K2.0. The courts of appeals have repeatedly indicated that they will scrutinize departures very closely, to prevent wholesale avoidance of the Guidelines. But in an extreme case, even absent the availability of the "relevant conduct" or "cross reference" approaches, the tactic of upward departure can be used by the district court to ensure that a defendant's sentence properly reflects the seriousness of his "real offense."

2. Sentencing Commission Policy Statements. The Guidelines contain the following Policy Statements explaining the Sentencing Commission's views about "real offense" sentencing and about departures:

"Chapter One—Introduction and General Application Principles
Part A—Introduction

"4. THE GUIDELINES' RESOLUTION OF MAJOR ISSUES (POLICY STATEMENT)

"(a) Real Offense vs. Charge Offense Sentencing.

"One of the most important questions for the Commission to decide was whether to base sentences upon the actual conduct in which the defendant engaged regardless of the charges for which he was indicted or convicted ('real offense' sentencing), or upon the conduct that constitutes the elements of the offense for which the defendant was charged and of which he was convicted ('charge offense' sentencing). A bank robber, for example, might have used a gun, frightened bystanders, taken $50,000, injured a teller, refused to stop when ordered, and raced away damaging property during his escape. A pure real offense system would sentence on the basis of all identifiable conduct. A pure charge offense system would overlook some of the harms that did not constitute statutory elements of the offenses of which the defendant was convicted.

"The Commission initially sought to develop a pure real offense system. After all, the pre-guidelines sentencing system was, in a sense, this type of system. The sentencing court and the parole commission took account of the conduct in which the defendant actually engaged, as determined in a presentence report, at the sentencing hearing, or before a parole commission hearing officer. The Commission's initial efforts in this direction, carried out in the spring and early summer of 1986, proved unproductive, mostly for practical reasons. To make such a system work, even to formalize and rationalize the status quo, would have required the

Commission to decide precisely which harms to take into account, how to add them up, and what kinds of procedures the courts should use to determine the presence or absence of disputed factual elements. The Commission found no practical way to combine and account for the large number of diverse harms arising in different circumstances; nor did it find a practical way to reconcile the need for a fair adjudicatory procedure with the need for a speedy sentencing process given the potential existence of hosts of adjudicated 'real harm' facts in many typical cases. The effort proposed as a solution to these problems required the use of, for example, quadratic roots and other mathematical operations that the Commission considered too complex to be workable. In the Commission's view, such a system risked return to wide disparity in sentencing practice.

"In its initial set of guidelines submitted to Congress in April 1987, the Commission moved closer to a charge offense system. This system, however, does contain a significant number of real offense elements. For one thing, the hundreds of overlapping and duplicative statutory provisions that make up the federal criminal law forced the Commission to write guidelines that are descriptive of generic conduct rather than guidelines that track purely statutory language. For another, the guidelines take account of a number of important, commonly occurring real offense elements such as role in the offense, the presence of a gun, or the amount of money actually taken, through alternative base offense levels, specific offense characteristics, cross references, and adjustments.

"The Commission recognized that a charge offense system has drawbacks of its own. One of the most important is the potential it affords prosecutors to influence sentences by increasing or decreasing the number of counts in an indictment. Of course, the defendant's actual conduct (that which the prosecutor can prove in court) imposes a natural limit upon the prosecutor's ability to increase a defendant's sentence. Moreover, the Commission has written its rules for the treatment of multicount convictions with an eye toward eliminating unfair treatment that might flow from count manipulation. For example, the guidelines treat a three-count indictment, each count of which charges sale of 100 grams of heroin or theft of $10,000, the same as a single-count indictment charging sale of 300 grams of heroin or theft of $30,000. Furthermore, a sentencing court may control any inappropriate manipulation of the indictment through use of its departure power. Finally, the Commission will closely monitor charging and plea agreement practices and will make appropriate adjustments should they become necessary.

"(b) Departures.

"The sentencing statute permits a court to depart from a guideline-specified sentence only when it finds 'an aggravating or mitigating circumstance of a kind, or to a degree, not adequately taken into consideration by the Sentencing Commission in formulating the guidelines that should result in a sentence different from that described.' 18 U.S.C. § 3553(b). The Commission intends the sentencing courts to treat each guideline as carving out a 'heartland,' a set of typical cases embodying the conduct that each guideline describes. When a court finds an atypical case, one to which a particular guideline linguistically applies but where conduct significantly differs from the norm, the court may consider whether a departure is warranted. Section 5H1.10 (Race, Sex, National Origin, Creed, Religion, and Socio–Economic Status), § 5H1.12 (Lack of Guidance as a Youth and Similar Circumstances), the third sentence of § 5H1.4 (Physical Condition, Including Drug Dependence and Alcohol Abuse), and the last sentence of § 5K2.12 (Coercion and Duress) list several factors that the court cannot take into account as grounds for departure. With those specific exceptions, however, the Commission does not intend to limit the kinds of factors, whether or not mentioned anywhere else in the guidelines, that could constitute grounds for departure in an unusual case.

"The Commission has adopted this departure policy for two reasons. First, it is difficult to prescribe a single set of guidelines that encompasses the vast range of human conduct potentially relevant to a sentencing decision. The Commission also recognizes that the initial set of guidelines need not do so. The Commission is a permanent body, empowered by law to write and rewrite guidelines, with progressive changes, over many years. By monitoring when courts depart from the guidelines and by analyzing their stated reasons for doing so and court decisions with references thereto, the Commission, over time, will be able to refine the guidelines to specify more precisely when departures should and should not be permitted.

"Second, the Commission believes that despite the courts' legal freedom to depart from the guidelines, they will not do so very often. This is because the guidelines, offense by offense, seek to take account of those factors that the Commission's data indicate made a significant difference in pre-guidelines sentencing practice. Thus, for example, where the presence of physical injury made an important difference in pre-guidelines sentencing practice (as in the case of robbery or assault), the guidelines specifically include this factor to enhance the sentence. Where the guidelines do not specify an augmentation or diminution, this is generally because the sentencing data did not permit the Commission to conclude that the factor was empirically important in relation to the particular offense. Of course, an important factor (e.g., physical injury) may infrequently occur in connection with a particular crime (e.g., fraud). Such rare occurrences are precisely the type of events that the courts' departure powers were designed to cover—unusual cases outside the range of the more typical offenses for which the guidelines were designed. . . ."

3.   The Guidelines and the Assimilated Crimes Act. Recall that the Assimilative Crimes Act—under certain circumstances—incorporates state criminal law into the federal criminal code, and allows federal prosecutors to prosecute defendants who commits crimes in federal enclaves for violations of what would otherwise be state criminal law. The Act states that, whenever the defendant commits an act that, although not punishable by Act of Congress, would be punishable under state law, then the defendant "shall be guilty of a like offense *and subject to a like punishment*." 18 U.S.C. § 13 (emphasis added).

In the Sentencing Reform Act of 1984, Congress enacted the following statutory requirement, now codified at 18 U.S.C. § 3553(b):

"In the absence of an applicable sentencing guideline . . ., the court shall also have due regard for the relationship of the sentence imposed to sentences prescribed by guidelines applicable to similar offenses and offenders, and to the applicable policy statements of the Sentencing Commission."

Moreover, the Sentencing Guidelines, at § 2X5.1, provide:

"Other Offenses. If the offense is a felony or Class A misdemeanor for which no guideline expressly has been promulgated, apply the most analogous offense guideline. If there is not a sufficiently analogous guideline, the provisions of [18 U.S.C. Sec. 3553(b), as quoted above] shall control."

In other words, under the Guidelines, it is now possible for a federal court to "find" an appropriate (federal) sentence for *any* federal crime—even one that does not appear anywhere in the Guidelines! The above statute and Guideline provide that, if there is no specific Guideline applicable to a particular crime, then the district court should apply either the "most analogous offense" Guideline (under § 2X5.1), or the Guideline that would apply to "similar offenses and offenders" (under 18 U.S.C. § 3553(b)).

To what extent, if any, does the Sentencing Reform Act implicitly "repeal" the Assimilative Crimes Act (or, at least, that portion of the Assimilated Crimes Act relating to the defendant's punishment)? What if the "most analogous offense" Guideline, or the Guideline that would apply to "similar offenses and offenders" in the federal system, happens to provide for greater punishment than would be allowed by the state criminal statute under which the defendant was convicted?

4.   Burden of Proof for "Relevant Conduct." All of the courts of appeals have now addressed the burden of proof for "relevant conduct" under § 1B1.3 of the Sentencing Guidelines. For the most part, the courts have uniformly held that such factors—even though they may require the judge to impose a (perhaps substantially) harsher sentence on the defendant—need only be established by a preponderance of the evidence. Moreover, the courts have also applied the same burden of proof to other factors affecting sentencing under the Guidelines, such as factors that trigger the use of a "cross referenced" Guideline, or factors that lead a court to depart from the Guidelines. See, e.g., United States v. Wright, 873 F.2d 437 (1st Cir.1989); United States v. Urrego–Linares, 879 F.2d 1234 (4th Cir.1989); United States v. Ebbole, 917 F.2d 1495 (7th Cir.1990); United States v. Restrepo, 946 F.2d 654 (9th Cir.1991)(en banc). The position taken by these courts, approving the preponderance standard, is generally consistent with the traditional view that sentencing courts (operating in the traditional "black box") are free to consider all relevant evidence, including uncharged and even acquitted conduct, before fixing a defendant's sentence; it is also generally consistent with the position taken by the Supreme Court in McMillan v. Pennsylvania, 477 U.S. 79 (1986)(a pre-Guidelines case upholding the use of the preponderance standard under a state statute enhancing a sentence for using a gun to commit a crime).

A few courts have indicated, however, that in special situations the preponderance standard might be insufficient to meet constitutional requirements. For example, in United States v. Kikumura, 918 F.2d 1084 (3d Cir.1990), the defendant was convicted of transporting explosives across state lines, with a Guideline range of 27–33 months in prison. The district court concluded that Kikumura planned to use the bombs to kill scores of people, and departed from the Guidelines upward to the statutory maximum of 30 years in prison. The Third Circuit vacated the sentence and remanded for further consideration:

> "Because less procedural protection is so clearly appropriate in the majority of sentencing cases, we sometimes tend to regard it as appropriate in all sentencing cases. However, legal rules—even rules that function perfectly well in familiar contexts when stated in categorical terms—cannot always be applied in extreme situations. ... Here, we are dealing with findings that would increase Kikumura's sentence from about 30 months to 30 years—the equivalent of a 22–level increase in his offense level. ... This is perhaps the most dramatic example imaginable of a sentencing hearing that functions as 'a tail which wags the dog of the substantive offense.' McMillan, 477 U.S., at 88. In this extreme context, we believe, a court cannot reflexively apply the truncated procedures that are perfectly adequate for all of the more mundane, familiar sentencing determinations.

> "Analytically, there are two possible approaches for providing sufficient process in such situations. The first would place some limit on the concededly broad power of legislatures to define, and courts to consider, conduct that is or could be criminalized as an aggravating factor at sentencing. In effect, this approach would require that, for sentencing purposes, certain findings in certain circumstances be made pursuant to the entire panoply of procedural protections that apply at trial. Neither here nor in the district court, however, did Kikumura advance [this] argument. . . .

> "A second, narrower approach to the problem would ratchet up certain, though not necessarily all, of the procedural protections

afforded a defendant at sentencing, so as more closely to resemble those afforded at trial. Kikumura expressly advanced such an approach at his sentencing hearing when he argued that in order to support a departure predicated upon his intent to commit murder, the prosecution must establish that intent by clear and convincing evidence....

"*McMillan* held that a preponderance standard was generally constitutional but suggested that a different question would be presented if the magnitude of a contemplated departure is sufficiently great.... For the reasons explained above, we hold that in such situations, the factfinding underlying that departure must be established at least by clear and convincing evidence. ... We hold that the clear and convincing evidence standard is, under these circumstances, implicit in the statutory requirement that a sentencing court 'find' certain considerations in order to justify a departure, ... and we reserve judgment on the question whether it is also implicit in the due process clause itself." 918 F.2d, at 1100–02.

To a similar effect, albeit by a different method, was the First Circuit's holding in United States v. Lombard, 72 F.3d 170 (1st Cir.1995). In *Lombard*, the defendant was initially acquitted in state court of murdering two men. Later, in a federal prosecution, he was convicted of firearms violations growing out of the same course of conduct. There was no statutory maximum sentence for the firearms violations. The district court relied on the "cross reference" provision of the Guidelines, § 2X1.1, to sentence the defendant to life in prison based on the Guideline range for the crime of murder, finding—by a preponderance of the evidence—that the defendant actually murdered the two men.

On appeal, the First Circuit acknowledged that a "sentencing court's operative factfinding is generally subject only to a 'preponderance of the evidence' standard." 72 F.3d, at 176. The court proceeded to vacate and remand, however, explaining:

"The consideration of the murders at Lombard's sentencing up-staged his conviction for firearms possession. The circumstances of this case that have combined to produce this effect raise grave constitutional concerns, although each doctrine considered separately might not provoke a second thought....

"The effect here has been to permit the harshest penalty outside of capital punishment to be imposed not for conduct charged and convicted but for other conduct as to which there was, at sentencing, at best a shadow of the usual procedural protections such as the requirement of proof beyond a reasonable doubt. This other conduct—murder—was surely of the most serious sort, but exactly the sort as to which our jurisprudence normally requires the government to meet its full burden of proof. When put to that proof in state court, the government failed...."

"That anomaly is heightened by the specific manner in which the Guidelines operated here. Unlike certain 'relevant conduct' guidelines that simply call for a determinate increase in a defendant's base offense level based on specified factual findings ... the cross reference provision that was applied in this case required the district court to calculate Lombard's base offense level as is his offense of conviction had been murder.

"The qualitative difference between the life sentence imposed and the term of years that Lombard might otherwise have received ... implicates basic concerns of proportionality both between the enhancement and the base sentence and between the offense and punishment as a whole. [T]he harshness of the life sentence in relation to the offense of conviction highlights the need for rigorous inquiry.

"Without impugning the principle that acquitted conduct may be considered in determining a defendant's sentence, the prior state court acquittal presents another concern in its interaction here. [I]t would ignore reality not to recognize that the federal prosecution arose out of and was driven by the murders, and that the prosecution was well aware that the Sentencing Guidelines would require consideration of the murders at sentencing....

"Here, the district court did not consider whether departure would have been appropriate under § 5K2.0. ... The court also did not consider whether the constitutional questions raised by the mandatory life sentence might warrant a finding that this case falls outside the heartland of the applicable guideline. Thus, we conclude ... that the district court erroneously believed it had no power to deviate from the sentence indicated by a straightforward application of the Guidelines.... Had such a downward departure been considered, the impact of giving sentencing weight to the acquitted murders could have been tempered by the district court's fact-based, discretionary judgment. That judgment would have been informed by the background principle that a sentence enhancement may not function as a 'tail which wags the dog' of the defendant's offense of conviction." 72 F.3d, at 177–85.

But pro-defendant rulings like those in *Kikumura* and *Lombard* are by no means a foregone conclusion under the Guidelines, even in extreme cases. In United States v. Masters, 978 F.2d 281 (7th Cir.1992), for instance, the defendant was convicted of both RICO substantive and conspiracy offenses, only one of which (the conspiracy to violate RICO) occurred after the effective date of the Sentencing Guidelines. The defendant argued that the Guideline sentence for his crime should be 33–41 months. The district court applied a "cross referenced" Guideline (for solicitation to commit murder) and then departed upward to the RICO statutory maximum, on the basis of a finding that one of the defendant's racketeering acts was the murder of his wife; this allegation was contained in the RICO indictment, but the jury did not include it on a list of racketeering acts that it specifically found the defendant had committed. The district court sentenced the defendant to 40 years in prison without possibility of parole.

On appeal, the Seventh Circuit, per Judge Easterbrook, affirmed. The court noted that the jury's silence on the murder allegation did not constitute an "implied acquittal"; in any event, "an acquittal means that the charge was not proven beyond a reasonable doubt; it does not mean that the defendant didn't do it." 978 F.2d, at 286. The court also rejected *Kikumura*'s suggestion that a heightened burden of proof might apply to cases of extreme sentence enhancement:

> "Although *Kikumura* expressed this conclusion in constitutional terms, it is impossible to square such a holding with *McMillan*—or with the history of discretionary sentencing in the United States. Before November 1, 1987, some federal judges regularly sentenced defendants to the maximum terms provided by law, and tacked sentences consecutively, on hunch and whim. A few even acquired sobriquets such as 'Maximum John' (Judge Sirica, of Watergate fame). Others rejected deterrence and desert as justifications of imprisonment and gave sentences reflecting disparate views about rehabilitation....

> "The guidelines represent a reaction against vesting such discretion in the hands of persons who may have dramatically different ideas about punishment. Yet they hardly exemplify a consensus that in 1987 what had been the norm in 20th Century sentencing became constitutionally repulsive. ... While sentencing practices have cycled, from fixed terms in the 19th Century to discretion in the middle 20th Century to guided discretion in the late 20th Century, the due process clause has remained the same. It is statutes, rules, practices, and ideas about criminology that have changed. Rather than treating the Constitution as paraffin that may be poured into a mold suiting current tastes, courts properly look to these statutes, rules, and practices. The living legal community, not an imagined decision imputed to those long departed, is responsible for contemporary sentencing practices.

> "No one can deny that the guidelines, coupled with recent increases in the maximum terms for many offenses, have increased the importance of sentencing vis-a-vis trials. We have indicated some sympathy with the conclusion that when sentencing becomes the dog and the trial the tail, judges should borrow some of the devices used at trial to protect the defendant's interests and improve accuracy (two objectives that are not always compatible). ... Neither the Sentencing Reform Act nor the guidelines specifies a burden of persuasion, so courts must devise their own. We are free to modify this standard as wisdom gained from experience suggests. But the preponderance standard remains the norm—in sentencing, as in almost all litigation, because it treats errors in either direction as equally costly. ... An excessive sentence

injures the defendant, but an insufficient sentence injures society, especially persons who may be victims of crime tomorrow if courts do too little to deter and incapacitate criminals today. . . . Finding murder by a preponderance of the evidence violated none of Masters' rights." 978 F.2d, at 286–87.

How should the courts identify the extreme cases that would warrant the use of a heightened burden of proof at sentencing, or perhaps some other combination of heightened procedural protections? So far, it appears that the only operative test is whether the "tail is wagging the dog." Is this test met when a sentence is enhanced from, say, 30 months upward to 30 years? How about from 30 months to 15 years? From 30 months to 10 years (i.e., a four-to-one enhancement)? Is the "tail wagging the dog" test at all helpful in answering these questions?

Witte v. United States

Supreme Court of the United States, 1995.
___ U.S. ___, 115 S.Ct. 2199.

■ JUSTICE O'CONNOR delivered the opinion of the Court. [CHIEF JUSTICE REHNQUIST and JUSTICE KENNEDY joined all but part III of the opinion, and JUSTICE STEVENS joined only part III.]

The Double Jeopardy Clause of the Fifth Amendment to the United States Constitution prohibits successive prosecution or multiple punishment for "the same offence." This case, which involves application of the United States Sentencing Guidelines, asks us to consider whether a court violates that proscription by convicting and sentencing a defendant for a crime when the conduct underlying that offense has been considered in determining the defendant's sentence for a previous conviction.

I

In June 1990, petitioner Steven Kurt Witte and several co-conspirators, including Dennis Mason and Tom Pokorny, arranged with Roger Norman, an undercover agent of the Drug Enforcement Administration, to import large amounts of marijuana from Mexico and cocaine from Guatemala. Norman had the task of flying the contraband into the United States, with Witte providing the ground transportation for the drugs once they had been brought into the country. The following month, the Mexican marijuana source advised the conspiracy participants that cocaine might be added to the first shipment if there was room on the plane or if an insufficient quantity of marijuana was available. Norman was informed in August 1990 that the source was prepared to deliver 4,400 pounds of marijuana. Once Norman learned the location of the airstrip from which the narcotics would be transported, federal agents arranged to have the participants in the scheme apprehended in Mexico. Local authorities arrested Mason and four others on August 12 and seized 591 kilograms of cocaine at the landing field. While still undercover, Norman met Witte the following day to explain that the pilots had been unable to land in Mexico because police had raided the airstrip. Witte was not taken into custody at that time, and the activities of the conspiracy lapsed for several months.

Agent Norman next spoke with Witte in January 1991 and asked if Witte would be interested in purchasing 1,000 pounds of marijuana. Witte agreed, promised to obtain a $50,000 down payment, and indicated that he would transport the marijuana in a horse trailer he had purchased for the original 1990 transaction and in a motor home owned by an acquaintance, Sam Kelly. On February 7, Witte, Norman, and Kelly met in Houston, Texas. Norman agreed to give the drugs to Witte in exchange for the $25,000 in cash Witte had been able to secure at that time and for a promise to pay the balance of the down payment in three days. Undercover agents took the motor home and trailer away to load the marijuana, and Witte escorted Norman to Witte's hotel room to view the money. The agents returned the vehicles the next morning loaded with approximately 375 pounds of marijuana, and they arrested Witte and Kelly when the two men took possession of the contraband.

In March 1991, a federal grand jury in the Southern District of Texas indicted Witte and Kelly for conspiring and attempting to possess marijuana with intent to distribute it, in violation of 21 U.S.C. §§ 841(a) and 846. The indictment was limited on its face to conduct occurring on or about January 25 through February 8, 1991, thus covering only the later marijuana transaction. On February 21, 1992, Witte pleaded guilty to the attempted possession count and agreed to cooperate "with the Government by providing truthful and complete information concerning this and all other offenses about which [he] might be questioned by agents of law enforcement," and by testifying if requested to do so. App. 14. In exchange, the Government agreed to dismiss the conspiracy count and, if Witte's cooperation amounted to "substantial assistance," to file a motion for a downward departure under the Sentencing Guidelines. See United States Sentencing Commission, Guidelines Manual § 5K1.1 (Nov.1994).

In calculating Witte's base offense level under the Sentencing Guidelines, the presentence report prepared by the United States Probation Office considered the total quantity of drugs involved in all of the transactions contemplated by the conspirators, including the planned 1990 shipments of both marijuana and cocaine. Under the Sentencing Guidelines, the sentencing range for a particular offense is determined on the basis of all "relevant conduct" in which the defendant was engaged and not just with regard to the conduct underlying the offense of conviction. USSG § 1B1.3. The Sentencing Commission has noted that, "[w]ith respect to offenses involving contraband (including controlled substances), the defendant is accountable for all quantities of contraband with which he was directly involved and, in the case of a jointly undertaken criminal activity, all reasonably foreseeable quantities of contraband that were within the scope of the criminal activity that he jointly undertook." USSG § 1B1.3, comment., n. 2; see also USSG § 2D1.1, comment., nn. 6, 12. The presentence report therefore suggested that Witte was accountable for the 1,000 pounds of marijuana involved in the attempted possession offense to which he pleaded guilty, 15 tons of marijuana that Witte, Mason, and Pokorny had planned to import from Mexico in 1990, 500 kilograms of cocaine that the conspirators originally proposed to import from Guatemala, and the 591 kilograms of cocaine seized at the Mexican airstrip in August 1990.

At the sentencing hearing, both petitioner and the Government urged the court to hold that the 1990 activities concerning importation of cocaine and marijuana were not part of the same course of conduct as the 1991 marijuana offense to which Witte had pleaded guilty, and therefore should not be considered in sentencing for the 1991 offense. The District Court concluded, however, that because the 1990 importation offenses were part of the same continuing conspiracy, they were "relevant conduct" under § 1B1.3 of the Guidelines and should be taken into account. The court therefore accepted the presentence report's aggregation of the quantities of drugs involved in the 1990 and 1991 episodes, resulting in a base offense level of 40, with a Guideline range of 292 to 365 months' imprisonment, see USSG § 2D1.1. From that base offense level, Witte received a two-level increase for his aggravating role in the offense, see USSG § 3B1.1, and an offsetting two-level decrease for acceptance of responsibility, see USSG § 3E1.1. Finally, the court granted the Government's § 5K1.1 motion for downward departure based on Witte's substantial assistance. By virtue of that departure, the court sentenced Witte to 144 months in prison, which was 148 months below the minimum sentence of 292 months under the pre-departure Guideline range. Witte appealed, but the Court of Appeals dismissed the case when Witte failed to file a brief.

In September 1992, another grand jury in the same district returned a two-count indictment against Witte and Pokorny for conspiring and attempting to import cocaine, in violation of 21 U.S.C. §§ 952(a) and 963. The indictment alleged that, between August 1989 and August 1990, Witte tried to import about 1,091 kilograms of cocaine from Central America. Witte moved to dismiss, arguing that he had already been punished for the cocaine offenses because the cocaine involved in the 1990 transactions had been considered as "relevant conduct" at sentencing for the 1991 marijuana offense. The District Court dismissed the indictment in February 1993 on grounds that punishment for the indicted offenses would violate the prohibition against multiple punishments contained in the Double Jeopardy Clause of the Fifth Amendment.

The Court of Appeals for the Fifth Circuit reversed. 25 F.3d 250 (5th Cir.1994). Relying on our decision in Williams v. Oklahoma, 358 U.S. 576 (1959), the court held that "the use of relevant conduct to increase the punishment of a charged offense does not punish the offender for the relevant conduct." Thus, although the sentencing court took the quantity of cocaine involved in the 1990 importation scheme into account when determining the sentence for Witte's 1991 marijuana possession offense, the Court of Appeals concluded that Witte had not been punished for the cocaine offenses in the first prosecution—and that the Double Jeopardy Clause therefore did not bar the later action. In reaching this result, the court expressly disagreed with contrary holdings in United States v. Koonce, 945 F.2d 1145 (10th Cir.1991), and United States v. McCormick, 992 F.2d 437 (2d Cir.1993), that when a defendant's actions are included in relevant conduct in determining the punishment under the Sentencing Guidelines for one offense, those actions may not form the basis for a later indictment without violating double jeopardy. We granted certiorari to resolve the conflict among the circuits, and now affirm.

II

The Double Jeopardy Clause provides: "[N]or shall any person be subject for the same offence to be twice put in jeopardy of life or limb." We have explained that "the Clause serves the function of preventing both successive punishment and successive prosecution," United States v. Dixon, 509 U.S. 688, 704 (1993)(citing North Carolina v. Pearce, 395 U.S. 711 (1969)), and that "the Constitution was designed as much to prevent the criminal from being twice punished for the same offence as from being twice tried for it," Ex parte Lange, 85 U.S. (18 Wall.) 163, 173 (1874). Significantly, the language of the Double Jeopardy Clause protects against more than the actual imposition of two punishments for the same offense; by its terms, it protects a criminal defendant from being twice put in jeopardy for such punishment. That is, the Double Jeopardy Clause "prohibits merely punishing twice, or attempting a second time to punish criminally, for the same offense." Helvering v. Mitchell, 303 U.S. 391, 399 (1938).

Petitioner clearly was neither prosecuted for nor convicted of the cocaine offenses during the first criminal proceeding. The offense to which petitioner pleaded guilty and for which he was sentenced in 1992 was attempted possession of marijuana with intent to distribute it, whereas the crimes charged in the instant indictment are conspiracy to import cocaine and attempted importation of the same. Under Blockburger v. United States, 284 U.S. 299, 304 (1932), "where the same act or transaction constitutes a violation of two distinct statutory provisions, the test to be applied to determine whether there are two offenses or only one, is whether each provision requires proof of a fact which the other does not." See also Dixon, 509 U.S., at 696 (emphasizing that the same inquiry generally applies "[i]n both the multiple punishment and multiple prosecution contexts"). Under the Blockburger test, the indictment in this case did not charge the same offense to which petitioner formerly had pleaded guilty.

Petitioner nevertheless argues that, because the conduct giving rise to the cocaine charges was taken into account during sentencing for the marijuana conviction, he effectively was "punished" for that conduct during the first proceeding. As a result, he contends, the Double Jeopardy Clause bars the instant prosecution. This claim is ripe at this stage of the prosecution—although petitioner has not yet been convicted of the cocaine offenses—because, as we have said, "courts may not impose more than one punishment for the same offense and prosecutors ordinarily may not attempt to secure that punishment in more than one trial." Brown v.

Ohio, 432 U.S. 161, 165 (1977). See also Ball v. United States, 470 U.S. 856, 861, 864–65 (1985)(explaining that, for purposes of the double jeopardy inquiry, punishment "must be the equivalent of a criminal conviction and not simply the imposition of sentence"); *Ex parte Lange*, 85 U.S. (18 Wall.), at 173. Thus, if petitioner is correct that the present case constitutes a second attempt to punish him criminally for the same cocaine offenses, see *Helvering*, 303 U.S., at 399, then the prosecution may not proceed. We agree with the Court of Appeals, however, that petitioner's double jeopardy theory—that consideration of uncharged conduct in arriving at a sentence within the statutorily authorized punishment range constitutes "punishment" for that conduct—is not supported by our precedents, which make clear that a defendant in that situation is punished, for double jeopardy purposes, only for the offense of which the defendant is convicted.

Traditionally, "[s]entencing courts have not only taken into consideration a defendant's prior convictions, but have also considered a defendant's past criminal behavior, even if no conviction resulted from that behavior." Nichols v. United States, ___ U.S. ___, 114 S.Ct. 1921, 1928 (1994). We explained in Williams v. New York, 337 U.S. 241, 246 (1949), that "both before and since the American colonies became a nation, courts in this country and in England practiced a policy under which a sentencing judge could exercise a wide discretion in the sources and types of evidence used to assist him in determining the kind and extent of punishment to be imposed within limits fixed by law." That history, combined with a recognition of the need for individualized sentencing, led us to conclude that the Due Process Clause did not require "that courts throughout the Nation abandon their age-old practice of seeking information from out-of-court sources to guide their judgment toward a more enlightened and just sentence." Id., at 250–51. Thus, "[a]s a general proposition, a sentencing judge 'may appropriately conduct an inquiry broad in scope, largely unlimited either as to the kind of information he may consider, or the source from which it may come.' " *Nichols*, ___ U.S., at ___, 114 S.Ct., at 1927–28 (quoting United States v. Tucker, 404 U.S. 443, 446 (1972)).

Against this background of sentencing history, we specifically have rejected the claim that double jeopardy principles bar a later prosecution or punishment for criminal activity where that activity has been considered at sentencing for a separate crime. *Williams v. Oklahoma*, 358 U.S., at 576, arose out of a kidnaping and murder committed by the petitioner while attempting to escape from police after a robbery. Following his arrest, Williams pleaded guilty to murder and was given a life sentence. He was later convicted of kidnaping, which was then a capital offense in Oklahoma, and the sentencing court took into account, in assessing the death penalty, the fact that the kidnaping victim had been murdered. We rejected Williams' contention that this use of the conduct that had given rise to the prior conviction violated double jeopardy. Emphasizing that "the exercise of a sound discretion in such a case required consideration of all the circumstances of the crime," we made clear that "one of the aggravating circumstances involved in this kidnaping crime was the fact that petitioner shot and killed the victim in the course of its commission," and rejected the claim "that the sentencing judge was not entitled to consider that circumstance, along with all the other circumstances involved, in determining the proper sentence to be imposed for the kidnaping crime." Id., at 585–86.

We then disposed of the petitioner's double jeopardy claim as follows: "[I]n view of the obvious fact that, under the law of Oklahoma, kidnaping is a separate crime, entirely distinct from the crime of murder, the court's consideration of the murder as a circumstance involved in the kidnaping crime cannot be said to have resulted in punishing petitioner a second time for the same offense. . . ." Id., at 586. We thus made clear that use of evidence of related criminal conduct to enhance a defendant's sentence for a separate crime within the authorized statutory limits does not constitute punishment for that conduct within the meaning of the Double Jeopardy Clause.

We find this case to be governed by *Williams*; it makes no difference in this context whether the enhancement occurred in the first or second sentencing proceeding. Here, petitioner pleaded guilty to attempted possession of marijuana with intent to distribute it, in violation of 21 U.S.C. §§ 841(a) and 846. The statute provides that the sentence for such a crime involving 100 kilograms or more of marijuana must be between 5 and 40 years in prison. § 841(b)(1)(B). By including the cocaine from the earlier transaction—and not just the marijuana involved in the offense of conviction—in the drug quantity calculation, the District Court ended up with a higher offense level (40), and a higher sentence range (292 to 365 months), than it would have otherwise under the applicable Guideline, which specifies different base offense levels depending on the quantity of drugs involved. USSG § 2D1.1. This higher guideline range, however, still falls within the scope of the legislatively authorized penalty (5–40 years). As in *Williams*, the uncharged criminal conduct was used to enhance petitioner's sentence within the range authorized by statute. If use of the murder to justify the death sentence for the kidnaping conviction was not "punishment" for the murder in *Williams*, it is impossible to conclude that taking account of petitioner's plans to import cocaine in fixing the sentence for the marijuana conviction constituted "punishment" for the cocaine offenses.

Williams, like this case, concerned the double jeopardy implications of taking the circumstances surrounding a particular course of criminal activity into account in sentencing for a conviction arising therefrom. Similarly, we have made clear in other cases, which involved a defendant's background more generally and not conduct arising out of the same criminal transaction as the offense of which the defendant was convicted, that "[e]nhancement statutes, whether in the nature of criminal history provisions such as those contained in the Sentencing Guidelines, or recidivist statutes which are common place in state criminal laws, do not change the penalty imposed for the earlier conviction." *Nichols*, ___ U.S., at ___, 114 S.Ct., at 1927 (approving consideration of a defendant's previous uncounseled misdemeanor conviction in sentencing him for a subsequent offense).

In repeatedly upholding such recidivism statutes, we have rejected double jeopardy challenges because the enhanced punishment imposed for the later offense "is not to be viewed as either a new jeopardy or additional penalty for the earlier crimes," but instead as "a stiffened penalty for the latest crime, which is considered to be an aggravated offense because a repetitive one." Gryger v. Burke, 334 U.S. 728, 732 (1948). See also Moore v. Missouri, 159 U.S. 673, 677 (1895)(under a recidivist statute, "the accused is not again punished for the first offence" because " 'the punishment is for the last offence committed, and it is rendered more severe in consequence of the situation into which the party had previously brought himself' ").

In addition, by authorizing the consideration of offender-specific information at sentencing without the procedural protections attendant at a criminal trial, our cases necessarily imply that such consideration does not result in "punishment" for such conduct. In McMillan v. Pennsylvania, 477 U.S. 79 (1986), we upheld against a due process challenge Pennsylvania's Mandatory Minimum Sentencing Act, which imposed a 5–year minimum sentence for certain enumerated felonies if the sentencing judge found, by a preponderance of the evidence, that the defendant "visibly possessed a firearm" during the commission of the offense.

Significantly, we emphasized that the statute at issue "neither alters the maximum penalty for the crime committed nor creates a separate offense calling for a separate penalty; it operates solely to limit the sentencing court's discretion in selecting a penalty within the range already available to it without the special finding of visible possession of a firearm." Id., at 87–88. That is, the statute "simply took one factor that has always been considered by sentencing courts to bear on punishment—the instrumentality used in committing a violent felony—and dictated the precise weight to be given that factor if the instrumentality is a firearm." For this reason, we approved the lesser standard of proof provided for in the statute, thereby "reject[ing] the claim that whenever a State links the 'severity of punishment' to 'the presence or absence of an identified fact' the State must prove that fact beyond a reasonable doubt." Id., at 84 (quoting Patterson v. New York, 432 U.S. 197, 214 (1977)). These decisions reinforce our conclusion that consideration of information about the defendant's character and conduct at sentencing does not result in "punishment" for any offense other than the one of which the defendant was convicted.

We are not persuaded by petitioner's suggestion that the Sentencing Guidelines somehow change the constitutional analysis. A defendant has not been "punished" any more for double jeopardy purposes when relevant conduct is included in the calculation of his offense level under the Guidelines than when a pre-Guidelines court, in its discretion, took similar uncharged conduct into account. Cf. *McMillan*, 477 U.S., at 92 (perceiving no difference in the due process calculus depending upon whether consideration of the sentencing factor was discretionary or mandatory). As the Government argues, "[t]he fact that the sentencing process has become more transparent under the Guidelines ... does not mean that the defendant is now being 'punished' for uncharged relevant conduct as though it were a distinct criminal 'offense.'" Brief for United States 23. The relevant conduct provisions are designed to channel the sentencing discretion of the district courts and to make mandatory the consideration of factors that previously would have been optional. United States v. Wright, 873 F.2d 437, 441 (1st Cir.1989)(Breyer, J.)(explaining that, "very roughly speaking, [relevant conduct] corresponds to those actions and circumstances that courts typically took into account when sentencing prior to the Guidelines' enactment"). Regardless of whether particular conduct is taken into account by rule or as an act of discretion, the defendant is still being punished only for the offense of conviction.

Justice Stevens disagrees with our conclusion because, he contends, "[u]nder the Guidelines, an offense that is included as 'relevant conduct' does not relate to the character of the offender (which is reflected instead by criminal history), but rather measures only the character of the offense." The criminal history section of the Guidelines, however, does not seem to create this bright line distinction; indeed, the difference between "criminal history" and "relevant conduct" is more temporal than qualitative, with the former referring simply to a defendant's past criminal conduct (as evidenced by convictions and prison terms), see USSG § 4A1.1, and the latter covering activity arising out of the same course of criminal conduct as the instant offense, see USSG § 1B1.3.

To the extent that the Guidelines aggravate punishment for related conduct outside the elements of the crime on the theory that such conduct bears on the "character of the offense," the offender is still punished only for the fact that the present offense was carried out in a manner that warrants increased punishment, not for a different offense (which that related conduct may or may not constitute). But, while relevant conduct thus may relate to the severity of the particular crime, the commission of multiple offenses in the same course of conduct also necessarily provides important evidence that the character of the offender requires special punishment. Similarly, as we have said in the recidivism cases, a crime committed by an offender with a prior conviction "is considered to be an aggravated offense because a repetitive one." *Gryger*, 334 U.S., at 732. Nothing about the labels given to these categories controls the use to which such information is put at sentencing. Under the Guidelines, therefore, as under the traditional sentencing regimes Justice Stevens approves, "it is difficult if not impossible to determine whether a given offense has affected the judge's assessment of the character of the offender, the character of the offense, or both." (Stevens, J., dissenting). Even under Justice Stevens' framework, the structure of the Guidelines should not affect the outcome of this case.

The relevant conduct provisions of the Sentencing Guidelines, like their criminal history counterparts and the recidivism statutes discussed above, are sentencing enhancement regimes evincing the judgment that a particular offense should receive a more serious sentence within the authorized range if it was either accompanied by or preceded by additional criminal activity. Petitioner does not argue that the range fixed by Congress is so broad, and the enhancing role played by the relevant conduct so significant, that consideration of that conduct in sentencing has become "a tail which wags the dog of the substantive offense." *McMillan*, 477 U.S., at 88. We hold that, where the legislature has authorized such a particular punishment range for a given crime, the resulting sentence within that range constitutes punishment only for the offense of conviction for purposes of the double jeopardy inquiry. Accordingly, the instant prosecution for the cocaine offenses is not barred by the Double Jeopardy Clause as a second attempt to punish petitioner for the same crime.

III

At its core, much of petitioner's argument addresses not a claim that the instant cocaine prosecution violates principles of double jeopardy, but the more modest contention that he should not receive a second sentence under the Guidelines for the cocaine activities that were considered as relevant conduct for the marijuana sentence. As an examination of the pertinent sections should make clear, however, the Guidelines take into account the potential unfairness with which petitioner is concerned.

Petitioner argues that the Sentencing Guidelines require that drug offenders be sentenced in a single proceeding for all related offenses, whether charged or uncharged. Yet while the Guidelines certainly envision that sentences for multiple offenses arising out of the same criminal activity ordinarily will be imposed together, they also explicitly contemplate the possibility of separate prosecutions involving the same or overlapping "relevant conduct." See USSG § 5G1.3, comment., n. 2 (addressing cases in which "a defendant is prosecuted in ... two or more federal jurisdictions, for the same criminal conduct or for different criminal transactions that were part of the same course of conduct"). There are often valid reasons why related crimes committed by the same defendant are not prosecuted in the same proceeding, and § 5G1.3 of the Guidelines attempts to achieve some coordination of sentences imposed in such situations with an eye toward having such punishments approximate the total penalty that would have been imposed had the sentences for the different offenses been imposed at the same time (i.e., had all of the offenses been prosecuted in a single proceeding). See USSG § 5G1.3, comment., n. 3.

Because the concept of relevant conduct under the Guidelines is reciprocal, § 5G1.3 operates to mitigate the possibility that the fortuity of two separate prosecutions will grossly increase a defendant's sentence. If a defendant is serving an undischarged term of imprisonment "result[ing] from offense(s) that have been fully taken into account [as relevant conduct] in the determination of the offense level for the instant offense," § 5G1.3(b) provides that "the sentence for the instant offense shall be imposed to run concurrently to the undischarged term of imprisonment." And where § 5G1.3(b) does not apply, an accompanying policy statement provides, "the sentence for the instant offense shall be imposed to run consecutively to the prior undischarged term of imprisonment to the extent necessary to achieve a reasonable incremental punishment for the instant offense." USSG § 5G1.3(c)(policy statement). Significant safeguards built into the Sentencing Guidelines therefore protect petitioner against having the length of his sentence multiplied by duplicative consideration of the same criminal conduct; he would be able to vindicate his interests through appropriate appeals should the Guidelines be misapplied in any future sentencing proceeding.

Even if the Sentencing Commission had not formalized sentencing for multiple convictions in this way, district courts under the Guidelines retain enough flexibility in appropriate cases to take into account the fact that conduct underlying the offense at issue has previously been taken into account in sentencing for another offense. As the Commission has explained, "[u]nder 18 U.S.C. § 3553(b) the sentencing court may impose a sentence outside the range established by the applicable guideline, if the court finds 'that there exists an aggravating or mitigating circumstance of a kind, or to a degree, not adequately taken into consideration by the Sentencing Commission in formulating the guidelines that should result in a sentence different from that described.'" USSG § 5K2.0 (policy statement). This departure power is also available to protect against petitioner's second major practical concern: that a second sentence for the same relevant conduct may deprive him of the effect of the downward departure under § 5K1.1 of the Guidelines for substantial assistance to the Government, which reduced his first sentence significantly.

Should petitioner be convicted of the cocaine charges, he will be free to put his argument concerning the unusual facts of this case to the sentencing judge as a basis for discretionary downward departure.

IV

Because consideration of relevant conduct in determining a defendant's sentence within the legislatively authorized punishment range does not constitute punishment for that conduct, the instant prosecution does not violate the Double Jeopardy Clause's prohibition against the imposition of multiple punishments for the same offense. Accordingly, the judgment of the Court of Appeals is

Affirmed.

■ JUSTICE SCALIA, with whom JUSTICE THOMAS joins, concurring in the judgment.

This is one of those areas in which I believe our jurisprudence is not only wrong but unworkable as well, and so persist in my refusal to give that jurisprudence stare decisis effect. See Planned Parenthood of Southeastern Pa. v. Casey, 505 U.S. 833, 979 (1992)(Scalia, J., concurring in judgment in part and dissenting in part); Walton v. Arizona, 497 U.S. 639, 673 (1990)(Scalia, J., concurring in part and concurring in judgment).

It is not true that (as the Court claims) "the language of the Double Jeopardy Clause protects against ... the actual imposition of two punishments for the same offense." What the Clause says is that no person "shall . . . be subject for the same offence to be twice put in jeopardy of life or limb," which means twice prosecuted for the same offense. Today's decision shows that departing from the text of the Clause, and from the constant tradition regarding its meaning, as we did six years ago in United States v. Halper, 490 U.S. 435 (1989), requires us either to upset well-established penal practices, or else to perceive lines that do not really exist. Having created a right against multiple punishments ex nihilo, we now allow that right to be destroyed by the technique used on the petitioner here: "We do not punish you twice for the same offense," says the Government, "but we punish you twice as much for one offense solely because you also committed another offense, for which other offense we will also punish you (only once) later on." I see no real difference in that distinction, and decline to acquiesce in the erroneous holding that drives us to it.

In sum, I adhere to my view that "the Double Jeopardy Clause prohibits successive prosecution, not successive punishment." Department of Revenue of Montana v. Kurth Ranch, ___ U.S. ___, 114 S.Ct. 1937, 1959 (1994)(Scalia, J., dissenting). Since petitioner was not twice prosecuted for the same offense, I concur in the judgment.

■ JUSTICE STEVENS, concurring in part and dissenting in part.

Petitioner pleaded guilty to attempting to possess with intent to distribute more than 100 kilograms of marijuana. At petitioner's sentencing hearing, the District Court heard evidence concerning petitioner's participation in a conspiracy to import cocaine. Pursuant to its understanding of the Guidelines, the District Court considered the cocaine offenses as "relevant conduct" and increased petitioner's sentence accordingly. Petitioner received exactly the same sentence that he would have received had he been convicted of both the marijuana offenses and the cocaine offenses. The Government then sought to prosecute petitioner for the cocaine offenses.

The question presented is whether the Double Jeopardy Clause bars that subsequent prosecution. The Court today holds that it does not. In my view, the Court's holding is incorrect and unprecedented. More importantly, it weakens the fundamental protections the Double Jeopardy Clause was intended to provide.

I

In my view, the double jeopardy violation is plain. Petitioner's marijuana conviction, which involved 1,000 pounds of marijuana, would have resulted in a Guidelines range of 78 to 97 months. When petitioner's cocaine offenses were considered in the sentencing calculus, the new Guidelines range was 292 to 365 months. This was the range that the District Court used as the basis for its sentencing calculations.[10] Thus, the

---

[10] After making offsetting adjustments for an aggravating role in the offense and for acceptance of responsibility, the District Court, pursuant to § 5K1.1, departed down-

District Court's consideration of the cocaine offenses increased petitioner's sentencing range by over 200 months. Under these facts, it is hard to see how the Double Jeopardy Clause is not implicated. In my view, quite simply, petitioner was put in jeopardy of punishment for the cocaine transactions when, as mandated by the Guidelines, he was in fact punished for those offenses. The Double Jeopardy Clause should thus preclude any subsequent prosecution for those cocaine offenses.

II

Despite the intuitive appeal of this approach, the majority concludes that these facts do not implicate the Double Jeopardy Clause. To reach this conclusion, the majority relies on our prior decisions that have permitted sentencers to consider at sentencing both prior convictions and other offenses that are related to the offense of conviction. The majority's reliance on these cases suggests that it has overlooked a distinction that I find critical to the resolution of the double jeopardy issue at hand. "Traditionally, sentencing judges have considered a wide variety of factors in addition to evidence bearing on guilt in determining what sentence to impose on a convicted defendant." Wisconsin v. Mitchell, 508 U.S. 476, 484 (1993). "One such important factor" to be considered in the sentencing calculus is "a defendant's prior convictions." Nichols v. United States, ___ U.S. ___, 114 S.Ct. 1921, 1928 (1994). Indeed, the prominent role played by past conduct in most guidelines-based sentencing regimes and in statutes that punish more harshly "habitual offenders" reveals the importance of this factor. As the majority notes, we have repeatedly upheld the use of such prior convictions against double jeopardy challenges.

However, an understanding of the reason for our rejection of those challenges makes clear that those cases do not support the majority's conclusion. Traditional sentencing practices recognize that a just sentence is determined in part by the character of the offense and in part by the character of the offender. Within this framework, the admission of evidence of an offender's past convictions reflects the longstanding notion that one's prior record is strong evidence of one's character. A recidivist should be punished more severely than a first offender because he has failed to mend his ways after a first conviction. As we noted in Moore v. Missouri, 159 U.S. 673, 677 (1895), " 'the punishment for the second [offense] is increased, because by his persistence in the perpetration of crime, [the defendant] has evinced a depravity, which merits a greater punishment, and needs to be restrained by severer penalties than if it were his first offense.' " See also McDonald v. Massachusetts, 180 U.S. 311, 313 (1901)(commission of a second crime after conviction for first "show[s] that the man is an habitual criminal"). Thus, when a sentencing judge reviews an offender's prior convictions at sentencing, the judge is not punishing that offender a second time for his past misconduct, but rather is evaluating the nature of his individual responsibility for past acts and the likelihood that he will engage in future misconduct. Recidivist statutes are

---

ward by 148 months and sentenced petitioner to 144 months' imprisonment.

consistent with the Double Jeopardy Clause not because of the formalistic premise that one can only be punished or placed in jeopardy for the "offense of conviction," but rather because of the important functional understanding that the purpose of the prior conviction is to provide valuable evidence as to the offender's character. The majority's reliance on recidivist statutes is thus unavailing.

When the offenses considered at sentencing are somehow linked to the offense of conviction, the analysis is different. Offenses that are linked to the offense of conviction may affect both the character of the offense and the character of the offender. That is, even if he is not a recidivist, a person who commits two offenses should also be punished more severely than one who commits only one, in part because the commission of multiple offenses provides important evidence that the character of the offender requires special punishment, and in part because the character of the offense is aggravated by the commission of multiple offenses. Insofar as a sentencer relies on an offense as evidence of character, the Double Jeopardy Clause is not implicated. However, insofar as the sentencer relies on the offense as aggravation of the underlying offense, the Double Jeopardy Clause is necessarily implicated. At that point, the defendant is being punished for having committed the offense at issue, and not for what the commission of that offense reveals about his character. In such cases, the defendant has been "put in jeopardy" of punishment for the offense because he has in fact been punished for that offense.

Under many sentencing regimes, of course, it is difficult if not impossible to determine whether a given offense has affected the judge's assessment of the character of the offender, the character of the offense, or both. However, under the federal Sentencing Guidelines, the role played by each item in the sentencing calculus is perfectly clear. The Guidelines provide for specific sentencing adjustments for "criminal history" (i.e., character of the offender) and for "relevant conduct" (i.e., character of the offense). Under the Guidelines, therefore, an offense that is included as "relevant conduct" does not relate to the character of the offender (which is reflected instead by criminal history), but rather measures only the character of the offense. Even if all other mitigating and aggravating circumstances that shed light on an offender's character have been taken into account, the judge must sentence the offender for conduct that affects the seriousness of the offense.

The effect of this regime with respect to drug crimes provides a particularly striking illustration of why this mandatory consideration of relevant conduct implicates the Double Jeopardy Clause under anything but a formalistic reading of the Clause. Under the Guidelines, the severity of a drug offense is measured by the total quantity of drugs under all offenses that constitute "relevant conduct," regardless of whether those offenses were charged and proved at the guilt phase of the trial or instead proved at the sentencing hearing. For example, as I have noted above, petitioner's guidelines range was determined by adding the quantity of marijuana to the quantity of cocaine (using the conversion formula set forth in the Guidelines). Petitioner has thus already been sentenced for an actual offense that includes the cocaine transactions that are the subject of the second indictment. Those transactions played precisely the same role in fixing his punishment as they would have if they had been the subject of a formal charge and conviction. The actual imposition of that punishment must surely demonstrate that petitioner was just as much in jeopardy for the offense as if he had been previously charged with it.

In sum, traditional sentencing practice does not offend the Double Jeopardy Clause because (1) past convictions are used only as evidence of the character of the offender, and not as evidence of the character of the offense, and (2) in traditional sentencing regimes, it is impossible to determine for what purpose the sentencer has relied on the relevant offenses. In my view, the Court's failure to recognize the critical distinction between the character of the offender and the character of the offense, as well as the Court's failure to recognize the change in sentencing practices caused by the Guidelines, cause it to overlook an important and obvious violation of the Double Jeopardy Clause.

III

Once this error in the majority's analysis is recognized, it becomes apparent that none of the cases on which the majority relies compels today's novel holding. In Williams v. New York, 337 U.S. 241 (1949), the Court held that the Due Process Clause did not prevent a sentencing judge from considering information contained in a presentence report. The Court's conclusion in *Williams* is consistent with my approach.

The *Williams* Court repeatedly emphasized that the information in the presentence report provided the court with relevant information about the character of the defendant. For example, the Court noted that "the New York statutes emphasize a prevalent modern philosophy of penology that the punishment should fit the offender and not merely the crime." The Court continued: "The belief no longer prevails that every offense in a like legal category calls for an identical punishment without regard to the past life and habits of a particular offender." Finally, the Court observed that "[t]oday's philosophy of individualizing sentences makes sharp distinctions for example between first and repeated offenders." Id., at 247–48.

Thus, the entire rationale of the *Williams* opinion focussed on the importance of evidence that reveals the character of the offender. Not a word in Justice Black's opinion even suggests that if evidence adduced at sentencing were used to support a sentence for an offense more serious than the offense of conviction, the defendant would not have been placed in jeopardy for that more serious offense.[11]

---

[11] The majority's reliance on Nichols v. United States, ___ U.S. ___, 114 S.Ct. 1921 (1994), is similarly unavailing. In *Nichols*, the Court permitted the inclusion of an uncounseled misdemeanor conviction in the calculation of a defendant's criminal history. However, as I have noted above, the inclusion of an offense in criminal history for sentencing purposes treats that offense as relevant to the character of the offender rather than to the character of the offense.

The Court also relies on McMillan v. Pennsylvania, 477 U.S. 79 (1986), suggesting that *McMillan* "necessarily impl[ies]" that consideration of "offender-specific information at sentencing" does not "result in 'punishment for such conduct.'" I believed at the time and continue to believe that *McMillan* was wrongly decided.

However, even accepting the Court's conclusion in *McMillan*, that case does not support the majority's position. In United States v. Halper, 490 U.S. 435, 448 (1989), we emphatically rejected the proposition that punishment under the Double Jeopardy Clause only occurs when a court imposes a sentence for an offense that is proven beyond a reasonable doubt at a criminal trial.

The case on which the Court places its principal reliance, Williams v. Oklahoma, 358 U.S. 576 (1959), is not controlling precedent. *Williams* was decided over 10 years before the Court held in Benton v. Maryland, 395 U.S. 784, 794 (1969), that the Double Jeopardy Clause "should apply to the States through the Fourteenth Amendment." Thus, *Williams* did not even apply the Double Jeopardy Clause and instead applied only a "watereddown" version of due process, see *Benton*, 395 U.S., at 796.

Moreover, in *Williams*, the State's discretionary sentencing scheme was entirely dissimilar to the federal Sentencing Guidelines, which require that "relevant conduct" be punished as if it had been proven beyond a reasonable doubt. The Court is therefore free to accept or reject the majority's reasoning in *Williams*.

The precise issue resolved in *Williams* is also somewhat different from that presented in today's case. In *Williams*, the petitioner committed two offenses, kidnapping and murder, arising out of the same incident. Though petitioner was convicted of capital murder, the judge imposed a sentence of life imprisonment. There is no reason to believe that the judge considered the kidnapping offense as relevant conduct in sentencing petitioner for the murder. Williams was then prosecuted for kidnapping. He did not raise a double jeopardy objection to the kidnapping prosecution—an objection that would have been comparable to petitioner's claim in this case regarding his cocaine prosecution. After Williams pleaded guilty to the kidnapping, the court considered the circumstances of the crime, including the murder, and imposed a death sentence. This Court affirmed. I agree with Justice Douglas' dissent "that petitioner was in substance tried for murder twice in violation of the guarantee against double jeopardy." Id., 358 U.S., at 587. In any event, I surely would not apply the *Williams* Court's dubious reasoning to a federal sentence imposed under the Guidelines.[12]

---

[12] I recognize that the Court in *Williams* stated that "the court's consideration of the murder as a circumstance involved in the kidnapping crime cannot be said to have resulted in punishing petitioner a second time for the same offense." 358 U.S., at 586. As I note in the text, I disagree with this statement. But even if it were correct, it does not dispose of petitioner's claim that he is being prosecuted for the cocaine offense a second time. The statement in *Williams* is directed only at the use of a prior conviction in a subsequent sentencing proceeding; it does not address whether the second prosecution

Given the absence of precedent requiring the majority's unjust result, the case should be decided by giving effect to the text and purpose of the Double Jeopardy Clause. Petitioner received the sentence authorized by law for the offense of attempting to import cocaine. Petitioner is now being placed in jeopardy of a second punishment for the same offense. Requiring him to stand trial for that offense is a manifest violation of the Double Jeopardy Clause.

IV

Though the majority's holding in Parts I and II removes the Double Jeopardy Clause as a constitutional bar to petitioner's second punishment, the majority does recognize that the provisions of the Sentencing Guidelines reduce the likelihood of a second punishment as a practical matter. The Guidelines will generally ensure that the total sentence received in the two proceedings is the same sentence that would have been received had both offenses been brought in the same proceeding. Moreover, as the majority notes, the departure power is available to protect against unwarranted double punishment, as well as to prevent any possibility that "a second sentence for the same relevant conduct may deprive [a defendant] of the effect of the downward departure under § 5K1.1 of the Guidelines for substantial assistance to the Government."[13] The Court's statutory holding thus mitigates some of the otherwise unfortunate results of its constitutional approach. More importantly, the Court's statutory analysis is obviously correct. Accordingly, I join Part III of the Court's opinion.

V

In my view, the Double Jeopardy Clause precludes petitioner's subsequent prosecution for the cocaine offenses because petitioner was placed in jeopardy when he was punished for those offenses following his conviction for the marijuana offenses. I therefore join only Part III of the Court's opinion, and I respectfully dissent from the Court's judgment.

NOTE ON *UNITED STATES v. WITTE*

Does the majority's last suggestion, that the departure authority discussed in § 5K2.0 of the Sentencing Guidelines can serve to mitigate any unfairness that might result from its double jeopardy holding, open the door (at least a crack) to precisely the same kind of discretionary sentencing that the Guidelines were designed to replace? What about the fact that such departure authority is explicitly limited to cases where a court finds "that there exists an aggravating or mitigating circumstance of a kind, or

---

is barred by the fact that the defendant has already been punished for the offense to be prosecuted.

[13] Of course, the safeguards in the Guidelines do not eliminate the double jeopardy violation. The Double Jeopardy Clause protects against the burdens incident to a second trial, and not just against the imposition of a second punishment. Moreover, a "second conviction, even if it results in no greater sentence, is an impermissible punishment." Ball v. United States, 470 U.S. 856, 865 (1985).

to a degree, not adequately taken into consideration by the Sentencing Commission in formulating the guidelines that should result in a sentence different from that described." See § 5K2.0 (policy statement). Did the Sentencing Commission "not adequately take into consideration" the possibility—indeed, the inevitability—that defendants would sometimes face situations like the one in *Witte*? Is that not the whole point behind the Guideline provision previously discussed by the majority, § 5G1.3, that addresses multiple prosecutions involving the same or overlapping "relevant conduct"?

SECTION 3: PLEA BARGAINING UNDER THE GUIDELINES

INTRODUCTORY NOTE ON PLEA BARGAINING UNDER THE GUIDELINES

When drafting the Sentencing Guidelines, the United States Sentencing Commission made a deliberate decision not to try to regulate plea bargaining directly. The Commission explained its view about the relationship between the Sentencing Guidelines and plea bargaining as follows:

"Chapter One—Introduction and General Application Principles Part A—Introduction

"4. THE GUIDELINES' RESOLUTION OF MAJOR ISSUES (POLICY STATEMENT)

"(c) Plea Agreements.

"Nearly ninety percent of all federal criminal cases involve guilty pleas and many of these cases involve some form of plea agreement. Some commentators on early Commission guideline drafts urged the Commission not to attempt any major reforms of the plea agreement process on the grounds that any set of guidelines that threatened to change pre-guidelines practice radically also threatened to make the federal system unmanageable. Others argued that guidelines that failed to control and limit plea agreements would leave untouched a 'loophole' large enough to undo the good that sentencing guidelines would bring.

"The Commission decided not to make major changes in plea agreement practices in the initial guidelines, but rather to provide guidance by issuing general policy statements concerning the acceptance of plea agreements in Chapter Six, Part B (Plea Agreements). The rules set forth in Fed. R. Crim. P. 11(e)[a] govern the

---

[a] Rule 11(e) provides, in relevant part:

"(e) Plea Agreement Procedure.

(1) In General. The attorney for the government and the attorney for the defendant or the defendant when acting pro se may engage in discussions with a view toward reaching an agreement that, upon the entering of a plea of guilty or nolo contendere to a charged offense or to a lesser or related offense, the attorney for the government will do any of the following:

acceptance or rejection of such agreements. The Commission will collect data on the courts' plea practices and will analyze this information to determine when and why the courts accept or reject plea agreements and whether plea agreement practices are undermining the intent of the Sentencing Reform Act. In light of this information and analysis, the Commission will seek to further regulate the plea agreement process as appropriate. Importantly, if the policy statements relating to plea agreements are followed, circumvention of the Sentencing Reform Act and the guidelines should not occur.

"The Commission expects the guidelines to have a positive, rationalizing impact upon plea agreements for two reasons. First, the guidelines create a clear, definite expectation in respect to the sentence that a court will impose if a trial takes place. In the event a prosecutor and defense attorney explore the possibility of a negotiated plea, they will no longer work in the dark. This fact alone should help to reduce irrationality in respect to actual sentencing outcomes. Second, the guidelines create a norm to which courts will likely refer when they decide whether, under

(A) move for a dismissal of other charges; or

(B) make a recommendation, or agree not to oppose the defendant's request, for a particular sentence, with the understanding that such recommendation or request shall not be binding upon the court; or

(C) agree that a specific sentence is the appropriate disposition of the case.

The court shall not participate in any such discussions.

(2) Notice of Such Agreement. If a plea agreement has been reached by the parties, the court shall, on the record, require the disclosure of the agreement in open court or, on a showing of good cause, in camera, at the time the plea is offered. If the agreement is of the type specified in subdivision (e)(1)(A) or (C), the court may accept or reject the agreement, or may defer its decision as to the acceptance or rejection until there has been an opportunity to consider the presentence report. If the agreement is of the type specified in subdivision (e)(1)(B), the court shall advise the defendant that if the court does not accept the rec-

ommendation or request the defendant nevertheless has no right to withdraw the plea.

(3) Acceptance of a Plea Agreement. If the court accepts the plea agreement, the court shall inform the defendant that it will embody in the judgment and sentence the disposition provided for in the plea agreement.

(4) Rejection of a Plea Agreement. If the court rejects the plea agreement, the court shall, on the record, inform the parties of this fact, advise the defendant personally in open court or, on a showing of good cause, in camera, that the court is not bound by the plea agreement, afford the defendant the opportunity to then withdraw the plea, and advise the defendant that if the defendant persists in a guilty plea or plea of nolo contendere the disposition of the case may be less favorable to the defendant than that contemplated by the plea agreement...."

In addition, Rule 11(f) provides: "Notwithstanding the acceptance of a plea of guilty, the court should not enter a judgment upon such plea without making such inquiry as shall satisfy it that there is a factual basis for the plea."

Rule 11(e), to accept or to reject a plea agreement or recommendation.''

Plea bargaining has, however, changed significantly in the federal system as a consequence of the Sentencing Guidelines—and not necessarily always in the "positive, rationalizing" direction foreseen by the Sentencing Commission. As set forth in Fed. R. Crim. P. 11(e), plea bargaining traditionally has involved one of two basic kinds of agreements: "charge bargains," or agreements about the charges to be filed by the prosecutor against the defendant, see Rule 11(e)(1)(A), and "sentence bargains," or agreements about the sentence to be imposed on the defendant, see Rule 11(e)(1)(B) and (C). "Sentence bargains," in turn, can lead to two different kinds of agreements: in the first kind, the prosecutor merely agrees to "recommend," or not oppose the defendant's request for, a particular sentence, see Rule 11(e)(1)(B); in the second, the prosecutor and the defendant agree that the defendant will receive a particular sentence, see Rule 11(e)(1)(C). Of course, the second kind of "sentence bargain," like all plea agreements, is subject to the trial judge's power to reject the agreement and insist that the defendant go to trial, see Rule 11(e)(3) and (4); but, prior to the Sentencing Guidelines, judges rarely exercised this power in connection with a Rule 11(e)(1)(A) or (C) plea agreement.

Under the Sentencing Guidelines, the prosecutor retains the discretionary power to determine the charges to be filed against the defendant, and can thus continue to engage in "charge bargaining" (subject to trial court approval, under Rule 11(e), if the agreement involves dismissal of charges already filed). However, the Guidelines virtually eliminate the prosecutor's ability to engage in traditional "sentence bargaining," because without regard to the prosecutor's recommendation or agreement, the trial judge now must generally sentence the defendant within the narrow sentencing range established by the Guidelines. The only "sentence bargain" that can truly survive the Guidelines is a "bargain" for a sentence that is within the Guideline range.

Given the virtual elimination of traditional "sentence bargaining," and given the generally limited scope of a trial judge's authority to depart from the Guidelines, there are only two paths that remain available to a defendant who wants to plead guilty and avoid the imposition of a harsh Guideline sentence. The first is for the defendant to provide "substantial assistance" to the government in solving other crimes; if the prosecutor certifies that the defendant has done so, then, under 18 U.S.C. § 3553(e) and USSG § 5K1.1, the trial judge is not bound by the Guidelines at all, and may impose any sentence within the range of sentences provided in the relevant criminal statute. The second is for the defendant to "accept responsibility" for the crime; the defendant who does so, under certain circumstances, will qualify for a two-level reduction in the applicable offense level for the crime. See USSG § 3E1.1.

The first three cases in this section deal with issues relating to the "substantial assistance" ground for departure from the Guidelines under

18 U.S.C. § 3553(e) and USSG § 5K1.1. The last two cases address the "acceptance of responsibility" reduction under § 3E1.1.

Wade v. United States

United States Supreme Court, 1992.
504 U.S. 181.

■ JUSTICE SOUTER delivered the opinion of the Court.

Section 3553(e) of Title 18 of the United States Code empowers district courts, "[u]pon motion of the Government," to impose a sentence below the statutory minimum to reflect a defendant's "substantial assistance in the investigation or prosecution of another person who has committed an offense." Similarly, § 5K1.1 of the United States Sentencing Commission, Guidelines Manual (Nov. 1991)(USSG) permits district courts to go below the minimum required under the Guidelines if the Government files a "substantial assistance" motion. This case presents the question whether district courts may subject the Government's refusal to file such a motion to review for constitutional violations. We hold that they may, but that the petitioner has raised no claim to such review.

On October 30, 1989, police searched the house of the petitioner, Harold Ray Wade, Jr., discovered 978 grams of cocaine, two handguns and more than $22,000 in cash, and arrested Wade. In the aftermath of the search, Wade gave law enforcement officials information that led them to arrest another drug dealer.

In due course, a federal grand jury indicted Wade for distributing cocaine and possessing cocaine with intent to distribute it, both in violation of 21 U.S.C. § 841(a)(1); for conspiring to do these things, in violation of 21 U.S.C. § 846; and for using or carrying a firearm during and in relation to a drug crime, in violation of 18 U.S.C. § 924(c)(1). Wade pleaded guilty to all four counts.

The presentence report put the sentencing range under the Sentencing Guidelines for the drug offenses at 97–121 months, but added that Wade was subject to a 10–year mandatory minimum sentence, 21 U.S.C. § 841(b)(1)(B), narrowing the actual range to 120–121 months, see USSG § 5G1.1(c)(2). The report also stated that both Guideline § 2K2.4(a) and 18 U.S.C. § 924(c) required a 5–year sentence on the gun count. At the sentencing hearing in the District Court, Wade's lawyer urged the court to impose a sentence below the 10–year minimum for the drug counts to reward Wade for his assistance to the Government. The court responded that the Government had filed no motion as contemplated in 18 U.S.C. § 3553(e) and USSG § 5K1.1 for sentencing below the minimum, and ruled that, without such a motion, a court had no power to go beneath the minimum. Wade got a sentence of 180 months in prison.

In the United States Court of Appeals for the Fourth Circuit, Wade argued the District Court was in error to say that the absence of a Government motion deprived it of authority to impose a sentence below 10 years for the drug convictions. Wade lost this argument, 936 F.2d 169, 171 (4th Cir.1991), and failed as well on his back-up claim that the District Court was at least authorized to enquire into the Government's motives for filing no motion, the court saying that any such enquiry would intrude unduly upon a prosecutor's discretion. We granted certiorari, and now affirm.

The full text of § 3553(e) is this:

"Limited Authority to Impose a Sentence Below a Statutory Minimum.—Upon motion of the Government, the court shall have the authority to impose a sentence below a level established by statute as minimum sentence so as to reflect a defendant's substantial assistance in the investigation or prosecution of another person who has committed an offense. Such sentence shall be imposed in accordance with the guidelines and policy statements issued by the Sentencing Commission pursuant to section 994 of title 28, United States Code." 18 U.S.C. § 3553(e).

And this is the relevant portion of § 5K1.1:

"Substantial Assistance to Authorities (Policy Statement) Upon motion of the government stating that the defendant has provided substantial assistance in the investigation or prosecution of another person who has committed an offense, the court may depart from the guidelines." USSG § 5K1.1.[b]

Because Wade violated federal criminal statutes that carry mandatory minimum sentences, this case implicates both 18 U.S.C. § 3553(e) and USSG § 5K1.1.

Wade and the Government apparently assume that where, as here, the minimum under the Guidelines is the same as the statutory minimum and the Government has refused to file any motion at all, the two provisions pose identical and equally burdensome obstacles. We are not, therefore,

---

[b] The full text of § 5K1.1(a), as amended through 1996, is as follows:

"§ 5K1.1. SUBSTANTIAL ASSISTANCE TO AUTHORITIES (POLICY STATEMENT)

"Upon motion of the government stating that the defendant has provided substantial assistance in the investigation or prosecution of another person who has committed an offense, the court may depart from the guidelines.

(a) The appropriate reduction shall be determined by the court for reasons stated that may include, but are not limited to, consideration of the following:

(1) the court's evaluation of the significance and usefulness of the defendant's assistance, taking into consideration the government's evaluation of the assistance rendered;

(2) the truthfulness, completeness, and reliability of any information or testimony provided by the defendant;

(3) the nature and extent of the defendant's assistance;

(4) any injury suffered, or any danger or risk of injury to the defendant or his family resulting from his assistance;

(5) the timeliness of the defendant's assistance."

[Footnote by eds.]

called upon to decide whether § 5K1.1 "implements" and thereby supersedes § 3553(e), or whether the two provisions pose two separate obstacles.

Wade concedes, as a matter of statutory interpretation, that § 3553(e) imposes the condition of a Government motion upon the district court's authority to depart, Brief for Petitioner 9–10, and he does not argue otherwise with respect to § 5K1.1. He does not claim that the Government-motion requirement is itself unconstitutional, or that the condition is superseded in this case by any agreement on the Government's behalf to file a substantial-assistance motion, cf. Santobello v. New York, 404 U.S. 257, 262–63 (1971). Wade's position is consistent with the view, which we think is clearly correct, that in both § 3553(e) and § 5K1.1 the condition limiting the court's authority gives the Government a power, not a duty, to file a motion when a defendant has substantially assisted.

Wade nonetheless argues, and again we agree, that a prosecutor's discretion when exercising that power is subject to constitutional limitations that district courts can enforce. Because we see no reason why courts should treat a prosecutor's refusal to file a substantial-assistance motion differently from a prosecutor's other decisions, see, e.g., Wayte v. United States, 470 U.S. 598, 608–09 (1985), we hold that federal district courts have authority to review a prosecutor's refusal to file a substantial-assistance motion and to grant a remedy if they find that the refusal was based on an unconstitutional motive. Thus, a defendant would be entitled to relief if a prosecutor refused to file a substantial-assistance motion, say, because of the defendant's race or religion.

It follows that a claim that a defendant merely provided substantial assistance will not entitle a defendant to a remedy or even to discovery or an evidentiary hearing. Nor would additional but generalized allegations of improper motive. Indeed, Wade concedes that a defendant has no right to discovery or an evidentiary hearing unless he makes a "substantial threshold showing."

Wade has failed to make one. He has never alleged, much less claimed to have evidence tending to show, that the Government refused to file a motion for suspect reasons such as his race or his religion. Instead, Wade argues now that the District Court thwarted his attempt to make quite different allegations on the record because it erroneously believed that no charge of impermissible motive could state a claim for relief. Hence, he now seeks an order of remand to allow him to develop a claim that the Government violated his constitutional rights by withholding a substantial-assistance motion "arbitrarily" or "in bad faith." This, Wade says, the Government did by refusing to move because of "factors that are not rationally related to any legitimate state objective," although he does not specifically identify any such factors.

As the Government concedes, Wade would be entitled to relief if the prosecutor's refusal to move was not rationally related to any legitimate Government end, but his argument is still of no avail.

This is so because the record shows no support for his claim of frustration in trying to plead an adequate claim, and because his claim as presented to the District Court failed to rise to the level warranting judicial enquiry.   The District Court expressly invited Wade's lawyer to state for the record what evidence he would introduce to support his position if the court were to conduct a hearing on the issue.   In response, his counsel merely explained the extent of Wade's assistance to the Government.

This, of course, was not enough, for although a showing of assistance is a necessary condition for relief, it is not a sufficient one.   The Government's decision not to move may have been based not on a failure to acknowledge or appreciate Wade's help, but simply on its rational assessment of the cost and benefit that would flow from moving.

It is clear, then, that, on the present record, Wade is entitled to no relief, and that the judgment of the Court of Appeals must be

Affirmed.

NOTES ON *WADE* AND PLEA BARGAINING UNDER THE GUIDELINES

   1. Mandatory Minimum Sentences.   Consistent with its support for judicial discretion in sentencing, the A.B.A. Project on Minimum Standards for Criminal Justice also took a strong stand against mandatory sentencing:

"[M]andatory sentences rarely accomplish the ends they seek. The certainty of punishment which is sought by such provisions is illusory.   There are numerous discretionary devices—ranging from acquittal of the guilty to reduction of the charge—by which the judge, if that is his purpose, can frustrate the effect of a mandatory sentence.   The experience with such sentences shows that such devices are very commonly employed, sometimes to the point of conviction of the defendant for an offense which could not possibly have occurred under the circumstances of the case in order to permit the imposition of a more realistic sentence. . . .   The only alternative in many instances is imposition of a sentence which under the circumstances of the case is much too harsh.   Neither emasculating the statute nor acquiescing in an injustice is to be commended.   Both effectively and understandably breed disrespect for the system."   Standards with Commentary, at § 2.1(e).

Nevertheless, many legislatures—including Congress—have recently enacted "mandatory minimum" sentencing statutes for certain crimes, usually (although not always) drug-related crimes.   These statutes have often compelled sentencing commissions to revise their guideline sentences upward in order to conform to the statutory "mandatory minimums."

   In Melendez v. United States, ___ U.S. ___, 116 S.Ct. 2057 (1996), the Supreme Court resolved a question that had been left open in *Wade* — namely, whether a federal prosecutor's certification of "substantial assistance" under § 5K1.1 of the Guidelines (which allows departure from the

Guidelines) also necessarily serves as a certification of "substantial assistance" under 18 U.S.C. § 3553(e). In *Melendez,* the prosecutor moved for a § 5K1.1 departure from the Guidelines, but successfully argued in the lower courts that this motion did not permit the courts to impose a sentence below the applicable statutory "mandatory minimum." The Supreme Court—rejecting the view of a clear majority of the federal courts of appeals—agreed with the Government that § 5K1.1 does not create a "unitary motion" system. Justice Thomas, writing for the Court, concluded that 18 U.S.C. § 3553(e) and § 5K1.1 instead implement a "binary motion" system, allowing the prosecutor "to authorize a departure below the Guidelines range while withholding from the court the authority to depart below a lower statutory minimum." Justice Breyer, joined by Justice O'Connor, wrote separately, agreeing with the majority that not all § 5K1.1 motions necessarily satisfy the statutory requirements of 18 U.S.C. § 3553(e), but arguing that the Sentencing Commission (of which Justice Breyer was an original member, before his appointment to the Supreme Court) intended the standard for "substantial assistance" under § 5K1.1 to be the same as that under 18 U.S.C. § 3553(e). Under Justice Breyer's view, a prosecutor's certification of "substantial assistance" that is sufficient to meet 18 U.S.C. § 3553(e) would also satisfy § 5K1.1, but a certification that is insufficient under the statute would likewise fail to authorize a departure from the Guidelines under § 5K1.1.

2. Increased Prosecutorial Leverage Under the Guidelines. The Sentencing Guidelines have greatly increased the severity of sentences for many crimes, especially drug-related crimes. This increase in severity is a product of three factors: (1) the Sentencing Commission's view of the relative seriousness of certain crimes; (2) the widespread use of "real offense" factors to enhance sentences, as discussed in the preceding section of this chapter; and (3) the enactment by Congress in recent years of numerous "mandatory minimum" sentencing statutes, especially for drug-related crimes, which have often required the Commission to increase the Guideline sentences for those crimes even further than the Commission desired (these "mandatory minimum" statutes will be addressed later in this section).

As John C. Jeffries, Jr., and John Gleeson have perceptively noted, the increase in sentencing severity under the Guidelines, combined with the restrictions placed on judicial discretion, have provided the federal prosecutor with substantial new leverage to put pressure on low-level members of drug conspiracies and other organized criminal ventures. This pressure helps the prosecutor to "turn" such defendants and thereby obtain "inside information" to help crack the conspiracy. Jeffries and Gleeson point out that, under the Guidelines, the federal prosecutor can now show a defendant precisely what his or her sentence is going to be upon conviction, even before a supposedly "lenient" judge, *unless* the defendant agrees to cooperate with the government; they refer to this practice as "cooperation bargaining." See Jeffries & Gleeson, The Federalization of Organized Crime: Advantages of Federal Prosecution, 46 Hastings L.J. 1095, 1121 (1995).

Not all observers view this development as desirable. For example, Judge Harry Edwards of the U.S. Court of Appeals for the D.C. Circuit has lamented the fact that the Guidelines "placed enormous power in the hands of the AUSA, effectively 'replacing judicial discretion over sentencing with prosecutorial discretion.'" United States v. Harrington, 947 F.2d 956, 963–70 (D.C.Cir.1991)(Edwards, J., concurring). "One wonders whether the guidelines, in transferring discretion from the district judge to the prosecutor, have not left the fox guarding the chicken coop of sentencing uniformity." Id., at 965 n.5.

3. "Fact Bargaining" Under the Guidelines. The new restrictions on "sentence bargaining" initially led some federal prosecutors to engage in so-called "fact bargaining," or the practice of declining to mention (or to highlight) certain facts that would be relevant to the determination of the defendant's Guideline sentence. One early study, conducted by a member of the Sentencing Commission in conjunction with a University of Chicago law professor, found such avoidance of the proper Guideline sentence in 20% to 35% of the plea cases studied. See Stephen Schulhofer, Assessing the Federal Sentencing Process: The Problem is Uniformity Not Disparity, 29 Am. Crim. L. Rev. 833, 845 (1992)(study conducted by Professor Schulhofer and U.S. Sentencing Commissioner Ilene Nagel). The Commission itself found evidence of manipulation in 17% of all cases, and 26% of all drug cases. See id., at 858–870.

In 1989, Attorney General Richard Thornburgh issued the following "Bluesheet" (a memorandum addressed to all federal prosecutors) emphasizing that plea bargaining practices should "support, not undermine, the guidelines":

"United States Department of Justice

"Plea Policy for Federal Prosecutors

"Plea Bargaining Under the Sentencing Reform Act

"In January, the Supreme Court decided *Mistretta v. United States* and upheld the sentencing guidelines promulgated by the Sentencing Commission pursuant to the Sentencing Reform Act of 1984. The Act was strongly supported by the Department of Justice, and the Department has defended the guidelines since they took effect on November 1, 1987. Under these guidelines, it is now possible for federal prosecutors to respond to three problems that plagued sentencing prior to their adoption: (1) sentencing disparity; (2) misleading sentences which were shorter than they appeared as a result of parole and unduly generous 'good time' allowances; and (3) inadequate sentences in critical areas, such as crimes of violence, white collar crime, drug trafficking and environmental offenses. It is vitally important that federal prosecutors understand these guidelines and make them work. Prosecutors who do not understand the guidelines or who seek to circumvent them will undermine their deterrent and punitive force and will recreate the very problems that the guidelines are expected to solve.

"This memorandum cannot convey all that federal prosecutors need or should want to know about how to use the guidelines, and it is not intended to invalidate more specific policies which are consistent with this statement of principles and may have been adopted by some litigating divisions to govern particular offenses. This memorandum does, however, set forth basic departmental policies to which all of you will be expected to adhere. The Department consistently articulated these policies during the drafting of the guidelines and the period in which their constitutionality was tested. Compliance with these policies is essential if federal criminal law is to be an effective deterrent and those who violate the law are to be justly punished.

"PLEA BARGAINING

"Charge Bargaining

"Charge bargaining takes place in two settings, before and after indictment. Consistent with the Principles of Federal Prosecution in Chapter 27 of Title 9 of the United States Attorneys' Manual, a federal prosecutor should initially charge the most serious, readily provable offense or offenses consistent with the defendant's conduct. Charges should not be filed simply to exert leverage to induce a plea, nor should charges be abandoned in an effort to arrive at a bargain that fails to reflect the seriousness of the defendant's conduct.

"Whether bargaining takes place before or after indictment, the Department policy is the same: any departure from the guidelines should be openly identified rather than hidden between the lines of a plea agreement. It is inevitable that in some cases it will be difficult for anyone other than the prosecutor and the defendant to know whether, prior to indictment, the prosecutor bargained in conformity with the Department's policy. The Department will monitor, together with the Sentencing Commission, plea bargaining, and the Department will expect plea bargains to support, not undermine, the guidelines.

"Once prosecutors have indicted, they should find themselves bargaining about charges which they have determined are readily provable and reflect the seriousness of the defendant's conduct. Should a prosecutor determine in good faith after indictment that, as a result of a change in the evidence or for another reason (e.g., a need has arisen to protect the identity of a particular witness until he testifies against a more significant defendant), a charge is not readily provable or that an indictment exaggerates the seriousness of an offense or offenses, a plea bargain may reflect the prosecutor's reassessment. There should be a record, however, in a case in which charges originally brought are dropped.

"*Sentence Bargaining*

"There are only two types of sentence bargains. Both are permissible, but one is more complicated than the other. First, prosecutors may bargain for a sentence that is within the specified guideline range. This means that when a guideline range is 18–24 months, you have discretion to agree to recommend a sentence of 18 or 20 months rather than to argue for a sentence at the top of the range. Similarly, you may agree to recommend a downward adjustment of two levels for acceptance of responsibility if you conclude in good faith that the defendant is entitled to the adjustment.

"Second, you may seek to depart from the guidelines. This type of sentence bargain always involves a departure and is more complicated than a bargain involving a sentence within a guideline range. Departures are discussed more generally below.

"Department policy requires honesty in sentencing; federal prosecutors are expected to identify for U.S. District Courts departures when they agree to support them. For example, it would be improper for a prosecutor to agree that a departure is in order, but to conceal the agreement in a charge bargain that is presented to a court as a fait accompli so that there is neither a record of nor judicial review of the departure.

"In sum, plea bargaining, both charge bargaining and sentence bargaining, is legitimate. But, such bargaining must honestly reflect the totality and seriousness of the defendant's conduct and any departure to which the prosecutor is agreeing, and must be accomplished through appropriate guideline provisions.

"*Readily Provable Charges*

"The basic policy is that charges are not to be bargained away or dropped, unless the prosecutor has a good faith doubt as to the government's ability readily to prove a charge for legal or evidentiary reasons. It would serve no purpose here to seek to further define 'readily provable.' The policy is to bring cases that the government should win if there were a trial. There are, however, two exceptions.

"First, if the applicable guideline range from which a sentence may be imposed would be unaffected, readily provable charges may be dismissed or dropped as part of a plea bargain. It is important for you to know whether dropping a charge may affect a sentence. For example, the multiple offense rules in Part D of Chapter 3 of the guidelines and recent changes to the relevant conduct standard set forth in 1B1.3(a)(2) will mean that certain dropped charges will be counted for purposes of determining the sentence, subject to the statutory maximum for the offense or offenses of conviction. It is vital that federal prosecutors understand when conduct that is not charged in an indictment or conduct that is alleged in counts that are to be dismissed pursuant to a bargain may be counted for sentencing purposes and when it may not be. For example, in the case of a defendant who could be charged with five bank robberies, a decision to charge only one or to dismiss four counts pursuant to a bargain precludes any consideration of the four uncharged or dismissed robberies in determining a guideline range, unless the plea agreement included a stipulation as to the other robberies. In contrast, in the case of a defendant who could be charged with five counts of fraud, the total amount of money involved in a fraudulent scheme will be considered in determining a guideline range even if the defendant pleads guilty to a single count and there is no stipulation as to the other counts.

"Second, federal prosecutors may drop readily provable charges with the specific approval of the United States Attorney or designated supervisory level official for reasons set forth in the file of the case. This exception recognizes that the aims of the Sentencing Reform Act must be sought without ignoring other, critical aspects of the federal criminal justice system. For example, approval to drop charges in a particular case might be given because the United States Attorney's office is particularly overburdened, the case would be time-consuming to try, and proceeding to trial would significantly reduce the total number of cases disposed of by the office.

"To make the guidelines work, it is likely that the Department and the Sentencing Commission will monitor cases in which charges are dropped. It is important, therefore, that federal prosecutors keep records justifying their decisions not to go forward with readily provable offenses.

"Departures Generally

"In Chapter 5, Part K of the guidelines, the Commission has listed departures that may be considered by a court in imposing a sentence. Some depart upwards and others downwards. Moreover, 5K2.0 recognizes that a sentencing court may consider a departure that has not been adequately considered by the Commission. A departure requires approval by the court. It violates the spirit of the guidelines and Department policy for prosecutors to enter into a plea bargain which is based upon the prosecutor's and the defendant's agreement that a departure is warranted, but that does not reveal to the court the departure and afford an opportunity for the court to reject it.

"The Commission has recognized those bases for departure that are commonly justified. Accordingly, before the government may seek a departure based on a factor other than one set forth in Chapter 5, Part K, approval of United States Attorneys or designated supervisory officials is required, after consultation with the concerned litigating Division. This approval is required whether or not a case is resolved through a negotiated plea.

"Substantial Assistance

"The most important departure is for substantial assistance by a defendant in the investigation or prosecution of another person. Section 5K1.1 provides that, upon motion by the government, a court may depart from the guidelines and may impose a non-guideline sentence. This departure provides federal prosecutors with an enormous range of options in the course of plea negotiations. Although this departure, like all others, requires court approval, prosecutors who bargain in good faith and who state reasons for recommending a departure should find that judges are receptive to their recommendations.

"Stipulations of Fact

"The Department's policy is only to stipulate to facts that accurately represent the defendant's conduct. If a prosecutor wishes to support a departure from the guidelines, he or she should candidly do so and not stipulate to facts that are untrue. Stipulations to untrue facts are unethical. If a prosecutor has insufficient facts to contest a defendant's effort to seek a downward departure or to claim an adjustment, the prosecutor can say so. If the presentence report states facts that are inconsistent with a stipulation in which a prosecutor has joined, it is desirable for the prosecutor to object to the report or to add a statement explaining the prosecutor's understanding of the facts or the reason for the stipulation.

"Recounting the true nature of the defendant's involvement in a case will not always lead to a higher sentence. Where a defendant agrees to cooperate with the government by providing information concerning unlawful activities of others and the government agrees that self-incrimination information so provided will not be used against the defendant, section 1B1.8 provides that the information shall not be used in determining the applicable guideline range, except to the extent provided in the agreement. The existence of an agreement not to use information should be clearly reflected in the case file, the applicability of section 1B1.8 should be documented, and the incriminating information must be disclosed to the court or the probation officer, even though it may not be used in determining a guideline sentence.

"Written Plea Agreements

"In most felony cases, plea agreements should be in writing. If they are not in writing, they always should be formally stated on the record. Written agreements will facilitate efforts by the Department and the Sentencing Commission to monitor compliance by federal prosecutors with Department policies and the guidelines. Such agreements also avoid misunderstandings as to the terms that the parties have accepted in particular cases.

"Understanding the Options

"A commitment to guideline sentencing in the context of plea bargaining may have the temporary effect of increasing the proportion of cases that go to trial, until defense counsel and defendants understand that the Department is committed to the statutory sentencing goals and procedures. Prosecutors should understand, and defense counsel will soon learn, that there is sufficient flexibility in the guidelines to permit effective plea bargaining which does not undermine the statutory scheme.

"For example, when a prosecutor recommends a two level downward adjustment for acceptance of responsibility (e.g., from level 20 to level 18), judicial acceptance of this adjustment will reduce a sentence by approximately 25%. If a comparison is made between the top of one level (e.g., level 20) and the bottom of the relevant level following the reduction (e.g., level 18), it would show a difference of approximately 35%. At low levels, the reduction is greater. In short, a two level reduction does *not* mean two months. Moreover, the adjustment for acceptance of responsibility is substantial, and should be attractive to defendants against whom the government has strong cases. The prosecutor may also cooperate with the defendant by recommending a sentence at the low end of a guideline range, which will further reduce the sentence.

"It is important for prosecutors to recognize while bargaining that they must be careful to make all appropriate Chapter Three adjustments—e.g., victim related adjustments and adjustments for role in the offense.

"Conclusion

"With all available options in mind, and with full knowledge of the availability of a substantial assistance departure, federal prosecutors have the tools necessary to handle their caseloads and to arrive at appropriate dispositions in the process. Honest application of the guidelines will make sentences under the Sentencing Reform Act fair, honest, and appropriate."

Despite the Thornburgh Memorandum, controversy over the immediate impact of the Sentencing Guidelines on plea bargaining continued, with many observers—including some federal prosecutors—taking the position that prosecutors, when plea bargaining, should continue to engage in individualized assessments of defendants and independent evaluations of the severity of Guideline sentences. Attorney General Janet Reno, in October 1993, issued a new "Bluesheet" stating:

"[I]t is appropriate that the attorney for the government consider, *inter alia*, such factors as the sentencing guideline range yielded by the charge, whether the penalty yielded by such sentencing range ... is proportional to the seriousness of the defendant's conduct, and whether the charge achieves such purposes of the criminal law as punishment, protection of the public, specific and general deterrence, and rehabilitation. Note that these factors may also be considered by the attorney for the government when entering into plea agreements."

After receiving a letter of protest from Senator Orrin Hatch, then-Ranking Minority Member of the Judiciary Committee of the United States Senate, Attorney General Reno wrote a reply reassuring Senator Hatch that "it remains the directive of the Department of Justice that prosecutors charge the most serious offense that is consistent with the nature of the defendant's conduct, that is likely to result in a sustainable conviction [and] that prosecutors adhere to the Sentencing Guidelines." See generally Special Issue, Justice Department Guidance for Prosecutors: Fifteen Years of Charging & Plea Policies, 6 Fed. Sent. Rep. 352–53 (1994)(Daniel J. Freed & Marc Miller, eds.).

United States v. Wallace

United States Court of Appeals, Fourth Circuit, 1994.
22 F.3d 84.

Before PHILLIPS, CIRCUIT JUDGE, and BUTZNER and YOUNG, SENIOR JUDGES.

■ PHILLIPS, CIRCUIT JUDGE:

James Darnell Wallace challenges on various grounds the sentence that followed his plea of guilty to a charge of conspiracy to distribute fifty or more grams of cocaine base in violation of 21 U.S.C. §§ 841(a) and 846. Wallace's primary contentions are that pursuant to a plea agreement he provided substantial assistance to the government's investigation of the criminal activities of other persons and that, upon his doing so, the government became obligated under the terms of his plea agreement to file a downward departure motion and, alternatively, that the government's refusal to make such a motion was based on unconstitutional motives, namely racial prejudice. We conclude that neither of these contentions, nor any other challenge to the sentence imposed, has merit, and we therefore affirm the sentence.

I

On several occasions during the spring and summer of 1992, Wallace sold cocaine base ("crack") to undercover law enforcement officers at various locales in Herndon, Virginia. In January, 1993, Wallace was arrested. In February, he waived indictment and pursuant to the terms of a written plea agreement pled guilty to a one-count criminal information charging him with conspiracy to distribute fifty grams or more of cocaine base in violation of 21 U.S.C. §§ 841(a)(1) and 846.

According to the terms of the plea agreement:

"The defendant agrees to cooperate fully and truthfully with the United States, and provide all information known to the defendant regarding any criminal activity.... The parties agree that the United States reserves its option to seek any departure from the applicable sentencing guidelines, pursuant to Section 5K of the Sentencing Guidelines and Policy Statements,[1] or Rule 35(b) of the Federal Rules of Criminal Procedure,[2] if in its sole discretion, the United States determines that the defendant has provided substantial assistance and that such assistance has been completed."

The defendant agrees that the decision whether to file such a [substantial assistance] motion rests in the United States' sole discretion. Shortly after his plea of guilty, Wallace was interviewed twice by special agents of the United States Drug Enforcement Administration (DEA). During the meetings, both of which lasted several hours, Wallace provided information concerning at least one, and possibly two, of his cocaine suppliers.

When, after these meetings, the government did not file a downward departure motion with the district court, Wallace made a Motion for Specific Enforcement of Plea Agreement. He asked the district court to direct the government to move for a downward departure pursuant to § 5K1.1 of the Sentencing Guidelines. In the motion, Wallace argued that he had complied with the terms of the plea agreement and was thus entitled to a downward departure based on having provided substantial assistance. He asserted that despite the fact that he "provided information to the government regarding the drug activities of an individual who is now the subject of an investigation," the United States "has refused even to submit Mr. Wallace's case to its Substantial Assistance Committee." In addition, Wallace's motion alleged that the government's failure to file a downward departure motion was based on his race; he is an African American. Finally, the motion alleged that the United States Sentencing Guidelines applied in his sentencing are inherently racist, and that the court should compensate for this bias by directing a downward departure.

The government, in its response, noted the plea agreement provisions leaving the decision whether the defendant provided substantial assistance to the government's "sole discretion." While admitting that Wallace provided information concerning two of his cocaine suppliers, the government contended that both were already targets of DEA investigations. Although Wallace's "cooperation and assistance, to date, has provided additional evidence against these suppliers, [it] can in no way be considered 'substantial.' Even if it were, the defendant has not 'completed' his cooperation as required by the express terms of his plea agreement." The government further argued that under Wade v. United States, 504 U.S. 181 (1992), the government's failure to file such a motion is reviewable only

---

[1] The relevant part of section 5K of the United States Sentencing Commission, Guidelines Manual (USSG) is § 5K1.1 which states in part: "Upon motion of the government stating that the defendant has provided substantial assistance in the investigation or prosecution of another person who has committed an offense, the court may depart from the guidelines." USSG § 5K1.1.

[2] Rule 35(b) allows courts, on motion of the government made within one year of the imposition of the sentence, to reduce a sentence to reflect a defendant's subsequent, substantial assistance in the investigation or prosecution of another person who has committed an offense.

when based on an unconstitutional motive, and no such motive existed here.

At Wallace's sentencing hearing, his counsel reiterated his argument that "crack" cocaine sentences are unconstitutionally disproportionate when compared with sentences for powder cocaine. And he again argued that Wallace gave substantial assistance and should be given a § 5K1.1 downward departure.

The district court denied Wallace's motion. It did so based on the fact that the plea agreement left the decision whether to file a downward departure motion in the sole discretion of the United States Attorney. As for the "cocaine-versus-crack argument," the court noted that it "has been made before, unsuccessfully." While expressing sympathy, the court observed that the issue was one for Congress not the courts and sentenced Wallace to a term of 120 months.

This appeal followed.

II

Here, as in the district court, Wallace challenges the district court's refusal to grant a substantial assistance downward departure on alternative grounds. First, he contends that he was entitled to it as a simple matter of enforcing his plea agreement with the government: the government promised to move for such a departure if he gave substantial assistance, and he had done so. Second, he contends that, independent of the plea agreement, he was entitled to the departure because of his proof that racial discrimination (he being black) was the motive for the government's refusal to make the required motion. We take these in turn.

A

The argument that the plea agreement obligated the government to move for a downward departure upon Wallace's provision of substantial assistance fails for a simple reason. Unlike the plea agreement in United States v. Conner, 930 F.2d 1073 (4th Cir.1991), on which he relies, Wallace's contained no binding obligation by the government to make the required motion. The *Conner* plea agreement in critical part provided that "[s]hould [defendant] provide substantial assistance[ ], then the United States will recommend ...," id. at 1074; the agreement in the instant case imposed no such binding obligation, providing only that "the United States reserves its option to seek any departure ... if in its sole discretion, the United States determines that the defendant has provided substantial assistance and that such assistance has been completed." The *Conner* agreement gave rise to an enforceable promise as a matter of simple contract law; the agreement in the instant case gave rise to no enforceable promise, explicitly reserving discretion rather than promising anything. Thus, even though the government conceded that Wallace cooperated "fully and truthfully," it did not violate its agreement by nevertheless concluding in its discretion that the assistance thereby given was not "substantial."

The district court therefore rightly refused to grant the downward departure as a matter of enforcing the agreement.

B

Wade v. United States, 504 U.S. 181 (1992), holds that without regard to whether substantial assistance has in fact been provided by a defendant, in the absence of a government motion a sentencing court may not grant a downward departure on that basis unless (1) the government has obligated itself in a plea agreement to move for such a departure, or (2) unless [sic], in the absence of such an obligation, it is shown that the government's refusal or failure so to move "was based on an unconstitutional motive." Id. In the first instance, the departure may be granted upon proof that the plea agreement has been breached by the government. In the second, upon proof of the unconstitutional motive. In either of these cases, a defendant is entitled to an inquiry by the court into the circumstances upon which entitlement turns; in no other case where there has been no government motion is any judicial inquiry warranted.

Here, as indicated, there was no enforceable obligation arising from the plea agreement; the government's refusal was a purely discretionary one. That left only the possibility that the discretionary refusal was unconstitutionally motivated by racial bias. As to that possibility, Wade imposes upon a defendant the burden to do more than merely allege unconstitutional motive in order to require judicial inquiry. A defendant must go further and make "a substantial threshold showing," failing which he is "not entitle[d] to a remedy or even to discovery or an evidentiary hearing." Id.

Here, the district court did not err in determining that Wallace had not made the required showing, and on that basis, in declining to give him the downward departure he sought as remedy. He made the allegation of racial bias, but he supported it with but a single instance of the same United States Attorney's Office having recently moved for downward departure in behalf of several middle and upper-class white defendants convicted of generally comparable drug trafficking offenses. We cannot find error in the district court's conclusion that evidence of this one episode was insufficient to make the required *Wade* showing.

III

Wallace also makes several other constitutional, and statutory, challenges to his sentence, all related to the use of "cocaine base" in 21 U.S.C. § 841(b).

First, Wallace charges that the demonstrated 100–to–1 sentencing ratio of "cocaine base" to "cocaine powder" in § 841(b) violates the Equal Protection Clause because African Americans are disproportionately sentenced under the stiffer sanction.[a] Second, he claims that the term

---

[a] The 100–to–1 sentencing ratio referred to by the Court of Appeals is the result of Congress's "mandatory minimum" sentencing statutes applicable to crack versus powder cocaine. Under 21 U.S.C. §§ 841(b), for example, in order to be subject to the same

"cocaine base" as used in 21 U.S.C. § 841(b) and U.S.S.G. § 2D1.1 is unconstitutionally vague. Third, he contends that the 100 to 1 sentencing ratio of "cocaine base" to "cocaine powder" in 21 U.S.C. § 841(b) constitutes racial genocide in violation of 18 U.S.C. § 1091. Wallace's first two claims are foreclosed by direct circuit precedent. United States v. Thomas, 900 F.2d 37 (4th Cir.1990); United States v. Bynum, 3 F.3d 769 (4th Cir.1993); United States v. Pinto, 905 F.2d 47 (4th Cir.1990). As for the third claim, Wallace offered no credible evidence that either Congress or the Sentencing Commission, when establishing the challenged sentencing ratios, did so with the "specific intent" of "destroying" African–Americans or any other racial or ethnic group. In the absence of such a proffer, this claim must also fail.

IV

For the foregoing reasons, we affirm the sentence imposed by the district court on James Darnell Wallace.

NOTE ON *WALLACE* AND CRACK COCAINE SENTENCING

Despite the Fourth Circuit's rather brusque dismissal of the argument in *Wallace*, other courts have expressed concern about the disparate treatment of crack and powder cocaine under the relevant statutes and Guidelines. For example, in United States v. Lattimore, 974 F.2d 971 (8th Cir.1992), the defendant argued that such disparity violated his equal protection rights. The district court departed downward in sentencing the defendant, based in part on the disparity. The Eighth Circuit reversed. Judge Myron Bright dissented:

> "Although statistics differentiating crack and powder cocaine do not exist on the federal level, in Minnesota (where Lattimore's crime occurred), 96.9% of the people charged in state court with using crack in 1988 were black. In the same year, 79.6% of the people charged with using powder cocaine were white. State v. Russell, 477 N.W.2d 886, 887 n. 1 (Minn.1991) [(striking down similar Minnesota sentencing guidelines under the Minnesota Constitution, based on disparate treatment of crack and powder cocaine)].

> "The Federal Judicial Center released a report this year documenting racial disparity among offenders in the federal system. Federal Judicial Center, The General Effect of Mandatory Minimum Prison Terms 20–21 (1991). According to the study, in 1984 the average sentence for blacks in the federal system, after controlling for several offense and offender factors, was 28% higher than the average sentence for whites. In 1990, that disparity had risen to 49%. Id.

five-year "mandatory minimum" prison sentence that would be imposed for possession with intent to distribute at least 5 grams of crack cocaine, a defendant would have to possess with intent to distribute at least 500 grams of powder cocaine. [Footnote by eds.]

"As the majority notes, the racial disparities created by the mandatory minimum sentences and the Guidelines are a 'serious matter.' Although such disparities by themselves may not violate the Equal Protection Clause, they constitute a mitigating factor which has surfaced since the drafting of the drug offense Guidelines by the Commission and on which the Commission has neither considered nor taken action."

In addition to the statistics mentioned by Judge Bright, a study published in 1994 by two research scientists, Douglas C. McDonald and Kenneth E. Carlson, found that disparity in sentencing between black and white offenders actually increased during the period from January 1989 to June 1990, as compared to the pre-guidelines period from 1986 to 1988. The study attributed most of the increase to a sharp rise in the proportion of black offenders who were sentenced for drug trafficking—from 19 percent of all convicted blacks in 1986 to 46 percent in the first half of 1990. The comparable proportion of white offenders sentenced for drug trafficking also rose, but not as much—from 26 percent in 1986 to 35 percent in the first half of 1990. The study also found that, in general, white and black offenders were treated equally when convicted and sentenced for the same cocaine trafficking crime (i.e., for either crack cocaine trafficking or powder cocaine trafficking). But, in the federal system, the study found that only 4 percent of all white cocaine traffickers were convicted of trafficking in crack, whereas 27 percent of all black cocaine traffickers were involved with crack. And the study revealed that 83 percent of all those federal offenders who were convicted of crack cocaine trafficking (and who were thus subject to the much more severe sentencing provisions mentioned in *United States v. Lattimore*) were black. See McDonald and Carlson, Sentencing in Federal Courts: Does Race Matter? Washington, D.C.: Bureau of Justice Statistics (1994).

In the Violent Crime Control and Law Enforcement Act of 1994, Congress responded—albeit in a very limited way—to concerns about crack sentencing and racial disparity. In Title XXVIII of the Act, Congress authorized a federal government study of cocaine sentencing in the federal criminal justice system. Based on the results of the study, the Sentencing Commission in 1995 proposed amendments to the Guidelines that would have eliminated the disparity in treatment between crack cocaine and powder cocaine. Congress, however, rejected the proposed amendments.

INTRODUCTORY NOTE ON CONTACTS BETWEEN FEDERAL PROSECUTORS AND DEFENDANTS

As Daniel C. Richman has observed, defendants—especially those who are part of a larger criminal enterprise—often are represented by defense attorneys who do not see their primary role as one of encouraging or facilitating cooperation with the government. See Richman, Cooperating Clients, 56 Ohio State L.J. 69 (1995). This can be for many reasons: an honest belief that the defendant will be best served by refusing to cooperate; a desire to avoid implicating other persons (who may or may not be represented by the same defense attorney, or another defense attorney in the same firm); a fear of possible reprisals by those other persons who might be implicated; and a general reluctance to be perceived as a defense attorney who is "cozy" with the government (a perception that might drive away future prospective clients).

In any event, defendants sometimes do not receive from their defense attorneys the kind of complete information about the Sentencing Guidelines and the possible avenues for departure that might prompt the defendant to cooperate with the government in hope of a reduced sentence. In some such cases, defendants have sought to make contact directly with the federal prosecutor, without the knowledge or consent of their own defense attorneys. This kind of contact implicates both the Sixth Amendment's right to counsel and DR 7–104(A)(1) of the American Bar Association's Model Code of Professional Responsibility (on which many state bar ethical codes are based), which provides:

> "During the course of his representation of a client a lawyer shall not: (1) Communicate or cause another to communicate on the subject of the representation with a party he knows to be represented by a lawyer in that matter unless he has the prior consent of the lawyer representing such other party or is authorized by law to do so. . . ."

The A.B.A.'s Model Rules of Professional Conduct also contain a provision, Rule 4.2, barring such contact.

United States v. Lopez

United States Court of Appeals, Ninth Circuit, 1993.
4 F.3d 1455.

Before FLETCHER, POOLE, and T.G. NELSON, CIRCUIT JUDGES.

■ POOLE, CIRCUIT JUDGE.

I.

Jose Lopez was indicted for conspiracy to distribute and distribution of cocaine and heroin in violation of 21 U.S.C. §§ 846 and 841(a)(1), and for aiding and abetting in violation of 18 U.S.C. § 2. While awaiting trial, Lopez was detained with a codefendant, Antonio Escobedo, at the Federal Correctional Institution at Pleasanton.

Lopez retained attorney Barry Tarlow to represent him. Tarlow informed Lopez that he believed that the defendants had a viable entrapment defense and that, in any case, it was his general policy not to negotiate a plea with the government in exchange for cooperation. Attorney James A. Twitty, who represented codefendant Escobedo, had agreed with Tarlow to coordinate a joint investigation on behalf of the defendants. In so doing, he often spoke to both Escobedo and Lopez by telephone and in person during visits to Pleasanton. In March or April of 1990, Escobedo telephoned Twitty and expressed his interest in reopening negotiations with the government. Concerned about his children, who he feared were being abused while in the custody of their mother, Lopez was anxious to be released from Pleasanton and thus echoed Escobedo's interest in a possible plea bargain.

Without informing Tarlow, Twitty twice traveled to Pleasanton in order to discuss the possibility of a plea bargain with Escobedo and Lopez. He spoke to both men about this possibility from five to nine times on the phone. Lopez apparently did not want to retain another lawyer to negotiate with the government because he feared that doing so would cost him Tarlow's services, and Lopez wanted Tarlow to represent him in the event the case went to trial. Lopez also was concerned about the additional expense of having Tarlow conduct plea negotiations. Twitty accordingly contacted Lyons on behalf of both Lopez and Escobedo. Lyons claims that Twitty informed him that Lopez did not want Tarlow present at any meetings with the government because "Tarlow didn't represent his best interest in this particular context." Lyons avers that he did not press Twitty on this point, but instead assumed that Lopez was connected to a drug ring which was paying Tarlow's fees, and which would endanger his family if Tarlow learned about the negotiations with the government.

Twitty, however, maintains that during his first phone conversation with the prosecutor about the proposed negotiations, he emphasized that Lopez's reasons for excluding Tarlow had nothing to do with concerns about the safety of his family. He stressed that Tarlow's fees were not being paid by anyone with whom Lopez was in the drug business. According to Twitty, he informed the prosecutor that Lopez simply feared that if Tarlow knew about the plea negotiations, he would resign as Lopez's lawyer.

Recognizing the sensitivity of a meeting with Lopez without Tarlow's knowledge or consent, Lyons contacted the district court ex parte. The court referred the matter to a magistrate judge, who conducted an in camera interview of Lopez on May 21, 1990. The magistrate judge warned Lopez of the dangers of self-representation, informed him that he could have other counsel, and cautioned him that Twitty, as Escobedo's lawyer, could not represent him. Lopez insisted on going forward with the meeting, and signed a waiver prepared by the government. Lopez, along with Escobedo and his attorney Twitty, met with Lyons in the prosecutor's office.

On May 30, 1991, Lopez was taken once again before the magistrate judge, who verified that Lopez wanted to meet with the government a second time without Tarlow. The second meeting also took place in Lyons' office, and was again attended by Lyons, Lopez, Escobedo, and Twitty. Following this second meeting, Lyons sent Twitty a proposed plea agreement for Escobedo, a copy of which Twitty provided to Lopez. After talking with Twitty, the two men rejected the proposal.

Tarlow found out about his client's discussions with the government indirectly. In August 1990, Lyons talked with Harold Rosenthal, who was the attorney for a third codefendant. Lyons alerted Rosenthal to the fact that the government had been negotiating with Lopez without Tarlow's knowledge. Rosenthal contacted Twitty, who urged him to refrain from informing Tarlow for fear that doing so would "mess up the deal." Nevertheless, Rosenthal called Tarlow. On August 15, 1990, Tarlow was permitted by the district court to withdraw as Lopez's counsel. Having retained substitute counsel, Lopez filed a motion to dismiss the indictment on September 27, 1990. Lopez alleged that the government infringed upon his Sixth Amendment rights as well as Rules of Professional Conduct of the State Bar of California Rule 2–100 (1988). Binding pursuant to Local Rule 110–3 in the Northern District of California, Rule 2–100 generally prohibits a lawyer from communicating with another party in the case without the consent of that party's lawyer.

After extensive briefing and six hearings at which Twitty, Lopez, and Lyons testified, the district court concluded that Lyons had violated Rule 2–100. United States v. Lopez, 765 F.Supp. 1433, 1456 (N.D.Cal.1991). The court rebuffed the government's attempts to invoke the "Thornburgh Memorandum," a Justice Department policy statement which purports to exempt federal litigators from compliance with the rule against communicating with represented individuals without the consent of their lawyers. See Memorandum from Dick Thornburgh, Attorney General, to All Justice Department Litigators (June 8, 1989). The court also determined that Lyons had not insulated himself from blame by obtaining the approval of the district court before each meeting, since he had "effectively misled" the court regarding Lopez's reasons for requesting to speak with him.

Since Lopez had been able to obtain competent replacement counsel for Tarlow, the court declined to say that the government's misconduct rose to the level of a Sixth Amendment violation. It also found, however, that Lopez had been significantly prejudiced, since he was effectively deprived of the counsel of his choice. Refusing to evaluate Lyons's actions apart from the Thornburgh memorandum which he invoked in his defense, the court condemned both as an egregious and flagrant "frontal assault on the legitimate powers of the court." Rejecting less drastic remedies as ineffective, the district court invoked its supervisory powers in order to dismiss the indictment against Jose Lopez.

The government, on appeal, has prudently dropped its dependence on the Thornburgh Memorandum in justifying AUSA Lyons' conduct, and has thereby spared us the need of reiterating the district court's trenchant analysis of the inefficacy of the Attorney General's policy statement. The government instead argues that Rule 2–100 was not intended to apply to prosecutors pursuing investigations, that the contact with Lopez was authorized by law, that Rule 2–100 did not apply since Lopez was exercising his constitutional right of self-representation, and that Lopez waived his rights under Rule 2–100. Finally, the government contends that dismissal of the indictment was improper, even if Lyons did violate the ethical rule.

II.

We review de novo the district court's conclusion that specific conduct violated court rules. The court's findings of fact, however, are reviewed for clear error.

Rule 110–3 of the local rules of the Northern District of California requires that:

> "Every member of the bar of this court and any attorney permitted to practice in this court under Local Rule 110–2 shall be familiar with and comply with the standards of professional conduct required of members of the State Bar of California and contained in the State Bar Act, the Rules of Professional Conduct of the State Bar of California, and decisions of any court applicable thereto; maintain the respect due courts of justice and judicial officers; [and] perform with the honesty, care, and decorum required for the fair and efficient administration of justice."

Rule 2–100 of the Rules of Professional Conduct of the State Bar of California governs communications with a represented party:

> "(A) While representing a client, a member shall not communicate directly or indirectly about the subject of the representation with a party the member knows to be represented by another lawyer in the matter, unless the member has the consent of the other lawyer....
>
> "(C) This rule shall not prohibit:
>
> > (1) Communications with a public officer, board, committee, or body;
> >
> > (2) Communications initiated by a party seeking advice or representation from an independent lawyer of the party's choice; or
> >
> > (3) Communications otherwise authorized by law."

Rule 2–100's prohibition against communicating with represented parties without the consent of their counsel is both widely accepted and of venerable heritage. The California rule tracks the language of Rule 4.2 of the American Bar Association's Model Rules of Professional Conduct, which in turn is nearly identical to its predecessor in the Model Code of Professional Responsibility, Disciplinary Rule 7–104(A)(1). A similar prohibition appears under Canon 9 of the ABA's Canons of Professional Ethics, which were promulgated in 1908. Not simply an American invention, the prohibition has roots which can be traced back to English common law. See, e.g., In Re Oliver, 2 Adm. & Eccl. 620, 622, 111 Eng.Rep. 239, 240 (1835)("When it appeared that Mrs. Oliver had an attorney, to whom she referred, it was improper to obtain her signature, with no attorney present on her part. If this were permitted, a very impure, and often a fraudulent, practice would prevail.")(Lord Denman, C.J.). Today some version of the rule is in effect in all fifty American states.

The rule against communicating with a represented party without the consent of that party's counsel shields a party's substantive interests against encroachment by opposing counsel and safeguards the relationship between the party and her attorney. As Tarlow's withdrawal upon discovering the secret communication between Lopez and the government exemplifies all too well, the trust necessary for a successful attorney-client relationship is eviscerated when the client is lured into clandestine meetings with the lawyer for the opposition. As a result, uncurbed communications with represented parties could have deleterious effects well beyond the context of the individual case, for our adversary system is premised upon functional lawyer-client relationships.

A.

The government argues, however, that Rule 2–100 was not intended to apply to prosecutors pursuing criminal investigations. Decisions of the state courts of California, which are binding on attorneys practicing in the Northern District of California through Local Rule 110–3, however, have held prosecutors to the rules prohibiting communications with represented parties. In People v. Sharp, 150 Cal.App.3d 13, 197 Cal.Rptr. 436 (1983), decided under the predecessor of Rule 2–100, the court noted that:

> "[b]ecause the prosecutor's position is unique—he represents authority and the discretion to make decisions affecting the defendant's pending case—his contact carries an implication of leniency for cooperative defendants or harsher treatment for the uncooperative. Such contact intrudes upon the function of defense counsel and impedes his or her ability to negotiate a settlement and properly represent the client, whose interests the rule is designed to protect." Id., 197 Cal.Rptr. at 439–40.

The court thus concluded that, by directing police agents to conduct a lineup without notifying the defendant's attorney, the prosecutor violated his professional ethical responsibilities. Id. at 440; see also People v. Manson, 61 Cal.App.3d 102, 132 Cal.Rptr. 265, 301 (1976)(holding prosecutor to ethical rules because he "is no less a member of the State Bar than any other admitted lawyer"); see also Triple A Mach. Shop, Inc. v. State, 213 Cal.App.3d 131, 261 Cal.Rptr. 493, 499 (1989)(assuming Rule 2–100 can apply to prosecutors).[1]

The cases advanced by the government in support of its position are largely irrelative. Starting with United States v. Lemonakis, 485 F.2d 941

---

[1] The government has speculated for the first time on appeal that the California Rules of Professional Conduct were not validly adopted by the Northern District of California, and that Local Rule 110–3 as adopted predates California's adoption of Rule 2–100. The government concedes that they failed to raise this issue before the district court, but argues that we may dispense with the rule that the issue is waived because it is a purely legal issue. We decline to do so, however, for the government's argument rests on the claim that the Northern District has not specifically adopted Rule 2–100, and that Local Rule 110–3 was adopted without proper notice and comment. Both of these claims are factual in nature, and we decline to review them without the proper development of a record. In any event, we have previously upheld the Northern District's adoption of the California Rules of Professional Conduct, and rejected the argument that attorneys practicing in the Northern District are not subject to the ABA Model Code because the

(D.C.Cir.1973), a number of courts have held that there is no breach of a prosecutor's ethical duty to refrain from communication with represented parties when investigating officers question or contact suspects prior to their indictment. Such cases have reasoned that criminal suspects should not be permitted to insulate themselves from investigation simply by retaining counsel. See, e.g., United States v. Jamil, 707 F.2d 638, 646 (2d Cir.1983); United States v. Hammad, 858 F.2d 834, 839 (2d Cir.1988); see also Pamela S. Karlan, Discrete and Relational Criminal Representation: The Changing Vision of the Right to Counsel, 105 Harv.L.Rev. 670, 701 (1992)("A broad interpretation of the no-contact rule would provide a powerful incentive for criminal actors to seek relational representation because having an ongoing relationship with an attorney could insulate them from several of the most effective law enforcement techniques for investigating complex crime."). In addition, they have noted that during investigation of the case and prior to indictment, the contours of the "subject matter of the representation" by [the suspect's] attorneys, concerning which the code bars "communication," [are] less certain and thus even less susceptible to the damage of "artful" legal questions the Code provisions appear designed in part to avoid. *Lemonakis*, 485 F.2d at 956; compare Rule 2–100 (barring communication "about the subject of the representation").[2]

The government's insistence that there are no salient differences between the pre- and post-indictment contexts for purposes of Rule 2–100

district's rules did not specifically adopt the code. Paul E. Iacono Structural Eng'r, Inc. v. Humphrey, 722 F.2d 435, 438–39 (9th Cir. 1983). Moreover, Rule 7–103 of the California Rules of Professional Conduct, which was in effect prior to the adoption of Rule 2–100, also prohibited communications with represented parties in almost identical terms.

The government has called our attention to Baylson v. Disciplinary Bd., 975 F.2d 102 (3d Cir.1992), which held that it was beyond the rule-making authority of the district court to adopt a state disciplinary rule governing the ability of federal prosecutors to obtain a grand jury subpoena. The Third Circuit's decision was founded on the fact that the rule in question was inconsistent with Fed.R.Crim.P. 17. See Fed.R.Crim.P. 57 (district court may adopt rules "not inconsistent with" the Federal Rules of Criminal Procedure). At the same time, the Third Circuit recognized that "[a]mong the rules which fall under the local rule-making authority of the district courts are rules regulating the conduct of attorneys practicing before them." 975 F.2d at 107. *Baylson* is thus not in conflict with our holding that

Rule 2–100 is applicable via Local Rule 110–3, since requiring prosecutors to refrain from communicating with represented defendants is not only consistent with the rules of criminal procedure, but implied by them. See Fed.R.Crim.P. 11(e)(1)(plea negotiations may be conducted between attorney for the government and attorney for the defendant).

[2] Although we do not reach the issue, we note that courts have been divided over whether the rule applies even in a pre-indictment setting. Three circuits have held that in custodial situations, the ethical rule prohibits prosecutors from interviewing defendants in the absence of and without the consent of their counsel: United States v. Thomas, 474 F.2d 110, 112 (10th Cir.1973); United States v. Killian, 639 F.2d 206, 210 (5th Cir.1981); and United States v. Durham, 475 F.2d 208, 211 (7th Cir.1973). See also United States v. Hammad, 858 F.2d 834, 839 (2d Cir.1988)(refusing to "bind[ ] the Code's applicability to the moment of indictment" since "an indictment's return lies substantially within the control of the prosecutor").

is puzzling. The prosecutor's ethical duty to refrain from contacting represented defendants entifies upon indictment for the same reasons that the Sixth Amendment right to counsel attaches:

"The initiation of judicial criminal proceedings is far from a mere formalism. It is the starting point of our whole system of adversary criminal justice. For it is only then that the government has committed itself to prosecute, and only then that the adverse positions of government and defendant have solidified." Kirby v. Illinois, 406 U.S. 682, 689 (1972)(plurality opinion).

In addition to focusing "the subject of the representation," indictment gives rise to a defendant's "right to rely upon counsel as a 'medium' between him and the State." Maine v. Moulton, 474 U.S. 159, 176 (1985). Thus, the Sixth Amendment guarantee would be rendered fustian if one of its "critical components," a lawyer-client "'relationship characterized by trust and confidence,'" could be circumvented by the prosecutor under the guise of pursuing the criminal investigation. United States v. Chavez, 902 F.2d 259, 266 (4th Cir.1990)(quoting Morris v. Slappy, 461 U.S. 1, 21 (1983)(Brennan, J., concurring)); see also Patterson v. Illinois, 487 U.S. 285, 290 n. 3 (1988)("Once an accused has a lawyer, a distinct set of constitutional safeguards aimed at preserving the sanctity of the attorney-client relationship takes effect."). Thus, beginning at the latest upon the moment of indictment, a prosecuting attorney has a duty under ethical rules like Rule 2–100 to refrain from communicating with represented defendants.

B.

The government next adopts the position that Lyons' conduct falls within the "communications otherwise authorized by law" exception to the rule against attorney communication with represented parties. See Rule 2–100(C)(3). The government argues that Lyons' contact with Lopez was authorized by statutes enabling prosecutors to conduct criminal investigations, and that the meetings were authorized by the magistrate judge's approval.

1.

The government reasons that federal prosecutors operate pursuant to a "statutory scheme" that permits them to communicate with represented parties in order to detect and prosecute federal offenses. Citing 28 U.S.C. §§ 509, 515(a) and (c), 516, 533 and 547, the government argues that Justice Department attorneys fall within the "authorized by law" exception to California Rule 2–100 and its counterparts.

The comment to California Rule 2–100 notes that:

"Rule 2–100 is intended to control communications between a member [of the bar] and persons the member knows to be represented by counsel unless a statutory scheme or case law will override the rule. There are a number of express statutory schemes which authorize communications between a member and person who would otherwise be subject to this rule.... Other applicable law also includes the authority of government prosecutors and investigators to conduct criminal investigations, as limited by the relevant decisional law."

Thus, the "authorized by law" exception to Rule 2–100 requires that a statutory scheme expressly permit contact between an attorney and a represented party. While recognizing the statutory authority of prosecutors to investigate crime, however, Rule 2–100 is intended to allow no more contact between prosecutors and represented defendants than the case law permits. We agree with the district court that the statutes cited by the government are nothing more than general enabling statutes. Nothing in these provisions expressly or impliedly authorizes contact with represented individuals beyond that permitted by case law. As discussed above, "the authority of government prosecutors and investigators to conduct criminal investigations" is "limited by the relevant decisional law" to contacts conducted prior to indictment in a non-custodial setting. Lyons' discussions with Lopez were not so authorized.

2.

The government also maintains that by obtaining the prior approval of a magistrate judge, Lyons brought his conversations with Lopez within the realm of the "authorized by law" exception to California Rule 2–100. We agree that in an appropriate case, contact with a represented party could be excepted from the prohibition of Rule 2–100 by court order. See Rule 2–100 cmt. (Rule 2–100 forbids communication with represented persons "unless ... case law will override the rule."). But, as in other areas of the law, judicial approval cannot absolve the government from responsibility for wrongful acts when the government has misled the court in obtaining its sanction. See United States v. Leon, 468 U.S. 897, 914 (1984)("[T]he deference accorded to a magistrate's finding of probable cause does not preclude inquiry into the knowing or reckless falsity of the affidavit on which the determination was based."); Franks v. Delaware, 438 U.S. 154, 165 (1978)(warrant affidavit must be truthful "so as to allow the magistrate to make an independent evaluation of the matter"). When seeking the authorization of the district court, the prosecutor had an affirmative duty to avoid misleading the court. Rules of Professional Conduct of the State Bar of California Rule 5–200(B)(1988)("In presenting a matter to a tribunal, a member [s]hall not seek to mislead the judge, judicial officer or jury by an artifice or false statement of fact or law.").

The district court concluded that the magistrate judge approved the meeting between Lyons and Lopez in the mistaken belief, fostered by Lyons, that:

> "Tarlow[ ] was being paid by a third party with interests inimical to those of Lopez and that Lopez feared that if Tarlow became aware of his client's interest in cooperating with the government, he would pass the information on to others who would harm Lopez and/or his family." 765 F.Supp. at 1452.

The district court thus concluded that the magistrate judge's approval could not legally authorize Lyons to meet with Lopez.

The district court found that Lyons materially misled the magistrate judge regarding the facts surrounding Lopez's request to speak directly with the prosecutor. We agree that the magistrate judge apparently did not have a full understanding of the facts surrounding Lopez's request. Without that understanding, she could not have made an informed decision to authorize the communications.

Although it is not necessary to our determination in this case to decide whether the district court erred in its finding that Lyons materially misled the magistrate judge, we suggest that the finding is not sustainable without resolving certain conflicts in the testimony of Twitty, Lyons, and Lopez as to what Lyons knew and when he knew it (the district court, for whatever reason, said it was not necessary to resolve these conflicts). On remand, were the district court to consider lesser sanctions than dismissal of the indictment, resolution of these conflicts would be essential.

C.

The government makes several related arguments regarding the effect of Lopez's waiver on its ethical obligations. We note initially that it would be a mistake to speak in terms of a party "waiving" her "rights" under Rule 2–100. The rule against communicating with represented parties is fundamentally concerned with the duties of attorneys, not with the rights of parties. Lyons' duties as an attorney practicing in the Northern District of California extended beyond his obligation to respect Lopez's rights. Consequently, as the government concedes, ethical obligations are personal, and may not be vicariously waived.

The government also argues, however, that Lopez created a form of "hybrid representation" by waiving his right to counsel for the limited purpose of negotiating with the government, while retaining Tarlow as his counsel for all other purposes. Since Lopez would be unrepresented for purposes of discussions with the government, it would presumably not be a violation of Rule 2–100 for the government to communicate with him directly. We have in the past held, however, that "[i]f the defendant assumes any of the 'core functions' of the lawyer, ... the hybrid scheme is acceptable only if the defendant has voluntarily waived counsel." United States v. Turnbull, 888 F.2d 636, 638 (9th Cir.1989)(quoting United States v. Kimmel, 672 F.2d 720, 721 (9th Cir.1982)). Representing a client in negotiations with the government is certainly one of the core functions of defense counsel, and there is no question that Lopez did not waive his right to counsel. In fact, the magistrate judge, following the hearing with Lopez, clearly communicated to Lyons that while Lopez was waiving his right to have counsel present while inquiring about the possibility of cooperating with the government, he was not waiving his right to counsel. The district court found Lopez did not wish to waive his right to have an attorney present. In *Kimmel*, we explained that: [w]hen the accused assumes functions that are at the core of the lawyer's traditional role ... he will often undermine his own defense. Because he has a constitutional right to have his lawyer perform core functions, he must knowingly and intelligently waive that right. 672 F.2d at 721. While we are not immediately concerned with the constitutional dimensions of Lopez's communications with the government, it is clear that the magistrate judge's intervention could not, as a matter of law, have created a form of "hybrid representation." To the contrary, Lyons was notified by the court that Lopez was still represented by Tarlow, and consequently he could not evade his duty under Rule 2–100 on this basis.

For the same reason, we reject the government's claim that enforcing the ethical prohibition against communication with represented parties would interfere, under these circumstances, with the party's constitutional rights. The government relies on the doctrine established in Faretta v. California, 422 U.S. 806 (1975), that it is unconstitutional to require a criminal defendant to be represented by an attorney. We see no conflict between *Faretta* and Rule 2–100. Of course, Rule 2–100 does not bar communications with persons who have waived their right to counsel, for by its express terms the rule only applies to "communications with a represented party." Because Lopez did not waive his right to counsel, *Faretta* is immaterial.

D.

We therefore conclude that the district court was correct in holding that Lyons had an ethical duty to avoid communicating directly with Lopez regarding the criminal prosecution so long as Lopez was represented by Tarlow.

III.

The district court dismissed the indictment under its inherent supervisory powers. Finding the government's conduct "flagrant and egregious," and believing that Lopez had been prejudiced through loss of his attorney of choice, the district court reasoned that no lesser sanction could adequately preserve judicial integrity and deter future governmental misconduct. We review the district court's exercise of its supervisory powers for an abuse of discretion.

There are three legitimate grounds for a court's exercise of supervisory power: "to implement a remedy for the violation of a recognized statutory or constitutional right; to preserve judicial integrity by ensuring that a conviction rests on appropriate considerations validly before a jury; and to deter future illegal conduct." United States v. Simpson, 927 F.2d 1088, 1090 (9th Cir.1991). We have recognized that exercise of supervisory powers is an appropriate means of policing ethical misconduct by prosecutors. United States v. McClintock, 748 F.2d 1278, 1285–86 (9th Cir.1984); see also United States v. Williams, 504 U.S. 36, 46 (1992)("[T]he court's supervisory power ... may be used as a means of establishing standards of prosecutorial conduct before the courts themselves."). We also have expressly recognized the authority of the district court to dismiss actions where government attorneys have "willfully deceived the court," thereby interfering with "the orderly administration of justice." United States v. National Medical Enters., Inc., 792 F.2d 906, 912 (9th Cir.1986).

It was therefore within the discretion of the district court to act in an appropriate manner to discipline Lyons if he subverted of the attorney-client relationship. We have no doubt but that federal courts are empowered to deal with such threats to the integrity of the judicial process. In the words of the Supreme Court, "[f]ederal courts have an independent interest in ensuring that criminal trials are conducted within the ethical standards of the profession and that legal proceedings appear fair to all who observe them." Wheat v. United States, 486 U.S. 153, 160 (1988).

At the same time, however, even assuming that Lyons did act unethically, we question the prudence of remedying that misconduct through dismissal of a valid indictment. To justify such an extreme remedy, the government's conduct must have caused substantial prejudice to the defendant and been flagrant in its disregard for the limits of appropriate professional conduct.

In United States v. Owen, 580 F.2d 365 (9th Cir.1978), we adopted the view that, in order to justify dismissal of the indictment under the court's supervisory powers, there must "be some prejudice to the accused by virtue of the alleged acts of misconduct." We explained that the idea of prejudice entails that the government's conduct "had at least some impact on the verdict and thus redounded to [the defendant's] prejudice." Id. at 368 (quoting United States v. Acosta, 526 F.2d 670, 674 (5th Cir.1976)); see also United States v. Larrazolo, 869 F.2d 1354, 1358 (9th Cir.1989) ("a defendant must be actually prejudiced in order for the court to invoke its supervisory powers to dismiss an indictment for prosecutorial misconduct."). Thus, in *Owen*, we found no grounds for dismissal where the defendant could not show any effect from the government's actions "beyond the vague claim of a strain in his relationship with" his attorney. 580 F.2d at 368.

The district court specifically found that the attorney Lopez found to replace Tarlow following his withdrawal "is very able and will provide him with outstanding representation." Without in any way wishing to disparage the importance of a criminal defendant's choice of counsel, we fail to see how Tarlow's withdrawal in these circumstances could be said to have substantially prejudiced Lopez in his defense.

Consequently, even if the district court's finding that Lyons misled the court is correct, we conclude that the district court abused its discretion in dismissing the indictment. We are sensitive to the district court's concerns that none of the alternative sanctions available to it are as certain to impress the government with our resoluteness in holding prosecutors to the ethical standards which regulate the legal profession as a whole. At the same time, we are confident that, when there is no showing of substantial prejudice to the defendant, lesser sanctions, such as holding the prosecutor in contempt or referral to the state bar for disciplinary proceedings, can be adequate to discipline and punish government attorneys who attempt to circumvent the standards of their profession.

Accordingly, the order dismissing the indictment is vacated. The case is remanded for proceedings consistent with this opinion.

■ FLETCHER, CIRCUIT JUDGE, with whom CIRCUIT JUDGE T.G. NELSON joins, concurring:

At issue in this case is the conduct of the government. Because it does not seem to me that the story began or ended with the prosecutor's misbehavior, I feel compelled to say a few words about the actions of Mr. Tarlow, Mr. Twitty, and the magistrate judge.

Tarlow told Lopez at the outset of the representation that it was his "general policy" not to represent clients in plea negotiations that contemplate cooperation with the government. United States v. Lopez, 765 F.Supp. 1433, 1438–39 (N.D.Cal.1991). In a declaration submitted to the district court, Tarlow elaborated that he considers such negotiations "personally morally and ethically offensive," and that, while he would have conveyed an offer of cooperation to Lopez, "another attorney would be willing and better able to arrange his informant activities." Although Tarlow apparently did not say so explicitly, Lopez took Tarlow's policy statement to mean that if Lopez wanted to negotiate, Tarlow would withdraw from representing him altogether.

Concerned about the welfare of his children because he thought his wife might not be caring for them properly, Lopez decided that he wanted to explore the possibility of an earlier release by cooperating with the government. Lopez also wanted Tarlow to try the case if it went to trial. Faced with a difficult dilemma that he may not have anticipated when he retained Tarlow as counsel, Lopez decided to meet with the government unrepresented. I question whether Tarlow's "general policy" was in the best interests of his clients generally, and Lopez's specifically.

A criminal attorney who is bound by the Rules of Professional Conduct of the State Bar of California ("California Rules") and California's standards of professional conduct, as was Tarlow by virtue of the Northern District's Local Rule 110–3, is not free to terminate his or her representation of a client at will, or for mere personal considerations, or without the permission of the court. People v. Castillo, 233 Cal.App.3d 36, 284 Cal. Rptr. 382, 392 (1991)(citing People v. Murphy, 35 Cal.App.3d 905, 111 Cal.Rptr. 295, 304 (1973)); see also N.D.Cal. Local Rule 110–3 (attorneys practicing in Northern District must comply with "the standards of professional conduct required of members of the State Bar of California and contained in the State Bar Act, the Rules of Professional Conduct of the State Bar of California, and decisions of any court applicable thereto"). Notably, although under the ABA Model Rules of Professional Conduct ("ABA Model Rules") an attorney may withdraw from representation if the client "insists upon pursuing an objective that the lawyer considers repugnant or imprudent," no comparable provision appears in the California Rules. Compare ABA Model Rule 1.16(b)(3) with Cal. Rule 3–700(C). See also Morris v. Slappy, 461 U.S. 1, 24 n. 6 (1983)(Brennan, J., concurring)(noting that continuous representation of a criminal defendant throughout trial court proceedings " 'affords the best opportunity for the development of a close and confidential attorney-client relationship' ")(quoting ABA Standards for Criminal Justice); Harold S. Lewis, Jr., Commentary: Shaffer's Suffering Client, Freedman's Suffering Lawyer, 38 Cath.U.L.Rev. 129, 133 n. 13 (criticizing Model Rule 1.16(b)(3) for allowing an attorney to withdraw for reasons of conscience because it "unfairly disappoints the client's reasonable expectations.") Because moral repugnance is not listed in the California Rules as a ground for permissive withdrawal, and because a criminal defense lawyer may not be entitled to assert moral repugnance to plea bargaining in any event, it is not certain, were a court to consider the matter, that Tarlow's general policy would prevail over a client's wish to pursue preliminary plea discussions with the government. See John W. Hall, Jr., Professional Responsibility of the Criminal Lawyer § 14.2, at 472 (1987)("If the nature of the case warrants it, defense counsel should explore plea discussions with the prosecutor."); cf. Mason v. Balcom, 531 F.2d 717 (5th Cir.1976)(ineffective assistance in part due to counsel's failure to plea bargain when his client may have benefitted); People v. Frierson, 39 Cal.3d 803, 218 Cal.Rptr. 73, 78–79, 705 P.2d 396, 401–03 (1985)(listing fundamental decisions over which the defendant, rather than his or her counsel, retains ultimate control; "the decision whether to plead guilty to a lesser offense ... frequently reflects strategic concerns, but a defendant nonetheless retains personal control over such a plea."); Cal. Rule 3–510(A)(1)("A member [of the state bar] shall promptly communicate ... [a]ll terms and conditions of any offer made to the client in a criminal matter."); ABA Model Rule 1.4 comment ("A lawyer who receives ... a proffered plea bargain in a criminal case should promptly inform the client of its substance unless prior discussions with the client have left it clear that the proposal will be unacceptable.")

Ideally, sufficient candor and trust are present in an attorney-client relationship such that a defendant does not feel compelled to resort to clandestine meetings with the government. Indeed, the model of a successful attorney-client relationship, as expounded in *Strickland v. Washington*, is one in which "[c]ounsel's actions are ... based ... on informed strategic choices made by the defendant and on information supplied by the defendant." 466 U.S. 668, 691 (1984); see also Campbell v. Kincheloe, 829 F.2d 1453, 1463 (9th Cir.1987)("The client's wishes are not to be ignored entirely."). Tarlow's relationship with Lopez fell far short of the ideal.

As for Twitty, counsel for codefendant Escobedo, his conduct was, undeniably, less than exemplary. Twitty had access to Lopez at Pleasanton correctional facility, where Escobedo was also incarcerated, because Twitty was responsible for what may have been an ill-conceived "joint investigation" of the two defendants' cases. In view of Lopez's problem with Tarlow, Twitty may have intervened in Lopez's affairs with benign intentions, but ultimately he ended up representing two defendants who had potentially conflicting interests. Although he informed Lopez that he could not act as his lawyer, Twitty nonetheless apparently advised both Lopez and Escobedo during the first meeting with the government, and may have pressured Lopez to provide information to the prosecutor during the second.

The Sixth Amendment contemplates that the assistance of counsel be "untrammeled and unimpaired by . . . requiring that one lawyer should simultaneously represent conflicting interests." Glasser v. United States, 315 U.S. 60, 70 (1942); see also Cal.Rule 3–310(B)("A member [of the state bar] shall not concurrently represent clients whose interests conflict, except with their informed written consent."); ABA Model Rule 1.7(b)("A lawyer shall not represent a client if the representation of that client may be materially limited by the lawyers' responsibilities to another client . . . unless . . . the lawyer reasonably believes the representation will not be adversely affected[ ] and . . . the client consents after consultation.") When an attorney represents defendants with conflicting interests, "the evil . . . is in what the advocate finds himself compelled to refrain from doing, not only at trial but also as to possible pretrial plea negotiations. . . . [T]o assess the impact of a conflict of interest on the attorney's options, tactics, and decisions in plea negotiations would be virtually impossible." Holloway v. Arkansas, 435 U.S. 475, 490–91 (1978).

Significantly, the government had apparently taken the position that a plea agreement would be possible only in the event that both Lopez and Escobedo agreed to cooperate. Assuming he felt that such cooperation was in his own best interest, Escobedo thus had an incentive to pressure Lopez to cooperate as well. Under these circumstances, Twitty was the wrong person to be acting on Lopez's behalf during plea discussions with the government.

Finally, there are the actions of the magistrate judge to consider. Although at the hearing before the magistrate the prosecutor apparently did not say anything about his suspicion regarding the source of payment for Tarlow's fees, the district court found that the magistrate "was operating under the mistaken assumption" that Tarlow was "being paid by a third party with interests inimical to those of Lopez." 765 F.2d at 1452. Because the prosecutor had previously communicated such a theory to the presiding district judge and because he failed to disabuse the magistrate of her erroneous assumption, the district court found that the government "effectively misled" the magistrate. The district court further found that the magistrate did not ask Lopez certain critical questions when he appeared before her, namely, whether Tarlow's fees were in fact being paid by someone with a conflicting interest, or whether Lopez feared for his or his family's safety should Tarlow learn of the pending plea negotiations.

The magistrate was confronted with a difficult situation. Unfortunately, her decision to allow Lopez to meet with the government ultimately led to Lopez's losing Tarlow as his counsel, the very result Lopez had sought to avoid. Although, as the district court found, her actions may have been "understandable" in view of her assumption that Tarlow was being paid by an interested third party, her judgment may have benefitted from a more thorough questioning of Lopez regarding the fee arrangement with Tarlow. Some different options might have presented themselves had she been convinced that the safety of Lopez and his family were not at stake.

In this era of guideline sentencing, when the applicable guideline often assumes more importance than the crime of conviction, it is not unreasonable that a defendant would want to find out what the government might offer. Various forces conspired to render that inquiry exceedingly difficult for Lopez. Contrary to the intent of the Sixth Amendment, he was left to face the " 'prosecutorial forces of organized society' " alone. Moran v. Burbine, 475 U.S. 412, 430 (1986)(quoting Maine v. Moulton, 474 U.S. 159, 170 (1985)). Others besides the prosecutor contributed to this regrettable result.

INTRODUCTORY NOTE ON "ACCEPTANCE OF RESPONSIBILITY"

Near the end of Attorney General Thornburgh's 1989 Memorandum on Plea Bargaining, he suggests that much of the plea bargaining discretion traditionally exercised by prosecutors can be retained under the Guidelines through the use of the "acceptance of responsibility" ground for reduction of sentence. Section 3E1.1 of the Guidelines provides for an automatic two-level reduction in a defendant's offense level if the defendant sufficiently acknowledges his or her "personal responsibility" for the crime. As noted by Attorney General Thornburgh, this can lead to a substantial sentence reduction (perhaps as high as 35% or more). The two cases that follow address the "acceptance of responsibility" sentence reduction. Do such sentence reductions constitute a useful way to reconcile plea bargaining with determinate sentencing?

United States v. Rosales

United States Court of Appeals, Ninth Circuit, 1990.
917 F.2d 1220.

Before GOODWIN, CHIEF JUDGE, and BROWNING and RYMER, CIRCUIT JUDGES.

■ GOODWIN, CHIEF JUDGE.

Adislado Rosales appeals his sentence upon his guilty plea to misprision of a felony (distribution of heroin) in violation 18 U.S.C. § 4. He contends that the district court erred in not reducing his base offense level for acceptance of responsibility and in considering the total amount of heroin involved in the underlying felony in setting his base offense level. We affirm the sentence.

DEA agent Pete Ramirez made arrangements with codefendant Enrique Mendez Pineda (Mendez) to purchase ten ounces of heroin for $22,000. Ramirez and Mendez agreed to conduct the transaction on May 23, 1989, in the parking lot in front of a Pay N' Save store in San Jose, California.

At the designated time and place, Mendez, accompanied by Rosales and another passenger, drove a pickup truck into the parking lot. Mendez met with Ramirez, who gave Mendez the $22,000. After counting the money, Mendez agreed to let Ramirez accompany him to the pickup truck to retrieve the heroin. Upon reaching the passenger side of the vehicle, where Rosales was sitting, Ramirez asked Rosales to show him the "thing." Rosales retrieved a grocery bag containing 230 grams of heroin. Mendez obtained the bag of heroin and walked with Ramirez to his vehicle. At the same time, Rosales drove and parked the pickup truck near Ramirez's vehicle. Ramirez gave the arrest signal to surveillance units, and Mendez was arrested.

Meanwhile, as the arresting agents arrived, Rosales attempted to drive away in the pickup truck. Following a vehicle and foot chase, Rosales was arrested and taken into custody.

Rosales was indicted on one count each of conspiracy to possess heroin and possession of heroin, and entered a plea of not guilty. A superseding indictment was subsequently returned. The charges against Rosales remained the same, and he again entered a plea of not guilty.

On October 11, 1989, a one-count information was filed charging Rosales with misprision of a felony (distribution of heroin) in violation of 18 U.S.C. § 4. He waived indictment by grand jury and pleaded guilty to the information.

A presentence report (PSR) was filed with the district court on December 4, 1989. Prior to the sentencing hearing, Rosales filed written objections to the PSR, arguing in part that he was entitled to a sentence reduction for acceptance of responsibility and that the PSR improperly calculated his base offense level of 17 on the basis of the entire amount of heroin contained in the bag.

The PSR calculated Rosales's base offense level of 17 in the following manner: The base offense level for misprision of a felony is [set by the Guidelines at] nine levels lower than the offense level for the underlying offense. United States Sentencing Guidelines (U.S.S.G.) § 2X4.1. The base offense level for the underlying offense, possession with intent to distribute 230 grams of heroin, is 26, U.S.S.G. § 2D1.1(c)(9), and thus the adjusted offense level for misprision is 17. The PSR recommended no offense level reduction for acceptance of responsibility.

At the sentencing hearing, Rosales reiterated his objections to the PSR. The district court accepted the PSR's determination that the base offense level was 17, and sentenced Rosales to 24 months of imprisonment and one year of supervised release.

1. Acceptance of Responsibility

At the outset, Rosales argues that the district court made inadequate findings under the Guidelines in denying him a two-point reduction in his offense level for acceptance of responsibility. He also contends that the district court's failure to make specific findings violated Fed. R. Crim. P. 32(c)(3)(D). Neither has merit.

In resolving objections to the presentence report, "the district court should make clear on the record its resolution of all disputed matters, and ... specific findings of fact are to be encouraged." United States v. Rigby, 896 F.2d 392, 394 (9th Cir.1990). The district court satisfies the above requirement by adopting the conclusions in the PSR. United States v. Corley, 909 F.2d 359, 362 (9th Cir.1990); *Rigby*, 896 F.2d at 394.

Here, there were no substantial factual disputes. The district court, for more than a month before the sentencing hearing, had Rosales's PSR, which recommended against an offense level reduction for acceptance of responsibility. The district court also had the benefit of Rosales's written objections to the PSR challenging the denial of an offense level reduction for acceptance of responsibility.

At the sentencing hearing, Rosales's counsel argued that Rosales was entitled to a two-point reduction for acceptance of responsibility. The government argued that the PSR should be followed. The district court accepted the government's position that the sentencing recommendation in the PSR should be followed, and proceeded to sentence Rosales in accordance with the base offense level of 17 calculated by the PSR. By adopting the PSR and its recommendations, the district court thereby denied Rosales a two-point offense level reduction for acceptance of responsibility. See *Corley*, 909 F.2d at 362 (district court made adequate findings in denying an offense level reduction for acceptance of responsibility where the district court indicated its acceptance of the government's position that the offense level reduction should not be granted and proceeded to sentence the defendant in accordance with the PSR's recommendations). As in *Corley*, " 'the record at the sentencing hearing reflects no confusion on anyone's part as to what the district court decided.' " *Corley*, 909 F.2d at 362 (quoting *Rigby*, 896 F.2d at 394).

We reject on similar grounds Rosales's argument that the district court failed to comply with Fed. R. Crim. P. 32(c)(3)(D). The district judge was presented with the PSR and Rosales's written objections to the PSR, gave Rosales an opportunity to argue at sentencing why he should receive the reduction for acceptance of responsibility, and adopted the presentence report's recommendation. No more was required under Rule 32(c)(3)(D). See id. at 362 (rejecting defendant's claim that the district court violated Rule 32(c)(3)(D) where it had the defendant's PSR before it, asked defendant's counsel whether there were any misstatements of fact in the PSR, and sentenced the defendant in accordance with the PSR's recommendations).

Rosales next contends that the district court erred in refusing to reduce his base offense level for an acceptance of responsibility. There was no error. Whether a defendant has accepted responsibility for a crime is a question of fact which this court reviews for clear error. United States v. Gonzalez, 897 F.2d 1018, 1019 (9th Cir.1990). The district court's determination will not be disturbed "unless it is without foundation." United States v. Smith, 905 F.2d 1296, 1301 (9th Cir.1990)(quoting U.S.S.G. § 3E1.1, Application Note 5).

A defendant is entitled to an offense-level reduction "if the defendant clearly demonstrates a recognition and affirmative acceptance of personal responsibility for his criminal conduct...." U.S.S.G. § 3E1.1. The defendant has the burden of showing acceptance of responsibility. United States v. Howard, 894 F.2d 1085, 1090 n. 4 (9th Cir.1990).

Rosales argues that he is entitled to the offense level reduction for acceptance of responsibility because he pleaded guilty immediately upon the filing of the information charging him with misprision of a felony.

While "a guilty plea may provide some evidence of the defendant's acceptance of responsibility, ... it does not, by itself, entitle a defendant to a reduced sentence...." U.S.S.G. § 3E1.1, Application Note 3. Here, Rosales pleaded guilty only after the original charges against him were reduced to misprision. Pleading to a reduced charge does not necessarily demonstrate an acceptance of responsibility. It is at least equally possible that the defendant has made a clever bargain. At no time did Rosales express remorse for his conduct.[3] Accordingly, the district court properly denied Rosales an offense level reduction for acceptance of responsibility....

Accordingly, the sentence is affirmed.

United States v. Acosta–Olivas

United States Court of Appeals, Tenth Circuit, 1995.
71 F.3d 375.

Before ANDERSON, LOGAN, and REAVLEY, CIRCUIT JUDGES.

■ ANDERSON, CIRCUIT JUDGE.

The government appeals from the district court's imposition of a seventy-eight month sentence on defendant Jesus Acosta–Olivas. The district court determined that Mr. Acosta–Olivas qualified for a downward departure from the statutory minimum mandatory sentence often years, because he met all the requirements of 18 U.S.C. § 3553(f).[1] This appeal addresses the scope of § 3553(f)(5), which requires defendants seeking relief from a statutory mandatory minimum to truthfully provide the government with "all information and evidence the defendant has concerning the offense or offenses that were part of the same course of conduct or of a common scheme or plan." 18 U.S.C. § 3553(f)(5). For the following reasons, we remand.

---

[3] Rosales's counsel conjectures that Rosales failed to clearly accept responsibility due to a language barrier. At the plea hearing, however, the district court specifically asked Rosales whether he understood his interpreter and he responded in the affirmative.

[1] The language of § 3553(f) has been adopted verbatim in the United States Sentencing Comm'n Guidelines Manual at § 5C1.2.

Background

On March 9, 1994, Francisco Javier Rosales–Quiroz, accompanied by his wife and small child, drove a 1990 Nissan Sentra to the United States Border Patrol checkpoint near Truth or Consequences, New Mexico. When questioned by Border Patrol agents about their citizenship, they produced documentation, and when questioned about the car, Rosales–Quiroz stated that he owned the car and had purchased it approximately fifteen days before. A Border Patrol agent apparently recognized the car as the type which was commonly used to hide contraband in its bumpers. When he inspected the rear bumper of the Rosales–Quiroz car, the agent noticed that mud had been placed on the bolts and brackets. With Rosales–Quiroz's consent, the agent removed the rear bumper and found fourteen plastic packages containing a substance which field-tested positive for cocaine. Rosales–Quiroz and his wife were arrested, and a search of their car revealed 23.4 kilograms of cocaine.

Rosales–Quiroz gave conflicting stories as to the details of where in Albuquerque the cocaine was to be delivered. However, consistent with what he had told one DEA agent, Rosales–Quiroz called a telephone number in El Paso, Texas, and was told to go to room 213 at the Howard Johnson Plaza Hotel in Albuquerque. A DEA agent supervised this phone call. When agents went to the hotel, they observed a man matching Rosales–Quiroz's description of "Willie," whom Rosales–Quiroz said paid him to deliver the cocaine. When Rosales–Quiroz and another agent drove Rosales–Quiroz's car to the hotel parking lot, Mr. Acosta–Olivas approached the car and asked the agent if he had the "produce." When the agent indicated it was in the car, Mr. Acosta–Olivas said he did not want to remove the drugs in the parking lot, and said he would follow the car to a warehouse where they could remove the contraband. When he returned to the parking lot to get into his car, after collecting his family from the hotel, Mr. Acosta–Olivas was arrested.

Rosales–Quiroz pled guilty to conspiracy to possess cocaine with intent to distribute. The government filed a motion stating that he had provided substantial assistance to the government under USSG 5K1.1, and he was sentenced to 24 months imprisonment. Mr. Acosta–Olivas also pled guilty, but refused to cooperate with the government. He did, however, provide the government and court with a letter describing his own involvement in the conspiracy.

Because of the quantity of cocaine involved, Mr. Acosta–Olivas was subject to the statutory mandatory minimum of ten years, under 21 U.S.C. § 841(b)(1)(A). He sought relief from the mandatory minimum under 18 U.S.C. § 3553(f). The district court determined that he qualified under § 3553(f) for relief from the minimum mandatory sentence and calculated his sentence as follows: the court adopted the presentence report recommendation that the base offense level was 34 under USSG § 2D1.1(c)(3), based upon the 23.4 kilograms of cocaine. The court also adopted the presentence report's recommendation that Mr. Acosta–Olivas receive the maximum three-level adjustment for acceptance of responsibility under USSG § 3E1.1(a) & (b). The court gave Mr. Acosta–Olivas a further three-level adjustment because he was a minor participant.[2] The court accordingly calculated that the total offense level was 28, which, with Mr. Acosta–Olivas' criminal history category, yielded a guideline range of 78–97 months. The court sentenced him to a seventy-eight month term. This appeal by the government followed.

DISCUSSION

The only issue in this case is whether the district court correctly determined that Mr. Acosta–Olivas met the requirements of 18 U.S.C. § 3553(f)(5). Section 3553(f) provides that a defendant can be given a guideline sentence, instead of the mandatory minimum prescribed by statute, if the court finds at sentencing that:

"(1) the defendant does not have more than 1 criminal history point, as determined under the sentencing guidelines;

"(2) the defendant did not use violence or credible threats of violence or possess a firearm or other dangerous weapon (or induce another participant to do so) in connection with the offense;

"(3) the offense did not result in death or serious bodily injury to any person;

"(4) the defendant was not an organizer, leader, manager, or supervisor of others in the offense, as determined under the sentencing guidelines and was not engaged in a continuing criminal enterprise, as defined in 21 U.S.C. 848; and

"(5) not later than the time of the sentencing hearing, the defendant has truthfully provided to the Government all information and evidence the defendant has concerning the offense or offenses that were part of the same course of conduct or of a common scheme or plan, but the fact that the defendant has no relevant or useful other information to provide or that the Government is already aware of the information shall not preclude a determination by the court that the defendant has complied with this requirement." 18 U.S.C. 3553(f).

The government argues that § 3553(f)(5) requires a defendant "to tell the government all he knows about the offense of conviction and the relevant conduct, including the identities and participation of others, in order to qualify for relief from the statutory mandatory minimum sentence." Appellant's Br. at 10. Mr. Acosta–Olivas argues that the section merely requires him to detail his own personal involvement in the crime, and he asserts that the district court correctly held that his letter met that standard. We review de novo the district court's interpretation of a statute

---

[2] The presentence report recommended no downward adjustment for Mr. Acosta–Olivas' role in the offense.

or the sentencing guidelines.[3]

Section 3553(f) was enacted as a "safety valve" to permit courts to sentence less culpable defendants to sentences under the guidelines, instead of imposing mandatory minimum sentences. As the legislative history of the section states, without such a safety valve, for "the very offenders who most warrant proportionally lower sentences—offenders that by guideline definitions are the least culpable—mandatory minimums generally operate to block the sentence from reflecting mitigating factors." H.R.Rep. No. 103–460, 103d Cong., 2d Sess. (1994). This would have the unfortunate effect that the "least culpable offenders may receive the same sentences as their relatively more culpable counterparts." Id. The legislative history does not, however, assist us in interpreting the scope of § 3553(f)(5). We conclude that the plain language of the statute and its implementing guideline, as well as the scheme of the guidelines, indicate that the government's interpretation is correct. The few cases addressing this provision with any specificity have so held.

As indicated, the statute and guideline themselves require the disclosure of "all information and evidence . . . concerning the offense or offenses that were part of the same course of conduct or of a common scheme or plan." 18 U.S.C. § 3553(f)(5). The phrase "all information and evidence" is obviously broad. The Application Notes to § 5C1.2 define "offense or offenses that were part of the same course of conduct or of a common scheme or plan" to mean "the offense of conviction and all relevant conduct." USSG § 5C1.2, comment. (n.3). "Relevant conduct" has in turn been defined to include "in the case of a jointly undertaken criminal activity . . . all reasonably foreseeable acts and omissions of others in furtherance of the jointly undertaken criminal activity." USSG § 1B1.3(a)(1)(B). Thus, the guidelines appear to require disclosure of "all information" concerning the offense of conviction and the acts of others if the offense of conviction is a conspiracy or other joint activity.

As applied to Mr. Acosta–Olivas, the guideline would therefore require disclosure of everything he knows about his own actions and those of his co-conspirators. See United States v. Rodriguez, 69 F.3d 136 (7th Cir.1995)(affirming district court's conclusion that defendant was ineligible for a § 3553(f) reduction because "he produced no information concerning the offense; if he did not know the identities of [drug suppliers or buyers], then he should have at least communicated that fact to the government");

---

[3] In this case, the district court interpreted the scope and meaning of § 3553(f)(5). We therefore review that legal determination de novo. We note, however, that a district court's application of the correct legal standard to a particular defendant, and the specific conclusion that the defendant is or is not eligible for relief under § 3553(f), would ordinarily be reviewed for clear error. See United States v. Rodriguez, 69 F.3d 136 (7th Cir.1995)("We believe that the district court's determination that a defendant is not eligible for the reduction permitted by sec. 5C1.2 ought to be governed by the clearly erroneous standard. The court's determination is a fact-specific one and will often depend on credibility determinations that cannot be replicated with the same accuracy on appeal.").

United States v. Wrenn, 66 F.3d 1, 3 (1st Cir.1995)(rejecting applicability of § 3553(f), stating defendant "did not provide the government with all of the information and evidence he had concerning the very crime to which he pleaded guilty [and observing] he claimed to have a number of reliable customers to whom he supplied cocaine, but he supplied nary a name to the government"); United States v. Saint Martinez, 1995 WL 328127 Dist. (D.N.J.1995)(holding defendant ineligible for safety valve because he "failed to provide information that was highly likely to be [in] his possession," including identities of co-conspirators); United States v. Buffington, 879 F.Supp. 1220, 1223 (N.D.Ga.1995)("Defendant is obliged to provide information relevant to his own course of conduct and his immediate chain of distributors, i.e., from whom he bought and to whom he sold, if he wishes to avail himself of the benefits of § 3553(f)."); see also Vincent L. Broderick, Flexible Sentencing and the Violent Crime Control Act of 1994, 7 Fed. Sentencing Rep. 128, 129 (1994)(describing § 3553(f)(5) as a " 'tell all that you can tell' requirement").

Mr. Acosta–Olivas argues that this interpretation has the effect of requiring him to become a government informant, and thereby renders USSG § 5K1.1 on substantial assistance redundant. As both parties point out, we should interpret statutory provisions and the guidelines in a way which gives meaning and effect to each part of the statutory or guideline scheme. In holding that § 3553(f)(5), and therefore § 5C1.2, require a defendant to disclose all that he knows concerning both his own involvement in the crime and that of any co-conspirators, we do not render any part of the guidelines superfluous or redundant.

Section 5K1.1 concerning substantial assistance operates very differently from § 5C1.2. Section 5K1.1 requires a motion from the government and the government's evaluation of the extent of the defendant's assistance is given "substantial weight." USSG § 5K1.1, comment. (n.3). Under § 5C1.2, by contrast, the court determines whether a defendant has complied with its provisions, including subsection 5. And the section specifically states that a defendant may still enjoy the benefits of the section even if the information he provides is not "relevant or useful" to the government. As one court recently observed, it:

> "eliminates the necessity for a defendant to obtain a letter from the prosecution under section 5K1 . . . in order to obtain a reduction of an otherwise mandatory minimum sentence. Instead, a defendant may come forward and furnish all available information and obtain consideration as a result if justified, regardless of the position of the prosecutor and regardless of whether anyone else can be prosecuted and convicted based on the defendant's disclosures." Shendur v. United States, 874 F.Supp. 85, 87 (S.D.N.Y. 1995).

Thus, § 5C1.2, if its directive that a defendant disclose "all information" is interpreted to require disclosure of the identities of co-conspirators, does not make § 5K1.1 redundant. See Broderick, supra, at 129 (describing § 3553(f)(5)'s "tell all that you can tell" requirement as "less draconian that the former reliance on letters from the prosecutors under § 5K1.1"). It operates differently anyway, regardless of whether a defendant must "tell all" or not.

On the other hand, Mr. Acosta–Olivas' interpretation of § 3553(f)(5) and § 5C1.2 renders USSG § 3E1.1(b)(1) concerning enhanced acceptance of responsibility largely redundant. Under § 3E1.1(b)(1), a defendant with an initial offense level of 16 or higher, like Mr. Acosta–Olivas, can qualify for an additional 1 level decrease if he "timely provid[es] complete information to the government concerning his own involvement in the offense." USSG § 3E1.1(b)(1). While § 3E1.1(b)(1) requires "timely disclosure," and § 5C1.2(5) requires disclosure "not later than the time of sentencing," Mr. Acosta–Olivas' interpretation of § 5C 1.2(5) to only require disclosure of his own involvement would make the two sections virtually identical.

In sum, § 3553(f), as repeated in guideline § 5C1.2, was clearly intended to permit courts to sentence relatively less culpable offenders to sentences below an otherwise applicable mandatory statutory minimum sentence. Besides requiring that a defendant seeking to avail himself of this safety valve meet certain objective criteria, the section also requires that a defendant truthfully tell all he knows to the government, regardless of whether this information is useful to the government. Presumably, this requirement assists courts in determining whether a defendant truly is relatively less culpable. We therefore hold that the district court erred in interpreting § 3553(f)(5) to require a defendant to reveal only information regarding his own involvement in the crime, not information he has relating to other participants.

For the foregoing reasons, we remand this case with instructions to vacate the sentence and resentence. If, at resentencing, the court makes a factual finding that, in deciding what information to disclose to the government, Mr. Acosta–Olivas relied upon the district court's interpretation of § 3553(f)(5), the court shall allow him the opportunity to comply with the statute as this court has interpreted it in this opinion.

NOTE ON *ACOSTA–OLIVAS*

The Eighth Circuit in *Acosta-Olivas* describes § 3553(f) as a "safety valve" allowing sentence mitigation without the necessity of the defendant obtaining a "letter" from the federal prosecutor. But does not the court's ruling effectively convert § 3553(f) into yet another useful tool for federal prosecutors seeking to increase their leverage over low-level drug conspirators?

SECTION 4: THE FEDERAL DEATH PENALTY

In 1972, the Supreme Court decided the landmark case of Furman v. Georgia, 408 U.S. 238 (1972), holding that all then-existing state and federal death penalty statutes violated the "cruel and unusual punishment" clause of the Eighth Amendment to the U.S. Constitution. Four years later, in Gregg v. Georgia, 428 U.S. 153 (1976), the Court upheld the newly enacted death-penalty statutes of Georgia, Florida, and Texas, explaining that Furman invalidated not the death penalty per se, but only the way that capital punishment was administered under the old statutes. The net result of *Furman* and *Gregg* was that the death penalty itself passed constitutional muster, but required the use of special procedures designed to minimize arbitrary, capricious, and discriminatory application of capital punishment. These special Eighth Amendment procedures are today known as "guided discretion."

Within a few years after *Gregg,* more than two-thirds of the states had enacted new death-penalty statutes containing the required special procedures. Congress, however, long declined to enact such curative procedural legislation. Thus, although many federal crimes continued to provide for a possible death sentence, the death penalty could not constitutionally be imposed for those federal crimes. The federal death penalty was, for all practical purposes, non-existent.

This situation changed when Congress enacted the Anti–Drug Abuse Act of 1988. In the Act, Congress authorized capital punishment for those who intentionally kill another person in connection with certain serious federal drug offenses. The Act contains its own special procedural provisions in response to *Furman* and *Gregg* (and numerous other intervening Eighth Amendment decisions). The first capital cases under the Act began to reach the Courts of Appeals in the early 1990's.

In 1994, Congress greatly expanded the possible application of the federal death penalty. In the Federal Death Penalty Act of 1994, enacted as part of the omnibus Violent Crime Control and Law Enforcement Act of 1994, Congress did two things: (1) it enacted generally applicable procedural provisions, in response to *Furman* and *Gregg*, to conform to the Eighth Amendment's "guided discretion" requirement and thereby "revive" existing but long-dormant federal death-penalty statutes, and (2) it added the death penalty as a possible punishment for a whole new range of federal crimes.

Moreover, in 1996, Congress enacted reforms designed to streamline federal collateral review proceedings and thereby reduce the average time between the imposition of a death sentence and its ultimate execution. The Antiterrorism and Effective Death Penalty Act of 1996, 110 Stat. 1214, implemented such changes in both 28 U.S.C. § 2254 (dealing with federal collateral review of state cases) and 28 U.S.C. § 2255 (dealing with such review in federal cases).

In light of the 1988, 1994, and 1996 statutes, it seems likely that, in the future, the death penalty will once again begin to play a significant role in the federal criminal justice system. Beyond the standard arguments for and against capital punishment, see Stephen Nathanson, An Eye for an Eye? The Morality of Punishing by Death (1987), what special problems are presented by the use of capital punishment for federal crimes? For example, is it appropriate for the death penalty to be available for federal crimes committed within states that do not have the death penalty (e.g., Wisconsin)? Is such an apparent anomaly tolerable, even if the capital crime under federal law is less heinous (relatively speaking) than many crimes that could not even lead to life imprisonment under the relevant state law? Should the federal death penalty perhaps be limited to crimes in which the intrusion against federal interests is significant enough, above and beyond any intrusions against traditional state interests, to warrant such an extreme punishment (e.g., treason, espionage, or murder of a Federal official)?

United States v. Pitera

United States District Court, Eastern District of New York, 1992.
795 F.Supp. 546.

■ RAGGI, DISTRICT JUDGE:

Thomas Pitera stands before the court charged in a twenty count indictment with racketeering, drug trafficking, and various firearms violations. Count Three of the indictment accuses Mr. Pitera of killing two persons, Richard Leone and Solomon Stern, while engaging in or working in furtherance of a continuing criminal enterprise. Such conduct carries a possible sentence of death. 21 U.S.C. § 848(e)(1)(A). The government has served notice of its intent to seek the death penalty if Mr. Pitera is found guilty of Count Three.[1]

Mr. Pitera challenges the constitutionality of § 848(e)(1)(A)'s death penalty provision. Joining in the attack as amici curiae are the Association of the Bar of the City of New York, the New York State Defenders Association, the National Association of Criminal Defense Lawyers, the New York State Association of Criminal Defense Lawyers, the National Legal Aid and Defender Association, and the New York Criminal Bar Association. Defendant and/or amici advance the following arguments: I. any form of capital punishment violates the eighth amendment's prohibition of cruel and unusual punishment; II. the particular federal statute at issue fails adequately to ensure that the death penalty will not be imposed in an arbitrary and capricious manner in that: A. the capital crime itself is both vague and irrational, B. the sentencing scheme relies on duplicative and vague statutory aggravating factors, C. the sentencing scheme permits reliance on unlimited non-statutory aggravating factors, D. the sentencing scheme impermissibly limits consideration of mitigating factors, E. the sentencing hearing is not governed by the Federal Rules of Evidence, and F. meaningful appellate review is not ensured; [and] III. Mr. Pitera was singled out for arbitrary and vindicative prosecution.[a]

Defendant asks the court to address these constitutionality challenges before trial since jury selection as well as defense trial strategy may differ considerably in a capital versus a non-capital case. See, e.g., Fed.R.Crim.P. 24(b)(providing twenty peremptory challenges per side if a defendant is charged with a crime punishable by death); 18 U.S.C. § 3432 (capital charge requires disclosure to defendant of a list of veniremen and place of

---

[1] This case is the first in the Second Circuit in which the United States seeks the death penalty pursuant to § 848(e)(1).

[a] In an omitted section of the opinion, the court also rejected the defendant's claim that Congress's failure to provide a specific procedure for executing a defendant pursuant to § 848(e)(1) violated the Eighth Amendment, and that any later attempt by Congress to provide such a procedure would violate the Ex Post Facto Clause. [Footnote by eds.]

abode three days before commencement of trial). This court has therefore carefully considered all arguments advanced by the parties and amici. It rejects the constitutional attack on 21 U.S.C. § 848(e)(1)(A). The parties were advised orally of this ruling on April 27, 1992. This memorandum details the reasons for the court's decision.

Statutory Background: The Anti–Drug Abuse Act of 1988

The Anti–Drug Abuse Act of 1988 makes it a capital offense intentionally to kill another person in connection with the commission of serious federal drug crimes. Specifically, 21 U.S.C. § 848(e)(1)(A) provides:

> "[A]ny person engaging in or working in furtherance of a continuing criminal enterprise, or any person engaging in an offense punishable under section 841(b)(1)(A) of this title or section 960(b)(1) who intentionally kills or counsels, commands, induces, procures, or causes the intentional killing of an individual and such killing results, shall be sentenced to any term of imprisonment, which shall not be less than 20 years and which may be up to life imprisonment, or may be sentenced to death....[2]"

The Act details procedures to be followed before a defendant can be executed. Initially, the government must serve notice "a reasonable time before trial" of its intent to seek the death penalty. 21 U.S.C. § 848(h)(1). If a defendant is found guilty of violating § 848(e)(1)(A), a separate sentencing hearing must be conducted, generally before the same jury that determined guilt. 21 U.S.C. § 848(i)(1)(A). The purpose of the hearing is to permit consideration of any "aggravating" and "mitigating" factors relevant to whether or not the defendant should be sentenced to death. 21 U.S.C. § 841(j). The information adduced need not conform to the Federal Rules of Evidence, so long as the court is convinced that its "probative value is [not] substantially outweighed by the danger of unfair prejudice, confusion of the issues, or misleading the jury." 21 U.S.C. § 848(j).

The process by which a jury is to consider sentencing factors is specific. Preliminarily, the government must prove beyond a reasonable doubt and to the unanimous satisfaction of the jury at least two of the aggravating factors expressly set forth in the statute (hereinafter referred to as "statutory aggravating factors"). 21 U.S.C. § 848(j) and (k). Moreover, it must advise the defendant a reasonable time before trial of which statutory aggravating factors it intends to prove. 21 U.S.C. § 848(h)(1). One of these must be from among the four listed in § 848(h)(1). The other must be from among those listed in § 848(n)(2)-(12). Absent proof of these statutory aggravating factors, a jury cannot vote to impose the death penalty. 21 U.S.C. § 848(k).

If a jury is satisfied that at least two such statutory aggravating factors have been proved, it may then consider any mitigating factors established

---

[2] The statute provides the same possible penalties for an individual who, in the course of committing certain drug offenses, intentionally kills or counsels, commands, induces, procures, or causes the intentional killing of a law enforcement officer. 21 U.S.C. § 848(e)(1)(B). That section is not at issue in this case.

by the defendant, whether from among those listed in § 848(m) or not, and any other aggravating factors of which the government gives notice in advance of trial (hereinafter referred to as "non-statutory aggravating factors"). 21 U.S.C. § 848(h)(1)(B), (j), and (k). Although non-statutory aggravating factors must be proved to the jury's unanimous satisfaction beyond a reasonable doubt, mitigating factors need only be established by a preponderance of the evidence. Moreover, any juror persuaded of a mitigating factors may consider it in reaching a sentencing decision; unanimity is not required. 21 U.S.C. § 848(j) and (k).

A jury that finds the required statutory aggravating factors proved must consider whether these factors, along with any non-statutory aggravating ones, so outweigh any mitigating factors as to justify a sentence of death in the discrete case. 21 U.S.C. § 848(k). Even absent any mitigating factors, a jury must still be unanimously satisfied beyond a reasonable doubt that the proved aggravating factors are themselves sufficient to justify capital punishment before a sentence of death can be imposed. Id.

Invidious factors cannot influence a jury's determination as to the death penalty. Indeed, each juror must sign a certificate attesting that neither the defendant's nor the victim's "race, color, religious beliefs, national origin, or sex" played any part in the deliberations. 21 U.S.C. § 848(o)(1).

Although a jury cannot vote for the death penalty absent the required findings and certifications just detailed, a jury is never required to impose a death sentence even if it finds sufficient grounds to do so under the applicable law. Indeed, a court must specifically so instruct the jury. 21 U.S.C. § 848(k).

The statute labels a jury's finding in favor of the death penalty a "recommendation." 21 U.S.C. § 848(l). In fact, it is determinative, for upon such a "recommendation" the trial court "shall sentence the defendant to death." Id. Absent a recommendation of death, the court must sentence a defendant to a minimum of 20 years and a maximum of life imprisonment. Id.; 21 U.S.C. § 848(e)(1)(A).

Appellate review of a death sentence is expressly provided by the law. 21 U.S.C. § 848(q)(1). Such appeal may be consolidated with a challenge to the judgment of conviction, and the case is to be given priority on the appellate docket. Id.

Discussion

I. The Death Penalty as Cruel and Unusual Punishment

Mr. Pitera contends that the death penalty is, under all circumstances, cruel and unusual punishment violative of the eighth amendment. He concedes, however, that this argument has been rejected by all current members of the Supreme Court who have had occasion to consider the issue. See, e.g., Gregg v. Georgia, 428 U.S. 153, 178 (1976)(opinion of Stewart, Powell, and Stevens, JJ.)(citing to two centuries of case law upholding the constitutionality of capital punishment); accord McCleskey

v. Kemp, 481 U.S. 279, 300–01 (1987). Moreover, he cites no objective indicia of any change in public opinion about this punishment that might warrant reconsideration of its constitutionality. See *Gregg*, 428 U.S. at 173 (opinion of Stewart, Powell, and Stevens, JJ.); Weems v. United States, 217 U.S. 349, 378 (1910). This court is, therefore, compelled to follow controlling case law and to reject the broad constitutional attack on the death penalty. See United States v. Pretlow, 779 F.Supp. 758, 777–78 (D.N.J.1991)(rejecting similar challenge to § 848(e)(1)(A)).

Instead, the court considers the specific challenges made to the capital statute here at issue. In so doing, it is mindful of Justice Holmes's admonition that constitutionality challenges to an act of Congress engage a court in "the gravest and most delicate duty" of the judicial branch. See Blodgett v. Holden, 275 U.S. 142, 148 (1927). A due respect both for the magnitude of the task and for the independence of Congress, which presumably "legislates in the light of constitutional limitations," makes it appropriate to construe a challenged statute so as to avoid a conflict with the Constitution if reasonably possible. Rust v. Sullivan, 500 U.S. 173, 191 (1991). These principles guide the court's analysis.

II. Arbitrary and Capricious Sentencing

The majority of the arguments advanced by defendant and amici contend that the statute at issue fails to ensure that the death penalty is imposed in a consistently reasoned manner. The single most important principle to be derived from the Supreme Court's recent death penalty jurisprudence, beginning with the various opinions in Furman v. Georgia, 408 U.S. 238 (1972), is that capital punishment is unconstitutionally cruel and unusual if it is imposed arbitrarily or capriciously. Thus, statutes must "genuinely narrow the class of persons eligible for the death penalty and must reasonably justify the imposition of a more severe sentence on the defendant compared to others found guilty of murder." Zant v. Stephens, 462 U.S. 862, 877 (1983). "[R]ational criteria" must be articulated "that narrow the decisionmaker's judgment as to whether the circumstances of a particular defendant's case" meet the "threshold below which the death penalty cannot be imposed." Payne v. Tennessee, 501 U.S. 808, 824 (1991)(quoting *McCleskey*, 481 U.S. at 305). Moreover, when, as in this case, a jury generally inexperienced in sentencing decisions is entrusted with "so grave [a] determination" as "whether a human life should be taken or spared, that discretion must be suitably directed and limited so as to minimize the risk of wholly arbitrary and capricious action." *Gregg*, 428 U.S. at 189 (opinion of Stewart, Powell, and Stevens, JJ.).

The means by which sentencing discretion can be narrowed and directed are varied. See id. at 195 (opinion of Stewart, Powell, and Stevens, JJ.). For example, a legislature can limit the types of murders for which capital punishment may be imposed. See Lowenfield v. Phelps, 484 U.S. 231, 244–45 (1988). Alternatively, it can require proof of specific aggravating factors. Id. In this case, Congress appears to have done both: limiting the type of homicide for which the death penalty can be imposed to intentional murders committed in relation to a serious drug crime, and providing for specific aggravating factors that must be found before a sentence of death can be considered. See *Pretlow*, 779 F.Supp. at 772. Nevertheless, Mr. Pitera and amici contend that the statutory scheme is constitutionally inadequate. The court addresses in turn the particular cited deficiencies.

A.   Vagueness of the Crime

Amici submit that the crime outlined in 21 U.S.C. § 848(e)(1)(A) is unconstitutionally vague. Specifically, they argue that the statute, in failing to specify the relationship to be proved between the defendant and the killing, between the enterprise and the killing, and between the defendant and the enterprise, risks arbitrary imposition of the death penalty. Amici further suggest that the statute violates due process in singling out certain drug-related murders for capital punishment when other equally or more heinous murders are not so punished. Neither argument has merit.

1.   Eighth Amendment Vagueness

Generally, a vagueness challenge to a criminal statute invokes due process and focuses on the adequacy of notice to a defendant that certain conduct is prohibited. See, e.g., Grayned v. City of Rockford, 408 U.S. 104, 108 (1972). An eighth amendment vagueness challenge to a capital punishment statute has a different focus. The critical inquiry is whether the statute so poorly informs the jury as to what it "must find to impose the death penalty" that there is a risk that it is left "with the kind of open-ended discretion that was held invalid in *Furman v. Georgia*." See Maynard v. Cartwright, 486 U.S. 356, 361–62 (1988).

This case presents no such risk. The statute plainly states the relationship that must be established between a defendant and the charged murder: a defendant must have himself "intentionally kill[ed] the victim" or he must have "counsel[ed], command[ed], induce[d], procure[d], or cause[d] the intentional killing." The latter clause, far from being ambiguous, as amici argue, parallels 18 U.S.C. § 2 and states principles on which juries are routinely instructed. In any event, the court understands the government's position to be that Mr. Pitera himself committed the two murders charged in Count Three. Thus, no jury confusion about his alleged involvement will arise.

The court further rejects amici's suggestion that § 848(e)(1)(A) is fatally vague in failing to define the relationship that must be proved between a defendant's efforts on behalf of a continuing criminal enterprise and the alleged killing. A common sense reading of the statute supports the conclusion that a defendant faces federal prosecution only for homicidal acts committed "[while he was] engaging in or working in furtherance of a continuing criminal enterprise...." Amici's speculation that the statute would permit federal prosecution of a drug kingpin who killed his spouse in a domestic dispute unrelated to his drug dealing is not only fanciful, it is jurisdictionally suspect. As between two possible interpretations of a statute, a court is, quite simply, obliged to adopt that which is not constitutionally defective. See *Rust v. Sullivan*, supra. The government, moreover, concedes that it must prove a relationship between the murders alleged and Mr. Pitera's involvement in the charged enterprise. The court understands this to be akin to that "vertical" relationship that must be proved between predicate acts and enterprises in racketeering cases. See, e.g., United States v. Minicone, 960 F.2d 1099 (2d Cir.1992). It will charge the jury accordingly.

Finally, the court finds no impermissible vagueness in the statute's description of the involvement a defendant must have in the charged enterprise. The government must prove that defendant was "engaging in or working in furtherance of a continuing criminal enterprise." How one "engages in" a continuing criminal enterprise is expressly defined in § 848(c). Moreover, courts routinely consider whether a defendant's actions are "in furtherance" of other criminal activity when applying Fed. R.Evid. 801(d)(2)(E)(co-conspirator hearsay exception). See United States v. Cooper, 754 F.Supp. 617, 627 (N.D.Ill.1990)(rejecting vagueness challenge to this aspect of § 848(e)(1)(A)).

Amici contend that "working in furtherance of a continuing criminal enterprise" can mean aiding and abetting it. They note that the Second Circuit has rejected aiding and abetting as a basis for finding a defendant guilty of violating 21 U.S.C. § 848(a) and (b). See United States v. Amen, 831 F.2d 373, 381–82 (2d Cir.1987); cf. United States v. Pino–Perez, 870 F.2d 1230 (7th Cir.)(en banc)(1989)(person supervised by drug kingpin cannot be guilty as aider and abettor of § 848(a) charge, but person not under kingpin's supervision who aids and abets the enterprise may be guilty pursuant to 18 U.S.C. § 2). This argument ignores the different concerns addressed by § 848(a) and (b) on the one hand, and § 848(e)(1)(A) on the other. The former sections focus on individuals who head significant continuing drug enterprises. Section 848(e)(1)(A) focuses on individuals who commit murders in connection with the most serious drug crimes, specifically, in connection with continuing drug enterprises or in connection with the importation or distribution of significant quantities of drugs. While, as the Second Circuit noted in *Amen*, there is something illogical about convicting an aider and abettor for criminal conduct that focuses directly on the leadership role a defendant plays in a continuing criminal enterprise, that incongruity is not present in Congress's express decision to punish severely anyone who actually kills or who counsels, commands, induces, procures, or causes the intentional killing of a human being in connection with large-scale drug trafficking.

In any event, this case does not require the court to resolve the scope of a defendant's liability under § 848(e)(1)(A) for homicides committed while "working in furtherance of a continuing criminal enterprise." The government here contends that Mr. Pitera did, indeed, head the drug enterprise. In short, this case will be presented to the jury on the theory that Mr. Pitera committed the charged homicides while "engaging in" a continuing criminal enterprise. Proper instructions pursuant to § 848(c) will ensure that the jury understands this concept.

2. Due Process/Equal Protection

Amici further argue that § 848(e)(1)(A) violates the equal protection guarantee implicit in the due process clause of the fifth amendment by irrationally singling out for possible execution a class of persons whose homicidal conduct may be no more, and possibly less, serious than that engaged in by others.

A party raising an equal protection challenge to a criminal statute proscribing conduct that does not implicate a fundamental right bears a heavy burden. At issue is not "whether the legislature made a correct judgment, but only whether it made a rational one." United States v. Richards, 737 F.2d 1307, 1310 (4th Cir.1984). Particularly when a challenge is to the punishment chosen for a given crime, courts must be mindful that " 'these are peculiarly questions of legislative policy.' " Gregg, 428 U.S. at 176 (quoting Gore v. United States, 357 U.S. 386, 393 (1958))(opinion of Stewart, Powell, and Stevens, JJ.).

In this case, the choice Congress made is rational. Drug trafficking is recognized as "one of the greatest problems affecting the health and welfare of our population." Treasury Employees v. Von Raab, 489 U.S. 656, 668 (1989). To address the concern, Congress has already provided for a potential sentence of life imprisonment for large scale traffickers. See 21 U.S.C. §§ 841(b), 848(a) and (b), 960(b). The Supreme Court has rejected the argument that such a severe sentence is cruel and unusual. See Harmelin v. Michigan, 501 U.S. 957 (1991)(upholding state sentence of mandatory life imprisonment for person trafficking in large amount of cocaine). One of the most troubling aspects of drug trafficking is, of course, the frequency with which it spawns crimes of violence, particularly murder. See id. at 1002–03 (Kennedy, J., concurring)(citing to studies linking drug trafficking to crimes of violence). In this context, Congress could reasonably have concluded that, when the risk of drug-related violence translates into the reality of an intentional murder, the death penalty is an appropriate sanction.

Amici are correct that drug-related violence is widespread, and not limited to large traffickers. Congress, however, may attack problems one step at a time. See Orleans v. Dukes, 427 U.S. 297, 303 (1976); United States v. Holland, 810 F.2d 1215, 1219 (D.C.Cir.1987)(rejecting equal protection challenge to statute prohibiting drug trafficking within 1000 feet of school); United States v. Agilar, 779 F.2d 123, 126 (2d Cir.1985)(Congress acted rationally in increasing penalties for drug trafficking near schools "in hope of providing further deterrence, whether or not such success is thereby achieved"). Congress could reasonably have concluded that the penalty of death was so severe that it should only apply to those whose homicidal acts occurred in the context of the sort of large-scale drug trafficking already punishable by life imprisonment.

Insofar as amici strain to read the statute to cover defendants peripherally linked to the drug enterprise who only aid in the commission of a homicide, this court need not address such hypotheses. As already noted, Thomas Pitera is alleged to have headed the significant drug enterprise charged in the indictment. He is alleged to have personally committed the homicides at issue. His prosecution for such conduct pursuant to § 848(e)(1)(A) does not violate equal protection.

B.   Statutory Aggravating Factors

The government has advised Mr. Pitera that, if he is convicted of Count Three, it will seek to prove three statutory aggravating factors. To satisfy its requirement under § 848(n)(1), it expects to prove that Mr. Pitera "intentionally killed Richard Leone and Solomon Stern." 21 U.S.C. § 848(n)(1)(A). To satisfy its requirement under § 848(n)(2)-(12), the government expects to prove that "defendant committed [the Leone/Stern murders] after substantial planning and premeditation," 21 U.S.C. § 848(n)(8), and that he committed these murders "in an especially heinous, cruel, or depraved manner in that [they] involved torture or serious physical abuse to the victims," 21 U.S.C. § 848(n)(12).

Mr. Pitera argues that the "intentional killing" factor is merely duplicative of an element of the charged crime, and thus serves no real narrowing function. Amici join in this argument and contend that the same defect pertains to the "heinous, cruel or depraved . . ." factor. Mr. Pitera challenges the latter factor as too vague to permit rational narrowing.[4]

1.   Intentional Killing

This court agrees that the "intentional killing" factor stated in § 848(n)(1)(A) mirrors the mens rea element of the charged crime. Defendant's suggestion that this duplication mandates a finding of unconstitutionality misperceives the purpose of statutory aggravating factors in a capital sentencing scheme. In *Lowenfield v. Phelps*, supra, the court explained that "[t]he use of 'aggravating circumstances' is not an end in itself, but a means of genuinely narrowing the class of death eligible persons and thereby channeling the jury's discretion." 484 U.S. at 244. In that case, the only aggravating factor proved, defendant's specific intent to kill or inflict great bodily harm upon more than one person, also duplicated an element of the charged homicide. Because the element itself narrowed the class of murderers that could be sentenced to death, the Court upheld imposition of the death penalty, noting that such narrowing could be achieved "by jury findings at either the sentencing phase of the trial or the guilt phase." Id. at 245.

As with the statute in *Lowenfield*, § 848(e)(1)(A) significantly narrows the class of murderers eligible for the death penalty at the guilt phase. A

---

[4] No challenge is raised to the premeditation and planning factor. 21 U.S.C. § 848(n)(8). See *Cooper*, 754 F.Supp. at 623 (rejecting argument that this factor was vague and duplicative of the intent elements of the underlying crime).

jury must be persuaded that a defendant intentionally committed homicide and that he did so in connection with large-scale drug trafficking. *Pretlow*, 779 F.Supp. at 772 (applying *Lowenfield* to identical challenge here at issue); *Cooper*, 754 F.Supp. at 622 (same). Moreover, Congress requires the finding of at least one other aggravating factor drawn from the list in § 848(n)(2)-(12) before the death penalty can be considered. This further defines and limits the class of persons eligible for capital punishment.

Defendant nevertheless seeks to distinguish this case from *Lowenfield* because § 848(k) requires juries to weigh aggravating and mitigating factors, whereas such weighing was not an aspect of the statute at issue in *Lowenfield*. The difference between "weighing" and "non-weighing" capital statutes involves more than "semantics." See Stringer v. Black, 503 U.S. 222 (1992). But the difference goes not so much to narrowing the capital class as it does to guiding the jury's individualized sentencing determination. Thus, in *Stringer*, the Supreme Court held that jury consideration of an unconstitutionally vague aggravating factor was particularly problematic under a weighing statute because "it creates the risk that the jury will treat the defendant as more deserving of the death penalty than he might otherwise be by relying upon the existence of an illusory circumstance." Id. at 235.

Mr. Pitera's challenge to § 848(n)(1)(A), however, is not vagueness. See id. (distinguishing *Lowenfield* as not involving a vague factor). Indeed, the Supreme Court has expressly held that a "highly culpable mental state ... may be taken into account in making a capital sentencing judgment." See generally Tison v. Arizona, 481 U.S. 137, 157–58 (1987)(even reckless disregard for human life can support imposition of death sentence). Mr. Pitera's complaint is simply that the factor is duplicative. A duplicative factor, unlike a vague one, does not risk the injection of an "illusory circumstance" into the sentencing process.

Defendant's real complaint is that a duplicative factor unfairly tips the sentencing balance by permitting the government to argue something in aggravation that really adds nothing new to the crime of conviction. This concern is easily assuaged by an instruction telling the jury that § 848(e)(1)(A) duplicates an element of the crime, and stressing the importance of the quality of the information adduced at the sentencing hearing rather than its quantity. The jury will, of course, also be instructed that it cannot recommend the death penalty unless it finds the aggravating factors to outweigh—in terms of severity not raw number—any mitigating factors. It will be told that even in the absence of any mitigating factors, the death penalty cannot be imposed unless the aggravating factors are themselves serious enough to warrant capital punishment. Finally, it will be told that it is never required to recommend a defendant's execution. The court is satisfied that these instructions are sufficient to safeguard against imbalance at the sentencing hearing. See *Pretlow*, 779 F.Supp. at 773.

2. Especially Heinous, Cruel or Depraved Manner Involving Torture or Serious Physical Abuse to the Victim

Defendant argues that the statutory factor permitting consideration of whether a defendant committed murder in "an especially heinous, cruel or depraved manner in that it involved torture or serious physical abuse to the victim" is too vague to constitute a real narrowing of the class of persons subject to the death penalty. The court must decide whether the provision adequately informs a jury as to what it must find to impose the death penalty or whether it invites the exercise of open-ended discretion. See *Maynard v. Cartwright*, 486 U.S. at 361–62.

By itself, the term "especially heinous, cruel or depraved," is too vague to narrow a jury's discretion in the manner required by the Constitution. See id. at 362–63; Godfrey v. Georgia, 446 U.S. 420, 428–29 (1980). Its modification in § 848(n)(12) by the phrase "in that it involved torture or serious physical abuse to the victim" does, however, provide sufficient specificity to withstand challenge.[5] See *Pretlow*, 779 F.Supp. at 773 (rejecting similar challenge to § 848(n)(12)); *Cooper*, 754 F.Supp. at 623 (same).

The conclusion derives directly from the Supreme Court's "expressed approval" of a definition that would limit an " 'especially heinous, atrocious, or cruel' aggravating circumstance to murders involving 'some kind of torture or physical abuse.' " Walton v. Arizona, 497 U.S. 639, 654–55 (1990)(quoting *Maynard v. Cartwright*, 486 U.S. at 364–65); see Proffitt v. Florida, 428 U.S. 242, 255–56 (1976)("especially heinous, atrocious, or cruel" factor not unconstitutionally vague when limited to "conscienceless or pitiless crime which is unnecessarily torturous to the victim"). Mr. Pitera notes that in *Walton* the court, rather than the jury, made the capital punishment determination. The distinction has no bearing on his vagueness challenge. The prior approval of a narrowing definition referred to in *Walton* was in the context of a jury sentencing decision. *Walton*, 497 U.S. at 364–65 (citing *Maynard v. Cartwright*, 486 U.S. at 362–65).

Moreover, in *Walton*, the cited aggravating factor was vague on its face. Defendant was simply alleged to have committed murder "in an especially heinous, cruel or depraved manner." The Supreme Court nevertheless upheld the death sentence imposed because (1) it was persuaded that the Arizona Supreme Court had, in previous decisions, construed the factor narrowly to meet constitutional requirements, and (2) it assumed that trial judges know and apply controlling law. *Walton*, 497 U.S. at 653. By contrast, § 848(n)(12) suffers no facial infirmity. By statutorily requiring proof of "torture or serious physical abuse to the victim," Congress has expressly narrowed the term "heinous, cruel or depraved manner" in a way specifically approved by the Supreme Court. See *Pretlow*, 779 F.Supp. at 773; *Cooper*, 754 F.Supp. at 623.

This court will, of course, instruct the jury as to its duties with respect to § 848(n)(12). The parties will have the opportunity to comment on the instruction to ensure against vagueness. Mr. Pitera already cites authority supporting an instruction that brutal conduct only qualifies as "torture" or

---

[5] Amici argue that § 848(n)(12) duplicates the crime because "[a] person of ordinary sensibility could fairly characterize almost every murder as [heinous, cruel or depraved]." See *Godfrey*, supra, "[T]orture or serious physical abuse," however, are not necessarily present in every murder. Thus, this court rejects the argument that § 848(n)(12) serves no real narrowing function.

"serious physical abuse" if it was inflicted before, rather than after, the death of a victim. See *Godfrey*, 446 U.S. at 431–32. At oral argument, the government advised that the conduct on which it would rely in seeking to prove this factor would have occurred before the victims' death.

Relying on the statutory requirement that "torture or serious physical abuse be proved," and confident that a sufficiently specific charge can be fashioned as to these elements, the court rejects defendant's vagueness challenge to § 848(n)(12).

C. Non–statutory Aggravating Factors

Defendant and amici challenge that part of § 848(j) permitting the prosecution to select the non-statutory aggravating factors that it will present for jury consideration at the sentencing hearing. Amici contend that the use of such factors always injects arbitrariness and capriciousness into the sentencing process. Mr. Pitera submits that, if non-statutory aggravating factors are weighed against mitigating factors, "proportionality review" by an appellate court is constitutionally mandated. He further argues that the discretion here afforded federal prosecutors constitutes an impermissible delegation of Congress's legislative powers and runs afoul of the ex post facto clause. The court is unpersuaded by these arguments.

1. Non–statutory Aggravating Factors Always Arbitrary and Capricious

Amici's contention that any consideration of non-statutory aggravating factors is constitutionally suspect has been squarely rejected by the Supreme Court in *Zant v. Stephens*, supra. In that case, the Court held that the invalidation of one of three statutory aggravating factors did not require reversal of a death sentence since the two remaining statutory aggravating factors supported the sentence, and since the information received pursuant to the invalid factor was properly considered as a non-statutory aggravating factor. The Court explained the different purposes served by statutory and non-statutory aggravating factors:

> "[S]tatutory aggravating circumstances play a constitutionally necessary function at the stage of legislative definition: they circumscribe the class of persons eligible for the death penalty. But the Constitution does not require the jury to ignore other possible aggravating factors in the process of selecting, from among that class, those defendants who will actually be sentenced to death. What is important at the selection stage is an individualized determination on the basis of the character of the individual and the circumstances of the crime." 462 U.S. at 878–79.

The statutory scheme here at issue similarly involves a congressional narrowing of the class of persons eligible for the death penalty, both as a result of the limited homicidal acts that Congress has labeled "capital" and by the required proof of statutory aggravating factors. Non-statutory aggravating factors are considered only after a defendant's membership in this narrow class is established beyond a reasonable doubt and only as a part of the jury's individualized sentencing consideration. Thus, although non-statutory aggravating factors cannot serve both to identify the class of capital defendants and to inform a jury's individualized sentencing decision, where, as in this case, the non-statutory factors perform only the latter task, their consideration does not render a capital sentencing decision arbitrary or capricious. See Barclay v. Florida, 463 U.S. 939, 957 (1983)("[I]t is clear that [there is] no constitutional defect in a sentence based on both statutory and non-statutory aggravating factors").

2.   Need for "Proportionality Review"

In capital punishment jurisprudence, "proportionality review" refers to appellate inquiry into whether imposition of the death penalty in a particular case is proportionate to the punishment imposed on others convicted of the same crime. See Pulley v. Harris, 465 U.S. 37, 43 (1984). In *Pulley*, the Supreme Court held that such review, while often useful, is not constitutionally required in all capital cases. Id. at 50–51. Defendant, however, insists that proportionality review is imperative whenever a jury weighs non-statutory aggravating factors. He cites in support of this argument a statement in *Zant v. Stephens*, supra, suggesting that the Court's approval of non-statutory aggravating factors in that case was conditioned "in part on the existence of an important procedural safeguard, the mandatory appellate review of each death sentence by the Georgia Supreme Court to avoid arbitrariness and to assure proportionality." 462 U.S. at 890.

Defendant overemphasizes [the] *Zant v. Stephens* reference to proportionality review. The Supreme Court's focus in the quoted passage was not so much on any particular aspect of the Georgia review process as on the fact that Georgia guaranteed meaningful appellate review in every capital case, thereby ensuring against arbitrary and capricious sentencing. See *Stringer v. Black*, 503 U.S. at 230 (emphasizing importance of "close appellate scrutiny" without reference to any particular type of review); *Pretlow*, 779 F.Supp. at 769 (rejecting argument that proportionality review is required in every case involving non-statutory aggravating factors).

This court is satisfied, for the reasons stated in Part II–F of this memorandum, that Congress has provided for full appellate review of death sentences imposed under § 848(e)(1)(A). Indeed, the court is convinced that the scope of this review is broad enough to permit appellate consideration of proportionality in an appropriate case, even though it is not required in every case. The government concurred in this suggestion at oral argument. To this extent, should Mr. Pitera be sentenced to death and should that sentence be premised on any non-statutory factor, he will be able to urge an appellate court to engage in proportionality review if that is necessary to ensure against an arbitrary sentence.

3.   Delegation of Legislative Powers

Article I, section 1 of the Constitution provides that "[a]ll legislative Powers herein granted shall be vested in a Congress of the United States." Mindful of the Constitution's separation of powers among the branches of government, the Supreme Court has derived from the quoted passage a "non-delegation" doctrine prohibiting Congress from transferring its legislative powers to other governmental branches. See Mistretta v. United States, 488 U.S. 361, 371 (1989). Defendant and amici submit that Congress has impermissibly delegated a part of its legislative power to fix sentence by permitting the prosecution to select the non-statutory aggravating factors on which it will rely at a capital sentencing hearing. The court finds no impermissible delegation in this case.

In identifying and presenting non-statutory factors for the jury's consideration, the prosecution does not intrude upon the legislative prerogative either to define the capital crime or to narrow the class of persons eligible for the death penalty. As already noted, that constitutionally-mandated narrowing has been achieved by Congress in limiting the types of homicides for which the death penalty may be imposed and in requiring proof of certain statutory aggravating factors. The prosecution's role is limited to that phase of the proceeding wherein the jury makes an individualized sentencing determination as to the defendant on trial. In the course thereof the prosecution engages in advocacy, not legislation.

This conclusion, which differs from that stated in the thoughtful opinion of Judge Harold Ackerman in *Pretlow*, 779 F.Supp. at 766–67 (prosecution's ability to select non-statutory aggravating factors constitutes a delegation of legislative authority), derives from a consideration of both Congress's power to fix sentences and the executive's power to enforce the criminal laws.

In an ordinary criminal case, Congress's power to fix sentence is absolute, as reflected in its ability to legislate mandatory sentences. See *Harmelin*, supra. Historically, however, Congress has rarely enacted mandatory sentences. Mindful of the general benefits of individualized sentencing, it had for many years delegated "almost unfettered discretion" to the district courts to determine what sentence should be imposed within a wide statutory range in a given case. See *Mistretta*, 488 U.S. at 364; Lockett v. Ohio, 438 U.S. 586, 605 (1978)("... in noncapital cases, the established practice of individualized sentences rests not on constitutional commands, but on public policy enacted into statutes"). Indeed, so commonplace had the exercise of such judicial discretion become that it was difficult to think of sentencing as a matter assigned by the Constitution to the exclusive jurisdiction of any one branch of government. *Mistretta*, supra. Of course, judicial discretion with respect to sentencing has been curbed somewhat of late through the enactment of sentencing guidelines. See 18 U.S.C. § 3553. Not insignificantly, these guidelines are not promulgated by Congress, but rather by a hybrid entity, the Sentencing Commission, to which Congress has further delegated a portion of its power to fix sentences. See 28 U.S.C. § 991 et seq.; *Mistretta*, 488 U.S. at 367–70.

Integral to Congress's delegation of a portion of its sentencing authority to the courts, whether before or after the advent of the sentencing guidelines, is the statutory requirement that sentencing decisions be based on a full and careful consideration of all relevant factors. Thus, "[n]o limitation shall be placed on the information concerning the background, character, and conduct of a person convicted of an offense which a court of the United States may receive and consider for the purpose of imposing an appropriate sentence." 18 U.S.C. § 3661. Pursuant to this statute, both the prosecution and defense routinely cite and argue factors that they think are relevant to the court's sentencing decision. See Fed.R.Crim.P. 32(a). The prosecution, in engaging in such advocacy, exercises discretion derived from the executive's enforcement powers, not from any delegated legislative powers. Such discretion is not static. In the first instance, it requires the selection from among different cases of those most appropriately prosecuted. It next requires the identification and presentation of evidence most likely to persuade a jury to convict. Finally and in the same vein, it involves a proffer to the court of further facts, sometimes not even admissible at trial, see, e.g., Fed.R.Evid. 404(b), about the character of the defendant or the crime committed, that may assist the court in exercising its congressionally-delegated sentencing discretion. The distinction between such prosecutorial conduct and the exercise of legislative powers is significant, for many statutes "depend on the discretion of some person or persons to whom is confided the duty of determining whether the proper occasion exists for executing them. But it cannot be said that the exercise of such discretion is the making of the law." Field v. Clark, 143 U.S. 649, 694 (1892)(quoting Moers v. City of Reading, 21 Pa. 188, 202 (1853)).

These principles are even more pertinent in the context of capital sentencing, for the individualized consideration that Congress has favored generally in the criminal law is constitutionally mandated when a defendant faces the death penalty. Quite simply, death is the one sentence that Congress cannot make mandatory. See Woodson v. North Carolina, 428 U.S. 280 (1976); accord, Sumner v. Shuman, 483 U.S. 66 (1987). It must delegate a portion of its sentencing authority, whether to the courts or to a jury, in order to ensure that a capital defendant is treated as a unique human being. Indeed, individualized sentencing is so important to the constitutional scheme that any legislative attempt to limit a defendant's ability to advocate mitigating circumstances to a jury is unconstitutional. See *Lockett*, 438 U.S. at 605. Neither Mr. Pitera nor amici suggest that the defense exercises "legislative" powers when it selects the mitigating factors to be presented and, indeed, there would be no reasonable basis for so viewing such conduct.

Although the Supreme Court has not required legislatures to permit jury consideration of all relevant aggravating factors in pursuing individualized capital sentencing, it clearly favors procedures that do "not ... impose unnecessary restrictions on the evidence that can be offered at [a capital] sentencing hearing. . . . We think it desirable for the jury to have as much information before it as possible when it makes the sentencing decision." *Gregg*, 428 U.S. at 203–04 (opinion of Stewart, Powell, and Stevens, JJ.). The Court recently reiterated this preference for full consideration of the defendant's character and the circumstances of the crime by overruling one of its own capital decisions curbing the use of aggravating factors. See *Payne*, 501 U.S. at 822 (limitation on prosecution's ability to offer victim impact evidence "unfairly weighted the scales in a capital case" in favor of the defense).

In enacting § 848(j), Congress both satisfies its constitutional obligation to provide for individualized capital sentencing and expressly endorses full jury consideration of all relevant factors, whether in mitigation or aggravation. The requirement that the prosecutor advise the defendant in advance of the aggravating factors to be presented is more reflective of a desire to ensure fairness to the defendant than to limit the jury's access to relevant information.

In identifying non-statutory aggravating factors pursuant to § 848(j), the prosecution plays virtually the same role in a capital sentencing proceeding as it does in a non-capital one. See Fed.R.Crim.P. 32(a)(prosecution entitled to be heard at sentence). It brings relevant facts to the sentencer's attention and urges it to reach a particular result. In a capital case, this advocacy will, in no small part, reflect the prosecution's considered judgment as to why the case was a "proper occasion" for serving a death penalty notice in the first place: an enforcement, not a legislative, decision. See *Field v. Clark*, supra. Such advocacy does not, however, involve the prosecution in the fixing of sentence. That remains exclusively the jury's function. Indeed, the jury remains free to reject imposition of the death penalty even if fully persuaded of the prosecution's position. The court thus finds no delegation of legislative authority to the prosecutor in § 848(j).

Even if § 848(j) did involve a delegation of legislative power, it would not be unconstitutional. See *Pretlow*, 779 F.Supp. at 767–68 (upholding § 848(j) as a permissive delegation of legislative power). The non-delegation doctrine does not bar Congress from obtaining assistance from coordinate branches of government so long as it articulates an "intelligible principle" by which the authorized body is to exercise its delegated powers. *Mistretta*, 488 U.S. at 372 (quoting J.W. Hampton Jr., & Co. v. United States, 276 U.S. 394, 409 (1928)). Although defendant and amici suggest that these principles must be "specific" when Congress delegates its criminal legislative powers, the Supreme Court has never formally adopted this standard. See Touby v. United States, 500 U.S. 160, 166 (1991)(Court finds "specific guidance" provided, without holding that such is required). *Touby* involved Congress's power to define crimes, an area where delegation has been both infrequent and circumspect. By contrast, as already noted, Congress has traditionally delegated its sentencing powers quite broadly. Thus, in *Mistretta*, the Court held that a delegation in this area need only set forth "broad general directives" to guide a coordinate branch. 488 U.S. at 372.

The court is satisfied that Congress has adequately provided such directives in this case. Although § 848(j) plainly contemplates a full individualized sentencing hearing, the law permits only non-statutory factors that are "more probative than prejudicial" to be submitted to the jury. In the capital context, probative information has generally been held to pertain either to a defendant's character or to the circumstances of the charged crime. E.g., *Zant v. Stephens*, 462 U.S. at 878–79. There is no reason to think that Congress intended any other meaning. It is, moreover, the trial court that determines whether proffered factors are more probative than prejudicial to exploration of a defendant's character and the charged crime. Such judicial review "perfects a delegated-lawmaking scheme by assuring that the exercise of such power remains within statutory bounds." See *Touby*, 500 U.S. at 169 (Marshall, J., concurring); see *Cooper*, 754 F.Supp. at 623 (prosecutorial discretion in selecting non-statutory aggravating factors under § 848(j) not unlimited given judicial determination of what is relevant).

The court thus rejects defendant's and amici's delegation challenge to the statute's provision for consideration of non-statutory aggravating factors finding (1) that if the jury finds proved both the crime of conviction and the statutory aggravating factors, the prosecution's presentation of non-statutory factors is an exercise in advocacy derived from the executive's discretion to prosecute, not the legislature's power to fix sentence, and (2) that, even if this limited exercise of prosecutorial discretion were deemed to constitute a legislative delegation, its exercise is sufficiently circumscribed, both by the statute and by judicial review, to ensure against overbroad application.

4. Ex Post Facto Implications

Article I, section 9 of the Constitution prohibits ex post facto laws. The Supreme Court has interpreted the clause to proscribe any legislation (1) making illegal that which was legal at the time of the alleged criminal activity, (2) increasing the punishment for a crime after its commission, or (3) depriving the accused of any legal defense available at the time the crime was committed. Collins v. Youngblood, 497 U.S. 37, 42 (1990). Mr. Pitera contends that any government reliance, in aggravation of the homicides charged in Count Three, on other murders he may have committed prior to passage of § 848(e)(1)(A) violates the ex post facto clause.

The argument is flawed in several respects. First, Count Three does not involve, as Mr. Pitera urges, a "straddle" crime. Such a crime holds a defendant accountable for conduct that occurs in part before and in part after the enactment of the relevant law. In straddle crimes—for example, racketeering charges involving one predicate act occurring prior to passage of the statute, and another after enactment—a defendant must be given clear statutory notice of what continuing conduct can resurrect his past misdeeds, for the earlier acts are themselves elements of the crime of conviction. See, e.g., United States v. DeStafano, 429 F.2d 344, 347 (2d Cir.1970). In this case, the government's reliance on other homicides in aggravation of those charged in Count Three does not make those earlier murders any part of the crime of conviction.

Neither does the government here seek to increase the punishment for any of the earlier homicides, as defendant also suggests. At most, it uses this earlier conduct as evidence of Mr. Pitera's character to assist the jury in determining whether it should impose the maximum sentence of death

for Count Three.   In Gryger v. Burke, 334 U.S. 728 (1948), the Supreme
Court upheld, against an ex post facto challenge, a statute permitting
enhancement of sentence for crimes committed before passage of the crime
of conviction.   The enhanced penalty was "not to be viewed as either a new
jeopardy or additional penalty for the earlier crimes.   It is a stiffened
penalty for the latest crime, which is considered to be an aggravated offense
because a repetitive one."   Id. at 732; Covington v. Sullivan, 823 F.2d 37,
39–40 (2d Cir.1987)(relying on *Gryger* to uphold enhanced sentencing
provision of New York law against ex post facto challenge).

   Moreover, this case differs from *Gryger* in that the death penalty is not
an enhanced punishment dependent upon the proof of non-statutory aggravating factors.   It is the maximum penalty, which a jury can recommend in
the complete absence of any proof of non-statutory aggravating factors if it
is satisfied that statutory aggravating factors outweigh any mitigating
factors.   Similarly, the jury is always free to reject the death penalty even if
persuaded beyond a reasonable doubt that defendant committed all the
non-statutory aggravating factors proffered.

   Viewed in this light, a jury's consideration of these prior crimes not
only does not implicate the ex post facto clause; it comes squarely within
the broad review of all relevant facts and circumstances that ideally
characterizes individualized sentencing.   Indeed, in a non-capital context,
the Second Circuit has specifically upheld a sentencing court's consideration of prior criminal conduct to which defendant pleaded guilty but had
not yet been formally sentenced.   See United States v. Sturgis, 869 F.2d 54,
56–57 (2d Cir.1989)(affirming upward departure).   Such conduct was found
relevant to a defendant's character, since it suggested he was more likely to
commit other crimes.   Id.   So in this case, a jury is entitled to consider
whether Mr. Pitera may not only have intentionally killed Messrs. Leone
and Stern, but also other individuals, which murders may have involved
torture or serious physical abuse to the victims.   These factors are relevant
to his character and his propensity to commit violent crimes.   Because such
consideration neither exposes him to conviction for criminal conduct of
which he was not given fair notice nor subjects him to further punishment
for earlier crimes, the court finds no ex post facto defect in the statutory
scheme.

D.   Mitigating Factors

   Amici's contention that the enumerated mitigating factors in § 848(m)
impermissibly limit what a defendant may present at a sentencing hearing
merits little discussion.   Section 848(j) expressly provides that a defendant
may proffer "any ... mitigating factors set forth in [§ 848(m)] or any other
mitigating factor...."   Thus, Congress has ensured compliance with those
Supreme Court cases holding that a capital defendant cannot be precluded
from proffering any factors relevant to his character or the circumstances
of the crime "which may call for a less severe penalty."   *Lockett*, 438 U.S.
at 65; accord, Penry v. Lynaugh, 492 U.S. 302 (1989); Sumner v. Shuman,
483 U.S. 66 (1987); Eddings v. Oklahoma, 455 U.S. 104 (1982).

E. Evidentiary Standard

The Federal Rules of Evidence do not apply at a capital sentencing hearing. 21 U.S.C. § 848(j). Mr. Pitera contends that this omission invites an evidentiary "free for all" lacking the heightened reliability essential to a death penalty proceeding. This issue may never surface in this case since the government advises that its proof as to aggravating circumstances will likely duplicate its evidence at trial and, thus, necessarily conform to the Federal Rules. Nevertheless, because it neither concedes the point nor expressly limits its presentation, the court considers defendant's argument.

It is undisputed that "[i]n capital proceedings generally, [the Supreme Court] has demanded that factfinding procedures aspire to a heightened standard of reliability." Ford v. Wainwright, 477 U.S. 399, 411 (1986). Should this case require a sentencing hearing, this court will be obliged to ensure such heightened reliability. The court is unpersuaded, however, that the standard can be met only through rigid adherence to the Federal Rules of Evidence.

The Federal Rules of Evidence are critical to the conduct of criminal trials to enable "truth [to] be ascertained and proceedings [to be] justly determined." Fed.R.Evid. 102. But the focus of a trial is singular: "whether a defendant is guilty of having engaged in criminal conduct of which he has been specifically accused." Williams v. New York, 337 U.S. 241, 246 (1949). An individualized consideration of sentence, by contrast, necessitates a broader inquiry into all aspects of the defendant's life and the crime committed. A simple example best illustrates why the concerns of the two proceedings are not always best served by the Federal Rules of Evidence. At trial, a jury generally cannot consider evidence of a defendant's past criminal conduct in deciding whether he has committed the charged offense. Fed.R.Evid. 404(b). That precise evidence is, however, deemed highly probative at sentencing. See U.S.S.G. § 4A1.1.

In *Williams*, supra, a capital case, the Supreme Court held that a sentencer should "not be denied an opportunity to obtain pertinent information by a requirement of rigid adherence to restrictive rules of evidence properly applicable to the trial." 337 U.S. at 247. *Williams* was, of course, decided before *Furman*, supra. Some care must therefore be taken not to read it so broadly as to impinge on a capital defendant's particular interest in the reliability of his sentencing proceedings. Thus, in Gardner v. Florida, 430 U.S. 349, 355–59 (1977), the Supreme Court rejected an argument that *Williams* permitted the use of confidential information at a capital sentencing proceeding. The reliability of information not subject to defense scrutiny and challenge simply could not be assumed. But neither *Gardner* nor any other case retreats from the basic holding of *Williams*: that the Federal Rules of Evidence do not control sentencing hearings.

Indeed, *Williams* was cited in *Lockett*, supra, to support the conclusion that no limitation can be placed upon a capital defendant's ability to present mitigating evidence. *Lockett* was extended in Green v. Georgia, 442 U.S. 95, 97 (1979), to preclude courts from mechanically applying rules of evidence to deny capital defendants the right to offer otherwise reliable information in a sentencing proceeding. Common sense suggests that Congress, in enacting that portion of § 848(j) expressly eliminating the need for strict compliance with the Federal Rules of Evidence, was seeking to bring the federal capital statute within the constitutional parameters outlined in *Green* and *Williams*.

This conclusion is not undermined by Supreme Court cases permitting different rules to apply to the parties at capital sentencing hearings. E.g., McKoy v. North Carolina, 494 U.S. 433 (1990)(fact that state required unanimous finding as to aggravating factors did not permit it to require unanimity as to mitigating factors).[6] The Court's concern has been less with the precise rules that legislatures apply to capital sentencing proceedings than with ensuring that any factfinding thereunder is highly reliable.

This court expects that in many circumstances reference to the Federal Rules of Evidence will be useful in deciding whether information proffered at a capital sentencing hearing is sufficiently reliable to be more probative than prejudicial. The Rules will not, however, be determinative. For example, they tolerate multiple layers of hearsay, without requiring judicial inquiry into reliability. See Fed.R.Evid. 805. The heightened standard applicable to capital sentencing proceedings may, however, demand further indicia of reliability before a court can say that the probative value of any such hearsay outweighs its prejudicial potential. Because of this heightened standard, a court's consideration of the probative value of information compared to its prejudicial impact may yield different results under § 848(j) than under Fed.R.Evid. 403. By way of contrast, certified judgments of prior convictions are highly reliable evidence and may be admissible at a capital sentencing hearing as probative proof of a defendant's character regardless of the limitations of Fed.R.Evid. 404(b).

The constitutional mandate is for a sentencing proceeding that ensures heightened reliability. The court is convinced that such a standard can adequately be factored into a consideration of whether proffered evidence is more probative than prejudicial. The court accordingly rejects defendant's challenge to the statute's evidentiary standard.

F. Meaningful Appellate Review

Mr. Pitera and amici both contend that meaningful appellate review is an essential element of any capital punishment scheme and that the review provided under § 848(q) is constitutionally inadequate. The government initially meets this argument by insisting that there is no constitutional right to appellate review. E.g., United States v. MacCollom, 426 U.S. 317,

---

[6] The distinctions that have been drawn have not gone uncriticized. See, e.g., *Walton*, 497 U.S. at 656 (Scalia, J., concurring)(suggesting that different treatment of aggravating and mitigating factors in various cases enhances the likelihood of random capital sentencing); *Lockett*, 438 U.S. at 629 (Rehn-quist, J., dissenting). But see *Walton*, 497 U.S. at 708 (Stevens, J., dissenting)(distinguishing between arbitrary definition of capital class and discretion to show mercy to those who come within properly-narrowed class).

323 (1976); Ross v. Moffitt, 417 U.S. 600, 610 (1974). While this may be true generally, it cites to no instance where a capital sentencing scheme without appellate review has been upheld. In case after case, the Supreme Court has identified meaningful appellate review as a critical element in ensuring against arbitrary and capricious capital sentencing. E.g., Parker v. Dugger, 498 U.S. 308 (1991); Clemons v. Mississippi, 494 U.S. 738, 749 (1990); *Gregg*, 428 U.S. at 198 (opinion of Stewart, Powell, and Stevens, JJ.). Thus, if the issue were really in dispute, it would by no means be obvious that the instant statute could survive an eighth amendment challenge in the absence of any provision for appellate review. See *Pretlow*, 779 F.Supp. at 763 (a capital statute that failed to provide for direct appellate review would be unconstitutional).[7]

In this case Congress has provided for appellate review. 21 U.S.C. § 848(q). The issue is thus whether the scope of that review is so limited as to cause the entire capital scheme to run afoul of the eighth amendment. Mr. Pitera cites a portion of § 848(q)(3) as evidence of such impermissible limitation:

"[T]he court shall affirm the sentence if it determines that—

"(A) the sentence of death was not imposed under the influence of passion, prejudice, or any other arbitrary factor; and

"(B) the information supports the special findings of the existence of every aggravating factor upon which the sentence was based, together with, or the failure to find, any mitigating factors as set forth or allowed in this section."

Not insignificantly, the section further provides that "[i]n all other cases, the court shall remand the case for reconsideration under this section." Id. Nevertheless, Mr. Pitera contends that, since no express provision is made for review of legal errors that may occur at the sentencing hearing, the law impermissibly requires affirmance of a death sentence even in the face of plain errors such as inflammatory prosecutorial remarks, improper jury instructions or unsuitable jury behavior.

Defendant's argument depends on a crabbed reading of the statute that ignores two important points. First, Congress has mandated appellate consideration of whether a capital sentence was infected by "any arbitrary factor." The term "arbitrary" has particular meaning in modern death penalty jurisprudence. As the Supreme Court cases relied on in this memorandum amply demonstrate, although the death penalty, per se, is not violative of the eighth amendment, any imposition that is arbitrary and capricious is impermissibly cruel and unusual. An arbitrary factor must perforce include errors of law that are not harmless, for such errors, particularly in the context of a weighing statute, may impermissibly tip the

[7] Indeed, the government conceded at oral argument that there would be a serious equal protection issue presented if Congress were to provide a right to appeal for all criminal defendants except those facing the death penalty. Since the capital statute in fact provides for appellate review, this court does not further discuss this point, which was argued by amici.

scales in favor of death. See *Stringer v. Black*, supra. Indeed, amici suggest that this is a reasonable interpretation of the statute and the government concurs. See *Pretlow*, 779 F.Supp. at 764 (review of "arbitrary factors" under § 848(q)(3) includes harmful errors of law).

Second, defendant overlooks the section immediately preceding § 848(q)(3), wherein Congress makes plain that appellate review of a capital sentence is to be exhaustive. On review of the sentence, the court of appeals shall consider the record, the evidence submitted during the trial, the information submitted during the sentencing hearing, the procedures employed in the sentencing hearing, and the special findings returned under this section. 21 U.S.C. § 848(q)(2). This court thus concludes that no aspect of a capital sentencing proceeding is impervious to appellate review. If any feature—whether the vagueness of a factor, or the sufficiency of the information adduced, or a court's instructions, or a prosecutor's remarks, or a jury's conduct—reveals that the sentencing decision may have been arbitrarily arrived at, remand is contemplated.

The precise form of review to be undertaken pursuant to § 848(q) is not specified. The statute is thus fairly interpreted to permit whatever review is reasonably necessary to ensure against arbitrary decisionmaking. At oral argument this court suggested, and the government concurred, that this could even include proportionality review in a case where the appellate court thought such was essential to ensuring that a capital sentence was not arbitrary. Although Congress has not expressly required proportionality review in § 848(q) for every capital case, neither has it forbidden it in any case.

Because this court finds no basis for thinking that the court of appeals will be limited in its power fully to review any sentence imposed, this court rejects this aspect of defendant's and amici's constitutional challenge.

III. Arbitrary and Vindictive Prosecution

Defendant contends that he has been arbitrarily and vindictively singled out for capital punishment in violation of the due process clause. The claim is without merit.

A. Arbitrary Prosecution

Mr. Pitera's arbitrariness complaint hinges on the government's failure to seek the death penalty against co-defendants Richard David, Frank Martini, and William Bright, all of whom were also charged with homicidal acts linked to drug trafficking.[8] The facts alleged in the case demonstrate

[8] Messrs. David, Martini, and Bright have all entered guilty pleas in the pending case. Mr. David pleaded guilty to racketeering, admitting participation in a marijuana distribution conspiracy and in the murder of Talal Siksik. He faces a maximum term of 20 years incarceration, pursuant to the pre-guideline sentencing scheme. Mr. Bright pleaded to drug conspiracy and racketeering, admitting involvement in the Leone/Stern homicides. Mr. Martini pleaded guilty to racketeering, confessing his involvement in the Acosta/Aguilera murders and in cocaine trafficking. The Bright and Martini pleas were entered pursuant to Fed.R.Crim.P. 11(e)(1)(C) and, subject to court approval,

that the four men are not, in fact, similarly situated. Mr. Pitera is the purported head of a significant drug enterprise. His three co-defendants are, at best, subordinate members of the enterprise. Mr. Pitera is alleged to have personally committed seven of the nine murders charged in the indictment, including the two that are the subject of Count Three. While various co-defendants assisted Mr. Pitera in one or more of these homicides, he is alleged to have been the principal actor. Moreover, the government contends that it was Mr. Pitera who instigated both the torture to which various victims were subjected before their deaths and the dismemberment that followed. Under the totality of these circumstances, this court cannot say that the government made an arbitrary decision in selecting Mr. Pitera alone, among the defendants in this case, for possible capital punishment.

Insofar as defendant and amici contend that any exercise of discretion by the prosecutor in selecting the defendants who will be charged with capital crimes necessarily implicates the eighth amendment's ban on arbitrary and capricious imposition of the death penalty, they pursue an argument explicitly rejected by the Supreme Court in *Gregg*, supra. There simply is no constitutional requirement that "prosecuting authorities charge a capital offense whenever arguably there [has] been a capital murder...." Id. at 199 n. 50 (opinion of Stewart, Powell, and Stevens, JJ.); id. at 225 (opinion of White, J., Burger, C.J., and Rehnquist, J., concurring). Thus, whether the crime is capital or not, "so long as the prosecutor has probable cause to believe that the accused committed an offense defined by statute, the decision whether or not to prosecute, and what charge to file or bring before a grand jury, generally rests entirely in its discretion." Bordenkircher v. Hayes, 434 U.S. 357, 364 (1978). Deference to the prosecutor "rests largely on the recognition that the decision to prosecute is particularly ill-suited to judicial review." Wayte v. United States, 470 U.S. 598, 607 (1985). Moreover, undue inquiry into prosecutorial decisions "delays the criminal proceeding, threatens to chill law enforcement [efforts] and may undermine prosecutorial effectiveness by revealing the Government's enforcement policy." Id. Concededly, due process will not tolerate a prosecutor's selection of defendants based on invidious factors. *Bordenkircher v. Hayes*, 434 U.S. at 364. But the defense does not contend that any such factors are here at issue.

The court therefore finds that the decision to file a death penalty notice against Mr. Pitera, but not against various co-defendants, was not arbitrary.

B.   Vindictive Prosecution

Mr. Pitera claims that the death penalty was sought in this case in vindictive response to his rejection of a government plea offer and demands for his cooperation. Although due process prohibits judges or prosecutors

expose each defendant to a maximum of 204 months incarceration without parole. Mr. Martini has, however, applied to the court to withdraw his guilty plea, which motion is still pending.

from vindictively retaliating against defendants who properly invoke their constitutional rights, including the right to a jury trial and the right to appeal, see North Carolina v. Pearce, 395 U.S. 711 (1969), there is simply no "objective evidence" before the court to support a finding of vindictiveness in this case. See United States v. Goodwin, 457 U.S. 368, 380 n. 12 & 384 (1982).

The chief prosecutor, David Shapiro, has filed an affirmation that (1) details his limited contact with Mr. Pitera on the day of the arrest, (2) denies any threat to pursue capital charges if defendant did not cooperate, and (3) recounts his conversations with Mathew Mari, defendant's original retained counsel, as to both the possibility of capital charges being filed, and the opportunity that would be afforded the defense to persuade the United States Attorney that such charges were unwarranted. In response, Mr. Mari files an affirmation that does not dispute these aspects of Mr. Shapiro's submission. Instead, it proffers a hearsay statement by Mr. Pitera attributing the offensive government conduct to unnamed officials other than Mr. Shapiro. Invited at oral argument to provide more particulars, the defense declined. Such vague hearsay is not the sort of objective evidence of vindictiveness referred to in *Goodwin*. See id.

Neither does defendant's claim give rise to a presumption of vindictiveness. Such a presumption has been applied to defendants who, after successfully pursuing appeals, are charged with more serious crimes on remand or are sentenced more severely after retrial. E.g., *Pearce*, supra. The presumption in such cases derives from a candid recognition of the "institutional bias against retrial...." *Goodwin*, 457 U.S. at 376.

No such obvious bias supports a pre-trial presumption of vindictiveness when charges are amended or increased. To the contrary, the Supreme Court has held that "[a] prosecutor should remain free before trial to exercise the broad discretion entrusted to him to determine the extent of the societal interest in prosecution. An initial decision should not freeze future conduct." Id. at 382. Thus, in *Bordenkircher v. Hayes*, supra, the Court upheld against a vindictive prosecution claim the filing of additional charges against a defendant who was threatened with same as the consequence of rejecting a plea offer. The Court explained that no "element of punishment or retaliation" was present since defendant was "free to accept or reject the prosecutor's offer." 434 U.S. at 363; accord Spinkellink v. Wainwright, 578 F.2d 582, 608 (5th Cir.1978)(applying *Bordenkircher v. Hayes* to capital case).

In contrast to *Bordenkircher v. Hayes*, it is not even clear in this case that Mr. Pitera was ever threatened with increased charges. As noted, he has declined the court's invitation to supplement his lawyer's hearsay submission in this regard. The matter is of no import. If Mr. Pitera was aware that by rejecting a plea offer he exposed himself to a capital charge, *Bordenkircher v. Hayes* precludes a finding of vindictive prosecution. If the notice was filed without any warning as to the possibility of a capital count, defendant's vindictiveness claim would be purely speculative. In *Goodwin*, the Court rejected such a basis for presuming vindictiveness, finding it lacking even the *Bordenkircher v. Hayes* predicate. *Goodwin*, 457 U.S. at 382 n. 15. Such a sequence of events may evidence an "opportunity for vindictiveness," but absent more is insufficient to give rise to a presumption. Id. at 384.

Mr. Pitera contends that his case is somehow different from *Bordenkircher v. Hayes* and *Goodwin* because the prosecutor purportedly knew all relevant facts at the time it first charged him. In fact, in *Bordenkircher v. Hayes*, the prosecution was similarly informed. Moreover, as the court noted in *Goodwin*, an informed prosecutorial decision depends not only on possessing the evidence, but on fully appreciating its significance and on carefully assessing "the proper extent of prosecution." *Goodwin*, 457 U.S. at 381. Little would be gained from a holding that encouraged prosecutors prematurely to file all possible charges in a criminal case. See id. at 378 n. 10 (noting potential prejudice to defendant). The claim of vindictive prosecution is rejected.

Conclusion

For the reasons stated in this memorandum and order, the court finds (1) that the death penalty does not constitute cruel and unusual punishment in all cases, (2) that the capital statute here at issue does not risk arbitrary and capricious imposition of the death penalty, [and] (3) that defendant was not arbitrarily and vindictively singled out for prosecution. The motion challenging constitutionality is, therefore, denied.

So ordered.

NOTES ON THE § 848 FEDERAL DEATH PENALTY

1. The Anti–Drug Abuse Act of 1988. As mentioned above, in the Anti–Drug Abuse Act of 1988, Congress authorized capital punishment for certain intentional killings committed in connection with serious federal drug offenses. The relevant portions of the statute are as follows:

"21 U.S.C. § 848. Continuing Criminal Enterprise.

"Penalties; forfeitures.

"Death penalty.

"(e)(1) In addition to the other penalties set forth in this section—

(A) any person engaging in or working in furtherance of a continuing criminal enterprise, or any person engaging in an offense punishable under section 841(b)(1)(A) of this title or section 960(b)(1) who intentionally kills or counsels, commands, induces, procures, or causes the intentional killing of an individual and such killing results, shall be sentenced to any term of imprisonment, which shall not be less than 20 years, and which may be up to life imprisonment, or may be sentenced to death; and

(B) any person, during the commission of, in furtherance of, or while attempting to avoid apprehension, prosecution or service of a prison sentence for, a felony violation of this subchapter or subchapter II of this chapter who intentionally kills or counsels, commands, induces, procures, or causes the intentional killing of any Federal, State, or local law enforcement officer engaged in, or on account of, the performance of such officer's official duties and such killing results, shall be sentenced to any term of imprisonment, which shall not be less than 20 years, and which may be up to life imprisonment, or may be sentenced to death.

(2) As used in paragraph (1)(b), the term 'law enforcement officer' means a public servant authorized by law or by a Government agency or Congress to conduct or engage in the prevention, investigation, prosecution or adjudication of an offense, and includes those engaged in corrections, probation, or parole functions.

. . .

"Hearing required with respect to the death penalty.

"(g) A person shall be subjected to the penalty of death for any offense under this section only if a hearing is held in accordance with this section.

"Notice by the Government in death penalty cases.

"(h)(1) Whenever the Government intends to seek the death penalty for an offense under this section for which one of the sentences provided is death, the attorney for the Government, a reasonable time before trial or acceptance by the court of a plea of guilty, shall sign and file with the court, and serve upon the defendant, a notice—

(A) that the Government in the event of conviction will seek the sentence of death; and

(B) setting forth the aggravating factors enumerated in subsection (n) of this section and any other aggravating factors which the Government will seek to prove as the basis for the death penalty. The court may permit the attorney for the Government to amend this notice for good cause shown.

"Hearing before court or jury.

"(i)(1) When the attorney for the Government has filed a notice as required under subsection (h) of this section and the defendant is found guilty of or pleads guilty to an offense under subsection (e) of this section, the judge who presided at the trial or before whom the guilty plea was entered, or any other judge if the judge who presided at the trial or before whom the guilty plea was entered is unavailable, shall conduct a separate sentencing hearing to determine the punishment to be imposed. The hearing shall be conducted—

(A) before the jury which determined the defendant's guilt;

(B) before a jury impaneled for the purpose of the hearing if—

(i) the defendant was convicted upon a plea of guilty; (ii) the defendant was convicted after a trial before the court sitting without a jury; (iii) the jury which determined the defendant's guilt has been discharged for good cause; or (iv) after initial imposition of a sentence under this section, redetermination of the sentence under this section is necessary; or

(C) before the court alone, upon the motion of the defendant and with the approval of the Government.

(2) A jury impaneled under paragraph (1)(B) shall consist of 12 members, unless, at any time before the conclusion of the hearing, the parties stipulate with the approval of the court that it shall consist of any number less than 12.

"Proof of aggravating and mitigating factors.

"(j) Notwithstanding rule 32(c) of the Federal Rules of Criminal Procedure, when a defendant is found guilty of or pleads guilty to an offense under subsection (e) of this section, no presentence report shall be prepared. In the sentencing hearing, information may be presented as to matters relating to any of the aggravating or mitigating factors set forth in subsections (m) and (n) of this section, or any other mitigating factor or any other aggravating factor for which notice has been provided under subsection (h)(1)(B) of this section. Where information is presented relating to any of the aggravating factors set forth in subsection (n) of this section, information may be presented relating to any other aggravating factor for which notice has been provided under subsection (h)(1)(B) of this section. Information presented may include the trial transcript and exhibits if the hearing is held before a jury or judge not present during the trial, or at the trial judge's discretion. Any other information relevant to such mitigating or aggravating factors may be presented by either the Government or the defendant, regardless of its admissibility under the rules governing admission of evidence at criminal trials, except that information may be excluded if its probative value is substantially outweighed by the danger of unfair prejudice, confusion of the issues, or misleading the jury. The Government and the defendant shall be permitted to rebut any information received at the hearing and shall be given fair opportunity to present argument as to the adequacy of the information to establish the existence of any of the aggravating or mitigating factors and as to appropriateness in that case of imposing a sentence of death. The Government shall open the argument. The defendant shall be permitted to reply. The Government shall then be permitted to reply in rebuttal. The burden of establishing the existence of any aggravating factor is on the Government, and is not satisfied unless established beyond a reasonable doubt. The burden of establishing the existence of any mitigating factor is on the defendant, and is not satisfied unless established by a preponderance of the evidence.

"Return of findings.

"(k) The jury, or if there is no jury, the court, shall consider all all the information received during the hearing. It shall return special findings identifying any aggravating factors set forth in subsection (n) of this section, found to exist. If one of the aggravating factors set forth in subsection (n)(1) of this section and another of the aggravating factors set forth in paragraphs (2) through (12) of subsection (n) of this section is found to exist, a special finding identifying any other aggravating factor for which has been provided under subsection (h)(1)(B) of this section, may be returned. A finding with respect to a mitigating factor may be made by one or more of the members of the jury, and any member of the jury who finds the existence of a mitigating factor may consider such a factor established for purposes of this subsection, regardless of the number of jurors who concur that the factor has been established. A finding with respect to any aggravating factor must be unanimous. If an aggravating factor set forth in subsection (n)(1) of this section is not found to exist or an aggravating factor set forth is subsection (n)(1) of this section is found to exist but no other aggravating factor set forth in subsection (n) is found to exist, the court shall impose a sentence, other than death, authorized by law. If an aggravating factor set forth in subsection (n)(1) of this section and one or more of the other aggravating factors set forth in subsection (n) of this section are found to exist, the jury, or if there is no jury, the court, shall then consider whether the aggravating factors found to exist sufficiently outweigh any mitigating factor or factors found to exist, or in the absence of mitigating factors, whether the aggravating factors are themselves sufficient to justify a sentence of death. Based upon this consideration, the jury by unanimous vote, or if there is no jury, the court, shall recommend that a sentence of death shall be imposed rather than a sentence of life imprisonment without possibility of release or some other lesser sentence. The jury or the court, regardless of its findings with respect to aggravating and mitigating factors, is never required to impose a death sentence and the jury shall be so instructed.

"Imposition of sentence.

"(*l*) Upon the recommendation that the sentence of death be imposed, the court shall sentence the defendant to death. Otherwise the court shall impose a sentence, other than death, authorized by law. A sentence of death shall not be carried out upon a person who is under 18 years of age at the time the crime was committed. A sentence of death shall not be carried out upon a person who is mentally retarded. A sentence of death shall not be carried out upon a person who, as a result of mental disability—

(1) cannot understand the nature of the pending proceedings, what such person was tried for, the reason for the punishment, or the nature of the punishment; or

(2) lacks the capacity to recognize or understand facts which would make the punishment unjust or unlawful, or lacks the ability to convey such information to counsel or to the court.

"Mitigating factors.

"(m) In determining whether a sentence of death is to be imposed on a defendant, the finder of fact shall consider mitigating factors, including the following:

(1) The defendant's capacity to appreciate the wrongfulness of the defendant's conduct or to conform conduct to the requirements of law was significantly impaired, regardless of whether the capacity was so impaired as to constitute a defense to the charge.

(2) The defendant was under unusual and substantial duress, regardless of whether the duress was of such a degree as to constitute a defense to the charge.

(3) The defendant is punishable as a principal (as defined in section 2 of Title 18) in the offense, which was committed by another, but the defendant's participation was relatively minor, regardless of whether the participation was so minor as to constitute a defense to the charge.

(4) The defendant could not reasonably have foreseen that the defendant's conduct in the course of the commission of murder, or other offense resulting in death for which the defendant was convicted, would create a grave risk of causing, death to any person.

(5) The defendant was youthful, although not under the age of 18.

(6) The defendant did not have a significant prior criminal record.

(7) The defendant committed the offense under severe mental or emotional disturbance.

(8) Another defendant or defendants, equally culpable in the crime, will not be punished by death.

(9) The victim consented to the criminal conduct that resulted in the victim's death.

(10) That other factors in the defendant's background or character mitigate against imposition of the death sentence.

"Aggravating factors for homicide.

"(n) If the defendant is found guilty of or pleads guilty to an offense under subsection (e) of this section, the following aggravating factors are the only aggravating factors that shall be considered, unless notice of additional aggravating factors is provided under subsection (h)(1)(B) of this section:

(1) The defendant—

(A) intentionally killed the victim;

(B) intentionally inflicted serious bodily injury which resulted in the death of the victim;

(C) intentionally engaged in conduct intending that the victim be killed or that lethal force be employed against the victim, which resulted in the death of the victim;

(D) intentionally engaged in conduct which—(i) the defendant knew would create a grave risk of death to a person, other than one of the participants in the offense; and (ii) resulted in the death of the victim.

(2) The defendant has been convicted of another Federal offense, or a State offense resulting in the death of a person, for which a sentence of life imprisonment or a sentence of death was authorized by statute.

(3) The defendant has previously been convicted of two or more State or Federal offenses punishable by a term of imprisonment of more than one year, committed on different occasions, involving the infliction of, or attempted infliction of, serious bodily injury upon another person.

(4) The defendant has previously been convicted of two or more State or Federal offenses punishable by a term of imprisonment of more than one year, committed on different occasions, involving the distribution of a controlled substance.

(5) In the commission of the offense or in escaping apprehension for a violation of subsection (e) of this section, the defendant knowingly created a grave risk of death to one or more persons in addition to the victims of the offense.

(6) The defendant procured the commission of the offense by payment, or promise of payment, of anything of pecuniary value.

(7) The defendant committed the offense as consideration for the receipt, or in the expectation of the receipt, of anything of pecuniary value.

(8) The defendant committed the offense after substantial planning and premeditation.

(9) The victim was particularly vulnerable due to old age, youth, or infirmity.

(10) The defendant had previously been convicted of violating this subchapter or subchapter II of this chapter for which a sentence of five or more years may be imposed or had previously been convicted of engaging in a continuing criminal enterprise.

(11) The violation of this subchapter in relation to which the conduct described in subsection (e) of this section occurred was a violation of section 845 of this title.

(12) The defendant committed the offense in an especially heinous, cruel, or depraved manner in that it involved torture or a serious physical abuse to victim.

"Right of the defendant to justice without discrimination.

"(o)(1) In any hearing held before a jury under this section, the court shall instruct the jury that in its consideration of whether the sentence of death is justified it shall not consider the race, color, religious beliefs, national origin, or sex of the defendant or the victim, and that the jury is not to recommend a sentence of death unless it has concluded that it would recommend a sentence of death for the crime in question no matter what the race, color, religious beliefs, national origin, or sex of the defendant, or the victim, may be. The jury shall return to the court a certificate signed by each juror that consideration of the race, color, religious beliefs, national origin, or sex of the defendant or the victim was no involved in reaching his or her individual decision, and the the individual juror would have made the same recommendation regarding a sentence for the crime in question no matter what the race, color, religious beliefs, national origin, or sex of the defendant, or the victim, may be.

(2) Not later than one year from November 18, 1988, the Comptroller General shall conduct a study of the various procedures used by the several States for determining whether or not to impose the death penalty in particular cases, and shall report to the Congress on whether or not any or all of the various procedures create a significant risk that the race of a defendant, or the race of a victim against whom a crime was committed, influence the likelihood that defendants in those States will be sentenced to death. In conducting the study required by this paragraph, the General Accounting Office shall—

(A) use ordinary methods of statistical analysis, including methods comparable to those ruled admissible by the courts in race discrimination cases under title VII of the Civil Rights Act of 1964 [42 U.S.C.A. § 2000e et seq.];

(B) study only crimes occurring after January 1, 1976; and

(C) determine what, if any, other factors, including any relation between any aggravating or mitigating factors and the race of the victim or the defendant, may account for any evidence that the race of the defendant, or the race of the victim, influences the likelihood that defendants will be sentenced to death. In addition, the General Accounting Office shall examine separately and include in the report, death penalty cases involving crimes similar to those covered under this section.

. . .

"Appeal in capital cases; counsel for financially unable defendants.

"(q)(1) In any case in which the sentence of death is imposed under this section, the sentence of death shall be subject to review by the court of appeals upon appeal by the defendant. Notice of appeal must be filed within the time prescribed for appeal of judgement in section 2107 of Title 28. An appeal under this section may be consolidated with an appeal of the judgment of conviction. Such review shall have priority over all other cases.

(2) On review of the sentence, the court of appeals shall consider the record, the evidence submitted during the trial, the information submitted during the sentencing hearing, the procedures employed in the sentencing hearing, and the special findings returned under this section.

(3) The court shall affirm the sentence if it determines that—

(A) the sentence of death was not imposed under the influence of passion, prejudice, or any other arbitrary factor; and

(B) the information supports the special finding of the existence of every aggravating factor upon which the sentence was based, together with, or the failure to find, any mitigating factors as set forth or allowed in this section. In all other cases the court shall remand the case for reconsideration under this section. The court of appeals shall state in writing the reasons for its disposition of the review of the sentence.

. . .

"Refusal to participate by State and Federal correctional employees.

"(r) No employee of any State department of corrections or the Federal Bureau of Prisons and no employee providing services to that department or bureau under contract shall be required, as a condition of that employment, or contractual obligation to be in attendance at or to participate in any execution carried out under this section if such participation is contrary to the moral or religious convictions of the employee. For purposes of this subsection, the term "participation in executions" includes personal preparation of the condemned individual and the apparatus used for execution and supervision of the activities of other personnel in carrying out such activities."

   2.   United States v. Chandler. In United States v. Chandler, 996
F.2d 1073 (11th Cir.1993), the Eleventh Circuit became the first Court of
Appeals to address the constitutionality of the federal death penalty provi-
sions contained in 21 U.S.C. § 848(e)(1)(A):

   "III.   Discussion

   "A.   Challenges To The Death Sentence

   "1.   Jury power to recommend a sentence other than death

   "Section 848(k) provides that, if the jury finds certain aggravating factors, the jury must then weigh the aggravating factors
against any mitigating factors to determine whether to recommend
'that a sentence of death shall be imposed rather than a sentence
of life imprisonment without possibility of release or some other
lesser sentence.' At Chandler's sentencing, the district court
instructed the jury that, in the event that it did not recommend a
sentence of death, it should not be concerned with the question of
what sentence he might receive. The district court also stated
that the judge alone would decide Chandler's sentence if the jury
did not recommend death.

   "Chandler contends that the district court violated § 848(k)
as well as the Fifth and Eighth Amendments by withholding from
the jury the authority to impose a sentence other than death.
However, at a pre-sentencing hearing, Chandler's counsel asserted
that 'I don't think they [the jurors] make a recommendation of a
sentence if they don't recommend death.' The proposed jury
instructions submitted by Chandler advised that, if the jury did
not recommend a death sentence, the responsibility for imposition
of a non-death sentence rested with the district court. Because
Chandler both argued for and submitted jury instructions stating
that the district court alone was responsible for sentencing Chandler if the jury did not recommend death, Chandler invited the
alleged error and cannot now, on appeal, complain that the instruction was erroneous.

   "Had Chandler not invited the instruction, the district court
properly construed § 848(k). When the language of a statute is
clear, the language controls any interpretation of the statute
absent a legislative intent to the contrary. United States v.
Turkette, 452 U.S. 576, 580 (1981). We must look to the language
and design of the statute as a whole in interpreting the language
at issue. McCarthy v. Bronson, 500 U.S. 136, 139 (1991).

   "The language of § 848(k) is not perfectly clear, and the
legislative history of the Anti–Drug Abuse Act of 1988 consists of
only a few debates on the Senate floor. Nevertheless, § 848(k)
can be confidently interpreted when it is read in the context of the
statute as a whole. Several provisions of § 848 suggest that
Chandler's interpretation is flawed. Section 848(*l*) provides:

'Upon the recommendation that the sentence of death be imposed, the court shall sentence the defendant to death. Otherwise the court shall impose a sentence, other than death, authorized by law.'

"The second sentence of this section instructs that the district court determines the sentence if the jury does not recommend death. Similarly, § 848(p) provides:

'If a person is convicted for an offense under subsection (e) of this section and the court does not impose the penalty of death, the court may impose a sentence of life imprisonment without the possibility of parole.'

"Thus, the statute grants the district court the discretion to sentence a defendant to life without parole if a death sentence is not recommended. These sections preclude an interpretation of § 848(k) that gives the jury the authority to impose a non-death sentence. Correspondingly, the responsibility for sentencing has historically resided with the trial court. In the absence of clear language in a statute to lodge the sentencing responsibility with the jury, we are reluctant to interpret the statute in a strained manner to reach that result. Hence, we find that § 848 grants the district court the power to sentence the defendant where the jury does not recommend death. ...

"2. Jury should have been informed of other sentences

"Chandler contends that even if the jury did not have the power to recommend a sentence other than death, under § 848(k) and applicable precedent, the jury should have been informed of the possible sentences Chandler would face if the jury did not recommend death. We review jury instructions de novo to determine whether they misstate the law or mislead the jury to the prejudice of the objecting party. The instructions must be viewed as a whole in the context of the trial record. Cupp v. Naughten, 414 U.S. 141, 146–47 (1973). Further, an error occurs only when there is a reasonable likelihood that the jury applied the instruction in an improper manner. Boyde v. California, 494 U.S. 370, 380 (1990).

"Initially, Chandler asserts that § 848(k) requires that the jury be informed that he would face some other sentence, including the possibility of a life sentence without parole, if the jury did not recommend the death penalty. Section 848(k) instructs that after weighing the aggravating and mitigating factors and determining that the aggravating factors sufficiently outweigh the mitigating factors, the jury may then exercise its option to recommend that a sentence of death shall be imposed rather than a sentence of life imprisonment without possibility of release or some other lesser sentence.

"At sentencing the district court instructed the jury:

> 'In deciding what recommendation to make, you are not
> to be concerned with the question of what sentence the
> defendant might receive in the event you determine not to
> recommend a death sentence. That is a matter for me to
> decide in the event you conclude that a sentence of death
> should not be recommended.'

"The district court also instructed:

> 'If you do not make such a recommendation, the court is
> required by law to impose a sentence other than death,
> which sentence is to be determined by the court alone.'

"Chandler's argument, in effect, is that the district court's instruction was inadequate because it did not inform the jury that the
'sentence other than death' included the possibility of life without
parole.

"We find that the district court's instructions adequately
informed the jury under § 848(k). The statutory scheme created
by § 848 provides that the jury alone has the power to recommend
a sentence of death. If the jury does not make such a recommendation, the district court sentences the defendant. Nothing in
§ 848 requires the jury to be informed of what sentence the
defendant might receive in the absence of death. The district
court's instructions were proper.

"Chandler also suggests that applicable precedent, mandating
that a defendant be allowed to introduce evidence relating to
mitigating factors, requires that the jury be informed of the
possibility that Chandler would receive a life sentence without
parole if death was not recommended. The Supreme Court has
defined mitigating factors as 'any aspect of a defendant's character
or record and any of the circumstances of the offense.' Lockett v.
Ohio, 438 U.S. 586, 604 (1978); see Skipper v. South Carolina, 476
U.S. 1, 4 (1986). The range of possible sentences that Chandler
might receive in the event the jury did not recommend death does
not fall within this definition. Accordingly, the district court was
not required to inform the jury of the possible sentences Chandler
might face.

"3. Return of mitigating findings

"Chandler urges us to rule that the district court should have
required the jury to return written findings of mitigating factors it
did or did not find to exist. At no time, however, did Chandler
request that the jury be instructed to return written findings of
mitigating factors or object to the lack of such an instruction.
Chandler did submit proposed jury charges that instructed the
jury that they should find two mitigating factors: (1) that Chandler lacked a criminal record, and (2) that an equally culpable
defendant would not receive the death penalty. These requested
instructions did not adequately bring to the district court's atten-

tion the issue now presented on appeal. Thus, we review for plain error. Fed.R.Crim.P. 52(b).

"The finding of plain error is a three step process: (1) there must be an error, (2) the error must be plain, i.e. clear or obvious, and (3) the error must affect substantial rights. United States v. Olano, 507 U.S. 725, 732 (1993). In most cases, the third prong of this test is met only when the defendant demonstrates that the error affected the outcome of the proceedings before the district court. If, however, the error affects the basic protections of a criminal trial without which a criminal trial cannot reliably serve its function, an effect on the outcome will be presumed. See Arizona v. Fulminante, 499 U.S. 279, 308 (1991)(distinguishing between trial type errors and errors which undermine the entire trial). If the defendant satisfies all three prongs, then we have the discretionary power to correct an error which seriously affects the fairness, integrity or public reputation of judicial proceedings. *Olano*, 507 U.S. at 736.

"We first determine whether an error occurred. We disagree with Chandler's interpretation of § 848 that the jury is required to return written findings of mitigating factors that the jury has either found to exist or found not to exist. Instead we interpret § 848 as providing the jury with the option of returning written findings of mitigating factors. Because the district court's instructions and verdict form foreclosed the jury's exercise of this option, the district court committed error.

"Section 848(k) is entitled 'Return of Findings.' It provides that the jury 'shall return special findings identifying any aggravating factors set forth in subsection (n) of this section, found to exist.' The section also states:

'A finding with respect to a mitigating factor may be made by one or more of the members of the jury, and any member of the jury who finds the existence of a mitigating factor may consider such a factor established for purposes of this subsection, regardless of the number of jurors who concur that the factor has been established.'

"The statute mentions special findings only in relation to aggravating factors. Also, the permissive language concerning the return of written mitigating factors, 'may be made,' contrasts with the mandatory language concerning the return of written aggravating findings, 'shall.' The jury is required to return aggravating findings and is permitted to return mitigating findings. Therefore, we find that § 848 requires that the jury be instructed that it has the option to return written findings of mitigating factors if it so chooses, but that it does not require the return of such findings.

"Section 848(q) does not require a different result. This section states that on review of a death sentence, 'the court of appeals shall consider . . . the special findings returned under this section.' 21 U.S.C. § 848(q)(2). The section also instructs, in pertinent part, that we shall affirm a death sentence if the information supports the special finding of the existence of every aggravating factor upon which the sentence was based, together with, or the failure to find, any mitigating factors as set forth or allowed in this section. 21 U.S.C. § 848(q)(3)(B). Neither of these subsections mandate the written findings of mitigating factors. They require only that we review any findings which are returned to ensure that the information presented during sentencing supports those findings. We hold that § 848(k) requires that the jury be given the option to return written findings of mitigating factors. Section 848(q)(3) requires that if the jury exercises its option, we must review those findings.

"This interpretation comports with the law as it stood at the time Congress drafted the Anti–Drug Abuse Act of 1988. The finding of mitigating circumstances is individualized; a juror is free to find a mitigating factor even if no other juror agrees with that finding. See Mills v. Maryland, 486 U.S. 367, 373–74 (1988). Congress may well have determined that forcing jurors to write down mitigating factors would discourage a lone juror from finding mitigating circumstances that the rest of the jury had rejected or disparaged. More significantly, by not requiring a juror to inform his or her fellow jurors of the mitigating factors that will be used in that juror's weighing calculus, the individualized determination of both mitigating factors and the appropriateness of a death sentence is protected.

"The district court in this case did not inform the jury that it had the option to return written findings of mitigating factors and the verdict form did not contain space for the optional findings. This was error. Moreover, the error was plain. The statute, as we interpret it in this opinion, requires that the jury be given an option to return mitigating findings.

"Accordingly, we must determine whether the error affected Chandler's substantial rights. We note initially that this error does not undermine the basic protections of a criminal trial without which a criminal trial cannot reliably serve its function, but instead is a trial type error. Chandler must therefore demonstrate that the error affected the outcome of the proceedings before the district court. Chandler argues that he was prejudiced because an appellate court on review cannot determine whether the jury found two mitigating factors which Chandler contends were beyond dispute: (1) that Chandler had no criminal record; and (2) that Jarrell was an equally culpable person who would not receive the death penalty.

"We are persuaded that the lack of written mitigating findings did not affect the outcome of Chandler's sentencing hearing. The government and Chandler stipulated that Chandler had no prior conviction on any felony or drug charge and that Jarrell would not receive the death penalty. These stipulations were presented at sentencing to the jury, and the jury was informed that they were stipulations. Moreover, the jury was properly instructed on how to find mitigating factors and the role of mitigating factors in their decision making process. The jury is presumed to follow the instructions they are given. See Richardson v. Marsh, 481 U.S. 200, 206 (1987). Thus, Chandler has not demonstrated that the lack of written mitigating findings affected the outcome of his case.

"In conclusion, the district court erred by not allowing the jury the option to return written findings of mitigating factors. However, this error did not affect the outcome of the sentencing hearing and was, therefore, not plain error.

. . .

"6.   Instruction on the weighing process

"Following the jury's finding of aggravating and mitigating factors, § 848(k) provides that the jury 'shall then consider whether the aggravating factors found to exist sufficiently outweigh any mitigating factor or factors found to exist, or in the absence of mitigating factors, whether the aggravating factors are themselves sufficient to justify a sentence of death.' Chandler assigns error to the district court's failure to instruct the jury that it was required to find that the aggravating circumstances sufficiently outweighed any mitigating factors either beyond a reasonable doubt or by clear and convincing evidence. Chandler contends that because the possible punishment under § 848 is the death penalty, the weighing process must be interpreted to require a heightened burden of proof.

"The clear language of a statute controls any interpretation of the statute absent a clearly expressed legislative intent to the contrary. In this case, the language of § 848(k) is clear and the meager legislative history is not to the contrary. The statute states that the jury must consider whether the aggravating factors sufficiently outweigh the mitigating factors to justify a sentence of death or if no mitigating factors exist whether the aggravating factors are themselves sufficient to justify a sentence of death. There is no language suggesting that the weighing process is governed by a burden of proof. Congress obviously knew how to assign burdens of proof to jury findings; it did so in § 848(j) for findings of aggravating factors (beyond a reasonable doubt) and mitigating factors (by a preponderance of the evidence). If Congress had intended to govern the jury's weighing process with a burden of proof, it could have done so. It did not, and we will not construe the statute to require one.

"That the jury need only be instructed that the aggravating factors sufficiently outweigh the mitigating factors is entirely appropriate. A capital sentencing scheme is constitutional even if it does not require that a specific burden of proof govern the jury's weighing process. Ford v. Strickland, 696 F.2d 804, 817–18 (11th Cir.1983)(en banc). The Supreme Court has also observed, 'we have never held that a specific method for balancing mitigating and aggravating factors in a capital sentencing proceeding is constitutionally required.' Franklin v. Lynaugh, 487 U.S. 164, 179 (1988)(plurality). Congress created a constitutional capital sentencing scheme by requiring the jury to find that the aggravating factors sufficiently outweigh the mitigating factors before a death sentence could be recommended.

"Alternatively, Chandler submits that even if the statute does not require a burden of proof in the weighing process, the district court erred in its instructions to the jury. The district court instructed the jury both at the beginning of the sentencing hearing, the preliminary instructions, and again at the conclusion, the supplemental jury instructions. On each occasion the district court provided the jury with a copy of the instructions that the district court requested the jury follow as the instructions were read aloud. Both the preliminary and the supplemental instructions discussed the weighing process five times. Three of those times the district court instructed that the aggravating factors must sufficiently outweigh the mitigating factors. Twice the district court instructed that the aggravating factors must outweigh the mitigating factors. The district court also gave the jury a verdict form. The form was to be signed by each juror and confirmed that the jury had found that the aggravating factors sufficiently outweighed the mitigating factors.

"We review jury instructions under the standard discussed above. In context, the instructions sufficiently charged the jury on the weighing process. The instructions communicated to the jury that it must find that the aggravating factors when balanced against the mitigating factors justified a sentence of death. The fact that the district court omitted the word 'sufficiently' two times does not render the instructions inadequate or erroneous. Moreover, the jury form that each juror signed stated that 'the aggravating factors unanimously found by us to exist sufficiently outweigh any mitigating factor or factors found to exist to justify a sentence of death.'

"7.   The weighing process

"A death penalty statute is constitutional only if the statue genuinely narrows the class of persons eligible for the death penalty and reasonably justifies the imposition of a more severe sentence on the defendant compared to others found guilty of murder. Lowenfield v. Phelps, 484 U.S. 231, 244 (1988)(citing Zant v. Stephens, 462 U.S. 862, 877 (1983)).

"Chandler argues that due to the breadth of 848(e), the finding of guilt under § 848(e) does not satisfy the constitutional requirement that a capital statute must genuinely narrow the class of defendants eligible for the death penalty. Instead, Chandler contends that the narrowing function occurs during the sentencing phase when the jury finds aggravating factors. Chandler further contends that because one of the aggravating factors duplicates a jury finding at the guilt phase, the jury's weighing process is skewed in favor of imposing the death penalty. He submits that the jury's deliberations are skewed because the jury will inevitably consider the number of aggravating factors during its weighing process.

"Section 848 establishes a two-step scheme that guides the jury's deliberations. At the guilt phase, the jury determines whether the defendant intentionally killed or commanded or procured the intentional killing of an individual while engaging in or working in furtherance of a continuing criminal enterprise. Before the death penalty can be recommended, the jury at sentencing must first unanimously find that the government has proved beyond a reasonable doubt the existence of aggravating factor (n)(1) and at least one other aggravating factor from the list in (n)(2) through (n)(12). Aggravating factor (n)(1) mirrors the intent element found at the guilt phase. The jury then considers whether the aggravating factors sufficiently outweigh any mitigating factors to justify a sentence of death. If no mitigating factors are found, the jury considers whether the aggravating factors are sufficient to justify a sentence of death.

"As long as a death penalty statute narrows the class of persons subject to the death penalty at the guilt phase of trial, the fact that the jury may find an aggravating factor that duplicates a finding made at the guilt phase does not render the capital statute unconstitutional. *Lowenfield*, 484 U.S. at 246. The statutory scheme of § 848 satisfies the requirements of *Lowenfield*.[4] Initially, the statute requires the jury to find that the defendant intentionally committed homicide in connection with large scale drug

---

[4] In *Lowenfield*, the jury, in convicting the defendant for first degree murder, found that the defendant had the specific intent to kill or to inflict great bodily harm upon more than one person. At sentencing, the jury then found, as the sole aggravating factor, that the defendant had knowingly created a risk of death or great bodily harm to more than one person. The Supreme Court determined that the statute narrowed the class of death eligible defendants at the guilt phase by narrowing the definition of a capital offense. The Court found that a capital statute is constitutional if it narrows the class of death eligible defendants at the guilt phase and at sentencing allows for the consideration of mitigating circumstances and the exercise of discretion. The fact that an aggravating factor in such a scheme duplicates the jury's finding at the guilt phase was not dispositive.

trafficking. The statute does not embrace anyone who committed murder, but only those who did so in connection with a continuing criminal enterprise. Thus, § 848(e) sufficiently narrows the class of death eligible defendants at the guilt phase. Moreover, § 848 requires that the jury find at least one other aggravating factor from the list of (n)(2)-(n)(12) before the death penalty can be imposed. The statute also requires the jury to consider any mitigating circumstances and allows the jury to weigh the aggravating and mitigating factors. This is all that *Lowenfield* requires.

"Nevertheless, Chandler suggests that the present case is distinguishable from *Lowenfield* because § 848(e) requires the jury to weigh the factors while the statute in *Lowenfield* did not. Chandler posits that the jury will be influenced in its weighing process by the number of aggravating factors. Although the Supreme Court has observed that the difference between a weighing statute and a non-weighing statute is 'not one of "semantics",' *Stringer v. Black*, 503 U.S. 222, 231 (1992), we have previously rejected the kind of argument Chandler now makes. *Johnson v. Singletary*, 991 F.2d 663, 669 (11th Cir.1993)(per curiam). Further, any such distinction was erased by the district court's instructions. The court's instructions made clear that the weighing process was not a mechanical one and that different factors could be given different weight. Thus, the jury was adequately instructed that it should not reach a decision based on the number of aggravating or mitigating factors. Accordingly, the scheme of § 848(e) was not improperly skewed towards a sentence of death.

. . .

"B.   Challenges To The Conviction On Count Three

"Count Three of the indictment charged Chandler with the murder of Shuler while engaged in and working in furtherance of a continuing criminal enterprise in violation of 21 U.S.C. § 848(e). Chandler contends on several grounds that his conviction on this count was improper.

"1.   Connection between the continuing criminal enterprise and the murder

"Section 848(e)(1)(A) states that 'any person engaging in or working in furtherance of a continuing criminal enterprise . . . who intentionally kills or counsels, commands, induces, procures, or causes the intentional killing of an individual and such killing results, shall be sentenced to any term of imprisonment, which shall not be less than 20 years, and which may be up to life imprisonment, or may be sentenced to death.' The government and Chandler agree that § 848(e) requires a connection between the underlying continuing criminal enterprise and Shuler's murder in order for the Chandler to be convicted under this statute. Chandler contends, however, that his conviction should be reversed because the indictment failed to allege, and the district court's instructions did not require the jury to find, a connection between the murder and the enterprise. Chandler posits that these defects allowed the jury to return a guilty verdict based upon a finding that Chandler was involved in Shuler's murder contemporaneously with his involvement in the criminal enterprise even if the murder was unrelated to the enterprise. Chandler contends that the jury could have found that Chandler solicited Shuler's death because of Shuler's abusive treatment of his family, yet still return a guilty verdict on Count Three.

"a. The indictment

"The indictment charged in Count Three that Chandler:

'while engaged in and working in furtherance of a continuing criminal enterprise, intentionally killed and counseled, commanded, induced, procured and caused the intentional killing of Marlin Shuler, and such killing resulted, in violation of Title 21, United States Code, § 848(e)(1)(A), and Title 18 United States Code, § 2.'

"The indictment was sufficient because it did require a nexus between the enterprise and the murder of Shuler. An indictment may track the language of the statute 'as long as "those words of themselves fully, directly, and expressly, without any uncertainty or ambiguity, set forth all the elements necessary to constitute the offense intended to be punished."' Hamling v. United States, 418 U.S. 87, 117 (1974).

"The language of the indictment is sufficient. The indictment tracks the language of the statute as written by Congress. Moreover, any reasonable reading of the indictment makes it clear that the government was charging Chandler with a murder in connection with, and not just contemporaneous to, the ongoing continuing criminal enterprise. The necessary connection between the murder and the enterprise was thus present in the indictment.

"b. Jury charge

"The instruction given by the district court to the jury stated,

'So count 3 is built upon count 2, which it is built upon count 1. Then goes on and charges on or about May 8, 1990 in or about an area known as Snow's Lake near Piedmont, Alabama in the Northern District of Alabama, the defendant ... while engaged in and working in furtherance of a Continuing Criminal Enterprise, intentionally killed and counseled, commanded, induced, procured and caused the intentional killing of Marlin Shuler....'

"The district court further instructed that:

'Section 848(e)(1) make[s] it a separate Federal crime or offense for anyone, while engaging [in] a Continuing Criminal

Enterprise such as the one charged in count 2, to kill an individual or to command or cause the intentional killing of an individual.'

"The court then enumerated the elements in a § 848(e)(1) offense:

'First, that while engaging in or working in furtherance of the Continuing Criminal Enterprise charged in court 2, the defendant either killed Marlin Shuler or commanded, induced, procured or caused the intentional killing of Marlin Shuler, as charged in count 3 and (2), that the death of Marlin Shuler resulted from such activity of the defendant and, (3), that such activity of the defendant was done knowingly and willfully.'

"Again, Chandler argues that these instructions allowed the jury to return a guilty verdict even if they found no connection between the enterprise and Chandler's solicitation of Shuler's murder.

"Chandler failed to request a jury instruction concerning the charge he now claims was erroneous, nor did he object to the charge that was given. Thus, we review the charge for plain error. Fed.R.Crim.P. 52(b). The instructions are reviewed under the standard discussed above.

"The instructions informed the jury that Count Three, the murder charge, was 'built upon' Count Two, the continuing criminal enterprise charge. The district court also instructed the jury that there must be a connection between the murder and the continuing criminal enterprise. The connection was described once as 'while engaged in and in furtherance of' the enterprise and later stated as 'while engaged in or in furtherance of' the enterprise. There is nothing vague about this clear and direct expression. Additionally, the prosecution introduced evidence and argued repeatedly that Chandler had solicited the murder of Shuler because Shuler had informed on one of Chandler's dealers.

"There is no reasonable likelihood that the jury believed that it could find Chandler guilty even if it found that he solicited Shuler's murder for reasons not connected to the continuing criminal enterprise. The instructions clearly conveyed to the jury that it must find a connection between Shuler's murder and the enterprise. The mere use of the word 'or' by the district court once during the jury instructions is exactly the type of 'artificial isolation' that the Supreme Court rejected in *Cupp v. Naughten.* 414 U.S. at 147. . . .

"4.   The offense in Count Three of the indictment

"Chandler argues that his conviction under Count Three of the indictment is invalid because § 848(e) does not define an offense. Instead, Chandler submits that § 848(e) is merely a sentencing provision that authorizes the death penalty without proscribing conduct.

"The Fifth Circuit has squarely rejected this argument, and the reasoning of that court is persuasive. United States v. Villarreal, 963 F.2d 725, 727–28 (5th Cir.1992)(rejecting claim that § 848(e)(1)(B) does not define an offense). Section 848(e) sets forth the elements of the crime (any person engaged in a continuing criminal enterprise who procures the intentional killing of an individual), the mens rea (intent), and a separate penalty (20 years imprisonment to life, or the death penalty). Similarly, the conduct proscribed in § 848(e) is referred to as an offense in subsections (g), (h), (i), (j), (n), and (p). We find Chandler's argument meritless."

The Eleventh Circuit upheld the statute, and affirmed the defendant's death sentence.

NOTE ON THE FEDERAL DEATH PENALTY ACT OF 1994

As indicated in the introduction to this section, Congress has recently expanded the potential reach of the federal death penalty. In the Federal Death Penalty Act of 1994, enacted as part of the omnibus Violent Crime Control and Law Enforcement Act of 1994, Congress adopted new procedures—for the most part similar to those contained in the 1988 statute authorizing the death penalty for drug kingpins—for the purpose of "reviving" the long-dormant federal death penalty statutes already "on the books." In addition, Congress added many new federal death penalty provisions to the U.S. Code. The list of new and "revived" federal death penalty crimes under the 1994 Act includes (but is not limited to) the following crimes[a]:

Aircraft and motor vehicle hijacking (18 U.S.C. § 34); Espionage (18 U.S.C. § 794(a)); Explosive Materials (18 U.S.C. § 844(d)); Federal Murder (18 U.S.C. § 1111(b)); Killing of a Foreign Official (18 U.S.C. § 1116(a)); Kidnapping (18 U.S.C. § 1201(a)); Mailing of Nonmailable Injurious Articles (18 U.S.C. § 1716); Wrecking Trains (18 U.S.C. § 1992); Bank Robbery (18 U.S.C. § 2113(e)); Hostage Taking (18 U.S.C. § 1203(a)); Murder for Hire (18 U.S.C. § 1958); Racketeering (18 U.S.C. § 1959(a)(1)); Genocide (18 U.S.C. § 1091 (b)(1)); Carjacking (18 U.S.C. § 2119(3)); Murder by a Federal Prisoner (18 U.S.C. § 1118); Civil Rights Murder (18 U.S.C. § 241 et seq.); Murder of Federal Law Enforcement Officials (18 U.S.C. § 1114); Drive-by Shootings to Further Drug Conspiracies (18 U.S.C. § 36); Foreign Murder of U.S. National (18 U.S.C. § 1119); Rape and Child Molestation Murder (18 U.S.C. § 2245); Sexual Exploitation of Children (18 U.S.C. § 2251(d)); Murder by Escaped Prisoner (18 U.S.C. § 1120); Gun Murder During Federal Crime of Violence or Drug Trafficking Crime (18 U.S.C. § 924); Homicide Involving Firearm in Federal

[a] Note that for most non-murder crimes, the death penalty is limited to cases involving intentional or extremely reckless killings that occur during the commission of those crimes.

Facility (18 U.S.C. § 930); Murder of State or Local Official
Assisting Federal Law Enforcement Official (18 U.S.C. § 1121);
Murder of Court Officer or Juror (18 U.S.C. § 1503); Retaliatory
Killing of Witness, Victim, or Informant (18 U.S.C. § 1513); Murder of Federal Witness (18 U.S.C. § 1512(a)); Offense of Violence
Against Maritime Navigation or Fixed Platform (18 U.S.C.
§ 2280); Torture (18 U.S.C. § 2340A(a)); Violence at International Civil Airport (18 U.S.C. § 37); Terrorist Act (18 U.S.C.
§ 2332(a)(1)); Use of Weapon of Mass Destruction (18 U.S.C.
§ 2332a); and Alien Smuggling (8 U.S.C. § 1324(a)).

Which, if any, of these new or "revived" federal death penalty provisions
constitute a meaningful response to the problem of violent crime in
America? How many defendants are likely to be affected by these provisions, given that the provisions can apply *only* to defendants who commit
their crimes within the scope of federal jurisdiction? Which provisions
seem to be primarily symbolic (or political) in nature and likely effect?

THE FIRST HOUSE DEBATE: H.R. 653 (APRIL, 1943)

H.R. 653, the bill that ultimately evolved into the Hobbs Act, went to the floor of the U.S. House of Representatives on April 9, 1943, and was the subject of extensive debate, extending for some 38 pages[1] in the Congressional Record. See 89 Cong. Rec. 3192–3230. It is neither possible nor desirable to reproduce the entire debate below, but its flavor is revealed in the following passages.[2]

Two major amendments to the bill were before the House. The first (the Committee amendment) was identical to what became title II of the Hobbs Act as enacted (see Chapter III, Sec. 1). Congressman Celler offered alternative language (the Celler or A.F. of L. amendment):

"That no acts, conduct, or activities which are lawful under section 6 or section 20 of an act entitled 'An Act to supplement existing laws against unlawful restraints and monopolies, and for other purposes', approved October 15, 1914 [the Clayton Act], or under an act entitled 'An Act to amend the judicial code and to define and limit the jurisdiction of the courts in equity, and for other purposes', approved March 23, 1932 [the Norris–LaGuardia Act], or under an act entitled 'An Act to provide for the prompt disposition of disputes between carriers and their employees, and for other purposes', approved May 20, 1926, as amended [the Railway Labor Act], or under an act entitled 'An Act to diminish the causes of labor disputes burdening or obstructing interstate or foreign commerce, to create a National Labor Relations Board, and for other purposes', approved July 5, 1935 [the National Labor Relations Act], shall constitute a violation of this act." (3220)

Excerpts from the debate follow. The first speaker was Congressman Halleck:

"Mr. HALLECK . . . I shall try in a few words to give . . . some idea of what I think this is about.

"In 1934 Congress enacted a so-called Anti–Racketeering Act. It was designed to bring about federal prosecution of people obtaining money or property by violence and threats of violence in connection with the movement of goods in interstate commerce. An exception was written into the

---

[1] Each page is three columns of small type that would print out to about 3½ pages in the type face used in this book.

[2] Particular attention has been paid in selecting these excerpts to colloquies or statements that may be relevant to the intended substantive scope of the statute. The page numbers from which quotations have been taken appear in parenthesis following each statement.

law which provided it should not apply to a situation where there existed a bona fide relationship of employer and employee.

"The celebrated 807 case in New York came on for decision by the Supreme Court. The case involved the conduct of individuals who stopped trucks going into the city of New York and in effect hijacked the drivers out of $8 or $9 per truck. The Supreme Court held that under the exception heretofore referred to by me, relative to the relationship of employer and employee, the prosecution would not lie in that case. I know a lot of good lawyers who disagree with that decision, and personally I disagree with it. . . .

"This bill seeks to supply the deficiency created by that decision. In a word, what this bill seeks to do is to superimpose federal jurisdiction or federal prosecution for robbery and extortion committed in connection with the movement of goods in interstate commerce. I say that is the objective, and as far as I have ever heard that is the sole objective of the bill. It is to stop the so-called hijacking and racketeering that has prevailed. . . .

"My view . . . is that we must legislate on the theory that the Court is going to interpret an act the way we write it and the way we intend that it be interpreted and applied.

"If any court or judge cannot see in these proceedings—cannot get a complete idea from what is going on here in the passage of this bill—that we intend that hijacking, extortion, and robbery in connection with movement of goods in interstate commerce be stopped, then I do not know what you can depend upon in the way of judicial interpretation.

"Another thing: It has been suggested that the four acts named [in the Celler and Committee amendments] authorize violence, but I do not so understand. For instance, take the Norris–LaGuardia Act. It specifically provides that conduct of labor organizations is legalized only when it is peaceful, nonviolent, and free from fraud. . . ." (3192–93)

"Mr. FISH. Mr. Speaker, the bill before us has for its purpose, according to its title[,] to protect trade and commerce against interference by violence, threats, coercion, or intimidation. No American citizen should object to such a proposal. There can be no real argument about legislating against robbery and extortion.

"Mr. Speaker, this bill—the Hobbs anti-racketeering bill—should not be opposed by Members of Congress, because it merely applies to labor what is already applied to all other groups among the American people. Its purpose is to do away with extortion, robbery, and practices that should be unlawful that have been used in the past by some union organizations in New York City extorting or attempting to extort fees from helpless farmers before permitting them to drive their produce truck to market. . . ." (3194)

"Mr. HOBBS. . . . [T]he decision of the Supreme Court in the *Local 807* case . . . has . . . decided that no matter how much violence a union man might use in seeking employment, he could not be punished under the 1934 Anti–Racketeering Act. If he commits murder, or if he commits assault with a weapon, it is all right under the antiracketeering law.

"Mr. HALLECK. [I]s it not true that that decision of the Supreme Court in the *807* case hinged upon the exception written into the act in reference to the bona fide relationship of employer to employee, and is it not also true that if this act becomes the law those words will be repealed, which will mean that the words upon which that decision depended will no longer be in the law?

"Mr. HOBBS. No. I do not so construe the opinion.... If I read that opinion correctly, and I have read it a hundred times, ... the opinion is based on both of the exceptions ..., the latter one of which is substantially in blanket form what is detailed in the committee amendment and what is also detailed in the A.F. of L. amendment. ...

"Mr. WRIGHT. I want to know how the gentleman can argue that both of these amendments are substantially the same, then say in the next breath that the Celler amendment emasculates the act and at least infer that the other one does not.

"Mr. HOBBS. I never said that. I said they seemed so at first reading. I submit that there is within the essence of the Celler amendment a phrase which seems to be in accord with our wishes as to stamping out the racket, but which does not result in that. It permits robbery or extortion because it does not deal truly with the status. It says that no acts, conduct or activity which are lawful under the four laws therein cited should constitute guilt under this law. And it implies that this is to be taken as true, no matter how unlawfully any of those lawful acts may be done. The four laws cited in the Celler amendment require the lawful acts in them enumerated to be done in a peaceful, lawful way. The Celler amendment, quite cleverly, omits any such requirement. ...

"Mr. COLMER. Will the gentleman explain how one can do an act lawfully and at the same time do it unlawfully?

"Mr. HOBBS. Of course, the question as framed contains a contradiction in terms. No one can act lawfully and unlawfully at the same time. But no such case is presented by the Celler amendment or its underlying meaning. There we have a lawful act done unlawfully. [T]hat is the effect of the construction put upon robbery committed while engaged in otherwise lawful conduct by the Supreme Court decision. No matter how much force is used, robbery is a perfectly innocent pastime, as Chief Justice Stone said, if the perpetrator be a labor-union member seeking employment." (3195)

"Mr. HANCOCK. ... This is a bill of general application. It covers the most heinous crimes the criminal statute book contemplates. It had its origin in the activities of the Dillinger gang. All this bill does is abolish the double standard which Justice Byrnes established and makes labor responsible for crimes just as well as those who are not laborers. That is all it does.

"Mr. CELLER. I wish the gentleman's interpretation were correct, but I fear that he is woefully in error. This bill is primarily aimed at labor. It has a label of racketeering, it has a label of extortion, it has a label of robbery, but it is an antilabor bill. Let us not delude ourselves, because were it not for the so-called Teamsters' Local decision by Mr. Justice Byrnes, a labor decision, we would not have had this bill. . . .

"This bill is not properly called an antiracketeering bill. Those opposing the bill, unamended, and labor opposing the bill cannot and should not be said to be in favor of racketeering. We disfavor any bill that interferes with legitimate labor acts under the guise of preventing racketeering. The language is broad and sweeping and is as broad as a barn door and may permit simple assaults to be converted into felones." (3201)

"Mr. GWYNNE. . . . The contention of the government [in *Local 807*] was, that . . . the exception in the statute did not apply, that this money was paid to these hijackers for protection, and not by way of wages. The Court overruled the contention of the government and held that the exception applied, and that is why we are trying to amend this law. . . . Putting it briefly, what this bill does if to rewrite the law and leave out that exception on which the Supreme Court's decision is based. So the net result would be that the same set of facts which existed in the case of the government against Local 807 would result in a conviction and punishment. That is title I. . . . Later on there will be some discussion about some proposed amendments.

"I believe it was not the intent of the committee in writing this bill to in any way interfere with the rights of labor, guaranteed in the statutes that are enumerated in these amendments. I think no amendment is necessary. There are those people who disagree and, in order to make it abundantly clear that we do not propose to interfere with the rights of labor under these statutes, some kind of an amendment will be offered, and the choice then will be between the so-called Celler amendment and the committee amendment. I prefer the committee amendment. . . . However, I am frank to say that I do not see much difference between these two proposed amendments. . . . There is nothing in any [of the four statutes referred to in the amendments] which authorizes the use of force and violence. . . .

"Mr. MARCANTONIO. Is it not a fact that the vital difference between the bill now before us and the Anti–Racketeering Act of 1934 is that this bill excludes two provisions which were inserted in the Anti–Racketeering Act of 1934 for the purpose of protecting labor, when it is engaged in militant labor activity, and those provisions, excluded from this bill, distinguished between a militant labor activity and a racketeering activity? With those provisions out, a militant labor activity such as a clash between strikers and scabs during a strike would be considered a violation of the provisions of this bill if it were enacted into law.

"Mr. GWYNNE. No. I cannot agree with the gentleman. This statute leaves out three provisions that were in the 1934 statute and words the remainder in a little different language.

"Now, here is the disagreement. I think the intent of Congress in the 1934 statute was to protect the lawful activities of organized labor. The construction put upon it by the Supreme Court would authorize unlawful acts—certainly never intended by this Congress." (3201–02)

"Mr. WALTER. Mr. Chairman, the reason for a law is the soul of the law. I think at the outset we might examine what is admittedly the reason for our being here today considering this legislation. I am about to read from the opinion of Mr. Justice Byrnes, that unfortunate decision that necessitates this legislation. . . .

"Now if the above stated facts [from the opinion] do not constitute racketeering, certainly the Congress, when it enacted this Anti–Racketeering Act, chose improper language. In my judgment, the decision was a bad one, and I ask you at some time to read the entire minority decision and you will have some idea of what Congress intended to do.

"Now, with the hope that my voice can be heard across the park, I want to state that it is the intention of the Committee on the Judiciary to enact legislation for one purpose, and one purpose alone, namely, to correct the unfortunate decision in the *Local 807* case. It was never within the mind of any member of the Judiciary Committee to take from labor any of those things that it has won. It seems to me that both amendments make that very, very clear. Both amendments, excepting from the operation of this act those things that are guaranteed to labor under [the four mentioned statutes]. As plain as we could select English, those exceptions are provided for. . . .

". . . We are amending the act of 1934 because the Supreme Court has, through the most tortuous decision that ever came from the pen of a justice, found something that the Congress never intended to be in the act of 1934.

"I do not know why labor is not willing to assist in putting its own house in order. I am always very much provoked when labor leaders take the position that labor, like the king, can do no wrong. . . . Farmer after farmer in the eastern part of Pennsylvania has been stopped at the entrance to the Holland Tunnel, compelled to get off his truck and give some man $9.40 to deliver that truck to a point where that farmer had been delivering his produce for a great many years; or he has been compelled to employ a pilot to show him where the market is; where he and his father and his grandfather have delivered their produce for a great many years. [A]ccording to letters I have received during the last week, . . . those slimy racketeers are engaged in the same shake-down that they were working when the case was brought to the Supreme Court of the United States." (3202–03)

"Mr. BALDWIN of Maryland. Mr. Chairman, I want to take just a few minutes to urge to the best of my ability the passage of this bill and the retention in it of the committee amendment, and the defeat of the Celler amendment which will be offered. Let me explain my reasons for taking this position. The Maryland delegation, including the two Senators, had a meeting with about 200 representatives of the C.I.O. of Maryland some two weeks ago. This bill came up for consideration. They were opposed to its passage except upon inclusion of the Celler amendment.

"Upon being questioned about the amendment, they admitted that it nullified the bill completely, and they were satisfied with it, because the bill meant nothing with the Celler amendment in it. That is the statement made by the C.I.O. leaders of Maryland, and I am sure they got pretty good legal advice when they proposed this amendment. . . .

". . . I know too much of what has been done by some men, possibly not with the sanction of labor generally, I may say in fairness, in my own state. I could stand here for a half-hour and tell you of instances of farmers' trucks hauling into Baltimore which have been stopped and made to pay exorbitant fees.

"I will give you one illustration of a milk transportation company in my county. It had five truck drivers who were farm boys. They tried to force them to belong to the union, but they refused. They oiled a curve on a sharp downgrade on the road, and ran one of their trucks in a ditch and wrecked it. Then one week after that, while unloading at the Western Maryland Dairy in Baltimore City, the driver was blackjacked, and knocked unconscious, his helper's throat was cut from ear to ear, and 22 stitches were required.

"Mr. Chairman, these things are disgusting, not only to everybody in this country, but to the decent, honest, law-abiding laboring people in this country. The main issue in this, in view of the generally acknowledged fact that this has happened all over this country, is this: Are we in Congress going to let that condition exist in this country because of a Supreme Court decision? We have one duty by this bill, and that is to tell the American people that by this act we are going to restore their respect and their confidence in the strength and the dignity of this government." (3203–04)

"Mr. GRAHAM. . . . If you will pardon a digression for a moment, this makes me think of a thing I once heard while waiting to argue a case before the Supreme Court of Pennsylvania. An attorney was arguing with some vigor and the Chief Justice of the court said, 'Mr. Blank, you are arguing from a dissenting opinion. That is not the law.' Unabashed, the attorney said, 'Well, if it isn't, it ought to be.' That is my comment in this case. If Justice Stone's opinion is not the law, in my judgment, it ought to be."

". . . Men have the right to strike. Of course they have. They have the right to collective bargaining, of course, and no one disputes that. They have the right to peaceful picketing, and no one disputes that; and they have the right to organize for better working conditions." (3204–05)

"Mr. KEFAUVER. . . . There can be no justification for what took place up there. These farmers, or men driving farm trucks, came in, and as has been explained, they were shaken down for $8 or $9. It might not have been so bad if they had been given an opportunity to join the union, but as was said by [a union attorney at] the hearings, they were not invited to join the union, they could not join the union, they were not eligible for membership. So they were confronted with a situation in trying to market their produce of paying a sum for the privilege of driving over the streets which they owned as much as anybody else. Down in Richmond, Va., a policy grew up where the apple farmers in bringing apples into the market could get within 100 or 200 feet of the place where they were going to deliver them, and then they had to employ a union truck, or a truck with a union driver, and take the apple boxes out of the farm truck and put them into the union truck, in order to unload them at the station. . . ." (3205)

"Mr. SADOWSKI. . . . The most highly publicized antilabor bill now before Congress is the Hobbs bill. The sponsors of this bill call it an Antiracketeering Act. We all agree that racketeering should be ended and that the punishments for racketeering should be severe. However, there is already an antiracketeering statute in federal law which is called the Anti–Racketeering Act of 1934.

"The trouble with the Hobbs bill is that it can be construed by the courts to prohibit and punish most of the legitimate activities of organized labor. Under its provisions a man who voted for a strike or walked a picket line would run the risk of being sentenced to a maximum of 20 years in prison or be fined $10,000, or both. Whatever the proponents of the proposed measure may say, the language of the Hobbs bill is so broad that it constitutes a serious menace to all that organized labor has struggled for, bled for, and even died for through many decades. . . .

"The Hobbs bill is a bad bill. It is a vicious bill. If passed, it would pave the way for the destruction of organized American labor. Let us not fool ourselves. Success of bills like the Hobbs measure will pave the way for fascism in America in exactly the same way Hitler fastened the bloody tentacles of fascism upon the unhappy people of Europe. . . ." (3207–08)

"Mr. RUSSELL. I cannot imagine any rubber material that could stretch as far as the imagination of mankind would have to stretch to reach such an erroneous construction. I say to the gentleman that [the bill] absolutely will not and it absolutely does not [penalize those who vote in favor of a strike or engage in peaceful picketing]." (3209)

"Mr. GIFFORD. . . . The gentlemen from New York (Mr. Celler) wants an affirmative declaration to provide for absolute exemptions. . . . Why do you lawyers insist on this 'Provided, however'? If we wish to stop racketeering, why do we not do it without providing loopholes. [B]eware of those lawyers who desire to complicate and provide too many defense provisions that they can make profitable cases for themselves." (3209)

"Mr. HANCOCK. [T]he Celler amendment is adroit and tricky. There is more to it than meets the eye. It provides that no act which is lawful under the various labor statutes which are specified shall constitute a violation of this act. Everyone concedes it is lawful to seek jobs. Under the Byrnes decision, it is lawful to use any amount of violence necessary to obtain employment. . . . The tribute . . . exacted [in *Local 807*] frequently amounted to all or a substantial part of the profit the farmer hoped to make on the sale of fruits and vegetables which he had raised by the sweat of his brow and which he had driven many long miles to deliver. . . .

According to that decision any thug belonging to a teamster's union may climb on a farmer's truck, beat him over the head with a club and extort a day's pay as a truck driver whether he performs any services or not....

"If that construction of the law is allowed to stand, a gang of teamsters can hold up every car and truck crossing the bridge into Virginia, and compel the owner or driver to hire one of them at his own terms to drive the car through the state." (3210)

"Mr. BUTLER. Mr. Chairman, this bill is an amendment to the antiracketeering law of 1934, but the only material change which the adoption of this amendment would make in the existing antiracketeering law is the elimination of the clause which protects trade unions, engaged in their legitimate functions, against persecution under it.

"I believe that every fair-minded person must recognize today that organized labor stands in the forefront of the successful prosecution of the war effort. The passage of this amendment would be an attack upon labor and would destroy much of the unity that now exists between employers and labor.

"The amendment is particularly dangerous because it seems reasonable enough that labor should not be permitted to racketeer, and to persons who do not know the facts, that seems all that this amendment would do, but the wording of the antiracketeering law is so wide that demands for increased wages could be considered racketeering. ...

"My objection to this bill lies in its wholly unwarranted reflection on the working men and women of our country. I think it very unfair to place them in the class of racketeers and enact a law to protect the country from their so-called crimes. Criminal antilabor legislation is not a suitable award for the loyalty and splendid cooperation of our laboring people. It seems to me that this bill, under the guise of protecting the American people against racketeering, has no other purpose than the persecution of organized labor." (3212)

"Mr. SUMNERS of Texas. Mr. Chairman, in the brief time allowed to me I want to discuss subsection (b), the robbery section, and direct your attention to the fact that in the amendment which it is proposed to offer, the four acts to which reference has been made, are specifically not repealed; and in addition to that, this word is to be found in the first sentence of that subsection:

"The term 'robbery' means the 'unlawful' taking.

"So when the government comes to make out its case it would have to prove even without the exception of these acts, that the term, 'robbery' means the 'unlawful' taking; not only the taking in the method detailed in this act, but if the defendant could find anywhere not only in those four acts, but anywhere in the criminal law, privilege or permission to take this money by the method resorted to, he would be entitled to a verdict of 'not guilty.' " (3213)

"Mr. HOBBS. Mr. Chairman, I am going to ask the undivided attention of the membership, while I close this debate. The first point I want to make briefly is that this is not an anti-labor bill, no matter who says it is.
. . .

"I want to call your attention to just one thing, if I may. I want everyone of you to listen to this, because it is my solemn pledge. If any man, woman, or child in the world will show me how any honest law-abiding member of organized labor can be affected by this bill, I will either offer an amendment correcting that threat, or I will vote against my own bill.

"Mr. MARCANTONIO. Mr. Chairman, will the gentleman yield.

"Mr. HOBBS. I only have 2 minutes for this.

"Mr. MARCANTONIO. I do not want to take the gentleman's time, but the gentleman has just asked a question which I would like to answer.

"Mr. HOBBS. I want it shown.

"Mr. MARCANTONIO. All right. In connection with a strike, if an incident occurs which involves—

"Mr. HOBBS. The gentleman need to no further. This bill does not cover strikes or any question relating to strikes.

"Mr. MARCANTONIO. Will the gentleman put a provision in the bill stating so?

"Mr. HOBBS. We do not have to, because a strike is perfectly lawful and has been so described by the Supreme Court and by the statutes we have passed. This bill takes off from the springboard that the act must be unlawful to come within the purview of this bill.

"Mr. MARCANTONIO. That does not answer my point. My point is that an incident such as a simple assault which takes place in a strike could happen. Am I correct?

"Mr. HOBBS. Certainly.

"Mr. MARCANTONIO. That then could become an extortion under the gentleman's bill, and that striker as well as his union officials could be charged with violation of sections in this bill.

"Mr. HOBBS. I disagree with that and deny it in toto.

"Mr. MARCANTONIO. Then, let us put in a provision providing against such an interpretation.

"Mr. HOBBS. To put in a provision covering every suggestion anybody can make on the floor after the committee has studied the bill probably a year is perfectly ridiculous. The gentleman, good lawyer that he is, knows that all that is needed and all that we are trying to do today is pass a law without leaving loopholes through which the guilty may escape.

"Now Mr. Chairman, let me make an orderly presentation of the case for H.R. 653. . . ." (3213–14)

Congressman Hobbs' remarks continue for some five pages in the Congressional Record. He began by describing in detail the plight of the farmers entering New York City. He then referred to some of the examples of similar behavior collected in 429 pages of hearings held on the predecessor to H.R. 653. One concerned truck drivers, themselves members of a union but not the right one, who were forced to pay $17.35 per truck for delivery of pipe to a New York pier. Another involved a union driver of a moving van, as to whom "the goons explained that he was a member of a local in New Jersey and had no authority to invade their exclusive province, since he was not also a member of Local 807." (3215) The perceived pervasiveness of the practice was revealed by this comment:

> "Information is to the effect that all railway-freight deliveries in New York City are covered by the same pattern of racketeering. The Chelsea Piers in New York City are also reputedly under the ban. It is further said that all deliveries to steamship and railway piers in New York City are paying tribute." (3215)

In another case armed Navy guards were called to a New York dock to supervise the safe unloading of "a critical piece of war equipment" by skilled union riggers in the face of demands by unskilled "goons." In yet another case, a trucker delivering steel bars was forced to pay in Newark, where two bars were dropped off, and again in New York City, where the remainder of the load was discharged.

Hobbs concluded by addressing three specific objections that had been raised against the bill. First, he suggested that "the states' rights argument is just another smoke screen" because Congress has the responsibility to regulate interstate commerce. Second, he defended the penalty structure on the grounds that "the crimes of robbery and extortion are ... major felonies, heinous offenses," that the penalties provided were maximum limits only and could be adjusted at the time of sentencing to fit the case before the court, and that the maximum fixed by the bill was about the average of sentences for robbery and extortion in state laws in effect at the time. "Take New York, for instance," he continued: "The definition of robbery in this bill is substantially copied from the New York statute.[3] Yet New York has fixed the minimum punishment for first-degree robbery at

---

[3] Later in the debate, an amendment was offered substituting another definition of "robbery" for that contained in the bill. Congressman Hobbs spoke in opposition to the amendment, in the course of which he said:

"I will tell you why robbery is defined as it is in this bill. The testimony before our committee in the 429 pages of hearings we took last year showed that about 80 percent of the holdups in the United States occur in New York City; that more than 100 trucks a night carrying fresh fruits and vegetables from the farms of New Jersey are held up and robbed there every night. Pennsylvania contributes about a hundred. There are many others running into the thousands a week. Therefore, in looking for the definition of robbery to be put in this bill, going on the old-fashioned principle that the hair of the dog is good for the bite, I copied the definition of robbery that is in this bill from the statute of New York, substantially. There are one or two words added which do not change the significance of it at all. Substantially, it is the same." (3226)

The amendment was rejected by a vote of 140 to 42.

10 years and the maximum punishment at 30 years." (3218) Third, he responded to the criticism that the bill was anti-labor. He recited his record on pro-labor measures, and suggested that it was enough to refute this criticism that the bill limits "the field of its condemnation to interferences with interstate or foreign commerce by robbery or extortion." (3218) He then concluded his remarks by quoting from the Star Spangled Banner and Elijah on Mount Carmel.

At this point, the bill was read and a series of motions and amendments were formally presented. The Celler amendment was the most vigorously debated. The debate began with this colloquy:

"Mr. CELLER. ... The difference between my amendment and the committee amendment is this: The committee amendment simply states that the so-called Hobbs bill in its entirety shall not modify or repeal the so-called Railway Labor Act, the Clayton Act, the Norris–LaGuardia Act, or the National Labor Relations Act. You might as well just say that the Hobbs bill does not affect or repeal the National Tariff Act, or it does not affect or repeal the White Slave Act or the Income Tax Act.

"My amendment embraces within the purview of the Hobbs bill all lawful acts and activities and conduct of trade-unions that have been made lawful under these four enumerated acts. It would preserve all legitimate labor activities. It would not place any approval upon racketeering or robbery or extortion or any conduct that the local teamsters' union was guilty of in New York City.

"Fear was expressed that what was done by the teamsters in New York, which was made lawful by the Justice Byrnes decision, would be made lawful by my amendment. That is not true. If you examine carefully the Justice Byrnes decision, you will see that it turns primarily on the significant words which are contained in § 3(b) of the old Copeland Antiracketeering Act:

"The terms 'property,' 'money,' or 'valuable considerations' used herein shall not be deemed to include wages paid by a bona-fide employer to a bona-fide employee.

"Justice Byrnes erroneously decreed that the payment of money, which to my mind was protection money, was in that case a legitimate and sanctioned activity under the Copeland Antiracketeering Act and set up a relationship between employer and employee in a bona fide manner. My amendment, since it does not contain such language, and since the Hobbs bill now contains no such language, would not by any wildest stretch of the imagination permit a recurrence of that which happened by virtue of the activities of the Teamsters Union. Nay, more such activity would be banned and branded unlawful as it rightfully should.

"What would happen if you did not accept my amendment and instead accepted the committee amendment? Let us say a man is indicted under the Hobbs bill as amended by the committee amendment. He might plead, 'What I did was excepted and made legal by a number of Supreme Court decisions, under, say, the Clayton Act, for example.' The judge might reply,

'No; you are indicted under the Hobbs Act, which does not embrace within its purview the Clayton Act and the exceptions under the Clayton Act as defined by judicial interpretations. Therefore, I cannot accept your plea.' The striker, or worker picketing or boycotting, would be held guilty. The exceptions under the Clayton Act as enunciated by these long lines of Supreme Court decisions are not part of the Hobbs Act, the judge would say, 'You are indicted under the Hobbs Act. If you were indicted under the Clayton Act, your contention would be sound.'

"For that reason, I say to the members of [the House] that you must accept my amendment if you want to protect labor in its honest endeavors, in its lawful, traditional activities such as collective bargaining, strike, picket, or boycott. . . .

"Mr. HOBBS. Mr. Chairman, I rise in opposition to the amendment.

"Mr. Chairman, almost any crime may be committed while the perpetrator is engaged in otherwise lawful acts, conduct, or activities.

"To snatch a child from the path of an onrushing automobile is not only lawful, but praiseworthy in the highest degree. But suppose that, while so engaged, the rescuer recognizes the child as one that he has planned to kidnap, and then does so. Would he be innocent of kidnaping?

"Because a man is engaged in the perfectly lawful conduct of striking, is he guiltless if he commits rape?

"Picketing is lawful. But does that mean that a picket cannot be punished for stealing?

"The right of collective bargaining is guaranteed by law. Does that give collective bargainers the right to murder?

"These questions answer themselves.

"Therein is the trick or joker in the Celler amendment.

"Honestly and peaceably seeking employment is not only lawful, but commendable. However, it is equally lawful for the one from whom employment is sought to refuse it. Does any sane and reasonable man contend that the lawful right honestly and peaceably to seek employment gives the seeker the right to force employment or to beat the refuser?

"The Celler amendment says 'No acts, conduct, or activities which are lawful under' the four major labor relations laws—Clayton Antitrust Act, Norris–LaGuardia Act, Railway Labor Act, and National Labor Relations Act—'shall constitute a violation of this act.' It wholly omits to require, as do these acts to which it refers, that the 'acts, conduct, or activities which are lawful' must be done lawfully and peacefully, and that no crime be committed while doing otherwise lawful acts.

"The committee amendment refers to the same four major labor relations laws and guarantees, as does the bill without the amendment, every right granted in them; but it does not grant the right to do a lawful act in an unlawful way, nor the right to commit crime under color of legality.

"In vain in the sight of the bird, is the snare of the fowler displayed.

"Organized labor was born and has grown great, strong, rich, and almost omnipotent under state and federal laws condemning robbery, extortion, murder, manslaughter, assaults, rape, larceny, and arson, with never a claim until 1934 that any right of labor was impinged or jeopardized by any one of them.

"Why does labor now seek to make itself above the law that applies to all others? Is there any reason why labor should be granted immunity from the penalties of the criminal law? Unless crime be committed, no one can be hurt by any criminal law. 'The guilty flee when no man pursueth.' If labor is innocent, how can this bill hurt them? If guilty, why should they be the only class seeking immunity?

"The answer to these questions is clear. The vast majority of the men of labor are as good citizens as America boasts. They ask no unfair favors or advantages. They are law abiding and have nothing to fear. But clients of lawyers sometimes commit crime. A few good men are misled into following bad advice.

"I submit that for these reasons the Celler amendment is dangerous, especially in view of the decision in the *Local 807* case, which held that no matter how much violence might accompany a request for employment it was all right and you are perfectly innocent under the antiracketeering law. The same thing is true here. No matter what may be said about the Celler amendment, it still does not require, as do the acts to which it points, that lawful acts, conduct, or activities must be done in a lawful and peaceful way. Without that or something like that the amendment should be defeated." (3320–21)

There was extensive additional debate on the Celler amendment. Among the comments were the following:

"Mr. WHITTINGTON. . . . It is maintained that the Hobbs bill is an attack on organized labor. There is no ground for such contention. It was not intended that labor unions would engage in the practices of gangsters or terroristic activities, but in the New York case union teamsters did engage in such practices. The purpose of the bill is to prevent a repetition of the criminal terroristic activities of racketeers, whether they are members of unions or not. They are not to be relieved because they are members of unions. They cannot hide behind the cloak of organized labor if they engage in gangster methods." (3222)

"Mr. FURLONG. Mr. Chairman, I rise to oppose this bill in its entirety. . . . Can anyone justify sending a union member to prison for 20 years for committing a misdemeanor during a labor dispute when a nonunion member, guilty of the same offense under different circumstances, would receive a fine of possibly $25?" (3223)

The Celler amendment was rejected by a vote of 167 to 126. After the Celler amendment was rejected, the Committee amendment was adopted without further debate and without a recorded vote. Further debate on other proposed amendments followed. One, to eliminate the words "or under color of official right" from the definition of "extortion," was rejected following a debate that is dealt with in connection with other materials below. Another, to reduce the authorized maximum punishment from 20 years to 10, was also rejected. A vote on the bill, as amended by adding the Committee amendment, was then held. H.R. 635 passed by a vote of 270 to 107, with 57 members not voting.

The Second House Debate: H.R. 32 (December, 1945)

H.R. 32, which was destined to become the Hobbs Act as enacted, came to the floor of the U.S. House of Representatives for debate on December 11–12, 1945. This time the debate continued for some 31 pages[1] in the Congressional Record. See 91 Cong. Rec. 11839–48, 11899–922. The flavor of the debate was much the same as the debate on H.R. 635 two years earlier. Excerpts from the debate follow:

"Mr. WALTER. . . . Now let us look to the need for [this legislation]. I do not know whether any committee ever held any more hearings than our committee held on this measure. The hearings consist of 429 pages. Of course, we did not hold any this year. This is not unusual because the problem is the same as it was when the legislation was first introduced. The testimony would be the same and the practices sought to be curbed are continuing.

"At the outset I want it distinctly understood that the legislation under consideration is designed to meet one situation and one situation alone. It is not the intention of the Committee on the Judiciary to interfere in any way with any legitimate labor objective or activity. . . .

"Let us see what the situation is. [At this point the Congressman described the facts of the *Local 807* case.]" (11842–43)

"Mr. MICHENER. . . . More than two years ago a bill was introduced to remedy the evil. Yet the practices on the past of certain members of labor unions sought to be corrected have continued. We are told that every day many, many farmers and truck drivers are prevented from entering New York City and other metropolitan areas because of the activity of certain individuals who are in truth and in fact committing extortion and highway robbery. . . .

"Extensive hearings have been held before the Judiciary Committee, not at this session of Congress but in the previous session. Further hearings will develop no new facts. I think that is conceded. . . .

"[Members of Congress who speak for organized labor] oppose this bill because they fear it might in some way impede legitimate strikes. . . . In my opinion, this bill will not interfere with legitimate strikes. It is not so intended. . . .

"Mr. SUMNERS of Texas. There is nothing in this bill dealing with persons connected with organized labor as such. It is just an attempt on the

---

[1] See footnote 1 in Appendix A, supra.

part of the Committee on the Judiciary to bring in a bill that will prevent this type of robbery in interstate commerce.

"Mr. MICHENER. That is all there is to it. The only way labor is involved is that if these offenders belong to the union, and if by robbery or exploitation collect a day's wage—a union wage—they are not exempted from the law solely because they are engaging in a legitimate union activity. Mr. Speaker, I cannot understand how any union man can claim that the conduct described by Mr. Justice Stone is a legitimate union activity. . . ." (11842–44)

"Mr. SABATH. . . . May I say further, Mr. Speaker, that hearings were held on the subject matter during the last Congress, nearly two years ago, at which time certain present Members were not Members of the House, and I do not think those hearings bearing on the then or previous existing condition should be used for the purpose of passing any law at this time." (11846)

"Mr. HANCOCK: . . . This bill has been labeled an antilabor bill. That is not true. It is not antilabor in purpose or in fact. This bill is designed simply to prevent both union members and nonunion people from making use of robbery and extortion under the guise of obtaining wages in the obstruction of interstate commerce. That is all it does.

"It is the function of Congress to regulate interstate commerce, and it is the duty of Congress to protect interstate commerce. That is the object of this bill, and there is not any other. . . .

"Mr. Chairman, this bill is made necessary by the amazing decision of the Supreme Court in the case of the United States against Teamsters' Union 807, three years ago. That decision practically nullified the anti-racketeering bill of 1934. In effect it legalizes in certain labor disputes the use of robbery and extortion, two crimes which are recognized as serious in every state in the Union and in every civilized country whether made use of by union men, nonunion men, professional racketeers, or plain hoboes. In effect the Supreme Court held that it was the intent of Congress and the meaning of that act that members of Teamsters' Union 807 in New York City were exempt from the provisions of that law when attempting by the use of force or the threat of violence to obtain wages for a job whether they rendered any service or not. In my judgment that is a gross misinterpretation of the law and a distortion of the intent of Congress. Of course, it was never the intent of Congress to legitimize crime; nevertheless, the decision of the Supreme Court in the teamsters' case will be the supreme law of the land until the Supreme Court reverses itself . . . or until Congress acts to correct and supersede the decision and adopts a new law written in clear and unmistakable language. That is all this bill does. We think a mistake was made by the Supreme Court, we are attempting to correct it through enacting a new law which will accurately and definitely reflect the attitude of the Congress, the general public and the honest, law-abiding members of labor unions. . . .

"I think the appended editorial from the Washington News of December 8 well summarizes and interprets the bill we are considering:

"The Hobbs bill is coming up again in Congress. This time is should become law. It is not, as some lobbyists would have you believe, an antilabor measure. It is a measure to protect honest labor and the public.

"This bill is a proposed amendment to the federal antiracketeering act. It says simply that whoever obstructs interstate commerce by robbery or extortion shall be held guilty of a felony.

"This amendment is needed because of a 1942 Supreme Court decision. Union teamsters had been waylaying out-of-state trucks as they entered New York City, and, by threats and physical beatings, compelling the truckers to pay a day's wages to local union drivers whose services were neither wanted nor needed. In some cases the local drivers, after collecting the tribute, refused to do any work for it. These facts were proved in a federal district court.

"But the Supreme Court held, in effect, that Congress had not meant the Antiracketeering Act to punish such conduct by a labor union or its members. . . .

"No member of Congress should be deluded into believing that a vote for the Hobbs bill is a disservice to unionism. It is a service. Honest workers do not need or want racketeering to be a specially protected exclusive right of organized labor." (11900)

"Mr. EBERHARTER. I am asking this question for information. It has been said by some opponents of this measure that if in the exercise of legitimate union activities in connection with organizing a group of persons or individuals who are not members of a union a truck, for instance, may be stopped, which truck is engaged in interstate commerce, then they would be subject to the penalties imposed by this act. In other words, they would be accused of attempting by threat, force, violence, or intimidation to extort money, whereas the intention may be only to convince the nonunion person that he ought to join the union. If the gentleman will clarify that I think it will be helpful.

"Mr. HOBBS. There is not a thing in the world to that statement. Title [II] of this bill exempts from the operation of this law any conduct under . . . the Big Four that have been termed the Magna Carta of labor. In addition, that cannot be seriously contended except as just a window dressing in opposition to this bill because there is nothing clearer than the definitions of robbery and extortion in this bill. They have been construed by the courts not once, but a thousand times. The definitions in this bill are copied from the New York Code substantially. So there cannot be any serious question along that line by the gentlemen from New York who are the leaders of the fight against this bill.

"Let me point out that when you are striking, when you are picketing, when you are organizing a labor union, or engaging in any legitimate labor function, then you are operating under some one of those four laws that are specifically exempted in this bill by title [II]. Aside from that there is absolutely nothing further from the mind of any proponent of this bill than to hurt labor. Did we amend this bill when the Teamsters' Union struck Washington? Not at all, no matter how much it hurt. It was not highway robbery. They were exercising their legitimate right to strike. The same thing is true of all the other legitimate activities of Labor, and I resent just as bitterly as you or anybody else does the aspersion cast upon organized labor that robbery and extortion are legitimate activities of organized labor. You do not believe that, I do not believe that, nobody does. . . .

"Mr. WALTER. In connection with the question asked by the gentleman from Pennsylvania [Mr. Eberharter], the gentleman should point out that the taking must be an unlawful taking.

"Mr. HOBBS. Certainly, sir. Thank you." (11900–01)

"Mr. CELLER. . . . If the proponents of this bill mean what they say, namely, that they do not wish to curtail legitimate activities of labor, then why not say so and leave § 6 [of the Anti–Racketeering Act of 1934] as it is?

"Read the provisions of the current bill and you will find that proviso is deliberately eliminated. Why? It was eliminated to hurt labor. The courts, if we pass this bill with that proviso eliminated, would have to construe that the so-called Hobbs bill actually does impair, actually does diminish, actually does destroy the right of labor to strike, the right to boycott, the right to picket, and does impair all of those rights which have been achieved by labor over the years with blood and sweat and tears. Only because of those rights have we achieved the high standards of living of the laboring men and women in this country of ours. That is to be destroyed at one full swoop. Why do they not leave that proviso in the pending bill? Why is it taken out? If they intend not to interfere with the legitimate practices labor why do they not leave that language intact? If we take the language out of the bill, then that is tantamount to saying to the courts, and particularly with reference to the definitions contained in the bill, that striking and boycotting and picketing is robbery and is extortion. Those crimes are so broadened in definition as to embrace fair and decent acts of labor. . . .

"Just as we are against sin, just as we are in favor of the Ten Commandments, we are against the crimes of robbery and extortion, but we are not against these crimes as they are defined in this bill. Those definitions are so broad as to permit one to drive a coach and six through them. Robbery and extortion may mean striking, picketing, demanding higher wages, boycotting. . . .

"[W]hen we discuss the instant bill we are not discussing the question of whether or not we are to have an antiracketeering law. We already have one which contains all of the substantial protections against racketeering which are needed, or, indeed, which this bill offers. When we discuss the Hobbs bill what we are discussing is what changes should be made in the present antiracketeering law.

"There are courts which have held that whenever workers seek to bring about a wage increase or other adjustment of their working conditions by a strike, however peacefully conducted, they are attempting to 'force' their employer to grant the wage increase or the requested adjustment of their working conditions.

"There are courts which would hold that since a union's sole method of inducing an unwilling employer to grant wage increases is the economic weapon of the strike, then the very posing of the demand by a union to the employer is a 'threat' of 'force.'

"Attorneys familiar with the decisions of the courts on question of picketing will recall that there are courts which have held that picketing, however peacefully conducted, is by its very nature an attempt to force the employer into action which he is not willing to take. It is on this basis that many courts have in years past granted sweeping injunctions against concededly peaceful labor activity.

"Attorneys familiar with the decisions of the courts on charge of 'violence' in labor relations can tell of the implications to labor in a statute worded as is the instant bill. There are courts which, in injunction cases and in disorderly conduct cases, have held name-calling or use of such terms as 'scab' to constitute 'force' or 'violence.' Whatever may be your views as to whether such name-calling should properly be considered disorderly conduct under local ordinances or statutes, it should be kept in mind that the pending bill is defining conduct which would become a felony, punishable by imprisonment up to 20 years; or by a fine of up to $10,000, or both.

"This problem has another aspect. It is generally recognized that some, if not all, labor disputes are unfortunately marked by heated tempers on both sides. It is unfortunately true that in some instances in the heat of labor disputes there will be minor altercations on the picket line. There will be occasional scuffles between partisans. And truly criminal conduct which may occur in the course of these altercations and scuffles is of course punishable by local disorderly conduct statutes or ordinances or other local laws. Under the Hobbs bill every such altercation is automatically raised to the level of a federal offense—a federal felony the punishment for which may be as high as 20 years in jail or $10,000 in fine.

"Nor is that all. Those dangers are not even limited to the persons who may take part in the strike or in the picket line and certainly not to the persons who may be actually involved in the altercations or in the name-calling or other incidents which under this bill would become felonius [sic].

"Section 3 of this bill makes equally felonious that conduct of those who 'conspire' with or 'act in concert' with others to commit the acts which are prohibited by the bill. Now, if a strike is 'force,' within the meaning of the other sections of the bill, then obviously not only the strikers are guilty of felony but all those who voted for the strike at the union meeting. Indeed all those who are members of the union may be involved, since by their membership in the organization they may be found either to have 'conspired' or to have 'acted in concert' with strikers. By the same token, all of the workers on the picket line, and indeed all of the members of the union, may be found to have 'conspired' or to have 'acted in concert' with the individual or individuals who may have become engaged in an altercation found to constitute a felony under the bill.

"All of these are not merely hypothetical dangers. They are not speculation. These are dangers which are found in the kind of construction which courts have in the past given to certain words in connection with their application to labor-relations problems.

"True, we have come a very long way from the kind of approach which is reflected in such interpretations. We may assume that there are very few today who would side with the courts of the first two decades of the 19th century which found the mere existence of a labor organization to constitute an unlawful 'conspiracy.' The fact is, however, that applied to specific strike situations and other specific labor-relations problems brought to the courts, there are many decisions now on the books and there are many judges now on the bench whose outlook may quite definitely be expected to result in holdings of the kind that have been outlined above.

"It is reasonable to assume our national legislators do not believe that legislation directed against 'racketeering' should be directed against a strike for higher wages or a picket line in support of such a strike. Certainly that was not the intent of the Congress which enacted the 1934 Antiracketeering Act. We doubt that the supporters of the pending bill would be willing to assert that this is their intention today. Yes; these are the results.

"So that many of the acts which accompany strikes, legitimate acts which accompany boycotts and which accompany picketing, come within the purview of this very, very wide definition of 'robbery,' this very wide definition of 'extortion,' and we must be careful before we leap into this egregious error.

"The gentleman from New York [Mr. Hancock] said that the purpose of this bill was to correct a difficulty that arose out of the so-called case of the teamsters' union local in New York. That teamsters' union was guilty of the vilest kind of offenses, and I hold no brief for that teamsters' union. . . .

"Mr. HANCOCK. A moment ago the gentleman said the threat of a strike came within the definition of extortion. This bill merely prohibits the wrongful use of force or threats. That cannot apply to a threatened strike because strikes are lawful, they are not wrongful. I wish the gentleman would show me a case to verify the wild statement he made a moment ago.

"Mr. CELLER. The statement I made is far from wild. The gentleman himself has been guilty of a number of wild statements. . . . I am willing to do anything in my power to prevent robbery an extortion, but when you tie robbery and extortion to the legitimate activities of labor, I am going to protest. . . ." (11901–02)

"Mr. GWYNNE of Iowa. . . . There has been some talk here of how this would affect the legitimate activities of organized labor. There is nothing to it, Mr. Chairman. Many of the Members of this House have been prosecuting attorneys. Here is what a prosecutor would need to allege and prove to get a conviction under this law if this bill becomes law:

"First, they would need to prove that the activity complained of in some way affected interstate commerce; second, they would have to prove that there was an actual, not a theoretical, taking of personal property; third, they would have to prove that the taking was by violence, by personal violence, or by actual threats of personal violence; and then, fourth, they would have to prove that the acts done—they might be violent, they might take something, but the government would have to prove in addition that the acts done did not come within the exceptions set out in title [II]." (11903)

"Mr. ANDERSON of California. . . . I happen to be a farmer in California. A lot of our produce is hauled into the city of San Francisco. The man who drives the truck, who hauls our fruit and produce into San Francisco, must belong to the teamsters' organization or he must pick up a member of the teamsters' organization, carry him on the truck to the point of unloading and pay him for all the time the truck is in the city of San Francisco.

"The farmers in the four counties I represent have been forced on many occasions, while hauling their own produce in their own trucks, to pick up members of labor organizations at the city limits of San Francisco, carry them on the truck to the point of unloading and back again to the city limits and pay them their wage for that period of time. This must be done in spite of the fact that the man who is thus paid does no work as far as driving or unloading the truck is concerned.

"Mr. Chairman, I say that is wrong. That is the sort of policy we must stop. Every farmer who hauls produce into the city of San Francisco or into any other large metropolitan area should be permitted to haul it in his own truck and unload it himself without paying tribute to any organization of any kind.

"I recall a time, back about 1938, when milk in the San Francisco milkshed was declared 'hot' and the members of the teamsters' union refused to haul the milk for dairymen. Because the farmers' milkers declined to join the dairyworkers' union, a secondary boycott was declared, and the teamsters left the milk to spoil instead of hauling it to the city for processing and bottling. As a result of such high-handed action the public went without milk and the farmers lost money. This ridiculous policy was carried so far in one instance in southern California that a farmer who fed his cows hay that was declared 'hot' because it was hauled by a nonunion truck driver also had his milk declared 'hot' and the teamsters' union refused to haul the milk.

"This bill seeks to prevent the legalization of highway robbery and extortion and I hope it will be passed by a heavy majority. . . .

"Mr. GRANT of Indiana. I am very much in favor of this bill. I voted for it on a previous occasion and expect to vote for it again. I have great respect for the gentleman's legal judgment, so I would like to ask him if he feels that this legislation that we are considering would reach the sort of case that the gentleman from California [Mr. Anderson] just related to the House?

"Mr. GRAHAM. I do. I think it will reach it." (11904)

"Mr. GALLAGHER. . . . [M]y friends, this bill is a declaration of war on organized labor or lack of trust in them and a declaration of the class struggle as vicious as any red advocate ever conceived. I know this bill was not taken from the constitution of Soviet Russia because Soviet Russia has a little conscience for the common man. The only place that it could have come from was the constitution of national socialism as advocated by Adolph Hitler. I want to say further that there is more racketeering on the heels and coattails of the Members of Congress in Washington than there is in the whole labor movement of the United States. It is about time that these people who are talking about home rule against the New Deal on account of these federal laws and the bureaucracy would be a little consistent and not try to socialize the laboring classes of this country." (11906)

"Mr. FELLOWS. . . . The so-called Hobbs bill is designed to make assault and battery and highway robbery unpopular. Its purpose is to protect trade and commerce against interference by violence, threats, coercion, or intimidation. It seeks to impress upon individuals who happen to hold a card of membership in some organization or other that there are obligations to recognize that other people may have certain rights. . . .

"A man, with his truck, taking food into the city of New York, is set upon by two or more men, who beat or threaten him with serious bodily harm and thereby compel the payment to them of a day's wage. It is admitted that in some of the instances these stick-up men disappeared as soon as the money was paid without rendering or offering to render any service. The man pays the money to save himself and his property. He does not feel that his assailants are fit men to be trusted with the driving of his truck with its load of food and rejects their offer of service. It is not clear to me how anybody could find in these facts an honest relationship of employer and employee, voluntarily entered into between the assailant and the assailed.

"Certainly this situation calls for correction." (11907)

"Mr. VOORHIS of California. . . . I should like to ask one or two questions of the author of the bill or the chairman of the Committee on the Judiciary. In the first place I would like to ask this question: Assuming that the bill is enacted into law and assuming thereafter the leader of a labor union walked into an employer's office and said to the employer: 'Our men are not getting enough pay; we want higher pay; we want to bargain with you for higher pay and unless we get somewhat better compensation than we are getting now there is liable to be a strike.' Is it possible, if this bill is passed, that under those circumstances a court could say that that was attempted extortion?

"Mr. SUMNERS of Texas. It is very difficult to say what a court might say, but it would not be extortion.

"Mr. VOORHIS of California. So that such an act would not be covered by this bill?

"Mr. SUMNERS of Texas. No.

"Mr. VOORHIS of California. May I say that with the provision in the bill which says that nothing in the act shall be construed to repeal, modify, or affect the National Labor Relations Act, and since the National Labor Relations Act was passed for the express purpose of protecting the right of collective bargaining, it appears to me it would be utterly impossible to construe this bill as affecting the collection of union dues or the collective-bargaining activities of a labor organization. If I am wrong about that, I would like to have somebody advise me. . . .

"Mr. WALTER. Out distinguished colleague from Iowa (Mr. Gwynne) pointed out the elements that it would be necessary to prove in order to make out a crime and I call the gentleman's attention to the fact that a mere threat does not constitute a crime. There must accompany that threat an unlawful taking.

"Mr. VOORHIS of California. I thank the gentleman. And certainly demands for higher wages or attempts to collect union dues are not unlawful acts by any stretch of the imagination. . . .

"Mr. SUMNERS of Texas. I may say to the gentleman from California that insofar as I can understand this bill, there is not a thing in it to interfere in the slightest degree with any legitimate activity on the part of labor people or labor unions, unless somebody thinks it is legitimate for them to rob and extort. If that is their notion, then this bill covers that activity.

"Mr. VOORHIS of California. Nobody believes that. My understanding of the bill coincides with that of the gentleman and I am taking the bill as I read it.

"Mr. HOBBS. May I add that the gentleman, in my opinion, is exactly correct and takes the proper position in his questions.

"Mr. VOORHIS of California. I thank the gentleman. I am just trying to make the record abundantly clear. I would like to ask the gentleman from Alabama a further question. In subsection (c) . . . there is the word 'wrongful.' Does that word 'wrongful' apply to the entire section?

"Mr. HOBBS. Yes; it qualifies the whole section." (11908)

"Miss SUMNER of Illinois. There have been complaints that in the case of strikes an attorney has gone in and asked an operator for something like $15,000 or $20,000 as a shake-down to stop a strike. Is there anything in this bill about that?

"Mr. JENNINGS. Not a thing. This does not have a thing in the world to do with strikes.

"This bill by express terms leaves in full force and effect every law upon the statute books passed for the protection of labor. If there were anything in here to the contrary I would not support this bill. The bill is one to protect the right of citizens of this country to market their products without any interference from lawless bandits." (11912)

"Mr. HOBBS. [I]f we had left in [§ 6] or any other part of the Copeland Act with all of its phraseology burdening down the Supreme Court, we would have exactly the same situation we had in the *Local 807* case, requiring the turning loose of everybody who had ever been convicted in New York state. . . ." (11912)

"Mr. WHITTINGTON. . . . The bill is to prevent a repetition of the physical violences by members of labor unions on those engaged in interstate commerce. It is to prevent a repetition of the assaults and attacks upon the drivers of trucks with produce entering New York City and similar cases. It punishes extortion and robbery no matter by whom committed. It pronounces the acts of those who assault and extort from the operators of trucks engaged in legitimate interstate commerce crimes with penalties.

There have been wanton assaults upon the operators of trucks by members of labor unions. No excuses have been offered for their crimes. They are exempt from federal prosecution because of a technical defect in the antiracketeering statute. The objectives of the sponsors of labor unions and organized labor are without merit. It is time for labor to clean house. The Antiracketeering Act should be strengthened and clarified. The pending bill will provide for punishing racketeers who rob or extort. There is no justification for labor unions opposing the bill as it constitutes no invasion of the legitimate rights of labor. Robbery and extortion by members of labor unions must be punished. Labor unions owe that much to the public. In demanding the protection of laws, labor unions should urge that those engaged in legitimate interstate commerce be protected from robbery and extortion." (11913)

"Mr. RESA. . . . This is another instance of objectionable duplication by the federal government of the functions and activities of the states. . . ." (11913)

At this point in the debate, the voting process began. Congressman Celler offered an amendment that would have added both the definition of "property" from § 3(b) of the 1934 statute and the proviso from § 6 of that statute to H.R. 32. In addition to several verbal altercations,[2] two interesting statements were made during the debate on the amendment:

[2] Congressman Granger said that "[s]ome members of the House are the most reactionary group on earth." When asked to yield by Congressman Cox, Granger said "no" and added "The gentleman who has just interrogated me is one of the gentlemen to whom I have been referring." Cox tried to interrupt again, and Granger added "Mr. Chairman, I do not yield further. The gentleman could not contribute anything that

"Mr. HAVENNER. ... At the risk of oversimplifying this issue, I would like to give the following illustration of its effect, if I understand it, upon the closed-shop agreements which have been established, by collective bargaining, between the teamsters unions and dealers in farm produce in the great cities of this country.

"The farmers of the country contend that they should have the right to haul their produce from their farms to the cities and deliver it in their own trucks to the produce dealers and merchants and warehouses in the cities. But in most of the cities of America the teamsters unions have, through collective bargaining, entered into closed-shop contracts with these produce dealers and merchants and warehouse proprietors to do all of their hauling for them. Obviously, if the farmers are permitted to haul and deliver their own produce to these mercantile establishments and warehouses, the effect of collective bargaining, closed-shop agreements between the merchants and warehouses and the transportation unions would be nullified, and a system of open-shop transportation would be established instead.

"This would be fatal to collective bargaining in the field of truck transportation.

"The proponents of this bill assert that it would have no injurious effect upon legitimate labor unions, and profess to be concerned only with racketeering and extortion. They would, inferentially, brand everyone who opposes the measure as sympathetic with extortion and racketeering.

"This sort of argument is, of course, too preposterous for serious consideration. What the bill really does is to classify as racketeering any effective effort by labor unions to insist that closed-shop arrangements which have been arrived at through years of collective bargaining shall not be destroyed by open-shop competition from areas outside of the areas where these closed-shop agreements are in effect. ...." (11915)[3]

"Mr. BIEMILLER. Mr. Chairman, I think it well to underline certain fundamental facts in the debate on this amendment. First of all, I think we ought to recognize thoroughly that those of us who are for the amendment and against the bill in its present form are the victims of a very good press agent trick. It is a cute trick to label a bill an antiracketeering bill and hence infer that any opponent of the bill is a person who therefore favor [sic] racketeers. But let us look at the true situation.

"Obviously there is no one in the House who favors racketeering. I am sure that I do not favor racketeering and I would not accuse any Member of

would be of very much interest to me." (11915) At another point, after a speech by Congressman Patrick in which he said that "no excuse remains for this legislation" because, in part, it violated states' rights, Congressman Knutson asked "Is the gentleman for or against the bill?" Mr. Patrick responded: "If the gentleman's deductions are so blunt that he cannot reach a conclusion, I cannot help him." (11916)

[3] The immediate response to Mr. Havenner's remarks came from Congressman Knutson, who asked: "[I]s all the time is to be taken by left-wingers?" Later Congressman Mercantonio asked for a definition of "left-winger," but no definition was forthcoming. (11916)

the House of such a position. Those of us who are opposed to the bill in its present form are genuinely fearful that the bill as it now stands can be used, as previous speakers have intimated, to infringe upon the legitimate rights of labor unions. I will add my voice to those we have heard earlier that where there is a clear case of extortion or robbery—I do not care if the individual belongs to a labor union or not—he is guilty and should be prosecuted. But in that respect I would like to point out that in Justice Byrnes decision, which has been talked about so much—and I recognize as a layman, I am sticking out my neck in invading that haunt that lawyers like to consider their private preserve, namely the interpretation of legal decisions—but I think there ought to be a point made about that decision that I do not think has previously been called to your attention. The decision says that under the existing law had the prosecutor handled the case correctly many of those who were involved in the case could have been convicted by the jury. I quote:

'And in several cases the jury could have found the defendants either failed to offer to work or refused to work for the money when asked to do so.'

"In that instance they are guilty under the present law. . . . If you read Justice Byrnes opinion carefully it rests in no small degree on the wrong procedure of the government prosecutor. I maintain that there is sufficient federal law under the Antiracketeering Act as it exists today, and certainly plenty of state law, to get at the kind of crimes that have been discussed on this floor today. In good faith the gentleman from New York has offered an amendment, and will later offer another, to protect the rights of labor. If either is adopted I will vote for the bill. I repeat that we are simply trying to protect the legitimate rights of labor organizations. We fear, for example, under the bill as it now stands, that a simple, unfortunate altercation on a picket line—and we all know that human beings are frail and when tempers are hot some trouble may develop—under such a situation you may send a man to jail for 20 years or fine him $10,000. . . ." (11916)[4]

After the Celler amendment was rejected, a colloquy occurred during which the following statement was made:

"Mr. BALDWIN of Maryland. . . . I am for the passage of the bill. . . .

"This bill would not have been presented to the House if organized labor had recognized law and order in striking and establishing their rights, as they have a right to do. Everyone can remember the taxicab strike in the city of Baltimore, which does not pertain to this bill, where cabs were overthrown, bricks thrown through the windows endangering the lives of people, innocent victims. Those were the tactics of organized labor which you people support outright and which organized labor sanctioned. The

[4] During the debate on the amendment, Congressman Rivers said of *Local 807*, in a statement later quoted by the Supreme Court,: "As one member of the bar, I disagree with the reasoning in this decision. I call the procedure referred to in this case, by the individuals involved, nothing short of hijacking, intimidation, extortion, and out-and-out highway robbery."

leaders were locked up and put in jail for participating in those activities.
. . .

"Mr. Chairman, labor has a right to strike, but when labor perpetrates that sort of thing, they are going far beyond the bounds of reason. Certainly, I do not take the position that labor has not the right to organize or to strike, but when they do they should abide by the laws of the land and the laws of decency. If they had done that, we would not have this legislation before the House today. . . ." (11918)

Congressman Celler then offered the same amendment he had offered to H.R. 653. After a short debate, during which Congressman Hobbs began his comments against the amendment by saying "Mr. Chairman, this is another good laugh" and concluded by saying "[t]herefore, we ask that this amendment be voted down, as usual," this amendment was also rejected. Congressman LaFollette then offered an amendment to substitute for H.R. 32 an amendment to the original 1934 Act:

"Sec. 7. The following definitions shall be binding upon all courts in construing this act:

"(a) The term 'the payment of wages by a bona fide employer to a bona fide employee' shall not be construed so as to include the payment of money or the transfer of a thing of value by a person to another when the latter shall use or attempt to use or threaten to use force or violence against the body or to the physical property (as distinguished from intangible property) of the former or against the body of anyone having the possession, custody, or control of the physical property of the former, in attempting to obtain or obtaining such payment or transfer.

"(b) The term 'the rights of a bona fide labor organization in lawfully carrying out the legitimate objects thereof, as such rights are expressed in existing statutes of the United States' shall not be construed so as to ignore, void, set aside, or nullify the definitions set out or the words used in or the plain meaning of subsection (a) hereof."

He explained that this was his attempt "in good faith . . . to prevent a reoccurrence of what happened in the Supreme Court opinion" and added:

"Of course, there is an element of coercion in strikes. It is the only right that labor has. I am not going to stand in the well of this House and affect that right in any way. But I am also not going to vote in this House for language which I am convinced can be construed against the organizing activities of labor. . . ." (11920)

After the LaFollette amendment was defeated, the bill itself was passed. There was no recorded vote.

†

1–56662–346–4

90000